BEN-GURION

BEN-GURION

The Burning Ground

1886–1948

Shabtai Teveth

HOUGHTON MIFFLIN COMPANY

BOSTON

1987

Library of Congress Cataloging-in-Publication Data
Teveth, Shabtai, date.
Ben-Gurion : the burning ground, 1886–1948.
Includes bibliographical references.
Includes index.
1. Ben-Gurion, David, 1886–1973. 2. Prime ministers —
Israel — Biography. 3. Zionists — Palestine — Biography.
I. Title.
DS125.3.B37T475 1987   956.94′05′0924 [B]   86-27485
ISBN 0-395-35409-9

PRINTED IN THE UNITED STATES OF AMERICA

S 10 9 8 7 6 5 4 3 2 1

To Raphael Recanati,
friend, ally, pioneer,
in admiration of his courage
and humanity

Acknowledgments

Many acknowledgments are in order. First, for the initial versions of the English translation of this work, I am indebted to Helen Sillman (chapters 1–9) and Jacqueline S. Teitelbaum (chapters 10–44 and Epilogue). The final version, which I translated, was ably revised by Stephanie Golden.

In collecting and sifting source material, I was assisted by a number of persons and institutions to whom I owe thanks: Mrs. Emanuel Gamoran, chairwoman of the Research and Archives Department at Hadassah, New York; Lois R. Brandwene, assistant librarian at the Zionist Archives and Library, New York; Abraham S. Peck, associate director of the American Jewish Archives, Cincinnati; Meir Avizohar, former director of the Ben-Gurion Research Institute and Archives, Sde Boker; Zehava Ostfeld, deputy director of the IDF (Israel military) and Defence Establishment Archives, Givatayim; Baruch Tor-Az, director of the Israel Labour Party Archives, Kefar Saba, Beit Berl; Elan Gal-Per of the Archives and Museum of the Israel Labour Movement, Tel Aviv; Shimon Rubinstein, curator at Yad Itzhak Ben-Zvi Historical Archives, Jerusalem; Nehama Chalom, curator at the Weizmann Archives, Rehovot; Michael Heymann, director, and Israel Philipp, former deputy director, of the Central Zionist Archives, Jerusalem; and Haim Israeli, former secretary to David Ben-Gurion and director of the Office of the Minister of Defence.

I owe particular gratitude to my former research assistant in New York, Michele Geldwerth-Zoltan, to my former secretary, Riva Oron, to my current secretary, Rachel Rader, and to my assistant, Tamar Gidron. They aided me through all the stages of composing this book with ability, dedication, and a sense of participation.

I am especially indebted to my friends at Houghton Mifflin, particularly to Wendy Withington and Austin Olney. Since the passage of the first six years of effort — and with them, of course, the contractual publication date of the book — delayed deadlines have followed in a seemingly never-ending sequence under Austin's petrified gaze. Yet, for thirteen long years, until the entire manuscript lay upon his desk, Austin manifested no impatience, but only encouragement. I dare say that such forbearance and understanding are not frequently encountered in publishing circles today. Once, when I could no longer contain my admiration, I wrote to Austin that, could my words paint, his portrait would emerge from my letter wearing a halo! Certainly his quiet, sure faith in this book strengthened my own. No words can properly express my thanks.

SHABTAI TEVETH
Tel Aviv, December 1986

Contents

Preface

Endurance and abundance are the hallmarks of David Ben-Gurion. He lived for eighty-seven years and two months, of which he devoted more than sixty-six years — from the day he joined the Warsaw Poale Zion in 1905 until his retirement from the Israeli Knesset in 1970 — to active politics. Given that he always held the highest offices — in the party, the Histadrut, the World Zionist Organization, and the Israeli cabinet — one is led to conclude that no other democratic system has ever known an elected leader who served so long in a central role.

Then, too, it would be hard to find another statesman whose field of operation spread over so many countries, continents, and regimes. Ben-Gurion began his political activity in his native Poland, then a government district in czarist Russia, and carried it on in Ottoman Palestine, Turkey, and pre–World War I Europe. From 1915 to 1918, he was politically active in the United States. Thirty years in Mandatory Palestine, during which he spent long sojourns in Britain and the United States, were followed by twenty-two years in the State of Israel.

As a diarist he also set records. From the outset of his public career in 1900, when Ben-Gurion was fourteen, he kept a diary; the early entries, however, were destroyed in a fire at his home in Istanbul in 1915. The diaries, in which he wrote in a clear hand almost daily from 1915 nearly until the day he died, December 1, 1973, are preserved among his papers. Once he completed an entry, he never altered it. The long process of editing these diaries for publication began comparatively recently; those for the War of Independence, October 1947 to October 1948, were published in Hebrew in 1982, in three volumes. Ben-Gurion's diaries will eventually fill at least fifty thick volumes.

In addition, in his lifetime Ben-Gurion published more than thirty books, which were translated into several languages; an incomplete bibliography of his writings between 1910 and 1959 contains twenty-five hundred items in Hebrew and other tongues. (In this volume, English-language quotations are cited as originally written.) From an early age, too, Ben-Gurion saved a copy of everything he wrote, and he carefully filed away nearly every note, document, letter, and press clipping concerning himself and his work. His archives at Sde Boker contain more than 750,000 items. Thus, in terms of industry, consistency, and self-appreciation, Ben-Gurion ranks at the top.

Such a plethora of documentation could be seen as an encumbrance to the would-be biographer. Some important persons have tried to erase, hide, or improve parts and episodes of their lives, both public and private, by means of silence, revision, and simple destruction of significant papers. But Ben-Gurion smoothed his over by inundation. The biographer accustomed to struggling with lacunae and well-buried sources, consequently seeking to overcome the scarcity of material at his disposal, encounters, in writing about Ben-Gurion, the opposite difficulty: a flooding reservoir of source material. A close look at it, however, reveals that for all its profusion it offers only a trickle of basic personal information and no gossip at all. To uncover details concerning Ben-Gurion's private and family life — the man's tastes in literature, art, or music, for example — one has to work very hard. Ben-Gurion compounds the problem of being unable to see the forest for the trees by providing such a profusion of data that his biographer can hardly see the trees for the leaves.

A different sort of obstacle for the biographer is the Israeli archives law, which proscribes the release of state documents for a period of thirty years. However, unlike Great Britain and the United States, Israel does not release cabinet minutes and armed forces archive material even after the thirty years have passed. Hence, essential material remains beyond the reach of the researcher. Thirty-eight years after the founding of the State of Israel and its War of Independence — Ben-Gurion's zenith — one is denied access to cabinet minutes and to the Knesset Defence and Foreign Affairs Committee hearings of that time. If, by dint of concentrated and prolonged effort, one can come to terms with the first difficulty, profusion, there is no telling when it will be possible to overcome the second, by which the biographer is denied an informed assessment of the political and social thinking, the positions and actions of Israel's first prime minister and minister of defense. In short, one is simultaneously afflicted by too much and too little.

For this reason it is virtually impossible to contain the life of Ben-Gurion in a single volume. To do so would require two modes of writing, with one based mainly on primary sources and other tools of the historian and the other relying heavily on oral testimony, press reports, and secondary sources. I find this inappropriate, and accordingly have contented myself with writing Ben-Gurion's story up to the establishment of the State of Israel. The reader will find a biographical as well as a scholarly rationale for this decision, for the pre-state Ben-Gurion differs decidedly from the post-state leader elevated in national status above his Israeli and Jewish peers.

In this book the reader will discover the story of the great life work of David Ben-Gurion: the establishment of authority. He undertook a task that could justifiably be called a mission impossible. After all, the problem of imposing a single authority on the Jewish people — to close their ranks and guide them along a single national course — has been the leitmotiv of Jewish history. The Bible is full of narratives indicating that prophets or kings — or even higher authority — were not always equal to this task. If this was the case when the Children of Israel were at home in their land, it must have been much more difficult once they had been exiled and dispersed among the proverbial seventy lands and tongues.

For some two thousand years of exile, the Jewish people had a dubious distinction: lacking their own land, they recognized no central authority. What every tribe, feudal fiefdom, duchy, or kingdom had was not possible for them. Even the Jewish religion, owing in large part to the Diaspora and also to its very nature, lacked what most other religions possess: an ecclesiastical government. In their dispersion the Jews obeyed, in matters temporal, the political authority that happened to govern their host country; in matters spiritual, they heeded their local rabbi, since no single rabbinic authority existed. Indeed, so vast was Jewish dispersion that there developed a genuine distinction between Eastern and Western Jewry; for example, the Jews of Yemen learned of the thousand-year-old Jewish prohibition of polygamy only a few decades ago.

The founders of the Zionist movement aspired to remedy this fundamental deficiency in the life of the people by returning them to their homeland and restoring their independent national life. If the chief contribution of Theodor Herzl was the creation of political Zionism and the establishment of the World Zionist Organization, and that of Chaim Weizmann was the achievement of the Balfour Declaration, the main work of David Ben-Gurion involved the founding of a secular authority, without which he could never have brought about the establishment of a state. This crowning accomplishment of his life warrants his singular place in history.

The initial premise for the authority Ben-Gurion strove to establish was his strong personality and equally strong sense of destiny. He himself was the mainstay of his enterprise. In the course of his struggle, Ben-Gurion summoned a rare and amazing power of concentration, so consuming as to make him, at times, quite oblivious of human needs. Over the years his natural sensitivity to others gave way to an imperviousness to anyone who stood in his way — or seemed to — toward the fulfillment of the mission Ben-Gurion had taken on himself. Friends, long-time companions, and even family bore the consequences of this weakness, which was no less essential to his overall achievements than were his wisdom, industry, tenacity, and endless patience. One is tempted to say that Ben-Gurion was able to bear his onerous mission thanks to this failing, which served him like blinders on a horse, by making him keep his eyes on the road. That which flawed him as a person enhanced him as a leader and statesman.

All his years as the Histadrut's secretary were directed toward building Histadrut authority over its members, the Jewish working public in Palestine. On his election to the Jewish Agency, Ben-Gurion strove to expand that authority throughout the Yishuv. One may surmise that, had he attained this objective in full, he would have attempted to expand that authority still further, from the Yishuv to the entire world. That he was only partially successful even in the Histadrut and the Yishuv does not in any way diminish his remarkable achievement.

History seems to have arranged a conjuncture that permitted the advent of Zionism but restricted the time span for its accomplishment. Ben-Gurion, who saw in Zionism the only solution for the problem confronting the Jewish people and the sole chance for their rescue, was utterly convinced that if Zionism was not realized at once, the Jewish people were doomed. This explains why, more than all his colleagues in the labor movement and the Zionist leadership, he was driven by an enduring sense that the ground was burning beneath the feet of the Jews, especially in Europe. Therefore, in his view, time was of the essence. He saw in the Jewish predicament a source of strength for the Zionist movement; he recognized the lack of an alternative that forever bedeviled the Jews as an instrument that could be used to accelerate the establishment of a state. For him Jewish hardship was a source of strength, and no one excelled him in tapping this "natural resource" that history had so lavishly bestowed upon the Jews. As the danger grew under Hitler, as disaster threatened the Jews of Europe and the clock began to run out on Zionism, this concept was put to the test.

From 1933 on, Ben-Gurion was guided in his judgments and actions by his sense of the burning ground, along with his drive to establish the authority without which rescue of the Jews in Europe would be impossible. Sadly, his fears were fully borne out by the Holocaust. Ben-Gurion found himself in a dilemma that no Jewish leader, perhaps no leader at all, had ever experienced: having to confront, helplessly, the destruction of European Jewry without losing faith in humankind and the Jewish people and without abandoning his confidence in the justice of the Zionist cause and its ultimate triumph.

Chronology

1886   David Gruen born on October 16, Płońsk, (Russian) Poland

1900   Founds Ezra youth group in Płońsk

1905   Joins Poale Zion, Marxist Zionist party

1906   Arrives in Jaffa, Palestine; elected to Central Committee and Platform Committee of Palestine Poale Zion

1910   Adopts Ben-Gurion as his name

1912   Enrolls in Istanbul University Law School

1915   Exiled to Egypt; sails to America

1916   Publishes *Yizkor* in New York; begins work on *Eretz Israel*

1917   Marries Russian-born Pauline Cora Munweis in New York

1918   Founds and leads American Jewish Legion Committee; joins Jewish Battalion of the British Royal Fusiliers; sails to Egypt to join expeditionary force in Palestine; Geula is born in New York.

1919   Achdut ha-Avodah is founded and DBG becomes the dominant member of its secretariat.

1920   Paula and Geula join DBG in Palestine. British Mandate in Palestine begins. The Histadrut is founded while DBG serves in London. Amos is born in London.

1921   DBG joins the Histadrut Executive Committee and the three-man secretariat.

1923   Visits Moscow but fails to change the Kremlin's hostility to Zionism

1925   Renana is born in Jerusalem.

1930   DBG builds his home in Tel Aviv; Mapai is established.

1931   Publishes *We and Our Neighbors*

1933   Elected to the Jewish Agency Executive at World Zionist Congress; *From Class to Nation* is published.

1935   Elected chairman of the Jewish Agency Executive at World Zionist Congress; Jewish immigration to Palestine reaches its peak of more than 60,000 people.

1936   Arab revolt against Jewish immigration, which lasts three years, begins.

1937   Peel Commission recommends partition of Palestine and termination of the British Mandate.

1938   DBG advances policy of combative Zionism and goes to America to raise money and support.

1939   Tripartite St. James's Palace Conference fails to bring accord between Arabs, Jews, and the British government; White Paper closes Palestine to immigration.

1940   DBG, in England and the United States as a self-appointed "Zionist preacher," presses the case of a Jewish state.

1941   Sets up Zionist Peace Program and War Program

1942   American Zionist (Biltmore) Conference in New York endorses Weizmann's and DBG's demands for Jewish state in part of Palestine after the war.

1944   In the wake of Allies' victories DBG visits Bulgaria; the anti-British struggle for the Jewish state begins under his leadership.

1945   DBG visits Jewish survivors in Germany.

1946   First postwar World Zionist Congress elects no president; DBG, as chairman of the JAE, is sole leader of the World Zionist Organization.

1947   UN Assembly accepts resolution to partition Palestine.

1948   DBG declares the establishment of the State of Israel and becomes its first prime minister and minister of defense.

1949   Elections to the first Knesset; DBG forms Israel's first elected government, in which he is prime minister and minister of defense.

1951   DBG initiates reparations agreement with West Germany for more than $2.2 billion.

1953   Retires to Sde Boker in the Negev to promote Israeli settlement in the south

1955   Returns to his post as minister of defense, in Moshe Sharett's cabinet, following the Lavon Affair

1956   Becomes prime minister and replaces Sharett with Golda Meir as minister for foreign affairs; initiates the Sinai Campaign against Egypt

1960   Cabinet committee exonerates Lavon.

1963   DBG resigns posts as prime minister and minister of defense and retires to Sde Boker to campaign for a commission of inquiry into the Lavon Affair.

1965   Mapai rejects DBG's demand for a commission of inquiry; DBG, with Moshe Dayan and Shimon Peres, forms a new party, Rafi.

1967   DBG resigns from Rafi, which rejoins Mapai, now named the Labour Party.

1968   Forms yet another party but wins only four Knesset seats in the 1969 elections

1970   Retires from the Knesset and from public life to write his memoirs

1973   DBG dies on December 1. In a state funeral, he is laid to rest in Sde Boker beside Paula, who died in January 1968.

BEN-GURION

1

Płońsk

H IS MOTHER loved him best of all her children. Sheindel Gruen
had passed on to her dearest child her features and slight stature. "Sheindel was small and so were her sons, but her daughters were tall like their father." Observant and God-fearing, she was
known for her goodness. Her neighbors in Płońsk called her Sheindel
the Righteous.

David-Joseph, the fourth child born to Reb Avigdor and Sheindel
Gruen, appeared on the world's threshold on October 16, 1886, during
the Jewish holiday of Succoth. He was a frail child who owed his survival, he believed, solely to his mother's love. All his life he cherished
the memory of her "overflowing tender love," which carried him
through his many battles with man and circumstances. On June 18,
1894, Sheindel was once more in labor. As she lay in one room, his beloved grandfather Zvi-Arie lay dying in another. Receiving the happy
news that Sheindel had given birth to a boy, Zvi-Arie remarked that he
had better die before the circumcision, so the child could be named
after him. On Sabbath eve he drank "L'chaim" with the guests, but the
following Wednesday, the day before the scheduled brith, both his soul
and that of his would-be namesake returned to their Creator.

David Ben-Gurion's later fear that the least breeze could snuff out
the life of the newly born therefore came, perhaps, from experience.
His mother gave birth eleven times, but only five of her children survived long: Abraham (1877), Michael (1879), Rivka (1881), David-
Joseph (1886), and Zippora (1890). These years formed an exhausting
chain of life and death, in which the gaps between the living children's
ages pointed to the absence of the dead.

Sheindel's last confinement came in 1898, when David was eleven
years and four months old. Intelligent, sensitive, and alert to the world

around him, he surely watched and listened in alarm to the escalating commotion as his mother succumbed to blood poisoning. She died on February 7, 1898, at the age of forty-one. His mother had given herself to her children — most of all to him — and as a result her own life had drained away. David-Joseph understood then that the creation of one new life could exact the destruction of another.

Ben-Gurion later said that when his mother was taken from him his world collapsed; without her, his life was in the balance. "My mother's death, when I was ten years and a few months old, was the cruelest blow of my childhood," he wrote in his memoirs. "The pain of this loss did not leave me for many years. Long afterward I'd see her in my dreams and talk with her. Sometimes I'd ask her, 'Why don't we see you anymore?' " They met like this throughout his eighty-seven years, virtually until his very last days. But as he confided to those close to him, something was amiss. He would beseech her to show him her face, because he couldn't remember how she looked and he longed to see her again. When she agreed and approached him — and the nearer she came, the greater his joy — the dream would fade and vanish.[1]

Although Ben-Gurion notes that he was "ten years and a few months old" at the time of his mother's death, he was actually a year older. Notwithstanding his powerful memory — he could remember that when he was two his bedroom stove was mended — Ben-Gurion could not bring to mind his mother's looks, whether her hair was curly, long or silky, worn piled up in a crown, dark or blond. Her face was forever withheld from him, and he was unable to conjure it up for even a moment. Other personal details about her were also lost to him. When he was married in 1917, he wrote "unknown" in the space for his mother's maiden name on the questionnaire for the New York city clerk. In his memoirs he once wrote her name as "Friedman" and once as "Broitman," even though in 1924 a copy of her birth certificate had been issued at his request. Preserved with his private papers, it clearly shows the name Broitman.

The summer after their mother's death, David-Joseph and Zippora went, as they had every summer when Sheindel was alive, to visit distant relatives in Roumbesh, a village in the country. There David-Joseph's grief overflowed; he ate nothing and lay awake at night. "I can't stop thinking about life in the next world and what it must be like there," he told one of his anxious relatives. In recalling his mother, Ben-Gurion always said she took him alone to Roumbesh, but Zippora, although three years younger, clearly remembered one holiday there: trips to the woods and her brother's nimble tree climbing to find a comfortable branch where he perched to savor the sugar crystals stuffed into little bags prepared by his mother. David-Joseph, however, had blotted his sister's presence from his memory; there is no trace of his two sisters and two brothers in his reminiscences of the entire period up to his mother's death.

This egocentrism was not groundless. He had received special attention from birth because his head was uncommonly large. On the one hand, this feature, a source of great anxiety, was cited to explain his chronic sickliness and bouts of fainting; on the other, it was a source of great expectations. The opinion grew in his family that his head, despite its unusual size, could not contain the vast range of his thoughts, which built up pressure and caused his fainting spells and general ill health. When David-Joseph was five years old his parents took him to a doctor in Płock, the provincial capital. The doctor, having felt the boy's head, told David-Joseph's father that its sheer size, the height of the crown, and especially the distance between the ears were signs of incredible talents.

The accuracy of this account, given by Ben-Gurion, is hard to judge. Phrenology, which had been fashionable in Europe in the first half of the nineteenth century, probably had its devotees in provincial Poland in the second half as well. It may also be that the Płock doctor spoke optimistically to reassure the parents. In any event, whatever its origin, the belief that a large head foretold a brilliant future took root in Ben-Gurion himself.

For Sheindel, the doctor's words were a fount of contentment and pride. Ben-Gurion remembered her saying to her friends, "Do I have a child!" She dreamed of his becoming a rabbi, while his father wanted him to be a doctor. Ben-Gurion himself wondered whether his mother loved him so extravagantly because of the great future in store for him — a future that seemed all the more probable since the doctor's prophecy was proving itself day by day. His quick mind and formidable memory brought endless delight to family gatherings. His talents were shown off by challenge; for so many kopecks, someone would say, "Let's see if you can learn this poem by heart." Without exception, he won the promised reward in half the time they set. For years afterward, people remembered and quoted Sheindel's saying, "I have two bright boys, Abraham and David. The whole town will hear of Abraham, but the entire world will talk of David." Those words were so widely broadcast that there can be little doubt that they reached David-Joseph's ears.

When Sheindel died, Reb Avigdor vowed that he would never marry again, but two years later he did. Tall and beautiful, Zvia Swistowski was a widow with two grown children. David-Joseph always referred to her as "aunt," for it was utterly unthinkable that she might replace his mother. For Ben-Gurion, the first things were also the final ones, and what filled his early years occupied his world forever. The foundation for his life's work was his formidable personality, composed of the virtues and failings with which he was born plus gifts from his mother that lasted his long journey through life: currents of tenderness and love, confidence in his singularity, and the glimmerings of a dream of the rebirth of Israel all combined in a mixture miraculously suited to his mission. So it seemed that when his mother died, her creation, so to speak, was complete.[2]

At the time of David-Joseph's birth there were just over four million Jews in imperial Russia, all confined to the Pale of Settlement, where, living in great poverty, they were forbidden certain occupations, including the liberal professions and commerce, and ownership of land. They found ways to commerce and farming through leasing franchises and freeholds from the landlords. Since the czarist government's policy was to keep Russia as free of Jews as possible, it delineated the Pale in such a way as to include only rural areas in western Russia and the Ukraine. Jews could live in the big Russian towns only by special permit, which was rarely granted. But the Pale did include all of Poland and its big towns. Whereas in Russia most Jews lived in small rural communities, in Poland they formed the majority in rural towns and cities alike. By 1905 there was a Jewish majority even in Warsaw.

In Płońsk, a subdistrict capital, Jews numbered forty-five hundred of a total population of seventy-nine hundred at the time David-Joseph was growing up. Płońsk's Jews supported themselves in tailoring and other craft workshops, breweries, flour mills, saw mills, and the like — all on a very small scale — bolstering their economy with a wholesale market in grain, timber, and farm produce. Despite all this and its proximity to the capital, Warsaw, 60 kilometers southeast, the town was isolated and self-enclosed. Travelers to and from Płońsk had to make do with horse-drawn wagons. By the time the Warsaw newspapers arrived, they were two days old.

At the time of David-Joseph's birth, Płońsk was at the peak of an economic boom. In 1862 there had been only 312 houses, most of them wooden, but by 1886 the number had risen to 361, of which 122 were in back-to-back terraces. Synagogue Street, on which two of Płońsk's four synagogues were located, was already cobbled, although it remained a dark and squalid alley with scattered holes that collected sewage. The buildings, usually two stories high, were supported by being built against each other, and the upper floors were further secured by wooden props.

Although there were two classes in Jewish Płońsk — the workers in the shops and the proprietors — there was hardly any real difference in wealth and standard of living; proprietors of tailoring workshops, for instance, worked side by side with their one or two employees from dawn to sundown. The Gruens, by virtue of Reb Avigdor's marriage to Sheindel, whose dowry consisted of some real estate, belonged to the proprietor class. The importance of the "class" difference despite (or most probably because of) the hardly noticeable economic disparity was borne out by Ben-Gurion's persistent claims that his family stood at the top of the proprietor class.

Several families in Płońsk shared the name Gruen, although no one knew if they were related to one another; neither Reb Avigdor nor any of the other Gruens could trace their ancestry much further back than one generation. While the majority of the Jews in Płońsk were Chassidim, Reb Avigdor's father, Zvi-Arie, was an extreme Mitnagged who regarded Chassidim and their rabbis as heathens. Driven by curiosity beyond the limits of Jewish Scriptures, he acquired some knowledge of the works of Socrates and Kant, as well as those of Rambam (Maimonides) and Ranak (Rabbi Nachman Krochmal, an early nineteenth-century philosopher and historian). At the age of thirty, Zvi-Arie had been a Hebrew teacher in Kuchary, a nearby town, and Płońsk; later he became a trader of sorts. He was never a property owner, and for about forty years he and his family were tenants in the house of a local notable. Toward the end of his life, he lodged in other rooms in Płock Street and finally moved in with his son Avigdor. He abandoned commerce, which had never favored him, to try his hand at something new: having a knowledge of Polish, German, and some Russian, he became "petition writer to government offices in general and to the courts in particular," writing legal documents such as permits and contracts of sale for the largely illiterate Polish farmers and peasants. He pursued this occupation until his death at the age of seventy-five.

For David-Joseph, his grandfather was next in importance to his mother. When the boy was three, Zvi-Arie sat him on his knees to teach him Hebrew. To the astonishment of the family, the child quickly learned the ancient tongue. Draping himself in a prayer shawl, he would launch forth into a sermon, aping his grandfather. In later years Ben-Gurion boasted that Hebrew, not the Yiddish used in the household, was his first language. The old man, who never failed to read the Bible before going to bed, bequeathed this habit to his grandson. From his grandfather David-Joseph thus inherited two of Zionism's precepts even before Zionism was founded: the love of Hebrew and the love of the Bible. Together these were the seeds of the love of Eretz Israel, the land of the forefathers. This accounts for Ben-Gurion's second boast, that he was born a Zionist.

*

Reb Avigdor, born June 26, 1857, the third and favorite of Zvi-Arie's four sons, referred to himself as his father's "spiritual heir." Zvi-Arie taught him languages and the skills of a petition writer; at twenty-one, Reb Avigdor was licensed to work on his own. Sheindel, the only daughter of David-Joseph Broitman, for whom Ben-Gurion was named, had, through dowry and inheritance, brought him her family's estate, which consisted of two houses and a large fruit orchard.

Compared with the two-story wooden houses in the town, Reb Avigdor's homestead appeared spacious. It was located at the far outskirts of town, next to the priest's orchard and a wall enclosing the Polish Catholic church. The family occupied only four of the downstairs rooms in the back house. The two remaining rooms on the ground floor were let to a ritual slaughterer. Upstairs, in what was little more than an attic, lived a couple who helped Reb Avigdor with the upkeep of the house and farm. The overcrowding lessened somewhat when David-Joseph was eleven and his elder brother Abraham married and moved to the front house facing the main gate, both floors of which had until then been let. The back house overlooked the orchard that stretched over three acres down to the banks of the river Płonka, for which the town was named. The courtyard opened onto an alley known as Kase Gessel, or the "goat track," a name expressing its former and sometimes present use.

From a tender age, David-Joseph saw his elders in close contact with the coarse, boorish country people. This in itself marked the family off from other Jews and contradicts Ben-Gurion's claim that his family was refined. The twice-weekly market days, when farmers and tradesmen flocked to town, were the most hectic for Zvi-Arie and his son. Their house teemed with strangers as well as local residents who sought advice or mediation and boisterously sealed their deals over a bottle or two of vodka. The working language was Polish, which at the time was known to only a few of the town's Jews. According to Ben-Gurion, Reb Avigdor had other business to attend to on these days as well: he used to let plots in his fields and orchards. Thus the picture Ben-Gurion painted of his father was that of a well-to-do landowner and sought-after lawyer.

Ben-Gurion stubbornly referred to his father and grandfather as "lawyers," and he stuck to this claim throughout his life: in 1912 on his application form to the law faculty in Istanbul, in 1918 on a questionnaire for the Labor Zionists in the United States; again on a questionnaire for his party in 1925; and finally in the several versions of his memoirs. It is certain, however, that Reb Avigdor was not a lawyer and could not conceivably have been one. There was no high school or yeshiva in Płonsk, not even in Ben-Gurion's day, and Reb Avigdor never studied elsewhere. Moreover, there was no law faculty in all of Poland when Reb Avigdor was a youth.

In point of fact, Reb Avigdor was a *Pokantny Doradca,* "corner advocate" in Polish. This was not a juridical title carrying with it special privileges; on the contrary, it contained a note of derision. That Reb Avigdor held himself up as a lawyer serves only to show how sensitive he was to its implications. To inflate his status, he sported a dashing appearance. Tall and lean, he was meticulously groomed, his clipped beard and mustache enhancing his handsome face. He dressed in stylish, tailored clothes, becoming one of the first Jews in Płońsk to abandon the traditional kaftan. The habits he acquired were fit for a man who had attained the rank of lawyer. Punctuality and discipline were his watchwords; he cut his daily quota of three cigarettes in half to give himself six smokes at precisely fixed times. Respectability, its pursuit and attainment, was the story of his life.[3]

Ben-Gurion also claimed that the local government offices and law courts sometimes commissioned Reb Avigdor to prepare documents and petitions for them. This made him a familiar figure to the government clerks, who were mostly Poles, and Reb Avigdor's status depended on the mood of the Polish magistrate. When he was in a good humor, he might allow Reb Avigdor to speak for a person who had trouble expressing himself or spoke a language the magistrate did not know. This would be a great day for Reb Avigdor, because he considered himself — and would perhaps be considered by others — to be a fully qualified lawyer pleading a case. For these occasions he donned a black gown over a snowy white waistcoat and wore a top hat.

Actually, the fact that Reb Avigdor rented out rooms suggests that petition writing left him struggling to make a living. In reality he had to hang around the magistrate's court touting for business. What is more, this familiarity had an effect exactly opposite from what he would have wished. Licenses and permits in czarist Russia, especially in governed Poland, were not issued strictly in accordance with regulations. Reb Avigdor had to flatter and bribe officials and justices; he participated in the conflicts between petitioners, who were quite capable of cheating on each other and then, when they were caught, claiming that Reb Avigdor had not written down what they had said; and he was in constant contact with peasants and with Russian and Polish officials who often behaved vulgarly and roughly. All this rubbed off on him and affected his behavior.[4]

Reb Avigdor was a Zionist, and since there was fanatical strife between Zionists and anti-Zionists in Płońsk, the anti-Zionists had extra cause to slander him: in making him out to be a scoundrel, they could discredit the Zionist movement as a whole. But even the Zionists spoke badly of him. Because he went about bareheaded, wore European-cut clothes, and enjoyed the literature of the Enlightenment, his entire household was suspected of "wantonness." He was charged with regularly holding card parties in his home. (To the Orthodox, card playing was sinful, a sign of bad character.) Others said he was willful and given to fits of anger. The story was told that one Sabbath in synagogue, he struck David-Joseph in the face for not taking part in the Torah reading; another story claimed that Reb Avigdor had once bought a live fish in the market and, with his fingers stuck in its eye sockets, carried it home still twitching, as if purposely to antagonize those to whom such a sight was objectionable.

Shlomo Zemach, Ben-Gurion's lifelong good friend and bitter rival, recounted that his father slapped him for visiting David-Joseph in his home and forbade him to go there again because of the card playing. Ben-Gurion maintained that the real reason for this ban was Reb Avigdor's Zionism, for Zemach's father was opposed to the nascent movement. But despite his vehement denials, there is incontrovertible evidence that Ben-Gurion did learn to play cards in his father's house. Reb Avigdor was evidently not in the first rank of Płońsk's community leaders, and his uphill struggle to win respect affected David-Joseph deeply; he felt bound to protect his father's honor. In Ben-Gurion's memory, Reb Avigdor was always one of the founders and leaders of Zionism in Płońsk, as well as one of the town's notables. Although the first claim is accurate, the second was unsubstantiated.

Sometimes David-Joseph's father would take him up to the ark in the New Synagogue and show him the beautifully carved wooden decorations, the citron, palm, and fruits of Eretz Israel, and tell him about the land of their fathers. One day David-Joseph said to him, "But these aren't real. I want to see the real ones, the ones in Eretz Israel." He had sensed the excitement surrounding the birth of Zionism.

Among the first words the child heard was Zion, amid discussions about the funds necessary to revive it, for he was raised in a seething atmosphere of furious arguments among the adherents of Hibbat Zion, "Love of Zion," a movement begun in 1882 by a group of Russian Jews who after the terrible pogrom of that year had left to settle in Palestine.

Hibbat Zion, the precursor of organized, political Zionism established by Theodor Herzl, developed into a movement, with branches all over imperial Russia, that expressed both the longing of the members for the land of the forefathers and their aspiration to return there one day to renew their life as an independent nation. The more difficult and oppressive life became in Russia, the more Hibbat Zion's tenets took hold among the more enlightened lay Jews in Russia — so much so that their yearning to flee the Russian hell turned into an expectation that a messiah of sorts would suddenly rise from their midst to show them the way to their redemption in Eretz Israel.

The Płońsk Hibbat Zion society was founded in 1890 by Reb Avigdor and his close friend Reb Simcha Isaac. Without understanding the substance of the arguments, David-Joseph absorbed the Zionist dream pervading his home. The first aspect he observed was the fervent collecting of money. No brith, engagement, wedding, or other celebration took place without his father and his friends' appearing to gather contributions. David's brother Abraham became a star in this field. Ten years David's senior, Abraham was small, puny, humpbacked, a deformity no one in the family acknowledged, and devoutly Orthodox. Without regular work, and with a father who supplied all his needs, Abraham had all the time in the world for religion and Zionism. In his long kaftan, he would rush from one celebrating household to another, darting among the wedding guests, rattling his collection box, and delivering an impassioned speech to anyone who paused to listen. At his own wedding party the guests contributed 2.27 rubles — a small sum — to the Płońsk Hovevei Zion, "Lovers of Zion," who, through the good offices of *Hamelitz,* a Russian Hebrew newspaper, passed on the money to the Odessa Committee, the headquarters of Hibbat Zion, which sent it to Palestine "for the benefit of the workers in the Holy Land." Somewhat puzzled, David-Joseph asked his father to explain why funds for Eretz Israel went first to Odessa. He thought the money should go directly to Eretz Israel.[5]

One day during prayers in the New Synagogue, he overheard something that cast an immediate and binding spell on him. It was 1896, the year Theodor Herzl's *The Jewish State* was published. From the excited talk he gathered that a messiah had appeared, "a miraculous man, head and shoulders taller than other men, with beautiful features and a luminous face adorned by a long black beard . . . in a certain foreign town a messiah named Herzl had arrived." Ben-Gurion remembered this episode all his life, and he repeated his account of it time and again, always in the same words, as if it was a melody he loved to hear.

This unforgettable event lighted up a vision for his own life — that he was destined to be the messiah's alter ego, a second Herzl. This conviction was not supported solely by his mother's singling him out and by her abiding faith in his future. Eight years later, when he was studying in Warsaw in 1904, an inquiry into the meaning of "the Chosen People" and "the Choice of Israel" inspired him to probe the role of the individual who is "chosen." According to the young Ben-Gurion, the "chosen" is not someone on whom greatness falls haphazardly; he

is rather one who while still in the womb is destined for a great mission
and blessed with the gifts necessary to carry it out. Writing to a friend,
he explained,

> God or nature (for our purposes it's one and the same, whichever is the
> true power) endows the genius with sublime talents, not out of love for
> him, but from a desire to bestow upon the world sublime creations . . . He
> brings into existence an intermediary . . . with the power to give such
> creations to the world. I trust in the future ahead of me; in my imagina-
> tion I see it outlined, magnificent and brilliant; great and sublime dreams.
> I dream of my future work (not for my own benefit). . . . I have deep long-
> ings for something but I don't know what this something is.

How he was to accomplish his dream he did not yet know, but there
was no doubt in his mind that he would do it in Palestine for the Zionist cause. Only after he had gone there, in 1906, did his ambition become well defined: to become a Zionist labor leader. But by then he
had learned how to hide it and to pretend he was following the movement's orders, and not the dictates of his heart.

As late as 1918 Ben-Gurion refused to divulge his specific ambition
and continued to refer to it in generalities and abstractions, even to his
closest kin and friends. He informed his new bride, Paula, that he knew
she was "capable of suffering with me for some great cause" and promised her that she would ascend beside him, "in tears and torment, a
lofty mountain from where a new world can be seen . . . a world of
sublime happiness . . . to which only the few shall be admitted." After
this he never again spoke directly about his own destiny or ambitions,
but in his writings, in his speeches, essays, and slogans — as a labor
leader, later as the chairman of the Jewish Agency, and finally as prime
minister of Israel — the linking of the destiny, vision, and mission of an
individual with those of a generation and a people is repeated countless
times.

Whether the ten-year-old David-Joseph already had a glimpse of his
destiny on the day he first heard about Herzl, or whether it actually
appeared to him later, what is important is that Ben-Gurion was
moved to antedate his awareness of his "task" to the earliest possible
age. Thus he saw himself as a Zionist from birth, as someone who had
made all his fateful resolutions while still on the threshold of life. "I
drank in the dream of Eretz Israel with my mother's milk."[6] When the
Płońsk Zionists elected their delegate to the second World Zionist
Congress in Basel at the end of August 1898, David-Joseph was inspired to persuade his cheder friends to save a kopeck a week from
their pocket money, so that after forty weeks they could purchase one
"shekel" — an emblem of membership — apiece to join their local
Zionist society. The project failed, since according to Zionist regula-

tions no one under eighteen was eligible for the shekel. Nonetheless Ben-Gurion later came to see in this childhood scheme the beginnings of his Zionist activity.

Time and again Ben-Gurion claimed that in speaking of his mother he was speaking of all mothers. Her very facelessness encouraged his failing to differentiate the individual from the abstraction, his living mother from his idealized one. This habit was most pronounced when he referred to a mother, whether offering condolences to a friend or addressing the Knesset on women's rights; it was always his own abstract mother whom he had in mind. But it also displayed itself when he dealt with national issues. This identification of the particular with the idealized abstraction lay behind his feeling, never explicitly expressed, that he and the Zionist movement, or he and the Jewish people, were one and the same. It was a trait that made him remote, not only in political matters but in private affairs as well, and especially in his relations with his wife. For him she was not so much Paula as Wife and Mother; he adored her, not only for herself, but for her role. Yet while this characteristic bedeviled his personal life, it was to be a major asset in his political career.

Płońsk's entire educational system was the cheder at its various levels. Ben-Gurion always said that his schooling in Płońsk comprised five cheders and one compulsory class in Russian. All he could remember about these, he said, was that two of the five were "reformed" or "modern," that is, they taught Bible and Hebrew grammar in Hebrew, not in Yiddish, as was done elsewhere. His memoirs contain little reference to his school life, because Ben-Gurion disclosed only what he wanted to. Most of what is known of his cheder days has come from other sources.

Five-year-old David-Joseph began his school career — a year later than he should have because of his sickliness — in a cheder run by his father's tenant Reb Aron Meir Grossman, a few steps from home, in which numerous children were crammed together with the teacher and his family. Every Sunday the teacher assigned a new portion of the Bible to be learned during the week, but David-Joseph knew it thoroughly the very same day.

At seven, David-Joseph went to his second cheder, Reb Kroll's, for just a year. Reb Feivel Oppenheim, his third teacher, took only a few pupils, and on Fridays he taught Bible and Hebrew grammar, a novelty that made his cheder "modern." Feivel's family lived in two rooms, one of which was used just for the cheder during the day. This classroom was spacious, quite clean, and noteworthy for the absence of the rabbi's wife and children. Reb Feivel was soft-spoken, a happy surprise for his pupils, who were used to shouting and uproar in cheders. The fourth cheder was conducted by Rabbi Shmuel-Joseph Lask, who had come from a large town to Płońsk. He had only one child, an important advantage because it meant peace and quiet during his lessons, which were held in one of the rooms where he lodged in the center of town. His was the other "modern" cheder.

The government Russian class was part of the Russianization policy in Poland, meant to ward off Polish nationalism. All cheder children, including girls, had to attend. Four grades were taught simultaneously: beginners in the front rows, intermediates in the middle ones, and advanced pupils at the back. The children had to participate in official celebrations such as the czar's birthday, so David-Joseph found himself singing, in Russian, "God Save the Emperor." Still, Ben-Gurion not only mentioned but commended this phase of his schooling. First he noted that learning Russian was entirely to his liking because "since my childhood I had resolved not to stay in Poland and therefore it was not necessary to waste my time learning Polish, for which I should clearly have no use when I grew up, so I was content to study Hebrew and Russian." Second, he praised the outstanding novelty of this class, the presence of girls. Here David-Joseph found his first love. In 1904, at eighteen, he wrote, "I was only a child of twelve, but I already knew love . . . my love was a soft spring bud. In time it grew and burst into flower — last summer I discovered that she loved me too." She was nine-year-old Rachel Nelkin, the stepdaughter of Reb Simcha Isaac.[7]

From the age of eleven until his bar mitzvah, David-Joseph studied with Reb Itzik Silberstein. This fifth cheder, held in the *beit hamidrash*, "study room," of the New Synagogue, was really more a Talmud study group than a cheder. It was there that David-Joseph met Shlomo Zemach, who was his bench mate. Płońsk's lack of a yeshiva meant that his schooling came to an end on his bar mitzvah, when David was thirteen. (And, as was customary, his double name disappeared at the same time.) The only higher education available in Płońsk existed in the person of Reb Tuvia Krieger, who taught Talmud at a scholarly level. Zemach called him "the oldest and wisest sage in Płońsk" and said he took very few students, no more than "three or four of the very best youths." Zemach studied with Reb Tuvia, but David did not. Was he considered less able? Zemach said he was. "David was never an outstanding logical thinker and that is why he dropped out of beit hamidrash. He could not cope with the abstractions of Talmudic dialogue." In fact the Płońsk beit hamidrash was not an exclusive club open only to the brilliant, and David was as capable as any other boy of learning Talmud. Why, then, was he not among Reb Krieger's pupils?

It was certainly not from distaste for further learning, because in

1901 Reb Avigdor wrote to Herzl about his "most diligent and excellent son" who was avid for knowledge but barred from all Warsaw schools by the *numerus clausus,* "quota system." David might have gone westward, to Germany for example, where there were no restrictions and where a large colony of Jewish students from eastern Europe had already gathered. The reason he did not appears in the latter part of the letter, in which Reb Avigdor asks Herzl for financial help so that David can attend the Israelitisch-Theologische Lehrnanstalt, the rabbinical seminary in Vienna, explaining, "I cannot support my own son, the apple of my eye." It appears that, at least from 1900 to 1904, Reb Avigdor was not even moderately well-to-do. This may be why David did not study with Reb Tuvia, whose tuition was very expensive; Zemach attested to his exceptionally high fees. This means that the myth Ben-Gurion later created about himself — that he did not study Talmud in his youth because it represented Jewish life in the Diaspora — unlike the Bible, which represented Jewish independence in its homeland, and which he loved — had no foundation. Advanced Talmud study was out of David's reach only because his father could not afford it.

Ben-Gurion's lack of even Jewish higher education may explain the cursory reference to his school days in his memoirs. But there is another likely explanation. In 1915 he forged a matriculation diploma from a Russian gymnasium in Poltava, a town he never set eyes on, to gain entry to the law faculty in Istanbul. This, he believed, discredited him, and he kept it secret throughout his life. The less known about his school career, the safer his shameful secret. In fact, he recorded nothing of the years 1900 to 1904, when he was fourteen to eighteen. What did David do in those "missing years"? He had completed his cheder studies and it is certain that he did not study elsewhere; Herzl had not seen fit to answer Reb Avigdor's letter.

To this question Ben-Gurion would give only a partial answer, one of which he was proud. In those years, he wrote in his memoirs, he was fully occupied with "Ezra." Fourteen-year-old David and his friends Shlomo Zemach and Shmuel Fox, both from wealthy, respected families, came to an extraordinary decision: to form a Zionist youth society named after Ezra the Scribe, the spiritual leader of the return to Zion from the Babylonian exile, bringing the wrath of the Chassidim down on them with full force. In the eyes of the Chassidim Zionism was tantamount to heresy, that is, interfering with the ways of the Lord. Their logic was that if the Lord so wished, the Jews would be returned to Zion just as they had been exiled from it. On the eve of Chanukah in December 1900, the three friends gathered about thirty boys in the beit hamidrash to discuss the society and its aims. They did not incite their followers to abandon Torah or its commmandments. "To remain within the people and to work for them" was their slogan. Even so, the doors to the hall suddenly burst open and about twenty young Chassidim rushed in. The light went out and there was a free-for-all.[8]

Ezra's primary aim was to teach the boys to speak Hebrew. They all swore to speak nothing but that language, and David, Zemach, and Fox actually did it. Their first step was to approach the students in the Talmud Torah, where children of less fortunate Jews studied. Ezra members asked the parents — porters, water carriers, and poor tailors — for permission to teach their children written Hebrew and Bible between prayer times, but the recruiting efforts were not wholly successful. More than once parents ambushed their children while they were talking with Ezra boys, scolding them for mixing with "goyim" and "criminals." Nevertheless, Ezra managed to assemble a few score of poor children for an hour and a half a day, teaching them to speak, read, and write correct Hebrew. Within a year the society had one hundred and fifty members; Ezra became a legend in Płońsk. In the wake of the Passover pogroms at Kishinev in Russia in 1903, Ezra boys went all over Płońsk to collect money for the victims.

David became Ezra's secretary and its moving spirit, guiding it along the lines of any other Zionist group, with membership dues and its own hectographed Hebrew publication. The editors were "Fox, Zemach, and David," whose writings completely filled the first and only issue. David first tried his hand at story writing but, realizing immediately that he had no talent for prose, switched to poetry. Fox's outspoken criticism persuaded him to stop that, too.

In contrast, Zemach's efforts received encouragement from the editor of the Hebrew paper *Ha-Zefirah* (The Dawn) in Warsaw. This paper, the principal organ of Polish Jewry, was edited by Nahum Sokolow and provided opportunities for new writers. Zemach had mailed it his first literary production, an essay on the Kishinev pogrom. Sokolow returned the manuscript with a note in his own hand encouraging Zemach to keep on writing, since he had in him "the holy spark of authors." Zemach's friends were awed by this "recognition" by the great Sokolow, and needless to say, it aroused David's jealousy.

Active as Ezra was, offering an outlet for David's imagination, energy, ambition, and organizing ability, its activities could not have occupied him for more than two or three hours a day, and then only in the late afternoon and early evening; the apprentices and poor youths whom he taught would have been working during the day. What did he do mornings and afternoons? Undoubtedly he read: literature, poetry, and science, anything he could lay his hands on. In Hebrew, he read the prose of Isaac Leib Peretz, Peretz Smolenskin, and Abraham

Mapu; the poetry of Judah Leib Gordon; and the essays of Ahad Ha'am. He read all of Berdichevsky — essays, satires, and novels, but the essays impressed him most and he counted himself one of Berdichevsky's fervent admirers. In his Russian reading he admired Turgenev, Dostoyevsky, and Tolstoy. The two books that left "formidable impressions" on him were *The Love of Zion* by Mapu and *Uncle Tom's Cabin,* which he read in Hebrew. Tolstoy's *Resurrection* moved him to take a vow, which he later broke, never to eat meat.[9]

Is it credible that, as Ben-Gurion's memoirs suggest, David occupied himself for four years solely with Ezra and voracious reading? While Zemach learned German in addition to his Talmudic studies, other Ezra boys had to work for a living, helping their fathers. This is likely to have been David's fate, too, especially since his father could not afford for him to study. Between 1900 and 1904 Reb Avigdor's lot was not a very happy one. He was burdened with an elderly, unmarried daughter, Rivka, a somewhat simple son, Michael, who got in his way and was fit only to run errands, and hunchbacked Abraham, who, although married, devoted all his time to religion and Zionism because he, too, was unable to earn a living. His five children, his younger stepdaughter, and his wife all depended on Reb Avigdor.

The fact that in none of his writings did Ben-Gurion let one word slip as to what he did in these missing years makes it reasonable to speculate that he, too, worked with his father, helping him write petitions. Just as his father had learned the skills from Zvi-Arie, so David acquired them from Reb Avigdor. If so, we may visualize him thus between 1900 and 1904: pale and delicate in a long, somber kaftan, traipsing about with his father to government offices and the magistrates' court, his pen, ink, and sheaf of papers stuffed into the capacious pockets of the kaftan.

The other possibility, that he was apprenticed to a craftsman, seems most improbable. Reb Avigdor would have been too proud to allow even his eldest son to learn a trade, so he would certainly not have sentenced the apple of his eye to the inglorious future of a tailor. What is more, had Ben-Gurion learned a craft it is very likely that he would later have made much of it to present himself as an authentic labor leader recalling his proletarian youth. It is fair to speculate that he clung so stubbornly to his claim that his father and grandfather were fully qualified lawyers because he had started out on their path; he could no more admit the truth about them than he could about himself. Without saying it in so many words, he depicted himself as having been a lawyer from the cradle, for this was the occupation he aspired to in adult life, the profession he chose as a springboard to his political career.

David's personality, talents, and ambitions caused him to be singled out from his friends. This boy — whose pale skin never tanned but only reddened under the summer sun, who had honey-colored curly hair, large brown-green eyes that looked at and through people at the same time, a wide thin mouth underlined by a chin that would become square and heavyset, and a nose neither large nor crooked but not quite straight — despite his slight build and generally fragile appearance was driven by tremendous energy and an incessant flow of ideas about what to do, where to go, and what to achieve. He already had a presence others took into account, which made older boys hold their tongue when he was speaking. He read much more than others and could render an informed opinion.

Fox, his elder by a year and a half, said he was "a leader who showed me a new way" and claimed that he had known from the beginning of their acquaintance that David "was destined to greatness." Shlomo Lavi, David's childhood friend, said the same in his autobiography. Even so it was not easy for David, the youngest of the three friends, to compete in their rivalry for Ezra's leadership. Fox, the eldest, modeled himself on Maxim Gorky's characters — barefoot, nonconformist, and rebellious — dressing and acting like them. David admired him and nicknamed him "the barefoot boy," but before long Fox returned to the fold. In May 1904, before leaving Warsaw for London, he posed with David for a farewell photograph. Sporting a thick, drooping mustache, Fox wore a conventional suit and assumed a mature and complacent expression. In striking contrast, David looked more like his son than a friend: not yet ready to shave, bony, swamped in clothes several sizes too big for him. Next to Fox's apparent self-confidence, David seemed unsure of himself, intense, wide-eyed with bewilderment, not unlike Charlie Chaplin's tramp.

Shlomo Zemach was considered aristocratic in looks as well as in lineage. His Chassidic family was by far the wealthiest in Płońsk. Shlomo's father, Abba Zemach, a merchant in timber, wool, and grain, objected to his son's Zionism for both religious and personal reasons; he wanted Shlomo to continue the family tradition of combining rabbinical scholarship and business. No other family enjoyed ancestors as illustrious, not only in Płońsk but throughout eastern Europe. The Zemach clan could trace its ancestry as far back as the seventeenth century, to Chaim ha-Levi, father of the genius Reb Abraham Abele Gombiner, one of the great scholars, the author of *Magen Abraham* (Dyhernfurth, 1692), a commentary on the *Shulchan Arukh*, a Judaic code still in use.

The town was full of reminders of the Zemach wealth: the beit ha-midrash for the town's prosperous Jews was founded by the family, and the government Russian class was held in a building they owned. Had

David wanted to rival his friend in Hebrew or Zionism, he would have had to compete with the prestige Shlomo acquired from having translated Moses Hess's *Rome and Jerusalem*. Little wonder that David was jealous of Zemach's beauty, wealth, and lineage. He liked to describe the time in his youth when Shlomo's father lost all his money and retrieved some of his past glory thanks only to a stroke of good luck in a lottery. "A quarter share in the 75,000 ruble lottery and he was rich again," wrote Ben-Gurion. In one version of his memoirs he mentions the elder Zemach's impoverishment and subsequent recovery three times on one page. Shlomo, on the other hand, envied the boy whose father was a petition writer, whose family boasted not a single rabbi, and who, although thin, weak, unattractive, and lacking in social grace, nevertheless had much more influence on their peers. Their rivalry was to last their entire lives.[10]

It is clear that not even a ripple from the wave of revolutionary fervor sweeping across Russia in those years reached Płońsk. In other Jewish communities, in the northwest and south of czarist Russia, societies were organized one after another, their names typically including the words *worker, guard,* and *new*. Their members were all followers of Marx, Plekhanov, and Martov. The Jewish Bund organized Jewish trade unions to hoist the banner of socialist revolution all over the Pale of Settlement, including Poland. But in Płońsk, where socialism was as yet unknown, the local youth founded Ezra. Nor was the social and political unrest in Poland, caused by resurgent nationalism, of much interest to the three Ezra friends, who were tied, body and soul, to Zionism.

In August 1903 Herzl brought before the Zionist congress in Basel his scheme to bring the more than one hundred fifty thousand refugees of the Passover pogroms to Uganda. There they would wait until Zionist diplomacy succeeded in obtaining from the Turkish sultan a charter that secured Palestine for Jewish colonization. Then the "overnight shelter" in Uganda, as Herzl called it, would be closed down and all its occupants would flock to the open gates of Zion.

On hearing of the Uganda scheme, David, Zemach, and Fox "wept bitterly," Ben-Gurion remembered. They identified themselves with the "Zion Zionists," who opposed Herzl at the congress and defeated him in the vote on the Uganda issue. For the three friends there was no "interim solution," not for a year, a month, or even a single day. They took an oath to go to Eretz Israel as soon as they could. Fox was the first to depart. In the summer of 1904 he set off for London to prepare himself, he solemnly said, for the right employment in Eretz Israel. Six months later, like many thousands of his brethren, he sailed, not to Palestine, but to the United States, where he became a dentist and lived in

Brooklyn to a ripe old age. At the end of 1904 Zemach became the second to leave. Unlike Fox he went directly to Palestine, where he became a farm hand. He was not only the first of the three to keep his oath, but also the first member of Ezra — and in fact the first of all the Zionists in Płońsk — to fulfill the Zionist commandment in his own person. David, then and later, found it hard to swallow Zemach's being there ahead of him and taking first place among Płońsk's Zionists.[11]

2

Warsaw

IN THE spring of 1904 David was living in Warsaw, preparing for
the entrance examination to a Jewish engineering school. His resolve to go to Warsaw seems, at least in retrospect, to have been
one of the many self-imposed decisions intended to steel his character
and will power and thereby shield himself from his emotional vulnera-
bility. He had made many such decisions before going to Warsaw, but
this was his chance to put them to the test. For example, his resolve not
to touch meat was so important to him that his first letter to Fox from
Warsaw gave the happy news that he had abstained for more than a
fortnight, "and I'm confident that I shall abstain from it in the future."
He vowed not to take financial help from his father and was so adamant that to keep this resolution he had to break another one: not to
earn his living by teaching.

To Ben-Gurion will power was man's sublime quality. His eulogy on
Theodor Herzl's death, in an August 1904 letter to Fox and Ezra members, reveals this. David compared Herzl's qualities to similar gifts in
others. In his judgment, Herzl had the heroism of the Maccabees, the
cunning of King David, the courage of Rabbi Akiva, the humility of
Hillel, the beauty of Yehuda Hanassi, the ardor of Yehuda ha-Levi; but
he found no human parallel for Herzl's will power. He credited Herzl
with "divine will power — the will power of the Gods." Given this belief, forging his own will power was essential if he was to act on a
"grand scale." He had decided that this ambition could best be fulfilled
through large-scale engineering activity in Eretz Israel — founding industries, constructing roads, bridges, and railways, establishing settlements and towns, and a great variety of other important projects. He
actually doubted that he had any aptitude for engineering. But through
will power, he believed, he could overcome this drawback. He was de-

termined, therefore, to be accepted in the engineering school "come what may." To Fox he swore, "I shall not budge from this aim."

David had intended to begin his studies in Warsaw in the fall of 1903. But in the summer of that year he was again in love with Rachel Nelkin. In Płońsk she was first called "the beautiful Rachel," and later simply "the beautiful Płońsker." Her stepfather, Reb Simcha Isaac, the leader of Płońsk's Zionists, allowed the living room at the back of his grocery to be used for Ezra meetings, and there Rachel and David saw each other regularly. She was thirteen, a tall, lissome, dark beauty with brown eyes. He, seventeen, disclosed his feelings to her, and when she told him she loved him too he had, he wrote to Shmuel Fox, a glimpse of paradise. Her words were "a source of life, an inspiration, a faith, a spring of eternal youth, and a soul of my soul."

Until midwinter he was the picture of happiness. Then the question "Am I really in love?" forced itself upon him and gave him no peace. Suddenly he became wretched. "My feelings scorched me," he wrote Fox the following summer, "and my soul was so troubled that time and again I was awake all night sobbing; I had realized that I could not stay in Płońsk any longer." For staying there, waiting for his beloved to grow up, meant eventually marrying and living out his life in his home-town, just like his brothers. David therefore had to weigh his ambitions against his love for Rachel; in this conflict ambition triumphed.[1]

David had arrived in Warsaw in spring 1904 and found lodgings in the heart of the Jewish quarter with a tailor's family. Almost penniless, he shared a room with two Płońsk students. But he managed to scrounge up enough money to acquire a European-style outfit, set off by a straw hat, to take the place of his Płońsk kaftan. This apparel was so daring that he could not gather the courage to show it off on his first visit home. He probably borrowed money for the farewell photos he had taken, first with Fox and then with other friends who immigrated to the United States. He quickly amassed debts of about twenty rubles.

True to his word not to take money from his father, he determined to become self-supporting by giving private Hebrew lessons. But students were not easy to come by, and until June he was in a perilous state. This, however, did not dampen his spirit: "I continued to believe in myself and in my strength." Salvation came when a friend who was immigrating to the United States bequeathed to David his position as Hebrew teacher in a Jewish school that was little more than a glorified cheder. David earned twenty rubles a month, out of which he spent only fourteen, so he was able to pay off some of his debts. He looked for better lodgings and changed his rooms in quick succession before fi-nally settling down with the Fernbuch family, who had a spacious apartment and two fine daughters. The younger, Jenny, took David's fancy, and he brought her with him on one of his visits to Płońsk. Except for the Fernbuchs, David had no friends in Warsaw, for all the others had sailed to America by July 1904. "The heart explodes with loneliness," he wrote to Fox.

David's reactions to his friends' departures were extreme. After saying good-bye to Fox at the railway station, David was gripped by so much emotion that he could not speak; he stood on the platform watching until the train was out of sight. Then, unlike Fox's other friends, who went about their usual business, he returned to his room feeling "as isolated as if I had been abandoned on a remote, uninhabited island." Finding no comfort in reading or thought, he rushed about visiting relatives, seeking distraction from his pain. This, too, failed, so he returned to his room to write a letter to Fox's brother, telling him all about Shmuel. Then he remembered that he had no money for a stamp, so he delivered the letter by hand. At last he borrowed some money, bought a new hat, took the train to the station nearest to Płońsk, and from there drove in a horse and wagon to his "aunt."

All that evening and the whole of the next day he poured out his heart to his family, until he could calm down a little and was able to return to Warsaw. A day or two went by and still no telegram had reached Fox's parents confirming that his passage, on a forged passport, had gone smoothly. Beside himself with anxiety, David ran back to his lodgings four times in one day to see if there was a letter from his friend. Not finding one, he repeatedly inquired of Fox's travel agent for news. Then he wrote to Fox, "You will never be able to imagine the fear which your long silence caused me; terrible thoughts filled our hearts every time we saw that there was no news from you."[2]

With Fox gone, Shlomo Zemach became David's only friend. Even though Zemach had remained in Płońsk, David made every effort to see him often. On November 20, 1904, on his way back from a resort town, Zemach made a detour to visit David in his room in Warsaw. There he confided for the first time his plan to go to Eretz Israel. Again David, thrown off balance, was unable to think clearly; he remembered that after receiving this news, letters poured from his pen "in a lunatic flow." If possible, his agitation was twice as great as when Fox had left him, because Zemach had told him that in going to Palestine he was defying his parents. On his way to Warsaw to pay some bills for his father, he had realized that he could use such money, the next time his father gave him a large enough amount, to finance his journey. Having resolved to do this, he was awaiting the first opportunity.

On December 6 David went to Płońsk for three days to help Zemach prepare for his trip and returned to Warsaw on December 9 to clarify certain travel details. Listing the things he did to help Zemach, Ben-Gurion portrayed himself as an accomplice to both the plan and its execution. On December 12 the opportunity arose. Zemach pocketed 580 rubles, with which he was supposed to settle one of his father's accounts, and hid in David's quarters. The following midnight he was on his way to Kraków, where he was to pick up an Austrian passport, and then to the port of Trieste to board the ship sailing for Jaffa.

After Zemach had gone, David, in a state of violent excitement, was stricken for more than a week with headaches and spells of faintness and finally collapsed into bed. He actually left a letter from Fox unopened, summoning up the strength to deal with it only thirty-three days later. On December 18 his hysteria reached such a pitch that he was rushed to a doctor. The prescribed treatment did nothing to help, and the doctor advised him to take two weeks' holiday in Płońsk. So on January 8, 1905, he went home. If anger with his friend for causing him the pain of loss or for getting to Eretz Israel first had brought on David's distress, the doctor gave poor advice. In Płońsk David had to face the admiration Zemach's clandestine, if not criminal, departure had aroused in Ezra. To add insult to injury, Zemach's daring was the talk of the town. It took ten days at home to restore David to good health; on his return to Warsaw he had a relapse.

A letter he wrote to Fox reveals his reaction to Zemach's feat. "Shlomo became the hero of the day and everybody, without exception . . . praised and revered him for his tremendous daring and his passionate love for his people," it began. But a clear note of jealousy crept into what followed. "Yes, there are some who achieve fame overnight." David also sneers at Zemach's mother.

> She can already see her son Shleiml a graduate of the agricultural college . . . and later of the Paris Academy and then the manager of all the settlements in Eretz Israel, with a salary of 10,000 francs per annum — no more, no less — for who could compare with her son Shleiml, a Hebrew scholar, a great idealist, an important manager. You cannot imagine the impression which his journey, and even more so his letters, are having on the young . . . It seems to me that he has halted immigration to America and turned it toward Palestine.

He then listed the friends who had determined to go to Palestine as a result.

Thanks to this one deed, Zemach was far out in front in their contest for leadership, and David was in a quandary: he had to explain to himself why Zemach, born into a Chassidic family, the son of an anti-Zionist, had picked himself up and gone to Eretz Israel whereas he, the son of a Zionist leader, stayed home. David's first answer was that by preparing for the engineering school in Warsaw, he was readying himself for a more significant role in Eretz Israel. "Had it not been for this aspiration," he wrote to Fox, "to work in our country on a *grand scale*, I would long ago have given up the idea of graduating from any college." But this self-justification could not withstand his own scrutiny, for as he knew full well his academic plans were uncertain. Therefore he came up with another one. "If I had had the wherewithal I would have made the journey this very winter," he wrote to Fox. But the fact was that other Ezra friends had made their way to Palestine, and not all of them were rich like Zemach. Indeed, Płońsk was never the same after Zemach's journey, which encouraged a continuous flow of immigration to Zion.[3]

Two traits in David's character emerged from this drama. One was his deep emotional dependence on his friends. His devastation over the loss of Zemach, which after all was expected to be only temporary, was such that he must have wondered how he would get through life if he did not manage to dull his extreme sensitivity. The other was his jealousy, so powerful that it could, given free rein, warp his memory and distort events beyond recognition. This is exactly what happened concerning a meeting David had with Zemach's father just before Zemach left. An earlier version of this meeting appears in a letter to Fox of December 14, 1904.

David related that Abba Zemach had become suspicious when his son did not return home to Warsaw on December 12 or the following morning. In the afternoon he set off for David's lodgings, arriving there in the evening. At that moment David was closeted in another room with his friend. "I went upstairs and found [Abba Zemach] sitting in my room," he said. "He talked calmly, with no visible signs of emotion. You can guess our conversation. I told him that Shlomo had already left. I don't know whether or not he believed me, but he didn't come back and it's certain he returned to Płońsk." In time this recollection underwent a profound change. Congratulating Zemach on his seventy-fifth birthday in 1961, Ben-Gurion, for no apparent reason, mentioned the meeting, adding that Abba Zemach had "implored me to bring the two of you together. When I hesitated, afraid to comply, he fell on his knees, clutching my legs and sobbing. I felt as though I would explode with sorrow and shame — Abba Zemach begging for pity from a boy my age."

Zemach was cut to the quick. It was most improbable that a proud, noble man like his father would have fallen on his knees to anyone, let alone a boy like David, and it was inconceivable that a man as pious as his father would abase himself except before God. To do so would have been tantamount to idol worship, the gravest of all sins. Nevertheless Ben-Gurion stuck to his story, and the older he grew the more distorted it became. He didn't admit his error until 1972, when he was eighty-six and had read the earlier version published in the first volume of his letters. On a visit to Zemach, who was convalescing from a heart attack, he apologized and asked for forgiveness. "You live in my memory forever as a handsome young man . . . my childhood friend, my beloved, my soul mate . . . brothers we are," wrote Ben-Gurion afterward. Zemach replied, "Brothers we are, the two of us . . . with a perfect love."[4]

So Zemach left David to his bitter struggle to enter the engineering school. Besides earning enough to keep body and soul together, he had to pay for private tutoring, without which he had no hope of passing the tough examination. He planned to take it in May of 1905, but this plan was shattered in September 1904, when the Jewish engineering school decided to admit Gentiles. This halved his chances, and he still had to face the fierce competition from the other Jewish candidates. His prospects had diminished to a point where he began to think of packing up for Eretz Israel, but instead he lowered his sights to a private three-year technological institute that offered three engineering courses. Unfortunately, only students under the age of seventeen were accepted, and his nineteenth birthday was approaching. He therefore did the commonly accepted thing: with his father's help he produced a new birth certificate, recording his birth date as February 18, 1887. Armed with it, he was very hopeful and announced to Fox, "I shall certainly be accepted."

Again he crammed math, physics, and Russian. But when his health deteriorated after Zemach's departure he lost this opportunity, too, and again focused on the engineering school. At the beginning of January 1905, beset by disappointments, frustrations, and premonitions about his uncertain future and torn between his vow to become an engineer and his desire to go immediately to Palestine, he succumbed to a series of illnesses and pains. His symptoms were similar to those of soldier's heart syndrome — anxiety neurosis — pain in the chest, high blood pressure, rapid pulse, and headaches. In his distress he wrote more often to Fox, his only real confidant. Unable to understand his sudden misery, David resumed his earlier habit of copying out Bialik's poems and even tried writing some of his own about the "uproar" in his heart and "a feeling of despair more terrible than death." In an effort to throw off his gloom he poured all his energies into forming a young Zionists' group in Warsaw that he ran feverishly until, after a recurrence of his symptoms, he was cast into black despair by his inability to achieve any of his aims.[5]

One event in Warsaw marked David forever: he witnessed the eruption of the 1905 revolution, which began with a railway strike at noon on Friday, January 27. Roaming the streets, David watched long lines of people waiting to stock up on essentials, noting that prices of kerosene, sugar, candles, and other basics had soared, and observed grim-faced workers preparing to meet the approaching storm. On Saturday the twenty-eighth the uprising began. Nearly everyone was out on the streets; at the huge demonstration in Zamkowa Place, where Government House stood, David saw the mob's attacks on the government buildings and watched while revolutionary agitators uprooted lamp-posts and screamed at the crowds about government despotism toward the hungry workers. Before long the streets were swarming with infantry and cavalry, the police shooting over people's heads.

On Sunday, January 29, David went out to learn about events elsewhere in Russia and Poland, moving from crowd to crowd, listening to the news. Suddenly Cossack cavalrymen were everywhere, brandishing whips and sabers, lashing out at anyone in their path. In Dzika Street where David lodged he saw three men and a girl student shot down and found himself in the middle of a ferocious clash between Cossacks and rioting students. When it was over there were two hundred dead and about two hundred and seventy wounded in Warsaw alone. David, however, estimated the slaughter at "six to seven hundred dead," which suggests how powerful an impression these events had made on him.

He wrote only once about this experience, and his letter, to two friends in Płońsk, betrayed no sympathy for the revolutionaries. In view of the Jews' hatred for the czarist regime, his lack of empathy with those trying to overthrow it may seem odd, but there are two likely explanations, both deriving from his Zionist faith. First, the Polish nationalist aspect of the uprising left him unmoved. He did not believe that Poland's liberation from Russian rule would improve things for the Jews, either in the short or the long term. Second, he felt no enthusiasm for the promises of social change offered by the revolutionaries; in fact, he despised the Jews who trusted that the revolution would solve the Jewish Question in Poland. Jews were a majority of its urban population — 58.2 percent in rural towns and 52.6 percent in the metropolitan areas — and 43 percent of the total urban labor force. Not surprisingly, Jewish membership in the Polish socialist parties was disproportionately high, even apart from the Bund, whose members were all Jews. The 1905 revolution, at least in Poland, was generally considered a Jewish revolution. David's apparent indifference to it concealed his anger with those Jews who were in the vanguard of the revolutionary and Polish nationalist movements. These, he believed, were not the causes for which Jews should dedicate themselves and risk their lives; he was convinced that for them salvation would be found only in Eretz Israel. He therefore loathed the anti-Zionism of the Bund, whose leaders argued that Russia and Poland were home for the Jews, who during their hundreds of years of residence there had contributed so much to economic progress and had the same rights as other nationalities in imperial Russia. This was a concept that David passionately rejected. "When the revolution broke out my heart was empty," he said later, "for I knew that the revolution might liberate Russia, but not the Jewish people."

He was so upset that he did not write to Fox about the Warsaw uprising, even though his friend demanded an eyewitness report. "It is very hard to describe once again the events I've already written about," he wrote, and instead sent Fox a copy of his letter to Płońsk. He did not keep his promise to write a second installment to his two friends, explaining that he had had a sudden fever on the day the uprising was brought to an end. This fever may have had a simple physical cause, but the fact is that throughout his life the same phenomenon recurred whenever he was agitated by some great event or decision. On some of the most important occasions in his political life, Ben-Gurion took to his bed.

Most likely David refused to relate again what he had seen in Warsaw to avoid stirring up the strong emotions he must have felt at the time. And the strange objectivity of his only written account of the revolution makes it look like another exercise in subduing his feelings. Years afterward, in his first autobiographical sketch, he declared of this period, "The revolutionary movement captivated me and I became a socialist." This stood in stark contradiction to the fact that he had not embraced socialism either during the uprising or immediately thereafter. Perhaps he back-dated his conversion to present himself as a veteran socialist in his campaign for leadership in the Zionist labor movement.[6]

In early February 1905 Reb Avigdor, worried about his son's ill health, ordered David home. In Płońsk his resolve to become an engineer revived and he decided to take the entrance examinations in May. In mid-February he was back in Warsaw, seeking private students for his upkeep, resolved as he had never been before, he wrote Fox, to gain admittance to the engineering school. If he was not ready for the May examination, he certainly would be ready for the August one.

But because of recurring ill health and the unrest all around him, he was unable to concentrate on his studies; nearly everybody he saw was actively working for a cause — Poland's independence, the socialist revolution, or Zionism. He gathered around him twenty young Zionists who put themselves "body and soul" at the disposal of the Zionist cause and in particular of the Labor Army, a scheme being floated by

Menahem Ussishkin, leader of the Russian Zionists, operating from Odessa. David announced his and his followers' readiness to enlist promptly in the Labor Army, set out immediately to Palestine, and obey all orders. However, nothing came of Ussishkin's scheme, and David was not even granted the courtesy of an answer from Odessa. As he waited in vain for one, his chest pains worsened, and his doctor ordered him to go home and rest. So ended his efforts to get a higher education and his resolve to become an engineer. For although he again set his mind on preparing for the August examination, his hopes were dashed when the political situation again became unstable.

The imposition of a constitution and the establishment of a Duma, or imperial Russian legislature, instead of pacifying the people aroused them all the more, since the limitations set on the Duma and the inadequacies of the constitution made Polish nationalists suspect that they had been devised simply to subdue Poland forever. The government sought to distract public opinion from the real political issues by inciting new pogroms against the Jews, but these tactics failed, and the renewed unrest stirred up by riotous protests against the proposed Duma resulted in the imposition of martial law. Warsaw was rapidly isolated from the rest of the empire, and in August all schools and universities were shut.

David found himself in a terrible predicament. He could not go to Palestine, because he would be following Zemach and other Ezra boys without being able to show any accomplishment for his delay. On the other hand, Ezra grew smaller and smaller as its members departed for Palestine, and his attempts to rekindle it while he was in Płońsk between April and August had not been entirely successful. Where was David to turn?

In Warsaw that August David must have become aware of a new phenomenon in the arena of Zionist politics, the creation of a party called Poale Zion (Workers of Zion). The previous May Ber Borochov — scholar of the history, economic structure, language, and culture of the Jewish people from a Marxist point of view and theoretician and founder of a Poale Zion party in Russia — had come to Warsaw on a recruiting campaign. He met with most of the prominent young socialist Zionists in the town and easily converted them to Marxist Zionism. "He became our teacher," proclaimed one of his first recruits, Itzhak Tabenkin. So David, pondering what to do next, could have concluded that Poale Zion was worth a second look.

This he gave it in the turbulent days of October, when he returned to Warsaw, probably for the specific purpose of joining the Jewish Social-Democratic Party (Poale Zion) and becoming a Marxist. In Poale Zion he must have seen a light and a way out of his predicament. It was a doctrine both Zionist and socialist — more and more the fashion for the young intelligentsia, the students, in the wake of the January revolution, and David surely counted himself among them. In addition, Poale Zion, following the example of the Bund and other Jewish parties, had begun to set up its own self-defense organization, which suggested to David new vistas of activity and a way to renew Ezra's ideological and organizational strength.

When David joined the party in October he was not a thorough convert to Marxist socialism; indeed, the thin patina of Marxism he acquired in Warsaw was to rub off very easily in later years, especially when he served as chairman of the Jewish Agency and prime minister of Israel. Yet whenever it was convenient, he presented himself as an ardent socialist, claiming that his socialism went way back, not only to the January revolution of 1905, but even further, to 1903, when, he said, he organized Ezra into a self-defense group in response to the pogrom in Kishinev.

So in October 1905, when David became a Marxist, at least in name, and a Poale Zion, his purposelessness came to an end. Suddenly he had a new faith, a new task, and a mission. He no longer aspired to become an engineer; his ambition to operate on a grand scale was from then to the end of his life to be carried out in the field of politics. Whether he realized this at the time — and there is no evidence to support the idea that he joined Poale Zion because politics seemed preferable to him — or whether it dawned on him gradually that politics was his vocation, this was his path for the future.[7]

Poale Zion clubs had first been formed in various parts of Russia at the end of the nineteenth century, each developing a separate ideology. In 1903 Ber Borochov set up his own branch in Poltava, his hometown, where he laid the foundation for his own doctrine of Marxist Zionism, on which he was able to organize, in 1905 and 1906, all the other clubs into one all-Russian Poale Zion party. Thus when David joined the Warsaw club it was already a branch of the Russian party.

The ideological basis for Borochov's Marxist Zionism — soon to be dubbed Borochovism — was set forth in his five-part essay, "On the Question of Zion and Territory." Borochov proved, to the satisfaction of his followers, that all Jews would be driven to Palestine, sooner or later, by what he termed "the inevitable process." His theory therefore allowed capital and capitalism to flow to Palestine — as this was part of the inevitable process — and, by building a capitalist economy there, at the same time ready the country for the socialist revolution. His logic was that the incoming capital would create a demand for Jewish workers and increase the proletariat, which under the guidance of Poale Zion would prepare and carry out the socialist revolution. To fulfill this role party members should go to Palestine even before the influx created by the inevitable process, to be ready for their calling.

David was attracted by Borochov's idea that a pioneering movement to Palestine of young men and women was a prerequisite for rebuilding Eretz Israel, but he did not much care for the Marxist arguments Borochov used to support the practical measures he advocated. Certainly David rejected out of hand Borochov's fundamental maxim that "historical necessity" would in itself ensure a Jewish flight from exile to Palestine. The "scientific" — that is, Marxist-Zionist — proof offered by Borochovism did little to convince David that this was the true road to Zionism. Neither did he accept Borochov's assertion that the "territorial vacuum" in Palestine — like many other Zionists of his time, Borochov held that Palestine was virtually empty, being only sparsely inhabited by the Arabs — made it the only country that could rescue the Jewish liberation movement from rejection by the Diaspora Jews. At heart David believed that only voluntary action, as embodied in Herzl's dictum "If you will it, Zionism will not be a dream," would bring the Jews back to Palestine.[8]

Itzhak Tabenkin, one of the founders of Poale Zion in Warsaw, argued, however, that historical determinism was not enough. He asserted that Eretz Israel surged through the veins of the Jews from the time of their birth, that their longing for their country was maintained in their genes as an innate love for their people coupled with the desire to renew its tradition in a new Jewish state in Palestine. These, he insisted, were the objective forces behind Zionism. But David rejected both Borochov's inevitable process and Tabenkin's "genetic objective forces"; he maintained a subjective approach that gave more weight to the spirit and argued that the aspiration to rebuild Eretz Israel was the fruit of the Jewish people's love for their heritage, which was why Zionism wished to resurrect national independence in the Jewish national homeland. As for the force that could bring the Jews to Palestine, David became one of the "voluntarists" who held that only their will would bring them, a concept Theodor Herzl had based on the ancient Hebrew axiom "Nothing can stand in the way of the will." In a way David's Zionism was messianic, with the difference that it would not be brought about by the will of God, or by devout prayer and observance of the commandments, but by energetic work in Palestine by those whose love for it, coupled with their will to return to it and rebuild it, was stronger than circumstances.

Although David was not an out-and-out Borochovist, he adopted Borochov's Marxist idioms. When he returned to Płońsk in October, many of his friends found him greatly changed: he appeared set on class struggle and seemed to be an ardent historical materialist. But it was a pose. In truth, David had not shed his heritage; he wrapped his small-town Jewish tradition around him like a cloak, and the feelings for Eretz Israel he had absorbed at home and with Ezra were in his bones. His Borochovist Marxism was merely a veneer, likely to peel off in time.[9]

He now divided his time between Warsaw and Płońsk, feeling it his duty to be home because of the widespread fear that the government would resort to its practice of inciting pogroms to divert public discontent. The bitter experience of 1903 had moved many Jews to prepare for self-defense, and David converted Ezra simultaneously into a branch of Poale Zion and a self-defense unit. He was one of the two instructors in the use of handguns, a skill he had probably acquired from his Warsaw associates.

Many of David's Płońsk contemporaries remember him as an orator and writer of handbills; overnight he had become a firebrand, an organizer, and an agitator. At public meetings he spoke bitterly of the anticipated pogroms and warned that "rivers of Jewish blood will flow in the wake of government incitement." Fortunately there were no pogroms, at least in Płońsk, and his self-defense group had to justify its existence by standing watch against rampages by drunken Polish ex-servicemen. The startling change in David's conduct was matched by an equally striking change in his appearance. Off came his Warsaw finery — high starched collar and bow tie — and on came the garb of a revolutionary intellectual — a high-necked Russian peasant *rubashka*, a peaked cap, and a gun stuck in his belt. To the delight of his young admirers, he once fired two shots inside the beit hamidrash, and another time he fired his weapon to impress Rachel as she rode by in a buggy.

David came of age as a revolutionary in December 1905, when he attended his first clandestine Poale Zion conference in Warsaw. There, behind closed doors, he saw the shiny coins amassed by his fellow members through "expropriation." While the threat of pogroms was imminent, Jews had gladly given to Poale Zion and Bundist defense groups, but as the danger receded, donations dried up. Warsaw's Poale Zion had about sixty guns at its disposal, which it used to "expropriate" money from the bourgeoisie to replenish its empty coffers. In a typical expropriation action a party militant in student dress, accompanied by two workers, called on a well-to-do citizen. The "student" would announce the amount of the levy he had been sent to collect as his two companions toyed pointedly with their weapons. It was a crude but effective ploy. The Warsaw expropriations were performed on a large scale by a *bojowka* (commando unit) formed for that end. The bojowka once "requisitioned" newsprint and took over a private press to print party literature. And when eighteen members, guns drawn, held up the railway station, emptying the cash box and leaving a receipt in the name of Warsaw's Poale Zion, they made headlines in the Warsaw papers.

Setting up a commando unit in Płońsk was unthinkable; the town was too small and too poor. David's expropriations there were perforce on a much smaller scale, but still successful. "We used to go to the house of a wealthy landlord, put our guns on the table in front of us, and start to discuss money. More often than not ten rubles would appear, but there were occasions when fifty materialized." One day David entered a store owned by a friend's father and aimed his gun, but the man humored him. "David, you don't need a gun," he said. "I'll give you the money anyway."[10]

At this "revolutionary" stage in his life, David was probably supported by his father, who fed and sheltered him, and by his party in Płońsk, which paid for travels to Warsaw and to small towns, where, on his own initiative, he was organizing Poale Zion chapters, and for his revolutionary apparel. That his party money came from expropriations one can be sure, since there is no evidence of other sources of income, or of David's earning his living by other means. By his own account he received arbitration fees that he donated to the party treasury, but how often he earned them, or how substantial they were, is unknown. Furthermore, these fees could easily have been a finer form of expropriation. One thing is sure: his bodyguards volunteered their services as a token of admiration.

David had adopted the Warsaw fashion of traveling with a personal armed guard. One of his bodyguards was a huge ruffian, a porter keen on gambling and drinking, quite an asset, since David was beginning to organize trade unions in Płońsk. However, before he could exercise a free hand in this, he had to deal with the Bundists and the Zionist non-Marxist socialists, both of whom had stolen a march on him by unionizing activities. As a nonrevolutionary party the non-Marxist socialists had little chance in those stormy days to attract youth seeking immediate action. They also had no leader to stand up to David. Poale Zion's combination of domestic and international appeal was hard to beat; it took a very strong ideology and a tight organization, like the Bund's, to counter David and his party. But while the Zionist socialists were easily vanquished, the Bundists put up a fierce fight.

There was an unbridgeable ideological gap between Poale Zion and the Bundists, who denied the nationhood of the Jews and claimed that there was no basis for the revival of a Jewish nation in Palestine. In their parlance "Jewish nation" meant simply those Jews living within the boundaries of the Russian empire as one nationality among many others, such as the Poles or Ukrainians. Since they sought a world revolution and a classless society, which would solve all national problems, they fought Zionism tooth and nail as a tool of the bourgeoisie that was drawing human resources into a particular national struggle and away from the general revolution. When David and the Bund clashed in Płońsk, it was a fight to the finish.

The Bundists' first appearance there had been welcomed by many. In early 1905, when pogroms were expected daily, it seemed that only the revolutionary movement, which promised redemption from anti-Semitism and class oppression, offered a safe future for the Jews. David was horrified at the Bund's initial success in his town, and when he returned there in October he threw himself into the fight to rescue its Zionist youth from the Bund heresies. He battled on two fronts — organizational and ideological. The main street in Płońsk became the site for organizing trade unions and the Great Synagogue the stage for ideological discussion.

David's success in converting Ezra into a branch of Poale Zion had alarmed the Bundists. A series of discussions was arranged, and from Warsaw they sent "some of [their] best speakers to storm Płońsk," including their star orator, Shmulik the Bundist. The legendary Shmulik, three years younger than David, was in such demand that he had to return to Warsaw directly after each of his performances in Płońsk. The debates aroused extraordinary interest. Shops were closed, and the large hall of the synagogue was placed at the disposal of the antagonists. The verbal exchange was staged like a duel.

David and Shmulik entered with their bodyguards, all flaunting handguns which, out of respect to the synagogue, were placed on the table. David was quite at ease on the dais; his Ezra experience and reputation as a lucid and witty speaker gave him confidence. Socialist theory was unknown in Płońsk, but Jewish learning and tradition were the stuff of daily life, so that David, reveling in the situation, scored a hit with this story: Once upon a time the people of Chelm wanted to build a magnificent new house. To do so they had to carry a beam from one side of the street to the other. But the beam was much wider than the street, so the people of Chelm pulled down all the houses in the street in order to get the beam across. That, he said, was what the Bund was doing.

Playing in this manner to his home crowd — some of his speeches sounding more like vaudeville sketches — David ridiculed the stranger from Warsaw, and Shmulik the Bundist's arguments fell on deaf ears. Finally Shmulik was licked. Płońskers said that David had hacked him to pieces, and David's name became a byword for a Bund-hater who would stop at nothing. The Bund's Vilna paper, *Die Volkszeitung*, reported the Bund ordeal in Płońsk. "The educated David Gruen apparently thinks that the workers' interests will be advanced by yelling at us, 'What are you doing here? Go to Bialystok and other towns where there have been pogroms; go there and join the hooligans in robbing Jewish property.' " The Bund leaders accused David of threatening their lives. "This same 'hero' shouted at us, 'We have weapons and we'll shoot you all like dogs.' " The report concluded, "The only question that remains is why should we go off to Bialystok when there is such a fine hooligan in Płońsk?"[11]

David was elated by his triumph, which left him free to continue organizing trade unions in Płońsk, but he was soon disheartened to find that this activity was not so grand as debating with the Bund. The available proletariat was simply not large enough to warrant a trade union movement or a socialist workers' party. Only one industry — tailoring — thrived. Płońsk's advantage in this fiercely competitive trade, low prices, was made possible by low wages and costs. The industry consisted of very small workshops whose owners worked with their two or three employees and apprentices; these, whom David labeled "needle workers," had become the targets of his unionizing. They worked from dawn to midnight, except on Thursday, when they kept going until 4:00 A.M. to make up for Friday, when work ended before Sabbath began. They resumed on Saturday evening after Sabbath had ended and worked until 2:00 A.M. Sunday morning.

David demanded that the workers' pay be raised and their workday shortened to twelve hours — from 7:00 A.M. to 7:00 P.M. — and to back these demands he called a strike of the needle workers. The date the town's and David's first strike began is not known, but apparently it spread slowly from workshop to workshop and lasted for some time, ending on the eve of Succoth, October 2, 1905. The strike coincided with the formation of the self-defense unit, whose weapons were probably used to dissuade employers from hiring scabs. No doubt some of Płońsk's Jews complained that weapons originally acquired for self-defense were being used by the Poale Zion youth to intimidate the "capitalists" who had paid for them.

The strike set the town afire, and the new beit hamidrash, Ezra's erstwhile meeting place, became the venue for organizers and strikers. It was a problematic strike because the employers worked just as hard as their assistants and did not earn much more. In one sense a twelve-hour day would benefit them as much as their hired hands. But a raise in pay would have required higher prices and wiped out the town's competitive edge in an industry that was rapidly being taken over by mechanized factories elsewhere. In the end the dispute was referred for arbitration to the Polish magistrate, who ruled in favor of the strikers. When the decision reached the town's Jews, they were celebrating Simchat Torah in the synagogues; that holiday was recorded forever as a day of victory for the Płońsk branch of Poale Zion.

Although this one achievement approached the grandeur of the Warsaw Poale Zion's actions, the potential for David's organizational and unionizing talents soon dwindled to next to nothing, as his second industrial action made all too clear. It centered around the women's section of the public bathhouse, where a job was vacant. The community council wanted to give it to a woman whom David thought was not needy enough; his own candidate was a poor widow. The council stood firm, so David summoned his ad hoc bojowka to stand guard over the bathhouse, refusing to let anyone in or out. The women, deprived of their baths, argued with him and cursed him, but he allowed no exceptions until the council gave in. This was not David's only encounter with women in his capacity as organizer. Small-scale as his actions were, they led Płońsk's housemaids to bring their troubles to the Poale Zion committee, with the result that the town enjoyed the first and perhaps only trade union for housemaids.

Some of David's industrial actions affected a single family business. Once he called out on strike a "knitting shop" whose employees were cheder teachers' wives who worked to help support their families. One of them implored Reb Avigdor to use his influence to get his son to call off the strike, but he would not interfere; this strike also ended in a victory for David. In another instance, with Rachel's help, he brought the "rope industry" of three people, owned by his sweetheart's widowed grandmother, to a halt: arguments broke out between the grandmother and mother and Rachel, who sided with David and was accused of having no consideration for her grandmother's precarious financial situation. The family's loss of money in this strike almost resulted in Rachel's having no new coat when she set sail the following year for Eretz Israel.[12]

Before long David's influence on Płońsk's economic and social life became a fact accepted by one and all, and David found himself settling private and public disputes. But his reputation in Płońsk was no help to his progress in Poland's Poale Zion hierarchy, partly because of his meager ideological background. David was not present at any of the Polish party gatherings in 1906; even after nearly all the Warsaw leaders were arrested on the eve of the empirewide Poale Zion conference in Poltava in the Ukraine on March 12, 1906, David was not named one of the two delegates from Poland. Consequently, he missed the opportunity to be arrested when the police raided the meeting and carried off most of the hundred twenty delegates.

For revolutionaries in czarist Russia, prison was a badge of honor. Some of David's colleagues, like Tabenkin, had had the good fortune to go to jail three times, for six months or more, a joy denied to David. He was detained eventually, but not for any revolutionary act. It seems that once when he was in Warsaw his revolutionary-style long hair had moved a squad of gendarmes to arrest him, and he was locked in a cell until his identity could be established, which was done as soon as his father turned up. A second arrest brought no greater glory. That August he took a boat trip on the river Vistula. As he disembarked a policeman arrested him for no reason at all, calling in German, "You dog!" Again his father came to the rescue and, with the help of a local rabbi, David was soon set free.

The truth was that there was not much left for him to accomplish in Płońsk or in Poland. Higher education was out, no place had been made for him in the top echelon of Poale Zion, and he could not make any further headway in politics from his small-town base. Eretz Israel beckoned as the one outlet for his ambition.

In aggrandizing and antedating his socialist past, Ben-Gurion needed to explain, in his reminiscences and memoirs, why a great socialist like him had not reached his party's upper ranks, especially after he made it appear that on his arrival in Palestine he was greeted as a well-known Poale Zion leader. He used the pretext that Polish Poale Zion had shunned him because of his agricultural policy line. True, the Borochovist Poale Zion thought little of establishing agricultural settlements in Palestine, because the prevalent primitive agricultural methods there could not raise a proletariat large enough to advance the class war.

But this excuse was given later, as at the time Ben-Gurion was not attracted to agriculture, as is evident from his letter to Shmuel Fox in November 1904. Tearing aside the veil of romance shrouding pioneer life, he wrote that he was not "looking forward to working on the land. It seems to me that it's high time we dropped this song of praise about the joys of a life on the soil, which experience belies. I willingly accept your argument about the need for physical labor, but your philosophy about the joy of farm life is somewhat absurd in its exaggerated naiveté."[13]

Apart from David's being at an educational and political standstill, something else was pushing him to Eretz Israel: the conspicuous increase in immigration there. The year 1906 had opened with a wave of immigration. In May one hundred fifty Jews, among them eight from Płońsk, left Odessa for Palestine on a single ship. This large group was followed by another, then by small groups in rapid succession. David, as head of Poale Zion in Płońsk, was naturally urging his followers to prepare themselves for a productive life in Eretz Israel, following in the footsteps of his good friends who had already gone there. When in May Shlomo Zemach returned home for a brief visit, David's announcement that he would accompany Zemach on his return to Eretz Israel surprised no one.

Although Reb Avigdor had still been hoping that his extraordinary son would have a brilliant academic career, his disappointment did not stop him from giving David money for his journey. Fortunately, thanks to his forged birth certificate, David would not be called up for the military service that, until 1908, czarist Russia required of young men by the time they turned twenty-one, which meant that he could leave the empire openly on his own passport. He planned to travel to Odessa and sail on the weekly packet to Jaffa with Zemach, along with Rachel and her mother, Shoshana, who were going to Palestine to join Reb Simcha Isaac. There he would be reunited with his old Ezra friends, who had been notified of his imminent arrival.[14]

On the eve of their departure, David and Rachel were given a going-away party by the Płońsk branch of Poale Zion. A group photograph taken there shows David and his friends assembled in front of his parents' house; Reb Avigdor and other members of his family looking out the windows are part of the tableau. David, in the center, sits ramrod straight, wearing a flat cap and a Cossack-style blouse, his jacket draped around his shoulders. Arms folded on his chest, Rachel at his side, he is the very model of a pioneering, revolutionary Zionist, sure of himself, of his chosen path, of his future.

The four took the train from Warsaw to Odessa, arriving on Friday, August 24. Before their boat sailed on Tuesday, they had time to put their papers in order and enjoy some sightseeing. Everything in the renowned port was new to David, and he eagerly reported it all to his father. Thus began a long correspondence in which David documented his day-to-day experiences and moods. In the seventh letter, he asked his father not to lose even one of his communications because "it is important to me to know in years to come what I thought about Eretz Israel every moment of my life." This request suggests that, conscious of his destiny, he was bent on preparing a record for posterity. What impressed him most in Odessa was the complete absence of any militiamen. Expecting to see signs of the terrible 1905 pogroms, he was astonished to find none. The police were "extremely courteous; it is incredible that the worst massacre took place here last October."[15]

On his last day in Russia he met the Zionist leaders in Odessa to whom the funds raised in his father's house since his infancy had been sent. He was deeply disappointed by their reception of him. Their looks seemed to indicate that they thought he was crazy, for at that time the Zionist leadership gave no encouragement to young immigrants without visible means. As the hour of sailing neared, he felt he was at last escaping the valley of death. In his final letter to his father from Russia he wrote, "A few more hours and I will have left the dark recesses of exile, and from the freedom of the high seas, on the way to the land of our rebirth, I shall send you my greetings. See you soon on the mountains of Zion."

David enjoyed the sea voyage, with its stopovers in Istanbul, Smyrna, Mersin, and Beirut. He and his companions slept on the open deck; Rachel's mother carefully interposed her bedding between that of her daughter and David. Aboard ship David first met Arabs, his future neighbors, and, he told his father, was encouraged to find that "they were easy to befriend and almost invariably good-hearted." The voyage also provided David's first encounter with Sephardic Jews, whom he scrutinized even more closely because they had been born in or very close to Eretz Israel. They dressed like Arabs and looked at him, an Ashkenazi Jew, with some suspicion, teasing him about his Hebrew pronunciation. He was very proud that after only a day or two his accent was hardly distinguishable from theirs.[16]

The day before their arrival in Jaffa, Rachel was sitting on deck, her eyes searching the horizon for land, wondering if she had been right to prod her mother to go to Palestine. While aboard ship she had heard from returning Eretz-Israelis that life in Palestine was no picnic; settlers faced hardships that included malaria and shortages of housing and everything else. Zemach, as though reading her mind, told her she had no idea what was in store for her: she would have to do hard physical work and suffer a great deal. His words made her soul-searching even more intense, and she asked herself if she had not been irresponsible to beg her mother to go with her to Eretz Israel.

When Zemach left her she was close to tears. David, seeing this, was alarmed and asked her what was wrong. To remove her doubts, he assured her that she was not alone, that he was at her side, a tower of strength. Even if he had to resort to teaching, he said, he would see to it that she and her mother were provided for. According to Rachel, David at that moment was ready to renounce the illustrious mission of the pioneer, the conqueror, and the redeemer just to support her and her parents. His assurances comforted her and she put her trust in him. All her life Rachel cherished the memory of this incident, which she did not disclose until shortly before her death in 1974, when she admitted they had a tacit understanding that might have led to marriage.

Their ship left Beirut for Jaffa on the evening of Wednesday, September 5. As it hugged the shoreline, David was able to identify the

mountains of Lebanon. His excitement mounted by the minute, and as
the ship neared Jaffa he was beside himself. Everything seemed symbolic and larger than life; he mistook a common sea gull for the bird
mentioned in Bialik's famous poem *To the Bird*. For a moment the gull
had been transfigured into the dove returning to Noah's ark. He even
wrote that it was the first bird they had seen throughout the voyage.
"In utter silence I stood looking out for Jaffa port, my heart pounding,"
he wrote his father. "Here I come."

At that time ships could not tie up at the Jaffa dock, so they anchored offshore all night. Then, at 8:00 A.M. on Friday, September 7,
1906, the ship eased into the harbor and was surrounded by innumerable small craft. Arab dockhands scrambled out of their boats, climbed
up the swaying ropes and gangplanks, and immediately began to unload passengers and baggage into the skiffs below. The noise was deaf-
ening, the scene confusing, and David was hard put to keep an eye on
his belongings. After briefly bargaining he agreed to pay one of the
Arab oarsmen the sum of two rubles to transport him and his possessions to the shore. At 9:00 A.M. the Arab porter who carried him ashore
put him down, and his foot first touched the land of his ancestors, Eretz
Israel. "Hurrah," he wrote to his father. He had accomplished the first
of what he later called the "three central deeds of my life."[17]

3

Jaffa

SCARCELY HAD DAVID Gruen set foot outside the customs shed
when he encountered the party war among the Zionists in Palestine. Poale Zion faithful tore him away from Shlomo Zemach,
who, in turn, was grabbed by members of his own group, Ha-Poel ha-
Tzair, and the two groups went their separate ways to Chaim Baruch's
Inn. There, waiting for them, brandy glass in hand, stood Israel Shochat, a Poale Zion leader who made it his business to inspect each
batch of newcomers. He was proud of his legendary ability to size up a
man at a glance, and after only a few words, Shochat invited David to
stay with him in Jaffa for a few days.

But David, straining for a first glimpse of the new Jews whose hands
were creating a new life in Zion, would not hear of it. The exotic, oriental town, with its narrow, winding alleyways, tamarisks, and reminders of earlier Christian, Islamic, and Napoleonic eras, stirred no
response in him. Only the "hills planted with cedars and palms . . . the
country's most beautiful trees" got a favorable comment. He spent exactly seven hours in Jaffa and its new Jewish quarter, Neve Shalom —
the nucleus of the first modern all-Jewish town, Tel Aviv, which was
founded three years later. "To me life in Jaffa is a more grotesque exile
than life in Płońsk," he told his father. "It's true that there is a street
with a Hebrew name, Neve Shalom, but it was full of Arab shopkeepers who sat about smoking narghilehs. There were a few Jews around,
but it made a bad impression on me." When he overheard Hebrew in
the streets and came across Hebrew shop signs, his heart swelled. "I
felt waves of joy sweep through me," for the use of Hebrew was one of
the "buds of rebirth." Later he explained that he couldn't stay in Jaffa
longer because he didn't like the dust that covered everything. The
miracle of national rebirth was taking place elsewhere, in the new

agricultural settlements, and he was impatient for a sight of them. His greatest desire was to see Petah Tikva, the "metropolis" of the "Hebrew republics," as he called the settlements.

At 4:00 P.M. on Friday, September 7, 1906, with Zemach, Rachel Nelkin, eleven others, and a donkey, David departed on foot for Petah Tikva. He was elated to witness another sign of the Jews' rebirth, a Jew riding on a donkey, which symbolized to him a long history of people closely tied to their own land. Whatever caught his eye looked wonderful. The party reached Petah Tikva at 10:00 P.M. The Płońskers went to the house of an Ezra friend, where they talked until the small hours.[1]

Palestine had 700,000 inhabitants, of whom 55,000 were Jews. Apart from 550 young men who had chosen to become field hands — called chalutzim, "pioneers" — the Jews were concentrated in the cities of Jerusalem, Hebron, Tiberias, and Safed. Palestine had been under Ottoman rule for nearly four hundred years, since 1516. The Ottoman Empire would expire in only eleven years, but such an event was inconceivable to the Zionists in 1906. They therefore geared all their planning for Jewish settlement to the political situation within the empire. This was no easy feat, for the Sublime Porte had a long-standing policy against any Jews, let alone Zionists, entering and settling in Palestine. Even before political Zionism had been established the Ottoman government suspected Jews coming to Palestine of conspiring to turn it into a Jewish state. A series of regulations, promulgated as far back as 1888, prohibited non-Ottoman Jews from buying land, building a house, or establishing a settlement. To prevent Jewish immigration in the guise of tourism, entry to Palestine for non-Ottoman Jews was restricted to a period not exceeding thirty-one days, and a guarantee of fifty Turkish pounds, paid on arrival and returned on departure, was required. In 1900 an additional regulation demanded that all Jews visiting from Europe be equipped with a valid passport that had to be surrendered to the port authorities and was returned when they left. On receipt of a passport the authorities issued a pink voucher as proof of legal entry; without it the passport would not be returned. But because there was widespread corruption these regulations had little effect; money and a ruse could get one anything. The Jews acquired land under the names of Ottoman Jews, exchanged money in lieu of passports or pink vouchers, and evaded building regulations by completing the roof of the house first.

Petah Tikva was founded in 1878 by seven members of the old Yishuv — Jews who had gone to Palestine for religious motives both before 1882, the year of the first Zionist aliyah, and thereafter — from Jerusalem. The first Jews to set foot outside the walls of the Old City, their aim was to lay a foundation for Jewish agriculture in Palestine. Their example was important, for until then Jews did not believe that they could farm under the regulations of Ottoman Palestine. The Petah Tikva settlers showed it could be done, and although they themselves were not Zionist, they influenced the Zionist pioneers who set up settlements in Judea and Galilee.

By January 1906 Petah Tikva numbered eighty households, which were supported by vineyards and citrus groves. What David saw that September was a thriving township of wooden houses painted white and a few stone houses, divided by tree-lined streets and one main boulevard. Its population of nearly fifteen hundred included two hundred pioneers of the Second Aliyah (1904–1914), who had flocked to Petah Tikva — renowned as the mother of the Jewish settlements — to "conquer physical labor" and to "create a new type of Jewish worker." By "new type" they meant Jews who did their work themselves rather than hiring Arabs to do it, as had become the custom in Petah Tikva and the other twelve agricultural settlements that followed its example. The Zionist pioneers maintained that if Arabs worked the land and did all the physical work, Palestine would belong to them forever.

Another aspect of the new type was their rejection of the philanthropy on which the thirteen Jewish settlements leaned heavily, for all were either owned or administered, or both, by the Jewish Colonization Association (JCA), a philanthropic project of Baron Maurice Hirsch, which he passed on to Baron Edmond de Rothschild. The JCA provided a subsidy that made up for the settlements' deficits and ensured some amenities. The first thirteen settlements were all built on land privately owned by either Rothschild or settlers' cooperatives subsidized by him, to which the young pioneers of 1906 also took exception. The settlements they intended to build one day would all be on land owned by the Jewish National Fund, that is, by the Jewish people. But in the meantime they had to work as day laborers in Petah Tikva to "conquer physical labor" and compete with the cheap Arab labor the settlers found it so profitable to hire from the surrounding villages. Their turnover was rapid, since only people fired by the loftiest ideals could weather this test.[2]

The morning after their arrival David and Zemach found a room for a monthly rent of five French francs, one of the legal currencies in the Ottoman Empire, and until the summer of 1907, with one long break, this room was David's home. His letters to his father, paeans of praise to Petah Tikva and to toil on the land, painted life as wonderful beyond belief. From his window, he wrote, he could see "the gleaming sea" —

a feat no human eye could actually have accomplished. In praising the economic situation, he told of a saddler who had arrived in Palestine with only the shirt on his back and had since saved thirty thousand rubles from his handiwork alone. He described his work for his first two days — manuring citrus groves — as a "clean, nice job" and made his eight-hour workday sound like a picnic: up at 6:00 A.M.; to the citrus grove at 7:30; a bath in the irrigation pool; work from 8:00 to noon; lunch with Zemach and a woman friend from Płońsk, who worked in a nearby orchard; a rest; then work again until 5:00 or 5:30 P.M.; another dip in the irrigation water; back to his room; and finally supper in the workers' cooperative kitchen.

His letters, depicting a land only half a step from paradise, were passed from hand to hand in Płońsk, and those who read them were captivated by his glowing picture of their homeland and the happiness it bestowed upon the Jewish tillers of its soil. These letters were worlds apart from those written by other Płońsk pioneers, who told of people dying of hunger, tuberculosis, and cholera, and before long David was asked to explain the discrepancy. At first he made excuses, saying, for example, that one of the complainers was disappointed in Palestine because he had not found the same amusements he had enjoyed in Warsaw. Eventually he was forced to concede that there were some bad things in Palestine, though he insisted that these were "only a drop in the ocean."

The truth, however, was quite different. Petah Tikva was not at all what David made it out to be. Some of the settlers depended on charity from Baron Rothschild; many were not Zionists at all, and those who were supported Herzl's Uganda scheme, which David opposed. Worst of all, in David's view, was the use of Arab labor. Beyond that, conditions were so bad in all of Palestine that, Ben-Gurion estimated, about 90 percent of the Second Aliyah despaired of the country and left — a fact he pointed out later. Even Zemach, who was firmly committed to settling in Palestine and had returned there, wrote that if the people of Płońsk had seen him "in the humiliation of my feverish convulsions, my spirit at its lowest ebb . . . and if they had known what I knew about Zion, its cities, settlements and farmers . . ." He let the sentence trail off. It was common for newcomers to come upon long lines of Jews going the other way and calling out to them, "You're the next victims." David never mentioned this in his letters. In his determination to picture Palestine as truly the Promised Land he differed not only from his Płońsk friends but also from such prominent Second Aliyah figures as Berl Katznelson, who became a labor leader and, in 1919, Ben-Gurion's closest collaborator. More than anyone else in Palestine, David had an almost mystical belief in the strength of Eretz Israel, in the Chosen

People, their resourcefulness, and their determination to triumph against all odds.[3]

In December, under incessant questioning from Płońsk, David let slip another scrap of truth to his father. He confessed that working with a shovel and carrying manure was not such an easy job and required much patience and perseverance, especially in one who, like most of the immigrants, had never done such work before. It was arduous, he admitted, to stand beneath the blazing sun all day, the sweat stinging the sores on his palms, his limbs turning slowly to jelly, while nearby strutted the Jewish overseer shouting "Yallah" ("Move it"). He had previously chosen not to reveal the existence of the overseer, nor the fact that all workers in Petah Tikva were hired only on a day-to-day basis.

He withheld from his father even longer the fact of his frequent bouts of malaria. In a letter of December 18 David denied reports that he had been very ill as a "total lie," making light of the fact that three weeks earlier he had been sick with malaria and a doctor had visited him at midnight, leaving him a prescription, but that "on the morrow, before I even had time to get it, I was absolutely cured." In fact, Dr. Menahem Stein had advised him to go back to Płońsk, advice David had rejected out of hand. As malaria continued to weaken him, his workdays decreased and his hungry days multiplied. But he believed he could conquer malaria with will power and faith.

Only much later did David admit the tribulations and despair of those first days. "I stayed in Petah Tikva and worked . . . but I was sick with malaria more often than not." On average he worked only ten days a month. His selective vision, which grew out of his strengthened determination never to disclose his feelings, never to acknowledge doubt, and never to give in to weakness, helped keep up his spirits, but it also made him insensitive and caused a rift between him and Rachel.[4]

On Sunday, September 9, he set off with her to manure the citrus groves. This was not a wonderful beginning for Rachel, whose hands were soon cut and blistered by the thin wire handles of the manure cans. Their weight made her stoop, and as she ladled the manure with a mug into the trench around the trees, acid stung her cuts, so before long she had to give up. The overseer promptly fired her. She was overcome with shame, certain she had disgraced not only herself but the whole of Płońsk as well. Remembering David's reassurances on the boat, she turned to him in her distress, but he reprimanded her for her lack of determination, telling her she must overcome her pain and weakness. She was stunned. "He was ashamed that I had failed, so I became a failure in his eyes," she wrote. His disappointment and anger were so great that he could not bring himself to comfort or encourage her, and for several days treated her like a stranger.

Rachel, too, subsequently fell victim to malaria. Unlike David she "did not know how to take the fever," but he made no attempt to comfort her when, because of her weakness, she was not rehired. Fortunately another Płoński, Yehezkel Beit-Halachmi, did not lecture her about determination; he helped her to bed, went for the doctor, and stayed with her, applying cold, damp towels to her burning face. When she was better he took her with him to work in the orchards and gently and patiently showed her what to do, never letting her out of his sight. He grafted the citrus shoots to the stock, then she bound it; he secured the supports for the new trees, while she did the easier task of pruning the old ones. Her heart cried out to David, but she found understanding and tenderness with Yehezkel. David did not seem to mind the loss of Rachel. Then or afterward, whenever he was engrossed in political thought, his friends, male or female, could not attract his attention. Rachel, who he felt had failed him, exited the center stage of his thoughts, and he saw her less and less.[5]

It is hard to tell whether the hardships in Petah Tikva or his flair for politics, attracting David to Shochat and to Jaffa, was the more potent force, but he returned to Jaffa on October 2, less than a month after his arrival, for the founding conference of the Palestine Social-Democratic Hebrew Workers (Poale Zion) Party. Although European members had been arriving in Palestine during the previous two years, they had not organized as a separate party or even thought of doing so: theoretically, they remained members of their old parties in Europe. But in October 1905 nine young men, Zemach among them, had founded in Petah Tikva the Federation of Young Workers, Ha-Poel ha-Tzair, an educational party with local roots whose mission was to shape the individual Jew into an independent Hebrew pioneer. Its anti-Marxist founders took strong exception to the use of Yiddish as the lingua franca of the Jewish working class and as an official party language.[*] Ha-Poel ha-Tzair members were adamant that without Hebrew, a Jewish renaissance in Palestine was impossible. Yiddish, which they sought

---

[*] The great majority of its members maintained that as a socialist workers' party, Poale Zion should use the language understood by one and all in its daily activity, literature, and propaganda. This meant that Yiddish for Ashkenazi Jews and Ladino for Sephardic Jews would be the party's recognized languages. This majority further held that these languages were the proletariat's only means of verbal communication, for Hebrew was known only to rabbis, scholars, and the well-off few who had been able to acquire it in their youth. In Poale Zion's terms it was the language of the bourgeoisie. If all the Poale Zion members had been Zionists first, socialists second, they would have chosen Hebrew as the exclusive language, but since many thought of themselves as socialists first, they did not want to give up the language necessary to rally the Jewish proletariat to the inevitable revolution or their ties with non-Zionist Jewry.

to eradicate, was the symbol of all that was negative in the Diaspora. By early 1906 Ha-Poel ha-Tzair was ninety strong, which goaded Poale Zion members to form their own Palestinian party.

There was a delay, though, because Shochat was not sure how he and his supporters would stand in the new configuration. The sixty-odd people the party could draw on were anything but united. Shochat and his followers considered themselves full-fledged Eretz-Israelis and, like Ha-Poel ha-Tzair, used Hebrew. Their opposition centered in thirty young men who had arrived in Palestine in October 1905 from Rostov in the heart of Russia. These self-styled Rostovians, having had virtually no Jewish education, had more in common with the Russian proletariat. The ideology they brought with them had been quarried in the 1905 revolution, and their Zionism was more a fashionable sentiment, a spontaneous response to a new life in a new country, than a coherent nationalist program. In Jaffa they formed themselves into a club, prompting Shochat to organize his own group with about twenty-five of his associates from the Lower Galilee. The eventual amalgamation of the two clubs seemed inevitable, and Shochat's only dilemma was how to ensure the dominance of his group in the joint organization from the outset. One reason he went to Jaffa port to inspect the new arrivals was to build additional support. When he spotted a likely prospect — David, for example, with his passion for Hebrew — he tried to win that person over. The strong first impression David made on him no doubt influenced Shochat's decision that the time was ripe to form a Palestinian Poale Zion party. He must have believed that with David on his side, his chances to dominate it improved substantially. So he wrote to David, inviting him to take part in the founding meeting. Later he remarked, "Ben-Gurion came and saved the situation."

David's success at the conference was astonishing: he was elected to both the central and manifesto committees. Elated over his triumph, David little suspected that the credit belonged to Shochat. A founder of Poale Zion in his hometown, Grodno, and the leader of one of the first Jewish self-defense leagues there during the 1903 pogroms, Shochat had reached Palestine on March 2, 1904, in the vanguard of the Second Aliyah. In the early days he had been drawn to Michael Halperin, a strange, mystical Jew who wandered the length and breadth of Palestine conjuring up such visions and wild ideas as the creation of a tribe of Jewish Bedouin, the formation of a Hebrew army, and fantastic plans for bringing masses of Jews out of Europe into Palestine. Shochat took Halperin as his mentor and, as a man of action, secretly believed he would be able to execute some of Halperin's improbable but prescient schemes. Having perfected the art of conspiracy, which he thought was the only way to get things done, Shochat made his first step toward his goal the formation of a secret cell. He had not yet decided whether David was fit to take part in the conspiracies he was hatching, but he was certain about the public role he planned for him.

Shochat, a bookkeeper, was exempt from physical work because he had asthma, although this affliction had affected neither his dark, manly good looks nor his commanding presence. His split-second understanding of a wink or a nod made him most at home in clandestine gatherings. In such situations he was truly charismatic, helped by his natural gift for picking loyal men. But he knew that his blindly adoring following was not enough to enable him to achieve his public ambitions and that he was hampered by personal shortcomings: he was not steeped in socialist theory, Judaism, or Hebrew, nor was he an orator. What he needed was a devoted deputy, and recognizing that David fitted the bill perfectly, Shochat chose him as his protégé and pulled the strings behind the scenes to ensure David's swift promotion.[6]

But if Shochat thought David would be content to serve as his mouthpiece, it was one of his few serious mistakes. For a time, however, David gave Shochat complete satisfaction, either because they were in full agreement on the issues that concerned them or because David had not yet found his sea legs. His first public tryout was the founding conference, which began on October 4 and ended on Saturday evening, October 6, 1906. In the party's annals it was known as a theoretical conference. Its most conspicuous feature was that every Poale Zion member in Palestine came and took part in the debates, which rapidly polarized between a Marxist socialist side and a Jewish nationalist one. The more devout Marxists gave preference to class struggle and therefore aimed at Arab-Jewish cooperation at all levels of party activity, a course that might eventually have led them to a binational state; the less orthodox Marxists stressed the Jewish nationalist aspect, restricting their socialism to the Jewish community, with their ultimate goal a Jewish socialist republic.

The first group, led by the Rostovians, insisted that any trade union organized by the party must be open to Jew and Arab alike, and they objected to the use of Hebrew as the party's official language. Their opponents, headed by Shochat and David, demanded that the principles of Zionism be incorporated in the party's platform, which meant a commitment to national pioneering — that is, the redemption of the land through labor — and the exclusive use of Hebrew. Any party-sponsored trade union had to be for the benefit of Jews only. It proved impossible to reconcile such profound differences at this or any later conference; thirteen years later the party split into socialist and nationalist wings.

David, appointed by Shochat to head the nationalist faction, became chairman of the conference. He addressed the gathering in Hebrew, forbidding translation of his speech into Russian or Yiddish, and word soon spread, in Palestine and elsewhere, that he was a Hebrew zealot. The other Hebrew zealots left the meeting very proud that Poale Zion had a Hebrew speaker to match their rivals in Ha-Poel ha-Tzair. The nationalists enjoyed another triumph when the meeting endorsed their demand that trade unions be for Jews only, and one of the party's aims became "the founding of a general trade union, dedicated to the improvement and betterment of the economic conditions of the Jewish worker in Palestine."

Shochat, with his conspirators' help, stage-managed the elections. The seventy enrolled members had to choose a central committee and a committee to draft the platform. Ten members were to be elected to the manifesto, or platform, committee. By successfully rigging the ballot Shochat prejudiced the committee in favor of the nationalists. Then he got the conference to approve his idea of segregating the committee members from all undue influence by sending them off to a cheap hotel in the Arab town of Ramla, paying their expenses out of funds he had diverted from European and U.S. Jews' contributions for other purposes. David never found out how the ten were elected to the manifesto committee, although he did record that, following the Russian custom, it was decided to have a secret ballot. Otherwise Shochat could not have gotten away with directing his supporters to vote for the names on a list he had drawn up.[7]

On October 8, 1906, the ten men arrived in Ramla, where, sitting on stools for three days, they debated their party's ideological platform; now and then an Arab brought them coffee in small cups, and at night they slept on mats. They seldom went out, except to get something to eat in the marketplace. Only on the first evening did they take a break to walk around and see the town's ruined fortress. David noted only the ruins and the scenery; he gave no thought to the Arabs, their problems, social conditions, or cultural life, nor had he taken time to find out about the other, much older, Jewish community of Eretz Israel. These realities did not impinge on David, who might as well have been drafting his party's program in Poland.

Predictably, the drafting committee split into nationalists, whom Ben-Gurion later termed "rightists," and leftists, that is, ultra-Marxists. David's faction "wanted to include a nationalist declaration, to refer to the universal Jewish problem and to spell out all the Zionists' demands concerning Palestine." Their opponents wanted the creation of a single Arab-Jewish proletariat that would lead the struggle for a socialist state to be paramount. David and his supporters argued that the Arabs had to wage their own class struggle, and if they did, an Arab proletariat would emerge separately from the feudal Ottoman economy. This idea, which was included in the manifesto, was the first mention of a segregation of the Jewish and Arab economies in Palestine, auguring the beginning of social, economic, cultural, and political partition between the Jewish and Arab communities. Since the nationalists prevailed, both in number and by argument, their positions appeared in the final draft.

The platform approved by the party at a meeting the following January was based on, but not identical with, the founding manifesto of the Russian Poale Zion. The Palestine manifesto had two objectives: its minimum goal was the creation of a Jewish socialist republic in Palestine, its maximum goal the establishment of a world classless society, unaffected by geographical, nationalist, political, or other divisions. The manifesto made it clear that Poale Zion was a political party with dogmatic, hard-line ideology. The fact that there were only five hundred fifty active pioneers did not weigh heavily on the party's ideologues, whose sights were set on the class struggle even though there was, as yet, neither capital nor classes to wage war. Whereas Poale Zion unrealistically set as its ultimate goal the construction of an independent socialist state, Ha-Poel ha-Tzair focused on the immediate needs of the pioneers and made it the party's task to increase their number and to improve their chances of employment in the Jewish sector.[8]

David and Shochat had come to know each other better as a result of their three days together in Ramla and afterward saw each other regularly at the weekly meetings of the central committee in Jaffa and sometimes in Ben Shemen, a model farm and school fifteen miles to the east, where Shochat worked. The lack of public transport turned David into an accomplished walker; he once got soaked to the skin on his way to Ben Shemen but walked on to Jaffa, where he had a recurrence of malaria. As soon as he felt slightly better, however, he was again on his way to Ben Shemen for a meeting at which he and Shochat set their policy for the January meeting of the party.

David arrived in Jaffa two weeks ahead of time for talks with the central committee and, more important, with Shochat. They conceived a spectacular project that included a party publication in Hebrew and a federation of trade unions, although there were no funds to finance these castles in the air. David's prominence in the party is clear from an official letter he wrote to the United States Poale Zion, recounting the founding of the Palestinian branch, setting out its future plans, and asking the American chapter to increase its contributions from 100 to 300 francs. This letter, published in the *Yiddisher Kemfer,* the American party's weekly, became David's first words to see print.

The address he gave for contributions was "D. Gruen, Petah Tikva," in spite of the fact that he was spending less and less time there. This was not only because his party work in Jaffa took up more and more of his time, but because Petah Tikva was not the same since Zemach had responded to a call from his own party and gone north to farm in the Galilee. Zemach had tried to persuade David to go with him to Sejera, but David, immersed in Poale Zion business, turned him down. Zemach and six other young men were given a rousing sendoff as they set forth on foot for the north, and David felt abandoned again. Having lost both Rachel and Zemach, he again confided his grief to Shmuel Fox: "I am so lonely although surrounded by so many comrades and friends." Shortly afterward he left Petah Tikva for Jaffa, to absorb himself in Poale Zion.

As Shochat became surer of David, he confided in him more and more, to such an extent that three days before the conference opened on January 5, 1907, David had already told Fox, in Brooklyn, that, in the summer, "I shall certainly take part in the eighth World Zionist Congress as a Poale Zion delegate," even though the party had not yet decided whether to take part in the congress. Indeed, the Rostovians objected to participating in this bourgeois institution, and even if their opposition could be overcome, the party had no money to send two delegates abroad. David's confidence that he would go could only have come from Shochat, the man with secret funds.[9]

When the conference got under way, the central committee's report sparked a raging debate — on the inefficiency of the committee and its political aimlessness — that culminated in all its five members' resigning. That action might well have been engineered by Shochat, since the outcome was the election of a new central committee composed of only two men, him and David. Shochat's account of the affair was that the party had wanted to appoint him as a virtual dictator until it was properly organized and financed — an improbable gesture with which the Rostovians would have flatly disagreed. Shochat claimed he refused the offer but did agree to serve on the two-man committee. In retrospect, it is clear how Shochat brought this about. The party was divided regionally, and each region sent one delegate to the conference, fifteen in all. Since the majority of Rostovians lived in two regions, the number of delegates they sent was disproportionate to their total number. All Shochat had to do to swing votes his way was gain acceptance of a plan for regional representation.

David did not return to Petah Tikva when the conference ended, because on January 9, 1907, David Wolffsohn, the chairman of the World Zionist Organization executive committee, was to arrive in Jaffa. On his first morning in Palestine, he held a reception for the representatives of all local Zionist bodies. Shochat had never needed a first-rate front man as much as now. David and Shochat went together to the reception, where Shochat made it clear that although he was senior, David would deliver Poale Zion's message. Despite the fact that David was a virtual unknown after four months in Palestine, his speech was prominently reported in the press. In his letters David treated Wolffsohn's visit as a royal occasion, honoring him with the title President and transforming his trips to the Jewish agricultural settlements into state visits to the "small Hebrew republics," with His Excellency enjoying the cheers of his loyal subjects. These scenes were more products of his imagination than reality, because David was not overly impressed by Wolffsohn.[10]

David made Jaffa his home and plunged into politics. Ha-Poel ha-Tzair noted, in its paper of the same name, that the Rostovian faction had retired from the battlefield and a new "leader" (it used the English word) had begun, somewhat haphazardly, to organize professional workers' unions. The writer described him as the "absolute leader" of Poale Zion, setting about his job in great haste to be in time for both the Socialist International in Stuttgart in March 1907 and the eighth Zionist Congress. Certainly David did not conceal his eagerness to go to his first congress, and he found his political work to that end thoroughly congenial. The first trade union he organized was in a shoe factory employing four workers. His second was a tailors' association numbering ten men, and his third a carpenters' union; a fourth was already in existence. He combined these groups into the Jaffa Professional Trade Unions Alliance. Ha-Poel ha-Tzair ridiculed this alliance, numbering not more than seventy-five workers, hastily created so that David could represent a large body in Stuttgart.[11]

On January 15 David wrote his father that he had moved to Jaffa, where, to support himself, he taught Hebrew as and when he could. His first opportunity as a labor negotiator arose in the wine cellars of Rishon Le-Zion, a Rostovian stronghold. When six veteran workers were fired for inefficiency, the Rostovians had reacted Russian-style, by calling a strike, closing the gates, and posting armed guards outside. The management's response was to shut down the winery. Shochat and David rushed to the scene to meet with the management. Although David held theoretically to the class struggle principle, he was much less militant than the Rostovians and Shochat and was repelled by their use of firearms. When Shochat stuffed a gun into his belt as they left Jaffa, David pointed out to him that he himself was armed only with arguments — certainly a change from his revolutionary Płońsk days. Indeed, shortly before the strike he had strongly condemned an expropriation which, he had good grounds to believe, had been carried out in Jerusalem by Shochat's men. At the winery David persuaded the management to reopen the plant and refer the dismissal of the six workers to arbitration.

The winery strike brought to the surface the fundamental differences between David and Shochat, who must have realized that David was too much his own man to offer the unquestioning loyalty he demanded. This brief period of cooperation seems to have been enough to open their eyes to the fact that they would never be able to work together. Three weeks later the two-man central committee dissolved itself, and less than three months after he had moved to Jaffa David returned to Petah Tikva. *Ha-Poel ha-Tzair* could not contain its glee. "The leader returned from the campaign and left Jaffa, and the 'alliance' which came into being with such pomp and circumstance has passed away in silence." The abrupt ending of the saga of Shochat and David came at exactly the moment that Itzhak Ben-Zvi was waiting in the wings to make his entry.[12]

Isaac Shimshelevich — better known to Poale Zion by several assumed names — arrived in Palestine incognito in April 1907 and registered at the inn with a new name — I. Ben-Zvi, meaning "the son of Zvi" — that stuck to him forever. He had visited Palestine once before and was returning as an emissary from the Russian party, so as soon as he had landed safely he set out to find the nonexistent Poale Zion central committee. On learning that David was in Petah Tikva, he wasted no time in finding him. Until this meeting their contact had been through letters; now they shared news and ideas about international and local issues. Ben-Zvi, a considerate man, did not want to offend David by replacing him, and offered to work jointly. But David did feel offended and rejected by Shochat and his men and turned down Ben-Zvi's pleas to return to Jaffa to take up party work again.

Ben-Zvi based himself in Jaffa, where he could devote most of his time to the party while earning his living by teaching, and turned himself into a new, one-man central committee. He visited regional branches, made decisions, and prepared for the party gathering to be held in May. Ben-Zvi had had a long career in the underground in Russia. Born on December 6, 1884, in Poltava, a district capital in Russia, he had been to cheder and gymnasium and had completed one year in natural sciences at the University of Kiev. His assets as a potential leader in Palestine included a thorough knowledge of Hebrew and Jewish studies; the fledgling party found in him the authority figure who could introduce new ideas, persuade the members that party policy was in line with the great Poale Zion centers in Russia, Poland, and

Austria, and appeal to conflicting factions. He had been Borochov's right-hand man in founding and organizing Poale Zion and had served with him on the first central committee of the Russian party. After Borochov was arrested in March 1906, Ben-Zvi stepped into his shoes and shifted the party's headquarters from Poltava to Vilna, where he founded the party's paper, *The Proletarian Idea*, as well as its publishing house, the Hammer. He traveled extensively on a forged passport, but after he had been arrested twice and put under police surveillance, Russia was unsafe for him. He therefore executed his plan to settle in Palestine, a decision that was reported to Borochov and to Poale Zion parties outside Russia.

Shochat was overjoyed at Ben-Zvi's arrival and could not wait to take him into his confidence. To crown all his other qualifications, Ben-Zvi was easygoing, unassuming, and modest almost to the point of humility, in spite of standing well over six foot three and having a voice nearly an octave lower than a normal bass. The Rostovians welcomed him as one of their own; Shochat, ever the opportunist, was willing to pay the price of reinforcement of their faction in return for an alliance with Ben-Zvi, and the nationalist element was pushed aside.[13]

In May 1907 the eighty Poale Zion members convened in Jaffa. David, the representative for the agricultural workers, walked from Kefar Saba, a small settlement twenty-five miles north of Petah Tikva, where he had been a day laborer, planting citrus. The warm-hearted, thoughtful Ben-Zvi waited near the well at the entrance to the town to greet each member, but the conference itself was not as congenial as he had hoped. The party's tilt to the Yiddish-Marxist camp as a result of his influence encouraged outspoken criticism of the former two-man committee, notably of David, who was blamed for not organizing the trade unions on binational lines. David did not respond at length to this accusation but said angrily that he would not get caught up in a fight and refused to justify his previous actions. Despite this hostility he still expected to be chosen as a delegate to the coming World Zionist Congress and was dismayed when he came in last of the five candidates. The winner was Ben-Zvi, with 64 votes, the runner-up Shochat, with 53.

The conference then chose a new central committee with two elected members, Ben-Zvi and a Rostovian, who had the power to appoint an additional one or two members at their discretion. Ben-Zvi, who had been most favorably impressed by David on their first meeting, and by what he had heard about him, immediately asked him to join the committee and David accepted. He stayed on in Jaffa and worked on routine matters, mostly information and propaganda, but his heart was not in it, because it had been a bitter realization for him that his party preferred the Russian Ben-Zvi. Rubbing salt in his wound, the conference had voted to publish a party journal in Yiddish and approved a dogmatic class ideology, thus moving Poale Zion away from being the broadly based socialist labor party he advocated. David stood by aloofly when the first issue was printed and refused to write one word for *Der Anfang,* the short-lived Yiddish organ.

His ill humor was intensified by a recurrence of malaria, which confined him to Chaim Baruch's Inn. Although his fever still ran high, by July 25 he was on his way on foot to Rishon Le-Zion to celebrate its twenty-fifth anniversary. He stayed for nearly two months to work in the winery, where, barefoot and half naked, he trod grapes. That he was accepted and liked is demonstrated by his central place among a group of fellow workers in the famous photograph taken there, his first in Palestine.[14]

His feeling of rejection turned his thoughts to his family in Poland and the question of how to bring them all, including his stepmother's family, to Palestine. He drew up a five-year plan to settle them in stages, with him in a new agricultural settlement whose livelihood would come from the cultivation of almonds, a project that had originally been devised for illiterate emigrants from Kurdistan.

Reb Avigdor received a letter from his pioneer son instructing him to sell his two houses in Płońsk; David would buy land with part of the proceeds, and the rest would pay the family's passage to Palestine, where they could support themselves by growing almonds, which David assured him was not difficult. Not surprisingly Reb Avigdor showed no enthusiasm for such a scheme, and his flat rejection left David at a dead end. His readiness to spend five years away from politics suggests that he was aware he would not fit in with the direction the party was taking unless he compromised his views. And since he refused to do this, there was no reason to return to Jaffa. But the season at the winery ended, and a party conference was to be held September 28–30 in Jaffa to hear the reports of the delegates to the Zionist Congress, so for lack of anything better to do, David walked there.[15]

Ben-Zvi and Shochat had returned from their trip to Europe as thick as thieves, having survived a number of mishaps on the outward and return journeys. They had run out of money in Trieste and been forced to spend the night in the Jewish cemetery, where each chose for a pillow the grave of a celebrated Trieste Jew; to earn their fare home they worked as porters. Their unavoidable intimacy had created the ideal conditions for Shochat to give Ben-Zvi an idea of his future plans. David probably sensed that something was in the air, for in his speech at the conference he condemned the growing Russian influence on the party, adding that certain members from Russia had "created a Russian party" instead of an Eretz-Israeli one. His several references to Ben-Zvi by name made the object of his antagonism quite clear. This speech was his parting shot; he had made up his mind to leave Judea and go to Sejera to join Zemach.

An event on the first night of the conference may have contributed to his decision. On September 28, the evening session ended unusually early. Although no reason was offered, it was clear that something important was afoot when Shochat and seven of his supporters met in Ben-Zvi's candlelit room. There they founded the secret society Bar-Giora, named after Simeon Bar-Giora, the military leader in the war against Rome, 66–70 C.E. The nine conspirators swore allegiance to their leader, Israel Shochat, and to the society's motto, "Judea fell in blood and fire; Judea shall rise again in blood and fire." The society's name attested to its triple objective: to form a Hebrew military force that would organize and implement an armed uprising to bring about its ultimate aim, the creation of an independent Jewish state.

The nine agreed that a small elite should operate as a command cell that would secretly initiate and manipulate a number of subordinate organizations. They swore to dedicate themselves unconditionally to the society's aims and unquestioningly to obey their leader's orders. All understood that the penalty for betrayal would be "death by snake bite," that is, sudden execution. The society's subordinate bodies were to be a watchmen's organization to undertake the protection of all Jewish agricultural settlements, which would be the nucleus of the society's future military force, and a countrywide network of shepherds to act as a cover for an intensive survey of the terrain. These two bodies would form new border settlements on the Caucasian model, combining farming and military training. The conspirators also decided to leave Jaffa and live together somewhere in the Galilee, to work out detailed plans for long-term projects. Only Ben-Zvi was excused from going north; he was to remain in Jaffa to run the party and act as Bar-Giora's secret agent.

Why had David been bypassed? What Shochat needed, he admitted fifty years later, was someone "who would be a friend and a teacher, as well as useful on the ideological front," that is, to reconcile the contradictions between Bar-Giora's secrecy and elitism and the liberal, democratic principles of Zionist socialism. One preacher was quite enough for this role, and Ben-Zvi, neither ambitious nor self-willed, had a high standing in Poale Zion's world body as well as in the Russian party. Moreover, he was completely trustworthy — Shochat's legendary eye had not failed him this time — whereas the same could not be said of

David. David, who wanted an integrated party that would act openly and democratically, was not Bar-Giora material. Not realizing this yet, but feeling slighted and rejected at having been left out of the secret, David departed for the Galilee in a bitter mood. Shochat, needless to say, left in a much different frame of mind, making his way north full of hope.[16]

4

Sejera

VISITING JAFFA at the time of the Poale Zion conference was Manya Vilbushevitz, a descendant of Comte Vilbois, an officer in Napoleon's army in Russia who had converted to Judaism and married a rabbi's daughter. Vilbushevitz, the daughter of rich parents, developed into an extraordinary person: slight of stature, a born rebel, ardent for a cause, and utterly fearless. In Minsk, as a member of the revolutionary movement, she was arrested in 1899 and subjected to interminable interrogations. Just as she was on the verge of suicide, a fellow prisoner near her cell, an attractive, intelligent-looking revolutionary with a sorrowful expression, offered her sympathy and solace.

Vilbushevitz fell in love with none other than the infamous agent provocateur Zubatov, an outstandingly successful officer of the Okhrana (secret police), who after their release created and led a new revolutionary group for the purpose of capturing her confederates. Trusting her beloved Zubatov, Vilbushevitz led many of her friends into his trap. Out of her mind with grief and guilt, and on the run herself, she took revenge on a door-to-door salesman who called at her hideout in Odessa, thinking he was an Okhrana secret agent who had tracked her down. Inviting him in, she shot him, then dismembered the corpse, packed the pieces in four suitcases, and dispatched them to four remote parts of the empire.

Vilbushevitz went to Palestine in January 1904, when she was twenty-five. What was to be a short visit turned into a very long one as she toured the country on horseback with some companions she had met, taking in Transjordan as well and being particularly impressed by the barren, black-rocked Golan Heights. It was during this trip that she first conceived the idea of founding a communal settlement for Jewish pioneers, but news of unrest in Russia, accompanied by new pogroms, caused her to go back there at the beginning of 1905 to help organize Jewish self-defense groups. In July 1905 she left again, never to return, to work on the project that had fired her imagination. The establishment of her collective — her dream settlement — became her only goal in life.

In realizing it Vilbushevitz had inexhaustible resources to draw upon, including 5,000 francs in gold from Baron Rothschild, to whom she had appealed, and excellent personal contacts arranged by her two brothers, one of whom was the foremost industrial engineer in Palestine and the other the editor of an agricultural journal published in Paris. After a visit to the United States to raise more money, during which she formed a long-standing friendship with Dr. Judah-Leib Magnes, a Reform rabbi and member of the U.S. Zionist Federation, she went to Europe to attend the 1907 World Zionist Congress in The Hague. In September she returned to Palestine as a friend not only of Chaim Weizmann but of nearly the entire Zionist movement, bringing back with her money and pledges of support for her collective.[1]

In Jaffa, Vilbushevitz was seeking Jews who were able and willing to take part in her project. Although both Poale Zion and Ha-Poel ha-Tzair were meeting there at the time, neither party responded positively to her proposal. Then she met Israel Shochat and his Bar-Giora men, and they seemed ideal for one another. She was looking for daring men; they were looking for a place and a cover under which to organize. Vilbushevitz, her collective project, her funds, and her connections were gifts from heaven for them. They agreed to establish the collective together, but instead of the Golan, they chose as their site the settlement project and training farm at Sejera in the Galilee as being perfect for their scheme. Thus the beginnings of Israel's collective agricultural movement — better known as the kibbutz movement — were wedded to defense. Shochat confided his secret to Vilbushevitz, and she agreed to have her collective serve as a reservoir of manpower and a camouflage for Bar-Giora.

Unaware of these plans, David Gruen arrived in Sejera after a three-day walk. The first Jewish agricultural settlement in Lower Galilee, as well as the JCA's first project of its kind, Sejera was a hilltop settlement comprising a model farm to teach Jews how to work the land and large plots of arable land that were leased on favorable terms to the best of the trainees, who became the settlers. The trainee-workers were housed in an old Arab *khan*, the farm's main building, which, set on top of the hill, was quite separate from the new white buildings, arranged in two rows on the hillside, which the settlers occupied.

David, having missed the hiring period for day laborers, stayed in

the khan as Zemach's guest, and they labored together night and day to
bring in the grain harvest. He was thrilled by the Jewish agriculturists
gathered in Sejera and the absence of non-Jewish labor and captivated
by the breathtaking landscape of hills encircling the settlement. The
Jordan River did not live up to his childhood imaginings, but he consoled himself with the thought that "quality does not depend on physical size." So intoxicating were the open fields, the plowing and planting, the certainty that the brown soil would again be adorned with the
soft green shoots of new life, that David felt himself "a partner in
the act of creation." At last he had found the Eretz Israel he had been
looking for. The contrast between Judea and the Galilee was so striking that he felt he had again experienced the passage from exile to redemption and finally found happiness. "At Succoth 1907, I left for
Sejera in the Galilee, where I worked for three years," he averred in his
memoirs.[2]

In fact Sejera was his home for merely twenty-five months — October 1907 to November 1909 — only thirteen of them consecutive, and
not all of them happy. Although in the early days he and Zemach rev-
eled together in the longed-for countryside, their joy was cut short
when Manya Vilbushevitz arrived with the announcement that at the
start of the new season the farm would undergo a profound change. On
Saturday, November 2, Shochat and his Bar-Giora troupe marched into
the settlement on either side of a wagon piled high with baggage. Zemach, seeing an invasion of swaggering soldiers of fortune, chests
thrust out, muscles bulging, sporting handguns, and slapping their
boots with their whips, became frightened. He, the intellectual aes-
thete, lover of beauty, serenity, and poetry, felt that a group of ruffians
were about to force themselves and their way of life on him. Shochat
and his men seemed to him a huge army taking over the countryside,
destroying the charm and "sweetness of tranquillity" of Sejera forever.

Under the new arrangement, the collective had contracted with
Eliahu Krause, the JCA representative in Sejera, to run the model farm
without supervision for one year and receive an agreed-upon sum for
its work, with any surplus revenue going to the management. This
meant that only the collective had the authority to take on new laborers; whomever it hired became a member. In this way the larger
collective could conceal the secret Bar-Giora cell within it. The collective was run as a domestic commune, pooling money and work. The
members' forty-franc monthly wage was kept in a common fund,
which paid for their food and other basic needs. Vilbushevitz, the liaison between the collective and the farm management, kept the books
and was paid eighty francs a month. Shochat became responsible for
the settlement's mill.[3]

Shochat invited Zemach to join the collective, but frightened by
what he saw, Zemach took to his heels in the dead of night, "as if I
were running for my life," he wrote.

Zemach, the aristocrat, found no virtue or grace in these strong men
or their bravado. He, David, and all the rest sensed that the new arrivals were a closely knit group, united in their common worship of Shochat, sharing a secret that involved arms and horseback riding; but
they could not guess what it was really about.

David was not asked to join the collective, was not hired, and therefore had no place in the farm; its 1907–1908 payroll for November and
December does not list his name among the new workers, all either
Bar-Giora or Poale Zion members. One reason was that he lacked experience as a farm hand. The most he could have contributed initially
was weeding or moving produce from place to place. Equally important was his distaste for Vilbushevitz's and Shochat's supervision. And
last but not least, Shochat was reluctant to allow David to get too close
to Bar-Giora, for fear that David might challenge his authority.

In January 1908 David was taken on as a trainee by one of the tenant
farmers. By the end of February he had become "a day laborer on one
of the farms." That year there were two hundred people in Sejera, one
hundred and fifty of them adults, a fairly large settlement for those
times. But the social life centered around the khan, where the collective members lived. About twenty people ate regularly in the communal dining room, and in the busy season the number rose to around
thirty-five. They were merrymakers, singing and dancing long into the
nights. There were very few women among them in the early days:
Manya Vilbushevitz, the first to come, was followed by six others. The
first wedding celebrated in Sejera was between Vilbushevitz and Shochat. Three of the women joined and found husbands in Bar-Giora; the
remaining three married Bar-Giora members but did not join. The
women's attraction to the romantic aura surrounding the men of Bar-
Giora meant that David and the other outsiders had little chance to
find a female companion, and David complained bitterly of his loneliness.

The Bar-Giora people became a tightly knit elite, the men affecting
ceremonial Arab dress — the soft riding boots, headgear (kaffiyeh), and
embroidered robes (abbaiya) that made up the costume of the fearless
Arab mounted guards or Circassians. They appeared to be glamorous
new Jews. Shochat, who resembled an Arab sheik, was respected by the
Bar-Giora and collective members, who responded eagerly to his commands. They learned to use firearms and followed a rigorous physical
fitness routine. David was allowed to take part in these activities, but
he must have felt like a pariah, for apart from an occasional meal in the

communal dining room and social evening in the khan, he was left on his own in his employer's home. Furthermore, as a field hand for Abraham Rogachevsky, he was paid only thirty francs a month.

Rogachevsky, who had been a saddler in Russia, had first joined the model farm in 1904 as a trainee. In 1907 he was, with his wife and two children, one of Sejera's twenty-three settlers. His purpose in hiring David was not to expand an already flourishing farm, but to free himself to return to his original vocation. Later he added cobbling to his skills, then bricklaying, and in the end was a jack-of-all-trades — except in farming, for which he had no aptitude whatever. Rogachevsky's house was built in two sections: the front for the family, the rear for livestock, produce, and farm equipment. He was kind enough to make room for his hired hand in the family section. David's day began at 4:30 A.M. He fed the animals, made his own breakfast, took his herd — "two oxen, two cows, two calves, and a donkey" — to the water trough, then returned them to their quarters. Just before sunrise, he was on his way to the fields. At 4:00 P.M. he returned to the farm, watered and fed his beasts, cleaned out their sheds, and bedded them down. The rest of the day, or what was left of it, was his own, except for one last duty — feeding the animals again before he retired.[4]

As a fervent Zionist David should have been happy, for in Rogachevsky's employ he truly fulfilled Zionism's most sublime tenet, the return to the land. But David and his employer had one thing in common: their hearts were fond of the idea of Jewish agriculture, but their minds were elsewhere. Rogachevsky loved to hold forth about Zionism, applauding Theodor Herzl and his policies; David was lost in thoughts of Jewish revival.

> How sweet and easy is plowing! The handle of the plow in my left hand, the goad in my right, I effortlessly follow behind the oxen, my eyes fixed on the black earth as it surfaces, then breaks up beneath the plowshare. In slow-measured step the oxen pace the field, as if they were prosperous landowners, with all the time in the world to think, to muse, to dream. When a Jew walks behind oxen plowing his ancestral soil and sees his fellow Jews nearby doing likewise, is it possible for him not to marvel?

Before long, David discovered that the life of a Hebrew farm hand was not as sublime as he had imagined it. He got no joy from his work, mostly because he could not find a quiet corner in Rogachevsky's home; babies and their noise never held his interest for long. He reported to his father that he was "completely enslaved from morning till night. . . . I hate the agrarian property which ties its owners and enslaves them, for with all my heart and soul I need to be free in body and mind." Shochat proved to be right in not asking David to join the collective.[5]

By March 1908 David was in very low spirits and began to amass debts, which soon amounted to forty rubles, the equivalent of three months' wages. The only item for which he is known to have borrowed was his Browning handgun; he took out a loan of seven and a half rubles, half its cost. Surely one reason for this extravagant purchase was his desire to be like the Bar-Giora members. This suggests that he had to borrow just to live, something he had done earlier in Jaffa. One expense beyond his means was his regular Friday trip to Tiberias to treat himself to a traditional gefilte fish meal, which was worth the one-fifth of a ruble it cost because it reminded him of the Sabbath in his father's home. "Many times, especially on holidays," he wrote his family, "I've longed to be with you, to settle down around the table and listen to all your voices, even for a minute."

Although he was growing weary of Sejera, there was one experience he would not have missed for anything: taking part in guarding Sejera with Bar-Giora. Determined to start the watchmen's organization, Shochat aimed to take over the guarding of the model farm and its surrounding fields. To do this, he had first to discredit the current watchmen, who were traditionally Circassians from nearby Kafr Kama. They had a contract with JCA for the job, which Eliahu Krause refused to cancel. Unlike Shochat, Krause could see no justification for risking Jewish lives for "abstract principle," especially since he doubted the capability of Shochat's men. But his greatest fear was that the Circassians, who considered themselves unmatched in bravery, would be insulted and revenge themselves on the Jews, destroying the peaceful relations between the settlers and their neighbors.

Shochat therefore resorted to trickery. One night when the attention of one of the guards wandered, Shochat arranged to have a mule taken from its stable and hidden. Then he woke Krause, reported the theft, and blamed the Circassian for the loss. The Circassian was sent away in disgrace and Shochat persuaded Krause to take on a Bar-Giora man as a replacement. The Circassians tried to intimidate the new Jewish guard by firing near him in the dark, but he was supported nightly by a different comrade, David taking his turn with the others. Before long Krause had added the guarding of the settlement to the collective's duties. Shochat's final victory came at the beginning of February, when the Sejera farmers let their livestock graze all night. Guarding the open fields at night was considered the highest proof of courage, so by taking on that task, the Jews proved that they were as brave as Circassians or Arabs.

A few years later Shochat and Ben-Gurion both hailed this guard service as the conquest of the first bridgehead on the way to a Hebrew army. Their claim was only partially justified, however, since Krause's concession to the collective did not last for two years, as they asserted, but only for the one year of its contract with JCA. Believing that peace depended more on a good relationship between Jews and their Moslem neighbors than on armed force, he reverted to his policy of avoiding provocation and making agreements, when possible, with the local Moslem sheiks. Accordingly, the Circassians agreed to withdraw a lawsuit they had filed and Krause told Shochat's guards to seek employment elsewhere. Shochat and his men moved to nearby Meskha, and the Circassian guards were reinstated in Sejera.[6]

David Gruen was not there to see the change. At the end of May 1908 he left Sejera for nearby Yavniel, where, the JCA records reveal, he was employed as a farm hand. From Yavniel he made many excursions to new settlements in lower Galilee and around the shores of Lake Tiberias, even finding time to revive his spirits with a little politicking. A few meetings of workers from all over the area were held at Kinneret, on the shore of the lake, and he took to the platform, delivered some speeches, raised some demands, and drafted resolutions. But before he could hit his stride, a letter from his father reminded him that he had to report for service in the czar's army; if he defaulted, his father would be fined 300 rubles. Just before his return to Płońsk, he went on a horseback excursion with a few friends all over the Galilee and as far north as Beirut. In June he sailed from Jaffa for Russia.

David stayed in Poland until the end of 1908. He spent three months in the army; then his father contacted a border smuggler to help him desert and escape the country. Reb Avigdor gave the smuggler an advance payment and left the completion of the transaction to his son who, naive to the point of recklessness, asked the first man he came across to take a message and the balance of the money to the smuggler. Luckily the stranger did as he was told. David sneaked away from his camp and traveled first to Warsaw, then on to the German border, where the smuggler saw him safely across. He returned to Palestine on a false passport, knowing that he would never again be able to enter the Russian empire under his own name.[7]

On returning to Jaffa Ben-Gurion had no clear idea of what he wanted to do or where he wanted to stay, although he did know that politics attracted him far more than farming. Furthermore, whatever he decided had to be suitable for his family, who had charged him with producing a satisfactory scheme for their settlement in Palestine, it having been agreed in Płońsk that Zippora would be the first to join him, by summer 1909 at the latest. But before choosing a permanent base, he decided to make a farewell visit to the Galilee and collect his possessions from Yavniel. What he had intended as a brief visit turned into a long one. Because he found Arab labor so prevalent in the nearby settlement of Menahemiya, he stayed on to prove that "we work much better." The farmer who hired him had two other workers, a Jew and an Arab, so David started a competition with the other Jew to spur him to greater efforts. The Arab, unable to keep up with them, begged them to slow down or he would be shamed. Later Ben-Gurion cited the incident as proof that Hebrew labor — *Avodah Ivrit* — would pay off.

After a short visit to Mitzpe, David went on to Kinneret, which had become a colony and model farm like Sejera. There he suffered a recurrence of malaria, which strengthened his inclination to make his home in or near Jaffa where, because it was drier, he believed he would be less susceptible. Although Ben-Gurion recollected staying in the Galilee a long time — "a few months in Kinneret . . . and a few months in Menahemiya" — his sojourn there lasted less than two months.

Before the end of February he paid his first visit to Jerusalem, where the sight of the Western Wall brought on such extreme emotional agitation that he remained in the city for a week. There he met with Itzhak Ben-Zvi, clearly the leader of Poale Zion, who had made it his headquarters, believing Jerusalem to be the best place for the party to grow and prepare a Jewish proletariat for its revolutionary mission. Apparently on Ben-Zvi's advice, and certainly with his blessing, David returned to Jaffa to join the party's district committee. Out of work and eighteen rubles in debt, David renounced his former vow and wrote his father asking for money, explaining that he did not want to find a regular job until he had returned to Sejera to attend the party's Galilee conference. That may have been true, but it might have been his desire to join Hashomer, the watchmen's association Bar-Giora was going to inaugurate after the conference, that persuaded him to ask for his father's help.

In Sejera David found a completely new situation. The Arab fellahs — peasants or agricultural laborers — had begun to object to the Jewish land purchases, freely contracted between the absentee Arab landowners and the JCA, because they resulted in the Arab farmers' eviction. The friction worsened as the Arabs' political expectations increased following a coup in Istanbul by the Young Turks and the sudden restoration of the constitution, which they believed would bring greater political and economic freedom to the provinces of the Ottoman Empire. The Arabs in Kafr Kanna and in Lubia seized by force land that had previously been sold to Jews.

As the conference convened in Sejera at Passover 1909, its delegates felt an explosive atmosphere enveloping the entire Galilee. During the communal Seder, everyone heard the story of the photographer who had been set upon by Arabs from Kafr Kanna while on his way to record the conference. Fearing for his life, he shot and wounded one of his attackers. The Sejera settlers were in a sober mood, for if the wounded Arab died, his family and village would have to seek a blood revenge. Everyone who owned one carried a weapon to the conference the next morning.

David, distracted by his own thoughts, sat in a remote corner and was surprised to hear himself elected chairman. But in the chair he could not concentrate on the ideological debate. "My mind and heart were on the immediate situation and my hand was glued to my Browning holster." When news arrived that a Sejera herd had been driven off by Arabs from Kafr Kanna, David ordered a recess to discuss the situation. The following morning it was learned that the Arab had died, and the conference was brought to an early end.

Many of the delegates quickly returned to their homes, but the Bar-Giora members — Ben-Zvi and Rachel Yanait, his fiancée, among them — who considered themselves experts on the Arabs, decided that the worst was over and went to Meskha for the inauguration of Hashomer, Bar-Giora's first offshoot. Their departure made the situation in Sejera even graver, since the settlers were ill prepared to defend themselves. David, who felt bound to remain to help them, wound up staying more than a year.[8]

While on the alert in Sejera, David did not lose sight of what was happening in nearby Meskha. He knew that Yanait, who had been in Palestine for less than a year and knew nothing of firearms, would be admitted as a full member to Hashomer and was mystified as to why he, with practical experience, had not been approached. Worse yet, four of the eighteen founding members were new faces, as if to emphasize the rejection of David the veteran.

In fact, Ben-Zvi and Yanait had jointly pleaded with Shochat to change his mind about David. Yanait later speculated that his self-isolation at the start of the conference, when David sat moodily aloof, signaled his awareness that he would not be invited to join. In any case, hurt beyond measure, he did not forget this insult for many years: even after he had achieved world fame, when Ben-Gurion encountered Shochat or any of his close associates, he would hiss in their faces, "You didn't want me!"

On April 12, as Hashomer's constitution was being formulated in Meskha, an agitated worker in Sejera reported to David and others that two unknown Arabs were on the hill beyond the settlement cemetery. They had asked questions in Arabic that he could not understand, so he had come to find help. Without waiting the worker rushed back to the two Arabs, who shot him dead. A pursuit developed into a confrontation between a large Arab crowd and the Sejera settlers. David, at the head of the pursuers, received his baptism of fire. As, gun in hand, he neared the two assailants, he heard his companion Shimon Melamed cry out, "I've been shot!" Melamed fell, and before David could drop to his knees beside him, he died. Thus did the Arabs take their revenge. After this incident, no one could doubt David's courage under fire, and he was appointed a guard in Sejera. His credentials for Hashomer were second to none; still no invitation came.

As tension between Jews and Arabs in the Galilee continued, David remained at his post, and the JCA invited him to an emergency meeting in Yavniel. "I was the delegate for Sejera," he wrote proudly to his father. At the meeting he was elected to a committee of ten set up to organize a defense group, to recruit more Jewish workers to the Galilee, and to strengthen the colonies' guards. No longer merely a field hand, he was one of the leading members of the Galilee Committee for Defense, whose aims did not differ greatly from those of Hashomer. The amount of energy he invested in his new task suggests that the thought of avenging himself by making his defense group overshadow Hashomer was one motive. "We buy as many weapons as we can afford," he reported to his father. "They are as important to a man here as the clothes on his back and the food in his mouth."

Happy in his new status and new job on the model farm, David resigned from the party's district committee in Jaffa. His timetable was different from that of his Rogachevsky days. To avoid the midday sun, he rose at 3:30 A.M., went to the fields at 4:00, harvested until 10:30, rested until 2:30 P.M., and then, when the sun was lower, returned to the fields and worked until 5:30. In his leisure time he played chess and chatted with Shlomo Lavi, an old Ezra friend who had recently arrived in Sejera. His only irritant was having no bed of his own, because he had not been hired at the beginning of the season.[9]

David now felt that Sejera was his home and it was time to send for his family. Figuring that they would get a good start from the loan of 25,000 francs for forty years, at the 2 percent per annum JCA provided its tenants, together with a house, a barn, and 250 dunams (about 63 acres) of arable land, he offered his family a three-stage plan to begin in the new agricultural year, not later than September 19, 1909. In the first, his two sisters would come at once to Sejera and he would take on a house and farm from JCA. He appointed Rivka housekeeper and assigned Zippora to a sewing machine; thus "our organized communal life will enable us to live cheaper and better." Zippora's earnings as a seamstress would supplement his income from the farm; with his own

hands he could clear stones, plow, plant, and reap. He would farm sci-
entifically, mixing crops and livestock — corn, chicken, ducks, cows,
vegetables, almonds, olives, and vineyards.

The arrival of his brothers would inaugurate the second phase, and
only "when everyone is here and has become familiar with the country
and skilled in agricultural work" and the farm was prosperous would
the third step be undertaken. "Our father will come to Eretz Israel."
Neither the scheme nor its three stages were definite, as became clear
when David addressed himself to the personal questions involved, such
as a match for twenty-eight-year-old Rivka. He pointed out to his father that because in Sejera there were thirty-five single men and only
five women, it would be much easier for her to find a husband there.
But if his father thought otherwise, he added, Rivka could stay in
Płońsk until she found a husband.

Like Joseph before him, David, the youngest, determined his family's future. He wrote without sensitivity for his siblings' feelings,
though they all read his letters; he could no more dissimulate his affection for his sisters than his disdain for his brothers. "Michael's interests," he wrote, "will always remain in Płońsk. . . . I have decided that
it is much better for him not to come. Work as a hired hand will be too
difficult for him, and if he's going to be idle, he will be better off at
home, where at least he earns a few rubles now and then. For in Eretz
Israel, in a settlement, among hard-working people, it's impossible for
a man to do nothing. Moreover, it's very difficult for a young man to
find a bride here. Of course, when our homestead is established, he,
too, will be welcome to come and some sort of work will be found for
him."

Humpbacked Abraham also played no part in David's program. Although Abraham wrote to David pointing out that he could earn his
living by selling lottery tickets, David ruled that Eretz Israel had no
use for such trades. Instead he invited Abraham to send his two children, promising to take good care of them. In short, David insisted that
his less able brothers had no place in Palestine in the near future. If, he
warned, they came despite his instructions, they must bring money, for
"I renounce all responsibility in the matter." But to his sisters he
wrote, "How great is my longing for you; how impatiently I wait for
you. Please fly to me, spread your wings, soar into the air, swoop down
on me, and then we can all look forward impatiently and longingly to
our father's arrival."

As for himself, David made it clear that he would settle permanently
on the land only if the family's good demanded it. If the plan came to
nothing, or if he could find someone else to run the farm, he would do

something else, for he had no ambition whatever to be a farmer. In fact, he was resolved to study law in Istanbul — an important step toward his Zionist mission — for he believed the new regime in Turkey and the restoration of the constitution would open up greater possibilities for the nationalities within the Ottoman Empire to take a more active role in the Ottoman government and parliament and move toward autonomy. This called for a better understanding of Ottoman laws and the working of Ottoman institutions. As a lawyer he could deal better, for Zionism's sake, with the administration, both in Istanbul and Palestine.[10]

While waiting for his sisters to come to him, he took part in Sejera's communal life and began to learn Arabic, in preparation for his eventual law practice, from a Safed-born Jew with whom he shared a room in the khan. But his heart was not in it and his progress was slow. Meanwhile he suffered another disappointment as JCA whittled away Sejera's defense scheme for fear it might provoke more trouble with the Arabs. By the beginning of July 1909 it was clear that nothing of substance would come of the Galilee Committee for Defense, whereas Hashomer had stepped up its activity and widened its scope. Nor was David's status in Poale Zion encouraging. In the party's election of delegates for the impending ninth Zionist World Congress, David received only one vote; Ben-Zvi got 167 and Shochat 146.

News from Płońsk was no more cheerful. An exchange of letters between Sejera and Płońsk usually took six weeks. When the eagerly awaited reply to his letter offering the settlement plan did not arrive on time, David lamented in another letter, "I am going out of my mind with worry." When the letter finally came, it did not contain the yearned-for news. His sisters insisted on more details, and he felt that his family did not care about him.

In a black mood, made worse by a labor dispute brewing between workers and management, he packed up his belongings and set off for Yavniel. En route he was waylaid by an Arab thief who threatened him at knife point and reached for David's gun. David received a knife wound as he struggled with the man, but though he managed to hold on to the pistol, the thief took all his possessions. There was nothing to do but return to Sejera empty-handed and wait forlornly for his sisters, who were now his only hope. Would they, after all, see the light and join him? As the closing date for admission to the next year's agricultural training schedule neared, his waiting became more and more painful. At last, eleven weeks after his reply to his sisters, another letter arrived with, alas, more questions, this time from his father, who admonished him that such a voyage could not be undertaken "in haste."

Deeply hurt, David retorted, "Stay at home and be happy there. I have just one small favor to ask — please don't cloud my mind with idle matters."[11]

Sejera's labor dispute, his sisters' interminable delay, and the improved security situation — relative peace had been restored after negotiations between JCA and the Arab sheiks — eliminated his reasons to remain in the colony. Reluctant to commit himself for a whole year, he declined a decent job offered him by JCA. In November he said farewell to Sejera and traveled on foot to Zichron Yaacov, near Mount Carmel.

5

Jerusalem/Istanbul

DAVID GRUEN HAD COME to Zichron, the pride of Baron Edmond de Rothschild's colonies, to study Arabic and improve his French, for both languages were used there. At first, as in Sejera, and before that in Petah Tikva, he found himself, by his own account, in the most beautiful settlement in all Palestine — indeed, in the whole world — "and if paradise even slightly resembles this place, then it is really paradise," he enthused to his father. Characteristically, he proposed Zichron as a suitable place for his family, at least for Zippora, because "there is a lot of work for a seamstress."

The wages in this so-called paradise, however, were the lowest in the country, and it was also unique because the Arab workers and their families lived on the farms with their Jewish employers — a blemish to David's eyes. Another defect that he neglected to mention was the settlers' use of Yiddish, not Hebrew, as an everyday language. If he omitted these deficiencies from his letters to point up only Zichron's attractiveness, he gained very little. His family's response was again unenthusiastic, and he said, "My plan to bring my family to Palestine came to nil."

David's schemes for his family were a product of his loneliness and desperate desire for a fixed base, emotional and physical, without which he could not direct his energy to the ambition that had taken definite form in his mind. "Either as a worker or as a lawyer," he told his father in January 1910, "I have only one aim: to strive for the Hebrew worker in Eretz Israel; this is the fabric of my life . . . the sacred mission of my life, and in it I shall find my happiness."

In the meantime, he justified his time in Zichron by continuing to learn Arabic, with poor results, and to improve his French, with far greater success. He could pay his tuition only by asking his father for ten rubles a month, with which Reb Avigdor obliged. David could have continued boring holes to plant trees and reading French for quite a while longer had not Itzhak Ben-Zvi invited him to the party's Passover conference in Jaffa.

It took him two days to walk the sixty-five miles from Zichron to the workers' club in Jaffa where the meeting was to take place; exhausted when he arrived, he slept for twenty hours. When he opened his eyes the conference was half over. Among other things it resolved to bring out a party newspaper, *Ha-Achdut* (Unity), for which Ben-Zvi wanted to appoint the best possible editorial board. Before the conference, he had turned to famed Poale Zion figures in Europe and America, but they had all declined, so Ben-Zvi asked the conference to elect local members. No one brought up David's name. Finally, three people were elected to the editorial board, with power to co-opt a fourth. In two conflicting versions of what happened, one claims that the three elected were Ben-Zvi, Rachel Yanait, and David. Ben-Gurion, on the other hand, asserts that Jacob Zerubavel was the third member and that he, David, was added later. This version would explain why he walked out in a sulk and returned to labor in the fields.

The essential difference between David's approach to the party as a Palestinian party responsive to the actual conditions in the country and that of the others, who still thought of it as a branch of the Russian party, was apparent when he outlined his program at the conference. To entrench and strengthen their political position so they could stand up to their enemies, the Jews had to unite and integrate all their organized resources in the form of committees, agencies, parties, and other associations. That is, Jews in all walks of life, in all parts of the Ottoman state, had to create and take part in a national, political organization that would be empowered to demand in the Ottoman imperial parliament and from the central government their civil, political, and national rights and to defend their economic and cultural interests. David wanted all Jews in Palestine, together with all other Jewish communities in the Ottoman Empire, to become Ottoman subjects and unite in one autonomous political body that would have the right to elect its own representatives to the parliament. He wanted to study law to groom himself for election to the Turkish parliament; he said that his plan was not only to be a member of the parliament, but to be a minister in the sultan's government, "so I shall be able to defend Zionism."

On his way back to Zichron he stopped at Ein Ganim, not far from Petah Tikva, to see Rachel Nelkin, who as Mrs. Beit-Halachmi was a very new mother. Finding her cradling a baby girl in her arms, David was overwhelmed. Rachel was more beautiful than ever, and her motherliness captivated him. Unable to conceal his feelings, he held her in his arms and kissed her. All the way back to Zichron and for a long time afterward Rachel's image haunted him day and night. Finally he wrote, commanding her to visit him "at once," saying it was her "duty" to see a place as beautiful as Zichron. In his naiveté he could not imagine that she could love him any less than he loved her; there was no doubt in his mind that they could still be together. But he waited for her reply in vain.[1]

When he received a note from Ben-Zvi inviting him to join *Ha-Achdut*, David expressed no joy, feigning surprise and claiming he had neither experience nor talent for such a job. Thinking he was playing hard to get, Ben-Zvi and Yanait doubled their efforts to convince him that they really needed him, and, mollified, he left Zichron for Jerusalem in June 1910.

Ben-Zvi invited David to share his room until he found a place of his own in Jerusalem. David must have been somewhat taken aback to find that Zerubavel, who had recently arrived from Russia, was already installed there and that there was only one "bed" for the three. None of them was selfish enough to take it, so they took turns sleeping on a mat on the floor while the bed, some planks balanced across two empty oil drums, remained unoccupied. There was no lack of time for discussing the future editorial policies of their publication, which would be dedicated to the interests of the workers and the Hebrew people in Palestine and elsewhere in the Ottoman Empire. The paper's name, Unity, was an echo of the Young Turks' pledge to bring together all Ottoman citizens and residents.

"It is clear to us," read the editors' note to the reader in the paper's first issue, "that all the strength of the Ottoman state, a state made up of many nations with differing races, languages, cultures, and histories, depends on the internal integration of its component nations." The fact that Ben-Zvi let Ben-Gurion give the opening address at the party's October 1910 conference, which served as the basis for discussion, indicates the nature of their relationship. Although Ben-Zvi was the party's uncontested number one, Ben-Gurion, with his more acute political sense, had an increasing influence on his colleague's political development, especially in adapting Borochov's political theory to the conditions of Ottoman Palestine.

David felt like a novice compared to Zerubavel, a carpenter's son who had grown up in Poltava, Ben-Zvi's hometown, had worked with him and Yanait in the Russian party, and was an experienced editor in its press. Sturdy and barrel-chested, he tried to disguise his lack of intellect with pompous words, pretentious phrasing — and by sporting a tremendous square-cut beard. It did not take David long to discover

that there was much less to Zerubavel than met the eye. Ahron Reuveni, Ben-Zvi's brother, soon turned up as a fifth editor. The printing
press had been set up in a house on Jaffa Street, near Floyd Court.
There David rented a windowless narrow basement room that included a well covered by a huge round stone. The only natural light
filtered through a glass door facing north, and the door had to be left
open for air to enter.

David, as proofreader and translator, was paid thirty francs a
month — not much, but within the accepted range for salaried party
workers. But it was inadequate for David, who had vowed to eat one
hot meal a day. This he took at the table of a woman who cooked meals
for regular customers; a month's board consumed his entire monthly
wage. His friends may have thought him extravagant — some supported a family on the same amount — but hunger was an acute problem for him. Although he reduced his morning hunger pangs by
sleeping late and then rushing over to Ben-Zvi's, where he could get a
bite to eat, there was no solution to his evening hunger "until I realized
that this couldn't go on and my pay must be raised to 40 francs a
month." When this was done, he had a few francs to spare. To augment
his income, he sought private pupils and finally found one — Rachel
Yanait's mother, to whom he taught Hebrew.

David rarely received his wages on time or in full and continued to
be extremely poor; the black overcoat he had brought from Płońsk
doubled as a blanket at night during the winter. His only escape from
loneliness in his dark basement was Shlomo Zemach's home on Jaffa
Street, a pleasant apartment financed by his wife's prospering brothers.
There David could drink tea and enjoy a game of chess. The handsome
Zemach was living in style. In Rehovot, in 1908, he had met the beautiful Hemda Polansky, who fell for him and married him secretly. On
her allowance from her wealthy family they had set up a well-ap-
pointed home where they held a literary salon. Zemach had given
himself over entirely to literary work and planned to go to France, to
study belles-lettres at the Sorbonne. One night when the two friends
were remembering old times, David told of his recent meeting with
Rachel Beit-Halachmi. The three of them sent her an invitation to visit
Jerusalem with her daughter. This time, too, Rachel chose to stay at
home with her husband.

Finally everything was ready for *Ha-Achdut*'s first appearance. The
initial run of a thousand copies was to be sold in Palestine, Europe, and
the United States. This would cover costs except for two hundred
francs a month, which was a small setback, considering that it was the
first socialist paper in Hebrew emanating from Jerusalem to the Jews
of the world. The first three issues came out monthly; after that the

paper was published weekly or twice a month as a double issue.

To mark his new status on the editorial board, David assumed a new name — Ben-Gurion — in conformance with the Poale Zion members' custom of taking names of national heroes and rebels. Shochat's secret society was named after the military leader Bar-Giora; Ben-Zvi added to his arsenal of pseudonyms the name of Avner, King Saul's army chief; Golda Lishansky finally settled on Rachel Yanait, after Alexander Yannai of the Hasmonean dynasty. Jacob Vitkin became Zerubavel, a Judean prince and scion of the royal house of David. David, wanting to preserve the phonetics of his family name, began with Ben Gruen, from which it was only a short step to Joseph Ben-Gurion, the renowned defense minister in Jerusalem at the time of the great Jewish rebellion against the Romans, an aristocrat with an uncrushable yearning for democracy, an honest man to whom freedom was priceless. This was greatly to David's liking, especially because his own middle name was Joseph.

His decision to take a new name was remarkable only because Ben-Gurion stuck to it, unlike so many of his friends whose name changing was difficult to keep up with. The plethora of bombastic pen names might well have led the casual *Ha-Achdut* reader to think that the old kingdom of Judea had come back to life. Ben-Zvi, for example, signed his political articles Categori. His brother signed his Wagman, reserving Reuveni for his literary output. The supreme name collector was Zerubavel who, in the absence of Ben-Zvi and Ben-Gurion, once wrote an entire issue by himself, signing each article with a different name. Although Ben-Zvi and Reuveni contributed three times as much material as Ben-Gurion, Zerubavel was the most prolific, writing four times as much.

In his first year with the paper, Ben-Gurion wrote fifteen articles, all dealing with organization or political matters. Jerusalem offered a number of public libraries whose books in Hebrew, Russian, and German he used to devour by the light of a kerosene lamp. He earned some extra money by translating Werner Sombart's *Socialism and the Social Movement in the 19th Century* from German for *Ha-Achdut*. Later published in one volume, his translation became the first book on socialism to be published in Hebrew.[2]

One theme recurred in Ben-Gurion's articles and speeches: the need to lay down foundations on which the Yishuv could develop into a "force." He argued that it was impossible to direct the implementation of Zionism from the outside, that it could be done only by the Yishuv itself. Therefore he insisted that the power vested in the Zionist organizations of the world be transferred to their analogues in Palestine. There was one main difficulty with this "Palestinocentric" approach:

not only were the Jewish people as a whole still outside Eretz Israel, but so, too, were the great majority of Zionists. How was it possible to deprive these millions of the right to direct Zionism the way they saw fit and bestow it on the few thousand Zionists who made up the Yishuv? Ben-Gurion's response, in line with his conviction, was a demand to increase the Yishuv systematically and to consolidate it into a political entity, for the strength of the Yishuv was the heart of the Zionist movement. Only by becoming a force would it be able to attain Zionism's goals, and to become a force it had to be vested with powers to direct its own course.

After four months Ben-Zvi warmed to Ben-Gurion's political ideas and rid himself of many Russian attitudes, becoming Palestinocentric and urging World Poale Zion to transfer its central agencies from Vienna to Palestine. Ben-Zvi became an ardent supporter of Hebrew as the party's only language in Palestine, clashing on this point with Zerubavel and other Yiddishists. For his part, Ben-Zvi brought Ben-Gurion closer to the inner party councils as his trusted friend and partner and in October 1910 asked him to chair the party conference on the most important issues. Their unanimity became a byword, and soon in Palestine and in Poale Zion the world over, they came to be affectionately called the *Benim*, "sons."

The year 1910 was one of despair for the Zionist labor movements in Palestine. Ha-Poel ha-Tzair was greatly disappointed in its campaign to recruit participants for the "conquest of labor" that was to have trained its members for agricultural work in settlements. Poale Zion was also dejected. The "inevitable process" had not come to pass as Borochov had predicted, nor had the belief in class struggle much scope for action in Palestine. Both parties were despondent because the World Zionist Organization had not yet recognized the principle of Avodah Ivrit or the employment of Jews by Jews. Even public works by Zionist corporations and other publicly owned companies were carried out by Arab labor. Beyond feeling ideologically and socially isolated within the Yishuv, Poale Zion and Ha-Poel ha-Tzair members were further depressed by the knowledge that more Jews were leaving than entering the country. This affected their party work, for it seemed that no one knew where to turn or what to do. Zionism had apparently reached a dead end.[3]

The pervasive atmosphere of despair led Ben-Gurion to decide that it was a good time to implement his plan to become a lawyer. While campaigning for new subscribers to *Ha-Achdut*, he came across Manya and Israel Shochat in Haifa. Shochat, too, was getting ready to study law in Istanbul, so that he would be able to handle personally any legal matters connected with Hashomer. He was not the only Poale Zion veteran preparing to study abroad; the seventh party conference held in Haifa in April 1911 was memorable for the announcement by Ben-Zvi, Yanait, and Ben-Gurion of their intention to leave. A new central committee and a new editorial board had to be elected, and Zerubavel's hour arrived: henceforth, he would be the leader of both. The conference also elected Ben-Zvi and Ben-Gurion as its delegates to the third world Poale Zion convention the following July, which coincided approximately in time and place with the World Zionist Congress.

Upon his return to Jerusalem, Ben-Gurion found that Zemach, too, had succumbed to the prevailing mood. He and his wife were planning to go abroad, and that spring they went to Płońsk, where, for reasons known only to themselves, they divorced. Zemach went alone to begin academic studies, first in belles-lettres in Paris, then in agriculture in Grenoble. At the same time Yanait and Ben-Zvi were discussing their plans. She was also to study agriculture in Grenoble while he would proceed to Istanbul to learn law. Ben-Zvi had received from Russia notarized copies of his matriculation certificate from the Poltava gymnasium and his freshman's certificate from Kiev University, the keys that would open the gate of the law faculty. The problem of supporting himself during his studies did not worry him too much, for his qualifications and experience as a teacher in the Hebrew gymnasium in Jerusalem would ensure him work in any Jewish school in Turkey.

Ben-Gurion's situation could hardly have been more different. His qualifications as a field hand were hardly recommendations to any institute of higher learning. Moreover, to pass the entrance exams he would have to study so hard that he would have no time to work for his living. He had no choice but to lay the entire financial burden on his father, making his father's cooperation central to all his plans. As it turned out, this made the plans difficult to execute, for Reb Avigdor had a tendency to promise quickly but delay fulfillment. In fact, had it been entirely up to his father, Ben-Gurion would probably never have reached Istanbul's law faculty. But his plan was rescued by a most unexpected event, which improved Reb Avigdor's financial situation overnight. In March 1911 Ben-Gurion's elder sister, Rivka, had married Abraham Lefkovitz, a wealthy Lódź merchant twice her age. Ben-Gurion nicknamed him "the old man" because he was not in good health and on his doctor's advice used to stop to take the waters at a spa en route to his frequent business meetings in Berlin. Rivka had rescued her entire family by her marriage. First, it took the heaviest load from Reb Avigdor's shoulders. Second, it meant that Zippora could study in Berlin, a city that suddenly seemed very close. Reb Avigdor could concentrate on finding a bride for Michael and consider Ben-Gurion's plans in Istanbul.

Before leaving for the party conference in Haifa, Ben-Gurion wrote to his father, listing all his needs. Rivka's unlikely wedding had yielded the means not only for his study, but also for new clothes. He intended first to visit Poland, where he would have a chance to enjoy his sister's newfound wealth, then go to Salonika in Macedonia to learn Turkish and prepare for the examinations. He asked his father to approve these plans by cable, making it clear that approval included sending the money necessary to carry them out. If he was to be ready for the new school year he had to move quickly. His plan was to spend much of the summer in Poland organizing for the next year, which included obtaining a matriculation certificate from a Polish gymnasium. But no money was awaiting him in Jerusalem when he returned from Haifa, and it was only a few days before the end of April. He wanted to go to Poland in May, but he could not arrange for the journey without the money.

Undecided whether to give up his room and his work in Jerusalem, he wrote his father again at the end of the month. No reply came, and Ben-Gurion began seriously to doubt that he could go at all. On May 8 he told a joint meeting of the central and editorial committees that his trip had been postponed, and on May 12 he wrote a bitter letter to his father, accusing him of not caring about his son's many difficulties, wondering if there was any point at all in writing. "Perhaps even these words of mine will change nothing." If he did not receive "a substantial telegraphic answer," he ended, "I shall not go. Of course, I shall lose a lot by this, but it's not the first time; with luck it will be the last." But it seemed that Reb Avigdor had telegraphed the money before receiving this letter, for on May 15 Ben-Gurion announced at an editorial board meeting that he would be leaving soon. At the end of May he set sail for Poland.

On June 13 he alighted from the train at Warsaw to find his entire family waiting to welcome him. They carried him off to his sister's home in Lódź, where he was given spacious living quarters. Because of his desertion from the army he had had to enter Poland on a false passport under the name Michaelson, and on no account could he show his face in Płońsk. In Warsaw, where he went to meet friends, he received a hero's welcome at his former lodgings with the Fernbuch family. Jenny, who knew of his heroic exploits in Sejera, gave him two autographed portraits of herself. Uppermost in his mind, however, was Rachel Beit-Halachmi, who had haunted him since their encounter in Ein Ganim, and who had come to Płońsk to rest with her family before the birth of her second child. He had written to her before leaving Palestine, and he wrote again from Lódź. Although he received no written answer, his sister Zippora, acting as go-between, confirmed that Rachel had received both letters. Rachel did write eventually to tell him all about a celebration in Płońsk. "How sorry I was that you couldn't have shared our joy, for I know how you would have liked to be here," she said. Encouraged, he wrote to her a third time: "I don't have to tell you how much I'd like to see you. You must understand this, and I believe that you want to see me. I shall be in Warsaw again during my four weeks in Poland. Is it possible for you to come to Warsaw for a few days? Please write if you want to and can, and then, any day you say, I shall come to Warsaw to see you. See you soon. Yours, David."

It is not known whether Rachel wanted to see him, but encumbered as she was by a two-year-old toddler and a newborn baby, she was certainly unable to come. She did send him a photograph of herself against an artificial background of misty forest — the comely, plump young mother he so longed for. Except for Rachel's absence, Ben-Gurion was content in his brother-in-law's home. Studying law in Istanbul was all sewn up, he announced to Jerusalem, and money was no longer a problem. Reb Avigdor had made a firm commitment to send him money, so he could enjoy the affluence in which he was living, especially after his sister and her husband went away, leaving him with their home all to himself.[4]

He arrived in Vienna on July 25 for the world conference of Poale Zion and left on August 22 for Palestine, where he had to make final arrangements before sailing for Salonika four weeks later. At Petah Tikva a letter from his father awaited him; it promised a monthly allowance and travel expenses and assured him that the financial arrangements agreed to in Lódź would be carried out. Consequently, he announced his resignation from *Ha-Achdut*. Four weeks elapsed, but the money failed to materialize. "This does not bode well," he wrote his father. "I fear the same thing will happen again." He was therefore delighted to hear that Zippora had won a scholarship to study in Berlin and would no longer need Reb Avigdor's support, making it easier for his father to help him; on October 28 he received a letter containing money.

The contrast between Ben-Gurion's and Ben-Zvi's personalities is apparent from the styles of their departures from Palestine. No farewell party was arranged for Ben-Gurion, and *Ha-Achdut* did not even report that he was leaving; his departure did not affect many. To Ben-Zvi's loving friends, on the other hand, his impending absence came as a painful wrench. He was given a number of farewell parties, some so well attended that the opportunity was taken to raise funds, and his leave-taking was reported in the press. Similarly, Ben-Gurion and Ben-Zvi both knew that Zerubavel was not competent to hold the reins of party and paper. Ben-Zvi left a stock of articles for the paper to draw on in his absence and continued to write prolifically from Turkey;

Ben-Gurion left nothing in Jerusalem, nor did he worry about *Ha-Ach-dut*'s survival until he knew Turkish well enough to feel competent to write about Ottoman affairs.

At dusk on November 7, 1911, Ben-Gurion's ship entered the calm waters of Salonika's harbor. The town — really an overgrown village — housed a unique Jewish community whose members were laborers and craftsmen engaged in all trades. Since most of Salonika's port workers and sailors were Jews, the port was closed on Saturday, a fact which, the legend went, had given the port its nickname, "the Jewish Port." Ben-Gurion asserted that it was there he realized that Jews were capable of all types of work, describing it as "a Hebrew labor town, the only one in the world." The throbbing of his heart as he watched the burly laboring Jews found no verbal expression, for he understood not one word of their Ladino tongue. In fact, his ten months in Salonika were among the quietest of his life, because his inability to communicate made him feel "as if in prison." He did not learn Ladino because he was determined to devote all his time and energy to his studies. His isolation was made worse by his feeling of strangeness as the only Ashkenazi Jew in town. Some of his neighbors turned on their heels when they saw him; others stared openly. Only at the end of his stay there did he find out that among Salonika's Jews it was common knowledge that all Ashkenazim earned their living as pimps or white slavers.

Out of his allowance of eighty francs a month, he spent fifty on board and lodging in the home of "a not so young widow." Once she had satisfied herself that her Ashkenazi lodger was pure in heart and deed, she treated him like a son and no longer kept her daughters out of sight. In her spare time she used to sit near him, wondering, according to his Turkish tutor, how it was possible that such a youthful, intelligent Jew could not understand her; it seems she was seeking his advice on how to go about finding husbands for her daughters. But his landlady's cordiality did not lessen his loneliness and longing for his father's home, his family, and its Sabbaths and festivals. But most of all, he longed for Rachel Beit-Halachmi.

The advantage of his isolation was that nothing distracted him from his formidable task. This had been one of his reasons for preferring Salonika to Istanbul; it was also much cheaper than the capital. He had thought, too, that he would be among Turkish speakers in Salonika, which would help him learn the language faster; but as it turned out his landlady's family knew almost no Turkish. During a single day, Ben-Gurion noted, he used or heard at least seven tongues: with his tutor, Turkish; in his lodgings, Ladino; with the landlady's children, who attended the Alliance school, French; German in his Turkish-language textbooks; Arabic, which he studied one hour a day because Turkish was still written in Arabic letters; Hebrew, in his correspondence; and Russian, when he read literature for relaxation at the end of the long day.

Each week Ben-Gurion had five hours of Turkish instruction, at a cost of ten francs, and he studied on his own from German textbooks day and night, greatly amused to discover that Turkish grammar made no distinction between the male and female genders. Joseph Strumsa, his teacher, a fourth-year law student in Salonika, said that Ben-Gurion "as a student was phenomenal." He had his first lesson two days after his arrival in Salonika and three months later could read the *Tanin*, the most important Ottoman daily. After four months he no longer needed Strumsa, whom he then taught Hebrew, gratis. Strumsa eventually qualified as a lawyer and became a Zionist, ending up as the legal representative for the Palestine Development Company.

In Salonika Strumsa soon observed Ben-Gurion's habit of suppressing his emotions, including discomfort. Once when they went to the theater to see a play that included scenes of Turkish defeats, a high-ranking army officer sitting near them sobbed uncontrollably. "That's disgraceful," Ben-Gurion whispered to Strumsa. "He should be thinking instead of crying." His accomplishments in Turkish, an exceptionally difficult language, boosted his confidence in himself; he was handicapped only by lack of daily spoken practice. At any rate, he informed his father, within a year he would have acquired, in addition to Turkish, a working knowledge of French and Arabic. In February 1912 he took three French lessons a week; by March he was reading a French newspaper.[5]

Although Ben-Gurion had much to be pleased about, his mounting personal debt caused him much anxiety. Before leaving for Salonika, he had negotiated a sizable loan from *Ha-Achdut*, promising to repay it out of his monthly allowance, which, however, rarely arrived on time. Consequently, he arranged another loan, this time from the World Zionist Organization's Palestine office, undertaking to repay it when he was a lawyer working for that same office. All the while he was running from one post office to another to see if his money had arrived. Eventually he discovered what was going wrong: sometimes the address was incorrect; sometimes the postal service lost the letter; and sometimes his father was not as punctual as he had promised to be. Outraged letters to his father did no good.

To be admitted to Istanbul University's law faculty, foreign students had to provide a matriculation certificate from a Turkish gymnasium in addition to one from a gymnasium in their country of origin, properly translated and notarized by the local Turkish consul. The first diploma presented no problem. In July 1912 Ben-Gurion sat for the Turkish gymnasium examinations in Salonika — Turkish language and literature, Ottoman geography and history, French, and introduction to jurisprudence — and achieved high marks, especially in the history and jurisprudence papers. The principal of the gymnasium, who tested him orally, was astounded on hearing that this David Gruen had not known one word of Turkish eight months earlier. "Incredible, sir, incredible!" he exclaimed repeatedly. But the second matriculation certificate was another matter. Ben-Zvi had taken it upon himself to get this document for his friend by appealing for help to friends and acquaintances in his native Poltava. When he was in Łódź in the summer of 1911, Ben-Gurion told his father that he would need sixty rubles, a sum three times his monthly allowance, to purchase it. It had to be paid in two installments: twenty rubles in advance and the balance on delivery. Ben-Gurion was cautious enough not to give the go-ahead for the first payment until he had won his Turkish diploma with flying colors.

Still another document — a passport — had to be produced for the university authorities. This was another ticklish problem. As an army deserter, Ben-Gurion could not obtain a Russian passport. He could have applied for Ottoman citizenship, something he considered personally and politically desirable, but this carried the obligation to report at once for army service, a grim prospect in the tense atmosphere heralding the Balkan War of 1912–1913. Exemption from military duty could be granted to university students, but only after they were registered as such, so Ben-Gurion was stymied. Even though the matriculation certificate had not arrived and his allowance was late again, he sailed from Salonika to Istanbul on August 14, 1912, to arrive in good time for the start of the new academic year on August 29. He badly needed fourteen rubles for his first year's fees; he had to register as a student immediately to be eligible for exemption from military service if he became an Ottoman subject. Penniless, he was hoping to borrow from Ben-Zvi and other friends in the city until his money arrived, so he was distressed to discover that Ben-Zvi had not yet returned from his summer vacation in Palestine. The insecurity of his situation enraged him, as he told his father in a very forthright letter.

By the time some money reached him on September 8, registration for the new term had been closed. Ben-Gurion tried frantically to find a way to rescue the year and might have succeeded had it not been for the outbreak, on October 14, of the First Balkan War between Greece, Bulgaria, and Montenegro, supported by Russia, and the Ottoman Empire. Expecting the war to last at least eight months, during which time he was sure he could do nothing useful in Istanbul, he decided to go to

Petah Tikva and prepare the first-year law curriculum on his own; he hoped, too, to chase down his Poltava diploma. On November 5 he sailed for Palestine, where he studied, worked for Poale Zion, and again contributed to *Ha-Achdut*. At last the forged matriculation certificate turned up, and, finding it satisfactory, Ben-Gurion sent it at once to his father to be translated and notarized by the Turkish consul in Warsaw — another expense for Reb Avigdor, who did not get this done as swiftly as his son wished. On March 13, when Ben-Gurion had returned to Istanbul, he again reminded his father of it. Eight weeks went by, and he wrote to his father describing his emotional anguish, his sleepless nights. It apparently never occurred to him that his father simply did not have the purse to match his desire to help his son. "Could this be simple inattention only?" Ben-Gurion wrote in his distress. "That I cannot imagine!"[6]

In April the Balkan War subsided into peace talks. Before these were concluded the law faculty, which had closed during the war, had opened its doors again; at the eleventh hour, the notarized diploma arrived from Płońsk. Indistinguishable from the authentic article, it was bound with tape, sealed with wax, and signed by the principal of the Royal Gymnasium in Poltava, the inspector of education in Poltava, and every member of the pedagogical council, including the secretary. This four-page foolscap parchment confirmed that David Gruen had been an excellent student during his four years at the school, and the grades listed showed that he had passed the exams in June 1908 with top grades. Flourishing this magnificent document, Ben-Gurion had no trouble registering as an ordinary full-time student; his failure to produce a passport was overlooked. The law faculty register records that starting June 1, 1913, the students included "David Gruen effendi, no. 134411094, son of Victor effendi (a lawyer)."

Ben-Gurion's two years at the law faculty were the most formidable test thus far for his will power and turned out to be one of the most severe tests of his life. His days were a continuous effort to learn. Thanks to his intensity of purpose he completed nearly three years of study in these two years, on an almost empty stomach, weakening himself so desperately that he came near death. He lodged first for a brief period in Galata, on the Turkish side of the Golden Horn, but then shared a room with Ben-Zvi on the second floor of the Pension Tatar at 12 Topcular Street in the Beyoğlu quarter on the European side of the water. For a while they were joined by Joseph Strumsa, who was in Istanbul to complete his law degree before moving to Palestine. He was penniless, too, so Ben-Gurion invited him to share the room, paying nothing, until February 1914, when he sailed for Jaffa. Strumsa never forgot Ben-Gurion's kindness.

In their long, narrow room, Ben-Gurion's and Ben-Zvi's beds were arranged along one wall and Strumsa's foldaway bed — always open — as well as a small table and two chairs, along the wall opposite. This plan created a passage so narrow that it took some effort to reach the teakettle and the three unwashed glasses at the far end of the room. Rachel Yanait, visiting, was astonished to discover that the spoons could be pried away from the sides of the glasses only with considerable difficulty. In fact, she could lift the glass by picking up the spoon. "Why wash up," Ben-Gurion asked, "since each of us has his own glass? The glass I used yesterday I shall use tomorrow and the day after." Nevertheless, they used to treat their guests to tea. Visitors remembered Ben-Zvi's gracious tea making, his lanky frame bending over the rickety Primus stove, while Ben-Gurion reclined on his bed, head cradled on his arms, miles away. They had no pillows; newspapers served that purpose. One iron rule applied in the room — only Turkish was spoken.

Although their life was so intimate, Ben-Gurion managed to remain impersonal. This is reflected in his letters to his father, which contained hardly any mention of his roommates or other friends; his father would not have known of their existence had Ben-Gurion not slyly compared his marks with theirs. He lived with Ben-Zvi for almost two years, yet he did not tell his father one thing about him. On sending his father a picture of himself with the *Ha-Achdut* editorial staff, he noted only that "the young man to my right is Ben-Zvi, my colleague."

Ben-Gurion was not impressed by the academic standards of the law faculty, which had been founded in 1900. In all subjects the teaching standard was "much lower than I'd expected." Most of the professors, he remarked, were absolute ignoramuses. Even so, the high marks he got were an extraordinary accomplishment, for he wrote the exams in flawless Turkish despite his rapidly deteriorating health. He proudly reported these marks to his father after each exam — all 10s, except for two 9.5s and one 8. In criminal law, twelve students took the oral examination. The professor was ecstatic over Ben-Gurion's answers to the questions fired at him and gave him a 10 on the spot. He could hear that Gruen effendi was not a Turk; and on learning that he was a Jew from Russia, he turned to the Turkish students and said, "This is our misfortune, that we don't have too many students of Gruen effendi's caliber. Had we ten Gruens, Turkey would look quite different."

In his reports, Ben-Gurion always included his friends' inferior marks, to highlight his own even more, as if he were still a child performing for kopecks. Yet he was also in his own way repaying Reb Avigdor, assuring him that his money was being spent in a good cause. He boasted about his marks to Rachel Beit-Halachmi, too, even before the exams were over. "This is the first time that any of the Russian students have gotten such high grades." Again he reported his friends' marks, adding that in the first two papers Ben-Zvi had gotten only 6, while Shochat had had to postpone one exam to the second test period and gotten only 8 in the other. It is little wonder that he was so proud of himself: he had come out first despite never having attended a regular school, well ahead of others with previous academic experience, and despite his bad health. Recurrent malaria would have been enough to affect his work, but the hunger pangs that had accompanied him throughout the year and by the end consumed him totally were worse. Insisting that spiritual effort could obliterate all physical needs, he had submerged himself in study as a distraction from the pain of hunger, but eventually the effects of near starvation told on him.

As early as April 1913, after the usual delay in the arrival of his allowance, he had experienced two weeks of "terrible torment in my mouth, and I couldn't eat or sleep." A doctor advised that the condition resulted from "chronic malnutrition." Ben-Gurion wrote his father that he had suffered from scurvy for three weeks, which had scarred his gums for life, but this was his own diagnosis and lacked any medical foundation; he had stomatitis periodontosis, or periodontic abscesses. His physical suffering coupled with his permanent anxiety about money threatened to undermine his moral strength. "Only an iron effort prevents a nervous collapse," he wrote. By the end of April he felt so much in need of a rest that he thought of going to his sister in Łódź, but decided not to. In the middle of the exam period he had a bout of malaria before the civil law paper, and doubted seriously if he had the strength to write it, so his mark, 10, was phenomenal.

During the weeks of the exams his health continued to deteriorate. In December 1913 he commented wryly to his father, "My health of late has not been all too good. From time to time malaria attacks me." In fact, he had never known a worse time. Finally his anguish overcame his reticence, and he wrote an accusing letter to Reb Avigdor.

> My health worsens daily and as always at the most trying moment I find myself penniless. Both of us have made a terrible mistake. You undertook something which is beyond you and I've agreed to live in conditions which may destroy my physical and moral strength. Forgive me, dear father, for causing you sorrow in this letter, but it is not out of joy that I write thus.

When this letter was shown to his family, his sister Rivka wrote immediately, inviting him to her home to recover his strength, after which he could make a future in Russia. She even advised him to report back to the army to complete his service, thereby canceling his deserter's status, adding that no matter what the cost, it was worth it to be "free." His father, too, urged him to continue his studies nearer home. Ben-Gurion was deeply hurt that his family should so misunderstand him. They thought he was suffering just for the sake of a legal career, whereas, he explained in his reply, his struggle was for rather more than that. "It is a matter of life," and only death would stop him from accomplishing his mission. Accepting his father's and sister's invitations would amount to moral and spiritual suicide. Of course, had his father been able to send him a larger, regular allowance, this misunderstanding would not have arisen.

Ben-Gurion's justification for his peculiar demands on his father bears examination. First, his roommate offers a striking comparison. Ben-Zvi had left Jaffa for Istanbul with a mere twenty francs, borrowed from his friends, in his pocket. He paid for his university fees and living expenses by teaching two hours a day in the Talmud Torah on the south bank of the Golden Horn. The trip there and back took an hour by streetcar. To economize, Ben-Zvi occasionally walked both ways. As Yanait pointed out years later, compared to Ben-Zvi, Ben-Gurion had it easy. Why, she asked, did he not work to support himself?

Ben-Gurion was quite aware that his father's financial situation was precarious: Zippora's engagement to a medical student in Berlin in July 1912, followed shortly by Michael's betrothal, had increased Reb Avigdor's obligations. Not only did his son David require a monthly allowance; his not-so-bright son Michael needed more support after his marriage than before; Zippora and her fiancé were impecunious students in Berlin; and his eldest son, Abraham, had embarked on the risky business of selling lottery tickets. Ben-Gurion knew he was a burden to his father. As soon as he heard that Zippora was engaged, he asked about the financial standing of her fiancé. The reply stung him to declare that if he was admitted as a full-time student in Istanbul, "I shall try to get myself some kind of a job so that you can send my allowance to Zippora instead. I've never felt such a strong desire as at present to earn a lot of money." He added that he felt his younger sister's want more than his own bitterness during his days of hunger and malaria. Although there was still old man Lefkovitz in Lódź, who possibly lightened his father-in-law's burden somewhat, his business was not doing well, either, for the nationalist movement in Poland had organized a boycott of all Jewish businesses, which harmed Reb Avigdor and his son-in-law alike.

However, when Ben-Gurion did not receive his allowance in March and April 1913, he blamed his father's irresponsibility. Only after he had read about the boycott in the Płońsk papers in April did it occur to him that there might be another reason for the delay, and he inquired whether its effect in Płońsk was as bad as elsewhere. His father replied that the *kupat milve* (savings and loan cooperative) he had founded in 1912 and of which he was managing director was in bad shape. Yet even after Ben-Gurion knew that the boycott had damaged trade in Płońsk, he acted as though nothing had changed. There is no doubt that he was egocentric, but it was an egocentrism of a special kind.

Ben-Gurion's complaint was that his father did not understand the importance of the punctual transmission of his allowance. This is not to say that he did not appreciate the difficulty of what he was asking his father to do. In his letter requesting money to register at Istanbul he wrote, "It is very hard for me to come to you with this request as I know that even without this you have a lot of expense just now (Zippora's and Michael's engagements), especially because I know that I shall never be able to recompense you for even one small part of what you sacrifice now for my studies." On another occasion he pointed out that he never asked for an addition to one month's sum to carry him over the delay until the next one arrived. While he actually wrote "Thank you very much for the money," only once, this cannot be construed as indifference or ingratitude. He recognized and appreciated what his father was doing for him, and it never occurred to him that his father did not take his appreciation for granted. "Since I was eleven, when my mother died, Reb Avigdor was both father and mother to me; he gave me a great deal out of love," he wrote after his father's death. Writing from Salonika, he imagined his family as one body with one soul and one heart. "Even if we are far away and scattered, we can feel one another's pulse. Without a word or a glance we still understand each other even though we are widely separated." But these feelings did not prevent him from making constant demands on his father, in the name of their "partnership": "To reach that goal which you and I have before us." His egocentrism had a certain childish quality, for in pursuing his own goal he did not see himself as a solo climber but as the personification of his family's aspirations. He wanted an unstinting partnership, first with his father, then, in order of precedence, with Zippora, Abraham, and the rest.

He saw the partnership with his father as founded on their common objective, realizing the Zionist dream. This, as Ben-Gurion — and to a large extent his father — saw it, called for a division of labor — Ben-Gurion to prepare himself for his future role as a leader, and his father to maintain and facilitate his preparation. "Not only by my poring over the textbooks, but no less by you bent over your account books will I be able to prepare myself for that enterprise which is so dear to us both," he told his father. This sense of partnership, the belief that he and his father identified completely with the cause, gave him the moral justification to reproach his father for not fulfilling his part of the deal, or to press him with fresh demands for more effort, promptness, and money. As Ben-Gurion understood it, the deal with his father expressly forbade him to do anything but study. Any distraction would mean that he had forfeited his commitment.

It would not be right, then, to regard this as simple egoism. Ben-Gurion believed in his mission and his capabilities. If proof is needed of his belief in his destiny, it may be found in the nature of his relationship with his father during the years he studied in Turkey. In later years he extended this attitude to his party, to the Yishuv, and to the entire Jewish people by identifying himself with their aspirations, so that his appeals to others became impersonal and indirect. In his favor is the fact that whatever part of the bargain he himself undertook, he fulfilled to the last letter.

Ben-Gurion's deteriorating health brought on more frequent bouts of malaria, followed each time by worse complications. When his second school term opened in December 1913, he was as weak and hungry as ever, and his allowance did not reach him until the end of the month, by which time he was exhausted from malaria. In early January 1914 his health was so bad that he had to go to the Russian Hospital in the Sisili quarter for a month and a half. From his hospital bed he wrote letters to his father, to Rivka in Lódź, and to Zippora's husband, Moshe Koritni. Alarmed, his relatives sent him money for the hospital bills, at the same time urging him to visit Lódź to convalesce. When he got the money for the trip from his father, he took the first boat. Once safely installed in Lódź, he complained that he was not allowed to study in peace. A constant stream of acquaintances, friends, and relatives — who, he considered, had nothing better to do than seek distraction from their boredom — came to disturb him, insisting that he play Klaberjass, a card game, with them. Nevertheless he managed to recuperate and study and on April 20 began his journey back to Istanbul. In Odessa, where he spent a few days with Zippora and his brother-in-law, he managed to lose all his possessions in the railway station and arrived in Turkey on April 26 with four rubles in his pocket.

Again his studies became "the only company in my life at the present." Without warning, and as though by sheer malevolence, the faculty added thirty-eight hundred pages to the syllabus. "The Lord knows if I'll be able to do it," he commented. Again, however, this mishap and the exhaustion that overtook him anew did not hinder him from excelling; years later the dean of the faculty remembered him as the "top in his class." At this high point, however, his academic career ended, for in July he sailed with Ben-Zvi to Palestine for the summer vacation, and while they were on the high seas, World War I began. It was ten years before Ben-Gurion saw Istanbul again, only to discover that all his books, diaries, and letters had been destroyed by fire.

In their three years in Turkey, politics had taken up very little of Ben-Zvi's and Ben-Gurion's time. In August 1913 the Benim had traveled to Kraków to attend the fourth World Poale Zion Conference, then to Vienna for the eleventh World Zionist Congress. Ben-Gurion's election as an alternate delegate gave him the opportunity to do some committee work at this, his first Zionist Congress, but nothing he did there was memorable. The Poale Zion conference had instructed the Benim to form party associations in the Ottoman provinces and in the capital. They failed completely to do this, however, not just because they were short of both time and energy, but because it took only a cursory look to conclude that "now there is no scope in Turkey for Poale Zion associations," as Ben-Gurion put it. Nevertheless the Benim — the "Eretz-Israeli pair," as they also came to be known — profited from their stay in Turkey, developing and consolidating their own political ideas.

Despite Turkey's losses in the Balkan Wars and the great upheaval that eventually brought the triumvirate of Talât, Enver, and Jemal to power, they were more than ever convinced that the Yishuv must remain loyal to Turkey. Without the European Christian nations it had formerly controlled, they believed, Asiatic Turkey would be more homogeneous and therefore stronger. Although smaller in area by a third and lower in population by a fourth as a result of its defeat, it would no longer be a multinational, chaotic mess but a virtually binational state of Turks and Arabs, tightly run and controlled.

Ben-Gurion was led to believe that Zionism might profit from the Arab threat to Turkish supremacy in the new empire. As he developed greater faith in the empire's durability — he did not doubt that it had the military strength to defend Palestine — he came to believe that Zionism's only chance rested with Turkey. It was vital to become Turkey's ally. For that purpose the Benim put forward their Ottomanization concept: the Yishuv and the Zionist movement must be pro-Ottoman, and all Jews residing in Palestine must become Ottoman subjects. The Benim matched their appearance to their policy, exchanging their Russian blouses for dark, striped, three-piece suits, stiff collars, and ties. The thin mustaches they had grown in Palestine were cultivated into luxuriant ones. The finishing touch was their new headgear — a red fez.

Before boarding ship in July 1914, Ben-Gurion sent his father a note. "When this card reaches you, the fate of Europe will be in the balance." His prediction came true on the voyage. The trip usually lasted one week, but this time it took them over three weeks to reach Jaffa as a result of the detour their Russian ship took to avoid the German cruisers *Goeben* and *Bresslau*. On August 16, 1914, after many hardships, the Benim came ashore, haggard, weary, but with their red fezzes cocked jauntily on their heads, and made their way to Jerusalem.[7]

6

Ottoman Patriot

T HE YISHUV of nearly eighty-five thousand Jews that David Ben-Gurion and Itzhak Ben-Zvi found on their return to Palestine was apprehensive and in disarray. With the Mediterranean blockaded, communication with many European countries was cut off. Funds from the Diaspora could not flow in and agricultural products could not be exported. While these economic consequences of the war were clear, its political significance did not become apparent until later. Turkey's secret alliance with Germany of August 2 had not been made public. Consequently the Turkish government's announcement on September 9 that the Capitulations — agreements between Turkey and the European powers that had granted Europeans special privileges for nearly four hundred years — would be abolished as of October 1 came as a bombshell.

At one stroke, the whole system of privileges that allowed foreign nationals to live in the Ottoman Empire, but outside the jurisdiction of the Ottoman legal system, collapsed. After October 1 all foreign post offices would be closed; European currencies would no longer be legal; goods imported by foreigners would no longer be exempt from import duties above 8 percent; everyone residing within the boundaries of the empire would become subject to Ottoman law. The extraterritorial consular courts were closed, and the consuls representing the Entente Cordiale powers and Russia were arrested. Most Jews in Palestine, as foreign nationals, felt particularly vulnerable, because had it not been for the consuls' protection, fewer of them would have returned to settle in a Moslem country whose rulers were notoriously arbitrary. The Yishuv also feared that the war, by diverting Turkish security forces, would release an explosion of Arab hostility toward Jewish settlers. The authorities reacted to this possibility by declaring martial law in all mixed towns, forbidding people to go out after dark without a lantern, and imposing a general curfew from 11:00 P.M. until dawn.

Unlike almost everyone else, Ben-Gurion, a freedom-seeking Ottoman socialist, rapturously welcomed the abolition of the Capitulations. "Turkey has freed itself from the yoke of tyranny and the domestic enslavement of absolute monarchy, and now frees itself from the chains of exploitation by the Great Powers," he wrote in *Ha-Achdut*. The immensity and sincerity of his joy were unique even among those who supported Ottomanization; he interpreted the event as a heaven-sent opportunity for the Jews in Eretz Israel to obtain Ottoman citizenship, which he thought was equivalent to official recognition of Eretz Israel citizenship. He was not oblivious to the distress of the Jews who suddenly found themselves on such thin ice. Although he could well imagine what was in store for foreigners, he told his friends, "Who cares? The future is what's important. The future is the main thing."

The distress of the Palestinian Jews was transmitted to the United States via Dr. Otis Glazerbrook, the American consul general in Jerusalem, and Henry Morgenthau, the American ambassador to the Sublime Porte. Funds raised in response to their pleas were promptly transferred to Palestine. Food, medicine, and bedding were shipped aboard two American warships, the *North Carolina* and the *Tennessee*, which kept up a sea train until April 1917. The Jews did not, therefore, hasten to adopt Ben-Gurion's advice to become Ottoman citizens, especially since they had reasons other than their worsening economic plight for not welcoming his Turkish savior. It quickly became apparent that the Ottoman governors in Palestine suspected the Zionists of subversion, and many were arrested and exiled. The use of Hebrew on commercial displays and signs was banned. In spite of this, Ben-Gurion continued to speak publicly in favor of the abrogation of the Capitulations, taking it upon himself to write a series of articles about how Jews should behave in economic matters during wartime. He and Ben-Zvi became energetic members of the Yishuv Ottomanization Committee.

Then, on October 29, Turkey's sudden entry into the war — two German warships thinly camouflaged as Turkish men-of-war had bombarded Russian ships at anchor in the Black Sea — automatically turned the fifty thousand Russian Jews in Palestine into enemy aliens. No one doubted that if these Jews did not immediately become Ottoman subjects, the Yishuv would be imperiled: the Russian Jews would have to leave Palestine voluntarily or they would be deported. Saving the Yishuv became imperative, but there was still no rush to apply for Ottoman citizenship.

The Jews knew that in Turkey the gap between the law and enforcement was vast. Indeed, when Morgenthau interceded, he was able to prevail upon the central government to cancel the locally issued detention and deportation orders shortly after their promulgation, suggesting that the central and local administrations did not see eye to eye on the Russian Jews. A further disincentive was the tax levied on a person who became an Ottoman citizen, which amounted to roughly one month's wages for a worker. Moreover, a man between the ages of eighteen and forty-five was liable to conscription in the Ottoman army, where conditions, especially the absence of sanitation, were abysmal. Finally, the local officials were not enthusiastic about Ottomanization; the two clerks employed in the narrow office designated for the procedures worked at a snail's pace. All in all, fewer than a hundred Jews were persuaded to become Ottoman citizens.

At first the Russian Jews thought all would be well if they flaunted red fezzes and patriotic expressions while praying silently for an Entente victory. But Ben-Gurion and Ben-Zvi shared absolute faith in an Ottoman triumph. Ben-Gurion wrote in *Ha-Achdut* of the advantages that such a victory would bring to the region, and Ben-Zvi gave an additional reason for supporting the Turks — that Russia was the Jews' worst enemy in the world. If an Entente victory were to result in Russia's getting a slice of the spoils, then Palestine might be made into another Pale. Ben-Gurion reinforced his case by pointing out that from an Ottoman defeat "only the Arabs stand to gain, and who hates us like they? We need a strong Turkey, which promises us both hope and a future."[1]

In Jerusalem Ben-Gurion and Ben-Zvi joined the *Ha-Achdut* staff commune in a house in Succath-Shalom. They shared everything, and as the economic situation worsened, the commune became closer knit. *Ha-Achdut* could not pay its editorial staff and printers in cash because its subscribers paid in kind, so Ben-Zvi recorded that the commune switched to "a barter economy." Near the beds and desks were heaps of wheat, honey, oranges, and vegetables. The staff was not overworked because shortages meant that the weekly could be published only every second or third week, leaving the commune with plenty of time for exhaustive discussion. Owing to the situation created by the war, the *Ha-Achdut* staff functioned as the party central committee, and party policy was made at the editorial meetings. Because of Ben-Zvi's position as number one and Ben-Gurion's influence on him, their ideas, for all practical purposes, were the party line.

Alexander Chashin, the new literary editor and a new face to Ben-Gurion, was a prominent participant. He had reached Palestine in 1912, having been ordered by his doctor to leave Russia because of a lung disease. Tall, thin, his pallor striking against his black hair, he was handsome in a spiritual way, exuding immense charm and boundless good humor. Although Chashin had been Ben-Zvi's close friend in Poltava, in Jerusalem he became more attached to Ben-Gurion. Ben-Gurion seems to have loved Chashin more than any of his other Poale Zion friends in Palestine — so much that he could forgive him for not toeing the party line. Chashin was loath to exchange his Russian passport for an Ottoman identity card or to apply for an Ottoman passport. "Where is it written," he asked, "that one can't hand the Turks a forged Italian *carte de séjour* affirming his Russian nationality?" If he had to apply for a Turkish passport he intended to hand over the forged document and keep his Russian passport in his pocket. He advised his friends that if Turkey lost and Russia found itself ruler of Palestine, Russian citizens who had, so to speak, betrayed Mother Russia during the war were liable to be tried and harshly punished. Apart from this possibility, relinquishing all proof of Russian nationality would debar them from Russia forever, including short visits to their families.

Chashin also declined to join the militia that Ben-Gurion and Ben-Zvi were about to form. They had been to the Ottoman commander in Jerusalem and registered as "volunteers" for the Ottoman army, proposing that he authorize a Jewish unit for the defense of Jerusalem. The commander had accepted, agreeing that it be a local militia open only to volunteers. Ben-Gurion and Ben-Zvi took his consent as irrefutable proof of their contention that service in the Ottoman forces would augment the Jews' claim to Palestine, which they would have helped to defend, and one commune member immediately announced to Poale Zion in New York, "Soon we shall be soldiers of Palestine." The Benim gave much time and thought to recruiting and training their militia. In his autobiographical sketch for the *Encyclopedia Judaica*, Ben-Gurion boasted that their call to the Turkish flag was answered by hundreds of volunteers; in fact, some forty Jews responded and began to train in the Russian compound in Jerusalem.[2]

As Ben-Gurion acted on his Ottoman concept, Ahmed Jemal Pasha, one of the ruling triumvirate and minister for the Ottoman navy, was, in addition to his other offices, appointed commander of the Fourth Army and governor of Greater Syria, which included Palestine. From the moment he made his headquarters in Damascus, the Palestinian Jews experienced a worsening in their treatment by local officials. Tel Aviv was encircled by troops, whose thorough searches found satisfactory proof — checks drawn on the Anglo-Palestine Bank, which was owned by the World Zionist Organization, and Jewish National Fund coupons — that the Zionists intended to establish a Jewish state. An order proclaimed that all branches of the bank be closed within ten days, that Jewish watchmen or guards were illegal, and that firearms owned by Jews be handed in. Land sales to Jews were prohibited.

A wide-scale mobilization of military and labor forces was suddenly announced, not primarily to recruit human resources, but to elicit ransoms accepted in lieu of service; payment in money or kind and supplying army animals with harnesses and fodder were customary ways to buy exemption from conscription. Thus these army requisitions were merely a transparent guise for robbery. The culmination of Jemal's vindictive policy toward the Yishuv came when he personally ordered that all enemy aliens who had not become Ottoman subjects must, by 4:00 P.M. on December 17, board the *Vicento Florio*, an Italian ship operating on the Jaffa-Alexandria line. Soldiers and police swarmed the streets seizing men, women, old people, children — whomever they came across — and marched them off to the police barracks. That night they were led to the harbor, where children were wrested from their parents, husbands and wives separated. These five hundred Jews were the first to be deported to Alexandria, Egypt. Other deportations followed.

The Jaffa deportations called Ben-Gurion's policy into question. He had already been made painfully aware of the discrepancy between his policy and reality in November, when Manya Shochat had been arrested and sent to Damascus for interrogation. At the time, Ben-Gurion explained the increasingly harsh Ottoman attitude to the Yishuv as the direct result of their alienation from the Ottomans. Had the Yishuv taken Ottomanization seriously and become good Ottoman citizens, the Turks would not have regarded them as suspect. Ben-Gurion therefore exhorted the Jews to Ottomanize before they found themselves in trouble with the authorities. His explanation held water as far as the first measures taken against the Yishuv were concerned, but the mass deportation of Jews from Jaffa was not so easy for Ben-Gurion to swallow. He found historical or political explanations inappropriate, and insisted on a protest.

At a meeting of *Ha-Achdut*, he asserted that the only acceptable response to the cruelty in Jaffa was to publish a protest, in spite of the censor. To those who hesitated, he declared, "There are moments when one should not pay attention to present circumstances; such moments make it mandatory to protest even if the protest achieves nothing, even if it makes matters worse." This was the first time Ben-Gurion displayed his talent for the "double formula" — one of his most original and consistent tactics of leadership — a response to those predicaments in which a choice had to be made between two evils. Ben-Gurion used it to bridge irreconcilable differences between his own perception of things and the external reality. In this instance, he both formulated a policy urging the party to insist on Ottomanization and the right to fight with the Turks as political equals as though no deportations had taken place, meanwhile insisting that the Yishuv must resist the deportations as though Turkey were not at war. While Ben-Zvi was hesitant to support this line, Chashin was utterly opposed to both Ottomanization and protest.

Ben-Gurion persuaded the *Ha-Achdut* staff to approve his policy, and while the cover of the December 30 issue heralded Ben-Gurion's call to join the militia, the inside contained a fierce protest against the deportations. On Monday, January 4, 1915, *Ha-Achdut* was closed by order of the censor and never appeared again. Policemen confiscated all copies and sealed the print shop's doors with wax. What was more, the call to arms was completely unwarranted, because on the very same day Jemal declared the militia illegal and personally ordered the Jerusalem commander to disband it. None of this deflected Ben-Gurion from his Ottomanization campaign.

Here one of Ben-Gurion's unique qualities was revealed: human suffering did not change his political thinking, and certainly did not induce any kind of emotionalism in him. Many thought it was a weakness, because it was inhuman, but more considered it a strength that made him a leader one could rely on in bad times or good.

The Jaffa deportations triggered an exodus from Palestine. Whoever could do so boarded the American warship *Tennessee*, which was to leave Jaffa for Alexandria at the end of December. On the day the ship sailed the train from Jerusalem to Jaffa was so packed that an extra train had to be put in service. Seeing the Yishuv disappearing, Ben-Gurion would, had he the authority, have "locked the country up." To try to reduce the numbers leaving, he became frantically active in the Ottomanization Committee. But Jemal Pasha had no patience for the slow Ottomanization of Palestinian Jews. On December 30 he ordered that "all Jews must become Ottoman subjects within three days, and those who have not done so by then must leave the country forthwith, taking their families." Since carrying out this order was administratively clearly impossible, it only accelerated the exodus. During the early war years the Yishuv decreased from eighty-five to sixty-five thousand or less. In the end, the fervent Ottomanizers themselves were caught up in Jemal's persecution of the Zionists. On February 9, 1916, the Ottomanization Committee's two secretaries were arrested. After a long and exhaustive investigation, Ben-Gurion and Ben-Zvi were jailed until Jemal could decide what to do with them.[3]

The report put on Jemal's desk by the investigators denounced Poale Zion as a clandestine association hostile to Turkey and recommended that their applications to become Ottoman subjects be rejected and that they be deported as enemy aliens. On his return from the Suez front, where his forces had been routed, Jemal concentrated his attention on the Zionist problem, and on February 26 passed judgment on Ben-Gurion and Ben-Zvi. From the high command of the Fourth Army headquarters in Jerusalem, cables were dispatched to Istanbul informing the appropriate authorities of Jemal's decision to deport them from "the state and from the precincts of the university." The law faculty followed with its own expulsion order.

When Ben-Gurion and Ben-Zvi were informed of the verdict on February 27, they decided to try to get the order set aside, to which end they addressed a memorandum to Jemal explaining that the charges brought against them were based on a misunderstanding. Since its inception, they argued, the party had acted openly. They had never joined an underground organization, and "all our actions, our thoughts, and our hopes, directed as they were to Jewish welfare, were no less aimed at the welfare of the empire itself." Consequently, the accusation that they acted against Ottoman interests was groundless, and they asked for justice and the cancellation of the deportation order. They sent their plea by registered mail, but receiving no acknowledgment, agreed that one of them should approach the pasha personally.

Any encounter with Jemal was hazardous because, depending on his mood, the drop of an eyelid could mean either liberty or death. How they decided that Ben-Zvi should take the risk is unknown. When asked, he said, "One had to go." Ben-Zvi became the topic of the day in the *Ha-Achdut* commune and much later was still so proud of himself that in his memoirs he set aside his customary modesty and let it be known, referring to himself by his initials only, that it was he who went alone to confront the pasha.

With the aid of a little baksheesh, he was let out of jail for a short while. Dressed in long, threadbare trousers and a stained jacket, a fez adorning his head, he managed to pass through the gates of the German hostel of Augusta Victoria in Jerusalem, where Jemal had set up his advance headquarters. He got as far as the inner courtyard and was just about to mount the steps when he heard a short order. Turning his head, he saw an entourage of army officers and high officials in gleaming uniforms. Two steps in front of them was Jemal. It had never crossed Ben-Zvi's mind that he might have to speak to Jemal in public, and he lost his nerve completely, wanting only to escape Jemal's preserve. But it was too late; the supreme commander caught sight of the long-legged fellow scrambling to hide behind a truck and ordered his soldiers to bring Ben-Zvi to him at once.

Asked what he was doing there, Ben-Zvi was too agitated to speak, which provoked Jemal to shout, "Don't you even understand Turk-

ish?" — as though Ben-Zvi could not comprehend human speech. The
encounter ended as badly as it had begun. "Your memorandum?"
Jemal snorted. "I threw it in the rubbish basket. Poale Zion has no
place in this country. You want to establish a Jewish state." While his
denials were to no avail, Ben-Zvi managed to present their request to
be exiled somewhere within the empire. But Jemal interrupted him.
"This you shall never live to see." The interview ended with the
pasha's ordering that they be deported to Egypt as soon as possible.
Ben-Zvi was glad to have escaped with his life.[4]

During his detention, in the courtyard of the government building
where he was being held, Ben-Gurion met Yahia effendi, an Arab from
Jerusalem who had studied with him in Istanbul and whom he regarded as a "close friend." Asked what he was doing in prison, Ben-
Gurion told Yahia about the deportation order. "As your friend I'm
sorry," Yahia replied. "As an Arab I am glad." As the years went by,
this exchange assumed increasing significance for Ben-Gurion, and he
recounted it hundreds of times, as if he had obliterated from memory a
statement he himself had made five years earlier, to Poale Zion's 1910
conference, which envisaged "a heavy war and a bitter rivalry" between the Jews and the Arabs.

He failed equally to recall his 1914 comment that only the Arabs
stood to gain from Turkey's defeat and chose instead to remember that
this Arab friend's words pained him more than the murder of his two
Jewish friends at Sejera, claiming that this was "the first incident in
which I met political hostility in an Arab." At that moment he foresaw
the future conflicts with the Arabs in Palestine. This experience laid
the foundation of all his political thinking, the principle that as long as
the Jews were in the minority in Palestine, they must be allied with the
ruling power in the region, to enable them to stand up to the Arabs;
this was more important to him than dialogue and understanding with
the Arabs.[5]

The deportation orders made a Poale Zion council meeting imperative, and Ben-Gurion and Ben-Zvi bribed themselves out of detention
to attend it. The meeting resolved that the Benim should go from
Egypt to the United States, where they would attempt to create an immigration movement to provide labor and defense for Palestine. The
recruited volunteers were also to be trained as an armed force to fight
alongside the Turks in Palestine.

On March 21 Ben-Gurion and Ben-Zvi were brought before the Jaffa
district commissioner, who handed them their boarding papers for the
Italian liner *Firenze*. They were taken aboard under guard, and the
ship sailed for Egypt the following day. Through the concern voiced by
Poale Zion parties in Europe and the United States, their deportation

brought instant fame to Ben-Gurion and Ben-Zvi, whose safety interested the World Zionist Organization. From Istanbul the German ambassador, Baron von Wangenheim, cabled the Zionist office in Berlin via the German consular service. Responding to the queries of American Jewish relief committees, Ambassador Morgenthau received from Consul Glazerbrook a running account of their arrest, interrogation, and deportation and sent it to the U.S. State Department in Washington, which notified the Zionist office in New York, which in turn handed the news on to the U.S. Poale Zion headquarters. The day the Benim arrived in Alexandria, cables were sent from Egypt to the Jewish National Fund offices in The Hague. In London the Yiddish daily *Die Zeit* was the first to write of the expulsion of these two "Palestinian leaders."

On their arrival at Alexandria the Benim underwent a scrupulous customs inspection, Ben-Gurion's Turkish books being held for further examination, and finally left the port at 4:00 P.M. on March 24. At the dock to greet them was Alexander Chashin, who had left Palestine of his own volition and was waiting for passage to the United States. Despite his desertion, the two, but especially Ben-Gurion, were delighted to see him. They remained in Egypt for almost a month to complete financial and practical preparations for their journey.

In Alexandria Ben-Gurion came up against the Zionist policy of Vladimir Jabotinsky, correspondent for a Russian liberal daily, who, with Joseph Trumpeldor, wanted to form the Palestinian Jewish refugees into a volunteer battalion to fight alongside the British. His initiative gave birth to the Zion Mule Corps, whose training and embarkation for the front the Benim witnessed. The corps was posted to Gallipoli, where its task was to supply water to the British combat forces. Ben-Gurion thought the scheme worse than foolish. The Jews would not be fighting to liberate or defend Palestine, and their collaboration with Britain would enrage the Ottomans, who would retaliate against the remaining Jews in Palestine and threaten the very existence of the Yishuv. His opposition, of course, was based on his conviction that Turkey would prevail in the war. Jabotinsky and Trumpeldor, on the other hand, believed that Britain would triumph in the Middle East and that if Jewish battalions fought with them, the Jews would acquire an additional claim to Palestine.

Ben-Gurion's position was not at odds with the official neutralist policy of the World Zionist Organization. Not only was the organization's head office located in Germany, but also, far more important, was the concern that Zionist support for England and France — and Jewish hearts were on the side of the democracies — would lead the Turks and the Germans to consider Zionism as their self-declared enemy, and both the Zionist organization and the captive Yishuv would find themselves in great danger, the latter in mortal danger.

Ben-Gurion devoted his last few days in Alexandria to teaching himself English. The difficult pronunciation, he said, was the main stumbling block to acquiring it rapidly. He also resumed the interrupted writing of his diary. On Wednesday, April 21, he wrote, "At long last I am leaving Egypt." Although Ben-Zvi had been with him every step of the way since their arrest in Palestine, the diary does not mention him at all.

An Italian ship took them to Greece, and after a few days in Rhodes and Athens they boarded the *Patros* on April 27, 1915. The ship was packed with Greek immigrants on their way to the New World. The sea was calm, conducive to studying English, philosophical speculations, and contemplating the future. Ben-Gurion resolved that his first action in the United States would be to meet with young Jews who had left Palestine because of the war, to prevent their assimilation into American life. He would also try to set up a temporary center to keep them in touch with happenings in Palestine and prepare them for "this great task which is the duty of each one of us if the great historical opportunities come to pass." He also planned to publish a Hebrew paper that would become a focus for Eretz-Israelis in America, attracting all readers of Hebrew and inspiring in their hearts a longing for "the land of their forefathers." If he and Ben-Zvi accomplished these objectives, he noted in his diary, then "our forced stay in America will have had some point." Nearing America, they ran into severe storms that slowed the ship and made Ben-Gurion feel like Noah. But on the day before their arrival the seas subsided, and the *Patros* sailed along as "though it was floating on pale blue crystal."[6]

7

New York

A T NOON on May 16, 1915, the *Patros* anchored alongside the quarantine ship waiting outside the port of New York. David Ben-Gurion noted his first impressions in his diary: Manhattan's skyscrapers seemed "absurd, resembling cages in a way." Jostled among the other passengers, he lined up for the health inspection. "We were told to expose chest, belly, and armpits. The first in line pass the inspection 'bare backed' and the rest watch. What's amazing is that even women are inspected in public." At 8:00 A.M. on May 17, the *Patros* passengers disembarked and went quickly through customs. The immigration officer treated Ben-Gurion "kindly, without much fuss," and when he asked Ben-Gurion his age, he was startled to hear English in reply. Ben-Gurion explained that he had taught himself during the voyage, a novelty that the official repeated loudly to a colleague.

The immigration files record Ben-Gurion as a "Russian (Hebrew)" student admitted as an "immigrant for permanent residence." Giving the Poale Zion New York office as his address — 79 Delancey Street, care of Hersh Ehrenreich — Ben-Gurion was out on the street by 10:30 A.M. Itzhak Ben-Zvi's interview, however, was not so short. Ben-Gurion waited several long hours for him and then, in desperation, went off to find Delancey Street by himself. By nightfall Ben-Zvi's absence was arousing alarm, and not until 7:30 P.M. did a representative from the Hebrew Immigrant Aid Society report to the Poale Zion office that he was safe and sound.

The local Yiddish press reported the arrival of the "noted editors," "famed members of Poale Zion," "labor leaders from Eretz Israel" as a great event, and their party comrades whirled them around New York, introducing them to all and sundry. "There is noise here," Ben-Gurion confided to his diary, "turmoil, confusion, activity, endless meetings, chaos." The two Eretz-Israelis rented a room near the eastern end of the Brooklyn Bridge, but during the first days spent much of their time at the home of Baruch Zuckerman, one of the top party leaders, on East Broadway.[1]

A reception organized by the party in honor of "Ben-Zvi (Avner) and Ben-Gurion, the noted founders of the Poale Zion party in Eretz Israel and of *Ha-Achdut,* and in honor of the famed publicist and literary editor of *Ha-Achdut,* Alexander Chashin (Zvi Auerbach)" was staged, but only a few members thought the event worth the ten-cent entrance fee. The only memorable aspect of the evening was the presence of a number of non-Zionist trade unionists, among them Congressman Meyer London and Max Pine, a union leader, who spoke in favor of a future understanding between the socialist movements in the United States and Eretz Israel.

From the beginning of the 1880s, Jewish immigrants had brought with them the nascent Hibbat Zion, and Zionism's development in the United States paralleled that in Europe; by 1889 there were eight active associations of Hovevei Zion in New York and other cities. In 1898, a year after Theodor Herzl founded the World Zionist Organization and its congress, the Zionist Federation of America was founded. Poale Zion emerged in the United States in the same pattern, immigrants forming their own factions within the Jewish socialist movement. In the wake of the 1903 Kishinev pogrom these factions strengthened and formed an independent party, Poale Zion of America, which by 1906 had its own weekly organ, the *Yiddisher Kemfer,* and in 1907 became a member of the World Union of Poale Zion.

Like the Zionist Federation, Poale Zion spread from New York to .other Jewish centers, first in the Midwest, then along the eastern seaboard and in Canada, and finally throughout the United States, although its total membership was only in the hundreds. The war in Europe gave a boost to all the Zionist parties, as well as to other Jewish organizations that initiated relief campaigns, but by 1915 this growth had not been substantial. In some instances a local branch could boast no more than seven paying members, and in New Palestine, Indiana, it comprised only two. Even the most generous estimate of the national membership at this time would not exceed three thousand, half of whom were located in the greater New York area.

It was not until May 29 that the Benim revealed their mission to the

U.S. Poale Zion Central Committee (C.C.), which subsequently issued a statement. "The comrades left Eretz Israel out of necessity. However, it was not necessity that brought them to the United States. Their visit is bound up with certain activities. . . . One of these is to establish an army of American pioneers — He-Chalutz — to go to Eretz Israel in time of need or immediately after the war." To this end a subcommittee of the C.C., the Palestine Committee, was formed. Its task was to organize a large number of volunteers to go to Palestine as quickly as possible to replenish the rapidly dwindling Yishuv and consolidate the Jewish people's rights to Eretz Israel by helping Turkey defend Palestine. Such a plan necessitated secrecy, so the C.C.'s deliberations were not recorded, and it was presented publicly only in the general terms that He-Chalutz would go to Palestine "to work it and defend it."[2]

The Palestine Committee had barely come into being before its members were deep in argument over whether to support the Benim's plans or those of Pinchas Rutenberg, a leader of the social revolutionary movement in Russia. Having turned Zionist, he wanted to establish a World Jewish Congress whose elected government would organize a Jewish military force within the British army to help wrest Palestine from the Turks. Ben-Gurion and Ben-Zvi embraced the congress but objected to the military plan. Like Rutenberg — and Jabotinsky — however, Ben-Gurion viewed the war as a unique historical opportunity. "The entire Jewish people must bear the responsibility not only of organizing for the purpose of claiming Eretz Israel, but also to prove their desire for Eretz Israel and their willingness to go there," he wrote in his diary after the C.C.'s discussion of the Rutenberg plan. A manifestation of the national will was "one of the duties of the hour."

The dispute over the military plans came as a blessing in disguise to the party's two paid officials, Hersh Ehrenreich and Shmuel Bonchek, secretaries to the Central and Palestine committees, respectively. A fierce controversy offered them a golden opportunity to act in their own best interests, which were not necessarily those of Eretz Israel. Thus the ground was laid for Ben-Gurion's and, to a lesser extent, Ben-Zvi's disaffection with the American party, which later developed into an open breach. Ehrenreich and Bonchek, his lieutenant, were remarkable for their devotion to the American party and their refusal to allow Palestine, or anything else, to distract them from what they believed was their duty to it.

Both were also experienced politicians, smart enough to realize that if ten thousand party members and sympathizers were to go off with He-Chalutz to Palestine, they would be left without a constituency. At the same time, they saw the benefits a good campaign for He-Chalutz could offer the party's branches: topics for debates, general activity, and monetary contributions. A lively campaign would increase party membership. Their task, as they saw it, was a delicate one: on the one hand to support the campaign for He-Chalutz, but on the other to thwart its fulfillment. According to Ben-Gurion's later account, Ehrenreich and Bonchek skillfully blocked a clear commitment to He-Chalutz by the Central and Palestine committees while undertaking to organize lecture tours by Ben-Gurion and Ben-Zvi to support it. Ben-Gurion reached this conclusion toward the end of his "exile," as he called it, in the United States, and used it to explain the failure of his and Ben-Zvi's mission. But there was more to the failure of He-Chalutz than just the narrow-mindedness and self-interest of Bonchek.

On June 28, 1915, the Central Committee sent its affiliates circular number 18, devoted entirely to the He-Chalutz project. It announced that Ben-Zvi and Ben-Gurion would visit "all our party's branches" and "discuss matters directly with our members." Organizing tours, the party's major tool for building up its membership and cementing its ideological cohesion, was equally important for fund raising. Most party members and sympathizers were European immigrants thirsting for contact with their past. A stimulating lecture and a few words with the speaker afterward went a long way to satisfying this need; moreover, a famous and "refreshing" speaker could draw upward of a hundred listeners, at a price of ten or fifteen cents a ticket. The proceeds were divided between the central office and the local branch, which bore the expenses of the tour. Friction between the local and central offices, always common, was notoriously bad over tours. Local activists desirous of increasing revenue as well as membership wanted only speakers of proven box office appeal, whereas the central office stressed a speaker's "morally" uplifting qualities, which to them meant the ability to bind the local chapters more securely to the central party in New York.

Bonchek and Ehrenreich therefore had a problem with Ben-Gurion and Ben-Zvi, whose only lecture topic was He-Chalutz. After watching the Benim closely at appearances in New York, the two officials concluded that, as an "asset to the party," the tall, pale Chashin, so attractive to women, was superior to either of them. His stories about Jewish literature and life in the old country, as well as in Palestine, enthralled his listeners; it is little wonder that Chashin was preferred to Ben-Gurion, who was loath to speak Yiddish and whose every topic boiled down only to the fulfillment of Zionism in Eretz Israel. Ben-Zvi's ap-

peal was not much greater. The branches reacted cautiously to circular
18. Winnipeg, for example, wanted to know:

1. Is Ben-Gurion a public speaker or a lecturer?
2. Will he help us in our local work and not only in setting up He-Chalutz?

Other branches, such as Springfield, Massachusetts, refused to have
Ben-Gurion. Bonchek tried to disguise He-Chalutz and its military
overtones with assertions about the general advantages Ben-Gurion's
visit would have for a local party, but in vain. Few branches were willing to gamble on Ben-Gurion's success when they had a certainty in
Chashin.

Another problem was that the party treasury was so low that the
C.C. risked bankruptcy as well as disaffection among its branches by
sending on tour two speakers who could not draw sizable crowds. To
minimize this risk Bonchek decided to finance He-Chalutz tours with
the funds of the Palestine Committee, that is, funds earmarked exclusively for Palestine. He had also warned the affiliates that they would
be deprived of "the comrades' visit" if they did not pay their share of
the expenses in advance. In the end each of them got fourteen cities,
with Ben-Zvi getting New York in addition.[3]

The tour was to begin July 4 and end some time in September 1915.
A schedule of sorts was arranged, and Ben-Gurion and Ben-Zvi, armed
with He-Chalutz registration forms, went forth to deliver their message, confident that it would produce a rush of applicants, but these
expectations turned out to be pure fantasy. While it was true that
"many comrades," as Ben-Gurion wrote in his diary, came at midnight
to greet him at the Rochester, New York, train station and engaged
him in conversation for hours, it was not about He-Chalutz. He
was soon whisked off to the Buffalo branch, which was completely
taken up with the third convention of the Jewish National Workers' Alliance, or Farband, then being held in the city. Ben-Gurion did his best,
bringing greetings to the opening session from the Jewish workers in
Palestine, but he was no match for Chashin, who "moved all present to
tears."

Ben-Gurion had hoped to enjoy more success after the convention,
but to his utter dismay, he fell ill with diphtheria and was taken to the
Ernest Wende Hospital, where he understood no one and felt as though
he was in solitary confinement. On his discharge two weeks later, he
was eager to leave at once for Detroit, to make up for lost time. But the
Buffalo comrades, observing his debilitated state, insisted that he recuperate first at a nearby Jewish farm. The kind Jewish farmer met him at
the station, and Ben-Gurion recorded a fragment of their conversation.

I asked him, "When did you become a farmer?"

"This is the first year."

"How did you acquire the skills?"

"Well, I truly don't have the skills."

"So how do you work?"

"I have a hired hand, a goy, and he does the work."

An old story. Jewish nature is the same the world over.

His harvest in Buffalo was one recruit for He-Chalutz, a stranger passing through who happened to hear him.[4]

The interruption in Ben-Gurion's tour necessitated a revised itinerary. Ben-Zvi was given Ben-Gurion's original cities of Milwaukee, Minneapolis, St. Paul, and Winnipeg, while Ben-Gurion was allocated Detroit; Toronto, Hamilton, Ontario, and Montreal; Boston and its shtetlach, "suburbs," and Providence. In Detroit, where he arrived on August 2, Ben-Gurion had his first real chance to prove his worth to Bonchek, who was keeping a close watch on him from New York. But although the Detroit party members did not take to Ben-Gurion either as a man or a speaker, they kept their views to themselves, so it was from Hamilton that Bonchek received the first written evaluation of Ben-Gurion's performance.

He gave us a most successful and almost scientific survey of the general situation in Eretz Israel. I regret to have to report that the first meeting with comrade Ben-Gurion, especially regarding He-Chalutz, was not a great success. That is to say, only one comrade registered.

For Bonchek, the professional, there was no worse verdict than "a scientific lecturer" or "an expert on the subject." Such speakers were, in his terms, "poison." The Boston and New Haven affiliates changed their minds and refused to have Ben-Gurion, and he was not favorably received in Toronto, which became the last stop on his tour. On August 24 he returned to New York with only nineteen signed He-Chalutz registration forms from five branches of Poale Zion. Ben-Zvi had fared better, having attracted forty-four volunteers in seven cities.

American Poale Zion held its convention in Cleveland in September 1915. Neither the inflated number of "approximately ninety" volunteers that Ben-Gurion and Ben-Zvi reported to it nor the praise lavished on the Benim in response could conceal the tours' sad results: there was no "army of pioneers" to replace the "ten thousand Jews who had had to leave Eretz Israel." Nevertheless, the convention called for greater efforts toward the support of Eretz Israel and decided to send the two friends on a second registration drive.

Ehrenreich and Bonchek were absolutely sure that party members and sympathizers would not flock by the thousands to He-Chalutz, so they felt they could give the Benim full support since they believed it to be highly beneficial to the party. In addition, Ehrenreich and Bonchek had feared that He-Chalutz would fall under the influence of the so-called Social Democrats, a faction of Poale Zion led by Ber Borochov — who also had sought refuge in New York for the duration of the war — which had threatened to break away from the party. If so, it is understandable that they were cool toward He-Chalutz until they were absolutely sure of the Benim's loyalty to the party. But by the time of the Cleveland convention they had satisfied themselves on that issue, and the party "machine" could afford to let them loose once again. Another factor, however, was that the official party line was one of neutrality in the war, which put Ehrenreich and Bonchek in a terrible quandary. They would have to pass up the prospects for party growth and prosperity offered by both the He-Chalutz campaign and the rival Rutenberg plan with its popular slogan, "Jewish Army! Jewish World Congress! Jewish Government!" Unwilling to lose these opportunities, they decided not to choose one over the other and tried as best they could to leave the options open for both. The C.C. members were nervous about endorsing a scheme that would certainly offend Turkey's opponents Britain and France and, therefore, the United States. This was what made Ben-Gurion suspect that Bonchek and Ehrenreich, as well as their elected bosses, were motivated primarily by the needs of the party in America, not by those of Zionism in Palestine.[5]

However, the second set of tours soon showed that other important factors were involved in the He-Chalutz disappointment. Four of its fundamental principles proved insurmountable obstacles: the demand that volunteers be ready to travel to Palestine at a moment's notice; the imposition of secrecy, to which many members objected; the military training; and the obligatory contribution of one dollar a week to the travel-expense fund.

Only in Toronto did Ben-Gurion find a pool of applicants from which to select. He deemed seven satisfactory, especially a man named Simon Julian, who, he noted, was "worth ten others." There was the further insuperable problem of finding a legitimate way to train the volunteers in the use of firearms. Even if such a way were found, what plan of training should they follow? A Milwaukee member put this question in a letter to Ben-Zvi, who replied succinctly, "You are to organize the exercise courses with the military drills that are most necessary." What type of drills Ben-Zvi, who had no military experience whatever, envisioned is hard to guess.

If the party members had had the will, they would doubtless have found a way to solve this problem. The truth was, however, that, as one volunteer explained in a letter to Bonchek, "our comrades love to talk but have very little affection for actually doing anything." The issue of He-Chalutz, not its implementation, fired their imaginations. Bonchek and Ehrenreich participated in this debate willingly. Bonchek assured a vegetarian who objected to He-Chalutz's military aspect that "we must become accustomed to defense, self-defense, no more, no less. There is no harm to an individual in that. Even if he is a vegetarian." And he hinted that, as secretary of the Palestine Committee, he was naturally a member of He-Chalutz and would go to Eretz Israel with the other volunteers. But this was not to be. Bonchek remained in the party office in New York for the rest of his long life, inheriting Ehrenreich's job on the latter's death.

Meanwhile the Benim were insisting that training start at once, to the puzzlement of many. "What's the hurry?" complained a member of Chicago's Lawndale branch. He, like many others, thought that the end of the war was far off, whereas Ben-Gurion and Ben-Zvi estimated that the "pioneer army" would move out within a year or so from its inception, that is, around autumn 1916. Ben-Gurion was so confident of this timing that he turned his attention to the question of what He-Chalutz would do on its arrival in Palestine, a matter he and Ben-Zvi had hitherto neglected. Their prospective recruits also wanted to know what arrangements would be made for their families if they were killed or wounded in battle. That question "requires clarification," Ben-Gurion noted in his diary.

Ben-Gurion's prediction that the Ottomans would avenge themselves on the Palestinian Jews if Jewish units were attached to the British army that fought against the Turks seemed validated when first Arab nationalist leaders and then Armenians were ruthlessly killed by the Ottoman governor of Syria. The Jews would be next, Ben-Gurion feared, and this would mean "the destruction of the very aspiration and idea of the revival of Eretz Israel, because without the Yishuv, the yearning for Eretz Israel is emptied of all meaningful content, and without this content, the entire movement will be destroyed." In July 1916, however, he was informed that Jemal Pasha might now allow some of the deportees to return to Palestine and, thinking that the hour for He-Chalutz had come, Ben-Gurion took immediate steps to get permission for himself and Ben-Zvi to return to Palestine at the head of their volunteers, to join ranks with the Turks. With Ben-Zvi, he wrote a memorandum that he asked Louis D. Brandeis, the former chairman of the Provisional Zionist Committee, to submit to the Sublime Porte through Ambassador Henry Morgenthau. But the request was either never received in Istanbul or rejected out of hand, and the hope for a quick departure vanished. Ben-Gurion had no choice but to start his second tour. Having learned from the mistakes of the first, he acceded to the machine's request not to restrict his topics to He-Chalutz and Zionism, though he felt no enthusiasm for this new arrangement, "because I hardly believe in the power of orators."[6]

Ben-Gurion set out on December 9, 1915, but, again, many branches showed no desire to receive him and nine rejected him outright. Ben-Gurion's inability to impassion his audiences created friction between the branches, eager for better speakers, and the Central Committee, which continued to impose Ben-Gurion wherever it could. He complained of loneliness, overwork, and poor organization, and was additionally plagued by lack of money. Like Ben-Zvi, he considered himself a party worker whatever he did and accordingly received a salary of ten dollars a week plus travel expenses.

Perhaps the worst feature of the tour for Ben-Gurion was the constant personal contact with strangers it entailed. Not only was there enforced intimacy with people with whom he had to stay because his hosts thought he was not worth the expense of a hotel, but before and after the meetings the comrades besieged him, especially in places where a speaker from Palestine was a novelty. Still he knew he could not avoid it. "After all, it is impossible to speak in a mechanical fashion — you have to inject some fire and warmth — and this isn't particularly easy when you have to talk and talk, day after day, without stop." He addressed nineteen meetings in the space of twenty-six days — all in small towns. This gave him another bone to pick with the machine, for he had no idea how Bonchek and Ehrenreich had had to struggle to persuade the large chapters to receive him at all. To get maximum value, they had filled the gaps in his itinerary by sending him to distant spots that other speakers usually bypassed.

Not every meeting was a failure. A few people were discerning enough to realize that although Ben-Gurion was no matinee idol like Chashin, he had something to say. Then, overnight, his reputation as an uninspiring speaker was transformed by his appearance at a mass meeting in Minneapolis, where he was confronted by members of labor unions who sympathized with the Bund, the sworn enemies of the Zionists. The war had forced some cooperation between these rival groups for the relief of Jewish war victims, but they still competed fiercely to attract new supporters. Ben-Gurion rose to the occasion, fighting as though he were back in Płońsk with Shmulik the Bundist, and routed his opponent. An admiring party member reported to Bonchek that "were it not for Ben-Gurion, the Poale Zion faction would have been defeated."

Ben-Gurion went on to consolidate his reputation as a brilliant debater in Galveston, Texas, when an anti-Zionist took the floor and alleged that Palestine was a country full of graves, beggars, and idlers. Ben-Gurion exploded, and the audience almost came to blows. He managed, however, to gain control of the two hundred Jews present and win them over to his side. Ehrenreich was duly informed of his magnificent victory, and Ben-Gurion proudly noted in his report, "They will have this lesson to keep as a remembrance."

These successes revived him, and he was very upset when the C.C. deleted California from his schedule. Nevertheless, his tour seemed set for a triumphant conclusion until he visited the Chicago branch, the second largest in America. The leaders there were itching for greater independence, but the machine would yield none of its power to Chicago and its five affiliates. The issue chosen for the struggle was whether the group should receive Ben-Gurion in accordance with Ehrenreich's demand. After much acrimonious correspondence and vacillation, Chicago said absolutely no. Nevertheless, Bonchek notified the branch that Ben-Gurion would be its guest from March 8 to 14 for a fee of only fifteen dollars. The affiliate stuck to its guns. When Ben-Gurion, unaware of the conflict, arrived in Chicago on March 7, he discovered that no preparations had been made for his visit. Attributing this to the C.C.'s incompetence, he wrote that he had no doubt that the party would have been ten times its size if only its leaders had talked less and done more. The day after he reached Chicago, he cabled Bonchek, "Am very tired want to stop tour." Although furious, he took part in some branch activities and then went on to his last engagement in Milwaukee, where he met Goldie Mabovitch, who later became Golda Meir. Ben-Gurion, she wrote in her memoirs, was one of the "least approachable men" she had ever met. On March 24 he returned to New York.[7]

8

Yizkor

FOR ALL their efforts David Ben-Gurion and Itzhak Ben-Zvi had recruited about a hundred men and women for He-Chalutz. Their trips to more than thirty cities should have shown Ben-Gurion how utterly wrong his premises were. Jews in the United States and Canada were not dormant Zionists waiting to be roused by a clarion call. Even if Hersh Ehrenreich, Shmuel Bonchek, and all the leaders of Poale Zion had supported He-Chalutz unequivocally, Jews would not have flocked to Palestine.

Ben-Gurion wondered if a lack of information about Palestine largely accounted for the lack of response to He-Chalutz, for both he and Ben-Zvi had been struck on their first tours by the prevalence of ignorance about the region. To remedy this situation, they began to prepare written materials for distribution by the party, contemplating an anthology on Palestine. Eventually the idea was shelved in favor of *Yizkor*, an album in Yiddish in memory of the workers and watchmen in Palestine who had given their lives in the service of Hashomer. Bonchek, always eager to promote a moneymaker, was quick to recognize a potential best seller and immediately devoted himself and the Palestine Committee to *Yizkor*'s preparation and publication. Starting in February 1916, the New York office was flooded with advance orders, but Ben-Zvi, head of the three-member editorial staff that also included Alexander Chashin and Zerubavel, resisted the pressure to go to press without the contribution promised by Ben-Gurion, who was still on the road. His article, "Selected Reminiscences — From Petah Tikva to Sejera," which arrived in March, was the longest in the volume, taking up fifteen of the 128 pages of text and illustrations.

Yizkor was an immediate success. The exploits of Jewish pioneers in Palestine and the valiant deaths of Hashomer men resonated in the hearts of American Jews. The entire edition of thirty-five hundred copies was snatched up overnight. Before long, "*Yizkor* evenings" featuring speakers, singers, and a reader had become more popular than any other Poale Zion activity. To see, hear, and talk about pioneers in Palestine was far more rewarding, it seemed, than joining them via He-Chalutz. Suddenly people were glad to give money for Hashomer, and the three editors and Ben-Gurion acquired an aura of the heroism they extolled. Reporting Ben-Gurion's appearance at a *Yizkor* evening in New York, the *Yiddisher Kemfer* said, "Comrade Ben-Gurion, in firm and measured sentences, remarked on the obstacles that the workers and watchmen in Eretz Israel had to overcome: the Diaspora mentality, the fear of death, and the self-doubt as to whether they would be able to achieve their goal. They overcame them, and a passionate, fiery idealism and belief were born that were strong enough to create the new life in Eretz Israel."

The praise for *Yizkor* was not universal, however. Under the headline THE JEWISH COLONIES IN ERETZ ISRAEL ARE BUILT UPON THE MISFORTUNES OF THE ARABS, the *Forward* published a trenchant attack by Moshe Olgin. "Heroes are always beautiful, especially when they die for that which is sacred and dear to them." Nevertheless, asked Olgin, "who are those Arabs" who had fought Hashomer? "The Arabs are the old owners of Palestine," and they were waging a just, obstinate, systematic, and prolonged national war against the Jews who wanted to oust them from their land. In short, Olgin concluded, the Jewish heroes commemorated in *Yizkor* had died in a war of conquest and suppression. Ben-Gurion, outraged that a fellow Jew should depict the Zionists in Israel as "robbers conducting politics of exploitation and oppression," composed a scathing reply calling Olgin's piece "hooliganist." When the *Yiddisher Kemfer* refused to publish it, Ben-Gurion declared he would not write for the paper again.[1]

In June the party decided to issue a second edition of *Yizkor*. Only Ben-Gurion and Chashin among the Eretz-Israelis were in New York at the time, and Ben-Gurion was unwilling to bring out a revised edition. He wanted a new book altogether, and further insisted on deleting Zerubavel's introduction to the first edition. Chashin, who shared Ben-Gurion's lack of respect for Zerubavel, sided with him. Bonchek, on learning of this intended slight to Zerubavel, seized the opportunity to create a split among the four former editors of *Ha-Achdut*. Counting on his habitual unwillingness to injure anybody's feelings, he wrote Ben-Zvi, under the guise of asking for his counsel, of Ben-Gurion's intention. Ben-Zvi immediately passed the information to Zerubavel, who flew into a self-indulgent rage, seeking in his distress the all too willing Bonchek's succor. Ben-Zvi, as expected, came out boldly in Zerubavel's defense, and Bonchek had achieved his purpose. He became, as though by the free choice of the four, their benevolent arbiter.

Bonchek, however, had omitted Ben-Gurion's tenacity from his calculations. Ben-Gurion saw the book as a means to inform and arouse the Jews about Eretz Israel, and nothing else mattered to him. In his view, Zerubavel's introduction was no good and therefore had to go. Bonchek and other Palestine Committee members were mainly concerned with their own petty rivalries. Chashin retired from the field to Montreal, where he limited his share of the editorial responsibility to editing new copy and writing the new introduction in accordance with Ben-Gurion's ideas and instructions. Ben-Zvi was staying with friends in Washington, D.C., claiming it was high time he acquired a thorough knowledge of English, a rather thin pretext to cover his displeasure with the machine. Zerubavel was happily touring the branches, which were all clamoring for his lively Yiddish oratory. Ben-Gurion used their absence to stiffen his demands, and Bonchek, eager to publish the second edition, was unable to prevent Ben-Gurion from doing as he wished. He wrote all the new material and directed the composition when printing began in mid-August.[2]

The title page had an illustrated heading that read "Expanded second edition, compiled by A. Chashin, D. Ben-Gurion." Ben-Zvi remembered the omission of his name to his last day. Fourteen thousand copies, printed in an album format, were bound in cloth embossed in silver; 190 pages included silhouette illustrations and drawings of the heroes who had died at their posts. The *Yiddisher Kemfer* headlined it as a "totally new book" and heaped congratulations on its editors. By November orders were pouring in from the West Coast, Rio de Janeiro, Manchester, Leeds, and Paris. Ben-Gurion's "Reminiscences" were translated in a French paper, and the *Judischer Verlag* in Berlin, which ordered 220 copies, sought permission to translate the book into German. The German edition, translated by Gershom Scholem and with an introduction by Martin Buber, appeared in 1918. *Yizkor II* was an international success, for which Ben-Gurion was quite justified in taking the credit. He earned for himself a fine reputation in the small but all-encompassing world of the Zionist labor movement and among the younger generation of Zionists in general. All proceeds from the book went into the party's coffers, and Ben-Gurion continued to receive his weekly pay.

Bonchek found himself in a dilemma. Although he was eager to follow the success of *Yizkor II* with yet another sequel on Palestine, he knew that only Ben-Gurion and Ben-Zvi could produce it well and quickly enough. But the Benim were at odds with the party, and the still greater fame such a book was bound to bring them might make it that much harder for the party to control them.

Indeed, the Benim's discontent had become an established fact. Ben-Zvi had settled in Washington, where he learned English and quietly pursued scholarly interests in the history of Jewish ethnology. Ben-Gurion remained in New York but withdrew from all party activity and institutions. He even resigned from the committee that the party had created to promote a World Jewish Congress, an idea very dear to him, and joined the Jewish Congress League as an individual. His experience with He-Chalutz and the party's various committees had strengthened his conviction that its activists were more interested in their own positions than in implementing Zionism.

Bonchek's solution to his dilemma was an anthology to be compiled and edited by many authors, leaving the Palestine Committee, the publisher, in control. So he announced the publication of a new book, *Eretz Israel — Land of Our Future*, to be written by "experts on Oriental issues, like I. Ben-Zvi (Avner) and D. Ben-Gurion, in collaboration with Dr. M. Sheinkin and other authorities." Ben-Gurion, free to devote himself completely to this project, embraced it with great joy, as did Ben-Zvi. In fact, they both considered it their own idea, conceived long before *Yizkor*. With Ben-Gurion in high gear, however, it was not long before the other "authorities" evaporated and the volume became the Benim's project; they dedicated all their time and energy to it for a year and a quarter. The party agreed to advance the publication costs and delegated the job of supervising the production to the Palestine Committee, that is, to Bonchek, who was paid twenty dollars a week, whereas the Benim continued to earn only ten. Even so, the Palestine Committee had overextended itself financially, and therefore decided to offer the book to advance subscribers at sixty cents per copy, instead of $1.20, the advertised price. By December 1916, $342 had been raised.

Though it was agreed between the Benim that each should write half the book, Ben-Gurion became the dominant author. Having undertaken to write the more political chapters, he spent days and nights at the New York Public Library at Forty-second Street acquiring a thorough knowledge of Palestine's history and demography. In the end he wrote the introduction and two thirds of the text. The gentle Ben-Zvi would have borne him no grudge had he not felt that Ben-Gurion had "snatched" from him the chapter on the fellaheen and their origins, a subject very dear to him, and one he had begun to investigate in 1908. In their long companionship, Ben-Zvi forgave and forgot many justified complaints against Ben-Gurion, but *Yizkor* and the fellaheen remained the two wounds that never healed. Ben-Gurion, for his part, regarded *Eretz Israel* as his own book. *Yizkor* opened his eyes to the importance of personal fame, and he was counting on *Eretz Israel* to enhance and extend it.[3]

However, the excitement of the *Eretz Israel* project was completely overshadowed by the events of 1917. February saw the Russian Revolution, and then, in rapid succession, the British government agreed to create Jewish battalions to fight in Palestine; the October Revolution took place; and, in November, the Balfour Declaration committed the British government to assist the Jews to establish their national home in Palestine. Like most other Jews, the members of Poale Zion were overwhelmed; there was no doubt whatever in their minds that these momentous events heralded nothing less than the redemption of man, Jew, and Zionist. Social justice would spread throughout the world once the revolution in Russia had triumphed; in the peace talks after the war Jews would gain equal rights all over the world; and in Palestine, the Jewish people would renew their national independence. *Geula,* the Hebrew word for redemption, a religious concept bound up with the coming of the Messiah, was on everyone's lips.

But even the common belief in imminent redemption could not overcome disunity. Poale Zion was torn between two conflicting forces. One pulled the members back to Russia, to take part in building the society that would bring the new order to the entire world; the other drew them to Palestine, to take part in building the new Jewish state that would gather in the entire Jewish people. In New York the *Yiddisher Kemfer* urged "support for our comrades in the Russian Republic" in the form of money and volunteers who could hasten to Russia. Borochov headed the Russian campaign, and he, Zerubavel, Chashin, and others eagerly made preparations to return to their homeland at once. Ben-Zvi was in turmoil. He had been informed by cable that the Russian Poale Zion, his alma mater, so to speak, had elected him to its Central Committee, but in spite of being drawn to Russia, he decided to return to Palestine. Nevertheless, he took an active part in helping the comrades who were preparing to leave for Russia on the first available boat.

Ben-Gurion, meanwhile, was seething with frustration because the party was using resources earmarked for Eretz Israel for the return to Russia. Outraged by the Palestine Committee's resolution to make its funds available to Zerubavel, to use as he saw fit, he wrote:

The new situation demands concentration from us — concentration of will, thought, action. Everything must center around one and only one

point — Eretz Israel . . . anything not directly aimed at Eretz Israel is out
of the question. From now on the Zionist slogan must be "Everything for
Eretz Israel — Nothing for anything else."

Somewhat unexpectedly, Bonchek reached the same conclusion,
though from other motives entirely. His fear was that not only would
American Poale Zion leaders themselves leave, but that they would set
an example for the rank-and-file members, depleting the party and rendering it insignificant. For the same reason, he later discouraged any
serious efforts to get people to leave for Palestine.

At that time, however, the only way to get to Palestine was to join
the British army fighting there. The British government's December
1916 decision to occupy Palestine and the first British victories in Palestine in March 1917 — crowned in December by the capture of Jerusalem — changed the Benim's political views, even before the Balfour
Declaration was made public. They now believed that Zionism's and
the Yishuv's future rested with the British, and in November 1917 Ben-
Gurion, having forgiven the paper, published this view in the *Yiddisher
Kemfer*. With the same fervor that had characterized their pro-Ottoman stance, they became pro-British and joined the Committee for a
Jewish Legion in Eretz Israel, organized to rally Jewish volunteers
from all over America and Canada to form Jewish units within the British army.

However, the committee placed one condition on General Wilfred
White, head of the British recruiting office in New York: that the Jewish units be used in Palestine only. But as late as February 1918 the
War Office was still instructing General White that while he was authorized to guarantee that "men of the Jewish faith from the United
States shall be employed in special Jewish battalions" in the British
army, "the theater of war in which they will be used cannot be
guaranteed." So in effect this route to Palestine was blocked, too.[4]

Nevertheless there was no doubt in Ben-Gurion's mind that since
this as well as other roads to Palestine would open soon, there was not
a moment to lose. He felt it incumbent on him to organize the Jewish
laborers for a mass exodus to Palestine. On November 23, 1917, he
presented to the Central Committee a proposal to enlarge its membership; create a special fund; set up a small action committee to carry out
an Eretz Israel project "among and by means of the Jewish workers"
under his leadership; and to convene an extraordinary conference to
reformulate the party's political line in view of the developments in
Palestine and Russia. Everything but the last item was agreed to, and
Ben-Gurion, among others, joined the enlarged C.C.

Three days later the Action Committee, composed of Baruch Zuckerman, Ehrenreich, Bonchek, and Ben-Zvi, with Ben-Gurion as chairman, was formed. A campaign on behalf of "the $40,000 Fund" was launched at once, to the amazement of all; no one had ever dreamed of appealing for such a huge sum. The new committee made its public debut on November 29 at a celebration of the Balfour Declaration in Cooper Union's Great Hall, where Ben-Gurion addressed two thousand people.

In the electric atmosphere generated by the declaration and the October Revolution, two resolutions were put to the vote. The first, a response to the declaration, called on every Jew to devote all his energies, "and if necessary, his life," to the establishment of a national home in Eretz Israel. The second, which Ben-Gurion had drafted, announced, "We, Jewish socialist workers and revolutionaries, pledge ourselves to be in the vanguard of our movement for national freedom, within the framework of the organized Zionist proletariat, and with all our power to aid the immediate enlistment of the Jewish proletariat to Eretz Israel, for Eretz Israel, and in Eretz Israel." He demanded a personal undertaking from everyone present to act, closing his resolution, "We solemnly pledge to follow in the path and continue the work of our courageous pioneers, workers, and watchmen who gave their lives for the freedom and revival of the Jewish people in the Jewish land."

Undeterred by the chairman's warning about the seriousness of this pledge, all two thousand approved the resolution with a standing ovation. The next day Ben-Gurion found that his fame extended beyond the Yiddish press — the *New York Times* printed his name for the first time, as one of the speakers who urged President Woodrow Wilson to declare his support for a Jewish home in Palestine. Inspired by the rapturous response to his call, Ben-Gurion worked tirelessly in the following weeks to spread it throughout the United States. Because, he said, the Action Committee was talking about a settlement project "not of families, but of a people," and not in the future, "but tomorrow," he wanted two things quickly and in great quantity — money and people. He needed "millions and billions," and since the Zionist movement had become a recognized political fact, he argued, it should have the right to obtain credit and loans just like "other governments."[5]

Not entirely unexpectedly, the party machine began to worry about the Action Committee's alarming activities. Ben-Gurion had to be stopped, lest party members who had not left for Russia depart en masse, with their money, to Palestine. An ingenious plan was concocted whose timing was determined by two concurrent differences of opinion inside the Action Committee. In the first, Ben-Gurion and Ben-Zvi maintained that all the money in the $40,000 Fund was earmarked exclusively for Palestine and should not be used for a proposed

Yiddish daily newspaper, to be called *Die Zeit*, for which they saw no need. Zuckerman, Ehrenreich, and Bonchek were strongly in favor of using the money to start *Die Zeit*, which they said would be a powerful boost for both party building and immigration to Palestine.

The second conflict involved the creation of a Jewish labor congress to aid in recruiting masses of Jewish workers to Palestine — Ben-Gurion's brainchild. He and Ben-Zvi wanted to convene it quickly, on a basis of obligatory pledges regarding Palestine; Zuckerman, Ehrenreich, and Bonchek wanted to organize it as a loose and non-binding framework, to assure that the party would benefit from it. These disputes reached a crisis, and at a Central Committee meeting on January 15, 1918, Ehrenreich and Bonchek and Zuckerman, the power behind them, accused Ben-Gurion of inaction. The C.C. decided unanimously to replace him, making Zuckerman chairman of the Action Committee. Outgunned, Ben-Gurion resigned from both committees.

The charge against him was outrageous. In the seven weeks of his chairmanship he had organized, from the new Poale Zion office at 266 Grand Street, lecture tours, mass meetings, and local Action Committees all over the United States; the activists he dispatched for that purpose visited seventy cities. The file for "aliyah registration" had fifteen hundred names of people who were ready to leave for Palestine at a moment's notice, promising to bring with them a collective sum of $3 million. The $40,000 Fund had already accumulated $25,000 and would easily have reached $50,000 if the operation had not been hobbled by the dispute. The innocent Ben-Zvi thought "petty intrigues" were the source of the conflict, but Ben-Gurion said explicitly, in his letter of resignation of January 18, that the criticism leveled against him had been motivated by personal considerations. In his view, Zuckerman, Bonchek, and Ehrenreich feared for their positions from the moment he attempted to broaden the base of operations. His resignation was immediately accepted and the *Yiddisher Kemfer* promptly announced the "reorganization" of the Action Committee.

Under Zuckerman's leadership the committee ceased all action on behalf of Eretz Israel and dedicated its efforts to raising funds for an American Poale Zion daily newspaper. Ben-Zvi, realizing that moneys which should have gone to Palestine were being used for this project, told the Central Committee on March 26 that "it is impossible for man to direct his energy and efforts in two different directions at once" and resigned from the Action Committee. While the party machine had welcomed Ben-Gurion's resignation, consternation followed Ben-Zvi's departure, and he was urged to reconsider. But he refused to retract his criticism and his resignation stood. Still, unlike Ben-Gurion, who withdrew from all party activity, including He-Chalutz, he continued to coordinate the He-Chalutz program in spite of Bonchek's petty attempt to retaliate by debarring him from signing checks drawn on the He-Chalutz bank account.[6]

The Action Committee dispute was concurrent with an even more severe conflict between the Benim and the party. Whether one triggered the other or was its result can only be surmised. This dispute concerned the copyright of the *Eretz Israel* book, whose length, production time, and costs had all greatly exceeded the original estimates. The slim volume Bonchek intended was to have taken three months to write as a means to satisfy quickly the public's curiosity about Palestine, which had been intensified by the Balfour Declaration and General Edmund Allenby's victories. But it had blossomed into "a great scientific work," as Ben-Gurion called it, that would take a year to complete. After long discussions the Palestine Committee had agreed to publish one weighty volume and raise the original price to $2 a copy. The party thereby hoped to recoup some of the publication costs, which amounted to a staggering $6,000.

The party's desire to exercise control over the book's sales until this sum was recovered may have influenced Bonchek and other members of the Palestine Committee to claim, on February 4, the copyright for the party, even though on January 4, when the committee had authorized the printing, it had indicated that the copyright belonged to the authors. Ben-Gurion felt as if he had been set upon by thieves. "Ben-Gurion is upset," reported Bonchek to his superior, "and claims that we want to rob him of his creation." Indeed, Ben-Gurion consulted a lawyer and wrote a long and bitter letter to the Central Committee, which had approved the Palestine Committee's copyright resolution. He demanded, "in the name of justice, law, and the honor of the party," that a plenary session of the C.C. revoke the decision. He agreed, however, to accept arbitration if the matter could not otherwise be settled, and at the end of March a mediator ordered the party to pay an insignificant sum to the authors for the copyright. The final production work fell entirely to Ben-Gurion, who supervised the proofreading and sent the finished galleys to Ben-Zvi, who had gone to live with friends on a farm on Long Island. At the beginning of April, the books entered the bindery and by May, sales were in full swing.

Eretz Israel — Past and Present, five hundred pages in a large format at $2 a copy, was a great success, rapturously reviewed by the Yiddish and English press. Within four months the entire edition of seven thousand copies was sold, and the book went into second and third printings. Altogether, twenty-five thousand copies were produced for $15,000, leaving the Palestine Committee with a net profit of more than $20,000.[7] Ben-Gurion, who had become one of the most famous members of Poale Zion in and outside the United States, was set to return to Palestine with Ben-Zvi as his equal, if not superior, in the party.

But this was not the only change that had occurred during his time in America. There was another, which profoundly affected his personal life.

9

Paula

POLITICAL FRUSTRATION had not been David Ben-Gurion's only
source of unhappiness in America; the man was also very lonely.
In his first year of "exile" he was on the road for long periods,
and when he settled in New York, Itzhak Ben-Zvi and Alexander Chashin were frequently out of town for months on end. He did not make
friends with any American, within or outside Poale Zion, and longed
for people he had known in the past. From a Poale Zion picnic at
Coney Island, which lasted well into the night, he sent a postcard to
Rachel Beit-Halachmi. "I stare at the skies, and I see as many stars as
people around me . . . but you aren't there." He vainly dispatched fe-
brile letters to the Ukraine, where she was caught by the war, imploring her to bring her babies and join him in America. He would pay her
fare and support her in comfort. Anything would be hers for the asking
provided she came posthaste.

There was only one place he could go to satisfy his need for warmth
and comfort. Dr. Samuel Ellsberg opened his home at 279 East Broadway to writers, community workers, socialist and trade union activists,
and Poale Zion in particular. In his clinic for general practice and
gynecology, which was in his home, there lived and worked Pauline
Munweis, a nurse. Her features were handsome enough, her figure
attractive. Warm, gay, and unreserved, she involved herself tactlessly
in other people's business. Responding to visitors with immediate familiarity, she became an integral part of the cheerful atmosphere of
the doctor's house.

Ben-Gurion first met Pauline, whom he called Paula, in the summer
of 1916 at Ellsberg's home and afterward at meetings and picnics arranged by Poale Zion. At the end of that year, he asked her to help him
with his research in the New York Public Library for *Eretz Israel* and
she copied out passages he selected in a clear hand.

She endeared herself to him because she was a compassionate nurse who cared for mothers and children and had a conspicuous maternal streak. With her he felt like "a young, foolish boy."

He was hungry for warmth, security, and attention, while she longed for someone who would accept her abundant attention, supervision, and care. Love, which both desired equally, came quickly, even though they hesitated to express it in words. He made love to a woman for the first time in Paula's bed, and if until then he had defined his feelings for her in terms of "want" and "need," once she had given herself to him, he added the concept of "sanctity" to their relationship. Only after three months of marriage was he able to declare his love for her. He wrote, "I feel as if I were in love with you for the first time . . . and I want . . . to stand by your bed, to bend over you, give myself up to your arms, and forget everything but you, as before, filled with joy by your love — together, arm in arm, lips to lips, heart to heart, forever in your maiden bed so holy to me."

The intense excitement generated by the Balfour Declaration was what had inspired Ben-Gurion to propose, after first warning Paula what to expect if she said yes. "You will have to leave America and journey with me to a small, impoverished country without electricity, gas, or motorized transport." Furthermore, he was considering enlisting in the Jewish Legion, should it be formed. Paula was opposed equally passionately to going to Palestine and to his enlistment, but she married him, confident that she could dissuade him, by fair means or foul, from both.

On Wednesday, December 5, 1917, Paula put on her best dress and the two went to City Hall. They submitted an application to register a civil marriage, paid two dollars, and were married by the city clerk in the office of the municipal judge, in the presence of two strangers who were good enough to lend their names and signatures to the formality. Ben-Gurion noted in his diary, "11:30 I got married." Nothing more. As soon as the ceremony was over he went off to chair an Action Committee meeting, then went to the *Yiddisher Kemfer* offices and placed an announcement in the paper. It appeared on December 14, in Hebrew, on page 7:

> Penina (Pauline) Munweis
> New York
> D. Ben-Gurion
> Jerusalem
> have married
> 20 Kislev 5678

The marriage took all their friends by surprise.

For three days after the wedding, Paula and Ben-Gurion continued to live apart — she with two of her co-workers, and Ben-Gurion with Ben-Zvi, in a red brick house at 243 Hewes Street, Brooklyn. They went about their ordinary business, she in the small Jewish Hospital at 270 East Broadway where she had started to work, and he in the public library. Then they moved into a small apartment at 531 Bedford Avenue in Brooklyn, where they spent five happy months together. Ben-Gurion gladly adapted his personal habits to his new status, and obediently accepted the regimen of cleanliness imposed by Paula. She was particularly insistent on his brushing his teeth, which she begged him to do every morning for her sake "and for the sake of our future." She treated his badly inflamed eyes tenderly and took care of his clothes, as she did for the rest of her life. With a full heart, he would wake her before leaving to carry on with his research or supervise the printing of *Eretz Israel,* "with kisses, a caress in your bare arms, and your eyes begging me to stay a little longer."[1]

Paula made it very clear to Ben-Gurion that she had made tremendous personal sacrifices in marrying him. Thus it seemed to him that in their relationship she was the giver and he the taker; he the winner, marrying up, and she the loser, marrying down. When she first met him, he was short, poor, lacking any distinction except for his fame as one of the editors of *Yizkor* — a book that held no interest for her, since she was utterly uninterested in Zionism, as she told him and everybody else; she had a diploma and was a well-established nurse from a noble family. "A refugee" was her first impression of Ben-Gurion. "No looks and no attractiveness, shabbily dressed, and his eyes watering badly," she told her elder daughter Geula. "But when he proposed to me, I knew I would be marrying a great man." She thus claimed to have been the first to "discover" Ben-Gurion.

Ben-Gurion never learned Paula's true story; only after her death in 1968 was it possible to reconstruct it. One of nine children, she was born in 1886 or 1887 to Shlomo Munweis, a grocer in Minsk, in White Russia. In New York, where she settled in 1904, she attended the evening classes offered by the city and state, for without a working knowledge of English Paula would not have been accepted into a nursing program. Always setting her sights high, she considered nursing a better occupation than a job in a sweatshop, offering a far better chance at a proper match. That Paula was pretentious — eccentric, some said — became evident immediately: she changed her first name from Penina to Pauline and added Cora as a middle name because she thought it went well with her high-born stock, for her family firmly believed that they were distant relations of Count Munves, a Polish aristocrat who never existed. Most probably, someone had joked about their ancestors, quoting from the Talmud, where the proselyte fourth-century King Monobaz of Adiabene, Mesopotamia, is mentioned, a joke they misunderstood. (In Hebrew, Munweis, Munves, and Mono-baz are spelled the same.) When her elder sister arrived from Russia with her family, Paula decided it did not befit her kinfolk to live on the Lower East Side and rented an apartment on Eastern Parkway, then a fashionable neighborhood in Brooklyn. When she registered her six-year-old nephew, Wolfe, in school, she changed his name, on her own initiative, to Will, and so it remained; when Ben-Gurion finally met Will Maslow he was the director of the American Jewish Congress.

Six years after her arrival in New York, Paula obtained certification from the Jewish Maternity Hospital that she had taken practical and theoretical courses in midwifery from April 20 to October 20 of 1910. She was hired by that hospital and later worked in a pediatric hospital on the corner of Second Avenue and Third Street. In 1915 she passed another nursing course at the Beth El Jewish Hospital in Newark, New Jersey, and a short while after that began working for Dr. Ellsberg.

In 1914 Paula had fallen in love with the handsome, romantic Isaac Zar, an unsuccessful medical student who was one of the leaders of Poale Zion and an editor of the *Yiddisher Kemfer* when they met. Their relationship was so intimate that Paula was considered Zar's fiancée by their friends, who expected them to marry soon. But Zar went to Minneapolis to study law, traveling between Minneapolis and New York and making tours on behalf of Poale Zion. He may have left New York for another reason: he told his friends that Paula was the one eager to marry, while he had evaded the issue, and they remembered him "breathing a sigh of relief" on learning of Paula's new lover.[2]

Paula did not tell Ben-Gurion about Zar, nor did she reveal her true age when they met, claiming to be twenty-four. Head over heels in love, Ben-Gurion believed every word she uttered, and repeated what she told him in writing, time and again, for himself, his family, and posterity.

She was born in Minsk, to a wealthy family, and while still a child, sailed to the United States. Her father sent her money to study medicine, but when he died, the family became poor and she could no longer continue her studies and became a nurse. She was not a Zionist. On the contrary, she inclined toward the anarchists and her ideal was their leader, Emma Goldman. She was sympathetic to an anti-Zionist socialist party.

Her position on Zionism, one is moved to suspect, was a preventive measure. If Ben-Gurion was supposed to be the first man she had loved, she might have found it necessary to deny any previous contact with Zar by calling attention to her indifference, if not outright antagonism, to Zionism. Subtracting several years from her age required other adjustments as well: in applying for the marriage certificate and in the questionnaire she filled out in 1918 so she could go to Palestine, she wrote that she had been born on the eighth and twelfth, respectively, of April 1892 and had arrived in the United States in 1908, dates she stuck to all her life.

But she need not have worried. Ben-Gurion never doubted her word that he was the first man she had loved in her twenty-four years, nor did he ever suspect her real age. He also accepted her other stories: that as "head nurse" at the "largest hospital in New York," she had nearly succumbed to the "professor of medicine" in charge of the surgical department, who was madly in love with her; that before meeting Ben-Gurion, she had been going out with intellectuals; and that the great Leon Trotsky had been attracted to her when she attended one of his meetings in New York. She repeated these stories endlessly to her friends and to her elder daughter, all to glorify her love for Ben-Gurion and magnify the sacrifice she had made in choosing him for a husband. When her family found out that she was going to marry him, Paula used to say, they were not pleased. "There are so many good young men, well established in New York," from whom she could choose, they said.[3]

It seems that there was no need for Paula to have gone to such lengths. Ben-Gurion was so grateful to her for having accepted him that it never crossed his mind to question her story or her motives in marrying him. He was utterly uninterested in such trivial details; what interested him was that she had accepted him. The idea that she had made sacrifices for his sake was not novel to Ben-Gurion, convinced as he was that his mother had loved him so much that she had sacrificed her life for him. He felt that by joining her life to his, Paula had given a priceless gift, which he could reciprocate only, and characteristically, by giving her equal share in his dreams and their achievement.

In early 1918, quite out of the blue, an opportunity presented itself to go immediately to Palestine. The British government sent to Palestine a Zionist commission, headed by Dr. Chaim Weizmann, to report on the situation and to prepare projects in the spirit of the Balfour Declaration. Two seats on the commission were offered to the American Poale Zion. Itzhak Ben-Zvi and David Ben-Gurion were the obvious choices for them, but Isaac Zar, backed by the Central Committee, was elected in their stead; the party actually gave up one place rather than send Ben-Gurion or Ben-Zvi. "This was a sad, a very sad chapter," commented Ben-Gurion, "one of political filth of the ugliest American kind, what is commonly called . . . by the 'famous' name of Tammany Hall." This episode completed Ben-Gurion's disillusionment with the American party's leadership. It was one thing not to accept his and Ben-Zvi's line in regard to Palestine, but it was another not to help them get there; this, he thought, was vengeance of the worst kind.

Soon another possibility arose. On February 21 General Wilfred White's instructions from the War Office in London — "You can give undertaking that Jewish battalions will be drafted to Jewish units in Palestine, if medically fit and when trained" — removed the last barrier to volunteering. As members of the Committee for an American Jewish Legion, Ben-Gurion and Ben-Zvi campaigned vigorously among the rank and file of Poale Zion and the Jewish public at large. They encouraged He-Chalutz members to enlist, calling on the branches to do likewise, and using for their letters Action Committee stationery; by February 28 the first volunteers were on their way to the British army depot in Windsor, Canada. But while, in theory, volunteering for the Jewish battalions had the Central Committee's blessing, the first enlistments among Poale Zion members made the party anxious. "The Legion has become more serious than we thought," Shmuel Bonchek reported to Hersh Ehrenreich. "Many comrades are joining . . . of course we cannot adopt a stand, but the party, in any event, will suffer terribly from it." Branch heads were no less panic-stricken. "Have they gone crazy?" one of them wrote to Ehrenreich. "Do they think that the party in America can manage without *all* of them?" Bonchek, for his part, informed the affiliates that Ben-Zvi's use of Action Committee stationery for the enlistment campaign was "the result of misunderstanding," for which Ben-Zvi was duly reprimanded.[4]

Ben-Zvi was the first of the Benim to enlist. Ben-Gurion did not find it so easy. His wife, four months pregnant, was more than ever opposed to his plan. But on April 26, he, too, signed up, then went immediately to tell Paula, who burst into bitter tears and cited the example of Arie Zvi Nelkin, Rachel Beit-Halachmi's brother and a friend from Ben-Gurion's youth in Płońsk, who had changed his mind and canceled his enlistment at the urging of his pregnant wife. Ben-Gurion felt that his heart would break, and he never forgot Paula's pain. He was no longer merely an impoverished man with nothing worth giving to the woman who loved him; he was an ogre who had knowingly perpetrated an injustice — an act of ingratitude, if not an outright crime — against a woman who had willingly sacrificed herself to him. He had turned an independent young woman into a pregnant one who might become a widow burdened with an orphaned baby, or, even worse, a woman whose husband's fate was unknown.

These fears were not groundless in wartime; but her personality, as well as the Jewish experience, made them much worse. Paula was convinced that Ben-Gurion, like every man, untrustworthy, would betray her, by either patronizing prostitutes or falling in love with someone else and abandoning her and her infant to their fate, as dire a disaster as widowhood. Only with great difficulty did he succeed in calming her. When her tears were dried, Ben-Gurion recalled, "she didn't tell me not to leave"; although she could not understand Ben-Gurion's motives, she must have found out, for the first time, that tears, taunts, or rage would not move him to change his mind. But he was wrong if he thought for a moment that she acquiesced.

Ben-Gurion did not leave without making sure that his wife and child would have enough money while he was away. He gave her $800 in cash, apparently the royalties from *Eretz Israel* and a loan he arranged against his army pay. She also received, by mistake, a weekly income of twenty dollars, twice the regular allocation to a soldier's wife — ten from the Zionist Organization and ten from the Jewish Red Cross, Magen David Adom, which helped the families of Jewish recruits. Ben-Gurion also insured his life for $2,500 — $2,000 for Paula and $500 so that "my dear father . . . can go to Eretz Israel and tour the country, at least once" — and asked his friend Nelkin to look after Paula, who moved into the Nelkins' large apartment in the Bronx as soon as Ben-Gurion left.[5]

On Sunday evening, May 5, a farewell banquet was held in Clinton Hall "for the Legionnaire comrades I. Ben-Zvi and D. Ben-Gurion." The master of ceremonies was Ehrenreich, the only senior party official present. "The few years they spent here in America were hard ones for them," said the *Yiddisher Kemfer*'s tribute to the Benim. "Their longing for their beloved land was too great. Their entry into the Legion is a liberation for them. . . . How will we manage without them? We owe much to the energy of Ben-Gurion . . . and how we will miss the gentle, friendly Ben-Zvi. . . . Our people need them. Our land needs them. Our party in Eretz Israel awaits them." The Central Committee was undoubtedly delighted to see them go.

On May 28 Ben-Gurion swore allegiance to the British Crown and received his first soldier's pay. A day later he and three hundred other volunteers of the fifth contingent assembled on East Broadway and marched to the British recruiting mission offices on Forty-second Street. Cheered along the way, they marched down Fifth Avenue to the Jewish Legion Committee office on Twenty-third Street, then turned west to the El station on Ninth Avenue and traveled to Pier 14 in Newark to embark on a boat that took them to Fall River, Massachusetts. From there they took a train to Fort Edward, Canada, via Boston, Portland, Bangor, St. John, Moncton, Truro, and Windsor. Crowds of Jews waited at each stop to escort them to the synagogue or a restaurant to be wined and dined by the local community and showered with cakes, cigarettes, chocolates, socks, and soap. When their train stopped in Bangor at 4:00 A.M., the Legionnaires were astonished to see "the whole town" waiting for them with an orchestra, flags, and mountains of sweets. On June 1 they reached Windsor, where they were given their final reception. At about this time the first copies of Ben-Gurion and Ben-Zvi's *Eretz Israel* were making their triumphant appearance,[6] and this knowledge, together with the emotional sendoffs to the Legion, further strengthened Ben-Gurion's belief that the path to Palestine was open and that the Jewish masses would soon follow on his heels.

What had the Benim achieved of their original goal to create an army of pioneers to come to Palestine and claim it for the Jewish people by tilling its soil and fighting for the Yishuv's security? Ben-Gurion's Labor Congress for Eretz Israel convened in the first week of June and, predictably, confined its activities to resolutions on paper. Certainly none of the waves of immigration that Ben-Gurion had so eagerly awaited emerged from it. The congress movement he had endorsed resulted only in another American organization controlled by the American Jewish establishment. And although the Benim showered extravagant praise on the recruitment in the Legion, it was misplaced. Ben-Gurion, for example, wrote that four thousand volunteers had enrolled, but in fact only twenty-seven hundred of the five thousand who had volunteered were accepted; of these fewer than twenty-five hundred reached Palestine, of whom only two hundred eighty settled there. Thirty percent of the Legionnaires belonged to Poale Zion and most of these were members who had already joined He-Chalutz or registered for aliyah. Between the years 1919 and 1923, which saw the first postwar wave of Zionist immigration, only six hundred people came from America. Such was the harvest that Ben-Gurion's and Ben-Zvi's mission to American Jewry yielded.

But this, of course, was something Ben-Gurion found out in due course. Meanwhile he trained to become a Royal Fusilier and read Paula's accusing letters. He needed no encouragement from her to feel guilty for leaving her alone. All he could do was justify his heartlessness on the basis of an imaginary pact like the one he had had with his father in his Istanbul days. By tying the realization of his self-appointed mission to her sacrifice and suffering he made her, like his father before her, an equal partner in his life's work. "I have already told you," he wrote her from Fort Edward, "that I don't know if I shall ever be able to pay you back in kind, but I shall work and work to do it, because I know you deserve it and our love deserves it."

Their prolific correspondence is a study in unrelated monologues. He wrote about "a great, shining, and joyous future," and she spoke of her everyday problems. Occasionally he was more practical, asking her to study Hebrew and read Heinrich Graetz's *History of the Jews.* She reminded him to dress warmly, to keep clean, and to brush his teeth every day. Before long her detailed accounts of her chronic sufferings had persuaded Ben-Gurion that he had married a martyr, if not a saint. He spared no words to convince her that his admiration for her was boundless. After the birth of their baby, he fused his images of the beloved, the wife, and the mother into one — Paula.[7]

She, however, was never deceived, for she could sense the anonymity and distance behind the passionate expressions in his letters. No personal detail connected these sentiments to her specifically, and she knew that she was essentially unable to reach or touch her husband. Soon after his departure, intent on not losing Ben-Gurion altogether, she tried to get to Palestine before him by volunteering for the Hadassah medical mission, claiming that she was only four months pregnant. But Henrietta Szold discovered that she was actually in her seventh month and refused her; Szold never forgot this attempted deception.

The more Paula's efforts to be with Ben-Gurion were frustrated, the more she lacerated him for abandoning her, escalating the accounts of her physical and emotional suffering to make it seem that she was at the point of death. Terrified, Ben-Gurion cabled at once for a report of her condition. The gist of her replies was that if he allowed her to join him, everything would be fine. She knew full well that while he was in the army this was impossible, yet she did nothing to assure his peace of mind. After the birth of their daughter Geula, she described in detail how she had taught their infant to feed herself so that she could survive without her mother.

He had one answer to all her complaints: her sacrifice would be more than compensated for them both. Two letters he wrote Paula exemplify his oft-repeated pledge.

> I know what a price you are paying, with your youthful happiness, for the sake of my ideal. The price is high . . . but this is the cruelty of deep love. On the other hand, if I had stayed with you now, I would not be worthy of the child you bear me, and all our life together would be ordinary, petty, and pointless. This is not the kind of life I want to live with you. . . . Keep well, be strong in body and spirit, for a great future, bright with light and happiness, is in store for you.

He wrote this letter after leaving for Fort Edward. When her grievances intensified, he wrote the other.

> I am certain that you are able to carry this heavy load of yours, that you'll
> climb, too, in tears and torment, a lofty mountain, from where a new
> world can be seen, a world of light and joy, bright forever with an ever-
> green ideal. There surely is another world, a world of sublime happiness, a
> magnificent universe, to which only the few shall be admitted. For only
> those whose souls are rich and whose hearts are deep are permitted to
> enter it. I know full well that your soul is rich and your heart large enough
> for this superior world and the superior life I want to prepare for you.[8]

10

Achdut ha-Avodah

O N June 6, 1918, David Ben-Gurion, nearing his thirty-second birthday, donned a military uniform and immediately had himself photographed. In his own eyes he looked younger, "like a lad of fourteen or fifteen," but fearing Paula would think he looked sick, he explained that if he did not look good it was attributable to fatigue. Having become a late sleeper, he had been terrified to learn that reveille was at 5:30 A.M. But after a few days of trial, he rushed happy news to Paula. "Not only do I not begrudge the sound of the bugle, I even take pleasure in rising with the sun and washing myself on the grass in the fresh air of the early morning. You were probably to blame for my not wanting to get up early at home."[1]

Though he had had a bout of fever after the smallpox and typhus injections and his eyes were puffy as a result of training in the sunlight, he found camp life not all that bad. He welcomed the two hours of daily exercise in the excellent weather; the food was all right; and the iron discipline did not weigh too heavily on him. Even the parades were entirely to his liking. He diligently brushed his teeth in the morning and took pleasure in washing his underwear. All in all, he enjoyed the life of a recruit, believing that within a month he would be a healthy soldier. He became tan, his face peeled, he smoked cigarettes, spent time at the YMCA, roamed the streets of the city with his buddies, and anxiously awaited mail and packages from home. Paula sent him cigarettes, newspapers, a fountain pen, and clothing. "Were it not for my longing for you," he wrote her, "I would be happy."[2]

Noting that Ben-Gurion had been chairman of the Legionnaires' Committee at Fort Edward, his commander wanted to make him an acting lance corporal; British army regulations allowed such assignment as a temporary local rank. The fact that the Legionnaires elected him their chairman and that the commander promoted him, and not Itzhak Ben-Zvi, indicates that Ben-Gurion proved to be the better soldier. For example, Ben-Zvi could not put on his puttees properly: he would bind his right and left legs in the same direction. To do them in opposite directions was beyond his power.[3]

Accordingly, Ben-Gurion was summoned to Company Sergeant Major Wilson and notified of his promotion, which meant he would have to sew one stripe on each sleeve and tie a whistle to his left shirt pocket. Still completely innocent of military discipline, Ben-Gurion warmly thanked Sergeant Wilson and explained that he could not accept the promotion because his moral authority in the battalion committee would be greater if he remained a soldier in the ranks. That, he assumed, was the end of the matter.[4]

But Major David Thomas Walkley, the commanding officer, thought differently. On an inspection parade Wilson pointed out Ben-Gurion and told Walkley why he had not accepted the promotion. Although Walkley, a veteran of the Royal Fusiliers' Regiment, well knew that refusal of rank was not a military offense, Ben-Gurion's excuse was one he had never heard before. He approached Ben-Gurion and explained sternly that in the British army there were no committees; leadership was the exclusive domain of officers and noncommissioned officers. As a private, Ben-Gurion would be useless to the rank and file, so that if he was concerned with their welfare he would do better to become an NCO. After four days of soul-searching, Ben-Gurion announced that "he had decided" to accept the promotion — against his will, he noted in his diary. Nevertheless, he enjoyed the NCO course he began to attend and wrote Paula, with ill-concealed pride, that from then on she should address her letters to "Cpl." instead of "Pvt." Ben-Gurion.

This idyll was not to last. The drills became harder and harder and the NCO course, which included not only lectures but supplementary training, became burdensome; incessant repetition of the same exercises bored him. Moreover, the extra training lasted until nine o'clock, an hour before lights out, and he sorely missed having time for reading, writing, and meditation. The longer he stayed at Fort Edward, the more dejected he became, and he anxiously awaited the departure for England, where they were to go for further training. At last the NCO course came to an end, and a few days later the Legionnaires were given sea fare allowance and boarded the *Caledonian Castle*, which brought them to England on July 22.[5]

After two weeks of training at the Eggbuckland army base, including bayonet and gas mask drills, Ben-Gurion was issued his personal rifle. However, he was a miserable shot, and his enthusiasm for army life completely evaporated. He and Ben-Zvi were seen mostly in each other's company, forever engrossed in long deliberations; the Legion-naires, picking up on their difference in height, nicknamed them Mutt and Jeff.[6]

Ben-Gurion spent his furloughs in meetings with Zionist and Poale Zion leaders in England, in receptions and public assemblies by which British Jewry honored the Legionnaires, and in sightseeing tours of London: Hyde Park, Westminster Abbey, Parliament House, the Tower of London, Buckingham Palace. In London an experience he never forgot contributed to his admiration for the British. He became aware that food was rationed when he entered a restaurant and was asked for coupons, without which he could have only eggs. He ate two, but was still hungry, so a Jewish soldier advised him to go to White-chapel. Not knowing what or where Whitechapel was, Ben-Gurion asked a taxicab driver to take him there. "I entered the restaurant. I was not asked for coupons. I was served bread and butter and roast chicken, as much as I wanted. They were Jews, of course. Although I was satisfied, I felt somewhat ashamed." Ben-Gurion was impressed with the fact that all Britons observed the austerity regulations of the war; to him it signified "statehood," something the Jews lacked. He re-peated this story about his encounter with the wartime black market whenever he reminisced about his army career.[7]

On August 13 the men of the 40th Battalion of the Royal Fusiliers were issued helmets, and two days later they sailed from Southampton to Cherbourg. They went on to Taranto by train, from there to Egypt by ship, and on August 28 disembarked at Port Said, hoisting high the Jewish flag. On September 1 the battalion camped at the Tel al-Kabir army base in the desert, midway between Ismailiyah and Cairo. Ben-Gurion's and Ben-Zvi's excitement heightened, both from being so close to Palestine and because they knew that Jewish volunteers from Palestine had reached Egypt and were camped at Halmiyyah, on the outskirts of Cairo.

The Benim were planning to take advantage of a three-day pass to Cairo to have a long awaited reunion with their Eretz-Israeli friends when, the day before the trip, Ben-Gurion became feverish, a symptom of the onset of acute dysentery. Nevertheless, on the morning of Sep-tember 5 he set out with Ben-Zvi for Halmiyyah, where he saw, among others, Shmuel Yavnieli, a friend from Sejera, as well as Berl Katznel-son, who in 1912 had founded a third, nonpartisan, workers' group that had come to be known as the Organization of Jewish Agricultural Workers. But Ben-Gurion's joy at the reunion was clouded by his ill-ness; his fever rose to 104 degrees, and unable to return to Cairo, he stayed the night in Halmiyyah.[8]

It seemed to be fate that Ben-Gurion was in Halmiyyah when Katznelson received copies of the anthology *Ba'Avodah* from Palestine, of which Katznelson's speech to the seventh conference of the agricultural workers in February 1918, "Toward the Future," was the main feature; it was to have a crucial influence on Ben-Gurion's future projects. When his fever had subsided to "only 101 degrees," he returned to Cairo, and a doctor friend brought him to the military hospital, where he was treated without delay. His dysentery required prolonged treatment, and he could not rejoin his battalion until October 5. Even this was too soon: unable to carry the full army pack during drills, he fell and was again rushed to the hospital, though this time he was discharged the next day.[9]

During his illness important events took place in his life, in Palestine, and in the world. A telegram from Paula brought the news that his daughter had been born on September 11. He wrote back immediately.

> God has given us a great, dear, and beloved gift, a gift which has added new meaning to our lives, and a great burden to yours, sweet, but heavy. . . . I would so much like to see you, at least for a moment, to embrace you, to hold you close, close to my heart, and to kiss and kiss you . . . to hear [the baby's] crying and to rock her to . . . sleep in my arms.

He did not write Paula about his illness and hospitalization until three days before his discharge, and did not receive her first letters from Bushwick Maternity Hospital in Brooklyn until late in November. "She is so clever," Paula wrote of the baby, "that she looks for her daddy dear." As he had requested before they parted, she named the child Geula, reminding him that he had promised "to try very hard to be reunited soon with mother and child."[10]

Meanwhile, General Edmund Allenby's expeditionary force routed the Turkish army in battle after battle during September. After the cavalry's entry into Afula, Ben-Gurion wrote in his diary, "I fear our battalion has lost the chance to take part in the conquest of Palestine." Indeed, Allenby's victory was completed while Ben-Gurion lay in his sickbed. In Europe, as well, the war neared conclusion, and on November 11, 1918, Germany and the Allied powers signed the armistice. The good news did not end there: as if to sweeten his return to his unit, all the volunteers from Palestine were transferred to his battalion.[11]

Ben-Gurion read "Toward the Future" with great interest, realizing that Katznelson's thinking was much like his own. "We are, in fact, of one mind," he said. Both thought that a great hour had arrived for the Jewish people, the hour of redemption and the beginning of the fulfillment of prophecy. Both considered the Balfour Declaration an opening of the gates to great masses of immigrants. Certainly they were not alone; many thought so. But Ben-Gurion, who, except for a few visits, had been away from Palestine since 1911, was overjoyed to find that Katznelson shared the views he had held since his first years there. Katznelson, too, criticized the Zionist Organization and its agencies and appealed for the centrality of Palestine in the Zionist movement.

Although Katznelson's moderate wording lacked Ben-Gurion's tendency to polarize by setting "Palestine Jewry" and "Diaspora Jewry" in sharp contrast, there was no doubt that Katznelson, too, upheld the right of Palestinian Jewry to show Zionism its way. As for the role of the worker in the implementation of the Zionist vision, they spoke with one voice. "The Yishuv will be built by the Jewish worker or it will not be built at all," Ben-Gurion had said in 1911, adding, while he was in the United States, "Palestine cannot be built except by pioneers"; Katznelson said that Palestine would be built by workers and pioneers, the true bearers of Zionist fulfillment whose future was the future of the nation. Both regarded Hebrew as the foundation of national rebirth.[12]

Their reactions to the Balfour Declaration and the Soviet revolution were also in harmony: a homeland is not given as a gift or by diplomatic guarantees, but is created and built by the people, especially the workers. Both regarded the worker-pioneer as the one to carry out the redemption and argued for his right to lead the way and be the decisive element. Likewise, both believed that Zionism and socialism were bound together and that Zionist fulfillment depended on the ability of those who implemented it to create a new, emancipatory, and highly progressive society.

If their singleness of mind was not perceptible at first glance it was because of the difference in their modes of expression. Katznelson, the product not of politics but of experience in the fields and a nonpartisan workers' organization, was a man of letters who could express ideas in unmatched Hebrew prose, whereas Ben-Gurion made much use of socialist and Marxist idioms and axioms. Ben-Gurion's "Republic" was Katznelson's "Society of Workers." Katznelson spoke with question marks, Ben-Gurion with exclamation points.[13]

Ben-Gurion felt that the British occupation of Palestine and the Balfour Declaration enabled Zionism, for the first time, to become political Zionism in the true and full sense of the word. He must have felt that his own time had come, too; and, being first and foremost a political animal, there was one thing on his mind: to turn the Yishuv into a political force both in Palestine and in the world Zionist movement. It had been impossible to achieve under the Turks; it was now not only possible but vital to do so.

The first step was to unify, to get rid of the many small parties that

bedeviled the Yishuv and create one major framework for all Eretz-Israeli workers. Ben-Gurion felt this was the only way to recruit and
group together all available human resources, which otherwise would
be wasted by interparty quarrels, and direct them to the nation-build-
ing task that was so close at hand.

Having long dreamed of a broad-based workers' party in Palestine,
Ben-Gurion had an abundance of time to work out the details as he lay
in bed. Such a party could be created by merging all the workers'
groups into one united party. Did Katznelson also think in terms of a
merger? There was no clear answer in his article. Ben-Gurion nevertheless believed that he had found a potential ally and made up his
mind to speak to Katznelson about merging the two workers' parties,
the organization of agricultural workers, and their respective affiliated
bodies. As soon as he regained his strength, he told Yavnieli that he was
of one mind with Katznelson and asked, "Why don't we join forces?"

Yavnieli took him to Katznelson's tent, but Katznelson was not as enthusiastic as Yavnieli. Katznelson objected on principle to parties and
therefore stipulated that they be abolished and replaced by an association of individuals.[14]

He believed that parties caused internecine quarrels and fragmented
the resources and efforts needed for Zionism's progress. He therefore
sought to create a general non–party worker organization that would
include a broad gamut of functions, from trade unions to health care,
from a school system to model farms, from publishing literature to retail shops. He had tried to realize this concept in the Organization of
Agricultural Workers, enabling members of conflicting political bodies
like Poale Zion and Ha-Poel ha-Tzair, as well as its nonpartisan members, to belong.

Ben-Gurion, grounded in the Marxist tradition, believed in the supreme role of the party, but he thought that Katznelson's idea of one
broad organization was a good start. Katznelson, however, doubted
that others in Poale Zion and Ha-Poel ha-Tzair would agree. Nevertheless, they reached an initial understanding that before going any further, they should first sound out the workers in Palestine, which both
had gotten leave to visit. They also agreed to keep their understanding
a secret, which gave credence to later accusations that their merger
scheme was born in conspiracy.

The meeting in Katznelson's tent proved to be a turning point not
only in Ben-Gurion's political life, but also in his personal relations, for
his partnership with Ben-Zvi came to an end. Of his scheme to abolish
his party and merge it with its great rival, Ha-Poel ha-Tzair, he said
not a word to Ben-Zvi. This duplicity manifested itself in early November, when, given ten days' leave to participate in a Poale Zion council

in Jaffa, they traveled together. But where Ben-Zvi's purpose was participation in the council, Ben-Gurion had an additional motive: to investigate the prospects for the merger.

In his diary Ben-Gurion described the journey in great detail, but, much as in his letters to his father from Istanbul, he never mentioned his traveling companion. Thus the November 13 entry, made during their return trip, said only, "It rained on the way; the freight car had no roof and the rain pattered on the trench coat with which I covered myself"; and, on the following day, "Malaria has again attacked me." Only from Ben-Zvi's letters can it be ascertained that they were together; on November 14 Ben-Zvi wrote to Rachel Yanait — who, after graduating as an agronomist from the University of Grenoble, had returned to Palestine during the war and become, in the absence of Ben-Zvi, Ben-Gurion, Shlomo Kaplansky, and Jacob Zerubavel, the actual leader of Poale Zion — "I'm feeling well despite the hardship of the road, only David fears a relapse of malaria and it seems as though the rainy night has affected his health." Ben-Zvi remained a true and concerned friend all his life.[15]

In retrospect the essential difference in the objectives of the friends at the Jaffa council, which lasted five days, is obvious. While Ben-Zvi resumed his function as Poale Zion's leader in Palestine, taking pains to chart a solid party line by adopting clear-cut resolutions, Ben-Gurion, to the best of his ability, strove to remove crucial topics from the council agenda and delay the adoption of far-reaching resolutions with the argument that they should be deferred until the establishment of the postwar order of the world, particularly as it concerned Palestine. He did not want his party to adopt any resolutions that might prove an obstacle to a merger at a future point. In the contest with Ben-Zvi and the other delegates, Ben-Gurion scored a partial victory, succeeding in quashing some draft resolutions which, had they been passed, would have been detrimental to the union project.[16]

Back at Tel al-Kabir and after more talks with Katznelson Ben-Gurion, weak and feverish, wrote to Paula, "I am elaborating on plans for our work in the future." As it happened, he had to suspend those plans, for Katznelson was not pleased by what he had seen on his visit to Palestine. The rivalry between Poale Zion and Ha-Poel ha-Tzair was virulent, and his misgivings regarding the practicality of Ben-Gurion's union project had not abated at all. Nevertheless, Ben-Gurion's enthusiasm was contagious, and Katznelson finally declared, "I have vowed to make every last effort regarding the association. . . . I do not know if I shall succeed. I accept this as one who is desperate, as a hope and a last attempt." In this statement Ben-Gurion first encountered a unique characteristic of Katznelson's, confidence in the face of doubt.

Katznelson said that his skepticism did not overwhelm his faith in an idea he believed sound. For Ben-Gurion that was sufficient; he was happy to hear Katznelson say dryly, "Very well, let's approach the men of Ha-Poel ha-Tzair." Those men wanted more details and proposed calling an informal parley of representatives of all of the parties in the battalion, so that Ben-Gurion and Katznelson could broach their plan to them. It was at this meeting, on November 24, that Ben-Zvi learned of his close friend's great and daring idea.[17]

There can be no doubt that Ben-Zvi was hurt. But realizing intuitively that his own era had ended, he was quietly clearing the stage for Ben-Gurion.

According to Ben-Gurion, the soldiers of the battalion responded to the union initiative "with great enthusiasm," but Katznelson detected fears, doubts, and suspicions. To a great extent, this was to be the difference between the two in the future as well. Yet, despite the sharp contrast in their personalities, they were not only the covert instigators of the merger but the engine behind it as well.

Katznelson discovered Ben-Gurion's fine political acumen. In Ben-Gurion Katznelson found a "healthy understanding of the questions," self-confidence, an urge to get things done, and the courage to do them, characteristics that, he well knew, he himself lacked. He was impressed most of all with Ben-Gurion's courage. Finding ardent supporters for both the abolishment of the parties and their subsequent merger presented no problem for Katznelson; he could find plenty of them among the nonpartisan members of his association of agricultural workers. Ben-Gurion, however, would have to carry on a fierce solitary battle in demanding his party's self-abolishment for the purpose of a union. Moreover, his Palestine party, which had not yet recognized Ben-Gurion even as number two, was only a small part of World Poale Zion. Katznelson therefore was fully aware that Ben-Gurion was taking on himself a burden inestimably heavier than his own. He expressed the utmost admiration for Ben-Gurion's strength. "One must understand the enormous difficulty facing Ben-Gurion, who, all by himself, a young man with ideas of his own, started his struggle within Poale Zion, while elder and more prominent leaders stood against him." Katznelson might have added his own skepticism and hesitancy to this list.[18]

To Ben-Gurion, Katznelson was a "revelation." Accustomed to the typically dogmatic, doctrinaire Poale Zion member, he was astounded to encounter this man, one year his junior yet immensely wise in the ways of people and the world, with the keenest common sense; a thinker by nature who made working the land his life's goal; one frail in body yet strong in faith, who personified the great future of the

Eretz-Israeli labor movement. It was impossible not to sense Katznelson's inner truth, which was reflected through his doubts.

Perhaps Ben-Gurion knew instinctively that the checks and balances he lacked could be found in a partnership with Katznelson. "Berl, how dear thou hast been to me, dearer than brother or kindred soul, ever since thou appearedst to me in uniform in the tents in the Egyptian desert," wrote Ben-Gurion at Katznelson's death. Katznelson was, Ben-Gurion said, a "teacher of the generation, one to enlighten all of the future generations; the mind, the conscience, and the voice of the movement . . . [a man of] foresight and profound vision, rich in knowledge and understanding, generous of advice and resourceful . . . who knew how to blend prudence and pragmatic shrewdness with creative initiative and revolutionary momentum."[19]

Katznelson had another trait that pleased Ben-Gurion, although he never referred to it. Intuition told him immediately that Katznelson did not aspire to power and authority and would never pit himself against Ben-Gurion for the crown of political leadership and was satisfied with having spiritual influence. Katznelson was the ideal partner for Ben-Gurion, and what was more, their partnership had from the outset the particular strength of having begun with a shared secret. From then on they planned everything together.

The next step — the decisive one in their work toward the association — could be taken only in Palestine, in the very midst of the parties and the organization of agricultural workers, whose members had to be persuaded to merge. They were both, however, inextricably stuck in the Egyptian desert, guarding prisoners of war and army installations and maintaining lines of communication. When the battalion was replaced by Indian units, the drills recommenced, and Corporal Ben-Gurion was especially busy training new recruits. He and Katznelson anxiously looked forward to the day the battalion would be transferred to duty in Palestine.[20]

On December 4 the long awaited order arrived, and the following evening, in torrential rain, the battalion bivouacked in Sarafand. Ben-Gurion's work load grew heavier. The camp routine, tent drying, more drills, and training were all the more loathsome now that his feet were at last on Palestinian soil. One morning his desire to accomplish his mission overcame military discipline; he left camp without permission and walked to Jaffa, a five-hour journey, where he met with Joseph Sprinzak of Ha-Poel ha-Tzair to broach the unity idea to him. The effort to convince Sprinzak led Ben-Gurion to stay that night in Jaffa, and the next as well. In his passion he was unaware that his absence was becoming longer and his offense more serious. Ben-Zvi, forever concerned for his friend's welfare, rushed a note to Yanait, with whom

Ben-Gurion had also met in Jaffa, asking her to give him the message that "he has already stayed too long, and might be severely disciplined."

When Ben-Gurion returned to camp after five days of being AWOL, he was informed that he would be tried before the battalion commander. His sentence, handed down on December 13, was demotion to private, deduction of three days' pay, and transfer to the lowest company in the battalion, most of whose members were facing dismissal. In separating him from his friends Ben-Zvi, Katznelson, Yavnieli, and others, the sentence constituted a clear warning that from then on he was to attend to public affairs only when on furlough. His sole recourse for getting leave was the Zionist Commission, headed by Chaim Weizmann, whose function was to guide the military administration in Palestine in the implementation of the Balfour Declaration.[21]

Weizmann, based in London, came to Palestine only for short visits; his stand-in there was David Montague Eder, the acting chairman of the Commission and a well-known psychiatrist, who had been raised and educated in England. Not knowing the languages spoken in the Yishuv — Hebrew, Yiddish, and Russian — he depended on a translator; and, like his colleagues on the Commission, he was unfamiliar with Palestine, did not think much of the Yishuv, and underestimated it as a partner in the Zionist enterprise. Blind to the potential of the workers' movement and to its strength, he did not think that unification of the workers' parties was a cause worthy of intervention with the military high command to obtain long leaves for Ben-Gurion, especially since he believed, with Weizmann, that Palestinian Jews were petty, vociferous, and bordered on the hysterical. Ben-Gurion's request was denied.

This was the starting point of Ben-Gurion's conflict with Weizmann. Ben-Gurion held that his leaves were "of vital importance to our work" and believed they would be easy to get. Eder and Weizmann considered Ben-Gurion a "political agitator" unworthy of their notice. Aware that strict army regulations governed the granting of furloughs, Eder must have wondered what kind of soldier this Private Ben-Gurion was who would not leave the heads of the movement and its Zionist Commission, duly recognized by the British government, to accomplish their work in peace. Moreover, Eder needed the good will of the British high command for important Zionist interests and was angered at being asked to waste the little good will he had acquired on trifles. His refusal must be seen in this context.

Ben-Gurion accused Eder and Weizmann of hostile intentions. Four days after being demoted, he wrote to a party friend in Jaffa that "one day someone will have to demand clarification from the Zionist Commission as to whether it is abusing us or not" and pressed him to ask Eder again for extended leaves for himself, Katznelson, Ben-Zvi, and Yavnieli. But it was quite unacceptable to Eder that four soldiers should be on His Majesty's payroll while dabbling in politics as they saw fit, which to him was the essence of their request. He argued that if they wanted to engage in public affairs, they would first have to be discharged, and he was willing to do everything in his power to help speed their demobilization. Thus, at the end of 1918 the four announced their wish to be discharged, but 1919 began and the release order did not come.

Ben-Gurion therefore had to make do with short and inadequate leaves. As a consequence, undisguised animosity grew between him and the NCOs in his company, until his demobilization in April 1920.

He started his work toward the establishment of Achdut ha-Avodah (United Labor)[22] by trying to convince the members of his party that it must disband itself. His argument rested on the premise that without the consolidation of the Jewish workers into a single body, "it is doubtful if [the Jewish worker] will be able to overcome cheap non-Jewish labor," and without such a union "the role of Jewish labor in building up the land is not guaranteed."[23] To understand Ben-Gurion's energy and readiness to do away with his party, one must recall his disappointment with Poale Zion. During his first years in Palestine the party had tottered beneath the burden of dogma and doctrine imported from Russia, which prevented it from becoming Israeli in the full sense of the word. Captives of the Weltanschauung peculiar to Russian revolutionaries, its members were unable to adjust to their new and completely different surroundings. Also, Ben-Gurion could not accept the fact that Palestine Poale Zion did not prevail in the world union and that Palestine was not the center of all consideration. His three years in America had taught him that local party interests came first whenever they conflicted with those of Palestine, and there he witnessed the splitting of the party resources between Palestine and Russia. He was intent on a Jewish Palestine construed not only as the center of the Zionist movement but as its sole leader, and saw no chance for it unless all the workers' parties in Palestine merged into one broad-based association that could focus all its resources in one direction. No longer bound by foreign dogma, such an association would be free to create an ideology from the realities of life in Palestine.

Obviously, he had a personal interest as well. The dismantling of the party and the creation of a new framework in its stead would, of necessity, change his fortunes. Instead of being, at best, number two in his party, he would become number one in his own creation. And, liberated from a rigid ideology, he would be free to openly address a wider public, as had always been his ambition.

The thirteenth convention of Poale Zion had one item on its agenda:

to resolve, on the basis of Ben-Gurion's motion, whether or not to dissolve and unite with Katznelson's nonpartisans. Its fifty-seven voting delegates gathered at the Spektor Hotel in Jaffa on February 21, 1919, in the presence of many guests, among them Katznelson, men in uniform, and volunteers from America. Even though he was about to celebrate his greatest victory in Poale Zion, Ben-Gurion could sense that Ben-Zvi was still number one in their hearts; of the three-man presidium, Ben-Zvi was elected unanimously, while Ben-Gurion was a distant second, with only twenty-five votes cast for him, eight against, and the rest abstentions.

He gave a speech whose core was that only a socialist association of the working class, which would set up a socialist society, would be able to fulfill Zionism and build Palestine. He emphasized that the hour pressed and time was short; if "we" do not build Palestine, he said, "others," that is, Arabs, would. The debate lasted two days, and at least thirty-seven delegates, whose words were recorded in the protocols, participated in it. Seventeen supported the merger proposal, three supported it conditionally, and seven were opposed. The rest straddled the fence. The reservations and objections raised involved concern for the socialist ideal of Poale Zion. Most of the participants in the debate, Ben-Zvi among them, were not ready to accept the fact that, as Katznelson insisted, the new association would not be a political party. This concept was not at all clear, particularly to anyone accustomed to viewing the party as the fundamental political vehicle. Both Ben-Gurion's speech and the replies he ably mustered against disputants earned him long and thunderous applause.

The fact that he succeeded in bringing Ben-Zvi around to his side, and was thus no longer fighting alone, influenced the delegates no less than his arguments. Moreover, Ben-Zvi was elected to the resolution drafting committee, which submitted the draft resolution — "the establishment of an association of workers as a sole socialist workers' party" — to a vote, and it was accepted unanimously. At the convention's conclusion the Poale Zion in Palestine was defunct and gone from the world. The few members who refused to join the union subsequently allied themselves with a new party, Poale Zion Left.[24]

The partnership between Ben-Gurion and Katznelson snowballed. According to a scenario they had drawn up on January 4, the inaugural session of another convention, the first of its kind — not of delegates but of the entire membership of the Organization of the Jewish Agricultural Workers in Palestine — was to be held on the evening of the closing session of the Poale Zion meeting. This convention was open to members of Ha-Poel ha-Tzair, whose leadership countered by calling a party convention of their own. At it they rejected the merger in an attempt to keep their members from joining the association. They feared that the ex–Poale Zion members, who stood for class war and socialist revolution, would have the upper hand in the union, and Ha-Poel ha-Tzair's particular cause would get lost. Moreover, as far as Sprinzak was concerned, the union did not have a chance; he predicted a quick and shattering downfall. "The future will tell which of us was right," he said to Ben-Gurion and Katznelson.

Katznelson claimed that Ha-Poel ha-Tzair insisted on its continued separate existence "without any theoretical or ethical foundation," thereby causing great and tragic harm to the building of Zion. Ben-Gurion ridiculed Sprinzak personally, and for the rest of his life argued that Sprinzak opposed the union solely because of a difference in style. And since style might have been defined as a manner of thought or action, he reduced Sprinzak's opposition to a style of speech only and would say that Ha-Poel ha-Tzair abstained from the union because of "different habits of speech." This was his revenge on Sprinzak, with whom he would one day travel a long road.[25]

Ben-Gurion and Katznelson never achieved their ideal, the unification of the entire working class into one general organization. The agricultural convention decided, as expected, in favor of the merger, but the majority of Ha-Poel ha-Tzair members there voted against it. Accordingly, only a few of them broke away from their party and participated in the founding convention of the association, which took place in Petah Tikva on February 28, 1919, with eighty-one delegates, representing 1,871 supporters, and many guests present. David Ben-Gurion opened and chaired the sessions, and, with Berl Katznelson and one other, was elected to the presidium. The debate over the union manifesto, authored by Katznelson, went on for two days. At the last session, in which the resolutions were adopted, a sharp controversy broke out concerning the name of the association. The delegates who had belonged to Poale Zion were committed to a resolution of the party's last convention to keep the word *socialist* and therefore rejected the name Working Class Association of Palestine, Achdut ha-Avodah, suggested in the manifesto. They also insisted that the association at least be called a party. The session lasted twenty hours. When Ben-Gurion realized that the convention was nearing a crisis he decided — at 5:00 A.M. on Sunday, March 2 — to recess, "in order for the delegates to rest and relax." He later prided himself on this action, which he believed saved the association. The following day he wrote to Paula, "I've never seen such tempestuous sessions. It's a shame you didn't see it with your own eyes. Then you would have been proud not only of your daughter, but of your husband as well."

The session reopened at ten in the morning, and the delegates compromised on the Socialist-Zionist Association of Workers of Palestine, Achdut ha-Avodah. They also determined its institutions: a convention as its supreme body, a council between conventions, an editorial board, and various committees. But Ben-Gurion, who was elected to all the important committees, was not present at this great hour. His rest had turned into a long sleep. By the time he returned to the meeting hall the convention was over; he won his struggle in his absence.

Ben-Gurion returned to his room to write to Paula. "I am sorry that you were not here with me these last two weeks. I think you would have been compensated for all you've been through. My plan for the union of workers [materialized] . . . I won . . . I will now begin great work." In his view, the creation of Achdut ha-Avodah was the second of the three major deeds of his life. The long road that led to the third, the establishment of the State of Israel, was both opened and made shorter by Achdut ha-Avodah, whose aim was to create a "commonwealth of workers" in Palestine, on both sides of the Jordan, that would absorb within itself "the Jewish people, returning en masse to their land."[26]

11

The Elected Assembly

WHEN HE WAS on leave from the army David Ben-Gurion worked and slept at Achdut ha-Avodah's temporary office on Nahalat Binyamin Street in Tel Aviv, where he served on both the nine-member executive committee and its three-member secretariat, in which only he and Shmuel Yavnieli were active. There was, however, little doubt in the minds of the members as to which of the two was the stronger man. Yavnieli was a zealous keeper of the association's ethics and ideology, leaving the management entirely in Ben-Gurion's hands, in practice, if not in theory. Within a short time his colleagues came to believe that nothing could be accomplished without Ben Gurion.[1]

In the executive committee he translated words into action. Berl Katznelson, Itzhak Ben-Zvi, Itzhak Tabenkin, and the rest of his colleagues were men of spirit to whom endless deliberations were not only a great delight, but an end in themselves. They must have been greatly relieved to realize how ready and willing Ben-Gurion was to take charge of Achdut ha-Avodah's administration and the running of its day-to-day business. He quickly acquired a reputation for organization, negotiation, and policymaking and became responsible for almost any problem that bedeviled the executive. Rapport with the Poale Zion in Europe and the United States — Ben-Gurion; resumption of negotiations with Ha-Poel ha-Tzair on the issue of the union — Ben-Gurion; the creation of new cooperatives and the settlement of newly released soldiers — Ben-Gurion; relations with the British Labour Party — "Ben-Gurion will have to go to London."

He was so delighted with his increased activity and so adept at solving problems that in February 1920 his colleagues proposed that Ben-Gurion alone be in charge of the secretariat; Tabenkin, in particular, was adamant about it. It was some time before this came to pass, but in practice it was accepted that the partnership of Ben-Gurion and Katznelson actually ran Achdut ha-Avodah, with Ben-Gurion in charge of practical matters, Katznelson, spiritual ones. The Balfour Declaration had created conditions demanding vigorous organizational activity and the formulation of clear Zionist policy and prepared the ground for the rise of Ben-Gurion and his partnership with Katznelson. At long last, Ben-Gurion was able to begin his "great work," "the grand design" of which he had dreamed since his youth. If only his wife and daughter could be with him, he felt, his happiness would be complete.[2]

When they had parted in New York, Ben-Gurion promised Paula that he would bring her to him in Palestine, "to a world of sublime happiness, a glorious universe," as soon as possible. This should have heartened Paula and brightened her lonely days, but in fact the promise proved counterproductive, since she insisted that he make good on it at once.

In her numerous letters, Paula painted a dark picture of her loneliness. She wrote him that she was ready to sacrifice everything in order to see him, but because she could do no such thing, the blame fell entirely on him. After the birth of Geula she terrified him with talk of imminent death. "If anything happens to me or Geula *it will be your fault* . . . probably we are not as dear [to you] as Palestine." One wonders whether Paula was beginning to show signs of hysteria, for she had family in New York and could easily have turned to her sister Raissa to help her with the baby.[3]

Did such thoughts occur to Ben-Gurion? Certainly not. In his eyes his "one and only" wife was not only faultless, but a great heroine to boot. "My messiah," he called her, meekly accepting the blame. Then he received her letter of April 2, 1919, in which she accused him of withholding the news that he and Ben-Zvi had long since been demobilized. She understood that he wanted to be free of her, she said. There was no need for him to exert himself, she would release him. On reading this letter his blood froze. He vehemently denied that he had been demobilized, trying his best to soothe her. "I don't blame you. The harsh words burst from your heart in a difficult moment, in a moment of desperation. You suffer too much, and if someone is guilty of this, it is I."[4]

All he could do was beg her to take it easy. "I don't want you to do the washing by yourself. That kind of work is much too hard for you." He promised her that in Palestine he would shower her with all the "comforts and conveniences of Brooklyn and the Bronx, at least until [Geula] wants to go to the Metropolitan Opera House."[5]

From the moment he arrived in Palestine Ben-Gurion had begun looking for ways to bring over his wife and daughter, but since Palestine was under military rule the entry of civilians was absolutely prohibited. Unable to bring her in as a member of the Hadassah medical mission, he tried to get Paula special permission as a soldier's wife. The Zionist Commission and the Zionist office in London appealed on his behalf to the high command in Cairo, but the answer was an unequivocal no.

Not one to give up easily, he tried yet a third tactic, repatriation, that is, bringing Paula in as a returning refugee. He was able to rally all the major Zionist forces to his support in a last-ditch effort that bore fruit. On August 1, 1919, the Zionist office in London informed him that the necessary arrangements had been made, a feat not accomplished according to the strict letter of the law, which allowed re-entry to Palestine only to those who could prove that they had been expatriated before or during the war.[6]

But Paula informed Ben-Gurion that winter was a better time for traveling than summer, which would be too hot, and the baby would suffer. If Ben-Gurion felt that their roles were now reversed and that Paula was holding back, he was not mistaken. She had it on good authority that "conditions are very bad at present in Palestine, especially for babies. Don't forget, dear, that . . . I must have very good milk for her, also ice to put the milk on." Ben-Gurion scolded her for listening to "all the old wives' tales about Palestine floating around New York." "Dear Paula," he wrote reassuringly. "Do you really believe that I would bring my daughter here in order to suffer? I will provide you with eggs and enough milk not only to drink, but to wash her all over if you so wish."

Paula, however, suggested that Ben-Gurion come to America, "for about 1 year," because her financial situation had worsened. The American Magen David Society had discovered that she was receiving support from the Zionist Organization as well and stopped sending her weekly $10 check. If he were there to watch the baby, she could go out and work, for she could not entrust Geula to anyone else. "Decide about your future," she demanded. "You did your share for your ideals, now consider your family if not me." He wrote back that he could not come. She understood, she responded, that the only thing preventing him was his friends in Achdut ha-Avodah, who were helpless without him, so she concluded that his friends were more important to him than his own flesh and blood. "If anything happens to me or Geula it will be your fault, as I am very weak and tired, have no strength to walk around, she takes all my health and strength away, and nobody to help. My money is almost all gone." The next day she wrote, "I am very sick this morning. I have a temp of 103, and baby is also sick. . . . In case anything will happen to me come and take baby as she is my life. . . . I am all alone, nobody to give me a cup of water. . . . Be well and happy, Paula and Geula." Later she informed him that Geula needed "a very small operation" on her nose, but that she would not hear of it in Ben-Gurion's absence, and again asked him to do his best to come to New York as soon as possible. When this imaginary operation failed to budge him, she revived a well-proven weapon, her impending death.

Ben-Gurion believed every word she wrote, and never doubted that death constantly hovered over his wife's head. "We parted unsure of ever seeing each other again," he wrote his father. "We both faced mortal danger." One can easily imagine his fear and anguish on reading Paula's letters; but returning to New York was impossible. He was still subject to army regulations, which Paula should have realized from his letters. She must have known that he stood guard and that in June he went through another series of musketry drills. In May he had written her that he did not yet know when he would be discharged, "but we must not postpone your coming until then."[7]

On September 30, on the instruction of the Foreign Office, the British vice consul in New York issued Paula a laissez-passer, which required, "in the name of His Majesty, all those whom it may concern to allow Pauline Ben-Gurion, Palestinian, to pass freely without let or hindrance, and to afford her every assistance and protection of which she may stand in need" on her journey to Palestine. Her national status was "Palestinian," born in New York. The fact that she needed this document proves that, contrary to all her later stories, Paula had not become a citizen of the United States and never held an American passport.[8]

On October 2 Paula and one-year-old Geula set out for London, where they obtained a military pass to Palestine. After a two-week stay in London they traveled overland to Trieste, where a first-class cabin had been secured for them on the *Helouan*. On November 12 they anchored in Alexandria, and on Saturday, November 15, 1919, they and their baggage arrived in Jaffa.

The voyage took six weeks and cost $900. "Paula had to travel first class," Ben-Gurion explained to his father, "because of the little girl, and even there the child sometimes suffered." The nature of this suffering will never be learned, and where he got the money to pay the fare also remains a puzzle. There is evidence to show that the Zionist office paid freightage and that the Zionist Federation of America accepted Ben-Gurion's life insurance policy as collateral for the return of a loan. The heavy debts he incurred in bringing his family to Palestine are further proof of his confidence in the Zionist future there, as well as in his own.[9]

In consideration of his family's arrival Ben-Gurion received a week's furlough from the army. He led them to the Spektor Hotel, and could not stop marveling at his daughter. "Without any bias as a father," he would tell everyone, "I can honestly say that this is one of the sweetest, loveliest, most charming, beautiful, and clever little girls that I have ever seen in my life." If she had suffered a rough passage, she and Paula nonetheless appeared to be in robust health.

The hotel room, like the room they soon rented on Ahad Ha'Am Street — like all of Palestine — was a far cry from the comforts of Brooklyn or the Bronx. Tel Aviv lacked not only gas, electricity, and public transportation — as Ben-Gurion had forewarned Paula — but proper bathing and laundering facilities as well. Furthermore, milk, butter, and ice were not easily available. Ben-Gurion could afford only small quantities of these on his soldier's pay, even with the supplementary $10 monthly salary (2 Egyptian pounds) he, like others of his colleagues in uniform, received from the Achdut ha-Avodah treasury. As far as Paula was concerned, Tel Aviv was a desert, and Ben-Gurion was forever grateful to her for consenting to follow him there. He dedicated the last volume of his book *Hazon va-Derekh* (Vision and Way) to her with a verse from Jeremiah 2:2. "To Paula with love. I remember thee, the kindness of thy youth, the love of thine espousals, when thou wentest after me in the wilderness, in a land that was not sown."[10]

With his family at his side, Ben-Gurion could focus his energy on the political work at hand. The future of the Jewish battalions was the most pressing issue on his agenda and on that of the Zionist Organization. The military administration of Palestine had already begun reducing the battalions, demobilizing the soldiers and sending them home. Of the four battalions only one, the First Judean, remained, thanks only to the intervention of Winston Churchill, a self-proclaimed Zionist. Two campaigns were then in progress — one in London for the continued existence of this last Jewish Battalion, the other in Palestine to settle demobilized soldiers and prevent their repatriation. Under the military administration this was the only kind of immigration available to the Zionists, and to this end Ben-Gurion directed all of his energies.

Ben-Gurion stated to his colleagues and to the Zionist Commission that in order to keep the four thousand volunteers in Palestine, it was necessary first to create the conditions for their absorption. This could not, however, be done in time to accommodate all the discharged soldiers, not only because of the Zionists' empty coffers but because

David Eder did not want the discharged soldiers to become a burden to the Yishuv and the Zionist Commission, which was forced to allocate funds from its meager budget to create jobs for the unemployed. Eder maintained that the Commission should be allowed time to properly plan the absorption of the ex-soldiers and not carry it out until the political status of Palestine was settled, that is, after the peace conference. He and the Commission wanted the ex-soldiers to return to their homes overseas and wait there until they were called back. Ben-Gurion, who did not want the ex-soldiers to fill jobs at the expense of the unemployed, yet wanted the ex-soldiers to stay in Palestine, declared that this could be accomplished by the creation of more new jobs.[11]

To that end he worked like one possessed. He would dash from his base in Jaffa — without leave, of course — to participate in meetings; to urge Poale Zion in the United States to send more money; to propose projects to the labor movement's People's Relief Committee in America; to conduct negotiations with the representative of the American Zion Commonwealth Federation, who wanted to settle ex-Legionnaires on its land in the Jezreel Valley; to check the possibilities for creating new jobs on private farms, national farms, and the railroads; and to draw up plans for cooperative factories. He termed his campaign an "assault," and the Zionist Commission, particularly Eder, was undoubtedly its target. The military administration agreed to permit those ex-soldiers who had been assured employment to remain in Palestine, but to prevent abuse, a certificate of employment from the Zionist Commission was required as proof. To Ben-Gurion such certificates seemed a mere formality, easily bypassed: the Commission — Eder, that is — could simply sign as many certificates as it could, or two certificates for one existing job, as long as the recipients of the certificates remained in Palestine. Eder could not believe his ears. Suspecting that Ben-Gurion meant to trick him by sending all the certificate holders to demand their promised jobs, he thundered "No!" He would not sign phantom certificates.

Ben-Gurion suspected that, beyond personal animosity, Eder was trying to make things as difficult as possible for those who wanted to remain in Palestine. On hearing that Eder had said all the American volunteers, including those who wished to stay, must be returned to America, Ben-Gurion cried, "What? Are they trying to walk all over us?" He had already made up his mind that the Commission was absolutely helpless, but when he heard Eder say that "the Commission is neither the father nor the stepfather of the battalions," he concluded that Eder was nothing less than a traitor to the cause.[12]

An explosion between Ben-Gurion and Eder was inevitable, and the spark to ignite it was provided by the so-called battalion mutiny — the soldiers' refusal to guard POW camps in Egypt, protesting that this order contradicted the guarantee that they would serve only in Palestine. After a court-martial, fifty-six men were sentenced to two to seven years' hard labor. Eder rejected out of hand the suggestion that the Commission submit a petition to King George V, requesting a mitigation of their sentences and protesting the national affront. Asserting that laziness and nitpicking, not loyalty and national pride, had motivated the mutineers, he argued that the "true" anti-Semites were not the officers, the judges, or the British, but "the soldiers who were ready to declare a strike because they lacked salt for their food." He called the American volunteers the scum of the British army, who "did not deserve to be Jewish soldiers."

Ben-Gurion was violently upset by these comments, which Eder made at a session of the Provisional Council of the Jews of Palestine (a body consisting of representatives of all the groups in the Yishuv, whose function was to prepare for an elected assembly). "The things he said were horrible, vilifying, and denigrating to the Jewish volunteers," he later wrote. Ben-Gurion controlled himself until Eder finished speaking, then, taking the floor out of turn, he announced that he would summon Eder to a court of honor, in defense of the battalion's men. Then he delivered his own version of the "mutiny," calling Eder a liar. On behalf of the soldiers of the battalion, Ben-Gurion demanded that Eder be removed from the Commission and from the Zionist administration altogether. To this Eder replied that his remarks were privileged according to English law because they had been made behind closed doors at the council session. Ben-Gurion then presented Eder with a written ultimatum: either Eder would retract what he had said and apologize, or Ben-Gurion would sue him for slander. He had four days in which to consider.

Eder was not alarmed. After three days he wrote Ben-Gurion a letter that read like a primer in democratic parliamentary procedure and freedom of speech. At the plenary session of the Provisional Council Eder had expressed his opinions as a democrat; Ben-Gurion's libel suit would "undermine the sacred and democratic right of free speech . . . and respect for democratic assemblies in which the freedom of thought and speech is one of the fundamental principles."

The chairman of the Provisional Council also felt that Ben-Gurion's action was improper and proposed that the matter be studied at a closed plenary session by the Provisional Council, and the entire affair could be hushed up. Ben-Gurion had no choice but to accept the proposal; his sole satisfaction was in the letter he wrote to Eder, who had assumed the stance of an Englishman who understood democracy bet-

ter than one educated in eastern Europe. It was now Ben-Gurion's turn
to act the part of one who truly breathed the spirit of democracy. "As
every enlightened individual is aware, the freedom of speech and the
freedom of scorn are entirely different matters. In England . . . the law
punishes slander and disparagement." Eder had charged that Ben-
Gurion's demand for litigation would undermine the nature of the
democratic parliament; Ben-Gurion, addressing Eder in the third person, returned a charge twice as damning. "His Excellency's evasion of
trial undermines the sacred right of every man to defend his honor
against slanderers. It undermines true freedom of speech as well."
With this exchange of insults, the affair ended.[13]

What was Ben-Gurion's purpose in trying to bring action against the
senior Zionist representative in Palestine? Was Eder his only target, or
did he also have Weizmann in mind? Of the seven witnesses Ben-
Gurion had summoned in case the trial should take place, five were famous for their criticism of the Zionist Commission and the London
Zionist office. Was Ben-Gurion going to air Zionist dirty linen in public? Was he trying to discredit the duly recognized Zionist leadership
for not fulfilling its role? Finally, did Ben-Gurion expect to profit personally from the trial? Playing the avenger, pitting himself against
Eder, pointing an accusing finger at him and, indirectly, at Weizmann,
he would have been seen in Palestine and worldwide as the pretender
to the Zionist succession. These questions certainly occurred to Ben-
Gurion's friends and foes alike.

There may have been other reasons as well. Litigiousness and the insistence on defending one's honor, or the movement's honor, were
characteristic of the entire Second Aliyah. For Ben-Gurion, this was
even more true; he regarded himself as a pursuer of absolute justice
and a born lawyer, the son and grandson of lawyers. Only a short time
before this conflict he had considered bringing suit against the heads of
Poale Zion in America because they had reduced funding to Achdut
ha-Avodah and spread rumors that he and Itzhak Ben-Zvi were "per-
secuting" the Yiddishist Legionnaires. Little wonder, then, that the affair strengthened Eder's conviction that Ben-Gurion was nothing more
than an irresponsible politician, eager to get publicity by means of
sensational trials.[14]

The fact was that from the moment Ben-Gurion took charge of Achdut ha-Avodah his energy and determination knew no bounds. He had
a sharp tongue and spoke in a tone of finality, and it was generally considered unpleasant to talk to him. Some, like Nellie Strauss, were afraid
to approach him. Strauss had come from America as the representative
of the American Zion Commonwealth Federation to establish a settlement of demobilized soldiers in the Jezreel Valley, to be called Bal-

fouria. For this purpose she brought an advance of $100,000, a considerable sum. One would think that Ben-Gurion would have had only praise for Strauss and those who backed her, but a conflict ensued.

Ben-Gurion wanted Achdut ha-Avodah to represent the settlers and decide who the settlers would be, while the Zion Commonwealth Federation wanted to deal directly with the settlers and decide for itself which of them were reliable and creditworthy. The company was leasing land it had bought for American investors, and it wanted to protect its investment. When Strauss met with Ben-Gurion he voiced his opinion that the name Balfouria, which had been decided without consulting the settlers, had been chosen exclusively for its publicity value to the Zion Commonwealth company, an "unseemly advertisement of an obstreperous name for a settlement that was not even in existence." Strauss, knowing Ben-Gurion's temper, said, "I would like to tell you something but I'm afraid you'll get angry." He promised he would not, so she continued. "There is one thing we don't like — most of the group considering settlement . . . are members of Achdut ha-Avodah." In other words, the members of Ha-Poel ha-Tzair had been left out. "You seem to have made a political maneuver, and you cannot imagine how it bothers us and holds up the works."

Very calmly Ben-Gurion explained that there were no party politics involved at all. Most of the demobilized soldiers who had opted to remain in Palestine were members of Achdut ha-Avodah. Nevertheless, the Zion Commonwealth company would not consent to share its authority with Achdut ha-Avodah and was ready to cancel the Balfouria project. Ben-Gurion's reaction was belligerent and openly menacing, and he made good on his threats with a worldwide "exposé"; the details of the negotiations and the annotated correspondence with Nellie Strauss were extensively published in *Kunteres* (Pamphlet), the mouthpiece of Achdut ha-Avodah. Ben-Gurion sent letters to the American *Yiddisher Kemfer*, the daily *Der Tag*, the Hebrew journal *Ha-Toren*, and other organs in the United States, England, and Argentina, as well as the office of the World Confederation of Poale Zion in Stockholm, with which Achdut ha-Avodah was affiliated; its press department issued news bulletins in French, German, and Yiddish. He also dispatched press releases directly to the Poale Zion newsletters in Czechoslovakia and South Africa and had material sent to the *Arbeiter Zeitung* in Poland. Within a short time Nellie Strauss, the Zion Commonwealth Federation, and its leadership found themselves in the spotlight of world Jewish opinion.[15]

Broadly speaking, the difference between the world Zionist leaders and organizations and the Eretz-Israeli ones was in temperament. The former wanted to encourage Jews, especially those in distressed areas like eastern Europe, to immigrate to Palestine, but only after adequate conditions had been created for their absorption; the encouragement consisted mostly of financial help. The latter called for a massive immigration from all parts of the world from all walks of life and for greater financial aid. Ben-Gurion and his colleagues referred to the former Zionism as philanthropic Zionism, whereas theirs was one of instant realization.

Soon, however, more important issues demanded the attention and energy of Ben-Gurion and the Achdut ha-Avodah secretariat: the self-rule of the Yishuv and the Arab opposition to the Balfour Declaration and its implementation. Although these were essentially different matters, they were linked by events. On his arrival in Palestine at the end of 1918 Ben-Gurion had maintained, as did the founding convention of Achdut ha-Avodah, that a Jewish state should be established under international guarantees and protection that would expire on the creation of a Jewish majority. At the Provisional Council of the Jews of Palestine there was no controversy over the first concrete step in this direction, the establishment of self-government among the Yishuv by setting up a founding assembly. There was, however, a great deal of altercation over the handling of elections. The Orthodox and ultra-Orthodox would not accept the resolution calling for universal, direct, and proportional elections by secret ballot. They denied women the right to vote and be elected, demanding that only men at least eighteen years of age be able to vote, and that candidacy be limited to men twenty-five and older. The Jerusalem ultra-Orthodox threatened to set up a separate house of representatives if women were enfranchised.

The elections were postponed several times, mainly as a consequence of this dispute. Ben-Gurion attacked those who put off the elections as "reactionaries," but it was clear to him that a separate religious assembly would preclude the formation of a single, indivisible national assembly. The only way he could rescue the national assembly was by compromise, at least with Mizrachi, the primary Zionist religious party, which was far less zealous than the ultra-Orthodox. Ben-Gurion had the exceptional ability to subjugate one important objective to another that he thought even more important, and in this instance he thought the creation of the assembly more important than Achdut ha-Avodah's socialist principles.

Ben-Gurion had an acquaintance in the rival Mizrachi party whose political views were similar to his own, and who would become his partner. He had met Rabbi Judah-Leib Maimon in 1915 in the Jerusalem jail where both awaited deportation by Jemal Pasha. Together they had founded the Association of Exiles in New York in 1916, and they had been of the same opinion regarding Eder's stand on the matter of demobilized soldiers. Owing in no small measure to this shared experience and opinion, Ben-Gurion and Rabbi Maimon were able to make a deal: if the assembly was not called a founding, that is, a constitutional, one — the religious Jews could not consent to a constitution and statutes that were not in accordance with the Halachah — the Mizrachi agreed not to oppose the vote for women. Each took it upon himself to convince his colleagues to go along with the compromise, and they did.

At Ben-Gurion's suggestion the Provisional Council elected a three-man committee, composed of Ben-Gurion, Rabbi Maimon, and a representative of Ha-Poel ha-Tzair, which, within an hour, proposed a new name that was immediately accepted, the Elected Assembly of Palestinian Jewry. After the elections, this body would succeed the Provisional Council. The new name was less binding and did not necessarily imply a future Jewish government in Palestine. Feeling obligated to defend this deviation, Ben-Gurion wrote, "The nature of the assembly and the scope of its activity do not depend on its name, but on its conveners and convened." Whatever it was to be called, he said, the assembly "has but a single task: to lay the foundation for the self-rule of the Yishuv."

As it turned out, Maimon's task was incomparably more difficult than Ben-Gurion's. In the six months preceding the elections, opponents of the women's vote aroused the Orthodox camp, calling the great rabbis — the Torah Sages, including Rabbi Abraham Isaac ha-Kohen Kook, who had just returned to Palestine — to their aid. Accepted by the Orthodox and ultra-Orthodox alike as the ultimate Torah authority, Kook would soon be appointed chief rabbi of Palestine. In a pamphlet issued on March 29 he came out strongly against the women's vote. Furthermore, he called a rabbinical emergency meeting in Jerusalem for only five days before the election, in which eighty-five rabbis from all over Palestine took part. At its close they issued a proclamation, signed by Rabbi Kook, stating that women's participation in the elections would be "in contradiction to the law of Moses and Judaism in particular, and to the national spirit in general. Until the eradication of the innovation, no observant Jew shall have anything to do with the Elected Assembly."

This manifesto came like a bombshell; the Elected Assembly seemed to be finished as the representative body of Palestinian Jewry. Rabbi Maimon, however, revealed rare courage. On the day following the manifesto's appearance, he published a statement he had made at the rabbinical meeting — "We do not submit to this resolution nor are we in need of it" — along with his view that the rabbis' proclamation, despite Rabbi Kook's signature, was nothing more than "a kind of advisory opinion and statement" and was by no means a rabbinical ruling or "an absolute ban." This opinion, said Maimon, was not binding on the Mizrachi party. Rabbi Maimon's decision to openly oppose Rabbi Kook et al., in the full knowledge that if the proclamation was not rescinded the elections would split the religious camp, rescued the future Elected Assembly as a national institution; following Rabbi Maimon's move the Mizrachi central committee gave its party members carte blanche to take part in the elections as their conscience dictated.[16]

After six deferrals the elections finally took place on April 19, 1920, with Yishuv-wide participation, except in Jerusalem, which had the Yishuv's largest constituency. There the Arabs rioted on Passover, and the elections were postponed until May 2. The effect of these riots was to rekindle the Jewish national spirit among the Orthodox; Rabbi Kook came over to Rabbi Maimon's side, accepting his view that the rabbis' proclamation was merely an advisory opinion and telling Rabbi Maimon that he saw the hand of Providence in its being interpreted as such. Rabbi Kook supported the elections, but since he would not cast a vote in the presence of women, he proposed special ballot booths for them to enable the Jerusalem Orthodox to cast their ballots sinlessly. Overjoyed by this development, the Mizrachi publicly announced that it too supported such booths.

Now it remained for Achdut ha-Avodah and the other groups to determine their positions. Segregation of the sexes was a contradiction of Achdut ha-Avodah's fundamental principles of equality, democracy, and socialist progress. Moreover, in consenting to such segregation, it would jeopardize its public image. All the lay parties had fighters for women's rights, for whom the main spokeswoman was none other than Ada Maimon, the rabbi's sister, a prominent member of Ha-Poel ha-Tzair. Rachel Yanait was her counterpart in Achdut ha-Avodah.

Again Ben-Gurion found himself on the horns of a dilemma: full national representation on the one hand, and women's equality on the other. True to his principle, he was prepared to temporarily sacrifice one objective for the sake of a more important one, and under the prevailing circumstances, parliament came first. He therefore agreed to negotiate with Rabbi Kook and, despite Tabenkin's fierce opposition, was able to bring his fellow members of Achdut ha-Avodah around to his position.

The meeting with Rabbi Kook took place at the rabbi's house in Jerusalem, on Tuesday, April 27, in the presence of rabbis, Orthodox leaders, and representatives of the center, that is, the secular middle class. Sympathetic to his interlocutors from Achdut ha-Avodah, who argued that women felt degraded by his proposal, Rabbi Kook cannily suggested that instead of segregating the women, they segregate the men, by creating special booths for them. Eventually an agreement that entirely dismissed the proposal for separate booths was reached. Each Orthodox head of family was given the right to vote on behalf of all the eligible female voters in his household. How Ben-Gurion was able to gain Achdut ha-Avodah's consent to having men speak for their wives and daughters remains a mystery, but the concession was a decisive step toward parliamentary democracy for the Yishuv. Immediately after the agreement Rabbi Kook publicly called upon "every upstanding man of Israel" to regard participation in the elections as "a sacred duty," so that no Orthodox vote would be lost.

At the close of election day the ballot boxes were carried to the election committee office to be sealed. The votes could not be counted until the number of women each Orthodox voter spoke for had been determined, so until that was done, Rabbi Kook took the Orthodox ballot boxes home for safekeeping. Later there was a festive ceremony, and Rabbi Kook was given the honor of opening the first box. Whatever the criticism of Ben-Gurion — and there was doubtless much — his joint achievement with Rabbi Maimon was impressive: the Yishuv acquired its first elected parliament, the Elected Assembly.

In the future there would be no more compromises at the expense of women's rights and elections were always universal, direct, equal, proportional, and by secret ballot. But beyond this, the Ben-Gurion–Maimon deal had far-reaching implications for the building of the State of Israel, twenty-eight years later, for the Elected Assembly served as a model enabling the Knesset, Israel's parliament and its supreme institution, to be established immediately.

Ben-Gurion was entitled to feel considerable satisfaction from the election results, which exceeded his expectations. Achdut ha-Avodah won 70 seats out of the 314 in the Elected Assembly, while its rival, Ha-Poel ha-Tzair, got only 41, and Achdut ha-Avodah emerged the largest of the parliamentary factions. He had ample reason to be proud of himself as well, for he personally received more votes than any other candidate in Achdut ha-Avodah, with Berl Katznelson coming in second.[17]

For the time being, however, these achievements remained on paper since the military administration prohibited the Elected Assembly from meeting. On October 10, 1920, the ban was lifted, and the Elected Assembly met and instituted the National Council (Va'ad Leummi), which functioned until the establishment of the government of the State of Israel in May 1948, as its executive body. Though the reasons for this prohibition remained unstated, it was clear that the

British feared the growth of Arab discontent and a worsening of the security situation, which had been steadily deteriorating since October 1919.

The situation in the north was especially bad. In February 1920 the threat of destruction hung over four isolated Jewish settlements in the Upper Galilee — Metulla, Kefar Giladi, Khamara, and Tel Hai, which were all surrounded by Arab villages. Ben-Gurion, who in January had joined the organizing committee of the Haganah, the Jewish underground defense organization established by Achdut ha-Avodah, was a party to the organization's hard line. Opposing those who advocated the abandonment of the four northern settlements, Ben-Gurion and Achdut ha-Avodah called for their retention and reinforcement with arms and manpower. The reinforcements, however, arrived too late, and on March 1 eight of the defenders of Tel Hai fell, their commander Joseph Trumpeldor at their head, in a heroic battle against hundreds of Arab raiders. Consequently, Tel Hai, Kefar Giladi, and Metulla were deserted; Khamara had already been abandoned.

The violence reached its second peak at Passover in Jerusalem. Arab rioters and marauders stormed the Jewish quarter in the Old City, killing six Jewish passersby and wounding more than two hundred. Weizmann, an eyewitness to this "bloody Passover," found it hard to believe that this "pogrom" had taken place not in Kishinev, under the Romanovs, but in Jerusalem, under the British, and called Lieutenant General Sir Louis Jean Bols, the head of the military administration, and Colonel Sir Ronald Storrs, the governor of the Jerusalem district, jackals. Nevertheless, he asked Ben-Gurion and his colleagues in Achdut ha-Avodah, who were calling for the dismissal of the military government's chiefs, to moderate their reaction.

Speaking for Achdut ha-Avodah, Ben-Gurion charged that the military administration was responsible for the "pogrom" on two counts: the dissolution of the Jewish Battalion and the stoppage of immigration. Had they set up new Jewish units, had they entrusted the maintenance of order and security to the Jewish settlements, or to a Jewish police force and the remainder of the Jewish units, the Arabs would not have taken up arms, neither in the Upper Galilee nor in Jerusalem, and there would have been no reason to ban the meeting of the Elected Assembly. Palestine would have been quiet and could have been opened to immigration; thousands of immigrants would have flocked to the Galilee and founded new settlements alongside the isolated ones; Tel Hai and its settlers would not have fallen and the four settlements would not have been abandoned. The malicious intent of the military administration in all it did and did not do was clear. On these grounds Ben-Gurion rejected Weizmann's appeal for moderation and accused

Bols and Storrs not only of halting immigration, but of conniving to partition Palestine by tearing the Galilee away from the Jewish National Home.

There was quite a difference between the attitude of Whitehall in London and the attitude of the military administration in Palestine in regard to Zionism and the National Home. Whereas Whitehall was sympathetic, full of good will and readiness to facilitate and expedite the building of the National Home, the military administrators were more sympathetic to the Arabs, for whom they felt a great romantic fascination. Furthermore, the military were witness to what Whitehall could not see — the small size of the country and its inability to accommodate two peoples in comfort; they were on the side of the Arabs as the country's inhabitants for centuries.

Ben-Gurion sought to bring down the military administration by means of an outcry that would prick the world's conscience. "The Arabs are preparing to destroy the Jewish settlements," he wrote in letters and long telegrams to American and British newspapers, the British Labour Party, and Poale Zion branches. He called for the opening of the gates of immigration, since "the immediate entry of thousands of young people is for us, now, a question of life [or death]." His cable describing the Jerusalem "pogrom" and the military administration's negligence found its way to the London *Daily Mail*, which carried it in full.[18]

Powerful as the outcry was, it did not lead to the dismissal of Bols and Storrs; Achdut ha-Avodah therefore believed that the danger to the Yishuv had increased. Tabenkin knew for certain that the Arabs were preparing "a general slaughter of the Yishuv" for the end of the month of Ramadan, so, as a preventive measure, Achdut ha-Avodah's executive committee decided to dispatch Ben-Gurion to London to ask for political and financial support and for the dismissal of the two officers. So urgent was this mission that Ben-Gurion's colleagues gave it precedence over his activity in Achdut ha-Avodah. On the eve of his departure, Tabenkin told Ben-Gurion that every day counted and beseeched him not to "get held up in quarantine."[19]

12

London and Vienna

D AVID BEN-GURION made his mission to London contingent on
his being accompanied by Paula and Geula. In May 1920
Paula was six months pregnant; for her to deliver alone a second time was absolutely out of the question. Despite its dwindling financial resources, Achdut ha-Avodah accepted this stipulation.

Ben-Gurion's departure was delayed, however, because his requests
for a passport and an entry visa to Britain were refused; the military
administration in Palestine was not at all pleased at the prospect of his
going to London. But at long last he got his papers, and on June first,
with his wife and daughter, he boarded the train to Alexandria. On the
tenth they set sail for Trieste, and from there traveled to England via
train and ferryboat, arriving at Folkestone on the twenty-second. Permitted to disembark on condition that they remain in the United Kingdom for a period not to exceed one month and report to the police at
regular intervals, they went to London and checked into a hotel.[1]

As it turned out, before Ben-Gurion had even left his hotel room, the
primary objective of his mission had been achieved. The British government had appointed Sir Herbert Samuel high commissioner of Palestine, and he was already on his way there. On Samuel's arrival in
Palestine on July 1, General Bols would retire from his post and a civilian administration would replace the military one. The changeover
was not, however, complete. More than a few of the military personnel
considered hostile to Zionism continued to serve under the new administration, among them Colonel Sir Ronald Storrs. Nevertheless, the
appointment of Samuel, a prominent Jew, Zionist, liberal, and renowned administrator, aroused the hope that the new administration
would be more sympathetic to Zionism and do all it could to help establish the National Home.

For Ben-Gurion, then, only two tasks remained: to secure the future of the Jewish Battalion and to raise funds for Achdut ha-Avodah. Regarding the former and more immediate task, Ben-Gurion lost no time in requesting an audience with Chaim Weizmann, for he was the de facto leader of the Zionist movement, and only through him could it be accomplished. Weizmann received Ben-Gurion without delay, at 9:30 A.M. on June 25; it was their first private meeting.[2]

The two were as different as east and west. At forty-six, Weizmann was twelve years Ben-Gurion's senior and at the height of his career, as both a chemist and a Zionist statesman. Since coming to Britain and joining Manchester University's chemistry department, he had been cultivating a wide network of personal connections with British soldiers, diplomats, and statesmen, including Lord Arthur James Balfour, the foreign minister. In 1916 Weizmann's important contribution to the British war effort — the invention of a process that yielded acetone, a solvent needed for the production of munitions — had brought him into contact with Winston Churchill, first lord of the admiralty, and David Lloyd George, minister of munitions, facilitating his access to Whitehall and the aristocracy. His personal influence reached its peak when Lloyd George, who considered Weizmann his friend, became prime minister in 1916. Indeed, the Balfour Declaration was attributed entirely to Weizmann's efforts. Considered one of the most brilliant diplomatic achievements of all time, since Weizmann accomplished it without the support of any government or large movement, it was certainly the greatest achievement in the history of political Zionism. Weizmann was, therefore, the undisputed, though unofficial, spokesman for the Jewish people and the Zionist movement. Tall, gracious, and captivating, he was the darling of his people. Wealthy and cultured, fluent in English, Russian, German, and French, he had an irresistible magic.

In sharp contrast was Private Ben-Gurion, recently discharged from the army, a member of the secretariat of Achdut ha-Avodah who could claim the support of 4,626 Eretz-Israeli voters. Despite his achievements, he was still just beginning his political career and was almost unknown outside Palestine. He had not yet participated in a Zionist congress as an elected delegate, his English was faulty, and his manners less than perfect; he was short, poorly clothed, and unimpressive looking. He was, nevertheless, quite sure of himself.

The two were not entirely unacquainted. In the autumn of 1918 Itzhak Ben-Zvi had told Weizmann about Ben-Gurion, then in the military hospital, and about their activities since being deported from Palestine. Most likely each nursed a grievance about the other. Ben-Gurion remembered the reluctance of David Eder, Weizmann's man, to get him furloughs, and Weizmann had probably been shocked to hear of Ben-Gurion's intention of suing Dr. Eder, which was as bad as wanting to sue Weizmann himself. They had met for the first time a month later, among many guests at a ceremonial gathering organized by the Provisional Council in Weizmann's honor. During the question and answer period after Weizmann's speech, Ben-Gurion had asked why Weizmann had not "simply [demanded] a Jewish state in Palestine"; whether "a National Home and a Jewish state are one and the same thing"; and what rights would "be granted to the Arab population." In fact he asked nine questions, many more than anyone else, giving Weizmann sufficient opportunity to distinguish him from the crowd and probably to remember his face. In any case, Weizmann had certainly not forgotten Ben-Gurion's name, for he had written to him and Berl Katznelson in Russian, as if to confidants, asking them to moderate Achdut ha-Avodah's stand against the military administration.

For his part, Ben-Gurion was quite familiar with Weizmann and his work. His charge against Eder indicates that Ben-Gurion had already marked Weizmann as his primary rival for the leadership of the Zionist movement. A week after their meeting at the Provisional Council gathering Ben-Gurion wrote to Reb Avigdor, "The World Zionist Organization has in Weizmann a dedicated, diligent, and multitalented leader. I do not agree with his politics. In my view he has not risen to the challenge. There is, however, no denying that he has done wonders. He has not demanded all that he should have, nor done all that he could have, but what he has done is enough to make his name immortal." In other words, it would be fitting and proper for Weizmann to relinquish his position to a man of the future generation. Ben-Gurion spelled it out to his father. "Why doesn't this intelligent and gifted man seize the opportunity to say 'I've done my share and now I'm leaving'?"[3]

The difference between the two men was even more striking when Ben-Gurion entered Weizmann's office. At the Provisional Council in Jaffa all members had felt like equals, but in London Ben-Gurion was lost in a strange new world. Class barriers closed the circle of London's cabinet members and top civil servants to him. He was a pauper representing paupers, while Weizmann appeared and behaved like an aristocrat.

Weizmann could have treated Ben-Gurion like a poor relation, but instead extended a hearty welcome and spoke with him as an equal, in his best folksy manner. Did Weizmann sense his guest's hidden aspirations and intend to disarm him with his irresistible magic? Not necessarily. For the moment Weizmann had no need to fear any opponent. He believed in being nice to people at the bottom, who would remember one kindly on reaching the top. Moreover, at that time he was entirely given over to preparations for the World Zionist Conference scheduled for July 4, 1920, in London, dubbed the Little Congress because it was the first world Zionist gathering to be held in seven years, since the outbreak of the war. Intending to consolidate his leadership of the Zionist movement at the conference, Weizmann used his charm left and right, seeking to blunt the opposition's attack.

Weizmann therefore went out of his way to charm Ben-Gurion, letting him in, as a start, on matters of global importance. He told him that the Supreme Council of the Entente powers, meeting in San Remo, had resolved to entrust Great Britain with the mandate for Palestine and that, as mandatory, Great Britain had created the consensus and political conditions necessary for the establishment of the Jewish National Home. Next Weizmann divulged a few items from the inner chambers of the British cabinet: first, that the gates of Palestine would be opened wide to immigration and the entry of fifty to sixty thousand Jews during the first year of Samuel's administration was to be expected. Second, the continued existence of the Jewish Battalion was secure. And to top it off, Weizmann said that the Zionist Conference would launch a drive for the collection of 25 million pounds sterling, which would accelerate the Zionist enterprise. Ben-Gurion's head spun — he had not dared dream of such enormous sums.

The Weizmann magic worked. For the moment Ben-Gurion clung to Weizmann as a blind man to the sighted and after the meeting optimistically wired Achdut ha-Avodah: "Political situation satisfactory. Battalion guaranteed. Implementation depends on Samuel." The overjoyed secretariat in Jaffa immediately telephoned the news to all its branches.[4]

At the beginning of July Berl Katznelson and Itzhak Tabenkin, the two other Achdut ha-Avodah delegates to the conference, arrived in London and, together with Ben-Gurion, worked out the position they would take, deciding to reject one-man leadership in favor of a triumvirate. During their deliberations they discovered that a good part of the information Ben-Gurion had received from Weizmann was false, something they attributed to Weizmann's putting too much trust in foreign powers and his own highly placed connections. All three agreed that Weizmann should instead have valued the forces at work in Palestine and thrown his political lot in with them. They decided to take a hard line against Weizmann, who already had the support of most of the delegates from England, the United States, and Russia.[5]

The conference opened with much pomp and circumstance. On Wednesday morning, July 7, the two hundred fifty delegates and approximately one thousand guests gathered at Memorial Hall, which was decorated in blue and white, with Union Jacks and a Star of David. Weizmann's opening address was greeted with waves of applause, each more thunderous than the last. Spirits were high, for the Jewish people's right to Palestine had been recognized in the peace treaty and in the law of nations. "That is the most momentous political event in the whole history of our movement, and, it is no exaggeration to say, in the whole history of our people since the Exile," he proclaimed. The opportunity now existed to turn Palestine into a Jewish country; work would begin immediately. Weizmann concluded his address with the good news he had previously imparted to Ben-Gurion.

As the conference settled down to business, the holiday spirit evaporated. Many, including Ben-Gurion, blamed the language problem, and interpreters were appointed at the delegates' request. The debate, proposals, and resolutions all had to be translated into English, German, French, Yiddish, and Hebrew, dragging out the proceedings, but the delegates would not hear of curtailing their oratory; the attempt to impose a time limit aroused mass indignation. Dr. Max Nordau, philosopher, cofounder of the World Zionist Organization, Theodor Herzl's right hand, and now an elderly Zionist dignitary, protested. "We have been waiting for seven years, and now you want to throttle discussion?" As a result the conference lasted two full weeks.

The medley of tongues was not the only problem. Weizmann had not prepared a comprehensive report on the activities of the Zionist Commission during its first two years in existence. He thereby killed two birds with one stone, withholding from the delegates data that might have been used in support of arguments against the Zionist Commission and saving himself the trouble of accounting for its mistakes. His "brief sketch" of the situation in Palestine afforded Weizmann the opportunity to shine and win over his audience, body and soul. Katznelson described his sketch as "light as a feather, keen, calculated, easy to digest — all in all a message of a leader" who wishes to win his listeners' support.

Weizmann blamed the Yishuv for all the mishaps and troubles that had occurred. The Eretz-Israelis, he said, were excitable, impulsive, and took themselves far too seriously; the parties in Palestine were unruly, and "the Jews there suffer from hypertrophy." By contrast, the British administration was stable and practical. Was it any wonder, then, that the administration had become on the whole anti-Zionistic, and perhaps even anti-Jewish?

Since most of the delegates had not come from Palestine, this witty address was greeted with laughter and applause. It was, of course, not at all to the liking of the Eretz-Israeli delegates. Those from Achdut ha-Avodah regarded this attack as proof of Weizmann's irresponsibility; his sketch epitomized the gap between the European and American Zionists, who were interested in public opinion at home and the good will of their governments, and the Eretz-Israelis, whose Zionism demanded personal commitment to immigration and pioneering and who relied on the Yishuv's potential.

Ben-Gurion delivered Achdut ha-Avodah's reply, and the forum turned into a battleground as he clashed with Weizmann. Ben-Gurion approached the rostrum with grim determination, and he spoke with passion and fury, presenting his case against Weizmann, Eder, and the Zionist Commission as if to a jury.

He began with Weizmann's misdemeanors and progressed to more and more serious offenses. The first charge was the absence of a proper report, for without information about the past, the future could not be discussed. Next Ben-Gurion pointed out that the Arabs, who had no Weizmann and no Commission, had gained much ground. They manned so many government posts that they administered virtually half of Palestine, not to mention that they had gotten a whole state in Transjordan. "And what have we got? Nothing." He then accused Weizmann of spoiling the relations between the Yishuv and the British administration. From the very beginning the Zionist Commission had been less friendly to the men of the Jewish Battalion than had the administration. Eder had called them traitors and sent them back overseas on demobilization, thus losing the opportunity to keep the thousands of soldiers already there. The Commission, which to Ben-Gurion's mind was synonymous with Weizmann, had been established as an intermediary between the Yishuv and the administration but had in fact "set up an iron wall between them and denied Eretz-Israelis access to the administration." In return for his privileged status, Weizmann had repaid the British by assuming a moderate line and making concessions. The result — here Ben-Gurion reached the gravest offense of all — was that the administration's sympathy had turned into an ever-growing hostility that served only to incite the Arabs to raids on Jewish settlements and pogroms in Jerusalem. Ben-Gurion placed the responsibility for the spilled Jewish blood neither on the Arabs nor on the British, but on Weizmann. To further dramatize this indictment, which lasted into the next day's session, Ben-Gurion compared the British to the Turks. In Ottoman times, he said, the Jews had been better off. At least they had been able to hold their own, and they had access to Jemal Pasha. A blacker slander of Weizmann's role was unimaginable. There can be no doubt that personal considerations and covert ambitions drove Ben-Gurion to such an extreme and unfair assertion.

While by his outrageous distortion of facts in blaming Weizmann for the bloodshed Ben-Gurion won some applause from the Eretz-Israeli side, his reference to the Ottoman days was a mistake. In Zionist rhetoric Weizmann had no equal. Even orators far more gifted than Ben-Gurion were bound to lose in a war of words with Weizmann, but Ben-Gurion's wild exaggeration ensured a resounding defeat. Weizmann dismissed Ben-Gurion's pertinent criticism as if it were a fleck of dust, saying that history, not the conference, would be his judge, and mocked Ben-Gurion at length. Ben-Gurion had recalled the "fleshpots of Egypt"; Weizmann picked up on this theme and ridiculed, in the style of the Haggadah, Ben-Gurion and anyone else who reminisced about the Turk. When the Turk did not let us build a home and we built it clandestinely — *Dayenu,* "It would have been enough." When the Turk banished us from Palestine instead of hanging us (with obvious reference to Ben-Gurion and Ben-Zvi) — Dayenu. And he went on. Thunderous laughter and cheers filled the auditorium every time Weizmann said Dayenu.

Unlike the Turk, he continued, the British had committed themselves to rebuilding Palestine, and now it was up to the Jews to prove themselves. Why were the Jews not flocking to Palestine? Weizmann pointed an accusing finger at the convention delegates. "The Jews merely held meetings and waved flags," he said, instead of immigrating to the National Home that had been given to them. In short, the Zionist Commission was not to blame, but rather the Jews' unwillingness to go to Palestine in great numbers and the resultant "lack of human material." In conclusion Weizmann raised his voice to ask, "I therefore turn to the nation and cry, 'Jewish People! What *have you* done?' "[6]

The speech made a tremendous impression. The delegates rose to their feet as one and gave Weizmann a seemingly endless ovation. Ben-Gurion's attempt to stand him in the dock might never have happened. Little wonder, then, that Ben-Gurion and Achdut ha-Avodah didn't demand Weizmann's resignation: they didn't stand a chance.

In this rush of feeling another important aspect of Ben-Gurion's challenge to Weizmann passed essentially unnoticed: the issue of the centrality of Palestine in the Zionist movement. In defending Dr. Eder, censuring the Yishuv, and calling the Eretz-Israelis excitable and impulsive, Weizmann was implying that the Zionist movement could be guided only from outside Palestine, specifically, from London. The conference not only crowned Weizmann the one-man leader of the Zionist movement, but embraced his external orientation as well. What was more, it endorsed his financial policy of raising funds from the few and the wealthy instead of from the Jewish people at large, as Ben-Gurion wanted.

When the conference adjourned, Ben-Gurion and his Achdut ha-

Avodah colleagues rushed to the fifth World Conference of Poale Zion in Vienna. There, in an altogether different setting, he continued to campaign for the centrality of Palestine. Since the day of its founding Achdut ha-Avodah had demanded a clear-cut resolution of this issue from the head office of the World Union of Poale Zion, but producing one was problematic because the union was in danger of division from the perennial question, Zionism or socialism? To what was Poale Zion, and every Zionist-socialist, committed — Zionism in Palestine or the promotion of worldwide socialist revolution? During his last year in the United States, Ben-Gurion had witnessed the growing immediacy of this recurrent question in the wake of the Bolshevik revolution, when prominent members of Poale Zion, among them his friend Alexander Chashin, had hastened to Russia to help set up the Soviet regime and spread word of the revolution to other lands instead of devoting themselves to the National Home in Palestine.

In the USSR, before Zionism was banned in 1928, Poale Zion had split into three leftist parties, of which the most extreme was the Jewish Communist Poale Zion Party. In neighboring countries, primarily Poland and Austria, large segments of the membership leaned toward the Russian parties' positions. Together they made up the bulk of the left-wing bloc of the World Union, which pressed for discussion of two fundamental questions: whether revolutionary socialist parties like Poale Zion could belong to the World Zionist Organization, which the leftists considered bourgeois, and whether such parties should not join the Communist International, or Comintern, and accept its authority.

Ben-Gurion and his colleagues had to prepare their stand should the majority at the conference proscribe allegiance to the World Zionist Organization and its Congress. In such an event, they thought, they would most probably split away. Katznelson, likening the left to gangrene that gnawed at the flesh of Poale Zion and threatened to lay waste its body, said he preferred a union, "small, but whole of spirit." The only thing that made them hesitate to break up the union immediately was their belief that such an act was tantamount to a division of the Jewish proletariat. They feared that Zionism in general, and labor Zionism in particular, would lose the greater part of their potential reserves, since the main source for immigration to Palestine was the Jewish working class in Russia and Poland.[7]

Ben-Gurion had time to ponder his tactics during the train ride to Vienna, which lasted three long days. He had to decide whether to urge division at once or to strive for a compromise that meant, at best, postponement of the schism. Later he admitted that he decided to create an immediate split, but in such a manner as to make it seem that

the left wing had forced his group to splinter off, thus enabling Achdut
ha-Avodah to carry away with it a greater number of followers. At
midday on July 29, he arrived at the Post Hotel in Vienna, in whose auditorium the third uneventful day of the conference was under way.
The storm did not burst until two days later, with the arrival of the delegates from Russia, red carnations in their lapels and on their lips the
demand to get on with the crucial issue of relations with the Comintern and the World Zionist Organization.

When Alexander Chashin arrived with the Russian delegation, he
and Ben-Gurion embraced like long lost brothers. For Ben-Gurion,
Chashin was more than a tried and true friend; he was one of the few
men he ever truly loved. However, this was not the same old Chashin,
and if Ben-Gurion had counted on his support, he was in for a bitter
disappointment. Chashin stood at the extreme left of his delegation, for
he had become a Communist and a member of the Jewish Communist
Poale Zion Party. He was still the same enthralling speaker, however.
His polished style and weaving of wit and puns into his speech made it
the conference's main attraction. It "glittered like all the colors of the
rainbow," wrote one of the reporters. Yet while his sharp quips amused
the gathering, the content of his speech was harsh: the members of
Poale Zion, like all workers, had only one homeland, and that homeland was to be found wherever the revolutionary flame blazed. Therefore they had but a single option, to join the Communist Party and
serve the revolution from its ranks. Only after the world revolution had
taken place and been securely established would Poale Zion members
be free to go to Palestine, which by that time would be free of any national conflict between Jews and Arabs. (Chashin's loyalty to the Soviet
regime and Stalinism turned out to be misplaced; despite it he was
purged and sent to Siberia because of his Zionist past. He died in a
gulag in the mid 1930s, before he was fifty.)

Unlike Chashin, Ben-Gurion saw no contradiction between Zionism
and socialism, and therefore rejected the question of priorities. We
have, he said to the conference, one conviction only, a Zionist socialist
one. We are Jewish socialists, and just as no one would demand that
British or German socialists serve the revolution outside England or
Germany, no one should demand that Zionist socialists serve it outside
Palestine. In place of that question Ben-Gurion posited another, which
to his mind was more fitting: In what respect were Zionist socialists different from other socialists? He answered it as follows: "The others
have a primarily political task, to seize power, overthrow the national
economy, and lay the foundations for a socialist one. Our primary task
is to create a national economy." Chashin's response was to call this
approach Platonic love of the socialist revolution.

The controversy focused not only on where to serve the revolution, but on how to go about it. The delegates from Russia and Poland were of the opinion that the instigation of a class war that would lead to the seizure of power in Palestine took priority over the creation of a Zionist socialist economy, which Ben-Gurion and Achdut ha-Avodah advocated. By the same token, the leftist delegates demanded that class solidarity among Jewish and Arab workers in Palestine take precedence over efforts toward Jewish national development. They considered the Comintern the sole framework through which class war and the realization of socialism could be achieved, which meant that the only way to make the interests of the Jewish proletariat identical to those of a Communist Party dictatorship was to join the Comintern.

Ben-Gurion adamantly opposed power seizure as a first step, with the argument that should a proletarian dictatorship be established in Palestine, where Jews were still a tiny minority, Palestine would go to the Arabs. It was possible to set up a proletarian dictatorship, he said, but then "Palestine would be rebuilt without us; socialism would be implemented there, with Soviets and Arabs, but no Jews."

Ben-Gurion did not denounce the Comintern, however. On the contrary, he said he regarded it as the world headquarters of the revolution, probably only to appease the left and those of its members who leaned toward Achdut ha-Avodah. But he quickly added reservations. "We cannot follow [the headquarters] blindly," he said, since it had considerations and politics of its own. For example, the Comintern supported the "Faisals" and "the other imperialist effendis," a policy he considered not only misguided, but anti-Zionist. His sharp political sense told him that Russian interests were more important to the Soviets than the interests of the world revolution, and that for the sake of Russian interests the Comintern was ready to support even the effendis.

If the Russians could support the feudal lords of the Arab world, why could not the Comintern support a bourgeois World Zionist Organization? "In order to advance the revolution in the East," Ben-Gurion maintained, with a sidelong glance at the left, "a center of Jewish labor in Palestine" must be created, which would be the natural bearer of the revolution to the East. The Comintern was not at issue, he argued, but rather the conditions for joining it, which of course was not at all true, but saying it enabled him to present himself as a conciliator. When the delegates from Russia and Poland urged joining it unconditionally, Ben-Gurion and Katznelson made it clear that they would have no further interest in Poale Zion unless Palestine was its central issue. The conference was on the brink of division; all that remained was for something to nudge it over the edge.

On August 8 the left put its own resolution to a vote, and 178 delegates voted in favor of it, while 179 — who would have voted for Ben-Gurion's proposal had he formally put it to the vote — abstained. The left solemnly declared that the fifth World Conference of Poale Zion had "decided to join [the Comintern] straightaway." Those who had abstained — mostly delegates from the United States, England, and Palestine — left the auditorium in a huff. Ben-Gurion's tactic had succeeded; by refraining from putting his proposal to a vote, and making sure all the delegates who supported him abstained, he made it seem that the left had forced the split by putting the conference in an untenable situation.

Ben-Gurion, who had learned how to hide in the first person plural, wrote his father that "we, the delegates of Achdut ha-Avodah, were the main instigators of this breach, as we did not wish to give in to those parties who, in our opinion, are drifting away from true socialist Zionism," which indicates that he was more ready than his colleagues to assume responsibility for this painful amputation. Though he knew full well that it meant the loss of Achdut ha-Avodah's richest manpower reserves, he firmly believed that it was in his and the organization's power to salvage large portions of them. The future had quite a few more painful splits in store for Ben-Gurion, but in Vienna in 1920 he formulated his guiding principle and found the strength to implement it forcefully. Like Gideon, who chose to set out with a force of three hundred carefully selected men, sending the anxious ones home, Ben-Gurion preferred a smaller active political body, united in its sense of purpose, to a larger but lax framework, paralyzed by internal strife.

As a result of Ben-Gurion's strategy and its post-conference efforts, Achdut ha-Avodah was able to salvage approximately half the membership of each party from Poland, East Galicia, and Bukovina, in addition to a few stragglers from the Austrian and German lefts — all who were convinced that the left was to blame for breaking up the conference and all whose loyalty to Zionism was greater than their enthusiasm for world revolution and who were not, therefore, willing to join a Comintern inimical to Zionism. These halved parties served Achdut ha-Avodah as the foundation on which to rebuild the pro-Zionist Poale Zion, and eastern Europe was not lost to socialist Zionism.[8]

The leftists continued the conference at the Post Hotel, where they founded the Jewish Communist Confederation (Poale Zion), or Komferband for short, and unanimously resolved not to take part in the World Zionist Congress but to request admission to the Comintern. However, the executive committee of the Comintern, which at first praised them for their eagerness "to wage a struggle against the bourgeoisie," later, "after careful scrutiny," decided that "trends incompatible with the principles of the Communist International still exist" within the Komferband, and therefore informed it that it was superfluous, since a Jewish bureau had already been established within the Comintern "which would handle all communist propaganda for the worldwide Jewish proletariat." The Komferband was short-lived; its remnants immigrated to Palestine and founded a new party called Poale Zion Left.

The right wing — composed mainly of delegates from the United States, England, and Palestine — gathered in the Bayerischerhof Hotel conference hall and decided to hold on to the old union, which Ben-Gurion and Katznelson were thenceforth able to direct as they saw fit; indeed, they had engineered the schism so that the union and its constituent Poale Zion parties would be the world arm of Achdut ha-Avodah, instead of the other way around. Ben-Gurion thus made an important stride toward realizing his Palestinian concept. What he had not been able to achieve in London he accomplished in Vienna: from then on the Yishuv would be the guiding force in the Zionist labor movement. He was only one step, albeit a difficult one, away from securing Palestine's centrality in the world Zionist movement. This, in turn, would lead directly to Palestine's becoming the focal point of world Jewry.

In accordance with the new situation, the rightists' conference decided to divide World Union activities between two offices. The one in Vienna was to strengthen what remained of the parties in eastern Europe, raise funds, and handle immigration to Palestine. A second office would be set up in London as a "political center" to handle international relations and World Zionist Organization affairs. Ben-Gurion and Shlomo Kaplansky, who had been the head of the World Union in Vienna, were elected to the London office, so Ben-Gurion's mission was extended by at least a year. To his father he wrote that he had agreed to be torn away from Palestine because the split, which was his own handiwork, had placed "the responsibility for the existence and strengthening of the divided union" on his shoulders.[9]

Ben-Gurion did not stay in Vienna to see the close of the deliberations, for Paula had wired him from London that she was nearly due to give birth. Hurrying to London by express train, he arrived there on the evening of August 20 to find that Paula was still in the hotel. She went into labor two days later and he took her to the maternity hospital in Clapham. After a difficult delivery, she gave birth on August 23 to a boy whom Ben-Gurion named after the herdsman-prophet Amos. When he sent the news of his son's birth to Reb Avigdor, Ben-Gurion apologized to his father for not honoring his request to name his first-born male as he suggested. And he added, "His head, much larger than usual, is promising."

The next day Ben-Gurion moved from the hotel to a boarding house at 75 Warington Crescent, near Paddington Station, and brought his wife and son there from the hospital. He was amazed at his son's light blue eyes — "I don't know where he got them from" — and at the size of his head, which reminded him of his own. He closely followed Amos's development, proudly and meticulously recording the results of each weighing. This, it seems, was his sole pleasure at the time, for he had to take care of two-year-old Geula and find an apartment large enough to accommodate his parents as well.[10]

It was more than six years since Ben-Gurion had seen his family in Płońsk. During this period hard times had befallen the town, and rampant inflation had hurt Reb Avigdor. Moreover, the fighting between Poland and Russia had disrupted transportation and postal services, so that he never got the money Ben-Gurion had sent him. In lengthy letters Reb Avigdor described his "critical situation" to his son. His income had been cut off. "The winter is approaching, I don't know what will be. Prospects are — not good." Ben-Gurion's heart "bled," he said, upon reading these letters, and he was saddened to see, in a photo his father sent, that Reb Avigdor's hair had turned gray. On his return to London he therefore entreated his father and stepmother, Zvia, to come there, taking care to emphasize that the invitation was from Paula as well.

Paula, however, was dissatisfied with the apartment he was about to rent, so only three days after sending his parents word of the room awaiting them in London, he had to notify them that the matter was not yet settled. He finally found a furnished apartment acceptable to Paula at 24 Westbourne Square. Ben-Gurion considered the two rooms plus kitchen and bath a bargain at three pounds a week, and they moved in on October 1.

From the beginning it was clear that there was no room for Reb Avigdor and Zvia there. Had this been Paula's intention when she rejected the three-room apartment that Ben-Gurion had previously found? Certainly it is possible that she was concerned with economizing, for Ben-Gurion's monthly income was fifty pounds, and saving five to nine pounds a month in the smaller apartment was no minor matter to her. It is also reasonable to assume that she was not overjoyed at the thought of having to tend to the needs of a befuddled elderly couple as well as her two babies. There can be no doubt that Ben-Gurion and Paula discussed the matter at length, for in the end Ben-Gurion pleaded with his father to come alone. In so doing he put his father in an impossible position, choosing between his son and his wife! Zvia was in poor health; who would attend to her? Certainly not Rivka's husband, Abraham Lefkovitz, for he had been reduced to poverty, as Ben-Gurion knew from Rivka's letters, which described "the heart-rending situation in Poland."

Reb Avigdor, almost sixty-four, asked repeatedly if he could bring his wife, even saying he would make do with less money for the journey, only 100 pounds. Ben-Gurion replied that although he and "especially Paula very much desired" that the "aunt" accompany him, two things made it impossible. For one, he could not get hold of 100 pounds, a sum "nearly twice my monthly salary," and for another, there was, regretfully, no room in the apartment. For a while it seemed that Reb Avigdor would agree to come alone, and Ben-Gurion arranged for his entry visa and furnished him with detailed travel instructions. In the end, though, Reb Avigdor opted to remain in Płońsk with his wife, and Ben-Gurion continued to send him money.[11]

13

The Either-Or Approach

THE BRITISH Poale Zion (Jewish Socialist Labour Party) operated out of two rooms on the second floor at 27 Sandy's Row, near Petticoat Lane, the famed secondhand clothing alley. The building's ground floor had once served as a club for exiled Russian revolutionaries, but all that remained of it was its cafeteria, still famed for its pickled herring. In late November 1920, David Ben-Gurion and Shlomo Kaplansky sublet one of the party's two rooms and set up the London Office of the World Union of Poale Zion, known simply as "the Office." The Office and the party had one telephone and one typewriter between them. Moshe Sharett, who was beginning his studies at the London School of Economics, worked there part time, after classes, translating the pair's letters and memos from Yiddish into English.

Ben-Gurion would take the bus or tram to the Office and wordlessly sit down to his paperwork, across from Kaplansky. The cacophony of haggling and peddlers' cries from the neighboring clothes bazaar infiltrated the office even when the windows were shut, but Ben-Gurion was imperturbable. His diligence and powers of concentration impressed the others in the Office, who nicknamed him "the great silent one." His dry, matter-of-fact manner was all the more striking beside Kaplansky's cheerfulness. Only at lunch at a nearby Lyon's Tea Shop were his office colleagues treated to his utterance of a sentence or two.[1]

Little by little, however, Ben-Gurion's mission in London lost part of its original mandate. The War Office's decision to mobilize five hundred new volunteers — one of the secrets he had learned from Weizmann — was never implemented, and within a few months the Jewish Battalion was no more. The Office's achievements in building up relations with the World Zionist Organization were hardly more impressive. Chaim Weizmann was unable to produce the huge operations budget he had promised, and the agricultural settlement allocation to Palestine was cut off.

When Ben-Gurion went to Weizmann's office to "forcefully protest this outrage," Weizmann sidestepped him by promising that half the budget had already been sent and would soon reach its destination. Learning that the sum was negligible, Ben-Gurion stormed back, but this time Weizmann requested assistance instead of lending it. He asked Ben-Gurion to cooperate in mobilizing the Poale Zion parties to increase donations to Keren ha-Yesod (Jewish Foundation Fund), and took Ben-Gurion's home phone number so that they could be in touch frequently. Nothing came of this either, and when in December the cultural budget was eliminated, Ben-Gurion boycotted the Zionist office altogether. Weizmann sent Dr. Leo Motzkin, a Zionist VIP, to appease Ben-Gurion, but in vain; Ben-Gurion saw no more of Weizmann during his stay in London, and focused on other matters.[2]

From the start it had been clear to Ben-Gurion that he had to raise money for Achdut ha-Avodah. He had enlarged the scope of its activity and obligations, and believed that the failure to obtain funds was due to the fact that the vision of Palestine had not been presented to the Jewish people at large. Ben-Gurion had the opportunity to prove this claim. He issued leaflets describing Achdut ha-Avodah's programs and in November 1920 he ordered from the Zionist office in London 678,000 shekels — membership tokens — for the twelfth Zionist Congress, scheduled to convene in 1921. But his high hopes were dashed; only 11,000 were sold.

The Zionist Organization was open to all Jews over the age of eighteen. To become a member one bought the shekel, which entitled one to vote in the elections to the Zionist Congress. All proceeds from the shekel went to the treasury of the Zionist Organization. In addition to individual purchasers, recognized world parties like Poale Zion or the Mizrachi could buy the shekel in bulk and sell it to their members, retaining the commission for their treasuries. The strength of a Zionist party was determined by the number of delegates it sent to the Congress; the number of delegates was decided by the number of votes, and only shekel holders could vote.[3]

Before his experience with fund raising Ben-Gurion had censured Weizmann's reliance on the wealthy few, regarding it as antidemocratic, leading to oligarchy and domination by an "evil group of capitalists . . . whose goals are inconsistent with the true interests of Jewish workers who aspire after work and freedom in Palestine." Reality taught him that Weizmann had turned to the rich simply because they were the only ones from whom he could get money. Even so, only a few donated to the Zionist cause. To his dismay, Ben-Gurion had not only to take back what he had said about Weizmann but swallow an even bitterer pill: to save Achdut ha-Avodah he had to resort to wooing the rich himself.

He had only one rich acquaintance, Major James Armand Rothschild, son of the renowned Baron Edmond, who had joined the Jewish Battalion during the war, making himself its patron. Ben-Gurion turned to Jimmy, as he was fondly known to his comrades at arms, to request a £4,000 loan for the consolidation of the cooperatives and *kvutsas** founded by Achdut ha-Avodah. Jimmy greeted Ben-Gurion warmly and listened attentively, then handed him a check for £1,200 as if it were petty cash. Emboldened by this success, Ben-Gurion later returned to request, "on behalf of the workers of Palestine," £60,000 on credit, to be used primarily as operating capital for the cooperatives of construction workers, which Achdut ha-Avodah had set up to contract for public works. In Ben-Gurion's estimate these projects would soon provide nine thousand jobs. Suddenly, the path to the Rothschild coffers, formerly so short, became long and winding; Jimmy wanted to submit Ben-Gurion's project to minute scrutiny by his experts. Five months later, by April 1921, Ben-Gurion had gotten only £2,200. He learned the size of the gap between his expectations and his ability to realize them.[4]

Forming and maintaining a liaison with the British Labour Party was also an important part of the Office's work, and therefore of Ben-Gurion's mission. In its War Aims Memorandum of 1918 the Labour Party had demanded that Palestine become a free state, with international protection and guarantees, and that Jews be able to go there to accomplish their redemption without interference from other races or religions. In March 1920 its leaders sent a signed telegram to Prime Minister David Lloyd George, then at the San Remo Conference, urging the British government to accept the mandate for the administration of Palestine to reconstitute a National Home for the Jewish people.[5]

During the same month the British Poale Zion (JSLP) became affiliated with the Labour Party; to pull more weight, it claimed a membership of three thousand, although it actually numbered only a few hundred, half of them in London. In any case, the fact that British Poale Zion was entitled to send representatives to the executive committee of the Labour Party fired Ben-Gurion's imagination. He envisioned Achdut ha-Avodah representatives, himself among them, filling these positions; parliamentary speeches and questions by Labour dele-

---

* *Kvutsa,* Hebrew for "group." In Palestine it came to mean a small communal unit, occupied with agriculture or construction. Today it means a small kibbutz.

gates would influence the British government, which in turn would affect the administration in Palestine. During his first months in the Office Ben-Gurion made every effort to get onto the party's Advisory Committee on International Questions, whose recommendations often determined the party's foreign policy.

The Advisory Committee had been founded in 1918 in the offices of the Fabian Society, which had left its mark on it. Sidney Webb, a founder of this society as well as the Labour Party and the London School of Economics, chaired the committee. Leonard Woolf was its secretary, and Arnold Toynbee, who then specialized in Greece and Greek cultural history, headed the subcommittee on Asian affairs. Ben-Gurion's hope of being accepted on this committee was based on his being a member of Poale Zion and on the committee's having already accepted a few foreign members, including the Belgian socialist leader Camille Huysmans.[6]

However, Achdut ha-Avodah and Ben-Gurion overestimated the Labour Party's sympathy, failing to realize that they themselves were the only ones who regarded the two as sister parties. They had not picked up the subtle difference between the sympathy for Zionism expressed so forthrightly by candidates seeking the Jewish vote and the guarded statements made by the party's ideologists and policymakers. Party candidates were eager to participate in Poale Zion gatherings and conferences. Through these Ben-Gurion met George Lansbury, a party leader and the editor of its organ, the *Daily Herald*, Tom Shaw, a Labour MP, and others. But the members of the Advisory Committee, as policy planners, kept their distance. Although the committee sympathized with Zionism in the abstract, the members had serious reservations concerning Zionism's realization in Palestine, which guided the recommendations they made. In fact, Sidney Webb, who as Lord Passfield would become colonial secretary in 1929, embraced a policy that was anti-Zionist and pro-Arab. Had Ben-Gurion known in 1920 the true political feelings of the more prominent members of the Advisory Committee, he would not have been surprised by Passfield's Palestine policy.

Ben-Gurion submitted his request for admission to the Advisory Committee with expectations that were dashed on September 10, when he was rejected. Undaunted, he still hoped to be invited as an observer, at least to the sessions about Palestine and particularly the issue of Palestine's northern border. The San Remo Conference had left the demarcation of this border up to Great Britain and France. Fearing that they might move it southward, Ben-Gurion composed a memorandum, "On the Boundaries of Palestine," which he and Kaplansky submitted in the Office's name to the Labour Party and the French socialist party on November 15, urging both to intervene. Without sparsely populated areas — primarily the desert zones east of the Jordan — which were needed for the settlement of the masses of Jewish refugees from eastern Europe, and without water for the development of agriculture and industry, it would be impossible to found "the Jewish Commonwealth" as a viable economic and political unit. The northern part of Palestine would therefore have to include portions of Syria and Lebanon, that is, "the west bank of the Litani, the sources of the Jordan up to Mount Hermon, and all of the Hawrān region until Wadi al-Áūjah, south of Damascus." In the letter accompanying this memo to the Advisory Committee, Ben-Gurion asked to meet with its members to discuss the issue, since it was a matter of great urgency.

But the committee neither considered the issue urgent nor granted Ben-Gurion's request. It did not discuss Palestine until the end of the month, after resolving to note that "the boundaries have already been fixed." Someone appealed this resolution on the grounds that such was not the case, and the committee agreed to discuss the matter further at its next session. This took place on January 19, 1921, when it was resolved "to point out that the question is settled" once and for all. Ben-Gurion and Kaplansky were denied the power they so coveted to influence Labour Party policy. Only after the committee discussed his border memorandum did Ben-Gurion realize that "there were individual members in the party who opposed the Balfour Declaration"; only a few, true, but they had considerable impact.

In sum, Ben-Gurion's success at his main task, to establish close ties with the Labour Party, was but partial; he made only casual contacts. Nevertheless the knowledge he acquired of the party laid the foundation for his future political dialogue with it. The only solid connection left to him and Kaplansky was their right to participate in the annual Labour conference, through the three delegates allotted to Poale Zion.[7]

Nor was there much contentment in Ben-Gurion's private life. At first his spirits were high, since he believed he would have time to continue the study of Palestine he had begun in New York; to this end he got a reader's card from the British Museum, where he read mainly about the history of the Eastern Church and the Druze in Lebanon. The museum was a sanctuary of light and warmth; he called it "a palace of humanity . . . a treasure of unequaled wealth." As Office matters became more demanding, however, he was left with little time for reading and study. Then he injured his arm, and suddenly his life hung in the balance as a result of first aid administered by Paula. His arm soon became inflamed; blood poisoning followed. For three days he hovered, as he put it, between two worlds, until his Office mates convinced Paula to call a doctor. With his health floundering and financial distress worsening, he felt as though the world was closing in on him, to such a degree that even after he was fully recovered he could find nothing much to brighten his life. London's treasures — the British Museum, the theaters, historical sights, and art masterpieces — seemed to slip beyond his grasp, and he missed his party colleagues in Palestine. "I'm in prison," he wrote in January 1921 to Itzhak Ben-Zvi and Rachel Yanait. "It is so cold here, empty, freezing, and boring, nothing to nurture the spirit." A few days later he shared his misery with all of Achdut ha-Avodah in a letter to the secretariat: "Ever since coming to London I have suffered awful torment."[8]

In March the World Union of Poale Zion decided, for lack of funds, to close the London Office and recall its staff to Vienna. After reassuring Paula that Vienna was not a place from which no one returned, Ben-Gurion began preparations to move there.

The trip to Vienna was expensive, despite his efforts to economize. He bought third-class train tickets and stocked up on food (£5 worth) so they would not have to eat in restaurants along the way — all of which, with transit visas, cost twenty pounds. However, he also shipped the books he had acquired in London and New York to Tel Aviv in two large crates; this, with insurance, cost twenty-four pounds. Ben-Gurion kept records of all these expenses, including the tip to the porter in the station. No doubt he needed them for reimbursement by the Vienna office, but there can be no doubt that the other purpose of such scrupulous attention to detail was self-documentation, in which he was always indefatigable.

On Saturday, March 19, 1921, Ben-Gurion and family, weighed down with packages and suitcases secured with new locks, straps, and ropes, took a taxi to Victoria Station. Their hand luggage contained plenty of bread, eggs, butter, coffee, and beef, as well as children's medication and a thermometer. Amos's new carriage was sent by freight, Amos being carried in his mother's arms while Ben-Gurion, sporting new pants and shoes, pushed Geula in her stroller. She was wearing a new coat and shoes. Paula had taken pains to make such purchases before the trip, for who knew what the future held? It seems that she bought only a pair of shoes for herself. The express train traveled via Dover and Ostend, stopping briefly in Cologne. They arrived in Vienna on Sunday evening and took a fiacre to a hotel.[9]

Ben-Gurion immediately cabled his father, inviting him to join them, and applied for his father's entry visa. But it soon became clear that apartments were a scarce commodity in Vienna. The family had to stay in one hotel after another. Ben-Gurion related Paula's complaints to his father: not enough milk for the children or sufficient hot water to bathe Amos. In short, life in Vienna was difficult, and since the World Union gave him no clearly defined assignments, he had no idea how long he would have to stay there. His family's situation was becoming so insufferable that he felt unable to remain in Vienna until the Zionist Congress, scheduled to meet there that summer. Moreover, he was burning to be at the center of activity in Palestine. When in April and again in May the executive committee of Achdut ha-Avodah demanded his immediate return to Palestine, he felt rescued.[10]

As a result the tables were turned: instead of Ben-Gurion's inviting Reb Avigdor to Vienna, Reb Avigdor came to his son's aid by inviting Paula and the children to stay in Płońsk until Ben-Gurion's plans were settled, for the union had objected to his returning to Palestine. Ben-Gurion accepted gratefully, and Paula and the children left for Płońsk in early April. Three weeks later he arrived there himself with some of the family's belongings. Father and son met for the first time in seven years, hoping to make the most of this long awaited reunion.

Ben-Gurion had originally intended to pay only a two-week visit, as he planned to depart for Palestine from Trieste on May 15, in a ship chartered to transport new immigrants. He had left some luggage in Vienna to take to Palestine with him. But on May 1 anti-Jewish riots erupted on the Jaffa–Tel Aviv border, and the news that twenty Jews had been massacred by Arabs and hundreds wounded made him determined to return to Palestine as soon as possible.

Apprehensive and short tempered, Ben-Gurion made his way to Trieste alone, where more bad news awaited him. Immigration to Palestine had been halted, and the ship, with hundreds of would-be passengers, was stuck in Trieste until further notice. He could have secured space on a passenger ship as a returning resident, but the Union was broke, and because of his own indebtedness he could not borrow the price of a ticket. Left with no alternatives, he returned to Vienna and feverishly set to fund raising to buy arms for the Haganah. What he intended as merely a stopover in Vienna turned into a three-month stay, and what was supposed to be a short separation from Paula and the children lasted nearly a year.[11]

It was a year of suffering for Paula, and her hosts as well. The room set aside for her and the children was "awfully damp" and "very dangerous" to health in general and the children's in particular, so she demanded that her in-laws keep the stove well stoked. Fuel was expensive, and her insistence seemed unreasonable. She insisted too that the Płońsk water was "unclean" and more dangerous than the dampness. She could not understand how "normal people use this muddy water," let alone drink it.

At his father's house Ben-Gurion tried to reconcile his loved ones in discussions. After parting from them, he wrote to explain to both Paula and his father that the root of the conflict was neither ill will nor lack of affection, but simple misunderstanding. "Two slightly alien worlds made contact."

But these peace efforts came to naught, and the conflict nearly soured the relations between Ben-Gurion and his father as both sides of his family fought for his sympathy and affection.

Two weeks after Ben-Gurion left Płońsk, Paula moved with the children to Roumbesh, using money that Ben-Gurion had borrowed in Warsaw and left with her. She explained in a letter that leaving Płońsk had been necessary because Amos was "sick with a temperature of 40 [104° F]" and the doctor had told her "to leave Płońsk immediately as the air of Płońsk doesn't agree with Amos." A week later she sent him the news that thanks to the pure country water and good healthy air Amos had recovered in the wink of an eye, and Geula too was beautiful. She pointedly mentioned that she found "the people in the country much better than in Płońsk."

Paula's departure hurt Reb Avigdor, and his pain intensified when he heard not a word from Ben-Gurion, for he interpreted the silence as a sign of anger. In his misery he wrote to his son expressing his frank opinion of Paula and reproaching him for having had a change of heart. Paula seems to have learned of this letter or had the gift of foresight, for she dashed off a letter to Ben-Gurion asking him to send mail to his father through her. But in this rivalry for Ben-Gurion's affection, Reb Avigdor held the upper hand, and Ben-Gurion wrote to him directly. He explained that he had been silent because of the immense pressure of work caused by the riots in Palestine and the suspension of immigration. "Did you really suspect that I am capable of being angry with you?" he wrote, adding, "Even if you had done some harm to me or mine — as if such a thing were possible — I wouldn't be angry with you."

This letter finally blessed Reb Avigdor with the demonstration of love and gratitude from his son for which he had waited so long.

Dear Father: You are very, very precious to me. I read your letter once, then twice — in great anguish . . . without a drop of resentment or anger. I regarded the hand that wrote those bitter things as the loving and caressing hand of both father and mother in one. . . . Believe me, my heart is filled with only love and adoration and respect and profound gratitude to you. I know that at times I have not fulfilled my obligations to you . . . but not because of a lack of love and respect. . . . No, my dear father. I have always been deeply attached to you, especially since leaving your house fifteen years ago. . . . Your image has always been treasured and imprinted on my heart, and the ambition to repay you a thousand times over and to make you content to the fullest of my ability has been the hub of all my thoughts and aspirations.

Paula, however, was a wily and stubborn rival. Ben-Gurion pleaded with her to return to Reb Avigdor's house and she did, but shortly thereafter went back to the country, singing a familiar tune: "The air of Poland doesn't agree with the children." To drive the nail home she added, "Amos is a wonderful by [sic] . . . but he looks very bad, he lost two pounds . . . he weighs only 23 pounds. Geula doesn't look well neither." In case this was not enough she unsheathed her old weapon, and asked Ben-Gurion to take Geula to Vienna in order to "make [her] an operation." He, however, having received a loan from the Haganah mission in Vienna, sailed to Palestine, and Paula stayed in Płońsk for nearly a year.[12]

When Paula had first arrived at Reb Avigdor's with her children, only Michael, who sold newspapers and was trying to save money, was living there with his wife and daughter. Rivka and her husband lived in Lódź, and the war had trapped Zippora and her husband in Russia. Abraham, his wife, Tauba, and their three children had also been caught in Russia by the war, but in July, three months after Paula's arrival, they returned to Reb Avigdor and Zvia's home.

With three daughters-in-law under his roof Reb Avigdor had not a moment's peace. He wished that at least his six grandchildren could enjoy equal treatment, but this, too, was impossible, because Paula was able to buy more for her children than her sisters-in-law could for theirs. The irritability of the children, and as a result that of their mothers, worsened when Michael's wife abandoned him, taking their daughter with her. Michael, forlorn, could no longer stand the other children's crying and scolded them fiercely.

In this troubled atmosphere each of the remaining daughters-in-law claimed seniority: Paula because of her New York background and her position as wife of the most successful and renowned of Reb Avigdor's sons, Tauba by virtue of her age and marriage to Reb Avigdor's first-born son. Paula, who demanded that Tauba treat her with respect, treated Tauba like a servant girl.

Relations went from bad to worse, from a spat over whose turn it was to wash the dishes to quarrels over money and possessions. Paula made no bones about her feelings in letters to Ben-Gurion. When Abraham asked Ben-Gurion for money for his daughter's studies, Paula wrote, "Don't send any money to Abraham, he has gold and silver and has more than we have." She also accused Abraham and Tauba of stealing a suit of clothes and a gold pin. The charge was absurd, yet on the basis of it, she continued to plead. "If you have any respect for me and the children don't send them anything." Finally, out of fear that Ben-Gurion would have to support them, she insisted that he refuse to help Abraham and his family immigrate to Palestine. "I will not have them in my house one day," she wrote.

To these supplications, which did not reach him until he returned to Palestine, Ben-Gurion paid no heed, and in his letters to Reb Avigdor continued to ask about his brothers and sisters and their families, promising to support Abraham's daughter, who was named Sheindel after their mother, until she finished school and came to Palestine. In one letter he sent her five pounds.[13]

On July 19, 1921, fourteen months after leaving Palestine, Ben-Gurion arrived at the port of Jaffa and checked into the Barash Hotel in Tel Aviv. The most important changes that had taken place during his absence were the establishment of the British Mandate and the government of Palestine, headed by British High Commissioner Sir Herbert Samuel, and its civil administration, which had replaced the military one. Another important innovation was the Histadrut (General Federation of Jewish Labor), which had been founded in December 1920.

Achdut ha-Avodah, seeking to counter the fragmentation of Jewish community life so characteristic of the Diaspora, had campaigned constantly for unification, and Ha-Poel ha-Tzair, its prime rival, could not deny that it shared the same goal of recreating in Palestine a working Jewish nation or that much benefit would derive from the joining of their resources. Finally, after much pressure, and moved by the heroic death of Joseph Trumpeldor in Tel Hai, Ha-Poel ha-Tzair accepted as the dead man's legacy his proposal to form a general federation of labor. It agreed to join a Histadrut (organization) that would pool all Eretz-Israeli labor resources and create and direct trade unions, but would also honor the political and cultural identities of its member parties. It also agreed that this federation would direct a good part of its resources to facilitating the absorption of new immigrants. While this did not fully meet Achdut ha-Avodah's desire to create an all-embracing association of Jewish labor, it accepted Ha-Poel ha-Tzair's conditions and the Histadrut was formed with a mandate to set up agricultural settlements, industrial cooperatives, and other constructive projects.

From its inception the Histadrut was the strongest, and largest, organization in the Yishuv. The other sectors — independent farmers, professionals, craftsmen, merchants, and the entrepreneurial class — were not yet organized, at least not to the same degree. But no doubt because they saw themselves as threatened by the Histadrut, this event hastened the development of their own organizations. From the moment of the Histadrut's creation, the Yishuv was divided into three major sectors: the Histadrut; the non-Histadrut, sometimes called the civilian sector; and the religious, which grouped under the name of the Torah all believers — workers, merchants, and rabbis.

Even though the organization was an exciting development, Ben-Gurion did not become a candidate for the Histadrut Executive Committee at the organization's council that convened in Haifa at the beginning of August, but instead deliberately chose Achdut ha-Avodah as his principal sphere of activity. His choice was ideological: the Histadrut did not abolish parties, Achdut ha-Avodah's foremost goal. Ben-Gurion perceived that the Histadrut, by its very existence, would inevitably drive Achdut ha-Avodah to become a party just like any other, and to him this spelled its death. Ben-Gurion made up his mind to take Achdut ha-Avodah into his own hands to rekindle its old spirit, which would in turn inspire the Histadrut and direct it toward Achdut ha-Avodah's original goals. A powerful additional motive was his desire to complete an unfinished job, implementing Achdut ha-Avodah's merger with Ha-Poel ha-Tzair, which, he knew, could be achieved only by working within Achdut ha-Avodah.[14]

In carrying out this program Ben-Gurion had no need to fear any power struggles in Achdut ha-Avodah. Indeed, his colleagues were in the midst of an identity crisis, struggling to define the rationale of their organization, which was becoming, against its will, a party in every sense of the word, and they gladly welcomed Ben-Gurion's readiness to assume a central role. At an Achdut ha-Avodah executive committee session that took place only three days after Ben-Gurion's return to Palestine, Itzhak Tabenkin proposed, as he had in 1919, that Ben-Gurion be elected sole secretary general, and this time Katznelson agreed with him; only one member of the executive committee opposed the proposal. Everything seemed to be progressing smoothly, for what could be simpler than charging Ben-Gurion with a task he wanted anyway? But Ben-Gurion said he would take the top position on one condition, which — following the code of political behavior prevailing among the Second Aliyah, according to which one did not speak plainly of one's motives — they had to divine by piecing together his casual remarks and by reading between the lines of an article he published in *Kunteres*. Ben-Gurion's ideology and private ambitions were equally embodied in this condition.

Its ideological side was based on a two-stage program. First, Achdut ha-Avodah would become a labor army, or a transitional commune — and there could be little doubt whom Ben-Gurion had in mind as its leader — grounded in military discipline. All members would have to obey the labor army's orders "concerning location, nature, and arrangement of the work." The labor army would then prepare for and direct the second stage, in which Achdut ha-Avodah's membership would grow so much that it would encompass most members of the Histadrut, which in turn would revamp itself into an even larger commune of producers and consumers alike. It would become one entity, directing and handling all nonpersonal affairs of its members, collectively and individually, both in the city and in the country, assuming ownership of all means of production, and taking over all channels of consumption, according to the rule of the socialist state. All Histadrut members would hand over their entire income, or produce, in the case of the farmers, to the Histadrut's treasury, which in turn would pay them, in money or in kind, according to their needs and look after their housing, health, education, and so on. "The *kvutsas* . . . contribute a maximum of grain, milk, etc., to the Histadrut, the tailors and shoemakers also contribute. Instead of a salary, everyone receives their needs from the Histadrut management." Later Ben-Gurion proposed a third and final stage in which the Histadrut commune would encompass all of Palestinian Jewry. For this final transition he coined a slogan: "From class to nation" — from the Histadrut commune to the socialist republic.

This plan was not entirely new, for as a youth in Warsaw in 1905, he had sought admittance with his friends to Menahem Ussishkin's Labor Army, which was to be open to all young Zionist men willing to enlist for at least three years, and to do all work in Palestine that they were told to do by the Zionist high command. The idea of a labor army, of voluntary acceptance of authority, stayed with Ben-Gurion all his political life and was the foundation upon which all his plans for the fulfillment of Zionism were built.

That this idea was not exclusively his own was already apparent, for in the fall of 1920 others had actually put it into practice, while Ben-Gurion was in London, in founding the Labor and Defense Legion, known as the Labor Legion. From its inception it constituted itself as a commune whose members contracted to pave roads and carry out other public works all over Palestine. Within the commune were separate groups, each comprising a company or a subcommune of the Legion. Furthermore, the Labor Legion held to the same two-stage plan, its stated aim being "the building of the land by the creation of a general commune of the Jewish workers of Palestine"; it intended one day to become the Histadrut itself, just as Ben-Gurion envisaged Achdut ha-Avodah's doing. Recognizing that the Labor Legion's plan was absolutely identical with his own, Ben-Gurion told Achdut ha-Avodah, "This idea, whose foundation is laid in my proposal, is not one individual's idea. . . . The cream of the new immigrants have already set out on this path and have organized themselves as the Labor Legion."[15]

Soon after his return to Palestine, Ben-Gurion visited the companies of the Labor Legion in different parts of the country to make the acquaintance of their members, young single men and women who were filled with the fervor of the Russian Revolution. They were people after his own heart: living in army surplus tents, they suffered from hunger and malaria; moved by great idealism and a will to sacrifice their young lives for the cause, they worked by day and sang and danced by night. Since many of them joined Achdut ha-Avodah, he and they easily found a common language, sharing the belief that the only sure and fast way to realize Zionism was to build a new society, by way of the commune and the labor army.

On the personal side, his plan stemmed from a need for absolute identification with the cause for which he worked, which could happen only if he had a hand in the creation of the body representing that cause and if he himself stood at its head. Neither the Histadrut nor the Labor Legion met these requirements. Both had been established in his absence, and the Histadrut was forbidden to engage in political activity. Finally, the Labor Legion had already found its leader in the young, charismatic Menahem Elkind, who personified it. Playing second fiddle was never a possibility for Ben-Gurion.

Achdut ha-Avodah, on the other hand, had come to life at his initiative and he was recognized as one of its two creators; that it could hardly make do without him was obvious from its decline. He felt that if it accepted his condition he could breathe new life into it and bring it to full flower in a brilliant future; as a labor army it would swallow up the smaller Labor Legion, then expand to become the great commune of all Jewish workers in Palestine, namely, the Histadrut commune. This development would be an entirely new enterprise, the fruit of his own labors, and his place as its leader would be only natural.

Ben-Gurion's condition, then, was that if within two months an Achdut ha-Avodah convention would convene and accept his program — for only a convention had the authority to transform Achdut ha-Avodah into a commune or labor army — he would agree to serve as secretary general. Meanwhile he assumed this office ad hoc, signing letters and circulars as secretary general in anticipation of positive results. When it became clear, however, that a convention could not take place in time, owing to the absence of prominent members, including Berl Katznelson and Itzhak Ben-Zvi, who had gone to Karlsbad to attend the Zionist Congress, Ben-Gurion settled for a council, which met on October 1 in Jaffa and listened to him elaborate his program before reaching a resolution.[16]

The first argument Ben-Gurion presented to support his idea was more efficient use and development of national and Histadrut resources. He considered the existence of individual cooperative economic units, with their profit-oriented management, not to mention private enterprises, an agonizing waste of the national and Histadrut capital invested in them. A general commune, on the other hand, would utilize and develop these resources inestimably better by making large-scale calculations as to how much to spend on individual and collective needs, that is, how much to invest in development. It would then be able to draw up a budget for the absorption of additional members to determine the number of new immigrants Palestine required.

Indeed, increased immigration was the basis of this program, as of Ben-Gurion's Zionist concept in general. A unified economy would better answer this need, and the labor army would impose military discipline to induce its members to receive new ones into their ranks. If any part of his program could gain Achdut ha-Avodah's acceptance, he thought, it was the potential for increasing immigration.[17]

The deliberations of this council and of Achdut ha-Avodah's executive committee left little doubt, however, that Ben-Gurion's colleagues were not enthusiastic about it. They regarded the axiom of voluntary obedience as too extreme. Some considered the plan a communist utopia, and others thought it was merely unrealistic or unsuitable to the public at large. Shmuel Yavnieli, despite his closeness to Ben-Gurion, thought that workers who were capable of grasping the commune idea and would not join it willingly should be taken into consideration. One council delegate directed Ben-Gurion's attention to the fact that the mass of workers was not homogeneous, that not everyone was imbued with the cooperative ideal. What would happen to those the commune rejected? Would the Histadrut expel them? It was also noted that the program did not mention Ha-Poel ha-Tzair, which opposed socialism on principle and would object to the labor army for ideological reasons. David Remez, an executive committee member and one of the six signatories of Achdut ha-Avodah's founding manifesto, put it best when he commented that "Ben-Gurion's doctrine is not encompassing enough" and that "any attempt to apply a specific system to Achdut ha-Avodah, even communism," did not do justice to its ideals.

The council, which the executive committee had called despite their reservations, because to refuse Ben-Gurion's demand would surely have caused him to resign at once, was unable to reach a decision for the same reason that had made it impossible to call a convention. The delegates to the Zionist Congress had not yet returned, and without their attendance, especially Katznelson's, it was impossible to make such a radical decision. Therefore Ben-Gurion's proposal was not put to a vote.[18] In response he resigned the office of secretary general, and all pleas and arguments failed to change his mind. Even the argument that as chief exponent of military discipline and voluntary obedience he should submit to majority rule did not sway him. He simply replied that from the start he had accepted the post for two months only. Even though he did not explicitly say so, it was clear that Ben-Gurion was confronting the council with an either-or proposition: either Achdut ha-Avodah accepted his proposal or he would resign. This, in fact, was their first stinging encounter with the either-or approach that Ben-Gurion resorted to again in the future to pressure them into accepting his ideas.

It seemed that his central role in Achdut ha-Avodah had come to an end. As if foreseeing the rejection of his program, he had begun to prepare for the Mandate's bar examination even before the council convened. Paula was very happy to hear that he would make a living as a lawyer. "About your examinations . . . I hope you will pass," she wrote him, "and then we will do everything for our children. It is fine to be independent." It is worth noting, too, that even though he advocated the commune as the sole solution for Achdut ha-Avodah, the Histadrut, and Zionist fulfillment, he himself preferred a legal office to a cooperative kvutsa.[19]

14

Reb Avigdor Immigrates to Palestine

SUDDENLY DAVID BEN-GURION changed his mind. He stopped preparing for the bar exams a month after starting, and on November 8, 1921, the Histadrut council elected him to both the executive committee and the secretariat. For fifteen years, until he became chairman of the Jewish Agency, the Histadrut would be his main area of activity.

This abrupt change was probably the result of several factors. It is reasonable to assume, first, that after cooling down a bit, Ben-Gurion realized that turning Achdut ha-Avodah into an army overnight was no simple matter. Second, since he believed that "historical providence has charged the working class of Palestine with the responsibility for immigration and building up the land,"[1] he could hardly fulfill his aspirations to leadership from a law office. To do that he would have to remain firmly in the midst of the working community. Most of all, he simply did not give up easily. It would have been easier to pry a bone from a bulldog than a true concession from Ben-Gurion. He was not unwilling to compromise, but his compromises, always the result of recognition of unaccommodating reality, were calculated to enable him to take a further step later. Although he was, in such cases, willing to strike a bargain, once it was done his compromise became his new hard line, pursued relentlessly. When he could not achieve what he wanted through Achdut ha-Avodah, he turned to the Histadrut as his tool to organize the workers and their economy as he saw fit.

This characteristic of being able suddenly to let go of a previously absolute and final position would manifest itself again and again in the course of Ben-Gurion's public life. In November 1921, without conceding his objective, he devised a different means of reaching it. Having made up his mind to join the Histadrut Executive Committee (HEC),* Ben-Gurion proceeded to pursue his plan with even more vigor from that position. He proposed it as a central issue for discussion at Achdut ha-Avodah's branch meetings, councils, and third convention, as well as at the councils and second convention of the Histadrut. In the course of the discussions the program's name kept changing: it was the General Commune of Eretz-Israeli Workers, then the New Society, then the Society of Workers; in the summer of 1922, an exasperated Ben-Gurion exclaimed, "Cooperative or commune — or any other name you want."[2] Whatever its name, the program's opponents had no chance of convincing Ben-Gurion to drop it from the agendas of Achdut ha-Avodah and the Histadrut, and in 1923, with its rough edges smoothed from all the battering, the name Society of Workers was accepted.

Therefore, Ben-Gurion allowed himself to be elected to the Histadrut secretariat. The November 1921 council accepted two of his proposals: to move the HEC and all the other Histadrut institutions from Tel Aviv to Jerusalem and to conduct a full and precise census of Histadrut members. Ben-Gurion argued that his proposal was designed "to concentrate Histadrut affairs" in one place, Jerusalem, the seat of the Mandatory government, the Zionist headquarters in Palestine, and the national institutions that served the entire Yishuv and the Zionist movement: the Zionist Executive, the National Council elected by the Elected Assembly as the internal governing body of the Yishuv, the Elected Assembly, and the Chief Rabbinate. Joseph Sprinzak, who had been re-elected to the secretariat, that same November became director of the Zionist Executive's department of labor in the Zionist office in Jerusalem. Nevertheless, the move was not made hastily, and throughout November, December, and January, Ben-Gurion shuttled back and forth between the Barash Hotel in Tel Aviv and the Varshavski Hotel in Jerusalem.[3]

He finally moved to Jerusalem on February 2, 1922. Though he had few personal belongings, he hired a truck, since his books were quite heavy. At 11:00 A.M. they set off without a hitch, but the truck's motor gave out on the uphill stretches, and they didn't reach Jerusalem until seven o'clock that evening, six hours late.

Ben-Gurion spent the night arranging his books in the two-room flat

---

* To distinguish it from other executive committees, that of the Histadrut will be referred to as the HEC.

he had rented, for five Egyptian pounds* a month, on the ground floor of a two-story house in the Yegia Kapaim quarter, and continued this task the following evening. On March 20 he noted in his diary that his personal library amounted to 775 volumes: 340 in English, 219 in German, 140 in Hebrew, 29 in French, 13 in Arabic, 7 in Russian, 7 in Latin, 2 in Turkish, 2 in Greek, and 15 dictionaries in assorted languages — his addition was off by one. On this foundation, laid in New York and London, he built a collection which, on the day of his death in 1973, contained more than 18,000 volumes and 5,000 periodicals. Throughout his life this library was his prized possession, and he tended it with great care and love.

In 1922 he had divided the collection into three sections. The first covered geology, archaeology, history, geography, ancient Middle Eastern history, biblical research, and Semitic linguistics. The second housed books on Judaica, Hebrew literature, Jewish philosophy and history, Chassidism, Kabbalah, and Zionism. The third, covering political economics, socialism, the labor movement, and workers' rights, included a small supplement of books on psychology and philosophy and a few volumes of belles-lettres.

The first section contained the largest number of books. Most of them were written by Christians, German and British scholars connected with institutes researching Palestine and the Scriptures. Ben-Gurion also bought journals published since the beginning of the previous century, such as *ZPDV* and *Mun,* put out by the German Society of Research on Palestine; *Palästina Jahrbuch* of the British-German Institute in Jerusalem; and *Quarterly,* published by the British Palestine Exploration Fund. He collected books by Julius Wellhausen and Hermann Leberecht Strack, orientalists and Old Testament scholars; Gustaf Dalman, linguist and scholar of Palestine; Eduard Meyer, historian of antiquity; Rudolf Kittel, Old Testament scholar; Paul Kahle, orientalist and scholar of the traditional annotation to the Scriptures; Emil Kautzsch, Semitic linguist and Old Testament scholar; Hermann Guthe, Temple Mount archaeologist; and Claude Conder, who headed the British mission that mapped and made archaeological and topographical surveys of Palestine. He also bought works by the Jewish scientists Hirsch Hildesheimer, scholar of Palestinian geography, and Samuel Krauss, scholar of the Talmud and Bible.

---

* From 1919 to 1927 the Egyptian pound was the legal currency. The Palestinian pound, which came into being in November 1927, was then equal to the British pound, valued at $5. On the day of the changeover, the Egyptian pound was exchanged for 1.026 Palestinian pounds; a Palestinian pound equaled 100 piasters, and one piaster equaled 10 mils.

The second section included both the Jerusalem and Babylonian Talmuds and the works of Maimonides, Yehuda ha-Levi, Ibn Ezra, Ibn Paquda, and Saadiah Gaon; historiography, studies on Maimonides, and comparative studies of Jewish manuscripts and Jewish philosophy, including the books of Simon Bernfeld. There were also books on the Kabbalah — *Ha-Zohar* with *Tikkunei ha-Zohar* and commentaries, and *Sefer ha-Yezirah,* an ancient discourse on cosmology and cosmogony, which occupied a central position in Jewish mysticism. The collection of Judaica included books by Moshe Moritz Steinschneider, an Arabist and one of the founders of modern Jewish scholarship; the historian Moshe Moritz Goodman, a scholar of medieval literature, Midrash, and Old Testament; Vilmos Becher, Simon Dubnow, of course, and others. Ben-Gurion owned Nahum Sokolow's *History of Zionism,* Shlomo Citron's *Life of Herzl* and other works on Zionism, and collected the Hebrew periodical *Ha-Tekufah* (The Season).

The third section included books by Karl Marx, Karl Kautsky, Franz Mehring, Werner Sombart, Franz Oppenheimer, and other writers on socialism. It is worth noting that in these years Ben-Gurion, who not long since had intended to become a lawyer, did not acquire a single book on jurisprudence.

In early 1922 Ben-Gurion's appetite for book collecting was further whetted by the combination of rampant inflation in Germany and an acquaintance with Gusta Strumpf, a young immigrant from Munich who worked in a room adjoining his at the HEC. Ben-Gurion was able to buy German books at bargain prices through her parents, ordering them from catalogues he found in the bookstore of Karaman the Greek. In February he bought Eduard Meyer's three-volume *Geschichte des Altertums* (Ancient History), published in 1884, for pennies, as well as Samuel Curtiss's book on Semitic religions, *Ursemitische Religion im Volksleben Heutigen Orients,* published in 1903, and two books by Julius Wellhausen.[4]

Ben-Gurion was also doing his utmost to prepare his apartment for his family's arrival. To give it a homey feel and appearance, he hired a mechanic to fix the sewing machine Paula had brought with her from America and a carpenter to put up bookshelves, and he had the clock fixed and bought a Primus stove and other household articles. He ate lunch at the Workers' Kitchen, but usually prepared breakfast and dinner himself until one February day of "tempest, rain, and hail," when he felt low in spirit. To fortify himself he indulged in the luxury of a bottle of red wine, but he could not shake off his loneliness and began to eat all his meals at the Workers' Kitchen.

On receipt of a cable announcing Paula's departure from Trieste with the children, he began to count the days and hours. On the day before their arrival he hired a maid to give the apartment a thorough cleaning and ordered fish for the Sabbath. On Wednesday morning, April 5, 1922, he had his shoes shined before taking the train to Lod, where he waited with bated breath for the train from Egypt to pull in, fearing they might not have managed to board it in time. When he saw them step out of the railroad car he nearly shouted, "They've arrived!" He watched them closely as they descended to the platform, ready for the worst; Paula's letters relating their distress in Płońsk and pleading for rescue had included extensive descriptions of the children's suffering. Of one-and-a-half-year-old Amos, for example, she had written, "Poor child nothing left of him. . . . He doesn't walk and doesn't talk yet because he is always sick." When at last he saw them, Ben-Gurion probably breathed a sigh of relief. "Geula is marvelous. Amos has an unhealthy coloring, but his body structure is strong. Paula herself looks thin and fatigued," he told his diary.

They took the late train to Jerusalem, and the next morning Paula sent Ben-Gurion shopping. Soap, lots of soap, was first on the list, then laundry powder and enough kerosene to heat large amounts of water. Later she asked for large amounts of milk, butter, cocoa, potatoes, and meat and ordered him to buy flour, eggs, almonds, wine, and delicatessen items to offer their expected guests on the Sabbath. While Paula energetically took charge of the household, for which Ben-Gurion allotted her two, sometimes two and a half, Egyptian pounds a week, he kept the record of expenses, which would no longer consist of entries for only herring and tea.

In Płońsk, Paula had begun preparing for her new home in Palestine, stitching coverlets, blanket cases, and clothes for every member of the family. For Ben-Gurion she bought blue material for a suit and enough cloth for six shirts and knitted socks for him. The list she gave Ben-Gurion that first day also included household essentials: glasses, an armoire, a table, and two beds. The family was inconvenienced until their belongings arrived from London, but the apartment still lacked elementary furnishings. In the absence of a sink, dishes were washed in a basin that sat on the kitchen floor, and not until January 1923 did Ben-Gurion bring home a heater, which he had bought on credit guaranteed by the HEC.[5]

Where had he found the money to help his family in Płońsk, bring them to Palestine, furnish an apartment in Jerusalem, and, above all, buy valuable books? As a start, he had a windfall: his discharge allowance of 16.61 Egyptian pounds from the British army, sent by the War Office in early 1921 and lost in the mail, suddenly appeared in April 1922. Second, his monthly salary of 25 Egyptian pounds from the HEC, despite the general postwar shortages and the rise in the cost of living, was a good one, from which he might have saved a handsome sum had it been paid on time. But the HEC treasury was empty; instead of regular wages it distributed small advances in arrears. At the Histadrut council in January 1922, Ben-Gurion proposed salary cuts for the HEC employees and a standardized pay scale for all Histadrut personnel, elected staff and salaried employees alike. His proposal was accepted and his salary accordingly reduced by 6 pounds a month, which obviously could not have met Ben-Gurion's needs; credit suggested itself as the only way to cope with them. The loans he obtained, before and after receiving his discharge allowance, totaled 25 Egyptian pounds, and that was only the beginning.

Unperturbed by the mounting loans, Paula set about arranging her living quarters. In one windowless room, whose walls were lined with books, she put the master bed; it would serve as a study for Ben-Gurion during the day and their bedroom at night. The room with a window was for the children. She put a couch and table in the entry hall, making it a dining and family room and, when necessary, a guest room as well. She had cold running water in the kitchen and cooked and heated water on a kerosene burner and the Primus stove. Laundry was boiled in a vat, rubbed on a washboard, and scrubbed in a tub, all in the courtyard. This was the lot of all the housewives in the neighborhood, but Paula had brought with her standards of order and cleanliness that were, given the means at her disposal, beyond her reach. Consequently, housework hung like a millstone around her neck.

When Geula began attending kindergarten Paula sent Amos, four months shy of two years old, with her. She hoped to make things easier on herself by leaving her mornings free except for bringing him milk and juice at ten o'clock. But to give it to him she had to catch him. The disturbances that ensued met with increasing resentment on the part of the teacher and the other children's parents. The teacher protested directly to Ben-Gurion, but his appeals to Paula were of no avail, and Amos continued to attend kindergarten, with her hot on his heels.

Since there was no improvement in the state of HEC finances, Ben-Gurion's salary was never paid on time, and since he was not always able to secure a loan, Paula needed miracles to make ends meet. Worse, Ben-Gurion's bibliomania did not abate simply because he had not a piaster in his pocket, and whenever he got some money his purchases in Germany came first. He also sent money to his family in Płońsk from time to time. All this meant that Paula's weekly budget was sometimes short, and her own debts piled up. At the beginning of June the milkman stopped delivering to her until she settled her account. At the grocery she became etched in people's memories as a shrew who demanded credit from the shopkeeper on the basis of being Ben-Gurion's wife.

Nevertheless, Ben-Gurion was able to settle into a routine. At the end of the summer he went abroad, marking the start of what would become the normal course of their life together: each year he left the country for an extended period of time — a few weeks or more — while Paula managed the household and looked after the family. When he was away she was dependent on his friends in the HEC, who fought for her to receive advances from the nearly empty treasury. In 1923, when Ben-Gurion was absent from August to December, she received sixty Egyptian pounds against his salary in fifteen separate payments.[6]

Reb Avigdor's family in Płońsk had been impatiently following Ben-Gurion's move to Jerusalem and subsequent homemaking. It was high time, they thought, that Ben-Gurion provide them with a short cut to Palestine. On his sixty-third birthday, in January 1920, Reb Avigdor had written to his children, "scattered in every corner of the world," that he longed to celebrate his sixty-fifth birthday in Palestine "with all my children [in attendance]." These included Abraham Lefkovitz, for the war had left him, the only rich member of the family, penniless, and Lefkovitz, brokenhearted, died shortly afterward, leaving Rivka destitute. So she, too, pinned her hopes on Ben-Gurion's bringing her to Palestine, describing her distress to him in "a heart-rending letter." Though he felt "her awful situation tugging at my heartstrings," Ben-Gurion doubted, he wrote his father, if "she could work or find suitable work," and it would be better if she stayed in Łódź.

The family had not recovered from this calamity when, in February 1921, Zippora was widowed in the Ukraine with two small children. She also asked Ben-Gurion to rescue her by arranging for her to come to Palestine. "No one else in our family is as dear and close to me as she is," Ben-Gurion wrote to his father, swearing to do "all that a man can do. . . . I will share my bread with her and adopt her children and be a father to them." Zippora and her children never forgot those words.

Reb Avigdor's anxiety was no less than his children's. At his age he found it difficult to cope with the economic and legal changes brought about by the war and Poland's newly won independence. In the new state his services as a petition writer were no longer required, and he was hard pressed to make a living. Eretz Israel was no longer just a life-long dream for him, but an immediate necessity. Although Rivka, Zippora, and Reb Avigdor were the urgent cases, Ben-Gurion's brothers Abraham and Michael, who had remarried, and their families were no

better off. However, since even in better days they had always seemed
to Ben-Gurion to be especially insolvent and in need of help, their
postwar plight was nothing new.

Ben-Gurion felt unable to come to everyone's rescue at once; he had
to choose. Should he first help those dearest to him or those most in
need? His guideline was clear and simple. The first to come would be
those able to earn their living; then, with their help, the others would
follow. Feeling that Zippora, as a widow, deserved top priority, he
advised that she and her two small sons, Arieh and Emanuel, and
Abraham's first-born, Benjamin, would be the first to come. This
meant securing the immigration certificates without which they could
not enter Palestine.* To obtain them for his family he had to use his
influence while attending the annual Zionist conference and the
Zionist Action Committee session, which met in Karlsbad and Berlin,
respectively, during August, September, and October 1922. He was
successful, and Benjamin, Zippora, and her two children were issued
certificates.[7]

The second step entailed financial assistance, at least for fare. As
Zippora was not in need of money, Ben-Gurion promised Benjamin in
August that he would shortly send him money to buy a ticket. But then
Arieh fell from a train in Russia and broke his leg, and Zippora had to
spend the little money she had saved working as a nurse. Swallowing
her pride, she asked Ben-Gurion for a short-term loan. "As you see,"
she wrote him in Berlin at the end of September, "I am now totally dependent on you, on your good will, and on your ability."

But before Ben-Gurion received Zippora's letter, he had been
tempted and fallen at the sight of all the important books he could buy
in Berlin at less than half price. In only seven days, from the third to
the ninth of September, he bought seventy-one books for three Egyptian pounds, and in all shipped home three crates of them. His passion
overwhelmed him to the point where he had no money left and had to
ask that funds be wired from Palestine for his journey home.

Unable to make good on the promise he had made to Benjamin
without going deeper into debt, he got credit from the Palestine office
in Vienna, increasing his debt by eight pounds four shillings. After
his expenditures in Berlin, he had to borrow five pounds ($25) from a
friend. Checking his accounts, he reckoned he could send Zippora no
more than two pounds, and he explained to his father, "To my sorrow I
cannot send any more. The expenses here are more than I originally

---

* The certificates, based on its "economic absorptive capacity," were issued by the Palestinian government according to quotas — schedules — decided twice a year. Their distribution was in the hands of the Palestine offices of the World Zionist Organization scattered throughout Europe.

expected and I am left without the means to return, though I thought when leaving Palestine that the funds I had taken would suffice for my return as well."

Ben-Gurion's empty pockets became Zippora's determining factor in making her travel arrangements. She sailed to Palestine at the beginning of 1923, taking only six-year-old Arieh and leaving three-and-a-half-year-old Emanuel in the care of Rivka, who had moved to their father's home from Lódź. Zippora had reasoned that since Ben-Gurion could not support her and both her children, she would manage better in Palestine without a baby to tie her down. Adults understood this, but how does one explain to a small child that his mother has abandoned him in favor of his elder brother? Until 1925, when at age six he immigrated with Reb Avigdor, Emanuel was told repeatedly that his mother had had to follow doctor's orders, because only the sun in Palestine could heal Arieh's leg, and that "since she had to make a living all by herself she couldn't take along two children."

Emanuel later described his reunion with his mother in Palestine. "They left me on the bed on which a woman was sitting. The woman began pleading, 'I'm your mother,' and I didn't know what to make of it. It took me a while to react. She cried but there was no answer from me. It is ingrained in my memory." Apparently the medical explanation for the preference given his brother had not put his mind entirely at ease, for while he was still a boy, his mother found it necessary to offer him another explanation, which was also untrue: that Ben-Gurion had been able to procure immigration certificates only for her and Arieh.

The separation from his mother left deep scars in Emanuel. Despite extraordinary gifts he was never able to settle down and raise a family, or even to earn a steady living. Until his death in 1982 at sixty-three, he lived alone in a rented room in Tel Aviv and barely supported himself by writing excellent books and articles on aviation, using as his office a café whose owners overlooked his tab. It never occurred to Emanuel, or, it seems, to his mother, to wonder if his life might have taken a different course had Ben-Gurion not spent all his money in Berlin. Ben-Gurion, brother and uncle, was the light of their lives. Zippora read her children the letter he had written to Reb Avigdor several times, and Emanuel remembered it by heart until his dying day. Although their last name was Koritni, Zippora and both her children changed it to Ben-Gurion, and Emanuel signed his books and articles Emanuel Ben-Gurion.[8]

The rule Ben-Gurion had laid down for the order in which his family would immigrate did not take his father's feelings into account. Since Reb Avigdor's logic told him that his son could afford to set up his father in comfort and in honor, he began to suspect that Ben-Gurion was putting off his father's immigration because he was afraid that Reb Avigdor would become a nuisance. Sensing this suspicion Ben-Gurion wrote his father in July 1924, restating his position more clearly.

I know that you are suspicious of me, but I promise you again that my hope and desire to see you settled in Palestine have not weakened even for a single day. It will be a great day when I can welcome you to our land. Were I privately employed instead of part of a movement and burdened with so much responsibility, I would have made your coming to Palestine possible long ago, as in such a case I would have directed all of my energies to this matter. But I have been charged with a weighty duty which I must fulfill, a duty which demands all of my thought and effort, which involves great responsibility and which leaves me bereft of personal freedom. I haven't the power nor the freedom of action to do what I *want* nor *how* I want to do it — only to do what I must in view of the movement's needs. On account of this I am unable to properly fulfill my obligations to my wife and children, and to you too, Father. This is the one and only reason why my bringing you to Palestine has thus far been prevented. . . .

I must take this opportunity to explain a paradoxical situation to you so that you will understand the state of things. My position in Palestine is such that every public institution, Histadrut or Zionist, is open to me, and each one would happily grant any request I might make to provide employment for whomever I request. This is precisely the hindrance to my using my influence for people close to me. . . . I am fighting, in the labor movement and the Zionist movement, against the customary nepotism, and I almost physically cannot make use of this system, even when I have the absolute authority to do so. That which I could do for a perfect stranger I cannot do for a relation. I do not want anyone to look [askance] at someone dear to me, who got a job only because of my intervention. I wouldn't want anyone in Palestine to think — after you had begun working in some institution — that you were working there not because you were fit for the job, but only because of me.

Therefore, I want you to be in Palestine long enough for people to know you, not as Ben-Gurion's father, but as yourself, and then you will get a job in your own right, not mine.

He then renewed his suggestion that his father sell the house in Płońsk; with the £300 to £400 he would get for it he would "be able to come to Palestine without any doubts or misgivings. It is imperative that you be able to support yourself in Palestine for at least a year. . . . I also hope you will be able to find a position appropriate to your qualifications and talents."

This letter exemplifies Ben-Gurion's directness, bordering on obtuseness; blinded by his principles, he had no sense of what and to whom he was writing. How could he have expected his father, at sixty-seven, to prove himself at a new job so he would be recognized in his own right, as though he were a young man just starting out?

Furthermore, Ben-Gurion had decreed that Reb Avigdor immigrate alone and leave his wife behind until he was settled and able to bring her to him. Practically, this meant leaving her with her relatives, since after the sale of the house she would have neither shelter nor means. In fact, after Reb Avigdor set off for Palestine she went to stay with her daughter in Lódź, where Ben-Gurion found her, in April 1926, "old and sick and lying in bed." Moreover, selling the house would dispossess Abraham and Michael, who remained in Płońsk without a firm financial base, of their maternal inheritance.[9]

This was pain enough for Reb Avigdor, and Ben-Gurion's rejection of nepotism only sharpened it. The fact was that Ben-Gurion did not fear for his father as much as for himself, lest people say he was overstepping his bounds in providing members of his family with jobs. Wrapped up in himself and his vision, he was unaffected by the normal human impulse to make exceptions for family members, to give them special treatment, with love and an outstretched hand. Since at the same time that he identified totally with the Zionist cause, and felt its needs intuitively, he was quite insensitive to the feelings and needs of individuals — be they wife, children, or colleagues — the fact that he was not helping his father did not affect him. The precedence of the national over the individual welfare came very naturally to him. Perhaps this example serves best to illustrate that his weakness as a person was his strength as a political leader.

Reb Avigdor began making arrangements to sell his house, and in March 1925 Ben-Gurion sent him an entry visa. Four months later Reb Avigdor arrived in Palestine with Emanuel; his wife was to join him two years later. Rivka and her brother Abraham and their families came in 1931, and Michael and his in 1933.

In a February 1922 letter Ben-Gurion promised his father that in his son's home Reb Avigdor would find "not only a loving and devoted son, but a loving and devoted daughter as well, as I know Paula better than you." On July 13, 1925, when he finally welcomed his father at the port of Haifa, Ben-Gurion was greatly excited, although he had his emotions so well in control that in his diary he noted briefly, "Father arrived." Eager to have Reb Avigdor live with him — and naively believing Paula's assurances that this was her wish as well — he took him to Jerusalem the next day.

But it turned out to be only a visit, for a few days with Paula convinced Reb Avigdor that he was not welcome. He chose to live with

Zippora, who was a nurse at the Histadrut Sick Fund in Haifa, where Ben-Gurion secured a job for him in the accounts department of Solel Boneh, the Histadrut construction concern. Most likely Ben-Gurion understood, on seeing his father face to face, how foolish he had been to expect this elderly man to manage by himself, and perhaps he went out of his way to make up for the coldness of Paula's reception of him. Reb Avigdor would one day tell his grandchildren that Paula never offered him so much as a glass of tea.

Unlike the rest of the family, Zippora had not met Paula in Płońsk and looked forward to their relationship with high hopes. Before setting out for Palestine Zippora wrote her warmly, as Ben-Gurion's beloved sister, "Let us be friends forever, as I've always dreamed I would be with David's wife." But shortly after their first meeting in Jerusalem, Zippora knew her dream would never come true. A proud woman, tall and strong, Zippora needed neither Paula's charity nor shelter in her home. As a graduate nurse, she quickly found work at the Sick Fund and rented her own apartment, first in Jerusalem and then in Haifa. Though she did not see Paula through the eye of the needy, she maintained from the beginning that Paula would not give any member of the family the time of day. In October 1923 she wrote Paula, "It seems that you haven't any feeling for family kinship."

Nor were Ben-Gurion's kin the only ones Paula alienated. In March 1924 her younger sister, Pessia, came to Palestine. Her elder sister had written that Pessia "hasn't anyone in Palestine other than you. You should look after her, you don't know what it's like to be alone. . . . Try to be family to her." Yet Paula met Pessia, twelve years her junior, whom she had not seen since 1908, coldly. She took her into her home, but assigned her cleaning chores and treated her more like a maid than a sister. Shortly thereafter Pessia moved to a kibbutz.[10]

In sum, Ben-Gurion's family considered Paula a woman of valor, a housekeeper par excellence, intuitive and perceptive, with a quick eye for appraising people and their weaknesses, but they agreed that she was "tough," "bad," and "a sourpuss." They never had the slightest doubt that she did her best to keep them apart from Ben-Gurion. According to his family — Paula's children included — Paula allowed them to sit down to a family Passover Seder only once in all of their years together. She preferred no Seder to sharing Ben-Gurion with kin.

In a way, Paula imprisoned Ben-Gurion in his own home and appointed herself sentry over him. No member of his family could reach him, either for deep discussions or idle conversation, without her prior approval and permission. Whether she loved her husband so much that she regarded his family as rivals; whether she believed that acting as his go-between endowed her with power and influence; whether she sought in this way to prove her worth and loyalty to him and avoid being replaced by another; or whether it was all of these, one thing is certain: Ben-Gurion's settling down was accompanied by the erection of a wall between him and his family, which grew higher and wider in the years that followed and increased his loneliness. Subsequently, the books shut up with him in his study were very often his only close companions.

15

The Quest for Predominance

FOR THIRTY-SIX-YEAR-OLD David Ben-Gurion, a new phase of life had begun. For the first time since his immigration to Palestine sixteen years earlier he had a home, regular meals, and immaculate clothes. His children filled the apartment with games and laughter, and his wife's vigilance guarded him from uninvited relatives and guests, giving him undisturbed peace and quiet to read, rest, and think. He could concentrate on consolidating HEC authority over the Histadrut.

At the time of its founding in 1920 the Histadrut had boasted 4,433 members. The workers' parties that united to form it had transferred their authority over all the bodies that they had established separately since 1907 to it. From its inception the Histadrut had a Labor Center, which served as a labor exchange and assisted in the absorption of new immigrant workers; an Agricultural Center for the communal agricultural settlements; a Sick Fund with urban and rural clinics; a supply and distribution company, Ha-Mashbir, which catered to farmers' needs in the country and supplied city workers through food co-ops; an Office of Public Works, which contracted to perform government jobs or subcontracted them to construction workers' cooperatives; the Palestine Workers' Fund (Kapai), which raised money abroad and helped establish and consolidate cooperative enterprises; a cultural committee that set up urban and rural schools for workers' children; and cooperative restaurants called Workers' Kitchens. "Histadrut institutions" were designed to strengthen the Histadrut and to serve its members and their families. But although they were theoretically owned by the Histadrut, their managements were chosen in elections held by the trade unions — the Organization of Agricultural Workers, the Organization of Construction Workers, and so forth — and the Histadrut council.

Bank ha-Poalim, established in the spring of 1921, was the first institution created by the Histadrut itself; its management was appointed by the HEC. These institutions made the Histadrut unique as a workers' organization: it encompassed industrial and farm workers alike, both individually and in cooperative groups; and it was more than a federation of trade unions, since it gave high priority to what it termed their "constructive role," that is, enlarging the economy to absorb more Jewish workers in Palestine and thereby implementing labor Zionism.

In practice the first HEC, composed of the three-man secretariat elected in January 1921 and the representatives of the Histadrut institutions, had functioned as a collegium in which each member had equal authority. Then the November council that elected Ben-Gurion to the secretariat had designated the second HEC explicitly as a nine-member collegium composed of the three-member secretariat plus six representatives from the central institutions. The council defined the HEC as "a coordinator and director of all the work and of all Histadrut affairs." In other words, the institution representatives would be the HEC's decision-making body while the secretariat would implement its resolutions.

In Ben-Gurion's view there was a contradiction between the HEC as an executive, as its name and definition implied, and its collegium structure, which, being based on a majority vote, gave more power to the institution directors than to the executive secretariat. He had addressed himself to resolving this contradiction by getting the November council to adopt his proposals to move the HEC to Jerusalem and to conduct a census. The census enabled the HEC to set up a central card index that registered name, residence, place of work, profession, and other personal details. The card index quickly acquired the nickname "the central directory"; out of it grew the bureau that issued membership cards. Another council resolution proposed by Ben-Gurion was that the Sick Fund and the Labor Center would "serve only card-holding, dues-paying Histadrut members."[1]

The connection between these resolutions and their objective was not immediately evident. Previously, directors of the Labor Center and the Sick Fund had rendered services to whomever they pleased. In their desire to enlarge their institutions they collected dues from people who weren't Histadrut members as well as those who were. With this system abolished, the secretariat, which controlled the central directory, would solely determine eligibility for assistance. Ben-Gurion's first important step on his long road to consolidating and enforcing the

HEC's authority embodied the essence of his voluntary subordination concept: work and medical care were of fundamental importance to the worker, particularly the new worker, but to receive them he would have to join the Histadrut, even if he was not so inclined.

In addition to the political purpose Ben-Gurion saw an important symbolic opportunity in the census and the directory: to assign Hebrew surnames to everyone who was counted. Had it been in his power he would undoubtedly have made all Histadrut members adopt Hebrew names, but he had to be satisfied with a name-changing committee that he established with Itzhak Ben-Zvi and David Remez, head of the Office of Public Works. This committee offered its services to Histadrut members who wished to register in the census, held on September 10, 1922, under new Hebrew names. This, too, was an important step in the long journey, which reached its goal when Ben-Gurion became prime minister and minister of defense of the State of Israel and ordained that all foreign ministry personnel and army regulars must have Hebrew names.[2]

Though he had neither powers of enforcement nor the apparatus of government, Ben-Gurion was able to count 16,000 workers, 8,394 of whom were Histadrut members, with the help of volunteers who conducted the census at 111 points. Considering that the census scheme was entirely his own and that not everyone was enthusiastic about it, this was an exceptional feat. The number of Histadrut members was also a basic reference point against which it would be possible to gauge his future organizational success. When Ben-Gurion retired from the HEC in 1935, Histadrut membership stood at 82,197 men and women, nearly all between eighteen and thirty-five years of age.

While there were no objections to a census and a directory in themselves, their overriding purpose — revealed by Ben-Gurion after his proposals were passed in a letter to Bank ha-Poalim asking for funds for the census and the directory — of improving the organizational and fiscal activity of the Histadrut and its institutions, which amounted to centralization, was far from acceptable to all, because it meant granting supremacy to the HEC, and more precisely to its secretariat, in the person of Ben-Gurion. That there was no actual dispute should be attributed to his colleagues' faith in the power of constraints that would foil his plan, rather than to their acquiescence. It was clear to them that full concentration of authority in the HEC and its enforcement were still a long way off, and that there was no sense in pressing their objections at this stage. They were wise enough to let Ben-Gurion find out for himself how impractical his scheme was under the prevailing circumstances.

Foremost was the HEC's poverty, which affected all of the secretariat's plans and activities. It stood out, as poverty will, precisely because it appeared against the background of a lavish event. February 10, 1922, was a great day: Ramsay MacDonald, the British Labour Party leader, came to Palestine for a ten-day visit as the guest of Achdut ha-Avodah and the Histadrut, Ben-Gurion hosting on behalf of both.

Ben-Gurion was satisfied with this visit for a number of reasons. MacDonald was the first tourist who came not to see the holy places, but to witness the Jewish revival. MacDonald declared that he and his party supported "the idea of the rebirth of the Jewish people in their land" and promised that his party would assist the Histadrut as much as it could. At the farewell party given in his honor at the HEC office in Jerusalem, MacDonald said that Palestine's spiritual and religious inspiration were now supplemented by "socialist and political inspiration" and then praised his hosts. "I have traveled in many lands but have never been treated with such hospitality nor embraced with such a welcome as I have among you." In a thank-you note to Ben-Gurion he added, "Very poor would our holiday have been but for your cars and your drivers and the comrades who came with them. . . . They have given us pleasure which otherwise would never have been ours, and we only wish they could share in the happiness which they brought to us when we were in Palestine."[3]

How much this visit cost and where the HEC found the money to finance it are unanswered questions, but Ben-Gurion's lavish hospitality undoubtedly exceeded its financial capacity; in fact, as soon as the guests dispersed, creditors descended on Ben-Gurion and David Zakay, Achdut ha-Avodah's second secretariat member.

The HEC landlord, trying to recover his money from the elusive Ben-Gurion and Zakay, chastised them in a letter. "Gentlemen: For an organization which aspires to make truth prevail in the world such behavior is not at all becoming." To placate him the two gave him a promissory note, but they never honored it. The landlord tried again. "What a private, respectable individual wouldn't do, the Histadrut shouldn't do either." In March 1925 he was still waiting. "Can it truly be that the time still has not arrived?" As a last resort, he proposed payment by installments, and was even willing to accept payment in goods from Ha-Mashbir.

Others who dunned the HEC included the Workers' Kitchen, whose patience lasted a year and a half; a bakery that held an unpaid IOU; and a woman who ran a nearby food and drink stand. She became impatient within only a few months and went to court, and the HEC had to pay its debt of 5.25 Egyptian pounds plus court expenses. Still other creditors included two cooperatives that had been proudly displayed to MacDonald, the shoemakers' To'elet in Tel Aviv and the machine

workshop Amal in Haifa, as well as Atid, a tailors' cooperative in Tel
Aviv. Amal's director, Shmuel Nativi — his surname, bestowed by the
naming committee, replaced his original Wagman — sent letters that
could have melted stone. He first explained that he needed the money
for the reception he was planning for his son's circumcision, and, eight
months later, for bringing his mother to Palestine. "She's had the visa
in her hands for almost a month and can't move because there's no
money."

Ben-Gurion's response was, "To our regret the HEC is, as usual,
penniless. As soon as we have the means . . . we will pay . . . what is
due." He could pay for neither the cabinet and desk that he had received from the central directory nor its typist. Zakay evaded her for
seven months with a thousand and one pretexts and asked her to accept
credit at Ha-Mashbir in lieu of payment, but she wanted her salary
paid in hard cash and threatened to sue the HEC for the sum of 2.30
Egyptian pounds.

In May the postmaster general, whose letters had gone unanswered,
served notice that if the HEC cable address fees were not paid within
ten days, the address would be invalidated. At times like these Zakay
turned to acquaintances for charity, that is, personal loans for a week
or two. But since the HEC couldn't hold up its end of these bargains
either, he finally had to ask a savings society for an interest-free loan of
fifteen Egyptian pounds, committing himself to return it on demand in
an explicit promise. "This time [the money will be repaid precisely on
time] as the law strictly requires." The press of creditors disrupted
normal work not only at the secretariat, but also at the adjoining Office
of Public Works, which implored the HEC to settle its accounts, because "the collectors show up daily, both inside and out of the offices,
demanding payment with threats, in voices fit to wake the dead . . . and
they keep us from working."

One reason behind the constant proliferation of creditors was simply
that the authorized signatories of the HEC, Ben-Gurion and Zakay,
who were charged with running its finances, had neither the vaguest
knowledge of financial matters nor the slightest inclination to acquire
it. Theoretically, Zakay alone was in charge of the treasury, but in
practice Ben-Gurion also made deposits and withdrawals. At times he
instructed Ha-Mashbir to pay HEC creditors in goods and charge it to
the HEC's account. Such steps were surely born of necessity, but they
brought havoc to HEC's finances. Their bookkeeping was equally un-
orthodox. For example, Ben-Gurion entered cash transactions, such as
money he loaned the HEC out of his own pocket to send a telegram or
buy stamps, or participation fees he received from Histadrut institutions, in his diary; one day he listed receipts of such fees on the same

page on which he entered his personal expenditures and various debts.
Zakay, for his part, kept the accounts in a little black book he carried
in his pocket, which also served as his personal diary. In the same column in which payment for the printing and distribution of *Pinkas,* the
first Histadrut organ, was entered, he listed personal expenses such as
"food" and "shoe shining." Needless to say, neither had a clear picture
of the financial situation.[4]

A more basic reason for the HEC's perpetual lack of funds was the
method the Histadrut had devised to finance the HEC budget.
Whereas its constituent institutions had money coming in — the labor
councils and the Sick Fund collected membership dues; Ha-Mashbir,
the Office of Public Works, and Bank ha-Poalim made profits on their
operations — the HEC had no direct income. The institutions were
supposed to pay "participation fees" to the HEC, but this arrangement
resulted in endless bargaining and haggling between the HEC, which
referred to them as obligations, and the institution directors, who were
against paying them. The institutions seldom met their obligations to
the HEC, arguing that the participation fees were beyond their means
and refusing to recognize them as commitments. Hence the HEC budget was under constant debate between the rich institutions and their
poor dependent, the HEC. This situation was too good for the institutions to give up, for they opposed Ben-Gurion's policy of centralization, and the more they contested the participation fees, the less power
the HEC could acquire.

In any case, the HEC's debts became so numerous that a committee
was appointed to examine them and come up with a recovery plan.
The committee found that within one year the HEC had accumulated
debts to the amount of 700 Egyptian pounds, but it couldn't conceive
of a way to make the HEC solvent. It was clear that as long as the HEC
had no sure and steady revenue of its own, or unless it retrenched its
operations, financial chaos would be its constant companion. In February of 1924 Zakay pleaded with the Agricultural Center to pay its
commitment within three days to prevent the HEC's telephone being
disconnected because of a three-month-old debt to the post office.*
Ben-Gurion added that the situation was "almost catastrophic": "We
are walking blindly towards the abyss." All in all, the institutions and
their directors had no need to fear that Ben-Gurion would be able to
put his centralization policy into effect.[5]

A second circumstance affecting centralization was that Jerusalem
did not become the center of Histadrut activity as Ben-Gurion had

---

* In Mandatory Palestine, as it does in the State of Israel, the post office provided all
telephone services.

hoped it would. Tel Aviv's rapid growth, the amazing development of the citrus orchards in the coastal plain, the building of a deepwater port in Haifa, and the settlement of agricultural kibbutzes and moshavs in the Jezreel and Jordan valleys made these regions the focus of economic activity and development. The construction of roads, industrial plants, urban housing, and farm buildings attracted the Histadrut institutions involved with them. Bank ha-Poalim, the Agricultural Center, and Ha-Mashbir did not move to Jerusalem despite the HEC's prodding, and the other institutions' local branches in Tel Aviv and Haifa became head offices. Perched atop its high mountains, Jerusalem remained distant and remote, as did Ben-Gurion's dream of a highly centralized Histadrut.

The prospects for centralization and proper coordination faded for the simple reason that it became harder and harder to bring the institution directors to Jerusalem for the HEC plenary meetings. The plenum met only twice each in January and February of 1922, and once each in March and April. The lack of regular plenary sessions left the secretariat without resolutions or directives; therefore, though it was expected to convene daily, it held only twelve sessions for which minutes were recorded. Joseph Sprinzak could take part in secretariat affairs only in the evenings after finishing his day's work in the Zionist Executive, and not always then, leaving the secretariat in the hands of Ben-Gurion and Zakay, which meant, for all practical purposes, in the hands of Ben-Gurion.[6]

Until Berl Katznelson, Zakay's close friend, elevated him to the secretariat, Zakay had taught Hebrew, his sole field of expertise and one remote from the realm of practical politics. In the secretariat he handled *Pinkas* and the correspondence, and, to his and everyone else's dismay, also served as treasurer. Had there been the slightest hope that his financial skills would improve, it vanished completely after an occurrence that widened the gap between his duties and his real interests. On the afternoon of March 23 he and Ben-Gurion were going over the galley proofs of *Pinkas* in a small printing house in Jerusalem. It was a clear, sunny day and there was no need of electric lighting. Suddenly, darkness filled the room. The pair ran out to the street in fright, only to witness a long-lasting solar eclipse. Ben-Gurion simply noted in his diary, "I saw the crescent moon in the sun," and went on as if nothing had happened, but Zakay was deeply agitated, mainly because the event had taken him by surprise. It changed his life profoundly, and to ensure that the sky would never again startle him so, he began to study astronomy. He bought a telescope to observe the stars, and forever after it was impossible to tear him away from them.[7]

Therefore, Sprinzak and Zakay helped Ben-Gurion only a little, if at all. "I am now the one in charge of all Histadrut activity," he wrote his father, "and this is a huge and difficult responsibility." Even if the institution representatives had agreed to accept HEC authority, the secretariat would not have had the resources to enforce it. Ben-Gurion grumbled that the HEC lacked "influence and access" and demanded that Achdut ha-Avodah, which was by far the strongest party in the Histadrut, step in and make a ruling. The outcome of the resulting party debate was a reiteration — purely theoretical — of the institution directors' recognition of the HEC's overall authority. That this was still open to differing interpretations became clear when Ben-Gurion signed a construction contract on behalf of the directors of the Office of Public Works, who were, as usual, absent from Jerusalem. While the office did not call for the contract's nullification, neither did its directors honor it.

This brought about one of the first clashes between Ben-Gurion and Remez, which developed into a controversy over Histadrut democracy: Was it to be built from the bottom up, or vice versa? Of special importance was the issue of labor council organization: Would it be handled on the local level or from the top, by HEC envoys? Remez took the middle ground: "We cannot maintain our institutions without meeting the urban councils halfway"; the labor councils and the local branches of the institutions "must all be run by the people on the spot." The HEC and other centers need not send representatives to supervise the local since "there are enough means to safeguard their control." Ben-Gurion dissented. "I do not agree with Remez's principal proposal," he declared. He was absolutely firm that the HEC appoint representatives to the labor councils and the institution branches, although "we will of course do things as much as possible with the locals' consent."[8]

He therefore moved wherever possible to strengthen the HEC's grip on both institutions and individuals. He intervened in a competition between the Office of Public Works and one of the Histadrut contracting groups for a construction job in Neveh Sha'anan, near Haifa; he demanded that the labor councils provide the HEC with a full weekly "summary of the matters that you handled in the course of the week and those on your agenda" for the next; he notified the Tel Aviv Labor Council, which had decided to hold a conference of all the labor councils, that "we strongly oppose your resolution . . . and suggest that you reconsider it, so that we won't have to advise all the urban councils to decline your invitation"; and he refused to sanction payment of wages to an employee whom the Jerusalem labor council had hired to work for the management of the labor exchange in its area because he had not been appointed by the HEC. "We decided . . . to hire someone to work at the exchange, at our own expense, who would be responsible to us and appointed by us, and as long as we don't appoint someone, we are not responsible for [paying his salary]." His use of the plural was absolutely majestic. It never even occurred to Zakay and Sprinzak that "we" included them.

He demanded regular progress reports from all Histadrut institutions and asked them to submit "details of the administrative budgets," including complete lists of all the workers and "each and everyone's" monthly salary, office expenses, and "the sources of revenue that cover these expenses" to the HEC "immediately." From Bank ha-Poalim he demanded a report of all transactions, large and small, down to bill discounting over 48 Egyptian pounds and requests for loans over 20 Egyptian pounds, whether they were approved or not. Needless to say, Ben-Gurion jealously guarded the HEC's right of representation, opposing all attempts by the government's labor department to get statistics directly from the labor exchanges. He instructed the exchange director in Tel Aviv to "categorically" inform the labor department that it would have to "address itself to the central body in Jerusalem, as only there will it receive the requested information."[9]

Still another obstacle to Ben-Gurion's endeavor to make the HEC "a central force" was the character of his colleagues — all the leaders of Achdut ha-Avodah and Ha-Poel ha-Tzair who were delegated by these bodies to the institutions, labor councils, and HEC. Although generalizations usually rest on precarious ground, it seems safe to point out two of their collective characteristics: a full, sometimes inflated, knowledge of their own worth and an unshakable conviction that they were in the right. Accompanying these two virtues were generous doses of sensitivity about their honor and indignation at views discordant to their own, the latter evidenced daily by frequent threats of resignation, interminable disputes, and litigiousness.

Even if Ben-Gurion had overcome Ha-Poel ha-Tzair's omnipresent fear of being shortchanged by HEC authority, were it ever to materialize, he would still have had to contend with the perpetual threats of resignation by envoys from both parties whenever a resolution they opposed was passed. On his first day at the HEC no fewer than four notices of resignation greeted him, and had the people involved not been mollified, four important institutions would have been left without leadership.

The Ha-Mashbir management was especially notorious for its threats of resignation, and when Ben-Gurion tried to put an end to this by pulling rank and appointing a supervisory committee, Joseph Aharonovitch, a codirector of Bank ha-Poalim, agreed to serve as its chairman only with reservations. "It is very much to be feared that at the first turning up of a nose I will make myself scarce." The directors of Ha-Mashbir did indeed turn up their noses, rejecting outside supervision. However, their united front against HEC intervention did not prevent them from quarreling among themselves, with attendant resignation threats. In the summer of 1923 the HEC received a message that "there is no possibility of cooperation between members of the administration." In a reconciliation meeting called by the HEC, one director said, "I resigned from the Ha-Mashbir management on the day I was elected." Aharonovitch himself resigned from Bank ha-Poalim because his codirector challenged him to a duel "to the death," swearing that "Aharonovitch won't supplant me as long as I live." During Ben-Gurion's fifteen years in the HEC there was not a single Histadrut official who did not resign his post at least once. In fact, until 1926 Ben-Gurion himself resigned, or threatened to, at least once a year.

These being the rules of the game, it is easy to understand why Ben-Gurion was unable to consolidate HEC central authority as quickly as he wished. The institution directors and their representatives in the HEC regarded themselves as equals among equals vis-à-vis Ben-Gurion, the secretariat, and the HEC as a whole. To Ben-Gurion, who was resolved to turn the Histadrut into a workers' state with one government, this was heresy of the first degree. The three labor councils in the big cities behaved as if they were "states unto themselves," as he put it, and he vehemently rejected the theory put forward by a Ha-Poel ha-Tzair leader that "the Histadrut is a veritable monarchy, handing out territories to its principalities." In Ben-Gurion's view such division of jurisdiction jeopardized Histadrut sovereignty.[10]

The major obstacle for Ben-Gurion, however, was the doctrinal controversy over the makeup of the HEC and his colleagues' insistence on running it as a collegium. Without a clear-cut constitutional ruling, which only the Histadrut convention was empowered to make, that the HEC was an executive, Ben-Gurion had no chance of overcoming the other obstacles. Therefore, at the end of 1922, after a year's experience in the secretariat and as the second Histadrut convention approached, he elaborated a proposal which conceived of the Histadrut as a state and the HEC as its government. "The HEC is the central executive of the Histadrut and of all its institutions and enterprises, and it is collectively responsible for its actions to the general council and convention of the Histadrut. . . . The HEC rules on all general questions of the Histadrut and its institutions and instructs its departments accordingly."

No longer a collegium, but a ministry, the HEC was to be divided into eight departments: Supply, to which Ha-Mashbir would be subordinate; Settlement, with authority over the Agricultural Center; Contractual Projects, to supervise all construction cooperatives and the Office of Public Works; Cooperative Industry, in charge of Kapai and industrial cooperatives; Culture, to guide the cultural committee and its network of schools; Health, responsible for the Sick Fund and other medical facilities; Aliyah, to supervise the Labor Center and the labor councils; and a Women Workers' Council. With a secretary in charge of each department, there would be eight ministers with portfolios who, with the three-man general secretariat, would constitute an eleven-member HEC, that is, the Histadrut government. The central authority would rest with the general secretariat, which would give political guidance to the HEC departments, thus placing a triumvirate at the head of the Histadrut government. As to who would be the strong man of this triumvirate, the prime minister, so to speak, there could be no question. To make his intentions perfectly clear, Ben-Gurion published the proposal in *Kunteres:* ". . . putting the Histadrut in command of all economic, cultural, and political affairs of the Jewish working community" in Palestine, that is, building the Histadrut into a workers' state.[11]

At the HEC session of January 1, 1923, both Achdut ha-Avodah and Ha-Poel ha-Tzair members hotly contested the proposal, refusing to subjugate the institutions they represented to departmental secretaries. Remez argued in favor of "differentiation." Katznelson, representing Ha-Mashbir, defended the collegium principle, declaring, "I am for differentiation," and adding that the Histadrut "needs to be a federation of economic units, submitting, of course, to the Histadrut general sovereignty" — to the rule of a democratic majority. Consequently, he thought, the powers of the HEC had to be narrowed, not broadened. The others, not surprisingly, supported Remez and Katznelson. Their reasoning was ideological: if a cooperative society was the Histadrut's ultimate ideal, participating members had the right to advise and consent in all Histadrut matters pertaining to them, individually and collectively, and this right should never be usurped. The institution representatives advocated an image of the HEC as a senior institution that they would recognize as a first among equals, but not as a supreme government, as Ben-Gurion intended.

This fierce struggle ended in compromise. The second Histadrut convention later that month accepted a literal definition of the HEC as "the central executive" but rejected Ben-Gurion's governmental proposal. Not only did the convention reaffirm its faith in the collegium principle, it added two more institution representatives to the HEC, expanding it to eight such representatives plus the three-man secretariat, whose incumbents were re-elected. The convention did, however, pass an amendment to the Histadrut constitution's definition of the

HEC. "The HEC has the right of decision in all the Histadrut institutions." So although it was denied governmental form and powers, the HEC was given the final say.[12]

Ben-Gurion's endeavor to establish a central Histadrut authority was as hopeless as it was daring, for from its beginnings the Jewish nation had had difficulty accepting any single temporal authority. Its journey in the desert, the struggles of the judges and prophets, the establishment of the monarchy with its problems, and the schism between the kingdoms of Judea and Israel all attest to this. If in its own land no sole authority could prevail, such a thing was all the more impossible in their dispersion and exile, and differentiation won out. Its splits became so deep and its conflicting factions so numerous in the struggles between messianic movements and their opponents — between Chassidim and Mitnaggedim, between Orthodox, Conservative, and Reform movements — that not even a single rabbinic authority, acceptable to all, had been able to materialize. How, then, did Ben-Gurion expect to establish Histadrut authority in one fell swoop? He could not have been oblivious to the difficulties facing him, and if he attempted to overcome them, it was because of his conviction that what was unattainable in quiet times was within reach in times of crisis and upheaval.

He considered his failure only partial, and his ardor lost none of its intensity. As for the little the convention had given him, he would foster and increase it, and what the convention had left out in authority he would make up for with the force of his personality. He would build HEC authority slowly and steadily, until there was no escape from recognizing it in the constitution. No longer, however, would he go to war with all of the "principalities"; he would wait for the opportune moment to take control of one of them. Thus the story of his years in the secretariat relates the inception, development, and consolidation of HEC authority.

Ironically enough, the first principality that chanced to present itself was the Labor Legion, the very group whose ideology and people were so close to his heart. Ben-Gurion was not alone in his fondness for these young people with torn shirts, who quarried and moved stones by day and sang, danced, and debated throughout the night. They were the darlings of the HEC and the whole labor movement as well. A perfect example to Zionist youth, ready to lay down their lives for their cause, they embodied the pure pioneering spirit. At the very first session of the secretariat Ben-Gurion had heard about the good relations between the Legion, the HEC, and the Zionist administration. Furthermore, the leaders of Achdut ha-Avodah were courting the Labor Legionnaires in hopes of recruiting them into the party. In March 1921 this courting led to a joint experiment in implementing Achdut ha-Avodah's plan to develop a "great kvutsa": a large commune in Nuris — the eastern part of the Jezreel Valley — which would be spread out over a large area and deal in agriculture, industry, and miscellaneous services. During Ben-Gurion's first month in the secretariat the HEC, the Agricultural Center, and the Histadrut council took it upon themselves to give the Legion preference for funds from the Zionist budget and for road building contracts from the government, to expedite the materialization of the great kvutsa. Construction began in the autumn of 1921; the first settlement went up in September, a hundred strong, pitching tents near the Harod spring. Most of its members belonged to Achdut ha-Avodah and were followers of Itzhak Tabenkin and Shlomo Lavi, the authors of the idea, who envisioned this great kvutsa as one of many economically and socially independent units that together would constitute a larger grouping, which later came to be known as the kibbutz movement. They joined the Legion for the purpose of this joint enterprise. A second settlement, composed entirely of Labor Legion members, went up in November on a spot an hour's walking distance from the spring. The two kvutsa settlements constituted two companies of the Legion, whose remaining companies were scattered in other parts of Palestine. By January 1922 there were more than 120 tents in the two settlements, one named Ein Harod, after the spring, the other Tel Yosef, in memory of Joseph Trumpeldor. Together the two companies created a joint communal unit.

When a conflict erupted between the Legion and the Office of Public Works because the Legion wanted to receive its projects directly from the government public works department, Ben-Gurion decided that HEC intervention was called for. Meeting Menahem Elkind, the leader of the Legion, for the first time in Tel Yosef in January 1922, he saw clearly that the Legion was not putting itself at the absolute service of the HEC, placing the fulfillment of its mission above all else. Elkind did not approach Ben-Gurion as a student before his master, and certainly not as a private before his commander, and the strength of his personality was apparent at first sight. A lean Russian émigré, he had a triangular face. The faint smile that perpetually hovered across his thin lips did not go too well with the steely gaze of his gray eyes. His acquaintances found him to be "a mixture of the Bolshevik commissar type and the Talmudic hair-splitter." Elkind had definitely decided to uphold the Legion's objective as formulated in its code of rules and regulations: "To fortify the workers' organization and guide it in the direction of the Legion." It meant that the HEC would not guide the Legion, but the Legion would guide the HEC on the path toward a general commune. This was exactly Ben-Gurion's own former idea that the labor army would grow and grow until it contained the entire Histadrut, but now he and Elkind — he and his former idea — stood on opposite sides of the fence.[13]

The Legion was not merely an ensemble of innocents and dreamers possessed entirely by the pure pioneering spirit, as it seemed from afar. At its head stood a leader whose vision and great aspirations included Zionist leadership. This was bad enough, from Ben-Gurion's point of view, yet something else bothered him even more. Achdut ha-Avodah and Tabenkin were not the only ones interested in the Legion; Israel Shochat and his Hashomer colleagues were too, but, as Ben-Gurion had learned secretly, with the important difference that Shochat and his followers had succeeded in secretly infiltrating its ranks from its inception.

Immediately after its establishment, Achdut ha-Avodah had resolved to dissolve the Hashomer underground defense force and had founded the Haganah in its stead. In its turn, the Histadrut had taken over Achdut ha-Avodah's responsibility for the Haganah. It was conceived as a broadly based underground organization open to all able-bodied Jews, a popular militia taking its orders from the Histadrut, which, as the supreme authority, would, through the HEC, appoint and supervise the command of both the regular Haganah cadre and its corps of volunteers. Shochat and his friends professed to have accepted these changes and become inactive. During the dispute over the Haganah's formation, Shochat had argued that it should be made up of a small restricted cadre of selected professionals who would handle all matters of security, a kind of small underground regular army, training and procuring arms on quiet days and fighting in times of crisis. The Histadrut council, according to Shochat, would fulfill its responsibility by having a representative in the high command and a supervisory committee. Ben-Gurion was familiar with Shochat's concept, having known since 1907 that it revolved around a self-appointed clandestine cell with arms branching into several areas, particularly defense.

Shochat and his group had only pretended to abide by the resolution. They transferred only a token quantity of Hashomer's arms to the Haganah and joined it simply for appearance' sake, since in fact they were set on continuing their secret existence within the rank and file of the Labor Legion, of which they were among the initiators and founders. As far as Shochat and his men were concerned, the Legion was simply a new incarnation of Bar-Giora, the collective, and Hashomer. In 1957 Shochat took credit for writing the Legion's charter, but in the twenties this fact was known only to his closest cronies, who had sworn on their lives to keep it secret, and to Elkind and a few of his confidants, who were equally tightlipped. Elkind was the Legion's leader in public, while Shochat occupied his favorite position — behind the scenes, pulling the strings. Since all the members of the Legion belonged to the Haganah (its full name was the Labor and Defense Legion) there was no doubt that Shochat had contrived to establish an underground within an underground that would be manipulated and led by his own secret cell.

There were two interwoven currents within the Legion: one social, in whose name Elkind spoke; the other secret, dealing mostly with security, which Shochat organized clandestinely. Ben-Gurion, with three of the Haganah leaders, all familiar with Shochat and his ideas, had no doubts as to where Shochat's intentions lay. Several facts reinforced the suspicion that Shochat and company were setting up their own "stronghold" within the Labor Legion. A consignment of arms smuggled into the country by former Hashomer men in the service of the Haganah disappeared and was suspected to be hidden in Kefar Giladi, the kibbutz established by Hashomer veterans on the northern border. Ben-Gurion and the Haganah top command knew that Shochat's secret cell, code-named the Circle by the latter, had run the whole operation and was Bar-Giora's direct successor, but they were unable to prove it for lack of evidence.

The combination of Shochat's separatist orientation in security matters and Elkind's in social ones — seclusion from the Histadrut, as it was called in a report that reached Ben-Gurion — certainly troubled him, but he kept the matter under wraps. It was still unproven, and in any case the public climate necessary for HEC intervention had not yet been created, although Eliyahu Golomb, the Haganah chief, demanded such intervention, threatening to resign if it did not happen. The fact that the HEC still lacked ultimate authority and the power to enforce it added another reason to put off such a confrontation. Meanwhile Ben-Gurion followed the Labor Legion's development with increasing anxiety, from time to time noting the growth in its membership — 665 at its peak, a very large force at the time — in his diary.[14]

Then, in 1923, a conflict that broke out between the two partners — the Legion and Achdut ha-Avodah — in the great kvutsa furnished Ben-Gurion with an opportunity to impose HEC authority on the socio-organizational side of the Labor Legion. Elkind had ordered that a certain debt of one of the Legion's other companies be paid out of the Zionist colonization budget funds earmarked for Ein Harod. This was certainly in accordance with the joint treasury principle of the Legion commune, in which all companies were to be absolutely equal, and of which Ein Harod was a participating company. However, Shlomo Lavi, of Ein Harod's secretariat, would not pay the debt, since he considered Ein Harod an autonomous entity and rejected the diversion of any of its funds for the use of other companies. Defending Ein Harod's financial "autonomy" in a general meeting of Ein Harod's members, he called for the dissolution of the Legion's joint treasury and its central organization, which was tantamount to calling for its liquidation. Elkind and the members of Tel Yosef countered by summoning the Legion council, which at their instigation passed a resolution expelling Lavi and some of his supporters from the Labor Legion, and hence from Ein Harod. Lavi and his friends, in turn, brought their grievance to the Histadrut council, which accepted their demand for Ein Harod's "administrative and financial autonomy" and denied the Legion's right to determine the settlement's membership. Acceptance and expulsion of members, the council resolved, would be carried out only with the Histadrut's consent, through the Agricultural Center. The Legion's general assembly, convening in Tel Yosef, rejected these resolutions with the well-founded argument that they were equivalent to "subversion of the Legion's foundations." Elkind and his colleagues said it was "imperative that those who disagree with the Legion's principles be expelled from the Legion," and, if worse came to worst, that Ein Harod secede from the Legion and divide the joint possessions of the great kvutsa with Tel Yosef.

Ben-Gurion, objecting to dissolution of the great kvutsa but perfectly willing for Ein Harod to secede from the Legion, as long as the members stayed where they were and held on to the property, which, he considered, belonged to the Histadrut, insisted on strict observance of the Histadrut council's resolutions. The Legion's threat of a "civil war" did not deter him. To him the issue was not "a question of the division of the settlements" but "the question of whether or not there is a Histadrut." Refusing to budge from this position, he presented the Legion with a choice: either it would commit itself, by signing a contract, to abide by the Histadrut resolutions, or its members would have to leave Ein Harod, and "if they don't, they will be expelled from the Histadrut."[15]

His HEC colleagues were not as rash as Ben-Gurion. News of the hard conditions in the Legion, especially the hunger, softened them. For the HEC to battle the finest of the pioneers, so honest and dedicated, was unthinkable. Ben-Gurion, however, held out for the integrity of Ein Harod and stood unflinchingly behind the council resolutions. Unlike his HEC associates who believed that with a bit of good will it was possible to meet halfway, Ben-Gurion would not take a step toward the Legion, unless it first announced absolute acceptance of Histadrut authority. At length the Legion gave in, declaring that it would yield and abide by Histadrut resolutions, as long as "the Legion's integrity" was not impaired. This declaration, though it did nothing to put Ben-Gurion's mind at rest, met with the approval of his colleagues, who granted the Legion's request to leave the decision to split or not to Ein Harod and Tel Yosef, by way of a referendum.

Two hundred fifteen — more than two-thirds — declared their loyalty to the Legion commune and 98 — less than one-third — stuck with Lavi and Tabenkin. In recognition of "the majority" decision the HEC, whose members wanted to end the mismarriage between Tabenkin and the Legion, decided to divide the joint two-site settlement "equally." Tel Yosef would from then on be composed entirely of those loyal to Elkind and the Legion, and Ein Harod's members would follow Tabenkin and Lavi, requiring some exchange of population. Historically, it marked Ein Harod's beginning as the first kibbutz in Palestine and as the cornerstone of the United Kibbutz Movement, led by Tabenkin. The split also marked the end of Achdut ha-Avodah's cooperation with the Labor Legion.

On the face of it the conflict should have ended then and there, but when it came to the actual division of possessions, the Legion company at Tel Yosef interpreted the HEC decision as applying only to territory, arguing that it was unjust to allot equal portions of the rest to two unequal factions. They therefore demanded that the HEC alter its resolution to read "equal partition of territory." The Legion council, which upheld this demand, also directed them not to consent to any "concessions or compromises."

Ben-Gurion, on behalf of the HEC, replied curtly that "the equal partition applies to inventory [and livestock as] well." To the Legion this was the epitome of injustice. Tel Yosef, it argued publicly, "would have to send away a lot of its members who have become attached to the place, who learned the work and put all their pioneering energy into the building of Tel Yosef, whereas the other settlement, which is short of people, will bring in outsiders" to keep its enterprise going. Disregarding the commission sent to supervise the partition, the Tel Yosef loyalists began to transfer livestock and inventory — everything that was not nailed down — from Ein Harod to Tel Yosef, both openly and in secret, leading to violent brawls. When the smoke cleared, all of Ein Harod's inventory, animate and inanimate, was at Tel Yosef. According to its leaders, Ein Harod was "without any means of livelihood."[16]

When he heard the commission's report — which included criticisms by Tel Yosef members of "the Histadrut's reactionary and antidemocratic behavior" that could be interpreted as directed at himself — Ben-Gurion could not remain indifferent to such gross disobedience to the Histadrut. His fury mounted, escalating when he found out that the Legion leaders in Tel Yosef had explained that they had not rebelled against the Histadrut as such, but only against "Ben-Gurion's Histadrut." However, anger alone cannot explain the steps Ben-Gurion took next; they must be seen in terms of the prevailing political context and, more precisely, against the background of another factor, the Legion's shift to the left, toward anti-Zionism and opposition to Jewish immigration.

The leftist inclination of the Legion leadership was first openly discussed at the HEC session of June 5, 1923, which dealt with the Tel Yosef affair. But although no one knows how many of the participants were aware of Elkind's and Shochat's increasing independence within the Haganah, there can be no doubt that leading members of Achdut ha-Avodah — Ben-Gurion, Katznelson, Golomb, and others — had long been aware of this development, and that this fact influenced the stance that they, and consequently the HEC, adopted toward the Legion in general and Tel Yosef in particular. It is also safe to assume that this stance was the central factor in the HEC's unanimous passage of an uncharacteristically harsh resolution, really an ultimatum. If within twenty-four hours the members of Tel Yosef did not carry out the partition commission's instructions, returning everything that was allocated to Ein Harod and abiding by the "equal partition" principle, all Histadrut institutions would "sever" relations with them.

Here, at long last, was the opportunity Ben-Gurion had been waiting for. If Tel Yosef rejected the ultimatum, all the Histadrut institutions would be operating in concert under the HEC's command, providing incontestable proof of the need for HEC authority over all the Histadrut institutions and members. He was primed and ready for battle.[17]

On June 6, 1923, the HEC ultimatum was conveyed to the Legion representatives, who instantly responded that the Tel Yosef general assembly, due to be convened on June 7, alone had the authority to deal with the ultimatum. Hence it was agreed to extend the deadline to Friday, June 8. The Tel Yosef assembly called the HEC resolution "an action beneath all criticism, in view of the internal principles guiding the Histadrut. . . . A severance of relations" meant "a severance of the day-to-day life line [to its members] and medical aid to the sick"; such a threat was a totally unacceptable action in negotiations "between the Histadrut's institutions and its members." (The Legion, too, conceived of the HEC as a peer among peers.) The assembly had therefore decided that Tel Yosef could not "comply with the partition demands under the threat of an ultimatum," the implication being that, were the ultimatum withdrawn, Tel Yosef would be ready to negotiate the return of property.

Nevertheless, on Sunday morning, June 10, before the HEC plenum had a chance to discuss this reply, Ben-Gurion, on its behalf, sent letters instructing all Histadrut institutions to break off their ties with Tel Yosef. He did this on his own initiative, without consulting any of his colleagues in the secretariat or the HEC. Severance from Ha-Mashbir meant hunger at Tel Yosef, and within one day the collective kitchen was left without flour or other basic provisions. The lack of cash and credit that followed severance from the Agricultural Center and Bank ha-Poalim prevented them from buying food elsewhere. Most serious of all was being cut off from the Sick Fund, for while other Legion companies could supply their comrades in Tel Yosef with food from their own meager and distant storerooms, they were clearly unable to provide them the medical help they needed. The health situation at Tel Yosef, as was widely known, was very bad. Poor nutrition sapped the members' strength and many were ill. Malaria and tuberculosis became rampant. A Sick Fund doctor predicted that "if the situation persists, only chronic invalids will be left in the camp." Even if this was an exaggeration it was clear that the suspension of food and medical aid to Tel Yosef came at a very bad time. The members considered this act not only a "cruelty" intended to bring them to their knees, but also a calculated step in "the evil attempt on the life of the Legion."

Ben-Gurion was pitting the HEC — and himself — against the hungry and the sick. The spirit of the members of Tel Yosef remained unbroken, and public opinion became more and more inclined to favor them; their bitterness and outcry against the cruelty sent a tremor through the labor movement and brought them sympathy and support. Two days after the severance, the company at Kefar Giladi wrote the HEC to protest "the illegality" and "the violence" of the boycott and in solidarity with Tel Yosef cut off its own connections with the Histadrut institutions, emphasizing that the HEC now had its permission to cut off its medical aid, too.

Within the HEC itself the winds blew in favor of the besieged, and explanations were demanded of Ben-Gurion. He argued that he had acted properly, since it was his duty as secretary to carry out HEC resolutions, but his colleagues accused him of deliberately ignoring the fact that there was an accepted procedural gap between saying something and doing it. It had not been necessary to begin the boycott with the Sick Fund and Ha-Mashbir. Had he written the members of Tel Yosef that the Agricultural Center would cut them out of the Zionist budget, the consequences of which they would not have felt until much later, they would have understood that the HEC meant business, and there would have been time for negotiations. This was what they had really had in mind, but Ben-Gurion had suddenly delivered the final blow behind their backs, taking them completely by surprise.

Five days after Ben-Gurion's boycott instructions the HEC convened in his absence to discuss the crisis. Joseph Sprinzak expressed his regret over the action, and David Zakay attested that immediately on learning of it he had told Ben-Gurion that it was "a reckless step and a blunder." All agreed that cutting off medical services was improper, and the HEC withdrew the ultimatum, postponing it "until the close of negotiations between Tel Yosef and the partition commission." As this had been their original demand, the Tel Yosef members could chalk up a victory in the struggle with "Ben-Gurion's Histadrut."

For reasons unknown, Ben-Gurion was absent from this HEC session, yet it appears that he emerged from the episode rebuked. Undoubtedly he knew, as did the others, that this affair would bring him recognition as a man of force, the strong man in the HEC who was able to enforce authority decisively and unrelentingly. Meanwhile, it seems, he listened to the voice of reason, which advised him to wait for further consolidation of HEC authority and an opportunity to renew his campaign against the Labor Legion and Shochat's Circle.

Ben-Gurion later called his boycott orders "a dreadful decision," which implies that he had been aware that his adversaries were pioneers in poor health because of their readiness to risk their lives for Zionism and the Histadrut, and that he did not think of them only as abstractions or pawns to be manipulated. Yet he was able to repress all empathy and sentiment, manifesting his singular attribute of being able to see his political objective clearly and pursue it relentlessly.

This event also made it clear to him that the Histadrut would never be the workers' state he had dreamed of with the existing HEC staff. Given, then, that absolute authority was beyond reach, he would have to strive for the maximum possible — a resolve that reflects another of his exceptional traits, the ability to continue working at full steam toward his goal, even with the full knowledge that it was only partially achievable. In January 1925, slightly disappointed, he noted in his diary that the Histadrut had been established "as a kind of workers' state."[18]

Messenger from
the Land of Wonders

DAVID BEN-GURION washed his hands of the HEC's renewed negotiations with Tel Yosef, whether because he did not want to become party to the withdrawal of his ultimatum or because he was nursing a grievance against his friends is open to speculation. However, another reason for his withdrawal was his absorption in preparations for a trip to Russia. In May 1923 the Histadrut was invited to participate in an agricultural fair scheduled to open in Moscow in September. After six weeks of weighing the issue, the HEC finally decided to accept and chose as its representatives Meir Rotberg, an agriculturalist and one of Ha-Mashbir's top officials, and Ben-Gurion. By the time the Tel Yosef affair was settled Ben-Gurion was on his way to Moscow.

His colleagues' reservations about the fair stemmed primarily from the short time the Histadrut had been given to prepare its display. Moreover, since there was not enough money for a proper pavilion, they were afraid that the Histadrut might become the laughingstock of the fair. Ben-Gurion, however, jumped at the invitation. Seeing much more in it than just the display, he was ready to forgo important events scheduled for the summer of 1923 — the Zionist Congress among them — to attend the fair. To him it had great political importance: his very entry into Russia "in a legal manner," as he put it, was a priceless political opportunity. He already envisioned using his trip "to establish economic ties with the Russian government" and to strengthen connections with Soviet Jews, and spoke with enthusiasm about "giving our work as much publicity in Russia as possible."[1]

It seems that in his efforts to bring his colleagues around to this view

Ben-Gurion became more and more convinced of the supreme political value of his mission, to the point where he armed himself with a special document empowering him to negotiate on the HEC's behalf "with all institutions in Russia relating to government, workers, cooperatives, and trade unions, on all matters of concern to the Histadrut, its institutions, and Eretz-Israeli workers in general." He was able to get necessary papers and permits from the Mandatory government for proposals he had prepared for a number of projects to give substance to any agreement on joint enterprises that he might reach with the Soviets. His projects ranged from the establishment of Zionist model farms and city workshops in the Soviet Union, to prepare He-Chalutz* youth for life in Palestine, to the sale of Bank ha-Poalim shares to Russian Jews and setting up a Russo-Palestinian Trade Company.[2]

To understand Ben-Gurion's excitement, his awareness of the importance of Soviet Russia's dual role in Zionist matters must be taken into account: on the one hand the political and "socio-moral" force, as he put it, of the Soviet government, and on the other, the Russian Jewish community, the third largest in the world after Poland and the United States. As early as 1920 he had suggested that the Zionists adopt a line intended to ensure that "these two factors won't become our foe, but rather the reverse, that they help us in our work." The great purpose of his trip was to bring the Soviets to recognize Zionism over the Comintern's head. He was sure this was in his power, or at least that the attempt was not entirely hopeless, but he did not breathe a word of it to his colleagues at the HEC meetings, where his trip was discussed. Only to his father did he intimate that there was more to this trip than met the eye. On setting out he told Reb Avigdor that "the time has not yet arrived for me to write about the goal of my trip and of my mission in detail. I will be able to do it only after my return."

The trip had the added attraction of his view of himself, the bearer of greetings to Russia's Jews from Eretz Israel, bringing back to his friends in Palestine eyewitness reports from the land of the revolution. How and to what extent the lofty ideals of the socialist revolution had been translated into everyday life were the questions that fired his imagination. In his diary he referred to himself as "the messenger from the land of wonders."[3]

The short time available for preparations and his own impatience left their marks on his trip. The pamphlet on the Zionist labor movement in Palestine that Ben-Gurion wrote for distribution at the fair was translated into Russian and printed, full of grammatical and typo-

---

*After the war He-Chalutz organizations were founded all over Europe and the USSR. The Soviet Union had not yet banned them in 1923.

graphical errors, in two days. The display items — seeds, fruits, oils, wines, cigarettes, chocolate, ornamental and fruit tree samples, photographs, and diagrams — were hastily crammed into crates. He did not even wait until everything was packed before delegating the handling of freight from Haifa to Alexandria to Rotberg and dashing off by train to Cairo. His sole baggage, apart from personal belongings, consisted of lists of regards to relatives and friends in Russia and, of course, lists of books to buy for himself and for David Zakay, who had implored Ben-Gurion not to forget him. He stayed in Cairo, reading the Bible with an eye for quotes he could use in his Moscow speeches, until July 7, then left for Alexandria, where Rotberg joined him. On July 12 they set sail for Istanbul, where they arranged entry visas to the USSR and waited twelve days for the Odessa-bound *Chicherin*. Ben-Gurion, as usual in times of stress or excitement, felt ill. "I've been attacked by malaria," he wrote his HEC colleagues, "and I am powerless to walk around, but the preparations are pressing, and only with the last of my resources can I move about."[4]

He recovered the minute he started talking with Soviet foreign trade ministry representatives in Istanbul, Hebrew-speaking Jews who received him genially. Although he felt, he said, as if he were dreaming, he was not too removed from reality to buy himself an overcoat, two "nice shirts," and a pair of shoes to improve his appearance for his Moscow exploits.

At long last, on August 4, the *Chicherin* lifted anchor with Ben-Gurion, Rotberg, and all their crates on board, minus one that contained pamphlets on the Histadrut in Russian, which had fallen in the sea during loading. His heart filled with anticipation, "fear and apprehension," Ben-Gurion neared the shores of the Soviet Union like someone approaching "a menacing mystery with many riddles." The sailors he met on board afforded him his first glimpse of the sons of the revolution, and he lost no time engaging them in conversation. "A typical Russian [sailor], innocent, straightforward, his eyes reflecting intelligence and honesty," told him that he understood his role in the new society as being "to work properly." Ben-Gurion could not make up his mind whether this sailor was an exception or the new Soviet type. The more he talked with the ship's hands, and the nearer he got to where the answers lay, the more curious he became.[5]

On disembarking in Odessa on Thursday, August 26, he felt that the "veil of mystery" had been lifted and the land of wonders opened for exploration. But from the moment he set foot on Russian soil Ben-Gurion made up his mind to be very cautious about relaying his impressions. He was wary of censors going through his mail and possibly abusing any candid observations to thwart his mission. He had also advised the HEC from the start to make sure that the Zionist press not be a party to "the campaign of lies and slander" aimed at discrediting the Soviet Union and its doctrine, and that there be "an immediate change in policy regarding Soviet Russia." Accordingly he wrote Paula that life in Odessa was "almost normal, like in any other place," and that there was no foundation "to all the horror stories about conditions in Russia." Meanwhile, he confided his true observations to his diary, noting that while swimming in the Black Sea he had seen the ruined buildings on Odessa's shoreline, which prompted him to muse on "the evil spirit of destruction that overran everything during the years of the revolution, sparing only the sea." He also wrote in his diary that Odessa was "dying, still and lifeless, worn out, grieving, and paralyzed"; in the silent harbor only "the screeching melancholy sounds" of the sea gulls were heard. People in the streets were dressed in rags, with only socks or nothing at all on their feet. By Sunday he could tell the secret police from the other citizens: they were the only ones whose clothes were unpatched.[6]

After two days in Odessa he left Rotberg to tend to the crates and went off to Moscow to prepare for the fair. He traveled third class by train for two days, received a "room slip" from the fair's head office, and had his first taste of Moscow. In contrast to Odessa this city was "bustling, with lots of people and pedestrian traffic, vibrant, active, and jubilantly alive." It had "automobiles, most of them with foreign number plates." Nevertheless, the capital looked like "a gigantic village." He watched the people as if trying to unravel the truth behind their appearance, telling his diary that the faces he had seen "express good will and exude vitality."

He could not conduct any deeper investigations because he was busy to the last minute with the fair, which opened on September 17. Lacking money for an entire pavilion, Ben-Gurion rented "a corner" in the eastern nations' hall, alongside Japan, Persia, Manchuria, and China. The display space — 5 by 5 meters (16½ feet square) — was so small that he feared there would not be enough room for all the exhibits. Nevertheless he managed to fit them in — the diagrams piled one on top of another — with enough room to spare for a small rostrum.

The corner was an instant hit; the Soviet experts showered it with compliments, not neglecting to put their praises in writing. But far more important was the influx of Jewish visitors, who arrived in throngs not only from Moscow and its environs, but from as far away as Petrograd, Kiev, Kharson, and other distant cities, proving that Ben-Gurion had been right in recognizing the fair's political significance. "In all my days I have never seen such admiration," Ben-Gurion reported secretly to the HEC in a letter entrusted to a Jewish traveler and hidden from the eyes of the censors. He spent his time standing on the rostrum to lecture at length on the Yishuv, escorting important visitors, wandering through the crowd, distributing his remaining pamphlets, answering questions, and, when Rotberg was away, explaining agriculture. What he liked most, however, was counting the visitors. On weekdays he estimated their number at between fifteen hundred and three thousand, and one fine Sunday ten thousand people showed up.

The fair afforded Ben-Gurion a means for meeting a great many Jews and a vantage point from which to observe their social status and problems. The picture that unfolded to him was of a Jewry ruined and torn apart by the Great War, the revolution, the civil war, and their attendant pogroms. "The flood of destruction and plunder," he wrote the HEC secretly, had soaked every bit of ground "from Odessa to Kiev with Jewish blood. [Literally] hundreds of thousands were slaughtered." The takeover by a new and incomprehensible regime, the confiscation of private property, the dread of the secret police, the banning of all traditional sources of Jewish livelihood, and the resultant poverty and hunger had all undermined the foundations of Jewish life — family, community, and culture — leaving the Jews "detached, empty, frightened, perplexed, and shorn of all spiritual and material assets . . . without support, without hope, without solace, without knowing where [to turn]."

Nevertheless, he divided this wretched Jewry into two categories. The elderly judged the regime by a single criterion, derived from their personal experience. " 'Pogroms — yes, or pogroms — no,' this is the yardstick that life has given them with which to assess the events in Russia," he wrote in his diary. Their lives were safe, and they were grateful to the Soviet government for putting a stop to the pogroms, but in a society officially divided into proletariat and bourgeoisie their economic plight was grave. Only a few of them were considered workers, the vast majority being classified as bourgeoisie, upon whom heavy state taxes were imposed. With their livelihood taken away from them, they were sinking beneath the burden of the taxes. A smalltime peddler whom the regime had classified as bourgeois epitomized the whole situation of the elderly for Ben-Gurion.

The younger generation, in contrast, had grown up without Jewish education or any knowledge of Eretz Israel. There was no longer a foundation of Jewish culture in which they could strike roots. The Jewish writers he met symbolized the condition of Jewish culture — they felt forlorn, "a lonely island in a sea of indifference and enmity toward the Hebrew language and its literature." Unconscious of their national tradition, the younger generation had grown up surrounded by dormant anti-Semitism that could erupt like a volcano at any minute; at the same time many of them had found jobs and even careers in the Soviet bureaucracy. Nearly all the officials Ben-Gurion met, beginning with those in Istanbul and ending with the fair's administrators, were Jews. He described one of them, Osipov, head of the foreign relations desk at the fair, at length. Unlike the others, he had not introduced himself as a Jew, and Ben-Gurion, who met with him more than with anyone else, was sure that this "devout Communist" was the only Gentile in the fair head office. Then one day an elderly Jew approached him in his corner, explaining that his son Osipov had "said that I'd be able to get hold of an *etrog* for Succoth here." Before he left Ben-Gurion learned the man's name and gave him some grains of wheat to show his friends. He noted later in his diary that "even Osipov is Jewish."[7]

The conclusion he drew, with a certain naiveté that was part of his genius, from all he saw and heard was that "Russian Jewry can again be the major building force in Palestine, both for its capital and its manpower," and Zionism should never "give up on Russian Jewry in desperation." This conclusion redoubled his faith in the main purpose of his mission, "to better inform the Soviet government" about Zionism and its enterprise in Palestine. While some members of that same class of young Jews who had made careers in the Soviet administration encouraged him to believe that this was attainable, another group, the Yevsektsiya — an acronym for the Russian words meaning "the Jewish Section of the Russian Communist Party" — did its best to foil him. It had its own Jewish pavilion at the fair, whose purpose was to show that the Jewish problem had been solved once and for all in the Soviet Union. Obviously the Zionist corner became its archrival. In this contest, Ben-Gurion thought, his exhibit held the upper hand. He reported to the HEC with satisfaction that visitors found the Jewish Communist pavilion boring, "without a drop of love or interest," and he thought its organizers were "jealous of our success." They tried but failed to prohibit the corner from unfurling the blue and white Jewish flag alongside the Histadrut's red banner. It was Osipov who allowed the blue and white flag, saying, "The Yevsektsiya is not Russia's overlord. . . . I am Soviet Russia's representative here."[8] Consequently, Ben-Gurion did not identify the Yevsektsiya with the Soviet administration and prodded the HEC to influence the Zionist movement to draw a clear line between the two, as if he hoped that in the battle between Zionism and the Yevsektsiya for Russian Jewry, Zionism would win the Soviet administration's support.

But if the Yevsektsiya was not Soviet Russia's representative, why did the administration make it "a part of the government," as Ben-

Gurion put it? His explanation was that the administration had made a great mistake by endowing the Yevsektsiya with legal status and power. He was convinced that the Soviet government was "untrusting and unsympathetic" to the Yevsektsiya but had "no other choice, because it has no other Communists working among the Jews." He thus relieved the Soviets of full responsibility, in effect blaming the Jews who ran the Yevsektsiya. Since according to the Bolsheviks' ideology the Jews were not a nation, but a religion, in their view Zionism, as well as religion in general, was nothing but a pawn in the hands of the capitalists and the imperialists, and as such the enemy of all revolutionaries. And the Yevsektsiya was charged, by the Communist Party and by the Comintern, with driving home these truths to the minds of the Jews, who, quite naturally, saw the Yevsektsiya, at least in the 1920s, as the archenemy of Jewish traditions and Zionism. Most likely Ben-Gurion accused the Yevsektsiya of being responsible for Soviet anti-Zionism because he could not believe that a reasonable person would regard the Zionists as a tool in the hands of anyone, least of all capitalists and imperialists, and he attributed such calumny to the Jewish self-hate that in his mind was the motive force of the Yevsektsiya and the root cause of the ill it boded for Judaism and Zionism.[9]

He held then, and ever after, that the interests of the Soviet state, rather than communist doctrine, dictated the policy of the land of the revolution — "These and these only are the sole factors of the new Russia's politics" — and these interests were not necessarily opposed to the Zionist movement and its enterprise in Palestine. Neither was opposition to Zionism inherent in "the actual Soviet system." Ben-Gurion believed Soviet recognition to be within the realm of possibility, and he advised the HEC and the Zionist movement to put their trust in his attempt to attain it.

His double formula — friendship with the USSR, war against the Yevsektsiya — was bold. Was it also the product of a defective view of reality? It is true that events in the next few years proved Ben-Gurion wrong, but he was certainly right about the important part of the Soviet reality. He believed firmly that "the Soviet regime is not transitory. It won't fall. There isn't anyone to bring it down. For better or for worse — it's all the same — there won't be another regime in Russia in the coming years." Moreover, the unlikely event of its downfall would be a terrible danger for Soviet Jews, "a new revolution in Russia — that would mean ruin and destruction for Soviet Jewry . . . the like of which Jewish history has never known." The memory of the pogroms during the civil war remained firmly impressed on his mind.

Ben-Gurion was not to discover his misreading of the Soviet Union's stand on Zionism and its enterprise in Palestine until five years later.

He set out to implement his formula, having in mind three immediate or "practical" plans to change the administration's attitude. The first was to use the fair to blaze a trail through the Soviet press. He asked representatives of Soviet institutions who visited the corner to write about it, gave interviews to local journalists, and wrote an article, which he sent to the *Ekonomichiskaya Zhizn* (Economic Life). This plan was a complete failure. The article was not printed, and the big papers did not take any notice of his display. Later, in a report to the Zionist Executive, Ben-Gurion attributed it to Yevsektsiya sabotage, because of which "these articles were not allowed to appear in Moscow. Only the provincial press mentioned us." As if to underscore this disregard, *Pravda* published an article in praise of the Yevsektsiya pavilion, noting how the victorious revolution marked a new page in the history of Jewish working of the land.[10]

Ben-Gurion's other two plans encountered just as many difficulties, but he was confident that he could overcome them. The private poll he conducted on behalf of the second one, selling Bank ha-Poalim shares, was very encouraging. He thought of these shares not only as a bond with Russian Jewry but was led to believe that the buyers would be moved to follow their money to Palestine. Estimating that £10,000 worth of shares could be sold in Soviet Russia — more than had been sold in the United States — he proposed that Bank ha-Poalim open a branch in Moscow. To this end the bank in Palestine wrote directly to Gosbank, the Soviet state bank in Moscow, requesting permission to establish a branch to sell its shares in the USSR. Expecting a favorable reply, Ben-Gurion made himself the bank's agent and sold $1,025 worth to a few of the many who were interested. Considering the Jews' poverty, this must have meant that he had both passed his enthusiasm on to them and assured them that they would be able to follow these last rubles that they had invested to Palestine with the blessing of the Soviet government. Having put much thought into complicated arrangements to get the money out of the Soviet Union, Ben-Gurion was nonplussed by the lax customs check when he left. Remorsefully, he told his diary, "I could easily have taken out all the money for the bank and the money they wanted to send with me myself, but how could one tell in advance?"[11]

His third and most ambitious plan, the establishment of a Russo-Palestinian trade company, faced a fundamental obstacle: the import of citrus fruits, wine, almonds, and the like into Russia was prohibited. What could the Histadrut export to the USSR in exchange for Russian imports? There being no answer, the rationale for such a company evaporated, but Ben-Gurion came up with an idea anyhow. "I've enlarged my proposal to include Egypt as well," he reported happily to the HEC. The company would conduct three-way transactions: the Histadrut would export farm produce to Egypt; Egypt would sell its cotton to the USSR; and in return the Histadrut would buy Russian timber.

The assistant director of the Soviet lumber export company was very enthusiastic about the proposal. After their meeting Ben-Gurion sent the HEC the news that "they want to do business with us very much," but he did not explain exactly how Egypt would become involved in such an arrangement. Palestine and the Histadrut were totally superfluous, since Palestine could export only farm products, of which Egypt, 90 percent rural, had no need. Meanwhile this proposal, like that for the bank branch, remained unresolved, awaiting authorization from higher up. Ben-Gurion saw fit to wait, and to this end requested and received a two-month extension of his Russian visa. "This is the minimum time necessary to carry out anything," he explained to the HEC.

The agricultural fair closed on October 21, and Ben-Gurion felt satisfied that he had "carried out his mission in full . . . to an extent that even I, the optimist, had not prayed for." In the notes he addressed to the HEC, he noted the "tears of joy" he had seen in the eyes of the Jewish visitors who had come to see the display and the sad moment of its closing. Young men and women packed the corner from the morning on, and "didn't move from the place all day . . . as if they were in a hurry [to take it all in] before the closing." The fair closed at exactly 6:00 P.M., in the presence of many Jews "who were still waiting to come inside."[12] The blue and white flag was taken down, not to be unfurled in Moscow again until twenty-five years later, when it would fly over the embassy of an independent Israel.

Ben-Gurion waited for meetings with the heads of the Soviet administration in his room at the Mamontov Palace, where, he erroneously believed, Napoleon himself had lodged "and had relished the sight of Moscow in flames." In fact it had been built after 1812 and was not a palace at all, but a rich merchant's old house in what had once been the aristocratic section of town, not far from the fairgrounds. Its wooden floors and staircases were appropriately creaky. Ben-Gurion decorated his room with snapshots of life in Palestine, of his days in the Jewish Battalion, and a large portrait of himself.

He paid $2.50 per day for his room, a slightly expensive "pleasure," as he called it, although it was cheap in comparison to the high prices of hotels. Since he complained about the high cost of living and had to cover the 250 Egyptian pounds' worth of the exhibit's expenses over the original budget of 300 Egyptian pounds from an HEC loan, there is no doubt that he was well aware of the cost of his extended stay. But he was convinced that the profit to be gained outweighed the cost. While he waited he was occupied with transmitting greetings and meeting with relatives. He persuaded Pessia Munweis, Paula's youngest sister, to immigrate to Palestine, helping her financially by borrowing from the Bank ha-Poalim funds. He had time, too, to browse through the bookstores. He bought a military library for the Haganah and shipped twelve crates of books to the Histadrut's central library. He did not, of course, forget himself, and bought about eleven crates' worth of books for his own library, in which he hid some of the money he had received for the bank shares and the documents of sale. In one bookstore he was overcome with a great longing for his friends and, remembering Zakay's plea, included "twenty-three books for Zakay, the writings of Chekhov," in his own consignment. On board ship going home, his homesickness evaporated completely, and Ben-Gurion realized that he had really bought all the books in his crates for himself alone. "It's a pity that I didn't buy even a single book for Zakay," he said in his diary two days before reaching port.[13]

He also had time for meetings with Zionist youths — "the last of the Zionists" — who described their terror of the secret police who kept "strict surveillance over all gatherings" and the impossibility of even "three people getting together." The stories he heard about agents infiltrating their ranks made him suspect every unfamiliar face he met. Ben-Gurion concluded that "the Zionist movement has been suffocated," but believed nonetheless that there was a good chance of reviving it; for in the opening days of the fair the He-Chalutz organization, which had been constantly persecuted, suddenly won "legalization" from the Politburo. This shift had followed prolonged efforts with the assistance of no less a person than Lev Kamenev, a member of the triumvirate that had taken over the Communist Party leadership when Lenin fell ill. Ben-Gurion regarded it as a tremendous achievement and significant corroboration of his judgment that there was a good chance of changing the Soviet stand on Zionism. He considered He-Chalutz "the most important and serious matter of all those at hand, and in itself worth coming here for," he wrote to the HEC, for he envisioned it as "a central stimulus" of Zionist activity in Russia. A strong He-Chalutz movement was "a precondition for a communal and moral revival within Russian Jewry."[14]

On November 7 (October 25, Old Style calendar), the sixth anniversary of the revolution, he woke early and staked out a spot near the platform in Red Square. Until then it had seemed to him that disappointment in the accomplishments of the revolution prevailed among the Russians, and that they had "autumn in their hearts." But in the square, surrounded by a sea of flags, slogans, and pictures of Lenin, the crowd acted as though the season had turned. Suddenly, however, he felt that a cloud had settled over this happiness, for in a copy of *Izvestia* he read that Lev Davidovich Trotsky, as Ben-Gurion thought of him, would not give a speech or even be present because of illness. Ben-Gurion, to whom the popular Trotsky, as Lenin's presumed heir and the foremost Jewish Bolshevik, was very important, felt "greatly disappointed," as though "the whole essence of the celebration had been taken away." He passed the information on to those standing nearby, and got the impression that for them, too, the holiday's "glory had departed."

Of the three speeches, that of Clara Zetkin, a sixty-six-year-old German feminist and socialist-communist leader who personified the KPD, the German Communist Party, moved him the most. He was attracted by the contrast afforded by the transformation of the sweet old lady who ascended the rostrum supported by two escorts into "a lioness, spitting fire and fury, insurrection and hatred" of the treacherous German social democracy. Her face at the end of her speech "lit up once again with the smile of a sweet little girl." Standing in bitter cold, Ben-Gurion watched the impressive military parade pass by, the air force fly overhead, and the "endless" march of workers, youth, and children. He left the square wearily while the march was still going on with questions gnawing at his mind. Why wasn't Lenin's name mentioned? Why didn't his disciple and close friend L. B. Kamenev mention him?

He had a great deal of free time and could read to his heart's desire. A book that revealed to him "the soul of the Russian Revolution more than all of the books I've read and things I've heard to this day" was the mimeographed report of the twelfth Russian Communist Party convention. "I didn't read it, I lived it," he told his diary, with overflowing emotion. "This revolution was made much closer, much dearer to me." Feeling the birth throes of "the new world" and pangs of desire for the world revolution, he suddenly understood his erstwhile friend Alexander Chashin and those like him in Poale Zion who abandoned Zionism "and rallied around the flag" of the Russian Revolution.

> It isn't good, it isn't human . . . to evade it and remain on the sidelines, because . . . this desire for revolution is unlimited and not defined by boundaries of land or nation . . . and if this revolution succeeds . . . it will carry you on its wings wherever you are . . . whether you like it or not.

He was so excited that for a moment he seemed to be only a step away from denying Zionism,

> and only the deep, spiritual need for internal wholeness . . . trickling forth from the depths . . . [the need] to live your own life and to die your own

death as well . . . forces whose meaning you don't know, which rule your destiny . . . only these stand between you and the powerful current which, with immense strength, sweeps away everyone whose soul is stricken with the disease of the revolution.

Apart from this he perused a series of articles in *Pravda* dealing with the organizational problems of the Communist Party and clipped out the sections devoted to party cells in industry, party activists, the work and status of the party's control board, "corruption" and "perks" in the party apparatus, the high standard of living of labor leaders, and the like, which he took back to Jerusalem.[15]

Since the official replies to his proposals were not forthcoming, he remained in Moscow waiting for an important meeting with a top Soviet official, trusting he could remove any hindrances to realizing them. He hoped to persuade the Soviet government through him that there was no conflict of interests between the Soviet state and the Yishuv, between revolutionary communism and labor Zionism. Perhaps he had set his sights on meeting with Kamenev, whom he believed to be number one in the triumvirate, calling him "Lenin's delegate," "Lenin's disciple and close friend," and the man "with the greatest influence in Russia, after Lenin" in his diary and letters. "Kamenev has no sympathy for us," he wrote, "but neither is he particularly hostile."

Ben-Gurion had looked forward to meeting Kamenev as early as the beginning of his visit, for he had been promised that Kamenev would honor the opening ceremony of the corner with his presence, in the company of Alexei Rykov, Lenin's stand-in as prime minister, and Leonid Krassin, the foreign trade minister. His disappointment was as great as his expectations: on that day Kamenev was out of town, Rykov was "very busy," and Krassin went abroad. No refusal of a request for a meeting — if he had directly submitted one — was included in the apologies offered to him, and Ben-Gurion could have interpreted them as just a temporary deferral. If so, it is reasonable to assume that he was waiting for another meeting to be arranged by intermediaries — whose names he never divulged.

Before setting out for Russia Ben-Gurion had believed that "all that is needed is someone who will raise the flag of Zionist socialism in Russia with firmness and pride, and I am sure that he will succeed in generating a large and mighty movement."[16] Now that some time had passed and there were no prospects for a meeting with Kamenev or any other Russian Communist Party representative, Ben-Gurion realized that the matter was far more complicated. He did not despair, however, nor did he acknowledge that his mission had failed or had been doomed from the outset. In fact, his conviction that it was both necessary and urgent became firmer than ever. He was driven by a strong intuition which told him that the invitation to the Histadrut to take part in the fair and the legalization of He-Chalutz pointed to a crack in the Soviet's stand on Zionism, which could be widened into an avenue through which Russian Jews would be allowed to immigrate to Palestine. Alongside his intuition was his growing fear that if the crack were not widened soon, it would seal up and never reappear.

He was set for a drawn-out endeavor of months or even years to change the Soviet stand on Zionism, but he had been in Russia nearly twenty weeks and his visa was about to expire. On December first, the last day of the extension, he left Moscow by train for Berlin to attend Zionist meetings. Thus did his first and last visit to the Soviet Union come to an end, although Ben-Gurion considered it not the end of the chapter but only its beginning. Not until October 1942 would he admit defeat, telling the HEC, in reference to this trip, that "although I found willing ears and my arguments were well listened to, there were no substantial results."

Since he believed that "only this administration can summon the strength to defend" the Jews from the enemies out for their blood, he worried about what would happen to them when Lenin died. He sensed the fierce struggle over the succession going on behind the scenes, but at the time he could not have known that, notwithstanding the conflict among Lev Kamenev, Grigory Zinoviev, and Joseph Stalin within the triumvirate, they were united in a power struggle with Trotsky. And he certainly could not have known to what extent Stalin, the party's general secretary since April 1922, had built his own power within the communist machine. But he understood that no man or triumvirate could fill the vacuum that Lenin would leave. "I don't know if there is any other party in which one man has fulfilled as decisive a role as the leader of the Bolsheviks in Russia." Lenin ruled "the hearts and the minds . . . his words, thoughts, and actions are a constitution, a command, a decree above all criticism," he had written in October on learning of the triumvirate's appointment.

December witnessed the deepening of his doubts as to whether, in Lenin's absence, the land of the revolution would blossom into that promised land of wonders. "Is not Lenin's fate . . . the fate of communist Russia?" he asked his diary.

> The great helmsman has been plucked away while still alive. How will the vessel, in battle with the elemental forces of nature, fare in the storm? Will it be able to muster up enough strength to reach the faraway shore of the mysterious land of wonders that no man has yet laid eyes on, amid the mighty breakers and the fathomless depths, while being continually eroded by conflicts [among the crew]? It is full of holes and splits, and

water from the mighty depths buffets the vessel with immense force, threatening to sweep the ship away and engulf it, since their sole support and guide will no longer be able to grip the helm, for his hand is wasted and the light of his mind has been snuffed out.

Ben-Gurion was even more concerned for the Jewish passengers on that same vessel, who "feel the suppressed hatred, the growing hostility toward the Jew"[17] all around them. Sensing that their fate, like that of the land of the revolution, would be decided within a short time, he felt all the more committed to his mission and vowed to return to Moscow in 1924.

In Berlin bad news from home awaited Ben-Gurion. A letter from Paula written months earlier informed him that she had fallen ill immediately after his departure. The Moscow fair had not yet opened when she wrote, "When do you expect to come back. . . . (I am better, but am look very bad) don't know what to do." Fifty people, she said, had come to a birthday party she had given for both the children, and ". . . They all brought nice present [sic] but you were not *there*." As in the past he admitted to having wronged her. "I know that you've suffered some, but believe me, dear, it wasn't in vain." Instead of staying two weeks in Berlin as he had planned, he stayed only one. After two days in Vienna — where he bought more gifts to add to those he had bought in Moscow and Berlin, among them a samovar — he left for Trieste by train and straightaway boarded the *Heluan*.[18]

Cruising among the Greek islands on a calm sea and under clear skies, he could devote himself to his notes and reflections undisturbed. One day he thought about Lenin, the next about Herzl, of whose diaries he had just bought the last volume, which he began to read. Thus the father of the Bolshevik revolution and the father of political Zionism, two helmsmen who died in the prime of life, engaged in a confrontation Ben-Gurion staged in his mind. Observing them, he was surprised to learn that they had far more in common than not.

The likeness between the two becomes clear, of course, only when viewed through Ben-Gurion's mind's eye, or, more precisely, through his concept of the ideal leader, perhaps the kind of leader Ben-Gurion himself aspired to be, which was a composite of the two. Since two decades separated his conceptions of the two men — he had first described Herzl in 1904 — one may conclude that his idea of the fundamental traits required by a leader — will power, tenacious loyalty to one cause, and cunning — had not changed in the course of twenty years. To Ben-Gurion the youth, who had not yet broken free of the dream world into which he had been born in Płońsk, Herzl "possessed the will power of the gods," uniting in his spirit "Maccabean valor with King David's cunning" and the tenacity of Rabbi Akiva, who upheld the unity of God to his last breath, proving his undying loyalty to the one cause. To Ben-Gurion the founder of Achdut ha-Avodah, Lenin was the "man of iron will," bound to "the one, the only, the unchanging goal," who scorned all obstacles and knew how "to crawl on his belly through the deep mire to attain the goal." Now he added a fourth characteristic, absolute identification with the cause, which he called the "fire" that inflames, motivates, and destroys the leader, all at the same time. In Herzl, said Ben-Gurion, blazed "a fiery love" for Zion that he had inherited from the twelfth-century Hebrew poet and philosopher, Judah ha-Levi; in Lenin burned "a red fire" of the Bolshevik revolution.

To Ben-Gurion at eighteen, Herzl embodied the nobler traits of the leader: the humility, love — of a "wretched" people and a "beautiful and widowed land" — and beauty; but the secretary of the Histadrut paid more attention to Lenin's characteristics: a lucid, "powerful mind" and the ability to read reality and speak its language. Lenin was graced with "the genius to look at life face to face, to think not in concepts and in words, but in the hard facts of reality." Without ever having seen him, Ben-Gurion discerned the same quality that Trotsky, who was close to Lenin, had defined: "The strength of Lenin lay, in very great measure, in the power of his realistic imagination."

Nonetheless, Ben-Gurion perceived Lenin primarily as an extension of his earlier image of Herzl. Herzl was the man of cunning who knew how to retreat, as he proved in the Uganda affair, only to amass a greater force for a new assault on the sacred goal. Ben-Gurion found this trait in double measure in Lenin. In his diary he quoted Lenin's speech at the Communist Party's seventh congress, in which "his intellectual and spiritual essence was embodied": "If you cannot adapt yourself, if you've no desire to crawl on your belly through the mire, then you're not a revolutionary, but a chatterbox, and I do not suggest this way because I like it, but simply because there is no other way." Hence, just as Herzl could outwardly deny that his intention was a Jewish state in Palestine and talk about a *heimshtat* and Uganda, so Lenin "would not be afraid to disclaim that which he had yesterday upheld and to uphold tomorrow that which he disclaims today." Both followed one true path, "the path that leads to the goal."

But while Ben-Gurion the boy attributed the 1903 meeting of Herzl with the man responsible for the Kishinev pogrom, the Russian minister of the interior Vyacheslav Plehve, to his valor and daring, the strong man of the HEC focused on Lenin's "iron will, which would not spare a human life, [which would shed] the blood of babes and innocents in the name of the revolution."[19] Ben-Gurion admired Lenin's leadership qualities almost as much as he had admired Herzl's, although the two stood for such different aims. Differences in opinions and political thinking were just as natural to him as differences in human appearances. The determining traits of great leaders were, necessarily, the same for all.

Zionism and its implementation, which were both the foundation of Ben-Gurion's social and political outlook and the test by which it could be measured, were a far different thing from Leninism and its implementation, as he witnessed them in Russian daily life. Voyaging homeward across the calm sea, he compared the USSR's achievements to the Histadrut's and proudly told his diary, "We have not been put to shame." In general, Soviet Russia seemed to him a land of irreconcilable contradictions. The nation that had called for a worldwide civil war to establish workers' rule everywhere was itself a nation "which denies human rights to all workers"; the nation that abolished private property also "develops the ugliest forms of speculation"; the nation that abolished capitalism also "in fact sustains class differences and privileges for men of property."

Ben-Gurion was moved by the paradoxes he saw there.

> The land of the blinding light and the impenetrable darkness, of sublime aspirations to liberation and justice, and the poor, ugly reality; the land of revolution and speculation, of communism and the NEP,° of saintly toil and profane corruption, of self-sacrifice and graft, idealism and avarice, new values and generations-long tyranny, the rule of labor and idols of gold. . . . You can never tell where the holiness stops and the wickedness begins, what is a relic of the past and what is pregnant with the future.

It was impossible to predict which of these aspects would "win out," but it seemed to him that the odds were not on the side of holiness. Nevertheless, he found it hard to conclude this summation without any positive prospects at all, so he ended it on the hopeful note that "the shadows do not black out the revolutionary light."[20]

While still in Berlin he was informed that he was scheduled to make two public appearances in Tel Aviv, one a report to the Histadrut council, the other a public lecture at the Eden movie theater. Although he was pleased at the thought of his friends' eager anticipation of hearing him, he was not at all happy about making many appearances. "I won't be able to discuss Russian affairs twice," he confided to his diary. His reluctance stemmed from his resolve not to speak disparagingly of

---

° NEP — Lenin's New Economic Policy, designed to win the farmers' support and cooperation for collectivism by allowing them to retain some measure of private property.

the Soviet system. Because he was planning to return to Moscow in 1924, he probably kept telling himself that discretion and a "balanced yet positive presentation" were called for in all he said or wrote publicly about his Russian trip.

He was given no rest from the moment he stepped off the night train from Egypt into the Lod railway station on Wednesday morning, December 19. Paula, Zippora, and Zakay met him on the platform and, to his surprise, accompanied him to Tel Aviv. About a week before his return, Paula wrote, she had gone there with the children, adding, "Amos is a little sick, the doctor's afraid it's typhus." But if he had a serious disease like typhus, how could he be only "a little sick"? Ben-Gurion wondered. Were they hiding some catastrophe from him? Since he had not yet caught on to Paula's habit of punishing him with wild medical stories when he went abroad, one can imagine his anxiety until he found out that Amos was far from mortal danger. Before he could regain his breath, friends, relatives, and acquaintances assaulted him all at once, eager to hear about the Soviet Union and its Jews.

The news of his public lecture at the Eden on December 22, only three days after his return, spread like wildfire, reaching a vast number of both workers and intellectuals. When he arrived at the seven-hundred-seat theater he found an audience of two thousand people; the doorways and aisles were packed. The daily paper *Ha-Aretz* found it necessary to explain this exceptional turnout to its readers. "Apparently the spiritual ties to the old homeland have not yet been cut, to say nothing of the tremendous hunger, of one and all, for greetings from our unfortunate brethren . . . in the 'Soviet' hell."

His lack of preparation alone can hardly account for what happened to Ben-Gurion at the theater. It seems more likely that the sight of the massive audience, all ears and afraid to miss even a single syllable he uttered, warmed his heart and loosened his tongue. In any case, in the course of two and a half hours he recounted not only the fair's success, the legalization of He-Chalutz, which was of "tremendous value to all of Russian Jewry," and the prospects "that the Bolshevik attitude toward Zionism will soon change"; he also told his eager audience about the hatred of Jews, "which had intensified among the Russian people to a frightening extent" and about the Soviet tyranny and oppression.

Two days later he was appalled to discover that precisely these negative aspects were what *Ha-Aretz*'s coverage of his lecture emphasized. The newspaper quoted Ben-Gurion at length as saying that the workers' soviets were nothing more than "mere decoration" and there was no such thing as the "Soviet government," for "the government is Lenin, and Lenin alone"; his influence was "the one and only decisive [factor], and not only in government affairs. All [Russian] hearts and minds yield to his boundless influence. The Soviet government stands on two things: one man and one idea. The man is Lenin and the idea is the proletariat dictatorship." But in truth the government was a one-man dictatorship, which suppressed "all freedom of thought, even that of the worker in that land of the workers' rule." *Ha-Aretz* made what Ben-Gurion meant as praise come out as condemnation — Balaam's curse in reverse.

Ben-Gurion was greatly alarmed, envisioning the frustration of his best laid plans by his own act, for he had urged the HEC and the Zionist Executive to go soft on Soviet Russia, and now it looked as if he himself was cursing it. He rushed off a letter to the editor protesting that the report was "nothing but a distortion . . . from beginning to end," and reiterating with emphasis the public stand that, to his mind, the Histadrut and the Zionist administration should take on the Soviet Union. "The whole libelous campaign to smear the communist regime that the Russian Black Hundreds and their members in all lands are waging against Soviet Russia is directed not only against the workers' rule but also against all of Russian Jewry. Anyone aiding and abetting this campaign is supporting pogrom organizers and those who thirst for Jewish blood."[21]

Anticipation of his speech to the Histadrut council was even greater. On the council's opening night, also Saturday, December 22, 1923, Joseph Sprinzak described the trip to Moscow as the most positive event of the year, a breach in "the Russian Chinese Wall," which shut out most of the Jewish people. By the time Ben-Gurion took the floor, on the twenty-fifth, the delegates were nearly faint with anticipation, but severe disappointment awaited them. Ben-Gurion, once burned, was not about to take any chances. His letter to *Ha-Aretz* had been printed that day, and he reduced his speech to the council to a bare minimum while insisting that no minutes be recorded and no summary be published in the Histadrut organ. The only section of his speech that was published was its opening, in which he accused *Ha-Aretz* of "intentional provocation." Moreover, also at his insistence, the council passed a special resolution expressing its "sorrow at the distorted account of his lecture" in *Ha-Aretz*. The paper, however, retracted nothing and called Ben-Gurion's contentions "unwarranted irascibility."

Although Ben-Gurion clearly wanted to throw a smokescreen over his impressions of the USSR, he had to give the Zionist Executive in Jerusalem an oral report, and he could not refuse the many individual requests made by Histadrut communal settlements. He therefore talked about his trip in three more places and then sealed his lips, except for an article on He-Chalutz in Russia, which he wrote and published in 1924. Brief sections of his letters to the HEC that had been

printed before his return — one in *Pinkas* and another in *Kunteres* —
were his only other published impressions.[22]

Not until 1944, at the height of the Second World War, when the
posture to be taken toward the USSR was one of the points of contention in the labor movement, did Ben-Gurion lift the veil from his journey to Moscow to prove that his attitude toward the Soviet Union had
been favorable from the start. This twenty-one-year silence from a
major labor leader on such a central issue could not have been unin-
tentional.

Lenin died on January 21, 1924, about a month after Ben-Gurion's
return to Palestine. Since Ben-Gurion noted in his diary that the HEC
had resolved to cable Moscow to express its condolences, it may be assumed that he had a say in the wording. Addressed to the nation and
the proletariat of Russia, the cable said that the workers of Palestine
shared "in the deep grief . . . over the death of your great leader."
Ben-Gurion eulogized Lenin at a closed meeting of the Tel Aviv
branch of Achdut ha-Avodah; not a word of what he said leaked out. A
cursory remark in his diary epitomizes his doubts about the revolution's future. "The leader and visionary of the Russian Revolution fell.
Can the revolution manage without its leader?"

Ben-Gurion believed that Lenin had suffered from "a malignant,
congenital, incurable disease." Since he never learned that it was arte-
rial sclerosis of the brain he began to suspect — starting when, he did
not say, but he lived with the idea for many years — that Stalin had
craftily and slowly poisoned Lenin, so craftily that the excellent doctors who fed and cared for him were fooled. With Stalin's rise Ben-
Gurion's hopes for a better understanding between Zionism and the
Soviet Union were shattered. He-Chalutz was banned, the erstwhile
crack disappeared, and the massive barrier dividing Soviet Jews from
the rest of their people finally became impenetrable.[23]

17

The Struggle for Authority

H IS COLLEAGUES had predicted that David Ben-Gurion would
return from Russia more of a centralist than Lenin himself, but
it seemed they were only partially correct, for he told the Histadrut council that while in Russia he had "learned how not to do
many things." Nevertheless, there were certain things he did learn,
some of which he remained silent about. He did carry around clippings
from *Pravda* containing ideas for more efficient organization of the
party, the Histadrut, and the labor councils and the interaction between them; and in 1925, the as yet invisible effect of his visit would
become manifest in the slogan "Organization, Labor, and Education!"

His associates, especially his adversaries, could easily have concluded, as some did in December 1924, that he was working toward
establishing in the Histadrut a Bolshevik-style personal dictatorship.
Nothing amazed or angered Ben-Gurion more than such allegations,
for all his thoughts and actions were directed at creating, by a purely
democratic process, a single dominant authority that would treat everyone equally. He believed that what prevented his HEC colleagues
from accepting his scheme for central control in the Histadrut was the
inherent absence of statehood in the Jewish Diaspora. This lack made
them confuse anarchy with democracy, and totalitarianism with authority. Ben-Gurion meant to correct it by educating Histadrut members about the meaning of statehood. He sought authority not for
personal gratification, but because he believed that without a central
authority the goal of Zionism would never be attained.

As for himself, he was not forcing his person on the HEC, and he was
ready to step aside if the Histadrut members so wished. But if they
wanted him, as was proven by election after election, he wanted to do

things his way. This condition was the foundation upon which his "partnership" with them rested.

Of the lessons he learned in the Soviet Union that he discussed openly at the Histadrut council, the most important was that "the time has come to venture out into a new field, industry, and to do so on a large scale, with large means and impetus, [we must] apply the same efforts and means to industrial development as we do to [agricultural] settlements. . . . We mustn't fear daring new undertakings." Supporting this idea was the confirmation of something he himself had been arguing since 1920, that socialist doctrine did not prohibit investment of private capital in state enterprises. "Russia does not impede certain property owners from helping its economy with their capital," he told the council, adding, "[In this matter] we should learn from Russia." He was ready to introduce the basic principles of Lenin's NEP, which he had severely criticized in his diary, adapted to conditions in Palestine.

This was a new direction for the Histadrut in more than one way. First, with private capital available for its undertakings, it would no longer be limited to its own resources in building and developing its enterprises. It would have recourse to conventional capitalist financing: bank credit, floating shares, joint ventures with private enterprise, and so on. Second, whereas the Histadrut had restricted its involvement in construction to agricultural settlements and small cooperative projects, it would now aggressively broaden it, according to Ben-Gurion, to large-scale industry, in cooperation with private capital. To dispel any doubts that what he was aiming at was neosyndicalism — workers' participation in management and sharing of profits — he expanded on his idea in a special article published in *Kunteres* in January, dubbing the new initiative "Histadrut capitalism."[1]

It was, in fact, the final avatar of his great commune idea. In January 1923 Ben-Gurion had presented the penultimate revision of his scheme for the Society of Workers to the second Histadrut convention. It bore the marks of nearly two years' experience in the secretariat and the scars of his campaign for "public rule," his phrase for strengthening HEC authority. The convention accepted his program, resolving that the entire Histadrut membership constituted the Society of Workers, not, however, as a great commune of individuals, but as a stock company, a legal entity. The Histadrut members were called on not to hand over their possessions and income in return for pay and services according to their needs, but to become the shareholders of all Histadrut companies without having to spend a penny. After the convention Ben-Gurion drew up a master plan for "parent and subsidiary" companies[2] that had taken shape in his mind. According to this blueprint, the Society of Workers, Inc., would be the holding company of all Histadrut enterprises; its constitution made every member the owner of one share. In this way the Histadrut conventions and councils were also to constitute stockholders' meetings of a sort, the delegates acting as proxies for members, at which the directorate of the Society of Workers was to be elected. The HEC and its secretariat were, ex officio, strongly represented in it.

After his return from Moscow his drive for centralization took on fresh vigor, as Ben-Gurion put the final touches on his concept of "Histadrut capitalism." He expected it not only to double the resources at the Histadrut's disposal for its constructive role, but also increase the HEC's, that is, Ben-Gurion's, control over the institutions that would need HEC approval to take private capital into their enterprises. He set about implementing it as soon as the December council adjourned.

On March 12, 1924, the Society of Workers, Inc., was officially registered with the government of Palestine's registrar of public companies, becoming fully authorized to found and administer companies in all fields — financial, industrial, banking, and commercial. Its subsidiaries were registered later in 1924: Nir replaced the Agricultural Center as the ultimate decision maker for all the kibbutzes and moshavs; Solel Boneh took over the Office of Public Works and became the Histadrut contracting company for construction and industry. Ha-Mashbir and Bank ha-Poalim remained the supply and retail company and the Histadrut banker, respectively. New subsidiaries, all founded by the Society of Workers, soon sprang up: Shikun Ovdim (housing), Yahin (planting and food processing), Ha-Sneh (insurance), Kur (manufacturing and heavy industry), Tnuvah (dairy and farm produce), to mention only a few.

The establishment of the Society of Workers and its subsidiaries was a decisive step in shaping the social and economic aspects of the Yishuv and later of Israel. Through these companies, and through private investment in their undertakings, the Histadrut became the major factor in Zionist economic development. For example, its share in new agricultural settlement reached nearly 100 percent. Some of the subsidiaries grew into conglomerates, the largest concerns in Israel — and obviously its largest employers — and some achieved world prominence. Bank ha-Poalim, for one, was cited by *Forbes* as the forty-first largest corporation outside the United States and the communist bloc. In 1958 the HEC secretary general likened the Israeli economy to a socialist sea upon which islands of private enterprise were scattered. Although in theory the parent Society of Workers and its subsidiaries belonged to all Histadrut members, in practice control of them was entirely in the hands of their managements and the all-powerful HEC. In 1935 the HEC finally attained the authority that Ben-Gurion had been preparing it for. In time it grew into a vast bureaucracy, beyond the wildest dreams of its founders; a Histadrut employee was regarded as a pioneer of the same order of idealism as the pioneers who drained the swamps. In 1924 Ben-Gurion's intent was simply to use the control given the HEC by means of the parent company and its subsidiaries to direct all efforts and mobilize all resources to increasing immigration, thereby enlarging the Yishuv and strengthening its economic basis. The Society of Workers endowed the Histadrut with the administrative, organizational, and political power with which to accelerate the realization of Zionism.

There is one other element without which the picture of the Society of Workers would not be complete: the Histadrut uniform pay scale, which Ben-Gurion considered a thousand times better than the differential pay system that prevailed in the land of the revolution and had partly been what prompted his pride in the Histadrut commune as compared to the Soviet one.

To Ben-Gurion it went without saying that equality must reign in the Histadrut. By being paid a uniform wage the Histadrut personnel, elected officers and employees alike, would prove their adherence to the equality principle and embody the vision of the future society. This was the concept underlying the family-based pay scale he proposed to the January 1922 Histadrut council, which voted to endorse it.

His pay scale was based on the same principle as the kibbutz: each member gives according to ability and receives according to need. The first need of the worker was to support his family; therefore the Histadrut salary consisted of two parts: the basic wage, uniform and fixed, plus a variable allowance in accordance with family size. The basic monthly wage of 10 Egyptian pounds was derived from two sources: the basic salary a "fair employer" would pay a regular worker, and the desire that the Eretz-Israeli way of life, especially the Histadrut's, be simple and austere. The variable family allowance consisted of 4 Egyptian pounds for an unemployed wife, 3 Egyptian pounds for the first child, and 2 Egyptian pounds for each additional child. This pay scale went into effect in March 1922 and became binding on all Histadrut offices, institutions, and enterprises, without exception. Accordingly, Ben-Gurion began receiving 19 Egyptian pounds per month instead of the 25 that he had been taking home. Reflecting on the cut in his salary, he said that instituting "the 'scale' was a great moral relief for me." He regarded equal wages — for new employees and veterans, for skilled and unskilled labor, for elected and hired workers — as an appropriate example for those who served the working class to set for the Zionist movement. All, from the highest elected official to the employee who swept the offices, were called Histadrut workers, that is, those who worked for the Histadrut's ideals. All were in the service of a poor nation rebuilding its land. The salary of the top five officials in the Zionist organization was 131 Egyptian pounds per month each, eleven times the wage of its lowest-level employees, who received only 12. The Histadrut strongly condemned the high pay customary in the Zionist institutions, which "did not at all befit the poor national resources and which undermined the Yishuv's economic existence."[3]

Ben-Gurion's vision had to undergo a few radical changes, as had his original vision of the great commune, before reaching its final form, because absolute equality in the Histadrut was difficult, if not impossible, to attain. Professionals — doctors, engineers, and others — claimed that their needs were greater and they could not make do with the standard pay. Moreover, the Histadrut did not operate in a vacuum; its professionals compared notes with colleagues who worked elsewhere. The Sick Fund, for example, constantly worried lest its doctors leave it to join Hadassah's medical staff. Some of the elected officers of the Histadrut institutions believed they deserved a higher salary on account of their "special merits." Ben-Gurion repudiated this attitude, maintaining that none of them had any special merits and there was no reason they should be paid more. And, he said, an elected Histadrut official got more out of the Histadrut than he could ever aspire to put into it.

In January 1923 the second Histadrut convention set up a wage committee to apply the uniform pay scale in all the Histadrut institutions and to inquire into "special cases," making exceptions if need be. Ben-Gurion conceived of it as a "sovereign" committee, "independent" and with "extraordinary" powers, and the council accorded it such a status, making it responsible to the convention only.

In theory the committee was disciplinary — the Histadrut's policeman, so to speak — and Ben-Gurion, ablaze with his great commune idea, expected it to keep all Histadrut members in line regarding matters of pay. Everybody — he and the HEC included — would obey its rulings implicitly. In fact, no committee could have done the job it was charged with, for as soon as it began its work it found that nearly everyone claimed to be a special case, and rightly so, to some extent. All Histadrut members were Jewish immigrants to Palestine — part of a minority within a minority of European and American Jews who had left their homes and jobs, sometimes giving up businesses or academic futures for the sake of Zionist ideals. These outstanding individualists, highly vulnerable and sensitive about their honor, were quick to defend their rights in the name of justice, and this characteristic largely determined their behavior.

There may have been several factors behind Ben-Gurion's belief that the Histadrut employees would, as one, willingly accept rulings from above on wages. First, Ben-Gurion still believed in the labor army concept of voluntary subordination as the only way to repatriate the Jews and, primarily, to change the Jewish character, along with the socioeconomic structure to which they were accustomed in the Diaspora. That he valued this purpose no less than the redemption of Eretz Israel, and that the changing of "the Jewish character" was paramount in his concept of socialist Zionism, are clearly evident from a talk he had in Berlin in 1928 with the Russian Jewish revolutionary Isaac Nahman Steinberg, to whom he described the Histadrut as undertaking to "transfer masses of detached, sterile, and parasitic Jews to creative work and to a constructive and revolutionary labor movement in Palestine. . . . We are not just creating national institutions in Palestine. . . . We are remaking ourselves [there], and this is not a means to an end, but the supreme end itself. No greater moral endeavor can be imagined than this one of reform and renewal of our lives, of ourselves."[4]

In some respects Ben-Gurion found himself in a predicament similar to that of Moses after the Exodus. Both were faced with the need to decide arbitrarily on a new starting point, which required that their followers accept entirely new rules and begin to act accordingly. Moses had called for the setting up of a hierarchy, with appointed chiefs of tens, hundreds, and thousands, and expected a people unaccustomed to self-government and internal order to obey them. Ben-Gurion expected the Histadrut members to voluntarily obey the rulings of the institutions that they themselves had chosen and to abide by regulations that they themselves had passed, completely disregarding their different backgrounds and upbringing. It was one thing to uphold democracy and equality and vote magnificent resolutions, but quite another to live by them, not because the members' hearts were not in what they had voted for, but because in everyday life they interpreted the resolutions in different ways and because of their strong sense of entitlement. But beyond the belief in equality as the true way to a happy social life in general, and the only way to the realization of Zionism, the deep sense of equality ingrained in the Jewish people since the Torah had been given to them on Mount Sinai was at play. The Mishnah said that all Jews were princes, because they were sons to the one and only King, the great Lord himself, needing no intermediary to reach him in their services and prayers.

Second, considering the strong spirit of volunteerism that marked the pioneers of the Third Aliyah (1919–1923), his expectation of a resounding response was not altogether groundless. Quite a few had already shown their readiness to abide by harsh rules that called for self-sacrifice and self-denial: the pioneers who set up frontier settlements, working and living in barren, desolate areas, and members of the Labor Legion who built roads and drained swamps under inhuman conditions, to name but a few. Ben-Gurion expected the Histadrut employees to follow their example and be satisfied with the bare minimum, uniform Histadrut pay.

Third, in his blindness to human frailties he thought that the others would understand and accept the new rules of the game just as he did. It never crossed his mind how circumstances shape the individual, that the same Histadrut members who had been ready to lay their lives on the line as road builders or swamp drainers would behave completely differently on becoming Histadrut employees in the city. And the more the Yishuv and the Histadrut grew, the more urban workers outnumbered the wilderness pioneers.

While at first the Histadrut personnel were completely dedicated to the good of the organization, their sense of self-interest gradually grew, to the detriment and at the expense of the Histadrut. They worked normal hours, demanded regular and better pay, more perks, and better positions. In 1923 only the first signs of this change were apparent; nevertheless it was beyond the committee's power to impose the pay scale on the Histadrut employees. The matter would have ended then and there had not Ben-Gurion, as always, been loath to give up on his brainchild without a fierce fight. So in his address to the Histadrut council after his return from the USSR, as if to lend more emphasis to having learned there "how not to do things," he called for reductions in the pay scale.

One of his arguments was that the scale actually discriminated against the great majority of Histadrut members, who were employed elsewhere. They did not work for any legendary "fair employer," and those they did work for could not have cared less whether they were married or had children or how many. They all received equal pay for equal work, and the only recognized differential was professional skill. Although a Histadrut official like Ben-Gurion, with a wife and two children, was not highly paid compared to Zionist officials, he still earned twice as much as a hired hand, single or married. And unlike the Histadrut employees, whose livelihood was secure, the hired laborer was constantly at the mercy of the economy, always fearing dismissal and unemployment. Out of consideration, the least the Histadrut employees could do was reduce their pay.

Hence the December 1923 council reduced the pay scale by a fourth across the board, cutting the basic monthly wage to only 7.5 Egyptian pounds and rearranging the family allowance: 3 Egyptian pounds for a wife, 2.5 for each child under three, and 3 for each of the rest. The sole special case remaining was that of dependent elderly unemployed parents, for each of whom 2 Egyptian pounds were added to a family allowance, although a ceiling of 20 Egyptian pounds per month per family was fixed. For good measure the council also made the pay scale apply specifically to professionals, whom the original version had been misinterpreted to exclude, and to restrict the wage committee's discretionary powers by allowing no exceptions. The new rates went into effect on February 1, 1924; Ben-Gurion's salary was accordingly reduced from 19 to 17 Egyptian pounds.* Zakay received 20.

It would seem that such forceful resolutions should have enabled the Histadrut wage to be implemented without a hitch, but, as Ben-Gurion had learned from experience, the Histadrut neither tried very hard to exercise its authority (what he liked to call "dominance") nor was it able to. Indeed, before the council closed it added an escape clause to its resolution: "An institution with sufficient cause to deviate from the pay scale must receive authorization in each instance from the wage committee." This tiny crack quickly widened into a breach, leading to the breakdown of Ben-Gurion's original principle of uniformity.

The wage committee and the HEC, who received reports from every institution on its employees and their salaries, were confronted with a wide variety of transgressions. The wage committee turned to the HEC for help in enforcing its rulings, but no assistance was forthcoming. Some committee members resigned and some stopped attending sessions, the result being that the whole problem ended up in the HEC secretariat's lap. Only twelve days after the new pay scale had gone into effect the secretariat issued a ruling on the major transgressor, the Sick Fund — which had been paying its doctors a professional increment of 5 Egyptian pounds per month, using the argument that otherwise they would all go over to Hadassah and "the institution would be done for" — in an unexpected about-face: "In consideration of the doctors' situation in Palestine, and of their working conditions in the Sick Fund," read the protocol, "[the secretariat] has resolved to sanction the Sick Fund's customary pay scale" until the Histadrut council's next session, scheduled for October.

This recognition of a professional increment was the first harbinger of Histadrut wage differentiation. The unskilled laborer and the professional were no longer equals in the eyes of the Histadrut. What was

---

* According to the pay scale, Ben-Gurion should have received 16.5 Egyptian pounds; no explanation has been found for the extra half pound.

more, at the same HEC session Ben-Gurion said, "It is impossible that a man who has worked for twenty years receive the same salary as someone just starting out," and demanded that seniority, too, be considered in fixing wages. This heralded the second differential component of the Histadrut pay scale: new workers and veterans would no longer receive equal pay.[5]

There were a number of reasons why Ben-Gurion abandoned the equal wage, about which he had been so enthusiastic just two weeks previously. He may have come to the conclusion that no uniformity was possible on realizing just how diverse the Histadrut's labor force really was. Just as he had rid himself of his great commune illusions on encountering the chill of reality, so he sobered up about his uniform wage vision. But it is more likely that his change of heart was caused by the realization that the Histadrut was neither ready nor willing to assume absolute "dominance" over its membership. This would explain his not coming to the wage committee's assistance. Had he stood up for the committee, whose elevated status he had asked for, and had he backed it up in its enforcement of the council's resolutions, a violent dispute would have broken out, in which he had no chance of victory, primarily because of the combined strength of his opponents: the institution managers, their representatives to the HEC, and the other HEC members who, as it happened, paid themselves more than the scale allotted them. Joseph Aharonovitch, director general of Bank ha-Poalim, took home 30 Egyptian pounds each month instead of the 13.5 due him according to the pay scale; the Kapai director received 35 Egyptian pounds; Itzhak Ben-Zvi got 16 from the HEC and another 15 from Kapai; Zakay, who received 20 Egyptian pounds from the HEC, earned an additional 10 monthly for editing the Histadrut paper.

To fight this battle both inside and outside the HEC at once was too much even for Ben-Gurion. Moreover he, who saw everything in political terms, was certainly not interested in a fierce confrontation with Aharonovitch, the only leader of Ha-Poel ha-Tzair who solidly supported him on all other HEC issues and whom he needed most in the efforts he was still making to merge Ha-Poel ha-Tzair and Achdut ha-Avodah. Therefore, quite in opposition to the wage committee's demand for enforcement, Ben-Gurion proposed to the HEC that the salary question be returned to the Histadrut council, "since this scale does not meet reality and the vicissitudes of life."

He himself was not in the mood to put forward a new one, however, since he was rapidly losing interest in the whole business, probably because he believed there was precious little he could do about it. So the HEC resolution to put the doctors' pay on the Histadrut council's agenda was forgotten and the wage committee became defunct, leaving the pay scale sanctioned by the December 1923 council in effect on paper only. This situation, lasting until January 1927, afforded Ben-Gurion the opportunity to show that he could practice what he preached. Could he stick to his guns and abide by the December 1923 rulings, which were all his own doing? At first he did; despite a rise in the cost of living, he continued to take home only 17 Egyptian pounds a month, even though his HEC colleagues were taking home between 30 and 35. The resulting financial distress led him to borrow money from everyone at hand. Then, in March 1925, under the guise of a cost-of-living allowance, all the institutions exceeded the pay scale, some requesting Histadrut authorization in advance and some not, some raising salaries by 10 percent and some by 15 percent. Eventually, without a peep from Ben-Gurion, the HEC also raised the salaries of its elected officers and employees by 15 percent. Transgression followed transgression, and the wage situation in the institutions got steadily worse until it bordered on anarchy. Handing out advances was a characteristic practice. Although neither the HEC secretariat nor Ben-Gurion himself raised their salaries arbitrarily, as did the institution managers, they did take loans from the HEC treasury, which by July 1926 reached a total of over 1,000 Egyptian pounds; of these Ben-Gurion's amounted to the largest, totaling 382.5, or about two years' pay.[6]

This issue and the attendant public scandal will be dealt with in the context of the third Histadrut convention and the events leading up to it in 1927. But in retrospect the existence of the secretariat members' debts clearly attests that, as early as 1925 and even earlier, Ben-Gurion with his equalizing wage formula had gotten both the Histadrut and himself into a terrible mess from which there was no way out within the confines of a democratic society. Any solution would have been so tortuous and discriminatory that it could hardly have been considered better than the problem itself. The result was that a pay system no one, not even Ben-Gurion, could comply with or fundamentally change remained in effect. What had seemed like a safe road to the egalitarian Society of Workers was in reality a trap that would hold the Histadrut, and later Israeli society, in its grips for years, for the Histadrut economy, which developed and spread much faster than that of the private sector, carried with it the Histadrut pay system and made it the prevailing one in the Yishuv, and then in Israel. Although it underwent a number of changes, its main feature — minor differentiation based not on excellence and productivity but on family size — remains to this day. In any case the history of the pay scale demonstrates that Ben-Gurion's management of the Histadrut could not have been dictatorial in any true sense, since he depended on the voluntary acceptance of the pay scale by the Histadrut membership.

His failure to impose the pay scale did not lead Ben-Gurion to abandon his efforts to establish a centralist administration in the Histadrut and to make the HEC a veritable executive, with himself at its head. Shortly after returning from the Soviet Union he tried a new approach, this time raising the question of the HEC's structure, not its status. He proposed dividing it into two branches, general and economic, the former to be a Histadrut directorate, in charge of all organizations, trade unions, and social, cultural, and political affairs, at home and abroad, and the latter the directorate of the Society of Workers, to "supervise all the Histadrut's economic activity." He claimed that this division was necessary for HEC office work to be handled properly. At an HEC meeting in April 1924 he argued that "letters go unanswered, secretariat members have to wander around, and office matters, often essential to the Histadrut, are not attended to." His real intention, however, was not lost on his colleagues. Had they adopted his proposal, all the institution representatives in the HEC would have been lumped together and isolated in the Society of Workers directorate, where they would be confined to economic matters, while the Histadrut directorate, under Ben-Gurion's leadership, would have full freedom of action in all other, more important areas. It was also clear that the Histadrut directorate, which would deal with general issues, would be the senior partner of the two and have the final word not only in political and social matters, but, by evoking the overriding importance of these issues, in economic matters as well.

Unwilling to concede their equal status to Ben-Gurion, the HEC members responded with an indirection that matched his own. Sprinzak said that there was no need to stand the HEC on its head in order to improve its office work, since "a good clerk would do the trick"; Ben-Zvi expressed the hope that in the course of time the secretariat staff would become more and more specialized in its skills and the office work would improve by itself. Only Zakay supported Ben-Gurion. "I haven't been the best clerk," he admitted to his colleagues, "but secretariat affairs won't be remedied by [one]." The HEC majority followed Sprinzak's lead, and each member suggested efficiency-improving proposals of his own. Berl Katznelson, as the sworn advocate of the "collegium system" and the one who had given it its name, was not going to watch Ben-Gurion's maneuvers idly. Their partnership, like any other, could last only so long as neither party was too strong. Yet he, too, like his friends, steered clear of plain speech or outright rejection, for the members of the HEC had made an art of saying no without ever using the negative. True to this habit, Katznelson did not reject the two-branched HEC but made a counterproposal, a better one, he thought, to divide the HEC into three branches of equal standing — one economic, another to handle organizational matters, and a third to deal with foreign relations. Decentralization and delegation of authority, he said, would go a long way toward improving office efficiency.[7]

The HEC did not reach an understanding on this matter, simply because Katznelson never showed up at the extra session scheduled for settling it. (Ben-Gurion noted this in his diary.) If Katznelson believed his absence was hint enough to Ben-Gurion to drop his HEC proposals, he was wrong, but so was Ben-Gurion if he believed that Katznelson would shirk confrontation. They both stood their ground and the proposals were forwarded to the June Histadrut council. The council, in its typical spirit of compromise, approved a scheme that was essentially Katznelson's, but it was couched in Ben-Gurion's terminology. It divided the HEC into three branches — the Society of Workers directorate and two secretariats, one for internal affairs and one for foreign affairs. Ben-Gurion was quick to agree to it, on condition that the two secretariats be manned by his nominees. The council did not object, but neither did it choose any of his candidates. In reaction, Ben-Gurion submitted his resignation from the secretariat, and the HEC structure remained unchanged.[8]

Did Berl Katznelson oppose Ben-Gurion's proposal and help kill it at the council only out of fear of tipping the balance of power too much in Ben-Gurion's favor? Probably, but there is no clear-cut proof. Almost certainly Katznelson was uncomfortable with the way their partnership was progressing. He regarded himself as a check on Ben-Gurion's power and undoubtedly realized that he was not being allowed to fulfill this role properly. All too often Ben-Gurion went ahead with his plans without consulting him.

Katznelson had first been made aware of Ben-Gurion's inclination to act on his own on May 1, 1919, when Ben-Gurion drafted and published an official Achdut ha-Avodah proclamation on the international workers' holiday without consulting with Katznelson or Achdut ha-Avodah's executive committee beforehand. Katznelson, who shrank from exaggerations, disliked the proclamation's pompous style, which stated that Achdut ha-Avodah "is already the strongest social force in Palestine." He sent off a sharply worded letter in reaction, but this was not enough to reform Ben-Gurion, who later circulated his labor army, or great commune, idea without consulting anyone. Nor did Katznelson approve of the Society of Workers program. When Ben-Gurion brought it up for discussion at the second Histadrut convention, he exclaimed to him, "Don't frighten the geese!" — that is, only geese would take him seriously. After the Tel Yosef incident he accused Ben-Gurion of causing "demoralization" in the Histadrut, and he was later heard to say several times that Ben-Gurion was "crazy."

If these were signals intended to alert Ben-Gurion to his partner's growing resentment they were wasted effort. Ben-Gurion was so immersed in himself, his activities, and his mission that it never even occurred to him that he might have hurt his partner or not been fair with him. Even had he noticed Katznelson's signals, they would not have had the desired effect. For example, on his return from Moscow Ben-Gurion devised his own strategy of what to say about the USSR and what to withhold, again ignoring Katznelson, who this time must have given Ben-Gurion the cold shoulder so pointedly that even Ben-Gurion got the message and took note of it in his diary. "For some reason Berl has distanced himself [from me] altogether — —." Why the dashes? Perhaps because only God knew why. These episodes, and more that followed, chipped away at their partnership. Katznelson was always the one who had to adjust to Ben-Gurion, never the other way around.[9]

In mid June 1924 the HEC held a reconciliation meeting at which Ben-Gurion explained the true reason for his resignation from the secretariat in strong language. "As long as there is no central power to coordinate all branches of [our] activity, there can be no improvement. It is imperative that there be an executive to defend the workers' interests, but there isn't any." Although these might seem to have been his parting words from the secretariat, the HEC members were unwilling to let him go, but not because they had suddenly had second thoughts about his proposal. They were just looking for a way to pacify him, offering one compromise after another. Hoping to tire the HEC into accepting his original scheme, he chose one that promised regular weekly "joint sessions" of the secretariat with the representatives of the major institutions and agreed to withdraw his resignation "for three months" only, to put the compromise to the test.

It was no secret that this was an honorable way out for Ben-Gurion, especially since in May the HEC had authorized his leaving on July 17 for a second three-month visit to Moscow to further pursue his efforts to reach an understanding with the Soviet Union. It was clear that Ben-Gurion yearned for this mission, and he could fulfill it only if he maintained his position in the HEC. In other words, he would not even have a month in which to test the joint sessions.

He went first to London, to arrange for a visitor's visa at the Soviet embassy there, meaning to proceed directly to the Soviet Union. But the embassy refused to issue him a visa, on the pretext of waiting for instructions from Moscow. This delay dragged out so long that Ben-

Gurion had time to take part in several conventions in Europe and America. After four and a half months he decided that his second mission to the Soviet Union had ended before it had begun and returned home in December, brokenhearted and empty-handed.

The one high point of the trip occurred when he flew, for the first time in his life, from Danzig to Berlin. Elated, he thought, "I parted from the earth." He was proud of himself for not showing fear or feeling ill in the tiny monoplane, in spite of warnings that he was taking his life in his hands. He even tried, unsuccessfully, to engage the only other passenger, facing him, in conversation. Imagining that he himself was flying, without the plane, he enjoyed himself immensely. "How sad that the flight is over," he concluded, immediately jotting down his impressions and emotions on a sheet of paper that he later attached to his diary.

In May 1925, after eight and a half months, Moscow finally granted two visas to Histadrut representatives for a brief visit in the Soviet Union, but by then Ben-Gurion was back at the HEC. He withdrew his candidacy for the mission and the visas went to David Remez and Levi Eshkol. Their visit to Moscow that summer was the last one to Russia by any Zionist representative for many years. Shortly thereafter Stalin's regime embarked on its campaign to wipe out Zionism, becoming its unforgiving enemy, and the Soviet Union shut its gates on its Jews. No one could get in or out.[10]

By the time Ben-Gurion returned to Jerusalem in December 1924, the three months of trial joint sessions had passed. The results, as expected, were dismal, primarily because of personal clashes, which had freed the litigious instincts of the HEC members. Ben-Gurion noted in his diary that "there hasn't been such anarchy in the HEC for a long time."[11] As a result, his resignation from the secretariat remained in effect. Theoretically, he was a member of the HEC plenum only.

Since his resignation had never been accepted, however, and he, in his capacity as plenum member, showed up from time to time in his office, making occasional decisions, and since no one else was called on to take his place in the secretariat, a singular situation developed, which gave Ben-Gurion the opportunity to test a subtle and daring tactic that he later used in the course of his many campaigns. Some of his rivals called it the driver's stratagem. Suppose that the Histadrut was a bus, the secretariat its driver, and the HEC its codriver; Ben-Gurion, having resigned as driver, remained at the wheel, but without gripping it. As long as the road ahead was straight there was no danger to the bus and its passengers, but inevitably it would approach an obstacle; someone would have to steer clear of the catastrophe, and the question would arise as to who it would be, the driver or his deputy? Whose daring, or responsibility, was greater, that of Ben-Gurion, who counted on the danger intimidating his colleagues into acquiescing to his terms, or that of the HEC, which stood by its resolutions?

The test of nerves was a long one. The fact that the HEC had a difficult and dangerous road ahead did not prevent its members and employees from devoting their energies to unending quarrels over legality and principles, forcing marathon sessions to settle intractable disputes of a personal nature. When the HEC could not sort them out, it handed them over to the Histadrut council, with the result that the HEC, and sometimes the council, too, was partially paralyzed. And as if this were not enough, the long-standing animosity between Ben-Gurion and Joseph Sprinzak was getting worse.

From the start it had seemed that their personalities were destined to clash, and party differences steadily fueled the fire until theirs became the longest and most irreconcilable conflict in the history of the Zionist labor movement. Both were short of stature, but the similarity ended there. They were complete opposites in every other way, from mode of dress to personality.

They had their first major bout at the second Histadrut convention. Sprinzak accused Ben-Gurion of "hysterics" and "inflammatory speech against those who aren't members of Achdut ha-Avodah," while Ben-Gurion spoke of "comrade Sprinzak's Christian tolerance" and accused him of cowardice. Nor did their work together in the HEC secretariat inspire any feelings of warmth between them. Sprinzak maintained that Achdut ha-Avodah, the Histadrut majority, had intentionally deprived Ha-Poel ha-Tzair of positions and power, accusing Ben-Gurion of placing party interests above those of the Histadrut. There is no doubt that Sprinzak regarded Ben-Gurion's efforts to turn the HEC into an executive as the manifestation of his ambition to take complete control, and his plan to split the HEC as one of his tactics to this end.[12]

Histadrut Week, held in December 1924 to mark the Histadrut's fourth anniversary with public meetings and celebrations, brought their relationship to the boiling point. The weekly *Ha-Poel ha-Tzair* accused Ben-Gurion of exploiting the Histadrut platform "for the good of his party's interests," and its editor, Itzhak Laufbahn, in a signed editorial, accused Ben-Gurion and Katznelson together of distorting the truth, being boastful and arrogant, and advertising their party at the Histadrut's expense, as well as of incitement and intrigue. What really cut Ben-Gurion to the quick, however, was Laufbahn's mocking comment, "The Histadrut — that's me; culture — that's me; literature — that's me; monotheism — that's me." Although the "me" was intended to refer to both Ben-Gurion and Katznelson as the joint personification of Achdut ha-Avodah, Ben-Gurion took it personally as an attack directed at himself, implying that he was aiming to rule the Histadrut alone.

Both wrote to the HEC, Katznelson giving notice of his resignation from *Davar*, the Histadrut daily newspaper, then in its last stage of preparations before publication, of which he was to be editor in chief, and Ben-Gurion giving notice of his resignation from the HEC plenum, unless the Histadrut took Ha-Poel ha-Tzair, meaning Sprinzak, to court. By a majority of the six Achdut ha-Avodah members against the four Ha-Poel ha-Tzair members present, the HEC voted to summon the editorial board of *Ha-Poel ha-Tzair* to the Histadrut supreme court.

To Ben-Gurion's great satisfaction, Sprinzak was alarmed. "Sprinzak, as usual, has begun to retreat," he noted in his diary. But his satisfaction was short-lived because Chaim Arlosoroff, an energetic young man from Germany who had recently joined the HEC and was Ha-Poel ha-Tzair's great hope, was made of sterner stuff than Sprinzak and, sparing few words, made it clear that prosecution of Ha-Poel ha-Tzair's editorial board was out of the question because the Histadrut lacked the power to pass judgment on a party. With this the matter came to an end.

Denied satisfaction, Ben-Gurion took his anger out on Sprinzak. Participating as an observer at a secretariat session in March 1925, Ben-Gurion remarked, in response to one of Sprinzak's customary reservations, that he didn't "attach any importance to comrade Sprinzak's grievances." At this manifest belittlement, Sprinzak walked out. "We have unfortunately grown accustomed of late to outbursts of venomous polemics," he wrote the secretariat, declaring that he would no longer set foot inside the secretariat of the HEC. True to form, he relented when the secretariat sent him a conciliatory note in Ben-Gurion's name.[13]

In the midst of all this, at the beginning of February, Ben-Gurion revived his proposal for the two-winged HEC. This utilized his driver's stratagem to perfection, for since his resignation the preceding June, the secretariat, lacking direction, had not been functioning properly. Because of preparations in Tel Aviv for putting out *Davar*, personal and partisan conflicts, and the dispersal of its members between Jerusalem and Tel Aviv, the plenum did not convene for six consecutive weeks, from February to April 1925, and the HEC members began to fear that, as one of them put it, public confidence in them was "on the wane."

On April 1 the plenum finally met to discuss the situation. The only remedy, to which the majority agreed, was to return the HEC to Tel Aviv "for the purpose of coordinating Histadrut activity and guidance of its institutions," which, the resolution said, would officially be based in Tel Aviv. Thus at least the plenum could meet in a regular fashion once a week and more. However, this action did not solve the secretariat question, nor that of Ben-Gurion's resignation from it, and without him at its center, it was no better than a wheel without a hub. Ben-Gurion, primed for this opportunity, restated his condition for withdrawing his resignation, the implementation of his scheme. This time it was Arlosoroff who rejected it forcefully, for partisan reasons. If Ben-Gurion's Achdut ha-Avodah colleagues feared he would personally assume control of the entire HEC by means of the political wing, Arlosoroff feared that the same development would put Achdut ha-Avodah in control of the entire Histadrut, to the detriment of Ha-Poel ha-Tzair. Both factions, for different reasons, voted down Ben-Gurion's scheme once again. As a result his resignation stood and the session adjourned at a stalemate. The nerves of neither driver nor deputy had yet betrayed them.[14]

On May 14, 1925, the HEC met in Tel Aviv for the first time. His chances of winning his campaign had become very slim, but Ben-Gurion did not back down until mid July. The Zionist Congress was to meet in Vienna from August 18 to 30, and most members of the HEC, Ben-Gurion among them, were elected as delegates, necessitating the appointment of functionaries from the lower echelon to a "provisional secretariat for the duration of the Congress."[15]

This proved to be the magic formula for breaking out of the vicious circle. Going to the Congress gave Ben-Gurion time to contemplate the situation, especially the move to Tel Aviv and the resultant changes in the HEC work pattern, and a new tactic suggested itself. Instead of confronting his colleagues, trying to take the opposition by storm, as it were, he decided that if he could not beat them he had better join them. From then on he would try to achieve a concentration of authority not by constitutional redefinition or a change in the HEC structure, but by tightening its organization. What he could not get by right or by might, he would try to get through finesse and his control of the apparatus.

When Ben-Gurion returned to Jerusalem he behaved as though his resignation was a thing of the past, forgotten in the hectic days of the Congress. In September he was back at the helm of the secretariat, moving full steam ahead in his new direction. Did his colleagues want the HEC to be composed of institution representatives, as equals among equals? Then what could be more proper than giving representation to all the institutions and other bodies that had grown up in the Histadrut's first five years? No one could object to this, and in December Ben-Gurion was able to increase the HEC membership to fifteen.

The secretariat, which had been increased from three to five members shortly before the HEC moved to Tel Aviv, grew, correspondingly, to seven. It became a very large plenum, including Remez from Solel Boneh, Katznelson from *Davar*, Moshe Beilinson from the Sick Fund, Golda Meir from the Women Workers' Council, and others, and ceased forever to function as an executive body.

As Ben-Gurion had expected, the HEC's dependence on the secretariat increased in direct proportion to its growth. Simultaneously, without his having to lift a finger, the secretariat became smaller. This was the change he had anticipated during his reassessment, since two of the five secretariat members elected in May were chained to other jobs in Jerusalem — Sprinzak to his department in the Zionist administration and Ben-Zvi to the National Council — precluding their full participation in secretariat work in Tel Aviv. In fact, the only three to remain were those who moved to Tel Aviv, received their salary from the Histadrut, and devoted all their time to it: Ben-Gurion and Eliyahu Golomb from Achdut ha-Avodah, and Jacob Efter from Ha-Poel ha-Tzair. These three became known as the smaller secretariat. (Zakay had long since left to join *Davar*'s editorial board.)

The smaller secretariat became the executive. For the first time, Ben-Gurion stood head and shoulders above the others in it; Golomb and Efter came from lower echelons in their parties and the Histadrut than Ben-Gurion, Katznelson, Tabenkin, Sprinzak, and Aharonovitch in theirs. In truth, Golomb and Efter were not Ben-Gurion's peers but his aides, one in organizational matters and the other as treasurer. As a result the impression was created that Ben-Gurion was secretary general, though no such position officially existed.

This fact acquired particular significance in view of what might be called Ben-Gurion's packing of the HEC and its becoming a mini-parliament that seldom met in full. Ben-Gurion's smaller secretariat quickly became the "general secretariat" of the HEC; it developed its own administrative apparatus, becoming a de facto executive that supervised all the Histadrut institutions, departments, and branches, which, by the end of 1931, employed thirty-three people full time and one part time. Six were directors of the departments of Aliyah and foreign affairs, policy, culture, statistics, Arab affairs, and finances; the rest included clerks, typists, and a messenger who also served tea twice daily. The part-time employee was Golda Meir's husband, Morris, who translated HEC overseas and government correspondence into English.

Ben-Gurion took great pains to establish what he called "the secretariat regulations" — its regimen, which consisted of an eight-hour workday, 8:00 A.M. to 6:00 P.M., with a two-hour lunch break. Ben-

Gurion, who liked to sleep late, preferred to begin at 9:00 and finish at 7:00. He was particularly stringent about requiring a set time for each activity: reading the morning mail, holding a general secretariat meeting at 9:00, being open to the public from 10:00 to 12:00 four days a week. The first half of the afternoon was devoted to correspondence, the second to preparing surveys and diaries. The days the secretariat was closed to the public were reserved for HEC sessions, secretariat meetings with institution representatives, and visits to the labor councils and Histadrut branches.[16]

With his customary love of order, Ben-Gurion created a system of diaries at the secretariat, hoping to endow the others with his own meticulousness. His own diary quickly became "public"; it did not contain personal speculations, for he did not intend it to be a reflection of his mind and thoughts. It was instead a record of meetings, a portable archive, aiding memory and work organization. The pages of the notebook in which he kept it were interleaved with carbon paper; he tore out the business pages, retaining the copies, and left in the private ones, such as personal letters. He would give the others in his office originals from his diary, and later demanded that they, too, keep diaries like his. Five copies were typed daily and became the secretariat master register, a kind of report that saved time, was always at hand, and served as a means of coordination. The other institutions learned from the secretariat's example, and the HEC administration and branches adopted Ben-Gurion's diary system.

Ben-Gurion's de facto status as the head of the general secretariat led to his becoming the Histadrut general secretary without his being elected to such a position and without the Histadrut convention, which still adhered to the collegium principle, seeing fit to create such a position. It was legally instituted only after Ben-Gurion had left the Histadrut, following the example he set in practice.

For him it was the man who made the job.

18

Paula's Jealousy

URING MARCH 1925, while his resignation was in effect, Ben-Gurion had busied himself with Achdut ha-Avodah matters, primarily editing its *Kunteres,* which he could do at home. He could spend more time with his family and help Paula, who was expecting their third child.

On March 29 she gave birth to a girl whom they named Renana (Hebrew for "exultation"); after their return from the hospital he kept a close watch on the welcome seven-year-old Geula and five-year-old Amos extended to their baby sister. "Geula was hysterically happy to meet Renana," he wrote in his diary, and "Amos, too, was jubilant, but quietly and moderately so." Fascinated with the phenomena of birth and growth, he made precise daily notations in his diary of Renana's weight, before and after nursing. He also took great pleasure in listening in on his children's conversations, taking one of them down in full:

GEULA: God wasn't born.
AMOS: He made himself all by himself.
GEULA: No. He already was. He couldn't make himself.[1]

This family bliss did not last. Ben-Gurion was soon torn away by a fit of feverish activity. Between May 14, when the HEC moved to Tel Aviv, and July 18, when he was to go abroad, he spent several days a week in Tel Aviv at HEC meetings, preparing for the two conventions he was to attend and looking for an apartment. In his hurried negotiations with the new landlord he got the apartment's vacancy date wrong and signed the lease just ten days before his departure. On July 14 he brought his newly arrived father from Haifa to his home in Jerusalem, on July 17 he gave Paula thirty-five Egyptian pounds, and the next day he left for London, where the British Empire Labour Conference was to meet, after which he was to go to Vienna for the Zionist Congress.

He had entrusted his family's packing and other arrangements to Shlomo Ze'evi, secretary of the Jerusalem Labor Council. But despite Ze'evi's dedication, energy, and organizational ability the move was plagued by a series of calamities, beginning when Amos came down with tonsillitis even before Ben-Gurion had set out. Shortly thereafter Reb Avigdor became ill, too. The packing took nearly three days because of all the books. Then, on the Tuesday when the family set out for the new apartment together — the healthy and the not-so-healthy — the real troubles began. The apartment at 64 Nahalat Binyamin Street — four rooms on the second floor for ten Egyptian pounds a month — was bustling with life, and the inhabitants did not seem ready to leave. Ze'evi had to handle both the truck driver and moving men, who wanted to unload and move on to other jobs, and Paula, whom he had to keep calm. After an exhaustive parley with the old tenants a compromise was reached: two rooms would be vacated immediately to store the furniture, and the entire apartment would be vacant on Sunday. Meanwhile, Paula, Reb Avigdor, and the children were to stay at the Barash Hotel, but then Geula came down with the mumps. Anxious about Renana, not yet four months old, and Amos, who had just recovered, Paula wanted to keep Geula far away from them. One of Ben-Gurion's old Ezra friends took Geula into his home "and saved the rest of the children," as Ze'evi wrote Ben-Gurion, adding, "But the devil's hand is ever poised [to strike]." The friend's wife, who had promised to take care of Geula, came down with a high fever, so Paula had to run back and forth between her baby at the hotel, Geula at the friend's home, and the new apartment, which needed her attention.

On top of all this she had to come up with the money for moving and plastering fees and the unforeseen hotel bill, amounting to more than eleven Egyptian pounds. "She was in a terrible state," reported Ze'evi to Ben-Gurion, absolutely determined to cable him to return home immediately — this time the cries of sickness and hardship were legitimate — and Ze'evi "needed the patience of Hillel the Elder," as he put it, to calm Paula down. After devoting "two solid weeks" to all of this he could inform Ben-Gurion, "I've made good on my promise to you [and] everything has worked out okay."

However, there was no peace between Paula and Reb Avigdor, and he went to live with Zippora in Haifa, so the spacious apartment housed only the immediate family. Paula embarked on what was then considered a bourgeois way of life, quite unlike that of most Histadrut members, who shared their living quarters. She set aside an entire room for the library and the living room for entertaining — for maintaining public relations as required by Ben-Gurion's position.[2]

The apartment was a short walk from the HEC offices, so when he returned from abroad Ben-Gurion could spend more time with his family and continue his close watch on Renana's development. In his diary he recorded the appearance of her first and second teeth, and in February 1926 he wrote, "Today we weaned Renana," as if he, too, had had a part in it. She could speak by her first birthday, and in May he wrote that she had begun to drink from a bottle. Soon the family became aware that Ben-Gurion's interest in Renana exceeded the normal interest of a father in his youngest, and that a special love was forming between them. Any doubts about this were dispelled when a severe illness sealed the bond between them forever.

On the evening of September 8, when Ben-Gurion was at the HEC planning his war against the Labor Legion and the Circle, Paula called him home urgently. Renana, who had come down with a fever that afternoon, had had a seizure. Seeing the girl he knew this was no false alarm. His intuition told him that she was deathly ill. Having as yet no telephone, he ran first to the home of Dr. Aaron Binyamini, a member of Achdut ha-Avodah and a top-notch physician. Not finding him there, he ran to the HEC office to telephone the Sick Fund clinic, which was closed. He next went to Ada Golomb, Eliyahu's wife, and together they ran to the renowned pediatrician, Dr. David Deutsch, who refused to go to Ben-Gurion's home because, he said, he was on his way elsewhere. "The little girl is dying!" Ben-Gurion cried, but to no avail. Deutsch referred him to another physician. Furiously he and Ada ran to Dr. Moshe Cohen, the Herzliya Gymnasium's doctor, who also refused to come at first, but changed his mind at seeing the dread in Ben-Gurion's face. "I wasn't sure I'd find her still alive," wrote Ben-Gurion afterward. Dr. Arieh Pokhovski, a surgeon and gynecologist whom Ada had also called in, arrived later on, and Binyamini came around midnight. The doctors could not diagnose the illness, but, following their advice, Paula and Ben-Gurion applied cold compresses to Renana's forehead and gave her cold baths throughout the night.

Ben-Gurion was still at his daughter's bedside the next day. She was better in the morning. Her fever had gone down and she spoke a little, but, Ben-Gurion wrote, "in the afternoon her condition worsened again. She had a terrible convulsion. She was blue all over and cold; her eyes were like glass, her teeth were clenched, and her mouth shut fast. It was impossible to force a hand or spoon into her mouth. Only foam dribbled out of her lips." Desperately, he again ran to Ada Golomb. On returning home he found the girl asleep. He noted that "injections of cold water and chlorine [*sic*] had quieted her," adding, "Paula's efforts restored her to life."

At dawn Binyamini returned and advised Ben-Gurion to consult a neurologist. That afternoon Dr. Deutsch finally showed up and said there was no danger; he diagnosed a simple case of the flu and suggested a diet of cereal, toast, and milk. Binyamini, who had returned that afternoon, was vehemently opposed to Deutsch's advice, so Ben-Gurion had to choose between two medical authorities. He opted to follow Binyamini's instructions, cold baths and a lab test. After reading the laboratory results Binyamini called Ben-Gurion and Paula to another room to say, "There's no hope. She's going to die." Paula screamed, "No! She won't die!"

On September 16 Ben-Gurion took Renana to Jerusalem's Hadassah Hospital, where meningitis was diagnosed. Until the discovery of penicillin it was usually fatal, and there was no particular treatment for her. Nevertheless, under Dr. Benno Greenfeld's care Renana recovered, but also forgot all she had known. On September 28 she returned home in her mother's arms.[3]

Although her speech returned, Ben-Gurion continued to give Renana special care until all remnants of the illness disappeared. Gradually a good part of Renana's care passed to him. He gave his daughter her daily bath, washed her hair, and sat her on the chamber pot. When she got sick in January and in November 1928, he stayed at her bedside until she was safe and well, and in the summer of that year he canceled his vacation for the same reason. Little wonder then if Geula and Amos nursed a grudge that Renana was the only one for whom their father would let everything else, even Zionism, go for a day or two. When she began school he would sit in her room, sewing buttons on her doll's clothes while helping her learn the alphabet. He also played charades with her, a game they enjoyed through her adolescence. He once devoted half of a short letter to Paula from abroad to her. "Dear Renanale, I received your drawings. They're very pretty, and I was happy to get them. Send me a lot more. Learn to write and write me a letter. I miss you, my sweetheart, and I love you very, very much." After signing it with "kisses, Daddy," he added a postscript. "And to Geula and Amos, too. Write me, children."[4]

As soon as they moved to Tel Aviv Geula had begun to attend the Herzliya Gymnasium; Amos followed a year later. Paula very much wanted her children to play the piano and registered Geula, the first victim of this fancy, with Moshe Hopenko, who taught violin and piano and owned the largest music store in town. His pupils were potential customers, and when the time came he sold Ben-Gurion's family a brand new Pleyel piano for 100 Palestinian pounds — more than five months' wages for Ben-Gurion — in installments of 2.5 pounds a month. Renana, too, later played this instrument; the only one to escape it was Amos, who fulfilled his musical obligation with an army bugle. Unfortunately the two girls' musical talent was limited, and they were never able to play for their parents anything sweeter than finger exercises. Michael's daughter was musically gifted, but once, when she sat down to play in his home while her famous uncle was in the library, she expected his praise. Instead, Paula hurried in and shut the lid on her hands — to keep her from disturbing Ben-Gurion, she explained.

The library served as a gauge of his disposition toward each member of his family. Paula and the older children were forbidden entry; Ben-Gurion would get angry at Paula when she swept and dusted there because she inadvertently mixed up his books and papers. Renana, on the other hand, was free to bother him as much as she liked. He often asked her to stop, but only once did he raise his voice to scold her. Amos, however, was rewarded with a slap when he was found there drawing in one of Ben-Gurion's old diaries. Although as a boy he was unaware of his father's public importance, Amos had more than ordinary respect for him. Ben-Gurion's aloofness, probably compounded by his preference for girls' indoor over boys' outdoor games, affected his son. Ben-Gurion once admitted that he had never played them and had no interest in tag, marbles, or soccer.

Amos quickly discovered that his father, unlike Paula, would give him money for candy or the movies, and he was forever impressed with Ben-Gurion's generosity. Yet, without games that they could play together they had no common language. For purposes of thrift Amos's birthday, which fell in August, was celebrated on Geula's, in September. Looking back on his childhood he could say, "I didn't have a bar mitzvah. I never had a birthday celebration." In contrast to this, the letters Ben-Gurion received from home when he was abroad were replete with remarks concerning his daughters and their birthdays, especially Renana's.

After Renana's first birthday, Geula wrote to their father for Amos and herself, "Yesterday was Renana's party and many people came and also many children. We participated a lot and then they gave Renana beautiful presents." People outside the family were also aware of his special weakness for Renana. British Labour Party delegates, who were invited to his home for her fifth birthday, brought her a doll, an item he saw fit to mention in his diary. Amos said that he did not remember receiving "even one present" during his childhood; his bicycle, for example, was a hand-me-down from Geula. He used to beat up his sisters, especially Geula, and was considered "a savage." Later the two sisters remembered that he was Paula's favorite and that their mother was easier on him.[5]

In July 1927, after two years on Nahalat Binyamin Street, the family moved to a larger apartment: four commodious rooms on the first floor of a new and impressive building at 10 Pinsker Street. The rent stayed the same in the new currency — ten Palestinian pounds a month. There was a large garden in front of the house and the apartment had enough space for a proper dining room. The library was spacious enough to serve as a work room and a place to receive guests, so that Ben-Gurion could invite visitors from abroad to dine at his table and hold large meetings in his home.

It seems that Paula should have been happy with her lot: her children were healthy and happy, her home new, spacious, and lovely. Ben-Gurion's salary — double a teacher's — should have been sufficient to support them comfortably, as befitted the family of a labor leader. His reputation had spread to the extent that two sculptors had modeled his head in bronze. In 1930, in a letter from New York, he hinted that he, too, thought her life had improved. "Several lady friends have told me that they envy you. I said that you're not at all proud of me and that you don't admire me so much. Did I tell them the truth?"

But Paula walked around gloomily, with bitterness shadowing her every move. First, her financial outlook was far from sunny. Ben-Gurion was up to his ears in debt to Bank ha-Poalim, cooperative banks, Kapai, Ha-Mashbir, and the HEC treasury. Although Ben-Gurion's salary had grown to 22.5 Egyptian pounds, including a small expense account, after subtracting rent, 4.250 Egyptian pounds' tuition for the two children, the piano teacher's fee, and the cost of Ben-Gurion's cigarettes — at his peak Ben-Gurion smoked eighty a day — Paula had hardly anything left with which to feed and clothe her family or repay debts. An additional debt of more than 23 Egyptian pounds accumulated at the produce department of Ha-Mashbir on Allenby Street, and in March 1927 Ha-Mashbir wrote to Ben-Gurion, "Apart from your large debt you owe our Allenby branch 4.410 Egyptian pounds," which he was asked to pay within the week. In March 1926 Paula wrote Ben-Gurion in Europe, "I cannot go out, no shoes, no dress." A month later she added that something was wrong with her heart and that the doctor had advised her to fortify herself with bananas and eight glasses of milk daily in addition to other nutritious foods, "but I will have to stop as my funds are too small for such a luxury." The heart ailment was, of course, a figment of her imagination.[6]

Paula did enjoy some material prosperity when her husband was on

his missions, since then she got his entire salary plus whatever was left
from the money given him by the HEC for expenses abroad. But although she would ask him to buy household goods on these trips, she
usually did not get everything she wanted. In April 1926, for example,
she sent a shopping list to him in France that consisted entirely of
items of clothing and urged him to buy a full-size down comforter for
the two of them. But Ben-Gurion bought two copies of his bronze head,
and since his mania for books consumed the bulk of his money, he
never bought the comforter. In August 1930 Paula would write him, "I
always wanted it and you have promised to fulfill my wish a dozen
times and you didn't keep it." In fact he spent only 788 francs on a
quarter or less of what she had asked for and 1,253 francs on 122 books.
His children remembered Paula's anger on receiving the shipments and
receipts. Geula apparently understood that "Daddy spent fantastic
sums on books. He didn't think that Mommy also had to support children." It was etched in Geula's memory that when the children sat
down to eat Paula told them that she would eat later with Daddy. But
when Ben-Gurion asked her why she did not eat with him, she would
reply that she had already eaten with the children. Her children remembered her as someone who existed on crumbs.

Paula was miserable in her privation and with her poor clothing.
When in 1930 the situation became intolerable, she wrote him,

> *You only think of yourself.* You have a good servant at home what do you
> care.
> I swear to you that some day will come I will kill myself, enough to suf-
> fer.
> I look so bad that people cannot recognize me. A lot you care, if you
> would care you would do different, the way you arranged things I have to
> beg every penny they give me, and when he gives me he thinks he gives
> me charity. . . . What do you care, you *play the part of gentleman. It is
> good to be a good actor.*

In 1927 — a bad year for everyone in Palestine — their situation
worsened. Even though Ben-Gurion rotated most of his debts, those to
Ha-Mashbir and a cooperative bank remained outstanding. He was behind on his municipal taxes and at the end of the year his debt to Tel
Aviv totaled 15.580 Palestinian pounds. With the addition of monthly
installment payments on the piano, Paula was in dire straits.[7]

In 1928 the HEC extricated him, assuming his payments to loan institutions against his promissory notes and the open-ended deficit listed
in the cashbook in his name. Of course, this manner of getting money
from the Histadrut treasury put Ben-Gurion in a bad light, since he was
using his position to get advantages precluded other Histadrut mem-

bers. Despite all these anomalies, however, his salary still amounted to less than half the customary wage at the Zionist administration and other public bodies, so he cannot be accused of wantonly taking public funds. It is also true that, had he wanted to, as Histadrut secretary, he could have allotted himself a higher salary from the very beginning, as all the institution directors had done. Certainly if he had received thirty-five Egyptian pounds a month, as the director of Kapai did, for example, he would not have amassed such debts and had to resort to irregular remedies. Nevertheless these excuses do not account for the fact that he could not practice what he preached. The worst part was that his own financial situation undermined his moral authority over others, a fact that had a decisive influence on the development of the Eretz-Israeli labor movement.

The creditors' touch reached his children as well. The Anglo-Palestine Bank, which discounted the Herzliya Gymnasium's bills, asked Ben-Gurion in writing to settle them promptly, and when he could not do so, Geula and Amos were pulled out of class and sent home. In Geula's memory this occurred frequently. "They sent us home every week because we hadn't paid tuition." This exaggeration probably derived from her pain at each public humiliation, and Paula's feeling at seeing the children come home with downcast eyes is easy to imagine.[8]

Another burden on Paula was Ben-Gurion's regular trips abroad, for three months and more, every year. In addition to her work load as a housewife with three children she had to shoulder the tasks that usually fell to a husband: worrying about money and supervising the family's moves. When they moved to Pinsker Street three days after the third Histadrut convention opened, Paula had had to take care of everything. In financial distress, without any help — except for a laundress two or three times a month — with neither friend nor confidante, and sometimes without a husband and a father for her children, she had every right to be bitter.

Nevertheless, not all her grievances were born of these woes. Ben-Gurion grew accustomed to the "fatal" illnesses that attacked Paula and her children each time he left home. In the spring of 1926, when Ben-Gurion was in Europe, Paula was still detailing severe illnesses in the children and writing that she herself was "sick of life." Amos, she indicated, had come down with typhus again; one night she herself "had an attack"; all the neighbors were called to the house and they rushed a doctor and nurse to her. Three days later Renana developed a fever as a result of a smallpox inoculation. Her arm swelled up and all day Renana called, "Daddy, Daddy," looking at his picture.[9]

Did Paula magnify the dangers to herself and the children to make Ben-Gurion notice her self-sacrifice, or did she simply not understand his life mission? Was she blind to the fact that his long stays abroad were, by and large, dictated by reality, necessitated by the Jewish nation's existence abroad? That the main activities of persuasion and organization needed to enlarge the Yishuv with many new immigrants had to be done in Europe and America? That if his ambition was to be a Zionist leader, a Jewish leader, Ben-Gurion had to be active abroad? While Paula had a right to begrudge her fate, her letters also seem to reflect fears and troubles not arising from her actual situation. Her greatest fear, that Ben-Gurion would abandon her, was, of course, reinforced each time he left. One way of binding him to her was to instill in him, as deeply as possible, recognition of his injustice and ingratitude to her.

The surprising thing about Paula's misery was that other women in similar situations were assisted by relatives and friends, mutual aid being one of the more prominent characteristics of the Histadrut community. Why was there no helping hand to care for the children in Ben-Gurion's absence and when Paula was laid up? Except for Ben-Gurion, she had no one in all of Palestine. Her sister Pessia had escaped to Jerusalem, and the sisters never closed the gap between them. Zippora, who had tried to make a sister of Paula, extended an invitation to Paula to come with her children for a rest to Zippora's apartment in Haifa. Of all Zippora's invitations to large family Passover Seders led by Reb Avigdor, Paula accepted only one — probably the same one Ben-Gurion's children remembered as the sole family Seder of their childhood.

There could be only two reasons for Paula's brush-off of Pessia and Zippora and the rest of Ben-Gurion's family. First, had Paula had any help from any of them, she would have lost her best weapon, her misery, which proved so effective on Ben-Gurion. Equally important was her desire that he not owe them anything or be grateful to them for any reason whatsoever. Because she wanted him to be all hers, she strove for exclusivity in his life. Only she knew what was good for him, and she toiled and troubled for his comfort and well-being at the cost of sacrificing her life for him.

Paula's insecurity had other manifestations. The rivalry for Ben-Gurion's affections raged not only among the children, but between them and Paula as well. Ben-Gurion usually came home from work late, but when Paula knew he would be home early she would send the children — ages twelve, ten, and five — to bed at 6:00 P.M., making especially sure that Renana went to sleep. Therefore, on his return, Ben-Gurion was all hers. "She always wanted him [all] to herself," said Geula, who was close to her mother and empathized with her.

Her jealous obsession knew no bounds; Paula appointed herself sentry outside Ben-Gurion's door. Her directive, "Don't disturb Ben-Gurion" (she never called him by his first name), was supposed to shield him from anything that might disrupt his work and his mission. But it also enabled her to keep everyone — except her — away from him. Only later did Amos realize that "Mommy is crazy about watching over Daddy," and ask her, "Why can't we disturb Daddy! Because Daddy wants to talk with us and you don't have that chance?"

As the years passed Paula's jealousy intensified. Did Ben-Gurion not sense this? Was he not aware of the tempest boiling around him in his isolation? If so, he never let on, even with a hint, but a change came over him nonetheless. After 1929 he wrote Paula no more letters referring to her self-sacrifice or declaring his indebtedness. No longer did he promise her "a world of sublime happiness." And, having become accustomed to the "illnesses" his departures caused her, he stopped writing her about his worries over her health.

Did he consider his marriage a good one or a miserable one? To this there is only one rather oblique clue. At the end of December 1923, after reading from Herzl's diary, Ben-Gurion noted in his own, "What a wretched family life this man had. Once he thought about his death, 'If I die soon my parents will grieve more than anyone, my children, consoled by their youth, less, and the entire Jewish nation will mourn.' He didn't mention his wife at all." Ten years later Ben-Gurion entered in his diary, as was his habit, the birthdays of all his family — his father's, his mother's, his own, and his children's, in that order. He left Paula's out.[10]

19

The Blood Wedding
with Ha-Poel ha-Mizrachi

O N HIS FIRST DAY in the HEC in 1921 the problem of unemployment was waiting for David Ben-Gurion, and it continued to
haunt him everywhere he turned, in private and in public. But
through it he would successfully consolidate his leadership and achieve
his goal of establishing the HEC's predominance.

Ben-Gurion believed in the principle that immigration creates work,
but a paradox confronted him. As immigration swelled, unemployment
grew, at least until the new immigrants were absorbed into the work
force. On the other hand, when immigration decreased — whether for
economic reasons or Arab opposition — construction, whose role in
creating new jobs was particularly important, slowed, and employment
opportunities diminished. In theory, and in retrospect, the concept
that immigration spurs development was correct, as shown by the fact
that the Yishuv and the Histadrut, followed by the State of Israel,
grew constantly, with the sole exception of the year 1928. But in fact,
in the HEC's day-to-day routine, unemployment was attendant on immigration and was therefore never struck from the agenda, at least not
during Ben-Gurion's first eight years in the secretariat. It was considered a concomitant to the growth of the National Home and the Histadrut's development.

Unemployment, which hurt primarily those who had just arrived in
the new land, which still lacked proper welfare institutions, was accompanied by much human suffering. But such suffering was also the
lot of more settled immigrants, for each bout of unemployment pulled
the ground from beneath their feet. Indeed, the clamor of the unemployed shook the walls of the HEC. In November 1921 Ben-Gurion

heard of people "standing on the brink of an abyss"; in November 1922, of "entire groups here for some time without work and going hungry." In February 1924 he noted in his diary, "The lack of work is ever increasing. Yesterday people were fainting in the office," and, in December, "The people are hungry and cannot work." In January 1925 the situation had so deteriorated that the labor exchanges, in desperation, referred job applicants to the HEC secretariat. At the height of the Fourth Aliyah, in 1926, seventy-four hundred immigrants left Palestine, as opposed to only thirty-five hundred in 1923. The HEC secretariat was informed of "thousands of workers" suffering hunger "for several months." In 1927 things got even worse, and the HEC secretariat turned to the Zionist Executive to budget funds to create employment, since this was "a question of life or death for eight thousand workers." In 1928 emigration canceled out immigration, and the annual growth rate of the Yishuv stood at zero for the first time in the history of the Zionist enterprise.[1]

Rachel Yanait described a meeting between Ben-Gurion and an unemployed man who burst into the HEC office and complained about his situation. Ben-Gurion looked at him in astonishment. "You're complaining? Don't you feel good? How can you not feel good in our land?" Unable to restrain herself, Yanait exclaimed to Ben-Gurion, "You think he feels, like you, that he's laying the foundations for the Jewish state? He's hungry." Ben-Gurion's sense of entitlement enabled him to face five thousand jobless and hungry workers at a rally in Tel Aviv in February 1928 and tell them, "There's no need to speak at length to this gathering about unemployment, and perhaps one who works and eats every day does not have the knowledge or the right to discuss it." Then he told them that they enjoyed a great privilege, taking part in the realization of the shared goal. "I have no work for you, but I do have a vision to give you," he said at these gatherings.

He must have learned how to cover his feelings with his Zionist optimism and cheerfulness, for he was anxiously keeping watch on the effects unemployment, particularly the dole, had on the individual. As a result his original opposition to the Zionist Executive's meager assistance to the unemployed through the Histadrut labor exchanges intensified. One reason was his fear that many might prefer the dole to the relief work created as part of the Zionist Executive's efforts to solve the problem, which he considered the best form of therapy. He was right; no jobless went out to plant forests or tobacco, jobs that paid ten Egyptian piasters (50¢) a day. The second reason was his belief that the dole would corrupt the workers. In his view the Zionist Executive's weekly handout demoralized its recipients, accustoming them to charity, which he found repugnant. According to him, by supporting this assistance his colleagues contributed to the increase not only of "many truly hungry people," but also of masses "of parasites." Ready to face the uproar that would rock the HEC in the wake of such action, Ben-Gurion first demanded the cessation of the dole in January 1924. "Better that windows be broken, that our offices be closed for a week or two, but we will not vitiate the people," he said. His HEC colleagues rejected this stance, not only then but each time he took it. The rebuff voiced by Joseph Aharonovitch — "You've eaten today, after all!" — echoed in the HEC and became the slogan for requesting contributions to the unemployment fund founded by the Histadrut, from which additional aid was distributed to the jobless.[2]

Even more worrisome than corruption of the people was his fear for the fate of immigration; High Commissioner Herbert Samuel had instituted a criterion for immigration schedules called the Economic Absorptive Capacity. Unemployment and its tale-telling Zionist dole were a clear sign that Palestine's economy suffered from a glut of workers and that there was no room for additional immigration until the situation improved. Unemployment was immigration's archenemy. Ben-Gurion's demand to stop the aid and thus spur the jobless to go to work in the tobacco fields and forests was intended primarily to prevent cutting the immigration schedule. This objective led Ben-Gurion in two contradictory directions — internally he used unemployment to trigger the raising of funds to create jobs; externally he denied the existence of such a problem and urged would-be immigrants to hurry to Palestine lest they lose the jobs awaiting them.

For example, on February 27, 1927, he wrote to Achdut ha-Avodah delegates at the Zionist Actions Committee session in London that "the scarcity of work opportunities and lack of security on which to base oneself firmly . . . is bringing hundreds of our members to desperation and depression — and many of them to emigration," telling the delegates to "take all measures" to raise the money necessary for housing projects to ease unemployment. On the same day he wrote the He-Chalutz central committee in Moscow that not only was "the employment situation in Palestine getting better," but that new tobacco planting would soon require a thousand more workers and, therefore, "we hope that a large number of pioneers" will quickly be forthcoming.

Unemployment beset Ben-Gurion even at home, as relatives, friends, and acquaintances camped out on his doorstep, asking him to put in a word for them or those close to them, so they could get jobs. Reb Avigdor, too, was honored with such pleas and in at least two instances he succumbed out of pity and took it on himself to intercede with his famous son. He gave two of his Płońsk friends letters of recommendation, addressed to Ben-Gurion at the IIEC, which his son Abraham also signed. But even in those most difficult days, Ben-Gurion could not be coaxed into granting favors to relatives, and he caused his father further sorrow by returning the recommendations with a reprimand and telling him not to give out any more. He wrote sternly that he and his colleagues in the secretariat were "dealing with the question *as a whole* — and I handle this [whole] only." Therefore he would not make "any exceptions for an individual just because my father or brother recommends him." The letter ended, "I'm not here to help individuals who have my relatives' 'protection' at the expense of *the public.* Yours, David."[3]

To present Ben-Gurion's attitude in the proper light it should be noted that he did not always completely shut out the problems of individuals. At times he was able to grant total strangers that which he withheld from his father and family. In one case, in October 1926, he asked the Tel Aviv dole office, "in an exceptional manner," to provide him with two Egyptian pounds "for a man with a large family whose pride prevents him from asking for it personally." Another case illustrates how he failed to divorce his feelings from his principles. One concerned Shaul Shaulov, a painter long unemployed, with seven mouths to feed. Ben-Gurion sent him to Jerusalem (the HEC paying his fare) with a civilly worded note to the labor exchange there. "Perhaps you could set him up with some painting work at the health center?" The labor exchange secretary in Jerusalem replied to Ben-Gurion in the spirit of the sages (charity begins at home). Since the only painting work in Jerusalem was at the new health center, "and all of the out-of-work painters have been anticipating it for several months," hiring an unemployed outsider would cause justified resentment on their part, and "therefore we must return Shaulov to Tel Aviv."

The secretary sent him back, fare in hand, but Ben-Gurion checked into the possibility of hiring Shaulov at the health center directly with the contractor, who granted Ben-Gurion's request, promising to give Shaulov the job reserved for his own son. Shaulov was again sent to Jerusalem, but the stout-hearted exchange secretary stood his ground: every job, new or vacated, belonged to Jerusalem's unemployed, he argued, spurring Ben-Gurion into the battle of principle, the battle for HEC predominance. "It is inconceivable that work, wherever available, be the closed, unconditional monopoly of the local labor council," he wrote the secretary. "The Histadrut is authorized to transfer a member from one place where no work is available to another where it is." This time he did not ask. He ordered that Shaulov be given work, but in vain. The secretary defied him, and Shaulov was returned to his benefactor. Ben-Gurion called the Jerusalem Labor Council, which was in charge of the exchange; only then did the HEC prevail and Shaulov take part in painting the health center.[4]

In general, it can be said that veterans of the Second Aliyah and the Jewish Battalion, the disabled of Hashomer and the Haganah, those who became sick and could not work, those who were unjustly laid off, and those whose lives were disrupted by other circumstances all turned to Ben-Gurion and were answered, and he saw to it personally that their requests were fulfilled.

It was not lack of compassion that prevented Ben-Gurion from offering his father and brother what he gave people like Shaulov, but the excessive worry that he would gain a reputation as a nepotist. He applied his principles to his family but tended to relax them with others.

One of the main characteristics that distinguished Ben-Gurion from his colleagues in the labor movement was his unusual knack for turning adversity into an expedient for furthering the goals he and the labor movement stood for. At times, when his exceptional ability was translated into action, he seemed to be on a kind of combat high, suffused with the joy of creation, and Ben-Gurion could be seen bursting with joy or energy among the sad faces surrounding him. The public first saw this aspect of his personality when he discovered what he considered unemployment's silver lining.

His belief that only the Jewish workers could carry out the Zionist enterprise led Ben-Gurion to the conclusion that the Histadrut's historical mission included not only a constructive but also a political role in the implementation of Zionism, one that could be accomplished only if the Histadrut became the sole representative of the Jewish workers of Palestine. In his mind unemployment and the Histadrut's struggle for exclusivity were a symbiotic match. As the sole representative of workers the Histadrut could best ease the unemployment situation, which in turn would help consolidate the Histadrut as the sole workers' organization.

An article Ben-Gurion wrote in the summer of 1922, "On the Situation," reveals the thinking that lay behind the tactics he used in his war with the leftists. Under the circumstances of unemployment and competition for jobs, which led to lower wages, the article explained, it would be extremely difficult to rally the workers and take strong, effective action on their behalf. This socioeconomic ground was fertile for the growth of the left, which was attempting to undermine the coalition of Achdut ha-Avodah and Ha-Poel ha-Tzair in the HEC. He drew a sharp line between "us" and "them," between the powers of unity defending "the Histadrut rule" and the powers of disintegration attacking it. In Ben-Gurion's view, the anti-Zionist left, an enemy a hundred times worse than unemployment, had to be destroyed. In this context the left consisted, first, of the factions that had won seven delegates (out of one hundred thirty) to the second Histadrut convention and that later became the Palestine Communist Party (PCP) and the Poale Zion Left Party, and second, of various groups of workers under different names.[5]

In May 1922 approximately fifty unemployed workers had burst into the Histadrut's Office of Public Works in Tel Aviv, where, after beating up the directors and kicking them out, they declared a siege, to be lifted only when the Histadrut began negotiating their demands for work and a different labor council in town. The members of the HEC, called to an emergency meeting, were divided as to whether to handle the intruders with leniency. Joseph Sprinzak favored moderation — treat them "not with force," he said, but "with reason and patience." Ben-Gurion was aggressively opposed. He identified them at once as "Borochov's gang," that is, those who had adhered to the leftist branch of Poale Zion abroad, and he believed that the issue was not "lack of work" at all. The besiegers were clearly "desirous of bringing the Histadrut to its knees" and therefore should "in no way" be given work. Sympathy would only fuel their inflammatory influence, and they would mobilize other workers to their cause and "wreck" the Office of Public Works' operation altogether. "There's only one remedy — not to comply with them, but to answer them with force," for the left had no place in the Histadrut. "We must declare their ouster from the Histadrut on the morrow" and "with force and determination" drum out the Communists who "knowingly undermine the Histadrut and slander it abroad." He rejected out of hand the moderates' proposal to call in the police; "I shall not be a member of a Histadrut powerless to defend itself."

No one at the meeting backed Ben-Gurion's stand entirely, and certainly not the Ha-Poel ha-Tzair members. Sprinzak was against "blows" — *geschlägerai*, he said in Yiddish — as undesirable and harmful. He proposed calling a workers' meeting in Tel Aviv with the besiegers, who would there be persuaded to abide by the majority's opinion. Only David Remez supported Ben-Gurion's proposal to create "a defense force for the Histadrut institutions" that would drive out the rebels. In fact, this controversy was academic; prior to the meeting Ben-Gurion had already instructed his followers in Tel Aviv to mobilize just such a force and put it on the alert.

The HEC voted for Sprinzak's proposal, and a workers' meeting was convened in Tel Aviv, at which Ben-Gurion was to speak. The force was hidden among the crowd. The besiegers' supporters had arranged for a rival workers' meeting at the same time and place, and the two groups soon intermingled. Ben-Gurion was unable to deliver his speech, for as he stood up on a table the crowd delivered a storm of shouts and catcalls until, according to an eyewitness, "battle was joined" between the two groups and a "really bloody fracas" ensued. Ben-Gurion's force had the upper hand, and the protestors of the left withdrew, resolved to hold a demonstration the next day. Ben-Gurion, who omitted the other aspects of this affair from his diary, noted with satisfaction that this demonstration never took place. "They were afraid to carry out their resolution." His conclusion that the force had accomplished its purpose is evidenced not only by this remark, but also by the repeated use he would make of it until the thirties, when it became an organized and disciplined body called the Hapoel Squadrons.

Ben-Gurion's harshness should be seen in the light of the dispute over the very essence of the Histadrut then raging between Achdut ha-Avodah and the left, which denied and condemned what the former called the Histadrut's constructive role, that is, the idea that the Histadrut's primary task was the implementation of Zionism. The left maintained that building a national economy — establishing agricultural settlements and factories, building housing complexes for workers, and so forth — had no place in a trade union federation, whose sole business was to fight the class war until the dream of a socialist society became a reality. To this end the left worked to replace the all-Jewish Histadrut with a federation of Jewish-Arab trade unions. Slogans advocating such an international federation were prevalent during the siege of the Office of Public Works and the workers' meeting.[6]

In opposition to the left, which demanded an increasing cut of private and national capital for both Jewish and Arab workers, Ben-Gurion aimed at channeling a growing share of Histadrut and national resources into economic development and productivity to create a greater "economic absorptive capacity" in the Yishuv and thereby a larger Jewish immigration. At the second Histadrut convention Ben-Gurion said that "our movement" was unique since immigration constituted "the ground upon which it grows" and "the source from which it . . . draws sustenance" and was its "primary motivating force" and ruler. "All traits and characteristics of our movement are derived from the process of immigration, its needs, and its strength." A delegate from the leftist factions concluded correctly, "Ben-Gurion said that the Histadrut was an immigration organization."

The left maintained that trade unions should be responsible to Jewish and Arab workers and therefore must of necessity object to the immigration, which caused unemployment and lower wages. In the summer of 1923 the leftists who adhered to such ideas formed the Palestine Communist Party, emphasizing their complete solidarity "with the Arab National Movement," which they upheld as an important factor in the war against imperialism. They condoned Arab acts of terror and denied the legitimacy of Jewish immigration. The less extreme left, whose members had organized as Poale Zion Left in the spring of 1923, remained within the Zionist fold but opposed cooperation between the Histadrut and the "bourgeois" Zionist Executive. They also called for remodeling the Histadrut as an alliance of independent trade unions, Jewish and Arab, whose aims were the betterment of working conditions and agitation for class war.[7]

Though Poale Zion Left supported Jewish immigration, Ben-Gurion and his colleagues argued that this group in fact opposed it in practice, if not in theory. At the second Histadrut convention Ben-Gurion accused both categories of leftists of being agents provocateurs who undermined "the Histadrut's existence," "exploited the hunger in Palestine," "incited the hungry" against the Histadrut Office of Public Works, and spread "libels against the Histadrut abroad." There was no room in the Histadrut for "traitors from within," he said, and called for the "purging of this evil in our midst." This infuriated Sprinzak, who held his tongue until he gained the floor, when he said, "It was hard for me to sit still and listen to Ben-Gurion's tone in speaking about the Faction.* . . . His was an inflammatory speech against everyone who isn't a member of Achdut ha-Avodah. Ben-Gurion didn't have to set feelings aflame. . . . We'll all be worse off for hysterical outbursts."[8]

While waging battle against the left Ben-Gurion also opened fire on a front on the right, calling it the struggle for organized labor, which demands explanation. Two principles, one national and one class related, were upheld by the Histadrut from its inception: Jewish labor, meaning that only Jewish workers were to be employed in the Jewish economy, and organized labor, meaning that their wages were to be regulated only by a Histadrut labor exchange and that they could be dismissed only with the consent of its trade union. As usual, Ben-Gurion differed from most on the scope and vigor with which these principles were to be applied in daily practice.

As early as 1921 it became clear to the HEC that the national principle, Jewish labor, and the class-related principle, organized labor, did not go hand in hand. Although there were employers who, for nationalistic reasons, hired Jewish workers even though they had to pay them more than Arab workers, they were usually unwilling to do so through the Histadrut labor exchange when cheaper Jewish labor was available.

---

* The anti-Zionist left in general, and members of the PCP in particular, were commonly referred to as the Faction, a euphemism deriving from their name on the election lists, the Workers' Faction within the Histadrut, intended to cloak its candidates' affiliation with the Communist Party, outlawed by the Mandatory government.

The eternal question of priorities arose. Which principle took precedence? Those who put Jewish labor first had to relinquish, readily or not, some of the Histadrut's claim as the sole representative of workers in Palestine and allow employers true to the Jewish labor ideal to hire nonaffiliated workers as well. By the same token, those who put organized labor first had to give up something of the labor exchange's all-Jewish nature and accept the idea of handling Arab workers as well.

But not Ben-Gurion. He stood for what he called "100 percent Jewish labor" *and* "100 percent organized labor," that is, uniting the two principles to create organized Jewish labor, which could be achieved only if the Histadrut was the sole representative organization of all the Jewish workers in Palestine. This, said Ben-Gurion, was in keeping with the Histadrut's full name, the *General* Organization of *Jewish* Workers in Palestine. Only by fulfilling the goal its name implied could the Histadrut also carry out its national and class roles properly and its authority become predominant.

In selecting the targets of this struggle, Ben-Gurion chose to start with what others relegated to last place. Establishing the Histadrut as the sole Jewish exchange in Palestine was first on his list. He took it on himself to ensure that all workers would obey the authority of a Histadrut labor exchange and its trade union and that all employers, willingly or not, would hire workers only through the labor exchange and follow the trade union's instructions on matters of salary, working conditions, and dismissal.

At first the campaign ran into difficulties on the home front. The members of the first HEC, lacking Ben-Gurion's far-reaching ambitions, had put the national principle first and ruled in 1921 that the exchange would serve Histadrut members only. As a result, before taking on the external rivals, Ben-Gurion had to open the Histadrut exchange to all Jewish workers, including non-Histadrut members. After two years of internal campaigning he got what he wanted, and in March 1923 the Histadrut council passed the following resolution:

> The Histadrut regards as vitally necessary the implementation of the demand that all workers, whether hired by the public institutions, the settlements, or by private employers, be employed through the Histadrut labor exchange. This demand stems from the need to set the worker and the immigrant on solid financial ground, and by so doing the possibilities for larger immigration . . . are improved.

While Ben-Gurion had convinced the majority of the council that Histadrut exchange domination was imperative for national reasons — so as not to hurt immigration — even before the council convened, he had also mobilized the support of the trade unions by using the class-related argument, calling on them to lend a hand "to secure the control of the Histadrut . . . in order to ease the weight of unemployment."[9]

His earlier battles, at the end of 1921 and 1922 and the beginning of 1923, had focused on the citrus growers, who preferred hiring Arab and unorganized Jewish workers, and on "the confederation of industry owners and employers" who rejected Histadrut conditions and reacted to the strikes Ben-Gurion called by shutting down their factories. Although he lost most of these battles, they gave him an opportunity to test his arsenal and acquire much-needed experience. So in March 1923, when the exchange was opened to the entire Jewish working community, Ben-Gurion was ready to bring out his heavy artillery. His stick was his firm resolution that the Histadrut not recognize or negotiate with separatist workers' organizations and that it fight them to the bitter end; the Histadrut labor exchange, which "stands apart from all parties," guided by the principles of organized Jewish labor and equal rights for all Jewish workers, was his carrot.

The first group to feel the weight of the stick was Ha-Poel ha-Mizrachi, the religious party's organization of workers, whose labor exchange handled Orthodox job applicants only. According to Ben-Gurion's reasoning this contravened the equal rights that were the foundation of the Histadrut exchange. Moreover, the religious exchange did not divvy up working days among its applicants in such a way as to provide for all, while the Histadrut exchange took the jobless into account, dividing, for example, sixty working days not among ten workers, with six days a week for each, but among twenty workers, allotting to each only three alternating days a week.

Ha-Poel ha-Mizrachi representatives rejected the Histadrut offer to set up a joint list of unemployed from which workers would be hired equally through the Histadrut exchange, an offer that was probably backed by a threat of force. But if Ben-Gurion thought this saber rattling was sufficient to subdue Ha-Poel ha-Mizrachi, he was mistaken. This engagement deserves a detailed description, for in his future campaigns Ben-Gurion was to replay certain aspects of it, as if following a preset scenario.

To forestall a confrontation between the Histadrut and Ha-Poel ha-Mizrachi as a whole — its workers' organization was only one part of it — that could easily have become a full-scale *Kulturkampf* between the religious and the nonreligious, Ben-Gurion engineered a limited engagement in June 1923. He confined the fighting to one battlefield, the construction site of the Shmuel David building on the corner of Mazeh and Allenby streets in Tel Aviv, all of whose twelve hired men were members of the religious camp. He also instructed that the war in the field be handled by out-of-work men who were registered in the Histadrut exchange. This way Ben-Gurion, the HEC, and the Tel Aviv Labor Council would all remain out of sight until later on. He staged it as a simple but bitter battle over bread between the unemployed who had been given work out of turn by virtue of their religious affiliation and the unemployed who had been deprived of their rightful place in line by the former.

Five days after the work began, twenty unemployed men showed up at the construction site, asking, according to the Histadrut, that they be hired by dividing the jobs between those already employed and themselves. Upon being refused, they declared a strike and sat down in the excavation. Ha-Poel ha-Mizrachi called in the police, under whose protection they went back to work. The next day the same thing happened, and so on for several days. But from then on, in the Histadrut's version, the Ha-Poel ha-Mizrachi men were guilty not only of stealing bread from the hungry, but of being scabs as well.[10]

Ha-Poel ha-Mizrachi did not believe for a minute that the strikers were acting spontaneously. Raising an uproar, it claimed that they were thugs sent by "the high officials" in the HEC and "the directors" of the Labor Council "to disrupt" the workers hired through Ha-Poel ha-Mizrachi's own labor exchange "with the power of the fist." Calling them rioters, it said, "This is the Labor Council's bojowka," a version of the Polish Poale Zion's commando squad of Ben-Gurion's youth. It is very likely that they were the same "defense force" Ben-Gurion had used successfully the year before against the leftists. In any case, the strikers certainly did not confine themselves to verbal action as *Kunteres* reported; there is no doubt that they knocked the Ha-Poel ha-Mizrachi people around. The religious organization put up posters saying, "The blood of Jewish workers was spilled today in the streets of Tel Aviv." The Labor Council angrily denied the allegation through the same medium, announcing its intention of suing those responsible for Ha-Poel ha-Mizrachi's posters.

The dispute did not remain a war of posters for long. Ha-Poel ha-Mizrachi sent about a hundred fifty of its members to a reception at City Hall to demand succor and an immediate session of the city council, in addition to threatening that if the Histadrut did not leave them alone, they would disrupt all the public works in Tel Aviv. The mayor's office complied by warning the Labor Council that if there were any more disturbances at the construction site the city would ask the British government "to take measures necessary to provide protection" to the religious workers. (Tel Aviv was the first town in Palestine run entirely by Jews.) The Labor Council replied instantly that it had not called that strike and that there was "no conflict" between itself and Ha-Poel ha-Mizrachi. "We have taken no side in this conflict, which has broken out between Ha-Poel ha-Mizrachi and the unemployed," its statement claimed.

The next day, Sunday, July 15, the "unemployed" returned to stop all work on the site. David Izmojik, a stand-in for the mayor, who was abroad, remained true to his word and called in the police, who arrested two of the strikers. Ben-Gurion, however, did not retreat. On his orders two hundred "out-of-work" men assembled the next day at dawn and spread out over the construction site, sitting on the sand heaps, casting molds, and concrete foundations. His ability to mobilize such a large number of strikers at such short notice indicates that they were members of his force. At 9:00 A.M., "All of a sudden . . . a line of vehicles came all at once from different directions," according to the Histadrut. This time it was not the police but the gendarmerie — under the authority of the British district commissioner, composed mostly of Irish and dubbed the Black and Tans — who, armed with rifles and pistols, arrived in machine gun carriers. It became clear immediately that this ambush had been planned, for Arab policemen, some on foot, others mounted, arrived simultaneously, sticks in hand. While the mounted officers surrounded the building site, the Irish and Arab policemen attacked the picketing strikers without warning, "and the whole place turned into a battleground," *Kunteres* reported. The Irish and the Arabs beat the strikers and the crowd indiscriminately with their rifle butts and sticks while the mounted police trampled them underfoot on the construction site and in the adjoining area. The Irish arrested twenty-two men and took them in their trucks to the Jaffa prison. Of the many beaten, some were seriously injured and required hospitalization, according to the Histadrut.[11]

Now Ben-Gurion emerged from behind the scenes. What he hoped for had materialized: the public could see that the Histadrut was not a violent and power-hungry organization, as its opponents painted it, but a community of day laborers and the unemployed, struggling to retain their dignity and elementary rights. More important, he had created the drama necessary to reach the minds and hearts of the people and convey to them that the Histadrut would fight fearlessly for its right to be the workers' sole representative.

To intensify the drama he operated in three arenas at once. He protested to the Mandatory government about the Arab police and the British gendarmerie, charging, "They beat the people in a cruel and barbarous way. . . . It reminded them of the pogroms arranged sometimes by Zarist [*sic*] Police in Russia"; he made the most of the word *pogrom* in other statements, too, including a letter to the British district commissioner of Jaffa, which included Tel Aviv. In a meeting with the commissioner he demanded an immediate, "energetic" investigation and that those responsible be brought to justice. The commissioner, however, politely refuted Ben-Gurion's version of the events, describing it as "in many points at variance with the actual facts"; the only man to be hospitalized, he said, had been struck while stooping to pick up a stone. "The arrests . . . were not made indiscriminately and the police only apprehended persons against whom there was definite evidence," as had been proved in court, where the twenty-two detainees were sentenced to a week's imprisonment each for disturbing the peace. In view of these facts he asked Ben-Gurion to "understand that your complaints have less ground than would appear to have been your belief at the time of writing your letter." The commissioner agreed with Ben-Gurion on only one point, that the Irish believed they had been called in to break up a "Bolshevist upheaval."

Ben-Gurion augmented this protest with a sensational appeal to British public opinion. "Jaffa police brutally attacked peaceful union picket Tel Aviv beating atrociously dispersing workers many wounded four severely. . . . arresting arbitrarily 22 workers," he cabled the Labour newspaper the *Daily Herald* and his friend Ramsay MacDonald, head of the Labour Parliamentary Party, asking MacDonald's help in Parliament to bring those responsible to trial. The telegram was followed by a registered letter describing Ha-Poel ha-Mizrachi as "a segment of the workers" that served "the employers very often as a whip against organized labour" and gave the same version of the incident that he had given the district commissioner, but with an added touch: "The police has attacked and beaten too [*sic*] sick people who waited for their turn near the office of the Sick Fund" alongside the construction site. The letter closed with an appeal to the Labour Party "for protection of our elementary human rights." His request was granted: the Labour Parliamentary Party raised the question in the House of Commons, which instructed the Colonial Office to conduct an inquiry.[12]

But Ben-Gurion's most crushing blows were reserved for the Histadrut's adversaries on the home front. He cast all the blame for what had happened on the civil, or rightist, and religious factions in the Tel Aviv City Council, singling out David Izmojik in particular. This move had been planned well in advance. By the evening of July 16 the Labor Council had already delivered an ultimatum to City Hall: release the detainees, "who have been imprisoned on its orders," within twenty-four hours and bring work at the controversial construction site to an absolute halt. When time ran out and only the latter demand had been fulfilled, the Labor Council called a public meeting "against the criminal municipality which summoned armed forces against a group of residents and caused blood to be spilled in the streets of Tel Aviv." A huge crowd assembled opposite the municipality building to hear Ben-Gurion speak, following which the Tel Aviv Labor Council met and passed a series of resolutions for a two-hour general work stoppage in Tel Aviv and another mass meeting of workers. Again Ben-Gurion delivered a speech to a crowd of thousands, which "unanimously" accepted a new series of resolutions. It was he, of course, who had drafted the Labor Council's resolutions, and it was also he who secretly wrote the resolutions voted on by the meeting.

The first read,

The meeting condemns the acts of . . . David Izmojik and his cronies in the City Council, who called in the non-Jewish police force from Jaffa to start a riot against Jewish workmen in Tel Aviv. This meeting regards the attempt to oppress Jewish workers with foreign policemen by leaders of the first Jewish city in Eretz Israel as a dangerous and shameful national provocation which undermines the foundations of the Yishuv's self-rule.

The meeting also resolved — "unanimously" — "to immediately bring David Izmojik and his cronies, who delivered Jewish workmen into the hands of foreign policemen and stripped the Jewish city of its honor, to a national and public trial." With a final vow "that despite the acts of terror [perpetrated by] the foreign police force and Izmojik's and the other Jewish informers' acts of provocation, not even a single worker will recoil from defending the rights and interests of the working class in our land," the resolutions ended and the meeting dispersed.

Now, at Ben-Gurion's signal, all the labor councils — like a well-rehearsed choir — raised their voices in support of the Tel Aviv resolutions. This shift in the focus of his attack from the separatist workers who were its original target was far-reaching not only in regard to the civil faction in the Tel Aviv City Council, but also in regard to the right in general. Izmojik and the mayor's office, trying to ward off the Histadrut's attack, published denials, refutations, and articles on bulletin boards and in the daily press. Moshe Smilansky, a beloved Hebrew writer and leader of the Farmers' Federation, took the Histadrut and "its leaders" to task in the pages of *Ha-Aretz*, particularly "certain leaders" (the reference to Ben-Gurion could not have been more pointed), whom he asked, "Did you really think you could set the Yishuv on the straight and narrow with fists, threats, and violence? . . . Didn't you know that violence breeds more violence?"

None of this stopped Ben-Gurion. He addressed a letter to the National Council of Jews of Palestine, enjoining it "to conduct a national public trial of David Izmojik . . . and his colleagues in City Hall, for handing the Jewish workers of Tel Aviv over to the Arab-British rule in

Jaffa and causing the notorious events" in Tel Aviv. The sole value of this demand was its publicity and its impact on less enlightened public opinion, since there was no legal or traditional basis for a national public trial, just as there were no grounds for branding the local Tel Aviv police "the Arab-British rule in Jaffa." Nothing came of this demand, as the legal-minded Ben-Gurion must have anticipated, yet he stuck to it until Izmojik's name became a household word, synonymous with the enemies of the Jewish worker and the Histadrut. Ben-Gurion had carefully chosen his foe to suit both goal and circumstances; certainly he did not want to aggravate his own and the Histadrut's relations with Ha-Poel ha-Mizrachi in particular and the religious camp in general, since from the outset he had aimed to reach an accord with them. Thus instead of censuring them, he hung Izmojik, who had no public importance whatsoever.[13]

Ben-Gurion's Figaro-like performance, his finger in every pot, did not end there. With the public storm he had generated still raging, he appeared in a different costume and another role, that of peacemaker. Contrary to all expectations, he consented to be a member of a three-man committee with representatives from Ha-Poel ha-Mizrachi and the National Council of Jews of Palestine, formed at Izmojik's request to look into the "Shmuel David Building Affair" and come up with a way to prevent another such incident in the future. Now it was Ben-Gurion who was restrained and moderate; he met the other two committeemen halfway in every respect. Their agreement, annexed to the conclusions signed by all three, stipulated that "the distribution of all jobs must be done on a proportional basis among all of the unemployed," whether registered at the Histadrut's exchange or at Ha-Poel ha-Mizrachi's. A two-man committee of representatives from both exchanges would oversee the distribution. Moreover, the annex enabled Ben-Gurion to demonstrate great magnanimity and generosity by allowing, as an exceptional case, that only 25 percent of the jobs on the Shmuel David building go to the Histadrut exchange, instead of the 50 percent demanded initially, and the remaining 75 percent to Ha-Poel ha-Mizrachi, which would willingly have agreed to these proportions if the offer had been made earlier.

How could Ben-Gurion, the staunch protagonist of Histadrut exclusivity, sign an agreement with another organization that conferred recognition and authority on it in absolute contradiction to his principles, and even yield on a fifty-fifty split between them? Simply because he had always intended such an agreement to serve as a first step toward incorporating Ha-Poel ha-Mizrachi into the Histadrut. He had correctly anticipated that his concessions would leave the other organization feeling satisfied and victorious, creating good will among its members, some of whom had voiced the wish to join the Histadrut even at the height of the dispute. At the same time, Ben-Gurion left no room for doubt that no satisfaction could be gained in grappling with the Histadrut when he was at its head. And indeed, within just a year and three months, in October 1924, the HEC concluded negotiations with Ha-Poel ha-Mizrachi resulting in "its merger" with the Histadrut, making the Histadrut and its labor exchange the sole, unchallenged representative of organized workers. Ben-Gurion could well have patted himself on the back over the success of the tactical rule he had laid down for himself — ruthlessness in war, magnanimity in negotiations.[14]

20

A Threat of Murder

THE FEAR that the Jewish immigration would bring throngs of "Bolsheviks" — a term very loosely applied then — from eastern Europe to Palestine was very much in the minds of the British press and His Majesty's government. In May 1921 the London *Morning Post* warned that "once Bolshevism spreads in Palestine it will quickly extend to other Arab peoples who are free" and endanger the empire in that part of the world. This fear was the source of the Mandatory government's law outlawing the Communist Party and making members and sympathizers liable to deportation. The Palestinian party, on its establishment in 1923, was immediately declared illegal and went underground.

The fear of Bolsheviks was equally lively in the Zionist Organization, because of the leftists' anti-Zionist extremism, and it, too, did its share — by screening would-be immigrants, for example — to minimize Bolshevik infiltration into Palestine. Its success could be only partial, for it could not control the minds of those true Zionists who had come to Palestine, stood its trials, and then begun to shift leftward.

Within the framework of this "external" campaign the Histadrut had to conduct an internal one against the "Mops,"* as the Bolsheviks were nicknamed, who, as a workers' party, found the Histadrut natural ground for propaganda and recruitment. A few days after the Histadrut's establishment, on December 30, 1920, the HEC discussed the Mops' infiltration into the railroad workers' union with the intention of turning it into an independent Jewish-Arab trade union. Berl Katz-

---

* In Hebrew, an acronym for the Jewish Socialist Workers' Party, which later became the Palestine Communist Party (PCP). The nickname was demeaning, as it means "pug" in German and Yiddish.

nelson and Itzhak Tabenkin were aware of the imminent danger and agreed that it was not to be ignored, but they stopped short of enacting "practical measures on this matter." Throughout 1921, the HEC was at a total loss vis-à-vis the left, which kept blasting the Histadrut for backing "the Jewish bourgeoisie supported by British imperialism," namely, the Zionist Organization.[1]

March 1922 marked David Ben-Gurion's first head-on collision with the Mops. After a prolonged effort during the course of a long and difficult strike at a large carpentry factory in Tel Aviv, Ben-Gurion was able to reach a compromise agreement with the factory owners, but when he assembled the workers to announce the strike's end, the Mops, who had considerable support in the woodworkers' union, protested and "didn't allow [the strike] to come to an end," he wrote in his diary. Hurting, he returned to the HEC and called for an immediate meeting to discuss this humiliation. But for various reasons, among them that his colleagues neither considered the humiliation so stinging nor the entire issue so urgent, this discussion did not take place until two months later. Then, on May 15, Ben-Gurion said, "Some of them must be expelled from the Histadrut," and he named two leaders of the Mops who were not workers at the factory and had had no direct part in the dispute.

But how were they to be ousted in the absence of a constitution? The constitution and bylaws were not to be drafted and enacted until the second Histadrut convention and the councils following it in January and March 1923. Second, how was Ben-Gurion to blame the two leaders for the acts of the woodworkers' rank and file? These and other questions left him undaunted; the Histadrut had to show its teeth and could not let such tampering with its authority go unpunished. He proposed improvisational measures: meetings at all workplaces in Tel Aviv to discuss what had happened and to elect delegates to a "special council," which in turn was to pass a resolution ousting the Mops leaders. "This very day," he told the HEC, "the troublemakers must be judged and sentenced."

Joseph Sprinzak, of course, was opposed. Street justice — the purport of Ben-Gurion's proposal — would start a public opinion war, and he had never approved of such, or of hanging a whole party for the sins of some of its members. "We don't have to fan the flames," he said, "and there's no one to blame for the disruption." He said he would go along with meetings as long as they were kept small and for the sake of information only, and most important, he dismissed Ben-Gurion's demand for charging the Mops leaders that same day, preferring "to concentrate" first on mediation and compromise, with a view toward bringing the strike to a quick close.

But no power on earth could stop Ben-Gurion. He brushed off Sprinzak's "gentlemanly airs" and "Christian forbearance" as nuisances, mere distractions when such a vital "Histadrut issue" was at stake. The question of how to charge the Mops leaders with the misdeeds of their followers was mere hairsplitting. "I read what they write," he said. "We must kick out all those who openly wish the Histadrut ill. Whoever doesn't obey Histadrut rulings is to be ousted." As was its habit, the HEC compromised. The Tel Aviv Labor Council was to bring charges against those who had countermanded the back-to-work orders at the carpentry factory; Ben-Gurion's move to bring the Mops leaders to trial at a "special council" was rejected. On the other hand, the HEC resolved, with Ben-Gurion's approval, "that no strikes be called anywhere without authorization from the HEC."

Undoubtedly Ben-Gurion had a hand in the unusual promptness of the Tel Aviv Labor Council, which on the evening of May 14 convened and suspended the guilty Mops from the woodworkers' union. Ben-Gurion, who was present at this summary proceeding, later noted in his diary, "The troublemakers were brought to trial." If the HEC resolutions and the Labor Council's speedy action pleased him, as this note implies, it was only because he knew in his heart that in the wake of these first steps all the rest would follow.[2]

Now he could settle his score with "the Borochov gang" whose members had besieged the Office of Public Works at the beginning of that same May. This time he chose a new judicial method, a committee of three. The letters of appointment that he wrote its members in July instructed them to investigate the disruptive action by "a certain group against the Histadrut" — he refrained from calling it by name for fear of giving them free publicity — and submit to the HEC "their opinion on the measure of penalty the culprits deserve . . . from permanent expulsion from the Histadrut to temporary suspension of privileges." When the committee reported, the HEC decided on the latter.

A suspension, not to mention expulsion, from the Histadrut was severe punishment. Without the Sick Fund's medical services, Ha-Mashbir's provisions, Bank ha-Poalim's credit, and the trade union's protection, the penalized and their families were vulnerable to disease, hunger, and unemployment.

Unfortunately this high-handed approach — in which the HEC appointed judges and served both as plaintiff and executioner — was interpreted by the Achdut ha-Avodah majority in the large labor councils as a license to take the law into its own hands. And the Tel Aviv council proceeded to oust the bakers' union, which had been founded by the Mops, in response to its calling itself an international union, that is, a Jewish-Arab one.

This time Ben-Gurion did not need his HEC colleagues' censure; he, as much as they, feared the anarchy that was liable to result from such overzealous pursuit of the line that he had marked out. The HEC secretariat notified the Tel Aviv Labor Council secretariat that "the Histadrut" had officially quashed its resolution, which was therefore null and void. "We think the ouster of the bakers' union members from the Histadrut unnecessary," wrote the secretariat to the council. Instead, it suggested, the council should notify the bakers' union that its name was unacceptable.[3]

Ben-Gurion was also quite aware that the HEC could easily be accused of abusing its authority. The public was already under the impression that he, not the convention, was the supreme authority of the Histadrut, and this was sufficient ground for not only the Mops but all Histadrut parties to rise up against him. The logic was simple. If Ben-Gurion considered party leaders accountable for the deeds or misdeeds of their rank-and-file followers, and if a labor council deemed itself empowered to expel a trade union on account of its name, then it was not altogether impossible that the HEC might disqualify an electoral ticket on the basis of its candidates' views. Such apprehension had already led the Mops to apply for a new name for their Jewish Socialist Workers' Party, and seek permission to campaign for the elections to the second Histadrut convention as the Workers' Faction.

This application opened Ben-Gurion's eyes to how far he had gone; instead of being addressed to the central election committee, or to the Histadrut council, it was addressed to the HEC. This was contrary to all of Ben-Gurion's principles and intentions; he strove to strengthen the council and the convention, increase their authority, and make the HEC the dominant executive body charged with enforcing that authority. He therefore referred the application to the central election committee, pointing out in his letter to the Jewish Socialist Workers' Party that according to the election regulations any group of fifty voters or more was entitled to make up an election slate. He closed his letter unequivocally. "The Histadrut is not involved with the founding of factions, it doesn't ban them (as long as they do not call into question the Histadrut's existence), and it doesn't sanction them. The Histadrut treats your faction in the same manner." Nevertheless — and he could not have helped it — Ben-Gurion was again speaking as the Histadrut's voice of authority, not as an interpreter.[4]

Ben-Gurion had to walk a fine line for the next few years. At this time, however, he was still seeking the proper combination of judicial process anchored in Histadrut law, as yet unlegislated, and the HEC's power to exercise administrative disciplinary action, which he wanted officially prescribed. This he managed to gain at the second Histadrut convention in January 1923, which established the Histadrut's basic constitution and the judicial guidelines for its courts.* The HEC was "empowered" — but not obligated — to bring cases of subversion and "breaches of discipline and malicious injury to the Histadrut and its institutions" before a Histadrut court. The convention also removed those "matters for which the HEC is responsible to the convention or the Histadrut council" from the member courts' jurisdiction while authorizing the HEC to determine what constituted such matters. The HEC was given the power to choose between using the judicial process and taking direct action of its own, thereby opening to Ben-Gurion many possibilities of administrative justice and disciplinary action.[5]

Of his two options Ben-Gurion naturally preferred the administrative process, an exemplary proof being the disciplinary action he took against the Tel Yosef Labor Legion. In 1924 his disciplinary moves turned into a general punitive expedition against the communist left.

The unity manifesto of the PCP, which affiliated with the Comintern in February 1924, stressed its complete solidarity with the Arab National Movement and promised to cooperate "in organizing joint actions." The PCP took it upon itself to organize the Arab workers into trade unions and tried to gain their trust by voicing its rejection of the "Anglo-Zionist" mandate and condemning Zionism as a bourgeois movement that had thrown in its lot with British imperialism. The party regarded Jewish settlement as having been built on the dispossession and exploitation of the Arabs and therefore considered fighting "proletarian Zionism" and Jewish immigration to Palestine as its sworn duty. Statements from the manifesto were translated into street language and disseminated in leaflets and posters. In November, after one Arab of a group that had thrown stones and shot at Jewish workers plowing fields in Afula was killed, the PCP put out inflammatory statements against the "Jewish land robbers." It was generally agreed in the Zionist labor movement that this was "the first overt show of treason by this Jewish party."

Even earlier, however, shortly before the Histadrut council at the end of April 1924, Ben-Gurion had begun a campaign to remove the Faction's delegates from all the labor councils. Since the PCP was illegal, it functioned underground using various covers. The Workers' Faction was only one of them; the Labor Legion, as has been seen, was another. The Faction delegates to the Histadrut opposed Ben-Gurion, and so did Menahem Elkind, who maintained, on behalf of the Legion,

---

* The Histadrut courts had no criminal or civil jurisdiction; they adjudicated only cases between the Histadrut and its members or institutions, and between the institutions themselves.

that only a general convention was authorized to oust Faction delegates from the Histadrut. Ha-Poel ha-Tzair, for the most part, backed
Sprinzak, who advocated strict adherence to the judicial process. Ben-
Gurion summed up their stand in his diary. "The evening meeting was
stormy and scandalized. The Ha-Poel ha-Tzair people think that justice
and the law don't allow for the purging of this filth without a trial."
Nevertheless Ben-Gurion prevailed, and the council passed the resolution he had drafted.

> The council of the Histadrut declares that the association masquerading
> behind the name "The Workers' Faction of the Histadrut" has proven it-
> self, through its schemes and machinations, to be an enemy of the Jewish
> nation and the working class in Palestine. The council condemns the defa-
> mation of immigration and the slander of the Jewish labor movement in-
> tended to deceive workers worldwide. The council resolves to invalidate
> "The Jewish Workers' Faction of the Histadrut" in all its sundry forms
> and titles. No slate [put forth] by the Workers' Faction or any of those
> who continue its activities will be accepted as an election slate to the
> Histadrut convention, its unions, and institutions. The council resolves
> that all the Faction's representatives and candidates appearing on its be-
> half are expelled from the Histadrut. The expelled have the right to ap-
> peal before the Histadrut Supreme Tribunal.

Just as the Mandatory government had outlawed the Communist
Party, so, at Ben-Gurion's instigation, did the Histadrut council.

The resolution gave the labor councils license to oust Faction members, and they were quick to make use of it. In May the Tel Aviv Labor
Council expelled nine men charged with "provocational activity" and
another who was found to be "a traitor in matters of the working
class," while the Jerusalem Labor Council ousted nineteen men and
sent their names to all the other Histadrut offices, which would then
refuse to provide them with jobs, in effect instituting a blacklist.

In the course of all this the question arose as to whether the expelled
should be allowed to retain their jobs. It came up before the HEC for
an in-depth discussion and the two adversaries stood opposed as usual,
with Sprinzak maintaining that "denying work . . . undermines the
Histadrut" and was "immoral . . . and unrealistic" and liable to bring
about the creation of two labor exchange systems on the one hand and
emigration from Palestine on the other. "If a worker is removed from
his job, what's left for him in Palestine? The Histadrut can't tell him to
go become a merchant." But Ben-Gurion saw no "social, ethical, Histadrut, or humane foundation" for an obligation to include Histadrut
rejects in the work queue. "We beg Histadrut members to be satisfied
with two workdays a week so that the hardships of unemployment
don't foil immigration. Now I ask, by what morality do we take this

tiny amount of jobs and hand them over to those who wish to destroy this mutual responsibility? . . . We have no right to take away even one day and give it to those who hate the workers. . . . They don't have a right to any of our work. We consider them traitors." The HEC voted accordingly.[6]

In his diary Ben-Gurion noted only, "Sprinzak demanded that the expelled Faction members not be deprived of the labor exchange's service; the rest of the members were all opposed to this," as if he himself had had no hand in it. His systematic playing down of his own role cannot always be explained, but in this case it can be described as shrewd nonadmission. He was not about to admit publicly that it was he who had convinced the HEC to close its labor exchanges to workers whose political opinions he found repugnant, and he did not wish his diary (which, as will be recalled, was read by everyone in the HEC office) to bear witness against him.

Nor did he intend that the closing of the labor exchange become public knowledge, as it soon did, since friends and fellow party members of the ousted spread it all over Palestine. Like others, Ben-Gurion was taken aback by the length of the list of names from Jerusalem. To withhold work from nineteen people, who because of their ouster were already without Sick Fund services, was an action the Histadrut was liable to pay for dearly, as Sprinzak had cautioned. Nevertheless, Ben-Gurion held his ground, advising his HEC colleagues that "we must do this with discrimination." He meant that the closing of the labor exchange to those expelled from the Histadrut should not be written everywhere in black and white for all to see.

With discrimination, but not cowardice. After the HEC meeting Ben-Gurion traveled the country to clear the Labor Council of all responsibility for closing the exchange and take it all upon the HEC, namely, himself. Thus he explained repeatedly, "If we had our own government, I could force them to fulfill all of the duties and allow them to work." But since the government was in the hands of the British the HEC had to defend the Histadrut with whatever means were at its disposal, including this painful expulsion. However, his adversaries, and even some of his followers, did not let him talk in such general terms. They told him bluntly how horrified they were by the means he had used, speaking not of expelling Faction members but of "denying work rights" and closing off a source of livelihood to rank-and-file laborers.[7]

Ben-Gurion fought fiercely, as if the very life of the Histadrut depended on his victory. At public meetings across Palestine he spoke against the Faction and communism, and in closed discussions at the labor councils and trade unions he demanded insistently that Faction members be driven out of the rank and file. His adversaries fought back with demonstrations, petitions, and calls to the labor councils and trade unions not to capitulate to the HEC's order. Mordechai Bentov, a leader of Ha-Shomer ha-Tzair, a Zionist socialist kibbutz movement, protested in *Kunteres*, crying out against the Histadrut leaders for not reprimanding "those members who saw fit to defend the Histadrut's honor with the power of the fist" and who drove out anyone they suspected of being a Faction member even from the Workers' Kitchens. Ben-Gurion angrily replied, "It's not by chance that most Faction members and almost all its leaders came out of Ha-Shomer ha-Tzair in Palestine."

Shut out, the Faction members tried to break in again with yet another name change. In the summer of 1924 they became an "Organization" and, a year later, a "Union." Ben-Gurion, however, in signed leaflets warned "all" Histadrut members to be vigilant and guard against the Faction's many faces. In 1926 a severe depression hit Palestine and the battle intensified. The Faction accused the HEC of being responsible for the grave unemployment caused by the new immigration encouraged despite the depression. This enabled Ben-Gurion to expose their virulent anti-Zionism, which made boycotting them easier. In May the labor exchange ban was broadened to include working youth who had shown an inclination toward the Faction. Publicly Ben-Gurion denied both the existence of a boycott and the expulsions, while privately he used all his authority to condone the administrative process that led to them. To the secretariat he tried to justify this discrepancy by arguing that "we do not oust a member for being a member of the Faction" — that is, for ideological reasons — *"but only a member guilty of perpetrating an act against the Histadrut."* But why, then, were the "guilty" not brought before the Histadrut judicial system, and why were those suspected of membership in the Faction not able to get work? He did not answer these questions, reiterating only that "in the Histadrut there was not and could not have been a general boycott."[8]

Not until the summer of 1927, shortly before the third Histadrut convention, was the ban eased, since by then opposition to administrative punishment had grown even in his own party, which demanded a reform of the Histadrut constitution to abolish it. But well before that Ben-Gurion had used it to settle his score with the Labor Legion.

The Legion's 1923 split, while bringing economic recovery to both Ein Harod and Tel Yosef, had increased the organizational and political isolation of the Labor Legion and the clandestine Circle of former Hashomer members in its midst. The danger inherent in this isolation was greatly increased, in the minds of Ben-Gurion and those who saw eye to eye with him, especially Eliyahu Golomb, by the Legion's growing leftist tendencies as well as its growing strength. In addition to Kibbutz Tel Yosef, the Legion had another settlement, Kefar Giladi, in the Upper Galilee, founded by former Hashomer men, which was now the Legion's stronghold and the Circle's most important power center. (Manya and Israel Shochat were full members, even though the latter stayed there infrequently.)

Two factors fostered the Legion's leftist politics. The first was the extremely difficult economic and social circumstances in which the Labor Legionnaires lived and worked. These acted as both a filter and a fortifier, for only the toughest, or most incurably idealistic, could survive the first few weeks in a Legion company, and those who did could stand up to any trial the Histadrut might put them through. The harsher it was, the greater would be their motivation to resist. They were mostly young, single people of the Third Aliyah, from Russia, Galicia, and Poland, all influenced by the October Revolution, which had inspired their idealistic search for a Soviet-like society.

The second was Shochat and his Hashomer* men, into whose arms the Labor Legionnaires had been pushed by the Tel Yosef–HEC conflict. (The Shochats' leftism had causes of its own, one of which was the fact that some prominent Hashomer members had been in Russia during the revolution and had ever after admired Lenin's regime on the strength of their experience in the war.) Manya had intentionally opened the Legion's doors to the left by requesting its parties to "place" some of their members in Kefar Giladi, a request met enthusiastically by the Faction, which used this opportunity to send members to other Legion companies as well, hoping to solicit recruits. The Faction's prize catch was Yerahmiel Luckaser, a graduate of the Herzliya Gymnasium in Tel Aviv, who had served during the war as an officer in the Turkish army and later joined Hashomer and then the Circle. While moving up in the Palestine Communist Party (to become a central committee member and coordinator of its Arab committee — all in secret), he also rose in the Circle's chain of command, proving himself an able and daring fighter.[9]

The Circle, meanwhile, was growing stronger and stepping up its underground activity. In November 1923 Kefar Giladi members attacked a carload of gold smugglers from Beirut near the northern border. The Chariot Coup, as this expropriation subsequently became known, put 15,000 gold sovereigns, then an enormous fortune, at the

---

* Theoretically Hashomer had ceased to exist in 1920 with the establishment of the Haganah, but since it continued underground, it was called "the former Hashomer," an awkward and imprecise name. For convenience I will call it simply Hashomer.

Circle's disposal, helping it begin the systematic implementation of Shochat's plan of establishing an armed and secret Jewish force. But this vision had undergone an essential change; while the force's role as defender of the Yishuv and its rationale as the foundation of a Jewish army to control Palestine had remained unchanged, it was clear to only a few which force was being warded off or for the sake of which ideological cause the army was being indoctrinated. These were very pertinent questions, for Manya and Israel Shochat and their comrades who had moved to the left had begun seeking understanding and friendship with Palestinian Arabs. Hence, their force would defend the Yishuv against Arabs incited to riot by the effendis and British colonial officers, but would not fight so-called peace-seeking Arabs. Although Manya, in 1925, joined the Brith Shalom (Covenant of Peace) association, which strove to make Palestine a binational state, Shochat did not go that far; his army was meant to take control of Palestine and establish it as a communist Zionist republic in which Jews and Arabs would live in harmony and further the socialist revolution in the Middle East. Accordingly Shochat and the Circle were ready to join forces with a foreign power with the same ideas, willing to help them build their underground force.

In the summer of 1924 Shochat and Luckaser went to Europe to buy, among other things, arms for the Circle's depots, especially for Kefar Giladi, where the central storeroom had been hewn 20 meters deep into the rock by a few of Shochat's most loyal men. Luckaser, who, in Manya's words, was to be "the first harbinger" of the Jewish Army, stayed on in Europe, taking private lessons in Berlin in the art of war from retired German officers and generals. In 1926, his education complete, he returned to Palestine and founded an officers' training school in Tel Yosef, where fifty Circle members trained in three three-month courses. Shochat stayed in Europe for a briefer period, with an equally grandiose mission in mind: to set up the beginnings of an air force. He nearly succeeded in gaining some of his men admission to flight training schools in France, but when this failed, he, too, went to Berlin, where he and another Circle man met with the Soviet ambassador. Introducing himself and his companion as socialist Zionists who pinned their hopes on Soviet support, Shochat detailed the Circle's plan and submitted a request for admission into the Red Army's flight schools. They supplied the ambassador with information about the Circle, gave him applications for entry visas to the Soviet Union, and returned to Palestine to await Moscow's response.

The following summer, 1925, Manya and Israel hosted a fact-finding mission from the Soviet Union, a husband and wife team who, in the guise of tourists, visited the Labor Legion companies. Was this visit the beginning of the Soviet government's response? Did it dispatch the couple to investigate the Circle and sniff out its real intentions? Shochat's contacts with the Soviet Union were kept top secret by the Circle's small leadership, Menahem Elkind among them, and most of them have not yet come to light. In any case, it is certain that Shochat's requests in Berlin did not go unanswered. In October 1925 Golomb got wind of a rumor that the Circle leaders had resolved "to maintain nonorganizational ties with the Comintern" in the belief that they could influence the Soviet leadership to change its attitude toward Zionism by making it realize that the movement encompassed the Circle, an influential group that could be of service to the Comintern.[10]

On learning only a smattering of what he later called the Legion's "separatist activity," Ben-Gurion feared its complete detachment from the Histadrut. To prevent this he sought private, secret meetings with Legion members in April 1924 in the hope that he could bring them closer to the ideas of Achdut ha-Avodah. But any such campaign was doomed from the start. The memory of Ben-Gurion's fierce encounter with Tel Yosef was still fresh, and the Labor Legionnaires rightly suspected that his primary motive was to convert them to Achdut ha-Avodah. News of his secret feelers was leaked and published, and all Legion companies — even those that had already accepted — were ordered to reject his requests for meetings. In his diary Ben-Gurion noted angrily, "The Legion stirs up intrigues with its agents, wishing for a split. Libels of all kinds are spread against me."

In December 1924, with remarkable fortitude, he went to Tel Yosef in person for a meeting with Elkind, hoping to sound him out, but in vain. Although their talk went on into the night, Elkind slipped through his fingers like sand, and Ben-Gurion was left with an unsubstantiated suspicion that the Legion's leftist tendencies were linked to a scheme to turn the Legion into a political party in its own right, anti-Histadrut and perhaps even anti-Zionist. Lacking proof, he could not bring the whole weight of his drive against the left to bear against Elkind and the Circle, but he tried yet another tactic to get his proof.

Although the Legion had agreed to abide by the Histadrut council's 1924 resolution, it had not done anything to rid itself of Faction members, even those who had been expelled from the Histadrut elsewhere. Now Ben-Gurion put the Legion to the test, knowing full well that it could not oust its Faction members without splitting up. He began insisting that the council's resolution be carried out to the letter, and as a result, in January 1925, the Legion was consumed by a controversy that split its ranks between right and left for the first time. Those who sided with Ben-Gurion's demand to oust the Factionists were called rightists and those who opposed it were called leftists within the Legion. In

February, when the majority of Tel Yosef favored the expulsion of its Factionist members, the line was drawn along which the Legion would shortly split. This could not have happened on its own since the Labor Legionnaires' social and ideological bonds were stronger than differences of opinion about banning the Faction. To hasten the rupture additional steps were called for, and Ben-Gurion believed that the time had come to take them, but his 1923 conflict with Tel Yosef had taught him caution, patience, and the need to prepare public opinion in advance.

The Legion was plagued with debts — to the Office of Public Works and to Ha-Mashbir — which its leaders asked the HEC to write off as "losses on account of members who had learned a trade in the Labor Legion and then left it." In essence, they maintained that these losses should by right have been paid for from the Histadrut's budget for the vocational training of new immigrants. Seeing in the debts an instrument for achieving his purpose, in January 1925, at an HEC meeting called to discuss them, Ben-Gurion brought up "the Haganah question, separatist activity abroad, the Legion's code of regulations, defiance of Histadrut regulations," and similar issues, turning the meeting into a discussion of the Legion's nature: "Is it a national kibbutz or a party?"

The HEC's consent to write off the Legion's debts was made to depend on the Legion leaders' answers to an essentially political-organizational question. They replied in a conciliatory manner, intending, Ben-Gurion thought, to mislead him. He therefore persisted, and the discussion of debts developed into a long controversy, requiring a second and then a third meeting. Time was on his side, and as far as Ben-Gurion was concerned, the longer it took, the better. In February, five weeks after the first meeting, the HEC, following his instructions, turned down the request, giving notice that the Legion was to repay its debts promptly.[11]

This was indirect economic pressure. Unless the debts were settled, the Office of Public Works, which had become Solel Boneh, would reduce the advances given the Legion companies on account for its contracts, and Ha-Mashbir would stop supplying them with materials, equipment, and food on credit. As a result the Legion's sources of employment would dry up and its debts would grow until it had to cut its members' food rations, meager though they were. Ben-Gurion's goal was not to starve them but to make them angry at their leaders, while also making it clear that without a firm bond to the Histadrut, which meant carrying out its resolutions, the Legion's very existence was at stake.

Ben-Gurion knew full well that this economic pressure would not produce the desired results overnight, given the Labor Legionnaires' devotion and strength of spirit. Therefore he set out to shake their faith in their leaders. He made a great show of unmasking the Legion leaders at public meetings and in the pages of *Kunteres,* as if he had caught them red-handed, claiming that "only a select few of the Labor Legionnaires" knew their leaders' "real platform," which made the Legion "a revolutionary, class war outfit." It demonstrated that the principal propositions of that same platform had been borrowed from the "party 'platform' of those who negate the kibbutz and settlement movement of the labor movement in Palestine" and oppose the Histadrut. He warned those Labor Legionnaires faithful to the Zionist labor movement against "the strong trend which prevails among an important sector of its members" to turn the Legion into "a political body, a party." He asked them again and again, "Where are you headed?" and demanded unequivocal answers regarding the Histadrut, the Faction, and the nature of the Legion — kibbutz or party?

Undaunted by his assault, the Legion leaders called him a thief. They filed a complaint against him, claiming that the propositions quoted in his speeches and articles "were lifted in a way unknown to us from the Legion secretariat's files." Furthermore, they said, these propositions had been filed away in the first place because in them "the national aspect does not get its proper emphasis." The Legion council's discussion on its standing in the Histadrut had not yet taken place. In fact, a large committee had been charged with drafting new propositions and bringing them up for final approval at the Legion's council as part of its platform. Ben-Gurion, for his part, hastened to make it known — unaware that he was contradicting himself — that the propositions had been passed on to him by a Labor Legionnaire "after they had put them to the debate in all the companies." But neither Ben-Gurion's exposé of the propositions nor his adversaries' accusation that he had pilfered Legion documents gave an advantage to either side. Despite the worsening economic situation in the Legion its leaders retained the members' loyalty.[12]

Ben-Gurion now needed irrefutable proof of the Legion leaders' anti-Histadrut and anti-Zionist stance. He waited for it patiently, and in the spring of 1926, when he was out of the country, it appeared out of the blue. In March the Soviet Cooperatives Center (Centrosoyuz) sent the Labor Legion an invitation to visit the Soviet Union. On April 2 the Legion secretariat notified the HEC in writing of its decision to send off within a week a delegation made up of Menahem Elkind, Israel Shochat, and Dov Mechonai to visit communal farms in Russia, adding, "If you have any messages for the above-mentioned institutions, please let us know."

In Ben-Gurion's absence the HEC was at a loss. None of its members had the authority or confidence to react instantly and sharply to this flagrant breach of the rule Ben-Gurion had worked so hard to institute, that foreign relations were the absolute domain of the HEC and no one else was authorized to conduct them without its prior consent. The best his colleagues could do was a formal expression of their puzzlement "that you write to us in such an offhand manner about a matter of great importance." They invited the Legion to the HEC to thrash it out. A meeting was held on April 7, in which Elkind explained cavalierly that the delegation's aims were to visit collective farms and study Soviet methods of child care and education. On hearing this, Golomb, then acting chairman of the HEC secretariat, responded angrily, "You could be more straightforward with the HEC" and not "play the innocent." He said it was common knowledge that the Legion had "no money for idle travels" and that "Israel Shochat isn't the man to study farms and child care." Evidently Golomb suspected a connection between this invitation to the USSR and Shochat's meeting with the Soviet ambassador in Berlin. Golomb knew of the meeting, but nothing about the information given the ambassador or the visa applications.

When it heard this account of the composition and goals of the delegation, especially Shochat's purported role, the HEC forbade its departure on the grounds that "foreign liaisons are generally, by the constitution, the domain of the Histadrut's executive committee." The Legion leaders defied this ruling. "How ludicrous that the HEC should proscribe things that are outside the realm of its authority," said Elkind, and after Passover he set out with the delegation. It arrived in Moscow before the May Day festivities and did indeed visit farms and educational institutions, but Shochat also met with the director of the foreign affairs department of the GPU, the KGB's predecessor, and proposed a deal. The Soviet Union "would look with favor on the establishment of a communist Jewish state in Palestine," and in return "an efficient force, able to take on" the British rule, would assist the USSR in the Mideast and throw the British out when the day came. In the meantime Shochat had a concrete request, "to find a place in the Soviet Union to train Jewish pilots." Nothing is known of the meetings Elkind had in Russia, but while his Moscow talks bore fruit, Shochat's reached a dead end. Mechonai remained in the Soviet Union to study medicine, never to return to Palestine.[13]

On his return to Tel-Aviv in June, Ben-Gurion was briefed on the Legion's contacts with the Soviets. Although the information pieced together by the Haganah was scanty he considered it sufficient for the all-out war he was ready to wage against the Legion, which was to last six months. His carefully planned strategy was divided into two parts, one overt and the other covert. For his overt battles he chose his favorite weapon, Histadrut dominance, which until then had given him all his victories. His choice of a theater of war was guided by an affair arising from Tel Hai's having joined the Labor Legion in 1924 and Kefar Giladi's consequent demand to merge the two settlements, a ten-minute walk from each other. For his covert battles he chose the inner sanctum of two committees of inquiry formed at his directive, the first by Achdut ha-Avodah, the other by the Histadrut. Both were to look into the separatist activity of the Legion leaders in political and security matters. His moves on both fronts were far too numerous and intricate to detail here; suffice it to say that he chose his gambits — interminable talks, nonstop joint meetings, and countless public committees — with public opinion heavily on his mind. He knew he had to create the impression that all his conciliatory efforts had failed if he wanted support which, once obtained, would enable him to deliver the final blow.

On the public front he stood by the small minority of Tel Hai veterans who opposed the merger with Kefar Giladi, arguing that they had been promised economic independence on joining the Labor Legion. The veterans complained that the majority had been artificially created by a host of new young members imported to Tel Hai by the Legion especially for the purpose of the merger. Though there is no reason to doubt that this was the Legion's objective, it was not the whole truth. Without the Legion's assistance and resources the small group at Tel Hai would have continued to dwindle. Second, Tel Hai's plots of land were scattered amidst Kefar Giladi's larger tracts. The proposed merger was, therefore, part of a recovery plan intended to create one large, uninterrupted unit of land, allowing for better agricultural planning, work methods, and crops. There was no question that economically the merger was sound.

But Ben-Gurion was not looking at it from an economic perspective. He and Golomb learned "that the Legion intends to liquidate Kvutsa Tel Hai and merge it with Kefar Giladi. Histadrut members are driven out and leftists are brought in." They were convinced that allowing the Legion chiefs to go on with their merger scheme would be tantamount to abandoning the entire Upper Galilee to a disloyal organization. Therefore only to the inquiry committees could Ben-Gurion reveal the true reason for their appointment: the national security risk of Kefar Giladi's takeover of the Upper Galilee, in which the merger with Tel Hai was only the first step. In other words, the entire northern sector of Palestine, through which ran the major smuggling route for Jewish immigrants without entry certificates and arms for the Haganah, would

PŁOŃSK

The marketplace at Płońsk, circa 1905.

Ben-Gurion, at right, with Shmuel Fox, Warsaw, 1904, before Fox's departure
to America

Ben-Gurion, sitting at center, arms crossed, with Rachel Nelkin at his right, on the eve of their departure to Palestine in the summer of 1906. Standing at the far right is Ben-Gurion's brother Abraham, and looking through the windows, on either side of the Poale Zion flag, are Reb Avigdor, Ben-Gurion's father, and Avigdor's second wife, Zvia.

The Gruen family in Płońsk, 1904: standing, from the left, are Zippora, Rivka, and Abraham; seated, second row, are Reb Avigdor and Zvia; seated in the foreground are Abraham's daughter, Sheindel, and Ben-Gurion.

RIGHT: Reb Avigdor Gruen, 1910

LEFT: Ben-Gurion as a student in Warsaw, 1905. RIGHT: Rachel Nelkin Beit-Halachmi, Warsaw, 1913. BELOW: Ben-Gurion with Warsaw friends on a visit from Palestine, 1911

A street in Petah Tikva, 1907

Editorial staff of *Ha-Achdut,* Jerusalem, 1910: standing, left to right, are Jacob Zerubavel and Alexander Chashin; seated, left to right, are Joseph-Chaim Brenner, Ben-Gurion, and Itzhak Ben-Zvi.

LEFT: Ben-Gurion, student of the Istanbul University Law School, 1914

The fifty-odd members who founded the Palestine Poale Zion Party in December 1906 in Jaffa. Ben-Gurion is seated at the far right of the second row.

RIGHT: Ben-Gurion, barefoot and holding grapes, in Rishon Le-Zion winery, 1908

BEN-GURION IN AMERICA, 1915–1918

Yizkor editors in New York, 1916: standing, left to right, are Shmuel Bonchek and Ben-Zvi; seated, left to right, are Zerubavel and Ben-Gurion.

Ben-Gurion, 1918

Golda Meir, 1918

A Poale Zion Pittsburgh conference, 1915: in the second row, seated, starting fourth from the left, are Nahman Syrkin, Kalman Marmor, Baruch Zuckerman, and Professor Chaim Fineman. Standing directly behind Marmor is Bonchek.

PAULA'S FAMILY

The Munweis family, Minsk, 1908, on the eve of Paula's departure to America. Paula is standing at the far right, her elder sister Raisa is seated at Paula's right, and her youngest sister, Pessia, is seated in the front row, holding a straw basket.

Ben-Gurion and Paula, New York, 1917

IN THE ARMY

First day at training depot, Fort
Edward, Canada, 1918. Ben-Zvi, in
uniform, is seated at Ben-Gurion's
right.

RIGHT: Ben-Gurion in training, 40th
Battalion of the Royal Fusiliers.
(Note the Shield of David on his
sleeve.)

Paula and Geula, 1919

In Płońsk, 1921: left
to right, Amos, Paula,
Ben-Gurion, and Geula

Ben-Gurion and family in Jerusalem, May 1925: left to right, Ben-Gurion,
holding Renana, Paula, Geula, Reb Avigdor, and Amos

Celebrating Reb Avigdor's eightieth birthday: seated, left to right, are Ben-Gurion, Renana, Reb Avigdor, and Abraham Gruen. In the second row, from left to right, are Zippora, Geula, Amos, Abraham Gruen's son and wife, and Rivka and Abraham Har-Melach.

fall into the hands of an isolationist, clandestine military group operating under communist anti-Zionist influence.[11]

After two economic study committees had presented their findings to the HEC and two long joint meetings of the HEC, the Agricultural Center, and the kibbutz movement leaders, plus three prolonged joint meetings of all of these with representatives from Tel Hai and the Legion — in addition to separate HEC and secretariat meetings — the HEC plenum concluded that the merger would lead to the minority's ejection, that is, the dispossession of veteran families with long distinguished pioneering records, and it considered "the minority's staying on as essential." This conclusion pleased Ben-Gurion, who could state that "the various Histadrut institutions' incessant efforts have not brought about a mutual agreement on cooperation between the two parties. The Histadrut has no choice but to make its decision." On June 30 his moment of decision arrived; following Ben-Gurion's lead, the HEC voted unanimously that "the Tel Hai kvutsa is no longer a part of the Legion and the Legion can no longer interfere in Tel Hai's affairs. Such affairs are from now on in the hands of the Agricultural Center."

As in 1923, the HEC arbitrarily and undemocratically intervened in a kvutsa's ability to conduct its affairs as it saw fit, but with the important difference that this 1926 intervention was harsher and entirely out of proportion. "According to what clause in the Histadrut constitution did the HEC assume the responsibility to determine who was a member of the Legion and who was to drop out of it?" asked the Legion leaders, certain that Ben-Gurion had no more tricks up his sleeve. The HEC had passed this resolution the day before the Histadrut council was to meet to discuss other matters. If they suspected that Ben-Gurion planned to bring up the resolution for the council's approval — to make it a Histadrut resolution — they underestimated his finesse. It was not he who wound up bringing it before the council, but rather the Legion. He begged the Legion not to go through with it, calling its representatives to yet another joint meeting with the HEC on the morning of July 1, a few hours before the council was to open.

This was the final refinement. At the joint meeting it was suggested to the Legion representatives "to accept the HEC's resolution" with the argument, which sounded more like a threat, that "the reasons behind the HEC's objection to the merger of Tel Hai and Kefar Giladi are such as do not lend themselves to public discussion." If the Legion appealed to the council, the HEC would have to tell the council members the findings of the Achdut ha-Avodah inquiry committee concerning the Circle's clandestine, separatist activity. The Legion representatives found themselves trapped. Bowing to the HEC resolution would result in a loss of face and hand Ben-Gurion a resounding victory, while rejecting it would immediately be construed as a flagrant violation of a Histadrut ruling, making them easy prey to Ben-Gurion's disciplinary fury.

Most likely it was here that one of Ben-Gurion's characteristic habits got its start. On seeing one of his weapons homing in on its target, he would suddenly step aside, pretending to be an uninvolved onlooker. In this case, the Labor Legionnaires acted exactly as he had anticipated, and on July 2 they appealed the HEC resolution. But if they had hoped to use the council's floor to arouse public opinion against the HEC's antidemocratic and unconstitutional intervention, they had yet another surprise coming: their appeal was not discussed in public. Citing the grounds that it involved sensitive security matters, Ben-Gurion persuaded the council to discuss the appeal behind closed doors.

From that point on events followed Ben-Gurion's scenario. The Legion and Kefar Giladi representatives voiced their complaints and Ben-Gurion and Golomb presented the HEC's case. Ben-Gurion told the closed meeting about the "existence of a permanent group dealing in defense . . . carrying out special operations, whose arms depots are neither open to the Histadrut's inspection nor placed at its disposal," recalled the Chariot Coup," and warned that, in view of the Faction's infiltration of the Legion, "there is a grave political danger in the negotiations that the Legion's delegation began in Moscow." After supplementary remarks by Golomb and long deliberation the council endorsed the HEC resolution by a majority of 21 to 4 with one abstention. The jaws of the trap opened wide around the Legion amid a total news blackout, except for a summary published in *Davar* that omitted any mention of the clandestine and military nature of the Circle.[15]

Ben-Gurion showed himself here as absolutely fearless, ready to put his life on the line in doing his duty. If word had leaked out of the council about who was responsible for the Chariot Coup, the police, working hard on the case, would have been knocking on doors in Kefar Giladi almost instantly. This alone could have convinced the Circle to issue a death warrant for Ben-Gurion as a provocateur.

It was clear to Ben-Gurion that his next move would be the dramatic action he had long been planning. If the Kefar Giladi members and the majority at Tel Hai defied the resolution, they would be thrown out of the Histadrut. But, perhaps because this time he contemplated a mass expulsion of scores of widely known and respected members, and perhaps because he had learned from the Tel Yosef affair that without thoroughly preparing public opinion even a well-timed action might appear hasty, Ben-Gurion did not hurry to spring his trap.

The Legion leaders and many members of Kefar Giladi and Tel Hai refused to heed a resolution that they believed trampled on justice and freedom. Unwavering in their conviction that the merger had economic and democratic justification, they established a united committee of both settlements and under its authority proceeded to carry it out. On July 25 and 26, despite strong opposition from the minority, aggravated by brawls, Kefar Giladi members plowed through Tel Hai's vegetable garden and fields. They stopped only when the minority families, the men, women, and children, lay down in the furrows.

A commission sent from the Agricultural Center requested the united committee to honor the Histadrut resolution, a request the committee turned down. Nonplussed, the Histadrut commission called the HEC for help. Only then did Ben-Gurion step out of the shadows and take center stage. On Friday, July 30, accompanied by Ben-Zvi, he went to Tel Hai, probably taking his life in his hands, since the things he had said at the closed meeting of the Histadrut had leaked out and led to rumors. One false rumor that had spread among the Labor Legionnaires had it that Ben-Gurion had accused the Circle of the 1924 shooting of Jacob Israel De Haan, an ultra-Orthodox anti-Zionist extremist from Jerusalem suspected of spying for the Arabs. Manya Shochat had been arrested on suspicion of the murder, which remained an unsolved case in police files. The truth, known only to a few, was that De Haan had been killed by order of the Haganah's Jerusalem command. The Circle people, who knew their hands were clean, suspected Ben-Gurion of intentional provocation against them — since he knew full well who was responsible for De Haan's murder — and articulated their threat in Hashomer terms, saying that he "would be dealt with like any other provocateur." Moreover, Manya, who was hurt most by the rumor, on July 23 sent him a curt registered letter in her own handwriting. "Ben-Gurion . . . I hadn't thought you were capable of using such means to hurt the Legion. I respected you too much as a person. The path you chose will destroy us and you. There's no forgiveness in my heart and I'm breaking off all personal relations between us. Manya Shochat."

Ben-Gurion put the worst construction on her letter. "Since you took upon yourself the important social mission of passing on to me the threat to destroy me, I wish to tell you that this threat raises in me some pity for those behind it, and nothing else," he replied with equal curtness by registered mail on July 26. It will never be known who started the rumor, but Ben-Gurion had real cause to fear for his life, not only because of the Odessa murder in Manya's past, but also because of the more recent murder of the Arab police officer Tawfik Bey by Luckaser, on Manya's orders, because the Circle held him responsible for the Jaffa massacre in 1921.[16]

Because of his apprehension Ben-Gurion took along Ben-Zvi, who, as a close friend of the Shochats and the Hashomer men, had their trust and could guarantee Ben-Gurion's personal safety and facilitate the talks with the united committee. Still, Ben-Gurion said, "I felt like the administration in an occupied enemy territory." Looking out of the taxi the HEC had hired for them Ben-Gurion and Ben-Zvi saw a horseman dressed like a Bedouin whom they identified as a member of Kefar Giladi on the lookout. The united committee knew when they arrived.

At Tel Hai the pair were welcomed by the minority members with open arms, but Kefar Giladi refused to let them visit. Ben-Gurion and Ben-Zvi thereupon invited the united committee to Tel Hai, where Ben-Gurion stated that its very existence and activity ran counter to "HEC and Histadrut resolutions" and warned the Kefar Giladi members "not to use force or violence, as such things are liable to lead to grave results." The united committee countered that it "does not accept the HEC resolution nor the council's, and will continue to carry out the merger . . . in the future as well." Ben-Gurion and Ben-Zvi spent the night in Tel Hai.

The next day, Saturday, July 31, Ben-Zvi received a letter from Nahum Horovitz, a pillar of the Circle and of Kefar Giladi, inviting him to come to Kefar Giladi alone. At Ben-Gurion's behest, Ben-Zvi accepted the invitation and returned three hours later with a new threat from the Circle. Ben-Gurion's remarks to the Histadrut council were a "provocation," and if he repeated them, "we will deal with him as with a provocateur."

Ben-Gurion and Ben-Zvi again invited the united committee to Tel Hai to caution them a second time against going ahead with the merger and using violence, and the united committee reiterated its previous statement. On Sunday Ben-Gurion and Ben-Zvi returned to Tel Aviv after sending a handwritten account of their adventures in Tel Hai to *Davar;* it was published anonymously the next day beside a report of a quarrel that had broken out there in the wake of the plowing of its fields. Any *Davar* reader would have had to conclude that the members of Kefar Giladi and the majority at Tel Hai had gone at least one step too far.[17]

In Tel Aviv Ben-Gurion convened the HEC and pushed through a unanimous resolution to dispatch a new deputation — two HEC representatives and one from the Agricultural Center — this time with the ultimatum that anyone who did not obey the council resolution would be expelled from the Histadrut. But he delayed the group's departure in order to convene yet another joint meeting of the HEC with the Legion's representatives. This, too, was probably necessary for the sake of public opinion.

The meeting ended inconclusively, and Ben-Gurion instructed the new delegates to set out. On the afternoon of August 7 the three deputies convened a general assembly in the courtyard of Tel Hai, urging all present to heed the Histadrut resolution with the warning that "a negative response to this demand will lead to expulsion of the members of Kefar Giladi and the majority of Tel Hai from the Histadrut." This created a storm of protests at the end of which the united committee replied on behalf of the majority that it would not honor the resolution. In keeping with Ben-Gurion's instructions the Histadrut deputies then announced the ouster from the Histadrut of the united committee members, the Kefar Giladi members, and the majority at Tel Hai, from a prepared list of one hundred names in alphabetical order, complete with membership card numbers.

The story of the expulsion was published the next day, August 8, in *Davar*. The material Ben-Gurion had prepared for the meeting, describing the patience the HEC had displayed before finally expelling the defiers of the Histadrut resolution, filled a whole page. In response the Legion secretariat sent the HEC a letter that it published the same day as a pamphlet entitled "An Open Letter from the Members of Tel Hai and Kefar Giladi" to Histadrut council delegates and "to all members of the Histadrut." It declared that the expulsion was "tyrannical and in poor taste," that the HEC's "iniquity and obduracy" were "enough to make heaven weep," and accused "certain leaders [Ben-Gurion and Golomb] of circulating venom and rancor." The letter closed with a summons "to court of all those responsible for spreading unfounded accusations and all kinds of slanders."

That Shochat and company understood the expulsion as Ben-Gurion's vengeance for their not taking him into Hashomer in 1909 was made clear in a paragraph that accused "certain leaders" of not judging the Tel Hai merger on its merits but of being interested in settling "old scores from ten years and more ago that remain unforgotten." "Ten years" referred to Golomb, who had joined Hashomer in 1916 but had had a difference of opinion with Shochat, and "more" referred to Ben-Gurion. The version of this letter received at the HEC was harsher. It called Ben-Gurion, who was its main theme, "an informer," among other things, because of what he had said at the Histadrut council and to the Achdut ha-Avodah inquiry committee.[18]

To Ben-Gurion this "letter of calumny," as he immediately tagged it, was a gift from heaven. He had long thought of setting up a Histadrut inquiry into the Circle, and the letter played right into his hands. He paid no heed to the Circle chiefs, who had second thoughts and proposed to Ben-Gurion, through Ben-Zvi, that the Legion "take back its letter," for it had given him the chance to kill three birds with the same stone. Since a storm of public opinion had already arisen over the mass expulsion and abrogation of the Tel Hai merger, Ben-Gurion took the opportunity also to liquidate the Legion's left and put an end to the Circle. On the day the open letter was circulated Ben-Gurion demanded that the HEC "appoint an authoritative committee" that same evening. It was urgent, he explained, because lives, specifically his own, hung in the balance. Manya and Israel Shochat, he said, had put in his mouth words he had never said at the closed council meeting and fabricated "dangerous slanders" about him, "which, if broadcast, are liable to lead to very grave results." To make sure the hint was broad enough he added, "Some of the leaders of the group in Kefar Giladi, who are also in the united committee, are now conspiring criminally against one of the HEC members, and are spreading false accusations and libels about him," and charged the Legion leadership with having a hand in this crime.

The HEC acceded to Ben-Gurion's demand and endorsed the seven members he had nominated for the "special committee, independent of all institutions." Its appointment was announced the next day in *Davar* as part of carrying out the Histadrut council resolution, which had charged the HEC with conducting a comprehensive inquiry, in cooperation with Legion representatives, into "all those questions, events, and relations which came before the council" in connection with the conflict over the merger. But there was no resemblance between the committee's role as described in *Davar* and the assignment Ben-Gurion gave it: to establish whether there was "an organized circle regularly conducting separatist activity in matters of security" among the Labor Legionnaires; whether it was responsible for the theft of arms hidden at Kefar Giladi, for the "gold robbery," and for the threat against Ben-Gurion's life; and finally, "if it's true that the Legion's delegation to Russia entered into political negotiations there."

As it turned out, of the hundred ousted, only eleven were Circle members, and some belonged to neither Kefar Giladi nor Tel Hai. But meanwhile Ben-Gurion had used the public's disapproval of the potential dispossession of Tel Hai veterans to counter its reaction to the mass expulsion and had managed to get rid of the Legion's leftists, who made up the lion's share of the expulsion list, as well as unaffiliated Circle members. What is more, under cover of the expulsion the ouster of individual leftists continued, until by the end of the year a total of 242 people had lost their Histadrut membership.

Ha-Poel ha-Tzair was disgusted by the whole affair, particularly by the publicity that accompanied Ben-Gurion's moves. Its central committee made public its opinion that this publicity put the Kefar Giladi affair in "a political light," expressing its "resentment at the sensational manner in which this matter was reported in our press." The committee stressed that it had opposed "and opposes today too" the administrative power of expulsion granted the HEC in the constitution, implying that Ben-Gurion had misused it since it was intended only "for instances of disciplinary offenses by individuals" and not for the expulsion of "groups of members . . . without a hearing or trial. In his paper Itzhak Laufbahn, editor of *Ha-Poel ha-Tzair* and long-time adversary of Ben-Gurion, mocked the "sensational publicity" intended to wrap Ben-Gurion in "a cloak of holy innocence," which cast his subordinates "as protectors of widows and defenders of orphans; all on account of the nine children and one widow who lay down in the furrows in the fields of Tel Hai . . . in an unsuccessful attempt to divert attention to sentimental points which in themselves have no bearing on the matter at hand."[19]

Ben-Gurion knew how to place himself at the center of public attention, an ability that would serve him repeatedly on the long political road ahead. Naturally he responded readily, in Histadrut forums and in print, to Ha-Poel ha-Tzair's challenge, with some support, though not so vocal, from Achdut ha-Avodah. In the process he revealed yet another exceptional talent, the ability to intensify the issues under public discussion — especially those he knew he was going to win   thus pushing his adversaries to extremes. In this instance he had little doubt of the outcome of the inquiry committee's investigation, while his detractors, who had not the vaguest idea what it was all about, continued to accuse him of misuse and abuse of his office.

After several postponements the committee took up its task, and Ben-Gurion attended to it with great industry as if apprehensive of the unexpected. He drafted its instructions, and he summoned witnesses and examined them, in his much loved role of prosecuting attorney. Day after day for five months he devoted time to the committee's work, except for one day when he took a sick Renana to the hospital. On January 27 the committee presented its report to the HEC. "The expression . . . 'we will deal with him as with a provocateur' can mean more than one thing, and it is not surprising that it should be taken as a threat of violent action." As to the principal issue, the committee found that Shochat and Elkind had conducted political negotiations with the Soviet Union and that the Circle had taken a separatist turn, obeying its leaders and disobeying the Haganah, and that it had also committed the actions alleged against it. The committee concluded that the Circle must be disbanded, absolutely and finally. Shochat, who had been summoned to the HEC to read the committee's report, protested vehemently but in the end, knowing the Circle was doomed, gave in, declaring, "My colleagues and I will submit to the conclusions." Ben-Gurion noted Shochat's words in his diary, quoting him twice as saying that he "will submit despite it all," a slight alteration that indicated Ben-Gurion's pleasure at his victory. After tortuous negotiations the Circle relinquished all its arms caches to the Haganah and, exactly twenty years after the inception of Hashomer, ceased to exist forever.[20]

When Ben-Gurion had been proved right and his detractors had to eat their accusations that he had shrouded himself in "mystery" and placed himself "above public criticism," the Legion's end also drew near. Its leftists, weakened considerably after the mass expulsion, lost more ground in the eyes of the public — greatly excited by leaks from the inquiry committee while its report was in preparation — and on December 17 the Legion split in two. Three hundred or so of its members, motivated by their loyalty to Zionism and the Histadrut, formed the right-wing Legion, and about two hundred, who followed Elkind, became the left-wing Legion. Tel Yosef, the Legion's first and largest kibbutz, joined the right wing, as did Kefar Giladi, where the majority followed Shochat. Its members expressed regret over their conflict with the Histadrut and took it on themselves to uphold all its resolutions. Shortly afterward, at Ben-Gurion's behest, the HEC decided to readmit them to the Histadrut, and Ben-Gurion delivered the news to them in person. The HEC took the additional step of proclaiming that the right-wing Legion was the one and only Joseph Trumpeldor Labor and Defense Legion "and the Histadrut will not recognize any other group by this name." The left-wing Legion was thereby stripped of its title — an important asset — and of a large part of its property and means of existence.

The left-wing Legion waged a bitter but hopeless struggle for the right of its members to stay in Kefar Giladi, Tel Yosef, and other settlements and to retain their property. Its petitions to the Zionist Executive went unanswered, and the severe economic depression that began in late 1927 made its situation even worse; its members abandoned it, and its decline accelerated. Ben-Gurion kept track of this development in his diary, although his dry, matter-of-fact notations did not reflect his inner feelings. That he had not acted coldly or heartlessly is illustrated by his describing to the third Histadrut convention the resolution to expel the members of Kefar Giladi as "dreadful."[21]

The end of the left-wing Legion was pitiful. Elkind returned to the Soviet Union, this time, it seems, to gain Soviet support for his organization. On the way an idea took root in his mind to settle his people in the USSR, where they would find a solid economic base and integrate into the ideological and social framework to their hearts' content. But most of his followers rejected emigration from Palestine. Only Elkind and sixty diehards, his wife among them, left for the Soviet Union in

1929 and founded a commune in the Crimea, near Yevpatoriya, which they named Via Nova ("new way" in Esperanto; they did not want to give it a Russian name, and a Hebrew one was out of the question). Their end was tragic: only the few who were disappointed early on returned to Palestine. The rest were purged by Stalin and exiled to Siberia, fell into the hands of their Tartar neighbors, or were destroyed by the Nazi armies that occupied the Crimean peninsula during the Second World War.

But in 1927, long before their fate became known, none of Ben-Gurion's explanations and arguments could silence the echoing of the cries of the ousted in the ears of Histadrut members who abhorred administrative punishment. They had been steadily gaining in strength and they found in Moshe Beilinson, the Sick Fund's representative to the HEC, a leader possessing the moral fortitude that enabled him to stand up to Ben-Gurion. At his lead the third Histadrut convention in July 1927 amended the constitution as follows: "Expulsion of a member from the Histadrut or the abrogation of his rights is possible only through a ruling of the Histadrut High Court."[22]

Nevertheless, at the beginning of 1927 it was clear that Ben-Gurion had succeeded in investing the Histadrut and its HEC with the predominance he had sought, as well as with the means and courage to enforce it. The uproar that accompanied his quest for Histadrut authority paradoxically strengthened, instead of weakened, his public image as a forceful, resourceful, and tenacious leader who knew what he wanted and how to get it. Furthermore, his showdown with the Legion had revealed another quality of his leadership: a talent for making his objective unmistakably clear to one and all by means of a dramatization so powerful, even sensational, as to rivet public opinion on it. Before the third Histadrut convention met he had a chance to employ this trait to still greater effect.

21

A Corpse at
Sprinzak's Doorstep

IN 1927 David Ben-Gurion was already thinking of "the conquest of Zionism," that is, the takeover of the Zionist Organization by the leadership of the Eretz-Israeli labor movement. To all appearances, he had accepted the prevailing Histadrut–Zionist Executive relations, as had his colleagues in Achdut ha-Avodah and the HEC, and consented, albeit with reservations, to an Achdut ha-Avodah representative, Shlomo Kaplansky, holding a position in the Zionist Executive, as did Ha-Poel ha-Tzair's representative, Joseph Sprinzak. When the time was ripe, however, Ben-Gurion used the unemployment situation as successfully against the Zionist Executive as he had against Ha-Poel ha-Mizrachi and the anti-Zionist left.

Ben-Gurion was constrained by the Histadrut's financial dependence. Its larger institutions had all been established, developed, and more than once rescued with Zionist funds. The Histadrut's entire agricultural-communal system depended on the Zionist colonization budget, to the point that it was impossible to draw up the Histadrut budgets until the Zionist annual budget had been determined. When the Zionist Executive's budget dwindled — a perennial phenomenon — "a catastrophe" threatened the entire Histadrut enterprise. At one HEC budget meeting Shmuel Yavnieli had asked, "Is it possible for us to continue in this manner, to depend on a miracle each time?" Joseph Aharonovitch answered, as if for everyone, "It would be better if we were able to tell the Zionist Executive we don't want its favors, but we're unable to do so."[1]

Ben-Gurion defined the Histadrut–Zionist Executive relation as a partnership in the implementation of a dream. He kept track in his diary of the ups and downs of the Zionist coffers and the allocation of funds from them to the Histadrut. When allocations decreased, unemployment rose, and he would speed to meet with Zionist Executive members in Jerusalem to ward off the catastrophe by urging them to raise more money. At the same time he and his colleagues stood between the masses of unemployed and the Zionist Executive, which seemed to be responsible for their difficulties. He had first taken this position on May Day 1922, when he forbade the municipal labor councils to call strikes and demonstrate against the Zionist Executive. Afterward, with his consent, the labor exchanges distributed relief on behalf of the Zionist Executive, acting as a buffer between it and the recipients.

In the face of the 1926 depression the Zionist Executive more than quadrupled its relief budget, of which Sprinzak, as director of its Labor Department, was in charge. The aid for all of 1923 had totaled 17,000 Egyptian pounds while that for January 1926 alone came to 7,750. To assure the weekly relief payments for the labor exchanges, Sprinzak shuttled between the banks in a desperate effort to get credit. "I've decided to demean myself once again," he told his colleagues, describing how he had gone back to one of the banks, "pleaded . . . wrangled," and made a "scandal," but had been unable to get money in time for the Thursday payment, so the unemployed had to welcome the Sabbath empty-handed.

Ben-Gurion could see the effect this situation was having on immigration. If unemployment continued or worsened, more people would oppose immigration, which would be the end of Zionism. Yet the Zionist Executive turned its development budget into relief, imperiling immigration and Zionism with it. "We need every penny for building up the land, not for relief," Ben-Gurion explained. If the new immigrants found no development projects waiting to employ them they would go back home. But if the Zionist Executive spent all its money on development and new immigrants there would not be enough for relief.

Ben-Gurion had a very simple solution to this dilemma: more money. If the Zionist Executive refused to understand the nature of its office and to raise sufficient money for development as well as relief, he asserted, "I would say that this Zionist Executive doesn't understand the situation and we'll find a way to kick it out and fight it." One way of doing so, which he proposed to the council, was to stop paying relief through the labor exchanges and refer recipients directly to the Zionist Executive. This would bring tremendous pressure to bear on the Executive, which would either collapse under it or get more money. In the meantime Ben-Gurion did not want the Histadrut to assist an Executive that wasted its money on relief alone. The HEC decided to discuss this proposal only after a joint "review" of the situation was held by the HEC and the Zionist Executive.

The review, which turned into a bargaining session, ended with the Zionist Executive's promising to step up productive projects and create new job opportunities. But the situation, instead of improving, got steadily worse: 10,000 Egyptian pounds were needed monthly for minimal relief to the unemployed. In spite of this Ben-Gurion was unable to bring his HEC colleagues around to his proposal; they still believed that all the Zionist Executive needed was a little more prodding to raise the necessary funds for large-scale public works and development projects. In January 1927 it looked as though this prodding had been successful, for a member of the HEC committee told the HEC, "I can reassure you that the question of the work shortage is about to be solved." The HEC members happily accepted his suggestion that they postpone the next Histadrut council for a week, since "it's no good to hold a council just to shout protests," and possibly because they knew Ben-Gurion was intent on passing his proposal through the council as a Histadrut resolution. The other members of the HEC and the committee wanted to have good news with which to head him off.[2]

When the council opened on January 31, no funds had been forthcoming, and Ben-Gurion launched his assault against the Zionist Executive. He called on the council delegates to resolve "that the Histadrut renounces all responsibility for the activity of the Zionist Organization and its Executive and demands that its members resign from the Zionist Executive until work is arranged for the community of workers in Palestine." After some explanatory words Ben-Gurion took the floor five more times to defend his proposal.

He maintained that the foundation of a true partnership was the equal responsibility of both partners. The Histadrut labor community's fault lay not only in its remarkable capacity "to endure, which is second to none, but also in its feeling of responsibility unparalleled in any part of the Yishuv and the Zionist movement." The Zionist Executive in Palestine, and particularly in London, "was unable to appreciate this quality of the working community and so reached the conclusion that there was nothing wrong; the situation could go from bad to worse until better times come along." During two and a half years the heads of the Zionist Executive had "hardly done anything except for the dole. . . . If the other side doesn't do its part responsibly," Ben-Gurion concluded, "we cannot do ours, either." His proposal was meant "to make it clear to them that they cannot sit for months on end in sessions while nothing changes" and to imbue them with "the feeling of responsibility that lives within us and the fear of loss of moral fiber" that results from living on the dole. Only then would they be compelled to make a "maximal effort," to find "the minimal means required to redress the situation." In short, "We must be claimants and claimants only."

Sprinzak defended his Labor Department and the Zionist Executive. "It's not true that the Zionist Executive has done nothing until now," he said. Ben-Gurion's "desperate cry" was out of place and "it is still too early to speak in apocalyptic terms." In a similar vein Shlomo Kaplansky defended the Zionist Executive and his Settlement Department. Both denied Ben-Gurion's claim that the danger of depredation and ruin hovered over "almost a third of the laborers in Palestine." "I won't say that Weizmann doesn't feel our claim and I certainly wouldn't say that about our own comrades in the Zionist Executive," Ben-Gurion responded, "but they aren't conscious enough of the danger to Zionism." If they were, they would be making "a desperate effort to get the loan" necessary for job-creating projects.

"Our people in Palestine are called on to save their souls, not just their bodies," Ben-Gurion said. He was not going to allow the callous Zionist Executive to ruin the souls of the workers, and he would employ the harshest means at his disposal to prevent it. "I don't think scandal is the appropriate word," he said, hinting at what he was planning to do, "but if there is to be one it will have to be a Zionist scandal, not an anti-Zionist one." In other words, before the extreme left started blaming Zionism, especially Jewish immigration, for the situation, and holding protests against the Zionist Executive, the Histadrut should hold its own to prompt the Executive to raise more money.

Ha-Poel ha-Tzair accused Ben-Gurion of "having lost his senses," and Sprinzak launched a counterattack. "Scandals won't put money in the till, nor can they be staged . . . Our people are aware of their Zionist responsibility and do not jump from disciplined behavior to rioting on order." He would soon learn how wrong he was.

Ben-Gurion won the vote by a nose: ten delegates supported his proposal, nine voted against, and three abstained. In the absence of a number of delegates, and in the face of the indecisive vote, the council did not feel empowered to decide two such important matters as calling for Sprinzak's and Kaplansky's resignations from the Zionist Executive and transferring relief distribution from the exchanges to the Executive. A second vote again showed Ben-Gurion leading by one, eleven in favor and ten opposed. The third time around he suffered a defeat: ten opposed and nine in favor.

The council closed on February 2 with the resolution that Ben-Gurion's proposal was to be decided by a referendum of all its delegates. In preparation for this Ben-Gurion pieced together his contributions to the debate into one article and published it in *Kunteres* under the title "Toward War Against Unemployment." He intended that the delegates, and the entire public, would see that his comments in the council were not made rashly or in the heat of the debate. Given the magnitude of unemployment, his argument went, the only course was to awaken the conscience of the Zionist movement and bring it to prompt the dormant Executive to action. The article did not spell out how to accomplish that feat, but in cold print some of its sentences read like veiled threats, leaving no doubt that Ben-Gurion had violent action in mind. "With our might we will compel . . . We must now shake up the Zionist movement. . . . We shall not allow Zionists to be silent." Finally, as if to dispel any remaining doubt as to what he was aiming at, he wrote that it was necessary to establish a Histadrut "action committee."[3]

Were these merely bombastic slogans, or were they calls to action over the heads of the Histadrut council? Several incidents that occurred before the referendum was held provide the answer. In Jerusalem, where unemployment had hit hardest, the start of construction of the Teachers' College, the Health Center, and the Hebrew University was anticipated as manna from heaven. But unfortunately for the labor council it became clear that the College Building Committee, headed by Colonel Frederick Kisch, chairman of the Zionist Executive in Jerusalem and hand-picked by Weizmann to be director of its Political Department, and including Menahem Ussishkin, chairman of the Jewish National Fund's board of directors, and David Yellin, former chairman of the National Council of Jews of Palestine, had not made the hiring of workers through the labor exchange a condition of bidding. This enabled a private contractor to submit a bid lower than Solel Boneh's and win the contract. What was more, construction of the Health Center was contracted to an independent group of construction workers, and it was doubtful that the building jobs for the university would be handled through the labor exchange. Fearing that all the major jobs in the city would be given to unorganized labor or to Arabs, the Jerusalem Labor Council posted notices asking, "Will the Hebrew College be built by non-Jewish hands?" If contracts for public buildings did not stipulate organized labor, the notices asked, what could Histadrut workers expect from contractors for private buildings? And what then would become of the Histadrut Labor Exchange, which handled the majority of the organized Jewish laborers, more than half of whom were registered as jobless and a quarter of whom received weekly relief?[4]

These posters were the first sign of Ben-Gurion's hand directing a campaign to bring about the change in HEC–Zionist Executive relations that he had not been able to bring about at the Histadrut council. He found the pretext he needed to stir up public opinion against the Zionist Executive in the fact that two of its members headed the College Building Committee. He turned a blind eye to the fact that this was a voluntary fund-raising committee and that the two National Council members served on it entirely apart from their official positions.

Two Labor Council secretaries, Itzhak Loewenstein and Israel Bar-Ratzon, both loyal followers of Ben-Gurion, took the field on his behalf in this battle. There is no doubt that without his backing these two subordinates would never have involved themselves in a fight of national dimensions, or have taken the extreme actions they took, which closely resembled Ben-Gurion's proposal to the Histadrut council. On February 15, as soon as the results of the bid on construction of the college became known, Loewenstein and Bar-Ratzon warned the Zionist Executive's Labor Department, that is, Sprinzak, in the name of the Jerusalem Labor Council that unless the contract called for organized labor hired through the labor exchange, relief payments would be transferred from the labor exchange to the offices of Kisch, Ussishkin, and Yellin. The next day they wrote Kisch, saying that thousands of unemployed "won't agree to giving this construction job to unorganized labor, contrary to the labor exchange's stipulation."

The Zionist Executive and Sprinzak protested that it was wrong to identify the Zionist Executive with the College Building Committee. There was no valid connection between the bid conditions and the Labor Council's resolution to transfer relief distribution to the Zionist Executive. Kisch responded to the Labor Council as chairman of the College Building Committee, expressing his hope that the contractor would agree to hire his work force through the exchange, and his feeling that it would be best if the Labor Council negotiated directly with him. "The numerous threats in the letters," added Kisch, who had served as a regular soldier in the British Royal Engineering Corps, "have no influence on me, as I have always aspired, and will continue to aspire, to attain a maximum of work for the organized community of laborers in Palestine under conditions appropriate to the economic rebirth in Palestine."

For a while the dispute was carried on by mail, with the Labor Council stepping up its threats and the Zionist Executive asking for time for talks and understanding. Then Loewenstein and Bar-Ratzon learned that the College Building Committee and the contractor had completed the deal and signed a contract that had no labor exchange clause. On March 8 they notified Sprinzak and his assistant in the Labor Department that they had resolved to transfer the relief distribution to the Zionist Executive, effective as of Thursday, March 10.[5]

From his HEC office in Tel Aviv Ben-Gurion closely followed the events in Jerusalem through copies of letters regularly provided by Loewenstein and Bar-Ratzon and through regular telephone reports, of which he made notes in his diary. However, the diary completely omits what he told them, as if to establish that he was no more than an innocent bystander. According to his one-sided version, they told him that Sprinzak had requested a deferral until he could talk the matter over with Kisch, who was in Haifa, on March 8. Absolutely certain that "if we get the Teachers' College, we can be sure of the Health Center and the University," they had refused the requested deferral since "we didn't see any effort on Sprinzak's part to settle the matter" — something inconceivable to anyone who knew Sprinzak and how hard he worked.

Beginning March 9 the diary entries bear witness to Ben-Gurion's involvement in what became known as the "Jerusalem Incidents." On Wednesday, March 9, the day before the weekly relief distribution, Ben-Gurion went to Jerusalem to participate in the Labor Council meeting, which discussed "the College question" and unanimously ratified the decision to transfer the relief distribution to the Zionist Executive. In his diary Ben-Gurion noted only,

> In the evening meeting of . . . the Jerusalem Labor Council . . . Bar-Ratzon reported that tomorrow the council won't pay out relief, in protest against the handing over of the College contract without the exchange's stipulations. A demonstration is feared. I proposed that they advise the relief recipients to send a deputation to the Zionist Executive in order to warn them and that a Council member accompany them, but that there should be no demonstration.

Six days later Ben-Gurion told the HEC secretariat that on that Thursday morning he had been in Jerusalem and told the members that on no account should anyone hold demonstrations, for if the HEC decided that there was a need for one, the Histadrut alone would conduct it.

In Jerusalem some remarkable things happened that he neglected to record in his diary. On Wednesday morning Loewenstein had sent word to the Labor Department of the Labor Council's withdrawal from distributing the relief. Sprinzak again rejected the connection between the Teachers' College Building Committee and the Zionist Executive and again requested, to no avail, a delay to clarify the terms of the contract signed with the contractor. Loewenstein went back to his office and phoned a report to the HEC in Tel Aviv.

That afternoon there was another meeting between Loewenstein and Sprinzak, at the latter's request. Sprinzak asked that he and Kaplansky be given the chance "to settle the issue during the course of the day," but Loewenstein still would not consent, and at 4:00 P.M. a notice was posted on the labor exchange's door referring all relief recipients to the Zionist Executive. This was the first public notice to that effect.

It is not known whether Ben-Gurion went to Jerusalem before the telephone report or after it, but it is clear that after Itzhak Ben-Zvi learned of the public notice the two of them met and then went to the Labor Council together. Ben-Zvi disagreed with its actions, but since he thought they had been taken in conjunction with the HEC, he did not protest them at that evening's meeting of the Labor Council.

Ben-Gurion stayed overnight in Jerusalem, and one can only speculate about whom else he met with that night or the next morning, when he returned to Tel Aviv. For Thursday, March 10, his diary contained the laconic notation, "I stayed in Tel Aviv this morning." That is, he stayed in his office and took part through reports in the events developing in Jerusalem, pleased by the knowledge that his work was being done without his visible involvement. By 8:00 A.M., following his suggestion, two stonecutters, members of the Labor Council, had stationed themselves in front of the Zionist Executive offices, accompanied by a contingent of out-of-work men. The appearance of the stonecutters instead of two Council secretaries signaled a break in relations. This was not a deputation but a fighting force, which put the Zionist Executive offices under siege. Sprinzak later told the HEC that on his way to the office he had "passed by straight rows of Georgians, among whom unemployment is particularly widespread, and others." He meant that these were not merely innocent men out of work, but a band of hotheads who had been brought in intentionally to use their fists. The conversation between Sprinzak and the novice Council representatives could not develop beyond a repetitious rejection of his requests. As a result Sprinzak consented to have the relief paid by the Zionist Executive's bureau of immigration, which was located apart from the Executive's offices; he asked that the lists of recipients be sent there and that the deputation go home. The stonecutters replied that "they hadn't brought the people there and they weren't going to take them away." They turned and went back to the Labor Council, according to Sprinzak, "but the crowd remained and besieged all entrances to the Zionist Executive offices." No one went in and no one came out.[6]

In the meantime a large crowd, nearly seven hundred strong, assembled at the labor exchange. Versions of what happened there also varied; Sprinzak was to argue that the crowd had been mobilized well in advance so they would have time to get fired up before the Council secretaries told them "that the Council takes no part in the distribution of the dole and everyone is free to do as he sees fit." Loewenstein and Bar-Ratzon disputed this, maintaining not only that the agitated crowd had assembled on its own but that they themselves had struggled against the Mops and Poale Zion Left, who had tried to hold a demonstration and had, to that end, elected an action committee on the spot.

Whether the crowd headed for the immigration bureau from the labor exchange on its own or whether it did so at the directive of the Council secretaries or the Council action committee, the outcome was undisputed. An immigration bureau clerk announced to the gathering crowd that disbursement would begin at 3:00 P.M., since a list of the recipients first had to be prepared because it had not been transferred from the labor exchange in time. According to Sprinzak, the "leaders of the crowd" demanded that the bureau clerks double the dole, to 50 rather than 25 Egyptian piasters, and pay it out immediately, even though that was plainly beyond their power.

The crowd stormed the bureau and "broke the doors, the windows, and everything within reach." The police were called, and the rioting came to an end, but only at the immigration bureau, for "after this victory the crowd was led from the immigration bureau to the Zionist Executive office" on Jaffa Street, Sprinzak said. While the action committee stirred up the crowd outside, scores of protesters burst into the finance department and even the treasury room "with shouts and threats." The police cleared them out by force. At the police captain's behest Sprinzak received from the protesters a "deputation" which demanded that the work on the Teachers' College building go to the labor exchange and made speeches about the class war.

From the start the besieged Sprinzak had tried to call the Council secretaries to his aid, but in vain: Loewenstein and Bar-Ratzon did not respond. In his distress he turned to the HEC in Tel Aviv, asking the secretariat members to hurry to Jerusalem "to take matters in hand." Jacob Efter of Ha-Poel ha-Tzair, who received the call, searched for Ben-Gurion without success until later that afternoon he finally found him in, of all places, the editorial office of *Davar.* In his diary, Ben-Gurion noted Efter's message. Sprinzak had telephoned "about a demonstration of the unemployed and a siege on the finance department. They had to bring in the police. . . . Sprinzak therefore won't be coming here today [to a scheduled HEC meeting] and he demands that the HEC secretariat come to Jerusalem." He told Efter that he would not go since he had just returned from Jerusalem, and that the other secretariat members could go if they felt like it. An HEC clerk who had helped Efter look for him asked Ben-Gurion, "How could you leave Jerusalem with the situation as bad as it is?" Ben-Gurion replied,

"When I left it there was absolute quiet." Afterward Sprinzak swore he would never forget "the disloyal attitude . . . The HEC secretariat didn't deem it necessary to come." And in truth, what good would it have been without Ben-Gurion?

That evening's HEC meeting was canceled because of Sprinzak's absence, so the secretariat could turn its full attention to the events in Jerusalem. The Labor Council had accused the Zionist Executive of having "met the workers with blows and arrests" instead of payments of the dole, making Sprinzak feel as though he had been stabbed in the heart. The accusation was followed by an ultimatum: the Zionist Executive had until five o'clock to declare its stand on the question of the labor-exchange clause in the Teachers' College contract. However vague the threat was, it clearly meant more violence. With the evening meeting called off, the natural thing to do would have been to hurry to Jerusalem — an hour-and-forty-five-minute drive away — as Sprinzak had requested. But Ben-Gurion decided that the secretariat could keep abreast of developments by telephone by maintaining an all-night vigil. As night fell the secretariat members left one after another to tend to other matters, until Ben-Gurion was left alone by the phone. At 9:00 P.M. he heard from Jerusalem that a vast crowd — "thousands of people," *Davar* reported the next day — had amassed in front of the Council offices and there were signs of "a gigantic demonstration" in the street. This was, it seemed, a part of the threatened action promised if the Zionist Executive turned down the ultimatum.[7]

Whatever else Ben-Gurion heard from the Council secretaries in Jerusalem and whatever he told them have not been revealed, but the next morning, Friday, March 11, when Bar-Ratzon phoned to report on the latest developments, Ben-Gurion made notes in his diary, including the comment "I didn't hear the end of what he said." Although in view of the gravity of the situation the conversation must have been important, Ben-Gurion did not bother to clarify why he hadn't heard — whether it was a bad connection — or why he had not tried to call Bar-Ratzon back. Later it became clear that he did hear everything Bar-Ratzon had said; but he chose to chronicle it in a way that would make him seem like a bystander.

That same morning an incident occurred which shocked both the Georgian community of the Nablus Gate neighborhood and the labor community of Jerusalem. On Thursday, the morning before, a Georgian woman named Gairan, twenty-three years old and the mother of two babies, one of them a month old, had hung herself. Her neighbors knew that she "was distraught and in the past few months she spoke of suicide a lot." It was rumored that for the past five months her family had been scraping along on relief only, "the shopkeeper stopped selling on credit, and the landlord was about to throw them out of the apartment." When her husband, Shmuel Ben-Moshe, left to stand on the dole line she took her life. If the start of the rumor was politically motivated, it accomplished its purpose. Gairan quickly became a symbol of the hungry victims of the Zionist Executive's incompetence.

Almost certainly Bar-Ratzon told Ben-Gurion about all this during their Friday morning phone call and asked for instructions, because the Labor Council assumed responsibility for Gairan's funeral, scheduled for Friday afternoon. It posted notices calling on Histadrut members to take part in it. Georgian funeral processions usually made their way from the deceased's home to the neighborhood synagogue via the Dung Gate to the Mount of Olives cemetery outside the city limits. This time, however, the procession took a different course — into the city, toward the Zionist Executive offices on Jaffa Street. Bringing the deceased to the Zionist Executive's doorstep — some wanted to drop the bier on the Executive's conference table — was outrageous. Ben-Zvi cabled Ben-Gurion to come immediately, but he stayed in Tel Aviv until Sunday.

Gairan's pallbearers and 150 mourners, with Bar-Ratzon at their head, marched past the Zionist Executive offices amid cries and shouted slogans, some of them anti-Zionist, gathering a large, unruly crowd on the way. The bier was then set down in front of the Executive offices, where a eulogy and speeches were delivered.[8]

Sprinzak could not allow such a dramatization of the Histadrut campaign, which he called a crusade, against the Zionist Executive to pass unchallenged. It was, he said, "a criminal act against Zionism"; he demanded that the HEC censure those responsible for Thursday's demonstrations and Friday's funeral, and announced that he would boycott all HEC meetings until these demands were met. Although it is almost certain that Sprinzak held Ben-Gurion responsible, he chose as his targets the two Labor Council secretaries. The full support of his party enabled Sprinzak to get what he wanted; in the second half of March, the HEC, sitting as an inquiry commission, devoted three long meetings to the Jerusalem Incidents, hearing Loewenstein's and Bar-Ratzon's accounts and the contradictory versions of Sprinzak and his assistant.

Sprinzak ridiculed claims by Loewenstein and Bar-Ratzon that the violent demonstrations and Gairan's funeral had been staged by the Mops and that it had been they who shouted slogans against the Zionist Executive while the bier was lying in front of its offices. Despite their significance as a militant and fiery minority, argued Sprinzak, the Mops could not draw such large crowds and lead them against the Zionist Executive. Pinning the blame on them was simply too transparent a ruse.

Ben-Gurion stood by the Council secretaries, backing up their account with the argument that the Council had taken the funeral under its wing in good faith as the only way of preventing the Mops from taking complete control of it. But Sprinzak insisted that the Council had organized the funeral and called on Histadrut members to take part in it. Even though some Mops had joined the procession, those who had guided the funeral past the Executive offices committed "the criminal act." Sprinzak demanded that the HEC reprimand the Labor Council secretaries.

It was clear to everyone that a reprimand of the Council was also a reprimand of Ben-Gurion. "I think that Sprinzak is accusing not only the Jerusalem Labor Council, but me and Ben-Zvi also," said Ben-Gurion at the start of the inquiry. Averse to linking himself alone with an entire institution, he most likely included Ben-Zvi for the sake of rhetorical modesty, even though Ben-Zvi told the HEC that he did not condone the line taken by Ben-Gurion and the Council. Eliyahu Golomb, too, understood Sprinzak's intentions and claimed that the Labor Council had acted with the HEC secretariat's knowledge and responsibility. Logically, that would have required censuring the HEC, a measure that was, of course, out of the question. Efter refuted Golomb's argument both at the inquiry and on the pages of *Davar*. Sprinzak and his party's central committee did not wait for the results of the inquiry but published the draft resolution they were about to present to the HEC in *Ha-Poel ha-Tzair* as a public statement. "The Jerusalem Labor Council committed an injurious and irresponsible act in providing the opportunity for demonstrations and an anti-Zionist scandal" and in so doing "undermined the enterprise of the workers' community and caused damage to all Zionist Organization activity in Palestine, and our Zionist responsibility compels us to oppose such acts and to condemn them."[9]

Ben-Gurion was confronted with a dilemma: by going along with the proposed denunciation he could wash his hands of involvement but would betray his faithful followers; by voting against it he would be admitting, at least indirectly, that he had had a secret part in the "anti-Zionist scandal." While the inquiry was still going on, the results of the referendum became known. Ben-Gurion's proposal calling for the resignation of Sprinzak and Kaplansky from the Zionist Executive had been rejected by a considerable majority. While Ben-Gurion had expected a majority of nineteen to thirteen, it turned out that only eleven delegates had voted in favor, fifteen — all the Ha-Poel ha-Tzair delegates and two members of Achdut ha-Avodah — were opposed, four abstained, among them Tabenkin, Zakay, and one more from

Achdut ha-Avodah. Two Achdut ha-Avodah delegates — one of them Berl Katznelson — did not even send a reply. After the results were published on March 21 two delegates, apparently under pressure from Ben-Gurion, phoned in his favor. By then, however, the news had already spread that not only had Berl Katznelson disassociated himself from the proposal, but also that most of the Achdut ha-Avodah leadership either opposed it outright or could not bring themselves to condone it.

This greatly strengthened his position, and Sprinzak probably surmised that his tactics were working quite well whereas Ben-Gurion had been hoist on his own petard. And that is exactly how it would have been had not Ben-Gurion taken a daring step. He charged right into the net Sprinzak had spread for him and ran away with it as if it were a bit of needlework. He denounced the denouncers and accused the accusers, calling the denunciation proposal of Sprinzak and Ha-Poel ha-Tzair a "disaster" and "a plot against a Histadrut institution." And he took full responsibility for the Labor Council's transferral of relief payments and declared that it had acted properly in taking charge of the funeral. "If the abdication from making relief payments is what is meant by 'the crime' and 'the provocation,' then I am responsible. The day before the incident I was in Jerusalem and I told them to renounce this duty." The cat was out of the bag. What Ben-Gurion had omitted from his diary was now revealed to all.

The Council didn't know then whether I was speaking on behalf of the HEC or merely for myself, but I did speak. . . . If another incident should happen tomorrow, I would still advise them to stop paying relief. . . . I don't know what they're attributing the Georgian's death to now. Possibly it's clear today that there's no connection between her death and hunger, but then we thought that she had died of it. . . . Regarding the funeral, Loewenstein and Bar-Ratzon did what they had to do. They had to call on the public, and the fact that the entire community, not just the Mops, participated was good. When such a death takes place on a day of trials and tribulations like this one — they had to act as they did and thus fulfilled their duty to the Histadrut.

All in all he gave the impression that the two secretaries had committed not a crime but a heroic deed, and that they should neither hang their heads in shame nor be reprimanded by the HEC but instead be treated as the praiseworthy individuals they were. The draft reprimand was dropped even before being put to the vote, since now it would mean holding Ben-Gurion responsible. Despite the exposure at the inquiry of his double role in operating openly as a member of the HEC secretariat and covertly and illegally as a leader of the action committee, it was still unthinkable for the HEC to hold Ben-Gurion responsible for "criminal demonstrations" and an "anti-Zionist scandal" or for "undermining the labor community's enterprise" and causing "damage to all Zionist Organization activity in Palestine."

If the HEC does not censure this "crime," said Sprinzak with the iron logic of the vanquished, "I must then assume that the act . . . was just and quit the Zionist Executive, and if this is not so then I must quit this body." Ben-Gurion responded that he had "permission to resign" since under the circumstances of unemployment it was "impossible that he hold down both of these jobs." Surely he was mocking Sprinzak, whom he must have thanked in his heart for not making his HEC job a full-time one. For political reasons he wanted Sprinzak — and Kaplansky — to resign from the Zionist Executive. But if Sprinzak refused to resign, Ben-Gurion warned, "the war against the Zionist Executive will continue to be waged in the future," and he would find himself caught between opposing loyalties again and again. Thus Sprinzak ended up back on square one.[10]

In writing in *Kunteres* before the Jerusalem Incidents that "we must now shake up the Zionist movement" with a scandal by means of a "Histadrut 'action committee,' " had Ben-Gurion been trying to bring about Sprinzak's and Kaplansky's resignations from the Zionist Executive regardless of what the Histadrut council delegates resolved? However Sprinzak did not resign, his resolution was not broken, and he did not flee the field. On the contrary, when the referendum results became public he demanded another referendum, this time among members of the HEC plenum. His reasoning was simple and right on target. The Histadrut council's rejection of Ben-Gurion's demand that he and Kaplansky resign from the Zionist Executive meant that it approved of the Executive, and therefore the HEC was likely to take the logical next step of adopting Ha-Poel ha-Tzair's draft denunciation as its own resolution.

Ben-Gurion, naturally, opposed this, and very sharply portrayed Sprinzak as the person most to blame for what had happened in Jerusalem. "Even if I, like Sprinzak, thought that the [Jerusalem Labor] Council had started a pogrom at the Zionist Executive I would still be adamant that the Zionist Executive was to blame for the Council being brought to such action," and Sprinzak alone was responsible for the transfer of the relief payment that led to the Incidents. This tirade, however, had no effect; on March 24 the HEC granted Sprinzak's wish and on March 28 it sent two draft resolutions to all the members of the HEC plenum. One was identical to Ha-Poel ha-Tzair's denunciation, holding the Labor Council, and Ben-Gurion by implication, responsible; the second fully supported the Labor Council and shrewdly cast "all responsibility for the incidents in Jerusalem on the members of the national institutions in the Teachers' College Building Committee, whose decisions straitened the working public in its hour of distress, and who delivered a blow to the Zionist Executive's reputation and also caused lawless acts on the part of irresponsible parties [the Mops]."

This denunciation extended to Sprinzak, too, as a member of the Zionist Executive. This second resolution was a shrewd move on the part of Ben-Gurion. He and his supporters explained that the first resolution, at least implicitly, accused Achdut ha-Avodah, the party in charge of the Jerusalem Labor Council, while the second draft defended it. Thus he turned an issue between the Zionist Executive and the Histadrut into a confrontation between the two Histadrut parties, relying on his party's support. This time all seven Achdut ha-Avodah members stood squarely behind Ben-Gurion, while the five Ha-Poel ha-Tzair members backed Sprinzak. For the sake of peace the resolution was never published, so the struggle ended in stalemate: neither Ben-Gurion nor his loyal subordinates were reprimanded, and neither Sprinzak nor Kaplansky was made to resign. The mistake Sprinzak made was to think that his dazzling rightness would blind Achdut ha-Avodah into backing him in the referendum, while Ben-Gurion calculated all his moves on the certainty that if he succeeded in turning his bout with Sprinzak into a party conflict, Achdut ha-Avodah, with its crushing majority, would back him to a man. When the choice was between party and justice, his acts implied, party came first. He could never get everything he wanted from his party, then or afterward, but he always knew how to get the most out of it, whether he was in the right or the wrong.

It is possible to argue that Sprinzak, Kaplansky, and the Zionist Executive ended up the losers, since they bore the damages without reaping any compensation. On the other hand, the Teachers' College Building Committee did not put the labor-exchange clause in its contract with the contractor, and the Zionist Executive steadfastly refused to add it to contracts for projects to be built with public funding. The conflict was eventually resolved by means of negotiations between the contractor and the Labor Council, just as Colonel Kisch had suggested at the very beginning.[11]

If Ben-Gurion was trying to establish the Histadrut as the sole labor organization and its labor exchange as the sole agent for hiring workers in Jerusalem with the blessing of the Zionist Executive, he failed utterly. But if, on the other hand, he was trying to give a new dimension to the relations between the Zionist labor movement and the Zionist Executive, he succeeded. The rivalry between them was to escalate until the labor movement became the dominant element in the Zionist Organization and its administration.

If one motive behind this bold campaign was Ben-Gurion's desire to correct the image of himself as being totally preoccupied with a struggle for authority and a war against the extreme left, the sensational drama he had created in Jerusalem certainly helped to build an image of him as a strong and decisive trade union leader. From then on, the public perceived him as a leader with one consistent aim, capable of incisive action, while among his party and the Histadrut workers he gained a reputation for standing behind his subordinates come hell or high water. Protecting those who stuck by him was a most important principle with him. They repaid him doubly with their loyalty, and the Histadrut and party infrastructure, which knew it could depend on him, consolidated itself around him, growing more and more powerful.

22

Indispensable

RAMPANT UNEMPLOYMENT also exacerbated the dissatisfaction with the inequities of the pay scale. The Histadrut salary, which included a family allowance, caused much resentment among industrial workers, who received the same salary whether they had families or not. Public opinion put the wage question back on the Histadrut council's agenda, and in January 1927 it selected a five-man committee, chaired by Moshe Beilinson, "to look into the scale and the payment of salaries in all the Histadrut institutions and bring its conclusions and recommendations before the HEC in a month." The wage committee was a strong one, since three of its members came from the top echelons of their parties and therefore had a good measure of authority. As a result, all the institutions' books were open to it, most notably those of Solel Boneh. It got down to business right away, and in such a complete and competent manner, that it took three months to finish its investigation.

Though it stated in its conclusions that no institution had adhered strictly to the pay scale, it also noted, with satisfaction, that out of 606 Histadrut employees "the overwhelming majority . . . some 500 men, live the life of a worker . . . which isn't at all easy, especially since in most of the institutions wages are not paid on time or in cash." It was, however, stunned by the salaries and perks of the other 100 employees, who "over the years have received salaries considerably in excess of the pay scale and have amassed substantial debts to their employing institutions." More precisely, between January 1925 and January 1927 these hundred, most from Ha-Mashbir and Solel Boneh, had run up a debt amounting to 4,309 Egyptian pounds, apart from the debt of over 1,000 Egyptian pounds amassed by the secretariat staff of seven. This group, the committee noted, was "composed of institution directors, the very people who stand at the head of the movement, who should be looked up to as an example to one and all.

"The responsibility for these transgressions," the committee added, "falls, in the public sense, primarily on the HEC," which had allowed such "complete anarchy" to reign. But owing to this very fact the committee found itself in a quandary when it discovered, to its horror, that following the recommendation of a previous committee headed by Joseph Aharonovitch, the secretariat staff's debts had been struck from the cashbooks in July 1926. David Ben-Gurion had owed the most, 283.462 Egyptian pounds (12.6 times his monthly salary), with Jacob Efter and David Zakay a close second and third, owing 259.023 and 201.999, respectively. Publishing these facts would violently shake the Histadrut public's faith in its leaders, including Ben-Gurion, and could give rise to a call for the dismissal of the entire secretariat, leaving a decapitated Histadrut whose financial ills would be even less amenable to cure. The committee opted to tend first to the head, the secretariat, quietly and discreetly before making its report public, and only then deal with the disorders of the body, namely, the institutions.

To this end the committee met with the secretariat members to demand that they reinstate their debts in the ledgers and cancel the March 1925 cost-of-living increment to their salaries, which contravened the pay scale, and arrange for repayment of their personal debts by April 30. This deadline was chosen so that the committee could prepare its report for publication in time for the third Histadrut convention, scheduled to meet in July.

The secretariat notified the committee that it accepted all of its demands, and on May 23 the committee officially handed the HEC its expurgated report. Theoretically the HEC could begin radical treatment of the "ailing" Histadrut, but the infection had so festered that the HEC had to step back and get a hold on itself before taking any action. Though the Histadrut basic wage stood at 7.5 Egyptian pounds, at Ha-Mashbir three directors and the main branch manager had been receiving an additional 5 each month (apart from the family allowance), while fifty-five employees had received bonuses and advances totaling 1,050 Egyptian pounds. Solel Boneh — itself on the brink of bankruptcy and up to its ears in debt to workers and suppliers — presented an even gloomier picture: 128 of its clerical staff had received various unauthorized pay supplements and its directors, in addition to inflated salaries, were given monthly expense accounts and travel expenses. Aside from this, senior Solel Boneh officials had, over the course of two years, received advances that totaled 1,130 Egyptian pounds. The committee regretfully noted that while salaries of "senior employees" were double those of the pay scale, the "lowliest employees" were paid wages well below it.[1]

Such a report would have been touchy even in the best of times, but in the great depression of 1927, with Solel Boneh withholding the salaries of hundreds of workers and unemployment at an unprecedented high, it was dynamite and liable, if not handled with utmost caution, to blow up the Histadrut. Late in May the members of the HEC and the wage committee met to decide how to deal with it. First, they looked for someone to blame. Most of those present supported the committee's conclusion that the HEC was chiefly responsible. As Berl Katznelson put it, the former wage committees had not done their jobs, the HEC had done nothing to get them moving, and as a result "a vacuum was created."

It was clear to all that in this case Ben-Gurion personified the HEC, and that the accusing fingers pointed at him. Since he was the father of the equalizing salary and had moved heaven and earth to justify and defend it, why had he not urged the committees into action and backed them up when they needed it? Ben-Gurion argued that from the very beginning he had maintained that the wage committee should be independent and responsible to the convention alone and laid the blame on the second Histadrut convention, which had invested the wage committee with "independent authority" but given it no teeth with which to enforce its decisions. The HEC was perhaps guilty of inaction when the committees had not done their jobs, but the state of affairs in the Histadrut had precluded any action by the HEC. From the manner in which Ben-Gurion spoke his colleagues could easily have gotten the impression that he was not so horrified by the findings.[2]

On the issue of advances, Ben-Gurion's great supporter in Ha-Poel ha-Tzair, Aharonovitch, whose salary as director of Bank ha-Poalim was thirty Egyptian pounds, spoke, taking a lenient position along the lines of "give a good dog a good bone." There was no Histadrut rule, said Aharonovitch, that forbade advances, and "you have to help an employee and give him an advance in time of need. It's morally wrong to withhold this from him." Outraged, the committee members retorted that it was morally wrong for salaried officials to get advances while wages were withheld from workers and day laborers; it was morally wrong for institution directors to receive perks while masses of unemployed went hungry. Katznelson chimed in, "There must not be a privileged class in the Histadrut which has not only secure jobs but free credit as well." Ben-Gurion said not a word.

Nor did he speak when the question arose of whether to hold institutions or individuals accountable. Some maintained that the institution administrations should be held responsible, while others believed that corrupt individuals should suffer the consequences; among these latter was Katznelson. There were even some who insisted that no mercy whatsoever be shown and that the entire hundred be penalized.

Ben-Gurion participated only when the pay scale itself came up for discussion. As it stood, the pay scale was acceptable only for elected Histadrut officials, he said. For Histadrut employees, a wage scale that included a professional component had to be implemented, for "we cannot handicap our economic system vis-à-vis the capitalist one . . . Why should a doctor at the Sick Fund receive less than elsewhere while a janitor gets three times as much? We do not live in a world apart." The wage committee had to become "a permanent control board." (These suggestions were eventually implemented, so Ben-Gurion may be considered responsible for seniority and professional increments of the Histadrut wage system and for incorporating the wage committee into the central control board of the Histadrut.)

After this the discussion finally got down to the practical and political question of whom to stand in the dock and how to handle the committee's report. The committee proposed bringing directors who received salaries of more than 20 percent over the pay scale and those who had received advances totaling more than two months' wages to the Histadrut court. Nowhere is it stated what the committee members' faces expressed when Katznelson, who had always stood for punishing corrupt individuals, rejected this proposal and instead proposed endowing the committee with adjudicatory "power to probe and decide." Regarding the second question, all those who had argued that the increments and advances were morally wrong and had demanded individual punishments were also in favor of full publication. Withholding information, they said, with the public in a rage amid rumors of corruption, would only lead to disorientation and loss of public trust.

Now Ben-Gurion rose to oppose them, acting as the shield of the Histadrut. Publication, he argued, would be tantamount to handing deadly weapons to the Histadrut's enemies on a silver platter. "We could do this only if we were able to publish all that goes on in other places too. Otherwise a distorted picture would emerge and the Histadrut would appear in a false light . . . this would be an unjust blackening of the Histadrut." His implication was that it would be best to bury the committee's report. As a safeguard for the future, he suggested, the HEC would from then on publish "a full list of all Histadrut employees and their salaries," making it clear that Histadrut salaries were still smaller by a third, or even a half, than Zionist Organization salaries.

Katznelson, in support of the committee members, again opposed him. "Publication is of vital necessity . . . The matter cannot be laid to rest in the Histadrut wastebasket." But, he immediately added, "for publication the report needs responsible revision." With this he once again outdid the HEC members in his virtuoso use of a trick they themselves were fond of, what might be called agreement by rejection. After this proposal was adopted, along with a second one "to express thanks to the committee for its arduous efforts," the joint meeting ended.[3]

On June 13 *Davar* carried the revised version, signed by the five committee members. All sections dealing with the HEC secretariat and its debts had been dropped, as had the passages quoted above and "the gravest cases." It said only that the HEC was indeed responsible, since it had not made "sufficient use of the investigative measures at its disposal." The sentence "The Histadrut pay scale was not strictly adhered to in any institution" was cut, and not even a hint remained of the committee's protest that it was precisely the institution directors, who should have served as models, who had sinned. Whereas the report had spoken of a hundred offenders, *Davar* referred to only seventy, all said to be from the middle and lower echelons of the Histadrut administration. And while the report dealt with all the institutions, the *Davar* version omitted Bank ha-Poalim, Kapai, and *Davar* itself (even Katznelson had received extra pay as the newspaper's editor). Katznelson rationalized this soft-pedaling by saying that the Histadrut wished to clean up the mess, not to take vengeance.

The committee, meeting as an adjudicative body, interpreted the rejection of its proposal to bring the directors to trial, the revision of the report, and Katznelson's rationale as a directive, and therefore found only "the ten gravest cases" guilty, while agreeing that the institution administrations were to be held accountable for the transgressions of six of them. Regarding the other four worst cases, all directors of Solel Boneh, the committee members were at odds. Two called for their dismissal, two said the HEC should decide their punishments, and the fifth abstained. In the end none of the hundred sinners was reprimanded, let alone penalized, nor were any names published. This protection infuriated many, and *Davar* was swamped by readers' letters.

The question that comes to mind is, What made Ben-Gurion, who in August 1926 had expelled a hundred members of the Legion and Hashomer for the crime of disobeying a Histadrut resolution, so lenient with wrongdoers in the bureaucracy in 1927? What had happened to Ben-Gurion the champion of the labor army, the great commune, and the Society of Workers, who had argued that "a moral endeavor greater than this one to reform and renew our lives is unimaginable,"[4] that a hundred wrongdoers, all officials, fared better with him than a hundred clean-handed pioneers, all frontier settlers?

The possibility that he acted as he did because the third Histadrut convention was about to open and his record since the second convention would be the focus of attention cannot be discounted. He would not have wanted to strengthen his opponents on the left and in the Labor Legion. It is also possible that since he, too, had been guilty he could not see either himself or the other sinners as corrupt, a conjecture suggested by one of his arguments for burying the report. "[Should] the committee publish the size of the debt the public will say 'theft,' and this isn't the truth. Absolutely honest people will be pilloried. These seventy men aren't criminals. It would be a sin to stigmatize people who owe money received officially through the administration. And aside from this, it would be a great loss to the Histadrut" if they were dismissed.[5]

However, this statement implies that he had not set himself apart from the wrongdoers, and, further, the inference is that since "these . . . men aren't criminals," neither was Ben-Gurion. Rather, it is the reverse: he was elevating them to his own level of innocence. Ben-Gurion was convinced of his own inculpability and incorruptibility, just as he was convinced that whatever he did within the Histadrut was done in the service of labor Zionism. The partnership begun with his father and continued with Paula had broadened to include the entire Histadrut, and the day would come when it encompassed the entire Jewish nation.

While Ben-Gurion gave himself body and soul to his mission, those who believed in this mission had to supply him with tuition, upkeep, a warm home and a family, books, and all the other things he required. From his perspective, the partnership adhered to the rules of equality that he had introduced in the Histadrut, namely, that all its members give to the Histadrut according to their abilities and receive from it according to their needs. In January 1928 he told the HEC, "For a person to give his job the maximum, he must be assured of his minimum."[6] This minimum was not fixed, and in Ben-Gurion's case it was larger, not because of his greater competence, but owing to his more demanding role. "If someone just wants to talk about equality out of some false morality," Ben-Gurion continued, "I am ready to fight it before the working public. A Yemenite* is not inferior to me, but he can do his job while living in one room whereas I cannot." Therefore, his larger salary, which was, in fact, the substance of his debt to the HEC, did not seem to him to violate either morality or propriety. This debt, although it was put back on the books, was never repaid, nor

---

* Yemenite immigrants were employed for manual labor and the reference here is to any unskilled worker.

were those of the other secretariat members. By projecting his own
values onto others Ben-Gurion could speak of seventy "absolutely honest people."

His siding with the hundred, even to the extent of singing their
praise, marked a change of emphasis in his Histadrut leadership: Ben-
Gurion gravitated more and more toward the political and organizational domain. Never again would he set his sights on lofty social projects or dream of social reform. What brought him to this remains
unknown. In any case, whether he reconciled himself to his weakness
as a social leader and recognized his value as an organizer and statesman, or whether he regarded organization and politics as more vital to
the Histadrut as far as realizing Zionism was concerned, the direction
he took was toward strengthening the Histadrut apparatus. Bureaucracy by its very nature is required primarily for an organizational or
political task, but by no means for social reform; on the contrary, a
powerful bureaucratic machinery is not only reform's archenemy, but
usually its first target as well. Ben-Gurion opted unequivocally for the
apparatus. The individuals in question were the most essential part of
the administration with which he wished to establish Histadrut authority, his organizational and political tool, loyal and obedient,
operating at his command. Moreover, he had nothing with which to
replace them and therefore had to guard them well. Thus when he said
that if they were dismissed, it would be "a great loss to the Histadrut,"
what he meant was a great loss to him and to all who shared his views.
Berl Katznelson understood this and helped him forestall a struggle
over the social character of the Histadrut by thwarting the execution of
judgment even for the four worst cases. He, too, regarded the political
price of their hanging as too high. And so, despite the criticism and the
public fury, the gravest cases, like the rest of the hundred, continued to
hold high office and remained the mainstays of the Histadrut and the
party bureaucracy. Some of them became Ben-Gurion's most loyal followers, who later backed him as chairman of the Jewish Agency Executive and then as prime minister of Israel.

Ben-Gurion's support of the bureaucracy was of course entirely new
to the Histadrut, not to say an aberration, or even a regression from the
dreams and principles of its founders. Ben-Gurion's wholly unexpected
behavior first came under attack in June, when the Achdut ha-Avodah
council met in preparation for the third Histadrut convention. But
something else had happened during the pay scale affair which, being
related to it, served to cover it up by becoming almost inseparable
from it in the council deliberations, at the convention, and afterward — the collapse of the flower of the Histadrut institutions, the
"glory of our might," Solel Boneh.

The public was only partially aware of this development, since a modest announcement in *Davar* on March 14, 1927, had stated only that "from now until further notice all documents" legal and binding on Solel Boneh "must be signed" by the three members of its new directorate, David Remez and Bar-Kochba Meyerowitz of the Histadrut and Eliezer Bavli of the Zionist Executive. Alert readers might have wondered why Solel Boneh suddenly needed the signature of a representative of the Zionist Executive, but in case this led to a suspicion of the true state of affairs, a public relations drive was set in motion to belie it. Large ads appeared in *Davar* portraying Solel Boneh as a thriving institution, signing new contracts and taking on new projects whose size was published in detail. There was not a hint of the banking consortium that had been set up a month before, on February 19, to save the institution. It was this consortium that appointed the new directorate, giving the Zionist Executive veto power over all Solel Boneh's activities. By the time the Achdut ha-Avodah council met in June, however, the whole truth had come out.

Solel Boneh, which had in 1924 replaced the Histadrut Office of Public Works, had expanded very quickly, but lack of share, capital, and other means forced it to resort to expensive credit and suppliers, which gobbled up its profits, increased its debts, and forced it to seek yet more expensive credit. Thus began a vicious circle, which its directors had sought to escape by rotating its debts, paying them off out of the following year's budget. Then the Fourth Aliyah, which began in 1924 and was to a great extent a prosperous one — composed as it was of smalltime and some well-to-do businessmen — brought an economic high tide that strengthened the directors' belief that they had found the road to success and that the bigger their operations and profits the more they would be able to reduce their debts from the previous years.

But the boom was short-lived, and in 1925 the first signs of a depression appeared. In 1926 and 1927 it worsened, and new and not-so-new immigrants returned to their countries of origin, among them some who had not paid off their commitments to Solel Boneh. When in 1927 the number of emigrants exceeded immigrants, construction came to an almost complete halt. This low ebb created a liquidity crisis so severe that Solel Boneh couldn't finish the projects it had started or be competitive enough to get new contracts. As its situation deteriorated, it could no longer rotate its steadily increasing debts, having nothing with which to pay them off. Bankruptcy seemed inevitable, and because it was Remez's worst fear, out of desperation he turned — without Ben-Gurion's or the HEC's knowledge — to the banks and the Zionist Executive, which set up the consortium and the new directorate as a last-ditch effort to save Solel Boneh.

Three factors brought Remez, the banks, and the Zionist Executive — and eventually Ben-Gurion and the HEC as well — to agree to this solution. First, the fallen enterprise had, from its inception, employed more than half of the men in the construction jobs done in Palestine by Jewish labor. At its peak, in September 1926, Solel Boneh employed about 15 percent of all Histadrut members, or about 22 percent of its urban members. Second, its fall was liable to drag down other Histadrut institutions, which were all greatly interdependent. It should suffice to note that 32.7 percent of all the loans granted by Bank ha-Poalim between 1920 and 1926 were to Solel Boneh and the Office of Public Works before it, and that the interest they paid the bank made up 32.3 percent of all its income during that time. The repercussions of the fall of Solel Boneh, and of the other institutions in its wake, would be felt throughout the Jewish economy, and as the ruins collapsed in the Histadrut sector, they would bury the whole.

The third reason — pertinent to the HEC and Achdut ha-Avodah in particular — was that the fall of Solel Boneh would be a knockout blow to the Histadrut vision. Solel Boneh had not been erected only to create jobs to increase Jewish immigration; it had been conceived for a far nobler mission. Just as the Agricultural Center had been created to found a new rural society of farmers in cooperative moshavs and communal kibbutzes, Solel Boneh had undertaken to create the parallel new urban cooperative society. The larger and stronger Solel Boneh became, the more it fed the hopes that it could achieve the sublime goal: the establishment of workers' cooperative neighborhoods in the cities.[7]

The collapse of Solel Boneh was by far the most difficult crisis Ben-Gurion had yet experienced and one of the worst he would ever know, since it called into question the viability of the Histadrut itself. The collapse could also have meant the end of his tenure as Histadrut secretary, since the responsibility for Solel Boneh's insolvency would certainly be laid on his desk, particularly since it was he who had unceasingly pursued centralization. And this might have spelled the end of his public career.

Those who put the blame on the HEC — read Ben-Gurion — had solid grounds for their argument that from its very beginning Ben-Gurion had been involved in Solel Boneh's affairs frequently, sometimes even daily. At times he delved into the details of technical problems or building contracts, and when the time came to register Solel Boneh as a public company, he sat with the Histadrut lawyers for long periods of time. As supreme administrator — Ben-Gurion regarded the relationship between himself and Remez as one between the chairman of the board and the company director — he was responsible for two important policies. In order that the institution belong not only to the Histadrut but also to its members, he limited the cost of a share to only one Egyptian pound, payable in installments, which accounted in part for Solel Boneh's inadequate capital. Even more important was his charging it with a mission to bring about the urban workers' cooperative neighborhoods and also to spearhead the development of the Histadrut economy and its expansion into various industrial fields. This was partially to blame for Solel Boneh's overrapid expansion.[8]

Ben-Gurion could have defended himself from the criticism that awaited him by arguing that his involvement in Solel Boneh matters was far less than met the eye. To begin with, like all the institutions, Solel Boneh opposed HEC intervention in its affairs. Ben-Gurion had complained more than once that the administration of every institution in the Histadrut constituted "a government in and of itself," and Solel Boneh most of all. He had demanded economic control of all Histadrut institutions, for example, by proposing in May 1924 a directorate that would "supervise all economic activity in the Histadrut." But Remez and the other institution directors had refused appointment to this directorate and rejected Ben-Gurion's plan for a two-branched HEC. Hence it was probably not in Ben-Gurion's power to have Solel Boneh's books examined regularly by the HEC without causing a crisis in the Histadrut and in Achdut ha-Avodah, of which Remez was a founding father.

Second, Ben-Gurion had not been a party to what was then euphemistically called "forcing the balance," the Solel Boneh directors' practice of presenting the annual balance "so that the magnitude of the losses won't be seen at its worst." Thus, for example, in April 1925 the balance sheet for the first year's operations showed 1,715 Egyptian pounds of "net profit," which had no basis in reality. The following year's account showed an even larger profit of 3,000 Egyptian pounds, which Solel Boneh reported to the Zionist Executive as well, receiving in return a letter of congratulations "for the good results of your activity in this past year." Though Ben-Gurion suspected something, he had no evidence, since the books had never been shown even to an HEC internal committee.

But complaints sent to the HEC in June 1926 by workers from whom Solel Boneh had withheld wages for months on end had roused Ben-Gurion's suspicion. He therefore conducted his own "private" investigation involving a meeting with Gusta Strumpf, who had once helped him get books cheaply in Germany and whose name was now Rechev. She was not only a member of Solel Boneh's directorate but Remez's mistress as well. On August 9 Ben-Gurion quoted her in his diary. "The situation at Solel Boneh is bad. At a standstill and regressing. The apparatus has become an objective in itself. A laborer who works one day a week — his pay is withheld, while all officials get advances. A screen has gone up between the institution and the public. Complex accounting. During a project it's unknown whether it's being done at a loss or not. Five thousand Egyptian pounds were invested in the Solel Boneh office building. There's no center. There's no more mutual trust. Solel Boneh employs 140 clerks." These terse statements drew an alarming picture of the institution's deterioration into an inflated bureaucracy where those at the top gobbled up funds in the form of advances while wages were withheld from workers who went hungry; it spent large sums on an office building while debts snowballed; and, lacking any business sense, it provided "no center" for the organization.[9]

The fact that this investigation was carried out behind Remez's back shows a measure of distrust; Ben-Gurion was not sure Remez would tell him the whole truth. But by the time Ben-Gurion learned of Solel Boneh's grave situation it was too late to save it, as Remez himself had confessed to one of his colleagues as early as June. Even if Ben-Gurion had been able to examine Solel Boneh's books openly and regularly, however, it is doubtful that they would have provided a clear picture of what was going on. The consortium, which was the first to see the books, was harsh in its criticism: no division of authority, with everybody in everybody else's way, involved in all matters, technical or commercial. "The directorate takes little notice of the expertise and data of the accounting department, leaning heavily on rule-of-thumb estimates and guesswork," while "the accounting itself is done in a manner which affords the directorate no possibility of getting to the bottom of the institution's financial situation itself," and "even after a contract has been signed, no detailed plan is worked out." In short, absolute chaos.

Finally, the consortium, too, had been set up without Ben-Gurion's knowledge. Only in December, at the earliest, did he learn of secret contacts that Remez and a handful of his intimates had maintained with the Zionist Executive and the banks. And only after these contacts had proved fruitful did Remez write the HEC, in January 1927, that "we hope to conclude negotiations with the banks in the near future."[10]

On this revelation of the sorry state of Solel Boneh, so far from fulfilling the vision for which it was created, Ben-Gurion despised Remez, whom he held responsible for this calamity that not only endangered the whole Histadrut but gave its enemies proof of its ineptitude in conducting its affairs — destroying its pretension to handle Zionist affairs as well. This enormous enterprise was tottering because of Remez, who had opposed HEC control but had not the vaguest idea of what management was about. The two had never been close, and of the five who had joined with Ben-Gurion to found Achdut ha-Avodah — Remez, Katznelson, Itzhak Tabenkin, Shmuel Yavnieli, and Itzhak Ben-Zvi — Remez was the furthest from Ben-Gurion in terms of friendship and outlook. This may seem strange, for Remez was intelligent, clever, and possessed of a wonderful sense of humor; the sparkle in his eye and his charm endeared him to all who knew him. Ben-Gurion regarded him as a man of merit — the fact that he chose Remez to stand in for him as secretary of the Histadrut attests to that — but nevertheless, there was no "chemistry" between them.

Ben-Gurion would not have found it personally difficult to publicly attack Remez for Solel Boneh's acting without the knowledge or supervision of the HEC. In fact, there is little doubt that his impulse to heap all the responsibility on Remez and those who had thwarted his drive for HEC predominance was very strong. Nevertheless, this was not the path he chose, and his defense against the criticism aimed at him was not built on diverting it onto Remez. Quite the contrary; throughout the year-long Solel Boneh crisis he took full responsibility, displaying exemplary self-control and discretion. Containing his wrath against Remez, Ben-Gurion stood beside him, defending him and his colleagues in Solel Boneh's directorate; not a word of censure or accusation passed his lips. He was probably motivated by the reasoning that if the crisis passed, such conduct would result in strengthening the HEC, while if he avoided responsibility or cast it on Remez alone, it would undermine it.

Supporting Remez was a bitter pill. He had to consent to the consortium and to the stipulation that went with the 20,000-Egyptian-pound cash loan it put up, namely, that representatives of the Zionist Executive join the supervisory board of Solel Boneh, with veto power over contracts which they deemed unprofitable. Instead of the Histadrut's "conquering" the Zionist Organization, the opposite happened, and the Zionist Executive acquired control — the same control that had been denied the HEC — over the largest Histadrut institution.

Nor was this all that Ben-Gurion had to swallow. He could read the derision between the lines of the Zionist Executive's letters to the HEC. One of these letters explained that the 20,000-pound loan, which the HEC had an obligation to repay within eight years out of funds raised by the Histadrut Appeal in the United States, was a truly dubious venture, "especially if we take into account that no one knows if the Histadrut Appeal will last another eight years." Ben-Gurion took this slap in the face without a word.

Ben-Gurion, along with his HEC colleagues, also had to consent to Remez's insistence that the consortium be kept secret until after it had started operating in March. While this breach of Histadrut democracy was bad enough, it forced the HEC into an even graver violation, not bringing up Solel Boneh's desperate situation for discussion at the January 1927 Histadrut council. This troubled their conscience and angered them. "Here is this matter of the consortium," said Sprinzak to the HEC in February, "and we haven't brought it up before the council. Nor did we get to the bottom of it ourselves. Why the whitewash?" He was particularly upset by the fact that he had to approve the consortium even though he was in the dark about Solel Boneh's true financial situation. "How can we conduct this ostrich policy, not knowing the situation?" Ben-Gurion, for once, did not fight him: "I agreed to the consortium not out of knowledge, but out of fear of catastrophe." Ben-Gurion later said that the HEC resolution he pushed through to accept the consortium and its stipulations was the second of the three most dreadful decisions that had been his lot to make as Histadrut secretary, the first having involved Tel Yosef.[11]

The resolution was dreadful not only because it impaired sovereignty over its largest institution but also because Ben-Gurion had to swallow his pride and crawl on all fours, like Lenin, toward his goal of rescuing Solel Boneh from court action. Many of its creditors were those very laborers, craftsmen, and small suppliers whom the Histadrut was supposed to serve. No party and no combination of forces could have done the Histadrut's reputation more damage than lawsuits from small creditors, because the court was liable to declare Solel Boneh bankrupt and issue liquidation orders. These two things were what Ben-Gurion, like Remez, sought to avert.

This was the consortium's only accomplishment. Eventually all likelihood of saving Solel Boneh vanished and its premises were turned over to the HEC, with Solel Boneh retaining only the basement to house its archives. There, with the assistance of an accountant, Remez labored for two years until he came to an agreement with most of the creditors. By means of the loan from the Zionist Executive, which had been raised to 25,000 Egyptian pounds, and other loans, and with money from the sale of property and equipment, the creditors all received at least 20 percent of what was due them and agreed to withdraw their suits.[12] Solel Boneh could continue its paper existence, with Remez and Ben-Gurion hoping it would one day rise like the phoenix, spread its wings, and take off again. Indeed, this did happen. In 1935 Solel Boneh rose from the ashes to become Israel's industrial giant.

But all this was still in the future when Ben-Gurion, in June 1927, went before the Achdut ha-Avodah council. In addition to leaks from the wage committee came the news of the concealment of Solel Boneh's approaching collapse and the consortium from the Histadrut council. All this, together with the withholding of workers' wages, incensed the delegates, who unleashed their fury on the IIEC — no one mentioned Ben-Gurion by name, although he was clearly their target — and clamored for justice.

Ben-Gurion's resolve to stand by Remez and the Solel Boneh crippled his ability to answer his critics, or, more precisely, to mollify them. Ben-Gurion found himself in the rare situation of not knowing what to say, particularly in regard to the advances. In desperation he simply repeated the questions that hailed down on him, in a tone of voice that suggested such questions would best be addressed to the Almighty. In the heat of his speech logic disappeared, but it could be deduced nevertheless that he was claiming that the truly guilty party was human nature, and more specifically that of his colleagues in Achdut ha-Avodah and the Histadrut. This, he said, was the source of all ills in the Histadrut and Solel Boneh, and there was but one remedy: the reform of the members' nature by Achdut ha-Avodah, through its very "travail" and "momentum."[13]

His words probably made no more sense to his listeners than they do to a reader today, yet they certainly helped him extricate himself from the council with minimal damage. In this hour of need he derived more than enough support from being completely at peace with himself in his deep identification with his mission, in his unshakable faith in the path he had chosen, and in his belief that he had done his best for the party's ideals, for the Histadrut, and for labor Zionism as a whole. So strong and radiant was his self-confidence that it infected his listeners with a conviction of his rightness, to the point where no one asked whether the collapse could have been averted if Ben-Gurion had made it his business to know what was going on in Solel Boneh, and no one doubted his fitness to stand at the head of the Histadrut. It was as if he had miraculously inspired Achdut ha-Avodah to accept its share in his peculiar brand of partnership, which in this case meant giving him the apparatus and forgiving it its frailties and imperfections. While he did not, of course, say this explicitly, he still got what he wanted: at his call the council voted to re-establish Solel Boneh when circumstances permitted, and following this it authorized, retroactively, all the steps he had taken to save it.

It would seem, therefore, that his defense of the apparatus was accepted at face value, that the delegates bought Ben-Gurion's unspoken argument that the apparatus was essential, and that without it Achdut ha-Avodah's goals would be unattainable. But some of the council delegates swallowed his defense with heavy hearts; surely this was so with Katznelson and Tabenkin. The former, as will soon be seen, eventually gave vent to his resentment; the latter, who concealed his opposition, never got over it, and the day came when it made a parting of the ways with Ben-Gurion unavoidable for him.

As for Remez, his heart was filled with unstinting gratitude to Ben-Gurion. He would never forget that precisely when he needed every drop of help, as he put it, Katznelson kept silent, thus discouraging the many who, Remez thought, were ready and willing to come to Solel Boneh's aid.[14] From then on Remez, though never a sycophant, could be counted among Ben-Gurion's faithful, a fact that manifested itself in one of Ben-Gurion's most difficult hours, the eve of the establishment of the State of Israel in May 1948.

The council served as a kind of trial run for the third Histadrut convention, in that it gave Ben-Gurion and his HEC colleagues a foretaste of what awaited them, since there was no doubt that the criticism of Ha-Poel ha-Tzair and opposition delegates would be even more scathing. Ironically enough, although Ben-Gurion was finally about to attain the great trial he had so desired since the founding days of Achdut ha-Avodah, he was not to be the prosecuting attorney, and his adversaries were not to be placed in the dock. On the floor of the convention he said, "They divided us into two camps; one was put in the dock, where I have the honor to be, and the other was given the prosecutor's seat."

Fearing a guilty verdict, and riots by the unemployed, the HEC members postponed the convention several times. It finally opened on July 5, 1927, in Tel Aviv's Beit ha-Am open-air theater. Because of the uproar that had preceded it, an unusually long period was scheduled for the deliberations, and the convention lasted sixteen days. It was a personal test for Ben-Gurion, not only of his record but primarily of the position he had built in the course of his seven years in the HEC. There was much evidence that he was becoming recognized as "first and foremost among equals." " 'The man' in the HEC is Ben-Gurion . . . Berl stands off to the side now," reported the sharp-eyed Ada to her husband, Eliyahu Golomb, who was abroad on Haganah business. With a certain pride, and a complete lack of humility, Ben-Gurion filled his diary with the requests he got from all Achdut ha-Avodah branches to come to their meetings and give them "direction." Even Kibbutz Ein Harod, Tabenkin's seat of power, invited him, so he noted in his diary, "to come and settle their differences."[15]

He had also become the biggest Histadrut name in the American Jewish labor movement. In 1925, after visiting Palestine, the editor of New York's Yiddish-language *Jewish Daily Forward* wrote:

> Ben-Gurion is a particularly intelligent man and a very practical man to boot. He's quick of perception and understands the world and its people. He impressed me as a man with a strong character. This is a man with

principles, which he works hard to realize. He's got a little humor, and is not without zing and zest. This is a real leader of workers (not the dime-a-dozen sort).

Ben-Gurion translated this passage from Yiddish into his diary, underlining the phrase "a man with a strong character."

Ben-Gurion's confidence in himself and in the support of his party was evident not just to the guest from America, but also to seasoned and skeptical local reporters. Reporting on the Elected Assembly in January 1926, *Ha-Aretz*, a paper that spoke for the anti-Histadrut middle-class opposition, offered this glimpse of Ben-Gurion.

His posture on the speaker's rostrum, hands in pockets, exudes awareness of his power. He always looks as though a great party stands behind him, and quite often he proves to be right. As he ascends the rostrum, someone jokingly remarks, "Now Ben-Gurion looks like an English lord setting out for Sunday's hunt." But at the sight of his serious face silence prevails in the auditorium. His strong and moderate voice begins to rise more and more. His words are weighty; he does not use a fiery style or big words, but from time to time he hits the right chords, now and then with a cutting quip. He always emphasizes the national aspect. He . . . associates the present with the past: there is history, there is continuity. He Judaizes his socialism, wrapping it in human morality and international justice."[16]

More important than his good press was the political asset that would gladden the heart of any party man: his success at the party polls. He was elected by a larger margin than anyone else to Achdut ha-Avodah's executive committee secretariat and to its central elections committee. In addition to this party recognition of his leadership was the external recognition manifested in the elections to the third Histadrut convention. For the first time Achdut ha-Avodah had an absolute majority in the Histadrut, 9,604 votes as against 7,970 received by all the other parties, or 53.2 percent of all votes, compared with 41.7 percent in the elections to the first convention and 47.1 percent in those to the second. The Histadrut had started with 4,500 members, grown to 8,500 by 1923, the year of the second convention, and by 1927 to 22,800; 56.5 percent of the growth between the first two conventions went to Achdut ha-Avodah, as did 56.2 percent of that between the second and the third. Furthermore, by taking into account Ha-Poel ha-Tzair's 26.7 percent share of the vote for the third convention, Ben-Gurion could claim that the great majority of workers had "demonstrated their devotion and Zionist loyalty on Election Day," since the two coalition parties received a combined total of 80 percent of the votes; adding those of two leftist Zionist tickets, the Zionist bloc could claim 94 percent of all Histadrut votes. This was very reassuring and Ben-Gurion was entitled to some satisfaction. Although the office of the secretary did not exist then, he was recognized and referred to by the public at large as the Histadrut secretary.[17]

Nevertheless, the convention would not be all clear sailing. The elections for it had been held in December 1926, before anyone knew of the salary scandal, the financial condition of Solel Boneh, and the consortium. This news was likely to hurt his position, which he had achieved by power plays no less than by persuasion. Ben-Gurion, who made no efforts to endear himself to his constituents or win their confidence, was appreciated for his exceptional talents and competence, which is not to say that people had no grievances against him. Perhaps this accounted for the paradox that although he was the most popular of the Histadrut leaders, he was the most controversial as well.

He also came in for censure both from prominent Zionists and from his colleagues. Colonel Frederick Kisch, chairman of the Zionist Executive in Jerusalem, regarded him as a schemer who placed his party above all and would stop at nothing to advance its interests. Sprinzak had spoken out against Ben-Gurion's "hysterics"; Laufbahn had accused him of arrogance ("The Histadrut, that's me"); Arlosoroff had portrayed him, with ironic understatement, as one who overvalued himself; and *Ha-Poel ha-Tzair,* voicing the party's position, accused him of occasional "loss of wits." Such personal criticism from any party, let alone the Histadrut's second largest, was enough to cause concern to any seasoned politician.[18]

There was much disagreement with his use of power tactics in the administrative expulsions from the Histadrut. In the Zionist Executive the word *dictatorship* was used to describe his labor-exchange campaign while others accused him of using violence to force adherence to Histadrut principles. Even in his own party there was no dearth of dissatisfaction; 120 appeals against expulsion without trial were addressed to the convention before its opening, and forty were added afterward. If sentiment in the convention welled up against his "dictatorship," would his party colleagues stand between him and the wave of censure, or would they join in and augment it?

Ben-Gurion knew that he was not entirely safe from the opposition, and therefore calculated a move that would enable the opposition to let off all its steam, preserving freedom of speech and action without doing any damage to him. He proposed to the standing committee — with a view to "clearing the air" — that the general debate — which normally would occur toward the end of the convention — start after he had presented his report on behalf of the HEC. One member of the committee warned him that such a discussion "will have to go into all the drastic issues. We may come out of it all in one piece, and then again we might not." To which Ben-Gurion replied, "There is a public in Palestine, not only parties, and it is unthinkable that its representatives not have a say or make their position known in regard to what has been done up to now . . . The debate is of value . . . the public is the judge."

Ben-Gurion also provided an alternative outlet by proposing that the agenda include, in addition to the regular Histadrut-related items, another item, "The Situation in Palestine and Zionism," which he wanted to follow immediately after the debate over his report. It was as if he was asking the convention not to spend all of its time rubbing salt into the Histadrut's wounds, but to turn its energy outward, mainly against the Zionist Executive. This was undoubtedly a brilliant move, but its significance was not lost on the representatives of the left on the standing committee, who were quick to divine his intentions and see how the HEC might evade punishment; instead of debating corruption and alienation of the worker, the convention would be occupied with the Zionist Executive and Zionist budgets. The Achdut ha-Avodah representatives, who had the same suspicions, were not overjoyed at Ben-Gurion's suggestion either, but factional discipline kept them from voting with Ben-Gurion's opponents. At the close of the deliberations, which lasted two days, the standing committee adopted the convention agenda just as Ben-Gurion wanted it.[19]

The success of this maneuver was borne out by the fact that 26 percent of the convention's time was spent on the debate over his report and 25 percent on "The Situation in Palestine and Zionism." Had he not put the second item on the agenda, the convention would have spent most of its time discussing the salaries, the advances, and Solel Boneh, and it is doubtful that Ben-Gurion would have come out of such a long roasting alive.

With much pride, and in the certain belief that it would gladden the delegates' hearts, Ben-Gurion presented them with a report of 700 closely printed double-column pages, a far cry from the 33 typed pages of the oral report he had delivered to the second convention. In fact, when two extra parts were added to it later, the delegates found they had 978 pages to deal with, not counting two entirely separate reports dealing with agricultural settlement and the Sick Fund, which together filled 272 pages. In his mind, the length of the report was proof of the vast achievement, which he thought should be credited to him.

Did the delegates think so too? Probably not. The first expression of their attitude toward the HEC came at the election for the convention presidium, when, alongside the standing committee's proposal for an eleven-man presidium representing all factions, the HEC proposed only three — Ben-Gurion, Sprinzak, and Remez. The HEC proposal gained a modest majority, and Ben-Gurion, who was elected with the widest margin, received 135 votes, or 67 percent, more than his faction alone could provide but far less than the 80 percent he would have gotten had all the coalition delegates voted for him. This implied that although he had retained his position as top man, he did not have the delegates' general confidence. Remez got only 91 of Achdut ha-Avodah's votes (45.2%), and Sprinzak, who also received votes from outside his faction, had a total of only 61 (30.3%). Both interpreted the vote as a show of inadequate confidence and stepped down from the presidium. This took some of the shine out of the convention's impressive opening, with 201 delegates and 800 guests in attendance.[20]

Immediately following the presidium elections the debate on the report began, and Ben-Gurion, whether he liked it or not, had to listen to every acerbic comment. As the sole remaining member of the presidium he had to conduct the convention meetings for three days, until a new presidium of seven, representing the three largest factions at the convention, was elected *en bloc*. Despite its length, the report was incomplete; it included only a shortened version of the wage committee's findings, and Solel Boneh was mentioned only as a limited stock company established and duly registered. One reason for this was Ben-Gurion's lack of verified information; when he wrote the report the HEC's internal committee had not yet finished its task, and even when it had its members doubted that they had been shown all the pertinent data. But what the report lacked the debate provided in abundance: almost all the participants vented their wrath on Solel Boneh, its directors' advances, and Ben-Gurion's "dreadful decision" to recognize the consortium. The cutting off of Tel Yosef in 1923 and the mass expulsion of 1926 were brought up by many critics, as were the Teachers' College Building affair and the scandalous demonstrations against the Zionist Executive in Jerusalem. When the thirty-five speakers finished, Ben-Gurion's image of a courtroom was complete.[21]

For the three days Ben-Gurion held the chair the invective he heard was like a pouring thunderstorm that soaked him to the bone. Everyone spoke of failure: the Histadrut's, the HEC's, Ben-Gurion's. The difference between Ben-Gurion's Achdut ha-Avodah critics and those from the other factions was that the former found Ha-Poel ha-Tzair partially to blame and covered for him slightly by using the HEC's name instead of his. Berl Repetur, one of the leaders of the future Tabenkin camp, told the convention that "the HEC's report" did not satisfy him and that the HEC should have known "Solel Boneh's true state of affairs six months, a year ago." He added that the HEC had overstepped both its authority and the rules of Histadrut democracy, since "it is forbidden to hand over Solel Boneh to the consortium without the Histadrut council's consent."

The only party colleague to praise Ben-Gurion wholeheartedly was Rachel Yanait, who said, "The four Histadrut years equal the twenty which preceded them." Katznelson, after some reserved praise of the HEC — "When I look over this tremendous account of the HEC . . . all the enormous growth to which the report attests . . . the vast scope of the things that were done, that were perhaps beyond our power" — aimed a dart directly into its heart, saying that "aside from the economic failure we have suffered another: a great moral failure, more serious than the economic one. This spectacle of advances, of excessive salaries, is in my eyes the more frightening. The truly severe loss is that of confidence." He then moved on to "the awful danger that has revealed itself" — which could in no way be deemed the public's responsibility — "the bureaucratization of the Histadrut." No graver "moral, political, or organizational danger" could have threatened the Histadrut more. Katznelson made his resentment of Ben-Gurion's patronage of the apparatus known, but he offered no action against the "danger." It is likely that he simply needed to let off steam and did not want to hurt Ben-Gurion, for he later expressed full confidence in his secretaryship, standing by him against the other factions' criticism, which was not much different from Katznelson's but far more caustic. Katznelson even chided them as an old teacher would his unruly students. "Is it becoming . . . to lower our differences to the level where . . . our people will depict their comrades in the HEC as thieves, as dictators?"

If Ben-Gurion's party colleagues did not spare him, his rivals far outdid them. The leftist factions claimed that the HEC regularly disregarded democratic procedures, which made democratic control impossible. Referring to the division of the Ein Harod–Tel Yosef settlement, they said, "The public was informed about it so suddenly . . . In whose name did the HEC resolve what it resolved?" The same objection applied to the mass expulsion. "The HEC made a resolution without the public's knowledge." Furthermore, the convention delegates were not told who was guilty in the matter of advances and salaries: "It turns out that we have no control in this matter either." The lack of democracy made control impossible and the leftists demanded "to uncover the filth," "to oust the guilty," and "to penalize them according to the strict letter of the law, going so far as confiscating their property."

Ha-Poel ha-Tzair's attack was particularly painful. Its delegates criticized Ben-Gurion personally, describing his secretaryship as "days of

torment." They then accused Achdut ha-Avodah of "excessive centralization"; the fact that 90 percent of the 600 Histadrut employees belonged to Achdut ha-Avodah meant that what Ben-Gurion called
"Histadrut rule" was nothing other than "party rule." Next, Chaim
Arlosoroff attacked Achdut ha-Avodah's approach to managing the
economic institutions. "Had Solel Boneh known its limits it wouldn't
have had fantasies of unlimited expansion. It would have grown slowly,
in a healthy manner, and fulfilled its purpose." In conclusion, Eliezer
Kaplan, who had recently joined the HEC as director of its Finance
Department, gave notice on behalf of Ha-Poel ha-Tzair. "We solemnly
declare that we shall not consent to a continuation of this situation . . .
We insist on democratic rule in the Histadrut and equal rights for all
workers." It was as if Ha-Poel ha-Tzair were joining forces with Poale
Zion Left, whose delegate had stated that "deep inside the Histadrut
absolutism and dictatorship reign . . . there is terror in the Histadrut
and the workers are afraid to open their mouths." Joseph Aharonovitch, to Ben-Gurion's enormous gratification, was the only Ha-Poel
ha-Tzair delegate to declare that the HEC was collectively responsible, adding, "I therefore take this responsibility [for all the HEC's actions and resolutions] on myself."

When at last Ben-Gurion could reply, he went after the Ha-Poel ha-
Tzair leaders who had accused Achdut ha-Avodah of being a "dictatorial majority." The assertions had infuriated him, and in mounting his
counterattack he became very personal and offensive. His remarks
about Chaim Arlosoroff were so caustic that Katznelson censored them
from the account that appeared in *Davar*. Ben-Gurion flatly rejected
Arlosoroff's accusation that it was Achdut ha-Avodah's policy of expansion, not the general depression, which had brought down Solel
Boneh. He declared, "If I could attribute 100 percent of the responsibility for what Solel Boneh did wrong to ourselves I would do so gladly
and with pride. I shall not do so because we didn't do it alone, and I
don't want to adorn myself with borrowed plumes." Solel Boneh in fact
had gone under because the Zionist Executive and others (clearly Arlosoroff and those who shared his view) had not understood that "the secret of our achievement in Palestine is in not being satisfied with little"
and had not supported the momentum of the great enterprise. "The
hour of the foot-draggers has come," Ben-Gurion said, oozing sarcasm.
"What they have foretold has come true, and they can celebrate the
victory. But what a woeful victory it is."

He continued with a warning against the danger of such foot-drag-
ging. "As I see it, the principal task of this convention is to fight to the
last of our strength against this reactionary type of victory and against
the bankrupt reality ruling in Zionism." He thus shifted the battle to

the Zionist front, the next item on the agenda. Before concluding he replied to Arlosoroff's accusation that the HEC had jumped ahead fifty years and behaved "as if" Histadrut rule already existed. "We don't see ourselves as a government . . . but in our concept the Histadrut is the beginnings of the Jewish socialist state, and who knows but we may succeed and have one?" He descended from the rostrum looking like a raging prophet.

The day on which Ben-Gurion made this speech, the convention's sixth, was the last time he actively participated in the assembly. Apparently he was already feeling poorly, as was customary for him during periods of tension and excitement, and only through sheer will power was he able to drag himself to the convention hall for a few more days. The inference to be drawn is that he was not only feeling under the weather but was also enraged and insulted. From the afternoon of July 14 until the convention's close seven days later, he was absent. *Davar* reported, "He's lying ill in his home in Tel Aviv. His illness isn't serious, but it is liable to last another week or two."[22]

Immediately following the convention's close, at dawn on July 22, the delegates and guests left in a procession, dancing through the streets of the awakening city to wish Ben-Gurion a speedy recovery and good health from outside his window and to give him the news that he had been re-elected to the HEC, that the convention had resolved to "approve [his] report," and that it wished to "express its confidence in, and esteem of, the HEC." This was an exceptional expression of confidence and respect, perhaps, on the part of most delegates, mixed with a bit of regret over the harshness of their criticism.[23] Ben-Gurion never wrote or said what he felt or thought when he looked out his window and silently waved to his many well-wishers, but he was probably grateful and touched.

This convention, which tested his position, was his last as secretary of the Histadrut; both of the fourth convention's sessions, in 1933 and 1934, were held when he was embroiled in World Zionist Organization matters. The intervening six years saw the development of a stronger Ben-Gurion in a stronger HEC. Although initially it seemed that the convention had effectively tied his hands by prohibiting expulsion without trial and by creating a central financial directorate and a central control board in the HEC, the consequence of its having asked what the HEC had done to prevent the Solel Boneh disaster was actually to recognize HEC predominance over all other institutions, including the two new ones. Ben-Gurion had at his disposal a loyal apparatus which, notwithstanding its past transgressions in wage matters, was by any standard clean-handed, devoted, and committed. Through it he could impose and enforce HEC predominance more

than ever. In re-electing him to the HEC the convention not only acknowledged that he was the top man, but also that he was indispensable, for in spite of the criticism and charges leveled at him no one
proposed, or even considered, electing someone else in his stead.

From here on, his indispensability would be the strongest and most
important factor in the consolidation of his leadership. In the final
analysis, the undying vote of confidence in his leadership, his integrity,
and his dedication constituted his party's endorsement of his style of
partnership, an endorsement that was the result neither of blind faith
nor of coercion.

This was both the secret and the basis of Ben-Gurion's leadership.
On the convention floor, Shlomo Lavi of Kibbutz Ein Harod analyzed
the constructive forces in the Histadrut that gave it its power. "In the
rebuilding of Eretz Israel we have nothing but the workers' loyalty and
dedication . . . Without this dedication those at the head of the institutions could not have done a thing."[24] This can be interpreted as a
warning to Ben-Gurion that he must retain the trust of the pioneering
public if he wanted to go on leading the party and the Histadrut. But
Ben-Gurion knew this all too well, and all his life saw himself as one of
the pioneers and workers who were willing to forgo comfort, and at
times their daily bread, out of dedication to the Zionist ideal; if he was
physically removed from them, and from the frontier, it was only because it was his lot to act in their name and on their behalf. That he
won their confidence and acceptance was perhaps his greatest political
achievement, for they truly regarded him as one of their own, the one
who could translate their accomplishments and sacrifices into political
objectives and outline the plans to achieve them. By virtue of this faith
they forgave Ben-Gurion and the HEC their mistakes.

They, too, accepted his style of partnership, an alliance that was as
strong as it was incredible. In return for their faith he made them the
pith of Zionism in general and of labor Zionism in particular. In party
councils, and later in Israel in the Knesset and in the government, they
were given representation that far exceeded their numbers. In his leadership Ben-Gurion succeeded in wedding two frequently conflicting
opposites, pioneering and bureaucracy, and this extraordinary blend
made it unique.

23

An Organization of Conquerors

IF BEN-GURION interpreted his re-election to the HEC secretariat as
a victory for his policy, the aftermath of the September 1927 Zionist Congress in Basel proved him right. As soon as it became clear
that nothing would come of the congress's resolutions, and that Chaim
Weizmann and his backers could not stop unemployment and would
continue the dole, Joseph Sprinzak and Shlomo Kaplansky resigned
from the Zionist Executive, as Ben-Gurion had long been advocating.
This agreement seemed to give Ben-Gurion the green light to step up
his campaign, on behalf of the Histadrut, to force the Zionist Executive
to mobilize funds for productive work projects.

Since the HEC was not eager to go to war with the Zionist Executive
even after the Congress, it adopted an either-or approach proposed by
Ben-Gurion: a formal statement was made to the Zionist Executive
that either it came up with work projects within a month, or the campaign for "Hebrew labor" in the agricultural settlements* would be accelerated. By 1927 unemployment had reached agricultural workers,
too, primarily those registered at the Histadrut labor exchange, because the times had forced citrus growers to hire the cheapest labor
available, Arabs or unregistered Jews.

The Zionist Executive was not forthcoming with projects, so in November the HEC focused on Petah Tikva, whose citrus plantations, in
which Ben-Gurion had worked twenty years earlier, were the largest in
the Jewish sector and employed mostly Arabs; the HEC estimated
their number at about three thousand. Ben-Gurion proposed "action,"
but the HEC members argued that they had not yet exhausted the pos-

---

*That is, *moshava*, in which the land and implements are owned by individual members.

sibility of dialogue with Petah Tikva's municipal committee and the agricultural committees that represented the growers, and they still hoped for an agreement on the Histadrut's two demands, that the growers hire only Jewish labor and do so through the Histadrut labor exchange, on its terms.

As a compromise to Ben-Gurion, the HEC decided on a warning action to speed up the talks. On November 13 a picket line stationed itself at the gate to one of the orchards, barring entry to its Arab workers. There was a skirmish, police dispersed the picketers, and the National Council rushed in to mediate between the local labor council and the agricultural committee. This failed, and Ben-Gurion revived his demand for action. In the first week of December, at the height of the fruit-picking season, he told the HEC, "We have to divorce ourselves immediately from relief and start the war this month . . . We must rouse public opinion." This time only two Ha-Poel ha-Tzair members opposed the action. Sprinzak argued that "harsh action should be avoided," as it would do more harm than good, and that it would be better to seek the assistance of the Zionist Executive and the National Council in holding talks. But Ben-Gurion called for an action that would "shake up Zionism," and the HEC adopted his proposal, with checks designed to soften the "shakeup." One stipulated that nothing be done without the HEC's knowledge and the other required a liaison who, they hoped, would keep the HEC informed and monitor Ben-Gurion's activity.

But Ben-Gurion shook off his restraints very quickly. He established direct, semicovert contact with the Labor Council, excluding the liaison from his secret conspiring with Council activists. The liaison, who began with very little to report, soon became silent.[1] Evidence attests to furtive visits by Ben-Gurion to Petah Tikva. On December 1 he spoke with the secretariat of the Labor Council, from whom he learned what "the enemy's" (the growers' agricultural committee's) intentions were, and that night he met with some workers and unemployed to establish an action committee; as usual, a planned "action" was to appear as a spontaneous outburst. He returned to the HEC in Tel Aviv the next day.

The results of this visit were not long in coming. On the evening of December 4 a thousand workers and unemployed assembled near the Petah Tikva Labor Council building for "a consultation." The crowd suddenly "went off, all by itself," according to *Davar*, demonstrating in the streets of Petah Tikva with calls of "Bread!" and "Work for the unemployed!" The demonstrators broke into the yard of the municipal council building, and their spokesmen made speeches from the second-story balcony. If this action was a trial run for the action committee, it was clearly a success. The National Council was called in and took it on itself to mediate between the Labor Council and the agricultural committee, but to no avail; the committee speaking for the growers refused to hire more than a handful of Jewish workers and insisted on employing them solely through its own labor exchange. On December 14 it set this handful to work picking fruit. That same day Ben-Gurion again visited Petah Tikva, meeting with the secretariat of the Labor Council as well as with the action committee; on his return to Tel Aviv he informed the HEC that "action has begun."[2]

On the fourteenth, picket lines were stationed at the gates of the orchards with Ben-Gurion's directive "to avoid, at all costs, a clash with the Arab workers" to whom they were barring entry. The police dispersed the pickets both that day and the next. Ben-Gurion was probably sounding out the growers, and when he realized that they were turning to the police, as expected, he was sure of his next step. On Friday the sixteenth the pickets were heavily reinforced and, at the gates of some of the orchards, faced hundreds of Arabs. Shortly after 10:00 A.M., as if following Ben-Gurion's plan, William Miller, deputy commissioner of the Jaffa district, arrived with a large force of Arab mounted police; another force, the Irish gendarmerie, was waiting unseen some distance away. At first, to ward off a "racial conflict," as he put it, Miller left the mounted Arabs near the settlement while he himself, escorted by a police vehicle commanded by a British officer, drove from orchard to orchard calling on the pickets to disperse. Receiving no answer, he ordered the mounted police to move in and open the gates. "The order was given," wrote *Davar* afterward, "and the Arab police ... carried it out with vengeful fury on the backs of the picketing men and women, inflicting head and face wounds on even those who turned their backs and took headlong flight. Their horses trampled the fleeing crowd." Of course, *Davar*'s account, which was Ben-Gurion's, made the worst of the situation, in comparison to the police account. Miller, in any case, later admitted that seven of their nightsticks had broken almost immediately, "either because they were of poor quality or because the blows were so strong." By 11:30 A.M. seventeen pickets, among them the secretary of the Labor Council, had been detained and taken to Jaffa. Of the wounded, fourteen needed first aid and four required hospitalization.

As news of the beatings and the arrests spread through Petah Tikva a public storm gathered. There is no doubt that what followed had been planned well ahead of time. A riotous crowd burst into the municipal council's building, destroying documents, office equipment, furniture, and anything else within reach. Miller called in the gendarmerie, and the Irishmen rolled into the village, taking positions behind sandbags and barbed wire. Soon Petah Tikva looked like an occupied town. Fearing to appear to be fighting the unemployed with the aid of British bayonets, the municipal committee members hurriedly initiated negotiations with the Labor Council, and by 6:00 P.M. an agreement was reached that within the week all the unemployed in Petah Tikva would be hired as pickers. Peace and order were restored, but only for the moment.

Ben-Gurion had promised the HEC to "shake up Zionism," and in his opinion this action was simply a fuse to set off an explosion of protest. On Saturday the seventeenth he went secretly to Petah Tikva to look at the situation and give the action committee further guidance. The next day a billboard war erupted. The Labor Council labeled the growers "defamers of the Yishuv, whose hands are stained with the blood of Jewish workers," and the agricultural committee responded by laying the blame "for staging events" on Ben-Gurion (who, as it turned out, was not able to remain anonymous), calling him and his colleagues "faint-hearted cowards." On his return to Tel Aviv late Saturday night, Ben-Gurion instructed all the labor councils to hold protest meetings "against the bloody attack by the police who were called in to Petah Tikva by the agricultural committee . . . and against the boycotting of Jewish workers for the fruit picking at this time of grave unemployment in Petah Tikva and throughout Palestine." The councils responded. Knowing from experience that there was nothing like a storm abroad to generate a greater one in Palestine, Ben-Gurion cabled his account of the events — an enriched version of what *Davar* had carried — to the British Parliamentary Labour Party and its organ, the *Daily Herald. The Times* of London also covered the story, and on December 21 four members of the foreign press, serving fourteen European papers, and a few representatives from the American press swooped down on Petah Tikva.[3]

Ben-Gurion knew full well that all the posters, the protest meetings, and the local and foreign press coverage would soon fade unless refueled by new events, and he knew that the seventeen pickets in the Jaffa jail were his best means of creating fresh drama: the longer the detention, the greater the public sympathy for the Histadrut, the champion of the unemployed and organized "Hebrew labor." To this end he worked both sides of the street. In public he forcefully demanded the immediate release of the detainees and instructed the action committee in Petah Tikva and all the labor councils in Palestine to call protest meetings and stir up a public clamor. The Petah Tikva Prisoners' Aid Fund, which Ben-Gurion had prepared long before the action began, went public and was instantly flooded with donations from everywhere. But privately, in his dealings with the authorities,

Ben-Gurion did everything in his power to prevent the prisoners' release on bail.

As early as December 19 the Jaffa district commissioner — at the behest of the high commissioner — offered to release the detainees if the Histadrut would guarantee their good behavior and an overall letup of the public outcry. Ben-Gurion rejected this out of hand. The high commissioner then turned to Colonel Frederick Kisch, who also failed to move Ben-Gurion. In fact, these negotiations played right into Ben-Gurion's hands, because while they lasted the police could not present a charge sheet, and the warrant for the arrest of the seventeen, originally for only five days, was stretched to twelve.

Not that Ben-Gurion was untouched by the prisoners' situation. To the contrary, his diary entries illustrate his concern and agitation on being informed that one of them had been beaten for refusing to do "demeaning chores" in jail. Nevertheless, he believed that the detention strengthened the Histadrut's campaign, and therefore the seventeen had to endure it. "We are amidst difficult conditions of war . . . Success is dependent on internal discipline," he told the action committee. Furthermore, he was aching for a trial at which the Histadrut campaign for the right to work and picket would be presented to all, a trial in which he himself, as counsel for the defense, would turn prosecuting attorney and take center stage.[4]

On December 28, twelve days after the arrest, the trial finally began. There, alongside the lawyers retained by the Histadrut to defend sixteen of the detainees, sat Ben-Gurion, with special authorization from the judge, as defense counsel for the Labor Council secretary. The trial proved to be "a sensation," in the words of *Ha-Aretz*. A huge crowd gathered in the courthouse yard several hours before it began and jammed the doorways. The paper depicted Ben-Gurion as the star of the trial, detailing his role in both the direct and the cross-examination of Miller and a police officer. Ben-Gurion, the hero of the day, was noticeably pleased with his legal role. When the sentence was handed down he patted himself on the back. His "client," the Council secretary, was sentenced to twelve days' imprisonment and in consideration of his previous detention released the next day. As for the rest, fifteen were sentenced to sixteen days in jail and one to an entire month.

But despite the sympathy and attention given to the protests and the trial, there was no escaping the sad conclusion that as far as unemployment was concerned, the action proved a failure. In the citrus groves economic interests — lower labor costs — prevailed over national or social considerations, and nothing came of the hasty accord between the Labor Council and the municipal committee. In a joint meeting with the Labor Council on January 6, 1928, its secretary told the HEC,

"There has been no change in the citrus groves. The number of Arabs grows steadily." A colleague of his added, "The working public knows we have suffered a defeat."[5]

Ben-Gurion's policy came up again in the HEC. Sprinzak, who two days before the trial had protested the action committee's having been set up without the HEC's prior knowledge, opposed any action. "I say that this war and its victories are dubious." But Ben-Gurion took a more extreme line. He attributed the failure to the fact that "we did not continue the action outside Petah Tikva as well." The war to win public opinion had to be a total one against all growers employing Arabs. "We can . . . create such an atmosphere that they will look no better than pimps." The Histadrut could not succeed, he said, unless it could "shape public opinion so that these people will be ostracized." The public, therefore, "must not be allowed to rest." Action had to be taken "so that everyone will know that the matter has not been settled."

He no longer was satisfied with passive pickets; the time had come for organized violence. Here he came into conflict with Berl Katznelson, who also considered winning over public opinion — not just organizing Hebrew labor in the agricultural settlements — the main objective of the campaign. Violence, particularly organized violence, revolted Katznelson. He upheld pickets as the only way to rouse public opinion, and only after the National Council was given more time for mediation. "If there was a way other than pickets we would have opted for it, but there is not, and I do not know why our people will not go to jail for one to two weeks for the victory," concluded Katznelson. By majority vote the HEC decided to go on picketing, but only "after a National Council meeting" and with the explicit condition that the Petah Tikva Labor Council, whose ties with Ben-Gurion had become so close, "take responsibility for making sure that the pickets will not turn aggressive."

Soon more shades of the differences between the two appeared: whereas in January 1928 Katznelson and the HEC majority approved a quiet and peaceful demonstration in front of the "black office" — their name for the labor exchange opened by the Petah Tikva growers — Ben-Gurion made known, in public as well as in the HEC, his position: "We will stand and fight as any man would for his life . . . If it is our destiny that our blood flow in this war, we shall not turn back."[6]

Ben-Gurion's appointment book for January 1928 reveals the thinking behind his words. Although he was heavily overworked — the diary records scores of discussions and meetings, including seventeen concerning fruit picking in Petah Tikva and three in connection with the trial's aftermath — he found time for Hapoel. This sudden interest in the sports association of the Histadrut did not spring from some awakening to the importance of physical fitness. Ben-Gurion first met alone with Joseph Hecht, national commander of the Haganah and an Achdut ha-Avodah member, asking him to set up strong-arm squads within the Hapoel framework. He then met with the heads of Hapoel, inviting them to move their head office from Haifa to Tel Aviv and instructing them that "acceptance of members must be entirely in the hands of the central committee, and every member must have the proper social qualifications, not only physical and athletic ones." "Proper social qualifications," he explained, meant "no Factionists." Instead of an occasional improvised force or temporary action committees, he sought a trained force always on the alert, which the HEC could send into battle whenever necessary. He laid the foundation for the Hapoel Squadrons, which reached their fullest development as the Histadrut's "defense force" in the early thirties.

But in the meantime, he had to make do with an improvised force. In January he demanded that the urban labor councils transfer their unemployed to the settlements and that the Tel Aviv Labor Council in particular "organize 200 loyal, reliable workers to go to Petah Tikva," as that town still had top priority in his mind. However, the economic tide had turned, the depression had passed, and instead of unemployment there was a modest shortage of hired hands in the settlements, even with the fruit-picking season almost over. But after he was told, on February 3, that there was no more unemployment in Petah Tikva, "except for 20–30 who are not working either because they do not want to or due to physical disability," he still pushed the transferral. On the seventh he directed the Agricultural Center, which was in charge of the agricultural workers, that "a bolder action must now be organized and the transferral of workers to the settlements must proceed briskly." Since there were hardly any jobless left in the towns, he sent the employed. In his diary he noted, probably with satisfaction, "They are taking workers away from building roads and sending them to work in the groves." He also ordered the Labor Council to cut off the dole to any single unemployed people left in Tel Aviv, since "as long as the dole exists they will not leave the city for the settlement." Thus he brought about a huge concentration of workers in Petah Tikva, among them the two hundred "loyal" ones.[7]

What kind of battle was he setting up? In a lecture he told Haifa workers, "We are now confronted with a shortage of workers in Palestine. The lack is felt particularly in agriculture." Commenting that this situation created a need for increased immigration, he explained his objective in Petah Tikva. "This was not a war solely for work . . . but war for Zionism and Hebrew labor." It was a political campaign designed to bolster the program for economic segregation between Jews and Arabs in Palestine that he had first conceived in his days of exile in America.

Toward the end of 1928, when the picking season was to begin again, Ben-Gurion prepared for battle against the black office by announcing Histadrut readiness to establish "a joint exchange" between the Labor Council and Petah Tikva's agricultural committee. He could have intended this as a real concession of Histadrut exclusivity and a gesture of good will to facilitate agreement, or, if it met with a negative response, a tactic to give the Histadrut an edge with public opinion, or both, although the second is more likely. In any case, the announcement led to a meeting in Petah Tikva on November 20 between Ben-Gurion, representatives of the Histadrut, and representatives of the agricultural committee. The latter group objected to a joint exchange, which meant, it said, accepting all the Histadrut's terms, and the meeting ended inconclusively.

The Histadrut invitation to renew the parley met with repeated postponement, which gave Ben-Gurion the opportunity to write to the agricultural committee, "We have approached you several times by telephone regarding a continuation of our talks and we have not been answered" and request that "negotiations be brought to a close as soon as possible." He could pursue war while giving the appearance of one who wished only for peace. Meanwhile the agricultural committee opened the black office.

As a result, the line of action was revived according to the familiar scenario. On December 17 the Labor Council held a demonstration at the office of the agricultural committee — according to *Davar*, the crowd gathered "on its own" — which ended with the demonstrators bursting into the office, breaking doors, shattering windows, and wreaking general havoc. The police again intervened; there were more arrests, trials, and another poster war, which this time was augmented by a public statement from seven citrus growing settlements against the Histadrut's "campaign of violence," pursued "solely for the purpose of imposing organized labor." The statement demanded that the Zionist Executive put a stop to the violence. The HEC again met to discuss the "events in Petah Tikva," the question again arose of how the HEC's unequivocal resolution banning violence had been breached, and the controversy was renewed.

Members of the Petah Tikva Labor Council also took part, averring that the war against the growers was a good thing in itself since it strengthened the Histadrut. "The continuing war is an absolute necessity," said one, adding that "in Petah Tikva the Histadrut has no other way to rally the working public around it." "Information and cultural activity by themselves will not do the trick," said another, "but our war for the workers will." In response Berl Katznelson and Moshe Beilinson condemned all forms of violence, and both rejected the idea that the war helped fortify the Histadrut. Ben-Gurion, for his part, tackled the issue affirmatively and negatively. While he said, "I do not believe that we will make the Histadrut stronger by breaking down doors every day," at the same time he noted, "There is some good in the black office in that it provides an object of war. This business may give impetus to organization and strengthening of the Histadrut in Petah Tikva." As he went on the contradiction became evident, and there was little doubt that he was hatching one of his "double formulas," this time using a double negative. On the one hand, he was saying, "First of all no violence, not against people and not against property"; and on the other, "But no peace either," for the war "cannot be waged only throughout the press and propaganda." Two weeks later, at the plenum of the National Council, called on January 9, 1929, to discuss the Petah Tikva events, Ben-Gurion said that, were he young and working in Petah Tikva, "I would not go to the agricultural committee building, but to the Pascals' house" (Perez Pascal was one of the larger growers in Petah Tikva), clearly implying that he would go to the grower's home "to break furniture and deal blows," in the words of one member of the Petah Tikva Labor Council secretariat, who proposed exactly that to the HEC.[8]

The closest of his colleagues could no longer doubt that Ben-Gurion was resolved to wage an all-out war for Hebrew labor, a war he would pursue even when unemployment was nil and the Histadrut exchange had no Jewish replacements for Arab hands. He was prepared to use violence to attain a political goal and made no secret of his belief that a war of this nature was a useful means to consolidate the Histadrut.

Since he was guided by this policy until he quit the HEC in 1935, and since it involved him in a struggle not only with citrus growers and their towns but even more with Vladimir Jabotinsky's Revisionist Party and its anti-Histadrut supporters in the heart of the Zionist movement, his further moves to implement it will be described here.

His struggle for Hebrew labor was only a part of an overall campaign for what Ben-Gurion called the "conquest of Zionism," by which he meant winning through political means a labor majority in the Zionist Organization and among its leaders. He had long been nursing this objective and, in 1927–1928, he made up his mind that the time had come to do something about it. But he still needed that same "broad-based labor party" he had been seeking since 1907. A merger with Ha-Poel ha-Tzair therefore became the order of the day.

In fact, not a day had passed since Achdut ha-Avodah's birth without

Ben-Gurion and Katznelson trying to win over Ha-Poel ha-Tzair, and with the passing of years the two parties had more in common than not. They ran on a joint ticket for the municipal and Zionist Congress elections; both had kibbutzes and moshavs; and their partnership in the coalition that ran the Histadrut narrowed, by force of circumstance, their differences in social and economic matters. Besides, socialism did not have a bad name with the younger Ha-Poel ha-Tzair members — Chaim Arlosoroff, for example, supported it — and by and large the party's stance against socialist Achdut ha-Avodah steadily weakened. It seemed that time and common experience in the Histadrut were preparing the ground for a merger that would one day simply fall into Ben-Gurion's and Katznelson's laps like ripe fruit. But this did not suit Ben-Gurion's temperament; Ben-Gurion believed that a bit of pressure could never hurt, and in this instance especially it could very well speed up the process.

Accordingly he brought pressure to bear on Ha-Poel ha-Tzair by efforts to boost Achdut ha-Avodah. As early as July 1922 he had told the executive committee of his party that "we have to stand out more." One way of doing so was by staffing the Histadrut apparatus and the higher-level positions with Achdut ha-Avodah members — that is, with more than the share allotted the party in the agreement which governed the coalition and upon which the Histadrut was established and run. Ha-Poel ha-Tzair's complaints and Sprinzak's protests accompanied every appointment Ben-Gurion made from his very first days in the Histadrut. In July 1922, four months after Ben-Gurion had talked of "standing out," Sprinzak told the HEC secretariat that "a kind of spiritual inquisition" was going on; he had the feeling that "someone fixed" the appointments, that Achdut ha-Avodah had decided them ahead of time, relying on its majority without taking Ha-Poel ha-Tzair into consideration, "and as a result [our] patience is exhausted." In April 1924 Sprinzak bemoaned the fact that the Solel Boneh directorate had been put together with "factional intentions," as indeed it had, for most of its members came from Achdut ha-Avodah. Three months later he protested Ben-Gurion's intention to appoint to the immigration center only one secretary, rather than two, who would likely exploit the opportunity to recruit new immigrants for Achdut ha-Avodah; in this case his protest was heeded and a collegium was set up to run the center. In March 1925 Arlosoroff denounced Achdut ha-Avodah men for starting factionally motivated disputes in the HEC. In the summer of 1926 Ada Maimon, whom Achdut ha-Avodah's Golda Meir was starting to supplant in the Women Workers' Council, accused Achdut ha-Avodah not only of filling Histadrut positions with its members but of giving preference to its own unemployed in the labor exchanges. She attributed all this to Ben-Gurion, adding that such actions by one "who always speaks in the name of the Histadrut's mission" were not done to warm the hearts of Ha-Poel ha-Tzair members toward his oft-repeated call for a merger.[9] Others in her party shared her opinion, and the merger was not supported in 1926 and 1927.

It seemed like a vicious circle: as long as he could not get the merger off the ground, Ben-Gurion worked to strengthen Achdut ha-Avodah, giving Ha-Poel ha-Tzair just cause for grievances and diminishing the chance for a merger, thus impelling Ben-Gurion to work harder to strengthen Achdut ha-Avodah even more. But was it really self-defeating? Some members of Ha-Poel ha-Tzair viewed things differently. Between elections Achdut ha-Avodah's strength increased under Ben-Gurion's leadership, and not only did its share of the votes soar from 41.7 percent to 53.2 percent between the first and third conventions, but its share of the Histadrut's growing membership increased by even more: it was 56.5 percent of those who joined the Histadrut between the first and second conventions, and a similar percentage between the second and third. If this went on, where would Ha-Poel ha-Tzair be, with its share of the vote falling from 29.8 percent to 26.7 percent between the first and third conventions? How would it fare in the fourth? Ben-Gurion and Achdut ha-Avodah were likely to conclude that they could run the Histadrut by themselves. Wouldn't it be better for Ha-Poel ha-Tzair to merge with Achdut ha-Avodah and share its rise in power instead of withering away? Gerda Luft, a Ha-Poel ha-Tzair intellectual, saw Ben-Gurion's pressure tactics as an important factor in the merger. "What decided the merger?" she asked after the fact, and answered, "Achdut ha-Avodah's factional takeover of Ha-Poel ha-Tzair in the Histadrut; that is what brought on the merger."[10] Another factor was the growing recognition within both parties that their quarrels hurt the Histadrut, and that the time had come to create a strong central political force that would guide the Histadrut, the Yishuv, and the Zionist movement.

In October 1927 the Ha-Poel ha-Tzair council resolved to open talks with Achdut ha-Avodah on the merger, and the two parties appointed representatives, Ben-Gurion and Katznelson among them, to a joint negotiating committee. The turning point came in 1928. As the rivalry between the two parties went from bad to worse, the joint committee, as if spurred on by it, went into high gear; Ha-Poel ha-Tzair came forth with a platform for a merger, to which Katznelson responded with one of his own. He was, however, prevented from presenting it by the unexpected.

On May 25, 1928, Ben-Gurion, his family, and Katznelson were injured in an automobile accident on their way to a conference in Ben

Shemen. Their driver had been racing another car and ran up a tree on the side of the road, throwing all the passengers into the adjoining field. A passing car whisked them to the government hospital in the nearby Arab town of Ramla. Two Arab doctors gave them first aid. "They wiped off the blood, stitched up the cuts, gave us injections against blood poisoning," noted Ben-Gurion later in his diary. Two doctors and two nurses from Hadassah transferred the wounded to Tel Aviv's Hadassah Hospital for further treatment.

As the news spread a deep anxiety took hold of the entire working community in Palestine. "An enormous crowd" congregated at the hospital's gate. "Exaggerated rumors intensified the sadness," said *Davar*. All the Jewish papers reported "the disaster" on their front pages. Katznelson had sustained multiple fractures and was hospitalized at Hadassah for several weeks. Ben-Gurion, Paula, Geula, and Renana (Amos had stayed at home) fared better, with just a few scrapes and bruises, and after treatment at the Hadassah were sent home, but two weeks passed before Ben-Gurion could return to work full time. Katznelson stayed away until the end of September. Seven months later they had another accident; on the way to Jerusalem their car collided with another. This time neither was hurt, and Ben-Gurion observed in his diary, "Apparently I must not travel with Berl."[11]

On September 20 Ha-Poel ha-Tzair reminded the joint committee that more than five months had passed since the party had put forth its platform and there was still no answer from Achdut ha-Avodah. Although assuming that the accident was the cause of the delay, it asked Achdut ha-Avodah for an immediate response. A practical consideration probably contributed to its sudden eagerness: the Tel Aviv municipal elections were scheduled for the end of December 1928, and Ha-Poel ha-Tzair was keen on running jointly with Achdut ha-Avodah.

Ha-Poel ha-Tzair's change of heart is further revealed by its consent to the creation of the new position of secretary of the Histadrut, and in November Golomb proposed giving it to Ben-Gurion. Here, at long last, was his heart's desire: not only the executive but a secretaryship all his own, the end of the collegium he so loathed, and an opportunity to run the HEC as he saw fit. But, astonishingly, instead of jumping at the offer he turned it down flat and proposed an enlarged secretariat: two paid secretaries, Eliyahu Golomb and Jacob Efter, plus another three, including himself. This meant that he would no longer be on the Histadrut's payroll or be a member of the smaller secretariat. Who, then, would pay his salary and where would he work? "*I will work in the party*," he stated in his diary, underlining the answer he gave Golomb and other inquirers; by "party" he meant the one to come out of the merger. Even in January 1929, when Eliezer Kaplan gave his consent on behalf of Ha-Poel ha-Tzair to Ben-Gurion's appointment as sole secretary of the Histadrut since he was "the only candidate for this job," Ben-Gurion still declined the office. His reason for doing so was that it might take up all his time, whereas his mind was already made up to work as hard as he could in the united party and make it into a new force that would carry out the "conquest of Zionism." He remained in the secretariat, lessening his duties there to create the time to carry out his plans for the future.[12]

Nevertheless, the question of the platform still stood in the way of the merger. Katznelson's wide-ranging twenty-two-point draft opened by drawing a parallel between Zionism and socialism. "At the center of Jewish history in our time stands Zionism and its total fulfillment," while "at the center of the modern history of humanity stands socialism and its total fulfillment." Both aimed at class and national liberation and abhorred subjugation and exploitation of either nations or individuals. The new "united party aligns itself with the Jewish liberation movement and the working class of the world, as an integral part of both; the united party will represent the Jewish working class in Palestine in the Zionist Congress, in Knesset Israel's* institutions, in the self-governing institutions in Palestine, and in the Socialist International." Achdut ha-Avodah approved the draft in full.

Ha-Poel ha-Tzair, however, rejected both the preamble and the articles outright. It would not accept class war or the "working class" formula, and therefore could not accept the World Union of Poale Zion, with which Achdut ha-Avodah was affiliated, as the representative of the world's Jewish "working class." Ha-Poel ha-Tzair took strong exception to Katznelson's thesis that socialism could be realized only through "struggle for the liberation of the working class" and that class struggle within Zionism was the "fruit of the movement of internal forces within the nation and the movement of social forces throughout the world." Most of all it repudiated the vision of working-class domination of state and society as a result of that struggle.

The sole concession it was prepared to offer was in the name. It agreed that the new party would be a "socialist" party, support world socialism, and take part in the Socialist International, which Achdut ha-Avodah had joined on its establishment. This provided Ben-Gurion with a spark of hope when, in May 1929, he tried to break the deadlock in the negotiations. In this he was assisted by two unrelated factors.

---

*Knesset Israel: in this context, the organized Jewish community in Palestine.

The Zionist Actions Committee, which served as the Zionist parliamentary body between the biannual congresses, was scheduled to meet in Berlin in June to set up the Jewish Agency, enabling Ben-Gurion to argue that without a prior merger the two parties would be unable to bring the full weight of their combined strength to bear at the meeting. In his diary he said explicitly, "The merger talks would not have ended so quickly had we not been about to sail off." The other factor was Katznelson's resignation from the joint committee for reasons of poor health. Ben-Gurion, now Achdut ha-Avodah's chief negotiator, went his own way as usual, acting first and getting party approval after the fact. In place of Katznelson's long draft, he produced a three-point platform of his own. The first two were the result of hard, relentless bargaining with Ha-Poel ha-Tzair; the third was made up of two of Katznelson's points, amended and supplemented.

This effort led at last to an agreement, and at 4:00 P.M. on May 17 David Ben-Gurion and David Remez signed the approved platform on behalf of Achdut ha-Avodah, with Joseph Sprinzak, Eliezer Kaplan, and Isaac Laufbahn signing for Ha-Poel ha-Tzair, all as members of what they called the unity committee. More was involved than a mere change of name. With the argument that time was running short — the June Actions Committee meeting was to be followed by a meeting in Zurich of the Zionist Congress on July 28, and it was essential that the new party appear there with its united strength — Ben-Gurion talked his committee colleagues into assuming the leadership of a party that had not been born yet. Thus the unity committee ran both parties, to all intents and purposes a single party, before the party members were asked their opinion on the merger.

The first article of Ben-Gurion's draft read:

Recognizing that "Achdut ha-Avodah" and "Ha-Poel ha-Tzair" are united in their dedication to the re-establishment of the Jewish people in Palestine as a free nation of workers, rooted in all branches of the economy . . . developing its independent Jewish culture; and in their solidarity with the struggle of the working class of the world to abolish class subjugation and social deprivation in any form; in order to nationalize the natural resources and the means of production; and to create a society of labor, equality, and liberty; the two parties resolve *to unite*.

The second article said:

The united party considers itself the standard-bearer within the Zionist movement of pioneering, and as a loyal member of the Zionist Organization and its institutions, the Socialist International, and Knesset Israel and its autonomous institutions. The united party aspires to embrace all workers in Palestine for the purpose of active, constructive pioneering in all areas of national life, the lives of the workers, and the Zionist and socialist movements.

The third affirmed that the united party aimed to "promote Zionist and socialist consciousness among the working public" and outlined the party's functions and purposes.

Compared with the 1906 Ramla platform and Achdut ha-Avodah's 1919 platform, the nationalist aspect was given much more prominence in Ben-Gurion's new manifesto. It made no mention of taking over the government by revolution or of the establishment of a Republic of Workers. Shlomo Kaplansky argued that it was not "socialist enough," and threatened to quit the party after the merger. Itzhak Ben-Zvi, too, torn between his loyalties to Ben-Gurion and to the principles of the Poale Zion of old, found the platform lacking socialist content. Class struggle was not explicitly called for; there was only the phrase "Zionist and socialist consciousness," with no elucidation of what it meant. But Ben-Gurion was confident of the path he had taken. And in mid June, a month after the committee had signed the manifesto, each party held a referendum, in which 81.6 percent of Achdut ha-Avodah's members and 85 percent of Ha-Poel ha-Tzair's approved the manifesto. Thereupon a joint secretariat of the two parties replaced the union committee and a joint ticket and platform were put together for the elections to the Zionist Congress, where for the first time a single labor bloc appeared. So the united party came a long way even before its formal establishment seven months later; another sign, most likely, of the burning ground beneath Ben-Gurion's feet.[13]

Two "winding-up conventions," as they were called, one of Achdut ha-Avodah and one of Ha-Poel ha-Tzair, met separately in Tel Aviv on the evening of January 4, 1930, twenty-four hours before the opening of the united party's founding convention. Ben-Gurion was the guiding spirit of his party's convention (Katznelson being in London for health reasons) and at that of the new one. He presided over the latter; delivered one of its two opening addresses (Sprinzak gave the other); read out the proposed manifesto, which was unanimously approved; delivered the keynote speech — a three-hour talk, "On Zionist Policy and the Arab Question," indicating his new field of interest; and chaired the closing session. On January 7 he declared, "The name of the party is the Palestine Workers' Party (Mapai)," and adjourned the convention.[14] Thus was born the largest and strongest party of the Yishuv and of Zionism, and Ben-Gurion's twenty-three-year-long endeavor to establish "a broad-based labor party" at last bore fruit. This was Ben-Gurion's historic enterprise, and it altered both the face of Zionism and its course. In retrospect, the steps he had taken — the fusion of Poale Zion with Katznelson's nonpartisans to establish Achdut ha-Avodah, the battle to establish the Histadrut's authority, the merger with Ha-Poel ha-Tzair to create Mapai — as well as the ones he had yet to take — the "conquest of Zionism" and the attempts to create a Jewish army in the Second World War — seem to be part of one grand design, entirely conceived to bring about the establishment of the Jewish state.

If Ben-Gurion felt this to be his greatest triumph, so did everyone else. As the convention ended, delegates and guests formed processions, singing and dancing through the rain-flooded streets, carrying their leaders aloft. In vain they sought Ben-Gurion, the hero of the day, to afford him equal honor. "They looked for Ben-Gurion and did not find him because he had made away without anyone seeing him," wrote *Davar*. As always at great moments, he was feeling poorly and had gone home. When the celebrants learned of this, at three in the morning, hundreds marched to his house to cheer him. They camped around his doors and windows, woke the sleeping neighbors, and dragged him out of bed into the street, "singing and cheering in a chorus under Ben-Gurion's direction."[15]

The merger altered the HEC and its secretariat beyond recognition. With 80 percent of the votes at its disposal, in convention and council alike, the new party had total control over the Histadrut, and there was no more need for coalitions or staffing on the basis of party quotas. Now that Ben-Gurion's position was so much stronger, the collegium format also fell by the wayside. It was as if the HEC had simply become the ministry for which he had struggled so hard in the past, and the post of secretary general was now his for the asking. But the Histadrut rule that he had coveted was no longer at the center of his thoughts; he was already looking to a new challenge.

In September 1929 he made this note to himself: "I see two main objectives in the near future: (1) strengthening the worker's position in Palestine; (2) activity abroad of important scope and content. These two are not easy but they are a question of life and death for us." In other words, he destined Mapai not only to direct the Histadrut in Palestine but also to lead the Zionist movement abroad, conceiving of these as inseparable parts of one vital task. "The primary motivation for the merger was not Histadrut matters," he wrote in January 1930, "but rather the great concern for the implementation of Zionism." The new party's objective, therefore, was "the concentration of masses of workers into a single political formation that can become the dominant force in the country and assume political power." It was not by chance that Mapai quickly became known as "the ruling party."[16]

This new challenge dictated that he had to free himself, at least partially, from the weight of his HEC duties, so he sought a stand-in. His choice was Remez, who at Ben-Gurion's request was elected to the HEC secretariat in August 1930 instead of Golomb, who would from then on devote all his time to the Haganah. Gradually Ben-Gurion passed on all his duties to Remez. By 1931 Remez was signing outgoing foreign correspondence as "Secretary General," and in 1932 he was issuing summonses to HEC meetings and signing HEC letters to the International Labor Organization, an area previously reserved exclusively for Ben-Gurion. Remez oversaw the HEC's move to its new and spacious quarters in a hotel converted to an office building at 115 Allenby Street. In 1934 Remez opened the fourth Histadrut convention's second session and delivered the HEC's report, and he chaired HEC meetings even when Ben-Gurion was present. In 1935, the year Ben-Gurion was elected chairman of the Jewish Agency Executive, Remez was elected secretary general of the Histadrut. Between 1930 and 1935 Ben-Gurion had more and more time to work on both the party-Histadrut front and the political-Zionist one.

The first thing he needed was a strong, consolidated Mapai, capable of vigorous expansion, and he had already created a formula for achieving this. As early as 1925 he had set his priorities with the slogan "Organization, labor, and education!" Seeking to make the Histadrut into a quasi workers' state, but lacking the power to legislate or enforce laws, Ben-Gurion put organization at the top of this list as their substitute. In his view this meant turning a voluntary organization — for anyone could join or quit the Histadrut as they pleased — into a disciplined one whose members would be required to respect its authority. "The Jewish worker will endure in Palestine only if organized," he said at the time, and to this end used the most effective tool at hand, the Sick Fund.

In Palestine, which had neither state nor private health services to speak of, or health insurance under either Ottoman or British rule, the Sick Fund, first established by the Organization of Agricultural Workers, was the Histadrut's senior institution. Proliferating and improving its services, the Fund became the largest and most important agent of health insurance and all medical services, to the point where membership in it was more important than getting a job, not only to the laborer but also to other wage earners, and to anyone who could not afford private medical care. "The Sick Fund is the one institution which gives the Histadrut some power," Ben-Gurion declared. That is why he had directed that only card-carrying Histadrut members whose dues were paid up were entitled to belong to it, and that anyone expelled from the Histadrut would automatically have his membership in the Fund revoked. Ben-Gurion thereby made the Fund the most effective organizing tool at the HEC's disposal, and its best moneymaker, as well, since it enforced the payment of dues. Anyone coming to a clinic or hospital had to go first to a special window and present his or her Histadrut membership card, a booklet, in which dues stamps* were affixed.[17]

Ben-Gurion did his best to use the other institutions, too, for organizational ends, including those involved with his second priority, labor. He connected it to employment organization: "Together with continuously maintained organizational effort . . . there must come the true and unceasing concern for employment." The Histadrut would fight with all its strength to enlarge and increase sources of employment in its own and other economic sectors, but it would also remain firm in its insistence on hiring organized labor through its labor exchange, on the trade unions' terms.

Regarding education, the last priority on his list, Ben-Gurion left no doubt that he meant political indoctrination: the organized and employed workers had to be enlightened in order to create "an organization of [labor and political] conquerors." He regarded the reformation of the Jewish character, the "shrewdness" of the Diaspora, as one of Zionism's loftiest goals. The Jews had managed to survive as a minority, he maintained, thanks to "a talent for adapting themselves acquired in the Diaspora"; but "such a talent is the exact opposite of the one we must acquire in Palestine, the talent of asserting ourselves." Ben-Gurion defined this as "the courage to be audacious, daring to initiate, to think and plan in national-state terms, to seek conquests; and the ability to meet the wide-ranging challenge posed by the need for economic, cultural, and social creativity. This is the mission and this is the nature of the *socialist education* which the Histadrut must offer the worker and the new immigrant," an education that would prepare them, ultimately, "to become a nation instead of a class." He aspired to replace passive (and, in his view, sometimes parasitic) Diaspora Jews with a new kind, namely, Jews who could assert their power over circumstances and adapt the environment to suit their purposes.

Within Achdut ha-Avodah as well he had stuck to the same strategy and the same priorities. In October 1925 he told representatives of the party's urban branches, "The party's organizational cell must be the

---

*The system was perfected in 1937 when uniform dues were implemented; one payment covered the various Histadrut dues — to the labor councils, Cultural Committee (in charge of Histadrut schools), the Sick Fund, and so on — and it was no longer possible to be remiss about paying any one of them. The Sick Fund's share of this single payment was 40 percent, so anyone who wanted its services paid an additional 60 percent for services he may not have needed or wanted.

workplace. We must put our people in those cells that haven't any of our members. Our members will go to work according to the party's directive . . . In investing our strength in the workplace we must . . . determine which places are more important and more in need of the party." Party organizing was "more important in the workplace than in the trade union." The effect of his visit to the Soviet Union manifested itself in his profile of Achdut ha-Avodah as "a party which always examines its direction by considering the spirit and needs of the time. Our action must be done in light of reality. If there is a need, we change direction."[18]

He assigned the Tel Aviv branch, which he considered especially important because "Tel Aviv is the most important center of workers," a primary objective, "to embrace half the organized workers in the Histadrut." This could be accomplished either through ideological persuasion or by preferential treatment at the labor exchange. This second method, which of course did not necessarily contradict the first, was faster and easier, but its disadvantage was that it could not be hidden from view. Rival party functionaries were quick to cry discrimination; in the summer of 1928 Ada Maimon wrote in *Ha-Poel ha-Tzair*, "All the 'minorities' silently voice their complaints, as one, that they are being deprived of their labor rights." But this did not deter Ben-Gurion.

Another important directive, which he gave the Achdut ha-Avodah urban branch functionaries in 1925, was that "our members in Histadrut institutions must be in our party's analogue institutions." In other words, whoever served as a delegate to Histadrut conventions should do so at the Achdut ha-Avodah conventions as well; whoever served on the HEC secretariat should also sit in Achdut ha-Avodah's secretariat; an activist in a trade union should also be the functionary in the party cell of that same union; and so on. There were two possible methods of going about this, too; either Histadrut employees could be elected to the party's corresponding institutions, or members of the party could be appointed to the Histadrut institutions. Either way, this move was intended to put Achdut ha-Avodah in control of the workings of the Histadrut, and again, the second was faster and easier, but it had the same disadvantage of being very much in the public eye. Ada Maimon took issue with this: "The Histadrut apparatus, even in the cities, serves, above all, that same majority on whose behalf B.G. speaks."[19]

In 1930 Ben-Gurion took up his strategy with renewed vigor, for if he had felt it was justified before the merger, it was all the more so afterward. One could say discrimination ends when it becomes total. By placing the Histadrut machinery in the hands of Mapai and by favoring its members regarding work opportunities, Ben-Gurion intended pri-

marily to bolster its majority in the Histadrut and to shape it as a disciplined political force. No sooner was the new party established than
Ben-Gurion took up an old habit — sketching in his diaries and notebooks columns and tables that represented the respective strengths of
his party and its rivals, in the city and the country. He wanted details
and went after them, finding that a considerable segment of the apparatus of the Histadrut institutions did not belong to Mapai. Faced with
this situation, Ben-Gurion asked Mapai's Central Committee "to
seriously discuss reforms, purging several places of work, and putting
the party in control of all workplaces in Palestine." In keeping with
this the committee was charged "to make sure that employees are
hired by the Histadrut institutions only with the party's authorization."[20]

With the creation of Mapai Ben-Gurion achieved his long-standing
goal of staffing the Histadrut machinery with functionaries of his own
party and bringing about a homogeneous apparatus. This done, he set
his sights further, on increasing Mapai's members and sympathizers in
the machinery of the Zionist Organization, to gain control over its administration and policy and eventually achieve "the conquest of Zionism."

At its birth Mapai was the strongest political force in the Yishuv, and
through Ben-Gurion's shaping it grew stronger. But something stood
between the party and the conquest of Zionism, a rival that sought the
same goal and also grew stronger, making a confrontation inevitable.

24

Toward a New Venture

"THERE IS NO DANGER of the working public in Palestine turning to the left," Ben-Gurion told the labor council secretaries in 1930, "but there is a great and actual danger of a turn to the right." He was referring to the five-year-old revisionist movement, describing it for the first time as a "danger" worthy of consideration, overcoming his earlier reticence.

What makes his reticence striking is that his colleagues had rapidly sized up the revisionist movement, which had been established in Paris in April 1925, after two years of groundwork. Moshe Beilinson and Eliyahu Golomb, for example, saw immediately that it was a radical-romantic movement, right wing and chauvinistic, which placed its trust in one leader; a movement which "blindly" emulated European nationalist movements, attracting followers by means of "colossal spectacles" and "rhetorical posturing" — ceremony, uniforms, high-flown words, mass meetings, and parades; a movement which favored "uprising and acts of terror" and whose goal was Jewish militarism. It was also clear that revisionism, which advocated a Jewish army, not agriculture and settlement, to deliver Palestine to the Jewish people, was hostile to the Histadrut and labor Zionism. Rejecting peace and diplomacy, it claimed that only through armed conquest and defense could the Zionist enterprise be accomplished. Although the resemblance to Mussolini's movement was obvious from the start, it was June 1926 before Histadrut members in Europe gave the HEC in Tel Aviv an explicit warning, on learning that the nascent movement was about to try to enlist the working masses. "In the course of time they will say that they are the true representatives of the workers, just like the Fascists in Italy."[1]

Ben-Gurion knew all this; in fact, his position in the HEC secretariat afforded him greater familiarity with developments inside the revisionist camp. Moreover, he knew Vladimir Jabotinsky, the movement's founder and leader, personally, and as early as 1918, when they were both serving in the Jewish Battalion, Ben-Gurion had noticed his love of military trappings and mocked it. There are no documents to prove that the repercussions from Jabotinsky's first public lecture, "Jews and Militarism," given in Riga in November 1923 — in whose wake Betar,* the revisionist youth movement, was founded — had reached Ben-Gurion's ears. Nor do we know whether he read either the theses Jabotinsky formulated and published in February 1924 as "The Militarization of Jewish Youth in Palestine and the Diaspora" or "Our Platform," a series of articles in which Jabotinsky expounded the necessity of preparing "broad-based cadres of organized and disciplined youth in Palestine and all the lands of the Diaspora, which will study the arts of war and be prepared to report for duty at the first call-up."

But Jabotinsky's January 1925 article, "The Left," could not possibly have escaped Ben-Gurion's attention, for this was Jabotinsky's first challenge to the Histadrut coalition of Achdut ha-Avodah and Ha-Poel ha-Tzair. Jabotinsky attacked their espoused principle of "building up the land." In his opinion a "revision" (hence the movement's name) was called for: a return to the style of political Zionism exemplified by Herzl's efforts to get a charter from the Sublime Porte for Jewish immigration and settlement in Palestine. Jabotinsky held that the Zionist Organization should see to it that the British government made good on its promise of dense Jewish settlement throughout Palestine by force of arms. If it did not, the Jewish people should do so with a military force it would build for itself. He derided the practical approach of Weizmann and the Histadrut parties, who did not wait for the British to show such good will, but added immigrant to immigrant, dunam to dunam, herd to herd, and settlement to settlement.

The adversarial relations between Jabotinsky and the labor leaders became more evident after the founding of the Revisionist Party. It not only opposed the principle of "building up the land," but also argued that this was too expensive, taking up too much of the Zionist budget and depriving non-Histadrut members of their share. The Fourth Aliyah brought many Jews, mainly from Poland, who came not to be pioneers but to continue their previous lives as small-scale shopkeepers. This influx made Jabotinsky more certain than ever that massive immigration to Palestine was in the cards and that there was no need to waste so much money training individual immigrants for life there. He demanded that the Zionist budget be channeled into private enterprise and settlement, not the Histadrut economy and Histadrut settlement.

---

* Betar is an acronym of the Hebrew for "Trumpeldor's Covenant."

When, in July 1925, his article "Basta!" a cry to halt the flow of funds from the Zionist budget to the Histadrut, was published, it became evident that Jabotinsky was as hostile to Ben-Gurion as he was to the Histadrut. The Histadrut, he wrote, abused its institutions "to establish the childish dictatorship" of its parties, which lasted only because the "Zionist Executive provides for them." If "dictatorship" was aimed at any individual it was Ben-Gurion. In August, writing that the Histadrut leaders needed the Zionist budget "for that same overblown Histadrut political apparatus," Jabotinsky specified Ben-Gurion by name, calling him and his HEC colleagues "cowardly, incompetent" leaders who constituted "a group concerned only with itself."[2]

The revisionist movement's most striking characteristic was its dual structure: it was a party both anchored in the Herzl tradition and subject to political Zionism's legalistic constraints and a radical, quasi-military youth organization bent on extreme activism. In April 1927 this militaristic side arrived in Palestine. First the "high command" and the officer ranks of Betar were set up — first- and second-class "chiefs of fifty," first- and second-class "centurions," and so forth, then the "battalions." On Herzl Memorial Day, July 20, the Betar battalions held their first parade in Palestine. Sixty strong, they wore their brown uniforms, complete with insignia, and carried banners. Perhaps this was the reason Ben-Gurion opted to let Jabotinsky's words pass, for they were still just words, newspaper articles and nothing else.

It was not, however, for its low numbers that the first appearance of Betar was noteworthy, but for its activity. On May 1, 1928, the Revisionists went into action. Following the example of the police, who, as usual, dispersed the May Day demonstrations with a mounted company and nightsticks, the Betar people, too, fell on the marchers, snatching the red flags from their bearers and tearing them to shreds. They were expressing their contempt for the red flag and May Day, and so for the Histadrut, whose symbols these were. *Davar* called the attack "acts of hooliganism by members of the Revisionist youth association," and *Kunteres* remarked, "We have been privileged to see the first fruit of the Revisionist organization's education." *Ha-Aretz* came out against "followers of argumentation and persuasion in the style of Rome," that is, of Mussolini and his Fascists.

The story was carried not only by the newspapers, but also by word of mouth through Palestine, and by the time it reached Ben-Gurion in Tiberias, it had grown out of all proportion. He immediately phoned *Davar* in Tel Aviv and was told that the Histadrut meeting in honor of May Day — attended by his children, his wife, and his father — had passed peacefully. In his diary he noted that Betar was "turning into a fascist band."[3]

After October 5, when Betar attacked a large meeting held by Poale Zion Left in Tel Aviv in honor of Jacob Zerubavel — wounding thirteen, three of them seriously — the group acquired the reputation of a gang of fascist thugs. One figure who helped make this label stick was Abba Achimeir, the founder, in 1927, and leader of the Revisionist Labor Bloc, who had begun publishing his column, "From a Fascist's Notebook," in *Doar ha-Yom*, one of Palestine's three Hebrew dailies, in 1928. When Jabotinsky arrived in Palestine that October 5, Achimeir extended the following welcome in his column. "Let 'Il Duce' not despair because only the few have gathered under his banner. This is the way of the world. The few will rule the many, in the full sense of the word *rule*, either by arms or by faith. 'Il Duce' ought to organize the few here who are capable of obeying his orders." Before 1928 was over, *Doar ha-Yom* came under revisionist control, with Jabotinsky as editor in chief.

Whether the fascist example was followed by many or just a few extremists who held it up as the standard of the movement — contrary to the taste and views of Jabotinsky, whose principles were merely anti-socialist and militaristic — it is still true that in 1928 no real attempt was made either by Jabotinsky or by Betar's commanders to shake off the fascist label. Therefore both *Davar* and *Ha-Aretz* diagnosed the two assaults as the first symptoms of the venom instilled by Betar's fascist indoctrination. But Ben-Gurion's reaction was entirely different. Even though he called them "a fascist band" in his diary, he did not yet label them as such in public, perhaps because he thought it wiser to fight them with actions than with words. He regarded the two attacks as the beginning of a campaign against Histadrut and Zionist institutions, which required action, not protest. Unlike Berl Katznelson, who held that "the worker in Palestine is strong enough to root out the source of the evil in its infancy" but was torn over the question — which he asked Jabotinsky and the public — "Do we want a *civil war* here?" Ben-Gurion promptly declared his own and the Histadrut's readiness to fight fire with fire. "The Hebrew worker will answer not only with words but with appropriate controlled actions, to root out these hoodlumist outrages."[4]

Indeed, Ben-Gurion saw clearly that the Revisionists had come to weaken Histadrut rule and the HEC's predominance in the working community, to destroy all his work. Did he also sense, as early as 1928, that the Revisionists would undermine the authority of the Zionist Organization, even after the labor movement, under his guidance, stood at its head? In any case, Ben-Gurion foresaw a bitter and protracted battle that at its peak would become a civil war, just as Katznelson had darkly prophesied.

Meanwhile, other salient events occurred which explain the hatred that intensified between the two camps and has not been forgotten to this day. On July 3, 1929, a special meeting of the Elected Assembly was held in Tel Aviv's Ohel Shem theater to elect the Yishuv's delegates to the Jewish Agency Council. Disregarding revisionist procedural objections, the Assembly decided to elect a three-man presidium. When the voting started Jabotinsky called out from his seat, "This is trickery, not voting!" at which the chairman reprimanded him, "Jabotinsky, have you no shame?" Interpreting this as an insult, the Revisionists clamored for the chairman to step down, creating a tumult. After a recess of several hours the meeting was called back to order by a new chairman, who apologized on behalf of the presidium for the "mistake" — his predecessor's unfortunate remark.

Ben-Gurion then asked permission to make an announcement. A revisionist delegate at once jumped up, interrupting him with the claim that he had been the first to ask for the floor. An even worse furor erupted, and this time the delegates went for each other's throats. The meeting was adjourned and did not reconvene until the next day, when it was held behind closed doors. Whether Jabotinsky was right in saying that the many labor delegates had ganged up on the few Revisionists, or whether Ben-Gurion was right in saying that a "mass" of Betar people, mustered ahead of time by Jabotinsky, had burst into the auditorium and taken part in "the event," everyone agreed that the first violent disturbance of the Yishuv's democratic process was started by Jabotinsky and his Revisionists. Their assault on the Yishuv's first parliamentary institution only strengthened the view that they were following in the footsteps of Mussolini. *Ha-Aretz* regarded their action as "a brutal attack on [the Elected Assembly's] honor and will," a result of "Il Duce's fascist methods," which did not spare "even the Elected Assembly from terror."[5]

If, as many thought, this attack demonstrated revisionist scorn for the Yishuv's parliamentary democracy, the "Wailing Wall Incident," which occurred next, convinced them that the Revisionists held Zionist Organization authority in equal contempt. The source of this incident was the Mandatory government's policy of recognizing Jewish rights of access to the Wall for the purpose of prayer only. Attempts to evade this restriction by blowing the shofar or by setting up a partition between men and women, which were generally made before Yom Kippur, led the Arabs to fear that the Jews were attempting to extend the bounds of their limited right. To defend their own interest the Arabs built a wall touching the Western Wall on one side and the Haram al-Sharif, their place of veneration, on the other. This innovation in turn spurred suspicions on the Jewish side that the Arabs were taking advantage of the situation to enlarge their rights in the holy place and to incorporate the Western Wall in their domain. At the same time the Arabs' complaints moved the British to act.

On Yom Kippur 1928 the authorities forcibly removed the partition between male and female worshipers that had been erected without a permit, and the spark of religious nationalist sentiment was lit in the Yishuv. Jabotinsky helped fan the flames by calling on the nation to mobilize all its efforts to attain full Jewish rights of worship at the Wall. Meanwhile, Ben-Gurion was trying to prevent a religious war. He exhorted the public to be wary of the trap set by the hostile British administration to draw the Jews into a "bloody war of religion," and at a National Council meeting he entreated his colleagues to downplay the issue of the Wall and holy places lest "we give our enemies an opportunity to spread the libel that Jewish settlement constitutes a threat to Muslim and Christian holy places."

In November the Mandatory government restated its position, reiterating Jewish rights of worship at the Wall and emphasizing that the area where the Wall stood belonged to a *waqf* (a Muslim religious endowment), which was therefore free to build on it. Construction started again, and the Muslims built a passageway through the courtyard in front of the Wall, leading to a joint response from the Zionist Executive, the National Council, and the Chief Rabbis in the form of a statement by the Zionist Executive (endorsed unanimously by the Zionist Congress in Zurich in July 1929) stating its fear that although the government had committed itself to preserve the status quo at the Wall, a mosque was being built there. A special deputation left the Yishuv for London to demand British Foreign Office protection of the Jews' right to observe the traditions of their faith.

As a result a cautious and balanced national policy was formulated: sharp protests to the British government combined with self-restraint concerning demonstrations at the Wall and in Jerusalem as well as other activities liable to be interpreted by the Arabs as a provocation. The apprehension was that the mufti of Jerusalem, Haj Amin al-Husseini, and his lieutenants, with the tacit approval of British officials, would use the Wall dispute to incite violent disturbances. As the fast day of Tisha be'Av, the Ninth of Av, approached, Ben-Gurion reminded the Yishuv of "the resolution of the Zionist Executive and the National Council" ordering restraint from demonstrations on that day. The only group to stray from the fold was the revisionist Zionists. Under their patronage "Wall committees" were organized and joined together in a single council, and the Betar commanders told their people to gather in Jerusalem for a demonstration.

On the Ninth of Av, August 15, 1929, some three hundred Betar members and sympathizers gathered in Jerusalem. With a permit from Harry Luke, stand-in for the high commissioner, at 2:00 P.M. they set out toward the Wall, in a procession flanked by numerous police. Violating their permit, the demonstrators raised the national flag in front of the Wall, made speeches, called out, "The Wall is ours," observed a moment of silence, and sang the national anthem, "Ha-Tikvah." On their way to the Wall and back they crossed the Muslim quarter and stopped in front of the Zionist Executive offices. In Zion Square they hoisted the flag and sang "Ha-Tikvah," then dispersed. Whether the rumors that reached the mufti's ears — that the demonstrators wanted "to capture the Wall," among other things — were exaggerated or not, the demonstration clearly served him as good cause for a counter-demonstration. The next day, the Muslim day of rest, a rally of two thousand Arabs, many from as far away as Nablus, was held. Led by the sheiks of the Al-Aqsa Mosque, they chanted slogans and waved flags. This was the harbinger of the riots of 1929, which spread throughout Palestine, leaving 133 Jews slain and 339 injured.

It was generally believed among Zionists and British alike that Betar was responsible for the demonstration in front of the Wall that provoked the Arabs to riot. Some forty years later Betar not only admitted its responsibility but also glorified the event as "the first act of revolt against the Zionist institutions and the British government," celebrating its bravery and congratulating itself for "the spirit of the national revolt." Ben-Gurion had been right in maintaining that the Revisionists' rejection of Zionist authority was a bad omen. A confrontation was inevitable.[6]

It started on the Histadrut level. In July 1929 Jabotinsky found it necessary to publish a "warning": "Zionism has no future . . . unless a social balance is secured." Since, in his opinion, the Histadrut had become so strong — "to an extent beyond compare . . . except in Russia" — it was imperative that the disproportion be redressed forthwith. He charged his party and its Revisionist Labor Bloc with the task of strengthening the propertied class and weakening the Histadrut in order to strike a proper socioeconomic balance between them. In the same warning Jabotinsky described the Histadrut as a limb of the Yishuv's body "that has swollen to seven times its natural size and weight . . . and in the end it will smother the body." He labeled Histadrut leaders "hacks, who in public matters behave like gypsy horse thieves in the market . . . writers who sold their conscience for a whore's fee . . . Mammon lords waving the red rag." They were *"canaille,"* despicable riffraff whose mentality led them "to pollute the air with the venom of cynicism and class hatred" and to suppress the other classes taking part in the building up of the land. After these harsh words Jabotinsky signed off with a prophetic warning. "This psychology will poison the entire Zionist enterprise unless we overpower its bearers. It will be impossible to breathe in Palestine if such as these rule." He called for the establishment of a new, "national" Histadrut to replace the "class" one.

Ben-Gurion, the leader of the canaille, returned no fire; for the moment, he was satisfied with a single punch. About two months after the warning, on behalf of Achdut ha-Avodah and Ha-Poel ha-Tzair, he made a public statement in *Kunteres* about the incidents of Av in which he said, "We must be on guard lest chauvinism inflame us. Like a putrid weed drawing sustenance from a befouled source, revisionism is liable to mushroom and spread in the Yishuv. . . . With all our moral strength we must rise against this false nationalist fervor, the diatribe and bravado which together cast a shadow over the emancipating and humanitarian content of the Zionist idea."

That he did not intend to waste energy on speeches and articles is evidenced by the fact that immediately following the attack on the Poale Zion Left meeting he began assembling a "dossier" on Jabotinsky: records of what he said to Zionist bodies, newspaper articles published by Jabotinsky on three continents and in four languages, and particularly proof that he was not the author of the idea for the Jewish battalions in the world war and thus did not deserve his popular title, Father of the Battalions. As the dossier grew thicker, material for ripostes and all-out attacks piled up in Ben-Gurion's hands, but only a tiny bit of it found its way into his scattered denunciations of Jabotinsky. He was saving his ammunition for a decisive battle.

At the same time he was aware of the strengthening of the Revisionist Labor Bloc, which, as the National Workers' Organization, would one day aspire to replace the Histadrut. "The Bloc" opposed organized labor on principle. It advocated a "neutral" labor exchange, administered and supervised by officers appointed by the national institutions, an exchange in which all would be equal, members of trade unions and nonmembers alike. The employers gladly encouraged this position, which created a new obstacle to Ben-Gurion's proposal of a joint Histadrut-employers labor exchange.

The signal for the start of this attempt to undermine the Histadrut was given in October 1929, when Betar's central command in Palestine announced the establishment of a new department for immigration and settlement, and in February 1930 it began to handle organized groups of Betar immigrants and send them to Rehovot, where a camp for their absorption was set up. Since Betar was organized in battalions, these groups became its work companies, which veteran Revisionists, who quit the Histadrut, also joined. This was probably what lay behind

Ben-Gurion's statement that the Yishuv was threatened by a dangerous shift to the right.

These companies, however, had only one hundred members in 1930, and their number remained small for the next three years. Breaking the Histadrut's monopoly on the labor market seemed quite beyond their reach. Nevertheless, Ben-Gurion and the Histadrut feared that this was just the beginning, that these companies would draw sustenance from Betar's growing strength abroad. In 1934 Betar had seventy thousand members, forty thousand in Poland. Ben-Gurion, apprehensive that there would one day be scores of companies scattered throughout Palestine, could not treat Betar lightly. As it turned out, no major organization was needed to threaten the Histadrut labor exchange's exclusivity; twenty-five Betar men were enough.[7]

In March 1930 the Betar command moved into action by sending a work company to Kefar Saba to reinforce the growers there who wished to thwart the founding of the joint exchange between the Histadrut and the agricultural committee. Seventeen Betar workers refused to register, saying that they were following orders from their central command, and on April 2, as prearranged, they went to work for these growers. "The workers of Kefar Saba could not, of course, agree to this," announced the Histadrut, which forbade them to begin work. Called to Kefar Saba, Ben-Gurion tried in vain to convince the Betar company leader that he and his men were "in the hands of those who fought the worker, whether for political reasons or out of opposition to organized labor." The Betar men were then "removed" from their work by force; in reaction, the growers imposed a lockout. Thus began one of the most severe and notorious labor disputes in the history of the Yishuv. Unlike its forerunners, it was a three-way controversy — between the Histadrut, the farmers, and Betar — in which for the first time workers — Betar workers — and employers stood shoulder to shoulder against the Histadrut in their call for a neutral exchange.

Ben-Gurion objected to this neutral exchange on two counts. The first arose from his faith in the Histadrut as the principal, if not sole, bearer of the task of implementing Zionism and its central mission of increasing immigration. Ben-Gurion suspected that the other groups, which a neutral exchange would have to take into consideration, were self-serving, concerned with temporary benefits only, and he feared that in the wake of an economic slump, unemployment, or any other adverse circumstance they would most likely opt for the easiest way out — cutting immigration. The other reason was practical: the national institutions — the Zionist Executive and the National Council — were not a government and had no means of enforcement at their disposal; obedience to them was voluntary. Moreover, the farmers and industrialists refused to honor not only their authority, but that of their own organizations as well, as had been evident in the Histadrut's negotiations with the agricultural committees over the issue of organized Jewish labor. If they would not toe the line for their own organizations, what was to make them cooperate with a neutral exchange?

Ben-Gurion regarded Jabotinsky's call for a neutral exchange that would accept national binding arbitration as intentionally misleading, for Betar defied the national institutions more than any other group in Palestine. Would these Revisionists, who had disregarded the institutions' explicit instruction, "respect the Zionist Congress's authority in labor matters?" asked Ben-Gurion. He lambasted the neutral exchange as "Jabotinsky's biggest lie yet," under cover of which he and his Revisionists were trying to render the Histadrut impotent.

Ben-Gurion had a third reason to object to the neutral exchange: Trigger-happy, ever ready to join a fight, even a losing one, he recognized it as the best way to make a cause tangible and rally the rank and file behind it. Unlike Berl Katznelson and Joseph Sprinzak, Ben-Gurion believed that a fighting Histadrut had a better chance of growing stronger than a complacent one. In discussing the Kefar Saba affair, Ben-Gurion called on the HEC to fight the joint exchange's opponents even though "we have a 50 percent chance of winning. Even if we lose I will not give up in advance. . . . We may take a beating in Kefar Saba, but that kind of beating can only strengthen us."

To his mind such a war became even more necessary after organized labor was also disrupted in the urban industrial and construction sectors, particularly in Jerusalem, under the influence of the Betar companies and the Betar and Revisionist Workers' Organization.* In 1931 and 1932 Ben-Gurion laid down two rules for fighting the Revisionists: public opinion had to be won over to organized Hebrew labor; and, as in any war, all tactics were allowable — it was imperative "to create the proper atmosphere and fight the war using any and all means, even harassment of those who defy organized labor."[8]

Yet he was not quick to move into action, for the Hapoel Squadrons, his answer to the Betar companies, had not yet reached readiness. This was partly because the party lost confidence in Joseph Hecht, handpicked by Ben-Gurion to build up the Squadrons in May 1929, and in 1931 he lost his position as Haganah commander in chief. Ben-Gurion

---

* The Betar and Revisionist Workers' Organization, which grew out of the Revisionist Labor Bloc, served as the basis for the establishment of the National Workers' Organization in July 1934.

opted to replace him with Israel Shochat, who had already proved himself an outstanding builder of clandestine organizations with a fine sensitivity to class issues.

Ben-Gurion had forgiven Shochat his former sins and had no qualms in reinstating him to a position befitting his experience and ability, believing that this time Shochat would accept Histadrut authority. He took the precaution, however, of making Shochat a member of a committee to establish the Squadrons, whose other members were prominent Haganah chiefs and Mapai functionaries.

But there was also an ideological reason for Ben-Gurion's delay. Not everybody in Mapai was happy with a Histadrut "defense force." Katznelson and Beilinson strongly objected to violence in general, and violence sanctioned by the Histadrut in particular. They joined forces with others in reaction to Ben-Gurion's explicit statement, in May 1932, that Hapoel "must carry out Histadrut tasks (on picket lines, in strikes)," and the HEC secretariat appointed a special representative to Hapoel's directorate. By that summer, lists of candidates for the Squadrons were drawn up, upsetting the people who opposed using a sports organization for political purposes.[9]

This opposition was neutralized by the Froumine strike in Jerusalem, which gave new impetus to the establishment of the Hapoel Squadrons. Early in October 1932, members of the Revisionist Workers' Organization took over the jobs of Histadrut members who were striking against the biscuit bakery. Skirmishes between revisionist scabs and Histadrut pickets, which continued for four months, captured public and press attention, inflaming passions. When the conflict began Jabotinsky was publishing the first of a series of scathing articles from Paris — he had left Palestine in July 1929, and the Mandatory government had prohibited his return — stressing the need to "break" the Histadrut's monopoly on the labor market. These articles so angered Mapai, the Histadrut, and large sectors of the public that Ben-Gurion could consider that his preparation of public opinion for the war — the proper "atmosphere" — had been accomplished for him by Jabotinsky.

The war he was priming for was different from all its predecessors. No longer would it be limited geographically or to a single issue. This one extended the length and breadth of the Histadrut in Palestine and of the Zionist movement throughout the world. Ben-Gurion considered it his premier appearance as a Zionist leader outside Palestine. Additionally, the immense proportions of the battlefield precluded his personal involvement in every stage of the conflict; he had to function as commander in chief. Embarking on the most prodigious venture of his career, he needed a solid party and a strong Histadrut with a "defense force" and, even more important, strength of body and soul and firm family support.

The vigor, audacity, and long hours — sixteen to eighteen a day — that characterized Ben-Gurion's activity and bore witness to his incredible capacity for work were also a sure sign of good health and unfailing strength of mind and body. As small as he was — five feet four inches in shoes and 131 pounds fully clothed — he was a human dynamo whose unflagging work pattern was hardly ever disrupted. The very fact that since his return from his mission to London not a year had passed without his falling ill at least once — some years two or three times — reinforces this conclusion. Had Ben-Gurion, a heavy smoker, suffered from a chronic disease or serious physical malfunction, his health would certainly have broken under such stress.

Even so, his third-class travel — no small feat in those days — and heavy work load left their mark. "I am worn down, my nerves have been destroyed completely, and my working capacity diminished," he complained in letters to his friends. As a result, in January 1926, "the doctors have forced me to check into a Sick Fund convalescent home in Motza." He was forced to take the first vacation of his life. Even then his colleagues were constantly telephoning, paying working visits, and calling him to meetings in Jerusalem. During one of these harried excursions he came down with a cold, but participated in an agricultural convention meeting in Haifa despite a fever.

Soon he was called to the He-Chalutz convention in Danzig and the immigration conference of the Trade Unions International in London. His doctors prohibited him from going abroad, "but who minds orders these days?" Ben-Gurion asked — with a touch of vainglorious self-sacrifice — in a letter to a friend, and he sailed off at the beginning of March. His plan to use his trips to and from meetings and conventions for recuperation proved abortive. He did little in the meetings he took part in and felt restless in the towns where he had hoped to find peace. Although he visited Płońsk and his sister in Lódź, he did not regain his strength. Finally, on April 20, he left for the health resort of Enghien-les-Bains, near Paris, where he stayed until the end of May. On June first he sailed for home from Marseilles, without having been to the immigration conference in London.[10]

In July 1927, at the height of the third Histadrut convention, Ben-Gurion took to his bed. His head ached and he ran a low, intermittent fever, which, despite medication, persisted through August. Blood tests did not help his doctors to diagnose his illness, and on August 16 they sent him back to Motza. Unable to determine what ailed him, the five doctors he consulted disagreed; three ordered him to stay in bed, while the other two maintained that he would be better off if he did travel — after his fever subsided — since he was not allowed to rest in Palestine.

On August 24 Ben-Gurion left for the Zionist Congress in Basel, but while he was at sea his fever returned. He meticulously noted his temperature in his diary two, three, and four times daily, betraying his anxiety. At its worst it rose to 100 degrees Fahrenheit. On the train from Genoa to Milan, three entries report, it dropped below 98.6, but it reappeared in Basel. "I had a temperature for most of the Congress, and now I must start recovering all over again," Ben-Gurion wrote to Golomb after seeking advice. Dr. Alexander Zelkind, an internist and director of the Hadassah Hospital in Jerusalem, a regular guest at the Zionist congresses, instructed him "to go immediately . . . to a place where it doesn't rain and it's not cold, to lie in bed all day, and walk around a bit until two weeks go by without a trace of fever."

He found such a place on September 16 — a boarding house in the town of Fontenay-sous-Bois, near Paris. On request the HEC gave him twenty pounds for his stay there. Ben-Gurion promised Golomb that he would remain "until I get rid of this fever once and for all." The fever did leave, but headaches returned to plague him, and for the first week he suffered insomnia. He stayed at Fontenay a month.[11]

No doubt Ben-Gurion needed diversion even more than physical convalescence, so after the headaches ended, instead of returning quickly to Palestine, he remained in Paris, overjoyed to discover that the trial of Shalom Schwartzbard for the assassination of Simon Petlyura was about to begin.* It opened on October 18, and Ben-Gurion dashed off a cable to *Davar* on an item he pulled from the Parisian press. The next day, learning that all the Jewish foreign correspondents had received press passes on referral of their consulates, he tried to do the same, but in vain. He could only report what he read in the Paris newspapers and what he heard from the Jewish correspondents. *Davar* touted him as a "special correspondent" and faithfully printed all his cables. On October 26, when the trial concluded, Ben-Gurion sent off the good news: "Not guilty!"

There is no doubt that he enjoyed himself thoroughly in this role and practically banished the Histadrut from his mind. But on October 28 two telegrams from Palestine asking for his return date drew him back to reality. After receiving twenty-five pounds for travel expenses and unpaid bills from the HEC, Ben-Gurion sailed from Marseille on No-

---

*On May 25, 1926, Shalom Schwartzbard, a young Russian Jew, had shot and killed Simon Petlyura, the founder of the Ukrainian Social-Democratic Workers' Party and the war minister of the independent Ukraine until the revolution of February 1917. Riots in which 100,000 Jews had been killed were attributed to Petlyura and his armies.

vember 4. He reached Tel Aviv on November 10; by the eleventh he was up to his ears in work.[12]

In April 1928 the headaches started again. In June Ben-Gurion, Paula, and Renana went to Rehovot for a brief vacation, but since Ben-Gurion was periodically called to meetings in Tel Aviv it was not very restful. During his annual trip abroad that summer he was constantly ill with stomach cramps and diarrhea, which he thought were dysentery and treated with large doses of Epsom salts. After six days he was better, but a few days later his fever and headaches returned, as if by appointment. In Berlin he confided to his diary, "I felt as though malaria had attacked me. The fever rose to 99.1° Fahrenheit; I was forced . . . to lie down."

In 1928 the unexplained syndrome of a low-grade fever, sometimes accompanied by shivers, and a headache struck twice in one year for the first time. The next year was a bit easier, and Ben-Gurion complained only once, in June, at the height of the Zionist Actions Committee meetings in Berlin, writing his HEC colleagues, "I was not feeling well and could not take part in the last meetings." By comparison, in 1930 the usual ailments were accompanied by a nagging pain in his leg and bluish spots on his thigh. On the basis of a blood test Dr. Aaron Binyamini diagnosed a renal problem. Paula made Ben-Gurion promise to get a second opinion from a renowned doctor in Paris, though her husband was satisfied with Binyamini's opinion, explaining his fatigue to his associates as being caused by the renal problem. But in July Ben-Gurion wrote them from Europe, "The pain in my leg . . . turned into a pain in both legs, which seem as though filled with lead, and walking is difficult. I will go to Paris and learn my fate." It could have been the first sign of lumbago, from which he suffered considerably in later years, but this simple diagnosis did not occur to any of his doctors.

He was examined on July 14 by the renowned Dr. Pierre Abrami, a disciple and research associate of Dr. Fernand Widal, a world-famous bacteriologist and pioneer in renal pathology. Abrami looked over Binyamini's letter and declared that he had no faith whatsoever in laboratory tests done in Palestine, which had shown a high level of albumin in Ben-Gurion's urine. This not only indicated kidney malfunction but was a sign of congestive heart failure; the result of Abrami's examination, however, showed that "the heart is sound and normal and no abnormality was found." Another blood test proved beyond doubt that there had been a mistake in the earlier test and, Ben-Gurion reported to Paula, "there are no signs of any organic disease, and I do not need treatment or a diet, but absolute rest for at least two months. Also, I must take no part in any issue that concerns me particularly and I should have clean air. The main thing is to slow down and rest."[13]

The doctor determined that Ben-Gurion's chronic sickness was a result of mental stress, not physical illness. Although Ben-Gurion took Abrami's advice seriously, his indisposition was never definitively diagnosed, most likely because a few weeks later it disappeared as mysteriously as it had appeared, and never recurred. Either the work and its concomitant stress were both the cause and the cure of his sickness or the knowledge that he was suffering from mental stress and not from an organic disorder resulted in a full recovery. In any case, not only did he not take a vacation in 1930, but from the Empire Labour Conference in London he went to another conference in Berlin, of the League of Labor Palestine, and after that to the United States for an exhausting speaking tour.

For the next few years his recovery was complete. He took no sick leave in 1931, or in 1932 or 1933 — the years of his great odyssey for "the conquest of Zionism" — or afterward. The sole drastic measure he took regarding his health was to quit smoking in 1940 when he was in London as the city braced for the war effort. He did it not because he was feeling poorly or on doctor's orders, but because of his son, Amos.

"If I stop smoking, will you?" Ben-Gurion had asked him.

"Yes," Amos answered. Then, turning the idea over in his mind, he'd added hurriedly, "But you're going to London. . . . You'll smoke there."

"I told him," said Ben-Gurion subsequently, "that if I smoked in London, I would wire him immediately, saying, 'You can smoke.' It was difficult not to smoke as I had for many years, seventy to eighty cigarettes a day. But when I remembered that I would have to send my son a telegram, I held firm and left off smoking." But Amos did not quit.[14]

After the wage committee reinstated the obligations of HEC members in 1927, Ben-Gurion's financial situation worsened considerably. In February 1929 his debts to the HEC totaled 195.235 Palestinian pounds. The sum he owed was composed of many small debts, none of which he could pay on time. Trying to help him, the HEC and other Histadrut agencies sometimes found him new loans to cover the old ones, and sometimes deferred payment on the old ones. Unfortunately, this made his situation worse, and he wound up deeper in debt. The HEC also offered to increase his salary from 22.5 to 26 Palestinian pounds, in accordance with a special clause permitting them to take into account any case in which "the wage is insufficient to allow for the worker's special situation and the institution cannot do without him."

But Ben-Gurion, who had had a hand in the HEC resolution concerning the pay scale, was unwilling to be such a "case" and accordingly notified the wage committee that he would accept only a salary "in strict accordance with the scale." To properly appreciate this it should be noted that Joseph Aharonovitch, the director of Bank ha-Poalim, and Shlomo Kaplansky, chairman of the HEC economic committee, demanded a monthly wage of 30 Palestinian pounds and refused to accept any cut whatsoever. That Ben-Gurion took pride in his stance is illustrated by a comparison he made in his diary between his and their wages. There can be no doubt that his refusal to accept the higher pay stemmed from his desire to serve as an example in the face of the rising tide of wage inflation in the Histadrut. On the other hand, the fact that his debts to the HEC and the Histadrut institutions continued to grow makes it clear that he derived certain benefits from his high office, though it was a modest fringe benefit.

From February 1928 on, therefore, Ben-Gurion was paid 22.5 Palestinian pounds a month, leaving him and his family too little money to live on after the deduction for his debts. Knowing this would happen, in refusing the wage committee's offer he had added, "Since this is not enough for me and my family to live on, I will have to take on another job, in journalism." But until extra money started to come in, he was forced to increase his debts. To make things worse, the HEC itself was in the red more than once, and since no wage could be paid nothing could be deducted. For this reason the HEC did not transfer Ben-Gurion's payments to the cooperative loan bank in June 1930, and the bank threatened legal action. His IOUs to Hopenko for the piano were three months overdue, and he borrowed 15 Palestinian pounds from the HEC thrift fund. How much more he borrowed is unknown, but in February 1931 his debts to the HEC totaled 229.136 Palestinian pounds — 40 more than in 1929, but 54.4 fewer than in 1927. Despite all this Ben-Gurion took on a new financial obligation, in the light of which all his past debts paled. In 1930 he undertook to build himself a house. Called Ben-Gurion House, it still stands at 17 Ben-Gurion Boulevard.[15]

The burden of securing the first loan to begin construction — 350 Palestinian pounds from Bank ha-Poalim — and of submitting the blueprints to the municipal building department fell entirely on Paula. After presenting a request for guaranty to the HEC, Ben-Gurion left for Europe. In his letters he pumped Paula for information. "What about the loan and the house? Did you start on this yet or are there new delays? Is the loan settled?" "What have you decided regarding the house? Will you start looking for a plan or wait for my return?" But Paula's health, as usual, began to falter the moment he left. This time her condition necessitated "surgery." The more letters he sent, the fewer he got. In mid August she wrote that "the matter of the house" would be settled within "a day or two," and then she would write again, even though she had already received the blueprints from the Solel Boneh technical office. In fact, on August 26 Paula had submitted them to the building department along with a signed request for a license to build. But to Ben-Gurion she wrote only of the dire straits she and the children were in.

Ben-Gurion, in Berlin, was shaken. "I don't know what has happened with the money. Can't you get the necessary sum — whatever it is — with the help of Golomb or Brudny [Itzhak Brudny of Bank ha-Poalim]? You must get a loan of 15–20 pounds at once, apart from my salary, so that you will be able to get everything you need." His anxiety over her need for "surgery" and his concern for the children left him in such a state that "I can hardly concentrate," and for the umpteenth time he wrote the lines that betrayed — at least to Paula — his egocentrism. "You must spend whatever is necessary to protect your health, which is one and the same as mine and the children's. I implore you, Paula, to do this for me and for the children if not for yourself."

Her physical condition did not keep Paula from going to the HEC to finalize Ben-Gurion's request for guaranty. On November 17 Kaplan brought it up again. This time the HEC resolved in favor and notified Bank ha-Poalim that "if . . . Comrade D. Ben-Gurion does not repay you what he owes on the loan for 350 Palestinian pounds, we hereby guarantee to make up the loss of half that sum." The bank would be responsible for the other half. The HEC guaranty was based on pay deductions of 4 Palestinian pounds monthly from Ben-Gurion's salary, to begin in July 1931 and continue until payment was complete.

Paula scarcely reported this important development to Ben-Gurion. The bulk of her letters was devoted to her misery and exhaustion. Ben-Gurion, who planned to go from London to the United States, wrote her, "I am very worried on account of your last letters. I hope that upon my return home you'll feel better and that you'll be able to rest also. Yours always, with love and concern."[16]

Paula's blueprint showed two rooms plus a kitchen and a bath on the ground floor, totaling 72 square meters (775 square feet), and one large room, about 41 square meters (441 square feet), on the second. Including the sun porch and verandah, the floor space totaled 134 square meters (1,442 square feet). Even though the plans were fairly conventional, the thickness of the walls on the second floor, the width of the staircase leading to it, and the location of a separate lavatory near the main entry betrayed intentions of future expansion on the second floor. Although the building department realized this, it was unable to reject the plans because of Ben-Gurion's political position, and they were approved with a restriction: "Construction of another story on this building will not be permitted." However, when — shortly after the foundations were laid — a second request was submitted, over Ben-Gurion's signature, to make the room on the top floor 7 square meters larger and to enclose the ground-floor porch, it was approved. The sun porch, of course, turned into an additional room. In the end Ben-Gurion's two-story home rose above the single-story houses alongside it and was the largest house in workers' quarters A in north Tel Aviv.

On June 5, 1931, Ben-Gurion and his family moved into their as yet incomplete new home. On the sixteenth he calculated "household accounts" in his diary: construction, the engineer's fee, insurance, taxes, legal fees, and so on, totaled 617.663 Palestinian pounds. Added to that was the cost of new furniture and the moving fee, for a grand total of 641.263 Palestinian pounds. He obtained a mortgage for 180 from a mortgage and credit bank and another, for 40, from another bank. Including the loan from Bank ha-Poalim, his total debt on the house came to 570 pounds, and the grand total of his debts amounted to more than 956 Palestinian pounds. It is clear that his debt did not upset him too much: the IOUs he had given the HEC treasury in 1927 for 198.5 Palestinian pounds, as an arrangement to repay half his debt, remained uncollected.

On June 18, 1931, Ben-Gurion, with a light heart, left for his yearly trip to Europe, which he could not have done without the knowledge that his HEC colleagues were putting their heads together to figure out how to get him out of the red. The HEC secretariat resolved to credit him with 82.5 Palestinian pounds for the vacations he had not taken for three years, although the more exacting Histadrut controller would acknowledge only 22.5 of credit. What was more, in May 1932 Ben-Gurion actually added a new deduction against his salary for payments on a life insurance policy for 200 Palestinian pounds.

Paula employed another form of credit. Her tab at the grocery was nearing its limit, so she begged credit from other stores. In May 1932 her housekeeping debts reached 37 Palestinian pounds. Left with no option, Ben-Gurion started borrowing from his colleagues in the HEC again, listing his scrounging in his diary just as he had in his first days in the secretariat: "I borrowed 2 Palestinian pounds from Eliyahu [Golomb]"; and "from Marom, 5 Palestinian pounds (2 for the municipality, 3 for Paula)." When this source, too, dried up he turned to the secretariat employees, borrowing a pound from this one and 25 piasters from that, and finally to the employees of the Tel Aviv Labor Council, from whom he would borrow sums as small as 10 piasters. He was clearly living at a deficit, and his only recourse was to arrange for new loans. In April 1933 he received a 10-pound interest-free loan from Bank ha-Poalim. This is just a rough sketch of Ben-Gurion's finances; the prospects of anyone's ever compiling a complete record of his debts and their repayment seem beyond the realm of the possible.[17]

As it turned out, his confidence in his ability to defray his debts by writing proved justified. His book *We and Our Neighbors*, published in June 1931, became a best seller. The articles he began publishing late in 1932 and throughout 1933 in the foreign press were lucrative indeed. He received £2.5 for an article in a London paper, $15 apiece for those in New York's *Morgen Journal,* and £2.5 apiece from the Warsaw *Hajnt.* In February and March 1933 alone his articles earned him $30 and £10 sterling, or 16 Palestinian pounds altogether. In the years that followed, his earnings from writing doubled.

The house also served as an important source of revenue. Paula rented it to tourists who came to the seashore while Ben-Gurion was abroad during the summers. She would pile herself and her children into one room, lock the library on the second floor, and leave the rest of the house at her tenants' disposal. Sometimes she earned some money by working as a nurse at the lifeguard station on the Gordon beach in Tel Aviv. Within a few years Ben-Gurion repaid all his debts, his account at Bank ha-Poalim accrued some interest, and he could improve and enlarge his home significantly.

This spacious house — only a very few of his colleagues had anything like it — was both a means and a symbol. Its small front garden and lawn were important to him, not only as an emblem of a warm, closely knit family caring for its well-ordered surroundings, but also as a reminiscence of — and expression of identification and solidarity with — the agricultural life he and his HEC colleagues had left behind. His 1932 and 1933 letters to Paula from Europe were full of questions like "Did you plant anything in front of the house?" and "What did you do with the flowers we planted? Have they all bloomed yet?"

The house was also a material expression of Ben-Gurion's soaring aspirations. Since his early days his grand design had steered his life's course. To him this was provided by his home, particularly by his study. Ensconced amid his many volumes, he felt rooted in the past, firmly planted by the springs of Judaism, ancient Palestine and the East, socialist doctrine and Western culture, assured of solid footing and recognition in the Histadrut, and ready to assault the targets of the future. The house also symbolized his elevated social position. Guests admitted to his home did not gain immediate audience with Ben-Gurion. To get to his room they first had to climb a staircase, and when they got there they could comfortably sit back in the 48-square-meter (516-square-foot) study, enlarged to 80 square meters (861 square feet) in 1946. He had come a long way since his efforts to make the Histadrut one labor army and great commune.

In his first year of guiding the Histadrut secretariat Ben-Gurion had mapped out the road before him. The establishment of "unity of the working class" was not Achdut ha-Avodah's ultimate objective, he believed, but merely a precondition for the realization of socialist Zionism. Once he regarded "Histadrut control over all labor issues" as complete and the "unity of the working class" as established, Ben-Gurion set out to achieve "workers' control of national life and society," to shape a third artifact — the Zionist Organization — and thereby inaugurate a further stage of development.[18]

It was as if, with the completion of his home, his leadership had crystallized and he had all he needed, in the personal and public spheres, to set the transition from class to nation in motion.

25

Conquests

I N 1932 forty-six-year-old David Ben-Gurion stood on the threshold
of a course different from any he had yet started, and though it was
a continuation of his past efforts, it was not necessarily their logical
consequence. The Ben-Gurion who began grooming his party to assume the mantle of leadership of the world Zionist movement was a
man of the world, no longer confined to a single way of life or a narrow
ideological, organizational, or ethical commitment. This change had
overtaken him almost simultaneously in both his public and private
life.

One of Ben-Gurion's basic tenets had always been that Zionism
could be fulfilled only by the power of the worker, and so the worker
had to lead the Zionist movement — and the Jewish nation as well,
once it opened its eyes and realized that its future lay in Zionism. Ben-
Gurion therefore spoke of the "conquest of Zionism," although he
never intended the worker to seize control by force. This was a sister
slogan to those coined by Second Aliyah pioneers. Just as the conquest
of labor meant adapting oneself to physical labor and the conquest of
the land meant no more than agricultural settlement, so the conquest
of Zionism was Ben-Gurion's call to his party to rally all its resources to
gain a majority in order to take over the Zionist movement by a democratic process.

His colleagues were of one mind with him on this issue, but many
differed on two essential points: when and how. Regarding the first,
there was a vague dread that history had allotted only so much time for
the implementation of the Zionist enterprise and that that time might
run out, never to return. David Lloyd George, British prime minister
and Zionist sympathizer, had expressed this best. The Jews had been
offered an opportunity by the Balfour Declaration and by the British

Mandate in the spirit of that declaration, and it was up to the Jews to respond to it and become the majority of Palestine's inhabitants. "You have no time to waste. Today the world is like the Baltic before a frost. For the moment it is still in motion. But if it gets set, you will have to batter your heads against the ice blocks and wait for a second thaw," he said to Chaim Weizmann in 1920, after the Mandate was confirmed. The dread was that British sympathy, a change of attitude likened to the thawing of a sea of ice, had a time limit, and that what Zionism — the vessel crossing that sea — failed to accomplish within this period of grace would be lost forever.[1]

Ben-Gurion had his own analogy for characterizing the historical opportunities that arise in the wake of great upheavals. Paraphrasing a Jewish legend that tells of a single moment in the year in which the sky splits and every wish is granted, he would tell his colleagues, "In this play of historic forces sometimes a great historic chance appears ... sometimes a movement must have the historical sense to seize that moment."[2] Ben-Gurion, by his very nature a man in a hurry, felt a premonition that time was short, to the degree that the race against time turned into the driving force behind his political thinking and actions. Nowhere did his anxiety manifest itself so acutely as in his resolution to conquer Zionism; the ground was burning under Ben-Gurion's feet.

As early as 1922 Ben-Gurion had said, "Until now we thought the Zionist Organization was the means by which Zionism would be fulfilled, and we have directed our activity accordingly. We have been disillusioned in this belief; I am absolutely clear on this. We must find another means. The only one capable of it is the workers' organization in Palestine." That December he told Achdut ha-Avodah's third convention, "The Zionist Organization is now merely a redundant, obstructive partition between the people and the real practitioners of Zionism." Therefore he urged Achdut ha-Avodah to become "a party whose prime objective is to put the Histadrut in control of all labor interests and the workers in control of national and social life." True to his nature he did not wait for a resolution from the convention before beginning to do so.

But his HEC colleagues, even those who believed in the Histadrut's historic and political vocation and longed for its achievement, did not feel the same urgency. Recognizing the primacy of the World Zionist Organization — the proof being that they participated in the Zionist Executive despite Ben-Gurion's protests — and trusting its chairman, Weizmann, to work for immigration in general and labor immigration in particular, they wanted the Histadrut to grow at a slower pace that would allow for fostering a society of workers faithful to class and pioneering principles through fundamental education and training of the individual and the collective. For the moment the Histadrut was neither large enough nor strong enough for the far-reaching national task Ben-Gurion wanted to assign it, and it would collapse beneath such a burden.

In 1927 his colleagues might have felt they could congratulate themselves for not being swept away by what seemed like Ben-Gurion's fantasy. Aware that without the Zionist Executive's financial support the Histadrut could not have established even a single agricultural settlement or industry, they saw during that difficult year that without the support, Solel Boneh would have gone down the drain, dragging the rest of the institutions with it. David Horowitz, who would eventually become the first governor of the Bank of Israel, expressed this feeling best at the third Histadrut convention. "We have established cooperative institutions with the pretension of being a state. . . . We were trying for something beyond our reach." Katznelson and Arlosoroff used similar language in taking the Histadrut to task for its pretensions, which were, by and large, Ben-Gurion's.[3]

Before further controversy over the Histadrut's ultimate goal could take place, however, Zionist fortunes took a turn for the worse. First, large numbers of the Fourth Aliyah — which Jabotinsky and the Histadrut's opponents called the wave of private capital and initiative that would prove itself equal, if not superior to, the Third Aliyah's workers, pioneers, and Histadrut followers — deserted Palestine. Other issues were the chill in British relations with Zionism and the partiality of its officials, in both London and Jerusalem, toward the Arabs; the imminent independence of some Arab states; the galloping anti-Semitism in Poland; and the United States' closing its doors to immigrants. These developments put pressure on Ben-Gurion to seek new and speedier ways to implement Zionism, and at the 1925 Zionist Congress in Vienna he first uttered the slogan "From class to nation" to the labor bloc. He called for the expansion of the labor movement into one that would embrace not only Histadrut members, hired hands in the agricultural settlements and trade unions in Palestine, and Histadrut supporters in Europe and America, but the entire people — shopkeepers, peddlers, small business men, and so on — turning them all into agricultural and industrial workers in Palestine.

He described the essence of what he called a "people's movement" during one of his visits to Berlin. Zionism was the bringing "of masses of feeble, unproductive, parasitic Jews to fruitful labor. . . . We intend to transform the entire nation, without exception . . . into workers in Palestine. This is the essence of our movement. . . . We are building not only a national framework in Palestine, but the individual, the society. . . . We are remaking ourselves, and this is not a means to an end but a supreme goal in itself." Though in agreement with his goal, many of Ben-Gurion's colleagues maintained that establishing such a labor society required a concentrated and prolonged effort. But Ben-Gurion thought that there was not enough time for this. In October 1926 he warned an Achdut ha-Avodah convention that "the objective situation dictates a quick implementation of Zionism. . . . If we do not go about carrying out our historic enterprise in Palestine quickly — in the very near future — who knows if we ever will."[4]

He marked out the parameters of the controversy, setting values against time. Only one course of action seemed plausible: bringing the largest number of Jews to Palestine in the shortest period of time — feasible only if the labor movement stood at the head of the Zionist Organization. This achieved, it could proceed to fashion the society of Palestine in its own image and according to its own values, however long that took. To Ben-Gurion, it was absolutely necessary that the labor movement become a people's movement at once so it could gain a democratic majority and lead the Zionist Organization.[5]

But here lay the hitch. Ben-Gurion's colleagues — Itzhak Tabenkin, who had settled in Kibbutz Ein Harod, foremost among them — held that the long, radical process required to create first the new Jew and then the new Jewish nation, a working nation, would only be disrupted by a premature conquest of Zionism. The Histadrut, on whose behalf Ben-Gurion spoke and on which he relied to bring about the miracle, had been in existence only six years, and it was questionable whether it had created an individual and society that could imbue the entire nation with its values. The kibbutz and the moshav, the labor movement's two most important social creations in Palestine, were still immature and in need of further support.

In addition, to become a people's movement the labor movement would have to turn to as wide a public as possible, one which did not necessarily believe in the Histadrut's pioneering, socialist Zionist ideas. Before it could change the people, the people would change the Histadrut. To win votes it would have to compromise on its principles and values, if not disassociate itself from them altogether. How then would the Histadrut be able to endow the entire nation with them or honorably discharge the task Ben-Gurion had allotted it with his slogan?

Whether because Ben-Gurion was unable to imbue his Achdut ha-Avodah colleagues with his sense of urgency, or for some other reason, the party did not respond to his demand for a plan to conquer Zionism, and the conflict between values and time eventually developed into the fault line along which Ben-Gurion and Tabenkin would one day split into separate camps. Meanwhile, Ben-Gurion continued to fight for the course he believed in.

Then, out of the blue, reinforcement arrived. Early in 1927 Ben-Gurion and the entire Zionist movement had to weigh a proposal by Weizmann to enlarge the Jewish Agency in Palestine by taking in non-Zionists. The term "Jewish Agency" had first appeared in Article Four of the League of Nations Mandate for Palestine. The intended function of such an agency was to aid and encourage world Jewry in the development and settlement of Palestine. At first the Zionist Organization served as this agency, so it was composed entirely of Zionists. Weizmann, wishing to capitalize on the resources of non-Zionist Jews to further the Zionist effort, in 1923 found a willing counterpart in Louis Marshall, long-time president of the American Jewish Committee. After years of negotiations the two agreed to set up the Jewish Agency and its Council on a parity basis: half its members would be Zionists elected by the Zionist Congress and the other half non-Zionist individuals and representatives of Jewish organizations who would be appointed, not elected, to these positions.

A proposal based on this agreement was on the agenda of the 1927 Zionist Congress. Ben-Gurion endorsed the proposed enlargement at the same time that he criticized Weizmann for agreeing that non-Zionists, who were not democratically elected to their positions, could join the Jewish Agency Council and its Executive. In an article published in February he wrote, "The ideal way of activating the Jewish people is undoubtedly by an elected congress of delegates sent from all over the world, on the basis of democratic elections and direct national responsibility." But as long as this was impossible, "enlargement of the Agency should not be ruled out." In view of the pressing needs and difficulties of the present hour "the mobilization of all the Jewish nation's forces and means for the rebuilding of Palestine is the Zionist movement's first and foremost basic obligation."

This was an important milestone in his political thinking. Although Ben-Gurion strove as before to put the labor movement in control of the Zionist Organization and considered what he called the Zionist half of the enlarged Agency its heart and soul, his very acceptance of the other half — to be composed entirely of prominent capitalists and businessmen ("notables," he tagged them sardonically) — attests to a shift of emphasis from class and pioneer interests to broader national ones. Although he continued to rail against the "landlordish" (bourgeois) Zionist Organization, such invective was thenceforth purely for effect. Achdut ha-Avodah approved the Weizmann-Marshall agreement, thereby putting the Zionist national interest before its principles and justifying cooperation with non-Zionists to accrue greater Agency resources. What then, Ben-Gurion asked, prevented it from cooperating with non-socialists in a people's movement to further the conquest of Zionism? This analogy between non-Zionists in the enlarged Agency and non-socialists in the proposed people's movement assisted his efforts to bring the party around to the idea of such a movement.[6]

Nevertheless, there still remained a solid pocket of resistance within Achdut ha-Avodah that was not restricted to Tabenkin and his United Kibbutz Movement. It reappeared in 1928, when Ben-Gurion reiterated his 1919 call to hold a World Congress for Labor Palestine. His plan was based on local committees for Labor Palestine, to be established worldwide by the Zionist labor parties. Each country would elect a national conference that would send delegates to the World Congress, which in turn would found a League for Labor Palestine. Through this league Ben-Gurion sought to pull together all resources in the Diaspora and link them to the Histadrut in Palestine. The HEC had given this idea its blessing early in 1923, and that summer seven such parties convened in Karlsbad, Czechoslovakia, committing themselves to set up an office and apparatus for Labor Palestine affairs. This was the beginning of the League for Labor Palestine, which incorporated local committees that eventually became Histadrut branch offices — embassies, in a way — in various cities in Europe and America. Ben-Gurion set aside the better part of his trips to Europe for furthering this organization, while his HEC colleagues dispatched emissaries from Palestine to the committees abroad and established a department within the HEC to coordinate their activity.

However, Ben-Gurion's political intentions for this effort — which involved bringing the leagues into an all-embracing labor Zionist movement that would conquer the Zionist Organization — did not meet with equal success. After visiting the Committee for Labor Palestine in Berlin Ben-Gurion wrote in his diary, in December 1923, "This little one will be big — from this the World Organization for the building of socialist Palestine will grow." Expecting quick developments, he told the Achdut ha-Avodah council in February 1924, "The old Zionism is dead . . . It will not come back to life . . . and we must see if it is in our power to set up a new Zionism . . . a socialist, Zionist movement to supplant the old bourgeois Zionism." On hearing this, his good friend Shmuel Yavnieli quipped, "No burials yet, please." That October Ben-Gurion wrote David Zakay that the time had come "to create the great socialist Zionist organization which will revolve around Achdut ha-Avodah and the Histadrut."[7]

But Achdut ha-Avodah did not agree. The members were prepared to accept the League, the committees, and their assistance to the Histadrut in Palestine with resources and manpower, but not a worldwide socialist Zionist organization, parallel to or substituting for the extant Zionist Organization. Even after Ben-Gurion refined his vision and is-

sued his 1925 call for a people's movement, his opponents remained
unmoved. They intended the effort invested by the Histadrut in the
League and its committees to produce a great many pioneers in Palestine, not an electoral majority abroad. Though his position was
strengthened in 1927 by Achdut ha-Avodah's backing the Weizmann-
Marshall agreement, Ben-Gurion still had to fight an exhausting battle
to persuade the HEC to consent to a World Congress for Labor Palestine in February 1928.

At long last, it seemed, Ben-Gurion could begin preparing for his
Congress, outlining its ideological, organizational, and personal features. In March he opened the Histadrut council with a long speech,
"Our Vocation to the People," and won a vote of support. But in May
his feverish preparations were brought to a standstill in the wake of an
auto accident. Nevertheless, in July, before fully regaining his strength,
he dashed off to Berlin, where the Congress was to take place, to continue the preparations. In early October he returned for the Achdut
ha-Avodah conference, where he gave a speech on the "hegemony" —
for the first time publicly using this word in this context — of the
workers' movement in Zionism. The clearer his intention for the Congress to become the first practical step in this direction became, the
more old doubts and hesitations were renewed among his opponents.
Would the Congress be a cornerstone of a new, socialist Zionist organization, competing with the Zionist Organization? Or would it be the
foundation for a people's movement that would storm the Zionist Organization and install the labor movement at its head prematurely?
Prominent among the nays was Beilinson, who called for abandoning
the idea altogether and instead begin quiet, grassroots activity. Ben-
Gurion, sensing defeat if a second vote on the issue was held, in one
breath threatened to resign from the HEC and demanded the convening of the Histadrut council. He could count on the council's support
on the basis of its former resolution as well as on the fact that he had
better standing in that forum. Knowing a good deal when it was offered, the HEC did not take another vote and satisfied itself with
electing "a committee on the Congress issue" (composed of Ben-
Gurion and three other HEC members, at least one of whom favored
the Congress), and avoiding both the threat of resignation and the call
to convene the council.[8]

At first 1929 smiled on Ben-Gurion, and he could congratulate himself on having gotten all he wanted. The merger of Achdut ha-Avodah
and Ha-Poel ha-Tzair — the key to the conquest of Zionism — seemed
assured. In the Histadrut council, which opened the year, he gave a
speech whose title, "Changing of the Guard," laid bare his intention.
"The landlordish class is doomed to extinction as the leader of the na-

tion, and the principal task, dictated by the process of national revival, will pass to a new class: the working class. . . . The call of the working class is to change from a working class into a working people." The new party that would arise from the merger in Palestine and the Diaspora should aim "to become a people's movement." This time the HEC was right behind him, and at the many meetings devoted to the Congress and the League for Labor Palestine it granted his demands, dispatching emissaries to Europe and the United States, allotting funds, and approving plans. This about-face probably occurred once Ben-Gurion made it clear, in his speech and in conversations, that the World Congress for Labor Palestine and the League were not to be "a rival organization to the Zionist Organization and the [Jewish] Agency, but a grouping of democratic and socialist elements around the workers' movement. Our aim is to increase its strength in Zionism and in the Agency."

But with the arrival of summer, his fortunes changed. Although Ben-Gurion had the HEC's energetic assistance, a preparatory conference held in Berlin in July did not go well as a dress rehearsal for the Congress for Labor Palestine. Instead of bridging differences and finding a common voice and purpose it degenerated, as Katznelson had anticipated, into bickering over trivialities.

As if especially to get his goat, Weizmann that year had an enormous success. At the August Zionist Congress in Zurich the Weizmann-Marshall agreement was ratified, and the labor representatives, Sprinzak and Kaplansky, went back to the Zionist Executive. Moreover, the inaugural Jewish Agency Council* meeting, held immediately after the close of the Congress, was everything Ben-Gurion could have wished his Berlin conference to be. Its opening ceremonies at the packed town concert hall were "grand and impressive, astounding and captivating, exceeding all expectations," wrote Ben-Gurion to Paula, adding, "The state of exaltation made a tremendous impression on one and all. . . . I myself was profoundly moved by this soul-stirring experience. All that is sublime and inspiring in the Jewish people was at this gathering, bringing out the loftiness and depth of the Jewish mind and spirit." As Ben-Gurion himself said, "This was a great and dignified opening of a new historic chapter in our lives — a great moral and political triumph for Weizmann."[9]

The delegates to the Zionist Congress and the Agency council were

---

*The Enlarged Jewish Agency for Palestine was simply called the Jewish Agency. Among the non-Zionist members of the Jewish Agency Council, 40 percent of whom were from the United States, were Albert Einstein, the writer Sholem Asch, Léon Blum, Sir Herbert Samuel, and Lord Melchett.

still in Europe on August 23, when the Arabs started the bloodbath following the events of Av, entirely changing the face of Zionism. Not only was the hope for Jewish-Arab peace shattered, but for the first time the British intent to withdraw from the Balfour Declaration was exposed. Its full official expression came in Colonial Secretary Lord Passfield's October 1930 White Paper, which stated that "for the present and with the present methods of Arab cultivation there remains no margin of land available for agricultural settlements by new immigrants," with the exception of negligible reserves held by Jewish agencies, and that unlimited immigration would be prevented. Not only had the interpretation of the Balfour Declaration as a commitment to the establishment of a Jewish state vanished, but the promised National Home seemed doomed.

Weizmann, champion of the Zionist-British alliance and chief spokesman for pro-British Zionism, resigned his office as president of the Zionist Organization in protest. The Basel Zionist Congress of July 1931 could have refused to accept his resignation by re-electing him, but under revisionist pressure and despite the energetic defense of Weizmann by Ben-Gurion and the labor bloc, it did not do so. Nahum Sokolow was elected president in his place. Weizmann therefore had to relinquish his chairmanship of the Jewish Agency Executive, which went with the presidency, just a little over a year after he had triumphantly established it. He considered that a slap in the face.

In less than two years, then, a new situation had arisen which, seeming to confirm his foreboding about the realization of Zionism, helped Ben-Gurion impart to his party his sense of urgency. In his view three dangers impended. The first was born of the disturbances of 1929, which filled him with a twofold dread: of the destruction of the Yishuv at the hands of the Palestinian Arabs, assisted by their brethren in neighboring countries — "For instance, a rush of Arab tribes from outside Palestine against the Jews within"; and of a renewal of Arab attacks that, even if the Haganah warded them off, would be sufficiently disquieting to keep sensible Jews away from Palestine. "The feeling that Jews are sitting on a volcano is liable to undermine the entire Zionist movement. The people will see Palestine not as a safe haven, but as a battlefield." The remedy he proposed to stave off the Arab threat was a massive wave of fifty thousand young immigrants within the year — the rapid realization of Zionism.

The second danger was the British retreat from the Palestine Mandate as confirmed by the October 1930 White Paper. Without Britain's aid, and especially against its will, how could large numbers of Jews immigrate to Palestine? No longer did the Zionists have ten years to set up the National Home, as Ben-Gurion had once estimated. They had not even a day. Against this peril Ben-Gurion proposed war — against the White Paper, against the British government, and if necessary, against the British Empire to boot. He likened the Jewish people to gunpowder, liable to explode if its will to live was threatened. From the pages of *Davar* he asked the British government if it wished "to test the powers of destructiveness underlying this will by stealing [the Jewish people's] last hope." At the Mapai council in October 1930, he elaborated. "England is a great world power, the mightiest of empires. But it takes only a little bit of powder to shatter even the largest rocks. Such powder packs tremendous force, and we, too, possess such force. If the creative genius that has been shown to be ours is choked by this vile empire, then our destructive force will be unleashed and we will blast away this bloodstained empire. . . . We shall be the ones to take up this war, and beware thee, British Empire!"[10]

The third danger was the rapid growth of the revisionist movement, which, unlike the two others, was an internal threat. Ben-Gurion was convinced that the Zionist enterprise could be achieved only through organized labor, and organized labor had no worse enemy. While the first two dangers subsided for a time, this one never slackened. Until 1936 there was no more Arab violence, and in February 1931, less than five months after the White Paper had been issued, Prime Minister Ramsay MacDonald sent Weizmann a letter, known as the MacDonald Letter, restating Britain's commitment to the Balfour Declaration. By contrast, the specter of revisionism grew more menacing every day.

Despite these dangers, Ben-Gurion's opponents did not relent. Mapai and the HEC were not at all enthusiastic about the Labor Congress to be held in Berlin. The date had been set, after several postponements, for the end of September 1930, and they gave Ben-Gurion money — by March expenses had reached 1,500 Palestinian pounds! — and assistance with preparations. Then, in his absence, just two months before the Congress was to open, the HEC decided on another postponement, to 1931. Moreover, a number of his colleagues either refused to go or evaded making a commitment. Ben-Gurion wished this Congress to achieve the status of a momentous event with the blessing of the entire labor movement, and therefore wanted all the top brass of Mapai and the Histadrut in Berlin. But late in July 1930, Arlosoroff refused to participate, telling the HEC, "Even today, the whole business of the Congress is a dive into the darkness." Berl Katznelson, once burned at the 1929 conference, agreed with him. Tabenkin was incommunicado in Poland, as if the earth had swallowed him up. But Sprinzak, Ben-Gurion's tried and true adversary, had an astonishing change of heart, turning from an opponent of the Congress into an ardent supporter. Ben-Gurion came to realize further that coolness toward the

Congress was widespread in Europe as well. In April 1930 he quoted two skeptical activists in his diary. "The Leagues [committees] are a fiction." But like a war horse at full gallop, he could not be reined in. He drew on an old, proven weapon, threatening to resign from the HEC, at which point Tabenkin was found and an HEC resolution obligating him to participate in the Congress was wired to him. Katznelson was also talked into going, and the opening date remained unchanged. Only Arlosoroff, billed as a speaker on the Yishuv and the Arabs at the Congress, remained adamant. On the pretext of expecting a visit from the undersecretary of state for the colonies, he stayed put in Palestine.[11]

And so, after three years of preparation, the Labor Congress opened on September 27 in Berlin's Prussian Landtag Hall, with 196 delegates and a thousand guests present, and concluded on October 1. In a series of resolutions it established itself as the supreme institution of the World League for Labor Palestine and its branch leagues in Europe and America and laid down their duties: assisting the labor movement in Palestine, namely, the Histadrut, and establishing an analogous movement in the Diaspora.

Ben-Gurion did his best to give the Congress an aura of grandeur and brilliance, as befitted an event of universal Jewish importance, making a great point of the attendance of celebrities at its opening: Albert Einstein, who also delivered a welcoming speech, the socialists Eduard Bernstein from Germany and Camille Huysmans from Belgium, the mayor of Berlin, and representatives from the Socialist International, the Trade Unions International, and the French Socialist Party. To his father he wrote, "The composition of the Congress, its echo in the Diaspora, and the participation of delegates from the Socialist International came off better than we could have hoped." To Paula he lamented, "After presiding over sessions on the first night and the first two days, in addition to which I also spoke twice, I have reached the final stage of exhaustion." To the Jewish news agency JTA he announced, "The Congress brought forth the idea of hegemony of the working class within the Jewish nation in the Jewish Renaissance movement. The League must turn this idea into a living, meaningful fact." More than ever, the labor movement would now be able to fulfill its task of "the conquest of the people."

But his secret heart held a different image. Most of the big names he had invited to the Congress had not shown, among them Sigmund Freud, Léon Blum, Martin Buber, Chaim Nachman Bialik, Simon Dubnow, and Lion Feuchtwanger. Despite all his efforts to include socialist Zionism's so-called sister party, the British Labour Party merely sent a congratulatory telegram. Weizmann did the same; Nahum Sokolow, his deputy, came in his place. Furthermore, the Congress was rocked by factional disputes and numerous disturbances, nearly falling apart more than once. Finally, except for Sprinzak and Kaplansky, the delegation from Palestine regarded it with such indifference that on his return to Palestine Ben-Gurion raised "objections" in the HEC about Arlosoroff, who had not come at all, and Katznelson, who "came as if the devil had twisted his arm."[12]

No, this was not Herzl's first Zionist Congress, nor even Weizmann's Jewish Agency Council. The only one who praised the Labor Congress was Ben-Gurion himself. *Davar* considered it no disservice to its readers to publish only a summary of the proceedings — except for Ben-Gurion's speeches, which were printed in full — two weeks after the fact. When they returned to Palestine the delegates did not deem it necessary to give the public any additional information. Had they done so they would have had to point out Ben-Gurion's exaggerations, for instance, that the Labor Congress delegates represented "hundreds of thousands" of Labor Palestine supporters, that a quarter of a million had bought Congress ballots to elect their delegates in Europe, and another quarter million in the United States had given the American delegation "power of attorney" to speak on their behalf. In fact, in a number of important countries, among them the United States, no elections to the Congress were held at all. Had the labor movement truly drawn half a million voters, the conquest of Zionism would have been assured without its having to lift a finger.*

The first Labor Congress was also the last, and no people's movement grew out of it. The League and its branches eventually became election campaign headquarters for Mapai, particularly in Poland and its neighboring countries, and as such they played an important part in future developments.

Two factors finally brought Mapai around to the conquest of Zionism. The first was the surprising strength of the Revisionists at the 1931 Zionist Congress, where they constituted the third largest faction among the 254 delegates (52 delegates, or 21%), after the labor faction (75 delegates, or 29%) and the General Zionists B† (59 delegates, or 25%). More important, they could influence the General

---

*A total of 535,113 voted in the elections of the 1933 Zionist Congress; of this number, 226,058, 44 percent of all valid votes, chose the labor movement — this after the leagues had been in action for three years. Just 300,000 votes would have sufficed to give the labor movement an absolute majority in 1933, and in 1931 it would have needed even fewer, since not as many people voted in the Zionist Congress election that year.

†The General Zionists were at one time the largest faction at the Zionist congresses, and despite their wide range of views they were capable of remaining firmly consolidated as a single faction. But at the 1931 Congress they split into two groups. One, group A (25 delegates), supported Weizmann and included moderate and progressive views, while the other, group B (59 delegates), opposed Weizmann and was more right-wing–extremist.

Zionists B and Mizrachi, the religious faction (14 delegates). Together these factions made up 125 of the total Congress delegates, and with such numbers, in addition to unseating Weizmann, they were able to disrupt the agenda and introduce a new item, what Jabotinsky called the final objective — a proclamation of Zionism's aim to establish a Jewish state in Palestine on both sides of the Jordan. Weizmann and his supporters, especially the labor bloc, were opposed, considering such a declaration premature and provocative. All of Mapai could clearly foresee that a continued buildup of the Revisionists' strength would help them establish an anti-Histadrut right-wing–religious–nationalist coalition that would wind up leading the Zionist Organization and constitute a right-wing conquest of Zionism.

The second factor was the worsening situation of the Jews in the wake of the 1929 crash, which generated a worldwide economic crisis. Ben-Gurion held that this hurt the Jews more than anyone else. In addition to economic difficulties, there was severe persecution of the Jews in Poland, with the official blessing of a government which made it perfectly clear that its policy was to reduce its Jewish population of 3,-275,000 as quickly as possible, via emigration. The Nazi power in Germany had grown by 1932 and with it a wave of intimidation and violence. In both countries many Jews were rendered destitute, resulting in masses of frightened, dispossessed people highly susceptible to the promises of the Revisionists, who recklessly pledged massive immigration and a Jewish state in Palestine forthwith. This won them the overt encouragement and assistance of the Polish government.

Concern for the fate of these European Jews and fear lest by virtue of their distress the Revisionists take control of the Zionist Organization underlay Ben-Gurion's first open demand that his party make up its mind to become the majority in the Zionist Organization. Ben-Gurion began his speech to the Mapai council in Kefar Yehezkel on July 2, 1932, on this note: "In Russia and America, in Poland and Germany, in the Balkans and the rest of the countries of the Diaspora, the economic and cultural deterioration of the Jewish masses is accelerating, the basis of their existence is crumbling, and the threat of physical and spiritual annihilation, of decline and destruction, looms over the Jewish people in their present state. There is no refuge." Their only hope, and only by means of a Zionist Organization under the control of the labor movement, was in Palestine.[13]

It is clear that when Ben-Gurion spoke of a "threat of physical . . . annihilation," he referred to the Jews of Poland and Germany and that he saw "economic and cultural deterioration" as the lot of the Jewish masses in other countries. At the time, of course, Ben-Gurion did not, and could not, foresee the Nazi Holocaust. Yet he was not talking merely for the sake of argument or to exhort his listeners. Since his September 1930 visit to Berlin, a growing anxiety for the fate of all of world Jewry haunted him. In January 1934 he would tell the Histadrut council that "Hitler's rule imperils the entire Jewish people."[14]

But in July 1932 the council did not easily accept his view that "our duty is to take over the Zionist Organization." The conflict between values and time was as sharp as ever, as was the council's opposition to a premature conquest. The Tabenkin camp, grounded in the kibbutz movement, unanimously opposed "taking Zionism in hand," as Ben-Gurion had put it, out of a clear concern for the movement's values. To struggle for a majority at this stage of its development Mapai would have to compromise its values to attract masses of voters. Tabenkin accused Ben-Gurion of not having faith in the Histadrut and its ability to carry out its ideals. Aaron Zisling, one of Tabenkin's lieutenants, countered Ben-Gurion's demand with the slogan "We will be built if we build our forces," which epitomized the position of Tabenkin's camp. The Histadrut's ideological and human resources were not to be invested in creating an image attractive to the masses and in managing the Zionist Organization, but in training pioneers, in communal settlements, in kibbutzes, and in the Histadrut's economic, cultural, and social enterprises.

There was no lack of opposition even among Ben-Gurion's followers. Some, like Yavnieli, feared that the Histadrut was not yet strong enough and could only fail if it took on national Zionist leadership all at once, while others were concerned lest it lose its socialist hue in becoming a mass movement. Itzhak Ben-Zvi was among the latter, arguing that "Ben-Gurion's words are at least twenty years before their time." Katznelson remained silent, which certainly did not help Ben-Gurion. Neither he nor Beilinson said a word for or against the conquest of Zionism for the duration of the council. To a certain extent this was characteristic of them. Katznelson never stood firmly behind Ben-Gurion in times of decision.[15]

It was primarily the "apparatchiks" who came to Ben-Gurion's aid. Some were top-level officials, but most were of second rank: David Remez, Abraham Hartzfeld, Eliyahu Golomb, Israel Marom, and others. Thanks to them Ben-Gurion's demand was not stricken from the agenda of the council or the central committee, to which it was referred for further deliberation. To avoid any misconception that it had been adopted, Itzhak Laufbahn struck the last sentence of Ben-Gurion's speech from the version published in *Ha-Poel ha-Tzair*, Mapai's organ since the merger: "The workers' movement is called upon to become the decisive force in Zionism, to constitute a decisive majority."[16]

There is no telling how long this stalemate would have continued had not Ben-Gurion taken the bull by the horns and capitalized on a resolution by the council to dispatch as many emissaries as possible — fifty or more — to the Diaspora to strengthen and expand the labor movement there. Even though the council had meant its role to be primarily educational, Ben-Gurion interpreted it as political, as though the emissaries had been put at the service of the movement's election campaign for the 1933 Zionist Congress. He simply took the resolution as an endorsement of his conquest of Zionism, and a few days after the council ended he set out, by way of London and Danzig, for the council of the League for Labor Palestine in Warsaw, where, as he declared, "I presented the conquest of Zionism as the central objective of our movement at this time."[17] Thus opened his great campaign that ended in triumph, placing Mapai, almost against its will, at the head of the Yishuv and the Zionist Organization.

While in London for a Zionist Actions Committee meeting in August, Ben-Gurion received a letter that cheered him very much. It came from Miss Rega Klapholz, who invited him to Vienna on the pretext that she wanted to discuss with him certain matters of interest to her. She had first seen him in August 1929, when she was twenty-two, and on vacation with her sister, Annie, two years her junior. They had come to Zurich to attend the Zionist Congress and see the celebrities gathered there, having financed their trip with earnings from various jobs and from work in the Congress office, through which they gained admission to the debate hall and proximity to the delegates.

Rega and Annie differed from the other female camp followers of the Congress and other Zionist events and their celebrated participants. First, they were young and pretty. The gay-spirited, charming Rega had silky brown hair, striking blue eyes, and a full, lithe body — a sight so rare at Zionist events as to hearten a weary delegate. Second, they were neither society ladies hunting prey for their tea parties nor hacks looking for advancement. Rega was a medical student and Annie studied architecture. Considering the general status of women at the time, these two were exceptional in their talents, daring, and ambitions. Third, they knew some Zionist grandees from their father's house. Haim Klapholz, a well-to-do businessman, had opened his home at 59 Tabor Street to various Jews and Zionists who happened to be in Vienna. Under their influence Rega had joined a left-wing Zionist youth movement (Ha-Shomer ha-Tzair), and Annie a more moderate one (Blue-White), and between them the sisters knew nearly all the members of the Palestine labor movement in Vienna. Joseph Baratz, one of the founders of Daganiah, the first kibbutz, and the Histadrut emissary to Vienna, had first introduced Rega and Ben-Gurion in Zurich in 1929.[18]

By that time Ben-Gurion, it seems, was open to a liaison with another woman. Two sources attest to this. One is the story of Rivka Katznelson (no relation to Berl), onetime editor of *Davar ha-Poelet*, the Histadrut women's monthly, and literary critic. Early in 1929, when she was twenty-two, she attended an Achdut ha-Avodah public meeting in Tel Aviv with a friend, who dared her to write Ben-Gurion a note. "Instead of sitting in a boring meeting, come take a walk with two girls," she wrote him, then went out. The folded note was passed from hand to hand until it reached Ben-Gurion in the first row. The two watched him turn around, searching for them. He left the auditorium, went straight to Rivka, and said, "You wrote the note."

The walk was the beginning of a relationship in which they discussed literature (she lent him a copy of *Lady Chatterley's Lover*) and went to see the silent version of *Ben-Hur*, one of the five or six movies that Ben-Gurion saw in his life. In 1931 Rivka visited him at home and met Paula, then forty-four. To her Paula looked worn out and "her expression was repulsive, primitive, bad." According to Rivka, Ben-Gurion showed up for their meetings "hungry": harried, aggressive, hugging, kissing, undressing; like someone looking for release and nothing else. Because of this, she said, "I did not give myself."[19]

The other source is Paula herself. The idea that male infidelity was axiomatic was already ingrained in her when she first met Ben-Gurion. The fear that he would desert her for another woman was explicit in her letters to him when he was in the army and in Palestine in 1918 and 1919. In the following years, such overt expressions disappeared from her letters, but in August 1930, she wrote Ben-Gurion, then in London, "Dear David, Your letters became more seldom, what is the matter, have you found new *attractions*?"[20] As if to protect herself by evoking his compassion, she immediately added that she had had an X-ray and would need another in a few days.

Was this the old panic reawakened, or a new suspicion with grounds to support it? It is certainly true that, if women in general are sensitive to their husbands' feelings and can sense their indiscretions, Paula had that intuition in spades. All who knew her agreed that she had a marvelous ability to "read" people. It would have been enough for her to find out that Ben-Gurion had been to the movies, or to notice a copy of *Lady Chatterley's Lover* lying around, to know that something unusual was going on, and she would have been vigilantly on the lookout for more clues. Although these two particular possibilities are pure conjecture, it is beyond question that in this area, at least, Ben-Gurion could not hide anything from her.

On July 21, 1931, after the Basel Zionist Congress, Ben-Gurion had gone to Vienna with Katznelson and Arlosoroff for talks with Weizmann. He had planned to stay for just three days, then visit Czechoslovakia before setting sail from Trieste for Palestine on July 29. But at the home of Mendel Singer, the labor movement's principal emissary, he encountered Rega. Whether this was a chance meeting or Rega had planned it — she was a frequent guest there — Ben-Gurion altered his travel plans drastically. His trip to Czechoslovakia forgotten, he left Vienna only when it was time to go home. He gave Rega a flattering snapshot of himself, on the back of which he had written "To Rega from D.B.G., 25.7.31," and a copy of his new book, *We and Our Neighbors*, inscribed "To Rega with fondness from the author, 28.7.31." A few days earlier Singer had noted in his diary that Ben-Gurion showed more interest in Rega than in Poale Zion.[21]

The closeness of their relationship can only be surmised. The inscriptions on the back of the photograph and in the book were highly unusual; labor leaders were generally careful to keep a low profile in their fleeting encounters with women and did not, as a rule, leave such clear tracks. The fact that Rivka Katznelson, by contrast, had no such tangible evidence of Ben-Gurion's attentions only stresses the intensity of his feelings for Rega. Second, in her letter of August 1932 Rega addressed him in the third person, as was customary in Europe, but in his reply (in Yiddish) he used the second person, saying "use of the third person is unwarranted between us."

Ben-Gurion's letter opens, "My dear, beloved Rega," and says, "Shall I tell you a secret? I wanted to see you — and now I want to see you even more. You wish to discuss subjects that interest you. Very well. I will do so with great pleasure. I, for my part, wish to see you. . . . I feel a need to see you, even if it is, to my sorrow, for a short time only." In his eagerness he forgot to be circumspect and made his purpose obvious by inviting her to Berlin for a few days, "and then we can travel together to Danzig." And if Berlin was too far, could she come to Munich? It was closer to Vienna and had not previously appeared on his itinerary. He signed off with "Perhaps it will become clear to you that I am impatient. If fault is to be found, you too must share in it. Yours, D. Ben-Gurion."[22]

He set out to conquer Zionism and the heart of Rega Klapholz at one and the same time.

26

Victory

O N AUGUST 11, 1932, Ben-Gurion sent a second letter from London to Vienna: "Rega, I have been awaiting your answer, and it hasn't arrived. Are you angry at me over my letter? I hope not. If so, I am deeply sorry." He explained his eagerness to have her join him. "Reading your letter was a joy for me, just as were the few short days in Vienna, which I have not forgotten." He assured her of how much he wanted to visit her. "This time, to my regret, other cities in Europe are on my schedule. I wish to come to Vienna only because it is your city, to see you and meet with you again. This time I have no other business in Vienna, but I will of course in any case weigh your request, though it conflicts with my itinerary. And you may write me as to a friend, without ceremony. Yours, B.G." In the margin he wrote his mailing address in Berlin, for which he set out the following day by train. He had packed in his suitcase five pairs of shoes, clothes, and undergarments he had bought for himself and his family, and a summer coat he had bought for Paula.[1]

After a few days in Berlin, he was off to Danzig on the eighteenth. Achdut ha-Avodah and Ha-Poel ha-Tzair had merged in Palestine, and their satellite parties in Europe were about to unite. The result was the founding of a world Mapai, which laid the foundation for a large united Zionist Labor Party in Europe. Although a necessary move toward "the conquest of Zionism," the merger was still, to a great extent, merely an agreement among the top echelons; the local parties — particularly in Poland and Germany — continued their independent existence and customary warring with each other. Ben-Gurion, therefore, had undertaken a double task: to iron out the difficulties among the merged parties on the municipal and national levels to make the world Mapai an effective practical reality, and to tighten cooperation among the participating groups in the League for Labor Palestine in preparation for the great role he had envisaged for it — getting a majority for the labor movement at the 1933 Zionist Congress.

In Danzig on August 19, Ben-Gurion wrote two letters in Yiddish, one to Paula and one to Rega. The former was a dry, businesslike account of the convention and of the speech he had delivered and those he had heard, as if Paula had no interests in life other than the tortuous road to a merger within socialist Zionism. The Hebrew P.S. to his children seemed rather perfunctory, a series of routine questions — for example, he asked Geula to "write [him] if Mommy buys herself something to wear." The second letter, though shorter, was wholly personal. "In London, and afterward in Berlin, I impatiently awaited your reply, and I did not know what to think of the silent Rega. I was truly perturbed, much more, perhaps, than you can realize." Then a friend came from London, bringing "your unexpected [but much hoped for] letter," dispersing the dark clouds that had burdened his heart. After a few lines about his role in the convention, Ben-Gurion told her he had decided to come. "I'll write you from Warsaw regarding the exact date of my arrival in Vienna, around the tenth to twelfth of September. In Vienna, thank God, I have no public engagements or meetings and will be entirely yours, B.G."[2]

Arriving in Warsaw on August 26, he gave his all to the council of the League for Labor Palestine in Poland, which opened the following day and lasted two more. There he delivered the same speech, "The State of Zionism in the Diaspora and in Palestine," that he had given at Kefar Yehezkel. He wielded it again and again like a battering ram against the wall of the Zionist Organization. After the council Ben-Gurion began a marathon round of meetings with all the parties, organizations, and splinter groups that belonged to the League, as well as all the bodies under their authority. He worked indefatigably from morning till night, seeing an unending stream of functionaries, filling his journal with their answers to his questions as to whether or not "getting a majority at the Congress was possible," with the statistics they supplied to give him an idea of the size of the force he would be heading when he stormed Zionism the following year, and with their claims and disputes. After taking part in a convention held by the Gordonia — a Ha-Poel ha-Tzair youth movement — he noted in his diary, "I spoke for two and a half hours about Zionism and socialism . . . and then *on the necessity and the feasibility of our conquering the Zionist Organization*," summarizing the message he imparted to all. In Warsaw, as in Kefar Yehezkel, the response was skepticism and disbelief.[3]

After a week he felt, he related to Paula in a short letter from Warsaw on August 31, that "my head is spinning, and I am almost unable to hear what is being said to me." He closed with the following lines: "The situation here is dreadful. The poverty grows from day to day. Everyone dreams only of Palestine. I've been told that there are many members of the Munweis family here, but I haven't met them." He summed up the rest of his journey by saying, "In two days I leave for Galicia, where it seems I'll have to spend ten or twelve days, and from there I'll return home."

In a shorter letter to Rega that same day, he described his itinerary in more detail. "Will you be free by September 6–7? I should like to spend at least seven days in Vienna, but if you're busy there's nothing for me there. Write me, then, straight to Lvov, when you'll be free and when is the best time for me to come."[4]

After a short respite of two days in Płońsk (although he no longer had family or friends there) and one day in the woods of the resort town Otwock, near Warsaw (where he had met Shlomo Zemach prior to the latter's journey to Palestine in 1904), he began another marathon in Galicia. On September 3 his plane landed in Lvov and once again he plunged into conferences, gatherings, talks, and disputes with functionaries and activists who had come from the far ends of western Galicia to meet with him, renewing his demand for the conquest of Zionism and again filling his diary with data. On September 7 the night train brought him to Kraków at 6:00 A.M. From then until 11:30 the following night he was busy with the Zionist labor movement in eastern Galicia, whose functionaries and activists had come to Kraków in his honor. This was the end of his political work, which he had driven at a furious pace in his desire to have a few days to spend with Rega.

Berl Locker, a leader of the World Union of Poale Zion, attested to his success in Danzig and Poland. Ben-Gurion had "made a strong impression," he wrote Chaim Weizmann, to the extent that in Danzig there was talk of his returning to Europe for an entire year "and many volunteered for the coming campaign." Locker was keeping Weizmann abreast of Ben-Gurion's rapid ascent in Zionist leadership. Ben-Gurion had already made up his mind to return to Poland in 1933 for a more extensive campaign. The unequivocal conclusions he drew from this visit were that a labor majority was feasible, and that if his party wanted it, it had to direct the major part of its electoral offensive at Poland, which had the largest Jewish community in Europe and the largest Zionist community in the world.[5]

But in the meantime he grappled with doubts about going to Vienna. There can be no doubt that it was his fondest desire, but he had not received the anticipated response from Rega. He was well aware of the twenty-one-year difference in their ages, and if she had taken flight at the last minute or changed her mind, he did not want to show up in

Vienna like a fool. He finally stuck his neck out and sent another letter from Kraków: "My train gets to north Vienna tomorrow evening at about 8:30. I don't think you will receive this letter before my arrival and I do not know if I will be able to see you as soon as I get in. Yours, B.G." In a postscript he added that he would be staying at the Bayerischerhof Hotel on the street where she resided and added, "I haven't told a soul in Vienna about my arrival and I don't wish it to be known until I leave."

On Thursday evening, September 8, at 11:30, he boarded the train in Kraków and arrived in Vienna the following evening. On Saturday, sitting at his hotel in the heart of the city, he wrote in his diary, as if for Paula's eyes: "Last night at 8:30 I arrived here without anyone's knowledge. *Perhaps* I will finally be able to be alone for a few days. To this end I have stayed far from the center of town." He dated this notation incorrectly, probably from excitement.[6]

This was the only entry he made during five stolen days in Vienna; except for an account of his expenditures, he wrote nothing until he returned to Palestine. Poale Zion members, and others, recognized him instantly in public, but when they tried to greet him they felt that he was distant.[7]

Ben-Gurion and Rega, in Annie's company, visited the romantic and historic spots of Vienna, sat in its famous cafés, had long talks, and went to the theater. But Ben-Gurion and Rega also had time to be alone. Ben-Gurion attempted to speak German, a language he had never used but in which Rega was most comfortable, which led him to tell her that the effort she had invested in learning the Hebrew characters to read his letters to her in Yiddish would best be applied to studying Hebrew. From then on he would write to her only in Hebrew. If he had invited her to Danzig to display himself in his full glory and impress her, and perhaps to make up for the fact that he could not offer her youth and beauty, Vienna gave him something priceless: the favor of a woman who appreciated him for what he was. When they parted on September 15 Rega had formed a high opinion of him. She thought him remarkable not only for his "quick perception, quick response," but also for his "warmth"; he was "friendly and tender" and "charming." Perhaps she was the first to see his still-dormant charisma, which would surface some ten years later. His subsequent letters amply document his feelings for her; they overflow with warmth and tenderness, opening and closing with "My Rega" and "Entirely yours, David." In February 1933 Rega sent him birthday greetings and admitted to having sneaked a look at his passport. Ben-Gurion implored her to speak "as one speaks with one's closest —" and informed her that he had been born on October 16, 1886, not in February 1887, as registered in his passport. "But it's not important. What is important and endearing is that you remembered, and for this I would like — in Vienna I'll tell you what I would like." Thenceforth Vienna was a permanent stop on his itinerary.[8]

From the day of his return to Palestine, September 21, until his next departure on March 29, 1933, Ben-Gurion had 191 days at his disposal. After that, until Election Day on July 23, he would have another hundred days in eastern Europe, mostly in Poland. This was not much time to prepare and carry out an election campaign on behalf of a party that was not yet entirely sure it wanted to conquer Zionism — that neither believed the feat was possible nor had a clear position and program to offer the electorate. Without these it was impossible to plan a campaign strategy. Therefore Ben-Gurion had to work on strategic as well as tactical objectives: getting his party to make up its mind, at the same time selling it a program and building the future campaign's electioneering and propaganda infrastructure, day after night after day.[9]

Two issues in particular were surrounded by growing controversy: education and immigration. In the Yishuv, and in Israel until 1954, there were three separate and distinct school systems: the Histadrut's (the labor trend), the National Council's (the general trend), and Mizrachi's (the religious). To qualify for financial support from the National Council a school had to adopt its curriculum and accept its inspection. In 1931 Ben-Gurion had proposed incorporating the Histadrut primary school network, the "labor system," into the national school system, which received most of its budget from the Jewish Agency and was administered by the National Council's Department of Education. He had a double purpose: freeing the Histadrut from a heavy financial burden and winning over the teachers politically. Once they went for labor they would impart the movement's values to all the Yishuv's schoolchildren. Ben-Gurion stuck by his struggle to abolish the three-school system until his concept was put into practice in 1954, with the introduction of state education in the State of Israel. In the early thirties, however, he was opposed by people who regarded his proposal as a concession of a supreme Histadrut value in return for the votes, in Palestine and abroad, of the great variety of non-socialist groups ("popular" groups, he called them) who feared Histadrut education as socialist indoctrination.[10]

Before his 1932 trip the HEC had been almost evenly split over his proposal, and on the day after his return the issue came up for further discussion at the Mapai Central Committee, but it was not resolved. Late in November a Histadrut council summoned for this purpose passed a long resolution whose effect was to preserve the labor trend's independence. In this defeat for Ben-Gurion, Itzhak Tabenkin and his followers were prominent, both in the kibbutz and in the city, and Ben-Gurion suspected them of having organized for this purpose as far back as the September Central Committee debate. A red light flashed in his mind. "Factions may form within the party. There is no danger in differences of opinion, but there is a danger in factions. . . . This situation is likely to move the rest of the members to organize into factions as well. It must be prevented." If this controversy had really triggered the formation of factions, it only goes to show how deep-seated the division over the conquest of Zionism was.[11]

The immigration issue was taken up by a special council in September 1932. Until then there had been no doubt that pioneering immigration was the foremost Histadrut goal, for which it spared no effort, allocating to it its own resources and those of the Zionist Organization. It set up training camps abroad, dispatched emissaries and counselors, and arranged for the pioneers — as the youth were referred to even before they set foot in Palestine — to be given preference in the immigration quotas set twice a year by the Mandatory government. Now Ben-Gurion, in his obsession with the conquest of Zionism, seemed to overturn the system by proposing broad-based "popular" immigration. He made it clear that he wanted to attract votes from all classes of people, particularly those deprived by the Polish government of their livelihood, who saw immigration to Palestine as a last hope and salvation. But to his opponents this was another shameful compromise of a sacred value. Instead of pioneers who would reinforce the socialist strength of the Histadrut, it would bring in people who lacked any socialist or class consciousness. They were not influenced by his argument that once the popular groups had put it in control of the Zionist Organization the labor movement would guide them along the path of socialist Zionism. No vote was taken, but Ben-Gurion probably would not have won it anyway; Tabenkin and his supporters were certainly stronger.[12]

Such dissension obviously prevented Ben-Gurion from drawing up "a plan for the entire Zionist movement . . . a *popular* Zionist blueprint for action, not just for *pioneers*, but for all the popular circles and for private capital, too." For the same reason the party rejected his other schemes for reorganization that were also intended to enable a labor movement majority. One involved "decentralization" of the Histadrut in Palestine — while concentrating political control of it in the hands of the party — and another called for establishing a world Organization for Labor Palestine, which individuals could join directly instead of having to become a member of one of the political parties in the League. Opting, in a sense, for prevention before cure, Berl Katznelson managed to squelch these ideas before debate began by cautioning, "We have enough experience of new tools that have not been put to use, and I mean the Labor Congress; a repetition must be prevented." The 1930 Berlin congress had left an indelible impression of a terrible waste of energy and resources on him.[13]

But despite the lack of faith and the reluctance of his party, Ben-Gurion did not flag in spirit and he did not weaken. Immediately following his return to Palestine he analyzed the results of the elections to the Zionist congresses of 1927, 1929, and 1931. These showed that nearly 40 percent of the electorate was in Greater Poland, including Lithuania and Latvia, from which came his slogan "Poland is the 'center of gravity' "; this percentage rose with the inclusion of nearby eastern and western Galicia. In 1931 the labor movement, namely, the League, had won 22,500 votes in Poland, and according to Ben-Gurion's calculations, trebling this number, concurrently enlarging the party in neighboring Galicia, Lithuania, and Latvia at the same rate, would be enough to gain a majority, or at least dominance in the next Zionist coalition. Having determined that he needed 75,000 votes in Poland alone, Ben-Gurion was confident that he could win them even without a clear party program and far-reaching organizational changes as long as he had enough money and a large number of campaigners.[14]

He got both of these thanks to the counterattack he was about to launch in the ongoing war between the Revisionists and the Histadrut. In 1931 the Revisionists had founded their own newspaper to replace *Doar ha-Yom* (which had been restored to its former owners), called *Hazit ha-Am* (National Front). Its editors, headed by Abba Achimeir, who proudly called himself a Fascist, led the "maximalist faction" (which laid claim to all of Palestine, including Transjordan and the Syrian desert) of Jabotinsky's movement and, in 1930, secretly founded Berit ha-Biryonim (the Covenant of Terrorists,* or just the Terrorists), an extremist nationalist group which, as its name indicated, advocated terrorism as a means to achieve its ends. From the very beginning the Terrorists were notable for their violent actions and polemics, and *Hazit ha-Am* was unparalleled in the annals of the Hebrew media for its invective and gutter journalism directed at the Histadrut, Mapai, and their leaders, particularly Chaim Arlosoroff, who chaired the Jewish Agency's Political Department from 1931 and supported Weizmann, also a top figure on the Revisionists' hate list. Mapai's apprehension that the Revisionists, under the Terrorists' influence, would

---

* The *Even-Shoshan Hebrew Dictionary* defines *biryon* as "a terrorist, a strong-arm man, one who uses violence to dominate. . . . Biryonim: the name of the freedom zealots during the Roman occupation who fought violently and brutally against the Romans without, and against the moderate Jews within."

follow in the footsteps of the Italian Fascists and the Nazis was confirmed in 1932.

Early in February, a few days before the inauguration of the Chair of Internation (Jewish-Arab) Peace at the Mount Scopus campus of Hebrew University, the Terrorists threatened, in writing, the life of Judah-Leib Magnes, chancellor of the university, who advocated a binational state as a peaceful solution for Palestine's Jews and Arabs. On the tenth, under Achimeir's direction, they stormed the opening ceremonies with fists and stink bombs. A large group of eminent persons was present for the speech, "Jerusalem, City of Peace," delivered by professor of law Norman Bentwich, who was to hold the chair. The Terrorists were demonstrating their readiness to use threats and violence to stamp out freedom of speech and silence differing views. Speaking in defense of Achimeir in the criminal action brought against him and the Terrorists, Eliyahu Zvi Cohen, his close friend and attorney, proclaimed, "Were the Hitlerites to remove their hatred of Jews from their program, we, too, would stand by their side. Had the Hitlerites not risen in Germany [it] would be lost. Yes, Hitler saved Germany." (And on March 30, 1933, two months after Hitler was made chancellor of Germany, an editorial in *Hazit ha-Am*, apparently written by Achimeir, presented a new defense of Nazism. "The various socialists and democrats are of the opinion that Hitler's movement is just a shell, but we believe it has both shell and substance. The anti-Semitic shell must be disposed of, but not the anti-Marxist substance.")[15]

The Revisionists' convention in Vienna in September 1932 made two things very clear: first, that Achimeir's faction had grown considerably, and second, that his praise of Hitler and the Nazis was a direct indication of his own political program. Even before it opened, Achimeir's men passed out leaflets among the delegates and guests deriding parliamentary democracy and procedures and claiming a need "to hand over the reins" of the revisionist organization to Jabotinsky's "dictatorship." At the opening session even revisionist sympathizers were taken aback by the efforts made to give it a Nazi aspect. As *Doar ha-Yom* put it, "The organizers saw that it was a spectacular event. They chose a magnificent hall . . . added brilliance with guards of Betar cadets." At the entrance of Jabotinsky (Il Duce, Achimeir called him), the curtain went up on "the military spectacle . . . A Betar corporal accompanied Jabotinsky to the dais, marching ramrod straight, his hand in a stiff salute at his cap brim." The Betar members, like the Nazis, wore brown shirts, and the rest of their uniform — cap, breeches, boots, and Sam Browne belt — was designed to match. Power in the revisionist organization, said *Doar ha-Yom*, had passed into the hands of the "Achimeir faction," whose "fascist leadership" was unmistakable.[16]

Under this regime the Revisionists had stepped up their war against the Histadrut labor exchange, all the while extolling their own "neutral exchange," which they also called the Blue-White exchange, after the national colors. Several labor conflicts, primarily in Jerusalem and the Sharon citrus settlements, turned into raging battles. Histadrut members, defending organized labor, and revisionist scabs — including members of the Terrorists and another strong-arm band called Ha-Egrof (the Fist) — touting the Blue-White exchange, engaged in combat.

Vladimir Jabotinsky, in exile in Paris, took a vital part in this battle through articles giving the revisionist warriors in Palestine moral support and ideological guidance. The most important — and bellicose — of these were published in October and November 1932 under the titles "The Red Swastika" and "Yes, to Break!" In the first, Jabotinsky sanctioned revisionist strike-breaking methods in Palestine: "On the authority of an honest man and an honest writer I hereby remove the stigma from the word *scab* on the ground of Palestine and in the building of the Jewish state." He also felt that "the leftists' takeover in Palestine [i.e., by the Histadrut and Mapai] has led to . . . knife fights, and I see no guarantee as yet that the process will stop at cold steel." He said the Histadrut was a "gross cancer in the body of the Yishuv, growing ever more malignant," whose every word in the press bears the "stamp of Mrs. Warren's profession." He solemnly vowed, "We will wage the war against this malignant growth until the end." Sharp as these words were, the title was harsher still, intimating that the Histadrut and Mapai were communist Nazis. In the other article Jabotinsky confirmed that his movement strove for nothing less than breaking the Histadrut as the sole representative organization of the workers. He called for all who found Histadrut methods displeasing to support the recently founded revisionist workers' organization "and to endeavor to make it the mightiest force in Palestine, one which will break, step by step — yes, break — the wretched and damaging system."[17]

Ben-Gurion's counterattack had long been in the making. Ben-Gurion had completed his task of collecting material to use against Jabotinsky late in September 1931. If he simply sat on this ammunition, leaving the lion's share of the war against the Revisionists to his colleagues, it was only because he was waiting for the time to be ripe. Jabotinsky's two articles, as well as an earlier one called "Pioneers and . . . Pioneers," apparently created what he was waiting for, the proper "atmosphere," in which public opinion had been sufficiently prepared for a massive assault to be effective.[18]

Ben-Gurion went into action on three fronts simultaneously. The first was the workplaces. To prepare for this battle he put the Hapoel Squadrons into final readiness for the violent clashes with revisionist strong-arm groups. On October 21, taking part in the national conference of Hapoel in Tel Aviv's Beit ha-Am open-air theater, he said, "Sport, for all its importance, is not an objective but merely a means." Hapoel was to serve as a "shield for labor," since "the character who professes sacred names and deals in scabbing has appeared." By the last day of 1932 he was able to gather a "committee meeting on the matter of organization" of the Hapoel Squadrons, which would "stand . . . at the disposal of the leadership for carrying out practical, day-to-day jobs" to "defend the class of organized workers and their achievements." On January 19, 1933, Ben-Gurion installed Manya and Israel Shochat in what could be considered the high command of the Squadrons, which then elected a tactical command that could take its orders directly from the HEC. At the same time, during the last months of 1932 and the first of 1933, Ben-Gurion increased the number of pickets in the Sharon citrus settlements who barred entry to the revisionist scabs and called for stepping up the struggle. On December 20 he himself marched on one of the picket lines "the entire day."[19]

The second front was his party, which he sought to win over to his conviction that the revisionist war was a life-and-death one and that violence had to be answered with violence. What was new about this argument was the extreme to which it took his either-or formula, which Ben-Gurion had first presented to the Central Committee on October 27. If Mapai did not design a plan "to become the majority in the Zionist Congress . . . the Revisionists" and their allies, from Mizrachi to the General Zionists B, would be the majority; they would "close off pioneering immigration and we will have to leave the Zionist Organization." Even so, the opposition to violence in Mapai, headed by Katznelson and Beilinson, remained unconvinced until Ben-Gurion made a comprehensive statement of his position at a Central Committee meeting on March 15, 1933. The following is a summary of what he said:

> Today's world is one of the beasts of prey; not only is this so in Germany, but in our own little world as well. While it is true that we have no storm troopers and secret police, our enemies fight us just as Hitler fights the workers. The difference is that our adversaries *cannot* carry out their designs. And there is another difference: the German people will not be destroyed by Hitler's actions, but we are liable to be ruined. All our work is destined for destruction unless we build a force to use against our own Hitlerites. They will use their majority to wipe us out, and they will cut us down brutally, with no holds barred. We face a war of life and death. This

time we must regard our preparations for the Congress as the central issue, vital to the entire movement. There is a danger that the elections will seem an everyday matter to us, but we must understand that this time it is a bloody game, and we must approach the elections as a war that will decide our fate. We can win this war and become the majority at the Congress.[20]

The third front was public opinion, and Ben-Gurion advanced on it at white heat. In January 1930 Ben-Gurion had spoken to Mapai about revisionism's "dark, reactionary character" and "its fascist tendencies, which imperil peace in the Yishuv." In a letter from Berlin about his impressions of the elections held in Germany that September, in which the Nazis gained nearly six million votes, he expressed the fear that the Revisionists, too, would reap major gains in the elections to the Zionist Congress. "I read . . . Hitler's organ, and it seemed to me that I was reading Jabotinsky in *Doar ha-Yom*. Same words, same style, and same spirit." After that he occasionally referred to the Revisionists as "our National Socialists" in letters and in closed meetings.[21] After Eliyahu Zvi Cohen sang Hitler's praises in February 1932 Ben-Gurion became less guarded about calling them Hitlerites; when he saw "The Red Swastika," the floodgates burst. Not only did he publicly call the Revisionists Hitlerites, but he dubbed Jabotinsky Vladimir Hitler at a huge mass meeting held in Tel Aviv in February 1933 to protest the Revisionists' having broken a large construction strike in Petah Tikva. Ben-Gurion, speaking under the open sky, said,

> What happened in Germany keeps Hitler's lieutenants in the Jewish community awake, itching to do the same. . . . In Germany, too, a cheap demagogue at first seemed ridiculous and laughable. . . . He knew how to capture . . . the hearts of millions of Germans from all classes with deceptive propaganda and rose to power. So let us not underrate the severity of this Hitleristic peril in the Jewish, Zionist street.

He applied this comparison to their respective organizations as well, saying, "Jabotinsky's wild propaganda feeds on street riots." The Terrorists and the Fist had been organized "for the sake of bloodshed" and were therefore capable of murder for political reasons.[22]

For the labor movement this represented a sharp escalation; until then it had behaved with restraint regarding the most venomous revisionist invective. Even Weizmann, a favorite target of revisionist diatribes, held his tongue, at least in public (though in a letter he called them "gangrene").[23] However, Ben-Gurion's derogatory labels did not become household words, and Ben-Gurion never repeated the epithet Vladimir Hitler. He probably had used it solely for dramatic effect, which he considered necessary not only to drive home to the public the main theme of the 1933 election campaign, but also, and primarily, to create the format of the campaign in Poland: a duel between himself and Jabotinsky.

This duel would not, of course, be conducted solely through public speeches. When Ben-Gurion learned that *Der Moment*, one of the two largest Yiddish papers in Poland, had gone over to the Revisionists, opening a column to Jabotinsky early in November 1932, he instructed Melech Noy, the Histadrut representative who headed the League in Poland, to discover whether *Hajnt*, the other paper, was prepared to carry his own articles. "To a great extent, the press will decide the outcome of the Congress elections," wrote the HEC to Noy in Ben-Gurion's name. The duel would be fought partly in print, from the pages of the two papers.[24]

Ben-Gurion held his first press conference on November 27, 1932, in his HEC office. He spoke about Jabotinsky and the Revisionists for three hours, making use at last of the files he had been accumulating. When he finished he thanked the reporters for their patience and said, "I am not tired, and will gladly answer any questions you have." The weary press had none. This heavy bombardment opened the campaign, making all that had preceded it seem like sporadic exchanges of fire. Ben-Gurion's remarks — cabled by the Jewish Telegraphic Agency to the ends of the earth, published at length in *Davar*, and distributed in myriad pamphlets in Hebrew, Yiddish, and English — provided both ammunition and guidelines to labor activists wherever the 1933 elections were to be held. Lengthy as they were, they can be summed up by Lincoln's famous adage, which Ben-Gurion quoted loosely: You can fool some of the people all of the time, and all of the people some of the time, but you can't fool all of the people all of the time. Jabotinsky and his followers were thorough demagogues whose words and doctrine were a huge and dangerous deception.[25]

Jabotinsky reacted to the press conference of "Mr. Ben-Gurion, one of the leaders of 'the left' in Tel Aviv," in a signed article published both in *Der Moment* and in *Hazit ha-Am.* "Only one of Ben-Gurion's charges is well founded, that I 'attack' the Histadrut," he wrote, adding that he intended to heighten his attack because it was imperative "to break . . . the unhealthy exclusive rule of the Histadrut and its claim to a monopoly as the representative of 'all' the Jewish workers."[26] Regarding Ben-Gurion's sobriquets Hitlerites and Vladimir Hitler, he kept his own counsel. No doubt he had good reasons for this, one of which was probably his disgust at the praise of Hitler and his doctrine spouted by Achimeir's fans and *Hazit ha-Am.* On March 17, 1933, he sent a letter to its editorial board demanding "absolute and unconditional adherence . . . not only to our campaign against Hitlerite Germany but also to our denunciation of Hitlerism in the full sense of the word."[27]

After the press conference Ben-Gurion began to scout for allies outside his party, groups such as Ha-Poel ha-Mizrachi and the General Zionists A. These efforts seem to have been designed to lend his campaign a positive aspect. He was seeking not only to destroy revisionism but also to build a responsible and progressive Zionist coalition. He was able to bring together those in his party who opposed "conquest of Zionism" slogans with the majority in supporting his efforts to create "a concentration" against a potential coalition of the Revisionists with Mizrachi and the General Zionists B.[28]

It is hard to tell whether Ben-Gurion made the war against the Revisionists the central theme of the election campaign on its own merits — out of his conviction that if victorious they would imperil the Histadrut and Zionism — or whether it was simply a stratagem designed to get around his party's reluctance to conquer Zionism. Certainly both motives played a part. In any case, that which Mapai had withheld from the conquest of Zionism it gave a thousand times over, in funds and manpower, when it came to battling the Revisionists and fighting for a "concentration." At the September 26 meeting of the Central Committee, Katznelson had complained that there was no money to send people abroad. If the party was concerned about the Diaspora, he argued, why not direct the party's press and literature at it? Sending correspondents abroad for the Histadrut young workers' journal and its children's weekly would achieve far better results than sending campaigners.

It is difficult to believe that Katznelson did not see through Ben-Gurion's maneuvers, but once Ben-Gurion escalated the struggle against the Revisionists and made it the central theme of the campaign, Katznelson no longer voiced doubts. Tabenkin, on the other hand, was more tenacious in his opposition to gaining a majority through electioneering; he not only saw through Ben-Gurion's stratagem, but he called it by name. At the March 15 Central Committee meeting, two weeks before Ben-Gurion's departure for Poland, Tabenkin announced that he did not believe in "political accomplishments," or that a majority at the Congress and a Zionist coalition would strengthen the labor movement, and rejected Ben-Gurion's either-or formula. "I do not accept the assumption," he asserted, "that there will be either a majority at the Congress or defeat. . . . I reject the idea of gaining a majority, because it implies an effacing of our identity. . . . Let us put forth our true self. Let us identify with no one." His position was unequivocal and intransigent. If the labor movement held on to its singularity through socialist pioneering and building up the cooperative agricultural settlements, and invested in these all its spiritual and material resources, Jewry would eventually rally 'round. "Broad-based popular groups will follow us, but only on the condition that we do not water down the essence of our movement." But even Tabenkin could not stand aside while a battle raged against the Revisionists. Eventually he and his followers came charging to the front line, forming an important contingent in the massive army of activists that the Histadrut and the party threw into the campaign.[29]

Nevertheless, despite entreaties and threats — in January Ben-Gurion notified the Central Committee that he would go to Poland "only if I can be assured that the party knows what it wants and if it can go before the masses with its own Zionist program" — Mapai did not accept the majority slogan and did not draw up a program. As far as the party was concerned, Ben-Gurion had set out to rout the Revisionists, not to gain a majority at the Congress and the mantle of Zionist leadership.

Although he told the Central Committee the day before he left for Poland that the lack of a program was "a worse setback than a lack of command," it seems he was not much upset by this. The absence of a program that might have clipped his wings, in conjunction with an abundance of money and personnel to do his bidding, gave him a freedom of action that made it appear more likely than ever that he would be able to confront his party with a fait accompli. There is, of course, no proof of this, but he did not carry out his threat, and all signs show that he never intended to.

Among the signs were his letters to Rega. On January 26, just two weeks after the threat, he had written her that he would be coming to Europe, "first to Berlin, from there perhaps to Danzig, then to Lithuania, and on Passover, to Poland. I will try to come to Vienna before Berlin *perhaps*, but I am not sure exactly when. But I will come to Vienna."

On March 16 he wrote her, "I leave Palestine on March 29. On the morning of April 4 (Tuesday) I will come to Vienna, where I intend to spend two days, and on April 6 I will leave for Warsaw." After that, he explained, he would be completely tied up with the campaign until the Congress elections in Poland, Danzig, Lithuania, and Latvia, and possibly other places as well. But between the elections and the Congress, he promised, "I intend to spend more time in Vienna. We will see each other, then, in another three weeks." He had opened his letter "My Rega" and closed "Yours, David." In the last line he had added, "For the time being don't tell a soul the date of my arrival in Vienna."[30]

On March 29 Ben-Gurion, without a program but with plenty of resources, set out on a campaign that would prove decisive in his political life as well as that of the Jewish people as a nation among nations. From Genoa he cabled Rega that he would arrive by train on April 6 at Vienna–South Station. But if he had intended to devote all his time there to her he was disappointed. The HEC had wired Vienna his arrival time, and large meetings had been scheduled for that night and the next day. And on April 9, his last day in Vienna, Ben-Gurion was called to a public meeting at the packed Continental Hall. Nevertheless, the short time he and Rega had together was pleasantly spent. To his delight she had already acquired a smattering of Hebrew and he could speak with her a bit in his beloved language; his enthusiasm encouraged her to try writing to him in it. At one scenic place in Vienna she took pictures of him with her box camera, one of the few times in his life that anyone close to Ben-Gurion had photographed him, and he was eager to know if they had turned out well. On receiving a letter with the snapshots enclosed, he wrote Rega, "I was doubly happy to receive your letter this time. It is good that you are writing in Hebrew, even if it leaves a lot to be desired. The pictures are good, especially the one with the shadow, and the second, the head in profile. If I could get two or three more of these I would be grateful." Ben-Gurion manifested his usual tactlessness, even to someone as dear to him as Rega.

The train out of Vienna Sunday night, April 9, brought Ben-Gurion to Warsaw the next afternoon; he was received by a group of welcomers and many Hapoel motorcyclists, who accompanied him from the station to his hotel in a noisy and impressive cavalcade. The following day, writing to Paula about his arrival in Warsaw, he explained, "I spent three days in Vienna. The comrades forced me to stay until Sunday for a public meeting that they had called a week before I arrived. They cabled Warsaw to insist that I remain. The Viennese thought the meeting a great success." This letter shows Ben-Gurion's awareness of Paula's watchful, if distant, eye, and his feeling that an account of his movements was in order.[31]

No answer came from Paula; instead Ben-Gurion received a letter from Geula informing him that Paula had fallen down two steps and was in Hadassah Hospital. Frightened, he wrote Paula two letters asking how she was, but then, although he wrote her several times more from Poland, he left off inquiring about her condition. He had probably become used to her false alarms and bids for attention and may have assumed that if something serious had happened, someone, either a family member or an HEC colleague, would have notified him. But it is more likely that he was so immersed in the election campaign that he forgot about his wife entirely. His last-minute cancellation of another meeting with Rega — he was supposed to fly to Vienna to see her in compliance with her repeated requests — bears this out. "I cannot leave the work in Poland now," he wrote her. "I am sorry that I did not notify you in time, as I am afraid you waited for me, and I am sorry I let you down. I wanted to meet, as you did, even for a short time, but the work is holding me up."[32]

The 108 days of his campaign trip were one intensive and almost superhuman effort. His base was Warsaw, where he spent thirty-seven days setting up the League as election headquarters, attending innumerable organizational meetings, preparing propaganda, writing articles, circulars, and letters, and, primarily, instructing activists from all over Poland whom, together with emissaries from Palestine, he put into action as a campaign staff answering to a single authority. He spent the rest of the time shuttling to twenty-five different cities, including some in Lithuania, Latvia, and eastern and western Galicia; he appeared at forty-one mass meetings, ten balls, forty-three regional activists' meetings, and countless other functions where he held many personal conversations.[33]

To a great extent his work was dictated by the nature of his duel with Jabotinsky, who also regarded Poland as the "center of gravity" and had arrived there before Ben-Gurion. Jabotinsky, who was making speeches and holding meetings in Warsaw in March, before Ben-Gurion had left Palestine, had two other advantages as well.

The first stemmed from a political victory within his own movement. In March the Revisionist Party Council, held in Katowice, Poland, owing to the opposition of a group led by Meir Grossman, had failed to adopt a resolution endorsed by Jabotinsky to secede from the Zionist Organization and found a new one. Twenty-four hours after the council ended, on the strength of his being the president of the Revisionist World Union, Jabotinsky issued a manifesto to the effect that he was assuming personal authority over the revisionist institutions. "You . . . will submit to all instructions of the president of the World Union of the Zionist-Revisionists and the permanent institutions approved by him," he ordered the Revisionists. To refute assertions by Grossman that this act constituted a putsch and dictatorship and prove the movement loyal to him, on April 16 Jabotinsky held a referendum in which Grossman was routed. Grossman founded a new revisionist movement and ran as its head in the Zionist Congress elections; he received only 11 percent of all revisionist votes.

The struggle to win the referendum served Jabotinsky as a dress rehearsal for the elections. The publicity he and his doctrine gleaned from it, and his great triumph over his rival, strengthened his position in his party and among the general public to such an extent that the

Polish government regarded him as the man who would lead the Zionist movement. Since it was eager to see the Jews emigrate from the country, it put the state radio at his service, on April 28, to deliver "The Word of Jabotinsky to the World."[34] Jabotinsky had great confidence in himself and his movement, which more than ever obeyed him to a man and served to augment his other assets.

Jabotinsky, who had been born in Odessa in 1880, was blessed with a gift for languages. As a young man he had mastered Hebrew, Yiddish, Italian, German, and English, in addition to Russian, his mother tongue. From an outstanding Russian journalist he became a Hebrew poet and author, some of whose translations into Hebrew of the poetry of Dante and Poe are considered classics; his novel *Samson,* first published in Russian in 1926, was translated into German and English, and it is still in print in Hebrew. But beyond all this Jabotinsky had another, more remarkable talent that made him truly extraordinary: he was undoubtedly one of the greatest, if not *the* greatest, orators ever to arise from the Jewish people. He knew and loved the craft of oratory.

The power of the word is mighty, and nowhere is it more so than in an election campaign. Among Jews, particularly in the Polish Diaspora, it had vastly increased. In their distress, bordering on hopelessness, the word, like a prayer, was a lone shaft of light in the darkness. With its power, itinerant preachers could brighten their gloom. It was enough to say "Jerusalem" in the right tone of voice to make downcast listeners stand tall. The 1933 election campaign in Poland was built entirely on the word, the spoken word in particular, a factor that seemed to work in favor of Jabotinsky. The great orator carefully matched his words with the right intonations, facial expressions, and gestures to make almost tangible to his listeners the image of a huge Hebrew army, all of whose soldiers were heroes of Maccabean proportions, ready to surge forth and establish a Jewish state on both sides of the Jordan. Listeners carried aloft on such rhetoric were led to believe they had merely to vote revisionist for the army and the state to become solid reality and assure their redemption.

Ben-Gurion was simply no match for Jabotinsky as a speaker, and knowing well that the long road to the realization of Zionism was fraught with difficulties, he found himself at a double disadvantage. A war activist cautioned Ben-Gurion about maligning his opponent the day after his first speech. "There is a feeling of admiration for Jabotinsky among the masses of Jews, the lower middle class. No one wants to hear a bad word about him." But Ben-Gurion's experience had apparently already taught him this, according to two anecdotes — among the few he ever told about himself — which he often retold. During the meeting at the Continental in Vienna, before he had gone to Poland, when he had spoken about Jabotinsky ("and of course I held nothing back," he would say) "a heckler in the crowd shouted at me, when I compared Jabotinsky and Hitler, 'Israel, although it has sinned, is still Israel' and left in protest." He demonstrated that this line of talk could be counterproductive. The other anecdote, revealing the unwillingness of people to hear the truth, concerned a speech Ben-Gurion had made in Riga. "The next day a man of about forty came to my hotel and told me that he had been to my meeting and heard for the first time the truth about Palestine — and stopped being a Zionist. I replied that at the meeting I had not exhausted all the difficulties I had met in my hard times in Palestine, yet my faith in Zionism grows stronger every year."[35]

Ben-Gurion knew exactly whom he had picked as his dueling partner.

Jabotinsky, one of the great stage actors . . . knew the weaknesses of the people, and through them wished to capture its heart . . . There has never been a more popular man among Polish Jewry. He was admired because there was a hunger for a national hero. They said, "Here is a hero." . . . Do not believe that anyone could disprove this with speeches. I do not say that out of modesty. The greatest of orators could not have stood up to him had it not been for the workers' constructive enterprise.

He wrote these words for *Davar* after the campaign. The strategy he chose to counter Jabotinsky was to expose the revisionist lies and demagoguery (an "easy Zionism") and to pit the truth against it — outlining the difficulties in implementing Zionism ("the necessity of pioneering efforts and unlimited devotion in the building of Palestine"). From this strategy, which he called the crusade against Hitlerism-revisionism, Ben-Gurion never swerved.[36]

If this was a risk, it was hedged by every means possible. Ben-Gurion made up for the strikes against him with organization and perseverance. He ran the election headquarters in Warsaw and its force of campaigners like an army. In his office he looked every inch the commander in chief, studying maps and figures. He instructed his subordinates "to find out about every Jew who might conceivably be a Zionist and get in touch with him," that is, sell him a shekel, which would enable him to vote. To this end he and his staff prepared a list of six hundred Jewish places in Poland, their associations and parties, and divided them into twenty-five districts. To each he assigned canvassers and had local campaign headquarters set up. He imposed shekel quotas on the activists and made them fill out weekly questionnaires: How many shekels had they sold in their districts? Had they filled the quota? Why not? How and when would they fill it? To keep up morale among his campaigners he gave speeches and pep talks, going to as many district meetings as possible, even by commercial flights, which were expensive but saved time. He was the first Zionist electioneer to discover the airplane.

The well-oiled machine he built brought his message to every corner where Jews lived in Poland, Lithuania, Latvia, and Galicia. It enabled him to duel with Jabotinsky more confidently, since the latter's sole ammunition was his silver tongue. Their combat began and ended in Warsaw, where they also met during its course, but all of Poland and its neighboring countries was their stage. They chased each other from city to city, from meeting to meeting, exchanging verbal blows, competing visions, and reproofs. The scale of this battle and its intensity were unprecedented, but had a most disturbing occurrence not taken place in Tel Aviv right in the middle of it, it is doubtful whether the campaign would have been enough to change wholly the face and course of Zionism.

On Friday evening, June 16, Chaim Arlosoroff, a leader of Mapai and head of the Jewish Agency's Political Department, was shot to death by two unidentified assailants. Three days later, Abraham Stavsky, a young Revisionist from Brisk and a member of the Terrorists, was arrested at Abba Achimeir's home and charged as an accomplice to murder. The affair acquired mammoth proportions among Jews in Palestine and Zionists worldwide and lasted for many years. (In 1982 the president of Israel's supreme court, at the behest of Prime Minister Menahem Begin, appointed a judicial commission of inquiry to finally put it to rest.) This affair not only left an imprint on the image of the Zionist camp and changed its course, it had tremendous influence on the 1933 election campaign and the contest between Ben-Gurion and Jabotinsky.

Many, perhaps the great majority in Palestine, were not surprised that a Revisionist was accused of the murder, since others besides Ben-Gurion and his fellow Mapai members believed that Achimeir and his Terrorists sanctioned and were capable of political murder. Moreover, among the moderate Revisionists there was even greater apprehension of an act of terror by Achimeir's people.

Shortly before Ben-Gurion had left for Poland, news reached Mapai that Betar members in Tel Aviv had told their friends that "Ben-Gurion won't return from Poland alive." When he arrived in Warsaw a safe house had been put at his disposal and bodyguards assigned to protect him. When on April 18 he delivered his speech from the platform of Warsaw's Nowošci Hall, a young Betar woman hurled a tin can at him from the balcony. Because he did not learn for a year that it was only a stink bomb weighted with sand, he was convinced that it was a bomb that had failed to detonate, an attempt to "liquidate" him. A few weeks later he left his secret quarters when their whereabouts became known to the Revisionists and moved into the Bristol Hotel. At his arrival in Vilna, on June 17, the local police assigned three men to his hotel, and secret police accompanied him everywhere, for intelligence had been received that the Revisionists intended to "assault" him.

Mapai reported Arlosoroff's murder to Ben-Gurion in a telegram it sent from the HEC on Saturday, June 17, to Warsaw, which reached him in Vilna shortly after he had checked into his hotel room. He felt faint when he read it. After recovering he wired the HEC, "What happened? Cable details," and rushed to the editorial office of Vilna's *Die Zeit* to phone the *Hajnt* office in Warsaw. Abraham Goldberg, the paper's editor, relayed the June 16 JTA dispatch from Jerusalem, which in essence said that on Friday evening Arlosoroff and his wife had taken a walk along the seashore. Two assailants accosted them in Hebrew, and after establishing Arlosoroff's identity and lighting his face with a flashlight, shot him once in the abdomen and fled. Arlosoroff died two hours later in the hospital. Melech Noy in Warsaw knew nothing more. Ben-Gurion tried to contact the HEC by telephone, but could not. *Die Zeit* published the story on Sunday, adding, "We have been told by Warsaw that Arlosoroff did not fall at the hands of Arabs." It is highly probable that Ben-Gurion also knew this detail.

Because the crime had taken place near Ben-Gurion's home and the assailants were not Arabs and had confirmed their victim's identity before shooting him, Ben-Gurion was convinced that the Revisionists — more precisely, the Terrorists — had assassinated Arlosoroff. He therefore cabled the HEC from Vilna: "Myriad pioneers mourn the loss to the nation and to the Jewish worker in the fall of Arlosoroff at the hands of brutes* thirsty for his blood. His memory will never vanish from our hearts and from national memory." This cable was printed in the special edition of *Davar* on Sunday, June 18.

Afraid that a civil war would break out in Palestine, Ben-Gurion decided to cancel the election campaign and return at once. Before boarding the train, hoping to forestall violence, he sent the HEC a tele-

---

* The Hebrew makes it evident that this word refers to the Terrorists.

gram: "Comrades, we will exercise restraint over our pain and seek no revenge." This cable was also printed in the special Sunday edition of *Davar*.

Ben-Gurion's conviction of the Terrorists' guilt was based on what seemed to be incontrovertible evidence. First, if a Betar woman had tried to kill him in Warsaw, as Ben-Gurion believed, why would Betar agents in Tel Aviv not try to murder Arlosoroff? Second, in a party whose leaders "educate their youth for bloodshed," he said, naming Jabotinsky and Achimeir, there had to be "a gang of murderers." The fascist indoctrination given Betar youth was the root of the evil. "Whoever breaks strikes and beats up workers is also capable of murder."

The same line of thought guided Katznelson in Palestine. He, too, regarded Achimeir's indoctrination of his followers as the "source of an impure, corrupt, and corrupting sect," and in his eulogy of Arlosoroff, delivered in the courtyard of the HEC building before the funeral procession set out, he said,

> Not by chance did Chaim Arlosoroff fall. An impure hand fired at his heart. . . . We live in troubled times when entire movements pretentiously claim to be changing history with unclean hands, shedding the blood of innocents, beheading leaders and thinkers. May every movement, whatever semblance it assumes, that takes this path, in which unclean acts are its tools, be damned.

With these transparent allusions Katznelson, too, without having exchanged one word with Ben-Gurion, pointed an accusing finger at the Revisionists and the Terrorists. They were the only ones to speak their minds so soon.

The following morning, June 19, detectives arrested Abraham Stavsky on the basis of statements made to the police by three people, one in Jerusalem and two in Tel Aviv, who had no connection to each other and did not know of one another's accounts. Revisionist leaders in Palestine officially dissociated themselves from Stavsky, informing the head of the criminal investigations in Jerusalem that he was nothing but a Communist who had been "planted" in Betar by the Comintern and had carried out the murder on Moscow's instructions.

The labor movement, led by Ben-Gurion, argued otherwise. Returning to Warsaw from Vilna at dawn on June 19, Ben-Gurion took part that afternoon in a mass mourning demonstration in Nowosci Hall, where he said,

> Certain circles are spreading rumors that the murder had a personal motivation; it is my duty to make it clear that this murder was political. . . . I am very well acquainted with [communist] subversive activity in the Yi-

shuv, but regarding Arlosoroff's murder I must make it plain that they are not to blame. . . . I do not accuse the Arabs of the murder either. . . . I do not accuse any party. I only think that this terrorist act against Arlosoroff was undoubtedly a political one.

Cables from the HEC persuaded Ben-Gurion not to return to Palestine, and for a few days he asked the committee to adhere to the line of restraint and no retaliation. It was nevertheless clear to all that in saying that the murder had been political, he was pointing a finger at the Terrorists, which meant at the Revisionists.

Jabotinsky perceived at once that a great danger threatened his party in the elections, as it tried to disconnect itself from Stavsky on the one hand and stood accused of the deed attributed to him on the other. On June 22 Jabotinsky published an article in *Der Moment* (distributed later as a newsletter in Palestine) in which he asserted two basic grounds for refuting the charge. The first was that it was unthinkable for a good Jew even to consider that one Jew could kill another; the second was that Stavsky was the victim of incitement. He laid the responsibility for making most of the public, including the Revisionists, believe Stavsky guilty at Mapai's doorstep. Just as Ben-Gurion, in Vilna, had intimated a murder plot by the Terrorists, so Jabotinsky, from Warsaw, pointed his finger at Mapai. He accused it of "trafficking in blood," comparing Abraham Stavsky to Mendel Beilis, the victim of a 1911 charge in Russia that was called a blood libel. Jabotinsky said that Mapai, to further its struggle against the revisionist movement in general and the election campaign for the Congress in particular, had falsely accused Stavsky and his friends — and by extension the entire Revisionist movement — of murdering Arlosoroff. This claim would be made repeatedly for over a generation and with innumerable changes of style, its central piece of evidence being Ben-Gurion's telegram from Vilna. The Revisionists deemed this cable urging restraint an indirect accusation that they were responsible for Arlosoroff's death.[37]

The murder investigation in Palestine and its ramifications, including illegal attempts to determine its course by both Mapai and the Revisionists, as well as two trials in 1934 (at the second of which Stavsky was acquitted, primarily because of a quirk in the Palestine criminal law), have no direct bearing on Ben-Gurion's biography. Suffice it to say that until the day he died, Ben-Gurion's belief in Stavsky's guilt remained unshaken. At the same time, the way he used the affair as a factor in the election campaign affords an insight into his way of thinking and working. Immediately after the murder he changed his tactics in his duel with Jabotinsky. On July 4 the League began to publish its own organ, *Dos Wort*, which Ben-Gurion had gone to great lengths to establish, and thus end his association with *Hajnt*, which wanted to censor the harsher opinions in his articles. Jabotinsky was publishing in *Der Moment* articles deploring the "blood libel," which were reprinted by other papers, stirring the readers to pity the innocent Stavsky and calling on them to donate to committees for Stavsky's defense. In response Ben-Gurion took the line of attacking Jabotinsky and his doctrine sanctioning political assassination. A letter he sent from Warsaw to Geula sums it up. "The guilty party is not Stavsky, but the mentors and leaders who pushed him along this course." In countering Jabotinsky's claim that one Jew could not kill another and that only Mapai was capable of such blood libel by Jews against Jews, Ben-Gurion did not mince words. First, he asserted,

> [There was] an unsuccessful attempt to liquidate Ben-Gurion. Yesterday, a successful attempt against Arlosoroff. Tomorrow, who knows against whom? . . . Must we wait until after a leader of the workers, at whom the incitement is directed, is injured by a deadly tin can thrown at him at a meeting in Warsaw, or by bullets fired in the night in Tel Aviv?[38]

This style of attack is puzzling in regard to the central question of whether Jabotinsky and his movement really had become strong enough to win the election or whether Ben-Gurion actually concocted the notion of their increased influence on the public and danger to Zionism and the labor movement only to rally his own movement and turn it more definitively to the conquest of Zionism. On June 15 Arlosoroff had told the Mapai Central Committee that in Poland, where he, too, had participated in the election campaign, he had found no "revisionist offensive" but rather that "our party is aggressive" because "the Revisionists are broken from within. . . . The period of revisionist sympathy in the Jewish community has passed. . . . The atmosphere I found in Poland was different from anything I had expected. I thought I would be walking into a revisionist ferment, but this was not the case."

That day Ben-Gurion had written in his diary, and to someone in the HEC, in a similar vein. "I estimate that in Poland we will receive approximately 50 percent of the votes — as long as . . . nothing unexpected occurs. There is the real fear that the Revisionists . . . will sabotage the elections and try to disrupt them in some manner as their panic continues to increase." He was so sure of victory that he vehemently refused to postpone the elections, as the Revisionists were demanding, and persuaded Mapai to do the same. On June 30 he was gladdened by the news "about the distribution of shekels. This proves that the possibilities were much greater than even I, the dreamer, had imagined." On July 3 he wrote in his diary and to one of his followers, "Our victory is assured." On the seventh he expressed a still greater hope. "It is not out of the question that we receive an absolute majority against all the other parties."

The Revisionists achieved only mediocre success in the elections, which they blamed on the Arlosoroff murder, or more precisely on Mapai's blood libel of them. The staff at Ben-Gurion's election headquarters also thought that the murder had helped Mapai at the polls because it forced the General Zionists B and Mizrachi, potential partners in the revisionist "concentration," to take a position on whether the murder was political, committed by Revisionists, or a sexual assault by Arabs, and to condemn it, and thereby "brought about the isolation of Jabotinsky's party in the election campaign." Itzhak Gruenbaum, leader of the radicals, was more reserved. In his view the murder did not influence the vote only in Palestine, but it seems there was a consensus that it had helped Mapai's cause worldwide.[39]

Only Ben-Gurion thought differently. In his view the murder and the charge against Stavsky helped the Revisionists. For one thing, many voters recoiled from the labor movement's belief that one Jew had killed another (which Jabotinsky played to the hilt); for another, many were affected by the revisionist charge of blood libel, or what Jabotinsky called the Beilisiad. This was a powerful tactic, as there was not a Jew alive who did not remember Beilis without a shudder. To reinforce the comparison Jabotinsky publicly asked the renowned lawyer Oscar Gruzenburg, who had defended Beilis, to take on Stavsky's defense. Jabotinsky convinced many Jews and non-Jews alike that Stavsky was an innocent victim being persecuted by wicked villains whose blind hatred was like that of the Black Hundreds in Kiev for the Jews or that of those who had slandered Beilis.

There were two good reasons for Ben-Gurion to adhere to his argument. One, of course, was that he truly believed it. For a short time Jabotinsky thought the same way, which supports this possibility. On June 26 Jabotinsky wrote to a friend from Warsaw, "I believe we will be victorious after all this incitement. . . . In Poland the mood of the public and of the masses has already turned against the slanderers. Circulation of *Der Moment* has grown enormously." Ben-Gurion, with his fine political instinct, seems to have read Jabotinsky's thoughts from afar. The next day he wrote in his diary, which he sent to his colleagues in Mapai, "Jabotinsky wants to be built up by the murder. For the time being he is succeeding."

But it is difficult to reconcile this evaluation with his unshakable certainty of an upcoming victory or rejection of the Revisionists' request to postpone the elections until a quieter time. Had Ben-Gurion truly feared that the charge against Stavsky was damaging to the labor movement he could easily have backed off on his assertions that Stavsky was a product of Jabotinsky's teachings. This consideration leads to the assumption that Ben-Gurion had a different reason: apprehension that his election victory would be attributed to lies and false accusations. On June 28 he wrote to the Mapai Central Committee in Palestine, "The Arlosoroff murder . . . is also a political disaster where the Congress is concerned. . . . They will now say [it is] a victory by murder . . . and I know the moral defeat that will involve."

To defend labor's triumph, Ben-Gurion had to refute the charge that tied the electoral victory to the murder and Stavsky's guilt. To this end he repeated his countercharge unceasingly, in letters and talks, in public and private. In July he wrote Paula, "Even Arlosoroff's murder has been an impediment to us. They have slandered us every day with news dispatches of calumny and defamation." He told an HEC functionary, who repeated it, "In the elections in Poland the Revisionists gained at least fifteen thousand extra votes thanks to an atmosphere created in their favor by various circles in connection with 'the blood libel.'" Later he put this figure at twenty thousand votes. Going over the election results at his home with fellow party workers, he reiterated his theory that the Revisionists had gained their extra votes "*thanks* to the Arlosoroff murder. . . . The murder served them as a rallying force and got them many people." Seven months later he explained once more to the Mapai Central Committee, "It seems that revisionism is getting more and more established, and the primary cause of this is the Arlosoroff murder."[40]

The victory he defended was prodigious, even greater than he had expected. In Poland he gained 91,055 of a total 214,388 votes; adding the votes in Danzig, eastern Galicia, western Galicia, Lithuania, and Latvia, he gained 149,498 of a total 365,724. His strategy was validated, for that total from the area he considered decisive constituted nearly 70 percent of the entire 535,113 votes cast in the 1933 election. Of these the labor movement received 226,058 (42%), of which 66 percent were from Poland and its neighboring countries. In Poland labor won thirty-eight of eighty-seven seats, and in the whole area in which Ben-Gurion campaigned it got sixty-three mandates, more than twice the Revisionists' twenty-nine. Three hundred six delegates were elected to the Congress worldwide, of which 132 came from labor, the largest faction (44%, according to the Congress's calculations). The revisionist faction numbered 43 (16%). Although he did not win an absolute majority — it is doubtful if he really believed that possible — Ben-Gurion did achieve his desire, the conquest of Zionism. Mapai would be the decisive factor in the new Zionist administration and remain so in Palestine for the next forty-four years, until 1977.

In his letters Ben-Gurion told Paula how overworked, tired, and tormented he was and about the obstacles piling up endlessly in his path. Paula's resentment over his prolonged absence — or her suspicions that his heart belonged to another — is evidenced both by her not writing to him and by his constant endeavors to write to her. From March 29 until May 11 he received only one letter from his wife. From an acquaintance whose friend had rented a room from Paula, Ben-Gurion learned that "you are back at home. I sent you letters the whole time, on the fifth of April, on the twelfth, the twenty-first, the twenty-fifth, and May 5, apart from newspapers — about my work and my appearances . . . and I am amazed that you write that in all this time you have received only one letter." Although he opened his letters "Dear Paula," they were really addressed to the whole family and signed "Kisses to all, Daddy," or simply "Daddy." A good portion of each letter was devoted to his exploits. For example, the government representative in Stanislav had compared his speech to that of Jabotinsky, who had visited there two weeks earlier. "With Jabotinsky — phrases; with me — seriousness. I had no idea that there were such discriminating people among the Poles as this one." By writing in this manner he was probably trying to make up to Paula for her suffering through his old partnership formula, and perhaps more because of a troubled conscience.

Rega, too, was brought into his partnership, and Ben-Gurion shared his problems and achievements with her to the point of making her his personal representative in Vienna. On June 3, for instance, he wrote her from Warsaw, among other things, "Phone Singer. . . . I want him to write me what's going on with him and with the shekel action also. . . . If Singer is ill and can't do anything new, let me know to whom I can turn regarding Congress action. Time is short . . . and if the task is not done now, the situation will be beyond repair." He signed these letters, "Yours, David." He also asked her to go to the Zionist Congress with him.[41]

He wrote to Paula of his intention "to rest" after the elections almost two and a half months before they were held. On June 13 he invited her to join him at the Congress: "It would be very good if you could come to the Congress. Travel a bit in Europe and rest. . . . Find out . . . how much it would cost. I'll try to make it possible, but what about the children?" This was obviously a halfhearted invitation given only to fulfill his sense of obligation. Even his questions about her and the house were vague and offhand. "Write me what Amos is doing. And what's going on in our neighborhood. Is the front lawn green? Are the children helping you out in the garden? I hope we'll see each other at the Congress." His interest in Rega was warmer and more personal. "Your well-being concerns me. What's going on with you, my Rega? When I come to Vienna you'll tell me everything, yes?" To Rega he also wrote that he was "very tired, working a lot, a bit beyond my powers," but hurriedly promised, "If I could see you at least once a week I would be much refreshed." But she wrote that she would not be able to attend the Congress, although she didn't say why, and on June 15 he asked, "Is it due to lack of money or some other reason?" On June 28 he wrote, "I wait impatiently for Election Day so that I can leave Poland and we'll have time to meet. We will suffer and live and love and do what we have to do — such is the command of life and fate. Yours, David."[42]

On July 1 he told Rega that the Congress was to meet on August 16 in Prague and asked, "When does your vacation begin? . . . Will you come to the Congress?" A week later he wrote her that although he was working a lot, "I have not for some time felt such an abundance of strength as in this war which I am now fighting. I believe it to be a decisive war and that we shall emerge triumphant." His letters to Paula, on the other hand, emphasized his fatigue and need for a rest. Sending Rega issues of *Dos Wort*, he said he would be coming to Vienna on July 25 or 26, and charged her with a small task. "I do not want to stay in Vienna because my colleagues won't allow me to rest, and I would like you to find me a nice place near Vienna where there are woods and mountains, costing up to 15–18 schillings a day including full board, and I will stay there for perhaps two weeks. But only on one condition, that you be there too. I want us to be together, if this is also your wish." Again he implored her to come to Prague for the Congress, closing, "Let Annie come too." On July 15 he wrote Paula from Warsaw, "From your last letter (9.7.33) it is not clear what you want to do with the children, especially with Renanale. I've already written you to leave her at home. If you don't you won't enjoy your travels abroad because you'll always be busy with her, since one cannot leave a small child in a strange city." He seems to have reminded her repeatedly and pointedly of the difficulties involved in traveling more than he urged her to come. In one letter he said, "After the elections I may come home. They will be held on July 23 here in Poland. I will leave on the twenty-fifth or the twenty-sixth, when the results are out." His phrasing could easily have given Paula the impression that he would start for home on one of these dates and was undoubtedly intentionally misleading. His last letter to her from Warsaw on July 25 gave her the good news of the "enormous victory!" which, according to the partnership formula, was her victory as well, but said nothing about his trip home. He found it sufficient to report that he was "awfully tired" and wanted "to take a two-week rest." Again he asked when she thought she would come for the Congress "and what you've decided to do with Renanale." And he sent her and the children many presents — witnesses to his troubled conscience.

On July 26 Ben-Gurion wired Rega, "I'm coming tomorrow morning at 11:05." He wrote party activists in Poland and Palestine that he was going to rest in the mountains outside Vienna for ten or twelve days. He arrived in Vienna by plane on Thursday morning, July 27. (He actually had eighteen days, until August 14, when he left for the Congress in Prague.) He revealed the location of his secret hideaway with Rega only to Mendel Singer, who provided him with a mailing address. But he could not avoid going into the city to meet with party members from Palestine at Singer's home (Singer was away on vacation with his family), leading some of them to believe he was staying there. One reported back to Palestine on August 8 that "Ben-Gurion has rested a bit and is fully energized for combat."[43]

With Rega and Annie he went to the theater, hiked in the mountains and woods of Vienna, and sailed the blue Danube. Snapshots of them, alone and together, show Ben-Gurion in an open collar looking rested, relaxed, and full of laughter. Rega, to whom Singer's wife had given a motherly warning against a broken heart, looks quite proud and happy. Not only did she have the great man to herself, but he had given her what he had withheld from his most loyal campaigners: he brought her one of the first copies of *From Class to Nation*, recently published in Palestine, inscribed, "To Rega from David." In her company Ben-Gurion got his warrior's rest and spent some of the happiest days of his life.

27

The Plan

BEN-GURION arrived in Prague on August 15, 1933, checked into the Grand Hotel Šroubek, and plunged into deliberations with party members who had gathered for the eighteenth Zionist Congress — "the decisive Congress" — which was to open on August 21. Ben-Gurion, however, was probably somewhat preoccupied by the tangle he would be in if Rega and Paula both arrived in Prague. Paula, unsure of his fidelity, had opted to keep him in the dark as to her plans, maintaining her silence even after he sent her £15 from Poland for the trip.

On August 10 he cabled the HEC from Vienna, "Has Paula set sail yet?" This roundabout inquiry had a dual purpose: eliciting the required information, while attesting — in case she had not yet left — to his having no doubt whatsoever that she was all set to go. The answer came soon: due to insufficient cash, Paula had not set out. He straightaway sent off another cable, this time directly to Paula. "I sent 15. If it's not enough borrow from Brodny [at Bank ha-Poalim]." But not until August 24, after the Congress had opened and Rega had arrived, did he receive a letter from Paula explaining that lack of money was not the only reason she had stayed home; she felt that Ben-Gurion was not all that eager for her to come. She had gotten the real message behind his invitations.

In his answer, Ben-Gurion dismissed her suspicions, going so far as to intimate that it was he who had been wronged.

> I don't know if you always take my opinions and wishes into consideration (you don't always have to), but I thought that this time you would and come to Prague. For this purpose I sent you £15 from Poland and after you wrote and cabled me that it wasn't enough I asked you to borrow from someone for the moment. . . . I would, of course, have repaid the

loan, and if you were here you wouldn't have to worry about money anymore. You would have rested here and found the Congress interesting. Regretfully, you did not do so. You got it into your head that I wasn't interested in your coming. I could not tear my heart out and send it to you so that you could see what was going on inside it. You also know that I must pass over in silence most painfully some of the things you write or say, as I do not wish to hurt you. Had you cabled me that you couldn't get a loan, I would have cabled Tel Aviv to give you one. I am very sorry that it was not our lot for you to be at this Congress.[1]

Nevertheless, he was undoubtedly relieved, as well as cheered, that this pleasure was Rega's lot. Rega spent two weeks in Prague, from the Congress's opening until its close on September 4, seeing Ben-Gurion at one of the finest hours of his life, as he ascended one of the highest crests of his political career. At the same time she was more careful than he to keep their relationship out of the public eye. After all, it was she who celebrated with him in the privacy of their hotel room. Ben-Gurion shared the leftovers with Paula in letters, when he had a free moment.

Actually, these were not insignificant; faithful to his partnership formula, he wrote her profusely. By parading his success he tried to prove to her that her suffering, past and present, had its due reward. In that way Paula was made a witness to the theatrics of his appearance at the Congress, especially when it set about electing the Zionist Executive. To the stupefaction of one and all, the man who had called on Mapai to conquer Zionism and who was responsible for its becoming, almost against its will, the largest faction at the Congress, in whose sole power it was to put together a coalition to stand at the head of the Zionist Organization, in Palestine and worldwide, announced — at the moment of his greatest triumph — "I shall stay in the Histadrut and shall not join the [Zionist] Executive."[2]

Those colleagues who knew him well and had heard him say in Vienna, before the Congress, "Under no circumstances whatsoever am I a candidate for the Executive," could not take these words at face value. Since 1929, when he had declined the sole leadership of the Histadrut on the premise that he wished to devote all his energy to the party, he had become increasingly involved in Zionist politics. After the 1929 Disturbances he had prepared a defense plan for the Yishuv and a constitution for a new biautonomous government in Palestine, or a federation of autonomies, under British aegis, for both of which he sought backing in the Zionist Executive.

He had drafted the rejoinder to Lord Passfield's White Paper and in January 1931 was elected the Yishuv's representative and had gone to

London to try to have it repealed. Joining with Weizmann in the struggle, he had had a part in the MacDonald Letter, which rescinded most of Passfield's decrees. In 1932 Ben-Gurion had put together his own Zionist political program and in 1933 called on his party to wage a "political war to change the scale of immigration," which was possible only with the British government's consent and cooperation. By 1933 he was up to his ears in Zionist politics, for which there could have been no more appropriate base than the Zionist Executive — more precisely its broader framework, the Jewish Agency.

But a more important reason for his colleagues not to believe Ben-Gurion arose from his fundamental principle, even before the election campaign, that his party not sit in the same coalition as the Revisionists. "Our war," he had told Ha-Poel ha-Mizrachi in March 1933, would be fought "against Hitlerism and scabs and it is unthinkable that we sit down together with them afterward." Later, at a National Council plenary meeting, he had argued, "There is nothing baser and more contemptible [than scabs] except perhaps for white traders and pimps"; and a few days before setting out for his Poland campaign, at a Mapai Central Committee meeting, he had rejected as coalition partners not only the Revisionists but also the parties close to them, the General Zionists B and Mizrachi.

However, the situation at the Congress, he said, was that "our faction is too big for anything to be done without our consent, yet we are not strong enough to do all we want by ourselves." To put together a coalition, Mapai needed the General Zionists B and Mizrachi, both of which he had already rejected. Would he then withdraw in the midst of this thorny situation that he himself had created? It was hard to believe.

First of all, twenty-four hours prior to the Congress's opening he announced at a labor faction meeting, with the press present, that the labor faction was ready to take charge of the Zionist Organization. Second, he himself frantically ran the negotiations for the new coalition — why would he have done so if he had not intended to join it? Third, Ben-Gurion's genius for politics was overwhelming; it was the breath of life for the man. Could he possibly turn his back on Zionism's supreme political body and return to construction workers' strikes and picket lines at the orchard gates? It would be like Beethoven's refusing to play the Broadwood piano made especially for him in England and brought to him in Vienna from Trieste, across the Alps, by ox cart. Convinced that Ben-Gurion's soul ached for the Zionist Executive, both his colleagues and the members of other factions implored him to agree to be elected to the Zionist Executive.[3]

He wrote Paula in great detail of these incessant entreaties. On September 2, he reported,

> I know the state of the movement well, and I am convinced that I have no right to quit the Histadrut now. I was certain that such would be our comrades' view. I am sure that, if questioned, every worker in Palestine would oppose my going to the Executive. But there is pressure on me here, and it grows stronger every day. . . . Katznelson demands it categorically. So does Tabenkin. Sharett makes it a condition for his own entry [to the Executive]. Dr. [Arthur] Ruppin is ready to join the Executive only if I do. And the faction demands that I join it. I have never faced such a trying personal question in my life. This is, I feel, a question of fate. My deep conviction stands at odds with the will of our movement.

Such reluctance was, to a certain extent, to be expected. The accepted form in the labor movement was for a man named to a high position to put up a show of refusing it, whereupon his associates set about entreating him to acquiesce to the "will" of the movement. Any display of eagerness for office or overt striving for it was disapproved. A pinch of humility was also considered desirable, so Ben-Gurion's description to Paula of his astonishment at the pressure brought to bear on him by the other parties — "I do not understand why Mizrachi, as well as the General Zionists, is demanding that I join the Executive" — was also bon ton.[4] But his humility and reluctance here went so far beyond the norm that the question arose as to what had pushed Ben-Gurion to such an extreme. He was not above taking pleasure in the ardent wooing, using it to impress on his colleagues how vital and indispensable he was to them and to Zionism. Nor is it too far-fetched to suppose that his proposal that Berl Katznelson join the Executive in his stead as the senior labor representative — a proposal forcefully reiterated — was meant to chide Katznelson, it being clear to Ben-Gurion and others, most of all to Katznelson himself, that he lacked the qualities and experience to be the strong, pragmatic, and fighting leader Zionism so badly needed. Katznelson, refusing the offered post and "categorically" clamoring for Ben-Gurion to accept it, seemingly avowed the latter's superiority and his inadequacy.

While Ben-Gurion was by no means immune to such pettiness, that alone could hardly explain his overblown resistance. Despite all the flaws in his character, Ben-Gurion was always a man of high purpose, unlikely to sacrifice it to satisfy a passing whim. And it was for a specific program that he had conquered Zionism. His insistence, before leaving for Poland, that Mapai put together such a program is evidence enough that he had already outlined one, for he would not have dreamed of spurring his party to adopt a plan not his own. As it turned out, his first weeks in the Executive confirmed that, and it was a plan to beat all plans. It therefore seems that he had brought the wooing ritual to such an unprecedented pitch in order to be able one day to tell his associates not to contest his position or program since both were of their own doing.

On September 5 the wooing finally came to an end, and the next day Ben-Gurion wrote to Paula.

> You already know the outcome of the Congress from the telegrams. To a certain extent it was a surprise; even as regards myself it was unexpected. I was always for a broad-based coalition — without the Revisionists — and to this end I put in a lot of effort. But it did not come to pass. The General Zionists B presented us with harsh terms and demanded broad concessions. . . . Mizrachi, too, made it difficult for us. . . . Over the last few days I have reached the conclusion that we must set up an Executive with a few close friends from the General Zionists A, and under these circumstances it has become absolutely necessary that I join the Executive. The difficulty lies in the impossibility of my leaving the Histadrut, so I agreed to join the Executive on condition that I receive no portfolio, and I will continue to live in Tel Aviv and work in the Histadrut as before, giving the Executive only one or two days a week. I will deal with political questions especially. To make this possible I must immediately have a telephone installed in my study, but the number is not to be given to anyone except Moshe Sharett and one or two others, so that they can phone me whenever necessary. Yesterday was the Executive's first meeting, and it was decided that I am to go to meet with Weizmann — he is now in Merano, Italy — and after that to London for negotiations with the Colonial Office on increasing immigration. . . . Shalom and kisses, Daddy.[5]

Just as he had joined the Achdut ha-Avodah secretariat in 1921, Ben-Gurion joined the Zionist Executive with one foot still in the Histadrut and with a stipulation. The stipulation then, that Achdut ha-Avodah become a labor army, had been spelled out, whereas this one was only hinted at. Nevertheless, his Mapai associates were probably well aware that he would continue serving as their man in the Zionist Executive only if he received their full support.

After the Zionist Congress elections of 1935, in which the labor faction made even further gains, almost accomplishing the full "conquest" (48.8% of the vote), Ben-Gurion again declined to join the Zionist Executive and to accept its chairmanship, with the claim that his place was in the Histadrut. "Tabenkin made me change my mind," he said afterward. "He sat and spoke with me for six hours, brought me to tears, and made me powerless until I was forced to listen to him and devote all my time to Zionist action." This time not Katznelson but Tabenkin, the man who headed the United Kibbutz Movement, forced the post of Zionist Executive chairman on Ben-Gurion. Ben-Gurion went out of his way to present himself as giving in primarily to the desires of the pioneering segment of the labor movement. That September he wrote his children, "Leaving the Histadrut for me is in fact like leaving Palestine. . . . My deepest desires and aspirations, my spiritual and human ties, my private and public life, my true worth as a man, a Jew, a worker, and an individual of our time — everything is tied in with the Histadrut. More precisely, with the Eretz-Israeli labor movement. I fear that if I stay in the Executive my responsibility in Zionist matters will grow, and I will be swallowed up in Executive activity and actually torn from the Histadrut."[6]

These letters to his children, like his diary, were sent to the HEC. More than once copies were made and distributed among members of the HEC and Mapai's Central Committee before they reached their destination, if they reached it at all. Amos, for instance, never read the most politically or historically important of them until they were published in book form, under the title *Letters to Paula and the Children*, or in Ben-Gurion's memoirs, thirty and forty years after the fact. Hence Ben-Gurion's letters to his family should not be read as an intimate account; at times they were intended as unveiled messages to his colleagues in the HEC and the party.

The more involved Ben-Gurion became in Zionist Organization affairs and the further he moved from the Histadrut, the more important his pioneering image became to him, and his outward modesty grew in direct proportion to his rising fame as a Zionist national leader. Theoretically he remained an HEC employee on loan to the Zionist Executive, demanding and receiving a much lower salary than the other Executive members. In response to the Histadrut census of 1937, by which time his name was known to all as chairman of the Jewish Agency Executive in Jerusalem, Ben-Gurion listed "the HEC" as his employer and "secretary of the HEC" as his "present occupation." In March 1938 he wrote Berl Katznelson,

> I have been held captive in the Zionist Executive for five years now. I had originally taken on this burden for two years . . . as I could not bear the sight of Moshe [Sharett]'s and [Eliezer] Kaplan's distress when weighty responsibility under difficult conditions fell on them for the first time in their lives. My membership in the Zionist Executive is a moral and human torment for me. A dual torment. I am absolutely cut off from the movement — and serving in a capacity which I cannot stand. After sticking my head in this noose I could not extricate it.

Ultimately, in the State of Israel's first official census in 1948, when Ben-Gurion was prime minister and minister of defense, he entered "agricultural worker" as his occupation, the image of himself as a pioneer being retrieved from his days in Sejera.[7] His stance as a "captive," shanghaied into servitude by the will of the movement, doubled his sway; powerful as his high office made him, his associates' perpetual courting of him increased his power.

An essential change in Ben-Gurion's partnership formula accompanied his rise to national leadership. Until 1933 both Ben-Gurion, as theoretician and executor, and his partners, as his aides, fulfilled their roles in the partnership willingly. His refusal to join the Zionist Executive signaled a new privilege for Ben-Gurion — to demand from his partners support even against their wills. Just as he (supposedly) subjected his will to that of the movement and took on a duty he did not want, so the movement would be obliged to support him always, unconditionally, even when differences of opinion occurred or when he was unable to take part in party deliberations and resolutions. This revised formula was apparently meant to strengthen his position in the labor movement's internal controversy. He had a gut feeling that this would escalate tremendously as the conflict between labor movement values and the necessity for action became more polarized upon his joining the Executive and taking steps to execute his plan — which his party had not yet approved.

If his colleagues accepted his new formula, even though they did not believe for a minute that Ben-Gurion had joined the Executive unwillingly, it was only because most of them had great confidence in his leadership. But Paula, who knew her man better than anyone, was aware that he was both proud and happy with his new status. Sure as he was of himself and the path he had chosen, something of the shtetl boy remained with him in his rise to the top of the world Zionist movement, and he considered his unlisted phone number and mission to Weizmann in Merano status symbols whose sweetness he shared with her in his letters.

On September 6, the day he had written to Paula, he had also written to Rega of his visit to Weizmann, but most of that letter was taken up with his fear that he would not be able to visit her in Vienna, though he had promised that if he returned to Europe within three months, "of course I will be in Vienna, too."

Ben-Gurion's refusal may plausibly have had yet another motive: to punish the party for not drawing up a program despite his repeated demands. In a special letter after the great victory at the polls, Ben-Gurion reiterated the need for a program and was prepared to return to Palestine to this end, though it would mean sacrificing his lovely days with Rega. But the Mapai secretariat informed him that "with all due respect, many members considered Ben-Gurion's return technically impossible." He next tried putting together guidelines for a program with some of his colleagues to be approved later by the labor faction in the Zionist Congress and the Zionist coalition that was created. But in a Vienna meeting to discuss strategy and Weizmann's return to the presidency, Katznelson showed no enthusiasm for the program initiative. Despite Ben-Gurion's insistence, additional meetings with him or others never came about. In fact, Ben-Gurion got the impression that Katznelson was evading discussion of a program or the need for one.

The reason for this must have been that while Ben-Gurion's program was broad in scope and sensational, the general desire in Mapai was to prevent a painful and, in the view of many, unnecessary confrontation. As far as the party knew his program covered the entire Zionist front, at home and abroad. Apart from allocation of Zionist means to significantly increase land acquisition (even if the expense held up further agricultural settlement) and concentration of political efforts to increase immigration from all sectors (including those who were not pioneers), he wanted to stand the Zionist Organization on its head. "The next objective," he had told the Mapai Central Committee prior to leaving for Poland, "is the restoration of the Zionist movement," and the more it became clear to them just what this "restoration" entailed, the darker their disposition toward it became.

Although in their view Ben-Gurion's program had neither a beginning nor an end, it stemmed from his intent to change the Zionist Organization from a federation of worldwide and national parties into a unified world organization. Any Jew who wished would be able to join the Zionist Organization in his own country directly. Ben-Gurion believed that the Zionist people's movement would encompass the entire Jewish people and the Zionist Congress would gradually become the "Congress of the Jewish People."

Second, he had in mind to put an end to the enlarged Jewish Agency in which nonelected, non-Zionist representatives served and which he termed "the biggest criminal and shameful mistake" that he himself shared responsibility for. He wished to abolish the partnership for settling Palestine that had been established by Weizmann between the Zionist Organization and non-Zionist Jewish bodies. His program involved absolute democratization of the Zionist movement. Its other bold propositions will best be discussed in the context of his activity in the Zionist Executive.[8]

The democratization that Ben-Gurion espoused, praiseworthy as it was, was not free of political and personal intentions. Not only did non-Zionists join the Agency Executive without being elected, but also, according to Zionist Organization regulations, members of the Zionist

Actions Committee automatically became Congress delegates by virtue of their position and were not obligated to undergo the test of general elections unless they wished to vote. (There were two kinds of delegates: those who could only make speeches, and those who could also vote.)[9] Ben-Gurion was aiming at the most prominent of these, the esteemed Dr. Chaim Weizmann. In his memoirs Ben-Gurion wrote, "He was the first leader whose original rise to greatness was not through election. . . . Weizmann's rise to the Zionist leadership was solely a consequence of his work in achieving the Balfour Declaration."

Ben-Gurion was both wrong and right. Weizmann had been duly elected to the second Congress on the ticket of the Democratic Faction, of which he was the founder and leader. But Ben-Gurion was correct in stating that Weizmann had no party of his own with which to fight for a particular course of action and on whose behalf he could speak to the Zionist Congress. It was Weizmann's habit to yield his vote to a candidate who had not been elected and instead take part in the congresses by virtue of his membership in the Zionist Actions Committee. That way he could claim to be a man of the entire Zionist movement, not a member of any particular party. The Jewish people were his constituency.

Ben-Gurion's associates could detect in the proposed democratization Ben-Gurion's ill-concealed motive of destroying Weizmann's power base and foiling attempts to restore Weizmann to the presidency of the Zionist Organization. Legally Ben-Gurion stood on firm ground, since Weizmann represented no one except himself at the Congress. On the other hand, nobody entertained the slightest doubt that had he wanted to Weizmann could easily have had his pick of any constituency. He could even have achieved election in Poland, the largest electoral district, in which — although he had never been there — his admirers in all walks of life were numerous. His standing among the Jewish people in general, and in the Zionist camp in particular, was so solid that even if members of Mapai had been inclined to side with Ben-Gurion in this matter, they probably would not have done so. Within Mapai Weizmann was considered one of a kind, which became clear in party deliberations before and after the elections, during the Congress, and in its aftermath.

Ben-Gurion knew Weizmann's power within Mapai and so had to camouflage his scheme. He employed his favored double formula. He was aware of Weizmann's great gifts and abilities, he said, but for the sake of "restoring" the movement it would be better if he were not president. At a Mapai Central Committee meeting in March 1931, six months before that year's Congress, he declared, "I am not against Weizmann. He has two fundamental merits: First, political intuition of near genius. He can captivate people; second, he is filled with a sacred awe of the enterprise in Palestine." But, "we need the movement," whereas "Weizmann neither understands nor loves [it]. And since at the moment this issue is central because the movement is in ruins — very much due to Weizmann — the situation will be much remedied if Weizmann stays out of office for two years." Nevertheless Mapai resolved to back Weizmann for the presidency. Although he had fought in the 1931 Congress against attempts by the Revisionists and their allies to depose Weizmann, in 1932 Ben-Gurion wrote in Mapai's organ that it was "an error of shortsightedness on our part to support Dr. Weizmann's candidacy at this Congress."[10]

On the eve of the 1933 election the question arose in Mapai as to whether the dismissed Weizmann should be restored to the presidency and whether this issue should take center stage in its campaign propaganda. Now that he could smell the conquest of Zionism, Ben-Gurion refined his strategy, arguing that "a uniform organization is more important than Weizmann's presidency," and that he in any event favored "abolishing the institution of the presidency." However, he was not prepared to do without the services and talents of Weizmann in an Executive under his own leadership. "There is no one like Weizmann for managing our political affairs and [we] must insist that he be engaged in these," he told the Central Committee in January. The longer the deliberations lasted, the clearer it became that Ben-Gurion meant to make Weizmann subordinate to the Executive. Sharett put it plainly: Ben-Gurion wanted "a coalition without Weizmann yet in contact with him." Sharett then warned against "the illusion that it is possible to leave Weizmann out and at the same time keep him working for the Zionist movement."[11]

But that was exactly what Ben-Gurion was determined to do, and before his trip to Poland he had presented it as follows to the Central Committee. "One point must appear in our program: abolition of the presidency, as there is no fitting candidate for this elevated position except for Weizmann, and at this time we cannot place him in this office. He must be brought to work for the movement without raising the question of his presidency." The party's eventual decision was something of a compromise between Ben-Gurion and those who wanted Weizmann back as president. One Central Committee resolution stated that the Zionist movement's major role was the "creation of an antirevisionist front," and that "the question of Weizmann's candidacy for the presidency" would not be brought up unless an accord was reached with all those "who will join with us in a settlement-oriented Zionist plan of action. We favor a working plan with room for Weizmann's active participation and an appropriate status for his activity."

At the same time another resolution stated that Mapai would "fight for the abolition of the presidency."[12]

This decision, as it turned out, was open to various interpretations. While there was no doubt that Mapai wished to include Weizmann in Zionist Executive activity and to afford him "appropriate status," it was not clear what "[fighting] for the abolition of the presidency" meant; should the Congress resolve otherwise, would Mapai back Weizmann's candidacy or nominate someone else? With respect to Ben-Gurion's goals, this was a significant question.

On March 28, a few days after its decision, the Central Committee named David Ben-Gurion, Berl Katznelson, and Joseph Sprinzak as representatives who were to "meet with Weizmann to discuss the coming Congress and his role in the campaign." *Davar* reported that the next day the three visited Weizmann in Rehovot and spoke with him at length. But Ben-Gurion, in his memoirs, claimed he had had no part in this meeting, "as I was forced" to leave that day for Poland. On Wednesday, March 29, he had boarded the train for Egypt, where he would set sail for Genoa on Friday. It is impossible to ascertain if Ben-Gurion could have delayed his trip to Egypt, an eight-hour journey, for one day. The Central Committee, which knew Ben-Gurion's travel plans, thought this possible; otherwise it would have named another for the meeting with Weizmann. Further, there is reason to suspect that Ben-Gurion simply did not wish to take part in the meeting, for he had already missed several meetings with Weizmann.

Weizmann, bitter about his dismissal and seeking retribution, did not attend the Prague Congress but stayed at the resort village of Zermatt, Switzerland. There he waited for news of developments and more specifically for the continuation of his talks with Mapai representatives. But Ben-Gurion and Katznelson, who was also no great fan of Weizmann, could reach no conclusion on the matter in their meeting in Vienna, and neither could labor caucus deliberators at the Congress. Since the Congress had no desire to see the presidency abolished, Ben-Gurion stuck to his position, which was, "Should Weizmann agree to serve the movement without being president, it would be desirable. . . . Weizmann has a great, far-seeing intuition, but he has no understanding of Zionist Organization matters. If the good of the movement is to be weighed against the question of Weizmann — the movement comes first." In a letter to his wife, Sharett reported, "The faction wants Weizmann, our Eretz Israel wants Weizmann, but people who count in the faction have entirely different opinions and feelings. Neither Berl nor Ben-Gurion is at all for Weizmann's presidency at the moment," and therefore "day after day there was talk of the need to go to see Weizmann, but nothing was done."[13]

Mapai's liaison with Weizmann, and the one keenest on seeing Weizmann reinstalled as president, was Sprinzak. He implored Weizmann that, if he was absolutely resolved not to come to Prague, he at least come somewhat closer than Zermatt to make consultation easier and less expensive. "There are many fine opening addresses and speeches at the Congress," Sprinzak wrote his wife, "but the spark, the central point, perhaps the central individual is missing. The Congress lacks content. Lots of figures and numbers spring forward to meet the eye, but not one idea. On all counts, it is Weizmann who is missing." This attitude, and the certainty that when the time came labor would vote to restore Weizmann to the presidency, kept Sprinzak's spirits up in his negotiations with Weizmann. But Weizmann asked Sprinzak to come to him for talks, "and then we shall see whether we move closer to Prague or not."

Weizmann very much wanted labor's support, since it was his sole hope of returning to the presidency, and he probably sensed that to do this he needed to win over Ben-Gurion. Consequently he wrote Berl Locker, a Mapai member of the Zionist Executive in London and as loyal to him as Sprinzak, that in his opinion Ben-Gurion should lead the Executive in Palestine. Until that time the Executive in Jerusalem had had a secondary standing and Weizmann had staffed it with his own hand-picked supporters. Now Weizmann was prepared to recognize the Jerusalem Executive under Ben-Gurion's chairmanship as equal to the London Executive under his own. The understanding of Ben-Gurion's aspirations and artful flattery evidenced by this proposal might have been a factor in the subsequent labor resolution to invite Weizmann to Prague for consultations. On August 15 he received a telegram signed by Katznelson, Sprinzak, and Ben-Gurion: "Situation requires immediat [*sic*] consultation urge strongly your earliest coming. Pray wire." But Weizmann sulkily continued to play the king, and in a letter summoned them to him.

Although it was his habit to show respect to older Zionist statesmen, Ben-Gurion did not come to terms with this development easily, and a week passed before he gave in to the party's urging and went with Sprinzak to meet with Weizmann in Zurich, nearly fourteen hours by train from Prague; Weizmann graciously met them there. On the morning of August 26, a few hours before they were to set out, Sprinzak asked a caucus for a clear guideline as to what they were authorized to offer Weizmann. "What are we going with?" Sprinzak asked, and proposed it be resolved that "[we are] going on the assumption that the Congress will adjourn with an Executive that has Weizmann at its head" and a program that recognized the Histadrut as the institution in control of all labor matters in Palestine and of the allocation of resources for maximal development. Ben-Gurion retorted that he did not see the election of Weizmann to the Executive as "the principal issue." Further deliberations got nowhere, and the caucus dispersed inconclusively. Consequently Ben-Gurion and Sprinzak were free to interpret their mission as they saw fit.[14]

The train ride to Zurich was costly in both time and money. They had to go via Munich, eight hours from Prague, where they had to get German transit visas. Ben-Gurion, always meticulous in documenting his movements and expenditures, recorded timetables and expenses. He also noted that they left Prague at 2:00 P.M. and on the way back reached Munich at 7:00 A.M. on August 28. At the Munich station they had to wait to change trains. He wrote these details without a word about their context.

Sprinzak was perfectly clear on their goal: to discuss with Weizmann "the issue of his presidency and the conditions of putting together the Executive." On August 27, after the meeting, he wrote his wife,

> We have already spent five hours with Weizmann. We talked and ate and came to no conclusion whatsoever. He is still hesitant, "will return in another two years," after the movement is cleansed. . . . He proposed the creation of an Executive in Jerusalem under Ben-Gurion's chairmanship, and that the Congress charge him, Weizmann, with a specific job — the rescue of German Jewry. This, of course, did not keep Weizmann from discussing in detail the terms under which he could be head of the movement. I am not sure that our mission will end with our returning to Prague with a program for an Executive with Weizmann at its head. In another two hours we are to meet again and see.

It might have been Ben-Gurion who was referred to on August 29 in a dispatch by the Palestine correspondent of the Jewish Telegraphic Agency saying that Ben-Gurion and Sprinzak had returned from a visit to Weizmann and that it was "known from a good source that Weizmann rejected the presidency categorically." If it was not, Ben-Gurion never said a word about this meeting.[15] All his diary shows is train schedules and ticket prices. The whole journey could have remained a passing episode had it not laid bare a raging internal conflict to which Ben-Gurion would never admit. Moreover, this journey is perhaps an appropriate marker of the beginning of the long and tortuous Ben-Gurion–Weizmann relationship that reached its climax ten years later with Ben-Gurion's resignation from the Jewish Agency Executive in protest against Weizmann's methods.

In December 1943, in explaining his resignation to the Mapai Central Committee, Ben-Gurion stated that, by 1931, he had seen that

Weizmann was headed for failure as a Zionist leader and statesman. Weizmann's defenders hastened to remind him and Mapai that there had been times when he had thought differently. "If in 1931 Weizmann was like that," asked Locker, "how is it that in 1933 Ben-Gurion traveled with Sprinzak to ask him to accept the presidency?"

Ben-Gurion said, "Heaven forbid. . . . I never went with Sprinzak to ask Weizmann to accept the presidency. This allegation is absurd. I did not go to Weizmann in 1933. It didn't enter my mind that he should be president."

Locker was ready to humor Ben-Gurion if the latter would make up with Weizmann. "Perhaps we erred," Locker said, "but I am not alone in this error." Sprinzak, however, could not let such a flagrant distortion pass, for setting the record straight was more important to him than placating Ben-Gurion.

SPRINZAK: Ben-Gurion traveled with me from Prague to Zurich to offer Dr. Weizmann the mantle of the presidency.

BEN-GURION: You are dreaming.

SPRINZAK: We set out, we got off at Munich, you bought *Mein Kampf*, and I went to buy cigarettes. We went to Zurich . . . to Dr. Weizmann. Why should I suddenly dream?

BEN-GURION: It's a dream.

SPRINZAK: Don't you dare deny it. We left the same day they murdered Lessing.* Ben-Gurion came along and with great courtesy tried to talk Weizmann into accepting the presidency.

The events Sprinzak recounted from that journey, the assassination of Lessing and Ben-Gurion's purchase of *Mein Kampf*, had made a permanent impression on him. As a rule, Zionist leaders steered clear of *Mein Kampf;* not only did they not buy it, they did not read it. Ben-Gurion never mentioned that he had bought this book (his reading of which helps explain his chilling prediction, made in January 1934, that "Hitler's regime puts the entire Jewish people in danger"[16] and further illuminates his struggle to turn the peril to German — and then all European — Jewry into a Zionist achievement in Palestine). There is no doubt that what Sprinzak said was accurate.

This being the case, the question arises, as it did again and again throughout his political struggles, as to whether Ben-Gurion denied having gone to see Weizmann in August 1933 for the convenience of

---

* Dr. Theodor Lessing was a professor of history and a philosopher and pacifist. Born in Germany, he was a convert who returned to Judaism and Zionism (he was a guest of honor at the Prague Congress), and one of the most active opponents of Hitler and Nazism. At 9:30 P.M. on August 30, 1933 (actually the day after Sprinzak and Ben-Gurion returned from their journey to Weizmann), he was shot in the head by a uniformed Nazi in his home in Marienbad, Czechoslovakia, where he had fled from Germany.

the moment or whether he had truly forgotten it. There is sufficient evidence to support the claim that he had banished this meeting from memory, it being a kind of admission on his part of Weizmann's superiority and therefore an unpleasant, if not humiliating experience for him. The proof is that he never mentioned it in his diary or his letters. On the other hand, a close reading of his words to the Central Committee suggests another interpretation: that he denied having asked Weizmann to return to the presidency, but not the journey to Zurich. Ben-Gurion made much of technicalities when it served his purpose; it is certain he did not want Weizmann to be president and believed that his absence from the Zionist Executive would aid the movement's "restoration." Why, then, did he not say so explicitly to the Central Committee instead of simultaneously resorting to insinuation and denial? In truth, no single explanation is sufficient; the answer most likely combines elements of them all.

In any event, Ben-Gurion's second journey to Weizmann that summer, of which he wrote to Paula, went off without complications, emotional or political. On its final day, September 4, the Congress elected Nahum Sokolow president and a nine-member Zionist Executive made up of a narrow coalition among Mapai, the radicals, and the General Zionists A, representing approximately 60 percent of the Congress's votes. The broad coalition initiative had been blocked since both the General Zionists B and Mizrachi held strongly to their anti-labor position. Believing that administering the Zionist Organization was beyond labor's reach, they refused to join the Executive in the hope that this would hasten its failure. In his memoirs Ben-Gurion quoted from the Congress protocol on the election: "Professor Zelig Brodetsky (thunderous applause); David Ben-Gurion (repeated thunderous applause); Itzhak Gruenbaum (thunderous applause)."

The Jewish Agency Council, which met after the Congress, ratified the appointment of the three non-Zionists who, with the members of the Zionist Executive, made up the twelve-man Jewish Agency Executive. In his new capacity Ben-Gurion had to speak to Weizmann solely about where and how he would cooperate with the new Executive. He documented this journey to Merano in the Italian Alps well, in his diary and in letters. Feeling rather pleased with himself, he mixed business with pleasure, in a kind of post-Congress picnic. From Prague he traveled to Innsbruck, and the next morning, Saturday, September 9, he left for Merano. He spent Saturday and Sunday on excursions and did not meet with Weizmann until Monday. To Sharett he wrote, "I spent three days in Merano, two touring and one talking. . . . The touring was somewhat more successful than the talking." He had found Weizmann "pessimistic" and unwilling to let Ben-Gurion use his political contacts, claiming that "his political ties are now few and weak. His friends are presently out of office, and those who are in are not that close to him." Nevertheless the two agreed that Weizmann would head the project to aid German Jews and do his utmost to create a political fund to be at the disposal of the Jewish Agency's Political Department. Weizmann donated £100 out of his own pocket on the spot.[17]

At the center of the program Ben-Gurion had proposed to Mapai lay the idea of "rule," which he had devised in January 1931. This purpose was behind the inclusion in his program of something new: guidance of public opinion. "The majority . . . charged with the destiny of the Congress and of the movement . . . will take in hand or put under its supervision the Jewish Telegraphic Agency,* and if this is impossible, it will found a new one. It will also cultivate an honest, educational, and loyal press in all countries; it will either put a number of extant papers under its supervision, or found new ones." This, too, was a product of Ben-Gurion's sense of the burning ground. For Zionism to accomplish its enterprise in the short time allotted it by history, it had to mobilize all forces and resources, even at the expense of absolute freedom of the press. Means and resources, he argued, were not lacking. On the contrary, "there is an abundance of forces and legions, mighty human resources. What is lacking is guidance, *generalship,* direction, *rule!*" It was, of course, obvious to all that he was the one graced with the necessary qualities to command and ready to step into the breach.

Yet Ben-Gurion refused the chairmanship of the Jewish Agency Executive in Jerusalem, as well as the directorship of any of its departments. The October 4, 1933, meeting of the Executive, held for the "distribution of posts," elected Dr. Ruppin chairman of the Jewish Agency Executive in Jerusalem, Moshe Sharett director of the Political Department, and Eliezer Kaplan treasurer and director of the Financial Department. "Mr. D. Ben-Gurion, who is domiciled in Tel Aviv, will assist Mr. M. Sharett and take part in the department's direction."[18]

Although Ben-Gurion stayed in Tel Aviv, he spent most of his time not at the HEC but in the Jewish Agency Executive, in Jerusalem and abroad. Zionism, not the Histadrut, stood at the center of his thoughts, so why would he not accept a position? A credible answer will not be found in anything he said or wrote. Instead one must consider that although he seemed by nature made to be number one, in 1933 his Mapai colleagues still did not consider him fit to head the World Zionist Orga-

---

* The majority owner of the Jewish Telegraphic Agency (JTA) was Jacob Landau, its chief director and editor, whom Ben-Gurion suspected of revisionist sympathies.

nization, and it is probable that he agreed with them. In his heart of hearts he must have known that he needed more experience. Yet he was simply not cut out to play second fiddle, especially to Nahum Sokolow; in the two years they worked together Ben-Gurion's attitude toward him deteriorated from mere indifference to outright disrespect. Besides, to move from being top man in the Histadrut to being head of an Agency Executive department would certainly have been a step down. The only solution was the one he found, which gave him the freedom to delve into all the Zionist matters he deemed important, enjoying an undefined yet unique status that made him a self-styled Executive member[19] "responsible for Zionist policy" — in effect Sharett's senior in the Political Department. Thus he attained complete freedom of action, which he could use to prepare the ground for his program and bring it from theory into practice. Meanwhile he would acquire diplomatic experience and make a name for himself worldwide in the Zionist camp and among the Jewish people. This was what he needed most if he was truly grooming himself for the inevitable showdown with Weizmann, whether at the 1935 elections and Congress or later.

It was a fine asset for Ben-Gurion — perpetually a man in a hurry, he nevertheless had the patience and the staying power to bide his time.

28

Peace Within
and Peace Without

AFTER HIS DISAPPOINTING talk with Weizmann in Merano, Ben-Gurion set out for London. In his concept of Zionism, immigration was always paramount, and on September 15, the day after his arrival, he met with two senior officials of the Colonial Office about the possibility of boosting it significantly. In his diary he noted later that 2,840 Jews had immigrated in 1931 and just under 10,000 in 1932; but in 1933, the year Hitler assumed power, 16,000 had arrived in Palestine by September. These figures served as a starting point against which he would one day be able to measure his success in the Zionist Executive.[1]

Another important goal of this visit was to prove that Ben-Gurion had contacts of his own that could serve the Zionist cause. He had met with Prime Minister Ramsay MacDonald three times before: in 1922 he had hosted the then M.P. in Palestine, and in July 1930 and July 1931 he was the prime minister's guest at Chequers; the third time he was Weizmann's envoy. Ben-Gurion, who believed in 1933 that the labor politicians spoke in good faith of their loyalty to Zionist socialism, hoped to reap political gains from this acquaintance. On September 18, 1933, he met with Malcolm MacDonald, Ramsay's son, also considered a friend to Zionism, whom Ben-Gurion had met at Chequers. He asked Malcolm, then parliamentary under secretary in the Dominions Office, to set up a meeting for him with his father, this time in his capacity as a member of the Executive.

Had Ben-Gurion been able to pull this off it would have greatly augmented his personal standing, even in the eyes of Weizmann. Unfortunately, Malcolm wrote a few days later, apologizing for his father, who was too busy to see Ben-Gurion, despite all the trouble he had gone to.[2] So Ben-Gurion's third meeting with Ramsay MacDonald had also been his last. Unlike Weizmann, Ben-Gurion was not received by a sitting prime minister or by a United States president until he became Israel's prime minister. Weizmann clearly had the edge as far as contacts and personal standing were concerned, which Ben-Gurion acknowledged only grudgingly but which lay at the core of their relationship.

On his return to Palestine on October 2, after an absence of six months, Ben-Gurion turned to the HEC, where a pleasant surprise awaited him: a cheering crowd had assembled in the courtyard to applaud him and his victory at the polls. Moved by this hearty display of affection, he addressed the crowd from the HEC balcony. "Greetings, friends, from a quarter of a million comrades in the Diaspora! For the first time in the history of our movement we have been charged with the responsibility for the fate of the entire Zionist movement . . . not victory but responsibility . . . and with faith in great things we will accomplish our difficult task."[3] At a meeting held in his honor by the Tel Aviv branch of Mapai he addressed the parties that had denounced the new Zionist coalition:

A flood of articles has been written, saying that we seized control and do not represent the people, and hence our victory is not valid. True, we [the labor movement] are still but a tiny speck in relation to the 17 million Jews. But we are the harbinger of a change and of a revolutionary transition to a productive and creative life. The vanguard is the true expression of the people's historic aspiration, and not in the metaphysical sense. The nation does not wish to submit to the extinction awaiting it in the Diaspora. . . .

This Executive is just the first step of a popularly supported administration in the Zionist movement, which is to become a mass movement. Our partial success in the elections is the proof that the movement is about to become a mass movement. We are the representatives of the nation not as it is, but as it will be. We are the vanguard of the nation not as it is, but as it wants and needs to be. This proclivity is only now beginning to gain ground.[4]

Although he continued to receive his salary from the HEC and was supposed to devote only one or two days a week to the JAE (as the Jewish Agency Executive was known), he was totally preoccupied with the latter. He dealt primarily with two issues — increasing immigration and reorganizing the JAE — which meant, among other things, transferring the Organization Department, which was in charge of the shekel and liaison with Zionist parties throughout the world, and the editorial board of the official Zionist organ, *The World,* from London to Jerusalem and establishing a propaganda bureau, press office, and news agency in Jerusalem. For this purpose he left for London again on November 24, just fifty-five days after returning from there, beginning a lifestyle that involved spending half his time in Palestine and half, and sometimes more, abroad. The Executive also charged him with the special mission of "finding a way to recruit a number of people for the political work of the Jewish Agency . . . Weizmann above all."[5]

Traveling by plane, train, and seaplane via Gaza, Cairo, Alexandria, Athens, Brindisi, Milan, and Paris, he reached London in only four days, writing letters at every stop. In Cairo he bought a few books, among them H. G. Wells's *The Time Machine*. So stirred was he by his own leap across the continents that Wells's vision of the future seemed tangible and within arm's reach. Without mentioning Wells, Ben-Gurion wrote Paula from Milan:

> I am certain that . . . travel will be obsolete one day. You'll be able to sit in your room and push a button and see whomever you like at the other end of the earth and talk with him the way people speak with each other in the same room. And perhaps not only on Earth but also on Mars. It is entirely possible that this will come about sooner than we think, provided a new world war doesn't break out in the meantime, destroying man and civilization, leaving only the blacks in the heart of Africa, and everything will have to start at the beginning. . . . Until then we must do what we must do, and whatever will be will be. Kisses to all, Daddy.

From Milan he wrote Rega:

> Have you ever read H. G. Wells's *The Time Machine*? . . . If no world war breaks out in the meantime . . . we will soon be able to meet without traveling at all. . . . I remember when it was impossible to go from Sejera to Safed except by donkey (or on foot). . . . Will I be able to see you this time in Europe?

At 11:30 A.M. on November 28, Ben-Gurion landed at Croydon, near London, and that evening he appeared at a public meeting.[6]

The next day he had "a hasty talk" with Weizmann, who agreed to assist the Executive with diplomatic contacts, participate in its strategy meetings, and embark on propaganda and fund-raising campaigns. He also agreed to use his personal contacts and invited Colonial Secretary Sir Philip Cunliffe-Lister to his home for dinner to meet Ben-Gurion. Further still, Weizmann raised no objection to influential people in the Jewish and non-Jewish world from his own circle — David Eder, Lord Melchett, Leonard Stein, Harry Sacher, Sir Simon Marks, Israel Sieff (the last two owned the Marks and Spencer chain of stores), and others — joining the public political committee that Ben-Gurion had been working to establish. Through them he wished to influence public opinion, in Parliament, and in contacts with the government, for the purpose of boosting the annual immigration quota to thirty thousand or possibly fifty thousand.

Weizmann opened the door to British politics for Ben-Gurion, although he continued jealously to keep his personal contacts for himself. For Ben-Gurion this was a great step forward, and he took care to spruce up his appearance for it. In preparation for the dinner at Weizmann's home on November 30 and for his meetings with other influential people he bought himself a new suit, a hat, a shirt, three collars, six handkerchiefs, three ties, and a pair of gloves; a few days later he added two shirts, a tie, three collars, and three pairs of cuff links. Elegantly turned out, he met Lady Erleigh, Lord Melchett's daughter and Lord Reading's daughter-in-law, who promised him her assistance, appeared at parliamentary debates, delivered a speech to a parliamentary committee, and held a large press conference.[7]

Despite numerous meetings in the Zionist office designed to transfer the Organization Department to Jerusalem, and despite feverish political and diplomatic activity, he felt terribly lonely in his room in the National Hotel on Upper Bedford Place. He longed for Rega. "I so very much regret the great distance between London and Vienna," he wrote her. "How I would like to see you, to be with you again, even if only for a brief moment. . . . If there was even a single day free I would come to Vienna, but I doubt that it will be possible." After his miraculously abridged journey the trip to Vienna probably seemed longer than ever, but precious time could be saved if Rega would meet him halfway. With Christmas vacation coming she would have time off from her studies.

> If you were free, I would suggest that you come to Italy for two or three days — Is it possible? Don't worry about expenses. . . . I believe you've never been to Italy. It takes only twelve hours to get to Venice from Vienna. I will wait here for your reply. It would be very hard for me to return to Palestine without seeing you. . . . Do you have a photograph of yourself? If you do, I'd like you to send it to me. . . . I reminisce and think of you perhaps more than you know. Yours, David.

The next day, December 13, he dashed off another letter to her. "It seems that I will be here longer than I had thought . . . maybe until the twenty-fifth of this month." After promising that he would do his best to stop in Vienna on his way to Palestine, he concluded, "It is very cold here both in the physical and the spiritual sense. I await your letter."[8] The spiritual cold and his longing grew with the approach of the Christmas season and the exodus of the elite from the capital for the holidays. On Monday night, December 18, he received a letter from Rega informing him that she would be unable to join him in Venice.

She also told him that she had celebrated her twenty-sixth birthday on the fourteenth. This milestone in her life moved him to address the question of their future.

I wish two things for you. The first is work that you value, that you can devote yourself to, and that will give you much satisfaction. I do not know the why and wherefore of life, or even if there is a why and wherefore of life and of the world, but I do know that we ourselves create the purpose of our existence in the work to which we dedicate our lives. We set ourselves a cause, and that cause gives life content and meaning, and we put all that is good within us at the service of this cause. I wish you one. . . . The second thing I wish for you is that your life is blessed with a great love, love for a man who will love you and whom you will love, since work alone cannot be the substance or the fulfillment of one's life. Perhaps love is a weakness, but it is a human failing for which there is no redress. Dear Rega, I love you with all my soul, but I can give you nothing. The happiness a woman needs — total love and devotion from a man — I hope you will find in your life from a man deserving of you. Will you accept these two wishes from me?

Dear Rega, I deeply regret that I cannot see you now. . . . I cannot make it to Vienna. It's a pity that you could not come to Venice. How happy I would have been had this small dream come true, but — Study and work, it matters not! Life has its bad moments, its problems, pain, and suffering. But there is also plenty to live, suffer, and fight for, and there is also love in life, and even if love, too, offers only suffering, it does not matter. I love you — what can I do? I do not want anything nor can I want anything. It does me good to see you now and again, for a little while. When I am lonely and sad I remember our meetings, I see your face, your pensive eyes, so dear to me. My heart beats from afar and I long and yearn for you (in vain, I know), and I pray for your happiness. Don't worry, the bad times will pass and other bad times — and good times too — will follow. Your whole life lies before you. I love you, my Rega, and it will make me happy to know that you are happy with your work and your love, which you will find in Palestine. You won't hold it against me if I love you, will you, Rega? Dear beloved Rega, I am yours, David.[9]

Laying bare his soul brought Ben-Gurion no release; on the contrary, committing his feelings to paper seemed to generate an emotional storm. On December 20, two days after mailing the letter, he found he could not bear his growing longing and came to a decision. That day he wrote Paula, "In two days I will go to Paris for a few days and on the twenty-seventh of the month I sail from Trieste." The presents he had bought for Paula were already packed — "a black suit in the size you sent me and a white silk blouse as well. . . . I haven't bought anything for the children as I didn't have enough money. I'll buy them presents in Palestine."[10]

The next day, December 21 (not December 22, as he had written Paula), he crossed the Channel. In Paris he had time to visit Baron Edmond de Rothschild, "Father of the Yishuv," in his home, marvel at the eighty-nine-year-old man's ability to speak "nonstop for an hour and a half," and listen to him say that "Germany is the great heater, Italy is dangerous — only England is worth consideration" as a reliable support for Zionism. He then bought eau de cologne for Rega and the next day got tickets to Vienna, wired Rega from the railway station, "Coming tomorrow 22:15 west," and boarded the train. He made the trip in one long haul of thirty-three hours, proving the power of love. Arriving in Vienna at 3:15 Saturday morning, December 23, he stayed with Rega until he left on Tuesday for Trieste.

On Wednesday he boarded the S.S. *Carnero*, and before Europe had faded from the horizon he wrote Rega.

> Who knows how many months will pass until I see you again — and where? I intend to concentrate on work in Palestine and not to go abroad for at least a year. I have at least two years' work packed into this one; if only I can manage to finish a part of it. You too have a lot of work ahead of you, but if you find a few spare moments from time to time to write me — be a good girl. Yours, David."[11]

Were bells of farewell tolling between these lines? Had they discussed their future or Ben-Gurion's earlier letter in Vienna? This shipboard letter seems to verify that they could not find a way to share their lives.

On January 1, 1934, he reached the shores of Palestine.

In February 1934 Ben-Gurion had more reason than ever to think of Rega. That month Austrian Chancellor Engelbert Dollfuss dissolved all political parties except his own Fatherland Front in order to consolidate his regime, which with the rise of Hitler in Germany became more and more inclined toward Nazism and acquired the epithet Austro-Fascist. On February 11 government forces and the Heimwehr (the "home guard" in whose ranks many Nazis served) raided the socialist headquarters in Vienna, leading to an uprising of the socialists and trade union workers, who had political control in Vienna, and the bombardment of the workers' housing units, where the socialist leaders were concentrated. In five days of street battles and house-to-house fighting, Red Vienna, backed by the Schutzbund (a paramilitary defense organization), fought for its life. On February 15 the revolt was put down with field guns and automatic fire and the Socialist-Democratic Party abolished; many of its members were either captured and sent to concentration camps or forced to flee. The press in Palestine reported the great fear that had fallen on the Jews.[12]

That day Ben-Gurion, in Tel Aviv, wrote,

Dear, beloved Rega, For the last three days my heart has been in Vienna in my worry, pain, and love . . . and Vienna for me, now, means both Vienna and you. . . . My heart was with you all along — even on the days I did not write you, and all the more when I did. Will you be able to complete your studies . . . or will you hurry to Palestine now? Entirely yours, David.

Upset, he called Mendel Singer's wife in Vienna (Mendel was in Palestine) on the sixteenth and asked her, among other things, about Rega, Annie, and their family. She told him they were all well. On the nineteenth he wrote Rega again, this time from a hotel room in Jerusalem. "If you were dear to me before today, these days you are seven times as precious. Let us hope that everything turns out all right! . . . My heart is altogether with you now, my dear, dear Rega — In never-ending love, Yours, David." In the margin he added, "How I would like to be hugging and kissing you right now!"[13]

Two central issues stood out in their correspondence: her anxiety over approaching final exams and her request for certificates — immigration permits — without regard to the waiting list, for friends in the labor movement who were in danger from Austro-Fascism. Ben-Gurion promised to secure them, and the JAE in Jerusalem directed the Palestine office in Vienna to set aside thirty such certificates. Ben-Gurion wrote and cabled Rega regarding them. At least one of the thirty recipients, a man named Walter, is known, but Rega and her family were not among them.

In the margins of his letter about the certificates Ben-Gurion explained its brevity by saying he was "very busy. . . . I only wish to add that you must try hard to pass your exams. It is very important; don't let your spirits drop. . . . Yours, with love, David." But while his concern for Rega weighed on his mind, the immigration question and other Zionist issues pressed him more, and his letters became less frequent. Rega called him "a bad boy" for not writing enough. "Your 'bad boy,' " he wrote back, "is not so bad. He devoured every bit of news he received from you. It's just that these last days have been filled with worries and work and more work, and I still have not managed to rest. . . . These days we are engrossed in this thing only" — that is, negotiations with the high commissioner and the government over a larger immigration quota. When she wrote him that she had passed her first exams he replied that he was "especially" pleased, "and I await the day you pass through all this hellfire and become a free individual and can finally leave that city and that country, which have betrayed you and spoiled life for so many — and start a new life *here.*"

His resolve not to leave Palestine in 1934 broke down in the face of new developments. "Most probably," he wrote Rega in April, "I will come to Europe in late July or early August for several weeks . . . and if all goes well I will, of course, come to Vienna. Will you still be there? . . . Write me in detail about your exams. When will they be over? Yours, David."[14]

But although he mailed her a Hebrew dictionary, he did not respond to her letters for almost three months. Then on July 8, overcome by guilt, he put pen to paper.

Dear beloved Rega —
  I truly am a bad boy, very bad — certainly much, much worse than you think. How many months have I gone without answering you — and yet every letter of yours is a holiday for me, particularly the letters about your exams, as I was very concerned . . . about your anxiety. And meanwhile during these last months so many things have happened here, one after another. I receive your letters, happy and ashamed, troubled and sorry. I get ready to set out and each time am forced to postpone, and I still do not know when I will finally be able to move from here. And now, all of a sudden, Vienna has once again become a center of attention — Bialik was lost to us there. . . . It's a pity you don't know enough Hebrew to understand what Bialik meant to poetry, to literature, to the Hebrew language. But Bialik was more than a poet of genius — we haven't had a poet the likes of him since the days of prophets — he was more than a great author. What Bialik left us in writing is but a fraction of the munificence of his soul and the greatness of his spirit. How wonderful it was to know that such a man walked among us. And how much poorer are we now that he has abandoned us — [but] shall we resent blind, cruel fate for robbing us of Bialik? Should we not rather be grateful to fate for giving him to us?[15]

On July 4, at the age of sixty-one, Chaim Nachman Bialik had died in Vienna following a gallbladder operation. Ben-Gurion had always had the highest esteem and admiration for him. In Płońsk he had copied Bialik's poems in a fine hand into notebooks he kept for just this purpose; he had given one to Shmuel Fox, another to Rachel Nelkin, and another to his father. When he was in the Histadrut he made sure to invite Bialik to every important event. News of the poet's death so upset him that he broke a lifelong rule and, for the first and last time, ranked a contemporary Jew as more important than others. In a letter to the high commissioner, Sir Arthur Wauchope, he accounted for the deep pall of mourning that had spread over the entire Yishuv.

Bialik was our greatest poet since the Destruction, and apart from the Prophets and the Psalmists he was the all-time master of the Hebrew language. . . . It was as if all stages of the more than three thousand years of the Hebrew language joined together in each and every one of Bialik's poems. . . . He was the spiritual leader of his people, the master craftsman of the revival of our language. No Jew of our time has had such a powerful impact on the life of his people. . . . In our eyes he was the bearer of the nation's legacy, of its ideals and aspirations. Fate has struck us in taking Bialik, the greatest Jew of our time, all too soon.[16]

Ben-Gurion took a central role in the commemorative services and headed the special delegation that left Palestine in mid July for Larnaca on Cyprus to receive Bialik's casket and accompany it to Palestine for burial. Of this, too, he wrote Rega.[17]

One factor preventing Ben-Gurion from leaving Palestine was his talks with Arab leaders. His interest in the Arab question — as the Zionists termed Jewish-Arab relations in Palestine — was of long standing, and his position on this important issue went through several revisions. From the start he was one of the few Zionists who wished to anchor Zionism's claim to Palestine not only in history and myth, but also in the argument — equally important to him — that Zionism was a movement of peace and justice, a blessing to non-Jews in Palestine and its neighbors as well. But Palestine's Arabs did not welcome the Jewish newcomers with open arms, and between 1910 and 1918 Ben-Gurion maintained that since there existed a conflict of interest between Zionists and Arabs, Zionism had no worse enemy than the Palestinian Arabs.

This view, which he held all his life, clashed with the principles of justice and peace inherent in his Zionist faith; therefore, although he knew that the conflict existed, for tactical reasons he had to deny it. He rejected Jabotinsky's teaching that the Jews would get Palestine only by force of arms. In 1916, implicitly acknowledging the conflict, he had written to himself, "It is possible to come to terms with the Arabs. This is a matter of strategy for the Yishuv." But after the revolution in Russia he began asserting that there was no conflict of interest between Zionism and the Arabs, since labor Zionism's vocation was to expedite the socialist revolution in the East. With the establishment of socialism in the region the conflict would disappear as if it had never been, since it had been created arbitrarily by the exploitative, feudal Arab effendis and clerics, who sought only to benefit themselves, fearing progress and the social and national liberation it would bring.

A Jewish socialist republic could be established in Palestine that would live in peace and harmony with its neighbors, the Arab socialist republics. This Marxist interpretation, which Ben-Gurion put into practice when he was Histadrut secretary, was based on the concept that the Arab residents of Palestine were but "a fragment" of the great Arab nation, and not a distinct national entity. This concept was bound up with another long-standing legacy of the labor movement: denial of the existence of the Arab national movement. The Zionists, including Ben-Gurion, claimed that the Disturbances of 1919 and the early 1920s — which constituted Arab protest in blood and fire against the Balfour Declaration, the Mandate, and Jewish immigration to Palestine — were no more than the work of vandals and mobs incited by the effendis and clerics, who feared Zionism as a liberating social movement that threatened their class privileges, and had the encouragement and assistance of British officials, who were also enemies of Zion.

After the riots of Av 1929, Ben-Gurion's concept underwent another transition. His class formula was laid aside and in its place arose a new formula of mutual reconciliation. He acknowledged the existence of the Arab national movement and, as he had not been formerly, was ready to meet with its spokesmen, the representatives of the same effendis and clerics whom he had once dismissed. He sought to convince them that there was no conflict of interest and that the two nations, Jewish and Arab, could live together in peace and harmony in the framework of a plan he had created to establish a Federal Palestine: a federation between a Jewish Palestine and its Arab neighbors, in which the Arabs of Palestine, even if they became the minority in the Jewish state, would not be a minority in the framework of the federation. In this manner the Arab "fragment" living in Palestine would not be oppressed since its national aspirations would be expressed within the framework. But Ben-Gurion could not approach Arab leaders about this plan — his party had not only not approved it but had held up publication of his book *We and Our Neighbors,* a collection of his views on the Arab problem that he thought would open the door to talks with the Arabs. But even after Mapai allowed its publication in 1931 and halfheartedly consented to his meeting with Arab leaders, he did not hasten to set up such discussions.

He was, it seems, awaiting the time when massive immigration would become a fact, believing that the larger the Yishuv, the stronger would be the Zionist position in any negotiation. This would be the starting point for talks in which he would win his Arab opponents over to his plan as the best solution for all sides: Arab consent to massive immigration in exchange for the Jews' assurance that Palestine would affiliate itself to the Arab federation, which the Jews would help to establish. If the Arabs did not agree, immigration would continue to grow anyway, Palestine would become Jewish despite all their protestations, and they would simply find themselves in the end with neither a country nor a federation.

Fear of massive immigration, thought Ben-Gurion, would induce the Arabs to accept his plan. In December 1933 he told Lord Melchett, "In the course of four to five years we must bring in a quarter of a million

Jews and the Arab question will be solved." To Sir Herbert Samuel, who had been the first high commissioner, he said that at a rate of forty thousand to fifty thousand immigrants a year "we can, in the course of a few years, arrive at a solution to the greatest problem we have in Palestine — the Arab problem"; the solution was possible despite the fact that the Arabs' opposition grew in direct proportion to increased immigration, for they "do not want Jews to come to Palestine. They want Palestine to remain Arab."[18]

Ben-Gurion's belief in this solution derived from his certainty that immigration would continue to grow, which in turn was based on four substantial factors: the increased pressure to emigrate being brought to bear on Polish and German Jewry; industrial development in Palestine, which led to a greater capacity to absorb immigrants; the new labor-dominated Zionist Executive, guided by Ben-Gurion's watchword "from class to nation"; and the policy of Sir Arthur Wauchope, high commissioner since 1931. Charged with carrying out the policy set forth in the MacDonald Letter, Wauchope made Jerusalem, rather than London, the center of British policymaking for Palestine. By virtue of his experience, understanding, and talents, he became a man whose word carried much weight in Palestine and Whitehall in everything connected with British policy toward Palestine. Although he was moved personally by the distress of the Jews, this was not the only factor that caused him to hasten immigration in his first five years in office. Wauchope was firmly resolved to carry out both obligations of the Mandate — to establish a National Home for the Jews and to protect Arab rights. Just as he was steadfast on increasing immigration, he was equally determined to set up the Legislative Council first recommended in the 1922 White Paper as a step toward more self-rule in Palestine, most of whose residents were Arabs, and to limit land sales to Jews. He probably felt that a strong Jewish population — making up 35 or 40 percent of the total population of Palestine, but not more — would be more inclined to participate in the Legislative Council than a weak Yishuv afraid for its life. While increased immigration* was a concession to the Zionists, the Legislative Council, which the Arabs were inclined to accept owing to their certain majority in it, was a concession to them.

In Ben-Gurion's first year in the JAE, immigration soared, but the satisfaction this gave him did not lessen his anxiety. At the fourth His-

---

* In 1930, 4,944 Jews immigrated to Palestine; in 1931, 4,075; in 1932 (Wauchope's first year in office), 9,553; in 1933, 30,327; in 1934, 42,359; in 1935, 61,854 (peak). By the end of 1931 the Yishuv numbered 174,606 (18% of the population) and by the end of 1935, 355,157 (29.8%).

tadrut convention in January 1934 the spirit of prophecy descended on him and he envisaged world war. "Hitler's rule places the entire Jewish people in danger," he said. "Who knows, perhaps only four or five years — if not less — separate us from that terrible day. In that period, we must double our numbers." In February he told the JAE, "Time is the decisive factor in our activity and our success in this period of severe crisis for Zionism."[19] Ben-Gurion was not one to hesitate to turn a crisis to his own advantage, or a Jewish disaster into a Zionist achievement. The time had come to begin talking with the Arabs.

Unlike other JAE officials who dealt with the Arab question, Ben-Gurion rejected political contacts with Arabs who favored Zionism for financial gain and openly espoused contacts with Arab nationalists, more precisely the heads of the pan-Arab movement. Since 1929 the star of the mufti of Jerusalem, Haj Amin al-Husseini, had been rising in the Arab community. The Jews held him responsible for the massacre and atrocities against Jews in the 1929 Disturbances. By 1933 it was clear that if anyone could claim to speak on behalf of Palestine's Arabs it was he, and Ben-Gurion focused on this man.

As a first step toward the mufti, Ben-Gurion approached Musa Alami, son of a wealthy and respected family and holder of a law degree from Cambridge. Until the end of 1933 Alami had been Wauchope's personal secretary, and from early 1934 he was assistant attorney general for the Mandatory government. Ben-Gurion said he was in search of an "Arab nationalist who cannot be bought with money or favors, but is not a hater of Israel." In Alami he found such an Arab, one who possessed other, no less important merits: his sister was married to Jamal al-Husseini, cousin and confidant of the mufti, and his wife was the daughter of exiled Syrian nationalist leader Ihsan al-Jabri. Together with the Druse emir Shakib Arslan, one of the leaders of the Arab revolt in Syria against France, Jabri headed the Syro-Palestinian delegation to the League of Nations in Geneva. The two also published a pan-Arab and pan-Islamic journal in French, *La Nation arabe*. Both had ties to the mufti in Jerusalem. Ben-Gurion chose Alami not only because of these family connections, but also because he regarded Alami — mistakenly, it turned out — as "an Arab politician who does not appear as such in public because he holds government office, but who is the man behind Arab policy in Palestine." And Ben-Gurion intended to open his talks with the Arabs quietly.

On March 20, 1934, Alami and Ben-Gurion met in Moshe Sharett's apartment in Jerusalem. Opening his remarks with the accepted Zionist claim that "we bring a blessing to the Arabs of Palestine, and they have no good cause to oppose us," Ben-Gurion received a shattering surprise. Musa Alami retorted, "I would prefer that the country remain impoverished and barren for another hundred years, until we ourselves are able to develop it on our own." Dauntless opponents had always found favor with Ben-Gurion, and he was pleased at this reply. "I felt that as an Arab patriot he was entitled to say what he said," wrote Ben-Gurion in his memoirs. It is likely that he also expressed the same sentiment directly to Alami at their first meeting, and a certain chemistry developed between them. The first talk, like the ones that followed, was frank and straightforward.

But their second meeting was delayed, for Alami served in the prosecution in the Arlosoroff murder trial, which opened April 24, and in the appeal that ended with Stavsky's acquittal on July 20. He then fell ill and was bedridden, and Ben-Gurion did not meet with him again for another five months.

Ben-Gurion was also chained to Palestine by the escalation of the conflict between the labor movement and the Revisionists, which was very much his own handiwork. Just three weeks after he had left for the election campaign in Poland, the Hapoel Squadrons had undergone their public baptism by fire. On the last day of Passover, April 17, 1933, they attacked a Betar parade on Allenby Street in Tel Aviv, dispersing it by force. Quite a few Betar men required medical attention. This action, taken without the party's knowledge, outraged the antiviolence faction in Mapai.

On April 20 Katznelson handed the Central Committee his resignation. "The events of the last day of Passover have given me the ultimate proof that I can no longer share in the responsibility of leading our movement." Joseph Aharonovitch, one of Ben-Gurion's staunchest supporters in the HEC, wrote in *Davar*, under the headline NEITHER SHALL YOU FOLLOW THEIR EXAMPLE, that "the use of force, other than in self-defense, is an abomination of our movement; it jeopardizes our work in Palestine and all the hopes of Zionism. Only he who has finished with Zionism, or a madman, can choose such a path." A meeting of the Central Committee that April heard harsh condemnation of those responsible for the attack. In a somewhat reserved defense of it, again in *Davar*, Shlomo Lavi, Ben-Gurion's old friend, wrote, "I would rather go to the worst hell with that Shmuel somebody [a youth who had justified the attack by reiterating Ben-Gurion's words, "We must war on Jewish Hitlerism!"] than to the best paradise with Aharonovitch."

Ben-Gurion's name did not come up, since by Passover Ben-Gurion was already abroad. Nevertheless it was obvious that the attack was in line with his thinking; this is why Katznelson spoke of sharing responsibility, by which he meant "with Ben-Gurion." In his first speech in

Warsaw's Nowoŝci Hall, just four days after the attack, Ben-Gurion did not denounce it at all but accused the Revisionists and Jabotinsky of "incitement against the workers of Palestine. At the head of this incitement stands a maniac whose life's ambition is to be the dictator of the Zionist Organization, and it seems to him that only the workers obstruct his path." When the minutes of the Central Committee meeting and the newspaper clippings reached him he supported the attackers, although indirectly. To an HEC member he wrote, "I was shocked at Berl's position, not with regard to the events themselves but to the personal conclusion he drew from them." To Sprinzak he wrote, "Although I do not at all agree with Joseph Aharonovitch it seems best to me that there be no controversy in the press over this article. Nor is there any need for a statement by the Central Committee as to whether Aharonovitch spoke on behalf of the party." Nevertheless he wrote to Lavi, "Well done!"[20]

The extent to which Ben-Gurion's spirit guided his followers and the Hapoel Squadrons, even in his absence, and how closely tuned they were to his cues from afar were demonstrated by a gathering of Hapoel on the festival of Shavuoth in Haifa, six weeks after the attack on Betar. The Betar leadership decided to hold a gathering at the same time and place, for which they brought in their own strong-arm men. The Histadrut leaders regarded this as a direct provocation and got ready for what was to come, issuing advance warnings. On the afternoon of May 31 Betar members paraded down Herzl Street, wearing their brown shirts, with Abba Achimeir — his arm in a full, smart fascist salute — at their head. With cries of "Down with Hitler" the Hapoel band fell upon them, and a free-for-all ensued. A day later *Hazit ha-Am* described "the red pogrom" in Haifa as "part 2 of the Tel Aviv pogrom."[21]

The murder of Arlosoroff in June had exacerbated the situation tremendously. Brawls on picket lines, disrupted gatherings, raids, and counterraids became everyday events throughout Palestine and even in the cities of Poland and its neighbors. When Ben-Gurion returned in early 1934 the Mapai Central Committee held an in-depth discussion on violence that extended over several sessions, ending in February. In the course of these meetings it became clear, without ever being explicitly stated, that Ben-Gurion approved of the violence and was determined to do his best to escalate it. The controversy over violence in general and the role of the Hapoel Squadrons in particular turned into an open showdown between Katznelson and Ben-Gurion, in which Katznelson found himself in the minority.

Tabenkin stood squarely behind Ben-Gurion, saying,

There is something new in the war between the parties, taken from Hitler's war: provocations, slander, mad incitement, and finally, even murder. . . . We cannot handle this attack with kid gloves. . . . At this moment our movement is not responding to the criminal means of war used against us as it should.

Ben-Gurion, concurring, added,

The growth of revisionism constitutes a grave danger to the movement of the workers and to peace throughout the Yishuv . . . and to Zionism as well. . . . The war against revisionism is one of the labor movement's central roles at this time. . . . Revisionist violence must be fought . . . with the full *class strength* of the working public. Every time a strike is broken it must be seen as an act of violence. It must be answered by organized force. . . . The war against revisionist violence must be waged by special formations under strict military discipline.[22]

The year 1934 saw an enormous increase in violent confrontations, in the press and on the streets, and Ben-Gurion saw fit to claim direct responsibility for one particularly violent and controversial incident. He and Mapai simply could not accept the supreme court's July 20 decision acquitting Stavsky on what they considered a legal technicality. Moreover, the celebration in the revisionist camp — as if the verdict had provided absolute proof of Mapai's blood libel — raised Mapai's collective blood pressure. The Central Committee met that day to plot its moves. Discussion had barely begun when it heard the staggering news that Stavsky and his accomplice, who had been acquitted at the first trial, were to be honored by Tel Aviv's Great Synagogue. The following day, a Saturday, they were to be called up to the Torah.

Once again Ben-Gurion and Katznelson differed. Katznelson ruled out violence categorically, arguing instead for passive defense, "a group of people to guard against acts of provocation. We must have a force to protect our institutions, our gatherings, etc., but no more. What they do in synagogues, in revisionist clubs, and in other places, need not interest us." For his part, Ben-Gurion demanded the mobilization of the Hapoel Squadrons.

Shall we allow a murderer to be so honored? . . . Since I have no guarantee that there will be a hundred Jews in the synagogue who will rise up against this show of respect to the assassin, we must send them there . . . There must be a disturbance. . . . I do not hold with nonviolence under all circumstances. That sort of a stance only facilitates the destruction of the Yishuv. . . . [We] must not accept the approach of withholding all reaction. . . . I am ready for this, even if something happens, even if there is a fistfight in the synagogue.[23]

After the meeting Ben-Gurion wrote a notice in the name of the Mapai Central Committee, distributed that day, in which Stavsky's acquittal was vehemently repudiated.

> This verdict, setting the murderers scot-free, reaffirms the gravest charges against them. . . . We know that Arlosoroff's murderers were but victims of ruffian incitement and corrupt revisionist indoctrination. Our quest to uncover the truth will not stop even now . . . We will fight more forcefully against the revisionist movement . . . and we will not be silent until the Zionist movement and the Yishuv are purged. . . . We will combat terror, strike breaking, and the civil war that the terrorist party has introduced into our lives, and we will go to the very heart of the Zionist camp to cleanse it.

Saturday morning a huge crowd gathered on the steps of the packed Great Synagogue. Scattered among the congregants sat members of Hapoel. The service began quietly enough, but when Stavsky approached the Torah, a roar of shouts of "Down with the killer!" arose, and stones rained down from the women's section at Stavsky in the pulpit. Hats began to fly, prayer books and Bibles sailed through the air, and all hell broke loose. The riot spread like a flash fire from the synagogue to the courtyard, from the courtyard to the street, and from the street throughout the entire neighborhood.[24]

Both the notice and the outbreak in the synagogue outraged the minority in Mapai led by Katznelson. Repudiation of the court's verdict and the renewed accusation of murder against an acquitted man were bad enough, but the desecration of the Sabbath and the synagogue scandalized the Zionist public as a sign that violence had broken all bounds and the Yishuv was headed for disaster. In October it was to reach unprecedented heights in Haifa, and the cries that violence only breeds violence became more and more insistent. Domestic peace seemed crucial to the continued existence and development of Zionism and the Yishuv. The demand for a truce gathered momentum within as well as without Mapai, so that the August 24 party council turned into a battlefield between Ben-Gurion and Katznelson and their respective followers.

Ben-Gurion, who always had more than one iron in the fire, found time to spare for external peace. On June 15, while Musa Alami was still involved with the murder trial, Ben-Gurion had met with the Lebanese Muslim leader Riyadh al-Sulh, and on July 18 with the leader of the pan-Arab Istiqlal Party in Palestine, Awni Abd al-Hadi. According to Ben-Gurion they, too, were well disposed toward — and Abd al-Hadi enthusiastic about — the proposed dialogue on his Federal Palestine scheme, in which the entry of four to six million Jews into Palestine figured prominently.

At the end of July Ben-Gurion was invited to Government House in Jerusalem. On this visit his friendship with Wauchope, whom he once described as the best English teacher he had ever had, deepened. Before dinner Ben-Gurion told him about his plan and the positive response it had received from the Arabs. That evening he wrote Paula on Government House stationery.

> It's midnight now, and it is quiet in Government House but I cannot sleep. My two talks this evening — one before dinner, the other after — tired me out but I can't sleep. I haven't as yet received an answer. The commissioner heard me out attentively, took notes on what I said, remarked that my position made sense, and promised to think it over and give me an answer. The conversation after the meal was informal and wide-ranging. We will see what happens in the morning. Yours, David.

His signature attests to a renewed closeness between them, which will become more evident later. From Ben-Gurion's report to the JAE it seems that the morning's conversation went well, since to his great surprise Wauchope asked him to continue his talks with the Arabs.[25]

He did. On August 14 he went to see Alami at his home in Sharafat, a village near Jerusalem, and visited him again on August 27 and 31. Alami and Hadi told Ben-Gurion things he had never heard before. He got a firsthand account of Arab fears and growing Arab pessimism. Although "a few are getting rich" from the development Zionism brought about in Palestine, Hadi told him, "the people are being dispossessed." These talks, Ben-Gurion believed, taught him to see Zionism and its enterprise "through Arab eyes" and to empathize with the Arabs. Ben-Gurion would later tell his JAE and Mapai colleagues that they saw only the terrible distress of the Jewish people, with the sword of Nazism dangling over their heads, but that he perceived the Arabs' distress as well and could sense their fear of growing Jewish strength in Palestine. He explained further that this fear was rooted in the prejudice that Jews ruled the world, having unlimited financial means at their disposal and omnipotent control over public opinion, the press, Parliament, and the British government. He said he understood how "the Arab fear" fueled the Arab national movement and its acts of protest and terror.

From these talks the irreducible conflict of interest between Zionism and the Arab national movement emerged very clearly, for the only solution perceived by his interlocutors for their problems was an end to Jewish immigration and land sales. "Our final goal," Ben-Gurion told Hadi and Alami, "is the independence of the Jewish people in Palestine, on both sides of the Jordan River, not as a minority, but as a community numbering millions," whereas "the goal of the Arab nation is independence, unity, and revival for all the Arab peoples in their lands." The main question he posed in the talks was whether these two objectives could be reconciled, and he believed they could. In exchange for Arab recognition of the Jewish right to return to Palestine, Ben-Gurion promised, speaking for the Jewish people, to recognize "the right of the Arabs to remain on their land, while the Yishuv is allowed to grow through the development of Palestine." The Jews would use their "political influence, financial means, and moral support to bring about the independence and unity of the Arab people," namely, an Arab federation.

What Arab countries were to join this federation? According to Alami, three blocs had to be considered. The first was Syria and western Palestine, the second, Iraq and Transjordan, and the third, Arabia — the Hijaz, the Negev, and Yemen. Although Saudi Arabia was part of this third area, Alami noted that there was no inclination on the part of Syria or Palestine to unite with the kingdom of Ibn Saud. And although the mufti and his followers did seek ties — in fact, unity — with Syria, the latter, including Lebanon, was still under French mandate, precluding such a union. In June Riyadh al-Sulh had remarked that the Arabs saw "no possibility of Syria's uniting with the other Arab countries except in the aftermath of another world war." For this reason, Alami commented, it was still too early to speak of a general federation, but only of one linking Iraq, Transjordan, and Palestine, all under British control. But Ben-Gurion could not accept this, since he saw Transjordan as an integral part of Palestine. There could be only a two-member federation consisting of Palestine (which, by including Transjordan, would be much larger than Jewish Palestine was at that time) and the state of Iraq. If, however, the Jews were guaranteed unlimited immigration and settlement in Transjordan, "we would be prepared to discuss a special status, either temporary or permanent, for Transjordan."

At the August 14 meeting Alami brought up the mufti, who was "the decisive force" in Palestine, promising to pass on to him the content of their talks and suggesting that Ben-Gurion meet with Haj Amin himself — secretly of course. Ben-Gurion got what he wanted and could congratulate himself for choosing the right approach. Nevertheless, he requested that this meeting be postponed until after he had conferred with the JAE in London. Meanwhile the connection continued through Alami, who kept his word and, in describing the Federal Palestine plan to the mufti, also raised Ben-Gurion's question. Was it possible to come to an understanding whereby the Arabs would agree to the establishment of a Jewish state in Palestine in exchange for Jewish consent to this federation?[26]

In August Ben-Gurion made a sudden about-face and joined those who favored making peace with the Revisionists. He, who had asserted that a truce with them was out of the question and that the only thing to do was "uproot the revisionist pestilence from the Zionist movement," now said the Revisionists were gaining strength because of the violence, and if there was no end to it they would "overrun" Poland. "The present situation in Zionism and the Yishuv must not continue unchecked," said Ben-Gurion, "for the repercussions are having far-reaching influence and doing us great damage." Since they were "not all of the same grain, not all veritable Fascists," he proposed that Mapai appoint two representatives to open negotiations with the Revisionists.

This 180-degree shift, which Berl Katznelson supported enthusiastically, roused much dissatisfaction among others in the party whose ears still rang with Ben-Gurion's battle cries against revisionist Hitlerism. Tabenkin and his followers in the United Kibbutz, whose influence in the labor councils had grown considerably, were particularly incensed. The controversy was so stormy that in August alone seven meetings were devoted to it, at the end of which the Central Committee appointed representatives to negotiate on labor relations and ending the violence. But those who opposed this move demanded a party council. Speaking to the council on August 24, Ben-Gurion tried to put his opponents' minds to rest with the assurance that his view of Jabotinsky, the Revisionists, and their deeds had not changed. To the contrary, he agreed.

> There is no cure for the Revisionists or Jabotinsky . . . since revisionism for him is not only breaking the Histadrut, not only acts of violence, and not even just strikebreaking; revisionism and Zionism for him are Jabotinsky. We won't change the man and we won't change the Jewish people. The Jewish people will not let this clown take control.

To allay fears that he was thinking of taking the Revisionists into the Zionist coalition and that making domestic peace was nothing but a covert step toward that end, Ben-Gurion swore that he was still adamantly against this. "Clearly, no coalition with the Revisionists can be considered. I do not know how anyone could have imagined such a thing." He sought domestic peace because he hoped it was possible to reform many Revisionists. "I do not know why thousands of Jews, who a year ago were not Revisionists, Jewish paupers like the rest of the Jewish masses, cannot be made to see the lies and distortions which motivated them to vote for the Revisionists. Why have we despaired of them? . . . We can save some of them." The controversy that followed was so intense that fears were voiced at the council that seeking peace with the Revisionists would split the party. At the end of two days and nights of nearly nonstop sessions, the council approved, with fifty-four votes in favor and four abstentions, an open statement by the party, addressed "to all sectors of the Yishuv and the Zionist movement," meant to open negotiations for "better relations in the Yishuv and the Zionist movement." This statement did not name the Revisionists, but a council resolution (approved by 33 to 22) forbidding "direct negotiations with the Revisionists" did. The council reversed the Central Committee's actions.

At these meetings Ben-Gurion's talks with the Arabs, and by inference his wish to meet with the mufti, were also examined. Although the discussion did not probe too deeply — Ben-Gurion's report was very sketchy — imaginary parallels were drawn between his efforts at domestic and external peace, and between the mufti and Jabotinsky as two instigators of murder. "I know the Revisionists murdered Arlosoroff," said Moshe Beilinson at the August 8 meeting of the Central Committee, adding, "We know that the mufti organized the riots against the Jews." Nonetheless, he went on, "had the mufti turned to us — even in the midst of the Disturbances — proposing to sit at a 'round table,' I would still have said that we must answer in the positive." In the council Katznelson also lent Ben-Gurion support, saying, "When I ask whether we can sit with the mufti after the pogrom, while I doubt the mufti's role in it no less than Stavsky's role in Arlosoroff's murder, I would say that I would meet with the mufti to discuss preventing pogroms and perhaps even for political negotiations. Is there anyone here among us who can call such a meeting dishonorable?" On August 24, 1934, Ben-Gurion received moral authorization from his party and its council for his peace initiative.[27]

On August 27 Ben-Gurion and Alami met again to discuss the meeting with the mufti. On August 29 Alami phoned Ben-Gurion in Tel Aviv with the news that he had seen the mufti and had answers to his questions. Two days later Ben-Gurion heard in Sharafat that his initiative had hit the mufti "like a bombshell." Haj Amin had no idea, or did not believe, that there were Jews who earnestly sought understanding with the Arabs. "He, for his part, did not oppose" Ben-Gurion's federal scheme. But as it had arisen so suddenly he naturally had to look it over first. In any event, he could do nothing behind his people's back. Since Ben-Gurion was about to go abroad, he agreed with Alami that Ben-Gurion would meet in Geneva with Arslan and Jabri, whose opinions the mufti held in high esteem. Alami would write them in advance of Ben-Gurion's impending visit and inform the mufti. When Ben-Gurion returned to Palestine, he would meet with the mufti.[28]

On September 2, 1934, Ben-Gurion set out for London, high hopes in his heart and Paula at his side. This was the first time she had accompanied him on a business trip and the first time in fifteen years that she had gone abroad. It seems as if along with Zionist and Arab peace, Ben-Gurion was also working to establish peace in his own home.

29

Disappointment

SAILING ABOARD the *Sphinx*, in sunny weather on a calm sea, passing the time so pleasantly, David and Paula Ben-Gurion might have felt they were on the honeymoon they never had. There was, nonetheless, a small cloud shadowing their peace of mind: mischievous fourteen-year-old Amos. Paula lamented to Ben-Gurion that he was out in the streets all day and would not listen to her. In May 1933 his school had expelled him for "poor behavior and carelessness about his studies." When the news had reached Ben-Gurion in Poland he exhorted his son, "Aren't you ashamed of yourself? You once told me that you wanted to work in the HEC like me when you grow up, but if you behave like that, neglecting your lessons and disobeying your mother, you won't ever be able to do my work." He ordered his son to shape up, to keep his mind on his studies, and to do what he was told. Amos was readmitted, but he did not live up to his father's demands.

At the end of the summer of 1934, Amos had to take extra entrance exams to the fifth form, having failed the first ones. He spent his whole summer vacation with tutors. Leaving nothing to chance, Ben-Gurion and Paula left him with their friends the Rittoffs, whose son was a model pupil. As consolation and incentive, they left Amos enough money to buy his heart's desire — a harmonica. On her first day aboard ship Paula wrote Amos — in English, as always to her children — asking if he was working hard and that he cable her if he passed the exams.

Autumn leaves and rainy weather greeted the Ben-Gurions in Paris when they arrived on September 9. From the Salvia Hotel, even before resting from the tiring journey, Paula sat down to write Amos. "How are you dear? I am so lonesome for my *bad boy*." Only after asking if he felt well, if the food at the Rittoffs' was good, and if they took good care of him, did she come to the point — "Did you pass your examinations?" — and ask him again to cable her the results.

The next day Ben-Gurion wrote to him.

> Did you pass your examinations? (Or will you be held back in fourth? You must pay more attention to your studies. It is unthinkable that you take examinations again next year.) . . . You have to get used to doing your homework as soon as you come home from school, and only after preparing your lessons may you go out and play. It's not that difficult — all you need is the will. If you devote two hours a day to your homework you could be the top student in school. Write to me in London what the exam was like, if you're studying, and if you feel at home at the Rittoffs'. . . . All the best, Dad. Did you buy a harmonica? How much did you pay for it?[1]

They wrote to Amos and his sisters separately, since Geula had remained at home alone and Renana was staying at Kibbutz Geva. If Ben-Gurion had brought Paula with him on this trip — she was to accompany him to Warsaw, too — to prove to her that he always wanted her, and none other, at his side, their shared worry over Amos's education seemed to complete the renewed family idyll.

But on September 10 Ben-Gurion sent another letter: "Dear beloved Rega, I am now on my way to London." After giving her the details of his itinerary — Geneva, Warsaw, then London again — he added that he would return to Palestine at the end of October.

> Will you be in Vienna all that time? . . . I do not know if you've finished all your examinations, or when you will finally set out for Palestine. I am afraid I will not be able to come to Vienna this time. Where will I see you, in Europe or in Palestine? . . . One of your letters gave me to understand that you are anxious over the new regulations soon to be issued in Palestine for doctors. Of course it would be best for you to hurry and come to Palestine before then — in fact, in any event you'd better move quickly. . . . Write to me in London. Yours, David.

Not a word about his not traveling alone this time — not the slightest hint about Paula.

In London they settled into the Galsworthy Hotel, and Paula immediately started shopping and writing letters, to Amos in particular. "What is the matter with you," she demanded on September 17. "Why don't you write. Did you pass your examinations? We have sent you 2 cables and received no answer." She continued in this vein until October 7, when the long awaited letter finally arrived with the news that Amos had passed all his exams. But despite his parents' entreaties, and regardless of the rewards he was given — a harmonica, a flute, an army bugle — Amos did not mend his ways. The summer and fall of 1935 were a replay of the same scenario: extra examinations, appeals for a letter or a telegram, and eventual success at the examinations.[2]

Ben-Gurion worked day and night at the Zionist office at 77 Great Russell Street, the seat of the Zionist Executive and the JAE. But he worked more on broadening the coalition than on restructuring the Zionist Organization on the basis of national associations. On his earlier visit to London, in December 1933, he had devoted his energies to transferring the Organization Department from London to Jerusalem and to establishing a worldwide information service and telegraphic news agency. But in spite of the resolution supporting these moves and promises of collaboration from his colleagues, his efforts had come to naught. The Organization Department remained in London and his budget request was rejected, leaving him with no means of hiring the personnel necessary for either the information service or the news agency. "I cannot appear as unreliable in the eyes of people I summoned to work or in the eyes of Zionist public opinion," he had written to his Mapai colleagues in the JAE on February 21, 1934, and therefore made up his mind "to return to the Histadrut." This was his first resignation from the JAE, which he accounted for by saying he was not willing to waste his time to no purpose. "The time factor is the essence of our work and our success in this trying and grave period of crisis for Zionism. Every day wasted is a loss never to be regained."

There could have been another reason for his resignation. Party members whom he wished to recruit for his program were not of one mind with him. Berl Katznelson had agreed to support him only if the proposed information department was a "*collegium* in charge of Zionist information policies." To Ben-Gurion it seemed that his partner-associates in the party were not honoring the IOU they had given him when they had forced him to join the JAE.

Eventually, however, he retracted his resignation, realizing that, just as Rome wasn't built in a day, so too his program needed time. Thereupon he plunged into what he called "internal political activity." Now in London in September, with a view to rallying "all the forces" called for by this plan, he put his mind to broadening the Zionist coalition. A large share of the meetings on Great Russell Street were devoted to this issue, where it was decided to act on Ben-Gurion's proposal and call all the parties to talks, the Revisionists first, on October 8.[3]

Between meetings Ben-Gurion dealt with other prospects — getting a development loan, bringing the Jewish Telegraphic Agency under JAE control, and establishing an airline as a foundation for a Haganah air force — all of which failed to materialize. The elections to the 1935 Zionist Congress were also very much on his mind. In stark contrast to the fear of a revisionist "landslide" in Poland that he had voiced to the

Mapai Central Committee, he now heard a rosy report from Itzhak Gruenbaum, a member of the JAE who had just returned from Warsaw, guaranteeing labor 50 percent and up to 60 percent of the votes; Ben-Gurion intended to check out this forecast on his upcoming trip to Warsaw. He used the little free time he had left to better acquaint himself with Weizmann's people, and perhaps to woo them as well. He met twice with a prominent member of Weizmann's circle, the historian Lewis B. Namier, author of *The Structure of Politics at the Accession of George III*, a good friend of Mrs. Blanche ("Baffy") Dugdale, niece to Lord Balfour and very close to Weizmann. In his diary Ben-Gurion said of Namier, "He is very bitter, an impossible man, but with many talents." As it turned out, it was this intellectual giant who in 1936 became the only one of Weizmann's circle to build a strong working relationship with Ben-Gurion.

Along with everything else, it was time to act on his Arab initiative. He had not yet gone to Geneva, as he was awaiting word from Judah-Leib Magnes, whom he had invited to take part in the meeting with Arslan and Jabri. On September 21 Magnes declined, and on that day Ben-Gurion submitted "a full report" (as it was called in the protocol under the heading "Understanding with the Arabs") to the JAE on his talks with the Arabs and the high commissioner. However "full," this report said nothing of Ben-Gurion's intention to meet with the mufti or plan to set out for Geneva the very next day.[4]

Would this trip also serve to camouflage a rendezvous with Rega? On the seventeenth Ben-Gurion received an answer from Rega to his letter from Paris. "The foolish little girl" longed to see him, she wrote, but could not leave Vienna. "Being in Europe yet so far from you is hard to take," he replied at once. "As much as you want me to come to Vienna — perhaps I want to even more. Apparently you still do not know how dear 'the foolish little girl' is to me and how much I want to see her and be with her. I am afraid that this time I won't be able to manage it." He described his heavy work load, again without mentioning that Paula was with him. Their next meeting, therefore, would have to be deferred until she arrived in Palestine. "Just don't settle in some far-off, inaccessible corner. It would be good if you could settle in Jerusalem, perhaps too good. How much easier my work would be, knowing that nearby sits a dear girl with whom, for at least a few moments, one can find peace and forget everything. Then again, when you come to Palestine, perhaps I will lose you altogether. . . . Never mind. I will nevertheless be able to love you — Yours, David."

He had just sent this letter and already his longing for her grew. Automatically his mind started devising ways to satisfy it, to steal some time to meet her without arousing Paula's suspicions. Parting from

Paula early in the morning of Saturday, September 22, he set out for Paris. In his haste he had time only to tell her that she would have to travel alone to Warsaw, where they would meet after he finished his business in Geneva and be together from September 27 to October 6. From Paris he wrote her instructions on how to get to Warsaw, mistakenly telling her to get off at the wrong train station in Berlin, as part of a suggestion that she stay in Berlin overnight. Were the haste, the error, and the suggestion all part of a ploy to manage a few days with Rega? It seems that just this suspicion sneaked into Paula's heart.[5]

Ben-Gurion's plan had been to take the 11:00 P.M. train from Paris to Geneva that Saturday night. From the Paris home of Mark Jarblum — his friend since the early days of Poale Zion — he was to set up the Geneva meeting for Sunday morning by phone with Jabri, whom he had met at Alami's home; unfortunately Jabri had no telephone. Emir Arslan, whose phone number they discovered only after an intense search, was not home. Shortly before eleven they tried again, this time successfully. But Ben-Gurion's satisfaction was not to be complete: Arslan was prepared to meet in his apartment the next day, but only at 9:30 P.M., not in the morning. Hence Ben-Gurion spent the night in Paris in talks and discussions, not getting to bed until 3:00 A.M., and there went one of the days he had set aside for Rega.

The next afternoon he and Jarblum left for Geneva. By that time the question had arisen as to why he had not invited Sharett, his partner in the Political Department, who spoke Arabic, Turkish, French, and English, to join him there. The probable reason was that Ben-Gurion was so sure of success in the talks that he was unwilling to share it. If he was to pit himself against Weizmann for the leadership of the Zionist movement he would need an achievement to match Weizmann's Balfour Declaration. A peace agreement with the Arabs would hit the mark.[6]

Promptly at 9:30 on Sunday evening, September 23, 1934, Ben-Gurion and Jarblum entered the emir's luxurious apartment for the first historic meeting between the Syro-Palestinian Delegation to the League of Nations and the senior representative of the JAE's Political Department. They started off on the right foot; Jabri heartily welcomed Ben-Gurion as an old acquaintance. Ben-Gurion later described Arslan in his diary as an old and slow-moving lion, still spitting fire as he spoke. After some small talk they got to the issue at hand. Ben-Gurion was asked to fill in the details of his talks with Alami, which Arslan and Jabri had learned about only sketchily from Alami's letters. For the next three hours the conversation deepened, without Ben-Gurion sensing that both sides were talking past one another. When they parted, each side understood what it wanted to understand.

There were at least three reasons for this. The first was the language barrier. They began in Turkish, but out of consideration for Jarblum switched to French. This was the first sustained effort Ben-Gurion made to converse in that language, his knowledge of which was far from perfect. To make himself understood he needed not only Jarblum's assistance, but also that of his two hosts, who came up with a missing word in German here and there when his French was lacking. Second, Ben-Gurion spoke from the assumption that immigration would grow from the forty thousand of 1934 to sixty thousand in 1935 and thereafter. On this premise he assumed that in five years the Jews in Palestine would number six hundred thousand. No longer would they compose 21 percent of the population, as they had at the end of 1933, but would reach 40 percent or more by 1938. The self-confidence this conviction gave him was interpreted by his hosts as arrogance. Finally, Ben-Gurion's proposed federation of a Jewish state in Palestine, including Transjordan, certainly did not endear him to his hosts, who regarded Palestine as southern Syria and supported their unification. In addition, they were strongly pro-Italy, and Ben-Gurion's appointment of Great Britain to the key role in his plan may well have put them off.

According to Arslan and Jabri, they heard Ben-Gurion out with a growing resentment concealed by smiles. He spoke of the absolute necessity of establishing a "Jewish homeland and Jewish state" in Palestine and Transjordan. In exchange for Arab agreement, Ben-Gurion declared, "we are ready to extend political and economic help to the Arabs." The political assistance would include the rallying of Jews to the cause of Arab Syria. By economic aid, Ben-Gurion meant "investments in Iraq, Saudi Arabia, and Yemen." Arslan and Jabri made it clear to Ben-Gurion that the Arabs did not yet need welfare from the Jews. Ben-Gurion could not expect the agreement of the Arab opponent to such grandiose, insolent, and far-fetched ideas. "We told Ben-Gurion that there was no point in continuing this chimeric talk," Arslan and Jabri reported in the November issue of *La Nation arabe*.

Earlier Arslan had described the talk in a letter to an Arab friend. By then he had even forgotten Ben-Gurion's name (so he wrote) and referred to Ben-Gurion simply as "he." "He sat with us for three hours and explained to me and my colleague, without so much as a stutter, that the Jews had come to Palestine, and that their numbers would soon reach six million," in a process that the Arabs could not prevent. "If this is so," asked Arslan and Jabri, "why did he come to inform us of his irrevocable decision?" Arslan dismissed Ben-Gurion's offer of aid for Arab development as "foolish proposals."

Ben-Gurion, blind to his hosts' resentment, actually left the meeting with soaring expectations, even though he heard Arslan say explicitly that the agreement had a chance only if the Jews undertook to remain a minority forever and that if, despite everything, the Jews succeeded in establishing a Jewish Palestine, "the Arabs will never reconcile themselves to this fact." What was the basis for Ben-Gurion's optimism? He felt that Jabri had taken a more temperate stand. This perception was based not so much on what Jabri had said during the course of the talk, but on the questions he had asked, which seemed to Ben-Gurion to be more accommodating and moderate. This distinction was strengthened when Jabri accompanied him to the train and assured him that what was said had not been the final word, and "the discussion will continue." In his diary, Ben-Gurion recorded this remark by Jabri: "Do not despair; the emir has not yet understood the importance of the matter." In any event, Ben-Gurion concluded that he was not alone in leaving the meeting with the impression that it had gone quite well. "The conversation made the biggest impression on ... Jarblum. He was truly astonished at such dialogue with the Arabs," he noted.[7]

Since there was no morning train to Vienna, Ben-Gurion lost another half day and spent the morning and afternoon of Monday, September 24, at the League of Nations, where protection of minorities was the topic of discussion. At 3:15, shortly before boarding the train, he wired Rega. "Tomorrow 15:20 station west David." Once again he was prepared to make nearly a full day's journey to be with her for a short while. When he arrived late Tuesday afternoon, he checked into the Metropol Hotel and could then concentrate entirely on Rega. On September 26 they posed for a photograph. Perhaps Ben-Gurion's radiance was due, among other things, to anticipation of another day or two of happiness in Vienna. By his reckoning, Paula would be spending that night in Berlin. The next day she was to leave for Warsaw, where she was supposed to arrive on Friday, the twenty-eighth. This left him time to relax in Vienna as well as to get to Warsaw before Paula and seem to have been waiting for her there for some time. But he was in for a bad surprise. Paula paid no heed to his instructions and did not get off in Berlin. With a heart full of dark foreboding she continued in the speeding night train straight to Warsaw. Only the strongest suspicion could have moved her to undertake such a journey, more than forty hours long. Arriving in Warsaw, she headed directly for the Bristol Hotel, only to find that Ben-Gurion was not there.

Exactly what happened next is not known for sure. Many years later Sara Noy, the wife of Melech Noy, head of the League in Poland, related that "when Paula arrived and did not find Ben-Gurion there was a perfect scandal. . . . I went to greet her and she threatened suicide." Apparently Melech Noy or Anselm Reiss, Mapai's representative in Poland, or perhaps both wired Ben-Gurion in Vienna to call him at once to Warsaw; both were aware of his relationship with Rega, but, like Mendel Singer in Vienna, they took this secret with them to the grave. According to Rega, Ben-Gurion suddenly told her that he had to drop everything and rush off to Warsaw since Paula had taken an overdose of sleeping pills. The train pulled into Warsaw on Thursday afternoon, September 27, but he was prevented from hastening to Paula by a large crowd that had gathered at the train station and was cheering him with cries of "Long live Ben-Gurion! Long live the Histadrut!" *Davar* reported, "The encounter between Ben-Gurion and the porters made a special impression. As he exited the doors of the railway station there was pressure from all sides from fans wishing to shake his hand and congratulate him." The 1933 elections had made him a great hero in Jewish Warsaw. At long last he got away from the reception and sped to Paula in the hotel. To his relief she was still alive. It is not known whether she actually took any sleeping pills, but if she was ever in any serious danger, it passed after the briefest medical attention. But when a rather frightened Ben-Gurion arrived on the scene and sat beside her bed she appeared to be hovering between two worlds. Those close to Ben-Gurion later spoke of Paula's "somewhat serious illness," owing to which the opening of one of the councils for which Ben-Gurion had come to Warsaw was postponed.[8]

Nor is much known of what passed between husband and wife in Warsaw. From Ben-Gurion, of course, nothing was ever heard. Just as he never mentioned the two days he had spent in Vienna in his diary, there was nothing about Paula's stay in Warsaw. The diary only records business as usual: gatherings, meetings, sessions. Paula, for her part, either said much and hid little, or vice versa, depending on her audience. She was torn between her desire to play the woman wronged and her pride, and her version of events was therefore the product of both. She told no one of her "suicide," not even Geula, who as an adult became her trusted confidante, privy to all her secrets. To relatives and friends who knew nothing of this episode in Warsaw she reported she had taken ill there. But to those she met in Warsaw and who saw her in her distress she wrote, in Russian, after her return to London, "Forgive my short letter, I am still tired and have not yet regained my strength." She did not say whether or how Ben-Gurion explained his sudden appearance in Vienna. In any event, Ben-Gurion found it no easy task to restore domestic harmony.

In a postcard to Amos that Paula sent from Warsaw on October 6 she wrote, "I am leaving today Poland for London" — first person singular. Had not Ben-Gurion added at the end, in Hebrew, "This evening we return to London," it might have been thought that Paula was making the return journey on her own. Probably he had to be very patient and tactful in trying to appease her. And indeed, on the day they reached London, despite her alleged poor health, she sat in on a meeting with the upper crust of Zionist women — Mrs. Weizmann, Mrs. Sieff, Mrs. Sacher, and others — and the next day she summoned enough strength to dine with Mrs. Weizmann. So she reported back to her friends in Warsaw, adding, "It was quite interesting, not like in Warsaw." She finally made up with Ben-Gurion; their letters to the children attest to this.[9]

Ben-Gurion's ten days in Warsaw were marked by efforts to broaden the coalition and gain a solid majority at the 1935 Zionist Congress. To this end Ben-Gurion embarked once again on a marathon of talks, councils, public gatherings, and meetings with the representatives of various parties. From the activists of his movement, some of whom came from neighboring countries in his honor, he demanded support for internal unity and for "the drawing in of the general Zionist and Mizrachi youth, a daily paper, a worldwide press and telegraphic information service . . . an *ideological* war against the Revisionists." At all his talks and meetings with party members he wanted to know if the party star was rising or falling and heard conflicting answers. He also set about financing renewed publication of the daily *Dos Wort.* Eventually he concluded, "We have a good chance of a *decisive* victory at the next Congress."

In both a press conference called the day after his arrival in Warsaw and a public speech at the Splendid Theater on October 1, he could not help but hint about the topic of his talks with the Arabs. "It is my duty to point out that there is no historic conflict between Zionism and the Arabs. We are not settling to their detriment, but helping them. Nor are there political conflicts. For us Palestine is everything, while for the Arabs it is only 2 percent of all Arab lands. . . . *Greater* Zionism will find a common language with the future *greater* Arab movement."[10]

On October 6 he and Paula took the evening train to Berlin, where they spent a few hours before continuing on to London. So convinced was he that an agreement was within reach that in a speech to the European Council of He-Chalutz in Berlin he suggested sending the JAE a telegram of congratulations. He himself drafted its text: "Great vistas have been opened to us. . . . We are convinced of the possibility of a far-reaching understanding between Jews and Arabs, and we welcome the initiative taken by the Jewish Agency to reach an accord between the two peoples."[11] They returned to London by second-class train and first-class ferryboat, a step up from their usual third-class accommodations and perhaps another token of Ben-Gurion's endeavor to pacify Paula.

On his return to the Zionist office on October 8 Ben-Gurion was asked to contact Pinchas Rutenberg, long-time Zionist leader, founder and director of the Palestine Electric Company, and a reputed enemy of Weizmann. Rutenberg vehemently told Ben-Gurion how serious Zionism's situation was and how much it needed a "united front," to which end he implored Ben-Gurion to meet with Jabotinsky. Then the unbelievable happened. Ben-Gurion replied that if Rutenberg "invites me to a meeting with Jabotinsky, I will accept."[12] When word of the meeting got out it fell like a bomb upon the outraged labor movement. Was he aware that shock waves were inevitable? His diary is silent. In any case, his move toward Jabotinsky was no more daring than the steps he had taken toward the mufti. At this stage Ben-Gurion was already quite capable of separating his political thinking from his emotions.

The reason that prompted him to take such an audacious step can easily be guessed. Returning to London, Ben-Gurion felt that great days were coming for Zionism. With his own eyes he had seen masses of Jews in Poland and Germany pinning their only hope to life in Palestine, bolstering his confidence that immigration would continue to grow and that within three to four years the Yishuv would double in size. Peace with the Arabs, therefore, was not far away. Ben-Gurion always believed that once the Arabs saw a strong Yishuv they would despair of destroying it and come to terms with the Jews. He expressed this high hope in a rather grandiose manner, proclaiming in October to the Jewish Agency Council in London, "We live in the days of the Messiah."[13] Perhaps he had assured himself that he who had the power to bring Zionism peace from without in such times could also bring it domestic harmony.

The report he delivered to the Jewish Agency Council and the letter he wrote to Magnes about his talks with the Arabs indicate just how sure he was that there were good prospects for an understanding by which the Arabs would recognize the Jews' right to immigrate to and settle Palestine and Transjordan, in the framework of an Arab federation. This seemed so certain a personal achievement for him that it appeared worthy of publication. One week after the Council report he granted the *Jewish Chronicle* an interview. "During a recent visit to Geneva," it reported, "[Ben-Gurion] was entrusted with the important mission of continuing discussions to bring about a more amicable relationship between the Jews and Arabs of Palestine. He had a number of talks at the headquarters of the Arab National Movement in Geneva with the leaders of the pan-Arab movement."

Ben-Gurion described the talks as "very satisfactory and interesting." When asked when the negotiations would bear fruit, he responded, "Permanent and enduring peace will not be brought about in a few days, weeks, or even months — it is a matter, perhaps, of years. There is still a good deal of suspicion and friction so far as the different interests are concerned. But ultimately I hope that the efforts for those who are working for Jewish and Arab cooperation will be crowned with success." He had acquired the glib tongue of the diplomat, always leaving room for either a retreat or further demands.

Along with the interview the paper carried a message to Jewish students in London. The agreement, Ben-Gurion told them, would not be attained by force of argument, either ethical or historical. No people had ever given up its land as a consequence of moral persuasion. The agreement would be within reach when the Jewish people had hard facts to back it up. "The question now is whether or not a great Jewish center can be created within a short time. With the present rate of immigration the creation of such a center could come about within a few years." He kept the news that he had spoken with the Arabs explicitly about a Jewish state in Palestine within the framework of an Arab federation to himself, remaining satisfied with references to a "great Jewish center." The *Jewish Chronicle* headlined the interview, TOWARD ARAB-JEWISH UNDERSTANDING; SUCCESSFUL TALKS PROGRESSING."[14]

Ben-Gurion's Arab initiative also came under review from an altogether unexpected source. The peace talks between the Zionist coalition and the opposition parties were to begin October 8. But although Ben-Gurion returned to London at dawn on that day to be in time for the opening of the negotiations with two representatives of the Revisionists in the office on Great Russell Street, he hardly took any part in them. Afterward he explained to his friends in Mapai that "instead of sitting and talking to the wind with two blockheads who are nothing but a phonograph in the hands of the man who runs the Revisionist Party," it was far better and more practical to negotiate directly with the "operator." And the next afternoon, at the height of the discussion with the two revisionist representatives, Ben-Gurion was called to the telephone. It was Rutenberg, calling to tell him that Jabotinsky was coming from Paris. Would Ben-Gurion be able to meet with him the next day? True to his word, Ben-Gurion replied that he would.[15]

So began one of the worst upheavals ever to rock the labor movement; it laid the fault line along which Mapai would split eight years later. Ben-Gurion must have been aware of the likely repercussions of this bold step, yet he was resolved to take it, without his party's consent, knowing full well he was acting against its will.

What was it that made Ben-Gurion willing to sit down with Jabotinsky? The two men had one thing in common: to both the realization of Zionism was more important than their ideologies. There is much ground to support the contention that, had Ben-Gurion thought that revisionism was a better vehicle for the advancement of the Zionist cause, he might have embraced it. The same is true of Jabotinsky; had he believed labor and the Histadrut the better instruments he would have discarded his militarist philosophy for them. This common virtue — or failing — made a dialogue between them possible. For they would be discussing tactics rather than strategy, as their talks proved.

Another reason for their willingness to meet was that each thought he could turn their new relationship to advantage. Ben-Gurion could see his Histadrut swallowing up the thousands of Revisionists, once their organization and leadership had weakened, as is bound to happen when a large, strong group links up with a smaller, weaker one, and did happen in 1924, when Ha-Poel ha-Mizrachi — the religious labor unions — joined the Histadrut. His power base in the coalition would then be broad and strong enough to eliminate the need to call Weizmann back to the presidency. Finally, he could see no ideological error in preparing the Histadrut to accept the Revisionists into its ranks, for from the outset the Histadrut had been a *general* federation of labor, open to all shades of thought. As for Jabotinsky, the agreements with Ben-Gurion could only enhance his influence in Palestine and in Europe, and might even provide him with a voice in the direction of major Zionist policies, specifically the launching of his petition. Once the petition had proved itself, it would be clear to one and all who was truly a leader of genius. In a man who believed in the power of words to win over Jewish hearts and minds, such a belief is not surprising.

Between October 10 and November 11, 1934, Ben-Gurion and Jabotinsky held twelve meetings in London; the talks conducted in the Zionist office, in which Ben-Gurion also took part, were merely a smokescreen for the other, truly important ones. They opened in Rutenberg's hotel, in a cold and official manner. When Ben-Gurion entered Rutenberg's room at 6:00 P.M., he found Jabotinsky already there. "I greeted him without shaking hands," Ben-Gurion wrote in his diary and later in a letter to Mapai. "He stood, offered his hand, and asked, 'Don't you want to shake my hand?' " Ben-Gurion mumbled something in astonishment and proferred his hand. They addressed each other throughout as "Sir," but gradually, in the course of the talk — which lasted, said Ben-Gurion, until midnight — "the formal barrier fell."

Moreover, in reviewing the principal issues of the Zionist world they found themselves in accord more often than not. "In the course of the conversation," Ben-Gurion noted in his diary, "it seemed as though we were not really at odds until we came to the area of joint activity." Nevertheless, their like-mindedness on so many important issues sparked a hope in each that they could overcome their differences and reach a full understanding.

This hope was so strong that by the middle of the evening Jabotinsky said, with great exhilaration, "If the two of us come to terms it will be a great day for the Jews, but such a day must be used for a grand project."

Ben-Gurion agreed.

"What project?" asked Jabotinsky.

"Massive settlement," replied Ben-Gurion.

Jabotinsky disagreed. "What is needed is a project the entire nation can participate in, a mammoth project that every Jew can give his hand to."

"Like what?"

"A petition," was Jabotinsky's answer.[16]

There could be no clearer illustration of the differences between them than this exchange. Ben-Gurion stuck to his belief that only deeds could create political reality, while Jabotinsky extolled the power of the word. The "petition" was his brainchild and it constituted the core of his political plan of action: Jews all over the world would sign two documents. The first would be a collective statement, for signature en masse, "praying for fundamental reforms in the administration of Palestine, and the introduction of measures consciously directed toward the re-establishment of a Jewish state." The second document would be a personal application "each signed by one single person demanding his or her own admission to Palestine." Both documents — petitions — would be presented to "the Crown and Parliament [of Great Britain] and governments abroad." Jabotinsky estimated that at least three million Jews would sign. This "project" had already been publicized in May 1934 and ridiculed, particularly by the labor movement.[17] Ben-Gurion regarded it as a propaganda gimmick, and he was therefore quite taken aback when Jabotinsky told him that it was the grand project he had in mind. Later he wrote his associates, "I felt ashamed for the humiliation of this man. He sensed my bewilderment and said, 'You, who have been a *Judenstattler* [supporter of a Jewish state] all your life, how is it that you neither understand nor appreciate the value of demonstration and slogan? Words and rhetoric have tremendous power.'"

"I felt we had reached the major bone of contention between us."

" 'If you lend a hand to this project,' he said, 'I will advise my associates to make the greatest sacrifice for peace.'

" 'What makes the petition important?' I asked.

" 'Participation by the entire nation, the fact that every Jew is demonstrating. This they [the British] will understand and it will work.' "

At this point their conversation flared into a debate over deeds versus slogans, a debate without end. "At this juncture the wall was raised. I saw that I had reached the roots of revisionism and that there was no way to steer them away from demonstration," wrote Ben-Gurion to his colleagues. But despite this wall he continued to believe firmly, as with the accord with the Arabs, that understanding and agreement were within reach. At exactly midnight they left Rutenberg and walked together to the nearby tube station. As fate would have it, they had to take the same train. Once inside Jabotinsky asked, for the second time, "Why didn't you shake my hand at first?"

"I didn't want to put you to the test."

"Would you be willing to see me tomorrow without Rutenberg?"

Ben-Gurion answered that he would, and each agreed to bring "a program in writing" to the meeting. Three stations later they parted. "I privately wondered what would happen tomorrow in Palestine and in the worldwide Jewish press if some reporter had found us talking with one another," wrote Ben-Gurion later to his colleagues. That thought returned to him on another occasion when they broke for lunch and strolled together to a restaurant.[18]

At their second meeting Jabotinsky accepted Ben-Gurion's federation plan as a solution to the Arab question. This undoubtedly encouraged readiness in Ben-Gurion to move toward his conferee on other issues. He was even ready to adopt the petition as the JAE's plan of action. But all their good will could not rescue them from an impasse over fundamental differences on two subjects. Jabotinsky would not recognize labor's right to strike, insisting that every industrial conflict be solved by binding arbitration, nor was he willing to obey the JAE or give up his party's independent political action. Still, they agreed to meet again. On one issue they saw eye to eye: disparagement of Weizmann. Rutenberg, never to be outdone on this score, suggested that they set up a "triumvirate" to head the Zionist Organization. Who would constitute it was one subject they never discussed, but the assumption that Rutenberg had Ben-Gurion, Jabotinsky, and himself in mind cannot be very far from the truth. Were they scheming to thwart Weizmann's return to the presidency? Kurt Blumenfeld, Ben-Gurion's nominee for the directorship of the propaganda bureau and a Weizmannite who knew well what went on behind the scenes in the JAE, regarded the peace talks with the Revisionists, and more so with Jabotinsky, as "a very shrewd strategy" to shut Weizmann out of the Zionist leadership.[19] However, Jabotinsky made it unequivocally clear to Ben-Gurion that even if their talks went well and peace reigned in the Zionist Organization, he would never join the coalition. Ben-Gurion must have believed him, for he had in the past accused Jabotinsky of equating Zionism with his own sole leadership. At the same time Jabotinsky also made it plain that he would not oppose his colleagues if they wished to join the coalition, which could equally prove an obstacle to Weizmann.

At this meeting, in Jabotinsky's hotel, they were able to work out two draft agreements, one of nonviolence between the labor and revisionist movements and the other a labor accord between the Histadrut and the Revisionists' National Workers' Organization. Together these drafts were called the little agreement. But "the big agreement" — covering a policy line and plan of action, collective responsibility of the Zionist Executive, restraint from separate political activity, acceptance of discipline by all members of the Zionist Organization, among other things — was beyond them. When they parted, however, the spark of friendship had been kindled between them, and probably because of that they believed they could swing the big agreement as well. Jabotinsky returned to Paris, seat of Betar's worldwide headquarters, to consult with his colleagues on the two draft agreements. He was so sure of their consent that he promised Ben-Gurion a renewal of their talks in London on October 16. Ben-Gurion, on the other hand, did not think the time was right to report to his colleagues in Palestine on this rather presumptuous step.

The bond between them quickly found expression in writing. Jabotinsky addressed Ben-Gurion as "Dear Sir" to tell him that at his return to Paris he had found "a bundle of troubles, mostly private ones," and therefore would not be able to come to London at the time specified but would try to get there before October 22. Their correspondence began in a formal tone, but Ben-Gurion's second letter opened, "Dear Jabotinsky, I hope you won't take offense that I address you as a friend, without the ceremonial 'sir.'" He signed it, "I shake your hand respectfully." In a flash Jabotinsky responded.

My dear friend Ben-Gurion! I just now received your letter of yesterday. It is difficult for me to tell you what an impression it made upon me. I am rather sentimental (and not ashamed to say it), but there is much more here than sentimentality if I am so moved upon hearing after so many years — and what years! — words like *my friend* from you. I had long since forgotten such language — perhaps I am to blame for the absence of such words between us. Their revival must be a sign and an omen of the dawning of a new era, and I will do my utmost so that it comes about. [He closed the letter,] Peace be with you. I shake your hand in absolute friendship. Yours, V. Jabotinsky.

By virtue of this closeness and mutual trust, as well as their political and personal aspirations, they were able to overcome those heretofore insurmountable obstacles in the path to an unprecedented agreement.[20]

Two more meetings — one in Rutenberg's office and the other in Ben-Gurion's hotel — prepared the ground for the fifth, decisive meeting. It continued for fifteen and a half hours, from 4:00 P.M., October 26, to 7:30 A.M., October 27, and during it both Ben-Gurion and Jabotinsky signed the nonviolence pact (agreement A) and the labor accord (agreement B). With regard to a discipline accord (agreement C) on the relations between the Zionist Organization and the revisionist movement, they prepared only an outline; final editing was put off since at this stage Ben-Gurion wished to consult with his colleagues in the Zionist Executive.

Ben-Gurion signed agreement A, entitled "Regulations Pertaining to Party Disputes," on behalf of the Zionist Executive, and Jabotinsky signed it "on behalf of the World Union of Zionist Revisionists." However, they signed agreement B, which they called the "Labor Relations in Palestine Accord," as private persons. Ben-Gurion would later explain that he had signed it "as an individual," as a draft agreement, which he had committed himself to bring up for Histadrut ratification, just as Jabotinsky had undertaken to bring it up to the National Workers' Organization.

After he and Jabotinsky parted Ben-Gurion noted in his diary, "I do not know if everyone in Palestine will accept this agreement with good will. In my opinion it is so important and augurs so well for the future that I still find it difficult to believe it will go through; it is too good to be true." That very morning he sat down to write to his party about the exciting development, in a letter which demonstrates that he very well knew he had committed the unforgivable. In the first part he nonchalantly described the session that ended with the signing of two documents "which I am sending to you" plus a third whose completion had been deferred "for a few days." Only halfway through did he let his Central Committee colleagues know with whom he had negotiated, slipping Jabotinsky's name in offhandedly, as if he had merely agreed to some clause in one of the documents. There followed a replay of what he and Jabotinsky had said until they reached a compromise. As if to appease his associates and assure them that he had held strictly to the party line, he said at the end, "Some in Palestine (and I hope not many) will probably be upset (to put it mildly) about the negotiations and the agreement, but what worries me is that the other side won't accept the agreement or that they will refuse to implement it, as it is still difficult for me to believe that this great miracle will happen, that the working public in Palestine will truly accept this agreement's authority." To the same end he added this icing to the cake: Jabotinsky had proposed, as early as their second meeting, that "both sides consider the Stavsky trial over and done with. . . . When I turned this proposal down flat [Jabotinsky] paled and asked me, 'Do you really think they might be guilty?' " He closed the letter by notifying his party friends that the nonviolence pact had been sent to JTA for publication and asked, "Will you stone me for committing these sins and treason in meeting with V. Jabotinsky?"[21]

On the night of October 27, before the morning papers had printed the JTA item on the nonviolence pact, Katznelson received "first notice of the agreement" from London and phoned Sharett to get an explanation from Ben-Gurion posthaste. Sharett cabled Ben-Gurion and immediately received a reply that Ben-Gurion would phone the HEC that afternoon to explain his actions. In that call — an unusual step in those days — Ben-Gurion related to Katznelson the content of the two signed agreements and the as yet unsigned outline for the third. But what he said only increased the bewilderment and consternation within Mapai, and a shower of harshly worded telegrams demanding more explanation rained down on him. The more details of his talks with Jabotinsky were learned in Palestine, the more imperative became the demand for his immediate return and calls for a party convention. Most urgent was a November 8 telegram from Katznelson. "The movement is wounded and the danger is great. What good is a miracle if the main tool to carry it through breaks? More negotiations will push the public to anarchy and destructiveness. . . . Don't commit yourself any further until your arrival. Come quickly. Every minute is precious. Berl."[22] Ben-Gurion ignored this entreaty. Still anticipating a "big agreement" with Jabotinsky, he had already informed the party's Central Committee and Katznelson on October 28 that because important matters would keep him in London he would not be able to return to Palestine any earlier than planned. His colleagues' furious reactions did not budge him one inch, and he welcomed the call for a party convention. After all, he had signed the agreements explicitly on condition that they be ratified by both Mapai and the revisionist movement.

Clearly Ben-Gurion was not upset or anxious about the abuse being heaped upon him. On the contrary, his query about being stoned attests to anticipation of the battle, and perhaps he even enjoyed imagining his colleagues' faces white with fury. There is, of course, no proof of this, but certainly in his diary there is no hint of regret or of sympathy for his stunned friends. Among the postcards overflowing with censure and protests he found letters from his children.

> I read in the paper that a peace agreement was signed between the Zionist Executive and the World Union of Zionist Revisionists [wrote sixteen-year-old Geula] and you were the signatory. I was very surprised. You . . . said that the party doesn't want to sit at the same table with the Revisionists, because the Revisionist Party has no place in the Zionist Executive, etc. And here it's as though you're contradicting yourself. . . . The whole working community, or more precisely, most of it, is against this agreement and is kicking up a fuss over it. . . . Before your trip there was a council . . . Most of the councilmen opposed peace and now despite that resolution you went and signed. . . . This will hurt the party.

If Ben-Gurion suspected that one of his colleagues opposed to the agreements was using Geula to put pressure on him, another letter, from his son, strengthened that suspicion. The same boy who wrote so rarely, always making do with a few hastily scribbled sentences, suddenly produced a long, well-composed letter. Between the lines allegedly penned by fourteen-year-old Amos one might read a hint of satisfaction that he could now give it to his father in return for all the moralizing.

> It seems to me that the working public is against the agreement with the Zionist Revisionists. . . . Why must we forgive them their crimes? Why should we forget about the Arlosoroff affair? Why should we forget about the strikebreaking? . . . Shall we let all this pass in silence? And you especially, who joined the Zionist Executive as a representative of the working community. I think you've neglected to fulfill your mission; the party council resolved not to enter into negotiations with the Revisionists, and then you and some other leaders went and did it on your own. And I do not accept your argument that you were sent by the Zionist Executive. You should not have taken on the role of mediator, for you are representing the party that opposes what you've done. . . . I doubt we will still be sitting in the Jewish Agency as we are now after the next Congress. I want you to answer me. Why did you do this and why did you forgive the crimes of those hooligans?

Not too long afterward, though, Amos wrote another letter.

> Dear Father, Please forgive me for the sharpness of my last letter. I was very upset by the whole affair with Jabotinsky . . . but after Marom explained (though very briefly) the need for peace and the present state of Zionism . . . and after I read your letter to Marom, my opposition to the agreement faded away almost completely. But here in Palestine there is a lot of resentment over it.[23]

(Israel Marom was one of Ben-Gurion's most loyal and devoted workers in the HEC.)

Ben-Gurion answered his children's letters thoughtfully and seriously, and on November 9, in a letter to the Mapai Central Committee, he reacted to the criticism.

> Of all the telegrams and messages I've received to date the most upsetting of all was the one I got from Berl yesterday. . . . I understand that something serious happened to deeply upset our comrades. [But] after further, profound consideration . . . I can find no *rational* reason for this. . . . With all the pain of Berl's telegram, I still have not lost my confidence that our public will weigh matters on their merits and our movement will overcome its confusion and emerge from the crisis stronger and more unified than before.

He had made up his mind to take this stand as early as October 28, the day he received the first wave of protests and calls for his immediate return.

Ben-Gurion met with Jabotinsky seven more times, and on November 12, the day after their final meeting, he left for Palestine with the third, signed draft agreement on discipline within the Zionist Organization in his pocket. While the big agreement remained unattainable, they still had great faith that the new situation engendered by the three small agreements, and their new mutual trust, would enable them eventually to realize this agreement as well. Their final talk took place in Rutenberg's office. Rutenberg again proposed a triumvirate, this time making it clear that he had in mind Ben-Gurion, Jabotinsky, and himself. In his diary Ben-Gurion did not mention his reaction, but he probably neither accepted nor rejected the idea.[24]

What Ben-Gurion was thinking on his way home with Paula is anybody's guess. Certainly he was full of pride and great expectations. Should fortune smile on his two initiatives — for peace within and without — Zionism would be freed of two of its most crippling problems and the process of its realization would gain incredible momentum. He was not alone in this thought; at a Zionist Executive meeting the director of the Political Department in London, Professor Zelig Brodetsky, said, referring to the agreements, "History will judge Ben-Gurion's action. This is a new era for Zionism."[25] And should history welcome domestic harmony, how much more would it approve of peace with the Arabs! The new horizons opening before Zionism under his leadership could put him in a class with Weizmann, and perhaps even Herzl.

If Ben-Gurion did think about his personal status, he could have found grounds to support his ambition to lead the Zionist movement. Of all the Zionist leaders he was the only one to devote time and energy to consolidating and restructuring the movement. He alone strove, by word and deed, to build a Zionist consensus, and he alone understood that without such a consensus Zionism would be unable to achieve its goal. This was the ultimate purpose of all he had done since he first put the conquest of Zionism on his party's agenda. His modus operandi was first to build a broad-based party, against whose rivals he fought mercilessly, forcing them to choose between joining or perishing. He used this method to expand this foundation into the Histadrut, the sole representative organization of workers, and he used it again when he set out to build the final part of his structure, a consolidated, disciplined Zionist Organization that would become a Jewish people's movement. It could be said of Ben-Gurion that in order to bring about peace he always set out first to make war. And he always argued that without peace and unity the only alternative — to the labor movement, to the Histadrut, and to the Zionist Organization — was loss and destruction.

He worked always to establish authority, first in the party and the Histadrut, then in the Zionist Organization. Both the negotiations he conducted to broaden the coalition after the 1933 Zionist Congress and his London agreements had as their goal what he called the institution of discipline — in other words, authority. And just as he had once tried to make a ministry, or an executive, out of the HEC collegium, so he now had it in mind to fashion a sort of government out of the Zionist coalition in preparation for the day when it would become a potential government of the Jewish people in all the lands of their dispersion.

But if Ben-Gurion thought that peace within and peace without were attainable and that he was only a step away from laying the foundations of Federal Palestine and a full Zionist consensus, reality proved him dead wrong.

His hopes came crashing down when he returned to his office in Jerusalem, on November 19. There he found the November issue of *La Nation arabe* on his desk. In it he was astonished to find an account of his talk with Arslan and Jabri, for they had agreed that the discussion would be secret. He immediately wrote a rejoinder, which he intended to send to *La Nation arabe;* instead he mailed the offending issue to Musa Alami. According to Ben-Gurion, Alami answered that he was "embarrassed and ashamed and cannot understand how it happened that they did not keep the matter secret." In his despair, Ben-Gurion seized on the publication of the talk in *La Nation arabe* as the cause of the breakdown in negotiations and the failure of his "Arab policy."

In 1936, he would say that his talk with Arslan and Jabri had been undertaken with the mufti's knowledge, and that "the negotiations were halted after these two gentlemen violated my trust and published our conversation (with distortions) in their French organ." But this face-saving explanation could not hold water; for in Warsaw, Berlin, and London, Ben-Gurion himself had mentioned the talks, particularly in his interview with the *Jewish Chronicle*. After the two Arabs' reactions to the Geneva meeting had been revealed in *La Nation arabe*, Ben-Gurion could no longer delude himself. The quickest route to the mufti had proved a dead end, and there was no other way.[26]

If Ben-Gurion was disillusioned and disappointed, at least he was saved from despondency, for the crisis generated by the London agreements kept him very busy. The hue and cry went on for half a year, and by the time it subsided Mapai was not the same. The main charges against him were that he had acted without the party's knowledge and against the August 1934 council's resolution; that his sitting down at the negotiating table with Jabotinsky legitimized revisionism as a partner in the coalition, and this legitimization strengthened fascism and weakened the labor movement's internal cohesiveness and fighting potential; that he had continued to negotiate with Jabotinsky despite urgent demands that he cease and return to Palestine immediately; that he had confounded the working public and led it to distrust not only him but the entire party administration; and that because of his action the party was in danger of splitting up. Itzhak Ben-Aharon of the Mapai secretariat had written him in London of Poale Zion Left's attack, of Ha-Shomer ha-Tzair's street bills against the "Ben-Gurion–Vladimir Hitler Pact," and of workers' meetings insisting that he resign from the Mapai Central Committee. He wrote, too, of the sharp confrontation between Katznelson, who defended Ben-Gurion at an October 31 Central Committee meeting, and Tabenkin, who attacked him harshly; in its wake Tabenkin resigned, taking with him some of his supporters in the committee.

The day after he returned to Palestine, at a Central Committee meeting on November 20, Ben-Gurion saw for himself the consternation over the negotiations and the fury over their signature. His total disregard of an explicit prohibition hurt his colleagues much more than he had expected. His claims that he had signed agreement A as a representative of the Zionist Executive, not of the party, and agreement B in a private capacity, not in the HEC's name, and that agreement C was still only a draft carried no weight. Nor did his reasoning that the agreements could open a new chapter in the history of the Yishuv and Zionism and that the present moment should be taken advantage of for "a great initiative before the situation changes." How would Zionism make use of this auspicious moment if "we are busy making war against our will . . . and all our energies are wasted as we walk forward into destruction?" he asked two days later at a joint meeting of the Central Committee and representatives of Ha-Shomer ha-Tzair.[27]

The heart of the issue, however, was the recognition by a considerable number of his Mapai colleagues that the agreements with Jabotinsky were meant to groom the Revisionists to be partners in the Zionist coalition. Central Committee member Abraham Katznelson put it plainly. "The London accords involved a specific attempt to reach a political alliance between Mapai and the Revisionists, between Ben-Gurion and Jabotinsky, perhaps for the sake of hegemony in the Zionist movement." This was also Tabenkin's view. "We are not working to isolate revisionism, but for an accord with it, in preparing it to join the Executive. How did we become so impatient that we cannot suffer opposition within Zionism, to the point where we must suddenly espouse the principle of a coalition of everyone, of peace with everyone?"

It was here that the conflict between values and the sense of the burning ground flamed highest. Ben-Gurion called Berl Katznelson, who supported agreement A, the nonviolence pact, and those who sided with him "the party of peace." In retrospect it seems that those who opposed Ben-Gurion — nearly all of the United Kibbutz Movement and a considerable number of Mapai members in towns — can be termed "the party of values." To the former, peace within Zionism and the Yishuv took precedence over the values of socialism and pioneering, whereas to the latter, peace was worthless if their singularity was diluted.

This issue was also the proving ground of Ben-Gurion's great partnership with Katznelson, who backed Ben-Gurion on agreements A and B (suggesting two amendments for B), opposing only the third one. Remez's loyalty was also put to the test; he supported all three. Of the four founders of Achdut ha-Avodah, all among the top brass of the Mapai Central Committee, Tabenkin was the only one opposed. The breach widened between Ben-Gurion and Katznelson on the one hand and Tabenkin and his circle on the other. Following his resignation from the committee, in protest against Katznelson, who had accused him of being "holier than thou" and leaning toward separatism, Tabenkin requested a broader forum to counter Ben-Gurion and the party of peace. Speaking at public meetings, he demanded a Histadrut referendum. Ben-Gurion consented, on condition that it be held after the December convention, at which he hoped to gain supporters for his agreements. But the Central Committee resolved to hold the referendum on agreement B (the labor accord) before the convention, and the HEC followed suit, setting the date for February 24, 1935. Nonetheless

Ben-Gurion managed to have it postponed to March 24, a week after the party convention, and the opponents had four months to campaign. During this time Ben-Gurion covered the length and breadth of Palestine, speaking at gatherings of all sorts, engaging in a tremendous struggle not only for his program — the conquest of Zionism, from class to nation, and Zionism as a popular movement — but also for his personal standing. But in the referendum Tabenkin scored an impressive victory: 60 percent voted against the labor accord and only 40 percent for it. Ben-Gurion was his own victim, undone by the hard line he had formerly taken against Jabotinsky and his movement. While he was capable of a sudden about-face, most of his fellow party and Histadrut members were not.[28]

Ben-Gurion accepted the majority decision, but he would remember that Tabenkin was able to block him when he chose to. Moreover, not only was he still convinced of being in the right, he still regarded Jabotinsky as a true friend. Following the referendum Jabotinsky wrote to him.

> Dear Ben-Gurion, I am not sure I will send this letter after I finish writing it. Even the most valiant spirits are sometimes influenced by their environment. . . . Perhaps you will read these lines with changed eyes. I fear that I, too, am somewhat "changed." I'll admit, for instance, that when I received the news that the agreement was rejected, something inside whispered relief, and I wondered if you had the same feeling at that moment. Regardless, my admiration of one Ben-Gurion and his aspiration has not changed.

In the same letter he asked how the referendum would influence the future relations between the two movements.

On April 24, 1935, Ben-Gurion responded.

> Dear Jabotinsky . . . It seems our labors in London have come to nothing, as regards the public. But beyond the public and politics there are still people. . . . It may be that we will have to remain on opposing sides, but whatever happens, our talks in London will always remain with me. . . . If we must battle each other, remember that among your "enemies" is a man who esteems you and feels your pain as his own. The hand you thought I withheld from you at our first meeting will be extended to you even in the heat of battle, and not only the hand.

To this Jabotinsky replied, "Go in peace. If you can, get your aides not to make the 'war' any more bitter than it has to be . . . I wish you success. In any event, as you wrote so shall it be: a scene the likes of which Israel has never encountered, war with two hands outstretched over the battlefield."[29]

All that Ben-Gurion had sought to prevent by means of the London agreements came about. Their rejection was the determining factor in

Zionism's fateful factionalizing and ongoing internal strife. The Revisionist National Workers' Organization, which would have been dissolved had the little agreement led to the big agreement, grew stronger. In 1935 Jabotinsky and his movement founded their New Zionist Organization. In the wake of this development the Haganah, too, split, and what was at first the Haganah B, with an undefined revisionist tendency, developed into the Irgun Zvai Leummi (National Military Organization), or just Irgun, under the leadership of the Revisionist Party. Thus rose two distinct and opposed Zionist entities: the organized Yishuv, comprising the Zionist Organization, the Haganah, and the Histadrut, and the "dissidents," the New Zionist Organization, the Irgun, and the National Workers' Organization. From then on Zionism would speak and act with two voices, in two opposite directions.

Thus, too, Ben-Gurion's dream of creating an all-inclusive Zionist-Jewish consensus evaporated. His hope of ousting Weizmann from the Zionist movement leadership also faded, for Ben-Gurion would need Weizmann to establish the broadest Zionist consensus possible.

30

The New Executive

TWO EXCURSIONS marked Ben-Gurion's return to normal activity after the London agreements fell through. On April 16, 1935, Ben-Gurion set out with Berl Katznelson and Eliahu Epstein of the Political Department, who specialized in Arabs and the East, for what they called their journey to Aqaba, intent on familiarizing themselves with the east bank of the Jordan and the Negev. In a chauffeur-driven car they went from Jerusalem to As-Salt and Amman, and from there through the desert to Ma'an, where they stayed at an Arab hotel. The next day, after paying a visit to the district commissioner, they set out on the poor road to Petra. At the sight of this city hewn in stone, words stuck in their throats. Katznelson noted in his journal, "Tremendous and awesome. A riddle." They also "climbed on the rock." All along the way they identified places and sights by their biblical names, feeling that they had gone back in time, to the days of the Exodus and Joshua's conquest. The fact that April 17 was Passover undoubtedly strengthened this feeling, and when they returned to their hotel in Ma'an they held a makeshift Seder.

On April 18 they drove to Aqaba and visited "its mayor," who was "barefoot. Cannot read or write. But smart. A politician," Berl jotted down in his notebook. A British officer they met "called upon [the Zionists] to come and plant oranges" (i.e., settle) there. They sailed in the gulf, strolled in the foothills, and spent the night in their car. On the second day of Passover they left Aqaba for Um-Rashrash, which in March 1949 was to become Israel's Eilat. On camelback they climbed Ras al-Naqab, then drove on desert trails — "as if on asphalt" — to Ksseima and Asluj, which they identified as Haffir. Katznelson noted in his journal, "We did not see a living soul the whole day until we came across the guard at the spring," in a place they identified as Kadesh-

Barnea. They spent the third night at the government house in Bir Asluj. On April 20, the third day of Passover, they left for Beersheba, returning to Jerusalem by way of Hebron, Beit Guvrin, Beit Shemesh, and Hartuv.

Ben-Gurion and Katznelson were not only among the first Eretz-Israelis to visit these reaches of Palestine — soon to play an important role in Zionist politics — but also, and more important, they were the only Zionist leaders who saw fit to do so. The historic significance of this "excursion" is suggested by the fact that when Epstein became Israel's first ambassador to the United States in 1948 he changed his name to Eliahu Elath. The trip reinforced Ben-Gurion's view that the barren Negev was a vital area for Zionist settlement; here there would be no friction with Arab inhabitants, as in the settled parts of Palestine, and here Zionism's goals of making the desert bloom could be fulfilled. In April 1969, thirty-four years later, Ben-Gurion wrote in his diary that when they stood alongside the Um-Rashrash police point he had whispered to his two companions, "Here we will establish our Eilat. I believe that in David's time it was Eilat, not Aqaba."[1]

On April 24 Ben-Gurion set out from the port of Haifa for an information campaign in the United States. On the twenty-ninth he got off the *Gerusalemme* in Trieste and cabled Rega in Vienna, "Coming tomorrow 9:17 south — David." This brief meeting was to be their last in Vienna, for on May 2 Ben-Gurion boarded a train that brought him to Berlin by the next morning. On the morning of May 4 he flew to Danzig for a meeting with Mapai representatives from eastern and central Europe in preparation for that year's Zionist Congress elections. On the afternoon of May 5 he flew back to Berlin for meetings with the heads of He-Chalutz, and at 7:00 A.M. on May 6 he flew to London. On the seventh he wrote Paula, "I spent three days in Berlin and one and a half in Danzig." This effort to keep his side trip to Vienna from her was apparently unsuccessful, for on May 12 Paula sent him the following letter. "I write these lines to you with trembling hands. If I'm not asking *too much*, please come home as soon as possible, after you finish your business in America. I hope you will honor *my wish*, love, Pauline." In the margin she added that she had awaited letters from Europe in vain, and begged him to write her "without vowels."* It seems she had taken offense at the letter he had sent to her and Renana from London, in which only the passages intended for Paula were scrupulously voweled.[2]

Ben-Gurion had parted from his wife in an atmosphere of marital

---

* Hebrew is usually written without the diacritical marks that indicate vowels, but they are sometimes added to make reading easier.

bliss and love — witness Paula's signing the name she had long since abandoned. Before the excursion to Aqaba he had found time to shower Paula with unprecedented attention. They spent a weekend together at the Kalia, an excellent new hotel on the Dead Sea, and in snapshots taken with Eliezer Kaplan and his wife they look like lovers. This being the case, what could have caused Paula to write him with "trembling hands," if not sure knowledge — at least a well-founded suspicion — of his furtive visit to Vienna?

Appearances suggest Amos as the cause. Geula reported to Ben-Gurion in detail how upset Paula was on Amos's account — "He doesn't do his homework, he roams the streets until late at night and refuses all discipline" — giving grounds for Paula's fear that in 1935 he would be left back. Ben-Gurion, fully aware of Amos's pranks and general unruliness, admonished his son before leaving for the United States. "I remind Amos once again to sit down and study, to quit the youth movement until my return, and to report to me once a week on his progress in school." However, had Amos really been the cause of her distress, Paula would have said so in so many words, as she had done more than once in the past. A letter from Renana dispels any suspicion that Paula did not choose her words carefully. After asking him "to write to me separately and a lot . . . not a couple of lines," Renana ended with this telling remark: "I don't know what's the matter with Mommy, she cries from morning to night and when I ask her what it is that makes her cry she doesn't answer but just keeps on crying."[3]

It can safely be assumed that her awareness of Ben-Gurion's visit to Vienna was what made Paula ask him to come straight home from America. If this plea was meant to keep him from stopping in Vienna again it was unnecessary. In May Rega had received her diploma and shortly thereafter set out for Palestine. By May 21, 1935, she was in Haifa, where her friends the Singers lived. A few weeks later she moved to Tel Aviv and took a position there with the Sick Fund. On July 9 she went to visit Ben-Gurion at his home, not realizing that he had not yet returned. According to his travel plans, which he had told her in Vienna, he should have been back, but something had come up in London and he did not return to Palestine until July 12, two weeks late. Paula, who was home, undoubtedly identified her rival instantly. According to a friend of Rega's, also a Sick Fund doctor, Paula had already scavenged plenty of information about Rega, and there was very little left to tell. Needless to say, the two women did not hit it off. Rega found the house to be "in great disorder," while for her part Paula lost no time in introducing Geula, who was also at home. Before they parted Paula gave Rega something to remember her by — three snapshots of her and Ben-Gurion in bathing suits, taken during their visit to the Dead Sea. She inscribed the backs of the photos "To Rega — from Paula, 7/9/35."[4]

Although Paula avoided an overt confrontation, her message to Rega was clear: Ben-Gurion had come back to his wife. Not one to take chances, Paula kept a sharp eye on Rega's movements, dropping in on her in her Tel Aviv apartment from time to time, ostensibly for a friendly visit. From this point on Rega and Ben-Gurion grew further apart, and their four-year love affair, which should have blossomed on Rega's arrival in Palestine, came to an end.[5]

Paula then did her best to ensure that she would accompany Ben-Gurion to the Zionist Congress, which was to convene in Lucerne. He spent the twenty-seven days before they sailed on August 8 in a seemingly unending chain of sessions in his party and the JAE and in another inspection of the Negev. At dawn on August 5 he left Jerusalem with Berl Katznelson, Moshe Sharett, Rachel Yanait, Dov Hoz, one of Ben-Gurion's closest and most loyal aides, Eliahu Epstein, and two others for Beersheba in two cars. This time they intended to tour the eastern Negev to see if the region of Arad was settled by Bedouins. From Rosh Zohar they looked over at Masada and the Dead Sea, which seemed to lie in the palm of one's hand, then made their way south, past Kurnub, then backtracked and spent the night under the stars, and returned to Jerusalem on August 6.

Everywhere they went they "looked for water and did not find any," wrote Katznelson in his little notebook. "The place looks as if the Creator had just finished it. The glory of nature is one thing and the settling of Jews is quite another. The difficult questions remain." According to Elath, Ben-Gurion and Katznelson did not converse much during the tour, but "looked, thought, meditated." Ben-Gurion's mind was firmly made up that the entire Negev was perfectly suited for Jewish settlement. The previous May, during his visit to America, he had met with Justice Louis D. Brandeis in Washington and handed him an exhaustive memorandum on the prospects of Jewish settlement in the Negev and Aqaba. Brandeis was so taken by the idea that he later sent Ben-Gurion a check for $25,000 to further the project. This made such a tremendous impact on Ben-Gurion that the sum subsequently grew in his mind to $100,000, and it became etched in his memory that the justice had handed him the check on the spot. Brandeis's donation, which led to the second tour by Ben-Gurion, was the first practical step toward realizing the vision of settling the Negev.[6]

On the evening of August 7 Ben-Gurion, Paula, and Katznelson left for Haifa on their way to the Zionist Congress. In the morning, since they had plenty of time before their ship was due to sail at 1:00 P.M.,

Ben-Gurion and Katznelson took a short tour of the area around Haifa. On returning to the port they found all the friends that had come to see them off in a tizzy, for the captain had been ordered by his company to lift anchor at noon. Katznelson wrote to his wife, Leah, "We almost missed the ship. . . . It seems that Paula's presence was to our advantage. Since she did not accompany us on our tour, she left early for the port with all the baggage, and there raised an outcry that it was out of the question to leave without her husband. . . . One can never tell from where one's luck will come." Paula became the continuing object of his bemused observation; from the port of Alexandria he wrote his wife, "Paula promises to look out for me, and Ben-Gurion says that he's all for it, so that she'll look out for him less."[7]

The trio had a pleasant passage; the S.S. *Ausonia* was luxurious and the sea calm. Nevertheless, Paula's chatter began to wear thin on Katznelson. When they reached Venice, Katznelson left the couple, deciding not "to do the sights" of the city of canals. "I sat down right away in the train," he reported to his wife, "as I wished to be left alone and also to get to Lucerne as early as possible." It was more likely that he had simply tired of their company, since they spent only nine hours in Venice and got to Lucerne's Schweizerhof Hotel on August 14, well before he did.

The nineteenth Congress opened on August 20 and closed on September 4, 1935, going on record as one of the most important in the history of Zionism. In the elections preceding it the labor movement's strength jumped from the 44 percent of the previous election to a new high of 48.8 percent. Consequently Ben-Gurion had much work ahead of him, both to prepare a plan of action to appeal to the broadest coalition possible, and to return Weizmann to the presidency of the movement and the Zionist Executive. On September 5 he wrote his children, "During the Zionist Congress I didn't write to you, because I didn't have a minute to myself. And when the Congress ended I was very tired. During the closing sessions I could hardly stand on my feet, and I felt mentally and physically exhausted. It will take a few days before I regain my strength, and meanwhile work has to go on, because when the Congress closes the Jewish Agency meets, and between one session and another there are the usual talks, clashes, and other bits and ends of the Congress."[8]

On September 8 Ben-Gurion and Paula cruised the Vierwaldstätter See, the "Lake of the Four Forest Cantons." From the boat he sent Geula and Amos this cry of victory: "The air of the mountains, the charm of the lake, the rest (imagine — no meetings!) are all marvelous after the weeks of tense conflict at the Congress." The next day they left most of their baggage at the hotel, sailed forty minutes across the

lake, rode up the mountain by funicular, and from there, carrying small
bags, went on foot — there were no motor vehicles — to the hamlet of
Burgenstock. There they rented two low-ceilinged rooms in a farmer's
cottage with walls covered with faded wallpaper, anticipating whole-
some, "good and satisfying" meals, walks outdoors, and perfect solitude. Ben-Gurion wrote to his children, "No one is here apart from the
two of us. Only trees and grass and hay and the mountain air." Paula
was to stay four days, then leave for Venice and home. "I'll stay on for
a week or ten days, walking and writing. Time will tell which will be
the busier, my pen or my legs."

On the day after the Congress ended Ben-Gurion had begun writing
to Geula and Amos about "what I hoped this Congress would achieve
and what it actually achieved." He now continued this project in his
retreat, sometimes sending two letters in one day. When he was
through, the account, published in 1968, filled fifty-four book pages.
He doubted whether his children would be interested in this long and
detailed narrative of all the divisions, strife, and politicking, and as was
his custom he sent the letters to the HEC, where they were read with
great admiration long before they ever reached Geula and Amos. After
reading them, Rivka Hoz, Sharett's sister and Dov Hoz's wife, wrote
her husband in London, "I doubt that Geula and Amos understood the
half of it, but it's good that they were written. Ben-Gurion's descriptions of the scenery made a huge impression on me and I read each of
them several times. What precision of expression, clarity and force of
language! What a pity that such a small portion of the letters was devoted to this subject."[9]

When he had a moment to spare from Zionism, Ben-Gurion could
enjoy the scenery and put it into words.

I walked between mountain and wood, discovering new trails. Pale vapors
hovered above the grass and harvesters were at work in the fields. Drying
hay sweetly scented the air. From the mountainside the reflection of "the
lake of the four forest states" was visible through the fading mists. Half
the sky is light blue, the other half veiled by rolling white woolen clouds.
Calm, tranquillity, and cool light — only the cowbells keep tinkling, and
one can nearly hear the damp grass sucking the soil beneath. The forest's
cypress and pine trees embrace each other, their tops seeming to interlock
in one endless green foliage. Solitary cottages redden the green mountain's sides — and I, a foreign wayfarer, walk trails I do not know, my
thoughts soaring beyond these tranquil, calming scapes.
   In a rich hayfield, bare to the sun, I lie down to rest my mind from
thoughts of the Congress. It is high noon and the bright sun lights up the
entire sky, but since the air is still chilly, its rays are softly caressing. The
lake glimmers with a greenish hue and the forest keeps its silence, with

the solemnity of tall, ponderous trees, confident of their staying power. Correct, huge, and close together they stand, making you feel it is their heritage from days immemorial. Here they have stood for ages, as did their ancestors before them, as far back as the primeval forests.

But the scenery captivated him for only a short while, as he admitted. Zionism was at the center of his thoughts no matter where he turned or looked, and it was the only theme of his letters to the children. If he wrote them of matters far from their hearts and minds, it was simply the result of his subconscious intention to include them, too, in his partnership formula. His letters revolved around himself and his feats; Ben-Gurion often repeated praise he had received — or entreaties that he take on a presidency or chairmanship, which were as good as praise — as if willing the children to understand that although he might be lacking as a father, their loss was their contribution to the goal that united the family.

The days spent in Burgenstock were perhaps Paula's happiest ever; Ben-Gurion was entirely hers, from morning till morning. On September 13 he accompanied Paula back to Lucerne. He had planned to have six more days of quiet, but when he returned to Burgenstock alone he grew sad, and on the fourteenth, when he finished writing up the Congress for his children, he felt even more lonely. The truth was that at that remote, all-too-peaceful place, without friends with whom to hammer out Zionist matters, he could not find the peace he sought. "Today it's chilly and rather sad. The material I need to write is at the Schweitzerhof, so I decided to return here," he wrote in his diary on the sixteenth, in his old room in Lucerne.

On September 17 Katznelson and Remez left Lucerne. At first Ben-Gurion decided to stay in his hotel for another three days, to prepare a summary of what he had said to the Congress for his colleagues, but he was too depressed and sad. "I wanted to write something for my colleagues," he later explained to Paula, "but I couldn't." He left Lucerne for Paris, but felt no better there, and on the twenty-third he flew to London, where he could engage in some much-needed activity. "We reached Croydon at a quarter to four. I headed immediately for the office," he noted in his diary.

There his spirits rose, to be boosted still further by Paula's cable that "Amos passed the examinations."[10]

The Lucerne Congress, which opened a new chapter in the history of Zionism, also opened a new chapter in Ben-Gurion's political life. Weizmann had been reinstated in his old posts as president of the Congress and of the Zionist Executive, and was back in the number one position in the Zionist administration and the Jewish Agency. Ben-

Gurion was elected chairman of the Zionist Executive and the JAE, filling the number two spot. A week after the Congress closed, the Revisionists, at a worldwide convention in Vienna from September 12 through 17, 1935, founded their New Zionist Organization (NZO), and the impending rift in the Zionist camp became a reality. At the head of one side were Weizmann and Ben-Gurion, and at the head of the other, Jabotinsky.

Ben-Gurion was prepared well in advance for these two developments; his trips to Danzig, Berlin, London, and the United States in May and June 1935 had laid the foundation for his plan. Among other things he was trying to show his party "why we, the largest party in Zionism, must set ourselves the role of uniting the Zionist movement and uniting the nation in Zionism — under the hegemony of the labor movement." On his arrival in the United States, on May 14, he had told reporters who came to welcome him aboard the *Aquitania* that he had in hand a plan to unite the Zionist movement in America. The Yiddish-language New York *Tag* printed this information on the front page, beneath a picture of Ben-Gurion, in an open shirt, beaming with optimism and confidence. To Zionist leaders he expounded on "the necessity . . . of unifying the Zionist Organization in America." Ben-Gurion firmly believed that what kept Jews away from Zionism, especially in the United States, was the requirement that they belong to a Zionist party and adhere to a specific ideology. If they could simply join the Zionist Organization as individuals, there would be an influx of new members. This was the basis of his "mass-movement" program. But he also had another goal in sight: if within the Zionist Organization, members identified themselves not with a particular party but with the organization itself, the parties would lose much of their power, and the influence of the Zionist Revisionists in particular would be reduced.

In his thirty days in the United States Ben-Gurion gave speeches in large Jewish centers in New York, Washington, Baltimore, Boston, Milwaukee, Chicago, Detroit, and St. Louis — places Jabotinsky had visited in January, trying not only to gain votes for the Revisionists in the Congress elections, but also to win people over to the NZO, which he was set on establishing. This was a repeat performance of their 1933 contest in Poland.

Ben-Gurion put a great deal of effort into the women's Zionist organization, Hadassah. Jabotinsky had spoken before Hadassah's National Board in late January, and Ben-Gurion did not want him to go unchallenged. Ben-Gurion had first paid attention to Hadassah in 1929, noting in his diary Golda Meir's praises of it. During his December 1930 trip to the United States, which had been devoted to the campaign against the Passfield White Paper, Ben-Gurion had found time to meet thirty top Hadassah leaders in the home of its president, Charlotte Jacobs. Addressing the Mapai council in February 1931 to summarize his impressions of the United States, he said, "Hadassah is the life line." His sharp political sense had told him instantly that this women's organization could serve him, and he was not mistaken. Had Hadassah not backed him in the many struggles leading to the establishment of the state, it is doubtful whether he would have prevailed as he did. Nonetheless, his evaluation of Hadassah was not based solely on political shrewdness. As a women's organization, Hadassah stirred Ben-Gurion particularly. The memory of his mother lived within him always, keeping alive a sense of the nobility of woman as beloved mother, rock of family stability, homemaker, educator of a generation, and social force. He had expressed his profound respect for women to Rachel Yanait in Jerusalem in 1910 when both of them were serving on *Ha-Achdut*'s editorial board. According to her, he "complained that women should not be satisfied to take second place to men, considering that they were stronger and wiser in so many areas of life. He said they should make themselves more evident and be heard more in party and national councils."[11]

Ben-Gurion went after Hadassah energetically, paying special attention to its two representatives present at his meeting with members of the executive committee of the American Zionist Organization. They repeated what he had said about the necessity of a unified Zionist movement at the next meeting of their National Board, and on June 5 he appeared before the board to speak on the political situation in Palestine and the prospects of a Jewish majority there within ten years. He concluded by emphasizing the necessity for a unified Zionist movement to achieve this goal. Although he was convinced he had defeated Jabotinsky in the minds of Hadassah's leaders (and cabled *Davar* that "the revisionist attempt to capture America has utterly failed"), he could not manage to turn the board into his ally. To Paula he wrote, "I wanted to set up a joint [American] ticket [for the elections to the Congress], but Hadassah is unwilling. It hopes to win many votes this time around. It has some 40,000 members — more than any of the other Zionist parties and organizations in America." Henrietta Szold, founder of Hadassah and its legendary leader, told him, "Hadassah fears losing its members."

Zealously guarding its integrity as an organization, Hadassah also refused to join the drive for shekel sales among the American Jewish community. Finally, at the Congress in Lucerne the Hadassah delegates joined not the labor faction, as he had hoped they would, but Group A of the General Zionists. If Hadassah was indeed "the greatest

[Zionist] force in America," as Ben-Gurion maintained, he still had ahead of him the difficult task of winning it over to his side.[12]

During the spring and summer of 1935, Ben-Gurion had also been busy working to restore Weizmann to the presidency. Ben-Gurion's about-face did not take place overnight. Before signing the London agreements with Jabotinsky Ben-Gurion had been interested in using Weizmann's status and diplomatic talents, but not in giving him the helm. At the March 1934 meeting of Mapai's Political Committee, Ben-Gurion had said explicitly, "I am in complete agreement with Katznelson with regard to the need to give Weizmann some share in the responsibility for Zionism's internal affairs" and proposed turning over to him the collection of funds for "the great settlement activity." There were those within the Political Committee who insisted that Weizmann be charged with more important roles, and eventually the committee resolved "to invite Weizmann to an in-depth discussion with the party Central Committee."

The London agreements made Ben-Gurion's associates suspect that he was thinking of excluding Weizmann totally from the decision making. While the agreements were in the making, Dov Hoz wrote him, "On the question of Weizmann you are inclined to seek a compromise at a time when this is undoubtedly one of those matters on which there can be no partial solution," and reasoned against "Weizmann's ouster." Before the referendum on the agreements took place this concern increased to the point where Ben-Gurion found it necessary to reassure Mapai and other Histadrut parties that "if a broad Zionist coalition is brought about, it won't be without Weizmann." Toward the end of 1934 he, along with Sharett, had taken the time to see Weizmann, and according to Ben-Gurion, "We discussed his return." In January 1935, with the referendum campaign still in full swing, he referred to Weizmann in an interview with Palcor (Palestine Correspondence, the news agency Ben-Gurion had set up in the framework of the Jewish Agency) as being "unique in our generation and beyond compare."

After the labor movement turned down the London agreements with the Revisionists, Ben-Gurion needed Weizmann, pure and simple, and courted him forcefully and single-mindedly. Not only was restoring Weizmann to the presidency the labor movement's express desire; without him there would be no chance of putting together a broad coalition. Weizmann, no less aware of this than Ben-Gurion, played hard to get. He was prepared "to stand again at the head of the movement" — as he put it to his suitors, Ben-Gurion among them — only "if allowed to man an Executive based on personal qualifications, regardless of party affiliation." Another condition was that the tenure of the Executive, as well as of the presidency, be extended from the usual two years — the time interval between congresses — to four or five years. And finally, he expressed the wish that for the duration of the first year of his presidency he not be forced "to take part in the day-to-day work of the Executive, but only in laying basic policy guidelines."

Such terms could be demanded only by one who felt that he towered above the rest, and indeed, the Balfour Declaration had endowed Weizmann with this status, and not only among the Zionists. Ben-Gurion's crowning him as "unique in our generation" did not then seem exaggerated; certainly it did not go as far as the tribute paid by Joseph Carlebach, the rabbi of Lübeck and an opponent of Zionism. In welcoming Weizmann at a public meeting in Hamburg, Carlebach greeted him the way the children of Het had greeted Abraham, "My lord: thou art a mighty prince among us."* [13]

The wooing of Weizmann was long and exhausting. On the eve of the Congress Weizmann suddenly announced that, owing to family, financial, and business reasons, he would not be able to accept the presidency. Taking it on would cost him an extra £5,000 sterling, which he did not have; moreover, his connections with certain chemical companies would be incompatible with such an office. However, he was willing to be elected to the Zionist Executive and to head the Political Department on one condition — that Ben-Gurion be president. In retrospect, it appears that this was probably a jest meant to pique Ben-Gurion and put him in his place, for Ben-Gurion did not have the support of even his own party for the presidency. When it was made clear that Ben-Gurion was not up for consideration, Weizmann suggested a second term for Sokolow. If Weizmann meant by this to remind everyone of his own worth and thereby up his price, his intention was completely lost on Ben-Gurion, who termed the proposal a "nearly ingenious idea." "All who heard it," he wrote in his diary, "believed this was a great step on Weizmann's part, a step which would serve to elevate his stature among the people and the movement more than any other possible action on his part, aside from the Balfour Declaration. We were all happy at this solution." Here, Ben-Gurion unknowingly betrayed his real intentions, for this entry makes it clear that he was overjoyed by the prospect of a figurehead president, with Weizmann a full member of an Executive chaired by Ben-Gurion, who would be pulling all the strings — Weizmann's included.

But Weizmann's friends thought otherwise, as did his wife, Vera, who played an important role in Weizmann's personal decisions. She would not hear of his subordination to any other president, certainly

---

* Genesis 23:6

not to Sokolow. Israel Sieff, a Weizmann faithful and a partner in Marks and Spencer, informed Ben-Gurion that Weizmann's proposal was out of the question and that his presidency depended on his prior stipulations, which had become even more stringent. "At this time," Sieff told Ben-Gurion, "Weizmann's political dictatorship is a must. He stands out as the only great man. He requires freedom, and he can work only with the people in whom he has special trust. Weizmann will appoint a political committee of Sieff, Sacher, Stein, Namier, and others, and he will be accountable to the Executive, but he won't sit on the Executive." Another friend of Weizmann's, David Eder, added pressure on Ben-Gurion with similar comments. Ben-Gurion rejected both. To Eder he said, "This is unthinkable. The movement will not consent to trust its policymaking to Weizmann outside the Executive," and he told Sieff, who asked to meet again for further negotiations, the same thing. Ben-Gurion went straight to Weizmann to sound him out, then consulted with his Mapai colleagues Katznelson, Tabenkin, Sharett, Kaplan, and others, and won them over to his position — Weizmann's terms had to be rejected.

At a more intimate party meeting Ben-Gurion explained why he himself could not join the Executive. "This time it would mean quitting the Histadrut," he said, "which for me is tantamount to leaving Palestine." This, then, was his gambit: Weizmann was not the only one who had to be courted; he, too, had to be wooed, and he, too, had his conditions. Like a circle within a circle, within the larger courting of Weizmann by Ben-Gurion and others, members of Mapai and other parties were entreating Ben-Gurion to declare his candidacy to the Executive and its chairmanship.[14]

The miracle happened. The Congress, overshadowed by "the Weizmann question," as Ben-Gurion put it, ended with the election of Weizmann as president and an Executive with Ben-Gurion its chairman — a broad coalition, yet a small Executive. Since the Revisionists had split away from the Zionist Organization, the coalition Ben-Gurion set up was all-inclusive, "wall to wall": the labor movement, the General Zionists, whose two sections had reunited as a liberal center, and Mizrachi. The Executive had only seven members — as opposed to the nine of the outgoing Executive — three from Mapai, three from the General Zionists, and one from Mizrachi. And the primacy of the six-man Executive branch in Jerusalem (three from Mapai, two General Zionists, and one from Mizrachi) over that in London (the president, Weizmann, and the third member of the General Zionists) was recognized. Following the election of the Zionist Executive, the Jewish Agency council met in Lucerne to elect the JAE: Weizmann, the seven members of the Zionist Executive, and three non-Zionists (who, under pressure from Ben-Gurion, had retreated from their demand for a fifty-fifty split), Morris Hexter and Julius Simon in the Jerusalem office and Maurice Karpf in London.

On the face of it, everything seemed to have turned out well, but the courting ritual and the stipulations proffered and rejected by Ben-Gurion and Weizmann had far-reaching effects. The differences between the two sharpened with time, developing into a dispute and finally escalating into an out-and-out feud. Although it was difficult to distinguish the personal from the substantive in their argument, the fact remained that their falling-out shaped the more important pattern of their work together for the next thirteen years, until the establishment of the State of Israel in 1948, to such an extent that their joint achievement may be regarded as nothing short of a marvel.

Ben-Gurion's attitude toward Weizmann was complex, a mixture of admiration bordering on envy for those qualities he himself lacked, and heartless, unrelenting criticism of Weizmann's shortcomings, whose antitheses he regarded as his own strong points. In his first two years in the JAE Ben-Gurion compiled a kind of catalogue of Weizmann's flaws and virtues, which he was never to revise. In Ben-Gurion's mind Weizmann was in a class by himself, "unique in our generation" and "of divine inspiration." Weizmann was the representative of the Jewish people in two senses. No one could voice as he did the Jewish tragedy, or embody as he did all that was fine and noble in the Jewish experience. Tall and spellbinding, an intimate of the mighty and the rich and a prince among princes, he was yet always the son of a persecuted and humiliated nation; no one, Jew or Gentile, could resist his deportment and charm, wisdom and unparalleled sense of humor. The appointed spokesman for the Jewish people, Weizmann was more courted than courting. To Ben-Gurion his diplomatic skill was invaluable. Lord Melchett had said that there were Jews in Great Britain, himself included, who could meet with the highest English ranks, but only "on a personal basis," whereas Weizmann could come to them on matters of state as well. Professor Zelig Brodetsky, director of the Political Section in London, who suffered from Weizmann's arrogance, claimed, as did Ben-Gurion, that only Weizmann could meet with Stanley Baldwin, deputy prime minister (who would follow Ramsay MacDonald to 10 Downing Street), Sir Philip Cunliffe-Lister, colonial secretary, and Walter Elliot, agricultural secretary, all three top Tories. Only Weizmann could assemble a political committee of big names in London, Jews and Gentiles, all from among his own circle. There were "people" in London, Ben-Gurion told the Political Committee, "but it is difficult to activate them without Weizmann . . . He is irreplaceable. . . . Without Weizmann our activity in London is worthless."[15]

In Ben-Gurion's catalogue, the list of Weizmann's faults was longer by far. It contained flaws of character and of conception. First, according to Ben-Gurion, Weizmann was ruled by his unstable temperament. Ben-Gurion regularly took note not only of what Weizmann said, but also of how he said it: "Weizmann is doubtful," "Weizmann is depressed," "Weizmann gave a pessimistic review." So alert was Ben-Gurion to Weizmann's moods that he considered himself able to read Weizmann's heart and innermost thoughts. After wooing Weizmann, Ben-Gurion noted in his diary, "I appreciate and understand Weizmann's mental condition and his difficulty in taking on this weighty responsibility again."

He attributed to Weizmann a certain frivolousness in that he was liable to act or speak for effect alone. "Weizmann could be very helpful," said Ben-Gurion to the Mapai Central Committee in February 1935, "but also very harmful. He might be swept away" by his own rhetoric and cause a setback. "In one speech he may cause irreparable damage." He also held that Weizmann was unable to distinguish between personal achievement — being received by government leaders whose doors were closed to other Zionists — and real political achievement. After describing a meeting with the colonial secretary, Ben-Gurion remarked in his diary, "Weizmann is always optimistic after a talk, but the situation, it seems, hasn't changed one bit."[16]

Ben-Gurion considered Weizmann's failure to distinguish between the essential and the unessential the gravest fault of all. "Weizmann has no sense of Zionist realities. He does not rank the immigration issue high." In contrast to Ben-Gurion, Weizmann was ready to yield on this point for the sake of peaceful relations with the British government and the Arabs. In August 1934 Ben-Gurion told the Mapai Central Committee, "We have suffered a major disaster in that we have very few people for this activity [immigration], among them only one man who is capable [Weizmann]. . . . But he lacks the proper understanding of the worth of large immigration." At another meeting he said, "Something happened with Weizmann so that he is untouched by the immigration issue. He has no feeling for large immigration . . . To Cunliffe-Lister he explained the value of half a million Jews in Palestine, but his heart was not in it." As a Weizmann "expert," Ben-Gurion went on to say that "his attitude may be understood psychoanalytically," by which he meant it could be explained by Weizmann's choosing to live in London instead of in the house he had built in Rehovot in Palestine.[17]

Alongside this failure stood Weizmann's lack of interest in or understanding of the Zionist movement. On the eve of the 1935 Zionist Congress, Ben-Gurion spoke to the Central Committee about "Weizmann's shortcomings, failing to understand the worth and strength of the movement, and neglect of the organizational side of the Zionist Organization." He blamed Weizmann for "the deterioration of the Zionist Organization" during his term of office. In a letter to his children from Burgenstock, after the Congress, he had summed up Weizmann's failings. "He does not understand the internal problems of the Zionist movement. He is moody and liable to make political mistakes . . . Many people in the Zionist movement . . . do not trust Weizmann politically. It is also not easy to work with him, as he is accustomed to people's taking his word as gospel."

"Weizmann's method" was to concentrate all information and political and diplomatic contacts in London, in his hands, and to let JAE members in on them when he saw fit. When the new JAE was taking its first steps, in September 1935, Ben-Gurion heard the familiar complaint again from Brodetsky. Weizmann had gone without him to his first meeting with Malcolm MacDonald, the new colonial secretary who replaced Cunliffe-Lister. Ben-Gurion asked Brodetsky "not to make anything of it, as ultimately the president is entitled to meet with the colonial secretary." But in his diary he commented, "It will be necessary to put the London office in working order."[18]

The "Weizmann question" had been on Ben-Gurion's mind long before he decided that Weizmann had to be reinstated to the presidency. In a December 1933 letter he had written, "If I weigh the positive and the negative, the positive wins, since Weizmann's shortcomings will be offset by the positive *might* of the movement and its people." Ben-Gurion was confident that Mapai and he himself could give Weizmann subtle direction, thereby making the most of what he had to offer while minimizing the damage his faults could incur. In February 1935 Ben-Gurion stated flatly, "We must make sure that those close to Weizmann . . . stay in contact with him and watch him. . . . He must be protected from himself." Berl Katznelson seconded that view, and this solution to Weizmann's reinstatement was almost certainly arrived at with his consent. In any event, Mapai and other groups accepted it as the best way of managing Zionist affairs.[19]

In March 1935 Ben-Gurion announced to the Mapai Central Committee, "I state plainly that I am for Weizmann's presidency, but not for a Weizmann regime." It was according to this formula that he tried to put together a new coalition at the Lucerne Congress. Part of the purpose of his trip to the United States was to mobilize supporters for it ahead of time. There he told Rabbi Stephen Wise and Judge Julian Mack, "Weizmann will not be the ruler and leader, and he knows it. The Executive will lead; he will be its head, but not its spokesman."[20] His formula was accepted, and from the Lucerne Congress on, "watching" and "coaching" Weizmann were considered primary tasks of the Zionist Executive and the JAE.

Upon whom would this "watchdog" responsibility fall? As early as August 1934 Ben-Gurion decided that "in fact, the London Political Section does not exist at all, and Brodetsky is not the right man." There remained Sharett, head of the Jerusalem Political Section, which was responsible for day-to-day political work, and Ben-Gurion himself, chairman of the Jerusalem Executive. Though Sharett was an industrious man of many talents, he was no watchdog either. He respected and revered Weizmann, both as a man twenty-one years his senior and as a master; Weizmann was closer to this disciple's heart than the outspoken Ben-Gurion.

Therefore Ben-Gurion alone was fit for the job. At first, when Ben-Gurion and Weizmann began working in the new JAE in London in October 1935, it seemed they would be able to pull together as a team. Weizmann, invited to lunch with Sir Arthur Wauchope, asked Ben-Gurion what points to bring up for discussion. But his report to Ben-Gurion on the luncheon produced only criticism. Wauchope had told Weizmann that he feared he would have to speak in public against the Jewish capitalists in England who were slowing down development in Palestine for their own profit, specifically Pinchas Rutenberg, the founder and director and a major shareholder of the Palestine Electric Company. Weizmann replied that Wauchope had already given that speech. To his diary Ben-Gurion remarked that Weizmann "shouldn't have said that to Wauchope." Two weeks later Weizmann invited Ben-Gurion to five o'clock tea with James MacDonald, American commissioner for refugee affairs from the League of Nations. Ben-Gurion's diary shows that he was amazed at the expertise revealed by MacDonald in Zionist office gossip, as well as irked by Weizmann, who unguardedly added to MacDonald's already impressive and unnecessary involvement "in internal Jewish conflicts."

Reporting to Sharett in Jerusalem on his first days with Weizmann in the London office, Ben-Gurion was unable to restrain himself. "I am enclosing the memo we handed Malcolm [MacDonald] and Weizmann's two notes to Malcolm and Wauchope. You'll notice that there is a difference in tone and content between the note to Malcolm and the one to Wauchope, as I wrote the first and Weizmann the second." Not only had Ben-Gurion composed a letter that carried Weizmann's signature, he even boasted of it.

In December another situation provided an opportunity to Ben-Gurion's liking. The high commissioner summoned Arab and Jewish representatives, on the twenty-first and twenty-second, respectively, to submit to them a new government proposal to establish the Legislative

Council. The first delegation included five representatives of the Muslim parties and two Christians. For the Jewish delegation, at the JAE's behest, Wauchope had originally invited the three members of the JAE — Weizmann (then in Palestine), Ben-Gurion, and Sharett — and the chairman of the National Council, Itzhak Ben-Zvi. After further thought the JAE resolved to include Rabbi Moses Blau, a leader of Agudath-Israel, the ultra-Orthodox, non-Zionist party, who was supposed to read a statement on behalf of his constituency.

The day before the meeting it was argued in Mapai's Political Committee that "there is something offensive in Weizmann's appearing before the commissioner with Rabbi Blau," and the suggestion was made that Weizmann go alone, as the sole representative of the Jews. But Ben-Gurion objected, saying, "I would not consent to Weizmann's going alone. Weizmann must go [with all the other Jewish representatives] to prevent the commissioner and the government from getting the impression that his view does not accord with ours on this matter. There is nothing wrong with Blau's joining us . . . He is important because he thinks the Council must be written off . . . He must come with us."

Six Jewish representatives — the last, a Sephardi, was added at the last minute by the National Council — appeared before the high commissioner. The commissioner spoke, then Weizmann; agreeing with what Weizmann had said, Ben-Zvi, Rabbi Blau, and the representative of the Sephardic and Oriental communities all gave their views. Afterward Ben-Gurion submitted his report (cited in his memoirs) to the JAE. It concluded as follows: "The united and forceful stand of the Jewish representatives made a deep impression on the government."[21]

But this idyll could not last. Weizmann naturally had felt slighted by what he considered an act of ill faith, as though he could not be trusted to be alone with the high commissioner. He had no desire to be "watched," and he certainly did not consider himself in need of Ben-Gurion's coaching. The differences between them were many and profound, and their personal ambitions far too fierce. It was only a matter of time before their initial cooperation turned into a steadily escalating conflict.

Weizmann:
A Danger to Zionism

T HE NEW EXECUTIVE was born at the time of a new age in Zionism. In 1935 both immigration and land acquisition peaked.
Sixty-five thousand immigrants, more than in the previous
twelve combined, arrived that year; between 1932 and 1935 the Jewish
population doubled to 355,157.* In large measure this impressive increase was to Sir Arthur Wauchope's credit. Ben-Gurion therefore not
only called him the best high commissioner ever, but also said he "admired Wauchope; I loved him." If immigration continued at that rate a
Jewish majority in Palestine would rapidly be achieved.

However, even before 1935 had ended Ben-Gurion began to fear
that the good years had passed, never to return. On November 13
Wauchope returned to Palestine after a vacation and consultations in
London, and Ben-Gurion felt that, politically, he was a different man.
"Since the commissioner's return I've sensed a change in course, and
this feeling is proving itself true more and more. The kind of strategy
we saw in the White Paper is being renewed. Aside from the Legislative Council, they are preparing far-reaching reductions in immigration and harsh restrictions on land acquisition." He told this to
Weizmann on January 16, 1936, during a consultation intended to prepare him for a meeting with Wauchope. Ben-Gurion restated his premonition at least four times that January; in February he noted it in his
diary and in a letter to Lord Melchett: "There is no doubt that Britain
is starting out on a new political course."[1]

---

* According to Mandatory statistics, the Jewish Agency counted 375,400 Jews. In 1935
Jews bought 72,905 dunams, more than in any other year of that decade.

Ben-Gurion was not blind to the reason for the "change of course": Wauchope's expansive policy toward Jewish immigration had also fueled the Palestinian Arabs' fear that they would become a minority in their land and made 1935 the turning point in the history of their struggle. The mufti proclaimed that immigration "jeopardized [their] very existence." In the face of this peril the Arabs joined forces politically for the first time. Two events triggered this change. On November 20 police surrounded Sheik Izz al-Din al-Qassām and his followers, who were hiding in the hills of Nablus after renewing their acts of terror against Jews. The sheik defied the police's call to surrender, and in the battle that followed, near Ya'bad, he and three of his men fell, guns in hand. Their heroic deaths inflamed the Arabs of Palestine, and the sheik's funeral in Haifa turned into a huge nationalist demonstration. Ben-Gurion was very impressed by al-Qassām's valiant last stand and foresaw its wide-ranging ramifications for the Arab national movement in Palestine. "This was the Arabs' first 'Tel Hai,' " he told the Mapai Central Committee two weeks after the battle. "Here was revealed a zealot, ready to die a martyr's death. At present there is not one, but ten, hundreds, perhaps thousands like him. And behind them stand the Arab people."[2]

The second event, which Ben-Gurion pinpointed as the turning point in the Arab struggle, took place on November 25. That day, in the wake of the great agitation over the sheik's funeral, a unified delegation of Palestinian Arabs submitted three demands to Wauchope: an immediate halt to Jewish immigration; a ban on land sales to Jews; and "the establishment of a democratic government," namely, an Arab government. These demands had surfaced often enough since 1920, but Ben-Gurion saw them in a new light. This was the first time that a delegation representing all the Arab parties had appeared before the high commissioner, signifying that the Arab camp was joining forces under the leadership of the mufti, Zionism's archenemy. However, Ben-Gurion was less apprehensive about the Arabs' demands and consolidation than he was about the British response, for he was no longer certain that the British government would reject them, as it had until then. And in replying to the demands in January 1936, the Colonial Office stated that it regarded the Legislative Council proposed by Wauchope as a practical step toward "a democratic government" and that it intended to enact a law prohibiting land sales unless the Arab landowner retained a "viable minimum" (lot viable), sufficient to afford subsistence for himself and his family. As far as immigration was concerned, a new statistical bureau was being established to gauge Palestine's economic absorptive capacity. This reply was interpreted as favorable toward the Arabs and a bad omen for Zionism.

This "change of course" — better known as Ben-Gurion's epithet "appeasement of the Arabs"[3] — derived from two sources. First were the changes in the international arena. Italy's conquest of Ethiopia, which had begun on October 4, 1935, aroused fears of war in the Mediterranean region, creating an overall specter of war in Europe. Consequently, the strategic value of the Arab lands grew in the British Empire's defense considerations. Italy's aggression in Ethiopia laid bare both the weakness of the League of Nations and the inability of Britain, the mightiest power, or France, its ally, to put a stop to it. Their loss of deterrent power became even clearer after the Rhineland confrontation on March 7, 1936, which led to a loss of prestige for both nations among the Arabs of the Middle East. In November 1935 anti-British demonstrations and riots broke out in Egypt and lasted a full week. In Syria a general strike began in January 1936 and lasted fifty days, accompanied by riots and disturbances throughout. Such direct action against the European powers reaped rewards both in Syria and in Egypt. At the end of February the French government summoned a Syrian delegation to Paris to discuss the signing of a treaty similar to the 1930 British-Iraqi treaty providing for Iraqi independence; and on March 2, 1936, earlier negotiations between Britain and Egypt over signing a treaty of independence were resumed. Egypt and Syria were soon to join Iraq in the ranks of independent countries. But the Arabs of Palestine had not only not advanced toward independence — they, too, wished to free themselves of the Mandatory power — their very existence, at least in their own eyes, was being threatened. They had learned that, in the battle for independence, there was no escaping violence. Britain, to save itself more such troubles and to strengthen its weakened position, considered it necessary to placate them.[4]

Ben-Gurion located the second source of the appeasement of the Arabs as the opening of a new phase in Wauchope's policy. When Jews constituted 30 percent of the overall population and held 1,317,000 dunams of land — of a total 6,544,000 dunams that the government considered fit for cultivation (the JAE thought there were 16 million) — Wauchope could assume that the National Home had been "crystallized" and would enjoy only moderate growth from then on, and that the hour had come to offer Palestine a new constitution, which would eventually result in Arab rule. On October 18 he received authorization to present the Jews and Arabs with a new, improved Legislative Council proposal: twenty-eight members and a British chairman with the power of veto. Fourteen seats in the Council were to be reserved for Arabs (50%), assuring them a good prospect of a majority. The Jews, who were to have only seven seats (25%), had no such chance. The rest of the seats were reserved for five British officials and two commercial representatives, also Englishmen. With their chairman, the British held eight seats. Hence the Jews' sole defense against the majority's alienating their minority rights was the chairman's right of veto. The establishment of such a Legislative Council was tantamount to perpetuating the Jews' minority status in Palestine and gradually establishing it as an Arab Palestinian state. The Arabs were well disposed toward this proposal, and it was certain that they would accept it after due negotiations.

But the Jews could not accept such a Legislative Council or its consequences, if only because of the growing need for immigration. In central and eastern Europe the situation of the Jews had worsened, and pressure to increase immigration and land acquisition for settlement had grown considerably. Ben-Gurion regarded the Nuremberg Laws, passed shortly after the Lucerne Congress, as a declaration of "a war of extermination" against German Jews. In October 1935 he noted in his diary that their situation was "alarming and shocking, liable to drive anyone who is not already insensate mad." At the end of December he wrote a Zionist activist that it was clear that "the tragedy awaiting German Jewry is much worse than it seemed two or three months ago." Yet he thought that Polish Jewry was in an even worse state. In 1933 he had told Wauchope that "the Polish government is abandoning the Jews to pogroms and dispossession . . . They must escape or else die of hunger." In the neighboring countries, particularly Rumania, Jews did not fare much better.[5]

To Ben-Gurion, Zionism was distilled to massive immigration. Appeasement of the Arabs, which meant reducing or even stopping immigration, was inimical to Zionism. Not only did the prospect of a permanent Jewish minority in Eretz Israel contradict Zionism's very foundations, it also, Ben-Gurion thought, perpetuated "the Arab question" — Arab objection to the Zionist enterprise in Palestine. He believed that this objection would vanish the moment a Jewish majority was achieved and the Arabs realized that they would be best off living together in peace. He also believed that should the Yishuv's growth be stunted and it remain a minority forever, the Arabs would eventually put an end to it.

What was more, the rationale for the very existence of the Zionist movement would be negated should the gates of Palestine clang shut before the Jews. What good was the movement if it could not provide the persecuted and tormented Jews of Poland, Germany, and Rumania with a refuge in Palestine? Here Ben-Gurion's Zionist ideology and his concern for the Jewish people fused. Zionism became for him not only a political solution to the problem of the Jewish people, but first and foremost the only way to rescue them, as he told Wauchope on April 2,

1936. "Were it possible to transfer the Jews of Poland to America or Argentina we would do so despite our Zionist ideology. But the world is closed to us, and if there is no place for us in Palestine either, our people have no other way but suicide."[6] To save the Jews, he was prepared to yield on Zionist principles; and if he did not do so it was only because Palestine was the sole lifeboat available to the Jewish people in Europe.

Ben-Gurion was right. In spite of Wauchope's denials, there had indeed been a change of course. But just as the suffering of European Jewry was not a major consideration in the making of British policy, neither was the Arab fear of dispossession. The decision to change policy had in fact been made by the British government while Wauchope was in London, the main ground for it being imperial strategy in light of Italy's war in Ethiopia. Even after the clouds of war seemed to have passed the government did not withdraw from its change of course and again, as in 1930, sought to back away from the Mandate and the Balfour Declaration. This time they were more successful, for as the waves of Jews in Poland and Germany asking for entry permits to Palestine grew and grew, instead of opening wide to accept them, the gates of Palestine began to close. In 1936 immigration was reduced to 29,727, less than half the previous year's figure, and only 18,246 dunams of land were sold to Jews, less than a third of 1935 sales. Unless the change of course was thwarted, Zionism held no hope of rescue for Europe's Jews.

Hence, upon joining the new Zionist Executive Ben-Gurion had first to design a policy to deal with the hardships he envisaged. One thing was clear to him: he would never, under any circumstances, accept a Zionism that could not save the Jews. Their rescue took priority over all else, including the reorganization of the Zionist Organization and the JAE.

His dark foreboding moved Ben-Gurion to work for two objectives in late 1935 and early 1936. He had to convince his colleagues in the JAE and Mapai, while there was still time, that a new political era had begun and to steer them toward the plan of action he would propose. The first task was not an easy one. While he was in London two events seemed to bear witness that Britain remained truer than ever to the MacDonald Letter. On October 16 the new colonial secretary, Malcolm MacDonald, his deputy, Lord Plymouth, and two of his top aides met with Weizmann, Brodetsky, and Ben-Gurion for dinner and talk. This get-together, incidentally, provides testimony of Ben-Gurion's sensitivity to his height. While MacDonald was proposing an agenda Ben-Gurion sized him up and mused, "It was a little odd that the youngest of the group, as well as the shortest, excepting me — Lord Plymouth is no shorter than [Sir Cosmo] Parkinson, and both are perhaps taller than Weizmann — was in command at the table." Whether Ben-Gurion truly thought it the way of the world that power was in the hands of the tall and strong, so that he termed MacDonald's predominance "a little odd" and to a certain extent projected the relationship between MacDonald and Plymouth onto himself and Weizmann, is a moot question. In any case, the conversation dispelled the Zionists' doubts and renewed their confidence. Such, at least, was Ben-Gurion's summary to Moshe Sharett.

> The meeting did not fulfill our expectations or provide any specifics for the time being. Nevertheless, there was no small progress. I hope for a significant change in the government's position on industry, possibly even something on land issues. As for immigration, there was nothing positive, but the meeting was perhaps indirectly helpful. . . . I was constantly worried that Italy's conflict would lead to our loss this winter of the schedule [the labor immigration quota]. It seems to me that this meeting, to a great extent, averted the danger.[7]

Four days later the Anglo-Palestine Club held a banquet in honor of MacDonald, during which further reassurance was given of Britain's loyalty to the Balfour Declaration. Among the five hundred guests were high-ranking clergy, Wauchope, senior civil servants from the Colonial Office, top military brass, the press, and important Zionists, James Rothschild among them. The many speakers praised MacDonald's friendship to Zionism and his valuable service in its support. Rising to make his remarks, Wauchope was met with a warm ovation. "Incidentally, the two most popular personalities there were Weizmann and Wauchope: both were received with thunderous applause," noted Ben-Gurion, concluding, "The banquet turned into a political event, a great Zionist demonstration." Anyone not privy to the secrets of the British cabinet could not have imagined that at the very same time a new policy was secretly taking shape.

What was more, in early 1936 the Legislative Council proposal was dropped in spite of Arab protestations and Wauchope's warning that this would inflame passions even more. From the start the British cabinet had not been united on the matter of the Council, and after Parliament harshly censured it as contradicting Britain's commitments and liable to obstruct the rescue of German Jewry, it gave up altogether. The parliamentary debate — first in the House of Lords on February 26 and then in the Commons on March 24 — was considered a smashing victory and a credit to the JAE's lobbying and political work. The Arabs, who failed to understand the impact of the Jewish plight on the parliamentary debate, attributed this victory to Jewish Mammon and were strengthened in their conviction that only violence could help them.[8]

But the Jews also misinterpreted the debate, smugly believing Britain to be the mainstay of Zionism. Consequently, not a man in the Mapai Central and Political committees or the JAE accepted what Ben-Gurion had to say. Although they did have fears that immigration would decrease or land sales be limited, none of them, not even Sharett, believed that there had been an actual change of course, Britain's disavowal of its commitment to the National Home.

Moving these nonbelievers toward his proposed response — his second objective — was therefore even more difficult for Ben-Gurion. He proposed nothing less than a great offensive on British public opinion and the government, not simply to thwart the change of course but primarily to persuade Britain to give Zionism active political, military, and financial assistance to expedite the construction and expansion of the National Home. More precisely, Ben-Gurion proposed demanding that Britain develop Palestine's economic absorptive capacity to a million Jews within five to ten years.

Had Great Britain agreed to this demand, a Jewish majority in Palestine would have been achieved within a short time. In Zionist jargon — well understood by both the English and the Arabs — "a Jewish majority" was tantamount to a Jewish state. On March 9, 1936, at a meeting of Mapai's Political Committee, Ben-Gurion called for "the launching of a policy which had the establishment of a Jewish state as its ultimate goal." Although he remarked that it had been Weizmann who said, several days earlier, "Now is the time to demand a Jewish state," the difference in phrasing stood out immediately. While Weizmann proposed "demanding" from British statesmen, Ben-Gurion called for "launching" an active policy. He ridiculed Weizmann's tack, saying, "One cannot simply approach [James Henry] Thomas [secretary of state for the dominions and supporter of Zionism] and say, 'Give us a Jewish state.'" Ben-Gurion's strategy was to inaugurate a public opinion campaign, in Great Britain and throughout the world, focusing on the demand that Britain actively assist in the immigration and absorption of one million Jews.

Here was an excellent indicator of the similarities and differences of Weizmann and Ben-Gurion. Although they were often in political agreement, their personalities and methods were miles apart. Weizmann had the ideas when the spirit moved him but was incapable of systematic work to carry them through, while Ben-Gurion worked relentlessly and indefatigably to realize his ideas. Here, too, appeared the cause of their falling-out over issues they agreed on. Weizmann's personal diplomatic approach held that Zionism would reap greater political rewards through discreet, first-name contacts, while Ben-Gurion maintained that the only tactic was to use public opinion for leverage.

Ben-Gurion hoped for the success of this new policy, laying his faith on British public opinion and its partiality to justice and fair play. If the public could be convinced that the change of course was both unjust to the Jews and damaging to British imperial interests, the government could be forced to rescind it. His reasoning rested on four basic premises. Since it had demonstrated great sensitivity over the worsening situation of German Jewry, the British public would also be affected by the state of Polish Jews, living as they were in "a permanent pogrom." Second, it could be convinced that the world was closed to the Jewish refugees and their salvation depended solely on Palestine, which had already proved its capacity for rapid development and absorption. Third, the public would understand that with war threatening, a Jewish Palestine was more essential to the British Empire than the Arab lands, and that it was in the empire's interest to enlarge and fortify it. Finally, it would accept the idea that there need not be any apprehension of Arab reaction, since increased as opposed to restricted immigration was the only solution to the Arab question.[9]

Growing concern for the fate of Polish, German, and Rumanian Jewry set Ben-Gurion on the course of "beginning a Jewish state policy" and gave him confidence in its success. This was his familiar tactic of using a disaster to advantage, and it is difficult to believe that it was not on his mind when he spoke of the tragedy as a "lever" — a term he was to employ very often between 1933 and 1939. He told the Political Committee that if the rate of immigration was reduced to a trickle,

> Palestine is liable to slip off the nation's agenda. . . . The main question is, What will happen in such a case to the Jewish people? [Therefore] we must begin working to turn Palestine into a Jewish land. The goal of our political action now is to get a million Jews [out of Europe] . . . and bring them to Palestine. . . . Since this need . . . is not only a matter of theory, but dictated by a reality which speaks in a language that the whole world hears and understands, I regard it as a lever for our political work.

Ben-Gurion wished to reorder the stages leading to the achievement of the Zionist goal. Since 1933 they had been (1) immigration, the means of reaching (2) a majority, which — provided (3) the Arab question was solved — would bring about (4) the establishment of the state, the key to opening the gates of Palestine to all Jews (the Return to Zion) — that is, (5) the realization of Zionism. But in 1936 his sense of the burning ground made it necessary to speed up the rate of immigration and force a state into being. Rescuing the Jews dictated a revised outline: (1) establishment of the state to allow for (2) mass immigration, which would create (3) an absolute majority, which would bring about (4) the solution to the Arab question and (5) the realization of Zionism.

This proposal was met with raised eyebrows in the Political Committee — not an unexpected response. Ben-Gurion, in a letter to Lord Melchett explaining the need to demand the entry of a million Jews within five to ten years, added, "Perhaps you will think this fantastic and that I've lost my senses." Not only did his colleagues deny that the time had come for such a policy, they also criticized him both for not having a plan of action and for lacking the means to carry out such a plan even if he had one. Berl Katznelson and Joseph Sprinzak were particularly harsh. The former, whose role in his relationship with Ben-Gurion was coming more and more to involve applying the brakes, now tried to check him again, hinting that with the heavy load already on his shoulders, Ben-Gurion was liable to break down if he embarked on a "Jewish State Policy." Katznelson quoted from the Bible: "Thou wilt surely wear away!"* Katznelson the skeptic, who was not at all pleased by Ben-Gurion's restructuring of the Zionist Organization, probably took this opportunity to discreetly express the opinion that "forgoing Ben-Gurion's political work is a luxury we cannot allow ourselves."

Sprinzak complained, as usual, that he was constantly being taken unaware. He wanted to know what he was doing in a Political Committee that met only when something came up and where information was received, but nothing was ever discussed properly. Even David Remez, who supported Ben-Gurion more than the others, remarked that the proposal was "incomplete." The committee adjourned after passing three resolutions, all with the best intentions: (1) Ben-Gurion was to work out the details of his proposal for the next meeting; (2) Discussion of it would continue at that time; (3) Meetings would be held weekly.[10] But none of these was ever carried out, either because Ben-Gurion did not have enough information to do more than call for a new direction or because new and rapid developments changed the entire Zionist agenda.

If the united Arab delegation's submission of its demands to Wauchope put an end to Ben-Gurion's hopes of reaching an accord with the Arabs, the dropping of the Legislative Council dashed Arab hopes of reaching their goal peacefully. Wauchope's warning was borne out: the Arabs chose violence. On April 19, 1936, an incited Arab mob attacked Jewish passersby in Jaffa, killing nine and wounding ten. The next day Arabs assaulted Jews in Tel Aviv, leaving seven dead and forty

---

* Exodus 18:18

wounded. So began the Arab revolt, which the Jews called the Events or Disturbances of 1936. On April 22 Arab political parties declared a boycott of the Jews and their products and called a general strike, to be ended only after Jewish immigration and land acquisition were banned and the Arabs were assured independent rule in Palestine. The strike ended on October 12, without their having achieved any of these demands, and thus ended the Events of 1936, in the course of which the Arabs killed eighty Jews, crippled transportation, uprooted orchards, destroyed property, and burned crops and forests.

Such was the backdrop for Ben-Gurion and Weizmann's work together in the new Executive's first six months. Ben-Gurion's primary purpose was not just to watch Weizmann but to activate him as a central implement to carry out policy with whose means or ends he often took issue. By January 16, 1936, Ben-Gurion had wanted to unleash Weizmann on Prime Minister Stanley Baldwin, while Weizmann argued that one "should not go to Baldwin above the high commissioner's head." It was ultimately decided to meet with the commissioner on January 26. Weizmann assumed that since he was authorized to meet with the P.M. alone, the same would be true with the commissioner. But Wauchope's door was open to Ben-Gurion, Arthur Ruppin, chief of Zionist agricultural development and settlement, and Sharett as well, so Weizmann found himself among a delegation of four. The sensitive Sharett later commented, "Apparently it also hurt [Weizmann] . . . that the others wanted to accompany him to the commissioner in order to share the responsibility, that they did not think him forceful enough."

Weizmann, the chief spokesman, was supposed to address the "land decrees" that restricted land sales to Jews, but his speech developed into a general reproof of Britain for not fulfilling its moral commitment toward the Jews and Zionism. Ben-Gurion was so impressed by this statement that he felt he had been struck dumb. "Weizmann," he later wrote a Zionist activist in Kraków, "told the commissioner things no English ear has ever heard. I do not know if a representative of a larger, stronger, armed, and more forceful nation could have allowed himself to speak in such a manner to an English representative. . . . This audacious and devastating attack left the commissioner speechless, and he had nothing to say for the duration of the meeting." In a letter to Zionist functionaries he again sang Weizmann's praises.

In the annals of the outstanding political activity of the father of the Balfour Declaration this talk has a *special place of honor*. It was a fine and brave assault, ably done, audacious and humble at once, mixed with the sorrow and anger of a representative of a small and hunted nation, fighting like a lion which has lost its cubs for its last hope, embittered and forceful, defending the justness of his cause and the vision of his redemption with the deepest faith.

Their differences did not diminish, however, and behind closed doors Ben-Gurion made no attempt to conceal them. Before the meeting with Wauchope, Ben-Gurion had insisted that immigration, not the Legislative Council or the land decrees, should be made the central topic, since it was the most important issue. At a Mapai Central Committee meeting after Weizmann's performance, Ben-Gurion commended it as "a great moral and spiritual display," but immediately added, "This does not change my view that Weizmann does not see what is happening and does not act according to the needs of the movement, but rather according to an accidental chance awakening. Certain political matters can be achieved only at a particular moment . . . and if this moment is gone . . . the whole matter is lost. . . . Weizmann's intervention undeniably left an immense impact on Wauchope, perhaps too immense."

Three days later, at another meeting of the Central Committee, Ben-Gurion asserted that Weizmann's performance had not been helpful at all, since personal diplomacy was powerless to change government policy, and certainly that of Great Britain. What was needed was a campaign to enlist public opinion.

> [But] for this we need people and there are none . . . The only man for this job is Weizmann, but Weizmann is no statesman. And I say this precisely after the greatest performance of his life, at the sight of which I myself was astounded. He is not a statesman. He does not weigh all the factors; an impulse brings to life all his gifts — and they are many. . . . He does not sense what a man like Lord Melchett, who is not half the man he is, senses, and at this time Melchett does not rest on the issue of Germany. Weizmann does not sense that this is the hour to move on this matter, and it is difficult to activate him in that direction.

Ben-Gurion's clear implication was that the only thing that had moved Weizmann to attack Wauchope on the basis of the proposed land law was Weizmann's personal involvement in that issue. Ben-Gurion considered the law a breach of the MacDonald Letter, the credit for which Weizmann rightly regarded as primarily his own. Ben-Gurion explained to Eliezer Kaplan,

> Weizmann does not weigh matters objectively; for him the personal aspect, for better or worse, overrides all others. In the conflict with the commissioner on the issue of restricting land sales he unveiled a tremendous readiness to attack, but as soon as he received the commissioner's letter [Wauchope needed a few days to recover before he could respond]

he cooled down, although, objectively speaking, nothing had changed. The personal satisfaction he got from the letter doubled as political satisfaction for him. And, in talks at which I was present, I have more than once heard him make an evaluation based not on the political content of the talk and its real outcome, but on the basis of a personal relationship and expressions of friendship. . . . I cannot repress the bitter and depressing feeling that at this time we have no supreme political leadership.

Nonetheless, Weizmann was incomparable, and any kind of activity in London without him was out of the question. Here Katznelson totally agreed with Ben-Gurion. "It is clear that Weizmann must be sent to London. He is indeed weak when it comes to pragmatic, constructive thinking, but he is the man to ward off an attack."

Early in February the JAE therefore decided to send Weizmann to London "on urgent business." Although "Sharett was asked to inform him of this decision," Ben-Gurion was undoubtedly responsible. But even in London, Weizmann's behavior did not ease Ben-Gurion's mind. In March Ben-Gurion repeated his old grievances to the Political Committee, adding, "And now I fear the same thing will happen again in London." But this time Ben-Gurion drew more sweeping conclusions. "Every mistake of Weizmann's has become a destructive force for the Zionist movement." Weizmann, that is, was a danger to Zionism. Once again, Katznelson backed up Ben-Gurion. "I am of one mind with Ben-Gurion that Weizmann's errors have caused many difficulties for Zionism and that something big must be done to reform the Zionist movement."[11]

Ben-Gurion had fallen into a trap of his own making: the exponent of authority was prevented from establishing it within the Zionist Organization. Weizmann could not uphold it, since his heart was not in the movement and he showed no concern for its organization. He was no statesman either, but rather worked when the spirit moved him. It is in the nature of things that one man cannot another's authority build. Nor could Ben-Gurion impose his own authority, for he was only number two. Had he tried to, it would have been interpreted as subversion, or an attempt to make Weizmann into a figurehead, and he would not have achieved authority but only wreaked general havoc and fragmentation. Between the man who was designated to exercise authority, but unable to assert it, and the man who was quite able, but undesignated, discord reigned. "I regard the lack of authority as the greatest disaster of all," said Ben-Gurion to the Political Committee in January. Later he claimed, "We now have no supreme leadership."

One possible solution, at least in theory, was for Ben-Gurion to unseat and replace Weizmann as president. But while Weizmann could not give the Zionist movement the sweeping leadership it needed,

Ben-Gurion lacked Weizmann's gift of reaching out and touching human hearts. This was probably why his colleagues thought Ben-Gurion unfit for the presidency; even Katznelson favored Weizmann over him. Had the pair come to terms with each other, as many must have prayed they would, the Zionist movement would have profited. But it was not to be.

An odd situation prevailed, with Ben-Gurion "watching" Weizmann, trying to guide him on the political scene as a choreographer directs ballerinas on the stage. But Weizmann did not follow instructions, and Ben-Gurion was caught in a bind. Weizmann may have been a danger to Zionism, but without him Zionism would fare far worse.

It was, for example, absolutely clear to Ben-Gurion that without Weizmann it would be impossible "to begin a Jewish state policy." Perhaps for this reason Ben-Gurion decided that after Weizmann was sent to London with the directive to demand "a fundamental change in the [British] political line" he had better leave him to do as he saw fit. "My going to London would hurt Weizmann because it was never discussed with him," he explained to Kaplan. "Weizmann is temperamental, and if we spoil his mood, we also impede his ability to work . . . and this must not happen, especially now, when he is charged with weighty matters." He intended to go to London only at Weizmann's invitation, which shows that when it came to a political purpose, Ben-Gurion, too, was gifted with tact and consideration of others.

For the moment, then, the answer seemed to be to guide Weizmann from afar, leaving him room to maneuver for "his very important work over the last weeks" in London. But an unfettered Weizmann was also free to decide how long to stay in London, and in early April he left, arousing Ben-Gurion's ire. "If [his work] ceases now, all the progress made thus far will be lost." On Weizmann's return to Palestine it became clear that the gap between the two men's views on British policy had widened considerably. Weizmann had no fears about a change of course; he radiated optimism, derived, Ben-Gurion suspected, from self-satisfaction over the way he had carried himself at the meetings. "Now that public opinion is with us, we're riding high," he reportedly told Ben-Gurion, who quickly noted it in his diary. "The government fears an attack in the House of Commons and won't dare do anything to harm us. . . . The government has learned a lesson, and now it will listen with awe." He therefore abandoned London and rejected Ben-Gurion's demand that he return there before May.

Ben-Gurion viewed the situation in an entirely different light. While English public opinion was very powerful, he told the Mapai Central Committee, "there is another force — the civil service — that rules the empire, and it is hard to tell which of them, public opinion or the civil service, will have the upper hand." Ben-Gurion respected public opinion but was well aware of its vagaries, and he could by no means share Weizmann's "exaggerated optimism."[12] Ben-Gurion realized that watching Weizmann from afar was not the answer either.

Events developed at an alarming pace. On April 26, 1936, all of Palestine's Arab parties united to form an Arab Higher Committee, authorized to manage the general strike until the November demands were met. By the end of April it was evident that this was no ordinary Arab protest. The economy was shattered, terror against Jews spread, and armed bands, known to the Jews as murderous gangs but dignified by Arabs and their supporters as guerrillas, roamed the country. In his efforts to restore order, Wauchope met on May 15 with the Arab Higher Committee, informing them that if the strike was stopped, a Royal Commission would be set up to examine the situation in Palestine and inquire into Arab and Jewish grievances. The Arabs replied that they would continue the strike until Jewish immigration was suspended.

At Wauchope's request, in May a battalion of the Royal Scots Fusiliers was sent from Egypt, beginning a steady buildup of reinforcements that continued throughout June and July. But the increased military presence, a curfew, and arrests were unsuccessful at restoring order, and the Arabs' demand for an end to immigration remained unchanged. To prove that His Majesty's government would not yield, as well as to lean on the Arab Higher Committee, Wauchope approved the biannual Labour Schedule of Jewish immigrants for June–December, a small quota of only forty-five hundred entry permits. On May 18, in reply to a question in Parliament, the new secretary of state for the colonies, James Henry Thomas,* stated that the government was resolved, as soon as order was restored, to appoint a Royal Commission, which, without bringing into question the terms of the Mandate, would investigate the causes of unrest. On June 16 and 20 and July 2, the government reasserted that the commission would not be sent until all was quiet.

Ben-Gurion was positive that the government would choose the path of least resistance and suspend, if not halt, immigration, at least for the duration of the Royal Commission; it had not done so already only through fear of losing face before the Arabs. Suddenly Zionism was faced by a grave crisis, and this time nobody doubted it. Ben-Gurion's forecast of a change of course and the appeasement of the Arabs had proved absolutely true. Even Weizmann realized that his optimism had no basis in fact and hurried back to London. Whether because of

---

* Thomas had replaced Malcolm MacDonald on November 22, 1935.

the gravity of the situation, or to watch Weizmann, Ben-Gurion followed on May 25.

On May 29 he found "a flood of telegrams" in the Zionist office that Weizmann had left unanswered. The reason for this became apparent when Weizmann walked in feeling "depressed" and said, according to Ben-Gurion, "There's nothing more to be done in London. He has already seen everyone. Now what?" In his diary Ben-Gurion commented, "The low spirits and despair I see in Weizmann and Lewis Namier are unfounded, as unfounded as [Weizmann's] runaway optimism after the parliamentary debate, as if public opinion, the press, and the British Parliament were in our pocket."

One ray of sunshine flickered in the darkness. On May 28, 1936, a new secretary of state for the colonies was named: Sir William Ormsby-Gore (later Lord Harlech), a friend to Zionism and a personal friend of Weizmann's since he had served as a liaison and political officer to the Zionist Commission on behalf of the British army in Palestine, after the war. Weizmann and his circle called him Billy. "With Billy, Chaim will be able to discuss everything, as with a friend," said Blanche Dugdale, according to Ben-Gurion's diary. In light of this prospect Ben-Gurion looked forward to fruitful cooperation with Weizmann and "his group" in the struggle for immigration.

Perhaps owing to the crisis, it seemed that this time the two were starting off on the right foot. But when Weizmann let Ben-Gurion in on his innermost thoughts, the latter nearly fainted. Weizmann maintained that Zionism would gain the favor of the British government and public opinion and, to a great extent, Arab good will, if the JAE took the initiative and offered to suspend immigration for a year of its own free will. Palestine would quiet down, the Royal Commission would go about its job, and it would be easier for all concerned to settle the conflict between Jews and Arabs. Ormsby-Gore, Wauchope, and the Colonial Office would all be indebted to the JAE for having gotten them out of a mess and repay Zionism a thousand times over.

Horrified, Ben-Gurion tried to show Weizmann his terrible error: what a tremendous victory it would be for the Arabs if through violence they achieved the suspension of immigration. From then on they would possess a proven means of enforcing their will on the Zionist Organization and the British government. Second, the suspension could easily develop into a cessation. Third, the hard-pressed German and Polish Jews would never understand such a gesture made at their expense. After "seriously" cautioning Weizmann on June 8 against such "sinful thoughts," Ben-Gurion repeated his protests the next day with redoubled force, believing that he had "killed Weizmann's dreadful idea."

Weizmann, however, was truly insensitive to immigration and its far-reaching ramifications, for both the persecuted Jews in Europe and others in the Zionist movement; that June, for example, he wrote to Felix Warburg in New York that, "although there are numerous problems outside Palestine which stir Jewry to its very depths [and] I do not believe that any rational solution for these problems will be or can be found . . . it is only natural that the Jewries interested should attempt to formulate at any rate some sort of a solution." He himself, however, would "be quite content if I am allowed to guide, to some extent, the destinies of the Zionist movement, and to bring our little ship into calmer waters." Without consulting anyone — and without Ben-Gurion's noticing anything amiss — Weizmann, in one day, did two things that came within an inch of sundering the JAE and the Zionist Organization.

On June 9, shortly after Ben-Gurion had complimented himself on killing Weizmann's "dreadful idea," Weizmann met with Nuri Sa'id Pasha, the Iraqi foreign minister, then in London to mediate in Palestine's conflict. It is most likely that at this meeting Weizmann told Nuri he was prepared to offer the government a year-long cessation of immigration to provide the Royal Commission the calm it needed to do its job.

That evening Weizmann, his wife, and Ben-Gurion dined at Dugdale's home, along with Lord Balfour's widow and Sir Austen Chamberlain, former secretary of state for India. At the dinner table Weizmann related his talk with Nuri Pasha, who was "ready to consent," Ben-Gurion wrote in his diary, "to a Jewish Palestine if the Jews lent their support to an Arab confederation." From here the conversation turned to the question of whether the Arabs would unite in a confederation, and Sir Austen asked if the Arabs were right in their apprehension that continued Jewish immigration would result in their loss of Palestine. No mention of his consent to suspend immigration passed Weizmann's lips.

Sir Austen and Weizmann then participated in a conference at the Royal Institute for International Affairs at Chatham House. Sir Archer Cust, a former senior official in the Palestine administration, took the floor after Weizmann to speak in favor of cantonization as a solution to a conflict. He elaborated on his scheme to create a Jewish canton from Jewish settlements along the coastal plain and in the Jezreel Valley. Haifa and Jerusalem would remain under British control. All the rest, including the Jewish settlements in the Jordan Valley, would make up an Arab canton. Weizmann apparently responded that this scheme was of great interest and worthy of further study.

The extent of Ben-Gurion's ignorance of the full content of Weizmann's talk with Nuri is shown by the surprise Ben-Gurion evinced at a meeting the next morning on learning that Weizmann still held to his dreadful idea, demanding a resolution that the JAE propose a suspension of immigration for a certain period "in order to assist the government." Of "the group" that Weizmann usually consulted — Dugdale, Namier, Melchett, and others — Dugdale alone supported him; all the rest were passionately opposed. In her diary Dugdale wrote, "Ben-Gurion's opposition was the most important." He said that Palestinian Jewry would never understand such a move, and not only would such a step break the Zionist movement "in twain," it would instantly start a civil war in Palestine, for nothing had kept the Jews from retaliating against Arab terror except for the determination to do nothing to stop immigration. Weizmann gave assurances that he would never do anything to split Jewish unity, "our chief asset." But after the meeting, alone in the privacy of his chauffeur-driven Rolls, Weizmann told her that "at present" he had no intention of bringing up his idea for further discussion in the Executive, but he "thought it would have to come."

The Weizmann-Nuri talk also came up at the morning meeting, though not in detail. In his diary Ben-Gurion wrote that Dugdale had later told him privately more "of Nuri's talk with Chaim." But she clearly had not told all, for otherwise it would have set off a storm at the meeting, and it is safe to assume that Weizmann had not told her the crucial information. She wrote in her diary, "Nuri Pasha has been in touch with Chaim the last day or two re plans for a Confederation of Arab States. Big things are brewing, but the way is dark and it is so easy to make false steps!" These last words were probably quoted from Weizmann himself, but there is no hint that Weizmann told her he had consented to the suspension of immigration.

When the meeting ended Ben-Gurion cabled Sharett to fly at once from Jerusalem to Cairo — out of British wiretapping range — and phone the London office. He did this in accordance with a resolution passed at the meeting. But while Weizmann wanted Sharett to approve his writing a letter "to Billy" informing him "that the Jews will facilitate the work of the Royal Commission" — that is, offer to suspend immigration — Ben-Gurion intended to call Sharett to London to keep a tighter watch on Weizmann, who had asked for an appointment with Ormsby-Gore and was expecting a date to be fixed. Eventually it was set for June 16.

Sharett could not get away from Jerusalem and Ben-Gurion, apprehensive about leaving Weizmann unattended in London, postponed a planned trip to Warsaw to "stand beside" Weizmann until his meeting with Ormsby-Gore. Ben-Gurion's premonition of impending disaster for European Jewry had come up against Weizmann's sense of having time for long-term maneuvering. On June 11 Ben-Gurion told Weizmann he was "in deep despair," knowing Weizmann still had a warm place in his heart for his "idea," which entailed "destruction inside and out." Weizmann replied, "A man has no control over his thoughts."

Ben-Gurion became more and more uneasy, as if he sensed that Weizmann was keeping something important from him, yet they managed to get along. It seems that Weizmann even took the trouble to put Ben-Gurion's mind at ease. On June 14 Ben-Gurion lunched at the Weizmanns' and at three o'clock the three of them drove to Churt, the home of David Lloyd George, the former prime minister, who had maintained a friendship with Weizmann. Without this gesture on Weizmann's part Ben-Gurion would never have met the great man. "The old man," reported Ben-Gurion to his diary, "is entirely gray, but his face is full of life. He received us most amicably." Lloyd George asked Weizmann his opinion of Ormsby-Gore. Weizmann replied that he had not yet seen him in action, "but his sympathies are well known." In his diary, in English, Ben-Gurion quoted Lloyd George, who hit the mark in more ways than one. "You don't need sympathy — you need courage, action, and driving power." Later on in the conversation he said, "The Arabs are afraid Palestine will become a Hebrew state — Well, *it will* be a Hebrew state." Two days later Weizmann reported to Ben-Gurion that Lloyd George had told him he was particularly impressed by Ben-Gurion's courage, adding, Ben-Gurion wrote to Paula, "If the Jews had people like [me], their future is assured." Weizmann was a master at winning hearts.

On June 16 Weizmann finally had his first interview with Ormsby-Gore. He returned "bursting with satisfaction," and reported to Ben-Gurion, who listened attentively, that "since Balfour he hasn't had such a good talk." In his diary Ben-Gurion added, "He found complete understanding for our cause. As usual, getting a full, clear report of the talk out of him was like pulling teeth." Nonetheless, Ben-Gurion felt he could breathe freely. They had a friend in the Colonial Office and Weizmann had not suggested suspending immigration. Parliament debated the government's policy regarding the Disturbances and Ben-Gurion had taken a good deal of trouble to brief the speakers, among them Lloyd George and Herbert Morrison of Labour. The Zionists considered the debate a victory because, apart from two pro-Arab members, all the speakers condemned the Arab strike and violence in Palestine and demanded the use of force by the government. They also praised the achievements of the Yishuv and asked for action to strengthen the National Home. Ben-Gurion finally felt free to leave, and on June 20 he set out for Vienna and Warsaw. On June 23 he flew back to London. The purpose of this lightning trip was "A. To get a sense of Polish Jewry's reaction to the Disturbances in Palestine. B. To update the largest Jewish center in Europe on our situation in Palestine and in England. C. To activate the Zionist forces in Poland." He accomplished all this in a nonstop succession of meetings with party leaders, functionaries, emissaries, and the press. He also found time to compose a long letter to the JAE, informing them of his impressions of Poland.[13]

All seemed in order, and Ben-Gurion might have complimented himself that his watch over Weizmann had paid off, but political developments have their own hidden logic. On June 20 Foreign Secretary Anthony Eden told the British cabinet of Nuri Pasha's visit to London and of his conclusion that "the only way of bringing the present troubles to an end and indeed of preventing their assuming far more serious proportions, was for some means to be devised to put a stop to the present immigration." Nuri had suggested to Weizmann that he make "a spontaneous offer to restrict immigration on the part of the Zionist Organization, [which] would go a long way towards easing the situation [and create] a measure of good will amongst the Arabs." At the same time, word had gotten out that Weizmann had agreed to Nuri Pasha's proposal. Eden had heard so from Sir George Rendel of the Foreign Office, who had met with Nuri Pasha in London, and Wauchope had heard it from the British ambassador in Baghdad, who had heard it from the mouth of Nuri Pasha. On June 20 Wauchope cabled Ormsby-Gore, seeking verification. On June 25 Ormsby-Gore wrote Weizmann to ask that he inform him "of the facts regarding the talk with Nuri Pasha," promising "strict confidence."

According to his diary, it was June 25 when Ben-Gurion learned of Weizmann's alleged consent. In response to his question Weizmann claimed that "not he but Nuri had made the proposal (?) and that in his talk with Ormsby-Gore, he had already made clear the impossibility of stopping immigration, and not to worry." Weizmann also said that if Ormsby-Gore asked, he would say just that. Nevertheless Ben-Gurion, disquieted afresh, was on the alert. The question mark in his diary indicates that he placed no great trust in Weizmann's version.

He had to renew his campaign against the dreadful idea, and tried to enlist the aid of Dugdale, because she was so close to Weizmann. On June 26 he invited her for a talk and explained "the danger of destruction inherent in stopping immigration," using Zionist, Jewish, and British imperialist arguments. He also emphasized that "apart from the overall disaster, this can also completely undermine Chaim's position in the movement." According to him, she promised to speak privately with Weizmann and "rid him of that idea."[14] To make sure, he decided to extend his stay in London and on June 26 wrote Kaplan, "To my great regret, I must continue to watch Chaim." On June 27 Ormsby-Gore's letter reached the office and an anxious Ben-Gurion telephoned Weizmann, who again denied the charge, putting the damaging words in Nuri Pasha's mouth. Ben-Gurion asked him to write as much to Ormsby-Gore at once, and Weizmann promised to phone in his response within the hour. But Ben-Gurion had no faith in Weizmann or his denial. He wrote Sharett, "This matter is very serious. Nuri did not dream it up. I also doubt if he will continue to keep it secret. Now we know it officially. Are we not also accountable? I am not at all certain that I can continue here, or that I can continue with Chaim at all. Can't these things happen all over again? Were we not in mortal danger I would undoubtedly come to the simple and inevitable conclusion, but an internal split now might destroy our political position . . . Consult with Kaplan and Berl and wire me your opinion."

Although it was difficult for him, Ben-Gurion said, "to be in the same room" with Weizmann, he stayed on the watch in London, doing his utmost to straighten things out. On June 28 he and Namier went to Weizmann's home to work on the formulation of Weizmann's denial. Ben-Gurion later commented in his diary, "It was a very painful talk. It is hard to look at a man in his disgrace. . . . Chaim is distressed through and through, and I no less." On June 28 and 29 Weizmann signed letters drafted in conjunction with Ben-Gurion and Namier and sent them to Ormsby-Gore and the British ambassador in Baghdad. He maintained that "Nuri Pasha's statement . . . must be based on a misapprehension [and a] wrong impression."

It seems that Ben-Gurion was willing to accept this conclusion of the Weizmann-Nuri affair, but another meeting between Weizmann and Ormsby-Gore on June 30 reopened the issue. This time Ben-Gurion went along, whether to watch Weizmann or because Weizmann's invitation was meant to appease him with an introduction to the new secretary of state for the colonies is not known. If it was the latter, the gesture did not succeed. At the meeting the secretary shocked Ben-Gurion by expressing an intention to halt immigration while the Royal Commission was in Palestine, and fixing a ceiling on immigration somewhere below fifty thousand a year. He also argued that political considerations should play a role in fixing the quota, instead of making economic absorptive capacity the sole criterion. Ben-Gurion considered this a reversal of the Balfour Declaration. So acutely were his political senses functioning that he let not the slightest detail of the meeting escape his notice. When Ormsby-Gore, thinking aloud, said he would prefer a governor in Palestine to a high commissioner, Weizmann let it pass as though he were deaf, but Ben-Gurion picked up the implication that, as he told Ormsby-Gore, the government "prepares a total break with the Mandate [and was] planning definite changes for Palestine."

Ben-Gurion left this interview, he wrote Sharett shortly afterward, "broken, miserable, and depressed." At the beginning of the meeting, when a memorandum from Cust, which was lying on Ormsby-Gore's table, was discussed, Weizmann was the speaker. But when the conversation turned to immigration, he said that "he was unable to offer a reply," and Ben-Gurion had to speak in his stead. "Chaim did not respond. I did, but neither Ormsby-Gore nor Parkinson could help but notice Chaim's silence." Although his response was very strong, he told Sharett, "After the Nuri affair no answer can help." He concluded the letter with his most stinging denunciation of Weizmann yet.

> Our main struggle now and in the future is immigration. Chaim has already failed us here; he is certainly not capable of future leadership. . . . I have seen not only the disaster that awaits us now because of this man — the cause of all our political failure in previous years has become clear to me as well.

Three extant documents allow us to judge the fairness of these harsh statements. One is the notes Ben-Gurion took during the interview. The second is Weizmann's report the next day, July 1, to the advisory Political Committee in London, which was also sent as a secret circular to a small number of Zionist leaders. The third is Ormsby-Gore's summary presented at the July 4 cabinet meeting. According to this last, he had begun the interview with Cust's memorandum, which reported that Weizmann had given Cust to understand that Weizmann's "Jewish associates" in America and Zionist labor interests "were prepared to acquiesce" to cantonization.

According to Cust, Weizmann had told him that there were 2 million Jews in Poland and central Europe who could be said to be homeless. Of this number Weizmann wished to be responsible for a third, say 700,000, whom he would settle in Palestine by immigration spread over a period of twenty years. Weizmann was prepared to accept a yearly quota of 35,000 immigrants, far fewer than Ben-Gurion's demand for a million within five to ten years, or 100,000 to 200,000 per year. However, Ormsby-Gore said that during their meeting he contemplated an annual immigration of 50,000 Jews over a period of fifteen or twenty years, to be determined by the economic absorptive capacity alone. On the question of suspending immigration while the Royal Commission was in Palestine, "Ben-Gurion expressed himself as strongly opposed in principle to any suspension of immigration. . . . Dr. Weizmann was disposed to be more helpful and said that the Jews might conceivably not ask for a labour schedule in October on the as-

sumption that the Royal Commission would be at work by then."
Weizmann had held his own and brought the dreadful idea to the attention of the colonial secretary, albeit in a somewhat revised form.

The three documents seem to show that Ben-Gurion was overreact-
ing in his letter to Sharett. Nonetheless, they do provide sufficient
grounds for his warning to the Mapai Central Committee nine days
after the meeting — "This could destroy the movement. It could be
politically disastrous: as if the movement's leadership was going off in
two different directions, one for stopping immigration and pro cantonization, the other opposed to these. This will be a terrible internal catastrophe."

The day after the meeting Ben-Gurion, behaving like a master correcting a rebellious pupil, hastily tried to undo the damage Weizmann
had done. He convinced Weizmann that he had to send another letter
to Ormsby-Gore to make clear his opposition to "setting a maximum
and suspending immigration." Ben-Gurion composed the letter in Hebrew, and Professor Namier and Rabbi Stephen Wise proposed alternate versions in English. After it had undergone much revision,
Weizmann signed the letter, and it was sped by messenger that evening
to the Colonial Office.[15]

Although Ben-Gurion and Weizmann made a point of keeping up
appearances, both were seething inwardly. Weizmann undoubtedly
resented Ben-Gurion's constant guidance and watchfulness, not to
mention having to sign letters composed for him by others. Ben-Gurion
must have known his feelings, for Weizmann went so far as to ask that
Sharett replace Ben-Gurion in London. Eventually Weizmann confronted his watchdog. "Chaim spoke bitterly again. They chose a
leader but they do not allow him to lead, rather they wish to lead him,"
Ben-Gurion wrote three weeks after the meeting. Weizmann, in a letter to Arthur Lourie, the JAE's political secretary in London, predicted
that if he continued to uphold his own views he would be called "a
traitor," and therefore he would be happy to resign before then. "He is
angry with us and with himself over the immigration-ending affair,"
explained Ben-Gurion to Sharett. "But beneath it all he feels he is our
prisoner. He said in jest, but was bitterly serious . . . 'The monarch is
absolute so long as he does our will.' "[16]

Ben-Gurion, too, was reaching the end of his rope. He wrote in his
diary on July 1, "I cabled Moshe [Sharett] to come at once to Cairo, so
as to pass the matter on to him [by telephone], and I decided to take
the first flight to Palestine" and stay there a few days. On the evening
of July 2 he called Sharett to tell him he was flying in the next day. This
enabled Sharett to set up meetings with Wauchope, the JAE in Jerusalem, and the Mapai Central Committee in Tel Aviv, all in the space of

this dramatic, short, surprise trip. And so, on Friday, July 3, at 12:45 P.M., Ben-Gurion took off from Croydon and at 10:05 A.M. on July 6 landed at Lod.

Barely off the plane, Ben-Gurion gave Mapai's Political Committee a summary of the two meetings with Ormsby-Gore. His treatment of Weizmann was moderate and indirect. "The situation of our circle in London is not all that good. Among the group of politically active people there is only one man with a more-or-less Zionist concept and some healthy common sense, Namier. . . . From a political or a Zionist standpoint he is more reliable than anyone else." Weizmann was included among the less commendable company of those "given to passing fancies, passing moods, and so on." During the next three days Ben-Gurion followed his usual routine in Palestine: meetings in the JAE and deliberations on current issues; he even found time for the personal grievances of the editor of *Ha-Olam*, the Zionist organ he had moved from London to Jerusalem. Only his greater-than-usual interest in the Haganah's munitions and manpower, the jetty under construction on the Tel Aviv coast, the Yishuv's economic situation in the face of the Arab general strike, and a talk with a water specialist — to whom he said that "the possibility of irrigation from the Litani [in Lebanon] should be considered" — showed that these were not ordinary times. He did get some encouragement from Wauchope, who assisted in training and arming the Yishuv in the face of Arab terror.[17] But Ben-Gurion could have tended to all these matters just as well from London. What lay behind his lightning visit?

A partial indication of his purpose emerged on the last night of his stay, in a July 9 meeting of the Mapai Central Committee. Its thirty members sat and listened to a bruising tirade against Weizmann, the likes of which had never before been heard from Ben-Gurion and would not be again for six years, until June 1942 in New York. He seemed simply to have lost all control, revealing to this broad forum top secrets that he had thus far shared only with Sharett. "I am doing this simply to ease my emotional stress of these past two weeks," he began. "We face a declaration of a cessation of immigration. There is almost no hope of averting the dreadful edict. It will probably be announced next week. Even our hands are not entirely clean in this matter" — Weizmann's in particular.

First he recounted Weizmann's plan to voluntarily suspend immigration — which "fell upon me like an ax blow" — and his talk with Nuri Pasha and the letter of denial that followed it. Then he related the exchange between Weizmann and Cust in Chatham House and described a subsequent letter to Cust, "a negative response on the canton issue," which Weizmann had signed. Ben-Gurion added that Weizmann had

had several further talks with Cust, but "he assured me that there was
no reason to worry." When Ben-Gurion had read Cust's memorandum
at the meeting with Ormsby-Gore, he said, "I nearly fainted for the
second time. It is evident that Weizmann had discussed cantonization
with Cust. . . . Weizmann said that this was an important proposal."
Ben-Gurion continued,

> Even before the cantonization business came up it became clear — and
> this was a very difficult realization for me — that Weizmann is dangerous
> to Zionism . . . It will be a terrible internal catastrophe. I do not know if it
> is possible to put the matter right, but I could not help but bring it before
> the movement's supreme body. I am aware of all the great service Weiz-
> mann can offer the Zionist movement in the future and that he is irre-
> placeable. But it must be realized that the first terrible political blow we
> are about to receive — the stopping of immigration, inherent in which is
> a decisive shift in our political situation — is not the product of the ad-
> ministration and the government alone. . . . We tried to discuss it today
> with the high commissioner, and he replied that this is a matter for the
> secretary of state for the colonies . . . and I fear we have lost on this. If
> they declare a stopping of immigration from the arrival of the Commis-
> sion through the duration of its stay, they will not take it back. . . . I am
> not at all confident that it will be possible to prevent such mistakes in the
> future.
>   It is impossible to accompany Weizmann everywhere, because it dis-
> heartens him, and without inspiration he cannot work. Weizmann's si-
> lence now could constitute a disaster for the Zionist movement. I tried to
> prevent him from making all kinds of mistakes, as well as from feeling de-
> pressed . . . But there is no guarantee that he will not make more such
> mistakes in the future. He is not capable of weighing matters, and we are
> in a terrible situation, faced with a life-and-death struggle. There can be
> no one other than Weizmann in command, but in his fickleness and lack of
> understanding he can hand us over.

The contradictions within this speech could have had but one meaning: that the only hope for the labor movement and for Zionism was
Ben-Gurion. Sharett, alarmed, hurriedly swore those present to secrecy. This constituted a reprimand of Ben-Gurion, who reiterated,
this time apologetically, "I had to bring the matter before the Central
Committee, I could not leave here with this burden. In London I felt I
was choking."
     Generally, Sharett, Kaplan, Katznelson, and his other colleagues in
the JAE and the party agreed with Ben-Gurion on his evaluation of
Weizmann's faults and the dangers inherent in them. But Sprinzak de-
murred. As far as he was concerned, Weizmann was blameless. "We
need not seek a scapegoat. It is all too easy to supply one." But if Ben-
Gurion had expected his colleagues to revoke Weizmann's presidency

on this account he was disappointed. The Central Committee determined that closer tabs be kept on Weizmann, and that "an ambience" be created around him to steer him in the right direction. To this end they were prepared to send more people to London, despite the burden that would impose on the party and the Zionist Organization. Two nominations were made — Dov Hoz to reinforce the political team and Berl Locker, a Weizmann confidant, who could help him see his errors without "depressing" or insulting him. Sprinzak, seeing no need for such measures, again protested. "If a mistake was made by Weizmann, Weizmann is the man to set it right."

Itzhak Tabenkin drew another conclusion. In his opinion Weizmann's mistakes were of secondary importance. The decree threatening immigration, he said, was just a harbinger of worse decrees to come, and therefore the JAE had to depart from its pro-British line, of which Weizmann was the founder and spokesman par excellence. "It is not enough to turn to England's conscience . . . The masses must be agitated against England. . . . We must put a stop to the unconditional loyalty of the Jews." Ben-Gurion, who was also pro-British, had not expected this. Such a reversal seemed to him immeasurably more dangerous than Weizmann. Without losing a beat he took the floor again.

> We must now watch Weizmann . . . I am charged with this task and I will fulfill it. I have done so to the best of my ability in these past weeks and will continue to do so in the weeks to come. . . . The people's trust in him must be preserved, if I myself have none. As one among 16 million I will not elect him my representative But he must be our representative now, for if not there will be a terrible catastrophe, within and without. . . . I caution against a campaign against England . . . against alienating the political wing that shelters us.

His words suddenly became quite precise and focused. "I believe the party must send a statement, to be signed by Berl Katznelson, Joseph Sprinzak, and Berl Locker, informing Weizmann that we have discussed [the suspension of immigration] and regard it as we do. . . . This is also important to me as I want him to know that it is not merely my private opinion, but that of the movement." The Central Committee agreed, and in addition to a resolution rejecting Weizmann's request that Sharett replace Ben-Gurion in London and reinforcing the watch over Weizmann by sending Hoz and Locker, it resolved to send "a telegram to Weizmann."[18]

Possibly Ben-Gurion had already consulted his close associates and been told that he had no chance of replacing Weizmann, which would explain why he did not launch his attack until the last day of his stay. The Central Committee meeting then confirmed that they were right. If he had really come solely to relieve his stress, or to demand of his colleagues a new IOU to back him in his future struggle with Weizmann, his intentions were fulfilled. But in December 1943, when the crisis in their relationship reached its peak, he seemed either to have forgotten those reasons or to have been embarrassed to admit them. At that time he gave the Central Committee a new pretext for his 1936 trip. "My objective was primarily to make a last-ditch effort to speak with Wauchope, to convince him that [the suspension of immigration] entailed danger." According to Ben-Gurion, Wauchope was convinced and "apparently sent a long and well-grounded report against stopping immigration," which included "parts of what I had told him." Either way, on the morning of July 10 he left for London, with everything just as it had been, ready to begin all over again.

Exploiting Disaster

THE ARAB REVOLT, which had begun on April 19, 1936, with the general strike, was, in the ensuing months, marked by sporadic violence. From the start Wauchope had tried to end the strike and the terror by peaceful means, but in August, left with no other alternative, he proposed to his government that the revolt be put down by force. On September 7 the British government announced its decision to significantly strengthen its forces in Palestine under newly appointed General Officer Commanding, Lieutenant General John G. Dill. The first military detachment arrived on September 22 and martial law was declared on September 30. At the initiative of the British Foreign Office, the "Arab kings" — the rulers of Saudi Arabia and Iraq, the emir of Transjordan, and the imam of Yemen — appealed for an end to the strike. On October 10 the Arab Higher Committee published the appeal, adding a plea of its own.[1] Two days later the Disturbances of 1936, the first stage of the Arab revolt, came to a close.

Concurrently, with no mention of suspending immigration, the government appointed the Royal Commission, whose members had been announced on July 20: the Right Honourable Earl Peel, chairman, who had served as a minister in several governments; Sir Horace Rumbold, a former ambassador; Sir Egbert Hammond, an expert on colonial affairs; Sir William Carter, former chief justice in Uganda and Tanganyika; Sir Harold Morris, a Jewish Zionist and former Liberal M.P.; and Reginald Coupland, a professor of colonial history at Oxford. This was by far the most important, highest ranking commission yet sent by the British to Palestine. Its mission was not only "to ascertain the underlying causes" of the Disturbances but to inquire into the manner in which the Mandate for Palestine is being implemented in relation to our obligations as Mandatory towards the Arabs and the Jews respectively; and to ascertain whether, upon a proper construction of the terms of the Mandate, either the Arabs or the Jews have any legitimate grievances upon account of the way in which the Mandate has been, or is being implemented; and if the Commission is satisfied that any such grievances are well founded, to make recommendations for their removal and for the prevention of their recurrence.[2]

On July 22 Ormsby-Gore had told Parliament that there could be no change in policy until the Royal Commission's report was issued. The Peel Commission arrived in Palestine on November 11 and held its opening meeting the next day.

The seven months between the outbreak of the Disturbances and the start of the commission's work were among the most important in Ben-Gurion's political career. At this time he outlined the guidelines for what he termed "launching a Jewish state policy" that provided him with both short-term positions and a strategy that culminated, twelve years later, with the establishment of Israel. In essence, his approach rested on turning to advantage two related misfortunes, that of Polish and German Jewry and that of the Jews of Palestine. Had Ben-Gurion not regarded immigration to Palestine as the Jews' sole salvation it might be said that he sought to exploit a Jewish catastrophe for Zionist advantage.

This approach to the advancement of Zionism had far-reaching consequences. The first involved Ben-Gurion's attitude toward the Arabs, which underwent a sharp change. On April 17, 1936, a year and a half after his last meeting with an Arab leader, Ben-Gurion had met with George Antonius,[3] a Christian Arab whom he described as the mufti's "chief aide," who was writing a history of the Arab nationalist movement.[*] They met a second time three days after the outbreak of the Disturbances and a third on April 29, four days after the Arab Higher Committee had been established, when the Disturbances and the strike were at their peak. On the face of it this seemed to be a further effort on Ben-Gurion's part to solve the Arab-Jewish problem. Ben-Gurion again brandished his Federal Palestine plan, while Antonius responded with a counterproposal for a "United Syria" that provided for a Jewish "Establishment," but otherwise confined its powers to a specified area, its boundaries to be negotiated. According to Ben-Gurion, he and Antonius were close to an agreement, but although they spoke for a total of eleven and a half hours they never touched on the strike or the terror

---

[*] His book *The Arab Awakening* was published in 1938.

that had all Palestine up in arms.⁴ These talks were no more than an academic exercise, for just as the Arabs were unwilling to make any concessions, Ben-Gurion remained true to a maxim he had first laid down in 1928 — "I am not willing to give up even one percent of Zionism for the sake of 'peace.' " In March 1936 he had told Judah-Leib Magnes, "The difference between you and me is that you are ready to sacrifice immigration for peace, while I am not, though peace is dear to me. And even if I were prepared to make a concession, the Jews of Poland and Germany would not be, because they have no other choice. For them immigration comes before peace."⁵

"Immigration before peace" was much more than a thumbnail formulation of Zionist policy, for given the circumstances it could mean belligerence. In June, in a letter to the JAE, Ben-Gurion said that in so many words: "Peace for us is a means, not an end. The end is the fulfillment of Zionism, complete and total fulfillment of Zionism in its maximum scope" — unlimited immigration and settlement throughout Palestine. Ben-Gurion's thinking had undergone a profound change which, if accepted — and accepted it was — would revolutionize the concept of Zionism as well. Because of the need to save Polish and German Jews by bringing them to Palestine, socialist Zionism, and Zionism as a whole, could no longer be a movement whose aim was absolute justice, with peace as an essential condition, but could strive only for relative justice, for which peace was merely a means. This conceptual transition from absolute to relative allowed Ben-Gurion to coin his pregnant formula. From then on rescue and immigration played an even greater role both in justifying the Zionist solution to the Jewish problem and in fortifying the Yishuv. At the same time, concern for absolute justice wavered. Whereas Ben-Gurion had previously maintained that the rights of both nations were equally important, rights would become functions of tragedies: the greater the tragedy, the greater the rights it conferred on its victims. Few except the Arabs doubted that the Jewish tragedy was the greater.

Arab opposition to immigration remained absolute, despite the Jewish calamity. Even before the Disturbances Ben-Gurion had foreseen that this would be so, and on April 16 had informed the Mapai Central Committee that "there is no chance for an understanding with the Arabs." In May he told the JAE that such an understanding was impossible, owing to a fundamental conflict. "We and they want the same thing. We both want Palestine." Given that he had reached this conclusion before the outbreak of the Disturbances, he certainly could not have expected his talks with Antonius to lead to peace, but they had other purposes. For one thing, Ben-Gurion maintained that, whatever the Zionist policy, the Arabs would always be the Jews' neighbors in

Palestine. In November 1935 he had told Menahem Ussishkin, "We should not, and cannot, drive the Arabs out by force." He regarded dialogue as essential, and Sharett defended the talks with Antonius to Wauchope in the same vein. "The attempt at an intellectual agreement is also of value to us."

Second, the talks with Antonius were aimed at the British public. The killing of sixteen Jews in Jaffa on April 19 and 20 had turned it, Ben-Gurion thought, against the Arabs. "After that wild murder, English public opinion will certainly not hand over legislative rule to this Arab majority," he wrote then. The image of the Jews as patient seekers of understanding and dialogue thwarted by an Arab boycott could only work to Zionist advantage. This "is a weapon in our hands," he told his party, one not to relinquish.

Ben-Gurion did, however, envisage peace of a kind with the Arabs. It would be attained, he explained to the JAE, "only when they despair of foiling a Jewish Palestine." He based his strategy on getting assistance from the British. After proposing in March to demand of Britain "a change [in its policy] with a view to turn Palestine into a Jewish state in the near future," on April 16 he told the Central Committee, "There is no chance for an understanding with the Arabs unless we first reach an understanding with the English that enables us to become the preponderant force in Palestine."

He told the party, "The Arab question has only two solutions. One is an agreement between us and the Arabs, and the Arabs don't want one. The other is reliance on England. There is nothing in between." How would such reliance lead to peace between Jews and Arabs? Here Ben-Gurion consolidated the political formula that would serve him until the end of his career: only a strong Jewish force in Palestine, one which the Arabs knew could not be beaten, would make them see that an agreement and peace were better than strife and war. Such a force could be established only with British consent and assistance. "Perhaps in another ten years," he said, "the Arab factor will be the most important, but for now, the British factor is paramount. . . . The key to the political strengthening of the Yishuv is to be found in British policy." And in January 1937 he told the Mapai council, "Attaining English assistance at this time takes priority over our negotiations with the Arabs."

Hence Britain was asked, in the name of peace, to assist in the Yishuv's development into a strong Jewish state, although not in so many words. "What can drive the Arabs to a mutual understanding with us?" he asked the Central Committee in April. "*Facts.* . . . Only after we manage to establish a *great Jewish fact* in this country . . . a Jewish force clearly immovable, only then will the precondition for discussion with the Arabs be met."

How did he figure on bringing about such a change in British policy? Ben-Gurion believed, as did Weizmann, that a strong Jewish state in Palestine would benefit Britain and that Britain would recognize this. But he did not base his strategy solely on imperial arguments. The plight of European Jewry, for which British public opinion displayed considerable sensitivity, was to be his mainstay. "I view the need to get a million Jews out of Germany and Poland as *the lever* for our political action."[7]

But meanwhile the Arabs were attacking Jews, and Ben-Gurion concentrated on present dangers without for a moment losing sight of his vision for the future. What distinguished 1936 from 1929 was that he no longer feared for the Yishuv's very existence; he felt it was strong enough to defend itself. All the same, he knew that the Yishuv needed British military assistance not only to prevent bloodshed but because without it Jews might shirk from immigrating and a strong Jewish state could never develop. "Our dependence on British gunboats puts us in a morally difficult position," he told the Central Committee, "but that is the situation, and we must see to it that those boats protect us and, above all, allow many more Jews to reach Palestine."[8]

This represented a drastic ideological change. Only seven years earlier, in reference to the Disturbances of 1929, he had warned, "It is impossible to stay long in Palestine, which needs building up, by relying only on bayonets, and foreign bayonets at that." Now, under the shadow of Jewish adversity in Poland and Germany, and faced with the danger that Zionism might be struck from the Jewish stage, as he phrased it, if it did not hurry to their rescue, he completely revamped his position. In a situation in which "Jews are drowning in a sea of blood, and their only salvation is Palestine," he told the Political Committee in January, there was moral justification for reliance on British bayonets and gunboats. So much for the moral aspect. On the practical side, did he believe it was possible to build up Palestine under cover of bayonets? The British Empire would not last forever, he had told the Central Committee in April, but "we are not concerned with 'forever.' We are concerned with the next twenty years. What happens during this time will be the decisive political factor" in the fate of Zionism, Palestine, and the Jewish people.[9]

Ben-Gurion now denied not only the liberal principles on which Zionism in general was founded but also those of labor Zionism, which regarded British imperialism as warmongering and largely accountable for world injustice and deprivation.

Even though he based his policy on the British, however, Ben-Gurion, more than any of his colleagues in the party and the JAE, understood the Arabs' feelings and was ready to acknowledge their rights. He took satisfaction in the fact that his meetings with Abd al-Hadi, Alami, Arslan, Antonius, and others had taught him to empathize with the Arab point of view. He pointed out this advantage more than once to his JAE and Mapai colleagues. His "Arab eyes" enabled him to feel "the Arabs' fear" of a Jewish buildup and to understand that this fear lay at the root of the Disturbances. "It really is difficult," he wrote the Jewish Agency in June, "for someone who has never talked with the Arabs to imagine the magnitude of their fear."[10]

Furthermore, he acknowledged the existence of an Arab national movement, and in November 1936 accounted for its origins in a letter to Ussishkin. "We ourselves, by our very presence and progress here, have nurtured the Arab nationalist movement." Such a movement would have arisen anyway, but Zionism had had a catalytic effect. In the same letter he presaged the conflict's future. "In these Disturbances we have already seen a mighty manifestation of a pan-Arab movement and military alignment . . . of the Arabs of neighboring countries for the Palestinian Arabs' war against the Jews."

Reviewing all of his statements at the time, one can see that the signs of recognition of a Palestinian people were clear. In 1930 Ben-Gurion had declared, "We wholeheartedly support the right of self-determination for all peoples . . . and that undeniably includes the Arab people in Palestine." He reiterated this view in February 1937 before the Histadrut council.

> The right which the Arabs in Palestine have is theirs as inhabitants of the country . . . because they live here, and not because they are Arabs . . . Arabs who do not live here have no rights in Palestine. . . . The Arab inhabitants of Palestine should enjoy all civic and political rights, not only as individuals, but as a national group, just like the Jews.

This acknowledgement of Arab rights necessarily determined his attitude toward the Disturbances. By early May 1936, a mere two weeks after they had broken out, Ben-Gurion reasoned at a JAE meeting that war was the Arabs' only alternative, since they regarded Zionism and immigration as a threat leading to their dispossession from the land of their fathers and their utter destruction. "The cause of the Arabs' war today is primarily their fear of Jewish growth in Palestine, in numbers and in strength that can bring about Jewish rule. And then they will face destruction."

Immediately afterward, at a Political Committee meeting, he had defended Wauchope against the criticism that he had not fully utilized

the troops at his disposal to suppress the Disturbances. "I cannot say
that the government has this military option. . . . It is not so easy to use
force against a people's movement." In September he said to the
Mapai Central Committee, "This people is fighting, fighting dispossession from its homeland . . . which others wish to turn into the homeland of the Jewish people. And the Arab fights in such a way that he
cannot be ignored. He strikes, he gets killed, he makes great sacrifices."
In February 1937 he said this publicly, to the Histadrut council, defining the Disturbances as war against the Jews and rebellion against
Mandatory rule, an interpretation he wished the entire labor movement would accept. "Let us not delude ourselves. . . . No government
in the world can prevent individual terror. . . . When people fight for
their land it is no easy task to stop them."[11] Ironically, Ben-Gurion repeated nearly word for word Moshe Olgin's statements in New York
twenty years before, which had so revolted him.

Consequently he found himself at odds with his Mapai colleagues,
who took him to task in both party forums and the press, in a controversy that lasted from May 1936 to February 1937. Berl Katznelson rejected the idea of the Arabs' fear and the existence of an Arab national
movement, did not see Arab terror as "war" or "rebellion," and therefore rejected Ben-Gurion's view that peace with the Arabs would never
be achieved as long as the Yishuv was not strong enough and therefore
necessitated "getting Britain on our side." Tabenkin, Beilinson, and
others agreed with Katznelson.

His colleagues adhered to the doctrine of Achdut ha-Avodah, which
had gained currency in the 1920s. Ben-Gurion, who more than anyone
else had been the principal author, became a victim in the present
to his power of persuasion in the past. The controversy was based on
differing evaluations of the Arab national movement. Katznelson still
regarded Arab violence as the work of "instigators" — clerics and effendis — and the result of the perfidy of British administrators. Therefore he denied the existence of an Arab national movement that was
the standard-bearer for the rights of Palestine's Arabs. "Can this be described as nationalism? Let's not believe it for a moment!" To his mind,
the hostility and terror stemmed from other sources entirely — the
malaise of the educated sons of the effendis, Arab savagery, and Muslim xenophobia. "The factor . . . of importance, which characterizes
the Arab movement in the East, is the desert origin, this deep
link with the desert which has not yet been severed." This, not "the
Arabs' fear," constituted "the true content" of the Arab movement.
Reprovingly, almost raising his voice, he asked, "Where is the *social
and progressive content* we saw in the liberation movements of Poland
and of the Czechs, in the protracted struggle against European rule in

India, and among all those who seek to liberate their culture? Not a trace." Katznelson rejected Ben-Gurion's premise that the Arabs were fighting against dispossession from the land of their fathers, as well as Ben-Gurion's view of Sheik Izz al-Din al-Qassām as an "Arab Trumpeldor." "In all these terrorist manifestations," wrote Katznelson, "one might find evidence of personal dedication to religious fanaticism and xenophobia, but we cannot discern anything else."[12]

By 1929 Ben-Gurion had found that a movement's political capacity is determined and measured by its ability to mobilize the masses. This was the ground on which he recognized the Arab national movement; Katznelson, on the other hand, judged a movement according to its "content." The Arab movement's "corrupt leadership," said Katznelson, disqualified it as a national movement. "Such is the Arab movement, and I say all the groping and sifting in the world is unlikely to change our attitude to its character." Tabenkin, Beilinson, and Kaplan also denied that the Disturbances constituted "war" and "rebellion." As far as they were concerned, these were nothing more than dastardly acts of murder, robbery, looting, and destruction, for which the sole accountability rested on the government. Naturally enough, then, they could not accept the British factor as the most vital of Zionism's interests. "I think this idea is far-fetched," said Tabenkin.

Ben-Gurion responded, "There are comrades among us who see only one enemy, the government. In their opinion, there is no uprising or revolt by the Arabs . . . I have a hard time understanding the astonishing blindness of people like Beilinson, Tabenkin, Kaplan, and others." He could not fathom, he said, their denial of such an obvious fact. In August 1936 he sent the party Central Committee a special letter on this matter. "I cannot ignore the harsh fact that there is indeed an Arab uprising in Palestine. . . . The Arabs fight with arms and strikes, terror and sabotage, mayhem and destruction of property. . . . What more must they do to make their acts merit the name of rebellion and uprising?" But the more he pounded away at his colleagues the more stubbornly and infuriatingly they held to their views. "Were I an Arab," he wrote Sharett in June 1937, "an Arab politically, nationally minded . . . I would rebel even more vigorously, bitterly, and desperately against the immigration that will one day turn Palestine and all its Arab residents over to Jewish rule."[13]

If Ben-Gurion was astonished by his colleagues' blindness, were they not also entitled to an equal measure of astonishment at Ben-Gurion's vision? And might they not take him for an opportunist? This possibility weighed heavily on Ben-Gurion, and he felt the need to demonstrate his ideological integrity. At the height of the controversy he confided to his diary, as if for his own eyes only,

In my opinion, there is no greater danger to political (and not only political) thought than inertia, devotion to an existing structure of outmoded thought. The world is never static, and certainly history is not. Powers and factors and constellations renew themselves from time to time, obliterating or fundamentally altering that which existed before. *Other* ways must be sought to attain the objective.

Ben-Gurion then went to great lengths to distance himself from outmoded thought. In June 1936 he had taken the rare step of confessing to an error, telling Mapai that his approach to the Arab question in the early years of Achdut ha-Avodah had been mistaken. To the Histadrut council in February 1937 he again admitted "a mistake I made . . . thirteen years ago."[14] If he did this hoping his associates would follow suit, he was disappointed. The disagreement deepened; at its center was the unspoken question of whether a Palestinian people truly existed. By remaining "blind," his colleagues were spared major ideological contradictions and could continue to regard socialist Zionism as a wholly just doctrine, for if there was no Arab national movement there could not be a Palestinian people threatened by dispossession.

Ben-Gurion, who could no longer claim, as he had previously, that the Arabs of Palestine were but a "fragment" of the great Arab nation and that therefore there was no conflict of interest between them and Zionism, found himself upholding a flawed doctrine. However, because he could not admit publicly that Zionism was not a movement of absolute justice, he stopped short of declaring that the Arabs of Palestine were a "Palestinian people." Only one argument could justify his avoiding this inescapable corollary of his new view: that Palestine was dearer to the Jews than to the Arabs because it was their only homeland. "And therefore the right of the Jews and the Jewish people to Palestine is not the same as the right of the Arabs and the Arab people." Moreover, the Arabs of Palestine had not yet declared themselves a "Palestinian nation," and Ben-Gurion, at the forefront of Zionism, was certainly not the man to do so for them.

All too aware of the contradiction implicit in his doctrine, Ben-Gurion sought to resolve it in his own inimitable way. His efforts would be directed at simultaneously implementing Zionism "in its maximum scope" and striving for good relations with the Arabs. He reconciled these two goals by means of one of his double formulas: the Jews would aspire to peace with the Arabs as though the Arabs were not fighting Zionism, at the same time working for the full realization of Zionism as though they did not aspire to peace. He sought to mitigate, if not resolve, the contradiction. For one thing, England would not assist a non–peace-seeking movement, certainly not one which claimed, as did Jabotinsky, that Zionism would be realized only by force of arms. The double formula was evident in a letter to the JAE in which Ben-Gurion spelled out the two necessary qualifications for the man who led the negotiations with the Arabs on Zionism's behalf:

A. He must uphold the sine qua non principles of Zionism, view maximalist Zionism as the absolute minimum for the Jewish people, and regard the implementation of Zionism as a question of life or death for them.
B. He must empathize with the Arab people, respect its national aspirations, and be capable of seeing matters through Arab eyes.

No great imagination was called for to identify the subject of this portrait.

At the Mapai council in January 1937 Ben-Gurion presented the policy dictated by the double formula. On the one hand, he maintained that the chance for agreement was very thin, rejecting vehemently the argument that it did not exist at all. On the other, he portrayed such agreement as vital to the achievement of the principal political goal, to "obtain England's support."[15]

But all this was more wishful thinking than a practical blueprint for political action. Ben-Gurion could debate and ponder how to obtain England's support and create *"a great Jewish fact,"* speak and write of these aims, and prepare himself and others for the future, but little could be done about them at the time. The Disturbances demanded attention and response, since the terror and general strike were intended as a protest against the Mandate and to destroy the National Home for which the Mandate was created in the first place.

For Ben-Gurion this was a heaven-sent opportunity "to begin a Jewish state policy." In this case it meant consolidating the Yishuv into a self-sustaining, impregnable island capable of self-defense and development in the Arab sea surrounding it. He identified three areas in which this work should begin: separating the economies, reinforcing Jewish defenses, and laying the groundwork for the government of the state-to-be.

Ben-Gurion had begun to apply himself to the first area at a time when the Disturbances seemed to pose a ruinous threat to the economy of the Yishuv. The strike and resultant transportation breakdown halted the supply of Arab farm produce before the Jews were capable of supplying their own. Many Jews found themselves without vegetables, meat, and dairy products. The strike and fear of vengeance kept Arab workers away from the Jewish sector, so that the industries that employed them were short of labor. The Jewish citrus industry was hardest hit, with ripe fruit left to rot on the trees. Many factories were stranded without raw materials, either because the strike had shut

down the ports at Haifa and Jaffa or because their supplies — most
building material, for instance — came from the Arab sector. The immediate result of the Disturbances, apart from the death toll, was
forced segregation of the two sectors of the population. The smaller
and weaker one, the Jews, was naturally hurt more. The economic aspect of this division was hardly encouraging.

Whereas most feared that the Yishuv would crack beneath the
strain, Ben-Gurion reacted as if he had discovered a treasure, and he
responded with a burst of imagination and energy. He worked first to
fortify the Yishuv as a separate economic unit, to make the temporary
segregation permanent. This tactic was consistent with his political
thinking from his earliest days in Palestine, when he had built the first
trade unions on this principle in 1906, and he had maintained it
throughout his years as secretary general of the Histadrut. His wars for
"Hebrew labor" were explicitly intended to create two clearly demar-
cated national economic divisions. It is therefore not surprising that he
took satisfaction in the Arab workers' absence from the Jewish sector.
"The first and principal lesson of these disturbances," he had told the
plenary national council only three weeks after the outbreak, "is that
we must free ourselves from all economic dependence on the Arabs."
Looking toward the establishment of the state, he explained, "This is
not merely a question of Jewish labor in the narrowest sense." He regarded economic segregation as "the fundamental issue of our existence and national revival," since a Jewish state could survive only
with a Jewish economy. "There will be a Jewish economy in Palestine
only if we build it with our own hands."

The need to reinforce Jewish defenses was more easily justified in
light of the bloody Arab attacks on Jewish settlements. The government expanded the Jewish supernumerary force under its control and
armed Jewish settlements. The strengthening of these legal sections of
what would become the Jewish state military naturally also increased
the strength of the illegal arm, the Haganah.

The Arab strike also triggered the development of one of its more
important state services, a Jewish port. The Arab dockworkers' strike
not only cut off the Yishuv's supply of iron and pipe for construction
and raw materials for industry, but it also halted the export trade. "It is
unthinkable that we in Palestine be in a position where those who hate
us can starve us, close off sea routes to us, and keep gravel and stone for
construction from us," said Ben-Gurion to the plenary National Council, and he called for the construction of a port in Tel Aviv. To him
nothing better symbolized the start of independence. "Economic freedom means a Jewish port, government institutions in Jewish population centers, Jewish agricultural produce for the Yishuv, and Jewish

raw materials, insofar as they exist in Palestine, for industry. If we want 100 percent Hebrew redemption, then we must have a 100 percent Hebrew farm and a 100 percent Hebrew port."

But here he encountered obstacles, the least of which were the lack of a natural harbor and of government consent to the construction of another port. These were far easier to overcome than hesitation and the opposition of economic interests in the Yishuv. In the wake of the Disturbances, many were apprehensive that when the strike was over there would be reprisals by the Jaffa port workers, who would suffer from the competition and lose clients. The Arab dockworkers and operators from Haifa would join their Jaffa brothers in a gesture of national solidarity and, for instance, refuse to load export shipments of Jewish-grown citrus fruit. Therefore Palestine's two large natural ports would be closed to the Jewish citrus growers, and it was doubtful that Tel Aviv's "port" — really just a small jetty at the beginning — could handle the traffic. If citrus exports were hampered, the Yishuv's economy would totter.

By virtue of the force of his vision, efforts at persuasion the like of which even he had never undertaken, and pressure, pure and simple, Ben-Gurion overcame the opposition. A jetty was built off the Tel Aviv shore and on May 16, 1936, lighters had begun to load and unload cargo from ships anchored in the open sea. This "inroad" into the sea, Ben-Gurion said, fired his imagination and he envisaged a great "conquest" of the ocean. Before returning to London he had visited the Tel Aviv port on July 10, 1936, reporting to his diary, "I visited the jetty. . . . The tanned young Jewish dockworkers anxiously asked if we would return them to Jaffa. One Jew asked me in Yiddish if there would be a port here. I said not only a port, but a kingdom [a Jewish state]."

A day later he concluded,

> The sheer sight of the jetty . . . is enough to encourage and dispel any pessimism and apprehensions. . . . Nothing better symbolizes our stand and our unique prowess in Palestine than this conquest in a time of Disturbances (or should I say war?). Had there been no loss of life, for which there is no recompense, all the economic destruction would have been worth it, and we would have had to award the rioters a prize for their share in this wonderful creation.[16]

Ben-Gurion had also succeeded in using the Disturbances to win over British public opinion and gain the sympathy of the British army in Palestine. From the very first day of the violence, he understood that the Arabs' indiscriminate killing could be turned to Zionist advantage. In his diary, he recorded that the mob killing in Jaffa represented "a great political setback for Arab policy," for, whether premeditated or spontaneous, it "besmirches the Arabs in the eyes of British and world public opinion." He set about at once to enlarge on this advantage. The funeral in Tel Aviv of one of the Jewish victims, at which mourners injured Arab passersby, provided him with a national audience on whom to impress his method of extracting gain from disaster, which he soon termed "the weapon of self-restraint" — avoidance of Jewish reprisal for Arab attacks. The Jews would limit themselves to self-defense and, as much as possible, to punishing the terrorists; under no circumstance would they harm innocents.

At a Jerusalem gathering on April 19 he had stated, "What happened in Tel Aviv ... beating up shoe-shine boys, breaking into a closed Arab shop, is a violation of that which is holy." He went on to note the bases of his future policy of response: moral and political considerations, the principle of nonvengeance, and avoidance of provocation. "I understand and empathize with all the bitterness voiced here ... but owing to the very gravity of the situation we must maintain clarity of thought as well as the moral and political principles which guide Zionism and the Yishuv. . . . If attacked we must not exceed the bounds of self-defense. . . . We must monitor ourselves so that we do not become the cause of a flare-up." He made it clear that the point of "self-restraint" was to avoid provocation and escalation. "I fear that those who today murdered our people in an ambush not only plotted to murder some Jews, but intended to provoke us, to push us into acting as they have, and turning the country red with blood. The Arabs stand to gain from such a development. They want the country to be in a state of perpetual pogrom." This early reaction, quick and right on the mark, presaged the position he took when terror became widespread.

Four weeks later, on May 15, Ben-Gurion had appealed to the JAE to guide the Yishuv in general and the Haganah in particular in keeping to this line of response, which formulated an official and obligatory stance. "We must do all that is necessary so that the public will know to restrain itself in the future as well and not exceed the boundaries of self-restraint, else we suffer a catastrophe." At the same meeting he coined an axiom of sorts. "Any additional bloodshed [caused by Jews] will only bring the Arabs political benefit and hurt us."[17]

The support of his JAE colleagues was not enough, and it was no easy task to convince the public and his own party to stop at self-defense when spilled blood cried for vengeance. Ben-Gurion had to call on his best powers of persuasion. He explained, with cool logic, that the Arabs could achieve their goals "only through revolt and rebellion," while for the Jews, the opposite was true. Revolt and terror would not encourage Britain "to assist in bringing the Jewish people to

Palestine and turning it into a Jewish country." Jewish counterterror would only feed the flames that would destroy the Zionist enterprise. "What we wish to achieve requires the help of the British; what the Arabs wish to achieve requires war on Great Britain." The conclusion: different ends dictate different means. "Our instruments of war differ," he said at a public meeting in Tel Aviv, describing self-restraint alongside striving for dialogue and negotiations with the Arabs as "front-line weaponry."

But no less important to Ben-Gurion than the political benefits was the image of the Yishuv's moral integrity, which soon came to be described by the phrase "purity of arms." In a letter to Wauchope, which he cowrote with Sharett, Ben-Gurion emphasized that it was not from weakness or fear that the Jews refrained from reprisals, but "solely out of a deep moral persuasion." At a plenary session of the National Council he said that a double standard was at work. "We are not Arabs, and others measure us by a different standard, which doesn't allow so much as a hairsbreadth of deviation. . . . Our strength is in defense . . . and this strength will give us a political victory if England and the world know that we are defending ourselves rather than attacking."

If this line met with resistance, the name he gave it — self-restraint — drew such violent criticism that Ben-Gurion was afraid the policy itself would be rejected. In 1938, when Arab terror was renewed with redoubled force and the controversy reached its peak, he conceded to the Haganah, the Yishuv, and the entire Zionist movement that self-restraint was a "stupid name" and instead proposed self-defense, for "we only defend ourselves and do not take revenge." But this had no effect, and in fact the label self-restraint stuck. His opponents' claim that the Arabs would interpret the policy as weakness and be encouraged to escalate the terror fell on receptive ears, as did their argument that a generation of valiant fighters could not be brought up on self-restraint or self-defense. Even those who accepted the moral imperative of not harming innocents feared that Britain would yield to the more aggressive side in the conflict and felt that the Haganah should emulate the Arabs.

Nevertheless, even though the controversy never abated for a minute, the call for reprisal and vengeance subsided. Ultimately the Yishuv and the Zionist movement as a whole, except for the Revisionists and their Irgun Zvai Leummi (IZL), created in April 1937, did practice self-restraint. In April 1939 Ben-Gurion concluded, "During these past three years . . . except for a very small and irresponsible segment [of the Yishuv], we did not spill the blood of innocent Arabs, although in a psychological sense it might have been justified." He harshly condemned the Revisionist Party, which was responsible for what Jewish counterterror there was, in 1938 going so far as to call it a Nazi party.[18]

His personal involvement in bringing self-restraint to bear gives a clearer picture of the efforts Ben-Gurion made along these lines. The first wave of terror diminished somewhat, then was revived on May 16 when Arabs fired into a crowd of Jews leaving Jerusalem's Edison cinema, killing three. One of the Haganah commanders in town hurried to Ben-Gurion's office to report the incident and asked permission to retaliate. According to Ben-Gurion, the news made his blood boil, but he nevertheless ordered the commander "not to touch innocent Arabs." The commander dutifully acknowledged the order and left, only to return a short time later. "My men won't obey me," he told Ben-Gurion and the JAE members with him. "Call them here and tell them yourself." The seconds in command were summoned and Ben-Gurion warned them not to "act hastily in defiance of discipline." They, too, accepted the order uneasily, left, then returned. Their subordinates, they said, refused to toe this line and needed to hear it from Ben-Gurion's mouth. A third talk was held, with the commander, his deputies, and the noncoms. Still the Haganah men demanded vengeance. Ben-Gurion at last threatened to resign if they took reprisals against innocent Arabs. Only then did they deign to obey. But the next day, at the victims' funeral, Sharett and Kaplan, who participated, were heckled.

Ben-Gurion later said that during his talk with the Haganah he had been close to breaking the rule that in politics it is "forbidden to act on momentary impulses, no matter how strong and just at the time. . . . Much political judgment was necessary," he added, "as well as no small measure of cruelty to ourselves and the comrades, since we felt just as they did." He must have struggled to quell his own raging desire for revenge against Arab terror, which did not discriminate between the armed and the defenseless. Returning to London aboard the *Marco Polo* from his urgent visit in July 1936, he had written in his diary,

> I have never felt hatred for Arabs, and their pranks have never stirred the desire for revenge in me. But I would welcome the destruction of Jaffa, port and city. Let it come; it would be for the better. This city, which grew fat from Jewish immigration and settlement, deserves to be destroyed for having waved an ax at those who built it and made it prosper. If Jaffa went to hell, I would not count myself among the mourners.

After Palestine had been calm for a while, he let it be known how strong his feelings had been, explaining that he had drawn the strength for self-restraint from his belief that "our crucial, decisive battle is not with the Arabs, but rather with the English," that "we must behave in this manner so as to attain the trust and assistance of the [British] army for the establishment of an armed Jewish force in Palestine, [and that] if a civil war breaks out in Palestine between Jews and Arabs *on our account,* the first thing to go will be Jewish immigration."

In July 1938 he told Mapai's Central Committee, "In the national war which the Arabs declared against us . . . we followed a certain line, one of self-defense, and this line stood us in good stead. We could not prevent casualties . . . but we prevented a political disaster. We prevented an undermining of our position."[19] The "weapon of self-restraint" proved effective against all the targets it was designed for: it helped blunt the conflict and left the door open for negotiations with the Arabs; it won the support of British public opinion; and it enabled the British to strengthen the Jewish security forces under their supervision and to arm Jewish settlements from government armories. The Yishuv emerged from the Arab revolt strengthened militarily, with a firm foundation created for the future Jewish army.

Ben-Gurion had returned to London on the evening of July 14, 1936. How he explained his lightning visit to Palestine to Weizmann is not known. To others he offered various explanations — apprehension of a panicky response in Palestine to the suspension of immigration, the gravity of the situation in general, and his wish "to give a little push to negotiations with the Arabs." He certainly could not share with them the secret he had divulged to Mapai's Central Committee — his distress and fears regarding Weizmann. In any event, if Weizmann's sources could not tell him exactly why Ben-Gurion had gone off to Palestine, he probably guessed the reason. When they met on the sixteenth Weizmann brandished the tried and true Zionist weapon, threatening to resign. Not explicitly, of course. As one pouring out his bitterness to his closest friend, Weizmann told Ben-Gurion that he was weary — "feeling the load of sixty-two years" — and unable to get any work done. He had no time for his beloved Hebrew University in Jerusalem, of which he was a founder; his office and his political work took all his time and energy and he had to neglect his chemical research. Weizmann "will not take on this weighty burden" again at the next (1937) Congress, Ben-Gurion concluded. Was Weizmann simply outflanking Ben-Gurion, who had gone to Palestine to get around him, by apparently offering on a silver platter what Ben-Gurion's party had refused him, in the full knowledge that the resignation would never be accepted? If so he got his wish, for after their meeting Ben-Gurion noted in his diary, "I told him that after the Disturbances were over, we would make things as easy as possible for him, but that the movement would not let him go." Weizmann had maneuvered Ben-Gurion into asking him to remain as president, albeit in the movement's name.

The talk cleared the air, even creating a camaraderie of sorts between them. Three days later they were lunching together at the Carlton Grill with Blanche Dugdale, discussing the possibility of jointly presenting their resignations to the Congress after failing — as they believed they would — to prevent a suspension of immigration, swearing never to acquiesce to it. Weizmann was a regular at this celebrated meeting place of British politicians, and thanks to him Ben-Gurion was introduced to the delicacies and manners of high society. To a certain extent, although he could never equal Weizmann, he, too, adopted the Carlton Grill as his luncheon meeting place. His once-flat stomach, which had so befit the head of the Histadrut, began to go to pot.

This domestic harmony also brought Ben-Gurion closer to Doris May, Weizmann's secretary. He had first met her in the summer of 1924, when she was working for Leonard Stein, an outstanding barrister and Weizmann's right-hand man until 1929. Ben-Gurion had been amazed that Zionism's two helmsmen were able to get anything done amid the rampant disorder in the Executive office — "One hand doesn't know what the other is doing." In all the "chaos" he beheld but one ray of light — the secretary, whose name he did not yet know. The gentle May kept things in order and was the only one, in the absence of Weizmann and Stein, who could say what was happening in the Executive. In his report to the HEC Ben-Gurion had commented, "A young Englishwoman. She's very nice, but doesn't quite comprehend all the strange things that pass through her hands." If this was true, it was only for a short time. She soon came to "comprehend" very well, and Weizmann commandeered her as his secretary. Miss May, as she was addressed by one and all, remained loyal to Weizmann throughout his five years out of office. When Ben-Gurion had been elected to the JAE in 1933, he began working with her, dictating to her in English. In fact, by that time she was not only going over the English Zionist correspondence, she also had a hand in its composition.

May was, second to Dugdale, the most important Gentile in the Zionist office. The two had little else in common, including friendship. They did not have equal status in the JAE or, for that matter, in society. May was of the middle class, although she had studied at Oxford and was proficient in French, Greek, and Latin, whereas Dugdale was strictly of the aristocracy, quite comfortable in the company of England's top politicians, some of whom were her relatives and personal friends. May, a devout High Church Anglican, was tall, blue-eyed, with light skin and auburn hair, and attractive in clothes she sewed for herself. "She looks and acts every bit the Englishwoman."

But the principal difference between the two was in their attitude toward the Zionist leaders. Dugdale held Weizmann alone in high esteem, bordering on worship. At the 1946 Congress, when Ben-Gurion had Weizmann dismissed from the presidency once and for all, she looked with dismay, even despair, at the Zionist leaders, for she thought that not a man among them could fill Weizmann's shoes and lead the arduous way to a state. Blind to Ben-Gurion's emerging greatness, she noted in her diary, "It is an age of pygmies." By contrast, May's respect for the men of the labor movement, and for Ben-Gurion in particular, grew by leaps and bounds. May put her trust in him in 1936, and by that summer she was addressing Ben-Gurion, Katznelson, Sharett, and others as "Darling." Her friendship with Ben-Gurion was such that she carried with her to Palestine presents he had bought in London for his family.

In his heart and mind Ben-Gurion remained convinced, as he had been in 1931, that the majority in the Zionist Congress of that year and in his party had erred in consenting to the Legislative Council proposed by Wauchope with the provision that it give equal representation to Arabs and Jews. But now, for the sake of harmony within the JAE, Ben-Gurion announced that he would consent publicly to the Council, provided it was established on a parity basis. He explained to his party's Political Committee that his change of position arose not from "political factors, but personal ones. I saw how distressed Weizmann was, how much his heart was set on this." Had Mapai backed his position he would never have taken Weizmann's mood into account, but since the party supported Weizmann, Ben-Gurion was prepared to support him too. "Weizmann is essential, and if he is depressed he cannot function"; he "thinks that this way he will rescue the situation." This shows how important it was to Ben-Gurion to keep peace with Weizmann at that time.[20]

Weizmann also made an effort. On August 31, after they had lunched together, he took Ben-Gurion, in a gesture of good will, to an interview with Ormsby-Gore. The colonial secretary read them a letter from Wauchope, in which he had proposed rejecting Arab demands and declaring martial law in Palestine. But he had also asserted the need to make some provision not to leave the Arabs bitter and angry, since otherwise they would rebel at the first opportunity. This left Weizmann and Ben-Gurion with the impression that his intention to suspend immigration to appease the Arabs remained unchanged, and they believed that Ormsby-Gore was capable of prompting the government to go ahead with the suspension plan. Although Weizmann rebuked Ormsby-Gore in strong terms and behaved coldly toward him throughout the interview, Ben-Gurion remained displeased.

"This talk did not go easily at all for me," he wrote Sharett. "I was dissatisfied at a number of things, but I couldn't start a dispute with Chaim in front of Ormsby-Gore, Shuckburgh, Williams, and Boyd. . . . I saw Chaim's strength in this talk as well — and his fickleness and irresponsibility with regard to vital issues, and how little he can be relied upon alone."[21] But this was just internal gossip between colleagues, not an omen of a new blowup. There was no time for one, for Wauchope's suggestion was accepted by the cabinet; immigration, contrary to expectations, was not suspended, military operations were begun to quell the Arab revolt, and the Peel Commission began preparing to get to work. The center of operations, as Ben-Gurion liked to call it, shifted back from London to Jerusalem, and he felt his place was there.

On the afternoon of September 4 Ben-Gurion flew from Croydon to Paris, and from there he went by train to Brindisi. The seaplane in which he had flown to and from Alexandria several times had gone down just two weeks before. On the morning of September 6 Ben-Gurion boarded its twin, not without fears: in his travel diary he twice mentioned the sinking of the *Scipio* near Mirabella, as if seeking God's hand in the affairs of men. On the morning of the seventh he arrived in Ramla safe and sound.[22]

Taking On
the Royal Commission

THE PALESTINE ROYAL COMMISSION — better known as the Peel Commission, after its chairman — was the Jewish Agency Executive's top concern from the day it was conceived by the British government in April 1936. To David Ben-Gurion and others, it was clear that nothing good could be expected of it. He believed that Chaim Weizmann might succeed in aborting it, and this was one reason why he pressured him not to leave London for even an instant.

Once it became clear that the commission was a reality, the question of whether the JAE should cooperate and appear before it arose. Should it cooperate despite the fact that all its predecessors, especially the Shaw Commission, which led to the Passfield White Paper, had proven inimical to Zionism, or should it announce a boycott? Even after the JAE resolved in favor of cooperation and began preparations, Ben-Gurion remained undecided.

There was no question in his mind that the commission was the evil fruit of a plan of Wauchope's. Sir Arthur Wauchope, Ben-Gurion argued, was "very desirous" of a commission, which he could use to achieve a policy to his liking. Later, Ben-Gurion's perception of the "change of course" increased his anxiety about "the danger" that a commission which was "the child of the Disturbances" would reopen the debate over "our status" in Palestine and question anew the Mandate and the National Home to appease the Arabs. Moreover, since this commission would enjoy "practically unlimited" authority and the power "to interpret" the Mandate, it could legislate restrictions on immigration and land acquisition. Therefore, he explained to the JAE, "from the moment we were aware of such a proposal we took a categorical, uncompromising stand against it."[1]

A commission that would make what he termed "a negative revision," that is, reread the Mandate in such a way as to nullify it, deserved to be boycotted. At the same time Ben-Gurion was sensitive to the fact that the Peel Commission would be "more important than all its predecessors," and its report would carry "enormous weight." Appearing before it could be an invaluable opportunity to present the Zionist case. He must have been torn between these two equally strong arguments, and between the camps that stood behind them. When he spoke of siding with "war against the commission" he gained support that in his opinion was too enthusiastic from Berl Katznelson, who called for a "storm"; and when he appeared ready to cooperate he found unwanted backing from Eliezer Kaplan, who claimed that the commission did not constitute a *casus belli*. Ben-Gurion remained on the fence even after the six commissioners were named and the decision to dispatch them to Palestine announced in Parliament. In July he wrote that the commission's potential dangers "should not be exaggerated," and said that "a boycott would do us no good," yet in August he came out for "war" against the commission. In September he proclaimed, "We are all against a boycott," but in October, though he remained "unenthusiastic" about a boycott, he did not eliminate the possibility altogether.

On another occasion he said that the JAE would appear only under circumstances that were not a priori inimical to Zionism, but the next day announced that he favored cooperation with the commission, since "this is an appearance before English public opinion." Early November found him still wavering, and it was apparently only on the ninth, just two days before the commission arrived in Palestine, that he finally made up his mind. While firmly convinced that the commission had been created to implement the change of course, two other arguments outweighed this and constituted his new stance, "A boycott is liable to undermine our already shaky position, [and] this is an opportunity afforded us, albeit against our will, to recount the saga of the Jewish people and Palestine."[2]

It is hard to tell what caused his uncharacteristic indecision; unquestionably several factors were involved. If Ben-Gurion was apprehensive that his feud with Weizmann would be unveiled before the commission, and ultimately before the world, this fear did not abate, becoming a pivotal factor in his preparations for the commission. For everybody knew that Weizmann would be Zionism's chief spokesman.

The commission was perceived as something of a court empowered to hear testimony and issue a decision. The JAE had to select its "witnesses" and elaborate suitable testimony for them. Although this was the terminology used at the time, the entire episode brings to mind a stage production. No one disputed that Weizmann would be the show's superstar, but Ben-Gurion's insistence that the Zionist witnesses adhere strictly to the script and follow the director's orders created a rivalry over who was in charge of the production. Ben-Gurion intended to be both writer and director, to guarantee a true and balanced portrayal of Zionism and its goals. Weizmann and his supporters, however, demanded these roles for Weizmann.

JAE preparations for the Peel Commission began in late June. Ben-Gurion wrote Moshe Sharett that in his opinion "the main thing now is preparation for the Royal Commission — read: preparation for war and not for harmonious cooperation." Accordingly Ben-Gurion drafted a letter, which Weizmann sent on July 1 to Sir William Ormsby-Gore, enumerating the JAE's stipulations for cooperation with the commission even before it was established: that it was not to call into question the terms of the Mandate; that the size of Jewish immigration be determined solely by the principle of economic absorptive capacity, and that no annual maximum be set, lest this arbitrarily hold up Palestine's development; and that there be no suspension of immigration.

Although Weizmann signed the letter, he did not approve of either its tone or its content, and his displeasure with Ben-Gurion's tactics increased as the JAE's preparations continued. From then on their personal rivalry grew, under the guise of a political-ideological battle that insiders chose to attribute to a tactical conflict between London and Jerusalem. Its unlikely beginning was an attempt at compromise, in the spirit of brotherhood that had marked their relations when Ben-Gurion had returned to London after his quick trip to Palestine. They agreed in July 1936 that Leonard Stein, who was known as a moderate and minimalist — one who did not support maximum immigration in the shortest time — would be appointed chief consultant on commission affairs and author of the memorandum to be presented to the commission by the JAE. Ben-Gurion went out of his way to meet Stein's demands for money and time, which ruffled tempers in Jerusalem. What made Ben-Gurion consent to this appointment? Was it only his high regard for Stein, whom in 1934 he had called "a great political talent"? Or was Ben-Gurion certain that he could bend Stein to his will, or at least effectively discipline him, although in 1924 he had said, "Stein is an institution in himself and dependent solely on Weizmann"? Ben-Gurion gave only one written explanation: he was afraid the JAE would have to refute the commission's report, "and there is no man in London who can do this successfully except Stein." Whichever was the case, at their first consultation Ben-Gurion informed him, "Our war against the commission will be aimed entirely against concessions made at our expense."[3]

In this spirit of compromise it was also agreed that the Jerusalem section of the Political Department would coordinate all preparations for the Royal Commission. To this end Sharett would form a committee in Jerusalem, to be divided into subcommittees that would prepare documentation covering a very wide area — "a great sea," Sharett said — relating to the questions of immigration, land, settlement, and policy. When Stein arrived in Jerusalem he would use this material to compose his memorandum, sections of which would from time to time be brought up for discussion and resolution in the JAE and the Small Zionist Actions Committee in Jerusalem.* In theory, control was centered in Jerusalem and Ben-Gurion was assured of the roles of author and director — or so it seemed. This was probably one of the underlying reasons for his consent to Stein's appointment and the generous consideration he showed Weizmann throughout the preparation period.

Stein, accompanied by May, who had been loaned to assist him, arrived in Jerusalem in early September. He went over the material gathered by the Political Department, sat in on JAE meetings and consultations, and at night drafted his memorandum. He proved to be so dominant a figure that some in the JAE wondered at the scope of his authority, and Sharett had to reassure them that "the sole body authorized to decide on the basics of our appearance . . . is the Executive" and that Stein was only its "chief consultant." On October 7 Stein and May left for London. He was to return to Jerusalem to apply the finishing touches in November, after the memorandum had been discussed in Jerusalem and London.

Ben-Gurion and Sharett understood Stein's paper to be only a "draft memorandum," expecting that after having obtained the comments of JAE and Zionist Actions Committee members, they would hammer out the final version together with Stein. This situation seemed to offer an ideal opening for cooperation between the JAE's London and Jerusalem branches and their respective chiefs as well. This, however, was not the case. After reading the first of the memorandum's three parts Ben-Gurion termed it "good, written with talent and expertise, [albeit]

---

* The Zionist Organization's supreme institution was the World Congress, which met every two years. Between congresses authority rested with the Zionist Actions Committee, but since its members, scattered all over the world, could not meet as necessary, at its Zurich session in August 1936 it delegated part of its authority to the Small Actions Committee of twenty-one members, all residents of Palestine. This was to be a temporary institution, authorized to decide questions of policy only.

in need of corrections here and there." But before he had a chance to read it through, London suddenly gave notice that "they were about to print Stein's draft" as is, without further consultations with Jerusalem. Sharett, who had read it in full, was probably the one who alerted Ben-Gurion to its "undesirable" sections. On October 18 Ben-Gurion heard, probably on the phone from Sharett, "several sections from the chapter on land," which in his opinion "must not under any circumstances be left as they stand." That same evening he and Sharett decided to demand that London not print the memorandum, or else "we will insert corrections and present a typescript to the commission." When Ben-Gurion finally read the draft completely he found that Stein had taken such unauthorized and damaging "political positions" that if London printed it, "we [should] have to burn all the material on account of a few phrases."[4]

By the eighteenth Ben-Gurion realized that asking London not to print the memorandum would not only "hurt" Stein and Weizmann, but also escalate the contest for the jobs of scriptwriter and director, and he opted for a more subtle approach. He would phone Lourie and Katznelson — then in London as Weizmann's watchdog — and ask them to persuade Weizmann and Stein not to print the memorandum. On the same day Sharett cabled Lourie at the Zionist office to expect a telephone call that evening. But Lourie was out and the cable was delivered to May, "who did not understand what was happening [and] in her innocence" told Weizmann of the forthcoming call. "And so we were forced," Ben-Gurion wrote to Katznelson afterward, "despite our wish, to speak . . . with Chaim, inadvertently."

However, Ben-Gurion could not speak frankly to Weizmann without causing an open break, while Weizmann for his part did not inform Ben-Gurion that on that very day London had approved a resolution that Ben-Gurion opposed even more, involving an essay written by Lewis Namier. Once again, Jerusalem compromised, so as not to offend Weizmann, and proposed that the memorandum be made up of "separate brochures" instead of being one comprehensive position paper. But London insisted that the memorandum be presented "in the form of one comprehensive position paper," and the battle over preparations went on as before, London and Jerusalem continuing to go their separate ways.

Meanwhile, the commission's arrival in Palestine drew nearer and May, afraid that the JAE might speak with two voices, found herself torn between Weizmann, to whom she owed her loyalty, and Ben-Gurion, whose leadership she trusted. On October 28 she made up her mind. She addressed a long cable, paid for out of her own pocket, to "Darlings" (it is uncertain if anyone other than Ben-Gurion and Sharett was included in this group), cautioning, "By the time you've reconciled your fundamentally divergent views commission will have left Palestine and probably reported. Do you really want our case go by default owing dilatories and internal discussion?" She concluded it, "Love and more power to your elbow," and signed it Dory, her nickname.

A long letter to "Dear B.G." followed immediately, in which she explained, "I've just sent you a damned impertinent telegram . . . and you're at liberty to sack me if you feel like it, or to call me all the names you please, or simply to ignore me completely, as no doubt I deserve. . . . I write to you because you have (I think) more of the makings of a dictator than Moshe [Sharett], and it's a dictator we're needing at the moment — somebody who will make up his own mind quickly and stick to it. . . . *You* have authority, *my dear* — authority which no one else has. *Please use it.*"

Like the prophet Deborah addressing Barak Ben-Avinoam, May broached to Ben-Gurion the idea that had inspired her "interruption." Since "you can't trust London," she wrote, "the only intelligent solution is for someone — preferably yourself — to be delegated as a 'plenipotentiary' to pay a flying visit to London, see the whole thing [the memorandum] in proof, and take the final text back with him by air to Palestine. By this means . . . we may hope to have something comprehensible in the hands of the commission by about November 20th, i.e., just before Charles's [Weizmann's code name] arrival in Palestine."[5]

Ben-Gurion's reply is likely to remain a mystery: May, loyal secretary that she was, destroyed all his personal letters to her. But there can be no doubt that he drew much encouragement from the faith this fine, erudite Englishwoman put in him — and she Weizmann's secretary to boot! It was probably this cable and letter that lent their increasingly close relationship its special character. Ben-Gurion did not fly to London as advised, but instead sent a wire urging Weizmann to come to Palestine for consultations. Their competition was also being expressed in the tug-of-war over when Weizmann should go to Palestine.

The uncertainty regarding the commission's procedure, and particularly its date of arrival, intensified the edginess in the Jerusalem JAE and the feeling that time was short. Consequently the demand that Weizmann come to Palestine became more and more urgent. During July the commission was expected in September; then it was put off until "after order had been restored." In mid October, after the Arabs called off the strike, a date was finally fixed. On November 6 Ben-Gurion told the JAE that the commission would arrive on the eleventh and hold its ceremonial opening session on the twelfth. It would hear government witnesses until the twentieth, the Arabs until the twenty-third, and then the Jews. This schedule was disrupted, however, when the Arab Higher Committee announced its boycott of the commission on November 7.

The sense of urgency in Jerusalem worked to Weizmann's advantage. He knew that the longer he postponed going to Palestine, the less time would be left for debating the JAE's ultimate stand. His power would consequently increase, and the chances of Stein's memorandum gaining the JAE's approval would improve. He would win all three major roles — star, author, and director. Without Weizmann the JAE could not appear before the commission; this was his decisive advantage over Ben-Gurion and he intended to maximize it. From afar he could wield his date of arrival like an ax to enforce his positions. A report Sharett made to Mapai's Political Committee in December described Weizmann's attitude in a rather understated manner. "He is well aware that he is the star witness . . . and he wants . . . to be in charge of the material we present to the commission."

Ben-Gurion found himself between a rock and a hard place. On the one hand, he was hard pressed by the JAE and the Zionist Actions Committee to come up with a line to be taken — "The Executive still lacks a position and has yet to deliberate and thrash out the question for itself," he told the JAE on October 11 — and on the other hand, his efforts to pressure Weizmann proved futile. The displeasure of Weizmann and his associates was brought home to Ben-Gurion in a secret letter from Blanche Dugdale, instructing him as a teacher would a pupil not only in manners, but also in political thinking. On October 14 he thanked her for her "kind" letter and for "writing so fully and so frankly." The intention in "urging him to come here" was not to make Weizmann uncomfortable; rather, "our purpose in asking him to come was to decide jointly the several fundamental questions connected with the preparation of our case for the Royal Commission which the Executive has to settle in the immediate future . . . It is indispensable that these questions be thrashed out in a joint discussion as soon as possible so that our memorandum to the Royal Commission can be put into final shape." In mid October Weizmann chose to explain his lingering abroad to Sharett by writing from Paris of the week-long medical treatment he had received there. He returned to London on October 17.

At the October 21 morning session Ben-Gurion told the JAE that a second wire urging Weizmann to come had not been answered. "If we receive word that Weizmann is coming . . . discussion will wait for his arrival . . . If Weizmann decides not to come . . . we will have to discuss these questions ourselves." He probably said this not because his patience had run out, though it would hardly be surprising if it had, but because he felt that deliberation, even without Weizmann's presence, was both justified and necessary at this stage. For him, this was also an opportune moment to sway the JAE's position his way. His statements to the JAE four days later attest to his intention. "The Executive will discuss the questions of immigration, land, constitution, grievances [against the conduct of the Mandate], and the Executive's directives and resolutions regarding these questions will be binding [upon the witnesses to appear before the commission]; whoever holds another position shall have to hold his tongue."

The proposal to discuss the JAE's stand in Weizmann's absence would have been impossible earlier. Even now some asked for additional information on Weizmann's timetable before consenting. As if to placate them Ben-Gurion and Sharett phoned London immediately after the morning session. At that evening's meeting Ben-Gurion reported that Weizmann intended to leave for Palestine between November 1 and 10, arriving either a few days before the commission or a week after it. "It is out of the question that we put off this fundamental discussion until then," Ben-Gurion maintained. But Weizmann's influence was much stronger than anticipated. Some members of the JAE held that even if Weizmann did arrive late it was best to wait for him. On November 6 Ben-Gurion complained in his diary, "Meanwhile our preparations are in bad shape." Nevertheless, he could mobilize no majority to determine a stance without Weizmann's blessing.[6]

Weizmann, for his part, held Jerusalem entirely accountable for the deadlock. The discord, on two issues in particular, was causing him "the gravest possible anxiety." In an October 31 letter to Sharett, he accused Jerusalem of "playing fast and loose" with Stein's memorandum, "trying to pick holes in it." Since Stein had been in Palestine, which had allowed ample time to discuss everything fully with him, it was unconscionable that "only now," three weeks after Stein had returned to London, "you begin to criticize it. It is an unheard of procedure." Although he agreed that there was room for additions, "the structure of the Mem[orandum] must not be interfered with unless you wish to disassociate me from it. I cannot take any responsibility for a hasty action at the eleventh hour." He regarded Jerusalem's "gross interference" as "tantamount to an expression of non-confidence and I feel sure that it will lead to disastrous results." He neglected to mention the fact that he had already had many copies of Stein's memorandum printed as it stood, without Jerusalem's knowledge.

The second bone of contention was the parity principle, which calls for some explanation. When Palestine came under British rule, Weizmann, Ben-Gurion, and the majority of the Zionist movement had expressed their agreement to the principle of "nondomination," according to which the Arab majority in Palestine would not rule over the Jews and the Jews, if they became the majority, would follow the same principle with regard to the Arab minority. In 1931, in response to the British government's demand to establish a Legislative Council in which Jews and Arabs would be proportionately represented according to their numbers in the entire population of Palestine, Mapai had adopted a parity plan as part of its political platform at the Zionist Congress that year. According to this plan, rule of Palestine would gradually be transferred to its residents on the basis of political equality between Jews and Arabs, regardless of their numbers. Mapai was prepared to accept the proposed Legislative Council on a fifty-fifty basis. The Zionist Congress backed the parity plan and Nahum Sokolow, who had then replaced Weizmann as president of the Zionist movement, publicly announced that parity was the practical interpretation of the principle of nondomination. Both the Congress's resolution and Sokolow's proclamation remained on paper, more a hope for the future or an ideological intention than a political plan of action.

While Weizmann supported the Congress's parity formula, Ben-Gurion objected to it, conversely calling for parity in the administrative branch, as opposed to the legislative. He preferred equality between Arabs and Jews in government as a transitional stage in conveying rule of Palestine to its residents. He was afraid that the British might impose parity in such other areas as population or possession of land as well, and that, despite parity, British votes or a British veto in the Legislative Council might result in restriction of immigration. Ultimately he despaired of getting his formula accepted by his party and the Zionist Organization and acquiesced to the majority.

Differences of opinion on this issue echoed throughout the fall of 1936, when Namier proposed using the Congress's resolution and Sokolow's proclamation as a political tactic. Zionism would be delivered of its tribulations, he believed, if the JAE publicly proposed that the Mandatory government adopt the political parity principle in Palestine. Such a step would refute the claim of the Arabs and their English supporters that because Zionist immigration dispossessed Arabs of their land it must be stopped at once. Namier wrote an essay on the subject "The Declaration of Parity," which London wanted to publish as the JAE's official position before the commission began its work. Jerusalem opposed the "Declaration," and on September 30 Ben-Gurion had cabled London his objection to publishing the essay. In his opinion the JAE would do better to confirm its adherence to the parity principle only if the Peel Commission itself brought it up. Resolution of this point of contention, which apparently revolved around tactics, not principle, was left to the Small Actions Committee.

Once again Ben-Gurion was forced to realize that he lacked the power to defeat Weizmann, even in Mapai. On October 12, after intense deliberations, Mapai's Central Committee resolved — as a compromise, to avoid a dispute with Ben-Gurion — to instruct its representatives in the Small Actions Committee to table a resolution in favor of parity, but to leave the decision on whether to make a prior proclamation that parity was the official Zionist position up to the JAE. On October 13 and 14, a dispute rocked the Small Actions Committee, as many opponents of the parity principle and of the "Declaration" rose to speak. Some feared the English would interpret it as a Zionist commitment to numerical equality between Jews and Arabs. Others regarded it as a declaration of readiness for partition or cantonization.

Ben-Gurion defended the parity formula in the dispute, for "I was mindful of Weizmann and Namier — it's very important to them . . . One must certainly do a lot for Weizmann." The minutes show that he fought like a tiger for a principle he opposed. But at the same time he managed to thwart London's desire to publish it in advance. Bringing up for a vote the resolution that "the Zionist Organization proposes that the Mandatory government guarantee political equality . . . in order to prevent either people's domination of the other," he specified, "This is not for the purpose of declaration but as a directive to the Executive for its political activity." The issue at hand, he stressed, was "an internal directive" for the Political Department. Thanks to the opponents of Weizmann and parity in the right-wing parties and the religious camp, the majority voted to send the subject back to the JAE for discussion and resolution, "after which, when necessary, it will be brought back here for a vote in our plenum."

Ben-Gurion's accomplishment here was complex, involving the constraints under which Zionism, as a voluntary movement, had to work. Since the Zionist leaders wanted to maintain a united front vis-à-vis the British, their differences were concealed by compromises. Had a vote been taken on parity, the divisions within the Actions Committee would have been exposed to the world at large. Ben-Gurion's objective was therefore to achieve his purpose and preserve the movement's unity at the same time. He sought a solution that would satisfy almost all sides: making parity an official position was avoided, but not rejected, by simply delaying the vote. As a result Mapai remained true to itself; the opponents of parity were pleased that it had not become the official position; and Ben-Gurion succeeded both in stopping the publication of Namier's paper (he had no idea that on October 18 London had decided that "[Namier's] essay be published upon Chaim's departure") and in showing himself loyal to Weizmann.[7]

But Weizmann was not to be led by the nose. In his October 31 letter to Sharett he described the controversy in the Actions Committee as "democracy gone mad . . . It is a piece of hypocrisy worthy of Hitler or similar demagogues." He did not specify just who these demagogues were. "You [in Jerusalem] have utterly failed us and have let us down terribly," he went on. Not believing that the issue had to be raised in the Actions Committee, he assumed this to be a ploy by Ben-Gurion and accused him of letting the entire movement down by preventing the proclamation of parity. He said, "If the Executive expects me to give evidence before the [Royal Commission]," he could only do so if he spoke as he believed. Otherwise "my evidence would be useless because insincere." He was prepared to "brush over" the material for his testimony, as well as to undergo a "dress rehearsal," but not to engage in arguments ("I'm not going to start discussions from Pinsker and Herzl"). He made it quite clear. No "amount of eloquence can shift me from this position. . . . If the Executive cannot support my point of view, which I thought was the *accepted* line, I [shall] go out at once and announce the reasons for it." Jerusalem had to come to a decision: if they weren't for him, they were against him. In closing, he announced — at last — that on November 14 he would leave Genoa on the *Esperia*.

Weizmann probably timed his letter to arrive when he was at sea and out of reach, reinforcing the effect of ultimatum and foiling any last-minute contravening of his wishes. Katznelson observed that "[Weizmann] fears he is a president in the French style," which perhaps prompted him to prove to one and all that he was a real president. Ben-Gurion was confronted with the dilemma of either giving in to Weizmann or going out on a limb — on the eve of the commission's arrival. He seems to have considered Weizmann's threat as just a bluff, since otherwise Weizmann would have sent the letter directly to the JAE or to Ben-Gurion, its chairman. Apparently Ben-Gurion mentally staged a confrontation in which Weizmann retreated, the beginning of the retreat being the "brushing over" and "dress rehearsal" to which Weizmann had consented. On November 9, in the closed forum of the Political Committee, Ben-Gurion came out openly against his rival's stand. "If we proclaim parity now, the English will interpret it as numerical parity. So our best option is to proclaim a nonproclamation." But his party, still believing in Weizmann's political judgment and taking the threat at face value, resolved unequivocally not to determine this or any other position before Weizmann's arrival. Ben-Gurion did not take this "no" easily.

It is evident to me that this resolution will only further complicate matters. First of all, between us [Ben-Gurion, Sharett, and their supporters in the Jerusalem JAE] and Weizmann. If we come to Weizmann without a position, Weizmann will not help us arrive at one. He has difficult moods, and precisely because I do not take them lightly, sometimes an excision must be made and he must be confronted with a clear position, in which case it is easier for him to give in. If we approach him without a position we allow an imbroglio to occur.

But his party associates could not be swayed. Not only did the outright Weizmannists in the JAE, like Eliezer Kaplan, line up behind Weizmann, but so did his severest critics, like Tabenkin. He announced that he "basically" favored parity and explained that "the internal feud in Zionism is not good for us now and we must make sure it does not flare up." David Remez supported Kaplan, saying, "We must not stand Weizmann before an iron wall." Even Sharett found it necessary to explain. "We do not now need a crisis in our relations with Weizmann, and it must be made clear that if the parity issue is dismissed, there will indeed be just such a grave crisis, and it will happen right before he goes to the Royal Commission. It will not remain a secret either, but will burst out. This is very serious and, moreover, it will cause us great difficulty with American Zionists."

Where did Katznelson, whose opinion carried the most weight with Ben-Gurion, stand? The comments he wrote Sharett on October 16 from his post at Weizmann's side were made known to many of Mapai's top brass and had considerable influence. "[Weizmann] must be imbued with the spirit of strength and faith, without sensing or suspecting coercion. The catch is that he is too intelligent and too sensitive not to see through the thin veil of adoration under which we conduct our struggle with him."

In fact, Weizmann and Ben-Gurion had a common problem: neither was able to bring the Zionist Organization to take his desired position before the Peel Commission. Yet Ben-Gurion felt intuitively that Weizmann was by nature more inclined toward retreat than assault, so he lay in wait for the opportune moment to strike again. His unique tactic of simultaneously fighting and wooing his rival would guide Ben-Gurion in the inevitable showdown that drew ever nearer as the *Esperia* sped through the waters, carrying Weizmann, Stein, Namier, May, Katznelson, and others.

Raring for battle, Ben-Gurion did not wait for the *Esperia* but set out to meet it. On November 16 Sharett flew to Alexandria, and on the seventeenth Ben-Gurion followed. On the morning of the eighteenth they boarded the *Esperia*, where their worst fear was confirmed. "They printed all of Stein's memorandums in one book in London, and now we have trouble," Ben-Gurion told his diary. "Several phrases and chapters will not do for the Jewish Agency and we are faced with that fact." When Weizmann asked "whether to stay in Egypt or go directly to Palestine," Ben-Gurion and Sharett advised him to "go directly." The entire company boarded the *Champagne*, which sailed for Haifa that evening. At night Stein worked out theses for Weizmann's testimony that gained Ben-Gurion's approval, but in "a joint talk" Weizmann repeated his threat that "without parity he shall not appear."

The confrontation was cut short the next morning when Ben-Gurion and Katznelson were greeted at the Haifa port with the news that Moshe Beilinson had just died, and they raced to the hospital in Petah Tikva.[8]

When they reassembled at Weizmann's home in Rehovot on the twentieth, only five days remained to settle the dispute. Despite the Arab boycott, the Peel Commission was to proceed according to schedule, except that the appearance of the Jewish witnesses, beginning with Weizmann, was postponed until November 25. But even with this extra time Ben-Gurion could not manage the kind of "dress rehearsal" with Weizmann that he wanted; if Weizmann had calculated his late arrival to afford him a dramatic entrance, he had succeeded.

Among the many questions left undecided, four were of particular importance: immigration; the underlying causes of the Disturbances; the "Declaration" of parity; and Stein's memorandum, a fait accompli. Beyond these issues, the differences in temperament and personality between Ben-Gurion and Weizmann mattered more at times than their differences of opinion. Weizmann was gloomy, complaining of old age and fatigue and all too ready to make concessions. "We shall not come out of this affair [the commission] without great concessions," he had told Katznelson in London. "We must be prepared for this; we must talk to our people." He responded vaguely when Katznelson asked what kind of concessions. "Why should we ensure all we want from now to eternity? We should leave something for our children. We had better guarantee what we can for the next ten years." Katznelson concluded, "He does not wish to fight; the need to always fight, press, claim is difficult for him . . . Only when he is forced against the wall does he strike out."

In contrast Ben-Gurion remained impassioned and eager for battle with the commission and its eventual report. His sense of urgency and fear of the destruction of European Jewry were much sharper than Weizmann's. From this contrast grew the difference in their proposed tactics. Weizmann would have been satisfied with the immigration of a million Jews within twenty or thirty years. Ben-Gurion doubted if Zionism had even five years at its disposal; he wanted one or two million Jewish immigrants brought into Palestine within five or ten years.

He would not concede, therefore, on the size of immigration. "There is no danger in other decrees," he had told Mapai's Central Committee in September, "because vast immigration will bring about Jewish rule in Palestine in not too many years, and when we become a greater power we can shred all the decrees." He was certainly not prepared to leave anything "to our children" lest there be none on account of their parents' spineless timidity. Twice in October, he flatly told the Actions Committee,

> No English commission can determine the fate of the Jewish people forever, but it can determine to a great extent what will happen over the next five years. . . . Five years are nothing next to "eternity," but not all years in history are alike, and in the next five years the fate of our generation may be decided, if not the fate of generations. . . . The situation of Jews in the world . . . the dreadful dangers bound up with the new world war, all point to a rapid growth of the Yishuv . . . The extent of immigration in the coming years is a question of destiny . . . In determining the principle of immigration [Britain] determines the fate of the people.[9]

This was probably the most chilling prophecy ever to be fulfilled; within eight to nine years a third of the Jewish people were cut down in Europe.

Another aspect of the conflict had to do with dividing the subjects of testimony between the two men. Ben-Gurion did not dispute Weizmann's being the lead and central witness on behalf of the JAE, or speaking in the name of both the Jewish people and the Zionist movement. Ben-Gurion would be a local witness, "a specialist" on current affairs in Palestine. Ben-Gurion wanted to testify on Jewish-Arab relations in Palestine, the causes of the Disturbances, and the lesson to be learned from them. Had Weizmann consented to Ben-Gurion's testifying on immigration, the controversy between the two would have been settled. But this issue was important to Weizmann's testimony as well, and Weizmann's view of its possible or desirable proportions was quite different from Ben-Gurion's. For this reason Ben-Gurion wanted to give his own evidence before Weizmann had finished giving his, thinking that if he made his points first Weizmann would have to agree with him for the sake of unanimity.

Ben-Gurion chose to strike first, on a narrow front — the issues of Stein's memorandum and the parity "Declaration." His strategy was to win Weizmann's aides over to his side, as a step toward persuading Weizmann. Dugdale had already changed her mind on the "Declaration." While Weizmann was on his way to Palestine, she had received a communication from one of her friends in the British government that influenced her to oppose it. Arthur Lourie, secretary of the London Political Section and a Ben-Gurion man, wrote Ben-Gurion of this development on November 12. It was very likely this information that enabled Ben-Gurion to change Weizmann's mind about parity without too much effort during a December 20 meeting at Weizmann's home.

On that occasion Ben-Gurion first spoke with Stein, then noted in his diary,

> I had a difficult talk with Stein. The conversation was later repeated in front of Chaim. I insisted on dropping the chapter on Zionist policy from the memorandum, as it does not accurately convey the movement's view. Chaim was hurt. Afterward we spoke of parity and Chaim agreed that we didn't have to bring it up, since it is better that it come from the commission.

With Stein, however, a real fight was unavoidable. As Sharett later told Mapai's Political Committee, he and Ben-Gurion made a lightning attack on both the memorandum's style and its content. The memorandum had been printed as a bound book, and Ben-Gurion and Sharett demanded that it be replaced with a loose-leaf collection of smaller memorandums written in Jerusalem on the questions of land, industry, the tie between the Jewish people and the land of Palestine, and the Yishuv's grievances against the Mandatory government, which Sharett termed "the catalogue of claims." Stein had prefaced the memorandum with a two-page introduction, but Ben-Gurion and Sharett opposed an introduction, "to emphasize that this is not *the* memorandum." They were equally harsh with respect to style. Stein, they claimed, had revived "the style of writing the government used" before Mapai had taken on itself the management of the Jerusalem political section and especially before Ben-Gurion had joined the JAE — a servile clerk's style.

But the battle at Weizmann's home reached its highest pitch over the chapter on Zionist policy. Since Stein wished to prove that Zionism had never intended the dispossession of the Arabs, he started out by "renouncing the idea of a Jewish state," quoting from Weizmann's speech to the 1931 Zionist Congress, in which he had said that even Herzl, when writing of the *Judenstat,* did not have in mind an actual Jewish state. There were further quotes in this vein from Weizmann's speeches as well. Ultimately the introduction was struck, the chapter on Zionist policy was "forcefully torn out," and papers written by others in Jerusalem were inserted in their stead. These corrections were made by tearing pages out of the book that had been printed in London and pasting in new ones printed in Jerusalem and by glueing paper over or crossing out with ink certain offensive lines. In this state

Stein's memorandum — if it could still be called that — was submitted to the Peel Commission; additional papers were presented separately. The JAE did not publish this version of the memorandum for two reasons: to prevent its falling into the hands of the Arabs, who might find in it arguments for their own use, and for fear that the Jewish press would criticize it, "as there are items that despite all our efforts we could not excise and they would undoubtedly raise a hue and cry," Sharett said.[10]

If Ben-Gurion was correct in saying that "we went over the basic lines of his opening address together several times" — and there is no reason to doubt it — one need not look far to understand Weizmann's gloom. There stood the king, but the book representing his policies was defaced and words were put into his mouth. Nevertheless, Weizmann's regal stature remained undiminished. Weizmann was president of the Zionist Organization and its chief spokesman to the Peel Commission, and his appearance before the movement's executive and parliamentary bodies was eagerly awaited. On Sunday, November 22, he took part in a JAE meeting, and on Monday he attended a session of the Small Actions Committee. But his visits at both institutions were no more than a perfunctory discharge on his part of democratic procedure. At the JAE he sat in on a morning session only, listening more than speaking. To Ben-Gurion's relief Weizmann did announce that he "agrees that it is a good idea to refrain from a solemn declaration of our consent to parity, but if they question on this we must answer affirmatively."

At the Actions Committee Weizmann also participated in the morning session only, for which he apologized. "Please forgive me if I do not take part in deliberations this afternoon . . . From this afternoon until Wednesday morning [the date of his appearance before the commission] I wish to be alone, and I am sure you will understand. Indeed, I face a difficult road, but I believe in the old saying, 'Those sent on a holy mission are never harmed.' " By virtue of his renowned personal charm he was borne out of the chamber on the wings of applause, without his statement to the commission having come up for debate and vote.

Weizmann most likely requested solitude not only to escape criticism and disputes, but also to allow his imagination the freedom it needed to produce the special flair expected of him, to invent those phrases and catchwords that he alone could pronounce with authority. Ben-Gurion recognized this aspect of his genius, as well as the need to afford Weizmann the conditions he required to mold his appearance into a great performance. "He is the man who can present our problems with that inspiration others cannot muster," Ben-Gurion told

Mapai, and he implored his colleagues in the Political Department to be considerate of Weizmann "so as to enable him to work up the appropriate inner fervor." Even so, Weizmann was not granted the seclusion he so needed. On Tuesday, November 24, Ben-Gurion — with Katznelson, Sharett, and others — sat with him until 11:00 P.M. Evidently Ben-Gurion did not consider his own presence a damper on Weizmann's inspiration.

As a ray of light breaks through heavy clouds, so inspiration found its way to Weizmann's heart. Weizmann's testimony or, as it was then recorded, "his public appearance" of November 25 was one of the most brilliant of his life. In a conversational tone, friendly and deferential, always using the first person and describing his own experiences as one who had stood over the cradle of Zionism and brought about the Balfour Declaration, who had negotiated with the world's great, from Arthur James Balfour and Lloyd George to King Faisal and Benito Mussolini, Weizmann unfolded a tale of woe of the Jewish people and their eternal bond with Zion, to the fascination of his listeners. He depicted the situation of German and Polish Jewry and the hopelessness of Jews in many other lands with feeling, yet not without humor. "The world," he told the commission, "is divided into places where [Jews] cannot live and places into which they cannot enter." In speaking of the difficulty of non-Jews in understanding Zionism and its goals, he mentioned Lord Passfield, "a very practical man, a great economist," who had told him, in 1930, "But Dr. Weizmann, do you not realize there is not room to swing a cat in Palestine?" "Many a cat has been swung since then," Weizmann went on, "and the population of Palestine has increased."

The next day Sir Laurie Hammond told Weizmann, "I think anybody who heard your eloquent speech, in fact moving speech, yesterday, would realize that it was your life work." *Davar*'s lead article, written by Katznelson, could not praise him enough.

> The Jews' representative did not shame his constituents. . . . Weizmann sat before the commission not as a defendant, accused . . . but as president of a people, first and foremost of the movement for freedom . . . without haughtiness or arrogance. . . . Weizmann's testimony has not been completed. He still has more to say.

Ben-Gurion, miserable with a bad cold, went to the Hotel Palace, where the commission held its sessions, despite pouring rain. Although there had been many rehearsals up to the last minute, he still did not feel wholly at ease, and, he said later, his "heart was pounding." Only when the session had ended could he breathe easily. In his opinion,

[Weizmann had to] speak in two worlds, to the English and to the Jews.
. . . And Chaim succeeded in both . . . but not in the sense that his state
ments will influence [the commission's] conclusions. I very much doubt if
even the finest presentation of our case will determine the policy. But he
explained the question to them, presented the issue in a broad scope, with
great power, and aroused their interest and respect. All the commissioners
. . . Hammond in particular, listened attentively . . . but if, externally, the
practical result is dubious, internally this appearance was a great deed.
Chaim has again left his indelible mark on Jewish history, and his statements will undoubtedly consolidate the movement which has so long gone
ununified.

Ben-Gurion, remembering that November 26 was Weizmann's sixty-
second birthday, remarked, "No more satisfying thing could happen to
Weizmann on his birthday." In bed, he noted all these things in his
diary; following doctor's orders he kept to his room that afternoon.[11]
It seemed that the JAE in Jerusalem and Ben-Gurion in his bed could
anticipate the rest of Weizmann's testimony with confidence. Their
method — guidance, surveillance, and freedom of inspiration — had
proved itself thus far in the best possible manner. But there was a
hitch: the commission wished to hear Weizmann's further testimony in
camera. Would Weizmann, unguarded, hew to the proper path?
Would the JAE be able to extract from him a full report on the investigation and his replies? To assuage these fears, Stein and Sharett accompanied Weizmann on the twenty-sixth, the former as a supporter, and
the latter as a sentinel. From them the JAE expected an accurate report on Weizmann's "secret appearance."
But even the best-laid plans may go awry. Weizmann and his escorts
had hardly sat down when the chairman, Lord Peel, explained that
when sitting in private the commission had always followed a rigid rule
that no one know what was said except the witness and the commissioners, to ensure the witness "absolute secrecy and full freedom of
expression." Weizmann assured the commissioners that he had confidence in his colleagues' "complete discretion" and that he had nothing to say that could not be said in their presence. A polite tussle ensued in which an adamant Peel commented on the fact that Wauchope
had given testimony completely unaccompanied. Weizmann thereupon asked his colleagues to withdraw. When this news reached Ben-
Gurion, in his bed, he wrote in his diary, "Until we see the mimeographed minutes, we won't know the content of the testimony."
Since the commission had promised its in camera witnesses complete
secrecy, a record of Weizmann's testimony could be procured in only
two ways: by Political Department agents, who more than once had
managed to get their hands on secret British documents, or by bugging.

In 1981 it was disclosed that, by order of the JAE Political Department, tiny microphones had been hidden in the light fixtures in the meeting room. Ben-Gurion and his colleagues thereby learned the content of the ostensibly secret testimony of Wauchope and other witnesses. Either way, it would be several days until minutes of Weizmann's statements were transcribed.

Meanwhile Ben-Gurion was extremely ill at ease. On the twenty-seventh he called Katznelson and Eliyahu Golomb to his bedside in Jerusalem for "consultations . . . on the situation in light of Weizmann's secret testimony." The monitoring agents had apparently told Ben-Gurion enough to reawaken his fears. He was still confined to bed, but on the thirtieth he went to a JAE meeting, in which Weizmann took some part, and returned home immediately afterward. Because he did not start working again until December 5, he once more summoned Katznelson and "several colleagues to look into the situation." By the eighth he was strong enough to chair the JAE.

When the full transcript of Weizmann's second appearance reached him on the ninth he read all forty pages closely. Afterward he reported in his diary, "I read and enjoyed, read and rejoiced, read and regretted, read and was ashamed. The testimony was mostly superb, well put and to the point. There are points which only Weizmann can make. But in this testimony all that is disgraceful in Chaim Weizmann's character came out, all his political frivolity, all lack of judgment and irresponsibility and all his fickle-mindedness." Weizmann's remarks were titled "The Underlying Causes of Conflict," the topic on which Ben-Gurion was supposed to give testimony.

However, this was not what mattered to him; Weizmann's readiness to make concessions saddened and infuriated him. Weizmann did not maintain that increased immigration was the way to calm Palestine. On the contrary, he told the commission that slowing down the pace of immigration was a fair price to pay for peace and understanding with the British and the Arabs. Hammond asked Weizmann if he would consent "to a standstill period," a kind of "truce," Peel called it, in the course of which immigration, Jewish development of the Yishuv, and Arab terror would come to a halt. This would enable both sides to learn to live together, after which development and immigration would begin again. Weizmann replied, "Will you let me give you an answer later?" Peel responded, "Yes, consider it, and let us have your answer." Weizmann said, "I will do that." What Ben-Gurion wrote was accurate: his version of Weizmann's private testimony was identical to the official one published many years later. Ben-Gurion was stunned.

Why did Chaim not realize that Hammond's suggestion of a standstill [was] fatal? First of all no such moratorium is possible — the citrus groves are near harvest and need extra hands. Where will they get them without Jewish immigration? From Hawran? And what will factories do when they need to expand and the workers and others want to build homes for themselves? Is a country an artificial thing in which it is possible to stop growth by decree? Isn't it clear that stopping immigration means either a severe financial depression or Arab immigration? And how will the Arabs be disarmed, and how will it be ensured that there are no riots? And how will they be educated for cooperation so that immigration may be renewed?[12]

This criticism was the merest hint of the anger that Ben-Gurion had thus far managed to suppress — anger at his JAE and party colleagues, especially Sharett, who did not accord him equal status with Weizmann as the JAE spokesman. Worse still, his colleagues accepted and did not appeal the commission's agenda, which treated Weizmann as the JAE's principal witness, relegating Ben-Gurion to the sidelines, to be heard only on Histadrut matters. His response to Weizmann's testimony — in which he kept his rage at his colleagues hidden — took a while to manifest itself, for he had undoubtedly planned his steps carefully, using his special talent for putting himself above suspicion of personal motives and unfailingly accomplishing his goals.

Mapai's Political Committee met the day after Ben-Gurion read the transcript. On its agenda, said Sharett, was "arriving at a conclusion on the issue of Ben-Gurion's appearance." Of all those present, Ben-Gurion showed the least interest. "We should discuss the issues," he said, "not who must appear." His party associates would subsequently learn to recognize such unselfishness as a sign that trouble was coming, but in 1936 Ben-Gurion had to be more explicit. "Behind this title [of Weizmann's remarks] lies a fundamental question: whether or not they will allow the Jews to grow in Palestine. . . . Weizmann testified regarding this subject, and will do so further. There is no need for two people to appear." Now his meaning was clear, and Sharett, to whom all eyes in the Political Committee turned, explained that the commissioners insisted on Weizmann's place in the agenda, "which cannot be changed." But Ben-Gurion's name had not been dropped from the list of witnesses. British witnesses had told the commission that a Jewish Palestine meant "a red Palestine," and Lord Peel wished to hear Ben-Gurion, and none other, address this subject, so Ben-Gurion was guaranteed a hearing. But on whose behalf — the JAE's or the Histadrut's? This question was significant.

Ben-Gurion told the committee that Weizmann, Locker, and a British friend had said to him, "Your evasion of an appearance before the commission makes you suspect" and would elicit surprise. Nevertheless, Ben-Gurion made sure that no date for his appearance was given by the Histadrut. Otherwise Weizmann alone would speak for Zionism and the entire Jewish people, while Ben-Gurion would be recognized merely as a local labor leader. He did not have to explain his refusal to testify on behalf of the Histadrut; his party got the hint and increased the pressure on him to testify on behalf of the JAE. Katznelson asserted, "In the chapter entitled 'The Underlying Causes of Conflict' Weizmann's appearance alone is insufficient . . . and Ben-Gurion must appear. . . . It is necessary that a member of the Executive appear who will present the issue in a style other than Weizmann's. Ben-Gurion is the man to do this." Others were vocal in supporting him. "There is not a man in the Histadrut or the Yishuv who would dream of Ben-Gurion's not appearing," said Remez, and Tabenkin added, "It is essential that Ben-Gurion appear. It does not matter if Ben-Gurion's appearance is identical to Weizmann's . . . his testimony can increase the effect, and cannot be discarded."

On Saturday, December 12, Ben-Gurion, Katznelson, Sharett, and Kaplan met with Weizmann at his home to rehearse him for his second in camera appearance. Earlier that day Ben-Gurion had said to his Mapai colleagues what he had refrained from saying to the Political Committee, that "Weizmann need not appear again in private." Kaplan the Weizmannist flatly rejected this demand. Katznelson and Sharett, although they saw eye to eye with Ben-Gurion regarding Weizmann's secret testimony, could see no way to stop him. From the silence Ben-Gurion maintained while listening to their arguments, they might have imagined he had given in. Only at the rehearsal at Weizmann's home did a hint of the storm gathering within him appear.

The outline Weizmann had prepared for his testimony, Ben-Gurion told them later, was excellent, "but the final conclusion on the principal issue was the opposite of what it should have been." Nevertheless, during the long rehearsal — "a monologue by Weizmann, in fact" — Ben-Gurion hardly opened his mouth, for "there are things I should not dispute with Weizmann, the question of immigration in particular . . . and we left this talk without settling what the position will be." The next day he told the JAE, "The primary responsibility at the moment is on Weizmann's shoulders, and what he says goes." Since it is unlikely that he had suddenly accepted Weizmann's position, his restraint is a further sign that the storm was still gathering force. On the fifteenth it broke in the form of three demands: first, that "Chaim must not be permitted to testify in camera"; second, that Ben-Gurion, too, would testify before the commission and say what Weizmann had left out, emphasizing the "main thing," the need to increase immigration and speed it up; and third, his testimony would have to come before Weizmann concluded his.

He thereby handed Sharett and Stein, who served as liaison with the Peel Commission, an impossible task. How would they prevent Weizmann from testifying privately when the date had been set for December 18? Even if Weizmann agreed to break off his testimony in the middle, how would he explain it to the commission? And how could Sharett and Stein arrange the commission's agenda so that Ben-Gurion would be heard before Weizmann had concluded, bearing in mind that the commission's heavy schedule was unalterable? Sharett and Stein were at a loss, but Ben-Gurion, just two days after he had agreed to testify, came up with a quick solution: he simply would not appear before the commission, he told them on the seventeenth. Was he punishing his colleagues for not speaking out enough on the wrong done him by Weizmann, or for failing to meet his demands? They did not have to wait long to find out. On December 18, just before Weizmann testified in private for the second time, a second preparatory session was held, in which Weizmann gave his word that in his testimony he would follow Ben-Gurion's line on immigration. But Ben-Gurion doubted that he would stick to it. On the twentieth Ben-Gurion denied the story Sharett had given the press of his coming testimony, and everyone knew that there had been serious trouble in the JAE.

Mapai's Central Committee, finding it had to step in, also met on the twentieth. First, Sharett related the whole "affair of Ben-Gurion's nonappearance before the commission." Sharett, too, believed that Ben-Gurion had been wronged. "When the JAE's political presentation was divided up, Weizmann wound up dealing with all the questions of major policy, while I dealt with the principal day-to-day questions. All the while I thought that Ben-Gurion's nonappearance was wrong." But, pleaded Sharett, "what could be done? Could [Weizmann's] appearances be stopped? This would indeed have been both an internal and an external catastrophe! Such a thing simply is not done." Sharett had wanted Ben-Gurion to appear before Weizmann finished testifying. This would be, he said, "flank defense," for Weizmann would know that Ben-Gurion "would not adopt Weizmann's positions, and if [Weizmann] contradicted Ben-Gurion's, this would only result in [revealing] discord before the commission." But arranging this, said Sharett, "was beyond our capabilities."

Ben-Gurion tried to convince the Central Committee that no personal motive lay behind his decision. "I always claim that we must explain the issues to the commission . . . It is not our business to present people." The issue on which he had wanted to testify from the beginning was "the growth of our strength in Palestine, without which we are in danger of destruction at the hands of the Arabs. . . . The principal question we must explain to the Royal Commission is . . . What conclusion must come from these Disturbances: reduction of immigration or the reverse, its increase?" Ben-Gurion knew that Weizmann "sometimes lacks the needed faith, and as this is the principal question I feared a terrible failure there." But since Weizmann had included this issue in his secret testimony, "I did not think it necessary to speak again on the same subject." Why? First of all, for fear of looking ridiculous. Ben-Gurion remembered being told by Harold Laski some time before,

> At the cabinet committee, in its time, Weizmann spoke for two hours and made a tremendous impression. Then Brodetsky wished to speak, and he destroyed the whole impression, leaving a sour taste, since he was speaking not because he had anything to add but just because he wanted to speak. . . . Even if I could speak with the same power as Weizmann, there is no reason to speak, as Weizmann has already said everything . . . This being the case, there is no sense in my appearing. I cannot make the Executive look ridiculous, and after immigration is discussed at three sessions of the commission I cannot come and discuss it once more, for the commission could simply stop me and say, "We've already heard this."

Until then Ben-Gurion had spoken like Jeremiah, reproaching, remonstrating, calling the Central Committee's attention to the severity of the situation, and admonishing its members for not meeting his demands. Then he suddenly changed to the hushed, subdued voice of one who, resigned to the inevitable, could do nothing but hope for the best. In the second preparatory session, before Weizmann's secret testimony of December 18, he said — as a ploy designed to provoke his colleagues to contradict him — "[Weizmann's] position changed." If Weizmann should take this stand in front of the Peel Commission as well, "no man in the Zionist movement can explain it as he can, nor make such a grand impression." As if to reassure those who had placed their trust in Weizmann, Ben-Gurion added that he had heard "that his appearance [on December 18] had made a tremendous impression," and as a result, "my apprehension has lessened a little." Since the commission wished to hear Weizmann again on the twenty-third,

> we must now take care that Weizmann, in concluding his testimony, takes a forceful stand on this issue and does not weaken when they start to press him. Since he left this appearance strengthened . . . I believe his power will not weaken on Wednesday [the twenty-third] either. Even so, we must watch, fortify, and encourage him . . . We must be certain that Weizmann will stand firm on the subject of immigration and demand its increase. If he does this . . . our principal battle will be over, and we will

have done all we can. This is not to say that the commission will accept our view, but the deed will have been done. And done well at that, if Weizmann is the man to carry it through.

The committee members might have thought Sharett was speaking to them. Ben-Gurion went on to say that Weizmann "is influenced by the criticism of his appearance and it hurts him deeply"; in order not to upset him he requested that the next scheduled Small Actions Committee meeting be put off. But lest his friends misread him, Ben-Gurion closed his pep talk with one final word of doubt. "As long as I don't read that he explicitly demanded that immigration not be decreased, I shall not be at ease." Katznelson immediately took the hint. "And if he doesn't say so?" he asked. Ben-Gurion replied, "If he doesn't say so, it will be very bad. It will be a catastrophe."

In this affair Ben-Gurion revealed his method of getting what he wanted from the party, a method he was to make into an art. First, he made himself appear to be a warrior for the issue devoid of any ulterior motive. Second, he made his colleagues understand that they had to divine his true intentions without his giving them so much as a clue. And third, by seeming to abandon his position, he brought them to accept it. Mapai, Zionism's largest party, could certainly not allow Ben-Gurion, its representative, not to speak on its behalf. The unanimous opinion in the Central Committee was that Ben-Gurion was "dutybound" to appear, and in the best tradition of the labor movement the rite of wooing him began: the staging of a general, "spontaneous" clamor among the rank and file to convince him that it would be best for him to submit to the will of the movement and agree to testify. Remez, who saw into Ben-Gurion's heart and sought for him an honorable path to that goal, demanded that Ben-Gurion testify publicly "so that the JAE chairman can state openly that the conclusion to be drawn from the Disturbances" was that the Yishuv's strength had to be increased.

In accordance with protocol Ben-Gurion gave in somewhat reluctantly, using the pretext Remez provided. "I doubt that this must be said in public testimony . . . However, if Remez believes *it is to the good of the cause* to say it publicly, it is another matter and must be considered . . . As to my appearance, I agree that two members be appointed to look over Weizmann's secret testimony, to see if there is a need to speak to the commission on immigration after Weizmann. I do not believe there is such a need."

Relieved, the Central Committee resolved to accept his proposal and elected Katznelson and Locker "to look over Weizmann's testimony and decide on the issue of Ben-Gurion's appearance before the commission." No one doubted what their decision would be. And there was no need to explain to Sharett that he had to get Ben-Gurion's testimony on the agenda before Weizmann concluded his.

Everything seemed to have worked. But on December 23 Ben-Gurion received the transcript of Weizmann's secret testimony of December 18 and was enraged. In his diary he wrote, "That which I feared came true. This testimony is a political disaster. . . . It is beyond Chaim's powers to stand firm before the forceful and courteous English. His will is not strong enough. His knowledge of the issues is inadequate and his faith and inner drive are on the wane." Weizmann had stuck to his former compromising positions and shown himself prepared, in the name of peace, to compromise on immigration. He had agreed with the commission that large-scale immigration was the cause of the Disturbances, and said that he would be "the first to seize upon" the Arabs' willingness to "quietly accept" immigration of thirty thousand or forty thousand a year as the first step toward an agreement. He had done his best, he added, to influence his Zionist colleagues "to make every sacrifice to assuage Arab fear." In his view the immigration of a million Jews to Palestine within twenty-five to thirty years "would be a respected contribution to the satisfaction of Jewish aspirations." The effort to "supervise" Weizmann and guide him had been in vain.

Two things fed Ben-Gurion's fury: the damage Weizmann had done to the Zionist cause and the fact that despite his pledge during their preparatory talk, Weizmann had gone ahead and expressed his own view instead of Ben-Gurion's. Ben-Gurion summoned Katznelson to Jerusalem "for consultation on the situation created by Chaim's testimony," but Katznelson had fallen ill on December 22. Ben-Gurion then turned to Sharett and Namier, saying, "It may be possible to reduce the damage somewhat — at least within the movement — by means of a letter signed by Weizmann and sent to the commission." He formulated eight questions for which a letter of explanation would offer "a well-founded and reasoned reply." But in signing such a letter Weizmann would be putting himself in the position of a wayward child making amends by repeating his teacher's lessons. Since Weizmann rejected this proposal, Ben-Gurion sent the following letter on December 24.

Dear Dr. Weizmann,

The love and esteem all my colleagues and I feel for you, and the personal loyalty I owe you as the people's chosen representative and the outstanding personality with whom I've had the honor of working, oblige me to inform you that I no longer see any possibility of my bearing active responsibility for the Executive. After difficult and bitter struggles it has become clear to me that my concept of Zionist policy does not coincide with yours. This first became apparent to me in London several months ago and was forcefully confirmed in the discussions preceding the Royal Commission.

I am aware of the heavy burden that rests upon your shoulders at this time, and I would have regarded it as a grave sin to weigh you down by even an ounce more, except that I could not remain true to my conscience had I withheld my feelings from you. It has become plain to me that our differences of opinion are not coincidental and temporary, but reach to the root of the issues, and I have come to the conclusion that there is neither benefit in nor any possibility of my continued participation in the Executive's political section.

Throughout the years, and particularly these trying times of late, you have made apparent your anxiety that the movement retain its solidarity and internal unity, and I wish to assure you that to the best of my all too slight ability I will assist you faithfully in strengthening the Zionist movement and its Organization. As previously I will stand, with my colleagues, at your service, and should you wish to hear my views on any question, even outside Executive meetings, I will do your bidding to the best of my ability.

Must I assure you that no political differences of opinion can obscure or weaken the respect, love, esteem, and loyal friendship I have felt for you ever since we met?

I deeply regret these differences of opinion but, as you told me in London, no man has control over his thoughts.

Yours in faith and love,

D. Ben-Gurion.

Although he added in a postscript, "Moshe [Sharett] is the only one who knows of this letter, and insofar as I can vouch for it no one else knows," obviously such a break in the Zionist Executive could hardly remain a secret for long.

This was the tactic Ben-Gurion had used so successfully in the HEC: abandoning responsibility at such a critical moment would constitute a pressure Weizmann and Ben-Gurion's colleagues could not bear. Fearing the ramifications of this breach in the Zionist Executive on the Peel Commission's conclusions would force them — even if they condemned his act as unconscionable irresponsibility — to compromise with Ben-Gurion. Predictably, Sharett, Kaplan, and Locker began immediate efforts at mediation and reconciliation, in which they were joined by Katznelson when he recovered. On the morning of December 30 Ben-Gurion and Weizmann met for a tête-à-tête, in the course of which Ben-Gurion reduced the controversy between them to two central topics: the pace and the goal. "At the center of our political war stands the necessity to *speed up* our activity — in other words, the increase in immigration, not just opposition to its decrease. Only in hastening the pace is there a solution to the Arab difficulty. And as to the goal: not a million Jews in Palestine, but a full solution to the question of the Jewish people."[13]

Weizmann could well afford to feel strong at this talk. The commission had nearly finished its work in Palestine. The Arab Higher Committee had canceled its boycott at the last minute, and on January 6 the mufti and other Arab witnesses would testify. Weizmann, who had already said his piece, had only a fourth and last private session with the commission to come. The question arose as to what benefit Ben-Gurion would gain if he got his desire and testified. Weizmann's three previous secret sessions would be neither erased nor changed, while revealing a split in Zionism on the very eve of the Arabs' appearance, or just after it, would hardly be beneficial. Nevertheless, Ben-Gurion held firm on two demands: that he would testify before Weizmann concluded and that Weizmann would write the commission a letter of explanation in which he would establish as definitive Ben-Gurion's positions, which were, said Ben-Gurion, the majority positions as well. Weizmann could hardly consent to such a step without damaging his own prestige and the JAE's status as well. Before they parted, therefore, Ben-Gurion made an unusual gesture: for the sake of appearances he would continue to bear responsibility for the JAE, but between him and Weizmann his resignation from such responsibility remained unchanged. In his diary he expressed it as follows: "The internal cohesiveness of the movement necessitates unity in the Executive, and I take part in all responsibility for the Executive, but between Weizmann and myself, I cannot accept the responsibility for the tenor of his secret testimony before the commission." Therefore, although Ben-Gurion's demands were not met, by his gesture of not publicly resigning but staying on like a loyal soldier of Zionism he managed to put pressure on Weizmann by creating a political debt.

As a result, efforts at appeasement and mediation continued, and in this war of nerves Ben-Gurion emerged the stronger. On January 3, 1937, the JAE notified the commission that "Ben-Gurion would appear on its behalf," and on January 7 he testified publicly in the morning and in camera in the afternoon. The next day Weizmann testified in camera for the last time. On January 13, when Weizmann reported on his testimony to the Small Actions Committee, Ben-Gurion did not criticize him, but neither did he support him against his critics; in fact he hardly opened his mouth, though he kept up the pressure on Weizmann, for on these issues Ben-Gurion had the weight of the party and the Actions Committee behind him. On January 19, two days after the commission left Palestine for London, Weizmann conceded on the second issue and sent Lord Peel a letter in which he upheld Ben-Gurion's positions on all points of contention. Weizmann was paid back in his own coin: having delayed his arrival in Palestine to escape parliamentary responsibility, he had to accept it retroactively, for the Actions Committee was called in to make its contribution to Weizmann's letter. Ben-Gurion, who never forgot this victory, included the long letter, which Weizmann signed but whose content was voted on by the Zionist Actions Committee, in the last volume of his memoirs, published shortly after his death in 1973.

His obstinate and extended battle over the central issue — in essence, as he saw it, over the right path for Zionism — was strenuous. He had challenged one greater and mightier than he in the eyes of the world and the entire Jewish people. This struggle was hardly free of a fierce personal jealousy so powerful that as a motivation it was second only to the force of the inner truth that ultimately guided him. As usual, the battle sapped him of emotional and physical strength and left its mark on his health. On January 25 he left to regain his strength in Cairo. In his diary he remarked, "I came here to find some rest. All the time the Royal Commission was in Palestine I hardly felt anything, but the day of its departure I felt how frazzled my nerves were."[14]

34

Grappling with Partition

OBSERVERS of the Peel Commission were treated to an apparent discrepancy when Weizmann and Ben-Gurion presented their views on Zionism's objective. The renowned moderate claimed that the Balfour Declaration intended the Jewish National Home to become a state, while the radical argued that Zionism's goal was not a state and that a National Home was preferable.

How could the same Ben-Gurion who had sounded the call "to begin a Jewish state policy" suddenly change his spots and become an advocate of the National Home, which meant the continuation of the British Mandate? There were probably three reasons for this: first, his conviction that a retreat from the Mandate was in the works led him to view the commission as a tool the British government would use to carry it out, so he made foiling it the JAE's primary goal. Later he said, "We went to the Peel Commission to fight for the Mandate." Demanding a state was tantamount to giving up the Mandate, and he feared that the concession would be accepted while the demand went unanswered and that Zionism would be left with neither Mandate nor state. The Mandate was still the only solid ground Zionism had to stand on.

The second reason involved his conviction of the importance of immigration. Unlike Weizmann, who agreed with the commissioners that Arab fear of immigration had led the Arabs to revolt, Ben-Gurion claimed — contrary to his private belief — that no such fear existed, that even if it did, there was no basis for it, and that in any event, it was not immigration that had caused the Disturbances. Either way, he told the commission, massive immigration was the sole solution to the Arab question as well as the way to end the Disturbances. But if the Arabs opposed immigration out of fear that it would bring about a Jewish majority and a subsequent state that would dispossess or deprive them of their rights, Ben-Gurion reassured the commission that Zionism's goal was not a state, so the Arabs need fear neither immigration nor a Jewish majority.

Again the tables seemed turned, for Weizmann had spoken of six million "homeless" Jews in eastern and central Europe who, unless they were rescued in time, would be reduced to "economic dust [and] destroyed," seeming to imply that only the Jewish state could save them. It is likely, however, that he did not intend such an inference, given his statement that Zionism wished to bring only one million of those six million to Palestine within twenty-five years. In the interim between his own public and private testimony Ben-Gurion was "shocked" to learn that Lord Peel had understood Weizmann to mean that Zionism aimed to bring to Palestine only one million Jews in all, including the 400,000 already settled there by 1936. That is why Ben-Gurion made it a point to tell the commission in camera that Zionism aimed for "at least four million." The following dialogue ensued.

> RUMBOLD: Four million in Palestine?
> BEN-GURION: Yes.
> HAMMOND: Total population, is that?
> BEN-GURION: No, I mean Jews . . .
> CHAIRMAN PEEL: Four million Jews?
> BEN-GURION: Yes, not in one year, or even in ten years, but perhaps in thirty or forty years.
> PEEL: How many Arabs are there in the country?
> BEN-GURION: At that time there will be about two million Arabs.
> PEEL: A total population of six million?
> BEN-GURION: Yes. I believe in time, with modern methods of industry, Haifa will be a town of one million Jews. It may sound ridiculous to you, and perhaps it is ridiculous, but we are an optimistic people. I remember that when I came to Palestine what is now Tel Aviv was sand.

He had had the figure of four million Jews in mind, he said, when he explained in his public testimony why a National Home in the framework of the British Mandate was preferable to a state. "A state means a separate political entity not attached to any other state unit. . . . For the solution of the Jewish problem, for our free national future, it is not necessary that Palestine should constitute a separate state and we should be only too glad if in the future, when the Jewish National Home is fully established, Palestine shall be eternally and completely free, but that it should be a member of a greater unit, that is, the British Commonwealth of Nations."

This turnabout was a landmark in Ben-Gurion's political life. Immigration was so important to him that he was willing to disavow the Jewish state, his heart's desire since his earliest days.

The commissioners apparently understood Ben-Gurion's Talmudic hairsplitting as intended to mislead British and world public opinion into believing that Zionism did not aspire to a state that would dispossess or dominate the Arabs. Perhaps one reason they were not impressed by Ben-Gurion, and now and then showed impatience with him, was their dislike of his dogmatic, emphatic, humorless style, which to them contrasted unfavorably with Weizmann's manner and appearance. The real fallout from his statements was among his labor movement associates, who demanded an explanation, but at the Histradrut council in February 1937, where he summarized his testimony, he made the fog denser.

> Just as the term "Jewish majority" does not define the Zionist desire, neither does the term "Jewish state" express it, and if a Jewish state on both sides of the Jordan was proposed to us on condition that no more than one and a half million Jews immigrate, enough to constitute a majority . . . we would have to reject such a proposal out of loyalty to the Jewish people and the needs of our redemption. A Jewish state of one and a half million Jews, unauthorized or unwilling to bring more Jews to Palestine, is nothing but a travesty and mutilation of Zionism. If we wish a Jewish majority, and if we wish a state, it is because we regard them as stages of Zionist realization, not as an end, but as a means to an end. We need a majority and we need a state so that we can take on the difficult and tremendous task of ingathering the exiles and, utilizing centralized governmental powers of our own, organize immigration and Jewish settlement on a broad scale. Zionist realization is more than a Jewish state. Zionism is the full and everlasting solution to the question of the Jewish people.

When it suited him Ben-Gurion could define his objectives clearly, and if he addressed the commission and the Histadrut with sweeping generalizations, it was intentional. He gave himself plenty of room to maneuver to achieve his primary aim of increasing immigration, whether through a continuation of the Mandate or a new state. And within just a few days he made use of this freedom and came out strongly for the exact opposite of what he had said on January 7. In 1958 he rationalized his about-face by saying that "private talks" with the commissioners had shown him that "from [then] on the fate of immigration very likely depended on the establishment of a Jewish state, not in the days of the Messiah and the far future, but speedily and in our days, as much as that was possible."[1] Perhaps his memory failed

him, for the recommendations of the Peel Commission — when he had
learned of them in January 1937, before their publication — hit him
like a bolt of lightning. He realized that if he had been right in sensing
a change of course, he was very wrong in thinking that the Peel Commission was a governmental tool to bring it about. In an instant the
stage setting of this political theater changed, rendering all the hard
work and preparations worthless; even Weizmann's disasters became
meaningless.

The Royal Commission's report, published in July 1937, recommended
the partitioning of Palestine into a Jewish state, an Arab state, and a
British Mandatory enclave. The first signal of the commission's leaning
in this direction had come during Weizmann's January 8 testimony,
when Professor Reginald Coupland suggested that, if there were no
other way to peace, the best final arrangement might be to "split Palestine into two halves, the plain being an independent Jewish state, as
independent as Belgium . . . and the rest of Palestine, plus Transjor-
dania, being an independent Arab state, as independent as Arabia."
Taken aback, Weizmann replied, "Permit me not to give a definite answer now. Let me think of it."[2]

Weizmann reported this exchange to the JAE and the Small Actions
Committee, adding his usual embellishment. On January 13 he had
told the latter, "During the last twenty minutes one of the commissioners said . . . Most of the Arabs now reside in the hills and the Jews in the
valleys. Let us partition the country: the bones to the Arabs and the
meat to the Jews, and thus a full-fledged Jewish state will be established legally and enjoy treaty relations with Great Britain. . . . This
will provide an excellent basis for you to conquer the Near East with
peace." On the same day Weizmann met in Nahalal with Professor
Coupland, who informed him that he regarded partition as the sole solution to the Palestine problem.

After the establishment of the State of Israel in 1948, some controversy arose among students of Zionism as to whether Weizmann or
Ben-Gurion first saw partition as political Zionism's way out of the
dead end it faced and as the best means to achieve statehood. According to the Weizmannites, immediately after his testimony on January 8
Weizmann had told his personal secretary that "the long toil of his life
was at last crowned with success." On the thirteenth, after his meeting
with Coupland, he said, "Today we laid the basis for the Jewish state."
There seems to be more legend than fact in these quotes. Except for his
talks with Archer Cust on cantonization, Weizmann's life work had not
been devoted to any partition-based solution. Had these statements

been attributed to Ben-Gurion the claim would stand up better, for the idea of partition was inherent in his very concept of Zionism, and over the years it had found myriad expressions.

Partition was latent in Ben-Gurion's principle of separating Palestine's population into two national structures, a principle that had manifested itself as far back as 1906, when Ben-Gurion had demanded that his party's trade unions be open to Jews only. The same idea fed the ideological premises he had laid down in America at the end of the First World War. After the war it had manifested itself in his credo that the Jews had not come to Palestine to dispossess or dominate the Arabs. In accordance with that belief he allocated the inhabited part of Palestine to the Arabs and the wilderness to the Jews, who would make it bloom. In the Histadrut, from 1921 on, he had put this idea into practice, dividing the trade unions, agriculture, industry, and services along national lines. Partition was next embodied in the idea of "100 percent Hebrew labor," which he had raised to a sacred principle in the 1920s and 1930s. Until then his idea of partition had applied only to Palestine's economy and administration, but Ben-Gurion's autonomy plans of the twenties added social, cultural, and constitutional partition. Further, Ben-Gurion's goal was to build Jewish settlement, under Jewish autonomy, by territorial contiguity, which amounted to geographic partition. Ben-Gurion had nearly used the word *partition* instead of *federation* for the plan he proposed for his party in 1929. The central concept of his plan for a Federal Palestine was two autonomous cantons which, with Britain, would establish joint tripartite rule. Even after the cantons became independent states Ben-Gurion wanted treaty relations with Britain.

Partition was also the basis of the Peel Commission's plan. Both Ben-Gurion and the commission put the holy places under British control. So similar were Ben-Gurion's plans and the recommendations of the Peel Commission that they seemed almost like the work of one hand. Accordingly, all that was required for Ben-Gurion to accept the partition idea was a mere tactical shift — from all of Palestine to a part of it.

Ben-Gurion never claimed that the partition idea had guided him from the beginning as a way to establish a state in part of Palestine or that he planned it as a state in Zionism's ultimate realization. Nor, probably, was he conscious of the comprehensive unity of his political ideas resulting from the combination of various fundamental elements in his thinking, as in a work of art. But in retrospect, the fantastic symmetry of Ben-Gurion's principles and the commission's proposal is obvious. Ben-Gurion recognized it the moment he heard from Weizmann that the Peel Commission was considering partition as a solution. It then dawned on him that "there is probably another way — not a Mandate but a state," by way of partition.[3]

If primacy is important, it would be better to ask which of the two reached this conclusion first. There is no doubt that Weizmann was thrilled with the partition idea. When Moshe Sharett was asked in Mapai's Central Committee meeting on February 5 what Weizmann had said to Professor Coupland in Nahalal, he replied, "We do not know exactly what he said, but it is clear that Coupland got the impression that there is something to talk about." Later Sharett added, "I was very apprehensive about Weizmann's quick enthusiasm in this matter, as if implying that this was our last chance and that if it fell through, we would be ruined."

Nonetheless, Ben-Gurion was the first to embrace partition as the basis of a new Zionist policy, as his JAE colleagues who had heard Weizmann's report on his testimony on January 8 attested. "When Weizmann told us these things, Ben-Gurion got very excited over the idea," said Sharett at a Mapai conference. On the same occasion, Eliezer Kaplan related that Ben-Gurion had said, "We must win over the American Zionists" to the partition proposal. Joseph Sprinzak, Weizmann's loyal follower, suggested to Itzhak Tabenkin, a leading opponent of partition, that he "investigate the matter well. It is still not clear to me who among us conceived of the partition idea, nor is it certain that the day won't come when Weizmann will say, 'You [Mapai] sowed and harvested this idea within me!'" Sharett's testimony agrees. According to him, Ben-Gurion's positive attitude "and my own [Sharett's] lack of 'don'ts' definitely encouraged Weizmann on the matter of partition, and Ben-Gurion and I are undoubtedly also responsible for [Weizmann's acceptance of it]." Kaplan, too, confirmed this in responding to angry naysayers who tended to accuse Weizmann alone of embracing partition without consulting either party or congress. "I attest before this assemblage that I cannot say our hands are clean and we are not guilty in the matter of the partition. We are guilty, and it does not matter how Weizmann spoke." It is reasonable to assume that Weizmann accepted the partition solution as the foundation of the new Zionist policy only after hearing Ben-Gurion's positive response.

It did appear to be a sharp reversal. In his April 1936 talk with George Antonius, Ben-Gurion had included all of Transjordan and the Golan in the Jewish state to be established within Federal Palestine. In January 1937 he not only became an adherent of partition, but he began to study the issue, day and night poring over maps and census figures and drawing up his own partition plan — the "two-state plan" — which he would present to Mapai's Central Committee on

February 5. Within Mapai, Ben-Gurion was thought to be the first to have seen the partition solution suggested by the Peel Commission as a cornerstone for a new Zionist policy.

At long last, the two captains of Zionism had a common strategy, with plenty of room for understanding and cooperation. It might have been anticipated that from there on they would pull together and Zionism would prosper. But this was not to be. Weizmann left Palestine for London on January 20, without having sat down with Ben-Gurion to thrash out their views on partition. Nevertheless, Ben-Gurion already knew that he did not "endorse Weizmann's consent to this plan, nor do I know what he consented to." Certainly their approaches toward partition and how to achieve it were worlds apart.

First of all, Ben-Gurion warned that while partition was the answer, "it is not the solution under all conditions. . . . I do not consent to *any* partition of Palestine; it depends on how it is partitioned." In order not to lose both state and Mandate, he tightened his hold on both. After the Peel partition scheme was published, Mapai could compare it to Ben-Gurion's two-state plan, whose guiding principle, he told Mapai's Central Committee, was "the desperate war against . . . the danger of strangling immigration." In contrast to the 4.84 million dunams in western Palestine allocated to the Jewish state by the commission, Ben-Gurion assigned it 4.38 million. To the Arab state he gave only 3.88 million, as opposed to the 20.67 earmarked by the commission. He added the 16.79 million dunams left over, consisting mainly of the Negev, to the 790,000 the commission had allotted the Mandatory enclave (Haifa port, a corridor to Transjordan, and the holy places), leaving a total of 17.94 million dunams under the British Mandate.* He wanted sovereignty, even over a tiny area, as long as masses of Jews — he spoke of three million — could be brought to Palestine and settled in the area he allocated to the Mandate (in which the Balfour Declaration was incorporated) as well, on the unstated condition that the Jews eventually inherit the desert they made to bloom. All he told the Central Committee was that if in addition to the area allocated to the Jewish state more territory was earmarked for future Jewish expansion, "then that is the solution." His division of the population was a clue to his drift: in contrast to the 545,000 Arabs the commission placed in the Arab state, Ben-Gurion put 213,000 there, only two-fifths as many. He put the other three-fifths in the Mandatory area.

Weizmann, on the other hand, demanded far less. In mid March

---

* The slight discrepancy between Ben-Gurion's total and the commission's apparently resulted from the use of different data.

Sharett learned that Weizmann considered a state having "enough room for the immigration of fifty to sixty thousand per year" and "absolute internal independence" as a satisfactory temporary solution for a transitional period of twenty-five to thirty years.

The second difference between the two revolved around the question of tactics. Both agreed that Zionist policy must be directed toward pressuring the commissioners to improve their proposal — to expand the area and authority of the Jewish state. But whereas Weizmann would have approached the partition proposal openly and enthusiastically, Ben-Gurion wished to conceal not only his excitement but also the JAE's readiness to accept partition, for fear the Arabs would reject it if it was good for the Zionists. Partition meant abolishing the Mandate, and if that was suggested by the Zionists, "Britain would probably accept it, but there is no guarantee that it would at the same time accept the establishment of a Jewish state." The Mandate had to be safeguarded until "something better" was given in exchange. "If this scheme comes up as a Jewish proposal," he told Mapai's Central Committee on February 5, "it is lost. It must come forth as *England's* plan." Mapai parlance referred to this strategy as "Ben-Gurion's method." Sharett, who supported the "method," added that the JAE should make sure it seemed that the plan was being "forced" upon it.

Weizmann did not act accordingly. Back in London on January 31, he began talking up the partition solution, even with Wauchope, who should have been the first to get the impression that all the Zionists rejected partition. Through him Weizmann led the British cabinet to understand that the Jews were all for partition. Meanwhile Ben-Gurion was signaling to the British government that it would come up against the Yishuv if it tried to enforce partition. At the Histadrut council of February 8 he described the force the Yishuv could bring to bear.

> Great dangers await us on every front, English and Arab. . . . Worldwide our strength is next to nothing alongside the mighty powers contending. We cannot turn the scales. But in this one small corner of our planet, Palestine, we are the *decisive* factor. We shall decide the fate of Palestine . . . because we are the only people in the world for whom Palestine is a question of life and death. . . . Many are the interests vested in this country. . . . What is our strength against gigantic powers . . . against the Arabs in their Arab countries . . . against the mightiest empire in history . . . the British Empire? . . . If the question of Jewish presence or nonpresence in Palestine were a question of *existence* for Iraq, Saudi Arabia, Syria, Egypt, a question of *life* or death for the British Empire, we would not emerge victorious.
>
> Our strength and security in this country are founded on the *unique-*

ness this land occupies in our regard . . . *on the uniqueness of the vital and fateful interest which binds us, and us alone, to this land.*[4]

To Ben-Gurion "the horrible suffering of masses of Jews in the Diaspora" was the central motivation of the Zionist enterprise. This massive suffering, together with the Yishuv's 400,000 Jews, would constitute the combined force with which he intended to back up the new Zionist policy. Ben-Gurion aroused considerable resentment in the London JAE. Blanche Dugdale, who in mid February had grumbled in her diary of "a tiresome split between Chaim and Ben-Gurion," early in March wrote, "What makes me most nervous is the growing rift between Chaim and Ben-Gurion — who is making most foolish and intransigent speeches in Palestine . . . We all try to soothe Chaim, who is very angry." Only after Sharett came to London and explained Ben-Gurion's method did Weizmann see its logic. Sharett then wrote, "We were all agreed that we must by all means avoid creating the impression that the plan is ours, so that we may be free to fight it." What won Weizmann over to the method was the internal argument that it was necessary not to provoke opponents of partition within the Zionist movement, who were liable, said Sharett, to create a "tremendous upheaval" within Zionism. But Ben-Gurion's act of rejecting partition was so convincing that Weizmann began to suspect him of switching sides and in June asked him directly about "your stand on the plan." Ben-Gurion recorded in his diary afterward, "To Chaim it seems I was once in favor of partition but recoiled after seeing the public's opposition."

The last cause of friction was that Ben-Gurion had no confidence in Weizmann as a negotiator. He wrote Sharett, "In political negotiations he is the most dangerous man to Zionism, in my opinion, because he can start with a plan like this and end up with land reserves."* Ben-Gurion made a point of meeting with Wauchope, who had returned to Palestine, to find out exactly what Weizmann had said to him. He had done this, he told Mapai and the JAE, because he was "full of anxiety. . . . There is partition and there is partition, and only a fine line separates a partition that saves from one that destroys." Hearing from Wauchope that "Weizmann is strongly in favor of this plan," Ben-Gurion played dumb, as if cantonization were the subject at hand. "I don't know what he favors now," he told Wauchope. "But before he went to London we had a similar plan before us, cantonization, and we all opposed it. Weizmann even wrote the Royal Commission that he rejected the idea." Then Wauchope put Ben-Gurion's fear into words.

---

* In 1936 Weizmann had thought to secure land reserves for the Arabs as assurance that Zionism had no designs to dispossess them.

"At present another plan is under discussion ... and I gathered that Weizmann was very much in favor of this solution." "You have no faith in Weizmann," Dugdale told Ben-Gurion, adding, "In many cases neither [did she]," which gave him "a nasty shock."[5]

But Ben-Gurion was not in London, which had once again become the main theater of operations. Weizmann was, and he alone, as even Ben-Gurion admitted, could negotiate on Zionism's behalf with the commissioners, as well as with British leaders, to secure the best possible partition scheme. Ben-Gurion had to be satisfied with offering Weizmann advice, convincing him of its soundness, and threatening parliamentary discipline if he strayed too far from the line. Weizmann held all the cards except one: without the authorization of the Zionist Congress, which was to meet in Zurich in August, Weizmann could make no commitment to the British government on any partition plan. To this end he needed Ben-Gurion, who held the key to a majority.

Their conflict of 1935 and 1936 replayed itself in 1937, with Ben-Gurion in Jerusalem trying to supervise and guide Weizmann, sending Sharett and others to London. But this time Weizmann was more defiant. He would not go to America to mobilize Zionist public opinion there for partition, as ordered by the JAE, and he would not stay in London to negotiate better borders for the proposed Jewish state. The news that he intended to leave London in April "stunned" Ben-Gurion. "His leaving," he wrote Sharett, "is a slap in the face to all of us." In better days Ben-Gurion would have reacted "more emphatically and effectively [but] at this time" he left it to Sharett to "do all in your power to prevent Chaim from taking such a step." Ben-Gurion felt that, during "the decisive days" of April, Weizmann had to be active in London in the hope that he would be able "to take a step that may determine the line."

But Weizmann did not regard April as "decisive," since he expected the city to shut down as it "began preparations for the coronation" of King George VI on May 12. In early April, Weizmann relaxed at Saint Moritz, then left for Belgium and France to meet government officials and members of the Mandates Commission of the League of Nations. When he returned to London on the eleventh he toyed with the possibility of a ten-day trip to America.

Ben-Gurion thought differently. Since the coronation would attract important personages from all over the world to London, he considered the time ripe for political action. With a great deal of trouble he managed to keep Weizmann in London during the second half of April, but he could not hold him there for the coronation. On May 4 Weizmann took off "for cure," he cabled Ben-Gurion, for a month, he told

Sharett. Nonetheless, Ben-Gurion spoke kindly of him to the Zionist Actions Committee. "I do not believe any member of the Jewish people bears so heavy a burden at this time or that in all the days of the exile there has been another Jew who shouldered a responsibility as weighty as that carried now by the president of the Zionist Organization." He had learned something about gaining friends and influencing people from Weizmann.[6]

Realizing once again that supervision and coaching from afar were not enough, Ben-Gurion left on April 29 to meet Weizmann in Paris. During their talk, all the errors Weizmann had made in a London meeting with Professor Coupland began to flash at Ben-Gurion like warning lights. "Chaim . . . did make notes of all the things we wanted him to ask, but he did not bring them all up. He argued principally against leaving any part of the Upper Galilee out of the Jewish portion, and Coupland remarked that he saw his point. Chaim insisted mainly on making possible the immigration of fifty to sixty thousand annually (a serious error — this schedule has nothing to do with partition, and it cannot determine the area). Coupland asked if 2 to 3 million dunams of irrigated land was sufficient, and Chaim answered in the affirmative. Coupland asked if he would be satisfied if the border reached Rafah, and the answer was affirmative. . . . From what Chaim has said it is evident to me that the area Coupland has in mind is much, much smaller than we need." Ben-Gurion reported all this to his diary, as if redeclaring open season on Weizmann's foul-ups.

On May 6 Ben-Gurion left for London and Weizmann for a vacation in Merano in the Italian Alps. He would return in early June for a dinner in his honor at the home of Archibald Sinclair, the Liberal Party leader, with the leaders of all the British parties, "and there Chaim will fire his parting shot" before the Peel Commission presented its report to the government. Until the dinner no important political activity was anticipated by the London JAE, which was typical of periods when Weizmann was away. During the days of the coronation London was, as Ben-Gurion had claimed, buzzing with important figures whom Weizmann could have met at receptions, dinners, and private interviews. As ever, it was clearly Weizmann who had all the contacts, and his absence suggested a father who locks the family inside and takes off with the house keys. Ben-Gurion, longing for action, could not meet with Coupland, Ormsby-Gore, or any other top statesmen. He spent his time buying books, talking with reporters from the *Times* and the *Herald Tribune,* and meeting with the Arabist St. John Philby, English and Eretz-Israeli Zionists (Leonard Stein, Harold Laski, Pinchas Rutenberg, Dov Hoz, and others), and with members of the Jewish Agency Council. He also went to a reception for Itzhak and Rachel

Ben-Zvi, who represented the Yishuv at the festivities. He spent the day of the coronation locked in the Zionist office — "I am the only one in London not . . . listening to the great scene [broadcast by the BBC]," he wrote in his diary — and phoned Rabbi Stephen Wise in New York. On May 23 he spoke to the English Zionist Federation, and the next day he met with Labour leaders Clement Attlee and Herbert Morrison. On May 25 he dined with Lord George Ambrose Lloyd, who headed the British Council and with whom he had had a long talk in Jerusalem early in 1937. Strangely enough, this pro-Arab lord, later to become colonial secretary, was the only British statesman with whom Ben-Gurion struck up a friendship.

Bad news from the Political Department's intelligence headquarters in Jerusalem — that the commission might tear the Galilee away from the Jewish state — led Ben-Gurion to press Weizmann to go immediately to Paris and enlist the aid of France's Jewish prime minister, Léon Blum. Blanche Dugdale and Doris May joined his efforts; even Vera Weizmann was called in and cabled her husband on the gravity of the situation. But Weizmann claimed there was nothing he could do at this point. Not until three weeks later could Ben-Gurion breathe a sigh of relief, as he wrote in his diary. "The two women's [Dugdale's and Vera's] cable influenced Chaim and tomorrow he arrives in Paris." On May 29 he added, "Chaim sees Blum tomorrow. . . . Chaim will be here tomorrow. Vera asked Arthur [Lourie] and me to come over tomorrow afternoon at five."

Present at tea at the Weizmanns' on May 30 were Arthur Lourie, secretary of the London Political Section, Blanche Dugdale, adviser in the Zionist office, and Dov Hoz, one of Ben-Gurion's men, who had been sent to London to open and nurture contacts with Labour and to supervise Weizmann. As always in London, Weizmann basked in the footlights while Ben-Gurion functioned from backstage, keeping a close watch on Weizmann's health and state of mind, which became major subjects of his reports to Mapai. "The rest in Merano did [Weizmann] good. . . . Chaim is ready to fight for the north and make it known that without the Huleh* we will wreck the 'plan.' "

Weizmann's sole contact with the Peel Commission was Coupland — Lord Peel had turned down three invitations to meet with Weizmann — and Ben-Gurion attached great importance to this channel, through which he hoped to get some of his demands across to the commission as it worked out its partition scheme. Therefore he had to know exactly what was said between Weizmann and Coupland, ver-

---

* A lake to the north of Lake Kinneret. Weizmann intended it to be drained and used for agriculture, and its rich peat deposits to be excavated.

bally and in writing. "Chaim read us Coupland's letter," he reported in his diary on May 30, after the tea. "The phrase I took down in my notebook from Vera, 'Things took a different turn,' is not in the letter." In this letter Coupland had also asked Weizmann to meet with him on the evening of May 30 at 9:00. After their talk Weizmann phoned Ben-Gurion, but he did not give him a fuller report until the next evening at 6:00, at a meeting Weizmann had called. Coupland had presented him with a choice: severing the Galilee or the Negev. "Chaim, of course, chose the Galilee. The town of Haifa will be included in the Jewish area and the English will get only the port. Jaffa, Lod, and Ramla will be part of the Jewish area and there will be a Mandatory corridor to Jerusalem." Later Ben-Gurion returned to his room at the Mount Royal — where he always stayed in London — and sat down to analyze his new data and plot the best course of action. This was also part of his function, as his diaries, pages of which he sent to Mapai in Tel Aviv, attest. "I fear Chaim's story is too good to be true. I find it difficult to believe that this will be the commission's proposal. The entire Galilee and all the way down to the potash works, and from there crosswise all the way to the sea, the coastal plain until Majdal, including Jaffa, and a corridor to Jerusalem to top it off. Is it possible?"

If it was true, he decided, "all efforts must be concentrated on the Negev, so at least half of the Negev from the potash concession south to Eilat will become English territory (Mandatory or otherwise)." But first he had to coach Weizmann, a task that proved difficult and frustrating, as he complained in a letter to Sharett. "As usual, Chaim regards as central some point that has captured his heart — this time it's the Huleh. And since he believes himself successful on this point, nothing else is important in his eyes and it's almost impossible to speak to him about anything else. Although he pretends to listen, it is like talking to a brick wall. And since he is our only means of contact the situation is very alarming." The situation was nicely summed up by Sharett, discussing Ben-Gurion's diary pages from London with Mapai's Central Committee. "Concerning the truly painful question, that all our contacts depend on Weizmann alone, it should be clear that as long as Weizmann heads the movement, no important Englishman in London will listen to anyone else . . . knowing that Weizmann said otherwise."

Worse still, Weizmann sought to enhance his superior status even further, jealously keeping his contacts to himself. It sometimes seemed that he treated his colleagues like poor relations. Zelig Brodetsky had complained more than once that Weizmann did not include him in his political contacts; on June 1 he "poured out his heart over Chaim's behavior" to Ben-Gurion. One October day in 1936 Weizmann had told Berl Katznelson that Walter Elliot (secretary of state for agriculture and Dugdale's friend and channel to the cabinet) and Leopold Amery (first lord of the admiralty, colonial secretary, and, eventually, secretary of state for India) would be joining him for dinner. "Chaim asked me to come," Katznelson wrote Ben-Gurion, "but then remembered to ask if I had a dinner jacket. Since I do not, we agreed that I would come to the after-dinner talk." Rutenberg had complained several times to Ben-Gurion that Weizmann had failed to invite him to a dinner at Sinclair's home on June 8, at which Winston Churchill was to be the prize guest. This dinner was intended to give Weizmann a platform for explaining why the JAE favored partition and to rally the dinner guests to support it in Parliament. To his diary Ben-Gurion revealed a hint of his own feelings: "I did not console him with the fact that I was not among the invited either."

Weizmann, as if handing out crumbs, gave an account of the dinner to the Zionist office staff, who gathered around him the next morning. "Everyone" had come, except for Lloyd George, who had apologized and promised to support in Parliament whatever decisions they came to. Everyone included Churchill, Victor Cazalet, and Amery, front bench Conservatives; Clement Attlee, Labour Party leader, and Josiah Wedgwood, former Labour government minister; James Rothschild, Liberal; and of course Sinclair, head of the Liberal Party — M.P.'s and declared Zionists every one. At the table, Churchill exhorted Attlee, "Weizmann is your master, and mine, and that of Lloyd George. What he says goes. It's true we left him on his own. It's easy for us to talk, but he carries the weight. If he consents to partition, I will not say a word . . . but I must speak my mind. A Jewish state is a mirage." Churchill then went into a long tirade against His Majesty's government, assuring Weizmann of his own support every time the government might try "to swindle" Zionism.

> WEIZMANN: I've seen you once in ten years.
> CHURCHILL: Yes, I am afraid to see you. After every meeting I am depressed for ten days, and I have to work for my living.

This is the way Ben-Gurion recorded Weizmann's version of the dinner in his diary. He was astounded, as the others had been, at what it seemed to reveal of Weizmann's stature in the eyes of his mighty friends, although, said Ben-Gurion to Zionists he met at Melchett House on the evening of the ninth, "the dinner will have been for nothing unless we mobilize the speakers" for the upcoming parliamentary debate. However, what the dinner actually turned out to prove was Weizmann's naiveté in trusting English politicians. Weizmann also described the dinner to Coupland, who followed Churchill's lead in flattering Weizmann, saying, "I knew we were all in your pocket."

When Weizmann repeated this in the Zionist office, Dugdale alone saw through it. She knew English aristocracy, and she knew Churchill's manner when he had a drink in his hand, and she pointed out to Weizmann that "these people were in no sense a team — [and] that they knew little or nothing about the subject." Churchill, she noted, had been "very drunk," and so, "in his most brilliant style . . . he fulminated . . . in favour of Zionism for three hours." Inwardly she was astonished that Weizmann was "oddly impressed by this performance, and anxious to exploit it in some undefined way." Having prevailed upon a reluctant Weizmann to let her get the impressions of some of the other dinner guests, she went with Ben-Gurion and Namier to the House of Commons to talk to Cazalet, "who *more* than confirmed my impressions of Winston's state, and wild talk."

Still another report on the dinner made it clear that Weizmann had omitted from his summary to the Zionist office the fact that most of the guests opposed partition. After Weizmann had made an opening statement in which he mentioned that the two ex–colonial secretaries — Churchill and Amery — had been unable to influence the administration to take a more pro-Zionist position, Churchill had replied, "Yes, we are all guilty men. You [to Weizmann] know you are our master — and yours, and yours [pointing to other members of the party] — and what you say goes. If you ask us to fight we shall fight like tigers." But once Churchill got started he began to voice emphatic disapproval of partition. Attlee was shocked at the idea of partition, which he considered a concession to violence, an admission of failure, and a victory for fascism. Wedgwood and Sinclair also disapproved of partition, but like Churchill and Attlee said they would not oppose it if the Zionists went for it. Only Amery backed it fully. Dugdale's fears had been well grounded. When, ten years later, Weizmann wrote his memoirs, he left out this dinner. But in June 1937, and for some years following, Weizmann and Ben-Gurion still put their full trust in these Gentile Zionist friends.[7]

The four weeks between the dinner and the publication of the Peel Report saw Ben-Gurion more tense and anxious than ever. Not only the future of Zionism, but his own as well, hung in the balance. Neither his party nor the Zionist movement had pronounced itself on partition, yet he had already committed himself unequivocally to a Jewish state in part of Palestine. The only question — the key question — which would determine his acceptance or rejection of the report, was the size of the portion given to the Jewish state. It was imperative that there should be no controversy within the JAE or between him and Weizmann.

As was his custom, Ben-Gurion tried to win Weizmann over through his aides, and on June 11 Weizmann's closest and most loyal aide invited him to five o'clock tea. "After tea Mr. Dugdale left and we were by ourselves," disclosed Ben-Gurion to his diary. He first shared with Baffy Dugdale his intense anxiety, "which had deepened particularly after the dinner." He then told her, "At this moment there are two persons whose stand counts, Chaim and Baffy ... In the mind of English public opinion Chaim is the Jewish people and Baffy his prophet." His anxiety, he continued, arose from three fears: that Britain would enforce the creation of a Jewish state in an inadequate area; that it would abandon the Mandate; and that Weizmann's mistakes would undermine Weizmann's position in the Zionist movement. "I shrink from the day there is a rift between Chaim and the movement, and between the Jews and the British government."

Dugdale tried to calm him. "We cannot do anything until the report is published ... When [it is] we will act." She said encouragingly that the creation of a state, even in the tiniest area, would be a useful step. Weizmann's description of a talk he had had with Coupland led her to an important conclusion. In response to his statement that Weizmann was ready to compromise on frontiers as long as this did not "break" the Jewish Agency, she had written in her diary, "But I think he may have to [break the Agency]. ... Great events lie ahead. The Jews in the plains — so it must be before Armageddon." A plan of action had crystallized in her mind, and on June 11 she said to Ben-Gurion, "If we get a state now, later we can settle all parts of Palestine. Having the state will give us the strength to reach an accord with the Arabs."

Ben-Gurion did not see her point at once, and replied, "I cannot share such optimism. Any partition, even one I consider disastrous, would rouse the Arabs against us." Dugdale became more explicit. "The Gentiles believe in [the Jews'] exceptional ability." Still missing the point, he responded, "And this belief is a good excuse to throw us a crumb, since even with a crumb we shall work wonders. But we cannot settle the Jews of Germany and Poland in Tel Aviv even if we build skyscrapers. A chopped-up 'scheme' will not only destroy the Yishuv and our future in Palestine, it will be a dreadful catastrophe for Jews throughout the Diaspora."

Dugdale said, "When in difficulty I always ask myself, what would A.J.B. [Lord Balfour] have said? And it seems to me that now he would tell the Jews, be brave. Take the risk. Prove what you can do with your state — the rest will come."

Finally Ben-Gurion saw the light. Whether or not Dugdale meant that a small Jewish state would expand with or without the Arabs' blessing, it seems that the idea of the militarily "expanding state" took root in his mind. It may have occurred to him earlier, but there is no evidence of that. In any event, only the legitimization this idea received from this British aristocrat, for whom he had great respect, and from the great Balfour as well, turned the spark into a beacon. More than before, he saw partition as the path to redemption. Profusely grateful, he said, "There has already been a time when our destiny rested in the hands of two persons, a man and a woman. The man was Barak Ben-Avinoam, the woman Deborah. You are our Deborah now."

On taking his leave he was more resolute than ever. In the dispute then going on among the ayesayers over whether the Jewish state should include the Galilee or the Negev, he chose the former, as long as the Negev remained in the Mandatory area, open to Jewish settlement. At a discussion in the Zionist office on June 14 he said that he did not insist on "the inclusion of the Negev in a Jewish state at the moment," for the simple reason that "we cannot now take it all in." The next day Dugdale, Namier, and Brodetsky collaborated with Ben-Gurion in drafting a letter that Weizmann reviewed, signed, and sent to Colonial Secretary Ormsby-Gore. In it Weizmann stated that he was "not in any sense committed to any partition scheme," but since he was "anxious as always to be helpful to H.M. Government," he briefly set out what in his view were "the minimum requirements for a Jewish state": the Galilee, the valleys and coastal plain (in Haifa, Great Britain "should retain whatever is required for the needs of the Navy, Army, and Air Force"), and a corridor to Jerusalem. As for the Negev, "We suggest that it will be kept under British control, while open to development and settlement by Jews." This represented the minimum area Ben-Gurion had sketched. "For me the main thing is the northern border [Galilee] and naturally sufficient area in the coastal plain, a recognized stake of the Jewish state in Jerusalem, and exclusion of the Negev from the area of the Arab state." If the government proposed such a plan, he promised, "I will fight for partition." On the other hand, should the government propose a scheme that was nothing more than a "crystallization" of the Jewish National Home in its present size, "I will fight partition, even if they call it a Jewish state." Since he was well aware that not only "among other parties, but also in my own, there will be many against [partition]," supporting the partition solution was one of the biggest political wagers he ever made.

Although Weizmann and he were then in the same boat, the duty of bringing it into harbor safely fell primarily to Ben-Gurion. He represented Zionism's largest party and it was up to him to guarantee a majority — a formidable, if not impossible, task. Of Mapai's three leaders he alone favored partition. Katznelson and Tabenkin rejected it outright, and their influence on the party, particularly on its younger generation, was immense. When in April he had brought his plan for a Jewish state in part of Palestine before Mapai's Central Committee for the second time, many argued that it was an improbable and fantastic dream, one which the English would never agree to and the Arabs would surely fight. Ben-Gurion retorted, "We must not underestimate Arab opposition, but neither should we overrate it. Every Arab revolt in this land . . . has thus far brought new gains for the Jews . . . This one would probably bring us even greater political gain." Although this debate did not blow up into a full-fledged controversy, it did not resolve the issue either.

Even the loyal Dov Hoz was shaken when in June, at a Mapai discussion of Weizmann-Coupland talks, he learned that before Mapai or the Zionist Congress had adopted any resolution, JAE representatives were discussing "not the essence of the partition scheme, but its details." Tabenkin went so far as to voice a veiled threat to split the party. "I find myself in great confusion, and I do not know if further discussion is worthwhile . . . Only a united front, absolutely opposed to this whole partition issue, could put things right. . . . Weizmann had no authorization to negotiate partition. The Jewish people gave him no mandate to do so." If Ben-Gurion, receiving the minutes of these proceedings in London, had any doubt that Tabenkin was accusing him and Sharett as well as Weizmann, Tabenkin's later statements resolved it. "The trust of the people in Weizmann is not *in him alone;* rather it is placed *in the movement,* in Weizmann, Ben-Gurion, and Moshe [Sharett] — that the movement *will not betray* that trust. . . . Weizmann was unauthorized and out of line to hold such negotiations." Ben-Gurion heard Katznelson's opinion over the phone on June 14, when Berl voiced his doubts that a Jewish state was viable at this stage of the Yishuv's and Zionism's development. It would be, he said, "a premature birth."

Ben-Gurion had to develop support for partition in his party and the Zionist movement in Palestine and abroad, particularly in the United States. Telephone calls, letters, and lectures became the order of the day. He told Rabbi Stephen Wise in New York, "The coming weeks will determine the fate of Palestine . . . We do not know what the six gentlemen are thinking . . . We assume it is partition or something worse." "Can there be anything worse?" Wise asked, and Ben-Gurion replied, "Undoubtedly: land reserves [for Arabs], restricted immigration to keep us an eternal minority." He wrote Mapai members in Palestine in the same vein, and to Ussishkin, the leader of those opposed to partition, he sent a long letter of persuasion.[8]

Weizmann, having no party to answer to, was free to take a week's rest at the Hotel Claridge in Paris. An envious Ben-Gurion wrote Paula on June 22, "Weizmann leaves today for Paris and will not return until week's end. If I could I too would escape for a few days to a quiet place, and gladly. My nerves are shot and I cannot sleep at night — and before us is perhaps another war, the likes of which we have never seen, and in another six weeks, the Congress. I am now trying in various ways to learn more of the report's content." To make things worse, he received a letter from Weizmann in Paris, written in Russian to "Dear B.G.," informing him that "Ussishkin and other zealots in Palestine are moving heaven and earth. . . . Zealots have always brought destruction upon the Jews," and urging him to increase propaganda in Palestine and London. It was signed, "With love, Chaim."[9] Another result of their new alliance was that when he returned to London Weizmann took Ben-Gurion along to his June 28 interview with Ormsby-Gore.

Meanwhile the minutes of the partition discussion in the Zionist office and a copy of Weizmann's letter to Ormsby-Gore reached Mapai and the Jerusalem JAE. Opponents of partition heightened their criticism of Weizmann and Ben-Gurion's conducting negotiations on the borders of the Jewish state even though the Zionist Organization had never sanctioned partition. The bonds of Weizmann and Ben-Gurion's forced alliance tightened as the attack on them grew stronger, and Ben-Gurion, a loyal ally, showed himself ready to hang for Weizmann's crimes. On June 22 he had written his colleagues in Jerusalem that he was in complete agreement with Ussishkin's reaction to the letter to Ormsby-Gore — "If Weizmann has to be tried in a court, military or otherwise, for this letter, I too must stand accused. . . . I am 100 percent accountable [for the letter], even if I do not side with its style or content. . . . But I now see it as my *sacred* duty . . . to stand beside him," either to assist him or prevent him from erring. To those who demanded that he return to report to the Jerusalem JAE and coordinate his actions with it, Ben-Gurion responded, "I know that there is a watch to be kept here and I have no business forsaking it. And until the report comes out I shall not budge unless the Zionist Executive or the party leadership asks for my resignation."

He fared no better in Mapai. Faced with the approaching elections to the Zionist Congress, Mapai had to determine whether it was for or against partition. The demand to convene the party council to resolve the issue, with or without Ben-Gurion, grew more insistent. At a Central Committee meeting that lasted through the night of June 20–21, Sharett did his best to block this move: "I cannot consent to calling a council now in order to pass a resolution and determine Mapai's stand on partition . . . without Ben-Gurion's participation . . . I . . . caution members against deciding without Ben-Gurion. Why not without him? Because he is the one on trial."

Tabenkin and the naysayers prevailed, however, and cabled a demand to Ben-Gurion to come at once. Ben-Gurion responded, "A council before the report comes out will not alter the situation. For the next three weeks it is out of the question that I leave. Consult with Moshe [Sharett]." When this consultation was held on June 23, Sharett again tried to block the council, and Tabenkin again prevailed. "Ben-Gurion continues to go his own way. At the first meeting at which the partition issue was addressed, the majority opposed it. And in spite of this we are witnessing one step after another on the road to partition. This is a tragedy for the movement . . . and so I urgently demand that a council be convened in a week's time, even if Ben-Gurion cannot make it."

It was resolved to hold the council on July 8, to allow Ben-Gurion enough time to get there, and to cable him the news. Ben-Gurion did not respond, but by telephone asked Sharett to make sure that the council "does not adopt any final resolution." Sharett wangled another day's delay, and on July 8 Katznelson and Golomb wired Ben-Gurion, "Our council tomorrow must adopt resolutions . . . If you are apprehensive about resolutions in general, you should come and we will postpone the council for a few days. There are far-reaching proposals for action that cannot be clarified without you. Wire." Ben-Gurion answered, "I cannot leave. There is no need for hasty decisions." The council thereupon convened on the ninth, lasted three days, and closed with a resolution rejecting the Peel Commission's partition scheme, which had meanwhile been published.[10]

It is probable that Ben-Gurion's indifference to the entreaties that he return to Palestine was not merely tactical or showed lack of concern for democratic principles. He was in the midst of a political process that demanded his maximum concentration and absolute solitude, like a poet or composer who is attentive only to the fleeting fragments of ideas within. Like them, he feared losing the creative movement of his thought if he diverted his attention for an instant. A hint of the absent-mindedness that had been apparent on the eve of his departure for London in May was his packing two pairs of pajama bottoms, without matching tops. He must have thought it would be nice to have his wife alongside him during these trying days, and for the first time in his married life, he sincerely beseeched Paula to join him.

Before leaving for London Ben-Gurion had discussed with her the possibility of sending Geula abroad for her eighteenth birthday, and in early June wrote his wife to get ready to go. "Geula will stay in Paris and you will be with me in London. . . . Write me at once if you agree to start out in two or three weeks . . . and what I have to arrange for

your trip." So began an exchange of letters and telegrams which make
it clear that Paula had sensed an unexpected windfall in her husband's
sudden need of her and was making the most of it. She wrote him that
she had to outfit herself properly, since she could not appear beside
him in London or at the Congress in old clothes. In addition she needed
money, but she was not sure exactly how much. On June 16 Ben-
Gurion began to show signs of impatience.

> I must ask you to please cable me how much money you need. . . . Re-
> garding clothes for you, I suggest you get them here from [Hirsh] Avra-
> ham, Perlmutt's brother-in-law [Perlmutt was a member of Poale Zion in
> London] — it will be fine and beautiful and inexpensive. If in any case
> you still want to shop in Tel Aviv before the trip — shop . . . but regard-
> less, you must come at the beginning of July. . . . Let me know immedi-
> ately by telegram how much money you need. . . . I'm not asking you to
> account for how you spend it. I've never asked you to, but I want to be
> sure that you leave for London at the end of the month. Next week may
> be a decisive one in our history. . . . Kisses, Daddy.

Apparently he did not think this letter was enough to get Paula moving, for he sent a telegram the same day: "Wire at once how much you
need. David."

But Paula was in no hurry, and her wardrobe took top priority. She
cabled Ben-Gurion that she and Geula would set out on July 8. "Why
did you put it off until July 8?" demanded an upset Ben-Gurion on June
22. On June 29 he sent her the following letter.

> It is difficult for me to explain to you my emotional tension and distress
> during these weeks in London. We face a complete revolution in our lives
> in Palestine, perhaps in Jewish history. And we do not know if we are
> standing before a major disaster or a great conquest. Both are possible.
> The report has been written but *we* do not know what it contains. . . .
> Matters are so serious and significant, and the subtle differences in various
> phrases so important, that without reading it through there is no way of
> knowing or estimating whether this is poison or cure. . . . Yesterday
> Chaim and I saw Ormsby-Gore. I am sending you — *and this is top se-
> cret!* — an English transcript of the conversation. This talk did not make
> us much wiser . . . The party members, as you must know, demanded that
> I come to the council. This time I could not fulfill their demand. I do not
> know if what I am doing is good or bad, but I feel I must be here during
> these crucial days, and although I know how important it is that the party
> cover all sides of this issue, and although I am aware that my participation
> in this is essential, I simply cannot leave here now.
>
> I wired you to leave this week, so that you would be here, perhaps,
> when we get the report. To my regret I see from your answer that you
> cannot leave this week. And what a pity! . . . Kisses, Daddy.

After he mailed this letter, insomnia got the better of him, most likely because of his forced alliance with Weizmann. Ben-Gurion was not blind to the fact that in taking him along to see Ormsby-Gore, Weizmann had made him a partner in the responsibility for his policy or, as Dugdale noted in her diary the day after the interview, "Ben-Gurion will now stand or fall with Chaim." On July 4 Ben-Gurion reported to his diary, "This is the fourth night that I can't sleep."[11]

But there were many other reasons why Ben-Gurion could have been nervous. First was the anxiety that the Peel Commission's recommendations would differ for the worse from what Dugdale had gathered from her friends in government and secretly told the London JAE. How would he and Zionism fare should the published report decree ceasing immigration and land sales? Second, he was afraid that at the last minute the British government would refuse to publish the report because it was too favorable to the Jews, representing a "political conquest and historic chance such as we've never had since the day our land was destroyed," as Ben-Gurion wrote to the Mapai council. This fear arose from a rumor and from his unceasing anxiety that the time history had allotted the Zionist enterprise would suddenly run out. "It seems the report will not be published on July 7 as we expected, but on July 14, and perhaps not even then," he wrote in his letter to Paula. He explained that the fall of Léon Blum's socialist government in France and the purge of generals in the Soviet Union had emboldened Hitler and Mussolini, and the tension between Germany and Italy and Britain and France had increased. He wrote, "There will be no war now, as England is not yet ready and is trying to placate Germany. But the situation is tense, and some think that under these circumstances the government will not wish to publish the report, as it is liable to lead to riots in Palestine."

His anxiety led Ben-Gurion to take a rather uncomradely step. On July 2 the Political Department in Jerusalem had received the report, Sharett said, "from two different channels at once." He had traveled to Cairo that day to phone a summary of it to the London JAE. "Chaim and Ben-Gurion were intensely relieved by it," Dugdale wrote in her diary, unaware that Ben-Gurion had leaked the summary to Palcor, the Jewish Agency's news service, which naturally forwarded its scoop to the American press. From there it spread to other countries. On the evening of July 4 Dugdale dined at the Weizmanns' and found Weizmann furious with Ben-Gurion for having "done it on his own." She later told Ben-Gurion that when they learned about the leak, "Chaim and Lewis [Namier] jumped as though a snake had bitten them."

Weizmann, in his fury, had no wish to speak with Ben-Gurion, although he gave Dugdale "leave to get him on the 'phone and tell him what I thought." She called the Zionist office, where Ben-Gurion, Lourie, and May sat decoding an endless stream of telegrams from Sharett in Jerusalem. That day Ben-Gurion noted in his diary, "Chaim and Lewis are angry about Palcor, (A) because it was done without their knowledge, and (B) because it may cause us unpleasantness with the government. With regard to B, they may be right, but A was done expressly so that Chaim could honestly say he had no foreknowledge of the affair." Ben-Gurion explained this to Weizmann on July 5, adding that extensive publicity was necessary "to quell the commotion liable to arise among the Arabs with the report's publication and . . . to prepare Jewish public opinion." He further acknowledged in his diary, "Baffy is right . . . just as she would throw no stone into the pool of Palestine without my knowledge, I should not have made waves in the English pool without hers." According to Ben-Gurion's account, this calmed Weizmann. The forced alliance was stronger than personal feelings. But Ben-Gurion probably did not tell them that another reason for his action was his suspicion that the government might bury the report and that by communicating it to the press he had sought to thwart any such attempt.[12]

But his fears proved unwarranted. On July 7 the British government published the Peel Report together with the statement that its recommendations were to become official policy At 10:00 P.M. an official copy was delivered to Ben-Gurion. Trying to get some sleep — "It's been two weeks since I've slept" — he decided to put off reading it until the next day. "But," he told his diary, "the trick didn't work; I couldn't sleep even without reading the report." When he did read it on July 8 and 9, he became even more worked up. A telegram from Paula finally informing him that she would arrive with Geula in Paris on the evening of July 14 may have promised some relief, but other news from Palestine did not bode well for his position at the Congress. All the Zionist parties in Palestine, including his own, had rejected the Peel scheme as published, each for its own reasons.

At midday on July 13 he took off for Paris, where the next morning he waited for his wife and daughter at the station, noting the exact hour the train arrived in his notebook. Geula remained in Paris, at Mark Jarblum's home, and the next day he and Paula flew to London. He was as warmed and overjoyed by her presence next to him on the plane as if he had just met her for the first time. As a token of his feelings he wrote in his diary, "I was amazed at Paula's courage; her face showed no fear and she never even flinched as the plane soared over land and sea."

But Ben-Gurion soon forgot how much he had missed Paula and

began to take her presence and ministrations for granted. He could direct all his attention toward getting ready for the Congress. Paula no longer fascinated him, and he no longer found her remarkable enough to mention anything she said or did in his diary, although they soon shared an experience no less unusual than their first flight together. After two weeks in London they returned to Paris, where they met Dov Hoz, who was preparing to drive one of Weizmann's cars, a Terraplane, to Palestine via Zurich. He invited Ben-Gurion and Paula to travel with him as far as Zurich. They would send their bags by train and motor unhurriedly in the fancy car through beautiful countryside. When they arrived in Zurich after a twenty-four-hour trip, including an overnight stop, Ben-Gurion noted in his diary, "I arrived here at 3:00 P.M. after an interesting and tiring drive. This was my first long trip in a car . . . and despite the fact that none of my suitcases were locked, I found everything in order at the Zurich station." There was no mention of Paula.[13]

35

First Seed

ON JULY 29, 1937, as soon as he and Paula were settled at the
Eden du Lac Hotel, Ben-Gurion set about producing a majority to support himself and Weizmann. Not only did the Congress open in just five short days, but he had had no face-to-face
contact with his party for three months. During that time, Berl Katznelson and Itzhak Tabenkin, with Menahem Ussishkin, Rabbi Meir
Bar-Ilan — head of Mizrachi in Palestine — Justice Louis Brandeis,
and the leaders of Hadassah in the United States, had forged a massive,
nonpartisan camp of naysayers encompassing a considerable part of
the labor movement — the entire left and much of Mapai — Mizrachi,
the majority of the American Zionists, and some General Zionists.
Ben-Gurion's ultimate triumph against these odds was primarily the
result of the political inspiration that had come to him in his days in
London. Inasmuch as political thought can be blessed with creativity,
inspiration, and even revelation, Ben-Gurion was graced during that
period. Late in life he said that at such moments he felt as though the
sky had suddenly split in two, revealing the solution to a complex
problem, leaving him no doubt as to which course to take. "A mighty
tremor would shake me from head to toe and I saw how it was going to
be. But this rarely occurred." It seems that one such tremor shook him
on the eve of this Congress.

The Peel Report described the promises given to Jews and Arabs as
irreconcilable and the Mandate in its existing form as unworkable.
Therefore the commissioners suggested, "Partition seems to offer at
least a chance of ultimate peace. We can see none in any other plan."
They devised a scheme of partition to which they attached a map outlining the frontiers of a Jewish state — the entire Galilee, the northern
valleys, and the coastal plain; an Arab state — all the rest, including

the Negev; and a neutral enclave in which the British Mandatory would safeguard the holy places in Jerusalem and Bethlehem. In the event the government rejected this solution, the Peel Commission recommended that immigration be regulated not only by "economic absorptive capacity" but also in accordance with political considerations. In their view the Mandatory should envisage a "political high level" of twelve thousand annually during the ensuing five years. Of these two alternatives the British government chose the former, and a White Paper, accompanying the publication of the report, stated that a partition scheme recommended by the Royal Commission represented the best and most hopeful solution to the deadlock.[1]

It might appear that all Ben-Gurion had to do was advise the Congress to embrace partition with open arms. But partition depended on acceptance by the Arabs as well as by the Jews; and since the Arabs demanded the whole of Palestine, not one Arab leader or government endorsed it. Those who doubted that Britain would force partition on the Arabs could discern a plot: the British would interpret Jewish acceptance of partition as giving up the Mandate and thereby creating a vacuum that the British would be happy to fill with a new constitution for Palestine. The Jews would lose both the state and the Mandate. Although Ben-Gurion shared these suspicions, he was ready to take the risk, especially since he had learned in his "private talks" with the commissioners that Britain wanted to get out of Palestine.

His "method" was to minimize the risk. It was not consent to partition that Ben-Gurion wanted from the Congress, especially after July 23, when the Arab Higher Committee rejected the Peel Commission's recommendations and the government's acceptance of them, demanding full independence for Palestine and the banning of immigration and Jewish land acquisition. He wanted the Congress to unanimously reject the proposed partition, but at the same time empower the JAE to negotiate a better partition scheme with the British government. His moment of inspiration in London had provided him with the perfect "line" — "Insist on the Mandate; negotiate for a better scheme." His formula called on the Jews to fight for the continuation of the Mandate as if they did not want a state, and induce the British to force a Jewish state with improved borders on them. Armed with this formula Ben-Gurion devised his strategy, dividing the coming battle into two aspects: internal efforts to gain approval of the partition scheme and an external facade of rejection in favor of perpetuating the Mandate. He said, at a closed session of the Congress, "As a sworn advocate of a Jewish state, not sometime in the future, but here and now, and not in all of Palestine, but even in a part of it, I am prepared to fight for the Mandate, and I regard such a war as vital until such time as the state is established." The Mandate was "the only real political asset we have."[2]

The second part was easy, and Ben-Gurion was happy with the resolutions of Mapai's council and of other parties and bodies, including the Small Actions Committee, to reject the partition scheme. On the eve of the Mapai council he had written to Sharett that "tactically, we must not give up the Mandate; the council's resolution should say as much." After sitting in on Weizmann's interview with Ormsby-Gore he had reported in his diary, "I went over the draft of Weizmann's response [to Ormsby-Gore] a second time and suggested omitting those phrases which imply consent to partition." In an effort to impress on British public opinion that the Zionist movement unanimously opposed partition he wrote an article for the London *Daily Herald*.

> The Jewish people have always regarded, and will continue to regard, *Palestine as a whole* as a single country which is theirs in a national sense, and will become theirs once again. No Jew will accept partition as a just and rightful solution. . . . Anything may be imposed on a defenceless Jewish people by the superior forces of the British Empire. . . . But they can never regard the proposal as something which is right and just in itself . . . The partition proposal excludes Jerusalem from the Jewish state. No Jew . . . will accept the cutting out from the Jewish state of this Jewish city. . . . The Jewish spirit is indomitable. Their purpose will ultimately be achieved.

The ink was hardly dry when those proud words were refuted by those in whose name Ben-Gurion ostensibly spoke. He wrote in his diary, "That which I feared came true. The rejoicing of Polish Jewry at the news of the Jewish state is plastered all over the English press. The news wires from Palestine as well show the majority of Jews' inclination to accept the scheme. Such information will not help our campaign for better frontiers. But it is difficult to keep the cat in the bag." Nonetheless he went to Zurich adamant, and the same day told his party colleagues, "We should at least be united on strategy: to continue and persist in our war for perpetuation of the Mandate." Seeing that the controversy between naysayers and ayesayers was liable to split Mapai only strengthened Ben-Gurion's faith in his formula, for it would also serve well to hold the party together. "The Congress will be able to pass a resolution," he told his associates, "only if we all uphold rejection" of the Peel scheme. But entirely for the sake of appearances.[3]

The hard part, of course, was the internal effort to convince the naysayers of the merits of "the new Zionist policy," of which partition was the linchpin and which in his opinion was nothing but the sequel to his "Jewish state policy" of 1936. This controversy was Zionism's longest and stormiest yet. It was not resolved by the end of the Congress; and it grew more heated afterward. It continued after the establishment of the State of Israel eleven years later, and it flares up with renewed vigor from time to time to this very day.

Ben-Gurion had to overcome three sets of arguments: the ideological or religious-historical, based on the indivisibility of Palestine, the Promised Land of the forefathers and of the Bible; the pragmatic, which maintained that the Yishuv and Zionism were not yet ripe for sovereignty, that a premature mini-state was no solution to the Jewish question, and that it would end in ruin; and the political, which suspected that partition was a British ploy to shrug off Britain's commitments under the Mandate and the Balfour Declaration. The naysayers believed that Zionism was capable of making Britain stick to the Mandate against its will, and therefore steered the Congress debate to what they considered to be the key question: whether there should be continuation of the British Mandate throughout Palestine or a Jewish state in part of it.

Ben-Gurion countered this reasoning with three arguments of his own: the theory of stages, historic opportunity, and the revolutionary approach. But first he blasted the premises of the various naysayers. The issue, he said, resorting to his battle-proven either-or formula, was between "the immediate establishment of a Jewish state in a small part of Palestine or curtailment of immigration and limitation of Jewish settlement to certain areas in accordance with Arab pressure. . . . Partition is a fact. Only one thing can annul this fact: Jewish consent to remain a permanent minority in Palestine. Anyone who does not see this is blind." To those who upheld the indivisibility of Palestine he responded with the theory of stages. "Our right to Palestine — to all of Palestine — exists now and forever," he told the Congress, and it could not "be expropriated under any circumstances. . . . Even the entire Jewish people has no authority to give up any part of Palestine. . . . Herzl would have accepted as a godsend a charter for any part of Palestine and put his stake in a Jewish state without any commitment that this and only this will always be the Jewish state. . . . Zionism is implemented in stages, stage upon stage," and a state achieved by partition was one of them.

"I see a state as but a tool . . . for the realization of Zionism . . . the supreme, most advanced, and potent tool imaginable." Even if the choice was simply state or Mandate, he would still opt for the state. "Through which option might we accelerate the Yishuv's growth? Through which can we get in the shortest possible time the most Jews in Palestine? Which gives us the most powerful lever for implementing Zionism in the coming stage?" he asked, and then answered, "How much greater will be the absorptive capacity [of the state's area] without an alien, unconcerned . . . hostile administration, but with a Zionist government making its own laws . . . and holding *the key to immigration* in its hand. If only for this I am willing to give up Mandatory rule." And if the partition scheme was really just a British ploy, he countered it with one of his own. "I am prepared to fight for the Mandate, which I consider vital as long as no state is established."

Ben-Gurion supported the proposed partition state, he said, not because he viewed it as the fulfillment of the Zionist goal — "Within this area there is no possibility of solving the Jewish question" — but because he thought sovereignty could decisively help achieve both short-term and long-term objectives. His sense of the burning ground made him view the saving of Jews from the destruction awaiting them in Europe as the primary, immediate objective. "For this reason the decisive factor," which he was unwilling to forgo, even in return for a truncated state, was "the area and the limits of authority . . . Will they serve to bring in one and a half million Jews within the next fifteen years? . . . I see time as the fatal, decisive, and crucial element. . . . I see the writing on the wall burning in letters of blood and fire all over Palestine."

The state could also achieve long-term objectives because "it would, within a very short time, establish the true Jewish force able to bring us to our historic destiny." The frontiers envisaged by the Peel scheme should also be regarded as a stage, for "no borders are eternal . . . and by the time we complete the settlement . . . of our state a lot of water will have flowed under the bridge." First, it would be possible to expand peacefully. "We shall break through these frontiers, and not necessarily by the sword." How? "We will bring into our state hundreds of thousands of Jews," "a million and a half," "more than two million," he said at different times. Then, "after we become numerous and strong," it would be possible to discuss settlement of the Negev desert, part of the Arab state, "making it worth the Arabs' while." Failing this, the state could be enlarged by other means. Two months after the Congress, in a letter to his son, he specified what these would be.

I do not doubt that our army will be among the world's finest, and then it will not be beyond us to settle in the rest of the country, either by mutual agreement and understanding with our Arab neighbors, or by some other way . . . We won't be able to bear seeing large tracts of unsettled land capable of absorbing thousands of Jews remain empty, or seeing Jews not return to their country because the Arabs say there is not enough room for them and us. Then we will have to use force, and this we shall do, without hesitation, provided we have no other choice! We neither desire nor need to expel the Arabs and settle in their place. All our aspiration is built on the assumption, proven throughout our enterprise, that there is enough room for ourselves and the Arabs in Palestine. If we must resort to force — not to dispossess Arabs of the Negev or Transjordan, but to guarantee our own right to settle in those places — we shall rely on our force.

While preparing for the Congress, Ben-Gurion had listed the stages of expansion as "immigration ... systematic, state-controlled settlement ... float a large government bond issue ... a Jewish army ... the chance to form an alliance with our northern neighbor [Lebanon] — a greater redemption than that of the days of Ezra and Nehemiah." And in conclusion, "I regard this scheme ... as a political conquest and our greatest historic chance since the destruction of our land ... a nearly decisive initial stage in our complete redemption and an unequaled lever for *the gradual conquest* of all of Palestine."

At the Congress he apparently felt he could not persuade those who were against partition with sheer logic, so he went on to warn that if they were not bold enough to seize the revolutionary momentum of the time they would lose this historic opportunity to realize their great dream.

I am all atremble, knowing that we stand before events likely to change the course of our history, events of a type that have occurred only two or three times over the course of our three-thousand-year history. ... This thing is so great and awe-inspiring that it seems to me but a dream. [He called on his colleagues to rise to the challenge and prove themselves worthy of] the days of the Hashmonaim. ... We must reckon this not against a background of daily affairs but against a revolutionary one — the profound historic crisis under way in Palestine. Historic crises have a logic all their own, fundamentally different from the logic of ordinary times, and we will miss the mark if we gauge things now by regular standards. ... A still, silent bay with a sheltered harbor bears no resemblance to stormy, thundering rapids breaking against rocky shoals over a vast abyss. Here there are altogether different perils, as well as a powerful momentum of a different kind.[4]

Although Ben-Gurion aimed these words at all the parties, the objections of those of his own party were of primary importance, since without them he had no chance of a majority. Katznelson did not oppose partition in theory, only in practice. In his view the partition scheme bore witness to "England's fatigue — her enemies have multiplied" and the ayesayers were deluded by any empty vision, "by the mirage of the state, independence, and luminous horizons opening for immigration." They were "like a silly pigeon rushing into the hunter's palm." His opposition was grounded in the recognition that Britain could not seriously offer a "good" partition — a territory affording a viable Jewish state — whereas a "bad" partition must be refused because it would "destroy or cripple" the Mandate. Both Katznelson and Tabenkin foresaw a long life for the Mandate — "The Mandate shall not be destroyed as long as we are not destroyed" — and therefore believed it best to enlarge the Yishuv in the old-fashioned way.

But while Ben-Gurion's conflict with Katznelson rested on the latter's doubts of the viability of such a stillborn state in too small an area of Palestine, Ben-Gurion's dispute with Tabenkin, who termed partition a "disaster," revolved around strategy and values. Tabenkin rejected the either-or formula outright. "We are told that the alternatives to partition are even worse . . . [but] it is inconceivable that our only alternatives are absolute victory or absolute defeat. . . . Nothing outweighs the importance of building another settlement and another, and hampering partition of Palestine. . . . The state," he said, "we will leave to future generations."

Here lay the essential contrast between the guardians of values, sworn to uphold them above all other considerations, and the man sensitive to the fluctuations of history. Tabenkin maintained that there were no substitutes for education and that only those thoroughly reared in socialist Zionist pioneering concepts could build a state true to those ideals. While Tabenkin claimed that Zionist socialists would educate the state, Ben-Gurion held the state to be a better educator of socialist Zionists. Tabenkin, to his dying day, remained true to the principles of Achdut ha-Avodah — an indivisible Palestine, socialist Zionism, and pioneering realization. Katznelson, on the other hand, eventually realized that European Jewry was in great danger and that Ben-Gurion's either-or hypothesis was appropriate to the situation. A year and a half after the Congress he admitted his error and crossed over to the ayesayers' camp.[5]

Ultimately, however, all Ben-Gurion's arguments were crowned with the inevitable threat of conditional resignation. "If Itzhak [Tabenkin]'s position is accepted, I will comply. Those members who believe in this path will be our representatives. This time . . . I am prepared to accept political office . . . on condition that I receive a clear and absolute mandate" to negotiate with the British government on a partition scheme, on the territory of the state and the terms of its establishment. After a stormy week of deliberation the hour of decision approached and formulation of draft proposals began. A few days before the Congress opened Ben-Gurion had made notes, as was his habit, titled "What I Want from This Congress." "In connection with partition, the Congress need not yet say 'no' or 'yes,' but it must authorize the new Executive to discuss with the government improvements in the commission's scheme." And should the Executive receive a reasonable proposal from the government, "a second session of the Congress will be called (I reckon in the middle of next winter) to discuss and decide." He said as much in his speech to the Congress as well, and this formula was proposed as a resolution.

The strain of imparting his deep conviction to others sapped his strength. While still in London, Ben-Gurion had felt so tired he could "hardly walk," and on the eve of his trip to Zurich he had been on his last legs — "I am barely able to do any work and taking part in discussions and debates is particularly hard on me," he wrote his son. Contrary to his expectations, his wife's presence did little to ease his tension, for Paula had little interest in the Congress debates and, with her husband occupied and no friends on hand, had little to do. Ben-Gurion found himself regretting that she felt "bad," "unhappy," and "dissatisfied."

Although he made a supreme effort to regain his strength during the Congress, he was nearing the breaking point as the vote approached on the afternoon of August 11. Such deep anxiety at this point could only have been due to fear that, despite all his efforts, the historic opportunity would be lost; for he foresaw not a majority, but at best a tie. Had he not come up with a formulation that even his opposing colleagues could vote for, and had not Katznelson and Tabenkin, and their followers in Mapai — with one abstention — crossed over to the pro-partition side for this vote only, there would have been a stand-off, not the victory of 299 in favor of Ben-Gurion's proposal, with 160 against and 6 abstentions. These Mapai members constituted between 60 and 70 votes that Weizmann, despite his senior position in the Congress and in Zionism, could not provide. The Congress rejected the Peel Commission's recommendations and authorized the Executive "to conduct negotiations to learn the specific content of the British government's scheme to establish a Jewish state in Palestine."

The re-election of Weizmann and all the members of the outgoing Zionist Executive could be taken as a vote of confidence. Ben-Gurion therefore got everything he had aimed for, except that the Executive would report back not to a second session of the 1937 Congress, as he had proposed, but "to a newly elected Congress." Ben-Gurion was so confident that the negotiations would bring positive results that he counted on this extraordinary Congress meeting in the summer of 1938 to sanction the establishment of the state and elect its provisional government.[6]

By all rights Ben-Gurion should have been elated, but two concerns, one involving Katznelson and Tabenkin and the other Weizmann, dampened his spirits. Katznelson, Tabenkin, and their supporters had given him their votes out of concern for party solidarity, and perhaps for the sake of their association as founders of Achdut ha-Avodah. This gesture was described by Katznelson as "a great sacrifice on our part," meant "to save the party from schism" and "to ensure the unity of our movement, so close to the edge of danger." Ben-Gurion, who was by this time, as Katznelson put it, "on the verge of a nervous breakdown," thanked him after the vote with a "glowing face" for "the sixty nay-sayers' votes," not forgetting to add that they were "very burden-some," for he was unhappily aware that he was indebted to Katznelson and Tabenkin. While he had borne the responsibility, his two partners in Mapai's leadership had not only failed to back him but boasted of their wisdom and guardianship of values, smug in their ability to mer-cifully throw him a life line in the hour of crisis. "Tabenkin hates England the way an anti-Semite hates Jews" and was no different from "people who think a Jew a demon," said Ben-Gurion in 1942, adding that anyone who thought all the English contemptible, "as does Ta-benkin, who has never even seen them," and did not understand that "Jewish politics must be based on love of the Jewish people and not on hate for the English" was certainly not competent to carry out any po-litical executive function.

Katznelson, for his part, was never to be blamed for either commis-sion or omission, and Ben-Gurion was undoubtedly fed up with his smug skepticism. On the eve of the Congress he had informed his diary that Katznelson "stands firm on his skepticism [regarding partition]. There are no small grounds for this skepticism, and no apprehension is a stranger to me, but skepticism alone accomplishes nothing." Never-theless he invited Katznelson to join the JAE's London section. Did he truly believe that Katznelson, who had yet to learn English, was fit for a diplomatic or political office, and in London of all places? And did he really want to share leadership of the JAE with him? Had Katznelson agreed, this would have been the result. Or did Ben-Gurion know full well that his invitation would be turned down? Perhaps he wished to teach Katznelson a lesson on the vast difference between the bearing of executive responsibility and the criticism and hindsight of an observer. Perhaps he thought that pinning executive responsibility on Katznel-son would make it easier, if not to silence him, at least to keep him under control. Katznelson probably thought so. In these critical days for Zionism, the Jewish people, and the entire free world, he chose to devote himself to perpetuating the memory of his friend Moshe Beilin-son and publishing the works of Nahman Syrkin. Writing this to his wife, Katznelson concluded, "I would rather engage in *my own* minor, unspectacular work than a glamour job in someone else's shadow." Although they never said it in so many words, from then on both probably knew the demarcations of their separate territories and responsibilities.[7]

Many of the naysayers, particularly in Mapai, came to regret their opposition to Ben-Gurion's position in 1937. Only afterward were their eyes opened to the reality that a Jewish state, even in part of Palestine, could have begun massive immigration and saved many Jews from the Holocaust. Golda Meir was the most famous of those who later recanted. In a television interview in 1977 she was asked, "Who was right?" She replied, "He [Ben-Gurion] was right. I have no doubt. . . . Had the partition scheme been shelved because of us, the naysayers, I would not be able to sleep nights on account of the responsibility for what happened in Europe." As a rule, Ben-Gurion refrained from emphasizing this aspect of his position, but in 1957 he wrote to one of the "negatives," "I was an adherent of the Jewish state in 1937 on the basis of partition, and had it gone through, the history of our people would have been different, and the six million Jews in Europe would not have been exterminated. Most of them would have been alive in Palestine."[8]

To understand the matter concerning Weizmann that affected Ben-Gurion, one must return to July 4, 1937, when, for no apparent reason, Sharett had included the following paragraph in a long and otherwise routine letter to Ben-Gurion, which he wrote at 4:00 A.M.

> You are surely aware of Coupland's praise for my testimony before the Royal Commission. He said I had done more for the Jewish people than any other Jews . . . (except Weizmann, of course). . . . But I want you to know that the privilege of reading your remarks on my testimony, of hearing them directly from your mouth, was in my eyes inestimably greater. . . . Your judgment is a moral backbone, and determines my stature. For years now I have measured myself, my achievements and failures, by your estimation. . . . In these last years I've had no guiding, directing, and driving force like your appraisal and criticism . . . although it has, more than once, embittered me. . . . For me you are not merely a senior colleague, not just the leader of the movement which is my life. For me you are a man whose moral and personal authority I have accepted from the very beginning. . . . Once . . . I made a list of those people whose moral soundness has been a guiding light in my life: first and foremost of these was my father . . . You were the second. . . . Since then many years have passed and I've gone through much . . . and there were the years of working with you. . . . I tremble to think what would have become of me had you not been at my side, leading the way. . . . And here we are in the midst of the battle . . . and I want you to know what you mean to me and how much I want you to be with me to the finish.

Deeply touched, Ben-Gurion showed the letter to his friends. On July 29, when he arrived in Zurich, he saw Sharett for the first time in three months, and at a party meeting that day he reciprocated. "The Jewish Agency's appearance before the Royal Commission deserves detailed evaluation. . . . I cannot but make note of the fine performance of our two principal witnesses: Weizmann for his great oration at the inquiry's opening and Sharett for his detailed testimony."[9] But if he expected Weizmann to return the compliment he was in for a disappointment. In his concluding address to the Congress on August 10, Weizmann barely mentioned Ben-Gurion and passed over his testimony and his major contribution to the preparation for the Peel Commission. At the same time he had already praised Sharett abundantly. "Here spoke a man before us," said Weizmann, "who remained unremittingly at the front of this war. His was a brilliant report, and we owe him our gratitude for making order out of our battle lines. Keep up the good work, Moshe Sharett!" Stepping down from the podium, Weizmann kissed Sharett.

As if this were not enough, in his closing address several days later, Weizmann was moved "to say thank you to my colleagues for their loyal, devoted, and unselfish assistance, for giving of themselves to the movement and myself . . . to my friends Professor Namier and Mr. Leonard Stein." He then mentioned Rabbi Stephen Wise and Professor Felix Frankfurter of the United States and Menahem Ussishkin of Palestine. His pointed omission of Ben-Gurion left Sharett dumbfounded. According to him, the audience caught on at once. To Eliezer Kaplan, who sat beside him, Sharett said, "Weizmann is doing a terrible thing." To his wife, Zippora, he wrote, "To be profusely praised to the humiliation of your friend, who is greater than you, is an unbearable agony. . . . I was miserable." Weizmann further manifested his high esteem for Sharett by picking him as escort when he went to Geneva to deliver the Congress's resolutions to the League of Nations. Katznelson noted, "[Sharett's] star is in the ascendant with Chaim. To take him to Geneva. Naturally without consulting with anyone." Weizmann needed no lessons from Ben-Gurion on how to use a rival's aides to advantage.[10]

Ben-Gurion was deeply hurt, and he tried but failed to hide it from his associates. Hence the question arises, To what extent did this affront influence his dealings with Weizmann? Following the Congress, the Jewish Agency Council convened in Zurich on August 18. Its main function was to elect an Executive and lay down its political guidelines. The dispute over whether there should be seven non-Zionists in the JAE, to match the number of Zionist Executive members in the wake of the 1929 agreement, or three, as before, was renewed. The

The Histadrut Pavilion at the 1923 Moscow Agricultural Fair

Ben-Gurion addressing Jerusalem workers, Lenin style, in April 1924, after his return from Moscow

A bust of Ben-Gurion by
Brzezinski, Paris, 1924

Ben-Gurion's photo on a
postcard of the 1929 World
Zionist Congress in Zurich

Ben-Gurion, center, in Aqaba (Eilat), 1935, with Berl Katznelson, at his left, and Eliahu Epstein, standing behind his shoulder

BEN-GURION AND THE LADIES

Ben-Gurion and Rega Klapholz, Vienna, 1933, taken by Annie Klapholz, Rega's sister, with Rega's box camera

Annie, Rega, and Ben-Gurion in woods near Vienna, taken by a photographer. On the back Ben-Gurion wrote, "To Rega," September 1934.

BELOW: One of the snapshots taken at a Dead Sea beach, which Paula gave Rega on July 9, 1935, with the inscription "To Rega from Paula"; Ben-Gurion and Paula are standing; Eliezer Kaplan and his wife are seated in the water, facing the camera.

Miriam Cohen (later Mrs. Eddie Taub), circa 1942

BEN-GURION, WEIZMANN, THE STATE

Berl Katznelson in New York, 1922

Cartoonist's view of the partition debate at the World Zionist Congress of 1937: Ben-Gurion, third from the left, and Chaim Weizmann, fifth from the left, lead the ayesayers; Menahem Ussishkin, fourth from the right, leads the naysayers. Berl Katznelson appears on each side.

BELOW: Weizmann and Ben-Gurion, Tel Aviv, 1936

The St. James's Palace Conference, London, February 1939: third and fourth from the left at the table in foreground are Weizmann and Ben-Gurion, heading the Zionist delegation. Sir Neville Chamberlain is seated in an armchair in the background.

Justice Louis D. Brandeis

World Zionist Congress, 1939, Geneva, a few days before World War II started. Seated from left to right in the foreground are Moshe Sharett, Ben-Gurion, Weizmann, and Kaplan.

Ben-Gurion declaring the establishment of the State of Israel, May 14, 1948, in Tel Aviv

American ambassador to Israel, James MacDonald, President Weizmann, and Prime Minister Ben-Gurion, Rehovot, 1950

Ben-Gurion chairing a cabinet meeting, 1952

Ben-Gurion at the government table at the Knesset, Jerusalem, 1950

Ben-Gurion with Weizmann on the reviewing stand at the first Independence Day parade, May 1950, in Tel Aviv

Ben-Gurion in 1950

novelty in 1937 was that the non-Zionists proposed that four Zionists of their choosing be added to their three representatives on the JAE so that both the principle of parity and the Zionist character of the JAE would be preserved. One of the proposed four was Rose Gell Jacobs, president of Hadassah and an American Zionist leader, who had represented the General Zionists at the Congress. But Ben-Gurion was not about to give in to the demand for what he considered fifty-fifty representation of the non-Zionists, at whose head stood Felix Warburg, financier (a partner in Kuhn, Loeb and Company and son-in-law of millionaire Jacob Schiff), philanthropist (the Jewish Theological Seminary, Hebrew Union College, the Juilliard School of Music, the New York Philharmonic, the Fogg Museum at Harvard), chairman of the American Jewish Joint Distribution Committee, and a leader of the American Jewish Committee. Ben-Gurion based his opposition on the claim that the non-Zionist delegates had not been elected democratically and did not represent the people.

Weizmann, for fund-raising considerations — one of his primary motives for adding non-Zionists to the Jewish Agency — was willing to compromise. Kaplan, Ben-Gurion's party colleague and head of the JAE's Finance Department, supported Weizmann for the same reason. But Ben-Gurion stood his ground: there must be no more than three non-Zionists in the JAE; among them "there must be one from labor," and in political matters they must go along with "resolutions of the Zionist Congress." "Eliezer [Kaplan], do not suspect me of not appreciating the value of money," he said, and forcefully rejected any compromise. Before the Jewish Agency Council met he found yet another argument, that the non-Zionists were all opposed to partition. "We stand on the threshold of the state, but from the threshold to the state there is still a long and dangerous way to go," Ben-Gurion claimed. One of the dangers was Warburg and those like him, who had never been cured of their Diaspora timidity and who "view a Jewish state as jeopardizing their property, status, rights, and influence." In this war against "the enemies of the Jewish state," as he called Warburg and his people, "we must divert attention from all other considerations, even if they are important and serious in themselves" — namely, the "fund-raising considerations" — even if the result was material and political damage to Zionism. "Just as none of us would dream of selling Jerusalem for all the money in the world, so we must not consider endangering in the least the possibility of establishing a Jewish state in exchange for the donations of Warburg and his associates."

Ben-Gurion's "great concern" was that "the enemies of the Jewish state would join forces with the opponents of partition among us" and tip the scales in the JAE on that issue. Ben-Gurion had no desire to see

Jacobs appointed to the Jewish Agency Executive by the grace of the non-Zionists, both as a matter of principle and because of her opposition to partition. He was prepared to allow the Jewish Agency to dissolve. "More than at any other time," he said, "the Zionists had best stick together and thrash out their issues in terms of purely Zionist considerations."

Weizmann was unmoved by this reasoning, Kaplan and Sharett did not support Ben-Gurion either, and Mapai wanted a compromise that entailed not parity, as Warburg had demanded, but five non-Zionists, three of them residents of Palestine, one of them Jacobs. Whether owing to fatigue, anger at his colleagues, or Weizmann's snub, Ben-Gurion behaved quite out of character at the Jewish Agency Council. Except for an interjection or two he did not open his mouth. Only toward the end of the Council, on August 21, did he stand up and declare that he would not sit on the JAE with Zionists who represented non-Zionists. Was he being faithful to his principles, or was his behavior the result of his resentment of Weizmann, an effort to show Weizmann how helpless he was without Ben-Gurion? Weizmann was obliged to renew negotiations with Warburg in an attempt to find a formula that would satisfy Ben-Gurion. All he could get, however, was a reduction of their original demand from seven members to five, which was not enough for Ben-Gurion. Mapai requested a short recess in order to talk Ben-Gurion into retracting, but got nowhere. Then Weizmann and Mapai simply ignored his intransigence and went ahead to include Ben-Gurion's name in the list of JAE members. When the meeting reopened and the Council voted, the nomination committee's proposal was accepted unanimously, for the members of the Zionist Executive could not vote: Weizmann was elected president of the Jewish Agency, and seven members of the Zionist Executive — Ben-Gurion, Sharett, Kaplan, Brodetsky, and three others — were elected to the JAE, along with five non-Zionists, Jacobs, who eventually moved to Jerusalem, among them. Apparently no one in Mapai or on the Jewish Agency Council would either support Ben-Gurion's principles or take his threat seriously.

But Ben-Gurion kept his word. He did not accept his election to the JAE and regarded himself as a member of the Zionist Executive only. He who had always fought for authority did not submit to that of the majority which put aside his claims and arguments. What brought him to abandon this principle, which had been the basis of all his service in the HEC? He must have had a very strong motivation, a suggestion of which may be gleaned from between the lines of the letter he addressed to Weizmann the next day.

My dear and esteemed Chaim,

I am very, very sorry, sorrier than I can express in words, that I caused you grief and sadness yesterday before the [Council's] close. All my life I've loved you, and every Jew has loved you ever since the great days of the Balfour Declaration. But you were dear to me sevenfold when I saw you after the 17th Congress [in 1931] in your pain and outrage. Then a new Weizmann revealed himself to me — not Weizmann the leader, magician, charmer, but . . . the man in pain, distressed, wounded, and downtrodden in suffering yet containing his anguish with supreme moral strength and standing at the service of the movement that wounded him, a loyal soldier in the line. Your "exile" lasted four years and during . . . those years I (and many of my associates) had the harsh and bitter feeling that we had contributed to the cruel caprice you were made to suffer. Your return to the leadership of the movement was to my eyes not merely a *political* necessity, but first a *moral* requirement. The Zionist Organization lost stature as long as it was tainted with the sin of "stabbing its teacher" . . . and so it was vital that you be re-elected at the 19th Congress. After I was privileged to work with you I saw you in a new light. I was never your blind follower, nor will I ever be. We have not always seen eye to eye, and when I felt I had to oppose you I did, and if I feel it is necessary I will do so again. But even in the thick of battle my love and respect for you will not fade by even a hairsbreadth, as I know you are the messenger of the people — not by virtue of your election by a majority, but because you were preordained for this, you are divinely inspired. In the last few months, since the great hope for the establishment of a Jewish state began to glimmer, I have seen this inspiration shine on you with a great new light. Grace and charm, and the vigor of youth such as I've never seen in you, have unveiled themselves. And whereas in these months I have taken issue with you on various matters, I knew that you now bear a historic mission, borne by no other Jew for two thousand years. I knew that every one of us owes it to you now, more than ever before, to stand beside you with all our hearts and all our might, so that you may successfully carry out this great and awesome task with which our historic Providence has charged you — the rebirth of the kingdom of Israel.

This task is great and difficult . . . and the obstacles and hurdles in your path are many . . . The enemies have multiplied as well . . . but in the face of these increased hindrances, our might has grown too . . . in Palestine . . . in the nation . . . in the world . . . and you are the human focus of this might. No man, no group of men within the Jewish people, now matches your strength. I do not believe in the shallow theory that history is made by great men, but I do believe that pre-eminent individuals represent the collective powers of the nations and working classes of history. . . . The Zionist movement has now reached the threshold of Jewish independence. The prolonged struggle between national denial and national faith in the life of the Jewish people is approaching the hour of decision. Its triumphant resolution will come with the establishment of the Jewish state. The eve of decision is here. There are still Zionists who are blind to the great and coming miracle. They . . . will not stand in the way — and the Congress proved it. But there are assimilationists who will not come to terms easily with reborn Jewish independence. We must, in my view, knock them out. . . . It is said that they have the money, influence, and clout with the world press and elite circles, and that we must avoid any clash with them. I am not on the warpath; I seek peace and am prepared to accept any compromise that will facilitate the work. But I deny the imaginary power of the Warburgs and Samuels° . . . They cannot hurt us now. You are the king of Israel, [and though] you have no navy or army, and Westminster did not anoint you, the Jewish people . . . see the shining crown of Israel upon your head. . . . The spirit of the Jewish people is on the path of deliverance — and they believe that the Zionist Organization, with Weizmann at its head, is about to inaugurate the dawn of redemption — their faith is a tremendous force. This is the reason I could not reconcile myself this time with the impudent efforts of prophets of the golden calf and their servants to press their will on the Zionist movement. . . . I saw that it was impossible for me to take part in an Executive not freely *elected* by Zionists and non-Zionists, an Executive in which some members were appointed by order of a New York lord. . . . I did not want to bother you with this matter, and I deeply regretted that you were charged, or that you charged yourself, to enter into negotiations with Warburg. I was even more regretful when I saw that it seemed as though I was standing in the way of setting up the Executive. There are, in Palestine, a hundred thousand Jewish workers, and I am nothing more than one of them. As one of them I held you dear to me as the nation's choice; as one of them I know I must stand beside you; as one of them I pray for your success. . . . When I saw your distress yesterday I was unbearably sorry, for I loved you with all my heart and with all my might. You should know that I did not intend for you to suffer. Let us hope that all will work out for the best.

Yours in faith and love,
D. Ben-Gurion.[11]

Ben-Gurion filled seven sheets of hotel stationery with one flight of the pen, never stopping to rewrite, except for one deletion and one insert. What could possibly have brought Ben-Gurion, who had called Weizmann "a disaster," refused him the title of statesman, and considered him irresponsible to suddenly compose this letter of adoration? Had he always secretly venerated him, not daring to express it? Or did he wish to demonstrate his magnanimity and prove to Weizmann that he was beyond insult and personal consideration, guided only by the

---

° Sir Herbert Samuel, the first high commissioner, opposed a Jewish state. In an address to Parliament, he proposed, in the name of peace, that the Jews remain a permanent minority, constituting no more than 40 percent of the overall population of Palestine.

matter at hand and the ultimate goal? There is no single answer to this enigma: a great man will manifest great contradictions. It is, however, evident that the momentousness of the hour was what loosed this flood of hidden sentiment. This may also explain the cold self-vindication and score-settling that lay behind those impassioned lines. For the letter brought back Weizmann's humiliation of 1931 and reminded Weizmann of who had restored him to the presidency in 1935 and broken through the naysayers' barricade at the recent Congress, offering the majority resolution from which arose the hope of a state. Although the letter called Weizmann "king of Israel," it also suggested that the creation of a Jewish state hinged as well on Ben-Gurion, who therefore offered himself as the king's lieutenant, ready to swear fealty the minute his worth was recognized — he was, after all, the leader of a hundred thousand workers — and his advice was needed. The implication was that Weizmann should know how fortunate he was to have at his side a man of Ben-Gurion's caliber, vision, and critical thought, beyond comparison with Weizmann's foolish courtiers. Most of all, Weizmann had better understand that it was best for the Zionist movement to rely on the Jewish people and their duly elected representatives, not to place its trust in "lords." Although Ben-Gurion had deserted the convoy to join the ranks of the simple folk, one word from Weizmann — a word of respect — and he would return to harness, to the JAE, and to their quest for the state.

If Ben-Gurion had expected Weizmann to come to him with open arms, waving a letter of veneration of his own, he was in for a letdown. Ben-Gurion received neither a letter nor a telephone call in response. Later he would discover that his confession of love had not only left its object dry-eyed, but that Weizmann, unforgiving, would become even more callous toward him, to the point of brutality.

It may be assumed that Ben-Gurion was considering a stronger measure than not joining the JAE, for Katznelson had found it necessary to hurry to his hotel after the vote, then meet him again the next morning, August 22. Katznelson said they had "a tranquilizing talk." He wrote a friend, "I had to bandage his wounds," and explained to his wife that Ben-Gurion felt "broken down; he is at the end of his rope . . . and I think I finally helped to soothe him and that he will get over it and return to normal." If Katznelson had tried to talk him into bidding farewell to Weizmann, he succeeded.

In the evening Ben-Gurion had headed for Weizmann's hotel, where he found a high-spirited crowd. Vera played hostess and Weizmann, all aglow, was jesting with the guests surrounding him, all members of Mapai: Katznelson, Sprinzak, Kaplan, Locker, Sharett, Hoz, and Golomb. In great good humor he unceasingly patted himself on the back for the kindness and patience he had shown over the past three weeks. From time to time he asked, "Am I not a fair man?" and remarked, "I really don't recognize myself." Weizmann felt that the Congress was all his, as did his adherents. "This time," wrote Sprinzak, "his worth and expression reached heights unprecedented at former congresses. He appeared as a statesman recognized in England and the world over, all his wonderful speeches were hits . . . and he was near and dear to all." Weizmann's sense of exaltation was heightened further, Sprinzak said, by "the fact that our faction was not behind Ben-Gurion."

This image of Weizmann — affable, lighthearted, and charming — had probably haunted Ben-Gurion as he returned to his hotel and, it is reasonable to assume, sat down to write his letter. The next day, Monday, August 23, the Zionist leaders dispersed, as was their custom, to various European resorts. Weizmann and Vera went, as usual, to Cannes on the French Riviera, and Ben-Gurion and Paula to Pont-Sainte Maxence on the river Oise, fifty kilometers north of Paris, to the summer home of a Poale Zion friend. There Ben-Gurion hoped to renew his strength before leaving that Saturday for the United States.

But on the first day of his holiday his depression was made worse by a headache, fever, and cough, and the next day Ben-Gurion suffered terrible pains in his back. "I cannot rest," he wrote in his diary. "When I sit I can't stand up, and when I stand I can't sit. . . . I've never in all my life experienced such pain." This was his first encounter with the lumbago that plagued him for the rest of his life. In addition, a toothache troubled him, and seeking treatment, Ben-Gurion left for Paris on August 27. The next day, Saturday, he said good-bye to Paula and left for Cherbourg where, in agony, he boarded the *Berengaria*.[12]

Although he shared a windowless inside cabin in second class, Ben-Gurion was able to rest during his six days aboard ship. He relaxed on deck, drinking in the fresh air, played in some friendly card games (he won $15), washed down his meals with red wine, and slept like a baby. Warburg and others who had attended the Congress and the Jewish Agency Council were also aboard the ship. Warburg waved hello to Ben-Gurion and approached him. At first he seemed sarcastic and resentful of Ben-Gurion's "dictatorial" tendency and disparagement of non-Zionists, but later "changed his tune and spoke cordially." He was the only one with whom Ben-Gurion had long talks, and by the time the ship reached New York he no longer viewed Warburg as a "lord" or "squire" whose sole desire was to "take over" the JAE. "I saw before me a man who undeniably loves Eretz Israel. He has a wholly Jewish heart, but he is a petty man and narrow-minded . . . Surrounded as he is by sycophants and servants, it is difficult for him to come to terms with a people's democratic movement and even more difficult for him to understand it."

An angry telegram from the secretary of the party in New York, who was surprised to learn that he was on his way to America, reached Ben-Gurion aboard ship, asking for details of the visit. Ben-Gurion responded, also by wire, "Short private visit, no public meetings." The word *private* meant that he had not been sent by the party or the Zionist Executive, and certainly not by the JAE. Except for Paula, Katznelson, and a few other confidants, no one knew of his plan. He had decided, probably in the last days of the Congress, to "meet with [Justice] Brandeis and his colleagues." This news made its way to Sprinzak through rumors and gossip, but he understood the gist of it well enough. "During the Congress [Ben-Gurion], on his own initiative, wired Brandeis to influence his followers — Stephen Wise and the Hadassah ladies — to vote in favor of empowering the Executive to negotiate the partition scheme." To this he added, not without a touch of malice, "One might have known from the start that a man like Brandeis cannot be moved like this ... [He sent back] a negative reply which strengthened the American naysayers. Now Ben-Gurion has gone to try to win Brandeis over."[13]

A far greater and truly momentous objective lay hidden behind his visit. As noted, Ben-Gurion was convinced that the Jewish state would soon be established and that the special Congress in the summer of 1938 would elect its provisional government. Based on his forecast that 3 million shekel purchasers would participate in the elections to this Congress, as opposed to 1,222,214 in 1937, he believed that "the Jewish people have never before stood so firmly behind the Zionist Organization" and that "the Zionist movement has now reached the threshold of governing the Jewish people." This seemed to him so inevitable that he considered it vital to ensure the continued "hegemony of labor" in the Zionist Organization. Even now, when he sensed the dawning of redemption, his mind did not stray far from cold political calculation. "If all of Polish Jewry attends the Congress we may lose power," he reckoned, "and only mobilization of the American workers will increase our strength." Furthermore, as one who felt responsible for the security of the state-in-the-making, Ben-Gurion intended to look into the possibility of training pilots and seamen in U.S. government academies.

He had only seven days, not counting his arrival on September 3 and departure on September 11, to accomplish these tremendous tasks. On his first day in New York it became clear that he could not have picked a worse time to come: the Jewish New Year fell on Sunday and Monday, September 5 and 6; the latter was also Labor Day. "For the next three days everything will be closed here . . . everyone is leaving the city," he wrote Paula. And to top it off a sweltering heat wave blanketed the city, ensuring a mass exodus lasting from Friday night through Tuesday.

His hastiness in making this trip and its miserable timing can be explained only by the enormous pressure he felt to prove his worth and the correctness of his diagnosis. Should his prediction that the creation of a state would sweep masses of Jews into the ranks of the Zionist Organization, making it a veritable people's movement — Ben-Gurion's long-time dream — prove true, he would become equal, if not superior, to Weizmann. But his reception at the port by Jewish journalists and others gave him a turn. "The interest in the Jewish state is not great," he wrote Paula. However, aside from the undoubted political importance of his trip, its primary effect was therapeutic. Activity and work healed his wounds, and therefore his spirits were not affected by the lack of response.

Given the short time at his disposal and in view of the circumstances, he could expect only to make a start on the goals he had set for himself. He checked into the Hotel McAlpin on Broadway and Thirty-fourth Street late that afternoon, hoping to get some rest on his first night in New York, for, having cabled Brandeis a request for an interview, he had hardly anticipated the rapid return wire inviting him to Brandeis's country home in Chatham, Massachusetts, at 9:15 the next morning. He spent six hours that night in a train bound for Hyannis, where Brandeis's son-in-law picked him up and drove him to his own home. After a breakfast spiced with gossip about Weizmann, the son-in-law took Ben-Gurion to Brandeis's home.

Ben-Gurion had two motives in meeting with Brandeis. First, he was very apprehensive that the next Congress would "give a green light to the state" while the Jewish Agency Council wouldn't. If Brandeis could be persuaded to back the state he could, by virtue of his exceptional public standing, bring over the Americans who had opposed partition at both the Congress and the Council. Second, Brandeis was Weizmann's sworn rival, and an alliance with him could only be to Ben-Gurion's advantage.

Ben-Gurion was pleased "to see this old man . . . standing erect as a fifty-year-old, walking with sure and steady steps," and he told him that his father was also "eighty-two and still going strong." As Brandeis had determined in advance, the talk was composed of two monologues, each an hour long, with a fifteen-minute recess. Ben-Gurion spoke first, comparing what Zionism could expect from Mandatory rule with the prospects a Jewish state would have of absorbing massive numbers of immigrants from Poland and Germany, even in just part of Palestine, and stressing his anxiety that Britain would back off from its policy of partition. At the end of the hour Ben-Gurion chatted with Mrs. Brandeis while Brandeis went for a quiet stroll in the garden. When the talk resumed, Brandeis spoke. In essence, his response was that the analysis is correct, the conclusions all wrong. "You are making Herzl's mistake," he told Ben-Gurion. "He saw Jewish suffering . . . and then came up with the Uganda proposal. That was the greatest mistake of his life." Brandeis remained totally unconvinced that a state would relieve the Jews' distress. "The dreadful circumstances of German and Polish Jewry must not be considered" an argument for the state. Immigration of 100,000 a year to the Jewish state would not solve anything, he insisted, since that figure equaled the natural increase of eastern European Jewry. Ben-Gurion's expectations of a state were unfounded; hence the Mandate must not be bartered for it. Zionism had to place its trust in the Mandate and the Mandate alone, and hope that England would overcome its weakness and delusions.

Had Ben-Gurion found even the slightest basis for an understanding with Brandeis, he would readily have postponed his return to Europe. But Brandeis proposed no follow-up talk and neither did Ben-Gurion. They parted, as Ben-Gurion phrased it, "in great friendship," and he returned to New York. Relating the episode to Rabbi Wise, with whom he breakfasted at his hotel on his last morning there — owing to the holidays, the rabbi had had no other time — he commented, "Violence now rules the world and time is of vital importance to us. We cannot wait for England to mend its ways. Maybe it will and maybe it won't; meanwhile the Arabs will grow stronger . . . and even if England changes its mind the prevailing circumstances will be against us." Wise agreed that Brandeis "lives in the world of the spirit and is not well enough acquainted with the facts."

Having had nothing else to do, Ben-Gurion devoted two days to himself. On September 5 he went shopping, buying clothes for Paula and Renana and books and a suit for himself. On the sixth he read his books undisturbed, and from the seventh until his departure on the eleventh he worked on an article for the *Jewish Daily Forward* on the imminent realization of Herzl's vision and the great opportunities the forthcoming state would make possible. He met with Judge Julian W. Mack and Robert Szold, both close friends of Brandeis, and with Rose Jacobs. Again both he and they held to their disparate views. And he questioned Dr. Meir Rosoff, a dentist, veteran of Poale Zion, and Zionist activist, on training opportunities for Jewish aviators and sailors in the United States. Such training is possible, replied Rosoff, provided they are American citizens between the ages of nineteen and twenty-five. Ben-Gurion exclaimed in his diary, "Where are the American Zionist youth?"

What remained for him to attempt was "mobilization of the workers," which he dealt with at a three-hour meeting of the Poale Zion Central Committee on the ninth. At a two-hour meeting the next day with Charney Vladeck, a Bundist who had become involved in Zionism and emerged as a major figure in virtually every area of concern to Jewish labor in the United States, Ben-Gurion talked of the importance of the 1938 special Zionist Congress, which might "have to appoint a provisional government. The composition of the Congress will determine whether the provisional government and the constitution of the Jewish state are socialist in character . . . and without the large working public of America there is no assurance that labor will not lose power." Vladeck promised him that should a "general unification" of all American Jewish workers' organizations — Zionists and non-Zionists, socialists and non-socialists — take place, and if the separate fund-raising operation of the Histadrut was dissolved, he could get two hundred thousand or perhaps a quarter of a million Jewish workers to buy shekels and vote in the elections to the special Congress. Ben-Gurion had calculated that ideally he needed three hundred thousand votes from the American workers, but even so, Vladeck's figures were music to his ears. Such a bloc of votes would guarantee labor Zionism an absolute majority at the Congress, and Ben-Gurion lost no time in sharing this good news with Katznelson.

Ben-Gurion invited nine members of the Poale Zion Central Committee to his hotel to his second breakfast on his last morning in New York. Without telling them the gist of his talk with Vladeck, he asked their opinion on three issues. "Is it possible to organize shekel sales on a large scale amid the masses of workers?" "What are the chances for the unification of all American Jewish labor for Zionist and world Jewish purposes?" And "Is it worth giving up the Histadrut's separate fund-raising operation?" His first question received mixed responses, whereas the second two got unanimous yesses, with the proviso that a major figure in Mapai be sent to New York to help organize the unification.

This most agreeable discussion made him miss his boat, but his travel agent put him on the luxury liner *Île de France.* Although he traveled tourist class he had a large and spacious cabin, with a private bath and a porthole, to himself. "This time," he reported to Paula, "I have absolute peace and quiet as well."[14]

*

Even though his campaign for the state had not been as productive as he had hoped and his article in the *Forward* had not drawn the attention he expected, Ben-Gurion felt he had grounds for satisfaction. His talk with Vladeck seemed to have assured a smashing majority at the special Congress, which would also serve as a firm foundation for continued labor hegemony, a united Jewish workers' movement in Palestine and abroad. Vladeck had promised that the money the movement would receive from the workers' organizations in exchange for abandoning the separate Histadrut Appeal would amount to a million dollars annually, many times more than the Histadrut had ever raised in America. This achievement was quite a feather in Ben-Gurion's cap, and he could anticipate that the train of events he had set in motion would prove that his trust in the broad appeal of the state had not been misplaced.

It is true that if this trip is judged by its immediate results, it may appear hasty and the product of mere fantasy, especially since what had seemed so possible turned out to be a mirage. Although the central committees of the American Jewish workers' organizations endorsed Ben-Gurion's agreement with Vladeck, when Katznelson went to America in November to negotiate the unification, he found it unworkable. "Vladeck is evading me," he reported. "He cannot make good on his promise to Ben-Gurion. Apparently his people have rebelled against him." The unification, and with it the money from American labor, remained unrealized. Nevertheless, Ben-Gurion's faith grew ever deeper that the Jewish people, for all their divisions, would awaken and rally together for a state. Indeed, ten years later, on the eve of the establishment of Israel, not only was a unified Jewish workers' movement that supported the state established, but it brought with it the much more powerful backing of the AFL and CIO. At that time, too, a corps of foreign volunteers was established which brought from America Jewish reinforcements for the fledgling Israeli air force and navy. A letter to Amos of October 1937 proves that Ben-Gurion foresaw this development. "If the Arabs declare war on the Jewish state we have a reservoir of millions in the Diaspora. All of our younger generation in Poland, Rumania, America, and other countries will flock to us in the event of such a conflict. . . . I have no doubt that our army will be among the world's finest."

The portentous seed he planted in 1937 was the first clarion call to American Jewry to come to the aid of the idea of a state. From there on his appeals to American public opinion, Jewish and Gentile, for political and moral support and material and manpower assistance grew more frequent.

As he left the shores of the United States in 1937, Ben-Gurion probably felt assured that his seed would yield a good harvest. He looked
forward to a well-earned rest, but in vain. A violent storm rocked the
ship. "The ocean is a horror itself," he wrote in his diary. "Quaking
mountains, gaping depths . . . the ship didn't glide, it lurched from side
to side." At the height of the storm a cable from Sharett was delivered
to him. "[British Foreign Secretary Anthony] Eden announced His
Majesty's government will appoint a commission to visit Palestine, negotiate [with] Jews and Arabs, and propose a detailed partition plan
with temporary borders. Permanent borders to be [later] fixed by a
special commission." A worried Ben-Gurion vented his fears in his
diary. "Should Eden's announcement be viewed as submission to the
pressure of Arab kings and the British administrators in Palestine? . . .
What is the meaning of negotiations with Jews and Arabs for the purpose of demarcating 'temporary' borders? . . . Should this announcement be seen as a 'melting down' of the scheme?" He could not write
much more, for the storm grew wilder and "the whole cabin reeled,
upward to heaven and downward to the depths." And so, it appeared,
did the prospects for the state, except that the partition scheme tum-
bled in only one direction — down, all the way to rock bottom.[15]

36

The Great Deception

TWO TELEGRAMS, one from Sharett and Katznelson in Geneva, the other from May in London, on Weizmann's behalf, reached Ben-Gurion at sea. He went straight from Le Havre to Paris, arriving at Mark Jarblum's home on Friday evening, September 17, 1937, exhausted after his stormy passage. When Jarblum gave him the bad news that "the commission sets out for Palestine in October, and will stay there four months," Ben-Gurion understood the urgency of his colleagues' wires. Weizmann, with whom he met Saturday morning, urged him to fly at once to Geneva, from where he himself had just returned, and Sharett phoned with a similar request. Ben-Gurion left for Geneva the same day.[1]

This urgent summons was triggered by Eden's statement at the League of Nations of his government's decision to dispatch yet another "body" to Palestine. Weizmann, Katznelson, and Sharett might have remembered that during the Congress Ben-Gurion had foreseen the possibility of a British turnabout. In a closed meeting he had said, "If one commission says the Mandate is unworkable, another could just as easily pronounce a state unworkable." But even if they had forgotten this prediction, they still relied on him to determine whether Eden's statement had created an emergency and decide what position to take. Was this an admission by Weizmann that he and Sharett could not defend Zionism's interests at the League of Nations? Ben-Gurion did not think so and apparently wondered why his colleagues had bothered to alert him, since when he arrived in Geneva he found that "in fact it was all over a week ago" and there was nothing left for him to do. He went for a drive in the mountains with Katznelson, attended a debate at the League, and left on Wednesday, September 22. He wrote Paula that he had wasted "four almost totally unnecessary days" in Geneva.

But there was probably another, no less important reason for his summons. Weizmann, Katznelson, and Sharett thereby demonstrated how highly they valued him, in an effort to encourage him to end his boycott of the JAE. In his diary, copies of which went to Mapai's Central Committee, and in letters to his party colleagues Ben-Gurion wrote that on August 21 he had acceded to Weizmann's request that he postpone publication of his decision for a month. On September 11 Rabbi Wise had also entreated him to delay it. Katznelson, too, felt that ignoring Ben-Gurion's resignation was the best way to nullify it; almost certainly the subject never came up during their drive. But Sharett was convinced that "he is firm and persisting in his decision [and that] a lack of response on our part is only liable to aggravate matters and make it more difficult to go back on," he wrote Katznelson. Therefore, "I did not follow your advice and grabbed the bull by the horns," asking Ben-Gurion straight out to reconsider. But "I realized . . . that this is a firm decision. . . . He is only waiting for Mrs. Jacobs's final decision. . . . In London . . . he will take part in talks but no meetings [of the JAE] . . . If [Mapai's] Central Committee tries to force him, he will leave the party. . . . He still hasn't decided if there's any sense in remaining in the Zionist Executive."[2]

In London, Weizmann continued to ignore Ben-Gurion's resolve, and on September 24 he wrote to "my friend Ben-Gurion" on routine matters common to the JAE and the Zionist Organization. But that day Ben-Gurion wrote Paula that he was still "functioning as a member of the Zionist Executive only. If by my return to Palestine Mrs. Jacobs's decision hasn't been made clear," he would not sit on the JAE. In that case he would not be able "to remain a member of the Zionist Executive . . . and then . . . I will be able to concentrate once again on my work in the Histadrut." As usual, his letters to Paula and the children were addressed to the HEC, so that his Mapai colleagues would read them. And it was they who brought his resignation up for consideration in Mapai's Central Committee. "We must discuss Ben-Gurion's frame of mind and his decision not to join the JAE. He brings this up time and again in his letters, and we cannot pass over it in silence," said Eliyahu Dobkin, who proposed "notifying him that after reading his diary the committee is of the opinion that it is unthinkable that he not join the JAE." On the committee's instruction Golomb wrote Ben-Gurion on October 11,

> We read in the diaries that you are firm in your resolve to resign from the JAE should Mrs. Jacobs accept the appointment. . . . We can in no circumstances accept . . . these conclusions of yours . . . on account of the danger attendant on your leaving the direction of political affairs . . . and we will not acquiesce to this decision. . . . We see no possibility of contin-

uing to bear the responsibility for the Executive and the [JAE] coalition if you yourself withdraw from it, nor do we understand how you can imagine that you can leave and others will remain.

This veiled threat of collective resignation must have seemed to Ben-Gurion an honorable way out of the impasse and so, despite the fact that Jacobs and Hadassah decided that she would join the JAE and settle in Jerusalem, he grudgingly returned to his post and his threat faded into oblivion.[3]

In the letter Paula sent Ben-Gurion on her return to Palestine in early September, she expressed her indignation with Weizmann for insulting him at the Congress and with Sharett who, in her opinion, had stolen Weizmann's praise. Paula's sympathy, concern, and demand for retribution moved him deeply. Although he disagreed with Paula's criticism, it nevertheless helped him resolve his attitude toward his two closest colleagues. He had no difficulty determining his position in regard to Sharett, his subordinate.

[Sharett] is no careerist. He takes matters to heart too and he does his work as best he can. His ability is limited, as is the ability of each of us, more or less. He is not a man of vision; he sometimes cannot find his way out of difficult and complex situations; he does not see far, nor is he capable of making up his mind on issues which demand great intellectual and moral fortitude. But he knows his job, and he is a man with many gifts . . . and it seems to me that he himself knows that he requires guidance. And he more or less gets this guidance.

His view of Weizmann was more complex. Whereas Ben-Gurion acknowledged the pre-eminence that stemmed from Weizmann's uniqueness, he also noted his own superiority, and saw himself as Weizmann's manipulator, much like one who played a fine and rare instrument.

Chaim . . . is a great man, with great merits and great faults. He has no devotion or loyalty to friends, nor is he always careful with the truth, and he can be quite light-headed . . . but he should be taken as he is, since there is no one else who can accomplish what he can. We must both protect and watch him, for he is essential to our movement, and I try to save him from the mistakes and failures he is capable of. What he thinks of me is of no interest to me. I am not dependent on him and I don't need his esteem. I see him as an important tool for our venture — and it is the venture, and the venture alone, which interests me.

Ben-Gurion's gratitude for the warmth that flowed from Paula's letter — "Every sign of love and intimacy from you is precious to me" — and his sorrow at the difficulties and misery she endured in her life with him — whose details she did not neglect to mention — moved him to bare his soul to her, revealing his feelings for her, his lifestyle, and his colleagues. For the first time he admitted how loneliness weighed on him and made the rare admission that under the cloak of Zionist faith he harbored gnawing doubts and tribulations.

> Life, Paula, life is very difficult. I have never complained, and I do not intend to start now. I know life, and I know that others suffer even more. I never feel apart from the people, but always a part of them, and I must bear the burden, be it light or oppressive. Throughout my life I have tried to do my work and play my part to the best of my ability, whether it was easy and pleasant or difficult, dangerous, and painful. But I am alone — notwithstanding my many friends and acquaintances. Perhaps my nature is at fault — but I am a lonely and solitary man, and at times I find it more difficult than ever. There are times my heart — tortured and torn apart by bitter and difficult questions — is about to explode and I have no one to turn to. I stand all alone — and a grave responsibility, sometimes too grave to bear, weighs upon me. Yet I bear it — with love, with all my strength. When I must, from time to time, steel the movement, give strength to my colleagues, fortify their faith and vigor — I am eaten alive by bitter, horrible thoughts of which no one else is aware. I love the movement and its members, and I love the work we do — but I alone know how much anguish, painful doubts, and tremendous effort it sometimes costs me. Never, I believe, have my colleagues heard me complain, but at times it is very hard, and a terrible feeling of loneliness attacks me, as if I lived in a desolate desert of ice, yet all is buried within. . . . Sometimes — without meaning to — you cause me pain, and my misery grows, and my feeling of loneliness is all the harder to bear. But such is life, and I accept it all with love.[4]

If loneliness and the burden of concealed doubts weighed heavily in ordinary times, how much more so did they when, as the plight of Europe and its Jews was becoming more foreboding day by day, Britain began considering a new solution for Palestine. Instead of promptly setting up a Jewish state that would open its gates to the Jews of Germany, Poland, and Rumania, the British government decided to send a "technical commission" to Palestine to study the problem further, or to conduct preparatory negotiations with Jews and Arabs. The lack of clarity that shrouded the establishment of the body was not incidental. Ambiguity and double-talk were part and parcel of the greatest policy of deception to which Zionism was ever to fall victim.

In short, because of strategic considerations in the event of war, as well as pressure applied by Arab states and pro-Arab British officials, the British government secretly reneged on its partition policy. To safeguard the Arab majority in Palestine the British had for some time been preparing legislation restricting immigration and land sales to Jews. This was the "change of course" that Ben-Gurion had so presciently foreseen in 1936. The British concealed their true intentions in a variety of ways. The first was by delaying the implementation of the Peel scheme with the argument that investigation of "the practical possibilities" of partition was necessary first. Not until January 4, 1938, four months after Eden's statement in Geneva, did His Majesty's government inform Parliament that the investigating body would be a commission of four, chaired by Sir John Woodhead. The terms of reference of this Palestine Partition Commission charged it to work out a practical and detailed scheme of partition on the basis of the scheme recommended by the Peel Commission; recommend boundaries for the proposed Jewish and Arab areas; and examine and report on the economic and financial questions involved in partition, including the administration of the railways and ports and postal, telegraph, and telephone services.

But the most important instruction was absent from the terms of reference: on December 8 the cabinet had authorized the colonial secretary to inform the chairman of the commission "by means of a personal communication" that "it was open to them to represent that no scheme of partition that they could devise was likely to prove workable." Once this personal communication was made, Woodhead and the other commissioners knew what conclusions were expected of them. Moreover, Prime Minister Neville Chamberlain had outlined a scenario for the commission. "The terms of reference might be so worded that the Commission would not be debarred from saying that if partition was to take place, this or that solution was the best, but that in their view no workable scheme could be produced." Woodhead and his colleagues fulfilled their mission to the letter. They went about their duties at a leisurely pace, as befitted a serious commission, spending four months studying background material in London and almost another four — April 21 to August 3, 1938 — in Palestine for an on-site investigation.

A noteworthy part of this deception was the furtive, surprise visit to Palestine of the colonial secretary three days after the commission's departure. On August 6 Malcolm MacDonald, who had replaced Ormsby-Gore on May 16, arrived in Palestine incognito, on a special plane, and stayed twenty-four hours. The information and instructions he came to deliver to Harold MacMichael, the new high commissioner, were so confidential that this was considered the only safe way to prevent a leak (the visit was exposed immediately, but not its purpose). Informing MacMichael of the predetermined recommendations of the Woodhead Commission, MacDonald also instructed him to use military force to put down the Arab revolt, which had flared up anew after publication of the Peel Report. Reinforcements for this purpose were already on their way to Palestine. Suppression of the revolt had a two-fold objective: to placate the Zionists with hard evidence that the government would neither submit to Arab terror nor adopt a policy of appeasement and to adjust matters so that retreat from partition and inauguration of a policy less favorable to the Zionists would become public at a time when Palestine was quiet.

When they returned to London the commissioners spent three months studying the Peel scheme, proposed a partition scheme of their own, and finally edited their report, arriving at Chamberlain's prescribed conclusion that even the best partition plan was unworkable. On November 9 — fourteen months after Eden's statement in Geneva — the government published the commission's report together with a statement adopting its recommendations as policy: His Majesty's government had reached the conclusion that

> the political, administrative, and financial difficulties involved in the proposal to create independent Arab and Jewish states inside Palestine are so great that this solution of the problem is impracticable. His Majesty's Government will therefore continue their responsibility for the government of the whole of Palestine. They are now faced with the problem of finding alternative means of meeting the needs of the difficult situation. ... It is clear that the surest foundation for peace and progress in Palestine would be an understanding between the Arabs and Jews ... With this end in view ... they propose immediately to invite representatives of the Palestinian Arabs and of neighboring states ... and of the Jewish Agency ... to confer with them as soon as possible in London regarding future policy, including [the] question of immigration. ... If the London discussions should not produce agreement within a reasonable period of time, they will take their own decision ... and announce the policy which they propose to pursue.

As there was no chance of both sides reaching an agreement, it was obvious that Britain was preparing the ground for forcing its policy on the Jews. In an effort to pacify them, however, it added, "In considering and settling their policy His Majesty's Government will keep constantly in mind the international character of the mandate with which they have been entrusted and their obligations in that respect."[5]

Despite Weizmann's and Ben-Gurion's different reactions to Eden's statement at the League of Nations — for one it came as an "absolute surprise," whereas the other was distraught because the change of course he had feared had become a reality — both men immediately suspected that His Majesty's government had gone back on its partition policy and was devising another solution. But by repeatedly emphasizing its adherence to the Peel scheme the British government reassured them, Weizmann more successfully than Ben-Gurion. At their London meeting on September 24, 1937, Ben-Gurion had found Weizmann "optimistic," believing that Eden had "committed the government unequivocally to partition," giving the Jews a "trump card," and that in general "the situation in the Arab countries is working to our benefit." Ben-Gurion, on the other hand, took the position of "let's wait and see." He "wholly endorsed" an editorial in *Davar* in January 1938 praising a government policy statement "denying the rumors . . . that the government is going back on the scheme proposed by the Peel Commission" and reaffirming that "the partition scheme . . . is the best and most hopeful solution" and that the duties of the Woodhead Commission were "to examine the facts and study the practical possibility of the partition plan." However, a few days later Ben-Gurion published a full-page article in *Davar* protesting the delay in executing the Peel scheme "for an unspecified and rather prolonged period of time." Between the lines can be read his suspicion that the government had reneged. Nevertheless he did not sound the alarm, satisfying himself with a vague call "to rally the forces of the working public and the Yishuv and enhance the Zionist movement's alertness and capacity for action."

If it is true that people see only what they want to see, the story of the Woodhead Commission shows that even one as sober and alert as Ben-Gurion was not completely immune to this failing. For him, standing firm by his original — and correct — analysis that the British had given in to Arab pressure would have been tantamount to admitting a delay that not only jeopardized his heart's desire but sentenced European Jewry to a life of desperation. As long as there was even the slightest chance that the government held to its partition policy, he preferred to cling to his belief in it. In mid March he poured his heart out to Katznelson. "Now, of all times, when partition is again a real possibility . . . I am afraid 'the dream' will prove false . . . Even after conditions have improved for the state (or the partition) in these last weeks and *days* . . . I am [still] afraid."

To Paula Ben-Gurion wrote that in tending to "the issue of the Jewish state" Weizmann had done "great and important work and to a certain extent he changed the atmosphere in the government from one of opposition to one of sympathy." An "immigration dispatch" sent by Ormsby-Gore on March 10 to the high commissioners — curtailing immigration but at the same time stating that His Majesty's government stood by the principle of partition (though it delineated two stages in its realization instead of one) — contributed significantly to this impression by seeming to indicate that "it is evident that the government is truly preparing to implement the partition scheme." The prospects for a state appeared even more real when the Woodhead Commission began its work, and the JAE energetically set about preparing a policy line, materials, witnesses, and memorandums. In short, it was a repeat performance of the Peel Commission, with appearances by Weizmann — who made "a tremendous impression" — Ben-Gurion, Sharett, and other star witnesses, and mountains of protocols, memos, and statistics. Would the British government have gone that far, and at such cost, to create a smokescreen?

That the commission's routine worked like the best sleeping potion is borne out by two facts. First, Ben-Gurion insisted that only ayesayers appear before the commission — so that the naysayers could not spoil the show — threatening to resign from Mapai's Central Committee. Second, the effort to expand the state's frontiers was renewed, and Ben-Gurion again felt it was his duty to activate Weizmann for this purpose.

So Ben-Gurion — back in London — and Weizmann, each in his own fashion, walked right into the trap the government had set. So thoroughly were they hoodwinked that even though the secret was out by September 1938 — on the third Weizmann had said at an Executive meeting that "partition is dropped" — they still did not move heaven and earth against the British tactic. As late as October 3 Ben-Gurion was still expressing some doubt. "If the Partition Commission was not just eyewash," he wrote the Jerusalem JAE, "if the whole partition scheme wasn't buried last winter . . . it may be assumed that the commission will bury it, and the government will come out of the affair smelling like a rose." He came to a clearly expressed realization only after reading the Woodhead Report, twenty-four hours before its official publication. On November 8 he recorded in his diary, "This was a crude and blatant deception."[6]

The Woodhead Report and the government's statement were not the only blows to strike the Jews. The following night was *Kristallnacht* (Night of the Broken Glass)* in Germany; it hit at 2:00 A.M. Thursday, November 10, only a few hours after the report's publication. This was the second time in 1938 that history, as if deliberately, had linked events that were portentous for the Jews. On March 14, in the wake of Hitler's invasion of Austria — which immediately increased Austrian Jewry's demand for shelter in Palestine — the "im-

---

* On that night riots were organized by the S.S. against defenseless Jews, in the course of which 20,000 Jews were arrested and sent to concentration camps, dozens were murdered in their homes, 195 synagogues were set on fire, 800 shops were destroyed, and 7,500 were robbed. Austrians joined their German brothers, and all of Vienna's twenty-one synagogues were set on fire.

migration dispatch" had been published and slammed shut its gates.

The blows rained down in pairs as if to emphasize how much the Jewish people and Zionism were bound together. In 1933, when Hitler rose to power, Ben-Gurion had viewed Jewish suffering as a principal lever in the realization of Zionism. Now that persecution escalated daily and public opinion in the democratic countries clamored for a solution, Ben-Gurion began to fear a new peril, differentiation — an attempt to separate the problem of the Jewish people from that of Palestine. If Palestine was no longer seen as the solution to Jewish suffering, Ben-Gurion feared, it and Zionism would "be dropped from our people's agenda."[7]

In an article in the *Jewish Daily Forward* in September 1937, Ben-Gurion had explained that the Jewish state "would be a state not just for Jews already living in Palestine, but for the entire Jewish people . . . that is, for every Jew who needs or wishes to leave his present residence and settle in Palestine . . . The rationale and purpose of the Jews' state will be to bring as many Jews as possible to Palestine within the shortest period of time." If British statesmen were misled into believing that other countries were prepared to offer refuge to the masses of Jews, the Zionist effort to convince Britain of the necessity of massive immigration and the state would fail. In July 1938 thirty-one countries responded to President Franklin D. Roosevelt's invitation to send delegates to Évian-les-Bains, on the shore of Lake Geneva, to discuss the emigration and resettlement of refugees persecuted because of their political beliefs, race, or religion, including prisoners of concentration camps in Germany and Austria not yet granted the status of refugees. But the Évian Conference proved that no nation was willing to lift a finger for the Jews. Not one, then or afterward, offered to shelter the Jews of Germany, Austria, and Poland. Zionism's claim that Palestine was the Jews' only refuge was substantiated and the danger of differentiation averted.

Ironically, then, the publication of the Woodhead Report in November made it clear that the state scheme was abandoned and the Mandate itself on its last legs. Palestine would not take in four million Jews within twenty-five years, or one to two million within ten, or a hundred thousand in one, or even thirty thousand as in 1933. Such dreams went up in smoke. Hitler, too, learned a lesson from the Évian Conference; it showed him that "the Jewish problem" could not be solved by emigration and that a different sort of solution had to be found.

By a seemingly supernatural disposition of history, the Zionist Actions Committee's two 1938 sessions, held in London, coincided with the two pairs of events just recounted. The first, which ran from March 9 to

14, was held without benefit of advance preparations. Retrospectively, it is unclear why Ben-Gurion put so much effort into calling this session, which would be remembered not so much for its content — nothing noteworthy came from it — but for the aggravation it caused him and the conflict that nearly ruined his relationship with Katznelson.

Those opposed to partition objected both to the timing of the session and to Ben-Gurion's insistence that it be held in London, where he wished to meet halfway "leaders from the United States who could not or would not come to Palestine." America occupied an ever more central place in his political thinking and plans. "It is possible that there will not be a war, but then again it could break out tomorrow," he told Mapai's Central Committee, "and then America will play a major role in our affairs."

Nevertheless, the naysayers, certain that Britain remained committed to partition, were furious with him. Tabenkin even developed a theory that the Woodhead Commission was an "imperialist plot" whose sole purpose was to implement partition against Zionism's wishes. Fearing that the Executive would consent to a state even tinier than that of the Peel scheme, the "opposers," led by Katznelson, announced that they would remain in Tel Aviv and boycott the session, disregarding Ben-Gurion's claims that the Executive had deviated not an inch from the line laid down by the Congress and was doing its best to negotiate an improved scheme and continue the Mandate until a state was achieved. Ben-Gurion took this as an affront and a vote of nonconfidence, and the conflict rapidly turned into a power struggle in which Ben-Gurion asserted the prerogative of the Executive to call a session of the Actions Committee, while Katznelson called into question Ben-Gurion's having done so in a way no one could "fathom."[8]

Twice during Mapai Central Committee meetings Katznelson had made comments — recorded in minutes sent to Ben-Gurion in London — that wounded Ben-Gurion in a way from which he never recovered. First, Katznelson accused him of focusing entirely on a state and no longer viewing immigration as "central to Zionist policy." Anguished at such an inference, Ben-Gurion protested that he saw the state primarily as a great instrument to create massive immigration; it was his master plan for the rescue of European Jewry. In addition, Ben-Gurion noted that it was Weizmann who dealt with the state in their discussions with the British, while Ben-Gurion handled immigration, meeting with Ormsby-Gore and Colonial Office officials and lobbying British members of Parliament.

Katznelson's second stab concerned the *mifdeh* (Hebrew for "ransom"), a progressive self-tax that Ben-Gurion had devised. Every Jew was to make a voluntary donation, according to his or her income, to the Zionist treasury. The session decided to send Levi Eshkol from Germany — where he was transferring Jewish assets to Palestine — to the United States to institute this mifdeh. Ben-Gurion wished to base the operation there instead of in Poland, as part of his contingency plan in the event European Jewry was cut off. Katznelson's reaction cut Ben-Gurion to the quick.

> It is in fact a *disgrace* that the Executive, with the situation in Austria being what it is, could not come up with anything more decisive now than proposing a self-tax. All eastern and central Europe is in danger. . . . Who is attending to the recovery of Jewish assets . . . ? At this time, to concentrate all our efforts on America and neglect central Europe is odd, to say the least. Negotiations with Hadassah should not take precedence now, but rather the mobilization of all forces for action in central Europe.[9]

The March session was noteworthy for another reason. While the annexation of Austria and Nazi brutality against the Jews naturally alarmed the delegates, just as a sinking ship will not make allies of a cat and dog, neither did the "Austrian disaster" move the Zionist factions to forget their old differences or their personal grudges. The leaders were not able to iron out their differences either. The longed-for unity remained unrealized.

Proof that this unfortunate phenomenon would not die even in the face of worse disasters came at Mapai's May 1938 convention in Rehovot. There both Tabenkin and Ben-Gurion, each in his own way, warned of the "destruction" looming over the Jewish people. Tabenkin asserted, "We need a party that will confront the coming dangers . . . lack of immigration . . . the destruction of the Jews . . . evil and the murder of humanity, culture, and spirit."

Ben-Gurion's description of the danger was far more comprehensive, nearly calling the coming systematic destruction of the Jews by the name it was later given, Holocaust. Ben-Gurion pointed to a "new fact, a war of annihilation against the Jewish people," the likes of which it had never seen. "This is not a denial of Jewish rights as there was in Russia; these are not the pogroms of the czar's day . . . [Rather] this is a state policy whose ambition, to be achieved by totalitarian, absolutist methods, is dispossession, destruction, and eviction on a massive scale."

Nevertheless, the dispute between the two and their factions continued unabated. In fact, the convention was occupied not with the approaching destruction, but with internal party questions that arose in the wake of the conflict between Tabenkin and Ben-Gurion. Tabenkin, saying that differences of opinion were a blessing, called for democratization, claiming that "comradeship" had given way to the bureaucracy of a ruling party. He yearned for another party. "Man also needs an environment, a home in which he can be bound to another man as a friend . . . by an idea, a light that binds . . . of the individual with a future, a national future . . . with a purpose in life." He still felt there was plenty of time and was more than ready to devote it to cleansing and rehabilitating the party. Ben-Gurion needed the party as it was, with all its shortcomings, for there was no time to waste on improvements; one does not repair the roof when the house is on fire. He kept his ear to the ground for what he called "the historic situation," which was always unique and never to recur. His conclusion, he told the convention, was that "the thrust of our efforts must be directed to the present, not to the future. . . . We must focus all our energies and efforts on this dangerous day that awaits us, lest we be destroyed . . . and we will discuss what to do later, when the fury passes . . . a fury neither Jewish nor world history has ever experienced."[10]

In spite of their common foreboding of the coming catastrophe they could speak no common language; instead of coming together Mapai's factions drifted further toward schism.

Before the Actions Committee's second session of November 9, 1938, Europe underwent another change for the worse. On September 30 the Munich Pact ceded the Sudetenland to Germany for the sake of "peace in our time." Czechoslovakia's loss gave the rest of the world a short-lived hope for peace. But for Jewry and Zionism, Munich represented another dark day, since Hitler was free to deal with the Jews, Britain's policy of appeasement having made it all too clear that no one would come to their aid. In May, as Hitler turned his attention to Czechoslovakia, Ben-Gurion had told the Rehovot convention that "this dreadful situation, where they want to destroy millions of Jews . . . might bring . . . world public opinion closer to the Zionist idea . . . [but] Jewish suffering does not show the way to Palestine." The British government was led in an altogether different direction, away from partition and the state.

These months probably constituted a decisive stage in Hitler's path to "the final solution." While no one foresaw the Holocaust, there is no doubt that Ben-Gurion, more clearly than others, had already perceived that "[Hitler's] sadistic, maniacal heart's desire is the destruction of Jews throughout the world"[11] and knew that in Germany and later throughout Europe their days of safety were drawing to a close. The hope for a speedy establishment of a Jewish state was crushed simultaneously with the sacrifice of Czechoslovakia's independence, both by Chamberlain's government, wiping out in one stroke the hope for peace in Europe by curbing Hitler and the dream of saving the Jews through their own state.

As a man with politics in his blood, Ben-Gurion had always meditated on history and the forces making it, but since the end of 1936, and especially in 1938, these thoughts had occupied him more than ever. A few examples from his diary and speeches reveal the trend of his thinking. "History has none of the certainty of physics or botany. Many factors and combinations of factors are at play here, precluding any accurate prediction of developments." "History never repeats itself." "History knows no 'never' " or any "final battle," and "there are no permanent solutions. Life and the changing and motivating historical forces are stronger than any political orders and conventions." Now, with the opportunity to follow closely one of the world's greatest conflicts, he devoured newspapers and stayed glued to the radio during news broadcasts, caught up in a real-life thriller (he was familiar with the genre from the detective novels he had begun to read). The role of outstanding men in history had also always intrigued him. At eighteen he had drawn a parallel between the "choice of Israel" and the individual who is "chosen," saying that the chosen is not someone on whom greatness falls haphazardly. "God or nature (for our purpose it is one and the same, whichever is the true power) endows the genius with sublime talents, not out of love for him, but from a desire to bestow upon the world sublime creations . . . He brings into existence an intermediary . . . with the power to give such creations to the world." And in 1937, in a letter to Weizmann, he had remarked, "I do not hold the superficial theory that history is made by outstanding men. But I do believe that outstanding individuals are the intermediaries of the collective might of the peoples and classes playing a role in history."[12]

In observing the great drama, Ben-Gurion focused to a large extent on the personal aspect, as if the confrontation were but a contest of will and nerves between Hitler and Chamberlain, and his comments about them reveal something of his own qualities as a statesman. On September 13 he listened to Hitler on the radio and concluded that his speech "was directed this time at France and England. This painter knows not only the shortcomings of the Germans, but also those of other nations, and he plays on their imagination. At the moment Hitler needs to divide France and Britain from each other and separate them from Czechoslovakia. He understands the order of things; when he has to tackle France, he will do so. When England's time comes, he'll settle the score with England. At present it is Czechoslovakia's turn — hence France and England must be placated."

Turning on the radio the next day, Ben-Gurion was shocked by the sensational news that on September 15 Chamberlain would fly to Berchtesgaden for a summit with Hitler. "If Chamberlain returns with war on his hands," Ben-Gurion told his diary, "the English people will rally around him as never before; and if he returns with peace? — It is hard to believe that Chamberlain's *beaux yeux* will change Hitler's mind. And who knows the price the Czechs will have to pay for this surprise flight of the British prime minister?" Nonetheless, Ben-Gurion admired Chamberlain's decision to meet with the führer in his nest, calling it "a daring and dramatic move." Before closing his eyes that night he posed a question in his diary: "War or peace?"

From the start Ben-Gurion was certain that giving in to Hitler would not bring peace, and he had grave forebodings for the world and the Jews. On September 20 he wrote Sharett, "The submission of the two great democracies to the Nazi spokesman, the rape of Czechoslovakia, the blow to the faith in pacts and guarantees, and the rise in Hitler's prestige" would merely whet his appetite for further conquests. "Hitler's star will rise higher, in Germany and the world, America will crawl inside its shell and isolate itself in disgust from the affairs of Europe, the nations of central Europe will rush to make peace with the Nazis, and a new, horrid catastrophe will crush European Jewry." He made a connection between Czechoslovakia and Zionism. "Czechoslovakia is unfortunately our affair too," since the spectacle of the British yielding to force and the policy of appeasement would "undoubtedly leave a profound impression upon the Arab world." Ben-Gurion feared that if war broke out "the Arab and Muslim world is liable to rise up . . . and the British Empire will be in danger." In such an event, Britain would certainly go even further to appease the Arabs to win them over, and the Yishuv would find itself under threat of destruction.

Two nerve-racking weeks passed before his question was answered. On September 26 he listened to Hitler's hour-and-a-half-long speech, during which he "roared, screamed, raged, vilified, degraded, threatened, intimidated, provoked, abused." Ben-Gurion concluded that the chances for war had increased and anxiously awaited Chamberlain's answer. Pressure had always suited his talents best, and once he felt war was at hand his mind began devising ways to exploit the disaster. This found very indirect expression in two letters he wrote that day. In the first, to Geula, he discussed the Yishuv's prospects in the event of war, asserting rather paradoxically, "I am, in fact, more optimistic here . . . We face new blows, but we are not helpless. Come what may, we will not be overcome . . . Hard days are ahead . . . A homeland cannot be gained without suffering and sacrifice." What would have made him "more optimistic" as war approached, if not the expectation of benefiting from it? In the second letter, to a Zionist activist in Poland, he declared, "I have more faith now than ever before in our future," explaining that in the face of "world upheavals" England will perhaps "need us . . . and the might of the Yishuv will serve as the principal basis of our political potential. We must simply hold our ground and keep our heads."

On September 27 he heard Chamberlain's answer. Chamberlain spoke for only seven minutes, "gently and softly," in understatements, but was "no less forceful and self-confident . . . although the man has thus far erred and sinned in his policy, even though he gave in — along with France — more than was necessary. He proved, this time, that he does not care only for peace; he is also prepared for war." Ben-Gurion pondered as to which of the two leaders had best represented his people. "Hitler spoke as an absolute ruler, and in his country not a single voice will be openly raised against him. Chamberlain will surely be met with harsh criticism, but a solid democracy was rather better expressed in Chamberlain's speech than totalitarian terror in the führer's."

He noted the feverish preparations for war under way. "In Czechoslovakia the whole army and nation have been mobilized. France is calling up the reserves, and Paris is being evacuated. In London they're digging trenches in the parks, distributing gas masks, and taking the children out of school. In Germany notice was given of mobilization tomorrow unless Prague responds affirmatively by 2:00." Although there was no sign of backing down, he wrote in his diary, "It is difficult for me to believe that there will be war now." As if the next step were up to him, he weighed the options of both sides and reached a conclusion.

> The key is entirely in Hitler's hands, and he would have to be crazy to go to war now. Without a war he is guaranteed a monumental victory — he'll get the Sudetenland, bring Czechoslovakia to its knees, control all of central Europe, augment his prestige among his own people and in Europe, grow still stronger, and with increased forces prepare for the decisive battle. Going to war now endangers his entire existence. This creature identifies himself with Germany, and in his view his loss is Germany's loss. And he stands to lose all in the event of war, to gain all with peace. Will he lose his nerve?

Here Ben-Gurion weighed the influence of Hitler's character — "He is a bully" — but countered it with the logic that his staff would have more sense: "Would they allow him to make this desperate move? . . . If Hitler does not want it there won't be war." His conclusion: war would not break out now; Hitler would wait for the right moment.[13]

On September 28 the tension peaked. The transfer of the Zionist office outside London in the event of war was discussed, and "We de-

cided . . . to mobilize a Jewish brigade." Weizmann was suddenly
called to the Colonial Office and Ben-Gurion proposed that the Yishuv
send a wire at once declaring its support for the British Empire at this
hour of crisis; these were first steps to exploit the disaster. At 3:30 —
after lunch at the Carlton Grill — Weizmann phoned to report that
war was imminent; there was only "a flicker of hope" for peace. At
once Ben-Gurion cabled Sharett in Palestine, "Situation grave." At
5:45 a faint ray of light appeared; the radio announced that Hitler had
postponed the mobilization in Germany for twenty-four hours and that
Chamberlain would fly to Munich. At 6:30 Ben-Gurion cabled Sharett
again, "It seems the crisis is over." On September 30 he wrote in his
diary, "The drama is over, for the moment. The horror of war has
passed. . . . My second prediction has also come true. On October 1
Hitler's hobnailed thugs will enter the Sudetenland. The wicked have
peace. Czechoslovakia pays the price."

When Chamberlain returned from Munich waving the white flag,
Ben-Gurion saw through his act. Chamberlain needed peace to pacify
British public opinion, which was outraged by his betrayal of Czechoslovakia. There were many signs of growing disapproval in the press
and in his own party; some even predicted that the public would
"rebel" against him. The first step in this direction, as Blanche Dugdale
said, was the resignation of Alfred Duff Cooper, first lord of the admiralty. But Ben-Gurion wrote to the Jerusalem JAE, "I do not believe
in this revolt." Even though "the whole nation was chafing over
Hitler's extortion," Chamberlain's sophisticated stratagem worked. Its
purpose was to bring home to the British "the fear of war . . . They distributed gas masks, evacuated the children from London, dug trenches
night and day in Hyde Park, spread panic that tomorrow or the next
day Hitler's planes would bomb London, mobilized the navy, and then
suddenly announced peace — and what a relief. No bombs, no destruction, no carnage, and the man in the street exultantly welcomed the
preserver of peace." The fate of Czechoslovakia, of Europe? "All that
is distant, alien, and unreal."

On the evening of September 30 Paula, who had escorted him on this
trip, left to return to Palestine. Ben-Gurion escorted her to the train
station. Back at the hotel that night, as London celebrated its release
from the danger of war, he felt a terrible emptiness within. "Were I a
child I would cry," he wrote thirteen-year-old Renana, and admitted,
"I am afraid." He described to her the horrors of war and of Hitler,
who would redouble in strength and then "lunge upon . . . his prey like
a raging beast."

Now that war was no longer imminent, Ben-Gurion's optimism
faded and he saw only dark horizons. "I fear our turn is next. All the

omens are bad ... True, one pretext for deferring the state has been eliminated — there is no fear of war in the immediate future — but will they fail to invent new ones?" Furthermore, if there was no war Britain would not need the Yishuv's help and the government might restrict Zionism, especially immigration, as it saw fit.[14]

To some of his party colleagues it seemed in September as though Ben-Gurion had little to do. David Hacohen, Mapai's liaison with the British army, who was close to Weizmann, spent more than two weeks in London and criticized Ben-Gurion harshly when he returned to Palestine. "I have the feeling that our people's efforts [in London] leave much to be desired in light of the gravity of the situation. Their workday is hardly packed full of activity ... In general our people are not all that industrious ... Statesmen (Chamberlain and others) ... work day and night. Not so our people," he told Mapai's Political Committee, and everyone knew whom he had in mind. In all the time Hacohen was in London "our people hardly met at all with politicians and other influential people there." With his good friends the "brothers-in-law" (Sharett, Golomb, and Hoz; the latter two were married to Sharett's sisters, Ada and Rivka) he was more caustic about "Ben-Gurion's idleness." In contrast to Sharett, whose "time was valuable [since] he is doing something, [Ben-Gurion] wasted his time and mine for nothing, so I know that his time is not valuable to him and that he's not doing anything."

This criticism can be attributed partly to a grudge Golomb carried against Ben-Gurion. Ben-Gurion's third resignation threat of 1938 had pressured Mapai's Central Committee to cancel an agreement between the Haganah and Irgun Zvai Leummi that Golomb had set up with Vladimir Jabotinsky, without Ben-Gurion's knowledge. This, at least, was Rivka Hoz's opinion; she had heard from her sister that Golomb was angry at Ben-Gurion and was behind "stories like David [Hacohen]'s, which serve to boost anti–Ben-Gurion feelings."

Nonetheless, the description of Ben-Gurion was not entirely groundless. His inactivity was also mentioned in letters between Sharett and Hoz, who was in London at the time, and to their wives and friends. The brothers-in-law candidly described Weizmann as working ably and energetically — "The main force at work is naturally Chaim Weizmann," wrote Hoz — and he enumerated Weizmann's many interviews with people in the upper echelons of British politicians and parliamentarians. In contrast, Ben-Gurion was described as "sour-faced and melancholy." No mention of his activity or admiration of him is to be found in their letters, but it does come through clearly that a new quarrel which erupted between Ben-Gurion and Weizmann in

September had deepened in October and November. A Mapai Political Committee resolution to dispatch Sharett posthaste to London attests to the mounting tension. The committee hoped that Sharett could "perhaps bring about more cooperation between Ben-Gurion and Weizmann." The cause of this conflict was Ben-Gurion's not being invited to participate in Weizmann's activities, particularly his talks with Malcolm MacDonald, which were the sum and substance of Zionist political activity.

On his way to London in August, Ben-Gurion had paid a visit to La Croix, Weizmann's rented villa near Cannes. There he found Weizmann "depressed, nearly desperate, [envisaging] a very bleak prospect": the Woodhead Commission would propose "an unacceptable scheme" that would be impossible to improve because MacDonald, the new colonial secretary, considered a friend of Zionism, had a "weak personality and a poor standing in the cabinet and nothing could be expected of him." Therefore, Weizmann claimed, he and Ben-Gurion had no choice but "to resign as soon as the report appears and convene a congress or convention in America to discuss the situation and set out for war," that is, for a battle against the expected proposal. Still, Ben-Gurion thought, they were agreed on a line of action. Weizmann would appear before the commission, speak openly with MacDonald, try to influence others in government, demand a speedy decision, and continue the fight for better frontiers and the inclusion of the Galilee in the Jewish state. "For the moment," said Ben-Gurion, "we must concentrate on preventing a bad report . . . It is still too early to discuss what steps to take in the event of utter defeat." Weizmann was apparently inspired by Ben-Gurion's optimism, for before they parted he promised to take Ben-Gurion to his next interview with MacDonald. Ben-Gurion noted this encouraging development to include him in high diplomacy in his diary with satisfaction, and then repeated it in a letter to Sharett. Armed with this "La Croix promise," he set out for London, ready to fight for the state shoulder to shoulder with Weizmann.[15]

In light of what followed, it seems that Weizmann made his promise in a moment of weakness. As long as he anticipated victory, Weizmann excluded Ben-Gurion from his contacts with Whitehall, but as soon as he sensed possible defeat he moved to share the responsibility with Ben-Gurion. There is no other explanation for his sudden, unexpected promise. The basis for this assumption is Weizmann's behavior the moment the pendulum of his mood swung back to high-spirited overconfidence in the British government. Weizmann went alone to the first meeting, held on September 1, with MacDonald and Sir John Shuckburgh, deputy under secretary and head of the Middle East Department in the Colonial Office. MacDonald told him he did not know what the Woodhead Commission's proposals would be and that in the event partition was not implemented, "another agreement will have to be made," remarking that "a Jewish-English-Arab accord would be best." Thus, two months before publication of the Woodhead Report, the ground was already being prepared for a round-table conference.

The La Croix promise was forgotten. A second meeting with Mac-Donald was set for September 13. While Ben-Gurion listened to Hitler's speech on the radio, Weizmann went to the Colonial Office, but MacDonald was called to an urgent cabinet meeting on Hitler's speech and their appointment was postponed until the next day. On the fourteenth Ben-Gurion again remained glued to the radio while Weizmann spent a few hours with MacDonald in the Colonial Office. The following morning Weizmann summoned Ben-Gurion to give him a brief account of his talks.

Noting MacDonald's statements in his diary, Ben-Gurion sought hidden meanings. "From what I could gather from Chaim," he wrote, "MacDonald believes the establishment of a Jewish state impossible." As in the past, Ben-Gurion had his doubts about Weizmann's report. He wrote Sharett,

> There is no way of knowing for sure just what was said, but the general drift is more or less clear: the Colonial Office is not particularly devoted either to the Mandate or the state. Both MacDonald and Shuckburgh assert that they do not know what the commission is up to. Maybe. But, jointly or individually, they are already looking for a third solution. This did not surprise me very much. I am ever apprehensive of one particular naysayer — the British government.

Weizmann, too, it is safe to assume, did not remain blind to this drift for long. Sensing defeat, he told MacDonald that he wished to include Ben-Gurion "in the continuation of the talks." MacDonald invited them both to his country house, Seven Oaks, in Essex, on Saturday, September 17.

Still resentful over Weizmann's backpedaling on his promise, Ben-Gurion first questioned Weizmann's Zionist faith. "The bitter surprise was that in these talks Chaim was far too easily reconciled to the new turn of affairs, even before we knew exactly what the commission's proposals and the government's official stand were," he wrote Sharett the day before the long awaited meeting. "During the past year I believed that on at least one issue he could be relied upon . . . the issue of the Jewish state. I saw his devotion to this plan and hoped he would stand up for it with all his might. What a harsh and bitter disappointment when I realized I was wrong even in this."

Owing to another extraordinary cabinet meeting, their interview with MacDonald was postponed until September 19, when it was held in Weizmann's home. The talk, which lasted three hours, until midnight, left Ben-Gurion angry and disappointed. He was angry with Weizmann for monopolizing the conversation and speaking "wearily, with no inspiration, not to the point, and a great deal of nonsense," despite the effort Ben-Gurion had invested in rehearsing with him an outline prepared at Weizmann's request. He was disappointed with MacDonald's statements and hints, which made it "more or less" clear that "the government has decided to turn us over to the Arabs; no state and no immigration." In retrospect it is easy to identify in MacDonald's words the general outlines of the policy that became manifest in the White Paper of May 1939: a drastic restriction of immigration and land sales to ensure that the Yishuv forever remain a minority in Arab Palestine.

After MacDonald left, Weizmann and Ben-Gurion sat with Vera and Dugdale, who had waited in another room, until 1:30 A.M. Then and the next day Weizmann disagreed with Ben-Gurion's unoptimistic evaluation. During the discussion Weizmann had shown no signs of disappointment, resentment, or rebelliousness but on the contrary had, according to Ben-Gurion, surpassed the boundaries of "good taste and political sagacity" with the personal compliments he showered on MacDonald, calling him his good friend. But at the JAE meeting two days later, Weizmann announced, to everyone's surprise, that he would take part in no further meetings with MacDonald. This fell on Ben-Gurion, he said, like a thunderbolt on a sunny day. "This time our roles are reversed," he wrote Sharett. It was now Weizmann who called MacDonald "a cheat, a traitor," announced that "there is nothing we can do now with the government of England," and exhorted his hearers "to prepare for war. Over the next three to four years we shall do all we can to undermine England's position in the Near East. We shall give her a bad name in America and meanwhile cement our position in Palestine as best we can."

Now Ben-Gurion insisted on continuing the talks with MacDonald, since "the decisive battle is not yet upon us." Furthermore, he said, "politics should not be directed by assumptions and suspicions." But he argued in vain. Weizmann remained obdurate; he "could not" meet with MacDonald, so it was up to Ben-Gurion and Namier to continue the talks with him.[16] There is no telling exactly what brought about such a sudden and radical change in Weizmann's mood at this crucial moment. One explanation could be his reliance on inside information about cabinet meetings obtained from trusted sources, chief among them Dugdale, who had many relatives and friends at all levels of society and politics. This information, sometimes clear and accurate, was just as often vague and misleading. There is good reason to believe that either type could affect Weizmann's disposition.

Only nine days later, the pendulum swung back again, and on September 28 a high-spirited Weizmann met with MacDonald once more, alone. On October 5, Yom Kippur, MacDonald called to invite him to his office. Ben-Gurion learned of this and, realizing he was not invited, noted in his diary, "Apparently Chaim wishes to go alone." But by then Ben-Gurion would not rely exclusively on Weizmann's report. "We arranged," he said, for Lourie to go with Weizmann, and "on Chaim's exit hear from him about the talk" before he could forget the details "and come at once to my hotel," where Ben-Gurion, Katznelson, and Locker were waiting. Ben-Gurion may also have hoped that the trusted Lourie would extract a more accurate version than Weizmann would have given him. But Weizmann must have guessed why Lourie had come — on Yom Kippur, of all days — for "Lourie did not get very much out of Chaim." From the little that he did, Ben-Gurion gathered that MacDonald had proposed that Weizmann meet with the Arabs — Iraqis, Syrians, and Saudis — to discuss a Jewish state in the framework of an Arab federation. Weizmann, quite pleased with himself for outwitting Ben-Gurion, telephoned at 9:00 P.M. to ask jubilantly, "Have you heard from Lourie yet about the talk?"

"From Lourie's story," Ben-Gurion responded, "it wasn't clear who brought up the idea of a Jewish state within an Arab federation, you or MacDonald."

"The answer was odd. 'We both said it,' " Ben-Gurion noted in his diary. The next day the JAE rejected this proposal. Meanwhile it was obvious that Weizmann's good mood was restored, as well as his confidence in Britain's good faith and his own ability to hitch it to the Zionist wagon. He still clung to the belief that partition had not been abandoned, but rather put on the back burner for only six months. (Weizmann told Ben-Gurion that MacDonald had said so, but in his diary Ben-Gurion wrote, "There is no way of knowing who said it.") Weizmann believed that if the Jews agreed to a mini-state, the British government could get Arab consent to partition. With great satisfaction Weizmann told MacDonald, "I see an important opportunity if you give us Tel Aviv and part of Haifa. We shall be able to create a great Yishuv by means of commercial enterprise, a sort of Venice of the Mediterranean." (Ben-Gurion shuddered at the mention of "the Venetian dream.") In addition, the "Turkey plan," whose outlines were soon to emerge, began to take shape in Weizmann's mind.

It seemed that his intention of excluding Ben-Gurion from his prospective glory was accompanied by a desire to pique him. It is inconceivable that Weizmann did not know what Ben-Gurion had been saying about him (confidentially, of course) to JAE members, particularly his assertion that Weizmann should not be permitted to maintain exclusive contacts with Whitehall and with important diplomats. Even Weizmann's most loyal admirer, Dugdale, told Weizmann that "in these difficult days he should not speak privately with the government and the Arabs."

"You don't trust me?" he asked.

"You should not trust yourself," she replied.

So she told Ben-Gurion, according to his diary. Confirmation that she, too, doubted Weizmann's talent as a negotiator and veracity as a reporter came in a wire Lourie sent in his and Dugdale's names to Sharett. "It is vital that you or Ben-Gurion participate in Weizmann's future interviews." Meanwhile Hoz, fearing "a grave crisis," reported to Sharett on the worsening relations between Ben-Gurion and Weizmann, who met alone with MacDonald twice more, for a total of seven meetings in September and October. Ben-Gurion "is in poor spirits, due to circumstances and our prospects at this time, as well as to the fact that he remains in nearly absolute seclusion during all the days of negotiations at this momentous time, [whereas Weizmann] is very active, works a lot, energetically, forcefully, but does all the work himself, without benefit of a partner, assistance, or the necessary control." Hoz also knew that "to put an end to the situation that has been created [Ben-Gurion was considering] as a last resort . . . taking a revolutionary course of action" — a constitutional challenge to Weizmann's authority as the sole decision maker — and flying to Palestine to "mobilize" the Jerusalem JAE. Ben-Gurion eventually opted for "open war," but it was prevented at the eleventh hour when on October 25 Weizmann invited him to his home for the second and final three-way meeting with MacDonald.

After this talk Ben-Gurion concluded, "The situation is bad . . . We must prepare for political war, primarily with America's assistance, and if this does not help, we still have our last-ditch support in Palestine." The next day he shared his fears with Weizmann, who retorted, "Cheer up!" but later phoned him. "Since you are full of fears, write a letter to MacDonald and tell him all that is on your mind."

BEN-GURION: I will take this opportunity to tell you what I never have before. Out of loyalty to you I do not contradict you before strangers, but in your talks with MacDonald you said many damaging things and I would have to contradict them. If I send him a letter he will think there are differences of opinion between us and that is undesirable.

WEIZMANN: Well then, write me a letter, and I will deliver it to MacDonald.

Ben-Gurion consented, but in composing the letter decided to send it directly to MacDonald and preface it by saying it was "the result of a discussion" between Weizmann and him. On October 31 the letter was delivered, but there was still no real cooperation between them. On November 4 Weizmann met with MacDonald alone, for the eighth and last time in 1938. From then until Ben-Gurion left London in late November, everything went downhill, and Weizmann left contact with the colonial secretary in Ben-Gurion's hands. On November 9 the Woodhead Report and the government's statement were published and the "eyewash" exposed for what it was.

If the ninth was a black day for Ben-Gurion, the days that followed were sheer hell. What went on within him can only be surmised, since for twelve days his diary "dropped out of his hands" — unusual under ordinary circumstances, but even more so at critical moments. His great dream of the state that would save millions of Jews and give momentum to the realization of Zionism vanished into thin air. The Yishuv could anticipate a difficult and bitter struggle against the severe restrictions of immigration and land sales. Amid the darkness that fell on the Jewish people the flames of Kristallnacht illuminated what the future held in store for them in Germany and Europe.

On November 21 Ben-Gurion finally found the strength to take up his pen again, even then jotting in his diary only unconnected phrases whose conjunction reflects the intensity of the preceding days: "Publication of the Woodhead Report; the pogrom in Germany; opening of the Zionist Actions Committee; meeting with MacDonald."

In the meantime Weizmann was preparing for a great venture. With MacDonald's blessing — and MacDonald must have been happy to see him go — he left with Vera and Sharett for Turkey to advance an idea for bringing it over to the Allies' side. This involved granting a Jewish loan of $250 million to Turkey in an attempt to ward off German influence. Once he had rendered this service, Weizmann believed — and "his face lit up" at the mention of it, according to Katznelson — the British government would be in his debt. This was the Turkey plan that had been largely responsible for his optimism with regard to Britain. Ben-Gurion termed the trip "a wild goose chase."[17] But Weizmann set out with a good measure of self-confidence. "We can save you," he told Horace Rumbold, a member of the Peel Commission. As World War II approached it became more and more evident that Weizmann was trying to repeat his achievement of World War I, when the Balfour Declaration was partly a reward for his contribution to the British munitions industry. Incredible as it may seem, this delusory scheme seemed to him the only way left to the JAE to restore the British government's Zionist sympathies.

November 1938

N OVEMBER 1938 was a decisive time in Ben-Gurion's life. The future Ben-Gurion envisaged was more terrifying than any of his colleagues could imagine. He differed from other Zionist leaders both in his foresight of political developments and in his adherence to the dream of a Jewish state that would be the salvation of European Jewry. The temporary peace achieved in Munich had not clouded his vision for an instant. He had no doubt that Hitler would move inexorably toward war and the destruction of the Jewish people and that Britain would betray the Jews just as it had Czechoslovakia. Ben-Gurion saw through Malcolm MacDonald's Zionist-sympathizer posturings whose purpose was merely to "cover up the betrayal." "At this time," he wrote the Jerusalem JAE, "we cannot rule out the possibility that they will abandon us."[1]

The Woodhead Report and its accompanying statement made it clear that the Peel Commission had merely postponed the change of course for two years. The report's significance was frighteningly clear: the harsh restrictions on immigration and land sales were tantamount to abolishing the Mandate and handing Palestine over to Arab rule, just as the Czechs had been turned over to the Nazis. As the sands of the hourglass measured out the last days of European Jewry, Zionism was simultaneously reaching the end of its rope.

Realizing this, Ben-Gurion felt pressed to find an immediate answer to two questions: If the state was not to be, how could Zionism save European Jewry from Hitler? And how could Zionism deliver the Jews of Palestine from the Arabs? Ben-Gurion was alone in considering these two questions a single problem. Originally he had seen the Jewish people from a Zionist perspective, as a vast reservoir of potential immigrants, but after he had embraced the idea of the state, his mind turned increasingly to the Jews' larger dilemma. This involved a global theater of action that was inestimably more complex than the Yishuv.

Beyond the duty of his incumbency in the JAE, these gifts of vision and character imposed a formidable task on him. Who was this man who, in November 1938, took on himself a charge heavier than that of any other Jewish leader? Moreover, where did David Ben-Gurion find the strength and resources to pit himself against the mortal threat to Israel — like that other David, but against foes mightier than Goliath?

In his way Ben-Gurion was an exemplary family man. He seems to have considered his bond with home a source of vitality from which he could draw moral sustenance and encouragement. Testimony to it are his repeated complaints to Paula and the children that they did not write often enough. "Why must you do this and add to my worries?" He made time, even in his most hectic moments, to write to them. His many letters show, paradoxically, that when he was absent from home his presence was felt more, since those dear to him received in letters the individual attention he denied them when he was in Palestine. Even so, there were moments at home with his family that were precious to his children. They all agreed that "he has an exceptional heart," being slow to anger and incapable of saying no. They could ask him for any amount of money, which they could not get from Paula, without being asked what it was for.

His children learned that his expressions of interest were cyclical. At one moment he would greet them with enthusiasm and inquire after their doings with keen concern; then suddenly his mind would be engaged in his own thoughts, so that even in his presence his children were left alone. In his letters, after writing a few personal lines he usually slipped into a lecture or an analysis of the Zionist or world situation. Only the letters to his darling Renana, the child of his "old age," were different. In them he displayed tenderness and an interest in frivolity, avoiding politics altogether.

Since he was absent so much of the time he had to devote a significant portion of his letters to sorting out the problems that arose as his children grew up. He was home when nineteen-year-old Geula married Emanuel Ben-Eliezer in November 1937, but he kept abreast of the beginning of her wedded life by mail from London. The young couple had three problems: employment, housing, and furniture. The last of these was somewhat aggravated when Ben-Gurion, feeling it was public money, angrily returned the JAE's gift of forty Palestinian pounds — quite a sum at the time — in spite of Paula's protests and Geula's tears. Instead of buying new furniture as Geula had dreamed of doing, she had to settle for secondhand. Nor was he pleased with her decision to become a teacher. He wrote her from London in February 1938,

> If from the start of your independence you get stuck in teaching, your world will shrink. You are fortunate that your financial situation does not force you to live off your earnings. You've already complained that Emanuel's salary isn't enough for the two of you, but you are lucky that you still have parents who are happy to help you. However, you are still my little girl, and it will take me a long time to get used to the idea that you are a grown woman taking care of herself. You are fortunate to have such a dear, gentle young man as Emanuel, and I am sure he would not want to see you chained to a job so soon either. I will buy you the dress with pleasure, but I need your size. If the things you want are available in Tel Aviv I'd prefer you buy them there. I don't like dragging things around with me, and it's better to spend money in Palestine than abroad.

He closed with an attempt to soothe her, employing the principle that misery loves company — he, too, had "a load of hard troubles": Czechoslovakia, Germany, and England.

Geula completed her teacher training against her father's wishes. In her letters to Ben-Gurion she described her problems in finding a position in Tel Aviv. On September 26, at the height of the talks with MacDonald, he wrote a long letter in response to hers, which he had read "with great sorrow."

> You're not yet twenty years old . . . and it's a little ridiculous that you are already trying to sum up your life. . . . You've only just completed your studies, in the midst of a terrible crisis [the Arab revolt] throughout Palestine, and while no one knows how long it will last, another, even worse crisis [world war] . . . might soon follow. But the riots in Palestine will not last forever, and what you've learned — in my opinion, only a little so far — will be of use to you, so why despair, why the wailing? . . . [Even if] you don't find work this year . . . I see no reason why a whole year should be wasted. You can and should continue to study. Fortunately, you don't depend on a job so terribly much. Neither your mother nor I — or Emanuel, I'm certain — feels that you should start earning money already, and if a paying job is not to be found, you have a much more profitable job — study. . . .
>
> You should read books to enhance your knowledge and enrich your spirit; read books on science, history, psychology; read English. It's not good that you aren't trying to master one of Europe's languages. If you need a private teacher, I'll be happy to pay for one — and read. . . . You should also study practical things: stenography and bookkeeping . . . If you learn Hebrew stenography I might take you on as my secretary.
>
> If you can only learn to make use of your free time, it won't go to waste . . . There is time for everything, and your time will come. And for the moment — study, study, study! Don't waste valuable time and get rid of

your childish philosophizing. Leave that to me. I'm an old man and I have to sum up the past. What's the matter with you? Read, study, and work.

But Emanuel also needed a job, and he wrote to tell Ben-Gurion so. Paula wrote, too, although she knew that no help would come from Ben-Gurion. It never occurred to him that Geula was asking him less for guidance than for his influence to get her a position. It was up to Paula to take the situation in hand, which she did by successfully seeking help for her daughter from Israel Bar-Shira, an attorney, neighbor, friend, and member of Mapai. Until she retired Geula was an outstanding elementary school teacher.[2]

With Amos, however, Ben-Gurion could not discharge his paternal duties by post, if only because Amos rarely wrote a letter. His father's absence seems to have left its mark. Amos's behavior may have been a desperate plea for paternal attention, since for all his good looks, "open mind," boyish charm, and appeal, when the spirit moved him he behaved like a savage. He loathed school and books and fought with his sisters at home. His jealousy of them is reflected in his not altogether inaccurate recollection of never having received a gift from his father, and never — and here he was accurate — having had his own birthday celebration or a bar mitzvah. Had Ben-Gurion been at home more often and spoken strongly with Amos, Geula thought, he might have taken his studies seriously and behaved toward his sisters. But no scoldings from Ben-Gurion, rare as they were and as stern as they could be, could help when the boy knew his father would soon leave again. On the other hand, it seemed to his sisters that Amos got encouragement from Paula, whose darling son was her favorite. Love him as she might, she could not control him, and her concern for him was expressed mostly in worrying about whether he ate properly. He took advantage of her fussing by getting her to promise him half a piaster if he finished his lunch or dinner; since he spent so much time in the street and at the movies, he hardly ever had enough pocket money.

Ben-Gurion could not help being concerned about his son's future, especially after Amos dropped out of school in the spring of 1936, announcing his desire to study at Kadoorie, a two-year government agricultural boarding school for boys at the foot of Mount Tabor, which was famous for its tradition of students governing their social and academic life, as well as its active participation in the Haganah.

Left with no choice, Ben-Gurion accepted this as an interim solution and began exploring future possibilities. "I want to know what Amos plans to do," he wrote Paula from London in June 1936. Had it been possible, Ben-Gurion would have enrolled Amos in a naval academy in

England when he completed Kadoorie. Meanwhile he hoped for the best and impatiently awaited Amos's matriculation. The question "When does Amos begin Kadoorie?" recurred in his letters. In August he wrote Paula, "I hope that at Kadoorie he'll change — work and study. In any case he won't hit Renanale anymore, and she will be like an only child." On August 22 he wrote Paula again, "When does Amos begin Kadoorie? Tomorrow is his sixteenth birthday, and I hope that now that he is a young man . . . he will work, study, and behave like a human being." But Kadoorie rejected Amos, and it was only through Ben-Gurion's direct intervention that at Chanukah in 1936 Kadoorie admitted Amos to its third class, which was to graduate in the summer of 1938.

Ben-Gurion's letters to Amos at Kadoorie generally went unanswered. Nonetheless, even though he never accepted the excuse Amos gave that he had no time, Ben-Gurion was somewhat comforted by the silence. "I know that you have enough work at school, both in the field and at home," he wrote in October 1937, "and I'm happy that you are buckling down to your studies." After graduating from Kadoorie Amos went to Kibbutz Na'an, where his favorite cousin, Israel Gruen, was a member; there he underwent agricultural training and served as a supernumerary constable.[3]

From Renana, Ben-Gurion experienced only joy. She wrote him most; when she was thirteen, he observed that "hers is a beautiful Hebrew." Her one fault was spelling — "She doesn't differentiate between *H* and *A*." Geula had had the same problem as a child, and it probably originated in Paula's incorrect pronunciation of her mother tongue — Russian has no *H*. In February 1938 Renana wrote Ben-Gurion in detail about a concert she had attended — she was continuing her piano lessons — and asked him to bring her pins, notebooks, pencils, statuettes, and artificial flowers. He read the list with interest and promised to bring her these items.

When Paula went to London in mid August 1938, she left Renana in the care of an acquaintance, Yonah Kahana. Kahana had only praise for the girl in her letters. "Renana will never be bored. She can always find something to do, and her happy nature has always helped her confront all kinds of obstacles." But Ben-Gurion had an issue to resolve even with Renana, for she declared that she was not on speaking terms with Paula and refused to write to her. "Ask Mother if I should have my teeth straightened or not," she directed Ben-Gurion. "If she says yes, I'll go to the dentist." Ostensibly this was because Paula did not write to her, for a simple enough reason. To her elder children, who had been born in English-speaking countries, Paula spoke and wrote English; Amos even wrote her back in English. But when Renana was born

Paula could already speak some Hebrew and had no further need of English. Apparently she was afraid to write her daughter in Hebrew lest Renana correct her in it.

But Renana's anger probably had a deeper cause: the social and political background of her host family. The Kahanas were shopkeepers, owners of a candy store on Allenby Street. They lived on Zevulun Street near the Levinsky market on the city's south side, far from the Ben-Gurions' home in the workers' neighborhood in north Tel Aviv. It is difficult to understand why Paula left Renana in the care of this family who lived in the heart of the right-wing, revisionist district, unless it was out of spite. Her efforts to convince Renana that the Kahanas were loyal followers of the labor movement show that Paula knew she was not being entirely aboveboard.

Renana's complaints made their way swiftly to Ben-Gurion in London. "Mother said they read *Davar* here. Tell her that it isn't true — they buy and read *Ha-Boker.**∗* And since I have no other newspaper, I read it also." Then, "Mother said they were leftists here but it's exactly the opposite. They are perfect right-wingers. Miriam (Yonah's sister) is always speaking against Mapai and saying to me 'your *Davar*,' and Mr. Kahana is also right-wing. I don't understand why Mother left me with Revisionists, of all people." On September 11 the girl finally addressed a letter to "Dear Mother and Father." But this was just a momentary truce.[4]

The most intractable of all the family was Paula. If in 1937 it had seemed that understanding and warmth, if not true love, had been restored, in early 1938 she made it clear that she still resented Ben-Gurion's trips abroad. Accompanying her husband more and more was not enough to satisfy her. She could not — or would not — join him on all his trips. She expressed her displeasure with his first trip to London in 1938 in a new manner: instead of dreaming up aches and fatal diseases, she took to making molehills out of mountains. In February she was hospitalized at Hadassah without letting him know. He learned of it only through Renana, who wrote him on the sixth, "Hello Daddy. . . . You know of course that Mother has to have some tests at the hospital. She'll be admitted on Tuesday, February 8." He waited in vain for further details from Paula herself and finally turned to the child. "My Renanale, I was very happy to have your letter, as it was the first I've received from home. I still haven't received a letter from Mommy and this worries and hurts me very much. Has she gone to the hospital yet?"

∗ *Ha-Boker* was the daily paper of the General Zionists and the merchants and industrialists.

Lack of further information made him more anxious, and on the eighteenth he wrote Paula,

To this day I haven't received a word from you. You apparently don't know how much this hurts me. Only through Renanale's letter did I learn that you're going into the hospital. You didn't even write me about that. I left Palestine with a concern perhaps greater and more serious than I have ever known before. All our work for the last fifty-six years, all our hopes of the last hundreds and thousands of years are in peril. . . . The situation of the Jews in the Diaspora is getting worse and worse . . . The work here is not easy and demands utter concentration of will and mind. Paula, I ask you, please write and don't cause me such pain.

But before Paula's letter arrived — the mail took five to six days to travel from Tel Aviv to London or back — Ben-Gurion received word from Renana. "Mother is still in the hospital; she will probably come home this week." He would most likely have been beside himself with worry had it not been for Renana's next few lines about Paul Muni's forthcoming visit to Palestine. "Mother said she might invite him over to dinner." Knowing his wife and her ways, he took great comfort in this information. The letter he finally received from Paula reinforced this feeling, although she still did not explain why she had been in the hospital. "My dear Renanale," he wrote on March 1. "I received your second letter. . . . I'm glad Mother is home again. But from her letter I understand that she still does not feel well. Therefore I've decided to come home as soon as possible — right after the Zionist Actions Committee sessions, two weeks from now." As soon as he was sure that Paula's life was not hanging in the balance, he no longer worried about her not writing. On the sixteenth he sent her his usual long letter, as if her entire interest lay in the Actions Committee sessions and his reasons for calling them. On March 22 he cabled her his departure date, the twenty-sixth.

In June, while Ben-Gurion was in Palestine, Paula was hospitalized to have her cecum removed. It is reasonable to assume that this was the source of her discomfort and hospitalization in February. However, she had another reason for wanting to punish him: her suspicions of other women had been rekindled, to the extent that she found it necessary to pour her heart out to Katznelson. There is a reference to this in his notebook entry of March 29, two days before Ben-Gurion's return to Palestine. If this was the case, she had an important objective in going to London in August — to unveil her rival, specifically, Doris May.

Probably the gifts Ben-Gurion sent with May late in 1936 had aroused Paula's suspicions, as if she assumed that a woman bringing presents from one's husband is as suspect as a Greek bearing gifts. Or perhaps one or more of Doris May's letters to Ben-Gurion since November 1937 had made its way into her hands. May wrote with an intimacy that went beyond ordinary office relations between secretary and boss. Most were written on her personal stationery; all began "My dear David" (one, from December 14, 1937, opened "My very dear David") and were signed "Yours ever, Dory." She was consistently frank about issues and people in the JAE, never attempting to conceal her affection for and admiration of Ben-Gurion; and she always assured him of "My love as ever." (Had Paula read Blanche Dugdale's letters as well, she would have realized that in England this style of address was not necessarily evidence of a love affair.) In the letter of December 14 she could have read that Dory was looking forward to a day when she would be able "to read a simple Hebrew letter (and then it will be *your* turn to try and develop a legible handwriting!). Meanwhile, I am quite prepared to acknowledge my sins — and to continue to struggle with the Hebrew." Paula would certainly have recalled Ben-Gurion's demand that she herself, and later Rega Klapholz, learn Hebrew; and May's remark would very likely have convinced her that the two were having an affair. It was as if Hebrew was the net into which Ben-Gurion invariably drew his loves.

Had Paula been unfortunate enough to come across May's letter of June 9, which included not only her address and telephone number but also a request to "please destroy," underlined twice, she would have felt that she had caught Ben-Gurion and May red-handed. These assumptions are supported by May's letter of November 29, when both Paula and Ben-Gurion had returned to Palestine. It opened, "David, my dear, I don't know if it is 'safe' to write to you, but if not, you will no doubt warn me in some way. Not that there will be anything in this letter that can't be cried from the housetops — or so I hope! Your departure leaves London a very empty place." Of all her letters this came closest to being a love letter. She closed it, "Bless you, my dear, and good luck to you, now and always. Try to take *some* care of yourself (though I know you'll do nothing of the sort!) And come back soon — and *safe!* Yours ever, D." The initial was written in Hebrew.

In London, Paula apparently found what she considered indisputable evidence of Ben-Gurion's indiscretion and announced her desire to return home. On September 21 Ben-Gurion wrote Geula, "Mother does not want to stay here anymore," and on the thirtieth he accompanied Paula to the train station, to see her off to Paris. The next day he wrote her how much he missed her. "When I went home from the station yesterday I felt terribly lonely, as if everything was empty. I am accustomed to solitude, but this time I don't know what happened. I cannot find a place for myself. Everything is cold and empty and silent. I wrote Renanale and Geula and Amos, poured out my heart to them, and am still not comforted." As proof that he was absolutely faithful and abided by her wishes, he wrote that he was adhering strictly to the diet she had prepared to keep him and their budget healthy. "This morning and this afternoon I ate in my room. I bought ham, beef, tomatoes, cucumber, lettuce, eggs, and cheese. I spent five shillings and I think the food will last me three days." In closing he asked her to write to him en route and ended with "Shalom and kisses, David."

In Paris Paula spent three days with the Fodiman family, relatives who showered her with gifts. On October 3 Joseph Fodiman wrote Ben-Gurion that Paula wanted him to make sure that she had no problems with customs in Haifa since "she's bringing along a lot of perfume and eau de cologne." Paula added to the letter, "Dear David! I am leaving Paris to night. Be well and happy. Pola." If Ben-Gurion ever sensed the hidden irony in these parting words it was only in retrospect, for he was totally unprepared for her next move.

Paula returned to Tel Aviv on October 10 and wrote to Ben-Gurion on the twenty-fifth. She had had two full weeks — during which she probably dwelled on how wretched her lot was — to ponder her chances against the formidable Miss May. Only then did she take pen in hand and write, in English:

> Dear David,
>
> I know I am a terrible person, but what can I do. You made me what I am, when I think of the past few months, I have no desire to live, eventually it will be so. Why, for what. To be in somebody's way and a burden to yourself. I could hardly keep the pen in hand. The image of the past is in front of me. I have no desire to be in somebody's way. Cannot keep it to myself and cannot tell to others. What will become of the children the children *seem* to need me, Amos was very happy when I came home with tears in his eyes he needs me. I look so bad, everybody asks me what is the matter with you, have no *answer*. Sama Aronowich, was to see me, he asked me, Paula, what is the matter with you, I am still looking for the answer. Probably *you* could answer *for me*.
>
> I must have rest, where shall I get it, cannot get away from *myself*. I wish I could.
>
> Amos is in Nana [Kibbutz Na'an], I want to go to see him, the comrades dont advise me, but I am going to-morrow, I wish it would happen The children would not need an explanation. Geula is still without work, Renana looks very well, she gets stout and looks very big. What is with you
>
> I hope you will be able to read my poor letter
>
> Paula
>
> P.S. Geula is writing you a letter. Renana will write tomorrow. It is so hard for me with Renana don't know which it will be next.

On October 28 Paula sent Ben-Gurion a vague telegram, the content of which is unknown. But if she intended him to think she was on the brink of suicide, she failed. On October 29 Sharett arrived in London with the news that he had seen her and she was in good health. Ben-Gurion's response to her cable was simply "I didn't know what to think," which prefaced a long report on a meeting he had had that day. Paula's suicide letter and the letters from his daughters did not reach him until November 1. If he had been at all alarmed by her letters, his alarm seems to have been brief; women resolved to take their lives do not, as a rule, stock up on French perfume, and he knew that the danger had passed. He wrote Geula immediately. "I feel better this morning since receiving letters from you and Mother and Renana after a prolonged silence."

When Paula returned to Palestine, a three-way quarrel developed between her and her daughters, triggered by Geula's jealousy of her sister. Geula had taken upon herself the responsibility for training Renana in housekeeping chores, looking over her homework, particularly her French lessons, and intervening when Renana asked her mother for a new coat and shoes. In London, Ben-Gurion heard about it from both, and he had to prove himself not merely a gifted diplomat, but also a wise judge. On November 4, 1938, at the height of the tension preceding publication of the Woodhead Report, he wrote them separately.

My dear Renana — I received your letter, with as many grievances as a pomegranate has seeds. . . . I wrote Geula not to make demands of you, but I don't agree with all you said. Some of your remarks against the French instructor's teaching methods seem valid to me, although I'm not a pedagogue or an education expert, but it seems to me that whereas you were partially in the right, I fear that the basis of your resentment is simply laziness, not wanting to work a little harder at your lessons. Particularly displeasing to me is your behavior toward Mother. I have no doubt that you love her very much, but you don't understand that love alone is not enough — you must behave yourself and never cause pain. You are causing Mother a lot of pain now. You know that Mother is sometimes edgy, and you are the only child still at home. You must make sure always to be a source of happiness and joy to Mother and not the opposite. You should help her around the house as much as you are able. . . . I am certain that if you just try a little harder you can be a good girl and diligent student . . . A little more consideration for Mother, a little more care around the house, and you will be a sweet and dear girl. Also, don't take it too personally if Geula makes a remark to you. . . . I am prepared to assume that you are sometimes in the right, but you know that Geula loves you and if she reproves you or reports you to Mother, it is not out of wickedness but out of love for both you and Mother.

Be more generous and patient. Learn to accept criticism made in love. And most especially take very good care not to cause Mother the slightest pain. . . . You must always obey her.

To his eldest he wrote:

Dear Geulik . . . Renana . . . has been contesting your remarks — particularly about her French lessons, and while I do not accept all of them, I must say that some of her observations were sharp, wise, and sometimes right on the mark. I knew she was no dummy, but in this letter she comes through as an intelligent and bright little girl. She claims, for instance, that they are given forty new words in each lesson, but that they aren't gone over in the following lesson and hence it is difficult to remember them. If this is so, in my opinion her grievance is justified. She also complains that some of the words aren't important, such as various nouns for socks and stockings, different types of pins, and here again, in my opinion her complaint is justified. They don't have to fill her with nouns for these insignificant things. She also complained that you are miffed when Mother buys her something. I don't know if this is true; again, if it is, she has the right to be upset. She herself admits, "In some things she (you, that is) is right, but even she [Mother] wouldn't do this, and she [Geula] has no right to be angry with me." As an older and wiser sister you ought to show a little more patience toward her. She is particularly upset when you say to Mother, "She's spoiled." She claims that Mother knows this already, and it would be better for you to tell it directly to Renana, but — she claims — "she doesn't have to say it constantly to Mother."

You know that I'm a pacifist. I want to spread peace in the Zionist movement and the Yishuv — and I would also like a little more peace to reign between my daughters. . . . As a teacher you ought to deal with a young girl accordingly, not strictly, or severely, but gently, with loving reproof, never in anger.[5]

Unlike Weizmann, whose power base was wholly personal, Ben-Gurion's lay primarily within his party. Weizmann's status as a world Jewish and Zionist leader rested on respect for his person, esteem for his past activity, and faith in his leadership for the future. Ben-Gurion, in contrast, drew most of his strength from his party in Palestine and the institutions in which he represented it, by virtue of which he was also the acknowledged leader of the Yishuv. The party, then, was of primary importance to him. However, if he was disappointed in his family as a source of private support, he was even more dismayed by his party. By November 1938 he had submitted three resignations.

The first grew out of the factional conflict within the Tel Aviv branch, his primary link with the party. Faction B, which was composed of Tabenkin followers from Ha-Kibbutz ha-Meuchad, fought Faction C, whose members leaned toward Ben-Gurion and Katznelson and came mainly from the ranks of the party. Between the two arose still another faction, D. The intramural struggle affected democratic procedure; factional tickets were drawn up for the elections to branch and party institutions instead of candidates running individually as in the past. Ben-Gurion opposed factional groupings on principle out of concern for party unity and declined — as did Katznelson, Golda Meir, and others — to join any of them. Before the elections for the May 1938 party convention the factional strife intensified, and members of the executive committee of the Tel Aviv Labor Council — Faction B's stronghold — submitted letters of resignation to the HEC and the branch secretariat. In April Ben-Gurion's motion in the party Central Committee to return the letters of resignation was rejected by a majority of 7 to 2, and Ben-Gurion announced his own resignation from the committee. The committee resolved on the spot not to accept it, but Ben-Gurion stood his ground and repeatedly stated in May and July that he was no longer a member of the Central Committee, which had vacillated on stamping out factionalism.

The Mapai convention in Rehovot discussed at length the threat to party unity posed by the factionalist regimentation of Ha-Kibbutz ha-Meuchad. Expressing his discontent with the convention for its ambivalence toward factionalism, Ben-Gurion did not stand for re-election to the Central Committee, even though he needed this status more than ever. At the same convention he called for giving the young military training and acquiring ships for illegal immigration — the incipient signs of his increasing militancy. Despite his refusal, the convention voted him in and when in October, in London, he received an official notice from the party secretariat referring to his resignation from the Central Committee, he pointed out its "inaccuracy. I did not 'resign'; rather, I did not accept election at the Rehovot convention." He reaffirmed this statement in December, and a year later, in December 1939, he argued at the Mapai council that he had not been a member since the previous council and that his status there was that of "a party representative in another institution," the JAE.

In June Ben-Gurion resigned from the HEC plenum because of the dispute over the Histadrut's position regarding the death sentence handed down for Shlomo Ben-Yosef, a Revisionist who in April shot at Arab vehicles on the road to Safed in retaliation for the March murder of four Jews on the same road by Arab terrorists.* Mapai opposed the death sentence on principle, but Ben-Gurion maintained, against the majority of the HEC, that the execution of a revisionist terrorist was an

---

* Shlomo Ben-Yosef was hanged on June 29, 1938, and became an IZL martyr. In the wake of his execution the IZL stepped up its counterterror operations.

inopportune occasion for mobilizing public opinion against capital punishment in general.

In September he threatened to resign from the JAE as well if Mapai sanctioned the pact between the Haganah and the Irgun Zvai Leummi (IZL). On September 29 he wrote Sharett, "You have two or three weeks to make the necessary arrangements in the Executive to replace me. You have a free hand in dressing up my exit and its cause in any way you see fit. When I get back to Palestine I will end my public life — my mission for the movement has come to an end." In November, however, *Ha-Yarden*, the revisionist organ, published an exchange of letters between Ben-Gurion and Golomb on the pact, which had been stolen. The pact was aborted, and as a result, Ben-Gurion said, he had deferred his resignation.[6]

This, then, was the state of affairs in November 1938 in his home and party, his two mainstays for bearing the onerous charge given him. For the party the future held further escalation in factional strife; in 1939 Ben-Gurion's ultimatums and resignations proliferated. It is likely that this was the result of his extended absences from Palestine and the nature of his political program. Just as he was unable, as head of his household, adequately to discharge family obligations by mail, so was he unable, as party leader, to unify Mapai from afar. Had he remained in Palestine the year round he would have seen for himself the extent of Mapai's flaws, so characteristic of a ruling party. He would have been aroused against its departure from its fundamental values, just as Tabenkin and his followers were. He almost certainly would have granted their central, repeated demand for "housecleaning" within the party and the Histadrut, to rid the apparatus and institution of their many irregularities. But his ever-lengthier trips abroad also prevented him from carrying out the necessary reforms. Even had he stayed in Palestine and agreed to the reforms, they still could not have been carried out, for faced with the dangers he had foreseen rapidly coming true, he needed the party as it was to establish a Jewish state in part of Palestine.

Despite the British actions that year, Ben-Gurion was convinced that partition was inevitable. From the moment the Peel Commission made its proposal, partition had become his definitive road to the establishment of the state. It was as if the commission had brought Ben-Gurion's two lines of action — his work to separate the economy, society, and culture of Palestine into two distinct national units and his initiative "to begin a Jewish state policy" — into one continuous track. On October 7, 1938, he had written his children, "Even if the partition scheme is dropped . . . it will resurface after a time, and the establishment of a Jewish state in part of Palestine will be inevitable." A few days later he had written Itzhak Gruenbaum, "For the first time, perhaps, I am of one mind with Weizmann in our political outlook on the situation and the action that must be taken. Weizmann maintains, as I do, that even if the partition scheme is shelved, they will have to return to it sooner or later." And a week after that he had written Dov Joseph, "As far as I can see there is no solution other than partition." In his policy a state and partition became synonymous.

But it was for just this reason that Tabenkin and other naysayers in Mapai opposed him, and a housecleaning within the party was liable to strengthen opponents of the state to the point that they could foil his policy altogether. Ben-Gurion had no option but to use his threat of resignation to get his way. Could Mapai truly go on without his leadership?

To make his lot worse, Ben-Gurion had no friends to lean on. What he had written in October 1937 — "Maybe my nature is at fault. . . . I am a lonely and solitary man . . . and I have no one to turn to. I stand alone, and a great burden weighs on me" — was even truer in November 1938.[7]

In trusting the adage "If a man is not for himself, who will be for him?" Ben-Gurion probably drew enormous resources from within and became his own strongest support. Just as he was sustained by his love for his family, so his intense sense of mission succored him in his lonely political struggle. Accordingly, September and October were not idle months, as David Hacohen had reported, but a time of creation in which Ben-Gurion formulated his response to the British government's "betrayal." On November 9, when the Woodhead Report was published, Ben-Gurion composed and issued an announcement on the JAE's behalf: the JAE could be expected to participate in further talks only on the basis of the Balfour Declaration and the Mandate. To the Actions Committee, which met in London immediately after publication of the report, he brought a "program for the coming political action" that involved "immigration, land, defense, maritime development, and negotiations with the Arabs," but "not on the basis of a Jewish minority." "The task before us at this time," he told the delegates, "is to fight for the fulfillment of the Mandatory commitment and for immigration."

This type of defiance of Britain was not exclusively Ben-Gurion's. In February 1938 Weizmann had said among his friends, "Those who think they can do anything to the Jews are mistaken." On September 21 Weizmann had announced his intention to sever his relationship with MacDonald and proposed that the JAE "prepare for war" against England. The difference between the two men lay in Ben-Gurion's tenacity. With Ben-Gurion the issue had gone beyond words and become a consistent, coldly calculated plan of action. "We must wean ourselves from empty rhetoric and clichés," he had written his colleagues in the Jerusalem JAE in early October. "Until now we knew only one means: crying. I doubt its power." In both scope and objective Ben-Gurion's program differed from anything Weizmann dared imagine.

In retrospect, it is clear that the first signs of Ben-Gurion's plan were revealed at Mapai's convention in May (where he hinted at ships and military training) and then more distinctly on September 19 and 21, 1938. After the first three-way talk with MacDonald, Weizmann had predicted to Vera and Dugdale that the British "are going to sell the Jews also" out of fear of the Arabs, Germans, and Italians. Ben-Gurion's first reaction, wrote Dugdale in her diary, was that "the Jews will fight." On Weizmann's intention of ending his relations with Mac-Donald, Ben-Gurion wrote Sharett, "What's the point . . . of severing this contact? In another month or two we may have to cut it off as an act of political war." He added, "The situation seems more or less clear to me: the government decided to turn us over to the Arabs. . . . I foresee circumstances in which we may fight England — a political war, and perhaps otherwise as well — but the aim of the war will have to be to obtain England's support."[8] Fight England in order to gain its assistance? Once the British deception was revealed, it became clear that this contradiction was the foundation of Ben-Gurion's most famous double formula.

On January 3, 1939, Ben-Gurion gave his new program a name, when he wrote in his diary, "We are faced, with the age of Hitler, with the necessity of 'combative Zionism.' Palestine will be ours if we want it and can take it by force." Although it was desirable to establish a Jewish state through peace with the Arabs and British support, if the other parties were not amenable, the state would be established in defiance of them, even if it came to war. By April 1939 "combative Zionism" had crystallized far enough for Ben-Gurion to declare the dawn of a new chapter in Zionist history. He told his party,

> Until now there have been two periods of Zionism. The first [the Ottoman], from 1880 until the outbreak of the world war . . . an attempt to implement Zionism with no legal basis. The second . . . the Mandatory period, in which Zionism was implemented on the basis of certain political rights. It is evident that we now stand at the threshold of a third period . . . a period of Zionist realization on the basis of state rule.

The marvel of combative Zionism was its birth at a time when the Jewish people had reached their lowest ebb and were more helpless than they had ever been. In 1938 militant Zionism was directed against the only government in the world that had shown sympathy for the Jews' misery. Could anything be sadder than the persecuted turning against their sole defender? Nothing better illustrates the Jews' plight at the time than the story of the JAE's request after Kristallnacht that the British government permit ten thousand children from Germany and Austria to enter Palestine, as a symbolic gesture. On November 22 MacDonald had informed the cabinet that although it was economically feasible for Palestine to absorb many Jewish refugees, and large numbers of small children could not be opposed on that ground, such a gesture would hinder the government's initiative to bring the Arabs to London for talks with the Jews on Palestine's future. The cabinet accepted his view, concluding, "We must not be dragged, in the wake of the persecution of Jews of late, into taking any action that could hamper the London talks." The success of its secret policy was more important to the British government than the rescue of the children.

The Jews, denied even a symbolic rescue of their children, were forced to take part in a stage play directed by their adversary. The Yishuv was up in arms, and many, including much of Mapai, demanded a boycott of the talks. Unlike Weizmann, who was "tremendously keen" on them, Ben-Gurion, in his heart of hearts, wanted them boycotted. Even so, he stood alone against his party's majority, insisting that they participate regardless of their feelings. He was well aware that these talks were little more than window dressing, but he was apprehensive of a boycott's turning public opinion in Britain and the United States against Zionism and making it easier for the British government to withdraw from its Balfour Declaration commitment. In addition, participation in the talks would likely provide Zionism with an international forum in which to prepare public opinion for combative Zionism.

On October 3 Ben-Gurion had written his JAE associates, "This is a period of power politics. . . . The world's rulers are deaf, unable to hear anything other than the sound of cannon, and the Jews of the Diaspora have none." He then exhorted them "to prepare to face the rule of evil and stand against it now, in our day, and in the days to come." In order to survive, the Jewish people needed force and cannon. Where would they find them? Ben-Gurion replied, "We have nothing but 'our Father in heaven,' the Jewish people itself."[9]

Creating power was the enterprise to which Ben-Gurion would dedicate the next decade, from November 1938 until the establishment of the State of Israel in May 1948. However, before opening this chapter in his life, the story of the deception needs to be completed. The British government proceeded with its strategy and invited Arab and Jewish representatives to London for talks. If no compromise was reached and no quick, durable solution found to the Palestine problem — and was there any doubt that there was none? — the British intended to force on Palestine a solution of their own design. "As far as the English are concerned, it is a wise move to bring both sides together for discussions before they do with us what they have already decided," Ben-Gurion said to Mapai's Central Committee in Palestine in December. He was certain that these negotiations were doomed from the outset and that "the liquidation of the Mandate" would ensue.

The Conference, as the talks were called, took place at St. James's Palace in February 1939. It was notable for its exposure of the Jews' helplessness and for the opportunistic and heartless way the British government used it in its attempt to force on the Jews the status of a permanent minority. At the February 15 session there was a sharp exchange between Ben-Gurion and MacDonald. According to the official protocol, Ben-Gurion said that without British bayonets the Arabs would be unable to stop immigration, and MacDonald replied that if Britain left Palestine, as Ben-Gurion wished, the result would be a bloody war whose outcome he did not dare foretell. Sharett noted in his diary that Ben-Gurion responded "very sharply," while in Ben-Gurion's memory the exchange took on dramatic proportions, illustrating MacDonald's answers less than his own frame of mind.

> MAC DONALD: How long do you suppose we will wield our bayonets in the service of immigration?
> BEN-GURION: By all means, if you so wish, take your bayonets away. Our immigration has no need of your bayonets, quite the contrary, it is solely by the strength of English bayonets that Jewish immigration can be stopped. If only you would not use your bayonets against immigration.
> MAC DONALD: And defence? Who will defend you? Don't you need our bayonets for the security of the Yishuv?
> BEN-GURION: We can do without your bayonets in defending the Yishuv. Permit us to protect ourselves. Don't stand in our way.
> MAC DONALD: Really? They have twice your numbers!
> BEN-GURION: That's our business.
> MAC DONALD: Not only that, they will bring reinforcements from Iraq, an Arab army.
> BEN-GURION: That cannot be helped, but we too will bring reinforcements. It is easier to cross the sea than the desert. . . . We are telling you, we no longer require your bayonets, neither for immigration nor for our security . . . both our immigration and our Yishuv will stand by virtue of their own strength and that of the Jewish people.

With this Ben-Gurion revealed something of the way combative Zionism was taking shape in his mind: boats would unceasingly bring immigrants to the shores of Palestine, where, by the thousands and tens of thousands, they would fight, weapons in hand, for their right to seek shelter and establish a state of their own in the land of their fathers.

This spectacle would awaken world public opinion to the Jewish people's essential need for a state of its own. He told his Mapai colleagues and the Jewish delegation at St. James's, "Our policy goal is a Jewish state"; this was to be made clear at the talks and become the backbone of Zionist policy. In these days when the hope for a state was crushed, Ben-Gurion redoubled his efforts to breathe life into it.[10]

At the outset of this struggle Ben-Gurion's position in both London and the Zionist world was considerably enhanced. One reason, though not the principal one, was Weizmann's absence — Weizmann was in Turkey from November 22 to December 11. During this time Ben-Gurion, as the senior Zionist, conducted the contacts with the Colonial Office and members of Parliament; he met with MacDonald three times, most notably on November 24, when Ben-Gurion sat in the visitors' gallery of the House of Commons and listened to a speech in which MacDonald announced, among other things, the government's rejection of the JAE's request to allow the immigration of the ten thousand children and to the debate that followed. Spotting Ben-Gurion in the gallery, MacDonald sent his secretary to invite him to his office in the House, where he asked for his comments, affording Ben-Gurion the opportunity to re-emphasize the gravity of the government's refusal and demand reconsideration. MacDonald promised to get back to him. Wauchope, too, was in the House and invited Ben-Gurion to lunch on November 26. It was at this meal that MacDonald's answer arrived, in the person of Sir Cosmo Parkinson, permanent under secretary of the Colonial Office, who conveyed MacDonald's reaffirmed refusal.

The other, more important reason for Ben-Gurion's greater strength was combative Zionism. As opposed to Weizmann's Turkey scheme, Ben-Gurion's, a fitting answer to the White Paper, was the only plan of action the JAE really had. After Weizmann returned from Turkey, he continued to pursue his old policy of trying to achieve concessions and favors through personal diplomacy. Ben-Gurion, on the other hand, turned toward the United States, a move that had far-reaching ramifications for Zionist policy and was a significant turning point in his long contest with Weizmann.[11]

38

The Kings of
the Jews in America

THE PLAN Ben-Gurion had conceived in May 1938 ripened in his mind throughout September and October. On September 20 he wrote Sharett, "We will probably have to use the little force we have in Palestine," and by early October he knew how to do so. At least that is the implication of the "analysis of the situation" he sent the Jerusalem JAE. Sending his children a copy, he wrote explicitly, "I only hinted at my main conclusion, since what I am aiming at one does without speaking, and I imagine you are bright enough to get my meaning." As usual, he had addressed this letter to the HEC, and Pinchas Lavon edited it for publication in the party's newsletter of September 24 with some omissions, among them the above quotation.

The letter was also read and discussed by the Central Committee, allowing Mapai leaders to congratulate themselves on their ability to understand a hint. Ben-Gurion explained to his children why he had revealed to them that which he had half concealed from his JAE associates. "Our party hacks, our fat cats, our clever ones, and our pragmatists will probably not display the necessary readiness to mobilize all the Yishuv's strength and use it unflinchingly, without recoiling for fear of losing life and property. But if they panic and give in, the youth — the young in age and the young in spirit — will rise up and unfurl the banner of rebellion." Perhaps Ben-Gurion wished to sound his children out and get a preliminary response from the youth on the role he intended for them. "The young in age and the young in spirit," those brave and daring individuals later known as the "activists," were a factor not previously counted on as part of Zionism's battle array. To them Ben-Gurion added another new element, American Jewry. These two groups increasingly became the targets of his appeals.

Ben-Gurion kept his plan secret for a while, which shows his apprehension of his colleagues' reaction. The first to be let in on the secret was Katznelson, to whom Ben-Gurion revealed his plan "in a night talk" on November 27, at the Lutetia Hotel in Paris. "I was primarily opposed to the internal rift [liable to rend Mapai] that would follow" its adoption, Katznelson commented in his notebook. On December 1 he and Ben-Gurion discussed the plan again on the deck of the *Marietta Pacha* as they returned to Palestine. Katznelson's measured words in his notebook — "fundamental talk with Ben-Gurion" — shed little light on what was said. Even after they reached Haifa on December 5, Katznelson remained the only one who knew about the plan, and on the tenth — the day before Ben-Gurion finally committed it to his diary in black and white, he added at the end of his entry, "The first man with whom I spoke of this plan was Berl. And this sworn skeptic told me after much thought, 'Maybe this is the way.' " But this reading of Katznelson's response turned out to be a sign that he still did not know his friend and partner that well. Later that day, Katznelson wrote in his notebook, "With Ben-Gurion, a third talk and there is progress. It's becoming clear what Ben-Gurion wants our policy to be, but not as regards the party." If Katznelson, who was close to Ben-Gurion in spirit and thinking, disliked the plan, his colleagues of Joseph Sprinzak's ilk hated it. At a Mapai Central Committee meeting on December 7, which discussed the wretched state of Zionism and possible responses to the new British policy, Ben-Gurion had made statements that sounded innocuous enough unless one got the "hint," saying that the center of gravity was to be found in the Yishuv itself, not in relations with England — "What counts is what we do." Either a whiff of the plan had already made its way to Sprinzak, or else he had picked up on Ben-Gurion's train of thought, for he said, "I returned from London broken, depressed, and an absolute mess. . . . Our situation lacks even a spark of hope or any out at this time. . . . I accept most of the statements heard here regarding the necessity of showing opposition if [the British] wish to hand us over [to the Arabs]. I assume that no one is contemplating lunatic opposition, but rather more calculated and carefully thought out opposition."[1]

Might that "no one" have been Ben-Gurion?

The main thrust of the "new policy" Ben-Gurion presented to the JAE on December 11 and to the Mapai Central Committee on December 15 was to gain substantial sympathy in Britain and the United

States, then to use it to impress on the British government that only a state could solve the Jewish problem. But the program's great innovation was the means it used for achieving these goals, "the immigration revolt," another Ben-Gurion tactic for militant Zionism. Preparations were to include military training of youth, establishment of a technical training apparatus, buying and renting small evasive vessels suitable for smuggling immigrants, creating a network of border smugglers in Germany, Austria, Poland, Greece, and Rumania, and readying Palestine to absorb the illegal immigrants. The revolt was to begin after the government's statement — expected at the conclusion of the St. James's talks — of a new policy inimical to Zionism. A world Jewish conference, to be held in New York, would then proclaim that "Palestine is our land" and that it was Zionism's intention to carry out "the mass return" of "hundreds of thousands of Jewish youths" to their homeland. "It is our right to bring the Jewish refugees to Palestine . . . for Germany's design now is to destroy not only the Jews of Germany but of the entire world." Following the proclamation the JAE would resign insofar as the British and Palestine governments were concerned — "The Jewish people would be taking matters into their own hands," choosing a policy of noncooperation with the British government in London and the Mandatory government in Palestine. The very planning of such a conference would affect the way the British handled the St. James's talks. "With these preparations in progress," said Ben-Gurion to the JAE, "we will be able to go to the talks in London with quieter hearts . . . the Conference . . . will also strengthen our hand in negotiations with the government and the Arabs."

In Palestine passive resistance would take place. Ships from Europe would arrive, one after another, unloading "thousands of young people from Germany, Austria, and other countries" onto the shores of Palestine, and Britain would be faced with "the necessity of shooting the refugees or sending them back," although there was no place to send them. "Immigration pressure" would be used against the British government, and would "to some extent offset the pressure of the Arab threat."

> Of course England is far stronger, but let's see what might happen. If she sinks our ships . . . if it is ordained that they and we die, they will die here. If it is ordained that they fight, they will fight here, for this is the only place for our war. . . . We will invite photographers to take pictures of the English shooting at the boats bringing refugees to Palestine . . . and returning Jews who came from Germany and Poland. [However,] this pressure is not intended for the sake of immigration itself, but only as a weapon . . . of the political war. . . . It is one that will, week after week, make the world press seethe.

The policy's culmination would be the establishment, by force if necessary, of a Jewish state in part of Palestine. This would require the conquest of Haifa, the mixed-population port city, to which tens of thousands of Jews would rapidly be transferred, with plants and services from other settlements, until the ratio of Jews to Arabs in the city was 2 to 1. Once the state was declared in Haifa, refugees could enter its ports en masse, legally and freely. Taking Haifa by force was not meant to harm England but to get it as an ally, wrote Ben-Gurion in his diary, not bothering to explain the paradox. "It is probable that in the present situation we can obtain England's support and sympathy only by making ruthless war against her."[2] Resolving this contradiction, as Ben-Gurion soon found out, would be a Herculean task.

Ben-Gurion often liked to speculate on his colleagues' reactions to his proposals, and he did so now. "I don't know if all JAE members will have the guts to accept this. I am certain of the support of Gruenbaum and Kaplan. Chaim will agree in theory, but I'm not positive he won't balk at the decisive moment. Ussishkin? . . . [Rabbi] Fishman will undoubtedly back me." Of course he also counted on Katznelson, but twenty-four hours later all his assumptions had been proved false. There was not much enthusiasm in Mapai or the JAE for the rebellion plan. The deliberations on it confirmed the doubts Ben-Gurion had expressed to his children with regard to "our clever party hacks and pragmatists." Almost without exception his colleagues chose to press instead for entry permits for the children from Germany and make the JAE's participation in the St. James's talks conditional on receiving them. That was as far as they were willing to go. Combative Zionism found no willing ears.

Even Katznelson attacked the plan, and only with difficulty did he manage not to sound sarcastic.

> Ben-Gurion spoke of "rebellious immigration." I do not know how many ships will come; a few will, with thousands of people on their decks, and they will stand alongside the shore, not permitted to enter Palestine. But it seems to me that the ten thousand children — whom the Yishuv wants badly and for whom certificates were refused on a technicality — offer far better cause for revolt than ships with thousands of people who reach Palestine but are barred from entering. I am not eager for a conflict with England. I would like to put that off as long as possible. I know how little support we can expect from the world in this conflict. Considering our lot in Germany and Italy and Poland it would certainly be no great pleasure to start a conflict with England. No world power is more just than she . . . yet Ben-Gurion has "plans." Undoubtedly they include important items . . . [but] I know . . . American Zionism and English Zionism will be panicked and terrified by his plans.

Of Ben-Gurion's entire program, only the world Jewish conference in America won approval. Even so, the JAE assigned the conference a different objective and left the final decision about calling it to the discretion of Weizmann and his colleagues in London. Nonetheless, the little Ben-Gurion got out of his party and the JAE was sufficient to encourage him in resuming preparations for the immigration revolt. Wise from experience, he knew that this was not the last word. More than once, plans he had offered that initially had been rejected later became the party's principal platform.

With the JAE's decision on December 15, and consent to his making a trip to the United States cabled from London by Wiezmann and Sharett, Ben-Gurion began a race against time. He immediately renewed his Palestinian passport, and on the seventeenth he set out for New York with the intention of persuading the Jews of the United States to accept not only the conference — the ostensible objective of his trip — but his wider-ranging goals as well. This time cables were sent to notify all concerned of his arrival.[3]

Landing at Croydon on the evening of December 20, Ben-Gurion was greeted by icy winds. In his diary he remarked, "Freezing and exhausted, I finally reached my warm room at the Mount Royal." The next day Sharett reported to him on Weizmann's latest talks with MacDonald, which reinforced Ben-Gurion's conviction that "nothing good can be anticipated" of the St. James's Conference, but that even so, "it would be a grave mistake for us not to participate." Ben-Gurion found Weizmann "understanding and in complete agreement with my action in America." But, he wrote to Kaplan, Weizmann had added "the Turkey worry" to his pack of troubles, asking him to find out "if it is possible to arrange for America to buy directly from Turkey — not via Germany, as has been done up to now — carpets, tobacco, raisins, and cotton." Weizmann still stood by the Turkish connection as Zionism's salvation. During his three days in London, Ben-Gurion also heard a report from Dr. Nahum Goldmann, head of the Zionist mission to the League of Nations, that American Jewry was ready for Zionist action. He concluded, he wrote Paula, that "we must now move in America, and I do not regret my decision to go there." Without naming his sources, he also passed along to the Jerusalem JAE the news that war was feared by March or April, along with a warning: "This rumor must not be spread in Palestine — but we must make ready." On the morning of December 24 he set out for Southampton, where he boarded the *Franconia,* to sail that afternoon.

"This is the first time in several years," Ben-Gurion wrote Paula from the ship, "that I have had absolute rest. I don't know any of the passengers and don't have to talk with anyone." He also found time to read, and he learned "a few important things" from the memoirs of Marshal Foch. Between books, Ben-Gurion devoted some thought to hammering out the new policy he was bringing to the United States, as evidenced by the fact that on January 3, the day after he arrived in New York, he detailed his plan in his diary. If the Yishuv could muster the strength to keep up the revolt for a year, he wrote, "England will be forced to yield . . . to combative Zionism.[4]

Fighting Zionism was the power formula Ben-Gurion had hatched in the days when the democratic powers had yielded to violence and their rulers turned a deaf ear to all but the sound of cannon. With what "cannon" did Ben-Gurion intend to arm the Jews, and what force would be put at the service of militant Zionism? Ben-Gurion had four pillars upon which to build: the Yishuv's capacity for endurance, the plight of European Jewry, British public opinion, and the Jews of America. The first three were old war-horses that had long been in harness to his political strategy. The most important of them, the Yishuv, had been steeled by what Ben-Gurion called "the war of life or death" forced on the Jews by the Arabs in Palestine, which had been in progress for thirty years and would continue, as he had told the Histadrut council in July 1938, "for perhaps hundreds of years." If in 1936, before the riots started, Ben-Gurion had held that the chances for peace were minimal, it became even more evident as the riots turned into the Arab revolt. As Arab hatred intensified, so did Ben-Gurion's fear that the Arab states would join forces with those of Europe "who wish to obliterate the memory of Jewry, and who are not so weak." In October 1936 Ben-Gurion had told the Small Actions Committee, "I cannot rule out the possibility of massacre and destruction of the Yishuv in Palestine." In August 1937 he had asked the Zionist Congress whether the Yishuv could withstand a coordinated offensive by the independent Arab countries, which would come to the aid of Palestine's Arabs in their war, bearing in mind that those countries possessed regular land and air forces and that Britain was engaged in self-defense against Hitler. In February 1938, Ben-Gurion had openly told MacMichael, "As a minority, we are liable to be wiped out."[5]

It was clear to Ben-Gurion that a strong Jewish armed force was the only guarantee of the Yishuv's security, so in February 1937 he had called the Histadrut council "to redouble our armed forces in one stroke." The line of restraint he had taken in response to Arab terror had borne fruit in that the Mandatory government had established and armed, for the purpose of self-defense, units of the so-called Jewish Settlement Police, as well as special anti-terror squads, which worked together with British troops and various other formations of "supernu-

merary constables." Both branches of the Haganah — underground
and overt — gained strength in numbers, weapons, and field training
during the three years of riots. In the autumn of 1937 the illegal organization had had twenty-five thousand members, men and women, deployed throughout the Jewish settlement, and the legal branch more
than twenty thousand uniformed young men authorized by the government to carry arms. To Ben-Gurion they constituted a considerable
force, a nucleus for future regular and reserve armies capable of fulfilling the principal task he assigned them, establishing the state.

Under ordinary circumstances the Yishuv would have drawn on the
Jewish people's support to reinforce and increase its military might.
But could this be counted on now? Of the world's 16 million Jews,
more than 11.5 million were incapable of such support, cut off from
any such possibility or in desperate economic straits. Those in a position to extend material aid, the 4 million in the United States, lacked a
strong, cohesive organization and, more important, the self-confidence
to stand against the prevailing isolationist tide of their country.

The Jews of Europe, rather than offering support to the Yishuv,
needed its help. But to render aid the Yishuv needed to strengthen itself first. This vicious circle could be broken only by turning weakness
into strength. How? Ben-Gurion seems to have viewed the situation as
follows. Zionism had changed. From an exclusive movement of pioneers, individuals who immigrated to Palestine through vision and
faith, Zionism had become an inclusive movement of people in need of
rescue. Were the gates of Palestine open it would have become a massive movement of immigrants overnight. But the gates were shut,
creating a situation in which greater and greater pressure built up until
central and eastern Europe resembled a sealed boiler, with the Jews
inside like steam, growing hotter as the fire of distress intensified.

Ben-Gurion had recognized the potential of this steam for creating
political and military strength. On January 19, 1933, eleven days before Hitler became chancellor of Germany, he had told Mapai's council, "From an abstract, Zionist ... perspective ... at the moment no
propaganda is necessary ... for Palestine. Jewish life in the Diaspora is
the strongest propaganda possible. It produces this propaganda with
the language of the utter destruction of ... tremendous masses. ...
Such Jews by the thousands are now bursting to come to Palestine." He
asked the council members two questions that were really one: "Is ...
it not high time that the great Jewish distress, the destruction of Jewry
in several countries, be turned into a lever?" and "Is there a possibility
of turning the Jewish disaster into a productive force?"

To acquire momentum for Zionism, Ben-Gurion meant to exploit

Jewish calamity as if it were a rich natural resource. The graver the Jewish plight, the more steadfast became his strategy. In May 1936 he had told Mapai's Central Committee, "It is in our interest that Hitler be wiped out, but since this is not happening, it is in our interest to exploit his existence for the building of Palestine." In August 1937 he had claimed that "whoever says that Hitler diminished our strength is not telling the whole truth." This approach reached its ultimate form after the outbreak of war, as Jewish misery and desperation grew in direct proportion to the spread of Nazi power. At a closed meeting of Haganah members in 1939, Ben-Gurion said frankly, "At the outbreak of the riots we saw it as a duty to ourselves and the Yishuv to use this disaster to further new conquests. It is the obligation of the military commander and the politician to turn each setback into an advance."

As he crossed the Atlantic Ben-Gurion thought about how to harness the energy of the steam in the boiler to the benefit of fighting Zionism. The only exit from the boiler was Palestine, and if the valve sealing the gates of immigration were not opened, one of two things would happen: the boiler would explode and the Jews would be destroyed or the steam would force the valve open as the Jews burst into an immigration revolt and stormed the shores of Palestine.

Unlike the first two pillars, the third — British opinion — lay completely outside the sphere of the Jewish people. Fair play, sympathy for the underdog, and freedom of speech, which stood at the foundation of Britain's democratic tradition, made Ben-Gurion an ardent Anglophile and were important factors in his assessment of the prospects of combative Zionism. Human suffering has social or political value only if public opinion can be influenced by it. This, it seems, was the root of his formula for turning disaster into advantage. Ben-Gurion believed that public opinion in Britain would not allow any British government to stand between stricken Jews and Palestine, since the issue was one of life or death. In April 1941 he would state this candidly in a lecture on Zionist policy. "Life or death — this generates tremendous, inestimable power . . . thus enormous might is at Zionism's disposal. . . . Only Hitler can oppose it, for he will sink ships . . . England cannot. And an English government that must fire on Jewish ships will not last even a week."[6] Hence public support was assured for a mass storming of Palestine's shores by Jews struggling for their lives and for a war there against forces seeking to send them back to the valley of death. This is one plausible explanation for Ben-Gurion's paradoxical statement that the British government must be fought in order to make it an ally.

But the British virtues were not the only basis for his hopes. In Ben-Gurion's calculations the Yishuv's military and economic potential played an especially important role. Although the Jews' standing had been undermined and weakened in the rest of the world, he had told the 1937 Zionist Congress, "In Palestine we have increased our strength, and thanks solely *to this strength* England cannot easily back out of its pledges and commitments to us." In his view this factor was of paramount importance. The Yishuv could prove very useful to the British war effort; its industry could be converted to military production, and it had great reserves of experienced, professional manpower, as well as soldiers. For this reason alone it was worth Britain's while to permit greater immigration from Europe. In the event of war, "which is not so distant," he had told MacMichael in February 1938, "if we are numerous in Palestine we shall be able to stand our ground, and perhaps be of support to you."

Ben-Gurion was already contemplating ways to exploit the coming war to establish a regular Jewish army and start a military industry in Palestine. His belief that a regular army was part and parcel of the state lay concealed behind words like *might* or phrases like "powerful tool," which he used to refer to the state. Ben-Gurion also courted British opinion to get support for his claim that the Jews had the right to fight their worst enemy and to overcome the opposition of those influential government circles that well understood that a Jewish army fighting Hitler would be a fine breeding ground for the future regular army of the imminent Jewish state. A few days after the war broke out he told a group of friends that "this goal [the state] must guide and direct all our actions and moves from now on . . . The first requirement for a Jewish state is the formation of a Jewish army." In July 1941, when he realized that for the time being there was no chance "of getting the English government to commit itself to a Jewish state," he made the creation of a Jewish army, within the framework of the British army, the first priority.[7]

The fourth and newest pillar, American Jewry, was a product of and complement to the rest. Ben-Gurion assigned it the role of assisting with materials and manpower and creating favorable opinion to influence British and American policies. Later this role would expand immensely, but in January 1939 the mere fact that Ben-Gurion turned to the United States was important, for this move marked not only the beginning of a reversal in the relationship between Ben-Gurion and Weizmann but, more significant, a decisive shift in Zionist policy. From then on there would be a lessening of Zionist reliance on Britain, counterbalanced by an ever-increasing thrust in America. In 1972, about a year before his death, Ben-Gurion summed up this shift.

I gave up on England when the Peel Royal Commission came to Palestine. I had a private talk with some of the commissioners, and it became clear to me that English rule in Palestine would last only a few more years. I no longer had any faith in England. At first the English government favored the Peel scheme. They endorsed it ... but then ... the government backed down and proposed something which neither the Jews nor the English [i.e., the Arabs] would hear of. Then I knew the game was up. Weizmann took a long time in coming around. Then I turned to the United States. I saw that nothing good would come from England anymore.

What is amazing, looking back fifty years later, is the historical accuracy of Ben-Gurion's reaction. By January 1937 he had urged Weizmann to go to the United States to mobilize public opinion against the Peel Commission's proposals, should they prove unsatisfactory. In the fall of that year he had again prodded Weizmann to persuade the American naysayers to support the partition scheme, and when Weizmann refused he went himself. In January 1938 he had insisted that Weizmann organize a large pro–Jewish state demonstration in the United States. Blanche Dugdale wrote in her diary, "This may be a good plan — but I think Ben-Gurion over-estimates importance of U.S.A. opinion on H.M.G." In August 1938, at La Croix, Ben-Gurion had again urged Weizmann to visit the United States to counteract British backpedaling on the Peel scheme, and in September Dugdale noted in her diary that Ben-Gurion "has become sadly anti-British."[8]

Weizmann, who had visited the United States several times in the 1920s, when a group led by Louis Lipsky that was in league with Weizmann ruled the Zionist roost, probably found it difficult to return when the rival Brandeis group had taken over the Zionist Organization of America (ZOA). Or perhaps Vera had kept him from crossing the Atlantic, for reasons she kept to herself. She may have feared for his health: Weizmann had aged quickly and in 1936, at sixty-two, was already moaning about the weight of his years. In April 1939, a month before publication of the White Paper, Dugdale had informed Ben-Gurion that "Vera said that [Weizmann] would go to America over her dead body." Whatever the reason, Weizmann declined the challenge Ben-Gurion proposed to him and did not set foot in the United States during the 1930s except for a brief visit in 1933 for the "Jewish Day" at the Chicago World's Fair. Ben-Gurion was better suited for action in the United States, and Weizmann stood aside for him.

In September 1938, as Ben-Gurion was developing the idea of combative Zionism, he also began looking actively into the possibilities presented by turning to America. On the fifteenth, in London, he had met with Benjamin V. Cohen, a Washington lawyer and member of an inner circle of advisers to President Roosevelt, mainly on domestic affairs. Ben-Gurion asked him straight out whether "American backing could be expected in one of two instances: (1) If in a few weeks we fight for an important amendment in the partition scheme. . . . (2) If we reject the partition scheme altogether and start fighting for broader immigration possibilities." The reply was discouraging. Ben-Gurion reported to his diary, "Ben Cohen doubts that any support would be forthcoming." Roosevelt, he said, would not lift a finger. Nonetheless, Ben-Gurion flew to Paris on the twenty-third especially to see Cohen again. This time he laid out two alternatives.

1. If war breaks out soon we will perhaps be entirely dependent on America for our existence. Our life line will be cut off, and enormous financial aid will be necessary, but not that alone. Our only chance of success in case of war will be the mobilization of a great Jewish army in Palestine, composed of men from Palestine and America. Without the backing of the American government it will not happen.
2. If war does not break out at this time, the month of October is likely to be "decisive" . . . and American aid would most likely tip the balance. He [Cohen], Louis Brandeis, and their friends would have to do all in their power to gain Roosevelt's friendly intervention. The question is not partition, but Jewish immigration to Palestine.

Cohen's answer was given laconically. Ben-Gurion recorded it in his diary. "Ben Cohen is uncertain, but they will make every effort. The situation is liable to change from day to day, and they will do what they can." And so, with no assurance of Roosevelt's support, only of "efforts" promised by Cohen, Ben-Gurion made his first attempt to activate his "cannon," the thunder of American Jewry. As a countermeasure to the British giving the Arab kings a voice in the St. James's Conference and leaking to the press an Iraqi initiative (stopping immigration, independent government, "equal rights for all citizens"), Ben-Gurion proposed to Weizmann that "an SOS telegram be sent to America" on behalf of the JAE. His draft of the wire called for the mobilization of "all our friends [to] make American voice heard through administration and press. Skipper [i.e., Roosevelt] should intervene British ambassador Washington instruct American ambassador London, take immediate action [against the] grave danger" that Britain would adopt a policy designed to stop immigration and establish an Arab state in Palestine. "Most urgent American Jewry issue statement Jews will not submit fate Assyrians [a minority wiped out in Iraq] and give up Jewish Palestine." On October 6, after managing to soften Ben-Gurion's draft somewhat — the references to Roosevelt and the genocide of the Assyrians were dropped — Weizmann agreed to send the wire to the ZOA's president, Rabbi Solomon Goldman, and to the two American Zionist leaders allied with him, Rabbi Stephen Wise and Louis Lipsky. To his own party in America, Poale Zion, for which he did not need Weizmann's imprimatur, Ben-Gurion sent off a more strongly worded telegram the same day: "Activate the press, the judge [Brandeis]. Assistance of [William] Green [president of the American Federation of Labor] in the White House and his telegram to the labor movement here imperative and urgent, also telegram leaders of Gewerkshaften [the Histadrut fund-raiser in America] to request opening of Palestine for broad immigration. Activate Abe Cahan [editor of the *Jewish Daily Forward*]."[9]

As the first protests echoed in America Ben-Gurion congratulated himself on his distress wire. "I believe my wire to New York . . . was the right thing to do, although Chaim was dissatisfied with it," he wrote in his diary. And indeed, as soon as Rabbi Goldman received the wire he went into action, uniting the Jews — Zionists and non-Zionists — in protest. An emergency committee* was set up to direct and coordinate it. Many of the important daily papers published sympathetic editorials and "more than 70,000 telegrams have already reached Washington," Goldman reported to Ben-Gurion on October 23; Brandeis visited the White House and spoke to Roosevelt "like a true prophet"; Bernard Baruch spoke with Churchill by telephone; delegations visited the British ambassador and the American under secretary of state, Cordell Hull; and "over the next two weeks" mass demonstrations would be held. Rabbi Goldman concluded his report on a note that gratified Ben-Gurion immensely. "This is truly the first time that American Jewry regards itself as standing on the front. If only this awakening would last."

This report fired Ben-Gurion's imagination, and he immediately urged Rabbi Goldman "to step up America's pressure," and not by words alone. "England is now negotiating for a trade treaty [with the United States]. If it is possible to arrange for them to feel here [in London] that loyalty to the Jews and allowing broad immigration are likely to facilitate the negotiations and improve their relationship with America, it would be a great thing." Ben-Gurion's letters and diary entries after this overflowed with admiration for the way American Jewry had flocked to the aid of the Yishuv. He believed that this flurry of protest had averted the dangers of halting immigration and the establishment of an Arab state "for the moment." On October 27 he wrote

---

* The National Emergency Committee for Palestine, headed by ZOA, Hadassah, and Poale Zion leaders, who were later joined by representatives of various non-Zionist bodies.

Rabbi Goldman, "If the Jews of the United States continue to support [the Yishuv] with courage and dedication, as they have in the present crisis, we shall be ever invincible."

After this first salvo of protest Ben-Gurion viewed the anticipated confrontation of St. James's with a lighter heart. To the JAE meeting of December 11, 1938, at which he first described his plan for "the revolt of immigration," he had said that, as a counterweight to the Arab kings, whom the British were bringing to St. James's to support the Palestinian Arabs, "we will gather the kings of the Jews in America."[10]

As the *Franconia* neared New York harbor, Ben-Gurion's resolve to place his trust in the United States grew ever stronger. It seems likely, however, that his political motive was accompanied by a personal one, although there is no knowing how much it weighed in Ben-Gurion's thinking; he never spoke or wrote of it. Nevertheless, a study of his life invites the assumption that he expected the new importance of America — with which he was more familiar than Weizmann, and where he had been more successful than Itzhak Ben-Zvi during the First World War — would also bring about a decisive turn in his rivalry with Weizmann for predominance in the Zionist leadership. Weizmann's advantage in Britain — his social standing and unmatched contacts with the policymakers — was to a great extent the product of the manners and class consciousness of the English. Weizmann's gifts and abilities were remarkably well suited to personal diplomacy — tactful, carried out behind closed doors with the proper language and manners. If it was true that Weizmann's appearance before the Peel Commission had been ten times more impressive than Ben-Gurion's, Ben-Gurion had very little chance of replacing Weizmann as the top Jewish leader in the British theater. In contrast, the classless United States, governed by public opinion, offered Ben-Gurion a theater in which he could use to the fullest his talents as a popular leader experienced in organizing and directing the masses. The reversal of their positions did not take place overnight, but Ben-Gurion's visit marked the start of the process.

On January 1, 1939, Ben-Gurion listed in his diary ten "matters I must attend to in America." The first was "the conference (organization, location, expenses, program)"; second, "security and ships." After these came other matters connected with the immigration revolt: "the Jewish Legion, aviation and naval training, etc. . . . immigration — the refugee camps . . . Haifa . . . land and the Jewish National Fund [speeding up land acquisitions before the ban went into effect] . . . United Jewish Appeal [financing for the immigration revolt and land acquisition, as well as] the talks" (bringing representatives of American Jewry to St. James's) and other things of secondary Zionist importance. Weizmann's pet plan was eighth on the list: "Turkey (tobacco, rugs, cotton, raisins)." These items alone contributed to a packed agenda for Ben-Gurion's nineteen-day stay, but as it turned out, more were added.

Although in the cables and letters announcing his visit it had been described as being "of a private nature," Ben-Gurion was met at the dock on the morning of January 2 by representatives of his party and by Morris Hexter, a non-Zionist member of the JAE. Unable to find his luggage under the letter *B*, he spent two hours in customs, where he was introduced to the common mistake in English-speaking countries of regarding Ben as a middle name. With Hexter's help he found one suitcase under *G* and two more under other letters. As they drove off in Hexter's new car — a fact Ben-Gurion found worthy of mention in his diary — Hexter told him what was going on with the non-Zionists, and by the time he registered at the Hotel McAlpin at 11:00 A.M., his trip was in full swing. He was handed a cable from Kaplan clamoring for him to "telegraph . . . possibility of increased financial action." Rabbi Goldman, who had made a special journey from Chicago, invited him to a meeting with Lipsky and Wise at noon. The party secretary was still talking his ear off with grievances and gossip when Baruch Zuckerman, a Poale Zion veteran, phoned and Ben-Gurion invited him, Levi Eshkol (the mifdeh representative), and Joseph Baratz (the Histadrut representative) to the meeting with Rabbi Goldman. There he found, as he said, "the whole gang," and he got to work at once, reviewing the situation, evaluating the prospects of the St. James's talks, and explaining that "we need the conference most of all to strengthen our position *during the talks.*"

"What about the non-Zionists," Wise asked. "Will they also help with the conference?"

"Let's assume they won't," replied Ben-Gurion. "Do you have the strength and the will to do it without them?" "Goldman answered affirmatively," he reported in his diary, "without convincing me of his seriousness. The others were doubtful. In Lipsky's and Wise's opinion, they [the non-Zionists] are liable . . . to take action in opposition. They fear anti-Semitism and want peace with the Arabs." That evening he spent two hours with Hexter, who explained why he would not take part in the St. James's talks and enumerated the dangers of a conference. Before calling it a night Ben-Gurion wired Brandeis to request a meeting. And so the differences of opinion were marked, the debate began to heat up, and the campaign to harness American Jewry to militant Zionism opened in high gear.

The next day Ben-Gurion learned from the previous Sunday's *New*

York Times's "Week in Review" section of Germany's demand to build
submarines equal in capacity to those of Britain's submarine fleet. This
information, which he interpreted as "a declaration of immediate
war," roused him "to see the facts as they are," and examine fighting
Zionism in the light of the lukewarm reception it had received on his
first day in the United States. Whereas "in Palestine there is at least the
psychological readiness to make provisions for the bitter day . . . among
the American Zionists" not only were the organizational and material
preparations still unattended to, but "psychological readiness is lacking," he wrote in his diary, beginning a comparison between what he
wished to find in America and what was actually there. "Besides the
sluggishness with regard to Zionism that has held sway here all these
years, inertia and laziness impede thought. They don't read the signs of
the time, and they live with outmoded ways of thinking. They still
don't realize that we have been confronted with the necessity of developing new ways to implement Zionism." Without saying so explicitly,
Ben-Gurion added an eleventh item to his list — curing the American
Zionists of their lethargy.

   If the Zionists had faults, so did the non-Zionists. Hexter was not
alone in his qualms about a conference. Cyrus Adler, leader of the
American Jewish Committee and one of its founders, had even stronger
reservations. Ben-Gurion went to Philadelphia especially to see him
for two hours. The October 1938 protest had left Adler with harsh
grievances against the Zionists — and against Ben-Gurion in particular. "They scared us," said Adler. "We were harnessed into action,"
and in the end "they saw no need to inform us" about how it had all
ended. "What do they think," he asked, "that the American is a yokel,
that you can push him around?" Refusing to put up with such inso-
lence and impudence anymore, Adler intended to resign from the
Jewish Agency Council. He was also infuriated by the Zionists' opposition to Felix Warburg's widow's taking his place on the Jewish Agency's
Political Committee. Ben-Gurion had to call on all his powers of diplomacy and his sense of humor to mollify Adler. But when Adler heard
Ben-Gurion's idea of inviting one hundred representatives of large
Jewish communities outside America to a conference and turning it
into "a sort of weapon" against the St. James's talks, his rage was
rekindled and he thundered, "So . . . you want a mass meeting . . .
five [or] six people will make speeches, vilify England, cry treason."
Although Ben-Gurion parted from him "in great friendliness," it did
not help incline the American Jewish Committee toward the conference.

   But in Washington, on January 5, a pleasant surprise awaited Ben-
Gurion. Brandeis was the only one who enthusiastically embraced

combative Zionism. "The old man," wrote Ben-Gurion in his diary, had aged considerably since their last meeting a year and a half earlier. "His face is shriveled, his hearing has degenerated, and his whole appearance bespeaks old age. . . . But his spirit is strong, his thinking lucid, his mind alert, and he still speaks with a young man's energy and fervor." "Neither the Arabs nor the English shall determine the future alone," Brandeis told Ben-Gurion, as if combative Zionism had been his idea. "Everything depends on us . . . We shall stand strong. This is war. We have support here. England needs America now. If we don't make any mistakes and don't give up, we shall triumph. The main thing is immigration. [We] must not yield on the question of immigration."

> BEN-GURION: I am happy to note that this time we are of one mind . . . but negative resolve is not enough — positive resolve is also imperative. We must continue immigration to Palestine under any and all conditions.
> BRANDEIS: Of course, of course. Continue as we are doing.
> BEN-GURION: What is being done now is not enough. It cannot go on like this forever. . . . We must proceed openly [with Aliyah Bet, the secret, illegal immigration that had begun in 1934], and let them [the British] step in with force. We have the strength to weather such a trial.
> BRANDEIS: We need action here, not words . . . The main thing is not to yield . . . Losses must not alarm us. They are the losses of war.

Brandeis agreed to the conference and was certain that the funds would be found for ships and the immigration revolt. "The wealthy Jews in America, too, are getting scared, and I believe that this time they will answer the call." As Ben-Gurion departed Brandeis reiterated, "Don't yield!"

The encouragement Brandeis's attitude might have given Ben-Gurion was unfortunately tempered by a meeting with Ben Cohen, who "threw some cold water" on his enthusiasm. Ben-Gurion privately concluded that Brandeis had been "a little too optimistic" about America's support, whereas Cohen "evaluates the situation here a little too pessimistically."

Ben-Gurion remarked that of all his meetings he got "much satisfaction" only from the talk with Brandeis. Of his ten original items, "Some went through, some did not, some partially." The conference came under the "partially" category. The non-Zionists had made a mountain of difficulties and the Zionists, except for Brandeis and Goldman, had shown little enthusiasm. "The former are scared . . . the latter are scared of the scared." To Ben-Gurion's mind the Diaspora timorousness of American Jewry and its leaders accounted for the non-Zionists' heeding the advice of the experts who claimed that the Jews and their organizations should avoid making themselves conspicuous, a view completely at odds with his concept of a conference. Ben-Gurion committed to his diary this axiom: "That which the non-Zionists oppose, the Zionists can do only with difficulty."

He found it hard to sell even the Zionists on his policy of fighting Britain to gain its support. Although he was careful to point out that militant Zionism did not involve anti-British terror but aimed ultimately to win Britain's friendship, everything he said in the United States was interpreted as a call for hostilities. Notwithstanding their isolationist mood, many Americans regarded Britain as a democratic stronghold and a champion of freedom defending itself against Hitler's Germany and therefore deserving of the fullest backing. Even when Ben-Gurion explained that with the outbreak of war "the fate of England" would "hinge upon the action of America," on which the Jews had influence, and that this influence could be used to strengthen the Zionists' position in their negotiations with the British government, he won no applause. There was not a chance in a thousand that the United States would embark on a Zionist, anti-British policy, and there was no sense in Jewish leaders trying to influence the administration to do so. Ben-Gurion also doubted Roosevelt's friendliness toward Zionism and did not pin great hopes on his administration. In October 1938 he had shared this feeling with his Jerusalem JAE colleagues. "This America did not stand up for the Czechs. Will it stand up for us? Quarrel with England on our account? As far as I know, Roosevelt does not believe in Palestine as a refuge for Jewish immigrants. . . . Ben Cohen, who is fairly close to the [president] . . . is very skeptical about American support."

If the prospects in America were so slim, and Ben-Gurion knew that Roosevelt, "a great friend of England," was not prepared "to pressure [it] the way we would like," why did he go there to call for assistance? An answer appears in a September 20 letter to Sharett. "It is most improbable that America will officially lift a finger for our benefit; it is also doubtful if American Jewry will join the fray now. But if everything is lost here in London, we must try to mobilize whatever is possible in America." There was no other option.

In recruiting American Jewry, Ben-Gurion had two more problems to tackle. The first was the Arab question. At nearly every turn he was asked if his state plan would promote peace with the Arabs. Although he never revealed the full extent of his Haifa plan, based on conquest by force, with some — particularly Adler, Brandeis, and Hadassah leaders — he discussed the idea of transferring a hundred thousand Arab families in Palestine to Iraq in exchange for $50 million with which to settle them. Peaceful relations with the Arabs was a key question for Hadassah, and even Robert Szold — Brandeis's right-hand man and a Ben-Gurion supporter — asked, "Between us, is there some chance or possibility for a Jewish-Arab accord?" Ben-Gurion's reply, "There is no possibility of such an accord under the present circumstances; the question will be decided only by force," was not what his listeners wanted to hear.

The second problem was the need to restructure the American Zionist movement so that it could "win the people, control American Jewry." Ben-Gurion sought to effect two changes, of which the first was the establishment of an inclusive framework that would unite the ZOA and all the other Zionist bodies, including Hadassah, Poale Zion, and Mizrachi. In addition, he wanted the United Palestine Appeal to engage in Zionist educational campaigns as well as in fund raising. This, he believed, would attract masses of people to the movement and make it more dynamic.

From Hadassah, which was so important to him, he received a mixed reaction on this and his other proposals. The Hadassah leaders favored the conference, as well as his negotiating positions for the St. James's talks — the establishment of a state in western Palestine, a "proposal for a transfer to Iraq," and inflexibility on the immigration question. They also responded favorably when he asked if it was possible "to raise a large loan," at least $5 million, for the Jewish National Fund to buy land. But when he asked whether Hadassah would be prepared "to take extraordinary measures" for illegal immigration, they wanted to discuss it first and give him an answer later. Was Hadassah for one united Zionist Organization? This question received the same response. The only definite answer Ben-Gurion got was from Judith Epstein, Hadassah's president, who invited him to her home for tea on January 7. In response to his question, "Is it possible to get hold of a million dollars for immigration purposes?" she said that outside the United Jewish Appeal (UJA), of which the United Palestine Appeal (UPA) was part, the Zionists could do nothing. "The rich are not in the Zionist fold, and he who pays the piper calls the tune."

He had no more success in his meeting with the ZOA chiefs. At his request, leaders from outside New York were also called to this meeting, held at New York's Astor Hotel. From the responses to his explanations of the conference and combative Zionism Ben-Gurion realized, to his surprise and regret, how deeply rooted was their fear that an all-Jewish conference on a political issue not directly concerned with America was "liable to increase anti-Semitism in America." Even when the plight of Jews hung in the balance, the gap between Zionists and non-Zionists was not that great. Robert Szold argued that "it would be better to hold an American conference, of Jews and non-

Jews." This suggestion met with considerable approval, and Ben-Gurion took the floor several times in an attempt to kill it. Ultimately, a resolution that he liked was adopted, but the debate echoed in his mind when he wrote later that even among the Zionists, "the conference . . . was not received very enthusiastically." If this was so, a positive response on thornier matters was surely too much to hope for.

Ben-Gurion probably had to restrain himself from calling "Cowards!" more than once. This is suggested by what he said in his talk with Ingrid Warburg, who lived in her late uncle Felix's house and raised money for refugee children in Nazi Germany. "Are you a coward?" he asked her straight out as he tried to win her over to his plan. "No," she replied. Learning that she knew wealthy Jews who were willing to help, he charged her to "find out if they are prepared to provide us with ships and means to bring over immigrants. And on my return from Washington introduce me to well-to-do young people." A few days later, when he met with her again, she told him that as long as the UJA was active, it was "impossible" to do much fund raising for Aliyah Bet. Ben-Gurion quoted her answer and his reaction in his diary: " 'They'll kill me if I try to raise large sums,' she said, not without cause. But I implored her to try to talk to some young, wealthy people with vision, if such exist."

Ben-Gurion kept up his heavy schedule of meetings — with a Jewish importer, to investigate the possibility of implementing direct U.S. trade with Turkey; with the Jewish Labor Committee, with which he had negotiated on his last visit through Charney Vladeck; with his party and representatives of B'nai B'rith, in his efforts to create a united Jewish front around the conference — despite a worsening ache in his mouth and throat, which had begun while he was still at sea and made eating and speaking difficult for him. At length he had to see Dr. Meir Rosoff, who pulled a tooth and made "a new man" of him. But although he could take on American Jewry with fresh vigor he achieved no better results.

At a United Palestine Appeal convention in Washington, Ben-Gurion had a long talk, on the morning of January 15, with Abba Hillel Silver, the renowned rabbi of Cleveland and chairman of the UPA since 1938. Unlike Silver, who favored maintaining the UPA's link with the UJA, Ben-Gurion had his doubts. In view of Zionism's growing needs, Ben-Gurion felt that the UJA, whose primary goal was to raise money for American Jewish welfare and aid associations, was not the appropriate framework for a Zionist emergency drive. "Isn't there a danger that Palestine will become merely a matter of donations and charity?" he asked Silver. "Aren't we subjugating ourselves to the American Joint Distribution Committee and weakening the Zionist movement?" He listed "the urgent needs that the Appeal cannot meet": a large loan to the Jewish National Fund "in order to buy land fast, since we do not know what will be in another few months"; and the large and growing "defense needs. We must get ready to defend the Yishuv in the event of war. And we need a million dollars for this purpose." These goals were beyond the capacity of the UPA, which received only two fifths of the funds raised by the UJA.

Following this talk Ben-Gurion was invited to be the "sole speaker" at the convention's closing session that evening. However, those who were supposedly "not to speak" but to say only "a few words" spoke at great length. Rabbi Goldman, who chaired the session, spoke fifteen times, Ben-Gurion recorded in his diary, "before and after each speaker . . . Silver also 'didn't speak' for half an hour." At 11:00 P.M., when the audience was tired after hearing all the "nonspeakers" and many were departing to make their trains, Ben-Gurion was called on to deliver his address. This was the first full speech he had ever made in English, and he was quite pleased with himself. Only one word — *traces* — slipped his memory. He felt he had held the audience rapt for an entire hour.

At this convention Ben-Gurion met Henry Montor, the executive director of the UPA, for the first time. On January 20 they had a serious talk, and Ben-Gurion was deeply impressed by him. American "Zionism is weak," said Montor, making Ben-Gurion feel that he was listening to himself speak, "for there is no leadership. In the community at large Zionist feelings are strong, and in any political controversy Zionists will win the day because our people are interested in Palestine." He also maintained, however, that the UPA's take would be less if it mounted a campaign separate from the UJA. One statement Montor made secured him a place in Ben-Gurion's heart forever. "Our leaders . . . do not understand the power of the press. What is written in the *Times* is more important than what is said to the president or a senator. . . . There is no open line to the American press . . . but an interview . . . [with an Associated Press correspondent] is worth an interview with a cabinet secretary." Because his dormant genius lay in the appeal to broad public opinion and to the media, which Ben-Gurion must have sensed, he saw Montor as a man after his own heart. Montor subsequently became a key man on his United States team, the one Ben-Gurion chose for the Israel bond drive. Meanwhile, before they parted, he asked Montor for "a list of American newsmen in London."

On January 20, the day before his departure, Ben-Gurion received a coded cable from Weizmann, advising him that the prevailing feeling in Whitehall was that war was near. Consequently, the Arabs' importance had grown. However, Weizmann also understood from discussions in the Foreign Office that Whitehall was vulnerable to American opinion, and the nearer war seemed to be, the stronger was that opinion's restraining effect on pro-Arab leanings. Weizmann pointed out the need for "our closest possible watch [on] Washington." This wire helped Ben-Gurion induce the Astor meeting to pass a resolution to open a political bureau in Washington as soon as possible. Established within the week, it was the first American Zionist (later Israeli) lobby in the U.S. capital. The next day the bureau's role was mapped out at a breakfast meeting in Ben-Gurion's hotel with Cohen, Wise, Lipsky, and Szold, after which they all saw Ben-Gurion off at the pier. At 11:00 A.M., in snow and with a forecast for heavy seas, Ben-Gurion set sail for London, for the St. James's talks, and for a bleak future.

Aboard the *Aquitania*, summarizing his visit in his diary, Ben-Gurion tried his best to assess its results in a balanced and realistic manner. Regarding "security and ships," on which he had spent a great deal of time with Szold, he wrote, "It seems to me that the decks were entirely cleared for a broader security drive." But, "for the time being nothing was accomplished as regards ships." The large loan to the Jewish National Fund for faster purchase of land was "given a push. Only time will tell if action will follow words." On Turkey, "No progress made." As for the "legion" — recruiting volunteers to Jewish battalions, on the model of the Jewish Legion in the First World War — "there is no doubt that if there is war we shall have volunteers, provided the administration gives us the green light . . . the idea for naval and air training also made some headway. But there's still a great deal of work to be done." Last, "On the whole the trip was worthwhile. . . . I prize the talk with Hadassah, which cleared up some misunderstandings."

These optimistic notes were dampened by the "weakness of the movement" on the one hand and the opposition he had met from the non-Zionists on the other. The Zionist movement was not central in the Jewish community and it lacked leaders of stature. So, for that matter, did the non-Zionists. "American Jewry . . . has no one of spiritual, intellectual, and political weight." Since Brandeis had quit the movement when he was nominated to the Supreme Court, "not one personality his equal in moral and intellectual stature has arisen." Felix Frankfurter, who had succeeded Brandeis on the bench on the day Ben-Gurion met with Brandeis in Washington, would be unable to succeed him in public Jewish and Zionist life as well. "He is learned in legal matters, but he hasn't . . . Brandeis's moral mettle. His life's ambition was . . . to reach the Supreme Court. His Zionism was only a desultory, secondary undertaking, not his heart's core." Perhaps this evaluation was made harsher by the fact that Frankfurter had refused, with the excuse of his appointment, to meet with Ben-Gurion. Wise did not possess the qualities of leadership either. "He is a typical American tribune, but he lacks political insight and his spiritual world is limited. He is capable of becoming the leader's mouthpiece, but not the leader himself." Abba Hillel Silver was just "a bad copy of Wise. Not only does he share Wise's lack of political insight, he lacks even Wise's moral fortitude and spiritual independence." The leadership of Hadassah did not escape his critical eye. "There are, it seems, efficient officials in this organization, as indicated by its expansion, good fund raising, and successful services. But Mrs. Jacobs, Mrs. Epstein, and even Mrs. Pool . . . are nothing more than middling functionaries with a practical turn of mind, but without the intellectual, spiritual light characteristic of a leader." None of the other Zionist bodies, including his own party, offered Ben-Gurion "one outstanding personality." The best of them was Rabbi Goldman, who "tops Silver morally and intellectually. He is more Jewish than any of them. He is the foremost Zionist functionary in America, rooted in Judaism and Hebrew culture. But I doubt if he has initiative, independence, or even minimal political flair."

If this was so, why was Ben-Gurion's resolve to rely increasingly on American Jewry strengthened? The first reason was his premonition that the United States would emerge from its isolationism and come to Britain's aid against Germany. "Our situation is likely to change for the better if Congress supports Roosevelt and makes even a minor amendment in its neutrality law, since then America's effect on English public opinion will immediately increase and England's fear of war will abate considerably." As Ben-Gurion had explained to Szold, Britain would no longer need Arab good will so badly, and Zionist influence on its policy would be enhanced. To Rabbi Goldman he had asserted that the argument that this was not the time for anti-British campaigns and that British support of Zionism was liable to provoke the world's Arabs and Muslims to rise up against England would prove to be groundless. Quite the contrary, if a Jewish army materialized, "nothing can safeguard England's position in the Mediterranean like sending 100,000 young Jews to Palestine, [for] the military worth [of the Arabs was] nearly zero."

Ben-Gurion's second reason was that American Jewry, for all its faults, was the only mainstay available for the Yishuv, the Jews of Europe, and Zionism. So its assistance "in our war" was imperative. This assistance would be obtained, Ben-Gurion wrote Rabbi Goldman, through a unified Zionist Organization, which would "demonstrate great Zionist strength." Through public opinion "[we must] activate our friends in government, Congress, the press, the church, the labor

movement. Not casually, but with perseverance and systematically . . .
After London, this is our political front."[11]

The six-day voyage to Southampton was pleasant, but Ben-Gurion got
no rest aboard ship. As if he did not have enough worries to give him
insomnia, his cabinmate — a professor of Semitic languages at the University of Chicago who took a liking to Ben-Gurion and related his entire personal history — went to bed late and snored so loudly that
Ben-Gurion was awakened and unable to shut his eyes again. "Only
when I reach London," he wrote Paula, "will I be able to catch up on
all the sleep I lost on the ship."[12] But in London the torture of sleepless
nights awaited him in even greater measure.

The Great Formula

O N HIS ARRIVAL in London on January 27, 1939, Ben-Gurion
found the mood there "more optimistic, or less pessimistic"
than before, "although the feeling that war is close remains."
The next day in the Zionist office he met Weizmann, who "displayed
a balanced, wise, responsible, and cautious approach." As he wrote
Paula, Ben-Gurion therefore looked forward to a little peace. This
turned out to be wishful thinking, for a trial more difficult than any he
had ever weathered was in store for him: the struggle to block, or at
least delay, the British government's use of the St. James's Conference
to force its own solution on Palestine.

On February 16 — an important day in the St. James's talks — Ben-
Gurion began having difficulty writing in his diary, and by the twenty-
second his pen lay untouched. On March 6 he wrote Paula, "During
these last three weeks . . . I couldn't write, and I haven't the strength
now to describe them." The days at St. James's, he said, had been the
most trying of his life, surpassing all "the extreme situations" that had
befallen him. "Never before have I been through what I've undergone
in these last few weeks." In his diary he wrote only, "The press of developments, the talks with the government, the internal disputes
among us, the tension increasing from day to day and hour to hour, the
nights of vigil and insomnia — all these made it physically and emo-
tionally impossible for me to continue writing." On March 4 he had
fallen ill and stayed in bed for a few days. He told Paula and his colleagues it was just a cold or a light case of the flu, keeping the doctor's
suspicions of something far worse to himself. Dr. Ben-Zion Kunin, an
intimate of the Zionist leaders, found "a high level of sugar in the
blood," and recommended that "he undergo a thorough examination"
when he got back to Palestine. (Ben-Gurion later spent three days in

Beilinson Hospital, where extensive examinations detected no abnormalities. Dr. Harry Heller, Palestine's finest internist, told him he was "all right" and that the high level of blood sugar found in London had probably been caused by "acute emotional stress.")[1]

In spite of this, the St. James's Conference saw Ben-Gurion's rise to a new status in leadership of the Jewish people. Since the Palestinian Arabs refused to sit at the same table as the Jews — only representatives of the neighboring countries met with them, and "informally" at that — most of the Jewish delegation's meetings took place with British government representatives. Thus, despite the participation of such high-ranking personages as the prime minister, the foreign and colonial secretaries, and their senior officials, the Conference can be seen as another in the long line of British commissions on Palestine, except that this time, in addition to delegates from the JAE and the Yishuv, there were also non-Zionist representatives, including Sholem Asch, Lord Melchett, and prominent rabbis and scholars. The "kings of the Jews in America" failed Ben-Gurion and stayed away. Of the Zionists, excluding Rose Jacobs, who was on the delegation as a JAE member, only Rabbi Stephen Wise and Robert Szold participated. Of the non-Zionists, not even the JAE representatives showed.

That Ben-Gurion regarded the Jewish panel as truly representing the Jewish people is evident from his argument to the JAE against the inclusion of Lord Herbert Samuel. "We are negotiating with the English government . . . on behalf of the Jewish people," whose redemption in its homeland Samuel had been willing to forgo, as evidenced by his declared consent to a Jewish minority in Palestine. In the vote he prevailed over Samuel's supporters. For perhaps the first time, he identified himself and Weizmann as the de facto representatives of the Jewish people who were entitled to disqualify other would-be representatives. He was also the one who named the panel the Jewish Agency delegation rather than the Jewish delegation. This implied that the Jewish Agency, of which Ben-Gurion was chairman, was the representative body of the Jewish people.

There was good reason to believe that Ben-Gurion's star was rising, and Weizmann, too, must have sensed the change. Coming into his colleague's office on the morning of January 31, Ben-Gurion found a different Weizmann, "fuming and depressed." With no preliminaries, Weizmann informed Ben-Gurion that he was "weary," that he was sixty-five years old, and "sixty is the time to retire"; in short, when the talks ended he would go not to America, but to Palestine, and return to his scientific work at his institute in Rehovot. He would "carry the burden no longer" and had no intention of being re-elected president.

Ben-Gurion and Sharett tried to talk him out of it, but Weizmann said, "Enough. My decision is final."

Like Ben-Gurion, Sharett was stunned by this inexplicable threat, and he attributed it to Jerusalem's rejection of a 2,000-Palestinian-pound grant from UJA funds to Weizmann's institute. Ben-Gurion was quick to adopt this explanation. In his diary he noted, "This was, clearly, a psychological error on [Eliezer] Kaplan's part . . . After all, Chaim is well 'worth' two thousand Palestinian pounds." The explanation had some merit, yet it did not account for the threat. Throwing his resignation in the faces of Ben-Gurion and Sharett with such vigor, at this critical hour, was certainly out of line if it was meant only to show Kaplan — one of Weizmann's oldest and most dedicated followers — that he was wrong. The rejection of the grant probably only aggravated Weizmann's growing bitterness and frustration.

Unlike the dejected Weizmann, Ben-Gurion was primed. He assessed the conference's prospects — much as in Omaha, Nebraska, in January 1916 he had assessed Arab-Jewish relations — and repeated his conclusions in a letter to Paula, which was also meant for his colleagues. Principally, it held that the danger of war with Germany had compromised the Jews' position; their support of Britain in the event of war was taken for granted. The Jews could not possibly side with Hitler; "England's defeat in war would be a disaster for all Jews." The Arabs, on the other hand, had to be bought if they were not going to join Hitler, "and therefore England is *now* compelled to do whatever it must to make up to the Arabs and secure their friendship at our expense." In sum, "The upper hand . . . is not ours," and nothing good could be expected of the St. James's talks. "We will come out of the talks worse off than we were to begin with, minus a Jewish-Arab accord and plus new decrees."

He saw two factors that could be to the Jews' advantage: "the American factor — there are in America anti-British forces, but they do not call the tune. America is a harsh critic of England, but it loves her and will not allow her to fall. England cannot dismiss the Jewish factor in America altogether, but this factor is (a) not the decisive one and (b) cannot, will not, has no interest in withholding America's support of England" in the event of war. The second factor was the Yishuv. "Relatively speaking, our strength in Palestine is great, but the danger of war is to our detriment. In ordinary days we could force on England basic changes in our favor, by means of open war. On the eve of war, that is difficult."

From this assessment came Ben-Gurion's position for the Jewish panel at St. James's: peace with the Arabs was possible only on condition that they agreed to massive Jewish immigration to Palestine, either by establishing "an independent Jewish state" within the framework of an "Arab federation," by a "cantonization of Palestine, as long as we have control [of immigration] in a sufficiently large canton," or on the basis of "a temporary agreement on the scale of immigration, on condition that we can bring in fifty thousand young people this year." Without saying so, Ben-Gurion was thinking of soldiers for the Jewish army. Since he saw no chance of any of these three stipulations being met, he turned them into bargaining positions at the talks with an eye to public opinion in Britain and the United States.[2] As for the main confrontation with the British government, he held in reserve a position of strength that was based on his second factor.

In January 1939 the Yishuv numbered 440,000 — 30 percent of the population of Palestine — of whom 45,000 bore arms or served as auxiliaries. Ben-Gurion saw the Yishuv and its "army" as a not yet decisive force but nonetheless one that could not be "disregarded." Suspecting that the British government intended to turn Palestine over to Arab rule by making it independent, he countered with this Jewish force. If the British did not give the Jews independence as well — through partition — the "force" would thwart the British scheme by preventing Arab independence.

If by the end of January Weizmann really sensed that Ben-Gurion's hour was approaching as his own passed, the talks made it clear that he was right. They opened on February 7 with great pomp, in the presence of the prime minister and senior cabinet ministers, but with separate ceremonies for each delegation: the Arabs arrived at and left St. James's Palace by one gate before the Jews entered through another. Despite the elaborate setting, the JAE's preparations were similar to those that had preceded the Peel and Woodhead commissions. But this time the shift in the balance of power between Ben-Gurion and Weizmann was evident. Not one but two stars shone at this performance, and Ben-Gurion's was brighter. Neither at the opening ceremony nor the next day did Weizmann rouse wonder or win praise as in the past. According to Ben-Gurion, Weizmann's address at the first working session made a "good general impression [despite] a few weak spots" in the middle. Perhaps its lukewarm effect resulted from its four drafts having been worked over by Sharett, Ben-Gurion, May, and Stein, as well as by Weizmann himself. Though Weizmann did not get the freedom and solitude he required to create his inspired speeches, there is no doubt that his irresolution was also a factor. But this was what subsequently cleared the stage for Ben-Gurion to be the only star.

Weizmann actually looked to Ben-Gurion for rescue on at least three occasions.

The government launched its offensive on the morning of February 10. MacDonald made a speech sympathizing with the Jews' distress and yearning for independence. However, he said, the Arabs had a claim too. "The British Government did not seek to avoid the obligations which it had undertaken to the Jews in Palestine, but ... the promise was a vague one." The term "Jewish National Home [was] ill-defined," and it was far from certain that the authors of the Balfour Declaration had meant to guarantee a Jewish state; therefore a British position ruling it out could not be taken as a broken promise. In addition, under the Mandate the British were required "to establish, in due course, 'self-governing institutions.'" As he went on it was no longer possible to doubt that the British intended to grant the rule of Palestine to the Arabs. In closing, MacDonald asked if the Jews wished to respond on the spot.

In the consultation that followed (MacDonald and his colleagues had left the room) Wise argued that it was best to weigh every word and prepare a careful and considered reply. Ben-Gurion, on the other hand, was against leaving the meeting without having answered: the Jewish delegation must not create the impression that the government had confounded it. Weizmann put the question to the vote, and the majority backed Ben-Gurion. Then came the surprise: Weizmann was not willing to deliver the response. In the absence of volunteers, Ben-Gurion consented to stand in and asked for a few moments to prepare himself. As he spoke Ben-Gurion consulted the notes he had made during MacDonald's speech; although he had not had the time to perfect and polish his words, what he said was right on target. He maintained that the Balfour Declaration had not been vague, that the British knew at the time that there were Arabs in Palestine, and that the Mandate obligated the British government neither to obtain the Arabs' consent to the establishment of the National Home nor to set up "self-government" in Palestine; it spoke only of "self-governing institutions," another matter altogether.

Sharett noted in his diary, "The general feeling was that Ben-Gurion had saved the situation, even if he sacrificed himself in so doing," that he had made himself vulnerable to having the British pick holes in his argument. The reverberations of this admirable performance soon reached Mapai's Central Committee in Tel Aviv, where it was said that Weizmann had insisted that Ben-Gurion answer and left him with no alternative. "Needless to say," said Dr. Dov Joseph, Sharett's substitute in the Political Department, who reported on the event, "the role thrust upon Ben-Gurion at that moment was not particularly easy." Katznelson acclaimed another appearance by Ben-Gurion, on February 15, as "tremendous."[3] It was most rare for this man, so stinting in his praise, to applaud Ben-Gurion over Weizmann.

On Saturday, the eighteenth, Ben-Gurion met with MacDonald for a "private talk," at which he unveiled his position of strength. Ben-Gurion argued for the partition scheme and the Jewish state.

> BEN-GURION: Not only would we be able to protect ourselves, but we could look after our own immigration.
> MAC DONALD: Even now, when the Arabs are twice as many as you are?
> BEN-GURION: Yes.
> MAC DONALD: Even so, could not the Palestine Arabs get reinforcements from Iraq?
> BEN-GURION: Of course they could, but so could we from other countries. We could easily bring in reinforcements by sea — hundreds of thousands of young men . . . not only from Poland; we can bring reinforcements from America, and I am certain that we could arrange to deal with the Arabs.

At the evening session of February 20, MacDonald detailed the government's proposals: annual immigration of fifteen to thirty thousand over five to ten years, allowing the Yishuv to grow only until it was 35 to 40 percent of the overall population; confinement of the Jews to a small area. Weizmann responded to these proposals and a verbal duel ensued, in which MacDonald, according to Ben-Gurion, held the upper hand. Although Weizmann kept to Ben-Gurion's line, his overarching principle was the need for peaceful relations; he still had not adopted Ben-Gurion's "immigration before peace" formula. The duel lasted two hours; before it could end in Weizmann's defeat, Ben-Gurion took the floor. There were "two sets of problems," he said, "one economic and one political." The Jews were prepared to discuss the former on its merits "if the data on which decisions were to be made were given them for examination," but not the latter. "On the political issue judgment had already been given when the nations who ratified the Mandate for Palestine, acting as an international court of justice, had given the Jews the right to come into Palestine . . . [The Arabs] had no right to reopen what was a closed question. The Jews were ready to discuss all political problems on this basis." If the British government backed off from the Balfour Declaration, as its proposal implied, the Jewish delegation would walk out.

Taking note of the division between the Zionist leaders, MacDonald leapt to Weizmann's support, pointing out that there was "a plain choice between following the policy of Mr. Ben-Gurion, deliberately alienating all Arab opinion ... or following the course in which Dr. Weizmann believes, and seeking Arab friendship. The latter is the policy of His Majesty's government."[4] If this was an attempt to strengthen Weizmann, it failed. The next morning Sharett found Weizmann "in a difficult mood after last evening's session" and felt it necessary to encourage him. Ben-Gurion remarked in his diary that "Chaim, in contrast to his mood a week ago, is immersed in a feeling of inferiority. He seems to be aware of his incompetence in yesterday's duel."

That morning Weizmann received an invitation from the foreign secretary, Lord Halifax, for 3:00 P.M. and another from MacDonald for 5:30; both stated that he was free to bring his colleagues. This polite but clear hint also bore witness to the shift in the balance of power in the Zionist leadership: whereas in the past Weizmann usually preferred to go alone, that was now out of the question. When Weizmann, Ben-Gurion, and Sharett arrived at Halifax's office at three, they found MacDonald there. Halifax invited them to sit in a semicircle facing the fireplace, as friends, and asked MacDonald to open the discussion. Their surprise at seeing him turned to stupefaction when he suggested that the JAE announce, "on its own initiative," that the Jews were "prepared to agree" to ten years of restricted immigration, and then no more. It was as though Ben-Gurion had never said that the Jews would take part in further discussion only on the basis of the Balfour Declaration and the Mandate. Did MacDonald hope for a favorable response from Weizmann and a split opinion within the Zionist leadership?

All eyes turned to Weizmann; Sharett was alarmed by his appearance, "so heavy was the cloud that darkened his brow." But Weizmann remained speechless, as though struck dumb, and Ben-Gurion found himself again occupying Weizmann's role of chief spokesman for Zionism and the Jewish people. "With intense emotion that nearly choked him," according to Sharett, Ben-Gurion turned directly to Halifax, as though MacDonald were not in the room. In his diary Ben-Gurion explained, "What I said to Halifax I could not and would not say to any other Goy," for he felt that despite "the objective hypocrisy in his philosophy," there was something of "the man of spirit" in him.

"Lord Halifax," said Ben-Gurion, "will you permit me for a few minutes to speak to you, not as the representative of the Jewish Agency to a Minister of the Crown, but simply as man to man?" He asked, "Have you ever wondered why a small people — scattered, persecuted, driven from pillar to post for nearly two thousand years, should have survived and retained its identity?" It had always been the very clinging to Zion that had saved the Jewish people from oblivion. As "inheritors" of the martyrs and the persecuted, the Zionists could not yield Zion, for otherwise "we should feel that all our past sufferings for fifty generations have been pointless." Hearing this, Weizmann took heart and spoke up. In his diary Ben-Gurion paid Weizmann the compliment of saying "[he] completed . . . [my address] nicely."

After the meeting the three strolled in St. James's Park, and Weizmann apologized for not being at the top of his form. He wondered aloud if it was the result "of a loss of direction or the strain and fear" bound up with responsibility.[5]

On the morning of February 24, Ben-Gurion presented to the Jewish panel three negotiating principles for the continuation of the talks with the government: "a continuation of the Mandate" since partition had been abandoned; independence for the Jews as well as the Arabs; rejection of any "institutions which symbolized minority status" for the Jews. He restated these principles later that day at a meeting with the British delegation that followed an "informal" tripartite meeting attended by representatives of Egypt, Saudi Arabia, and Iraq. At both these meetings MacDonald brought up proposals of his own for a constitution and the establishment of "self-government" in Palestine. The following day Ben-Gurion asked MacDonald if the British government's declaration of July 1937 that there was no intention of making the Jews a minority under an Arab government in Palestine still held. His demand for an unequivocal answer angered MacDonald but had no effect on the preconceived British plan. On the contrary, MacDonald asserted that the Jews' rejection of his plan had worsened their position. The transition period preceding independence would be less than ten years, and annual immigration would be less than fifteen to thirty thousand.

Worse yet, attached to the official protocol of the meeting of February 24, which the Colonial Office sent to the Jewish delegation on the twenty-sixth, was an appendix entitled "General Summary of British Government's Suggestions." This was the first time that the British proposals to end the Mandate and create "an independent Palestine State" had been printed in an official document. This "Summary" — also sent to the Arab delegation — was leaked, and its publication raised a furor. The shocked Yishuv was plunged into grief and anger.

Ben-Gurion wrote a proclamation, "To the Yishuv," which was cabled to Palestine and published in *Davar* the next day.

> There is a scheme afoot to liquidate the National Home and turn us over to the rule of the gang leaders. This scheme shall not materialize!
>
> The valor of the Yishuv, the plight of vast numbers of Jews in the Diaspora, the conscience of fair-minded England, and the moral and political support of the nations of the world will blot out the evil intentions of our oppressors.
>
> Do not be alarmed!

Your representatives are here on the watch, fully confident that each and every one of you will stand up to the supreme test with loyalty, unity, discipline, and strength.

David Ben-Gurion[6]

On February 26 the St. James's Conference reached an impasse when the Jewish panel boycotted the ceremonial dinner the government held in its honor at the Carlton. An apology from MacDonald, explaining that the "Summary" was just a draft mistakenly sent out by a junior official, did not mend matters. The next day Weizmann delivered a bitter address, enumerating each of the British proposal's negative points, and read a statement prepared by the JAE that rejected the British suggestions and refused to accept them as a basis for further negotiations. When MacDonald opposed publication of the statement, Ben-Gurion emphasized that the delegation would not continue the negotiations on the basis of the "Summary." Halifax then took an unusual step: he spoke. Sharett reported to his diary,

Lord Halifax, who was at first silent as usual . . . suddenly opened his mouth . . . and true to form . . . he spoke in abstractions, on a very high moral and intellectual level, but . . . his meaning was sharp as a dagger: England had done its best to try to help the Jews. If in spite of this the Jews withdrew from the talks with England, England's helping hand would be considerably weakened. This seemed an open threat: beware, Jews!

The controversy that flared up the next day at the Zionist office between those who demanded withdrawal from the talks and those who favored continuing them was settled by acceptance of Ben-Gurion's proposal to inform the government that although the Jewish delegation would not discuss any suggestions the British had brought up so far, it was willing to consider new proposals they might present. From then on the talks were held "informally," with reduced Jewish representation, in MacDonald's office. However, from the moment the Arabs learned of the suggestions in the "Summary," the government was no longer in a position to withdraw them or offer the Jews any improvements. As far as the Jews were concerned the St. James's talks — the Anglo-Jewish Conference, Ben-Gurion called it — had lost their purpose.

To Ben-Gurion, who by February 11 had written in his diary that "matters are nearing their end in London; our center of action will soon be moving to Palestine and America," this came as no surprise. He did not insist on breaking off the talks, both because he wished to preserve the unity of the Jewish delegation and domestic harmony with Weizmann and because "I had to take into consideration the needs of Jewish unity and loyalty to the leaders of the Zionist movement." But on March 3, with great sorrow, he told the Jewish panel, "If the rights of the Jews . . . [to immigrate to Palestine] are taken away, we have no further business here. We should tell the government that the negotiations have reached the breaking point and issue a press statement." Nevertheless, the vote went against him; the "informal" talks continued and Ben-Gurion, for the sake of unity, took part in them.[7]

The government presented its suggestions to the delegation in their final form on March 15, and the Conference ended on March 16. Since the Arabs as well as the Jews rejected its proposals (the Arabs fearing that if they did not object the Jews would wring concessions from the British), the Chamberlain government considered itself free to formulate and enforce its predetermined solution.

These difficult days steeled Ben-Gurion and strengthened his resolve with respect to combative Zionism. On the evening of February 28, he went to Sharett's room, in the same hotel as his, to tell him that Britain's promise of independence to the Arabs was "not just a weapon against us — it is a weapon in our hands also. The government made a commitment to the Arabs which it cannot fulfill without our cooperation. We have a tremendous lever for war." This was the uniqueness of Ben-Gurion: even when his morale was low, the fighting spirit did not desert him and his will to turn disaster to advantage remained undiminished. The time had come, he thought, to put the kings of the Jews in America to work.

At a March 3 meeting he spoke with Wise and Szold about the urgent need to raise money in America for land acquisition in Palestine "as long as [it] is permitted." Aware that this was part of his anti-British campaign, they reacted indignantly, and when Ben-Gurion urged Wise to cable Louis Brandeis to appeal for Roosevelt's intervention in asking Britain to suspend its new policy, Wise refused, making it clear that he would not fight the British government. He and his colleagues had insisted that the United States administration stand beside Britain in the conflict with Hitler, and as long as Hitler existed they could not change their position. Sharett wrote in his diary that Wise's response "depressed all assembled." When Ben-Gurion learned that Brandeis was to meet with Roosevelt, he entreated Szold to cable his mentor guidelines for the talk. But Szold refused, saying that it was unthinkable for him to advise Brandeis, who knew all there was to know. So Ben-Gurion took Sharett's advice and did it himself. That day, he sent Rabbi Solomon Goldman the following signed cable in Hebrew: "Ask the Justice [Brandeis] on my behalf to urge the president in his meeting with him tomorrow to appeal to the director here [the prime minister] in favor of immediate large-scale immigration, against condemning us to a minority, for putting off the decision on the Palestine question."

So began his battle against the White Paper, the first stage of which involved delaying its publication in the hope that this would make it possible to enlist America, among others, in an attempt to weaken its provisions. But even the prospect of a conference there soon faded, as Weizmann expressed doubts that he should participate in a meeting whose object was, or appeared to be, mobilizing American opinion against the British government. Without Weizmann the conference would be worthless. None of this, however, could dishearten Ben-Gurion. On March 15 he noted in his diary, as if trying to strengthen his own convictions, that Britain's acquiescence to the Arabs grew out of Chamberlain's global policy of appeasement. "Today Hitler's troops entered Prague, and this evening the government delivers [to the Jewish delegation] its proposals for the liquidation of its National Home policy." The negative reactions of Wise and Szold made him understand that America would not readily raise a protest against the prospective White Paper. On March 19, a touch of despair seems to have stolen in.

> To all intents and purposes, our hands are tied. Satan himself couldn't have come up with a more oppressive and menacing nightmare. They've got us locked up and silenced. A sentence that we won't be able to appeal has been passed on us. There will probably be a debate in Parliament — but who will find heart now to defend an old promise to a helpless people who cannot speak out against England in their own defense?

This was, however, just a passing thought. Ben-Gurion was utterly resolved, as he wrote Paula on March 6, that "if we don't repeat Czechoslovakia's mistake, Czechoslovakia's fate won't befall us." After the St. James's Conference closed, he wrote her and his JAE colleagues, "We came out of the London Conference beaten, but not vanquished."[8] Combative Zionism would kick back. If so, the true test of the Conference would be whether the British government could establish an independent Arab state in Palestine in defiance of the Yishuv's will, or if the Yishuv and the Jewish people could force the government to agree to partition.

On March 28, Ben-Gurion, Weizmann, Katznelson, Dugdale, and other members of the Jewish delegation set sail aboard the *D'Artagnan* from Marseilles to Haifa, determined to speak of anything except the Conference and its aftermath. Dugdale was the first to break this vow. The picture of Weizmann leaving one of the Conference sessions "all broken to pieces" haunted her. She asked him about his spiritlessness, which was obvious to her, and he poured his heart out. She then related to Ben-Gurion what Weizmann had told her. "At the next Congress he will resign. He wishes to become an elder statesman. He will guide the movement but not from elected office." He wished Ussishkin to be his successor, only for two years, and "afterward the charge will fall upon Ben-Gurion."

In truth, the weakness that had assailed Weizmann before and during the Conference burdened him well after it. In this he was no different from Ben-Gurion. Both were affected by emotional reactions. But whereas Weizmann's derived to a great extent from a sense of personal affront — in turning its back on its commitments under the Balfour Declaration England had betrayed not only Zionism but the declaration's progenitor — Ben-Gurion's resulted primarily from the burden of responsibility he himself had assumed. In Weizmann the weakness followed his recognition of personal failure, of the fact that his policy had reached the end of the road and that he was unable to suggest a new one to replace it. For Ben-Gurion, his increased strength came from his not being identified with the prior policy to the extent Weizmann was as well as from his resourcefulness in devising a new course of action. Furthermore, at the very moment when Britain's betrayal had robbed Weizmann of his self-confidence, the importance of the Yishuv, Ben-Gurion's power base, had increased and was continuing to grow. Weizmann's spirit was weakened further as he watched Ben-Gurion's ascent.

It was obvious to the inner circle of the JAE and the upper echelons of Mapai that Ben-Gurion was closing the gap, and it became evident externally, which was important for strengthening his position in his continued political activity. He had first made the acquaintance of the top British leaders at the London Conference, meeting twice with the prime minister and twice with the foreign secretary in exclusive sessions and several times privately with MacDonald. In the general meetings, too, he had taken a major role; more than once, Sharett said, "he handled the debate for our side almost single-handedly."[9] But what made a rising leader of Ben-Gurion was his stringent and unequivocal message that the Yishuv had power and would not hesitate to use it, if it had no other option. "For the first time in the history of Zionism and the Jewish people after the destruction," he wrote Paula, "we stood our ground against a great power, standing tall without pleading for mercy or merely demanding justice. For the first time we used a new argument: our strength in Palestine . . . We told the government with determination and self-assurance that they could not set up an Arab state in Palestine and that the Arabs were not strong enough to rule Palestine against our will." In his opinion, what he termed the "revelation of *our strength*" in a letter to the Jerusalem JAE was not merely "the principal, if not the only innovation" in the British-Zionist dialogue, but also "a significant positive aspect" of the Conference in London.

For his fellow delegates and JAE members the sense of Ben-Gurion's rise in stature was connected to his faith in the strength of the Yishuv and the Jewish people to endure the trials ahead; he radiated the confidence of one who knows his way. This above all set him apart from Weizmann. Even Kaplan thanked him in a letter for "the encouragement we found in your remarks, in the display of faith in our strength, in the showing of self-confidence in the negotiations." The British further acknowledged his new status by honoring him with the attention of their secret agents — at the London Conference he first became aware of being tailed and suspected that his letters were being opened. In his March 6 letter to Paula he explained that he was not writing to her in detail "because I am not certain you will be the first to read this letter."[10]

During the St. James's Conference Ben-Gurion had laid down two principles that in retrospect reveal themselves as the most important aspects of the policy that led to the establishment of the State of Israel. The first — especially daring — was that of the strength of the Yishuv. The second was the inevitability of partition. Ben-Gurion reiterated his message in letters to Palestine.

"We must . . . concentrate all our efforts on increasing our strength in Palestine — *quickly, with all the means available to us and in every way*": bringing to Palestine the greatest number of young people trained to bear weapons; maximal arming of the Yishuv; rapid acquisition of land and entrenchment in Haifa, the Galilee, and along the river Jordan; military training of He-Chalutz members in Poland; training (in land, sea, and air operations) of military cadres in America; and preparations "for the establishment of a Jewish army in Palestine, America, Poland, France, England, and the dominions." At the same time greater unity was necessary within the ranks of the Zionist movement. This meant "creating better relations within the Yishuv" itself and forging "stronger ties . . . with the Diaspora, particularly in Poland and America." The primary instrument for accomplishing these objectives was Mapai. From it he demanded "increased strength" through "unity within the kibbutz movement and among youth, and reinforcement of party discipline," by purging its factions and strengthening its central leadership. These tasks that he set for himself awaited him in Palestine.[11]

Aboard the *D'Artagnan* the question arose as to whether the harmonious relations between the two leaders meant that they were at last following the same path. As opposed to that of the days of the Peel and Woodhead commissions, their cooperation at St. James's won them much praise. David Hacohen told Mapai's Political Committee that "the fine relations within the Jewish leadership deserve special note . . . In my opinion Ben-Gurion plays a large part in keeping up the relations . . . Ben-Gurion stays on the watch, often exercising restraint on issues that could lead to clashes." That is why he had not broken off the talks on March 10 in Weizmann's absence. Mention of the unity of the Jewish delegation as one of its successes allows the assumption that Ben-Gurion's role in preserving it was considerable. It was probably not difficult to bring about, since the good relations within the delegation owed less to mutual agreement than to the shift in the balance of power between Ben-Gurion and Weizmann. Ben-Gurion knew that Weizmann toed his line unwillingly.

At St. James's it became clear — although Weizmann's adherents and adversaries were probably unaware of it — that when the British turned hostile to Zionism, Weizmann's leadership faltered, and all the advantages that had given Weizmann his special status vanished. He was no leader for a Zionism that had to adopt a policy of noncooperation, not to mention outright conflict. On March 15, the day Hitler's troops marched into Prague, Weizmann told Ben-Gurion, "Beneš is responsible for the fall of Czechoslovakia; he should have fought" — suggesting that he was reconciled to taking the hard line of militant Zionism. This tendency seemed to be gaining ground when, on the deck of the *D'Artagnan*, a friend of Weizmann's told Dugdale and Ben-Gurion that Weizmann had said, "England betrayed us, and we must fight her until she falls. The Jews should align themselves with the isolationists in America and condemn England's machinations and hypocrisy. [Weizmann] will devote the rest of his days to this war." Seeing the look of deep sorrow etched on Dugdale's face, Ben-Gurion told them, "There is no doubt that these words were blurted out on the spur of the moment . . . Insofar as I know him he is constitutionally incapable of a hostile stand against England, and a slip of the tongue during a passing mood should not be taken seriously." Ben-Gurion, who was as dubious of Weizmann's intention to fight Britain as he was of Weizmann's determination to resign, was soon proved correct.[12]

According to Ben-Gurion's original plan, the conference in America was to proclaim the "immigration revolt." Then, a year later, when more fighting power and supplies had been made available, shiploads of immigrants were to begin landing in Palestine and carrying out the takeover of Haifa and other parts of Palestine, leading to the establishment of a Jewish state. But this plan fell through. Lacking a strong voice to spur them on, the American Zionist leaders opposed the plan so strongly that any chance of a conference — the starting point of the immigration revolt — was destroyed. On March 23 Ben-Gurion wrote Rabbi Goldman, "I am going from here not to America, as I thought two months ago, but to Palestine. You have apparently not made arrangements for the conference as we planned, and it is not clear whether you want to hold it. This is a very sorry situation. It is unthinkable that after publication of the new policy the Jewish people would not offer an appropriate and impressive reaction, one which could have come only from America."

On March 24 Ben-Gurion received a seemingly encouraging wire from Goldman and Wise, who were back in the United States. "We saw the President, whose intervention secured postponement [of publication of the British policy]. Hope his continued intervention may avert decision." Although Ben-Gurion still sought support from the U.S. administration, both houses of Congress, the media, and influential people and organizations, he did not really expect America to intervene in British policy. "Only a simpleton," he explained to his JAE colleagues, "could think that even the friendliest American administration would identify itself with our position." Roosevelt was certainly "a friend of the Jews . . . but Roosevelt is not a monarch. Public opinion in America is regressive and backward in international affairs . . . and he will not take a step that is likely to arouse great resentment in the people. . . . Like any progressive American [Roosevelt was] a great friend of England and is concerned about its welfare and position. And he is not prepared to ignore the difficulties and fears that brought about the shift in British policy." Perhaps, too, Roosevelt identified with the political argument that dictated Britain's new direction — the necessity of appeasing the Muslim world.

Another reason for his probable nonintervention was that Roosevelt knew that America was not prepared to trade places with Britain and send its troops to Palestine or other Near East countries. Therefore, strengthening "the front in Palestine" was of primary importance; Ben-Gurion had not "a single day to waste," and American Jewry, he wrote Rabbi Goldman, would have to offer not only political assistance, "but also — and most important — financial aid: for land, immigration, defense, and operations on the sea."[13]

Before leaving London, Ben-Gurion had revealed to Paula, in his March 6 letter, something of the nature of the struggle about to begin in Palestine. He was not an advocate of strikes and demonstrations, he wrote; he was entirely opposed to such forms of protest, which he regarded as "a sign of impotent anger. . . . We are not without force by any means . . . *It is in our power to foil* [the plot] to turn Palestine into an Arab state." He thought of doing this with two tactics: "sit still and do nothing" and "get up and take action." Ben-Gurion, calling this type of struggle by the English word *noncooperation,* got the JAE and its advisory committee to approve it. The more he meditated on it the more he believed it could succeed, for he was sure that a policy as wicked as that set out in the White Paper was bound, in a country as fair minded as England, to backfire. "A more malicious, foolish, and shortsighted policy is impossible to describe. I have no doubt that this policy will not last long."

On April 3 Ben-Gurion, loaded down with books and presents, went ashore at Haifa. He summoned Mapai's Political Committee to a meeting on April 5 to discuss his plan. First, he told his colleagues, "we will make a list of things we *shall not* do and will fight against: terror, strikes." Second, "there are a number of things for which the time has not yet come: refusal to pay taxes, settlement by force." And third, "we will determine the things we will do right away: [establish] organizations for irregular activities" within the Histadrut, the Yishuv, and the Zionist movement, and initiate "action to increase immigration" illegally. This last he regarded as the principal "weapon" against the government's policy; "this immigration is not intended solely or particularly to enlarge the Yishuv, but rather for fighting the policy aimed at establishing an Arab state in Palestine."

At the same time, Ben-Gurion re-emphasized, "we take no part in any action of terror against England," for his plan did not involve civilian resistance or guerrilla warfare. Noncooperation was to operate in two areas only: immigration and settlement, and on two levels. "Sit still and do nothing" was a command to the politically active; they would refuse to discuss immigration and settlement with British representatives or to participate in the preliminary institutions for the independent Arab state. "Get up and take action" was directed at the people of the Yishuv; they would deliberately disobey the directives for immigration and settlement by bringing more Jews to Palestine and in due course establishing new settlements with the help of the organizations for irregular activities, in full defiance of the government. Undoubtedly the government would adopt "measures to liquidate the Balfour Declaration . . . in one form or another," Ben-Gurion told the Political Committee, and "then we shall be called on" to offer a political answer. "The answer is a Jewish state." Noncooperation had to begin, on both levels, with the coming publication of the White Paper.

Although Ben-Gurion felt considerable time pressure, the British stole a march on him, and he again had to step up his pace. On April 6, the day he was admitted to Beilinson Hospital for the tests Dr. Kunin had recommended, the high commissioner was empowered to set a "political high level" for immigration, as he saw fit. The significance of this ordinance became clear on April 12, when it was published in the *Official Gazette* along with an immigration schedule for April of one thousand immigrants, total. If this figure implied an annual schedule of twelve thousand, it meant that the restrictions known to be in the White Paper had become effective before its publication. Ben-Gurion was dismayed by the argumentative letter of reaction written by Dov Joseph to the high commissioner. "Such a letter," he wrote in his diary, "should be written to sound like 'drums of war'. . . beaten by the Jewish people for its right to Palestine."

On April 13 Ben-Gurion dashed off a letter to Harold MacMichael in which he stated that the ordinance was "a cruel and unjustifiable blow to the Jewish people in the most tragic hour of its history"; breaking the fundamental principle of economic absorptive capacity, forcibly restricting immigration, "undermines the very basis of the Jewish National Home." Moreover, the ordinance shut Jews out of Palestine, "although their admission or exclusion may be a matter of life or death to them," and prevented Jews living in Palestine "from rescuing their fathers and mothers, their brothers and sisters from countries of persecution." On behalf of the JAE, Ben-Gurion asked the high commissioner to pass on its appeal against "the new ordinance's moral and legal validity" to His Majesty's government. This was a polite way of rejecting the ordinance — of reopening discussion of it — making it clear that the JAE would conduct no further negotiations with the government or bargain with it over immigration schedules as long as the political high level was in force.

This letter was not approved by Ben-Gurion's associates. Sharett, who had remained in London, argued that the JAE would do better to negotiate with the Colonial Office, to ensure that if the Yishuv was unable to absorb the full quota in a given year, the balance would be added to the next year's schedule. At a JAE meeting, however, Ben-Gurion said, "It is out of the question that the Executive negotiate with the government for the amendment of some detail or other. We are fighting the principle." The JAE ruled with him.[14]

Publication of the White Paper on May 17, 1939, came as no surprise to Ben-Gurion and his JAE colleagues. Not only was it the embodiment of the "change of course" he had foreseen in 1936, and not only had its general lines been adumbrated by Malcolm MacDonald in the talks of September and October 1938, but Dugdale and the Political Department had been receiving from their sources secret information to the same effect. In December — more than a year before the Land Transfer Regulations were enacted — Ben-Gurion had noted in his diary that "the Palestine administration has already prepared the 'scientific' data upon which to base the fatal decree prohibiting the Jews from acquiring land outside the cities and the withdrawal from the Balfour Declaration in all the agricultural areas of Palestine." The White Paper announced the government's intention to establish, following a transitional period, an independent Palestinian state. The first part of the White Paper said that the British government had lived up to its obligation to the Jewish people and the National Home, evidenced by the fact that its "population has risen to some 450,000, or approaching a third of the entire population of the country." As soon as peace and order were restored the transitional period, during which Palestine would remain under British rule, would begin. At the end of five years, "an appropriate body representative of the people of Palestine and of His Majesty's Government will be set up to . . . consider and make recommendations regarding the Constitution of the independent Palestine State," which would safeguard the holy places, the rights of the Jewish minority, and Britain's foreign relations and strategic interests. His Majesty's government would "do everything in their power to create conditions which will enable the independent Palestine State to come into being within ten years."

The second part of the White Paper dealt with immigration during the transitional period. The Yishuv would be permitted to increase to approximately one third of the total population — 75,000 Jewish immigrants would be admitted. For each of the first five years, 10,000 would be allowed. Additionally, "as a contribution towards the solution of the Jewish refugee problem, 25,000 refugees will be admitted" above the cumulated yearly totals. However, if any Jewish immigrants entered the country "illegally" their number would be deducted from the yearly quotas. Further, the totals were subject to the criterion of economic absorptive capacity, determination of which was to be the ultimate responsibility of the high commissioner. After the period of five years, no further Jewish immigration would be permitted unless the Arabs of Palestine were prepared "to acquiesce in it."

Finally, the third part, which dealt with land, decreed, "There is now in certain areas no room for further transfers of Arab land [to Jews]." The high commissioner was to be given "general powers to prohibit and regulate transfers of land. These powers will date from the publication of this Statement of Policy and the High Commissioner will retain them throughout the transitional period." When, on February 22, 1940, the Land Transfer Regulations were published, Palestine was divided into three zones. The ban on Jewish land acquisition covered all of Samaria and large parts of the Gaza and Beersheba regions. The second zone, in which sales were permitted by authorization of the high commissioner, included the Jezreel Valley and the Galilee, part of the coastal plain, and the southern Negev. Most of the coastal plain, the Haifa district, and other urban areas made up a third zone — only 5 percent of Palestine's area — in which Jews were free to buy land from the Arabs.

In the four months until August and the Zionist Congress, which Ben-Gurion wished to harness to fighting Zionism, he devoted himself day and night to discussions, directives, and other preparations focused on defeating Britain's policy. These included a report from a three-man committee which, in December 1938, he had charged with looking into "how to organize a tax rebellion, if such a need should arise," and another, "most secret" report entitled "The Question of Supply in the Event of Politics of Noncooperation," presented to him by the Economic Research Institute established by the JAE. His major effort was devoted to the three fronts of the war against the White Paper: strategic settlement, the immigration revolt, and the Haganah. Readying the Yishuv turned Isaiah on his head — the order of the day was to beat their plowshares into swords, and their pruning hooks into spears, as Ben-Gurion issued a call to turn villages into military positions, their populations into military reserves, and their farming implements into tools of war. He saw no other alternative, for not only did he have no other force available, but beneath the watchful eye of the Mandatory government preparations for war could not be carried out openly.

On April 14 he addressed Mapai's council about the coming struggle and then set about making the preparations. On the nineteenth he began a series of meetings with the Haganah command, looking into "the structure of authority, functions, budget" and military procurement and development. He was briefed on "our aviation enterprise" and at another meeting suggested that "we have to establish a fishing school (with a view to camouflage for illegal immigration). He demanded that the JAE move to an emergency budget — increasing the Zionist budget by means of loans and devoting half of it to combative Zionism. The spearhead of his plan was the special Organization for Illegal Immigration (Mossad) set up secretly within the framework of the Haganah. Settlement points near the shore were charged with receiving and hiding illegal immigrants. Ben-Gurion filled his diary with detailed information about the shore, anchorage points, and settlements and about fishing boats, which were to be outfitted with steel plate armor and radios. His entry for Saturday, April 22, reveals something of his state of mind and intentions. It also reflects a rare trait so important in a wartime leader: high spirits, with a touch of humor at decisive moments.

That Saturday he had arranged a sea tour in order to see for himself the scene at which the immigration revolt would take place. Despite the forecast for a stormy sea he was unwilling to postpone the expedition, for "who knows if I will be free some other Saturday?" The high points of the tour, as planned by the Haganah command, were visits to anchorage points and an exercise in smuggling in "illegals." At 6:00 A.M., Ben-Gurion, with the Haganah chief of staff, three senior commanders, and an entourage, set out for Atlit in two cars.

Apparently the expedition had not been well coordinated: the fishing boat *Peled* (Hebrew for "steel"), bought with funds provided by the Histadrut and the special fund set up by Ben-Gurion for the immigration revolt and put at the disposal of a Haifa fishing company, arrived late. "Here we were supposed to meet the motorboat of the *ogen* [company], but it was late in coming. Meanwhile we climbed the Crusaders' fortress and a dozen Arab children sprang out of one of the rooms and peeked at us in fear and anger." According to Haganah intelligence, only one Arab family was living in the fortress, but, Ben-Gurion remarked, "the children were almost all the same age and they didn't seem to be the offspring of a single father." The *Peled*, accompanied by a four-horsepower motorboat, finally arrived. By then Ben-Gurion's entourage numbered thirty. They all took off their shoes, rolled up their pants, and got into a rowboat, from which "they helped us on [the motorboat], not without difficulty." The humorous aspect of the gap between the lack of means and the lofty aspirations did not escape Ben-Gurion: it was a poor man's sightseeing tour, acted out as though the Yishuv were already a military and naval power challenging the ruler of the waves, with a group of dreamers behaving like the general staff of an imperial army. In this vein he referred to the *Peled* in his diary as a Dreadnought (Britain's foremost class of battleship). The two vessels turned south, the motorboat keeping close to shore while on its flank, as escort, "the *Peled* sailed 'the mighty seas' far from the shore." The tour's organizers very much wanted to gratify Ben-Gurion with the sight of "the grace and splendor of our fishing boat," but when they maneuvered it near the motorboat, "it collided forcefully with the [motor]boat, and we nearly capsized. The great crash sprayed sea water all over us, but except for a passing panic nothing happened."

With the help of maps, Ben-Gurion surveyed the shore and took note of tiny inlets "that the British fleet cannot pass through, but that will not be dangerous for fishing boats and small freighters." Near Caesarea, Jewish guards who were semaphoring were sighted through binoculars. But "the GHQ of the generals who accompanied us" did not have even one flag to answer with; to enable them to communicate with the guards on shore, the boat dropped anchor, and one of the men jumped into the water and swam to shore, returning with the warning that for security reasons they "should not go ashore in [Arab] Caesarea" but rather stay right where they were. However, Ben-Gurion insisted on anchoring in the port of Caesarea and sent the guards there.

> With the *Dreadnought* to our right and the guards to our left, we set our course to "the enemy" fortress, the ruins of the city built by Herod in honor of Caesar. At 1:00 P.M. our boat entered the port . . . All the Arabs of the place came streaming to the shore. While we dropped anchor and set up the little boat to take passengers to shore the land force arrived in the town and took up strategic positions — in the central buildings of the city and at all the exits and entrances in the area. Three by three we left in the little boat, while the dumbfounded Arabs stared in fear and puzzlement at the unexpected guests.

After an extensive tour of the ruined and half-desolate city and the land surrounding it, owned mostly by PICA,* Ben-Gurion concluded, "From here it is possible to control the sea between Tel Aviv and Haifa," since most of the land was in Jewish hands and "only a small number of poor wretched Arabs live in this place with so rich a past and so great a future." At the same time "the staff officers," as Ben-Gurion called the Haganah commanders, worked out "a plan of operations" and agreed that "it is possible to put a group of forty to fifty boys in the empty northern port and in the line of ruined houses on the shore without uprooting even one Arab." This was how Kibbutz Sdot Yam got its start. It settled in that very place in February 1940, for the purpose of sea operations, fishing, and training seamen in bringing in illegals. Ben-Gurion and his entourage returned to the shore "while the eyes of the stunned Arabs followed us in silence." On the boat a surprise awaited him. "An unexpected order was given; scores of guns were raised in salute simultaneously and scores of young men in uniform stood at attention" until he was on board. This was an expression of gratitude and support for his leadership, an oath of allegiance to the state to come — an omen of his future as the first defense minister of Israel.

Under the hot sun the motorboat was tossed from wave to wave of the rocking sea, but Ben-Gurion remained calm, since "the *Peled* is watching us, if from afar." He felt a touch of fear when "the skippers," through their binoculars, sighted a police patrol boat approaching. But it kept straight on its course to Haifa, while Ben-Gurion, to his relief, saw "nice shadows on the sand . . . our land force" making its way to the last stop of the tour, an exercise in clandestine unloading of immi-

---

* Acronym for the Palestine Jewish Colonisation Association, founded in 1924 by Baron Rothschild.

grants held alongside Hepzibah. Ben-Gurion got a clear sense of what was in store for the illegals who would come to Palestine according to his plan as two bronzed and powerful young men, wearing only loincloths, "picked us up one at a time on their shoulders and set us down on the shore of Hepzibah." A crowd of swimmers from the nearby beach watched the goings-on and "came to see the unexpected procession" making its way through the sand dunes. But the cars waiting with their motors running a kilometer from the landing site sped away.

When he got home, sunburned "crimson," Ben-Gurion completed his diary notes with great satisfaction. "We shall establish on this empty shore tens of fishing villages, and Caesarea will be their mother city." Later, giving instructions on how to respond to the expulsion of illegal immigrant boats, he said, "We shall fight for immigration with immigration. . . . There will be no quiet in Haifa . . . A 'newsworthy' spectacle — riot, protest — will be organized . . . The English and American press interests me . . . Action must be planned to cater to the taste of this press." About a month after the expedition this formula was translated into a plan to bring in a thousand Jews a week, amounting to an annual influx of fifty thousand, as in the peak year of 1935. As far as Ben-Gurion was concerned, Aliyah Bet was worthwhile only if it reached those or greater proportions.[15]

Had he been able, Ben-Gurion would have met the White Paper on the day of its publication with shiploads of immigrants storming the shore and new settlements going up without authorization. But lack of the time required to make the arrangements was not the only obstacle; not everyone in Mapai and the JAE agreed with him. Disobedience was liable to generate too harsh a conflict with Britain, the main security against Hitler. In February, Ben-Gurion had asked the archaeologist Arnold Walter Lawrence, a critic of the British Foreign Office, "What will happen if we immigrate by force? Will they shoot us?" Lawrence replied that a British government that shot at Jewish refugees as they came to Palestine "would not last a week." This sentence remained etched in his memory, and Ben-Gurion repeated it as a central argument in favor of his plan. But Sharett was not reassured by this reply. "It can be so arranged," he told his diary, "that the British won't fire at us, but we will have to shoot at them. What then?" Then the papers would be filled with stories not of the British shooting at Hitler's refugees, but of the Haganah fighters shooting at British soldiers mobilized to stop Hitler.

Although none of Ben-Gurion's colleagues could come up with a better plan, they thought that with militant Zionism Ben-Gurion was asking the impossible. The dilemma of how to fight England and gain its friendship at the same time, as well as another poser loaded with contradictions — how to exploit (Ben-Gurion's word) disaster for advantage — came up endlessly in party and private meetings. His colleagues had always feared that Ben-Gurion was capable now and then of doing something extreme, even insane. They remembered that in 1936, after the Arab general strike, he had said, "The matter of the strike is not all that simple. We have . . . three fronts in the strike: the government front, the Arab front, and the Jewish front, and our interest in each is different. This is similar to the issue of Hitler and Palestine: we are interested in seeing Hitler destroyed, but as long as he exists, we are interested in exploiting this fact to build up Palestine." To them, mentioning Hitler in any even remotely positive sense was anathema.

The ability to think and act in two different directions at once was undoubtedly one of the most outstanding of his collection of exceptional traits, and Ben-Gurion again had to find a double formula. But this time it was not easy to devise. At a Political Committee meeting on April 5, and again before the Central Committee on May 28, he reiterated, "We shall not fight England," but otherwise kept going around in circles, not finding the redeeming epigram. At the Zionist Congress, convened in Geneva in an atmosphere of imminent war, during deliberation on the battle against the White Paper, he was still groping, although getting closer to his target. "Perhaps tomorrow or the day after the lot will fall and the decision will come in blood and fire — and with this decision we shall stand beside England. But we shall not conceal or make indistinct . . . that on Palestine's political front we have a grave and tragic quarrel . . . We shall not give in or shrink a hairsbreadth." Only when the war broke out did he find what he needed. On September 12, 1939, he fired off his most famous epigram. To Mapai's Central Committee he said, "We must support the [British] army as though there were no White Paper, and fight the White Paper as though there were no war." A week later, in the JAE, he broadened this formula. "[We must] offer England all possible support. To the extent that the White Paper materializes we shall fight it as though there were no war in the world." In December Ben-Gurion explained to the Small Actions Committee,

> The war forces us to double our considerations; on one hand we must consider the White Paper, on the other, the war . . . This double accounting is . . . a difficulty without equal, but we must accept it, since if we take only the war into consideration we shall deny the hopes of the Jewish people. If we consider only the White Paper and block out the war, we deny all, both the hopes of the Jewish people and of humanity. . . . We have been confronted . . . from the start of the war with a tragic situation that has no

equal. While with all our hearts and our souls we sided with England and France against the most terrifying enemy ever to rise against the Jewish people ... the state which leads the war against Hitler regretfully proclaimed war against the hopes of the Jewish people. This spiritual conflict has also become a great political entanglement for us since the outbreak of this war.

Ben-Gurion's colleagues seem to have repeated and polished his formula, and in the way a folk song or proverb is created, the famous version emerged: "War against Hitler as though there were no White Paper, and war against the White Paper as though there were no Hitler." Ben-Gurion ultimately made this version his own. An official notice published by the JAE in May 1940 included the slogan "War against the Nazis as though there were no White Paper; war against the White Paper as though there were no war against the Nazis."[16]

40

Struggle within a Struggle

D URING THE "days of the White Paper" Ben-Gurion became the
Yishuv's leader, a step away from heading the world Zionist
movement. If the partition scheme had made the Peel Commission and the 1937 Zionist Congress "Weizmann's," as Joseph Sprinzak had put it, the battle against the White Paper made the St. James's
Conference and the 1939 Congress "Ben-Gurion's." "Combative Zionism," as the only existing Zionist policy, was the only one that could be
presented to "the organized Yishuv" — particularly to its younger
generation — with any chance of gaining support. Militant Zionism, a
political expression and continuation of the course already begun in
the areas of settlement and illegal immigration, also gave expression to
the "activist" spirit that had become the driving force in the Yishuv.

On May 18, 1939, the day following publication of the White Paper,
there were general strikes, mass meetings, and Haganah-led demonstrations. A pronouncement defying the immigration and settlement
laws and calling for noncooperation with the institutions to be established under the White Paper was read at the meetings. Police clashed
with the demonstrators in Jerusalem, leaving many wounded and a
British officer dead. The next morning the Yishuv's leaders were summoned to the headquarters of Lieutenant General Sir R. H. Haining,
commander of British forces in Palestine and Transjordan, who admonished them without allowing them either to sit down or reply.
After that meeting, Ben-Gurion composed the answer he had been unable to offer to Haining in a letter which achieved acclaim.

> We deeply deplore and condemn unreservedly the shooting of a British
> constable which caused his death. . . . With all due deference, I must,
> however, take exception to your statement this morning that the blood

which may be shed will be on the head of the Jews. For the past sixty years, including the period of the present disturbances, the Jewish community has by its conduct proved conclusively that its methods of achieving its national aspirations are methods of constructive effort and concern for the welfare of the country as a whole. The Jewish people is now confronted with a new policy of His Majesty's Government which constitutes a breach of faith and a surrender to Arab terrorism. . . . The Jewish demonstration of yesterday marked the beginning of Jewish resistance to the disastrous policy proposed by His Majesty's Government. The Jews will not be intimidated into surrender even if their blood will be shed. In our submission the responsibility for what may occur in this country in the course of enforcing the new policy will rest entirely on the government.

An even greater response was generated by an analysis of the White Paper — "a superb analysis" in Sharett's estimation — which Ben-Gurion had begun writing on May 1 and finished May 18. His *Great Betrayal Analysis: A Policy Statement* was first published in the Hebrew press and later distributed by the Jewish Agency Executive in thousands of pamphlets in Hebrew, Yiddish, and English. An address to the Tel Aviv Labor Council, a speech to the Zionist Congress, and other speeches he made were widely circulated and applauded throughout Palestine and the Zionist world. A condensation of his spoken and written remarks at that time would read something like this.

We must thwart the government's design. We are entering a period of emergency . . . [that] will demand of us other dimensions of activity, both productive and aggressive . . . Our war is harsh and complex . . . and will not be won by words. Only deeds will decide, and the deeds will require of us will power and many daring sacrifices.

This government enjoys an enormous majority in the world's finest Parliament, and at its service stands the great power of the press, the civil service, and of arms. In contrast, the victim of its policy — the Jewish people — stands powerless and defenseless. It has no navy, no army, no government, not even a tiny strip of land of its own. The world's rulers seem to believe that anything can be foisted on this helpless people. But there is one thing that not even the mightiest of governments can do to the Jewish people, and that is to lead it astray with winning words and deceitful rhetoric. . . . We shall not engage in moralizing to the Mandatory government; it is deaf. . . . Nor shall we engage in futile efforts. Our strength is not quite nil and we need not resort to the only means we have ever had throughout our long Diaspora — preaching morality, appealing to conscience and compassion alone. . . . We will not reverse these decrees solely by appealing to the conscience of humanity; rather, by means of our will and strength, we shall overcome them ourselves.

We are not powerless . . . for at our disposal are two forces far stronger than that which stands behind the decrees: first, the pressure of the Jewish people storming Palestine; second, the strength of the Yishuv in Palestine

. . . This is the answer to the fateful question, Where lies our strength? It lies in our lack of choice. There are Jews who have no choice but to storm Palestine, regardless of the White Paper, be the gates open or shut. . . . Palestine is part and parcel of their existence; it is a question of life or death for them. No power in the world, except death, can stand in the way of Zion's returning exiles' . . . treading the path of illegal immigration to Palestine . . . Only with warships and machine guns will England be able to stop the Jewish youth, the pioneers of our people. . . . Only with these can the road to the homeland be blocked.

Nor does the Yishuv have a choice. Locking the gates of Palestine, establishing a territorial ghetto, spells its death sentence . . . and no matter what power stands behind this sentence . . . a living Yishuv shall not yield. It has the strength to thwart and undo this sentence. The Yishuv is capable of foiling the White Paper if it considers the defeat of such a policy . . . just as the refugees of the Diaspora regard their immigration to Palestine, as a matter of life and death. The Jewish people have created a position of strength in Palestine . . . Two principles must be established: the main front against the White Paper is in Palestine; the engine for this war is *the Jewish youth* in Palestine.

Palestine constitutes less than 2 percent of the British colonial empire . . . less than 2 percent of the vast areas in the hands of the Arab peoples. But for the Jewish people it is the world . . . and for the millions of Jews in the Diaspora it is the last hope of salvation. The only power that can decide the eventual fate of Palestine is the creative and fighting will of those Jews in Palestine and the Diaspora who have but one choice: the redemption and building of Palestine.

We shall act as though we were the Mandatory in Palestine . . . We alone must conduct ourselves as though we were the state in Palestine, and we must carry this through in order that we become the state in Palestine . . . until we are the state.

Hard days have come, but they can also be days of glory . . . It depends on the Jewish people, led by the Yishuv in Palestine, to confront the betrayal with all its might, not with words but with action appropriate to its aspirations and enterprise, its distress and dignity.[1]

The Yishuv — the youth in particular — ate it up. Ben-Gurion's flair for turning despair into hope and faintheartedness into vigor and mostly his ability to give his listeners the feeling that this narrow impasse was a field broad enough for freedom of movement and strategy electrified them. The two dominant themes of his speeches — youth as the standard-bearers of the war and the sure victory of a just war waged through lack of choice — were so deeply impressed on the collective mind of the Yishuv that they became the premises of the struggle for the state. Ben-Gurion could not but sense the waves of esteem and gratitude that met him at every turn. His image as a daring leader took root in the public mind, and his charisma — which was to grow steadily in direct proportion to the intensifying struggle for the establishment of the state — began to manifest itself. There is no doubt that the days of the White Paper were his finest hour.

His speeches were not mere rhetoric. Ben-Gurion devoted most of his time and energy during the five months between his return to Palestine in April 1939 and the outbreak of war in Europe to preparing the Haganah to defeat the White Paper. First, he established the ironclad principle that the Haganah fell entirely under the JAE's authority, and he placed at its head a civilian board of representatives of all sectors of the Yishuv, except the Revisionists, casting the Yishuv in the mold of a democratic state whose military was responsible to elected authority. In this way he differentiated between the Haganah and the IZL (as well as the Lehi, which later split off from the IZL).

Second, with the "war budget" he demanded from the JAE, as well as with funds from taxes and Kofer ha-Yishuv* fund-raising drives, he expanded and enlarged both arms of the Haganah, intending to demand of the Zionist Congress "a budget ... that will free" the Haganah from its dependence on funds raised through the Kofer ha-Yishuv. He created a mounted reconnaissance unit and a signals course. For training sailors, Ben-Gurion investigated the possibility of having members of the Yishuv drafted into the Royal British Navy; with an air force in mind, he encouraged the development of Aviron† and the establishment of a workshop for plane maintenance and repair in Lod.

To prepare for their major role in the struggle, he called for the youth organizations to join in a program that would include all the young people in Palestine and train them in sports, seafaring, and "all activity that falls within the category of resistance [and] the institution of national discipline." He wanted "a mobilized Yishuv" — as opposed to one that was merely "organized" — bound to "firm discipline" and obeying the authority of the elected institutions. (The important test of this authority involved terrorist activity carried out by the IZL without the knowledge and in defiance of the JAE and the National Council; Ben-Gurion was able to demand that the Haganah adhere to the JAE's line in opposing "the Jewish gangs.")

At his request the Haganah drew up plans for three forces: one to

---

*Kofer ha-Yishuv (the Yishuv ransom), established on July 24, 1939, was the Yishuv fundraiser for security. The principle behind the name was that those who could not physically fulfill their obligation to the Haganah would pay a "ransom" to its treasury. The money was collected by means of a tax on luxuries, restaurant bills, cigarettes, and so on. The Yishuv ransom was abrogated with the establishment of the State of Israel.

†Aviron was a company established in 1936 by the JAE and the HEC to advance Jewish aviation. When the war started it had four light planes and six gliders.

handle local security, one for regional and countrywide security, and one a semiregular army of fifty-seven battalions to defend against general danger. In mid December Ben-Gurion was presented a scheme for "setting up a navy." Were the Yishuv larger, he calculated, it could establish the state within a few years. This is probably what he had in mind when he told Mapai's Central Committee in July that "ten or twenty thousand more young men in Palestine could be the decisive factor in determining its fate in the event of war."[2]

The struggle to unify the Yishuv was not Ben-Gurion's alone. From all sectors and parties the cry was sounded for "a Yishuv-wide accord" — the formation of a national coalition whose leaders would be forceful and inspire confidence. Some suggested including the Revisionists and their sympathizers in the National Council; others came up with a "Supreme Committee," whose authority would surpass that of the National Council; still others, led by Katznelson, proposed a "Committee of Five" — composed of representatives of the five large parties — in which all Yishuv and Haganah matters would be discussed before being brought up for resolution in the national institutions.

In these and other proposals the name of Pinchas Rutenberg, who worked tirelessly to promote his own candidacy, figured prominently. Menahem Ussishkin went so far as to suggest that he be appointed head of the Yishuv's financial and political affairs and made "security chief." It is no wonder then that Rutenberg considered himself a candidate for the leadership of the Yishuv, a kind of prime minister. The prevailing opinion was that such a strong figure — a financial entrepreneur and leading industrialist, a political independent accepted by workers and farmers, Histadrut and Revisionists, yet a forceful man with a mind of his own — would win the loyalty of the entire Yishuv and could unify and lead it in this time of emergency. Starting in October 1938 Berl Katznelson and Ben-Gurion had met with Rutenberg to sound out his views and win him over to theirs in preparation for the central role he might be charged with. It soon became plain to Ben-Gurion that peace with the Arabs was Rutenberg's primary aim, since Rutenberg was convinced that once this was achieved, the British government would no longer need its anti-Zionist policy. He had his own strategy for this, which involved "buying the Arabs" — beginning with Nuri Sa'id, the Iraqi foreign minister, and ending with Fahri Nashāshībī of Jerusalem, the secretary of the Arab Defense Party. The more Ben-Gurion told Rutenberg that the Arabs who could be " 'bought' were worthless [and that] those who determine policy cannot be 'bought,' " the more resolute he became. On January 29, 1939 — his sixtieth birthday — Rutenberg reiterated his plan. After the meeting Ben-Gurion noted in his diary, "It seems to me that he doesn't recognize the impotence of money in certain corners of life," adding that Rutenberg left the impression of a "motor without a driver."

Although Rutenberg accepted Ben-Gurion's plan for the "conquest of Haifa" and promised to work for the "Judaization" of the city, he vehemently opposed the immigration revolt. When Ben-Gurion asked him "what to do about the White Paper, and how to unify the Yishuv for action," Rutenberg showered him with "complaints and grievances" instead of answering the questions. Even after speaking with Rutenberg's candidates for the National Council and other Yishuv institutions, Ben-Gurion was none the wiser as to how Rutenberg planned to conduct the struggle. He began to suspect that Rutenberg "wants to control the Yishuv — not directly, by accepting responsibility, but through puppets he will introduce into the National Council to do his bidding and stand against the JAE, which is not subject to Rutenberg's authority." Given this suspicion, Ben-Gurion was not pleased that Katznelson was campaigning to give Rutenberg a central role in the Yishuv leadership, or with the support that this initiative won him in Mapai. Joseph Sprinzak even proposed making Rutenberg chairman of the Supreme Committee.

On May 28 Ben-Gurion told Mapai's Central Committee, "Like Berl, I highly esteem this man, his concern . . . for issues. . . . This man . . . is great by virtue of his dynamic resources and influence in economic affairs, but he sticks his nose into political affairs. . . . I see danger in his entering politics, particularly in the Arab area." Shall we put a man who does not know what to do on a Supreme Committee? asked Ben-Gurion. He let it be known that if Rutenberg was appointed to an executive position he would resign. On June 4 he repeated his threat to the JAE. On the sixth, in another talk with Rutenberg on "the basics of the line," Ben-Gurion told him, "I am ready to work with any man and vacate my position for anyone who is prepared to do what must be done, in my view, to save Zionism, but I am not prepared under any circumstances to work in an agency with people who adhere to a different line of action." However, he never did resign.[3]

How could Rutenberg, an independent with no status in Mapai, have brought Ben-Gurion, who was practically the crowned leader of the Yishuv, to threaten resignation? Although Ben-Gurion's policy was the only one that really spoke to the public, among Mapai's leaders and the JAE many still expressed reservations and were inclined toward a different course. The fact that no alternative was presented in a clear, coherent form or put on the Zionist agenda for discussion and resolution did not lessen the strength of those who united to block principal points of fighting Zionism and the immigration revolt.

There was no disagreement about land acquisition and agricultural settlement, particularly on the frontier. Beginning in 1936 it had been agreed by all that Zionism's fate hinged on rapid land acquisition and that the success of the effort to speed it up would determine the borders of the future state. But there was a shortage of funds as well as opposition by the Arabs and the British to land sales to the Jews, and acquisitions slid from 62,000 dunams in the peak year of 1935 to 27,000 in each of the next three. As for settlement, in both 1938 and 1939 seventeen Jewish settlements were established; but whereas only one important frontier settlement was founded in 1938, six were created in 1939. This "strategic settlement" was a common objective, and Ben-Gurion's role here was primarily to urge greater momentum.

But this was not the case with illegal immigration, which had been begun by both the labor movement and the Revisionists in July 1934. Between then and late 1937, the two movements undertook five journeys in small vessels and brought to Palestine approximately 536 illegals. In 1938, fourteen such voyages were made. The establishment of the Mossad for Aliyah Bet in April 1939 gave illegal immigration great momentum: 1939 saw five voyages in the first four months and twenty-nine in the next eight. According to one estimate, 21,630 illegals were brought into Palestine between 1934 and 1939, most by sea. But despite this considerably increased rate, Ben-Gurion was not satisfied, for his idea of illegal immigration was much different from that of his colleagues. "I opposed Aliyah Bet," said Ben-Gurion to the Mapai council in April, "because it destroys scheduled immigration." Most of the illegals were intercepted and their number deducted from the yearly total by the British, so illegal immigration contributed very little to the growth of the Yishuv. Faced with Britain's Royal Navy and land forces in Palestine, Aliyah Bet had no chance of bringing in more immigrants than the British would allow.

The bone of contention between Ben-Gurion and his opponents could be reduced to one question: What was the objective of Aliyah Bet? The heads of the Mossad and the Haganah, ardently supported by Katznelson and Itzhak Tabenkin, viewed the struggle to reach the shores of the homeland in terms of internal, moral, and pioneering values. They believed that every immigrant was a world unto himself, and they hoped that every ship that reached the shore would be a banner drawing more people to come illegally. Ben-Gurion rejected this approach, which he regarded as an outdated "sneaking in" of a few individuals who would not serve the purpose. "Now is the time of Hitler," he cried, "and immigration today is a question of life and death for hundreds and thousands of Jews." At the April council Ben-Gurion stuck to his insistence that if Aliyah Bet did not smuggle in at least fifty thousand illegals annually, it had no real value. He opted for the immigration revolt, for if it forced open the gates and immigration were legalized, it would be inestimably more productive than Aliyah Bet, even at its most daring.

But the capture and impounding of boats that was expected during the immigration revolt was unacceptable to the chiefs of the Mossad and Haganah and the great majority of Mapai. The few boats at the Mossad's disposal had sailed to Palestine more than once — the *Atrato*, for example, had carried approximately 3,150 people in seven voyages, from November 1938 until it was captured on May 28, 1939, with 400 illegals on deck. Anyone who knew how difficult it was to obtain boats was not prepared to sacrifice them for the sake of a spectacular dramatization with dubious prospects.

These differences came to a head over the *Colorado* affair. This ship, which had brought in 379 illegals in June, on July 28 was caught at sea by a British destroyer, which proceeded to escort it and the 377 people on board to Haifa port. When Ben-Gurion learned on August 1 that the British intended to deport the *Colorado* and its passengers, he thought it a golden opportunity to inaugurate the revolt by landing the immigrants by force, in defiance of government orders. To this end he summoned Katznelson and Eliyahu Golomb to a consultation. Katznelson refused to come, and two days later Golomb showed up alone. "He opposes my intention to land the immigrants," reported Ben-Gurion to his diary. "He thinks it would be better if the boat went back, took on more immigrants, and returned."

Thereupon Ben-Gurion went behind Golomb's back to Jacob Dori, the Haganah commander in the north, asking him to submit a plan of operation. He called a JAE meeting for August 3, but Moshe Sharett and Eliezer Kaplan — his two other party colleagues in the JAE — as well as Itzhak Gruenbaum, opposed him. Ben-Gurion next turned to Mapai's Political Committee, but there Tabenkin's formidable opposition stood in his way.

Years later Ben-Gurion recounted his version of the *Colorado* controversy. "My proposal," he told students in Jerusalem in 1961, "was to bring the ship to Tel Aviv. We would have brought in hundreds of armed Haganah men and taken the illegals ashore by force; if we had had to fire on the army or the police — we would have fired . . . but we had a Political Committee in the party . . . and the majority decided against it." In the end the *Colorado* was impounded and the illegals — along with the Greek crew — were imprisoned in the Atlit detention camp, while the captain was tried and jailed in Acre. However, he and his men were liberated by a special task force of the Haganah and returned home in a Haganah motorboat.

Ben-Gurion's willingness to use the misery of the illegals to heighten the drama was revealed on April 23, when the JAE discussed the government's request that the JAE supply food for 450 illegals aboard another captured boat, the *Asimi*, whose passengers were about to be deported. "There is no place here for mercy pleas," Ben-Gurion argued, "since when they capture a ship and send it back it makes no impression whatsoever on the world" and would not do so unless the Jews responded in a way that would create a dramatic confrontation. So he notified the government that "we will not provide food for [the illegals], although we are ready to care for persons delivered to our care. If they are sent back hungry, their blood will be on the head of the government."

But when Ben-Gurion made it clear that he was not put off even by the prospect of loss of life, resistance to his strategy redoubled. "The action will require many sacrifices of us," he said in speeches during May and June. Minutes were not recorded for most of the discussions on this matter for fear of the British secret service — some of whose information came from Jewish informers — so it is difficult to quote Ben-Gurion or his opponents on this dispute. However, the few documents that do exist indicate that Ben-Gurion had either been deliberately misleading when, in late 1938 and early 1939, he told the JAE and Mapai, and particularly the American Zionists, that he had no intention of using arms against the British in the immigration revolt, or simply changed his mind. In any case, on August 18 he revealed to members of the labor faction at the Zionist Congress a scenario in which a bloody battle would be waged to suit the taste of the world press.

> BEN-GURION: The struggle has a simple meaning: cannoning that fire!
> MEIR YAARI (leader of Ha-Shomer ha-Tzair): That's a new interpretation.
> BEN GURION: The new meaning is correct for the hour . . . When they do not want to let us enter, we will go ahead with the little strength in our hands. We will defend ourselves . . . with the only means — the rifle — which does not fire when it need not, but does when it must.

In the dispute over Aliyah Bet neither side proved to be correct in practice. As it turned out, Ben-Gurion's prediction that Aliyah Bet would fail to enlarge the Yishuv came true. During the war years, from 1940 until May 1945, fewer than 10,000 illegals were smuggled in by sea, and nearly all were deducted from the immigration schedule; of the nearly 108,000* who entered Palestine illegally by sea over the

---

*In all, illegal immigrants totaled 122,000, including 5,500 by land, 150 by air, and 8,500 with forged certificates.

fourteen years until the establishment of Israel, approximately 69 percent did so in the three years after the war and the Holocaust, at which time the operation was carried out Ben-Gurion's way: fighting detention and deportation in full view of the world media. At the same time, the doubts of Ben-Gurion's opponents about fighting immigration were justified. Britain had no compunctions, in March and April 1939, about turning back the illegals aboard the *Sando* and *Asimi*; in March, opening fire on the *Aghios Nikolaus* and killing one of the illegals on board; or, in July, requesting the assistance of European countries in the effort to prevent illegal immigration.[4] Although the British government did not issue a standing order to the Royal Navy to open fire on illegals' ships, as Ben-Gurion had predicted, no media event resulted when it did not hesitate to shoot. It is almost certain that the immigration revolt would have achieved no better results than Aliyah Bet, and it surely would have cost lives. The immigration revolt, planned to erupt in March or April 1939 and finish within a year, would never have had a chance, for events overtook Ben-Gurion's plans: the Germans invaded Poland on September 1 and the war began. In the new circumstances both the immigration revolt and militant Zionism were shelved.

The differences between Ben-Gurion and Katznelson deepened when Ben-Gurion formulated his policy of war against the White Paper from a pro-British position, which he brought up before the party council in April. Rejection of his strategy, he argued, would spell death for Zionism. Katznelson, however, who had thought Ben-Gurion's formula absurd from the start, asked the council to refrain from debating and voting, since he believed that such a debate was unnecessary and would push the party toward a split when there was enough of a consensus to make decisions on such important issues as "immigration, land, the organization, preparation, and education of the nation, and many other important items." Furthermore, while the cautious Katznelson was fearful of the party's accepting so extreme a policy, he did not want it rejected altogether. He preferred to wait and see how things went, instead of making a premature commitment. Ben-Gurion then offered the council the following analogy:

> Imagine a man sentenced to death . . . but the verdict is not to be implemented for a month. Two friends visit him in prison. . . . One says, "During the interim you should breathe the air . . . eat, sleep . . . walk . . . read a book. As for . . . what happens when they lead you to the gallows, we shall see." . . . The second says, "Yes, you should breathe the air, walk, sleep, read a book; but aside from not despairing, you must do other things to save your neck."

Although Katznelson's intervention at the council hints at a controversy that ran far deeper than what may be called the operational level, the actual dispute seems to have centered on Ben-Gurion's demand that a smaller body be made responsible for carrying on the battle against the White Paper. His sensitivity about secrecy had intensified in reaction to, among other things, the discovery of Jewish spies in the service of British intelligence. This had an important effect on his mode of operation because he did not wish to reveal his specific plans for the war against the White Paper except to such a special body. The Central Committee of thirty and the Political Committee of seventeen seemed to him too broad and clumsy and presented too much of a security risk. "There are things I shall not speak of at this gathering because their hour has not come, and it is the carrying out of these things, not the speaking of them, that is important," he told the council. The small "forum" would be "the deciding body," and it would not require the sanction of either the Central Committee or the party council.

At first the council was inclined to agree to elect a "deciding committee," but there was protest. Katznelson again did not want a vote taken because he did not consider the small body to be necessary at that time and wanted to avoid the controversy that a vote would create. His opposition was decisive, and the council resolved that "the party's Political Committee be the deciding committee."

Since he never revealed his plan to his party for its sanction, Ben-Gurion could not bring it before the JAE, and assuredly not before the Zionist Actions Committee. Criticism was heaped on him when he spoke to the Small Zionist Actions Committee at its June session. After hearing him out, Shmuel Zakif of the General Zionists proclaimed, "Gentlemen, I believe I shall need the services of a doctor in the next few days. Apparently I am stupid. I do not understand anything that is going on here." Joseph Baratz, a member of Mapai, accused Ben-Gurion of "speaking ambiguously [when] the Yishuv needs a day-to-day program." Ben-Gurion continued to speak in innuendos and abstractions, and his war plans remain shrouded in mystery.

Quoting phrases from his addresses and articles — "We are entering a period of emergency," "national rebellion," "another framework for action," "institution of strict discipline," training the youth "for any activity that falls within the category of resistance" — a number of party members suspected that Ben-Gurion wanted the special body not only for security but because he aspired to authoritarian leadership. On this point fierce controversy erupted in his party, as well as in the JAE and the Zionist Actions Committee. A rally of youth organizations held in Jerusalem at Ben-Gurion's initiative, without their going through channels in their parent organizations, and at which Ben-Gurion spoke of the "unification" of the youth, gave the impression that he intended to create one all-inclusive youth framework which would answer directly to a single national authority. This idea infuriated Meir Yaari, who, at the June 1939 session of the Zionist Actions Committee, accused Ben-Gurion of trying to assume dictatorial powers, saying, "I have no call for dictators, even for those nearest me. I believe they are a disaster."[5]

Ben-Gurion's statement "We shall behave in such a way as to become a state in Palestine . . . until we are in reality a state" led some of his opponents to believe that he wanted to exploit the disaster of the White Paper to establish a state immediately, but one that lacked both Parliament and parties. The naysayers opposed a Jewish state in part of Palestine and flatly rejected Ben-Gurion's proposal to act as though the Yishuv were already a state. In his attempt to create the framework of a state during a crisis — without elections and with a controlled press — Ben-Gurion repelled those for whom democracy was axiomatic.

Despite the harsh differences of opinion in Mapai, Ben-Gurion returned from the Geneva Zionist Congress optimistic, having gotten his Haganah budget, set for a violent struggle against the White Paper, and certain of victory. He was confident in the "force" that he worked so diligently to nourish and in the rallying of the Yishuv around the struggle. "If not for the outbreak of the war, all memory of the White Paper would have been wiped out," he told a gathering of soldiers in 1943. But the war changed the situation, he maintained, and the hour for the immigration revolt had passed.

On September 8, 1939, he assembled some members of the Haganah command and mapped out their roles in the new situation. The Haganah had developed and been strengthened in three stages, he explained. The first had begun on April 19, 1936, with the outbreak of the Disturbances. The second had started on May 17, 1939, with publication of the White Paper. "We had to be prepared to defend with all our might, in body and spirit, our basic rights — immigration, settlement, self-defense, and independence" without recoiling from "any sacrifice or any enemy, however powerful." The third stage was just beginning. Ben-Gurion believed that the war had brought about an improvement in the political situation of the Yishuv, leading him to broaden his vision to embrace the entire Jewish people. "It can be said that the circumstances have changed in our favor . . . The change affects the evaluation of and attitude toward Jewish strength." He saw the Yishuv's strength as the core around which a great and powerful

Jewish army would arise in the course of the war; by virtue of the existence of such an armed force, its establishment seemed to him to be within reach. So he said to the Haganah staff,

> The First World War brought us the Balfour Declaration. In this war we must establish a *Jewish state.* . . . Our objective . . . must guide and direct all our moves from now on . . . and sometimes our very being, behavior, efforts, and attitudes toward the government . . . The first condition for a Jewish state is the formation of a Jewish army, above all in Palestine and for Palestine. We must establish Jewish military units, Jewish regiments, in every country where we can. . . . The heart of our strength is in Palestine, and the right kind of Jewish army in Palestine is likely to decide the fate of Palestine, the fate of the Jewish state. . . . The possibility exists of setting up a Jewish state in the near future, before the end of the war. Obviously, we will not do anything now that might worsen our relations with the government . . . but this does not mean that we will not do anything until we receive official sanction for the establishment of an army.

What they would do was pressure the British to form a Jewish military structure — quickly. It seemed to Ben-Gurion that from a Zionist perspective the gain from a second world war would surpass that of the first one. Where once the Jewish Legion had been established, this time an entire division would come into being. He was filled with hope that the war would put off implementation of the White Paper and the land regulations. "It is doubtful that the government will now commit this criminal folly and put the land regulations into effect," he told his listeners. "And it is almost sure that during the war the government will not institute the constitution guaranteed in the White Paper." But of course he could give no guarantee. Therefore, he said, "We must see this as an interim period. What we did and planned to do several months ago, and the ways we took and planned to take, are no longer valid. We must revise the Haganah in accordance with the new situation and requirements."[6]

This forecast of renewed cooperation with the British government at war with Hitler was accepted by many, and the integration of Rutenberg — vehemently pro-British and a personal friend of Sir Harold MacMichael, the high commissioner — into the Yishuv leadership seemed more essential than ever. Who could better reap the benefit for the Yishuv and Zionism from the state of war as Britain's need of Jewish industry in Palestine, with its potential for war production, steadily increased? And so — either to placate Katznelson and Rutenberg's many adherents, or because he felt sure he could impose his authority on him (since Rutenberg had pledged himself to accept it and work as part of a team), or because he was certain that his coming on board would unify the Yishuv — Ben-Gurion joined the effort to recruit Rutenberg into the service of the Yishuv. They all tried to dissuade Rutenberg from his "absurd" (Ben-Gurion said) ideas, discussing with him "the question of unifying the Yishuv . . . and reforming the institutions" to reach a compromise with his positions on this matter. On September 17, 1939, Rutenberg was elected president of the National Council over Itzhak Ben-Zvi, who remained chairman.

In supporting Rutenberg, Katznelson may have been seeking a brake on Ben-Gurion. If this was his intent, Katznelson could be sure of Mapai's support, and even more of that of the other parties. This made any arguments by Ben-Gurion useless. Having accepted that Rutenberg would be appointed, Ben-Gurion turned his attention to getting him under his own control and supervision. Promising him "cooperation" between the JAE and the National Council "even on political issues" Ben-Gurion proposed, to this end, establishing "a small war cabinet of three" — similar to the forum he wanted to set up in Mapai — composed of Ussishkin, chairman of the Zionist Actions Committee, Rutenberg, president of the National Council, and himself, chairman of the JAE; Rutenberg accepted the proposal subject to minor conditions. However, Ben-Gurion reserved the direction of "political affairs" exclusively for the JAE — himself — since it was the representative body of the Jewish people, charged with its Zionist policy, whereas the National Council represented the Yishuv alone.

On the face of it, a new chapter had begun in the history of the Yishuv, based on the inclusion of the Revisionists, the farmers' union, and other groups in its leadership. Rutenberg instituted an "emergency tax drive" — to fight unemployment and poverty — which began actively on all fronts. For a time all seemed to be for the best, especially since both the Yishuv and the British had a lot of faith in him. His friend MacMichael expressed this in a letter to Malcolm MacDonald. "Ben-Gurion is something of a fanatic, determined and honest in his convictions. To Sharett it would be a crime not to turn anything and everything to short-term political account. The pair between them can exercise a vast deal of authority and pressure. Rutenberg is longer sighted and a bigger man; he has annexed the National Council."

However, it soon became clear that Rutenberg's outstanding characteristics — a strong personality, political ambition, independence, and self-esteem — proved stronger than the man's pledges, and one after another of Ben-Gurion's doubts about Rutenberg were justified. In the economic sphere Rutenberg reached the conclusion that "the main problem before us in the political war is the raising of financial means"; he told Ben-Gurion that "no one else could raise funds" abroad. In the political sphere, Rutenberg admitted, "The main thing is raising an army," but he wanted it to be "under my control": he would shape its personnel, conduct negotiations with the government, and in general "direct the army." When Ben-Gurion remarked, "We favor team work as opposed to individual work," Rutenberg replied, "We shall decide together and I will carry out the decision." Ben-Gurion objected that "in the course of carrying it out there are things that must be decided." When Rutenberg asked, "Why don't you trust me?" Ben-Gurion responded unequivocally, "I don't trust your political judgment." Ben-Gurion was the last man who would have devoted his life to building up authority only to hand it over to someone else.

Each day made it plainer that Rutenberg, this man of free enterprise, did not recognize the parliamentary and coalitionist system and was not capable of working within its bounds. Not a month had passed before he despaired of the coalitionist constraints that restricted his moves and demanded the establishment of an executive of four above the National Council and the heads of the parties. Prevented from doing this, he dipped his oar into all areas of activity, including those that lay within the sphere of the National Council and the JAE, and began negotiating — with the high commissioner, army commanders, and government officials in London — on political issues. By his second month in office he had responded to objections to these actions with threats to resign. And by November 2 Ben-Gurion was saying that he was "deeply worried over Rutenberg's appearance before the authorities," particularly since "his intervention is not amenable to supervision and guidance." Ussishkin, Kaplan, and Gruenbaum also evinced their disappointment. In January 1940 Rutenberg was censured by Mapai's Political Committee. Rutenberg's intervention in political affairs had evoked "grave fears," said Ben-Gurion, and "it will be very unnatural if a situation is created within the Yishuv where political relations with the government are left in the hands of one man without control." A chorus led by Kaplan arose, urging Katznelson to get involved in National Council affairs since "he is one of the few people to whom Rutenberg listens. Rutenberg now meets with the government more than all the members of the JAE combined. He resides in the King David Hotel, where all the military leaders are quartered, and he meets with them every day and discusses scores of matters. It is impossible for committees to supervise him and keep him from running afoul." The faith in the ability of Katznelson to control Rutenberg derived from their mutual esteem and affection. Rutenberg claimed that "in Palestine only two men understand the situation" — he and Katznelson. Ben-Gurion, too, regarded Katznelson as "the first place to turn" when it came to Rutenberg.

But when Katznelson finally spoke, he defended Rutenberg: the problem was not Rutenberg or his faults, but the National Council, which had become the "lightning rod and shield of the Jewish Agency. All the arrows are now aimed at the National Council since it is weak." Despite his faults, Rutenberg was worthy of more trust. "I can say that I know of hardly a man in the Zionist movement for whose mistakes we have not paid and continue to pay in order to exploit his talent. This holds for Rutenberg as well." This barb was apparently directed at all the complainers, especially Ben-Gurion. Katznelson was prepared to help guide Rutenberg only if he did not have to go to meetings in Jerusalem, and the overwhelming majority of them were held in that city.

Visiting London in May 1940, Rutenberg praised MacMichael, whom the entire Yishuv regarded as an enemy and whose resignation it was demanding. "Here something happened which spoiled our plan [to get rid of MacMichael]," Ben-Gurion said at a JAE meeting. "The president of the National Council went to London, and meeting with [Colonial Secretary] Lord Lloyd, praised the high commissioner, offering thanksgiving that the Jews were fortunate to have such an excellent commissioner." To drive home the extent of Rutenberg's irresponsibility and political folly, Ben-Gurion pushed his point a little too far in Mapai's Central Committee. "The Jewish people have three enemies. I shall enumerate them in order of their importance: the first is Hitler, the second MacDonald, and the third MacMichael."

Eleven months after the Yishuv had decided to hitch its wagon to Rutenberg's star, the star faded and winked out. In August 1940 Rutenberg again made known his intention to resign; this time he meant it. Fear that his resignation (Sprinzak described it as a "catastrophe") would result in a loss of confidence in the Yishuv leadership led to all-out efforts to dissuade Rutenberg, which failed. On August 18 he sent Ben-Zvi a letter to the effect that illness compelled him to resign from the presidency of the National Council, adding that he had done his best to give the Yishuv "effective" leadership, but that internecine party squabbling had precluded it. On August 29, he made the letter public, and in November his address to a press conference generated a storm in the Zionist and Jewish world. Rutenberg recounted all the "plagues of the Yishuv," blaming them on political parties and concluding with a call to replace party leadership with a nonpartisan national administration.

His illness, however, was not a diplomatic pretext; Rutenberg had cancer of the esophagus, which was kept secret. In July 1941 his condition worsened and he was confined to bed. On January 1, 1942, he sent his chauffeur to bring Katznelson to his deathbed to say farewell, and on the third he passed away at dawn. Ben-Gurion grieved and wrote a eulogy. But to Paula he had revealed an opinion that he did not make public: the Rutenberg case "proved that good intentions — although in and of themselves very very important — are not enough if one wishes to lead. Rutenberg's failure was in his not knowing what had to be done. The man knew only that he was the one who had to do it."[7]

The Rutenberg episode is noteworthy in this context because of its implications for Ben-Gurion's status, and for the light it sheds on Ben-Gurion's relations with his party. From the start Ben-Gurion had known that Rutenberg's appointment would cause him difficulties, which is why he tried to avert it by threatening to resign. But even had he believed that Rutenberg would fulfill the hopes invested in him and become a sort of prime minister of the Yishuv — overshadowing and outshining Ben-Gurion himself — it is doubtful whether he could have prevented the appointment in the face of the broad support it received both in Mapai and the Yishuv as a whole, despite the many reservations concerning Rutenberg's ideas. It was finally not with Rutenberg that Ben-Gurion settled his score, but with his party and his colleagues.

In December 1939 Ben-Gurion's skies had again turned gray: it became evident that the British government was resolved to implement the land regulations. Ben-Gurion meant to issue a sharp response, but he received no support from his party. The resolution in favor of his policy failed to come through, and the controversy of the previous April was rekindled. Therefore on December 15 Ben-Gurion notified Mapai's council, "I am not a member of the council," explaining that he would take part in its meetings as a party representative to the JAE only. As far as he was concerned, all his former resignations — from the HEC and the party institutions — were still in effect.

In November Ben-Gurion had gone to London for eight days to accelerate the battle "to tear up the decree" over impending land regulation while there was still time. The battle's central axis was the Labour Party, from which a delegation, under Clement Attlee, met with Neville Chamberlain. Ben-Gurion again became enraged with Weizmann. "I could get no clear-cut information as to whether there was hope of putting off the regulation," said Ben-Gurion to Mapai's Central Committee. "Only on my last day in London did Weizmann recall that in his talk with [Colonial Under Secretary R. A. B.] Butler, which had taken place long since, Butler had told him that publication of the regulation probably would not be postponed. Weizmann forgot all about it." Therefore Ben-Gurion could not anticipate any success. On November 23, 1939, he wrote in his diary, "I fear the regulation will be published. If the regulation is published, we shall have to go on acquiring and settling land, if only Arabs can be found to make it possible."

In December he told the Small Actions Committee that "the government's approach to land regulation" would be "the touchstone": if that decree was published and implemented it would show that the British intended to implement the White Paper in full.[8] On February 12 the British war cabinet decided to put the land regulations into effect, and on February 28 they were published in Palestine in the *Official Gazette*. Thereupon the grave question of how to respond became an item on the Yishuv and Zionist agenda. As usual, the change in circumstances induced a switch in Ben-Gurion's policy. On January 29 he had written in his diary, "If the regulation is passed we must draw conclusions, be ready to continue our settlement under all conditions." But he no longer thought in terms of fighting Zionism and the immigration revolt. "What we did and planned to do several months ago is no longer relevant," he went on. "We must adjust the Haganah in light of the new situation and requirements." He meant that a harsher reaction was required. The same day, discussing the Haganah with Mapai's secriat, he demanded "new procedures" that would give the leadership more powers in the face of "the discovery of internal corruption — the reality of a network of Jewish spies willing to turn over the defenders of the Yishuv."

On February 26 the draft of the land regulations was given to the JAE by the chief secretary of the Mandatory government.[9] The next day Ben-Gurion sent a letter to the high commissioner, which was published in most of the Jewish newspapers on February 29, in contravention of British censorship directives. *Davar*, *Ha-Tsofeh* (the organ of the Mizrachi Zionist religious party), and *Ha-Aretz* (nonaligned) were closed by government order "until further notice." Only *Ha-Boker*, the General Zionists' organ, obeyed censorship orders and was not shut down, demonstrating how far the Yishuv was from Ben-Gurion's dream of unification. Like the *Great Betrayal Analysis* and Ben-Gurion's speeches after publication of the White Paper, this letter moved the people and became an integral part of the legacy of their struggle. In essence, it said,

> The effect of these regulations is that no Jew may acquire in Palestine a plot of land, a building, or a tree, or any rights in water, except in towns and in a very small part of the country. The regulations deny to Jews equality before the law and introduce racial discrimination. They confine the Jews within a small Pale of Settlement similar to that which existed in czarist Russia before the last war and now exists only under Nazi rule. They not only violate the terms of the Mandate but completely nullify its primary purpose. . . . This attempt to frustrate the age-old aspiration of the Jewish people to become rooted again in the soil of its ancient homeland is made at a time when millions of Jews are being mercilessly perse-

cuted by a cruel enemy. This blow is being inflicted by the government of a great nation, which undertook to restore the Jewish people to their Na tional Home. The Jewish people will not submit to the conversion of the Jewish National Home into a ghetto, nor can it believe that Great Britain would consciously be responsible for such a travesty of an international obligation.

The day the letter was published, a protest meeting of the Small Actions Committee was held, and protest demonstrations, which lasted until March 6, began throughout Palestine. Three Jews were killed, in clashes with the British police and army, in Jerusalem, Haifa, and Tel Aviv.[10] But for Ben-Gurion this was not enough; the "disorder" had to continue until the decree was annulled. Moreover, it constituted only the beginning of the response, whose specifics he made known only to Katznelson and a few others. Undoubtedly Ben-Gurion meant to institute the second part of his double formula — war against the White Paper as if there were no war against the Nazis. There is no doubt that this entailed taking advantage of the firepower of the Haganah to support the "defiant settlement" and broad-based resistance movement of the youth and the "mobilized Yishuv"; in London, Blanche Dugdale heard that Ben-Gurion wanted to break with the British government. The exact details of what he proposed to do cannot be determined. Because Mapai refused to grant him the small forum he wanted, he stood his ground and did not explain to any group, even in general terms, what he thought the response to the land regulations should be. In March 1940, when he finally described it to the Zionist Actions Committee, he still spoke vaguely. Even so his speech was so stirring that Herzl Rosenblum remarked that in twenty years of listening to Zionist speeches, "only at a few have I been so moved as at hearing Ben-Gurion's address." But, he added, "Ben-Gurion went through all the letters of the alphabet, stopping before Z. Why didn't he say Z? . . . I had the impression that he did not want to say it in such a forum."

Although Ben-Gurion had many talks with Katznelson — they never met as often as they did during the days of the White Paper and the land regulations — and Golomb, the substance of their discussions remains a secret. Since no one knew what was going on, there was general puzzlement when, on February 29, 1940, at the opening of a Small Actions Committee session called to discuss the response to the land regulations, he announced his resignation once more.

With the outbreak of the war I said that the war of England and France against the Nazis was our war too and that we must lend England and its army all the assistance that we, as Jews, can give and are asked for.
This has been my position throughout.

But yesterday something happened, and we can no longer live and act as we have done up till now. As of yesterday a Jewish ghetto was set up in Palestine. As of yesterday we Jews have been put, as the Czechs were, in a "protectorate." . . . This was done by the Mandatory government. . . . As chairman of the JAE I was empowered . . . to represent the people to this government and enter into negotiations with it. I must tell you that I cannot be true to myself and go on holding this office, so I am stepping down.

Ussishkin, the president of the Zionist Actions Committee, immediately responded,

I deeply regret that you have not acted in accordance with procedure. The president must be notified of every announcement in advance. I saw no such notification. And had I seen it, as chairman I would not have allowed it . . . to be read. Now, since you have made this announcement, I say we did not hear it. Meeting adjourned.

At the JAE meeting immediately following, Ben-Gurion's colleagues expressed resentment and remarked that his resignation was an "uncollegial move." Gruenbaum said it was "liable to break up the entire Executive," and proposed rejecting it. But Ben-Gurion, though apologizing for the shock he had given them, did not give in. He had reached his either-or stage. "The Zionism we knew exists no . . . longer . . . [my] brand of Zionism was [my] own," he said, without making it clear whether he intended it to be only a liberation movement or a democratic one as well. Those who remembered a dictum from one of his famous White Paper speeches — "nor shall we engage in futile efforts" — understood his either-or: either they let him do work that was useful, or he quit. "His mind is made up"; "his conscience does not allow him to resume his office" in a way not his own.[11]

The resignation was directed primarily at Katznelson and Tabenkin, who had the power to harness Mapai to his plans. With it, it seems, he was waving in their faces the IOU they had signed the day they made him leave the HEC to join the JAE. With it he called into question their unwritten partnership, which stipulated — he believed — that he would serve as the party's representative in the JAE and do his best for Zionism, while they did their share in the party and guaranteed him their backing. Ben-Gurion saw developments in a different and much more portentous light than did his two senior partners. The burning ground, which affected him so much more than they and brought him so much closer to compromising on values — even on the wholeness of Palestine — blazed with a white heat. Faced with the looming annihilation of European Jewry, if they did not soon find refuge in Palestine, and of the Yishuv, if it was not permitted to increase in order to withstand the Arabs who wished to destroy it, compromising democracy was a small price to pay.

But Katznelson, Tabenkin, and the majority of Mapai opposed the concentration of power and authority Ben-Gurion wanted, and they doubted that any good would come of the policy of response that he demanded, fearing that the Jews would pay its price for nothing. At the April 8, 1940, JAE meeting, Ben-Gurion reiterated, "We must . . . determine that the war against the White Paper now takes first priority . . . and we must oppose the government's policy and not recoil from possible damage. . . . Resistance means damaging [the British] as much as we can . . . There are also other things to be done . . . fierce and prolonged disorder in Palestine . . . a sharp response to any repression of Jews in Palestine, fine for fine, punishment for punishment."

But all his colleagues opposed giving the war against the White Paper "first priority" over the war against Hitler, or over the democratic process in Zionism and within the Yishuv. As for the concentration of authority, the non-Zionist Werner Senator said, "In my opinion Mr. Ben-Gurion's method is nationalist fascism." Gruenbaum, who chaired the meetings after Ben-Gurion's resignation, said that at the moment he saw not "even one soul in the Zionist movement in whom the entire movement has enough confidence to warrant his deciding [matters] on his own." Rabbi Judah Leib Maimon, usually a Ben-Gurion supporter, agreed. "It is out of the question that one of us shall determine." Although Ben-Gurion asserted, "I never asked for that," his colleagues suspected him of wanting exactly that.

On the practical level, they feared that this was one of Ben-Gurion's wild schemes that would bring the Yishuv into conflict with the British and do more harm than the White Paper. "Ben-Gurion is a most talented individual, of good intentions," Arthur Ruppin later wrote in his diary, "but a zealot liable to drag us into the abyss." Gruenbaum opposed "disorder in Palestine, which would certainly lead to breakdown," arguing that "first it must be ascertained whether Mr. Ben-Gurion's proposals have a chance of success or if they harbor danger of destruction." Sharett's remarks were the most cutting of all. "I cannot accept the proposal of perpetual disorder in Palestine. . . . I do not fear the injury to Britain at all, rather the injury to us . . . It would be so great that we should not be able to stand our ground." In a cable to the London JAE, Sharett explained Ben-Gurion's resignation as follows: "The ostensible reason is his personal inability to resume the contacts with the government that are still necessary. The true reason is that most of the Executive and the Actions Committee do not accept his policy of response to the land decrees. [Mapai's] Central Committee is divided."[12]

Ben-Gurion's resignation resembled a three-stage missile. Nearly six weeks passed between the firing of the first stage — the announcement to the Zionist Actions Committee — and that of the second — a letter Ben-Gurion presented to the JAE on April 8, 1940. During that period he went about his business in the JAE, theoretically awaiting his replacement. Expecting that Katznelson, Tabenkin, and a majority of his party would eventually see that he was right, he therefore gave them time for thought. However, Katznelson anticipated equally that Ben-Gurion would cool off and his resignation, unaccepted and unpublished, would be forgotten, as had happened more than once before. Therefore he kept the Central and Political committees from discussing the resignation. Itzhak Ben-Aharon, of the party secretariat, was told that this was best, since "the matter might resolve itself." But when the test of nerves came, Ben-Gurion wielded his driver's tactic, and no one in his party could face him down. On April 9 he wrote to Mapai's Central Committee that, with his departure from the JAE the previous day,

I am entirely out — until the right time — of all political activity, formal and informal, official and unofficial, inside and outside the party. I have reached the conclusion that the good of the movement and the party demands that I do not explain the reasons for my resignation in the party institutions or in any other forum. For a short while I will continue to tend to the business of the Haganah.

It was apparently no longer possible to table discussion of the resignation. After reading the letter to the Central Committee Ben-Aharon chastized it for its silence. Ben-Gurion's resignation was being discussed everywhere, he said, and all kinds of conjectures were being made, yet in the Mapai Central Committee no one knew the why or wherefore of it. Shmuel Yavnieli, Ben-Gurion's greatest disciple, spoke in support of his mentor's policy, and then said that Mapai should make sure that steps were taken to "move the earth. If we do not . . . others [the Revisionists and the IZL] will." Nevertheless, the meeting still did not discuss the issue fully, as if a hidden hand were preventing it. If it is true that this hand belonged to Katznelson, perhaps it was because he saw in the last sentence of Ben-Gurion's April 9 letter a sign of an additional reprieve. But the third stage was fired on April 12, when Ben-Gurion directed his secretary to refer questions on Haganah matters to Sharett.

His colleagues finally accepted his resignation and thought he was really and truly preparing himself for kibbutz life. Sharett and Golomb seem to have believed that, for Rivka Hoz wrote her husband, Dov, that Ben-Gurion had "asked Paula if she was ready to move to a kibbutz. After consulting with Moshe [Sharett] and Berl [Katznelson] she answered yes, and he was happy as a child." But Katznelson was not for a moment fooled into believing that rural life attracted Ben-Gurion more than his political office. Katznelson took part in creating this facade — which became a myth of the labor movement — knowing full well that despite his declared love of his bygone days as a field hand, Ben-Gurion pined for his public work in the city. It was quite plain to Katznelson that all that was required for Ben-Gurion to forget his resignation was patience and the provision of an honorable out.

The rumors of Ben-Gurion's stepping down and the controversy that caused it took wing and traveled far. The *Daily Jewish Courier*[13] in Chicago wrote of a "sharp controversy in the JAE, saying that Ben-Gurion had resigned because the aggressive policy he proposed had been rejected. He was depicted as a leader of vision, a brave and daring fighter whose power was sapped by his petty partners, for whom the good of the moment outweighed the disaster that the next day would bring. Among the Yishuv activists, particularly the youth, Ben-Gurion appeared to be a courageous giant bound to the earth by numerous cowardly political hacks, and he won substantial popular sympathy and support. When his day came several years later, it would be remembered that the main fault with the policy he had proposed in 1939 and early 1940 was that it was ahead of its time.

41

An Ultimatum for Weizmann

THE MAJORITY in Mapai was not enthusiastic about the double formula. Golda Meir was subsequently to say that the only reason they "didn't laugh" at it was that Ben-Gurion had proposed it. Another Central Committee member remarked, in 1941, "This slogan is a good epigram, but hardly a political program." And the war, the major factor in the Yishuv's life, belied the second half of the double formula. Realistically there could be no war against the White Paper without war against the British. In the middle of a world war, such a battle had not the slightest chance of success. Furthermore, the British seemed to be pitting a double formula of their own against Ben-Gurion's: war against Zionism — against illegal immigration, settlement, striving for a state — as though Britain were not in the midst of war against Hitler, and as though the Jews were not his primary victims. Since Britain was stronger, this crushing formula, as set forth in the White Paper, was the one that was put into operation. The British government was well aware that the Yishuv had no choice, and it soon became evident that of the two parts of Ben-Gurion's formula, only one remained: cooperate with Britain in the war against Hitler as though there were no White Paper.

Only after Italy entered the war in June 1940 (by September Italian planes were bombarding Tel Aviv), and particularly during 1941 and 1942 — when the anti-British revolt broke out in Iraq, France's Vichy government put Syria at the service of the German army as a bridgehead to the Middle East, the German armored force sped through the Western Desert and reached El Alamein at the Egyptian border, and all the Middle East was in danger of conquest by the Axis — did the British move to cooperate with the Haganah. At the same time, all

forms of the battle against the White Paper — "defying settlement"*
(or "conquering settlement," in Ben-Gurion's phrase), Aliyah Bet, and
noncooperation — faded away, not to be renewed until 1944, when an
Allied victory over the Axis was assured. Then, as the situation in the
Middle East improved and the Germans retreated from the Western
Desert, British cooperation diminished. In 1943, the pivotal year of the
war (spanning the Stalingrad victory and the Allied invasion of Sicily),
British cooperation with the Haganah almost ceased entirely as the
latter went back underground and the White Paper policy reared its
head anew.

It can therefore be said that during 1941–1943 there was a tacit
agreement — an unwritten truce — between Britain and the Yishuv,
which in practical terms meant postponement of the conflict between
them in order to defeat Hitler. Ironically, it was the original rejection of Ben-Gurion's aggressive response policy that made possible its
later success. The Yishuv was given a respite that enabled it to build
economic, organizational, and military strength, so that after the
Holocaust in all its horror was brought to light, and its survivors
began making their way to Palestine, fighting Zionism and the immigration revolt suddenly emerged as the force that Ben-Gurion had envisioned.

Until then, given the miserable situation of the Jewish people, there
could be only one policy — enlist in the fighting forces and work for a
speedy victory. But the British government heaped obstacles in the
way of its realization, and resisted the Yishuv's demand, presented by
Ben-Gurion, to be allowed to fight Hitler as a nation among nations by
establishing Jewish fighting units. That which the Yishuv wished to
gain — most of all a Jewish army within the framework of the British
army — was precisely what the British government wished to prevent.
The effort to persuade the British to accept the Yishuv's assistance in
the war effort, to form Jewish fighting units and group them in a brigade and possibly a division, spearheaded the Jewish Agency Executive's political battle.

During this period of delicate balance, Ben-Gurion, as in the past,
lost center stage. When it came to getting the British to agree to establish a Jewish fighting force, Weizmann was once more the star. While
Ben-Gurion toyed with the idea of retiring to a kibbutz, or serving
Zionism "as a rank-and-file soldier," Weizmann regained his old status
and glory. Yet it was also a gesture from him that enabled Ben-Gurion

---

* After the outbreak of the riots in April 1936, the Mandatory government had forbidden
the establishment of new Jewish settlements without prior government sanction. After
publication of the White Paper, in accordance with its noncooperation policy, the JAE
stopped giving the required advance notice.

to extricate himself from the mess in which his latest resignation had landed him.[1]

In March 1940 the JAE had come up with a face-saving proposal that he go to London "to consult with Weizmann," hoping he would get caught up in political activity and forget his resignation. In an April 9 cable to Weizmann in London, Sharett requested his intervention. Weizmann, who also needed him inside the JAE, wired Ben-Gurion on April 13, "Beg you defer decision come London." Dugdale also sent a cable. "Implore you consider effect on proposed step stop love." Doris May thought such a cable was useless, she wrote Sharett. "When he has achieved his 'inner certainty' he's such a Rock of Gibraltar!" Nevertheless, on April 18 Ben-Gurion wired Weizmann, "Unable leave immediately will try meet you London before your departure America."

Obviously he, too, was seeking an honorable way to back off from his resignation, having woven through his statement a fine thread of compromise: in the nonpolitical area he was at the JAE's service. The idea was that he would go just for a few days to keep the London office informed — "He is obliged to do so for the sake of explaining the political situation and our work in the future," the JAE minutes for April 21 put it — as well as talk to Weizmann about his own plan.[2]

Not that Ben-Gurion expected much from Weizmann. While it was true that both supported an alliance with Britain, Weizmann did not believe that it would be achieved through violence. He had opposed Ben-Gurion at the Geneva Congress as if he belonged to the "opposition" to Ben-Gurion within the labor faction. Ben-Gurion had accused Weizmann of turning his Mapai colleagues against him, saying that "he was always a divisive factor in our movement." After the Congress, Ben-Gurion argued in Mapai's Central Committee that the London office lacked an "Eretz-Israeli, Zionist climate" and that "if political action is undertaken without the sense of Jewish independence, it [the London office] is liable to become a stumbling block." This dart was aimed at Weizmann, and had probably been at least partly inspired by Weizmann's closing his home in London and taking up residence in a suite at the luxurious Dorchester Hotel. Perhaps Ben-Gurion thought that the Dorchester's ambience had influenced Weizmann's optimistic November 1939 forecast that "this war will not last long."

As ever, Ben-Gurion saw Weizmann as a "tool," capable, under certain circumstances, of moving mountains, "but a tool whose capacity for work, value, and direction depends on a guiding hand." In this case, however, it seems that the "guiding hand" was forced to go to London so that Weizmann could lead him back into his office. On April 25

Ben-Gurion left Haifa for London via Paris, arriving on May 1, 1940. On his return in February 1941 he was to tell the JAE, "I left Palestine . . . for ten days, and was gone . . . ten months." These months — during which the war spread to the Middle East as well as Britain — were among the most exhilarating in his personal life, but the most frustrating of his political career.

Paris was still peaceful, and Ben-Gurion, in high spirits, could browse through bookstores, picking up volumes on military affairs, history, and philosophy. In London he stayed, as usual, at the Mount Royal Hotel and by May 2 had already taken part in a meeting at the Zionist office. Weizmann, in the chair, opposed one by one his arguments for a policy of more "active" resistance and in the debate that developed all supported Weizmann, leaving Ben-Gurion in total isolation. However, as Dugdale noted with satisfaction, Ben-Gurion and Weizmann spoke "with utmost dignity and feeling of responsibility," and therefore, it seemed, although "Ben-Gurion wants to resign from the Executive," hope grew that "we can dissuade him."

"On each of the six days I've been here we held long meetings, and the debate is still not over," Ben-Gurion wrote Paula, but added, "I am satisfied with my visit. We didn't agree on everything here, but I found more understanding, concern, and independence than I expected. Outside the general meeting I had two private talks with Chaim. On several matters we are at variance, but the distance is much smaller than that between myself and some of the colleagues in Jerusalem (and T.A.)." Weizmann had recently returned from a visit to the United States, his first in years. Having "rediscovered" America, as Ben-Gurion put it, he planned to return for a more extensive visit in five or six weeks. Pleased by this, Ben-Gurion wrote Paula, "As for the plan of action in America, we reached a nearly complete understanding."[3]

However, in the end understanding proved elusive; the differences between them hardened and also leaked out, gaining increasing attention from the British secret service and air time on Radio Berlin's broadcasts in Arabic. But even this indirect external pressure could not bring them to any agreement; the hope that Ben-Gurion would come back into harness evaporated, and he expected to return to Palestine as soon as possible. "I saw no reason to extend my stay in London," he said. Nevertheless, whether because he still hoped to get Weizmann to accept his policy of resistance or because no honorable way to retract his resignation had been found, he did not seem delighted by the prospect of returning home. But then, as if in answer to his prayers, a major event altered the entire situation overnight, justifying his remaining in London. On May 10 the Chamberlain government fell; it was replaced by the coalition government headed by Churchill, which seemed to open a new phase in the battle to raise a Jewish fighting force.

The hope of participating in the war was rekindled, for the so-called friends of Zionism and its enterprise in Palestine were among the new government's central figures: the Conservative Winston Churchill, prime minister and minister of defense and considered a personal friend of Weizmann, who had reiterated his enthusiastic support of the Jewish army idea; from the Labour Party, Lord Privy Seal Clement Attlee, Minister of Labour Ernest Bevin who in 1930 had had a hand in the MacDonald Letter, and Minister of Supply Herbert Morrison; the Liberal Secretary for Air Sir Archibald Sinclair, another friend of Weizmann's; and last but not least, Lord Lloyd, MacDonald's replacement at the Colonial Office and the one British statesman with whom Ben-Gurion had struck up a friendship. This stroke of luck caused Weizmann to put off his trip to the United States and Ben-Gurion to extend his stay in London. On May 14 he cabled Paula, "Under changed conditions must stay longer than intended inform Sharett."[4]

At first Ben-Gurion regarded the new government with caution and reserve. In a congratulatory letter to Lloyd on May 13, he wrote, "There are in Palestine now tens of thousands of young Jews who are eager to fight as the devoted allies of Britain. . . . All our technical, economic, and scientific resources . . . will gladly be placed at the disposal of the British Government if and when required. I pray that under your guidance a new chapter may be opened in our relations with H.M. Government, a chapter of sincere and helpful cooperation." But he was not certain his prayer would be answered, and on May 14 he wrote Paula that although "better conditions have been created . . . we must be watchful." Similarly, on May 31 he wrote the JAE that there had been a "change for the better," and that "now there is a listening ear, even in the Colonial Office there is someone we can talk to, [but] in fact nothing whatsoever has changed, and I am not sure anything will change soon, [since] the key people have their concerns . . . and carry a serious and awesome burden, and will not be easily able to turn to our affairs, which in comparison to what is going on in France now, seem third and fourth priority." Most important, White Paper policy had not been altered in the slightest. Only several months later did Ben-Gurion write in his diary, "Never before was there a prime minister more capable and inclined to understand us, never before have there been in an English government better and more sincere friends."

As he explained to himself and others, Ben-Gurion decided to stay in London to assist in "raising a Jewish army in and for Palestine." He regarded this as "the only important task we have at this moment . . . and as long as there is any chance that it can be accomplished, I feel I have no right to leave this battle." The chance arose from Churchill's having agreed in principle to a Jewish army in Palestine, but a "battle" was still needed to overcome the opposition and obstacles presented by Anthony Eden (in the War Office), Lord Halifax (in the Foreign Office), and Lord Lloyd (in the Colonial Office), who, despite his friendship with Ben-Gurion, remained solidly pro-Arab and anti-Zionist. To Ben-Gurion these three secretaries and their senior civil service staff were like a "wall" that had to be broken down, and he intended to remain in London until this was accomplished or he became convinced that "there is no hope."

Under the influence of this new prospect, Weizmann and Ben-Gurion cooperated. On May 12 Weizmann published in *The Times* a public proclamation on the will and readiness of the Jewish people to assist Britain as a nation that included a slogan created by Ben-Gurion: "The Jews will be allowed to fight as a nation." Weizmann also renewed to Field Marshal John Dill, chief of the imperial general staff, a proposal that had been rejected by Chamberlain's government, based on the plan sketched by Ben-Gurion during his visits to the United States in 1938 and 1939: the Yishuv would offer fifty thousand volunteers, to whom the JAE would add Jewish volunteers from the United States, Canada, and South Africa and from among the refugees of Europe. The JAE would also supply professional manpower — doctors, chemists, and engineers — for technical units, while the Yishuv would develop a war industry to aid the British war effort.

On May 15 Weizmann invited Ben-Gurion to accompany him to an interview with Lord Lloyd in the Colonial Office. Ben-Gurion — who despite his friendship with Lloyd could not have gone alone on official business without Weizmann's assent — imagined that Weizmann, pleased that he had stayed in London, was sharing personal and political contacts with him in a combined effort to break down the wall. But within a short time their relations deteriorated, and both realized once again that they were not made to work in tandem. As usual, more than one reason lay behind this latest breach.[5]

First of all, at this period before the Holocaust became known, Weizmann saw the Second World War as a repeat performance, on a greater scale, of the First World War. He believed that the same means that had enabled him to bring about the Balfour Declaration would enable him to achieve a greater feat: if not a state, at least the repeal of the White Paper and the building of the longed-for Jewish force. As in 1914–1917, it seemed briefly in 1940 as though Britain needed Weizmann's talents as a chemical inventor and especially as an unsurpassed shaper of public opinion who could obtain increased American support. This time, too, a revolutionary Weizmann invention* might speed the Allied victory; in December 1939 Ben-Gurion had told Mapai's Central Committee that "the issue here is his chemical invention, of great value to the war effort. If this invention has worth — and in the opinion of experts it does — we will have our quid pro quo . . . political benefit."

Even greater political gain was anticipated from Weizmann's second talent. In June, Churchill asked Weizmann to go to the United States as soon as possible to build support for Britain among Jews who could then influence public opinion at large. "Such a request, at such a time," Weizmann answered, "is equivalent to a command." But he set a condition: for such a mission to be successful he would first need Britain's consent to a fighting Jewish force as proof that it valued the Jewish effort. This mission strengthened Weizmann's position not only with the British, but most of all among the Zionist leadership, at a time when he and Ben-Gurion were the chief protagonists in a controversy over how the Jewish force should be structured and deployed.

The second reason for the break between Weizmann and Ben-Gurion was that the concern for the existence of the Yishuv, which motivated everything Ben-Gurion did, was only secondary for Weizmann. Since the outbreak of the war two nightmares had vied for preeminence in Ben-Gurion's mind: the fear that the pro-Nazi position of the Arab national movement in Palestine (bordering on admiration for Hitler), manifested by the strengthening alliance between Hitler and the mufti, would spread through the entire Middle East and prompt the Arabs to attack the Yishuv while Britain was engaged in a battle for its own life; and the fear that Axis armed forces would invade Palestine. Either of these possibilities was bound to result in the destruction of the Yishuv. Ben-Gurion therefore concluded, in November 1939, that if a Jewish army was not raised soon the days of the Yishuv were numbered. May, familiar with his state of mind, wrote Arthur Lourie in late August 1940 that "[David] is very depressed, convinced [Eretz Israel] is doomed, and chafing to get home. . . . I do hope he . . . gets home safely, (and finds a home to get to, when he *does* get there!) Myself, I think that if his gloomy forebodings are right, he's already too late to get home at all." Within a year Ben-Gurion was proved correct: in 1940 the British army was defeated on the western front and England was laid open to German invasion by sea and by air; in the spring of 1941 a pro-Nazi rebellion broke out in Iraq under the leader-

---

* This was a process called aromatization, a sort of catalytic cracking of heavy oil leading to higher yields of benzine, toluene, and so forth, developed at the Weizmann Institute in Rehovot. It was eventually rejected.

ship of Rashid Ali; in the summer of that year Germany established a
bridgehead in Syria; and from a base in Italian-controlled Libya the
Axis armies moved through the Western Desert toward Egypt. The Yishuv, threatened with encirclement and destruction, had to depend on
a Jewish fighting force for its defense.[6]

Weizmann's approach to the Jewish force was vastly different. In
November 1939 he interpreted the sympathy shown to the idea by
Chief of the Imperial General Staff Field Marshal William Ironside to
mean that he had the force in his pocket. Believing that the Zionists
had to act quickly and strike while the iron was hot, Ben-Gurion demanded that the JAE publicly propose to the British government that a
brigade be mobilized in the Yishuv and sent into action immediately
wherever it was needed. He dispatched Berl Locker to Jerusalem to
report that "Chaim's star is rising in government circles. We are close
to Foreign and War offices. The chief of staff gives his absolute pledge
that he will raise a Jewish army." But this report, said Ben-Gurion,
only made him want to see what was going on at first hand, to save
himself and his colleagues from "the pleasures of a fool's paradise." He
saw a great gulf between the optimism in London and the reality in
Jerusalem and thought that "the good spirits in London are liable to
prove our downfall." This had been an additional reason for his November 1939 visit to London.

Weizmann held to the same position even after the Churchill government took power. It is safe to say that, in the face of the obstacles
created by Eden, Halifax, and Lloyd to raising Jewish units — and considering that his primary objective was the renewal of the British-
Zionist alliance of old — Weizmann would have been satisfied with
Britain's consent to any Jewish fighting force. From his perspective it
was inconsequential whether the force was recruited from the Yishuv
or the United States and other countries; he did not care where it was
stationed, as long as its officers were all members of the Yishuv, to guarantee its Zionist character.

By contrast, Ben-Gurion saw a dual problem. Although he never
made his position completely clear, it seems to have been that since the
Jews had the right and the obligation to take part in both the defense of
Palestine and the war against Hitler, they had to make a double demand. The primary one was the creation of a Jewish military force in
Palestine, to be stationed on its frontiers or somewhere in the Middle
East, for the purpose of defending Palestine. This position did not lack
contradictions. Ben-Gurion admitted that raising a Jewish division in
Palestine would incite "an Arab revolution," the last thing that Britain
wanted. He also argued forcefully that it was the right of the Jewish
people to fight Nazi Germany as a nation among others. He was con-

sumed by "the moral necessity of taking part in the destruction of this preying beast which has persecuted the Jewish people for seven years and wishes to destroy them with no conditions or restrictions." But Ben-Gurion never specified the connection that would exist between the two forces or how they were to be raised and deployed. Only his priorities were unquestionably defined: the Jewish army for the defense of Palestine was to be raised first.

The vague nature of this controversy was probably at least in part the result of Ben-Gurion's fierce jealousy, which made him contradict Weizmann simply for the sake of contradiction. He, who saw past the formidable obstacles to the certain, short path to the state and was sure of his ability to lead Zionism along it, was not the man in charge. Was it not simply human for Ben-Gurion to be consumed by jealousy when he knew with every bone in his body that the state was within arm's reach and saw fate choose another to deliver it to the Jewish people?

At times during the battle for the Jewish army, Ben-Gurion seemed to take positions opposed to Weizmann's only to catch him in a mistake and prove that he had to take him to meetings, heed his advice, and submit to his supervision. But why should Weizmann share this great privilege to make history with him? What was to prevent the man who had laid the cornerstone for the state in World War I from calling the crowning glory of its formation following World War II his own? Did such a man need the advice or surveillance of Ben-Gurion? Indeed, the more Ben-Gurion tried to guide him with advice and criticism, the more Weizmann saw him as a pest and a bother and kept his contacts close to his chest. From his arrival in May until Ben-Gurion left London for the United States on September 21, his entire diplomatic activity consisted of two meetings with Lloyd in Weizmann's company, two private meetings with Lloyd — one to say good-bye — and one meeting with Dudley Danby, Lloyd's private secretary. He found himself distanced and isolated more and more, and for perhaps the first time in his public life he had an abundance of free time on his hands.[7]

Ben-Gurion learned soon after his arrival in London that Weizmann was not going to let him share his diplomatic work, so to occupy himself he set about to acquire a basic understanding of ancient Greek. His diary records that a friend at Oxford taught him the alphabet, and after buying a textbook for beginners and a Greek-English dictionary, he began teaching himself the language on May 19. He was soon buying and reading books, including the Septuagint translation of Genesis; chapters of Plato's *Republic*; five quarto volumes of Aristotle; *Outlines of Pyrrhonism* by Sextus Empiricus; parts of the *Meditations* of Marcus

Aurelius; the first part of Homer's *Iliad*; and a number of others. With the help of the dictionary he translated several poems of Sappho and Anacreon into Hebrew. In the first two months he was very pleased with himself and thought that he had Greek in the palm of his hand, but then he realized that he knew very little, "and that the task is not easy." But he was resolved to continue his independent study until he could read Aristotle fluently, without the aid of a dictionary. On the evening of September 26 he began reading the second-century B.C.E. *Wisdom of Ben Sira (Ecclesiasticus)* of Jerusalem. To test himself he translated it into Hebrew and checked his work with the dictionary.[8]

However, his diary systematically conceals the help he received from May, probably to allay the suspicions of the ever-watchful Paula. They had continued to be very fond of each other. A few days after the war began May had written to apologize for leaving the Geneva Zionist Congress without saying good-bye, "And now who knows when I'll see you again?" After describing a bleak London at war she closed, "Good-night, my dear, my love to you, as always, D." She wrote her initial in Hebrew. It is safe to assume that they were very happy to see each other when he arrived in London and spent as much time as possible in each other's company. Ben-Gurion invited her to see G. B. Shaw's *The Devil's Disciple,* one of the few plays he attended in his life.

It was also May who introduced him to the "friend at Oxford," Chaim Raphael, a lecturer in post biblical Hebrew, author, and civil servant, whom she wished to recruit for the Zionist office; it was she who lent him the Greek grammar for beginners, and it was with her that he read Genesis and other books. Thanks to her classical education, their friendship took on a dimension that strengthened it. Her detailed letters to Arthur Lourie, her long-time friend and colleague in the Zionist office, who had been transferred to New York and offered his home in Maida Vale to Ben-Gurion, offer a humorous picture of their relationship between May and September 1940, the period of the Battle of Britain and the great air raids.

On June 11, May introduced Ben-Gurion to the renowned Blackwell bookshop at Oxford. They were supposed to take the 6:30 A.M. train to Oxford, but when she arrived at Paddington Station at 6:25 he was not there. Unable to find a taxi, he had taken a subway to the wrong station. They finally took the 9:15 train, standing for two hours. "I confess," May wrote to Lourie, "I had not fully appreciated the results of introducing David to Blackwell's." At 11:30 she "parked him in the Classics section" on the second floor and went off to sit "among the modern poets" on the ground floor to give her feet a rest, "skimming happily" through her favorites. At 1:30, wondering what had happened to her friend, she "found him in Bay 2 of Classics (there are six bays) with a step-ladder, an impressed assistant, and an imposing pile of classical education rising rapidly on the floor beneath him!" It took her "some five minutes to catch his eye," and when she did, "he said plaintively that he was 'tired and hungry.' " Telling the assistant that he would be "back in half an hour," he grabbed May and "charged out into the street, ejaculating in high spirits: ' . . . Why did you never *tell* me about this bookshop?' 'It is the bookshop of my dreams.' " After a quick bite they returned to Blackwell's; Ben-Gurion wandered with his stepladder into the Foreign Department on the first floor where, at 5:30, "he hailed with delight the Collection des Universités de France [classical texts interleaved with a French translation]." During this visit Ben-Gurion bought books that amounted to £15, a third of his monthly salary. They returned to London "in silence . . . dog-tired," and parted at Paddington Station. In the next three days Ben-Gurion made May phone Blackwell's three times to ask about the delivery of his books.

May also took Ben-Gurion to an ophthalmologist for an examination, since "his eyes," she wrote Lourie, "are protesting, at long last, against perpetual study of Greek texts in bed: he admits, he doesn't sleep well and often reads till 3 or 4 A.M. . . . What can one do with a man like that?" The doctor made up two pairs of eyeglasses for him, one for reading and the other for the street. As if to return her attentions, Ben-Gurion noticed her new permanent, expressing his disgust. The "poor dear," she wrote, "is still under the impression that he dislikes any suggestion of artificiality!"

Hilda, the Louries' housekeeper, had stayed on, so Ben-Gurion was able to entertain his friends, writing Paula of the luncheon he had given at "his" home for Dugdale and Berl Locker and his wife. But he did not write her that on June 23 he had invited May to dinner.[9]

May visited Ben-Gurion at least twice more. In a letter of September 2 she related how, while she was waiting "to take dinner and some final instructions from David," the sirens began. It was after 9:00 P.M. and the antiaircraft guns were roaring. She rose to leave and Ben-Gurion insisted on accompanying her to the underground station, but while they argued this point at the doorstep a passing warden ordered them to go back inside at once and take cover. Her second attempt to leave also failed, the same warden still being on watch, and she agreed to stay the night. She described that night "of Victorian domesticity" to Lourie: "David at your desk, muttering gently to himself over the *Iliad* and a Greek dictionary, self in armchair knitting winter vest; Hilda hovering watchfully between kitchen and radio — and producing tea punctually at ten P.M. . . . After which, silence descended, broken only by David's murmurings, and the distant woof-woof of the AA barrage."

Thus passed the minutes until midnight, when Ben-Gurion "suddenly awakes to his 'social responsibilities' and startles me by saying abruptly: 'Shall we read a chapter of St. John?' We do; reading the Greek — as in my youth — verse by verse, antiphonally." It was the story of the miracle at Cana, the village neighboring Sejera, about which Ben-Gurion had often reminisced to her. As he told her the Hebrew words for the Greek spoken in the Gospel, May stole a glance at him and wondered "when — if ever — these eyes will look again at Cana's clustering red roofs." Then, saying "I always read a few words of Marcus Aurelius before I go to bed," Ben-Gurion began reading to her from the passage in which Aurelius adjures the reader "to remember, on rising each morning, that this day you will meet with the fool, the charlatan, the arrogant and boastful man, the liar, the idler, etc., etc. . . . but that they are as God made them; it is not their fault but their misfortune; to you has been given wisdom — not to judge them at all but to be patient."

May asked if he had chosen this passage with certain colleagues in the Zionist office in mind, but Ben-Gurion denied it, saying that was simply where he had stopped the night before. At length it was time for bed: "And so — for the second time in a week — to the inappropriate promiscuity of your bed, and D's pyjamas!" When she awoke at 7:30 the next morning, Hilda told her that a "whistling bomb" had fallen in one of the back gardens opposite, and that the wardens had waked all the neighbors at 4:00 A.M. looking for it. Ben-Gurion said he had been "waked by some knocking somewhere but had gone to sleep again." "David is a darling to have around in air raids," May also wrote. "He takes it so beautifully" and was among the few who never went down to the shelters. In general, even "at his worst he's still a nice person." He had captured Hilda's heart, May added, and she missed him quite a bit after he left.

The study of Greek reawakened Ben-Gurion's bibliomania, and it reached unprecedented heights. Ben-Gurion began the wholesale buying of classics from catalogues, and May, groaning beneath this new burden, supervised the purchase and delivery. The list of classics in his library fills sixty typewritten, double-spaced folio pages. Two Greek quotations were always displayed beneath the plate glass covering of his desk. One was from Plato: "Therefore we ought to try to escape from earth to the dwelling of the gods as quickly as we can; and to escape is to become like God, so far as this is possible; and to become like God is to become righteous and holy and wise." The other was a popular proverb that Ben-Gurion chose for a guideline: "With brave men, the fortress is secure."

Ben-Gurion's interest in Greek language and literature worked its way into his diplomatic activity during the summer of 1940, curtailed though that was. In particular he discussed his interest at length with Dudley Danby, who had once worked as a teacher in Greece. Danby remembered that in their first meeting they "talked mainly about Greece — ancient and modern." Together they made lists of ancient Greek words and their modern equivalents. "His studies were, I believe, more than just a diversion from his work. He had really got interested in ancient Greece and he speculated on the possibilities of how far some of the Greek ideals could become those of a future homeland/state. . . . In a peculiar way Judaism had got mixed up with Hellenism."[10]

Ben-Gurion maintained that studying Greek brought him a double relief that he had not anticipated: "The Greek classics made me forget two troubles: the enemy airplanes and the failings of Great Russell Street." It is easy to tell which of these two was the more trying; not only did the air raids over London hardly seem to bother him, but he actually enjoyed this opportunity to see the war close up and live this extraordinary experience to the fullest. He listened equally to Radio Berlin and Radio Rome as Norway, the Low Countries, and France fell one by one. Regarding as a supreme test the stance of the British in the months when invasion seemed imminent, he identified with them, since even in this fateful hour they had not turned their backs on democracy but replaced the Chamberlain government with one which was "committed to triumph." He followed the British retreat and rescue operation at Dunkirk and admired the nation's perseverance in fighting until victory even when it remained alone in the war.

After a month in London, he wrote Paula, "As it happens I was called here during days that will not quickly be forgotten by history." On July 1, he added, "I know of no other two months in history reminiscent of these." His identification with the British stand made the sounds of war seem like music in his ears. "No concert or chorus in Palestine gave such pleasure as the thunder of the guns that shake the four walls of my room for hours on end," he wrote Paula from the Mount Royal. On September 11, at Lourie's home, he reported in his diary, "Tonight the guns thundered like never before. From eight until two (though I fell asleep and heard nothing until this morning) the thunder and lightning never paused. The house shook to its foundation — but it was nice to know that the guns were greeting the emissaries" of the devil. "Now it is a quarter after eight, and the 'chorus' has begun," was the mode in which he opened many of his letters to Paula. "I estimate that it will last, as usual of late, until dawn. But I almost never hear it after one or at the latest two in the morning, since by then I am restfully sleeping." If May was surprised by his calm during the air raids — "I envy that man his ability to concentrate," she wrote Lourie after seeing him study Greek grammar during the din — Ben-Gurion, for his part, admired the phlegm of the English. During his visit to the United States he praised their cold-blooded courage with admiration bordering on amazement, and on his return to Palestine praised them profusely in press conferences, speeches, and articles. "Not only did I love London, but London became sacred for me . . . It is the noblest of man's visions, expressing man's greatness and moral beauty. . . . I saw the sublime in man."

On a Sunday he accompanied Dugdale to a church designed by her architect father and constructed on the ruins of the first Church of Scotland in London, which had been built for James I. "Outside the guns roared," wrote Ben-Gurion afterward, "and the explosion of bombs was heard (when we left we learned that a Nazi plane had fallen not far from there), but the vicar didn't seem to hear anything of what was going on outside, and the congregation did not stir. After the sermon various hymns were sung — quietly, calmly, and as if nothing had happened — and when the service ended at the scheduled time, the congregation tranquilly went their separate ways." After church they went for a walk and in passing a train station were told matter-of-factly that "a Nazi plane has just been shot down in the station yard." Throughout their walk the guns continued to roar "until we got home — to Baffy's house, for lunch."[11]

The Greek classics, however, did not really make Ben-Gurion forget the "aggravations of the Zionist office." His anguish over the danger he foresaw for the Yishuv focused on Weizmann, and the longer he stayed in London the more angry and jealous he became. Overestimating the importance of the proponents of the Jewish fighting force, led by Churchill, and underestimating the importance of its opponents, led by Lloyd, Eden, and Halifax, Ben-Gurion blamed Weizmann's characteristic "light-mindedness" and irresponsibility for the failure to obtain government consent to raising the force. Churchill welcomed the JAE's proposal mainly because he feared a German invasion. He thought that Palestine's Jews could be armed and trained rapidly to replace most of the infantry battalions that had been garrisoned in Palestine since the Arab revolt, allowing these to be transferred to the home front. On May 23 he therefore instructed Lloyd to issue the Jews arms for self-defense and to organize them in military formations.

But Lloyd, who was convinced that, in return for military support, the Zionists would claim Palestine for a Jewish state, insisted that no action conducive to the creation of a Jewish force or in contravention of the White Paper be taken. Despite interventions by Churchill, he managed to scuttle the force through his ally General Haining, who had become vice chief of the imperial general staff. After a talk on July 15, Weizmann reported that Haining had accepted the plan for training a corps of officers and that implementation could begin as soon as Field Marshal Archibald Wavell, commander in charge of the Middle East, received instructions to that effect. Weizmann cabled Sharett to start preparations. But Haining refused to send these instructions, saying only that it was his understanding that Wavell was contemplating the formation of both Jewish and Arab Palestinian units as garrison companies, but that he himself would take no further action in the matter. He stressed that any recruiting of volunteers that Weizmann intended in the United States "in no way concerned the War Office." In a telegram to Palestine Ben-Gurion notified Sharett to "ignore Weizmann's wire."[12]

This episode had ramifications for Ben-Gurion's relationship with his son as well as that with Weizmann. In September 1939, when the war broke out, nineteen-year-old Amos had answered the call for general mobilization. As a British subject by birth, Amos was eligible for any British force, including a combat unit, whereas men with Palestinian citizenship were permitted to volunteer for service units only. Amos's ambition to excel drove him to volunteer for the Royal Air Force. Paula liked the idea of Amos as a pilot in this prestigious service, and with her support he registered at the recruiting office without Ben-Gurion's knowledge. When he was turned down, Paula asked David Hacohen, the central liaison between the Yishuv and the British army, to intervene. He promised Amos a personal interview with the RAF commander in the Middle East. After a long wait, Amos began to detect his father's hand behind the delay. Ben-Gurion had always done his best to prepare Amos for service to the nation, as befitted the son of a Zionist leader. As in 1938, when he had intended to enroll Amos in a naval academy in England so he could serve in the immigration revolt, Ben-Gurion wanted to see him in the Jewish army. In his diary Ben-Gurion wrote, "Until now I have kept him from volunteering for just anything, since I anticipated a Jewish unit in Palestine."

But Amos was intent on going his own way and at his request Paula cabled Ben-Gurion in London twice, "Amos is pressing for immediate instruction." On June 7 Ben-Gurion wrote her a letter saying, "There has been no real change in our affairs . . . the main thing, a Jewish unit, is still up in the air." The letter was intended primarily for Amos's eyes. However, Haining's apparent acceptance seemed to open the gates of heaven to Amos, and on July 16 — a day after receiving Weizmann's cable — Sharett cabled Ben-Gurion, "Paula asks your opinion on Amos. He wants to be a pilot. As a British subject by birth he is perfectly qualified, although if they agree to recruit him hc will have to undergo tests. The general mobilization for aviation for citizens of Palestine is for land service — drivers, mechanics, etc. Wire." When Haining's true attitude was revealed, Ben-Gurion, to Amos's grief, returned to his first position. On July 19 he wired Sharett, "Against Amos's present design. Await decision on main issue." But in early August Ben-Gurion received another cable from the Political Department in Jerusalem: "Amos firm original intention, unless you cable him otherwise." Ben-Gurion again replied, "Please tell Amos to await my return." Amos went on banging on the recruiting office door in vain.[13]

As for Ben-Gurion's relationship with Weizmann, the Haining episode seemed to prove his old claim that Weizmann lacked the statesman's knack for negotiations and that his understanding of a situation and reporting on it were not trustworthy. On July 28 Ben-Gurion "burst out . . . against Chaim's policy," as Dugdale put it, notifying her and Lewis Namier that he would not take part in any more meetings at the London office and would return to Palestine at the first opportunity. From then on Ben-Gurion limited his participation in the Zionist office's work to writing memos and letters to Weizmann and his aides, most of which he dictated to May. Since her job was not merely technical — aside from rendering documents into excellent English she made a significant contribution to their content — and her status not that of a secretary but that of a good friend and adviser, privy to many secrets, she was in a delicate position.

The extent to which she was cognizant of the ins and outs of the personal relationships within the JAE and understood Ben-Gurion's true feelings about his colleagues is manifest in a letter to Lourie about a memorial service held by the JAE for Vladimir Jabotinsky, who had died on August 4 in New York State. Ben-Gurion, who attended alongside Weizmann, spoke of Jabotinsky as a personal friend and political opponent. Berl Locker regarded this as a betrayal of principles, she wrote, and "quite fails to understand that [Ben-Gurion] will *not* be insincere in paying tribute to Jabotinsky's memory." The more the Weizmann–Ben-Gurion relationship deteriorated, the more May was obliged, in keeping with her values, to draw a line between her feelings for Ben-Gurion and her duty and loyalty as personal secretary to Weizmann, for whom she also had affection and admiration. The line, fine from the start, became more so after the summer of 1940. She seems to have found it hard to contain her growing tension, and sought an outlet by sharing it with Lourie. Her letters show clearly that she, too, mistrusted Weizmann's report on his July 15 talk with Haining, describing it as "a bit too optimistic"; whereas she considered a memo

Ben-Gurion dictated to her on July 17 for a meeting the next day between Weizmann and Halifax to be "admirable," adding that Halifax
thought so too. She was also impressed by Ben-Gurion's English, particularly its concision. "He is one of the few foreigners who manage to
escape verbosity." After Ben-Gurion and Weizmann had separate
meetings with Lloyd, May wrote Lourie that they "continue to bring
back diametrically opposed reports" on the prospects of raising a Jewish force.[14]

Although at first Weizmann ignored Ben-Gurion's "boycott" of the
meetings, by August 19 he found it necessary to refer to it, in a letter
dictated, naturally, to May. "Dear Ben-Gurion, I understand that you
will soon be travelling to Palestine via America. I therefore find it necessary to ask you to participate in an Executive meeting as soon as possible. Weizmann." Ben-Gurion agreed. At the meeting, held on August
21, he was asked to support a plan proposed by Ernest Bevin, who was
thought to be friendly to Zionism and had been recruited to the effort
to break down the wall. Having almost total control over British manpower, Bevin had an interest in anything that would increase the country's manpower reserves and hence in the replacement of the British
garrison in Palestine with a Jewish force. Bevin had proposed that the
Jewish volunteers who exceeded the number of Arab volunteers for
service in the Palestine units (the Colonial Office insisted that equal
numbers of Jews and Arabs serve in separate Jewish and Arab units in
Palestine) be sent for training to Egypt or anywhere else in the Middle
East. Ben-Gurion agreed to this plan, and for a time it seemed that a
thaw had set in not only in the Weizmann–Ben-Gurion relationship,
but also in the matter of the Jewish force.

But it was not so. The wall began to undermine the new plan too. On
September 3 Weizmann had lunch with Churchill at 10 Downing
Street and received his enthusiastic consent to five proposals involving
the formation of Jewish combat units in Palestine, the Western Desert
(the idea of Colonel Orde Wingate), and Britain. Still, however, the
wall blocked the way. Eden summoned Weizmann for a talk on September 9, for which Haining had outlined a series of arguments against
the Churchill-backed plans. Feverish consultations were held in the
Zionist office, the most significant of which was on the morning of September 9, in preparation for the important meeting that day with
Eden.[15]

Ben-Gurion, well aware of all that was happening, maintained his
boycott and stayed away from the consultations in the Zionist office.
Weizmann paid him back in kind by not reporting to him directly, and
Ben-Gurion refused to hear any secondhand reporting from Namier.
May, who thought this refusal justified, nevertheless wrote Lourie, "I

do wish D. had been behaving better lately." On September 6 Dugdale observed in her diary: "David Ben-Gurion still behaving like
Achilles and boycotting the [meetings] for no ascertainable reason."
The same day May wrote Lourie that even though things seemed to
be moving in the right direction, "David is simmering over with barely
suppressed indignation against Ch., and Ch. is peevish and nervy
about David." Ben-Gurion, who was "a darling," was now also like a
"fretful porcupine. . . . I've spiked myself on the quills several times
lately!" One night he made her listen to a tirade against Weizmann
until she "got stuck, because by the time D. had got through, the
AA barrage had started good and proper. . . . The outpouring took
the form of a long and confused 'j'accuse' letter," which "totally
failed to make clear, at least to me, what he is really so distressed
about — other than the fact that Ch. is what we all know he is, and
prefers to govern by 'boudoir.' This is no news to D. or anyone else,
and why he has to burst out *now*, when things are just beginning to
move, I can't imagine."

May did her best to soothe Ben-Gurion and managed to stop him
from sending his tirade to Weizmann; it was buried in his diary. He did
send Weizmann another and, she wrote, she might "have toned it
down too much. . . . I'm afraid D. is finding me a good deal of a broken
reed, these days, for I can't conceal that I think he's not behaving at all
well." She thought that if only Weizmann took "a little more *trouble*
over him," they could straighten things out, since "D. is terribly susceptible to the famous charm, in spite of himself." However, Weizmann was "in no mood to take trouble over anyone just now, and over
David least of all." She felt sorry for him. "I hate to see D. making
himself miserable, and getting himself hated all round. And there isn't
a darn thing I can do about it!" When Weizmann noticed Ben-Gurion's
absence from the meeting of September 9, he sent him the following
letter:

My dear Ben-Gurion,
    I was very much surprised not to see you here today when we had a dis-
cussion preliminary to my seeing the Secretary for War and the Chief of
Imperial General Staff.
    You will remember that you asked me for an opportunity of discussing
these matters, and I replied that I was prepared to have such a discussion.
. . . I asked Miss May to ring you up and say we had better leave our talk
until after the appointment with Dill was actually fixed — not, as you
seem to have understood, until after the interview. . . . I asked Miss May
to inform you that we would be having a meeting at 12.15, and I would
have liked also to have a discussion with you personally — in fact I was
holding myself free for it.

Ben-Gurion replied the same day, in a letter dictated to May, which she also "toned down."

Thank-you . . . I am really sorry that among your anxious pre-occupations at present, you should have been worried about such matters. I hope to be able to leave London very soon, and in case I should not see you again here, I would like to take this opportunity of wishing you a heart-felt godspeed. It is no mere courtesy when I say that all I wish you is every success in your work. I shall always be ready to give whatever help I can, whenever my assistance should be required, and wherever I may happen to be.

Ben-Gurion regarded this as a friendly letter of farewell, from which Weizmann "should have understood that I have no intention of seeing him ever again." He later explained his terrible rage at Weizmann — which to his colleagues appeared rather sudden — as a consequence of two events that took place on September 9. The first was the Italian air raid on Tel Aviv, in which 127 people were killed. To Ben-Gurion this meant that the Yishuv was paying the price for being allied with Britain without receiving in exchange the opportunity to raise an army for its defense. In his diary he wrote that the raid "seemed to come as 'compensation' for the diligent attention [Weizmann's, of course] to the question of the Yishuv's defense." The other was Weizmann's interview with Eden and Field Marshal Dill, in which Weizmann again brought up the idea of a desert force, as well as other subjects in which he was not well versed, instead of exploiting the momentum Churchill had provided for the military force to defend Palestine. On September 10, reading Weizmann's report on this interview, Ben-Gurion wrote in his diary, "I was stunned. After we actually had Churchill's consent on the main points of our military demands, he went to Eden confused with Orde's new idea, and instead of discussing our Jewish demands, baffled Eden with Orde's strategic idea, which he hadn't digested, as if it was his job to decide what the Jewish army (which still doesn't exist!) will do, instead of demanding that there be one."

Nevertheless Ben-Gurion decided to see Weizmann one more time. On the morning of September 11 he walked into Weizmann's office and said, "I was about to depart — now I want to stay here, if you will agree to my demand not to speak to anyone about the Haganah and the Jewish army, and not to conduct any negotiations whatsoever without my participation and consent." Weizmann asked "what brought on" this demand. "Two things: your interview with Eden" and the bombing of Tel Aviv, Ben-Gurion replied, and explained to him "the mistake you made . . . in the talk with Eden." Weizmann protested. "Throughout I wanted you to take part but you refrained." And Ben-Gurion retorted, "I have no desire to waste time discussing the past, and am prepared to take all the blame upon myself. What interests me now is the future." Weizmann "said he concurred, and tomorrow morning there will be a meeting." Ben-Gurion recorded all this in his diary on September 11, without realizing that he had confused the chronology and revealed the true motive behind his "letter of farewell."

Ben-Gurion's simmering rage had been apparent to Dugdale and May on September 6, before the two events. The silent vow not to see Weizmann again was the fruit of Ben-Gurion's anger at not sharing Weizmann's contacts with the government and military leaders. But his pride would not allow Ben-Gurion to offer this wholly personal explanation for so extreme a reaction. He must have realized that this was a lame excuse, and in his diary attempted to reinforce it, at least in his own eyes.

> I knew throughout these last four months that he doesn't understand the situation, is incapable of conducting any serious political negotiations whatsoever, and lacks the expertise and understanding necessary to discuss the Yishuv's defense. But I had no idea he would display such light-mindedness and irresponsibility. We have never had such a justifiable demand as that for a Jewish army in Palestine (and abroad), never have the objective circumstances been so favorable to us, never has there been a prime minister more capable and inclined to understand us, never was an English cabinet made up of better and truer friends (along with a number of opponents and enemies) — and a special "talent" is needed to lose the battle under these conditions. Chaim, apparently, has this talent.[16]

Ben-Gurion was happy to encounter Locker after leaving Weizmann, because by telling him of their talk he acquired a witness to Weizmann's consent to his demand. However, the true worth of this consent soon became clear, since while they were talking Weizmann phoned Danby to make a lunch date for the next day, without a word to Ben-Gurion. Ben-Gurion noted this in his diary, adding, "He is used to words being nothing but words. Either he doesn't make a move without me on matters of the Haganah and the army, or he'll never see my face."

May, who heard about their conversation from both of them, wrote Lourie that to a certain extent Ben-Gurion was right to accuse Weizmann of "being light-minded and irresponsible, and half a dozen even less complimentary adjectives," since Weizmann was "*not* giving his whole mind to this part [the Jewish army] of his work." She described the understanding they had reached as "a temporary — and I fear very fragile — truce, based on Ch.'s agreement not to see anyone without D. (can you see him doing it?)." No sooner had Ben-Gurion left the room, she continued, than Weizmann asked her to arrange a confidential and exclusive interview for him with Haining, telling her to keep quiet about it. Immediately afterward she went off to tea with Ben-Gurion, where she probably said enough for him to understand that Weizmann was not being true to his word, for he told her, "What I *won't* stand for is that he say yes and act no." If he did say this, perhaps he did not actually hear Weizmann phoning Danby, but said he had to protect his source of information. May, for her part, maintained her loyalty to Weizmann by telling Ben-Gurion only that Weizmann had invited Danby, a person of lesser rank than the vice chief of the imperial general staff, to lunch.

On the afternoon of September 11, Locker, his wife, and Dugdale had lunch with Ben-Gurion, who told them of his talk with Weizmann. He probably wanted to enlist Dugdale's influence with Weizmann to keep him to his word. "I have the impression," Ben-Gurion told Dugdale, "that Chaim gave me a positive answer all too easily, perhaps because he didn't take my position seriously." Hence he thought she should speak to him. She claimed that Ben-Gurion was being unreasonable since "[Weizmann] cannot accept such a demand," but nonetheless promised "to explain" it to Weizmann.

What Dugdale said to Weizmann was not recorded, but further developments led Ben-Gurion to conclude that, instead of water, she had thrown fat on the fire. In their talk on the morning of September 12, Weizmann was sullen and spoke with restrained anger. He had always made Ben-Gurion a party to everything, he insisted, and did not know when he had failed to do so; Weizmann then made a list of all the meetings that had taken place, crossing off all those to which he had been invited to attend alone. Finally he admitted that maybe he should have taken Ben-Gurion with him to see Halifax, but claimed that this was not reason enough for Ben-Gurion's distemper. As was his custom Weizmann complained of fatigue: he was an old man, he had worked for some forty-five years, and at the next Zionist Congress he would step down. But an ultimatum such as Ben-Gurion had given him the day before was more than he could take. Ben-Gurion argued that he had not given any ultimatum, but had merely explained "under what conditions I feel I can be at all helpful in London, since for the past four months I have seen, to my regret, that all my efforts to be of help failed." The talk ended with nothing having been accomplished.[17]

Ben-Gurion's next step is hard to explain. At his insistence, the London Political Committee was summoned to thrash out "the question of the military unit." If all he had wanted was to convince everyone that Weizmann was to blame for the Jewish army's not having been established, he did not need to have it out in this forum: in the weeks and months that followed, Ben-Gurion was to repeat this unjust accusation ceaselessly. If he had wanted to force Weizmann to include him in his contacts, it was unrealistic for him to expect support from this committee, whose definition eluded even him, since it was a group hand-picked by Weizmann that had no official status. Ben-Gurion opened the meeting by saying that "what he wished to know was whether the recruitment of Jews in Palestine, for the defence of Palestine, was still their policy. In his opinion it should be. All the more so because Egypt was being invaded [the Italian invasion from Libya had begun in early September] and because of the recent bombing of Tel Aviv . . . It was not necessary to prove to him the importance of units outside Palestine." They must, he said, demand of the government two things: (i) that Jews in Palestine be allowed to defend themselves . . . (ii) that the Jews should be given the right to fight as Jews against Hitler, irrespective of Palestine."

He himself, said Ben-Gurion, intended to go to the United States, as the main reservoir for recruitment was there, and he "would try to mobilise a Jewish unit to fight wherever the British high command might decide." But he could not possibly call on the Yishuv to join "an army not destined to fight in Palestine," on the basis of Weizmann's "impression that they would be sent to the Middle East." Before he left England, he wished "to know exactly where Dr. Weizmann stood."

Weizmann replied that had he been aware of Ben-Gurion's position, he would not have negotiated at all, and "now he felt himself to be in an intolerable position." In his opinion, it had been agreed that a Jewish army would be raised to fight wherever required, "but it was quite obvious that the authorities meant to send that army, after training, to the Middle East." As far as he could tell, "even if their men were to fight in France as a Jewish army, they would be fighting for Palestine." Here the confrontation reached its height. Ben-Gurion put forth an either-or formula — either a Jewish army to defend Palestine and a Jewish army for the war against Hitler, or nothing — and Weizmann responded with one of his own. "They had to decide whether to reject what was offered to them . . . or to take what was given them and ask for more afterward." The agreement to the principle of raising a Jewish army was in his view like the Balfour Declaration, "merely a frame into which the Jewish people had to put something which would be eternal." If Ben-Gurion was unwilling to explain this to the Jerusalem JAE and the entire Yishuv, Weizmann would go to Palestine and do it himself. Hearing this, Ben-Gurion said that he had been equally unaware that Weizmann's outlook on this issue was at variance with his, and walked out of the meeting. Weizmann vented his disgust for Ben-Gurion's behavior at lunch with Dugdale and Namier at the Dorchester.

When he read the minutes Ben-Gurion realized that unless Dugdale and Locker, who had remained silent, opened their mouths to speak against the others, who had all taken Weizmann's part, he would find himself in "splendid isolation." While he felt he could understand the others who opposed him, he could not get over how strongly Dugdale supported Weizmann. Her diary, however, shows that he was an equally bitter disappointment to her. In demanding a guarantee that the Jewish force not leave Palestine he was, she thought, "unreasonable to the utmost." By contrast, Weizmann "rose to his greatest heights in warning him that he is refusing to cooperate in the greatest hour of the Jewish people." Compared to Weizmann, Ben-Gurion offered "a sad exhibition on the part of a great and noble fellow, only he has no common sense."

For his part Ben-Gurion noted in his diary how she had let him down. "Not the spurious and insincere arguments that she tried. And not her stand that *Chaim* alone should decide on Zionist questions. This morning I learned something I never suspected: this woman has an ambition to rule Zionism by virtue of her hold over Chaim." In casting this aspersion he revealed that his quarrel with Weizmann and the bill of divorcement he had thrown in his face were to a great extent the result of a power struggle for the Zionist leadership, which was accompanied by, if not fed and nourished by, a consuming personal jealousy. Otherwise Ben-Gurion would have seen clearly that the blame for the delay in raising a Jewish army for service in any theater of war rested entirely on the White Paper policy, whose diehard supporters in the government proved more steadfast than Prime Minister Churchill. The announcement of the establishment of Jewish battalions was put off until August 1942, and not until September 1944 did the government publish its resolve to establish a Jewish combat brigade. But Ben-Gurion clung to his accusation against Weizmann as a weapon in his battle against him, in which he had nearly been defeated. With nothing to do in London, he set his sights on returning home via the United States. On September 21 he left for Liverpool, to board the ship that would take him to New York.[18]

Owing to the war, the struggle for leadership had taken an unusual turn: the Yishuv, Ben-Gurion's power base, was cut off, while London, Weizmann's base, was restored to center stage. In this situation, when it was impossible to convene the movement's supreme institutions, Weizmann was for all intents and purposes an absolute ruler, as in the days of the First World War, a situation Ben-Gurion wished with all his heart to alter. Since both he and Weizmann were agreed that a state in part of Palestine was within reach and that only with a Jewish army could it be established, the struggle between them turned into a personal contest to determine which would be the founder of the state. Although they never admitted the existence of such a competition, it is hard to believe that they were not aware of it.

There is solid evidence that Ben-Gurion was apprehensive lest Weizmann become the absolute ruler. Before his departure, he "instructed" Locker and another Eretz-Israeli, a "close aide" who had taken part in the Political Committee meeting, "to stand guard." He himself met with Weizmann for a "parting talk."

> I told him of my grave concern about the situation of our representation in London — since in effect he is all by himself, and only Lewis [Namier] is capable, to a certain extent, of evaluating political developments independently — and that Palestine will not accept Chaim's judgment if on a serious matter he sets a policy not to the liking of the Yishuv without consulting it first. Chaim asked to have someone sent from Palestine, but even if that was possible the situation wouldn't be remedied . . . A remedy is possible only if a body of independent people is formed in London to prevent Chaim from making any political commitment and talking with the government alone. . . . I see no such possibility at present; hence for the time being there is no remedy for London.

In leaving last instructions, not unlike writing a will, Ben-Gurion did not forget Amos. "I understand . . . that it is hard for him to sit with his arms folded at such a time and to wait interminably," he wrote Paula. Some headway was being made in Weizmann's negotiations with the government on recruiting volunteers in Palestine for Jewish combat units. Although Ben-Gurion claimed that from Weizmann's oral report "I couldn't tell exactly how things stood, especially with regard to the question that interests me — What will our boys do after training," be deployed in Palestine or sent to the front in Europe? — he "instructed Amos to consult with Moshe [Sharett], who knows the situation. On the basis of consultation and information he may have freedom of action."

Amos joined the eighth company of the Buffs, as the Royal East Kent Regiment was called, in December. Ben-Gurion's son-in-law, Emanuel Ben-Eliezer, who had become a father in June when Geula delivered Ben-Gurion's first grandson, Yariv, was unable to volunteer because fathers were not yet being inducted into the British army. He enlisted a year later.[19]

After passing many obstacles caused by bomb damage to the tracks, Ben-Gurion arrived in Liverpool. In the Zionist office few tears were shed at his leaving. Among those relieved at the restored tranquillity was Weizmann, who wrote his wife, "Ben-Gurion has gone off, and so — an irritant less." Not so May, who wrote him a few days after they parted as follows:

David my dear,
    You can't think what a gap you leave here. (even though you weren't so much at the office!) It's quite beastly without you — no sense of security or decency at all.
    You see there's no one here now on whom, *as a person* one can rely at all, and I feel more deserted than I can remember. . . .
    Be well my dear, and try not to worry.
                                    Much love, D. [initial in Hebrew]

If Ben-Gurion also felt forlorn, his heart was not warmed by this letter until he reached New York. He boarded the *Scotia* and spent four days on the ship before it set sail, on September 24, in a convoy. This delay seemed symbolic of the holding position he had created by his resignation and conflict with Weizmann. But — as he had proved in 1911 when he left Poale Zion to study law — his ability to bide his time was, despite a seeming contradiction in his turbulent nature, one of his more prominent characteristics. So he was able to take pleasure in an "astounding sight such as I've never seen . . . a huge armada of merchant ships coming toward us from the New World to England. I counted more than forty. No, England will not be vanquished or starved. My eyes couldn't get enough of this great and wondrous sight. I was sorry I couldn't photograph the glorious scene."[20]

42

Zionist Preacher

T HE ORIGINAL GOAL of Ben-Gurion's trip to America had been to recruit volunteers for the Jewish fighting force, to be deployed wherever the British saw fit. However, as his day of departure from London drew near, he had added others. One was to get a close look at America's Jewish community. "I want to see with my own eyes what we can expect from America in wartime," he wrote Paula in August 1940, a month before he left. "Only two groups of Jews can play an important role during the war: the Yishuv and the Americans . . . and I want to know the extent of the contribution America's Jews are prepared to make for the life of their own people."

Still another objective went beyond the Jewish community. The presidential race was on, and he was certain that Roosevelt would win by a landslide, ensuring that America would increase its aid to England, thereby increasing its political influence. "America's added material aid will lead to wider prospects for us as well. The aim of my trip to America is to study and prepare the ground for these prospects," he wrote Paula a week before his departure.

Ben-Gurion detailed one such prospect in a memo entitled "Our War Programme," which he had submitted to the London Jewish Agency Executive on September 12. He proposed that once a Jewish unit was approved by the British, an unofficial body should be set up in America — even though the United States had not yet entered the war — which, without "infringing the neutrality laws, would seek some practical means of mobilizing Jewish youth in the Americas, and of organizing large-scale military training for all services, but especially for the air force." One can only guess whether Ben-Gurion also harbored one further objective: to acquire allies among the American

Zionists, particularly Brandeis's followers, to tip the scales in his contest with Weizmann.[1]

When the *Scotia* lifted anchor Ben-Gurion believed that British approval of the Jewish troops was imminent, and he expected to be met in New York with that good news. The encouragement this belief gave him left him free to cast his mind back over his previous trips to America. In 1915 he and Itzhak Ben-Zvi had founded He-Chalutz, whose members were meant to fight beside Turkey for the defense of Palestine; in 1918 he had recruited volunteers for the Jewish Legion of the British army, with which he sailed to Palestine to assist in liberating it from the Turks. Did not his present trip prove that Zionist history repeated itself? But if Ben-Gurion imagined himself sailing from America at the head of a formation of volunteers, as in 1918, his reception in New York provided an inauspicious beginning. The two cables announcing his arrival had been delayed, so that when the ship dropped anchor on the morning of October 3, the first day of Rosh Hashanah, no one was there to greet him. He aroused the suspicions of the immigration officer on duty, who found it hard to believe that in wartime someone with nothing to hide would travel from England to Palestine via America only for the sake of "meeting with some friends." While waiting to be sent to Ellis Island for further questioning, Ben-Gurion observed a man from the Hebrew Immigrant Aid Society (HIAS) dealing with immigration officers, seeing in his submissive manner a symbol of Jewish timidity in America.

At length Rabbi Stephen Wise, coming directly from his synagogue, guaranteed that Ben-Gurion would present himself upon demand before the immigration board on Ellis Island. At 3:00 P.M. Ben-Gurion was permitted to disembark, and by evening had taken up residence in the Winthrop Hotel on Lexington Avenue, where he fell onto his bed drained and exhausted. He was summoned to Ellis Island a week later and questioned for over an hour. The most difficult query to answer, he later recounted, was "What are the duties of the chairman of the Jewish Agency?" To one unfamiliar with Zionism, the name sounded more like that of an advertising agency than a representative body of a worldwide movement. Finally, however, his passport was stamped.[2]

During this visit Ben-Gurion reinforced the foundations he had laid during previous trips and, primarily, prepared the ground for the next one. He met with various leaders and groups, mostly Zionist, and with young people whom he wished to affiliate with the "unofficial body" suggested in his memorandum. The day after his arrival he told the Yiddish press about the anticipated Jewish fighting force, asserting that "the future of the Jews of Palestine is dependent on the establishment of a Jewish army." He said that Britain had begun to understand that the half million Jews in Palestine could be of more value in the war in the Near East than millions of Arabs.

However, in his meetings he emphasized that he was in America "for the purpose of studying the situation in Zionism, in Jewry, and in America in general." He said that he would work to recruit volunteers only if the British government approved the mobilization of a Jewish army and the United States government did not oppose such recruitment. "If these two conditions are fulfilled," he said, "I shall dedicate myself to raising the unit with or without the support and good will of all the groups and parties." He was convinced that raising a Jewish fighting force would "serve to unify" American Jewry.

At a meeting of the Zionist Emergency Committee, which had been founded by American Zionist groups late in 1939, his remarks were not well received. He was again confronted, he believed, with the "Jewish timidity" symbolized for him by the HIAS man. The sight of this Jew "trembling before some official" was etched deep in his mind, surpassing all he "remembered or imagined possible only in czarist Russia." The fearfulness, which had struck him during his previous visit, became so important to him that he made curing it his first task. At a gathering of his party at the Astor Hotel, he argued that the Jews of America had to rid themselves of "the fear Hitler and his agents have inspired even in American Jewry" and raise a "daring Zionist leadership" that would demand the establishment of a Jewish army and, in due course, a Jewish state. Again, his remarks created only resentment and indignation, but Ben-Gurion held his own.[3]

After a month's stay he wrote Paula, "One thing has become clear to me: the Jews in America are in a state of fear. They fear Hitler, they fear Hitler's allies, they fear war, and they fear peace. During the election campaign they were afraid Willkie would be elected, and they were also afraid to back Roosevelt openly. The Zionists fear the non-Zionists, and the non-Zionists fear the non-Jews." Nevertheless he remained unshaken in his conviction that the true voice of American Jewry would be heard if they were called on to act boldly for the Jewish people and for the Yishuv. "There is conscience," he wrote Paula, "and there is ability and a feeling of a common fate — and if we know how to define and state our demand, I am certain we shall be answered."[4]

Ben-Gurion impatiently awaited a green light from London to begin recruitment. As the news was slow in coming he imparted to the Zionist leaders his "heavy fears" that the British decision would prove less than hoped for. "Chaim did not understand how to present the issue," he told them, so he was not certain that the decision would assign the force to the defense of Palestine and grant the five points assuring its national identity that he had specified in London: language (Hebrew), command (Jewish), allegiance (to the Jewish Agency), flag (blue and white), and anthem ("Ha-Tikvah"). Nonetheless, said Ben-Gurion, "if a miracle occurs and the decision is affirmative . . . the raising of the Jewish army will be the major task of Zionism at this time, particularly in America."

In his anxiety, he sent Locker a telegram pressing for news, and he learned from the reply that the government was still considering the Jewish force, but that the London Jewish Agency Executive had resolved "unanimously" not to propose his five points. Ben-Gurion vented his fury in his diary. "I doubt if what has befallen our people has been the lot of any other people at a fateful moment — that its leadership backed off from its most urgent need. Winston saw the justice of our demand and consented to it — then in came Chaim and for some reason dropped it. What happened?"

On October 15 Locker wired Ben-Gurion that Colonial Secretary Lloyd had informed them orally that the cabinet had decided in favor of the force but did not want to make it public before the elections. An official letter was expected any day. It was assumed that the unit would be sent to the Near East, but there was no guarantee. "Things are done so slowly in London," Ben-Gurion complained in his diary. "If only the Italians and Germans don't beat us to the Near East." As if to reinforce his apprehension, a cable arrived from Paula asking if he thought Geula and her baby should go to the United States. He responded, "Myself consider inadvisable but leave decision Geula with you."

Roosevelt's election to a third term, which he had predicted, seemed to Ben-Gurion to constitute "England's first great victory in this war and the hardest blow yet to fascism in the world and in America. The star of democracy has risen anew and the power of a free nation is revealed." He made a new prediction, which would also prove true: the war would last "longer than four years" and "in this dreadful battle a tremendous, perhaps decisive role is reserved for America." Anticipating America's increased material and military aid to Britain, he believed that this was the hour of opportunity for recruiting volunteers for the Jewish army. But his hands were tied. "The elections are over," he wrote Paula on November 9, "but the news I am awaiting from London hasn't arrived yet, and I have no assurance that the decision will be either affirmative or soon in coming."[5]

Without London's go-ahead Ben-Gurion could not begin recruitment, and when he realized that the delay was likely to be prolonged, he had to fill his time. On October 15 he listed with great precision the names of all the Greek books he had bought in New York — sixty-five volumes costing $179.25 — and on November 26 he spent more than $382 — equivalent to almost $2,900 today — on books dealing with the culture, history, and language of ancient Greece. He found time to check catalogues, browse in bookstores, list his purchases in his diary according to subject, and even read some of the volumes. A few days before leaving America he wrote Lourie asking him, as a "personal favor," to buy four more books (whose catalogue numbers he specified alongside the titles) and included a check for $15.[6]

Ben-Gurion's recruitment plan relied on the Zionist youth organizations; he expected their members to form the first wave of enlistment. The pessimism expressed by his party's youth organization leader on October 4 — "Our young people won't go into the army out of patriotism [to America] and egoism" — did not affect him. "For some reason," he wrote in his diary, "none of this pessimism convinces me." And indeed, four days later he was told by the leader of Young Hadassah that in his opinion the youth would answer the call. Ben-Gurion therefore made a list of all the Zionist youth organizations in the United States and set about meeting their representatives. He found the remarks of the man from Ha-Shomer ha-Tzair particularly pleasing. "His associates would volunteer for a Jewish army if it was to be deployed in Palestine . . . or even in the Near East, but not for just any Jewish army." Summing up his meetings he concluded that "the response is better than the colleagues predicted — [the youth] are ready to volunteer, and willingly accept the idea of aviation training." He decided not to wait any longer for an official statement of the cabinet decision but "to get started within a short time . . . on aviation training for scores of Zionist youth and paramilitary training for a larger number still." First on his list was He-Chalutz, whose leaders, however, received his directive with skepticism. The budget allotted He-Chalutz by the JAE was barely enough for the upkeep of the existing training farms and their day-to-day activity. But Ben-Gurion was adamant and at his behest, with the full backing of the Emergency Committee, the JAE allocated additional funds for the organization. The first flight course started in December 1940, and in February 1941 the Zionist Organization received word of a historic landmark: "At the Cream Ridge training farm they are now flying solo."

As the danger of Axis armies invading Palestine from Syria and the Western Desert increased, Ben-Gurion decided to investigate the possibility of recruiting American youth for the Haganah, in preparation for the day the Jewish army was established. "This war will go on for some time," he told William Ziff, a young Jew from Chicago, whom he had asked to help raise a volunteer army and broaden the air training, "and what we do not accomplish now we shall be able to later." His concern about "the situation in the Near East and the fate of the Yishuv" led Ben-Gurion to give the nonexistent Jewish army a new goal: the reconquest of Palestine. To Ziff he said, "There will be a Jewish people even if the worst disaster happens in the East, and American Jewry will have to see to raising a Jewish army to reconquer Palestine." But even if Hitler did not capture Palestine, "I do not rely any longer on assurances and declarations. Our policy must be so directed that at the war's end we take Palestine." And so, with neither British approval for raising the army nor a guarantee that the American administration would sanction the recruitment, Ben-Gurion began his one-man recruitment and propaganda drive, which involved meetings and talks, press conferences, and articles and interviews in American newspapers, including the *New York Times*.[7]

Ben-Gurion had to do it all by himself, for not only was he unable to win over Wise and Lipsky, who were Weizmann adherents, but Louis Brandeis and his group proved equally intractable. On October 15 he went to Washington to meet with Justice Felix Frankfurter in the Supreme Court Building. After recounting his London experience, he brought up his volunteer army plan. The look on Frankfurter's face, the questions he asked, and the fact that he voiced no opposition led Ben-Gurion to believe that Frankfurter approved. The eighty-five-year-old Brandeis, Ben-Gurion's only American friend of long standing, welcomed him warmly, although he spoke little. Ben-Gurion told him of the heroism and moral fortitude of the English nation and went so far as to add that "it is good to know that we are associated with such a nation — one which has the two noblest of traits: fairness and courage" — comments that greatly impressed the Anglophile Brandeis.

According to Ben-Gurion, Brandeis gave his full consent to raising a Jewish army in America, and wrote to Robert Szold, a close follower, "Ben-Gurion was most reasonable with me," by which he probably meant that Ben-Gurion had made a strong argument for the army and that Szold and others should listen to him. At the end of their meeting he asked Ben-Gurion to come to him after the elections, since until then nothing could be done with regard to the army. But as things turned out, this was their last meeting; Brandeis died a year later, on October 5, 1941. Ben-Gurion next laid his plan before Ben Cohen, in the Department of the Interior, putting more emphasis on America's part in the Jewish army. According to Ben-Gurion, Cohen said that in his opinion "the government will not raise obstacles," a statement Ben-Gurion also interpreted as consent.

These three men could create important contacts for Ben-Gurion within the administration and with Roosevelt himself. Weizmann had

had an interview with Roosevelt in January, and for Ben-Gurion to achieve equal status, a tie with the president was vital. The trio could also help him within the Zionist establishment, particularly with Hadassah, whose leaders held Brandeis in deep esteem. The efforts Ben-Gurion invested in his meetings with Hadassah's National Board and its leaders attest to the importance he attributed to this organization, the largest of all Zionist groups in the United States: in 1940 it had 74,000 members (as opposed to the 43,000 in the Zionist Organization of America). The Hadassah membership — which had previously not favored his policies and suspected him of discriminatory treatment of non-Histadrut groups in Palestine — seems to have been more open to him, thanks to the support Brandeis gave him, and they invited him to their convention in Cincinnati at the end of November.

This convention was an important landmark in his courtship of Hadassah. His speech at the closing session aroused great indignation, for he praised the Zionist enterprise in Palestine in simplistic terms, as if speaking to children or tourists (for example, describing the milking of cows in the kibbutzim as an unmatched achievement). The delegates, expecting a political analysis, and particularly insights into the Arab problem, attacked him with a flood of questions. Although it was 1:30 A.M., the closed convention was reopened, and Ben-Gurion had the opportunity to explain Zionism's political situation "in a fundamental manner." He answered questions until five in the morning; no one in the audience left. Concluding, he was thanked with thunderous ovations and a kiss from Etta Rosensohn, then Hadassah's treasurer and later its president. Although the convention passed resolutions that were too mild for his liking — highlighting support to Britain as the major line of Zionist policy and drawing attention to the need for better Jewish-Arab understanding — his appearance did foster good relations with Hadassah. Most of its leaders were impressed by his intellectual honesty, originality, and fortitude, and the National Board thanked him "for a thought-provoking speech."[8]

Up to this point Ben-Gurion had been sailing a calm sea, as though cooperation with Britain in the war was the only Zionist policy and he had altogether forgotten his double formula. In November, however, a chain of events created a storm within the American Zionist establishment. The Mandatory authorities were zealously pursuing the White Paper policy: they interned any illegal immigrants they caught at the detention camp at Atlit and released them only in accordance with the immigration schedules. When the quota was filled, they decided to deport the remainder. When the *Pacific* and the *Milos* were intercepted at sea, their 1,771 passengers were transferred to the *Patria*, which was to take them to the island of Mauritius in the Indian Ocean. On November 11 a special meeting of the Elected Assembly was called, and ten days later it declared a general strike in the Yishuv.

Ben-Gurion learned something about the November 11 events in Palestine and prepared to move heaven and earth with the aid of American public opinion. But on November 18 he received a cable from Weizmann, explaining that Lord Lloyd intended to turn away all ships carrying illegals. Lloyd's argument was that the Nazis were using the ships to introduce "German *agents provocateurs*" into Palestine. Weizmann directed Ben-Gurion to "prevent rise of feeling which may complicate situation" and set back the Jewish army project. Ben-Gurion cabled in reply that although he "recognized the need not to embarrass H.M.G.," deporting the illegals was not the right way to make sure there were no German agents among them. He had, he added, "reliable information as to their bona fides . . . They should be allowed to land."

The JAE offices in Jerusalem and London joined in the fight to revoke the deportation decree, and New York was asked to do its part. Ben-Gurion began putting members of the Emergency Committee into action, which resulted in, among other things, a cable of protest being sent by the president of the American Federation of Labor, William Green, to Minister of Labour Ernest Bevin. After reading the British government's statement of its decision to deport the illegals in the American press, Ben-Gurion noted in his diary, "The most deplorable part of the statement is the announcement that even after the war these refugees will not be permitted to come to Palestine." His proposed response was, however, unanimously rejected by the Emergency Committee on November 22, as was his demand to call protest rallies in American cities. The only thing the committee agreed to do was send a delegation to the British embassy, on condition that it behave with due restraint. After the meeting Brandeis, too, expressed his opposition to publishing any response to the deportation decision, in line with Weizmann's directive not to embarrass His Majesty's government. Weizmann and Ben-Gurion were once again at odds. Ben-Gurion found a little pleasure and some release from his frustration at the annual convention of the Histadrut fund-raising organization, which opened in New York on November 22. There he was allowed to speak uninterrupted against the British deportation policy and to declare that, just as he had returned to Palestine after Jemal Pasha had banished him forever in 1915, so would the deported illegals. The convention condemned the British policy.

In Palestine, meanwhile, the deportation created an uproar, and a prolonged controversy between activists and moderates erupted. The mood in Mapai's Central Committee was closer than ever before to

Ben-Gurion's policy of response, and faced with the preparations for the deportation, even the Jerusalem JAE drew closer to a more forceful reaction. Hence it was important that Ben-Gurion sway the Zionist leaders and public opinion in America toward the line taken in Palestine. On November 19 Sharett had sent him two cables — one on behalf of his colleagues who missed him and one on behalf of the JAE — "begging" him to remain in the United States. Apparently his colleagues enlisted Paula's aid, for she sent Ben-Gurion an uncharacteristic wire saying "Children myself miss you very much but fully appreciate importance your remaining." The meaning of these cables became clear on November 25. The Haganah, with the JAE's approval, had placed explosives on the *Patria*, intending to blow a hole in the bottom of the ship to cause a leak and cancellation of the voyage. But when the blast went off the ship sank within minutes, and some two hundred of the deportees drowned. This disaster, however, had only a slight effect. As a gesture, the British permitted the survivors to remain in Palestine, but no changes were made in the deportation policy. On December 9 the *Atlantic*, with 1,645 illegal immigrants aboard, set sail for Mauritius. These events, which horrified the Yishuv and the entire Jewish world, exemplified better than anything else the desperate situation of the Jews.

Once again Ben-Gurion found himself in isolation. Not only were the members of the Emergency Committee against any response that might upset or embarrass Britain, but Brandeis, Frankfurter, and Cohen told the committee that they opposed any announcement liable to put stress on the United States' relations with Britain. This was Ben-Gurion's first hint not to trust Frankfurter's facial expressions. Later Frankfurter made it clear that he wanted a Jewish army to be recruited not in the United States but "in other countries," and he expressed his "reluctance to speak in America on this issue." Only then, Ben-Gurion told Mapai on his return to Palestine, "did his [true] position become clear to me."[9]

Ben-Gurion was therefore in a terrible spot. His political instincts told him that a storm of public opinion in America, which the British government would be forced to take into account, would make it possible to prevent the deportations, defeat the White Paper, and raise a Jewish army. But this option was blocked by Jewish timidity. Any hope that may have been left in his heart was destroyed at an Emergency Committee meeting on November 29, when a proposal he made to issue a press statement on the Emergency Committee delegation's visit to the British embassy on November 26 was opposed. Wise claimed that the embassy talk had left him with a favorable impression that secret diplomacy had a chance of bringing about helpful cooperation with Britain, and they must not spoil it with a press statement. It was not this particular instance of silence that worried him, said Ben-Gurion, but the principle behind it. He could not accept the idea that no action should be taken by the American Zionists solely out of fear that a public protest might be disapproved by the British and U.S. governments. At the end of the debate the majority voted with Wise, and Ben-Gurion's proposal was rejected.

The controversy continued in further meetings of the Emergency Committee and spilled over into other forums — exchanges of letters, conventions, meetings, and the pages of *Opinion,* Wise's organ. It was an expanded version of the controversy that had existed during Ben-Gurion's previous visit, when he had presented his plan for combative Zionism, and centered not only on the approach to England and the double formula but on all the possible means of response available to the American Zionists. Supporting restrained response, Wise took a familiar Weizmann-like line: the Jews had an obligation to help Britain win the war against Hitler and ignore the White Paper, for if Britain fell the Jews would fall with it, and if it emerged victorious, "we have a chance." Ben-Gurion's double formula was "folly" to him. With characteristic pathos he declared, "To add even the smallest weight to the backbreaking burden Britain carries would be a sin against the Divine Spirit." His trump argument, which Ben-Gurion took to be his primary one, was to warn against an outbreak of anti-Semitism should the Jews forcefully and publicly oppose Britain.

Ben-Gurion gave his own argument a new turn on December 5, at an unofficial meeting of Zionist leaders that he called at his hotel. "As much as the world at large depends on the attitude of America, perhaps even more the fate of the Jewish people may depend on the attitude of American Jewry," he said.[10] He then proposed a new, primary goal: to provide American Zionists with a forceful political line that they would fight for, publicly and courageously, even at the price of a wave of anti-Semitism. "After looking into the situation," he said on his return to Palestine, "I reached the conclusion that the Zionist activity I had to undertake was not to try to convert the non-Zionists to Zionism, but rather to make Zionists out of the Zionists, their leaders first of all, and in this I invested not a little effort."

Paying no heed to those who wanted him to soft-pedal the demands for a Jewish army and Jewish state, he insisted openly that American Jewry support these two goals. At meetings of the Emergency Committee; at United Palestine Appeal committee meetings and conventions; at a gathering of the representatives of the four largest Zionist groups (Hadassah, the Zionist Organization of America, Poale Zion, and Mizrachi) on December 22; and at a Zionist Organization of

America Administrative Council meeting in Philadelphia on January 5, 1941, he pressed for this policy. At first he used the terms "state" and "commonwealth" interchangeably, but from January 5 on he made sure to use only the latter in the United States. "Commonwealth" sounded softer and less controversial to him; it was also, he explained to the Small Actions Committee, a word that President Woodrow Wilson had already entered into "the authorized political lexicon of America with regard to Palestine, hence it is an asset which must not be underrated."

The only real support he got, however, was from Rabbi Abba Hillel Silver; Ben-Gurion later said to Mapai's Central Committee, "I found one exception to the all-pervasive Jewish timidity in the United States — Rabbi Silver." But Rabbi Wise, whose influence was greater than Silver's, remained steadfast; in *Opinion* he issued a call to "do all for Britain," and under the headline BRITAIN FOREVER, he initiated an American Jewish aid to Britain movement. Ben-Gurion seems to have had Wise in mind when he later summarized his visit by saying, "I did not find willing ears in America. My arguments were taken for idle talk. They heard me out patiently, but they took no account of what I said."

Meanwhile — because Ben-Gurion's feverish activity suggested that he had forgotten about his resignation or because the announcement of the British decision was still being delayed and thus there was no use in trying to recruit volunteers in America, or perhaps simply because he was missed in Mapai and the JAE — his colleagues in Tel Aviv and Jerusalem began imploring him to return home as soon as possible. As usual, this request was sung by a chorus of voices from the party and the JAE, and by Paula, whose cable said, "Emanuel still without work. What's to be done. Cable." Ben-Gurion wired Sharett and Paula that he had decided to leave early in January 1941, and to Paula he added, "Will see about Emanuel [at] home."[11]

On January 13 he flew to San Francisco, on his way to Palestine via the Far East. Before leaving he met with Dov Joseph, who had been sent to replace him, to prepare him for his mission; he put his papers in order and sent them to Arthur Lourie in New York for safekeeping; and he wrote a "peace program" and a "war program," in which he formulated his political plans for action.

The peace program called for the "establishment of Palestine as a Jewish commonwealth" for the purpose of "organizing a state-directed mass immigration of millions of Jews from Europe (and other countries) and their settlement . . . in Palestine." With Britain's consent the Jewish "commonwealth" would join the empire "as one of the dominions"; failing this, "it will stand entirely on its own." Should the Arabs consent to its establishment and its becoming a member of "an Arab-Jewish federation in the Near East it will join . . . such a federation."

The war program stated that "the Jewish people participate in this war through a Jewish army, as a military ally of England, under the same conditions applying to all other Allied armies." The army's first and second tasks were to be the defense of Palestine and the Near East, its third, taking part in all war theaters. The JAE would recruit the army from among the Jews of Palestine, the British Empire, refugees, and "from Jewish citizens of all countries, subject to the laws of these countries." Among the latter he included the United States, disregarding Frankfurter's advice. A double formula was also incorporated in this program. On the one hand American Jewry was to offer "all the moral assistance England needs . . . [and] support the American administration's efforts to give England military aid," while on the other it was to support "the battle against the implementation of the White Paper . . . publicly and by mobilizing all possible support from American public opinion." Finally Ben-Gurion enumerated the tasks of the Emergency Committee, beginning with "unfolding before the Jewish and American peoples the Jewish question in all its tragedy . . . as one of the central, universal issues of democracy, peace, and justice" and ending with aiding the recruitment of the Jewish army and the training of Jewish youth in all the arts of war, especially by sea and air.

In spite of all his disappointments, Ben-Gurion believed that "in essence, Zionism is alive and well among American Jewry. All these leaders, quarreling with each other, nevertheless have a Zionist spirit." He was determined to return to America to instill his program in the hearts of Zionists and non-Zionists alike and get them to close ranks around it. This three-and-a-half-month visit was, therefore, the prelude to another, longer visit. The action that had to be taken in the United States, so unlike the tactic used in Britain, had become clear to him. "I reached the conclusion," he informed the JAE on his return, "that the way to win over the American government is by winning over the people, winning over public opinion. . . . To this end extensive, continuous action with great momentum is called for . . . We must tackle the American people, the press, members of Congress, the churches, the labor leaders, the intellectuals, and when all these are with us, the government will also be with us, and Roosevelt will help us. The way to Roosevelt is through the American people."

On January 18 he took off for Honolulu, and twenty-six days later, after circling the globe, he landed in a seaplane on the Sea of Galilee.[12]

His stay in London in 1940 was, Ben-Gurion maintained, one of the times a mighty tremor shook him and he realized intuitively that the very destruction wreaked by the war would make the Jewish state possible. Because he never for a minute doubted the Allies' ultimate victory and was convinced that the British commonwealth and the United States of America would thereafter determine the destiny of Palestine and the world, he conceived a plan that went as follows: the first step in winning over Churchill and Roosevelt, who had the power to implement it, was to win over every member of Mapai. Then, in a chain reaction, the party would transmit its will to the labor movement and the entire Yishuv, and eventually gain the support of the Zionists and all the Jews, who would pass it on to public opinion in the free world, particularly in the English-speaking world. Since democracy ruled there, the prime minister and the president would accept the will of the people and act accordingly. His return to Palestine marked the beginning of a massive assault, which ultimately ended with the approval of his political plan by the Biltmore Conference in New York in May 1942 and later by the Jerusalem JAE.

From February 13, the day he landed in Palestine — and also met with Berl Katznelson — until he left again for London on July 28, Ben-Gurion covered ground like a tornado in his effort to convert souls. "Zionism's political objective at this time," he would say, was the rapid transfer of millions of Jews (he usually said five, and once even eight million) to Palestine at the end of the war "and their settlement in Palestine as an independent nation." The only instrument capable of carrying out such a vast operation in so short a time was a state. "The Yishuv and the nation" were committed to prepare the ground for the establishment of the state when the war ended, and at the same time to prevent, "by all the means available to them," the continuation of White Paper rule, the conversion of Palestine into an Arab state, and the acceptance of other solutions to the Jewish problem, which would thwart forever the triumph of Zionism.

But whereas in America Jewish timidity prevented acceptance of the plan, in Palestine the problem was indifference and a "dreadful blindness." Shocked to find the Yishuv behaving as if there were no war and as if it did not know that Europe was witnessing the destruction of the Jewish people, Ben-Gurion, like a raging prophet, poured blazing reproof on the Yishuv. There were, however, other obstacles to his plan, one of them clearly his own fault. When asked by Mapai and the JAE how to translate it into action, he could offer no clear-cut answer, and the plan began to dissolve into mist. His vague call for "Zionist alertness," which he often repeated as a slogan, or as a goad to prod the Yishuv out of its indifference, was neither specific enough to prompt action nor completely understood by anyone.[13]

Ben-Gurion saw clearly only the last mile of the road, without knowing exactly how to get to its beginning. Even so, he was one up on his colleagues, who were groping in total darkness, unable to see even the distant flicker of light that guided Ben-Gurion. A one-eyed man among the blind, even he, the best sighted, could see no path to salvation, especially as, with Italy's entry into the war, the Mediterranean became a theater of war and there was a real threat of Palestine's being overrun. To the north the Nazi armies were in Syria, and in early May apprehension grew that they would take Haifa ("There is no strength to meet tomorrow," wrote Katznelson in his notebook). Later that month Field Marshal Erwin Rommel reached the Egyptian border, threatening Palestine from the south, and to the east, Rashid Ali, at the height of a coup d'état, declared Iraq Germany's ally. Ben-Gurion, like Churchill, thought that the Germans' main thrust would be directed to the east with its fuel resources, and the fate of the Yishuv would be sealed either by the German armies or by a pro-Nazi uprising by the Arabs of Palestine and its neighbors. Nevertheless, Ben-Gurion fought unreservedly for his plan, goading his colleagues to agree to an immediate declaration that a Jewish state would be established after the war.

They, however, saw no sense in such a declaration, and his call to use any and "all means" to halt the rule of the White Paper and prevent Palestine from being turned into an Arab state seemed to them a contradiction of Mapai's and the JAE's stated resolution calling on members of the Yishuv to volunteer for the British army despite the fact that a Jewish army had not been approved. The situation was desperate and, as in all such situations, a mass of contradictions: even though the British went ahead with their White Paper policy, closed Palestine to Europe's Jews, and rejected the Yishuv's demand to fight in the war as a nation, the Yishuv, in order to defend Palestine, had only one option: to cooperate with the British army, enlist in its ranks, and assist in any way possible in the effort to defeat Hitler.[14]

Cooperation did increase, one example being the participation of Palmach scouts, among them Moshe Dayan, in the invasion of Syria on June 8. The Allies' takeover of Syria and suppression of the uprising in Iraq removed the Nazi threat from the north and east. Hitler's invasion of the Soviet Union, which began on June 22, suddenly shifted the thrust of the German war effort to eastern Europe, and on June 29 Ben-Gurion told the JAE that this was "a relief, but not a salvation" for the Yishuv. Until the start of the decisive Battle of El Alamein and Rommel's retreat from the Egyptian border in November 1942, the Yishuv feared desperately for its life, while the invasion of Russia cast a shadow over the fate of that nation's 3,250,000 Jews. "The front . . . now . . . is . . . the Pale of Settlement, and millions of Jews . . . face destruction," Ben-Gurion told Mapai in July.

It was against this background that Ben-Gurion had to act; it proved to be a major factor in the rejection of his plan. An equally important factor was the situation within his party, which had apparently been the central topic of Ben-Gurion's talk with Katznelson on the day he arrived. If he expected a division of labor — with him conducting the struggle for a Jewish army and a state and Katznelson keeping Mapai united and strong enough to take on the historic task awaiting it — he was clearly disappointed. Katznelson was, by nature, not the man to organize and discipline the party. Called the teacher of the generation, he made his name, more than by anything else, by educating the youth. However, his position was steadily weakening, largely because Tabenkin, the leader of Faction B and Ha-Kibbutz ha-Meuchad, was gaining influence over a significant portion of Mapai's younger generation.

Incessant factional infighting was bringing Mapai closer and closer to a split between the larger Ben-Gurion–Katznelson camp, which drew its strength mainly from the party and Histadrut apparatus and from veteran members in the cities, and the Tabenkin camp, backed primarily by kibbutz members, laborers, and young people who regarded themselves as guardians of the labor movement's values. In late January, Israel Galili — a promising member of the younger generation who, only a few years earlier, had been nicknamed "the little Ben-Gurion" — had told Katznelson privately that he was joining Faction B, nearly breaking Katznelson's heart. As Mapai's internal conflict escalated, the struggle between Katznelson and Tabenkin for the souls of the younger generation became more ferocious, and as it became evident that the youth preferred Tabenkin, Katznelson, feeling his loss of power, kept to his bed because of real or imaginary weakness.

Without a strong central authority during Ben-Gurion's absence, the factional infighting had spread from Tel Aviv to other branches, including the large ones in Haifa and Jerusalem, until it encompassed the entire party. One manifestation was Faction B's demand for greater representation in the party and Histadrut institutions. To enforce this demand, its members engaged in protest actions that nearly incapacitated party branches and institutions. Tabenkin himself protested by absenteeism. He had dropped out of the party's secretariat in September 1939, and from then until the beginning of the split in the summer of 1942 he had hardly participated in meetings of the Central and Political committees and boycotted even the party council. This absence was emphasized by his regular and biting commentary in Ha-Kibbutz ha-Meuchad's deliberations and in its newspaper, *Mi-Bifnim*. From time to time resolutions were adopted urging him to return to his work in the party institutions, but they were fruitless.[15]

Therefore, instead of moving to exploit the unique, historic opportunity to achieve a state, Ben-Gurion was compelled to drag his feet through the party mud. During the five and a half months Ben-Gurion spent in Palestine in 1941, he invested tremendous energy in attempting to rehabilitate and consolidate the party that was so important to him as an implement for inducing the labor movement and the entire Yishuv to accept his political program. Eleven days after his return he had proposed holding a convention at once, for the purpose of increasing "within the movement the following three things: harmony, democracy, control." At a party council in March, amid a storm of controversy, Ben-Gurion, who was still technically without a mandate, agreed to be elected to the secretariat, whose stated role was to prepare for the convention. His objective was to cleanse the party of its factions by means of a convention resolution banning them, at the same time setting up smaller party institutions. "The movement's capacity for action demands a *compact executive*," Ben-Gurion had declared shortly after his return, thereby renewing his old demand for a special forum. He thought the new body should have seven members; after all, the British Empire was run by a seven-man cabinet. In preparation for the convention he published in the party newspaper an organizational plan according to which the convention would meet annually and elect a council to meet monthly and receive the executive's report.

For a time it seemed Ben-Gurion would get what he wanted, but the March council rejected his plan. Instead, it elected — "until the convention" — a nine-man secretariat with "full authority to administer party affairs and resolve all matters." Faction B, however, opposed this "authorized secretariat," and Tabenkin, who was elected to serve on it, stayed away. It was dissolved in June, before the convention. Both in theory and in practice, all Ben-Gurion's proposals and demands were rejected. The factional dispute had given rise to claims of discrimination, for which the only answer was to broaden, not constrict, the institutions.

This failure apparently had two principal causes, both arising from the inherent conflict between the sense of the burning ground, which propelled Ben-Gurion, and labor Zionist values, the safeguarding of which Tabenkin saw as his mission in life. Tabenkin demanded that the party and the Histadrut undergo an immediate housecleaning — that they be purged of their bureaucracy and its accompanying corruption and be staffed by members "loyal to the fundamentals of the Histadrut" and its values. When Ben-Gurion met with representatives of Ha-Kibbutz ha-Meuchad he understood that they were demanding that his people be replaced by Tabenkin's. Had it not been for the fact that the goal of a state was within reach he might not have found anything wrong with this. However, Tabenkin was loyal not only to labor Zionist values, but also to the idea of an undivided Palestine, which had been made sacred by Achdut ha-Avodah's founding platform. He opposed partition on principle, and hence Ben-Gurion's Jewish state in part of Palestine.

Tabenkin's absolute distrust of Britain and his inclination toward the Soviet Union made matters worse. Had the controversy been merely a question of purging the apparatus and reaffirming the old values, it would almost certainly have ended long before with agreement and good will. But as things were, it was merely a veil concealing the deeper dispute over partition, and the two adversaries read each other well. "We will understand each other no matter what words or language we use. Even if I speak in Turkish he will understand me, since we know what's behind it all," Ben-Gurion put it.

Ben-Gurion had managed to convince Katznelson to support partition, and on January 9 he announced for the first time his backing of Ben-Gurion's concept, repeating it word for word. "We must raise the flag of the solution of the Jewish question — of *a Jewish state* . . . The state, more than a goal in itself, is *an essential implement* for the achievement of those things that are essential to the life of the people," he told Mapai's Central Committee. But this support from Katznelson, whose position in the party was steadily weakening, was not enough to rally it around Ben-Gurion's plan. Ben-Gurion more than ever needed the support of the party apparatus he had built over the years and which remained loyal to him; in accusing Tabenkin and his faction of blindness he was trying to protect this apparatus. At the Central Committee meeting of March 19 Ben-Gurion remarked,

> Party members who in all innocence, out of blindness . . . believe they are the only group loyal to socialism, to Zionism, to the party, to its unity, to the people . . . [ignore the fact] that what we must do will be done only with the efforts of all the people in all of the Zionist movement . . . Every member wishing to assist in thrashing out matters in the Histadrut and correcting them will be welcome among us. The party apparatus will not stand in their way; rather, it will be pleased to welcome them . . . There are always the day-to-day affairs . . . But now there is a war, there is destruction of the Jewish people, there is a danger that after the war there will be confusion among the Jewish people, all sorts of witch-doctor solutions will come forth, and there will be a great catastrophe. If a carefully considered effort is not made now by all of us, we will have to suffer the consequences in the future.

Ben-Gurion's sharpest barb was aimed at the absent Tabenkin. "Each and every member, in light of the tasks that stand before us, must lend a hand; he must not run away. This is war. Taking to one's heels at a time of war is the vilest crime."

Ben-Gurion made many attempts to bring about a reconciliation, including frequent convenings of party institutions: in March, the council in Jerusalem, the central committee in Ayanot, and a mass meeting in Nahalal; in April, a study month in Rehovot and another council in Tel Aviv; and finally the party convention in June — all devoted not to discussion of the political program, as Ben-Gurion would have liked, but to hammering out the party's internal affairs. However, all his efforts failed.

In May 1941, Faction B had reached such a level of organization that Ben-Gurion found it necessary to test the balance of power between himself and Tabenkin by means of a referendum held along with the elections for the convention. Of the four referendum questions three went to the heart of the faction issue: Should "members of the party institutions be elected by the delegates at the convention" or by factional tickets? Did the authority of the institutions apply to everyone? And most important, Should the party "do away with the factions within it?" Since Faction B opposed the referendum and its members took no part in it, their relative weight in the party could be reckoned: although 17,746 party members voted in the convention elections, only 13,142 took part in the referendum, the overwhelming majority of whom opposed factions and favored the party's central authority. These results enabled Ben-Gurion to estimate the relative size of Faction B at 25 percent or more of the party, if some of the abstainers were taken into account.

Faction B was therefore an important bloc in the party, and its members believed that their power would be even greater if Ben-Gurion brought his political program up for resolution at the convention. With the addition of the opponents of partition among the majority supporting Ben-Gurion, Faction B was capable of accumulating more than 25 percent of the votes against his program, and its acceptance as the party line would inevitably lead to schism. Furthermore, if he had so many opponents within his own party, it was doubtful he could gain the broad support in the Yishuv that he needed to win the approval of the JAE and the Zionist movement. Therefore Ben-Gurion settled for presenting his plan at the convention in general, noncommittal terms; instead of using the word *state*, he spoke of "independence and ingathering of the exiles into the homeland," a formulation acceptable to all.[16]

The JAE was no more favorably disposed to the plan than the party. Over many meetings the criticism that both the program and what was needed to carry it out were not as clear as they should be was often repeated. Some remarked that it was not different from the plan Ben-Gurion had proposed before his departure. Dr. Arthur Ruppin, for instance, did not understand whether it was a plan of action, a basis for internal education and propaganda, or directives for external propaganda. Rabbi Maimon posed the thorny question of why Ben-Gurion didn't come right out and plainly say "state." It would be better, he said, to make explicit "what his goal is." Ussishkin claimed that it was not clear whether the program involved a sovereign, independent state, one affiliated with an Arab federation, or a member of the British Commonwealth. It is possible that Ben-Gurion avoided giving an unambiguous answer because he lacked his party's authorization and therefore could not give details of the plan to the JAE; but the most probable reason is that he still did not see the road clearly himself.

The JAE had other reasons for rejecting the plan. The opponents of partition raised their old argument that at this stage a state could arise in only a small part of Palestine, and would constitute a concession of the right of the Jewish people to all of Palestine. Ussishkin asked how Ben-Gurion's program differed from the Revisionists' demand at the 1931 Zionist Congress for a decision on a "final aim," of which Ben-Gurion had been a leading opponent, implying that the reasoning he had used so well then against it was no less relevant in 1941. And was not a state a double-edged sword? In a sovereign state majority ruled, and an Arab majority would certainly prevent the immigration and settlement of masses of Jews. If Ben-Gurion's intention was to impose a Jewish state by force, Kaplan added, he opposed "military conquest." There were also many doubts: Would five million Jews be able to immigrate to Palestine? Would they want to? Was it possible to bring them there and absorb them within a short time? What grounds did Ben-Gurion have for thinking the nations of the world would consent to his proposals? And in general, it was thought that wartime was no time to make such sweeping plans. It would be best to wait until the situation stabilized.

In response Ben-Gurion rebuked the JAE for behaving like "a business administration" instead of assuming the stature of "the Executive of the Jewish people." In April he threatened to bring his plan to the Small Actions Committee as a private proposal on his own behalf, and under this pressure the JAE appointed a committee to examine it in depth. But the committee never met, and on May 11 Ben-Gurion again demanded "a decision on policy," complaining that the JAE had delayed discussion "for a month now." To no avail. Four members of the JAE proposed programs of their own in opposition to his plan; the JAE was unable to decide which one to adopt and bring before the Zionist Actions Committee. When the committee convened on June 17, Ussishkin announced that five proposals were on the table and gave the floor to each of their authors in turn, a procedure that left the JAE open to criticism. "We were a laughingstock," Rabbi Maimon said later to the JAE, and all agreed that it had been "a disgrace."[17]

In the course of all this the question of the status of Ben-Gurion in the JAE was raised anew. If his colleagues regarded his participation in their deliberations and putting his plan up for debate as a sign that he had rescinded his resignation, they were not entirely correct. "For the time being," Ben-Gurion informed them, "I regard it as an obligation to be something of a Zionist preacher among the Jews of Palestine." But he did not take the directorship of a department or any other routine work, nor did he act as chairman. He assigned himself the single role of representative of the Jewish people. "It is my duty to tell the Zionists what I saw . . . what must be seen: destruction of the Jewish people and the possibility of their salvation," he said in February, and in March, "Every issue has someone working on its behalf [a department in charge] . . . but one which is fundamental has no spokesman: the Jewish people."

Ben-Gurion assumed the status of a member of the Zionist Executive — from which he had not resigned — taking part in JAE deliberations but not in its work. Like his political plan, his new role remained ambiguous. Would he work to create that missing "Zionist alertness" so that the Jews would be ready "to leap at the right moment" and establish the state, or did he intend to start a new movement or an intraparty body with his preaching? Certainly this was the implication of such comments as "I will gather together people [from all the parties] . . . who see what faces the Jewish people, and which only Zionism can rescue them from . . . and we shall do the work." This may have seemed like a threat to capture the hearts of the people over the heads of the JAE, but it was perhaps directed more at his party.

In his new role Ben-Gurion set up meetings with various parties and organizations — from Poale Zion Left to the Association of Immigrants from Germany and Austria — and held a "Gathering of Zionists for Unity in the Yishuv" on April 13 in Jerusalem. And there his mission to the Yishuv ended, for to his grief the public at large disappointed him. Although, as a political genius, Ben-Gurion intuitively foresaw the possibility of establishing the state after the war, he could not explain it logically in a way that would win him the necessary support.[18]

The impasse between Ben-Gurion and his party reminded him of the days when he had fought alone for the "conquest of Zionism," a program that had also lacked clarity. He was determined now, as he had been then, to put his program into action despite all obstacles. Unable to proceed according to his original plan — moving from the party to the free world — he reversed it. From then on he would work to convince the English-speaking countries, and from that direction enforce his plan on the Yishuv and the party.

His primary target was the United States, which, from a Zionist perspective, Ben-Gurion now regarded as more important than Britain, since "effective [Jewish] political" strength was to be found only there. "With mere explanatory propaganda to the people of the government in London we will not succeed . . . Without pressure from the United States we will not be able to stand our ground against the hostile attitude of the English government toward us." American pressure "could be decisive" in raising the Jewish army (it was possible to explain to the Americans "what it means to leave the Yishuv without defense when it wants . . . to defend itself"). Much could be gained by influencing U.S. public opinion to believe that making Palestine a Jewish state was "the only solution to the Jewish question, which has been made more critical by the war in Russia."

In April he told Mapai that American Jewry must not be left without an emissary from Palestine and demanded that a delegation of three be dispatched to the United States "at once." He wanted Katznelson to lead it, and he nominated Golda Meir, Ben-Zvi, and Sprinzak to it. However, Mapai and the JAE thought the emissary should go not to Washington but to London and that there was no better man for the job than Ben-Gurion himself. But Ben-Gurion insisted that *the center of gravity of our work is at present not in England but in America,"* and continued to insist that unless a delegation headed by Katznelson went to America, "there was no sense" in his going to London. He said this again privately to Katznelson, who commented in his notebook, "I said, 'I do not consider my trip of much importance, but I am prepared to do anything as long as Ben-Gurion goes.' " In the JAE, too, Ben-Gurion reiterated that "no talks in London will do any good without public activity in the United States," and that Weizmann had to be on the alert in London "to take advantage of the pressure that will come from the United States." Finally, on June 2, the JAE compromised; instead of dispatching two separate delegations it asked Ben-Gurion "to go to London for a short time and from there to the United States." He agreed and on June 27 he detailed his objectives for the Central Committee. Earlier he had defined Britain's position in his thinking. "We are contending with the worst of nations and with the best of them," he said on one occasion, and on another, "If England is defeated, we are lost, but if it wins, we will not necessarily win." Now he added that "England's victory is a precondition but not a guarantee." Therefore in London he would push Weizmann and the JAE toward making "desperate attempts" to prevent "further commitments from being given to the Arabs." This would be done by threatening that, because of the

Yishuv's opposition, "they will hardly be able to accomplish anything, [for] we shall fight . . . with all our strength." It was also incumbent on the JAE to emphasize to the government that "after the victory the question of justice [for the Jewish people] will come up once again.

In his heart of hearts, however, Ben-Gurion knew, as he later wrote to Paula, that in London "there is nothing . . . much to do"; he pinned his hopes on the United States, where, aside from getting the Jews to "work for a Jewish state," he intended to open "a public offensive" against the anti-Zionist policies of the British government.[19]

Ben-Gurion was so swamped with work during his five months in Palestine that only twice, it seems, was he able to get away from world affairs and Jewish problems and enjoy himself a little: at the birthday party of his year-old grandson and in a visit to the opera house in Tel Aviv. Remembering his first opera, in New York as Hadassah's guest, Ben-Gurion told Mapai's council, "This time I did not go out of obligation, which is not always pleasant. I went as an ordinary human being and had a most enjoyable evening."

On July 28 he boarded the train to Cairo. When his plane landed in Lagos on August 1, he discovered that his passport was missing (it remained with the flight crew), and as a result missed the weekly flight to London. "Here I am in the most dreadful place I have ever seen," he wrote Paula in English, and described the filth and degradation that made animals of men. "It's really a nightmare." While there he learned that Amos had been made an officer. On August 11 he finally took off for Freetown in Sierra Leone, where he spent the night aboard a Royal Navy warship, a night he remembered for many years. "I have never met such people!" he wrote Paula. "I was very impressed by the fresh, open, and clean faces of these naval officers, and from the warm and friendly reception." From Freetown he took a fourteen-hour flight to Lisbon, where, for the first time since leaving Cairo, he was able "to really get washed up" in a hotel. He reached London on the fifteenth, and stayed, as usual, at the Mount Royal Hotel. He was to be away from Palestine for more than fourteen months.[20]

43

"An Act of
Political Assassination"

T HIS TIME no one in London knew the purpose of his visit.
Ben-Gurion told May he had come only to gather information,
and on his return to Palestine told Mapai, "I went to the United
States via London." This stopover, however, lasted three months, since
German submarine fleets made leaving Britain by sea perilous, and air
travel required high priority status. On November 12, 1941, Ben-
Gurion finally flew from Bristol to Lisbon, and on the fourteenth he
boarded an American ship bound for New York.[1]

Perhaps his uncertainty over his departure accounts for his seemingly lackadaisical efforts to use his time well. He had only a few important meetings, with the new colonial secretary, Lord Walter
Edward Moyne; Secretary of State for India Leopold Amery; Soviet
Ambassador Ivan Maisky; Arthur Creech Jones, Labour member of
Parliament (who, in 1946, would become colonial secretary); Professor
Harold Beeley of Oxford from the Foreign Office Research Department (later to become adviser to the foreign secretary on Palestine);
and James Middleton, a Labour Party leader and friend since 1920. He
also had luncheons and dinners with the Zionist old guard — Leonard
Stein, Sir Simon Marks, Harry Sacher, James Rothschild, and others.

His contacts with the press were limited to two. He had a "long and
fundamental discussion" with the London bureau chief of the *Manchester Guardian,* which he considered a coup when the next day's editorial quoted him nearly word for word:

> Any scheme which gives still further satisfaction to the Arabs must in-
> clude justice to Palestine, the abandonment of the White Paper . . . and
> the establishment of a well-based independent Jewish state. . . . We ought

to let the Jews fight . . . as Jews (as the Poles do and the Czechs), to orga-
nise them more thoroughly for the defence of their own country. . . .
Without such a State, which it is our duty to assure, there can be no lasting settlement [to the Jewish problem].

This, however, was not such a great achievement, for the *Guardian* still
adhered to the pro-Zionist line of its editor Charles Prestwich Scott,
one of Weizmann's first supporters in England, who had died in 1932.
It was the only newspaper that published Ben-Gurion's praise of the
Yishuv's war effort at a press conference on October 4, which was attended by correspondents of *The Times* and the *Daily Telegraph*,
among others.[2]

For want of anything better to do, Ben-Gurion made desultory efforts to broaden the Jewish Agency Executive's political foundation, although there was no demand for him to do so. He held two talks with
revisionist representatives on the possibility of their party's return to
the Zionist Organization and two meetings with the secretary of the
ultrareligious Agudat Israel and its central committee in London, with
whom he discussed the possibility of its joining the JAE. Members of
Mizrachi in the JAE were at a loss to explain these contacts, and Moshe
Shapira commented mockingly that "Ben-Gurion began negotiations
with Agudat Israel on broadening the Jewish Agency, but it doesn't
make sense: the leaders of Agudat Israel are in Palestine; only the secretary is in London, and the negotiations are held with him, which does
not leave a very serious impression . . . The secretary wires here, asking
for instructions." Even propaganda for Zionism, which should have
occupied a central place in his thoughts, occupied little time for Ben-
Gurion. The most important event in this category was a dialogue between Zionists and non-Zionists initiated by Weizmann. The minutes
of this meeting, held at New Court on September 9, were among the
documents in Ben-Gurion's possession that British secret service agents
chose to photocopy.[3]

Like Ben-Gurion, Weizmann, during his visit to the United States,
had tried to find some common ground between the Zionists and non-
Zionists as a basis for dealing with the problems that would face the
Jewish people in the aftermath of the war. The dialogue at New Court
was an extension of this effort in Britain. The Zionists were represented
by the London JAE and its advisers and intimates, and the non-Zionists
by Sir Anthony Rothschild, Lord Victor Rothschild, Lord Horace Samuel Bearsted, and other notables. They debated how to relieve the distress of European Jews after the war: by instituting equal rights and
preventing discrimination, as Anthony Rothschild argued, or by means
of a Jewish state in Palestine to which masses of Jews could immigrate,
as Weizmann and Ben-Gurion proposed.

Weizmann reckoned that there were some eight million Jews in Nazi-conquered territory, and that it would be necessary "to deal with at the end of the war — perhaps six or seven million" whom he feared would be found "stripped of everything and physically broken." His statement that there was "physical destruction going on — at what rate they could not determine" did not imply any suspicion — for no one yet suspected it — of the systematic annihilation of six million Jews; like Ben-Gurion, Weizmann expected the situation of European Jewry after the war to compare with that which followed the First World War, only in far larger dimensions. This time, however, the Jews of Poland and Germany would not be able to return to their homes. Weizmann estimated that some of them would emigrate to North or South America after the war, and that therefore "in the best of circumstances there would still remain some two and a half or three million Jews" — Weizmann's repetition of the figure Ben-Gurion had used at the press conference did not go unnoticed by Lord Moyne, who received a report of the proceedings — for whom Palestine would be the sole refuge, and who would have to be brought in at the rate of a hundred thousand annually. However, this was not feasible without "(i) Free immigration into Palestine; (ii) Freedom of land purchase; (iii) Fiscal autonomy" and, added after Ben-Gurion's speech, "(iv) The right of self defence. . . . To all intents and purposes this meant a State."

Ben-Gurion had originally presented the state idea as a Zionist vision and the aspiration of generations as well as a unique and effective means of rescuing the Jews. Weizmann now borrowed this argument, which was in part intended to pacify the non-Zionists who opposed a Jewish state because of the dilemma of dual loyalty it would pose for Jewish communities the world over. To reach some common ground at New Court, Ben-Gurion said, he would not "insist on the name 'state' " but would be satisfied with a "Jewish Administration," which would be able to bring in an annual immigration of 100,000. However, after "two million Jews [had] been brought into Palestine," they would constitute a majority capable of defending the country and would become a self-governing community. They could then establish a state, calling it "Judea or Eretz Israel."[4]

Lord Bearsted's pertinent question, "What was to happen to the two millions during the 20 years or so which it would take to move them to Palestine at the rate of 100,000 per annum?" received only a lame reply from Weizmann (they would be put in training centers), but on the whole the meeting concluded favorably. The JAE was mandated to compose a memorandum based on it, which its participants could then debate. For Ben-Gurion the meeting constituted excellent preparation for his further efforts to bring America's non-Zionists to a "joint front," as May put it, with the Zionists in the demand for a Jewish state. He devoted Rosh Hashanah eve, September 21, to composing a "plan of action for united Jewry in America," specifying its goals during wartime ("the war program") and afterward ("the peace program"). These notes were also photocopied by the British secret service, as were others in which he detailed his secret strategy.

> Once we have succeeded in getting America behind a Zionist solution of the Jewish problem, all the present difficulties — whether real or imaginary — will fade into insignificance. If Jewish Palestine interests were to conflict with the really vital interests of the British Empire, then perhaps even the support of America would not overcome British resistance. But even the most extreme among the British opponents of Zionism have never claimed that Zionism is in itself against British interests; the differences of opinion were not between pro-Zionists and pro-British, but between pro-Zionists and pro-Arabs. When the war is over, and Hitlerism and Nazism destroyed, and England and her allies victorious, there can hardly be any doubt which will prevail with a British Government, the American view or the view of an Egyptian King or an Iraqi P.M. American support for a Jewish State in Palestine is thus the key to our success.

Ben-Gurion still had plenty of free time for Greek, book hunting, and going with May to Sunday morning mass and to see the "ruins" of London, "the worst damaged parts of the city." He had the highest praise for the fortitude of the English in the face of the air raids, and he wrote Paula, "I saw the results of the enemy's bombardment, but London is as it was, bleak and steadfast, exuding confidence and courage."[5]

This visit might have passed as just a "stopover" that lasted a bit longer than expected had Ben-Gurion not harbored two objectives for it. He had come for information, he told May, but what he meant was information about Weizmann's plans. On his first day in London Ben-Gurion had met with Weizmann at his suite in the Dorchester Hotel. "I described the situation in Palestine and heard a little from Chaim about America. He intends to visit Palestine in the fall, and from there go on to the United States early in 1942," he wrote to Paula, adding an account of the next day's activities. "I picked up some reading material at the office and managed over the weekend to get something of a grip on our situation here."

However, his remarks to the Central Committee on his return to Palestine make it clear that he had not read documents only to catch up on current affairs, but had also delved into documents from 1940.

> I looked over all the notes from the interviews, I read all the protocols, and I have a good memory for such things, I remember them, and I found that [Weizmann] saw ministers, spoke with them on various issues, but

said not one word on the defense of Palestine or a Palestine army, not even the barest mention, and this was at a time when we thought invasion imminent and had already agreed what to do if it happened. If in September 1940 I found him unfit politically, now I find him morally crippled as well.

It seems that one of Ben-Gurion's objectives on this trip was to store up ammunition for a confrontation with Weizmann.

Although there appeared to be harmony between them, it is reasonable to assume that one of Ben-Gurion's meetings with Lord Moyne, at which Weizmann was present, did not please Ben-Gurion. Moyne had been disturbed to learn from the report he received of the New Court meeting that both Weizmann and Ben-Gurion had spoken of an immigration of two to three million Jews to Palestine. As an alternative, he proposed finding "some other territory" to absorb Jews after the war. Perhaps Weizmann's response that he knew nothing of the report Moyne had seen and that all the JAE asked was freedom of immigration upset Ben-Gurion. Certainly Moyne's statement — when the talk moved to the Jewish army — that the government "had to give every possible aid to Russia, and in the circumstances it would not be possible for them to form a Jewish Division outside Palestine" infuriated Ben-Gurion.

Moyne's argument was a transparent pretext that Weizmann should long before have disproved as nonsense. If Weizmann had lived up to his responsibilities in 1940, Ben-Gurion believed, there would have been a division and Zionism would be marching vigorously down the road to a Jewish state, instead of being lectured to about alternative territories. After this meeting they apparently had words. What was more, Ben-Gurion's attitude toward Weizmann extended to the entire London JAE, whom Ben-Gurion regarded as Weizmann's "court" and despised as such. May wrote Lourie on October 30, "David says he has shaken the dust of 77 [Great Russell Street] from off his feet, and is present with us no longer," although he was not due to leave London until November 13. She also reported that Ben-Gurion was "considerably disturbed" by a change in Weizmann's plans. "Ch. now intends . . . to come now to the States, i.e., about the end of November, and continue round the world to Palestine in the spring." May, who well knew that Weizmann preferred that any confrontations should take place in London, doubted he would ever get to Palestine, but perhaps, she added, "I'm a pessimist."

If Ben-Gurion was irked by the prospect that he and Weizmann would be in the United States at the same time, he was not alone. Sharett, who apparently, like Locker, wished to forestall a confrontation, got Mapai's secretariat to resolve "to appeal to Ben-Gurion to reconsider his decision to go to America, and ask Weizmann to make every effort to come to Palestine." This appeal, however, had no effect at all. In a letter to Sharett, Locker described Ben-Gurion's relations with the London JAE. "At last those who sit here have developed a certain way of thinking and modus operandi. You can either work with them or replace them, but you cannot just order them around." Furthermore, "David was in a difficult mood and sometimes it is not a simple matter to understand what he's getting at and explain to him his adversary's opinion."[6]

Ben-Gurion's second and more important objective was to prepare for a face-to-face meeting with Roosevelt. The reputation of John Gilbert Winant had reached Ben-Gurion in Jerusalem, and through Ben Cohen, who was attached to the London embassy, he hoped to make contact with this Lincolnesque Republican, the deeply religious, Anglophilic former governor of New Hampshire, who had replaced Joseph Kennedy as United States ambassador to St. James's and become an intimate of Churchill. Through Winant, Ben-Gurion hoped to reach Roosevelt, who took Winant into his confidence. Ben-Gurion's original plan fell through when he arrived in London and found that Ben Cohen had fallen out with Winant and returned ("very wounded," according to Ben-Gurion) to the United States. "For me this was a hard blow, as I had great hopes for this contact," Ben-Gurion wrote to Paula.

But he soon recovered and on August 27 appealed directly to the ambassador, who agreed to meet him that afternoon in his office. The chemistry — or "atmosphere," as Ben-Gurion termed it — between the two was right from the start, "as if we had known each other all our lives." Ben-Gurion found Winant to be "a man by far exceeding his reputation." As soon as he began to describe the Yishuv's war effort, Winant "set up two chairs in the middle of the room and an intimate chat began," during which Winant affirmed that he was "ready to assist in any way he can." The name of Brandeis, a friend of both, also helped create a meeting of minds. The talk turned to world affairs and lasted an hour and a half.

Ben-Gurion was very enthusiastic afterward. "I saw," he wrote Paula, "that this man has one concern above all which does not let him sleep: the fate of humanity in our time and how to motivate his country to give maximum assistance. Before me was revealed a rare individual the equal of whom I have not often had the pleasure to meet, and certainly not in such a responsible office." He also shared his impressions with May, to whom Ben-Gurion described Winant as a "pure idealist." Ben-Gurion had not forgotten to mention that he was en route to America and that Winant had asked him to visit again before his departure. Meanwhile Ben-Gurion sent Winant a summary paper entitled "Jewish War Effort and War Offers," which he later published in the November issue of the *Jewish Frontier* in America.

When Brandeis died on October 5, Ben-Gurion invited Winant to the memorial meeting held by the Zionist office, so Weizmann met him too. At this meeting Winant again invited Ben-Gurion to call on him before his departure. On November 6, "something glimmered" in his mind on the subject that interested Winant most — the fate of humanity — an idea which, Ben-Gurion told Paula, was likely to facilitate his meeting with Roosevelt. "I knew that if he's the man I think he is and listens to what I have to say to him, he will ask a certain thing of me." "Certain thing" was an allusion to a meeting with Roosevelt, not spelled out for fear of the ever-watchful secret service.

Winant received him that day, and in the course of their talk, which lasted from 5:00 until 7:20 P.M., told Ben-Gurion that he should see the president "as soon as I get to America" and assured him that Roosevelt would call him. Ben-Gurion wired Sharett that "this was perhaps the most effective talk" he had ever had, and that it had been "worth coming to London" if it meant he could have "a man-to-man talk" with Roosevelt, as he had had with Winant. What was the idea that assured him of a meeting with Roosevelt? Ben-Gurion made only a few vague remarks about it to the JAE on his return to Palestine. "I told him my view of world affairs as regards the three fighting powers, England and Russia and America": there was no trusting the Soviet Union, "since Communism will probably be her goal, not the redemption of humanity, which task will fall to America, [which had] to play a decisive role in this war."

Their meeting occurred on Ben-Gurion's last day in London, an hour and a half before he left for Bristol. The ambassador seems to have reiterated his assurance that he would arrange a meeting with Roosevelt, for Ben-Gurion said so to May, who was part of the entourage that accompanied him to the railway station. She thought that "D. takes with him, I fancy, a very nice letter to the skipper [Roosevelt]." He said the same to Locker, whom he charged with relaying this news to Weizmann, who was very insulted that Ben-Gurion had not taken leave of him in person. May, aware of Weizmann's feelings, must have mentioned this to Ben-Gurion, who dashed off a letter of farewell from his hotel in Lisbon.

Dear Weizmann,
  Before departing Europe I send you warm regards. The day I left I went to the office to take my leave of you but there I learned that your son was home on leave, and I did not wish to spoil your happiness.

Although I was not particularly encouraged when I left London, I was not in despair. We shall overcome the difficulties if we continue to do our best, above all in Palestine: land, immigrants, recruits. . . . I was happy to hear from Locker that you are renewing your effort to go to Palestine. Your visit will greatly encourage the Yishuv and may have something to offer you as well.

I wanted to tell you something fairly important concerning my talk with Winant . . . but since I did not see you I asked Locker to do so.

My regards to Mrs. Weizmann and all your family. Be strong and of good courage! Yours in faith, D. Ben-Gurion.

The letter left no doubt that Ben-Gurion preferred that Weizmann go to Palestine rather than the United States, and behind its veil of warm wishes lurked distrust; Winant's promise to arrange a meeting with Roosevelt had been given a week earlier, allowing more than enough time for Ben-Gurion to tell Weizmann about it. This omission had far-reaching repercussions. May described the two men as "oil and water, so D. goes off bitter and disgusted, and Ch. remains a pattern of long-suffering innocence of all offence."[7]

The ten months Ben-Gurion spent in the United States, November 21, 1941, to September 18, 1942, were among the most decisive in his political career. His objectives could not have been clearer: to create a unified Jewish front of Zionists and non-Zionists that would demand a Jewish state and a Jewish army, and to convince the government of the United States to back these demands. And this time he also had his strategy mapped out: Zionist preaching and the establishment of an "unofficial body," which he would direct. The question of his status — still officially resigned from the JAE — did not trouble him. It was enough for him, he wrote in his diary, to conduct "political Zionist propaganda . . . as a minister of Zionism and on its behalf." Even though no institution had authorized him as such, so high was his confidence in himself and in his task and so deep his desire not to miss the hour of opportunity that Ben-Gurion constituted himself his own authority.

His visit opened with a flurry of activity. While still at sea he was invited by telegram to lecture to the Pan-American Conference, at which representatives from Canada, the United States, and sixteen South and Central American countries were to participate. The ship had barely docked on the afternoon of November 21 when American Jewish Committee members whisked him off to Baltimore, where by 8:30 P.M. he was addressing the delegates and fifteen hundred guests. The audience was rapt as he delivered his speech, and when he finished they burst into "Ha-Tikvah." The next day's Yiddish press ran headlines saying that at the end of the war Europe would hold "millions of homeless Jews" and that since only Palestine could be the solution to this problem, a Jewish state had to be established. Ben-Gurion proudly reported his triumph to Paula, intimating that the next speaker had "made himself scarce" because his own act was so hard to follow.

In New York he stayed at the Winthrop Hotel, and the next day he opened an assault on the media with two press conferences on succeeding days, the first for the Yiddish press and the next for the English-language papers, including the *New York Times, P.M.*, and the London *Daily Telegraph.* In the course of singing the praises of the Yishuv's war effort, he openly called on Jews to help build pressure on the British government to raise a Jewish military force and abolish the White Paper. AMERICAN JEWRY CAN WIELD A POWERFUL AND DECISIVE INFLUENCE ON THE ENGLISH GOVERNMENT read the front-page headline of the *Jewish Daily Forward.*[8]

On November 27 Ben-Gurion began what was to develop into a long series of talks with non-Zionists on the subject of defining the Jewish people; on November 28 he addressed the Emergency Committee on the plight of Zionism in Palestine; and on November 30 he left for Washington with Emanuel Neumann, the Emergency Committee's public relations director, to open his contacts with the administration. (Weizmann had once described Neumann as "a most untrustworthy individual," and Ben-Gurion suspected him of having fascist inclinations.) They met with Colonel William Donovan, director of coordination and information (an intelligence service that laid the ground for both the Office of Strategic Services and the Central Intelligence Agency), who had just returned from a presidential mission to the Middle East. Ben-Gurion explained to him the fundamentals of "the issue of the Jewish Military Force in both its sections, in Palestine and the diaspora," finding him a sympathetic listener. Donovan asked for a one-page memorandum and a longer, more detailed one, and promised to get them to the president, the State Department, and the British. For all his efforts, however, Ben-Gurion could not boil everything down to one page and ended up with four and a half pages.

On December 2 he went to Felix Frankfurter's home, where he met Frankfurter's friend William C. Bullitt, a senior American diplomat, ambassador to France until mid 1940 and an enthusiastic supporter of lend-lease. Bullitt was about to leave on a mission to the Middle East to investigate the military situation and supply needs on behalf of Roosevelt, who was in close touch with him and valued his opinions. Roosevelt, as Ben-Gurion knew, did not regard Palestine as a solution for all the Jews who would have to start new lives after the war, and Bullitt wanted to clear up the question of Palestine's absorptive capacity. Ben-Gurion, for his part, wanted to win American aid for the development of chemical, iron, and electrical industries "for the war effort." Ben-Gurion, arriving at Frankfurter's home a quarter of an hour late, found the two friends settled with whiskeys in hand. He turned down the offer of a drink, and for the next hour and a quarter detailed for Bullitt the "paradoxical" situation whereby the Yishuv was forced to abet a war effort despite the hostility of the Colonial Office and its opposition to a Jewish army. In response to Bullitt's question as to how many the Yishuv could mobilize in addition to the ten thousand who had already volunteered, Ben-Gurion said, "Another thirty thousand; we can staff three divisions." Bullitt received the impression that Ben-Gurion regarded the raising of a Jewish army as "the essential object." When the conversation turned to absorptive capacity, Bullitt suggested that all the Arabs be "expelled" from Palestine and a Jewish state established. Ben-Gurion replied, "There is no need to evacuate the Arabs, since Palestine just as she is can absorb millions, on condition that control is in our hands."

Returning to New York that night, Ben-Gurion was surprised to learn that the Jewish Telegraphic Agency had released the news that "David Ben-Gurion and Emanuel Neumann, representing the Emergency Committee for Zionist Affairs, today conferred with a number of high officials . . . The main subject of discussion was the Jewish army . . . Both Jewish leaders seemed satisfied with the results of their conversations." It could have been inferred that Ben-Gurion was responsible for this leak, because Neumann had accompanied him only to the meeting with Donovan, not to Frankfurter's home, and he rebuked Neumann, who, he believed, was the source, in writing. Neumann, however, was not "impressed," and told Ben-Gurion with a grin, "Weizmann does the same thing."[9]

In New York Ben-Gurion met with American Zionist leaders, with representatives of Jewish youth organizations, and was again taken to the opera by Hadassah members, this time to Mozart's *Marriage of Figaro*. On December 4 he went to Washington for a talk with Frankfurter, and returned there to see Ben Cohen on December 7, 1941, the day that changed the war and the face of the world. Hearing on the radio that Japan had attacked Pearl Harbor, Ben-Gurion wrote in his diary, "America is at war." This was the moment he had anticipated in his confident belief that United States involvement in the war would increase its influence, on Britain particularly, improving the prospects for the Jewish army and state. Back in New York the next day, he decided not to await Roosevelt's call there but to settle in Washington to expedite it. As was his custom, Ben-Gurion veiled his objective even in his diary, describing his new move as follows: "For the sake of political activity I must reside in Washington . . . gather around me a group of young people and find a way to reach the progressive and radical circles in the government, beginning with [Vice President Henry] Wallace."

That his decision would stir up resentment was probably brought home to him on December 8, at a meeting of the Emergency Committee's public relations committee. Neumann suggested opening a bureau of the committee in Washington, to be run by one man — he had himself in mind — since in the capital "there are [approximately] a thousand people . . . with whom contact should be maintained." Ben-Gurion did not announce his intention of moving to Washington at this meeting, but apparently weighed the matter for two weeks before reaching a final decision. Later he told Frankfurter, "I decided to settle in Washington and take the work upon myself while I am here. I am aware of the difficulties and of my own shortcomings, but I know our case and have faith in its justness and feasibility. My situation is that of a delegate of the Jewish people . . . without authority, status, or power. But I have a case I believe in and for which I've worked all my life, and responsibility for it is now mine, and I must do what I can."

On December 22 he visited the Zionist office in Washington and looked into renting an apartment and getting office help. It soon became clear, however, that this was "not at all a simple matter" and he was offered the use of the central office at the Zionist Organization of America (ZOA). "But," he wrote in his diary, "they have no Hebrew typist (although there is a Hebrew typewriter)." He turned down this generous offer either because he wished to keep his anticipation of Roosevelt's call secret or because he wanted full independence of action, and elected instead to work out of the Ambassador Hotel on the corner of Fourteenth and K streets. It was a second-class hotel, old and not large by American standards, which charged a thousand dollars a month for a two-room suite and secretarial services. On December 30 Ben-Gurion cabled Kaplan, treasurer of the Jerusalem JAE, presenting him with a fait accompli — "Residing Washington Hotel Ambassador require up to $1,000 monthly for secreterial [*sic*] office expenses cable your views." He packed his books and belongings and took the train to Washington.

The first to learn of Ben-Gurion's decision "to settle in Washington for the sake of Zionist political propaganda in this city, as the representative of Zionism and on its behalf, in full contact with the Emergency Committee," were Dr. Nahum Goldmann, Neumann, and Lourie, the senior staff of the Emergency Committee, whom he had told on December 23. In his diary Ben-Gurion wrote, "I did not get the impression that the three of them received this news happily," but to his surprise they said nothing. Only Goldmann asked "if I would inform the Emergency Committee [officially], and naturally I answered yes." He did so at the end of an Emergency Committee meeting that afternoon. As Stephen Wise was excusing himself to leave for another engagement and the committee members were putting on their coats, Ben-Gurion asked for "one moment" to announce that he was "moving to Washington."[10]

As he expected, the move angered the Emergency Committee and the Zionist leaders. Two delegations — from the Zionist leaders and Hadassah — visited him to ascertain "the nature" of his intentions, find out why he had not consulted the Emergency Committee "before the fact," caution him against duplication of efforts, and demand a commitment to cooperate and report in full. Ben-Gurion replied that as a member of the JAE it was his right "to conduct political activity in any country, including America," that his place of residence was his own affair, and that "for the time being I wish to study the situation and promote the Zionist cause as much as possible." There could be no doubt, he said, that he would work "only in conjunction" with the Zionist movement in America, but he would not commit himself to disclose to the Emergency Committee the names of the people with whom he was to meet, although he would do so "after the fact"; nor would he report on secret talks. He did agree to inform "a small political committee (of no more than three)" of all his confidential talks and activity. This hardly satisfied the Emergency Committee. Ben-Gurion's request to Jerusalem for office expenses was also a bone of contention, especially since the money was to come from funds raised in America.

On January 5 the committee met to discuss his move to Washington, which Ben-Gurion, disregarding advice from Lourie, did not attend. In his absence the committee was told that Ben-Gurion was contemplating opening a "separate office" of the JAE in Washington and decided that the matter "should be taken up with Mr. Ben-Gurion without delay." The committee also heard that Ben-Gurion had arranged to meet with "a small group of Jewish Government officials" and instructed Neumann to participate in it. Accordingly, Neumann asked Ben-Gurion the meaning of "the activity" he wished to conduct in Washington, expressed disapproval that Ben-Gurion had sent a memorandum to the president (the short one he had given Donovan) "without anyone's knowledge," wondered that he should arrange a meeting with government officials "without informing us," asked to participate, and was refused.

Thus began a struggle widely publicized in the Jewish press, which unanimously took a hostile view of Ben-Gurion's actions. In Toronto's *Yiddisher Journal*, for example, the headline read, BEN-GURION TO SET-TLE IN WASHINGTON, CHALLENGES THE EMERGENCY COMMITTEE. The article related that Ben-Gurion had wired Palestine for "extra money" and was "looking for a two-room office," but probably would not get far "since both the American administration and the British embassy would not choose to deal with him in preference to the Americans." His recent experience in press relations enabled Ben-Gurion to detect Neumann's hand in these headlines, as well as in what he called a whispering campaign.

But the result was merely to whet his appetite for battle. On January 10 Ben-Gurion went to New York for a meeting of the Emergency Committee, where he said he was "requesting [from the Jerusalem JAE] authorization to spend up to $1,000 a month for [his] expenses in America," and that he would travel anywhere for the purpose of promoting the Zionist cause, meet with anyone who could aid him in it, and act on behalf of the Executive. He was prepared to report to the Emergency Committee directly on any talks he might have on the subject, except for cases involving confidentiality. In short, he refused to give an inch on independence of action. The Emergency Committee called a second meeting on January 15, for further discussion, but Ben-Gurion wrote from Washington that he could not take part, "as I must write and think."[11]

The "whispering campaign" spread — to the delight of the Revisionists, who threw more fat on the fire — to the West Coast and across the Atlantic, manifesting itself on the pages of San Francisco's *Jewish Standard* and London's *Jewish Chronicle*, and Ben-Gurion found himself awash in a flood of cables and letters from London. To a wire from Locker he responded that he was working in harmony with the Emergency Committee, not opening a separate branch of the JAE, and that the fuss was nothing but malicious rumormongering. From Jerusalem, Sharett and Kaplan cabled him, "Executive appreciates importance your settling in Washington approved your proposal [for expenses] but trusts coordination Emergency Committee assured [would] appreciate information this regard. . . . Suggest use far as possible Zionist offices Washington." They also asked that he make an effort to keep expenses at a minimum. Ben-Gurion replied with a short telegram, similar to the one he had sent Locker, saying he was working in close cooperation with the Emergency Committee and had never intended to open a separate office. He next got wind of a news bulletin to be released by the Independent Jewish Press Service: "The story goes that American Zionists are making it so unpleasant for Mr. Ben-Gurion that he is planning to return to Palestine soon by way of the Atlantic, instead of

retaining planned HQ at Washington." Although previously he had
preserved his equanimity with respect to press reports, he asked Lourie
to find out who was behind the campaign.[12] He was learning that
American Zionists could deliver quite a sting.

At fifty-five, Ben-Gurion, more than ever, yearned for female companionship, a longing he had managed to stifle by immersing himself in
work. But at the Emergency Committee office, or perhaps earlier in
the offices of Hadassah, where she worked as secretary of the Palestine
Committee, he had seen Miriam Cohen, an attractive woman of
thirty-four, taking the minutes at meetings. There is no doubt that he
found her appealing, for no sooner had he settled in his hotel in Washington than he wrote to Lourie in New York, on January 1, 1942,

> I want you to *"lend" me Miss Cohen for a few days* — until next wendes-
> day [sic]. . . . I have some dictation, and until I find my way here I need a
> trusted, confidential help, and I believe I can rely on her. I don't know . . .
> whether I will need a permanent secretarial [sic]. . . . But I need her *now*.
> So if you and she are both agreed let her take the earliest train tomorrow
> and come over with pencil and paper. . . . I will "return" her to you next
> week and then we will see.

According to Miriam, "We were all taken aback and I nearly
fainted." Since she was dedicated and reliable, the Emergency Committee was not willing to part with her, and she, after weighing the
matter, decided it was best to turn Ben-Gurion down. Ben-Gurion,
however, rejected all other secretaries offered him, and when he appeared before the Emergency Committee on January 10, he again requested that Miriam act as his secretary "for a period of ten days."
After "considerable discussion" the committee agreed to "loan" Miss
Cohen to Ben-Gurion and continue to pay her salary and expenses.
Faced with this pressure, Miriam could not refuse and went to Washington.

In her room on the seventh floor, she quickly discovered the disad-
vantages of the Ambassador Hotel. Claiming a sudden spate of ideas
that must be committed to paper, Ben-Gurion would use the hotel telephone to summon her to his fourth-floor suite at two or three in the
morning. Because the elevator did not work in the middle of the night,
she would run up and down the stairs, her heart pounding from fear of
being arrested for loitering. But if Miriam got used to his erratic schedule, she did not respond to his advances. As she put it, she "could not
abide" Ben-Gurion and told him she would resign.

As a typical incident, Nahum Goldmann requested her to go to the
State Department to secure American visas for his refugee relatives.

Ben-Gurion, outraged either because Miriam had helped Goldmann ("If Goldmann's character matched his brilliance, that would be a wonderful combination," he told her) or because he loathed personal intervention on behalf of those fortunate enough to have influential connections, criticized her for it. "These are living people," she retorted with tears in her eyes. Adding that she would not work with him any longer, she went to her room and phoned Goldmann to say she "would not return to Washington." But Ben-Gurion followed her to her floor, begged her forgiveness, told her he "loved a good fight" and that she had exonerated herself handsomely. He added that he had no one to help him with his inadequate English. Although she thought he was "the most impersonal person I have [ever] seen," she withdrew her resignation.

Still, Miriam was certainly no comfort to Ben-Gurion in his loneliness. In the United States he felt, he wrote Locker on January 26, "like a fish out of water," and it was unbearable. "I am now living in terrible loneliness," he wrote Sharett on February 8. Ben-Gurion spilled out his misery to May in a letter. "I am altogether alone, among so many people — and a desert! . . . In lonely sleepless nights I am still with my Plato — I just finished reading the whole *Politics* — what a wonderful . . . book!"[13]

The main reason for his move to Washington had been the chance to meet Roosevelt; Ben-Gurion wished to make himself available for the call from the White House. He did not take on this mission in Washington, which was "a new world" for him, without apprehension. Addressing Frankfurter, he said, "I came to you as to Joseph — true, not in Egypt and not under the Pharaoh — for two things: guidance and aid." Ben-Gurion told Frankfurter of Winant's undertaking, of his desire to establish "an unofficial body" and organize young people to help him with administration and information, and particularly of the need for "work" in Washington. He said, "I will not take this upon myself unless you tell me that you can help me, that you will guide me in American affairs." Frankfurter thought a moment and replied, first, that he agreed there was a need for "systematic work" in Washington; second, that he believed Ben-Gurion was capable of doing it; and third, that he would help him — "Let's have a committee, and we will consult together."

Frankfurter suggested his friends Ben Cohen and David Niles, both Jewish senior officials close to Roosevelt. Niles, a presidential aide on domestic affairs, labor, and appointments and a member of the White House inner circle, was, said Frankfurter, "meek and modest, but an important man, knows everything, sharp, wise, well connected . . . He will be able to help you. He will put you in contact with the necessary people." Certainly Frankfurter and his two friends were the greatest potential assets in the support system Ben-Gurion created to prepare for and follow up on successes. When Miriam arrived in Washington his cadre was complete. With her assistance he could produce all the memos and paperwork his advisers requested in correct English.[14]

On December 31, 1941, Frankfurter invited Ben-Gurion, Ben Cohen, and David Niles to lunch in the Supreme Court Building. Ben-Gurion spoke to them in simple terms — Frankfurter had asked him to speak as if they were "ignorants" — of the work in England and America for the establishment of a Jewish army and of a Jewish state after the war. Cohen displayed great pessimism and challenged the need for such an army. "Why fight as Jews?" he asked. "I will answer you separately," said Ben-Gurion, for he wished to concentrate on the new man, Niles, who did not show much interest. Despite their reservations, the three assured him of their assistance and Ben-Gurion, much uplifted, left. But his expectations came to nothing: Frankfurter was unable to set up a meeting with the president. "Frankfurter took it on himself to find out, but as of today he's done nothing," he wrote Sharett on February 8. "Before going to Washington I consulted with Frankfurter. Assurance of his assistance was a primary condition for me. He gave it — but he has not lived up to it. . . . He lacks Brandeis's deep involvement as well as any serious and consistent attitude to our cause, and he did not keep his promise."

Nevertheless, Ben-Gurion met important people who could be of great assistance through Frankfurter. An assistant librarian in the Semitics Department of the Library of Congress showed him around the library and promised to help him prepare a bibliography on the Jewish and Palestine issues. Henry Morgenthau, Jr., secretary of the treasury, displayed sympathy and great optimism for the future of Zionism. From the Churchill-Roosevelt meetings — Churchill had visited the White House for three weeks beginning December 22, 1941 — Morgenthau learned that "these two men are your friends." Three members of Colonel Donovan's staff — Professor William Langer (director of research), Dr. Walter Wright, Jr. (chief of the Near East section), and a Mr. Wiley (chief of the Foreign Nationalities branch) — asked questions that "shocked" Ben-Gurion: Was there no danger that Jewish spies in the service of the Gestapo would infiltrate Palestine if immigration was permitted? Could tiny Palestine absorb massive immigration, and would not large numbers immigrate to Germany or America after the war? And would not the "imminent collapse" of the Jewish economy in Palestine "have serious consequences for Jews everywhere"? Ben-Gurion realized that they had been nurtured on anti-Zionist propaganda.

Ben-Gurion came closest to Roosevelt when, in New York on January 29, he met with Judge Samuel Rosenman, whom he described to Sharett as "the skipper's best friend, his intimate adviser for some twenty years, speech writer, and regular visitor at his home and in the inner sanctum." The few questions he asked made it clear he knew very little of Palestine. Yet Ben-Gurion got the impression that "on the question of the Jewish army he displayed absolutely sincere sympathy. On the question of the future of Palestine, I requested control of immigration, development, self-defense; he was 'non-committal,' but not unsympathetic," and he asked Ben-Gurion for a short memo on the subject. With great effort Ben-Gurion prepared one, showed the first draft to Frankfurter and Ben Cohen, and sent it on February 10, with a request for another meeting "soon." The memo said that

> [the absorption] of the maximum number of immigrants in the shortest possible time [could be accomplished only by] a Jewish administration — an administration completely identified with the needs and aims of the Jewish settlers and wholeheartedly devoted to the building of the country. . . . Jewish immigration on a large scale is bound to result in the not distant future in a growing Jewish majority . . . and in the establishment of a self-governing Jewish Commonwealth. . . . The Jewish Agency for Palestine . . . should have full control over Jewish immigration and be invested with all authority necessary for the development and upbuilding of the country and the maintenance of internal defense. To secure the homeland for homeless Jews, Jews themselves must be entrusted with its reconstitution.

Rosenman did not respond to the memo and almost certainly did not pass it on to Roosevelt, as Ben-Gurion had expected him to do. In any event, no invitation came from the president. Ben-Gurion's second meeting with Rosenman, in the White House, did not take place until six months later, on August 11, by which time Ben-Gurion had given up hope of meeting Roosevelt. What was more, neither Rosenman nor Niles joined Frankfurter and Cohen on the "advisory committee" to open doors for him.[15]

The worst disappointment was served him by Winant, from whom he had parted as "a friend and brother." Winant had been "quite adamant (naturally there was no objection on my part), and as far as I know he is neither rash nor does he speak lightly, and I am certain he did what he promised." Convinced that there had been some mishap, Ben-Gurion racked his brains for a plausible explanation. "I could not figure the thing out." On January 19 he wrote Winant, "What you asked me to do before I left London, I have not been called upon to do here — at least thus far. I need not tell you how happy I will be to do it at any time." To his consternation, he received no reply.

The most likely reason for his pervasive loneliness and heartbreak was the shattering of Ben-Gurion's hope for this long awaited interview and the chance to lay before the president of the United States the only solution to the problem of the Jewish people. The extensive network of contacts Ben-Gurion had worked so hard to develop failed to produce an interview; the ten-week stay in Washington, which created resentment in all the Zionist leaders, was no more productive. Ben-Gurion, after attending to other business en route, returned to the Winthrop Hotel in New York on March 9. Ironically, Winant had arrived in New York that very day. The *New York Times*, reporting his visit, added that Winant had met with Roosevelt on March 10. There is nothing in Ben-Gurion's papers to indicate that he knew anything about this development or had read it in the *Times*.

Ben-Gurion probably wanted his meeting with Roosevelt to take place before Weizmann's scheduled visit to the United States, and the feeling of lost opportunity could not help but add to the pressure building inside him, in spite of Weizmann's frequent postponements of his departure for the United States. The last of these was the result of news received on February 12 that his younger son, Michael, a fighter pilot in the Royal Air Force, had not returned from a mission over the Bay of Biscay.

Weizmann, the bereaved father with whom everyone sympathized, arrived in New York on the evening of April 14 and checked into the luxurious St. Regis Hotel on Fifty-fifth Street. Ben-Gurion, suffering an attack of lumbago so fierce he found it "difficult to move . . . It was nothing short of a miracle that I could get in and out of taxis and planes," returned from "important talks" in Washington, with, among others, Soviet ambassador Maxim Litvinov. His hope of seeing Roosevelt had been rekindled that morning. Frankfurter had phoned with the news that Winant had again arrived in Washington, and Ben-Gurion immediately cabled Winant at the State Department, saying "Felix" had asked that he "get in touch with you at once on an urgent matter. Wire me when I can see you." When, to his surprise, he received no reply, Ben-Gurion began a feverish search for Winant. The White House referred him to the State Department, where he was told that Winant was at the Hotel Washington, which said Winant had checked out.

Ben-Gurion and Weizmann met at 6:00 P.M. on April 15 and again on April 17 and 18; neither mentioned what, as it turned out, were their rival efforts to reach Winant. It appears that ever since Ben-

Gurion had reported to Weizmann about his promising meetings with
Winant in London and their developing friendship — and especially
Winant's promise to set up a meeting for him with Roosevelt — Weizmann decided to cultivate Winant himself. Weizmann invited him to
dinner at the Dorchester, wished him a happy New Year, thanked him
for his "kindness and consideration," saying it was a "privilege to be
able to speak to you so freely, and to find so much comfort . . . in these
dark days," and got his assistance in arranging his flight to the United
States. Now that he was in New York, Weizmann, too, sought Winant
and managed to contact him. They met in Washington on April 22 and
23, and Weizmann gave him a short statement on the Jewish military
force. Ben-Gurion, when he learned this, must have felt that the rug
had been pulled out from under him.[16]

Ben-Gurion could find comfort and understanding only with Miriam.
She told him she had learned some Hebrew and Greek, and he was able
to talk with her on subjects dear to his heart, as well as those which
disturbed him. Their deepening relationship did not remain a secret,
and Arthur Lourie, who kept his eyes open, wrote May a humorous account of it in March, interspersed with other bits of gossip. "Your account of D. has kept me chuckling inside all day," she wrote back, and
from London waved a cautionary finger at him. "If your Miriam isn't
really nice to him, my curse will follow her all the days of her life!"
    Although Ben-Gurion turned down her invitations to go to the
movies or the theater — "He was always immersed in Zionism and in
Greek" — his misery touched Miriam; she took walks with him and invited him to her apartment at 23 East Eighth Street and for weekends
at the country home of her cousins Harold and Bertha Linder in Olivebridge, New York, in the foothills of the Catskill Mountains, which was
surrounded by 400 acres of forest. Ben-Gurion, seeing such an estate
for the first time, asked, "Do all these trees belong to one man?" It was
probably on Miriam's advice that on April 24 he went, for relaxation
and escape from the disappointments and backaches that had been
plaguing him, to Beaver Lake House, an inexpensive resort on the
shore of Beaver Lake, near Olivebridge.
    In his four days there Ben-Gurion wrote Miriam four letters, which
he sent via special delivery to New York. That they hit their target and
captured her heart can hardly be in doubt, for through them she discovered a side of Ben-Gurion previously unknown to her, and for that
matter to anyone else: a man in whom the adolescent lived, musing,
questioning, probing, and wondering, crying out for the sublime and
the unattainable in an attempt to impress the object of his affections
and gain her understanding and support, and maybe her love.[17]

Four letters, excelling in neither literary grace nor philosophical depth — perhaps even a bit affected — reveal, in an English that is rich, if faulty in spelling, a burning desire to communicate with a kindred soul and express a vibrant need for human contact. In the first letter Ben-Gurion discovers nature, with which Americans living in New York (which he perceives as Sodom and Gommorah) are necessarily unacquainted. Ben-Gurion describes it to Miriam as to a little girl whose hand he holds as he guides her through the mysteries of nature, like a Greek pedagogue of old — every line draws heavily on Plato's dialogues — and he bewails her ignorance of Hebrew, the one language in which heaven's celestial glory can be adequately described.

Miriam —
Here I am.
   It is a real "here" — it exists and lives its own life, and has a nature — a real nature, not the one out of a dictionary — of its own. Shall I try to describe it?
   The first thing — there is here a sky, a real sky, and not a blue or grey patch somewhere above forty-second street [where the Emergency Committee office was located]. Here it is gods own sky — big, high, enormous, almost limitless. . . . It is not very blue — I am sorry to say . . . very . . . deep . . . There is one [such sky] somewhere in a little country, far away, very far away — and so near though! — it is a country of my own — would you believe it? . . . [The sky] entered my hearth . . . the first time I saw it (was it yesterday or many-many years ago?) and whenever I am away and lonesome and sad I look at it (never mind how I do it!) . . . we have also a sun. . . . I mean the real one . . . a divinity — Only in my own little country and also here there is a genuine Sun — and it pours out generously, indiscriminately, gracious by its warmth and light. . . . [I] could tell much more about it — were you not so ignorant of the only language which can properly deal with these divine matters as "The heavens declare the glory of God"* (or is it my ignorance of your American language?). . . . And there [are] also here cows. I doubt whether you have any idea of such a creature. Perhaps you saw it in the — dictionary. But it is not the same thing. There it consists of three letters: C-O-W. It is quite different here. First of all it has no letters at all! It cannot even read — neither english nor hebrew! — But I will try to explain to you what it is.

Here he embarks on a lengthy discourse on milk, and the difference between the milk Miriam is familiar with and the genuine article. To his regret neither time nor paper is sufficient to describe "all the wonderful things I found here" at Beaver Lake House, like the grass, the frogs, and "the wonderful symphonies . . . the trees standing up and standing down . . . the mountains, the stones and the silence and the

---

* Psalms 19:2

birds and the fields and all other marvels" which Miriam, living "in that empty, forsaken desert called city of New York," has never seen. In the next letter, he promises, he will tell her "about my distinguished companions here," whom he doubts she has ever met.

In the second letter, dated April 25, Ben-Gurion offers an account, again at length, of his "Athenian friends" — Plato, Socrates, "Glaukon," "Adeimantos, Palemarchor," and "Alkibiados," among others. He describes their discourses and activities in contemporary, plain language, like a teacher to his students. The bitter memory of his disappointments with Winant and Frankfurter seeps into this letter in his distinction between his "Athenian friends," who were first and foremost men of honor who respected their promises, and the Americans, as different from these ancient Greeks as the sky, the sun, and the cows are from their poor imitations in New York and in the dictionary. After reading it, Miriam, on whom all this had had the desired effect, called Ben-Gurion from New York to thank him for his wonderful letters. "Yesterday I was rung up by a friend," he wrote her, encouraged, in his third letter, "and while I had a shrewd suspicion that that voice — it was merely a voice and non of Athenian friends could explain how and whence this voice is reaching me — is coming from that dreadful place (I forgot its name) where there are all kinds of Committees useful and otherwise — I was rather . . . glad to hear it, and wonder: will I hear it again to day?" In this letter, along with derisive references to the Emergency Committee and another installment of the adventures of his "Athenian friends," Ben-Gurion included the following lines:

> I am certainly *not* in America — at least not in U.S.A., as you call it. First of all nobody seems to speak [English] here . . . they . . . seem to speak something like German. But I don't believe that I am in Germany. I have still a faint memory from the days I was *there* [New York], with you, that there is in Germany a crazy and wicked fellow — his name is, if I am not mistaken, something like Hitler, and he amuses himself by attempting to annihilate Jews, and I can hardly imagine myself going there just now. I know too that I am not in my own country, in that little marvellous piece of heaven and earth with the most ansient long-bearded, humble, wise men and the most young brave enterprising, fearless, determined, single-minded, purposeful, visionary and efficient toiles and warriors . . . Whenever I leave it . . . I put it in its entirety completely (you see it is a little country) in my heart and I carry it, not *with* me . . . [but] *in me.*

In his last letter Ben-Gurion recapitulates his distinction between "here" and "there," the former good, beautiful, and pure, and the latter ugly, wicked, and fallacious. He also describes the newest friend to join him and his group of Athenians, and in the process defines for Miriam the meaning of love.

I meet often — several times a day, — a good friend. He is much taller than any of the Athenians, very upright, poised, fresh-looking, always deep thoughts, sure of himself, unmoved although very sensible. . . . I had with him a long interesting conversation — not on war or Emergency Committee, oh no, he cares nothing about *these* things. His speech is peculiar, hardly produces any syllable — but is nevertheless very expressive and clear. . . . He . . . never uses any of these long-winded, empty, high-sounding words used by your orators *there* . . . and can you imagine that? He never tells a lie! He [is] very much alive to what is going on around him and is a great admirer — some say even a worshipper — of the sun, and of the earth too, not like your people there. And he told me his love story, and what real life is and about heaven and stars — he sees them more than anybody els, and has such a deep understanding of them, although he never read a single book on Astronomy. . . . And how deep is his knowledge of the earth — more that of the must accomplished Professors of Geology. He told me — rather whispered — wonderful story of mysterious drops falling from the heavens, of refreshing, caressing breezes, of unspeakably beautiful and generous rays of light, of hidden springs beneath the earth and many other enchanting stories — they are true, all of them, unlike the stories one may here *there;* What a pity I can't bring my friend with me, he cannot leave his place here — and he shouldn't, there is no use for him *there* anyhow. Nobody is going *there* to talk to him. But if you will one day come here you will find him — just where I conversed with him, as he is always there — being a tree, a true, living, evergreen tree, deeply in love with the earth, which he dos not want to leave for a single moment. Is not that true, dear love?[18]

These four letters, which laid the foundation of their relationship, were the beginning of a long correspondence. Ben-Gurion signed the first "David," but by the end of the second letter he felt close enough to sign only "D." In all his past correspondence with his women friends the latter signature had always denoted a higher level of intimacy, surpassed only by the woman's addressing him as "D." and signing her initial in Hebrew. As with her predecessors — Paula, Rega, and Doris — Ben-Gurion pleaded with Miriam to study Hebrew, and soon Miriam, too, was opening her letters to him "Dear D." and signing them with her Hebrew initial.

Fully aware, however, of Paula's unerring intuition and incomparable resourcefulness in detecting forbidden correspondence, Ben-Gurion, after he returned to Palestine, introduced something new: the opening lines, in which they called each other by name, were written in pencil, so they could be erased. Moreover, from the beginning he instituted a code all their own. His first four letters from Beaver Lake House were referred to as "the BL papers," and Miriam was accordingly referred to as "friend," "correspondent," or "the keeper of the

Beaver Lake papers" (as in the third letter where he wrote, "Yesterday I was rung up by a friend") and always referred to in the masculine. Ben-Gurion, the man of nature and "Athenian" — as distinct from the Zionist leader — was "the Beaver Lake papers-man" or simply "BL."[19] All, alas, to no avail; Paula tore the veil off Miriam's identity in record time.

These letters to Miriam offer the only opportunity to discover how Ben-Gurion viewed himself.

You ask me about the Beaver Lake papers-man. I know somewhat that fellow. He may be sometimes very disagreable and has a large number of shortcomings, but you can absolutely rely upon him, as he means every word he says, and he rather says less than he means. . . . He sometimes seems rather narrow-minded, but once something got into his head or a similar place — it sticks there, and time and distance do not exist at all as far as he is concerned. Being rather obstinate it is remarcable how much he yilded to his assistant and was quite willing to learn and to adapt himself to new requirements which he always overlooked.

In another letter:

As you know I meet from time to time BL. He is as you know a queer fellow (although not as bad as some people think) but there is one thing about him — *he is reliable,* and you can take his word.

And last:

You, I imagine, want to hear something about BL. I don't see him to often, and he is as you know rather busy . . . little communicative, somethimes brooding, sometimes being entirely, unreservedly absorbed in his work.
I really dont know after all what his work is about — , very seldom talking about himself. . . . And as I have — I am afraid — less sympathy for him than you have, I can hardly tell you any more about him.[20]

Ben-Gurion attributed that quality he so esteemed in BL, reliability, to Miriam as well, writing, "Your information is invaluable and reliable" and that he could "entirely absolutely rely on him." Once the BL code is broken, there is little room for doubt that after Ben-Gurion's return to New York they became closer still, and their love grew deeper and stronger. Miriam, now his private secretary, visited him in his room at the Winthrop Hotel (another code name for Ben-Gurion) and accompanied him on his trips to Washington and Chicago and "to two-three summer places." They spent his last twenty-four hours in New York together, before he set out for Palestine on September 18.

On the anniversary of this parting he wrote her, "It was one of the numerous departures I took and may still take, but things which happened during the twenty four hours before that departure as well as days and weeks and months before it make it a living tresure unique in its kind." The bell in the New York airport signaling him to board his flight never stopped echoing in his ears, he wrote her. "We were waiting for the departure of the plane rather a long time, and then suddenly a bell rung . . . and never in my life have I experienced such an intense feeling of sadness and loneliness as at that moment, — and I don't know why — I often hear or rather feel the same bell ringing accompanyed by the same feeling of anguish and sadness and bewilderment, as if I were suddenly left alone, entirely alone."

During a stopover on the way to Palestine, he dashed off a letter to her, asking, "How are you, dearest?" and after reaching home he wrote her that he could "make out more or less accurately what [BL] is thinking or feeling," promising her that he hadn't changed "a bit, and Winthrop is alive for him now" as ever. Furthermore, it "seems that he is expecting something rather violently — you know his passionate habits." Love taking wing between a man and a woman always seemed like a miracle to him. Longing for her, he wrote, "But for . . . the present nothing more is left with you than those unforgettable hours of work together, of those talks and discussions . . . meetings and memoranda and those unexpected, more than unexpected, things which happen by a miracle." Several times, in his desire for her, he wrote, "The main thing I wish to tell you I leave to your imagination."[21] In his eyes a woman's voluntary submission was an act of astounding largesse, a symbol of unselfishness and nobility of the soul. He termed Paula's maiden bed, in which he had first known a woman, "sacred," and, twenty-five years later, Ben-Gurion once again could not rest until he came up with an appropriate expression of Miriam's saintliness. Therefore he designated her one of the "thirty-six Justs."*

> Tell him . . . that I can absolutely rely on him (although God only knows why I deserved such a thing) and I believe I knew — from the moment I met him — his deep humanity, nobility of heart and generous mind. When I knew him better I learned to admire his insight, sympathetic understanding and something more valuable and undefinable quality of saintliness blended with healthy worldliness. . . . He is one of those rare people who by their sheer existence make life more bright and worthwhile. You feel in their presence that faith, devotion, unselfishness are not merely items in a dictionary. They are not many, but they *are,* in true

---

* According to Jewish tradition, these thirty-six constitute the minimum number of anonymous, hidden saints living in the world in every generation, on whose merit the world exists.

life. . . . In hebrew they are called *Lamed vav* which means 36. . . . But one of them is quite sufficient to radiate all the human glory to make your life worth living.[22]

Just as Ben-Gurion read and reread Miriam's letters, so she pored over those of "the person I love best." Her letters to him were also filled with double meanings, and after explaining how essential a man of his stature was to the Emergency Committee and to Zionism in the United States she continued,

But you are so very far away; so utterly remote. Sometimes I wonder whether I just dreamed there was such a one — that he said thus and so — that he stood for this and that — that all the loyalty and faith on which I seem to have built my world, is built on something which I imagined once in a moment of ecstacy [*sic*] and revelation. Perhaps the long, long weeks of solitude have confused me and I no longer know what is real and what is imaginary. . . . Sometimes I have a flash of insight and understand in every pore of [*sic*] what the Psalmist meant when he said: How long, O Lord, how long! . . . I'm here for whenever you need me — wherever it is, for whatever I can do.
   Perhaps if you can't or don't write, you'd send me a cable every once in a while. Let me know your plans, if you can. . . . Yours, M. [initial in Hebrew][23]

She, too, regarded the love that bound them as the fruit of a miracle, but when his letters were long in coming, she wrote,

It is hard to believe that, busy as you are, you haven't any time to write to me at all. It is next to impossible to believe that it is not a more or less deliberate act of cruelty. . . . I know that you would not be deliberately cruel. And if you count on me more than anyone has a right to count on anyone — without one word of response, one line of encouragement, one word of reassurance — I am glad that you do. On the other hand, maybe you don't, and expect me to have sense enough to understand that from your silence. I honestly don't know what to think or do, or to infer. I am afraid I haven't much sense. Like children, I believe in miracles and fairy tales, even when the miracles occurred a long time ago in never-never land, which may never have existed, except in my own imagination. . . . The past year and a half has seemed an eternity. Yours, M. [in Hebrew][24]

One question remains unanswered: Did BL promise Miriam a life together, or were her hopes for this nourished by the hints and inferences of their impassioned correspondence? Did Miriam look forward to a fulfillment of this promise or merely to another reunion, projecting further and further into the future? Was Ben-Gurion's appraisal of himself as a man of his word less than a declaration of his intentions? "[BL] used to tell me," he wrote, "(I was the only person to whom he told it) that never before has he met such a trusted and reliable collaborator, and that he will never feel quite as happy in his work (and his work means everything to him) until that collaboration is reestablished." Did this bespeak a pledge? And what conclusions might Miriam have drawn from his writing that since he had met her he "always regretted why I did't meet [her] before, and at the same time I felt as if I knew [her] all my life"?

Even the airport bell, which he perennially recalled, seems full of promise. "Perhaps you remember a bell ringing one friday after- noon — it seems to me ringing still, and may it not mean also arrival as well as departure? I don't know at what end it may be — there or here but I cannot imagine [no meeting] at all." In describing his longing to her, he wrote, "And you are left even more to yourself to your brood- ings and memories (will all this be merely memories?)." But no explicit promise was ever made in his letters, and even his aching for a renewal of their "collaboration" has an air of helplessness: "And while unable for the moment to continue the same work, I feel it was no mere pass- ing, temporary occupation of momentary effect. Whenever you meet that friend of mine please tell him that I will never forget what we have done together and that I look forward for a renewal of that collabo- ration — when — where — I don't know."[25]

Still, no obstacle or doubt could dim their yearning to be together, and — if only for this reason — the promise, if unspoken, held firm. In 1944 Ben-Gurion again wrote her that "[BL] *is reliable*" and had told Ben-Gurion that time would overcome distance "in a not too-distant future" and that "23 [Miriam's house number] must return, and I trust him, and so can you." But Ben-Gurion did not return to the United States in 1943 or in 1944, and with the passing of time his letters be- came less frequent and less impassioned, and whatever promise may have existed withered and died.

May, who followed the romance through her correspondence with Lourie, asked him in April 1945 what "Miriam Cohen's young man [is] like" and — not without the sigh of relief of a jealous woman — wired Ben-Gurion, who already knew, that Miriam was about to be married. In June 1945, Paula was at Ben-Gurion's side and Eddie Taub at Mir- iam's when the two met again in Miriam's new home in Washington.

Nevertheless, their correspondence continued. On June 27, 1973, Ben-Gurion wrote her a letter that began by hand with "Dear Miriam" in Hebrew and continued on an English typewriter. "I received your letter from April 29. Peace to Israel is growing . . . I would like to see you here, in Jerusalem." On August 26, answering her response, he wrote his last letter to her. Following "Dear Miriam" in Hebrew, writ- ten with a shaking hand that betrayed painful arthritis, were three

typed lines in English, in which he expressed hope of seeing her in Sde
Boker, his Negev retreat. He signed his full name in Hebrew with a
hand still shakier. He died three months later.[26]

It was fortunate that the BL letters won Miriam's heart and sympathy;
from April 27, the day Ben-Gurion returned to New York, until he left
for Palestine on September 18, and even afterward, he needed every
last bit of sympathy and support in the fiercest of his battles with
Weizmann. As was their custom, the first round opened and closed in
cooperation and shared enthusiasm. Sharett told the Jerusalem JAE
that "Weizmann arrived in the United States rather dejected but after
a long talk with Ben-Gurion was encouraged and got down to work."
Weizmann had two objectives in coming to the United States. First, he
wanted the process he had invented for manufacturing synthetic rubber to be developed on an industrial scale by American companies for
the war effort. He thereby hoped to gain sympathy for Zionism from
the White House and in Whitehall, as he had done during the First
World War. His second purpose was to participate as a principal figure in an all-Zionist conference that would make the establishment of a
Jewish state after the war the goal of Zionist policy. This was the conference that Ben-Gurion had been advocating since he had devised
"combative Zionism" in 1938. After a December 5, 1940, meeting at
the Winthrop Hotel, he had suggested that a "Zionist conference to
include all groups and bodies should be held to present to the Jewish
and general public a clear picture of what Zionism means." No longer
satisfied with "Zionist unity" but aspiring to unite all Jews in America,
Ben-Gurion worked indefatigably to produce a "common platform,"
whose key demand was the establishment of a Jewish state, which both
the Zionists and non-Zionists would back. With the United States'
entry into the conflict, the great opportunity offered Zionism by the
war was finally a reality. For some time Ben-Gurion had maintained
that "what is impossible during ordinary times becomes possible in
times of upheaval; and if at this time we miss the opportunity and do
not dare to do what can be done only in such great moments as these,
we forfeit an entire world." Ben-Gurion could view as personal
achievements both a proposal Weizmann had made during his July
1941 visit to America for an "international Zionist conference in the
U.S.," to serve as "nuisance value for Great Britain just as the Arabs
are," and the American Zionists' willingness to hold such a conference
and demand a state.

   This conference, which Weizmann was to convene in April 1942,
"could not replace a Congress," but it "would be the next best thing,"
and it was meant to formulate policy and adopt "binding resolutions."

Delegates were to come from the Americas, South Africa, Palestine, Britain and the dominions, and "other countries still accessible." Ben-Gurion looked forward to it, and when in December 1941 a cable from Jerusalem requested that he attend to the preparations, he got down to work with great energy. In March he wrote Paula, "We are now preparing for a conference of all the Zionists in America to discuss Zionism's present problems and formulate Zionist policy for the near future and the coming peace." He was in agreement with Weizmann on the conference's goals, and in Emergency Committee discussions he backed Meyer Weisgal, Weizmann's right-hand man in America, who was in charge of the conference's organizational side. Weisgal's telegrams to the would-be delegates included "regards" from both Weizmann and Ben-Gurion.

Of 586 credentials, 519 were distributed to American delegates and 67 to honored guests from Canada, South America, and Palestine. The event became not "the next best thing" to a congress, as Weizmann had hoped, but rather a general conference of American Zionists, the first of its kind. The Extraordinary Conference or Pan-American Zionist Conference, as it was variously called, opened with great ceremony on May 9, 1942, at New York's Biltmore Hotel at Madison Avenue and Forty-third Street and closed on May 11 with a "Declaration," as its resolutions were termed. In the first six paragraphs the "American Zionists" reaffirmed "their unequivocal devotion to the cause of democratic freedom and international justice"; gave expression to "their faith in the ultimate victory of humanity and justice over lawlessness and brute force"; offered "a message of hope and encouragement to their fellow Jews" in Europe and in Palestine; recounted the history and achievements of the Zionist enterprise; declared on behalf of the Jewish people "readiness and . . . desire . . . for full cooperation with their Arab neighbors"; called for "the fulfillment of the original purpose of the Balfour Declaration and the Mandate which 'recognizing the historical connection of the Jewish people with Palestine' was to afford them the opportunity, as stated by President Wilson, to found there a Jewish Commonwealth"; and affirmed their "unalterable rejection of the White Paper," which even Churchill, in May 1939, had regarded as " 'a breach and repudiation of the Balfour Declaration' . . . in its denial of sanctuary to Jews fleeing from Nazi persecution."

The first six paragraphs, which laid the ideological foundations, were based on an address Weizmann delivered at the conference opening, as well as on statements by Ben-Gurion, and the last two, the operative ones, were taken, almost in their entirety, from Ben-Gurion's policy address of the second day of the conference; they were the familiar points he had been expounding in his role as Zionist preacher.[27]

These two paragraphs, the seventh and eighth, delineated a new Zionist policy:

7. . . . recognition must be given to the right of the Jews of Palestine to play their full part in the war effort and in the defense of their country, through a Jewish military force fighting under their own flag and under the high command of the United Nations.

8. The Conference declares that the new world order that will follow victory cannot be established on foundations of peace, justice, and equality, unless the problem of Jewish homelessness is finally solved.

The Conference demands that the gates of Palestine be opened; that the Jewish Agency be vested with control of immigration into Palestine and with the necessary authority for upbuilding the country . . . and that Palestine be established as a Jewish Commonwealth integrated into the structure of the new democratic world.

It would seem that Ben-Gurion should have felt gratified, not only by the actual assembling of the conference but by its adoption of his policy and by receiving public recognition of his importance in it. For the first time he made headlines in the *New York Times,* over a long story on the conference: BEN-GURION OUTLINES PROGRAM FOR SOLVING PALESTINE PROBLEM; MANDATE FOR JEWISH COMMONWEALTH, WIDE POWERS FOR ZIONIST AGENCY AND EQUALITY FOR ALL ARE LEADER'S SUGGESTIONS. Just two weeks later, however, it became clear that there was no joy in Ben-Gurion's heart and that anger and increasing resentment of Weizmann had replaced Ben-Gurion's spirit of cooperation. The first outward manifestation was the announcement on June 10 that Ben-Gurion would not attend a meeting of the Emergency Committee, which Weizmann called at his hotel for June 16.

The second manifestation was his resolution to return to Palestine immediately after the Biltmore Conference, either to avoid clashing with Weizmann, or because Ben-Gurion felt redundant. On May 1 he had asked Frankfurter to help him get a flight — "as I may have to return to Palestine soon" — and after the conference cabled this intention to London as well. To Paula he wired, "Hope return soon inform Sharett, love David." In response, the JAE's telegraphic chorus, with Paula as soloist, was reawakened. On May 31 Sharett cabled, "Deeply perturbed by your intention return stop thought you had initiated fruitful activity internal external stop." This was followed by an uncharacteristic telegram from Paula, "Cable whether this is your final decision." So far Ben-Gurion had made no real preparations to leave, but, receiving a second wire from Paula on June 7, he answered the same day, "Leaving as soon as plane accommodations available love David," and sent the same message to Sharett.

The Jerusalem JAE met that day for an urgent discussion, with all present wondering at the meaning of this sudden return. "When Ben-Gurion informed us he had decided to go to the United States he said it was imperative a member of the Executive be present on this important front," said the non-Zionist Werner Senator. "He owes us an explanation for his return to Palestine." Itzhak Gruenbaum expressed surprise that after the JAE had granted Ben-Gurion's request to set up a "special office" in Washington it should suddenly be told that he was leaving. "This should not be passed over in silence ... [We] want to know if the work begun by Ben-Gurion is finished, and if not it is desirable that he remain in America until it is." Sharett, from whom the members of the JAE expected an explanation, could say only that Ben-Gurion was coming home because "in his view he should be in Palestine now. The telegram is not very enlightening." The only one to hit the mark was Rabbi Maimon. "The probable reason for his return is a difference of opinion between him and Weizmann, who is also in America." They finally decided to notify Ben-Gurion that "for all our desire to see him among us, the Executive believes he should finish the work he started in the United States."

One possible reason for Ben-Gurion's behavior could have been the tension created by his outward acquiescence to Weizmann's predominance (as long as Weizmann continued to cooperate fully) and his inability to come to terms with his number two status, which kept him at a distance from top diplomacy yet compelled him to observe the top man's lapses. Certainly there is evidence of it. On December 18, 1941, Ben-Gurion reported in his diary that "in Weizmann's absence I am the representative of the Jewish people in America — without any official status or powers of representation." Three days later he said the same thing to Frankfurter. It seems that he had intended to be active in the United States only "until Weizmann's arrival," he wrote to Locker in London. When he returned to Jerusalem he told the JAE, "When Weizmann arrived I decided not to continue any longer on my own on behalf of the Executive, and my work in Washington came to a stop." He showed himself to be perfectly willing to turn the field over to his senior. However when, two weeks after his arrival, Weizmann informed Wise, head of the Emergency Committee, that since the United States was the "center of gravity" for Zionism, "I am proceeding ... to set up, at once, what will be known as the Office of the President of the World Zionist Organization" to act as liaison with the various government agencies in Washington, and that for this purpose "a considerable fund will be needed to be placed at my disposal ... forthwith," Ben-Gurion was enraged. He not only felt threatened by this move, which could have added the United States to Weizmann's London power base, but was also concerned lest the primacy of the Jerusalem JAE be compromised. Weizmann yielded to his opposition and agreed to Wise's proposal to establish a New York office of the Zionist Executive.[28]

Still, inability to reconcile himself to Weizmann's senior status does not seem to be a sufficient reason for Ben-Gurion's rancor. Was it envy? Certainly some of the events associated with the conference were such as to incite envy even in one whose heart was made of granite. In January 1942 the prestigious quarterly *Foreign Affairs* published Weizmann's article "Palestine's Role in the Solution of the Jewish Problem," in which Weizmann argued that only a Jewish state could absorb two million Jews after the war. This, of course, was the heart of Ben-Gurion's position, and the article, which was meant as a platform for the Zionist conference and won universal attention, stole the thunder from Ben-Gurion's political address to the conference. Even before the conference opened, Rabbi Wise, chairman of its presidium, emphasized Weizmann's pre-eminence in a letter to the delegates. "We are to welcome our beloved leader Dr. Chaim Weizmann. . . . We shall also have an opportunity to hear a full report by Mr. David Ben-Gurion." Wise opened the conference by addressing "Dr. Weizmann, ladies, and gentlemen" and stated, "This conference could not more fittingly open its deliberations than by making record of its gratitude to him who is by right of uncancellable service, the great leader of the World Zionist Movement, Dr. Chaim Weizmann." Thereupon the delegates rose to their feet, applauded, and sang "Ha-Tikvah."

Not until several moments later did Wise mention Ben-Gurion in the same breath with Weizmann as two men from whom the conference could draw inspiration. Turning the floor over to Weizmann, Wise introduced him as "our beloved Weizmann," and the audience again honored him with a standing ovation. Even Ben-Gurion's fellow party member Chaim Greenberg, who chaired the conference's third meeting, introduced Weizmann as "a man that was introduced to you by destiny and not by the chairman." When Weizmann concluded his address the audience again leapt to its feet, cheered, and sang "Ha-Tikvah." Although Ben-Gurion was also rewarded with a standing ovation after concluding his remarks, "Ha-Tikvah" was not sung in his honor.

But the love and admiration that poured forth for Weizmann at the start of the conference and during its course were nothing compared to its dramatic and emotional close. The minutes tell the story:

WISE: Dr. Weizmann, beloved leader and friend, you it was who . . . won the Balfour Declaration from Great Britain (Applause). You, it was who pleaded with the Paris Peace Conference in 1919, that the British Government be given the Mandate for Palestine. I believe, Dr. Weizmann, it will be you, who will again from Britain, the U.S. and the U.N., at the Victory Peace Conference win a charter for the Jewish Commonwealth. (Applause and cheering.) Some years ago, through the generosity of a group of friends, there was presented to me a ring, worn and held, up to the hour of his death, by the immortal founder of the Zionist Movement, Dr. Herzl. Dr. Weizmann, at the peace conference, when you present the claims of the Jewish people, I want you to have in your hand, on your finger, the ring of your predecessor in the leadership of the Zionist Movement, and as you wear the ring of Theodor Herzl, God give it that to you, and through you, to us, your people, there comes the charter of the Jewish People, of the Jewish Commonwealth in Palestine, and God give it, that for years and years you wear it in health and strength and triumph, this ring of Theodor Herzl, your great predecessor. (Dr. Wise hands ring to Dr. Weizmann as they embrace. The audience arose, applauded and cheered, as Dr. Weizmann arose.)

Thus did Wise crown Weizmann the true and only heir of Herzl. It had been Ben-Gurion's idea to convene a Zionist conference in America, and now that it had finally been held and had adopted the resolutions he had initiated, all the laurels went to Weizmann. No wonder, then, that he was green with envy. Nevertheless, it was not envy alone that propelled him into round two with Weizmann, for after the conference they met several times, with the Emergency Committee and alone, and worked in close contact and harmony. On Saturday, May 23, they met again in preparation for a trip to Washington, and at the Wardman Park Hotel there they got together once more on May 27, privately.[29]

It was almost certainly at this meeting — after which Ben-Gurion wired Paula and the London Zionist office of his hope to "return soon" — that something happened to bring to a head all his growing resentment, frustration, and jealousy and cause a flare-up that lasted several days and on June 1 finally detonated the ultimate explosion in Ben-Gurion's relationship with Weizmann. In his diary Ben-Gurion wrote only that Weizmann told him of his efforts to get him priority on a flight to Palestine, but did not report to him anything of his activities and meetings in Washington. There is no doubt that the diary does not reflect everything that happened between them. Ben-Gurion knew that Weizmann was working hard to secure an interview with Roosevelt, and the Winant mystery, which had tormented him since his arrival in the United States, returned to plague him again. He suspected that Weizmann knew something he did not. "I mentioned Winant," Ben-Gurion said in his report to the JAE in Jerusalem, and the mystery was solved.

In their talks of April 22 and 23, Winant had asked Weizmann to tell

Ben-Gurion that "he was very sorry" he had not kept his promise to set up a meeting for him with Roosevelt. Winston Churchill had come to Washington shortly after Ben-Gurion had moved there, and Winant "knew that the president would be busy with Churchill then." But that Winant "is now ready" to arrange matters, if Ben-Gurion is still interested in the meeting. Weizmann had forgotten, he said, to deliver Winant's message for over a month. Winant had departed for London on April 29, so Ben-Gurion would have had four or five days, at best, to arrange a consultation with him. Ben-Gurion explained to his colleagues that Weizmann had asked Winant "to arrange the thing . . . since Weizmann himself wished to see Roosevelt at the same time." With this the Winant affair ended. Meanwhile Weizmann met three times with Vice President Henry Wallace, with government officials, with New York State governor Herbert Lehman, and ultimately — thanks to the intervention of Under Secretary of State Sumner Welles — with Roosevelt himself on July 7, only five days after requesting the meeting, for a short talk devoted to the process Weizmann had invented for the production of synthetic rubber.[30]

It was natural for Ben-Gurion not to believe that Weizmann had simply forgotten to relay Winant's message; had he not always accused him of jealously keeping diplomatic and political contacts close to his chest? It seemed to Ben-Gurion that Weizmann had deliberately undermined his chances to meet with Roosevelt. In a telephone conversation on June 10, Ben-Gurion turned down an invitation to lunch and repeated to Weizmann that, since he no longer regarded himself as associated with him, he would not come to the meeting at the St. Regis on June 16. A letter he sent the next day — after writing several drafts — reiterated that he no longer considered himself Weizmann's associate. Ben-Gurion explained this decision by accusing Weizmann of consulting and cooperating only with people he felt a personal liking for, as one does in one's private life, even though the World Zionist Organization (WZO) constitution prohibited this and it was not in the best interests of the movement. If Weizmann could not offer his "wholehearted support [and] assure the necessary common and united action," Ben-Gurion doubted that he could be of any use in the United States and refused to share the responsibility for political activity. Sharett received a copy of this letter, and Lourie sent one to May, who wrote him that "Darling David persists in refusing to play ball . . . [I am] referring to perfectly idiotic letter of June 11, 1942 — which should never have been sent (and would never have been sent if he had tried dictating it to me!)." The dig at Miriam could not have been more obvious.

In his response, sent by courier on June 15, with a copy to Sharett, Weizmann rejected all Ben-Gurion's arguments and termed his letter a "rather amazing document." He could not defend his actions, he said, for he was unaware of any guilt on his part. If there was guilt, "it is rather with the accuser than with the accused": he had done nothing without prior discussion and consultation, whereas Ben-Gurion had absented himself from meetings and consultations. And as if to dispel any doubts regarding the difference in their status, he reminded Ben-Gurion that "contrary to your opinion, I am charged with the responsibility of conducting Zionist political affairs." As to whether his actions were in the best interests of the Zionist movement, Weizmann thought, "We can safely leave this for time to decide." Ben-Gurion's accusations were "aimed by indirection to cover up the failure of a mission, which was, I believe, rather nebulous in its nature and without set purpose." Weizmann saw "no justification whatsoever" for Ben-Gurion's letter, which he regarded as "merely the result of a temporary mood, dictated . . . by an imaginary grievance caused undoubtedly by the many heart-breaking disappointments" — an allusion to Ben-Gurion's fruitless efforts to meet with Roosevelt — "which all of us must face in this crucial hour."

Ben-Gurion responded the next day with a short letter, also sent by courier, with a copy to Sharett. First he challenged Weizmann to state "the dates and occasions when I was asked by you for any consultation on any matter and chose to absent myself." Second, in stating " 'contrary to your opinion, I am charged with the responsibility of conducting Zionist political affairs,' " Weizmann had left out "the all important word *alone*. . . . I maintained," wrote Ben-Gurion, "and still maintain that you are not authorized to conduct political affairs *alone*, and it is also my considered view that it is not in the best interests of Zionism and Palestine that you conduct affairs alone." The same day, the Emergency Committee canceled a meeting called by Weizmann at the St. Regis and called a plenary session at the Astor Hotel, in which both adversaries took part, making the Emergency Committee witness to a further altercation between them. On June 17 Weizmann responded in writing to Ben-Gurion's second letter, stating that "in writing you before I had in mind not only your [absenting yourself from meetings and consultations] here, but also in London." However, he did not think that "any useful purpose will be served by continuing our correspondence further."

Being talked down to only enraged Ben-Gurion further, and he brought this "matter of extreme gravity" to Rabbi Wise's attention in a letter he delivered personally. Weizmann, wrote Ben-Gurion, was jeopardizing the current political objectives of Zionism and undermining the unity of the movement. "I made several attempts to dissuade Dr. Weizmann from this unfortunate course. . . . I have had to inform Dr. Weizmann that I do not see that I am any longer associated with him." Unless "this disastrous situation" was remedied, Ben-Gurion saw "no other course . . . left for me than to ask the Executive and the Actions Committee in Palestine to call for his resignation." Before taking "such grave action," Ben-Gurion felt "bound to bring the matter before the Zionist leadership of [the United States]." He would be grateful, he said, if Wise would arrange an informal meeting of the American Zionist leaders and members of the Zionist Executive in New York with Weizmann, and concluded, "You may, if you wish, send a copy of this letter to Dr. Weizmann."

Wise first tried to soothe Ben-Gurion by "saying . . . as a friend and fellow worker" that since his fears that Palestine would be invaded were not "unjustified . . . I cannot believe that we ought to spend a moment's time . . . [on] the problems you feel have arisen between Dr. Weizmann and yourself." But when Wise realized that Ben-Gurion would not be pacified, he quickly arranged the informal meeting for Saturday, June 27, at 4:00 P.M., in his home at 40 West Sixty-eighth Street.

Wise asked the two antagonists and the other seven present — including Miriam Cohen, who took the minutes — to be seated in his study. He sat at the head of the conference table, Weizmann and Ben-Gurion faced each other in the middle, and the duel began. Ben-Gurion could count on the sympathy of two participants, Chaim Greenberg of Poale Zion and Robert Szold, as well as the silent encouragement offered by Miriam. Weizmann had three supporters: Rabbi Wise and Louis Lipsky, long-time admirers, and his assistant Meyer Weisgal. The two remaining participants, Nahum Goldmann and Judge Louis Levinthal, the new president of the ZOA, were undecided. But when the meeting ended that evening, everyone present sympathized with Weizmann, the noble, charming, and long-suffering president, the prince sporting Herzl's ring like a royal signet, the man who embodied the distress and vision of his people, and the bereaved father silently bearing his grief. Ben-Gurion, railing harshly and heartlessly against Weizmann, stood alone, his accusations impressing the others as groundless and wholly unjustified. Miriam, like the others, regarded his attack on Weizmann as a form of lèse-majesté.

The minutes — Ben-Gurion, usually fastidious in recording his words and deeds in his diary, passed over this historic confrontation in silence — do not reflect very well the violence of Ben-Gurion's attack attested to by other sources. According to the minutes, Ben-Gurion opened by declaring how painful it was for him to say what he had to say, but perhaps "when I finish you will understand" that necessity. He recounted the story of his relationship with Weizmann since 1931 and lately in London and New York, in the course of which he detailed Weizmann's faults and their recent correspondence. In summary, he stated that he would no longer be associated with Weizmann, who "since he came to America . . . has acted entirely on his own, consulting and cooperating from time to time with people of his personal choice, as one does in one's private affairs," and established a "personal regime." Ben-Gurion rejected Weizmann's statement that time would judge his acts. "In all humility I differ. I do not think that what Dr. Weizmann says or does is not a matter for discussion. . . . I certainly have a right and a duty to discuss what he does, and Dr. Weizmann cannot leave it to the future." Furthermore, "(1) Dr. Weizmann is not authorized to act alone. (2) It is not in the interests of the movement that he should act alone." Whereas he had always considered Weizmann "the first man in Zionism," his modus operandi was harmful to it. For two years Ben-Gurion had tried to avoid the issue, hoping that Weizmann would change his ways and make good his assurances. But Weizmann did not do so, and, Ben-Gurion said, "I was eliminated, but he says I eliminated myself."

Ben-Gurion went on to relate his aggravation in turning to Weizmann time and again for cooperation and consultation, to no avail. If he had returned to Palestine, he said, he would have had to tell his JAE colleagues that he had seen in the minutes of the Emergency Committee that Weizmann had had important political meetings, yet when asked, "What did he say?" he would have had to reply, " 'I don't know.' Each time I went to see him I asked whether he had anything to tell me and he said no. . . . The story is incredible." This was the moment for Ben-Gurion to use all the ammunition he had accumulated in London in his industrious study of the Zionist office files, and he listed Weizmann's omissions, negligent reporting, and deficient conduct of negotiations. One accusation he flung at Weizmann bordered on treason: he claimed that Weizmann had told Lord Halifax — who was no friend and should be considered the father of the White Paper — that he would report to him on all his meetings with American officials. "I want to be there when Weizmann sees Halifax. I know what one incautious phrase can do." Ben-Gurion offered proof that Weizmann was responsible for a Jewish military force's not having been raised, and finally he came to the Winant affair. He concluded this stage of his remarks by saying that he considered himself Weizmann's devoted friend, "whatever he may think."

Weizmann's rebuttal was offered in an elegantly supercilious manner. "You do not expect this to be a tribunal to pass judgment on charges which Mr. Ben-Gurion has made," he said, so "out of respect for [those assembled here]" he was limiting himself "to a few points, not by way of justification, but by way of correcting facts. And for the rest, I will leave it to whatever will happen." He was glad to see that minutes were being taken, for "there were a great many facts mentioned which are new to me [in the] long speech of Mr. Ben-Gurion, meant with the greatest sincerity and no personal pique." There were, however, "misinterpretation, misunderstanding, and in a great many cases, misstatements." Ben-Gurion's leitmotiv was that "I am acting alone. I am not aware of it." He had never taken it on himself "either to initiate a policy, or even to execute it . . . on my own." Although he usually did go to interviews alone, he always reported them "faithfully and honestly, according to the best of my ability. . . . No one else in my position would agree to act differently. . . . Whether one has always to run in couples is something the wisdom of which must be decided; whether I need a *mashgiach al kashrut* [overseer of the ritual purity of foods], I must leave to you or to the Congress or whoever wishes to decide." In conclusion, Weizmann dismissed Ben-Gurion's charges as unfounded, untrue, unjust, and unfair. "As to the other remarks, they really can't be taken seriously."

Wise asked Weizmann if he had ever promised Halifax a full report on everything. Weizmann responded, "What I did say and I repeat is, 'Whenever I talk to an American, I talk as if Halifax could hear it.' . . . I think Mr. Ben-Gurion suffers from some hallucination about my relations with Lord Halifax and with the English." Defending himself against Ben-Gurion's insinuation that he never did or said anything that might be disagreeable to the British, he went on, "I have said no to many. . . . This peculiar statement [is] based on a sick imagination. . . . He sees ghosts and has produced a picture which led him to the conclusion which he put before you."

In the second part of the meeting, the disputants stated their positions on America. Ben-Gurion claimed that America was more important than England, although "I do not think we should write off England." America was "the decisive power, and the political work in America is of decisive importance for the army. If America says a word, [the British] will have to hear it . . . Without the support of America our work cannot be done." But Weizmann did not agree "that the world begins and ends with America. I think we should do our level best — as much as it is in our power to do — to get England and America to cooperate on our problem. . . . I am glad that Ben-Gurion has not written off England. I believe that the combination and focusing of Anglo-American interest on our problem is the right way to go about it. Whether we can do it or not is a different matter."

From these exchanges of views the antagonists proceeded to verbal blows: the dispute grew heated, and Weizmann lost his calm. He said that if Ben-Gurion had come to be a "mashgiach, he will not expect me to work with him." Ben-Gurion replied that Weizmann heard what he wished to hear and his optimistic reports were entirely out of line with reality; he accepted empty gestures as political promises. It was not in the best interests of the movement that Weizmann act alone, and therefore the JAE operated on the principle that someone had to stand beside him. If no solution was found, Ben-Gurion said at last, and "if Weizmann can do the work only in the way he is doing it, it is better that he should resign." And if the JAE did not agree, he would go to the Actions Committee.

Weizmann answered that he was unaware that another member of the Jerusalem JAE "was always sent to England to watch that I should not make mistakes." The "whole construction of [Ben-Gurion's] charges . . . is painfully reminiscent of purges. When Hitler or Mussolini want to make a purge they bring up a whole host of charges, brought up out of the void." He came to the inevitable conclusion that this "host of imaginary charges" was intended "to culminate in an act of political assassination." Unable to speak without humor, he remarked, "The future corpse is delighted that it should be so." He would continue to act as he had been, and if he chose to see people alone, that was to be left to his discretion. Before concluding he repeated twice that Ben-Gurion intended "political assassination."

Ben-Gurion is remembered as having made far harsher, more shocking statements and calling Weizmann more offensive names than appear in the minutes, probably because Miriam, overwhelmed, shirked her duty; there is evidence that, from time to time, she neglected to take down what was being said. In her record there is no mention whatsoever of Ben-Gurion's stating that Weizmann acted like a führer — a story that was passed by word of mouth among the Zionist leaders of America as a carefully guarded secret. It became confused in the telling, so that the ultimate tale had Ben-Gurion calling Weizmann Pétain, although Weizmann is recorded as having said, "I reject the offensive statement that I am a Fuehrer."

Had Miriam, consciously or not, tried to soften for posterity what she herself termed Ben-Gurion's "attack"? She recalled that his remarks had fallen on her "like a bombshell. . . . I wished that the earth would open and swallow me . . . None of us thought he was capable of such behavior; no one had ever seen him in so belligerent a mood or heard him speak so harshly." In May 1944, leafing through the papers left her by "the person I love best," among them the minutes, she wrote Ben-Gurion that it was regrettable that so much suffering and real damage had been caused which could have been avoided "with a little more generosity of mind and an approach of a little more understanding and tolerance." Like the others, Miriam did not understand what had motivated Ben-Gurion to attack Weizmann with such ferocity. If he had wanted the meeting to condemn Weizmann and his methods, the result was perversely Weizmann's triumph and his own discomfiture. According to Miriam, Ben-Gurion had been aware of this and was "down and dejected" as a result.[31]

But Miriam was wrong. Quite to the contrary, Ben-Gurion was eager to continue the fight. The next day Wise invited everyone back to his study for another attempt at restoring peace, but fruitlessly. Ben-Gurion had nothing further to add, and Weizmann rejected Wise's suggestion to strike the previous day's remarks from the minutes. For Weizmann there was no question that "this careful choosing of the ground for the delivering of a blow at a time when I was trying to grope in the maze of America-at-war," he wrote the JAE, "was nothing short of an attempt at political assassination, carried out deliberately, calculated coolly, and with a zeal and energy worthy of a better cause." All further attempts to reconcile the two, including one in mid July by Nahum Goldmann, who engineered their last private meeting, in New York's Commodore Hotel, failed.

The rivalry between them became a war. If the meeting in Wise's home had been the scene of Ben-Gurion's grand offensive, the months that followed witnessed Weizmann's counterattack. If it was not immediately evident to their associates, it was only because they employed different weapons. Weizmann used more sophisticated ones; he operated with his personal charm and gift of winning his associates' confidence and love. Weizmann's principal ammunition was Ben-Gurion's harshness and the poor impression his adversary's attack had made on those who had witnessed the confrontation. Nor did Weizmann hesitate to exploit Ben-Gurion's failure (for which he was partly responsible) to meet the president and other important statesmen.

Under the guise of readiness to cooperate with Ben-Gurion, Weizmann went so far as to distribute copies of Ben-Gurion's letters to him to JAE people in London, New York, and Jerusalem. His finesse is especially evident in the style of his letters, each carefully and individually composed to win over a particular addressee. To the forceful and direct Lewis Namier, Weizmann described Ben-Gurion — on the day of the confrontation — as "grumbling and grousing ... and it is extremely difficult to determine what he has been doing and what he has achieved, aside from repeating the same speech about the army." There was no point in trying to talk to him, "as I think the man suffers

from some mental aberrations." To the sensitive and refined Rabbi
Wise Weizmann apologized. "[If] what I said on Saturday seemed to
you too sharp . . . Of course it was not my intention to cast any reflection on Ben-Gurion's personal integrity." He said he believed "it is
possible to work together [and was] hopeful that whatever differences
may exist will eventually be removed [since] a continuation of this unfortunate controversy will only . . . result in untold hurt to the movement."

In his campaign to shift the war to enemy territory, Weizmann
wrote frequently to Berl Locker, Ben-Gurion's party colleague and a
Weizmann supporter. In mid July Weizmann wrote that he had not yet
succeeded in establishing collective authority in American Zionism,
largely because of "the attitude and general incomprehensible behav-
iour of our friend, B.G.," and he expressed doubt that "the office of the
Executive . . . will last long [on account] of B.G.'s antics." The same
letter contains lines that he subsequently excised from his memoirs and
which the editors of his collected works omitted from the volumes of
his letters.

> He is in a constant state of jitters, nervous tension, which reduces every
> meeting, either in the Emergency Committee or elsewhere, to the gyra-
> tions of an insane asylum. Now he has gone off the deep blue with me in a
> manner which is utterly bewildering not only to myself but to every per-
> son who is aware of the situation.

In early August Weizmann notified Locker, "There will never be
any more cooperation between us and I'm quite certain that [Ben-
Gurion] is developing fascist tendencies and megalomania coupled
with political hysteria."

Sharett was also among the Mapai allies Weizmann wished to enlist,
but his comments to this prospective comrade in arms were guarded.
Testing the waters, he wrote Sharett that Ben-Gurion was making arrangements to return to Palestine. "No doubt he will tell you his own
story, whatever it may be worth. All I can say is, neither here nor
in London has he been an unqualified blessing." In October — in a
long letter he sent directly to the JAE in response to Ben-Gurion's
charges — Weizmann emptied his armory in a frontal attack, a
counter "political assassination."

> I have watched Mr. Ben-Gurion carefully during his stay here. His con-
> duct and deportment were painfully reminiscent of the petty dictator, a
> type one meets with so often in public life now. They are all shaped on a
> definite pattern: they are humorless, thin-lipped, morally stunted, fanati-
> cal and stubborn, apparently frustrated in some ambition, and nothing is
> more dangerous than a small man nursing his grievances introspectively.

Mr. Ben-Gurion is in a constant state of exaltation and tension, obsessed by a mission in life which is bending down his shoulders. He alone, apparently, is the self-appointed guardian of pure Zionist principles. He alone knows and represents the views of the Executive. He alone has the solution to the Zionist and Jewish problem, he alone is conscious of the tragic plight of our people. . . . Anybody who is unfortunate enough to question some of his statements is simply jumped upon and shouted down and he terrorizes his audience by interminable ranting speeches. . . . He had nothing to show by way of achievement after having spent in America the best part of the year. . . . As to Ben-Gurion's ideas about the necessity of an army, I can only say that Jabotinsky's views were merely milk and water compared to his. . . . We have battled against revisionism for years under the leadership of Jabotinsky. It would be a calamity to have to fight a new and more dangerous brand of fascism under the leadership of Ben-Gurion.

This escalation of hostilities by Weizmann was undoubtedly a response to Ben-Gurion's having hit sensitive targets. The charges that Weizmann cultivated a "personal regime" by means of deficient reporting, "holding court," and distancing his JAE colleagues from his personal and diplomatic contacts were accurate, even if this was not clearly appreciated in the United States. May, who followed the battle through Lourie's letters, asked huffily what Ben-Gurion wanted to prove "beyond a complaint that Chaim is Chaim?" Ben-Gurion's accusation that Weizmann had not been devoting all his energy to the Zionist cause was not refutable. Weizmann himself admitted years later, in his memoirs, that for "the first few months of my visit I was almost completely absorbed by my chemical work and its attendant problems. . . . I permitted myself some Zionist activity; not very much, to be sure . . . but enough to maintain contact with external and internal developments." Even the demand that Weizmann include Ben-Gurion in his political contacts was well founded, since, after all, it was Ben-Gurion who had brought Weizmann party support and thereby made his leadership possible.

But for the time being envy was not the emotion that directed his steps. Ben-Gurion knew in every bone in his body that a state was within reach, and he acted from a powerful synthesis of accurate political vision and strong personal motives. He regarded the Biltmore Conference as an instrument that would place the entire Zionist movement firmly behind his own political policy, which came to be known as the Biltmore Program. He chose the moment to open his campaign to destroy Weizmann politically with cool judgment and cold-blooded calculation. Ben-Gurion was not heartless or unsympathetic toward Weizmann's bereavement, and his war against Weizmann did not erase Ben-Gurion's feeling of friendship and love for him. Rather, in the heat of his race against time to reach the goal, Ben-Gurion knew no consideration, mercy, or compassion; pity the person who stood in his way. In his drive to accomplish the mission, the institution came before the individual and the goal before the man. Whenever political genius came into conflict with human feelings, genius had the upper hand. There was no doubt in his mind — and time would prove Ben-Gurion right — that Weizmann was incapable of guiding Zionism down the tortuous road to a state and was not built to lead the Yishuv and the nation in the war to establish it. Ben-Gurion had not the slightest doubt that he was the only man who could take on these tasks. From a historical perspective his struggle against Weizmann was wholly justified, and the only valid criticism of Ben-Gurion involves the insensitive manner in which he waged it. Weizmann could not mobilize public support for the Biltmore Program among all the parties in Palestine and in the confusion that encompassed the Zionist movement, nor could he exploit calamity to advantage or use its few survivors effectively to influence public opinion worldwide. Ben-Gurion, who knew this, was capable of doing what had to be done.

One of his important advantages in his battles with rivals was that Ben-Gurion always knew how to suit his attack to the arena he chose. His charges regarding Weizmann's faulty reporting and keeping his contacts to himself were employed as ammunition rather than expressions of frustration and envy, as were his complaints about Weizmann's fickleness and political blunders. What the shocked observers of the confrontation in Wise's study thought was a sudden "attack," and what May had regarded the year before as a loss of self-control, was a calculated, carefully staged performance.

It might have seemed that in the confrontation in Wise's study Ben-Gurion had been licked, but this was only the first of many battles in a war for the establishment of the state. And after — as it appeared — Ben-Gurion had cooled off, he continued to act consistently, single-mindedly, and tirelessly to unseat Weizmann. To this end he "forgot" that he had resigned from the chairmanship of the JAE. On June 29, 1942, he signed his name to a letter to John McCloy, assistant secretary of war, "D. Ben-Gurion, Chairman of the Executive Jewish Agency for Palestine." The position of chairman, which he had needed for the status it conferred, he now needed as a means of exerting pressure as well.

Little by little his associates would find out why he had quietly resumed his office. To their horror, he soon treated them to the most daring and frightening performance of his driver's tactic to date. In the middle of the war — during the worst catastrophe ever to befall the Jewish people — when the Yishuv was under threat of destruction and Zionism was helpless, Ben-Gurion would, shortly after he returned to

Jerusalem, brandish anew his tried and true weapon, threatening to resign from the JAE unless it unequivocally demanded Weizmann's resignation.

This time it took nearly four years for the tactic to accomplish its goal. Weizmann, who was not re-elected to the presidency at the 1946 Zionist Congress, well knew that this was the result of Ben-Gurion's driver's tactic. In a passage excised at the last minute from his memoirs, he attributed his defeat, at least partially, to the confrontation in Wise's study.[32]

In all probability, Ben-Gurion had decided on his tactic well before that confrontation. The very taking on of the formidable Weizmann in 1942 reflected his confidence in himself and in his sense of destiny. He felt that he alone was capable of recruiting public support for the Biltmore Program, and he set out to do so in Jerusalem. Herzl had written, "In Basel I founded the Jewish State," and Ben-Gurion could write that in New York he had ensured the State's being.

44

Disaster Means Strength

THOUGH BEN-GURION had stayed away from meetings in London the previous fall, after the clash at Wise's home, he displayed an impressive willingness to work. For nearly three months, until he received his flight priority, he participated in all discussions and put tremendous energy into diplomatic contacts, the Palestine Defense Appeal, and negotiations with the non-Zionists. At the same time he made it his business to antagonize Weizmann.

Picking one of the arguments Weizmann had used in his June 15 letter — "Even the organizational form of my activities was decided upon after long and serious discussions with all our colleagues" — he set out to publicly demolish it by tirelessly pursuing "all our colleagues" in writing and in person. He asked Rabbi Stephen Wise, Dr. Nahum Goldmann, ZOA president Louis Levinthal, Robert Szold, and others if they recalled such a decision and had taken part in it. A letter to Wise of July 15, for example, said, "I will be grateful if you will let me know whether you have taken part . . . in a decision about the organizational forms of Dr. Weizmann's activities in America, and, if so, what the decision was." The embarrassed Emergency Committee members tried to avoid offending Weizmann, but Ben-Gurion did not let up.

In another letter he informed Wise that since Weizmann was determined to "continue to act in the same way . . . I will have to inform the leaders of the Zionist parties officially of the . . . irresponsible action of Dr. Weizmann." In deference to Weizmann, who found the heat and humidity of the unairconditioned office difficult to bear, Emergency Committee and other meetings were held at the St. Regis Hotel. Ben-Gurion would not attend these meetings, but when a few with Weizmann were held in the office, as Ben-Gurion wanted, he would disrupt them with sudden and irrelevant questions, all about Weizmann's activity. A meeting on August 3, for example, was supposed to discuss establishing a Jewish Agency Executive office in New York. Nahum Goldmann — who, by agreement, acted as chairman to prevent further friction between the two — had barely begun to announce the day's agenda when Ben-Gurion declared, "A letter has come from Palestine, from Eliezer Kaplan, asking about Dr. Weizmann's activities," and asserted, "I would also like to know what Dr. Weizmann has been doing." When the discussion turned to the makeup of the New York JAE, Ben-Gurion repeatedly demanded to "know what Dr. Weizmann was doing in America," and did not relent until Weizmann was compelled to reply.

> WEIZMANN: I have made no secret of what I have been doing. I have reported from time to time.
> BEN-GURION: I have never heard a word from Dr. Weizmann as to what he is doing in America.
> WEIZMANN: I can return the compliment . . .
> LIPSKY: There will be found in the minutes of the Emergency Committee continuous reports of Dr. Weizmann's doings.
> BEN-GURION: It is not in the minutes and I do not want to have reports from proxies.

Left with no choice but to mollify Ben-Gurion, the members resolved to prepare a report on Weizmann's activities, which exasperated Weizmann and put him on the defensive.

To prove that the JAE did not rely exclusively on Weizmann's judgment and negotiations, and to keep up to date, Ben-Gurion also conducted diplomatic activity parallel to Weizmann's. He distributed memorandums on the Jewish army and the war effort in Palestine and its defense to all the high officials he met. However, he could not penetrate above the level of assistants and under secretaries; he had three meetings with Under Secretary of War John McCloy on naval matters, one with Under Secretary of State Sumner Welles, and two with Assistant Secretary of State Adolf Berle.[1]

What was more, his report to the JAE that with Weizmann's arrival he no longer wished to meet Roosevelt had not been strictly accurate; while Weizmann was trying to set up a meeting with the president through Sumner Welles in early July, Ben-Gurion renewed the race to the White House. Frankfurter had an appointment with the president on July 3, and on the second Ben-Gurion wrote him from New York, "Is it possible that I should see the President for ten or fifteen minutes? . . . Were it not on a matter of such momentous gravity to the whole of the Jewish people" he would not make such a request when the president was so burdened. He attached a memorandum to the letter, outlining briefly what he wished to say to Roosevelt, adding, "I doubt whether the written word can adequately convey the tragic, concrete realities of the situation in Palestine. It is for this reason that I ask you whether such an interview is possible." Frankfurter promised Ben-Gurion on the telephone that he would give the president the memorandum and ask him to receive Ben-Gurion.

Elated, Ben-Gurion hurried to Washington the same day to enlist Ben Cohen's help in polishing the memorandum and sent a second note to Frankfurter.

> After the President has read the memorandum how will we know what his reaction was and whether he will do anything? . . . I am not going to thank you for what you are doing. But if you succeed tomorrow, the Jewish people will owe you more than thanks.

In the memorandum Ben-Gurion warned,

> [The] invasion of [Palestine] by Hitler, even temporarily, may result in the complete annihilation of the Jewish community there — men, women and children — and the total destruction of their work by the Nazis with the help of the Mufti. To the Jewish people throughout the world, this will mean more than the massacre of some 600,000 Jews; it will be the ruin of their Third Temple; the destruction of their Holy of Holies.

Frankfurter's intervention led only to a request from Roosevelt for another memorandum, and Ben-Gurion lost the race to the White House. When the president saw Weizmann on July 7, he confined the meeting strictly to Weizmann's invention; with respect to the Jewish army, he asked for yet another memorandum. Ben-Gurion never got further than Roosevelt's confidant Judge Samuel Rosenman, with whom he met for a second time on August 11, the only occasion on which he set foot in the White House.

In his report to the JAE, Ben-Gurion glossed over this failure.

> Frankfurter advised me: these things [defense of Palestine and a Jewish army] must get to the President. But I knew that Weizmann was trying very hard to reach the President, and I did not wish to try myself as well for an interview with Roosevelt. However, said Frankfurter, write these things down and tomorrow I will present them to the President. I prepared the memorandum, this was on July 2 . . . and on the third the memorandum was in Roosevelt's hand, and he gave instructions to [General George] Marshall. What this accomplished I could not find out . . . Three days later Roosevelt received Weizmann for an interview that Sumner Welles arranged for him, and Roosevelt told him he had given an order for action.[2]

Ben-Gurion reserved the main thrust of his energy for what he called unity of action by American Jewry on the Palestine issue — the problem of reaching an accord with the non-Zionists. To this end he met no less than a dozen times with the president of the American Jewish Committee (AJC), the banker and philanthropist Maurice Wertheim. In early June they arrived at a draft agreement on Palestine's role in "a program of action by a united American Jewry." In the draft Wertheim agreed, on behalf of the committee, to aid the JAE

> in maintaining Jewish rights under the Mandate in Palestine for the immediate future . . . to aid in securing the fulfillment of the original purpose of the Balfour Declaration, whereby through unrestricted Jewish immigration and large-scale colonization, under a regime designed for this purpose, Jews, upon constituting a majority in Palestine, will establish an autonomous commonwealth.

Two subclauses specified that in this commonwealth "all the inhabitants without regard to race and religion shall enjoy complete equality of rights" and that the establishment of the commonwealth "will in no way affect the political and civil status of Jews who are citizens of any other country." For the Zionists, the draft required the ratification of the Jerusalem JAE and Zionist Executive and the New York Emergency Committee, and for the non-Zionist, the approval of the American Jewish Committee.

The Emergency Committee endorsed it on June 5, and an elated Ben-Gurion, cabling its contents to Jerusalem, anticipated that everyone would understand the significance of his achievement. "Cable view Executive," he asked his colleagues in the wire. In Jerusalem, however, the draft elicited much controversy, since it was not clear to the members of the JAE whether this was a "joint program" to which Ben-Gurion had committed the JAE or merely a "unilateral act" or statement that he had extracted from the non-Zionists as their "minimum program." As a result it was resolved "to request further clarification" before the draft was brought up for debate in the Zionist Executive.

Nor was Weizmann enthusiastic, although he had initiated contacts with the non-Zionists. He may even have regarded Ben-Gurion's "frequent talks" with Wertheim with suspicion or envy. "I was a little amused at the thought of long discussions on Zionist affairs between the wealthy non-Zionist Mr. Wertheim and the leftist Zionist Ben-Gurion," he wrote his friends. Apparently only Sharett saw Ben-Gurion's point and understood the importance of this accord, that "a united front of American Jewry is essential immediately, this very day, for the continued Zionist struggle in America." Otherwise, said Sharett, Ben-Gurion would not have "invested such effort in Wertheim [and] that for the sake of this unity . . . a political program, a framework, is essential, to serve as the basis for action."

If the importance of unity had not yet been grasped in Jerusalem, that was even more true in the American Jewish Committee, for which the question of "dual loyalty," which would arise with the establishment of the state, was of the greatest concern. Instead of being quickly endorsed, the draft accord bogged down in discussions and debates that lasted several years. Judge Joseph Proskauer, who in 1943 would succeed Wertheim as president of the AJC, headed the opposition and threatened to break up the committee over it. Wertheim reported this to Ben-Gurion, who replied, a few days before leaving for Palestine, as to a comrade in arms, that in spite of everything he had "not yet given up the hope of seeing full-fledged unity of action among all groups in American Jewry." Though it was rejected in 1942, their draft accord later helped facilitate the establishment of the American Jewish "front," which in 1946 and 1947 put forward the claim for a Jewish state.[3]

During this period Ben-Gurion also had his worries at home. On May 13, 1942, Reb Avigdor died in Tel Aviv at the age of eighty-seven. The news reached Ben-Gurion in New York the next evening, right after the Biltmore Conference and just before a meeting with Weizmann. That night he wrote to "dear and beloved Paula, Geula, Amos, and Renana" a short biographical sketch of his father, in which this message stood out: "From my eleventh year onward, when Mother died, he was a father and a mother to me. He gave me much, very much, always out of lavish love." The letter ended, "It is sad that he passed away without my being able to attend his deathbed in his last moments . . . On my return home I shall see him no more. Never shall I be able to see him."

True to form, Paula had not left him in peace. The news of his Washington office, and of Miriam Cohen's working for him, reopened not-so-old wounds, and she reacted immediately with proven and new weapons. After a letter she sent on December 5, enclosing pictures of their grandson, Yariv — May described to Lourie how proud Ben-Gurion had been, showing her a photograph — Paula did not answer his letters. She thereby kept from him news of his son-in-law, Ben-Eliezer, who had volunteered for the British army; of Geula, who was left alone with a baby; and of Renana, who was preparing for her matriculation examinations. Paula did not send him a photograph of Amos in his officer's uniform, which he had repeatedly asked for, though she did cable him that Amos had been hospitalized, without specifying the cause. The vague cable caused him untold worry. On receiving a second wire saying that Amos had pneumonia, Ben-Gurion consulted with New York doctors and cabled Paula on February 25 that he was "advised by experts try 5 grams daily sulfadiazing or sulfathiazol." But Paula sent no further news. When his patience ran out he cabled her on March 28, "Cable whether Amos still in hospital how is he send his portrait, love." When no answer came, he wired Sharett on April 22, "Please cable how is Amos." A few days later Sharett's reply calmed his fears: "Amos is perfectly alright." In late March 1942 Ben-Gurion wrote Paula, in English.

> I cannot imagine that all letters were lost. . . . I know that at least some of my letters you received, as I know that their contents became known to Moshe, Berl and other friends. I know there is no use in my complaining. . . . I wrote you asking to send me Amos picture, and write me whether Yariv is already walking and talking. I send you yesterday cable inquiring Amos'es health and asking again to sent me Amos'es picture . . . I am anxious to know what Geula is doing while Emanuel is away, ho Renana is behaving in school and at home. . . . I must ask with all earnestness to write me "more often," and to send the letters by Atlantic Air Mail. . . . With love yours, David.

Like other men who trust that they can hide a love affair, Ben-Gurion underestimated his wife's capacity for quick intelligence gathering, and he was inattentive to her signals. A telegram in January asking him to get a copy of her nursing diploma and send it to her was the first sign of her intention to begin a new, independent life, and perhaps instill in him the fear of divorce. Ben-Gurion, unaware that her diploma had never existed, charged Lourie with this hopeless task. By the end of April Lourie gave up, and Ben-Gurion wired Paula, "Regret nursing diploma unobtainable." On May 19, her fiftieth birthday — according to her reckoning — Paula wrote her will, leaving all her possessions equally to her three children. She asked that Ben-Gurion

> honor my wishes in this will and waive his legal rights to the possessions I am bequeathing the children . . . fully cognizant of the fact that our house and property are registered in his name. Nevertheless, I hereby leave the house and property, together with all our possessions, exclusively to the children, and I ask him to respect my wish and waive all his rights for the good of our children. . . . I herein request that I be buried in the old cemetery in Tel Aviv and that the children visit my grave often and remember me in their lives and deeds, as I devoted my whole life to them.

Israel Bar-Shira, the Histadrut lawyer who was also a neighbor and Paula's friend, drew up this will, which aimed to deprive Ben-Gurion of ownership of his house, his only possession, and asked for Paula to be buried in the city's most exclusive cemetery. This will was a new device to drive home to Ben-Gurion Paula's state of desperation. Paula

used it as a vehicle of reproach. Although she enjoins her children to
visit her grave, and remember her, she makes no such demand of Ben-
Gurion, of whom she expected nothing. Paula probably chose Bar-
Shira, despite his lack of expertise in wills and testaments, because she
expected him to pass word of it to his colleagues in the HEC, from
whom it would leak, directly or indirectly, to Ben-Gurion. If this assumption is correct, Bar-Shira, the small circle of Ben-Gurion's confidants in the HEC, Renana, Geula, and probably Amos knew of the will,
and at least a rumor of it must have reached Ben-Gurion in the United
States.

The day Paula signed it Geula wrote Ben-Gurion, "Mother is ill
lately and has been diagnosed as having arthritis. She needs absolute
rest, but of course she hasn't the chance as Renana doesn't help her,
and she has to do everything herself. . . . Mother alone arranged and
paid for the funeral [of Reb Avigdor] and the burial." In June, Paula
asked in a telegram if she could rent out the house, and Ben-Gurion replied, also by cable, "You may let the house if you like but lock library.
Cable where going and how you are." Paula did achieve independence
for a time, working as a nurse on the beach in north Tel Aviv and renting the house for the summer to a group of children who had been
brought from Jerusalem to be by the sea.

Renana's prolonged silence undoubtedly hurt Ben-Gurion more than
anything else, but it never occurred to him that Paula was to blame.
On June 17 Paula cabled him that Renana had passed her exams successfully, that she and her friends were spending the summer working
on a kibbutz, and that in the fall she intended to begin studying biology
at the university. Such an important development in the life of his beloved daughter and not a word from Renana herself? Had he asked
Renana about her silence she might have answered that Paula had
told her daughter "many things." Subsequently Renana recounted, "I
thought betrayal a dreadful thing . . . and Mother was hysterical. . . . I
was angry at him because of what Mother told me, and I wanted to
fight with him . . . but you cannot fight with a smart man who does not
want to fight."[4]

In addition to these worries, Ben-Gurion felt a deepening concern for
the fate of Europe's Jews. What has been found of his diary does not
cover much of the years 1942–1944,* and therefore it is not known ex-

---

* For fear that the British secret services might read them, Ben-Gurion did not take all his
papers with him on his trips during 1941–1947, but left them in various places for safekeeping. Some were lost or have not yet been found. The diary for January to mid September 1942 is missing; short sections exist for 1943, but for 1944 the diary is continuous
only through November; for 1945 it covers May through November; and for 1946 it is

actly how and when he learned the extent of the Nazis' destruction of
the Jews. There is, however, no doubt that he knew what was happening. From items published in the media he could learn of the mass murder on the Russian front carried out by the special *Einsatzgruppen*, of
the emptying of the Lódź and Vilna ghettos, and similar news. Much
significance was attributed to three revelations that Ben-Gurion could
not have missed. A letter from Soviet Foreign Minister Vyacheslav
Molotov to the United States government was published in March
1942. It included eyewitness accounts of the murder of some hundred
thousand Jews in a few days. It was the first official confirmation by
an Allied government of the systematic killing of Jews and of the connection between their transport to eastern Europe and their murder
there. A second item, which also received worldwide attention, was
published in June: a white paper presented to the Allied governments
and parliaments by the Polish government in exile stated that the
Nazis had begun the physical extermination of the Jewish population;
700,000 had already been killed, mainly by shooting and by carbon
monoxide fumes piped into sealed vans, and a wave of murder was
spreading from Soviet territory into Poland. The third followed on
June 30, when a spokesman for the World Jewish Congress announced
over American radio networks that at least a million Jews had been
killed.

His awareness of the fate of European Jewry is also attested to by
events and discussions in which Ben-Gurion participated. The Jews'
desperate plight was most poignantly manifested by the *Struma* affair.
This little ship set sail from Rumania to Palestine with 769 refugees on
board. Stuck in Istanbul port when its old engines broke down, it was
held up there for over a month. The sanitary situation was appalling;
disease spread easily in the overcrowded and stifling ship. The passengers took turns going on deck to breathe fresh air. The JAE implored
the British authorities to allow these refugees, especially the children,
to enter Palestine. The British used delaying tactics, and by the time
they finally agreed to accept the children, the Turks had towed the
ship from the port into the Black Sea. Sharett's efforts to recall the ship
and take the children off to bring them to Palestine by a safer route
were fruitless. The Turks' temporary repair of the engines had been
faulty, so the ship was immobilized. After a tense night, it exploded
at 9:00 A.M. on February 23, 1942, and all the passengers save one
drowned. The cause of the explosion was unknown; the Turks claimed

---

continuous only for January through March. Part of the 1946 diary, dated April 21, was
found in the possession of a person who claimed to have acquired it at a rare book shop in
Paris. For 1947 there are only a few pages for every month; for part of that year Ben-
Gurion kept a pocket appointment calendar.

a Russian submarine had torpedoed it. Three days later the Emergency Committee discussed making a public protest over the sinking and accepted Ben-Gurion's proposal to send protest letters to the British prime minister and the American president. Ben-Gurion also made a speech at a protest rally at the Mecca Temple in New York.[5]

Information about the situation in Europe was generally passed on in Emergency Committee meetings, and there is no reason to believe that Dr. Goldmann, who continually received reports from the World Jewish Congress representative in Geneva, Gerhart Riegner, did not relay them to Ben-Gurion. On July 9 Ben-Gurion met someone with firsthand knowledge, Francis Ketuni, a Catholic Arab who had spoken in London with the head of the Polish government in exile, General Władysław Sikorski, and other Polish leaders. According to Ketuni, they told him (Ben-Gurion reported to the JAE, adding that he was "shocked" to hear it), "We rely on Hitler to solve the Jewish question; by the end of the war there will be no more Jews in Poland." On July 21 Ben-Gurion participated in a mass protest demonstration against Nazi atrocities held at Madison Square Garden and honored by Churchill with a special message.[6]

Nevertheless, Zionist leaders in the United States and Palestine, including Ben-Gurion, greeted news of wholesale slaughter with a certain amount of disbelief. They thought that Europe was witnessing a repetition, on a larger scale, of the pogroms that had ravaged the Jews during the First World War and that the deaths of Jews, even in staggering numbers, were the result of locally initiated actions and wartime conditions imposed by the Nazis. No one could yet stretch his imagination to believe that a plan existed to systematically annihilate the entire Jewish race. Moreover, when news of the Final Solution did filter through, it was considered suspect as Soviet "atrocity propaganda" against Germany, like that propagated by the West during World War I to encourage hatred of the enemy. Even in Palestine the press cautioned readers against being swept away by propaganda and the tendency of the news agencies to blow every rumor out of all proportion.[7]

There is probably no unequivocal answer to the question of whether Ben-Gurion, while in the United States, heard about the telegram Riegner sent Wise, reporting that in Hitler's headquarters a plan was discussed according to which "three and half to four millions should after deportation and concentration in east be at one blow exterminated in order resolve once and for all Jewish question in Europe."[*]

---

[*] This was the first indication that the Final Solution had been discussed at the Wannsee Conference in January 1942.

The action was reportedly planned for autumn, and possible methods of execution, including prussic acid, were under consideration. The wire was sent from Geneva by the American consul on August 8, but it was held up by the State Department in Washington by order of Sumner Welles and did not reach Wise until August 28. He and Goldmann, coleaders of the World Jewish Congress, immediately contacted Welles, with whom they met almost every week from then on. At his request they agreed not to publish the wire until the details could be verified by American sources.

Ben-Gurion was in New York and met with Wise several times before leaving the United States on September 18. Although there is no proof that Wise showed him the wire or told him of its content, it is highly probable that he did — indirect evidence to support this assumption can be found in an HEC discussion of late November. On that occasion David Remez said, "From Ben-Gurion I learned that in America there was very alarming news well before it reached us." Eliyahu Dobkin, deputy chief of the JAE Immigration Department, added, "Ben-Gurion tells us that in America it was thought that this was a method of *gruel* [German for "horror"] propaganda." These comments suggest that Wise and Goldmann first doubted the reliability of the information. Edvard Beneš, the Czech president in exile in New York, also warned them that Riegner's telegram should be regarded as horror propaganda. A letter from Wise to Weizmann in late October, in which he sided with him in a new dispute with Ben-Gurion — perhaps generated by the wire — also bears witness to his disbelief.

On the eve of his departure from the United States on September 17, Ben-Gurion summoned the Emergency Committee, as if in a last attempt to instill his policy in it. Attacking Weizmann's "gradualist" philosophy, he announced that when he got to Palestine he would demand Weizmann's resignation from the JAE and the Zionist Executive, and he brought up a new project: American support for a transfer of some two million Jews from Europe to Palestine, in one massive operation. Riegner's telegram had probably aroused in him an instinctive response, a desire to make a revolutionary and far-reaching move that would fit the new circumstances, sound the alarm, and thereby break through the routine Zionist incremental immigration policy. He had probably conceived this idea before the Biltmore Conference in May, as in his address he had mentioned the transfer between Greece and Turkey after the First World War. In opposition to Goldmann, who warned that after the war Jewish survivors might emerge so "broken down mentally and spiritually" that they would reject both Zionism and Palestine, Ben-Gurion maintained that "after this war Jewish immigration to Palestine will be both in numbers and pace immeasurably greater than after the last war."

To Weizmann the transfer idea was merely another of "Ben-Gurion's antics," intended to impress Zionist public opinion in America. Responding to Wise's October letter, he denounced these "mock heroics" as disquieting and harmful and thanked Wise for his support. Wise responded by offering Weizmann more ammunition for his attack on Ben-Gurion. "We must face the tragic fact that there will be no millions to migrate, assuming that a goodly part of the Jews, who may survive, will wish to return to the countries whence they came."

Riegner's telegram, therefore, prompted no changes in the position of the Jewish leadership in the United States. Wise, Goldmann, and Weizmann still doubted that there was a plan for systematic mass extermination and tended to believe that the obstacle facing Zionism after the war was won would be not a scarcity of Jews but their unwillingness to go to Palestine.[8]

The journey home — via the Caribbean, Brazil, Liberia, Nigeria, the Sudan, and Egypt — lasted three weeks, during which Ben-Gurion was cut off from all contact with the world; he arrived in Palestine on October 2. From then until he went to Bulgaria in November 1944 — more than two full years — he stayed in Palestine, except for a one-day excursion to Syria.[9]

He had left the United States with the intention of using the American Zionists' adoption of the Biltmore Program as a lever for getting his party, the JAE, and the Yishuv to adopt it as well, making it the official policy of Zionism. The day before leaving New York he had written in his diary what amounted to an oath or stipulation: "If forced to resign, I shall serve on as a soldier." If the JAE did not accept his plan, he would once more announce his resignation. With Ben-Gurion it was all or nothing.

In Palestine he immediately resumed the JAE chairmanship, to the relief of all his colleagues. At first, as if tackling one thing at a time, he concentrated all his efforts on the program, not to the tragedy of European Jewry. He maintained a puzzling silence about what was taking place in Europe and Riegner's telegram. The first three JAE meetings in which he participated, on October 4, 6, and 11, were devoted to reports on his activity in the United States and debate on the Biltmore Program, ending in its endorsement. Although he knew that Tabenkin and his faction would reject the Biltmore Program, he pressed for a party convention.

He was prepared to split the party for the sake of the program, believing that the majority would follow him and that a small, effective tool was superior to a large, defective one. At the convention, which met on October 25 at Kefar Vitkin, the first crack appeared, heralding a fissure in the party: in the vote on the program, Itzhak Tabenkin's Faction B abstained as a body. With the party technically behind him, Ben-Gurion could turn to enlisting other parties, and on November 1 he wrote Miriam the good news that the three major parties — Mapai, the General Zionists A, and Mizrachi — had assured him of their "unanimous" support for the program.[10] In truth, however, the Mapai convention had set in motion a process leading to Faction B's forming a separate party, which in the elections to the Histadrut convention and to the Elected Assembly in August 1944 ran on an independent ticket under the historic name the Achdut ha-Avodah movement. These two parts of Mapai would not reunite for twenty-six years.

Sketchy information about the ongoing destruction of European Jewry had been accumulating at the office of Gruenbaum and the committee of four, later to become the Rescue Committee. A full replay of the scenario surrounding Riegner's telegram took place in Jerusalem. The wire itself did not reach the JAE, and nothing in the minutes suggests that Ben-Gurion mentioned it in his reports on America, although it is clear that he told his close colleagues, in secret, what he knew. The same information, however, was passed on to Jerusalem by Richard Lichtheim, the JAE representative in Geneva. A report he wrote on August 30 and sent after two weeks of hesitation reached Jerusalem in late September and "shocked" Gruenbaum. On October 6, the second day of Ben-Gurion's report to the JAE, Gruenbaum wired Lichtheim to "do everything possible to verify." Lichtheim's reply came in two cables: on October 8, that the information was already confirmed and that it was difficult to obtain further confirmation, since "for obvious reasons there are no eyewitnesses, and the exact figures aren't known. Therefore do not publish"; and on October 10, that as a fellow skeptic "I can easily understand that you don't want to believe." Chaim Barlas, a representative of the JAE Immigration Department, brought affirmation and more news when he arrived in Jerusalem from Istanbul in late October. Also in October, Anselm Reiss of Mapai received a wire from Abraham Silberschein, the World Jewish Congress representative in Geneva and a colleague of Riegner's, describing mass murders in special death chambers from which human fat and bones were salvaged for industrial use. Subsequently Reiss said that "the wire was so horrific" and its accuracy so doubtful that it was withheld from publication.

It seems that Gruenbaum — like others — found it difficult, if not impossible, to believe the Germans were perpetrating deliberate genocide, and thought it best — and again, he was not alone — not to publish the reports. Did he also keep them to himself? That is hard to believe, yet there is no evidence that he shared them with Ben-Gurion. Not until October 25 did Gruenbaum inform the JAE of "rumors" and that he had cabled "to various places," always receiving the same answers: the Jews were being "sent to forced labor and vanishing." Ben-Gurion was absent from this meeting, not having finished preparing his speech for the Mapai convention, which was to open the same day. Whether Gruenbaum reported the rumors to him before the convention or Ben-Gurion read of them in the minutes on his return to Jerusalem, it seems that they did not constitute sufficient reason to alter the JAE routine, and the meetings Ben-Gurion chaired on November 1, 8, and 15 had nothing to do with the ongoing massacre in Europe. Ben-Gurion, too, found it difficult to believe the rumors — for all the Zionist leaders found the Holocaust difficult to comprehend, even after it was fully documented at the end of the war.[11]

His principal address to the Mapai convention reveals how little Ben-Gurion knew of the extermination and its implementation.

Hitler and his cronies have already enslaved more than a fifth of the human race . . . More than a third of the Jewish people are in Nazi concentration camps, tens of thousands are put to death in the darkness of forests, on the roads, and in closed vans, and the rest are abandoned to starvation, plagues, disease, forced labor, and the desecration of their humanity and their Judaism.

By decoding German ciphered messages, British intelligence had learned of ten death camps, including Auschwitz, the largest, as early as the spring of 1942. But Ben-Gurion, ignorant of the death camps, spoke only of concentration camps. He had perhaps learned about the "closed vans" from the Polish white paper, which described the killing of Jews in Chełmno, ninety people to a van, by exhaust fumes rechanneled into the cars. He still referred to "tens of thousands put to death in the darkness of forests" when such executions, begun with the German invasion of Russia in the summer and fall of 1941, had been discontinued by the spring of 1942. His lack of knowledge illustrates the tragic impotence of the Jewish people and their leaders, from whom reliable information of the most fearsome of calamities ever to befall them was kept. They were victims of the diversionary tactics and deceptions of the Nazis and the withholding of the truth by the British, who kept their knowledge of the death camps secret.[12]

The turning point came with the arrival in Palestine of sixty-nine "exchangees": Palestinian Jews — among them kibbutz members, scientists, and veteran Zionist activists — who had been held in Europe by the war and exchanged for German nationals residing in Palestine. They came from various cities in Poland, Holland, and Belgium, and from Hamburg, Berlin, and concentration camps in Germany. Dobkin spent two days questioning them at the detention camp in Atlit, and in his report to the JAE on November 22, and later to Mapai's secretariat and the HEC, described them as "people of sound judgment and comprehension, with no interest in distorting the facts." He was particularly impressed, he said, by the accounts the children gave — a remark that shows how suspicious the JAE was of information coming out of occupied Europe. At the JAE meeting, Dobkin spared his listeners "the blood-curdling descriptions" and "the dreadful details," but asserted in no uncertain terms that the Jews of Europe were being systematically wiped out.

Three facts, said Dobkin, were substantiated by the testimony of the sixty-nine: a special committee visited Poland's cities, organizing the destruction; "slaughter of the young and the old en masse" was occurring; mass deportation of Jews to the east was taking place in all of occupied Europe. Dobkin did not know the fate of these Jews; they had vanished, and "there is no news of them whatsoever." With regard to these mass deportations, added Dobkin, who became extra cautious, "there are all kinds of rumors in Poland, and it seems they are well founded. There are stories of large concrete buildings on the Russian-Polish border where they are gassed and cremated. One woman from Oświęcim, in western Galicia, told of three furnaces for cremating Jews which were built in that town." This was the first reference to the Auschwitz death camp.* A few of the other exchangees had witnessed the killing of some thousand children in Radom. "When I told a woman from Radom I couldn't believe it," Dobkin recounted to the Mapai secretariat, "I was slapped in the face and did not ask any more questions." The next day the JAE issued a press release that generated a public storm and evoked harsh accusations that the JAE had known of the extermination and deliberately kept it quiet. On November 30 Reiss warned Mapai's secretariat, "This won't pass without a public trial."

Ben-Gurion was also absent from the meeting at which Dobkin's report was heard. A letter he wrote to Miriam on November 23 explains, "I got a light cold and for the second day I am in bed — left alone to myself," since Paula had gone to Tiberias to ease her arthritis in the hot springs. Nonetheless, there can hardly be a doubt that the accounts of the sixty-nine reached him at once, for from his sickbed he sent tele-

---

* Auschwitz is the German name for Oświęcim.

grams to Frankfurter and others to alert them to the annihilation. On November 29 he chaired the meeting which discussed what actions the JAE should take and issued a call "to save every Jew who can be saved," particularly children. At this meeting Dobkin, who took issue with Gruenbaum's amazement at the Jews' lack of resistance as they went to their deaths, first applied to them the phrase "like lambs to the slaughter." The National Council announced a three-day work stoppage and mourning period. Ben-Gurion agreed with his party and JAE colleagues that the world's conscience should be awakened with a great outcry, and at a special session of the Elected Assembly to mark the days of mourning, he addressed himself to "the conscience of mankind." The picture he drew of the Jewish misfortune was far harsher than the one he had offered in October.

> We do not know exactly what goes on in the Nazi valley of death or how many Jews have already been slaughtered, murdered, burned, and buried alive and how many others are doomed to annihilation . . . Only from time to time does news of atrocities break through to us . . . the screams of women and children mutilated and crushed. But we do know what Hitler has in store for our people and what he wrote in *Mein Kampf* and what he has done and is doing to us . . . before the war . . . during the war. . . . We do not know that the victory of democracy and freedom and justice will not find Europe a vast Jewish cemetery in which the bones of our people are scattered . . . and our bleeding nation calls the conscience of humanity to trial before the judgment of history. . . . We are the only people in the world whose blood, as a nation, is allowed [to be shed] . . . Only our children, our women, our brothers, and the aged are set apart for special treatment, to be buried alive in graves dug by them, to be cremated in crematoriums, to be strangled and to be murdered by machine guns . . . for but one sin . . . because the Jews have no state, no army, no independence, and no homeland.

His last remarks were aimed directly at Britain and the United States.

> As long as the gates to our land are closed . . . your hands, too, will be steeped in Jewish blood. . . . Give us the right to fight and die as Jews . . . We demand the right . . . to a homeland and independence. What happened to us in Poland, what, God forbid, will happen to us in the future, all our innocent victims, all the tens of thousands, hundreds of thousands, and perhaps millions . . . are the sacrifices of a people without a homeland . . . We demand a homeland and independence.

In conclusion, he pledged an oath to the Jews of Europe.

> Let us tell our dear brothers, martyred and tortured in the Nazis' ghettos: your tragedy is our tragedy, your blood is our blood . . . We shall have no

rest until we redeem you both from the Nazi hell and from the debilitating exile and bring you . . . to the land we are building and redeeming, to our land.[13]

Ben-Gurion received further confirmation of the situation in Europe directly from the deputy prime minister of the Polish government in exile, Professor Stanisław Kot, who visited Jerusalem. At the JAE meeting of December 6, which heard "far worse" news and adopted various resolutions on rescue actions, he said, "It is our duty to do everything and we must not say a priori that rescue is impossible." As a practical first step it was resolved to set up a joint committee of the JAE, the National Council, and organizations outside the framework of the Zionist Organization to "handle all questions connected with the rescue of European Jewry." As if to support and encourage this committee Ben-Gurion added, "The committee must discuss every proposal offering even the smallest hope of saving Jews." The Rescue Committee was established in January 1943 under Gruenbaum's chairmanship.

In accordance with the proposals made at the meeting, Ben-Gurion cabled Lourie in New York on December 8, asking that Miriam send the following letter to Frankfurter, "on behalf of Amos's father" — Ben-Gurion's new code name in communications with the JAE and Haganah.

Hitler's decision to destroy Polish Jewry is apparently the first step in the genocide of the Jews in all occupied countries, and we will undoubtedly receive confirmation of unthinkable acts of atrocity against women and children. . . . Our information is that the massacre is not being carried out by the army, but by the Gestapo and special storm troopers of the Nazi party, and a warning by the president to the leaders of the German army, that they will be held personally responsible for atrocities, will probably influence them. There may also be a possibility of saving children and perhaps women as well by exchanging them for German national women and children residing in the Allied countries. . . . Special actions should be taken to rescue the Jews in the Balkans, Hungary, and western Europe, where the Nazis do not rule directly, or where the Nazi regime does not yet act with the same brutality it displays in eastern Europe. A warning to the governments of Hungary, Rumania, and Bulgaria from America is likely to influence them . . . It is certainly possible to save at least the women and children from these countries, and pressure must be brought to bear on the English government to permit the entry of all the children to Palestine.

In December 1942, therefore, Ben-Gurion knew the truth about the extermination and had made the connection between the deportations and the death camps. But his rescue efforts in 1943 and 1944 amounted to no more than speeches, wires, discussions, and participation in passing resolutions. His direct contribution was essentially limited to arousing the conscience of the world and preaching to the Allied governments, an activity that repetition eventually reduced to clichés. He who had argued that the time for raising a clamor had passed and that the time had come for action — the originator of combative Zionism — reverted now to that vintage Jewish weapon, the cry for help. This is the only conclusion possible.

In spite of the certainty that genocide was being carried out, the JAE did not deviate appreciably from its routine, and Ben-Gurion, the chairman, left all its rescue efforts completely in the hands of Gruenbaum, Sharett, and Kaplan, not even taking part in the Rescue Committee. Two facts can be definitively stated: Ben-Gurion did not put the rescue effort above Zionist politics, and he did not regard it as a principal task demanding his personal leadership; he never saw fit to explain why, then or later. Instead, he devoted his efforts to rallying the Yishuv and Zionism around the Biltmore Program and to the preparations for its implementation.[14]

Why didn't Ben-Gurion head the rescue from the moment his sober predictions materialized beyond expectations? Was it not this vision of disaster that had led him throughout the 1930s to decisive and urgent conclusions? The more his forebodings seem corroborated and the clearer it appears that, from the start, he had had no illusions about Hitler's true plans for the Jews, the deeper this mystery becomes.

In August 1933 Ben-Gurion bought a copy of *Mein Kampf* and after reading it announced to the Histadrut Council, in January 1934, that "Hitler's rule endangers the entire Jewish people . . . Who knows, perhaps just four or five years — if not less — stand between us and that terrible day." That January he and Sharett confronted Sir Arthur Wauchope with the threat of destruction hovering over the Jews of Germany and Poland. In April 1935 he asked the Zionist Executive, "Is there a man today so blind he does not see the catastrophe of the Jews?" That year he forewarned the Zionist Congress of "the greatest perils in store for the existence of the Jewish people all over the world . . . the days of the Inquisition . . . and the Crusades . . . are back." In November he told the JAE, "From the fearful situation of the masses one gets the feeling that even the little it is possible to do at the moment will not be possible a short time from now. We must work as fast as we can to save the maximum." And in December 1935 he said, "Destruction is lying in wait for our people in all the lands of its dispersion . . . A war of ruination has been declared against the captives of the Nazis."

In a letter to Kaplan in March 1936, Ben-Gurion spoke of "the destruction in store for the Jews of Germany and Poland and the other countries of eastern Europe," and several days later prophesied to Mapai's Central Committee that "the situation of Polish Jewry will be worse than that of German Jewry." In October 1936 he warned the Zionist Actions Committee, "There are forces in Europe that seek to blot out the memory of Judaism." At the Mapai convention in Rehovot in 1938 he spoke of "a war of extinction against the Jewish people," saying that Germany had "engraved upon its flag the obliteration of the Jewish people." In November he wrote Malcolm MacDonald that "millions of our people are facing annihilation." He did not keep his forebodings secret from the public at large; at a meeting of representatives from throughout the Yishuv in December 1938 he announced that one of Hitler's goals was "the absolute eradication and physical destruction of the Jewish people, not just in Germany but all over the world." The approach of the world war strengthened his belief in his prediction, and in June 1939 Ben-Gurion told the Zionist Executive, "This war could bring down catastrophe upon us . . . in this we can trust Hitler . . . If there is a world war . . . he will carry this out. First of all he will wipe out the Jews of Europe."

Thus, the extermination could not have come as a surprise to him. But while his warnings and admonitions were unremitting before the war, after it broke out they let up considerably, practically ceasing. In December 1939 he had been using the same language. "Hitler is a preying beast who wants to devour . . . the Jews all over the world," he told the Histadrut council. Then, as if a curtain had fallen over Europe, hiding it from his view, until late 1942 his remarks were confined almost exclusively to the destruction the Yishuv could expect in the event of a German invasion of Palestine.[15]

For nearly two years — from March 1941, when Italy entered the war, until Rommel's defeat in December 1942 — Ben-Gurion was more concerned for the fate of the Yishuv than for that of European Jewry. Ben-Gurion repeatedly stressed that the importance of the Yishuv went far beyond the individual Jews of Palestine. As people they were not more worthy of salvation than the Jews of Poland, and Zionism's first consideration was not their individual fate. The Yishuv's importance lay solely in its being "the vanguard in the fulfillment of the hope for the rebirth of the people." Its destruction would be a greater catastrophe than that of any other community of Jews, for one reason: the Yishuv was a "great and invaluable security, a security for the hope of the Jewish people."

Why didn't Ben-Gurion, who so accurately predicted the catastrophe, take charge of the rescue efforts after the extermination became a fact? This is the central question about his leadership during the Holocaust; the answer is not simple. His approach to the rescue was the complex product of his philosophy of what might be called the beneficial disaster; his difficulty in drawing the line between this beneficial disaster and a total calamity; his basic disbelief, as late as June 1944, that an actual genocide was in progress; and finally, his lifelong rule of dealing only with the feasible. Although all these factors were interwoven and concurrent in his mind, they can be crudely separated, thematically and chronologically.

First, Ben-Gurion's early prediction of the tragedy formed in his mind a concept of which he became a captive throughout the war. Regarding Jewish adversity as a source of strength had always been at the foundation of his thinking. In March 1928 he told the HEC that "in order to start a movement in America, a great disaster or upheaval is needed." Since Hitler had come to power, Ben-Gurion maintained it was imperative to "turn a disaster . . . into a productive force" and asserted that "distress" could also serve as "political leverage": "the destruction" was a factor in "expediting our enterprise [and] it is in our interest to use Hitler, [who] has not reduced our strength, for the building of our country."

Ben-Gurion regarded even a "no-alternative" situation as a source of Zionist strength. In July 1939 he wrote in *Davar*, "Our strength is in the lack of choice," and in June 1941 he told the Mapai convention, "We have no alternative . . . but this, too, is a fountain of strength, perhaps the main source of our strength." "We have no power," he said to Mapai's Central Committee in March 1941. "All we have is the Jewish people, beaten, persecuted, diminished, and impoverished." He told the JAE, "The harsher the affliction, the greater the strength of Zionism." He saw the danger of defeatism as far greater than that posed by Hitler. It is probably this statement that most clearly distinguishes Ben-Gurion from his colleagues and highlights the difference between him and Katznelson, who wrote in his diary in May 1941, "There is no strength to meet the morrow."

Did he ask himself, when confronted with information on the systematic physical extermination of the Jews, whether history was playing a cruel joke on him, testing the courage of his convictions? He might well have answered yes, for the terms "destruction," "extermination," "ruin," "catastrophe," and "extinction" had had an entirely different meaning before the Holocaust, the putting to death of six million Jews, was recognized for what it was and named. When Ben-Gurion spoke in January 1933 of the "annihilation" facing German Jewry, he meant terrible living conditions imposed on them by Hitler.

In April 1935 he defined "ruin" as "economic and cultural impoverishment, the weakening of a people as a whole, political devastation, the eradication of civil rights." Even at the Congress in the summer of 1937, he said that "physical destruction and material impoverishment endanger the existence of the Jewish populations of many countries." And when he wrote Miriam from Beaver Lake in April 1942 that Hitler aimed "to annihilate" the Jews, he was thinking of political and economic ruin, not genocide. Until late 1942, when he used the terms "obliteration" and "devastation," Ben-Gurion, like his colleagues, visualized large-scale pogroms, not the Final Solution.

Nothing better illustrates the relatively mild significance these words had than Weizmann's speech at the Biltmore Conference, in which he predicted that at most a quarter of eastern Europe's Jews would be victims of "liquidation." These would be "the passive casualties, through torment, starvation and enslavement, over-exploitation, and mere simple brutal killing." How many would be left, who would find themselves in limbo after the war, Weizmann found difficult to determine. "If one can speak of two or three or even four million, it isn't an exaggeration. There will still be left enough to continue the great tradition of European Jewry." He concluded on an optimistic note, a ray of sunshine beaming down Hollywood-style on the field of carnage the morning after the victory, for which he received long and thunderous applause:

> Those who will be physically destroyed will be destroyed, but those who will survive will carry the torch proudly, and we shall all be proud of them, and may God speed the day when we can see them and take them by the hand and say, "You have suffered more than anybody else, and to you belongs the place of Honor."[16]

If there was a line in Ben-Gurion's mind between the beneficial disaster and an all-destroying catastrophe, it must have been a very fine one. For although a distinction was made after the Holocaust between the massive death caused by premeditated starvation, deprivation, disease, and large-scale killings and the massive death by industrial implements that took place after the Wannsee Conference in January 1942, this distinction concerned only the Germans. From a Jewish, Zionist point of view it mattered little whether the six million died by typhus and shooting or by gas and crematoriums. Hence it was difficult for Ben-Gurion to draw a line beyond which this destruction would threaten both Jewish existence and Zionism. Had he realized sooner that an industrial, systematic genocide was taking place, he would have understood that time was of the essence and might have reacted differently. But, as must be repeated forever, such annihilation was far beyond his grasp and that of his generation. He, along with everyone else, was thinking in terms of a relatively modest catastrophe that his Zionist concept defined as suitable for exploitation, not the full-fledged one that actually occurred. He foresaw destruction, but not the Holocaust, and this imperfect forecast predetermined his actions. He worked out his plans in accordance with his conception of the world at that time, its faults and its surprises; the world of evil spawned by Hitler was unthinkable to him in the literal sense of the word. He believed that the Jewish people had been cast into an abyss of darkness, but that the beacon of Zionism would direct them up into the light. He did not understand that there would be no exit, no salvation, and no hope of escape from Hitler's inferno.

This incomplete vision was what allowed Ben-Gurion to become so attached to the concept of turning a Jewish misfortune into a Zionist asset. Acting accordingly, he fell victim to his own idea. Having successfully turned such disasters as the Arab riots of 1929 and 1936 to advantage, he became a grand master of this political skill, to the point that he considered himself ready to take on Hitler. Each disaster, Ben-Gurion might have said, has its rewards for Zionism, and given that Hitler was the worst disaster until then, Ben-Gurion was determined to make it yield the greatest prize.

The advantage Ben-Gurion had sought after publication of the Nuremberg Laws was a Jewish majority in Palestine; he therefore demanded "commencement of activity to turn Palestine into a place of refuge for the masses of Jews, who will in turn make Palestine a Jewish country . . . *to get a million Jews* out of [Poland and Germany] and direct them to Palestine. . . . I regard this as *the lever* for our political activity." In January 1937, having adopted the partition solution recommended by the Peel Commission, Ben-Gurion reversed the order of his strategy, and instead of trying first to create a Jewish majority and then establish a state, he wanted to exploit the disaster of Hitler to obtain first a state, which could then absorb masses of the persecuted. When the partition solution was withdrawn in November 1938, at the very hour when the anticipated devastation was, in his view, a certainty, Ben-Gurion came up with combative Zionism, which was also based on the disaster created by Hitler.

In February 1941 Ben-Gurion connected the disaster of Hitler with the disaster of war and, again trying to exploit them, with renewed vigor called for the state as the sole means of rescue, devising a plan for the rapid transfer to Palestine of five to eight million Jews who "after England's victory [would] remain uprooted and ruined in Europe." Until publication of the land ordinances he hoped that for the sake of defending the Middle East the British government would overlook the White Paper and permit massive immigration during the war. "Eight million free Jews," he enthusiastically assured Mapai, "can help destroy Hitler. This is real strength, greater than that of the Poles or the Czechs."[17]

The war picture that developed in his mind in 1941 mistakenly included the possibility that the tormented Jews would break out of the Nazi hold and through the British blockade to Palestine. In May and June 1941, he described his vision of the masses putting their lives on the line in attempting to get through to Palestine. "With the help of the immigrants storming through from the Diaspora," the Yishuv would acquire great strength with which to oppose the land ordinances and the White Paper. The two forces upon which Zionism rested — the Yishuv and immigration — would become still more powerful when the cannon were silenced, Ben-Gurion believed. So convinced was he of the power to be achieved by exploiting this disaster that in London in October 1941, before his departure for the United States, he wrote himself the following note, which the British secret service later got hold of.

> In my opinion, we must make it perfectly clear that we want no less than all of western Palestine. The scope of the Jewish problem, the size of Jewish immigration in the future, the suffering and injustice inflicted on the Jewish people, the need for a "new deal" after the war, the sweeping changes that will be necessary throughout the world, the spacious and sparsely populated Arab countries which will win independence after the war, the smallness of Palestine, and the fact that it is the only corner of the world the Jewish people may call home — all these considerations prove that the establishment of a Jewish state in Palestine is both imperative and possible.[18]

There is no doubt, therefore, that in October 1941 Ben-Gurion saw the catastrophe, in its pre-Holocaust sense, as a source of strength and momentum and a powerful accelerator of the realization of Zionism. He did not hope for the disaster, needless to say, but since he was not in a position to prevent it, he used it to help solve the Jewish problem.

Did he still think this way once he learned that the Germans were carrying out systematic, full-scale genocide? When he returned to Palestine Ben-Gurion did not know of the existence of the death camps, and his remarks to the Zionist Executive on October 15, 1942, should be understood in this light. "Disaster is strength if channeled to a productive course; the whole trick of Zionism is that it knows how to channel our disaster not into despondency or degradation, as is the case in the Diaspora, but into a source of creativity and exploitation." The same spirit infused his speech to the party convention on October 25.

We ... reject the doctrines of the ghetto and the assimilationists that we and our strength are nil ... We knew it was possible to turn even adversity, disaster, and catastrophe from a source of decline, degradation, and destruction to a source of vitality and creativity. This is our Zionist message: to pour the Jewish disaster into the molds of redemption ... We have strength ... A great disaster means strength. An idea can spark disaster into redemption, can turn the disaster of millions into the redemption of millions.

But once it became evident to him, in late 1942, that his prophecies were coming true beyond all expectation, he fell silent on the strength of adversity and did not mention it again for three years. He could not struggle against the Holocaust; from it he could expect no strength or reawakening. Extermination would cancel out the need for a solution to the Jewish problem and, for that matter, the need for a state. "The extermination of European Jewry [meant] the end of Zionism, for there will be no one to build Palestine," he told the JAE in December 1942.

Only in the final stages of the Holocaust, hoping that a remnant of European Jewry would survive, did Ben-Gurion revert to his "adversity is strength" formula. The war and the Holocaust were not in his power to control, but he again resolved to extract the greatest possible benefit from the catastrophe. If the Jewish people had to suffer such a calamity, it was better that they gain a state in its aftermath than nothing at all. In December 1943, therefore, Ben-Gurion told Mapai's Central Committee that the tragedy would help create worldwide sympathy for the Jews. "The Zionist case rests not merely on the reality we have created here thus far, but also on the reality of the Jewish catastrophe ... The world must be made to see this."[19]

Like the concepts "disaster" and "destruction," "rescue," too, took on new meaning. In Zionist thinking, the word *rescue* had always carried a negative connotation, as it was taken to mean the antithesis of *redemption* — the code word for Zionism's ideal — implying that there were solutions to the Jewish problem other than Palestine, or that individual distress could be alleviated while ignoring the problem of the people as a whole. Ben-Gurion considered such rescue as something that undermined Zionism; it was the duty of every Zionist to reject this temptation at all costs. He gave the highest priority to a rescue that would function as a lever to advance the Zionist cause and as a source of strength. In November 1935 he had said,

Our movement will be doomed unless it exerts the greatest effort to salvage the absolute maximum of Jewish assets for Palestine, in the absolute minimum of time. ... To the disaster of German Jewry we must offer a Zionist response, namely, we must convert the disaster into a source for the upbuilding of Palestine, we must save both the lives and the property of German Jewry for Palestine's sake. *This* rescue takes priority over all else.

In accordance with this concept, Ben-Gurion demanded, even as the war drew to a close, that restitution be given "not to individuals, not to those Jews harmed personally, but to the Jewish people." In his view rescue "for Palestine's sake" was the only rescue. Alternative solutions — equal rights, emigration, territorialism, socialism — he considered nothing more than "witch doctor's medicine," which would only perpetuate the condition of the Jewish people. In April 1936 he had told Wauchope, "Were there a possibility of transferring Polish Jewry to America or Argentina we would have done so, regardless of our Zionist ideology. But the whole world is closed to us. Had we not room in Palestine, our people would have no choice but suicide."

The Évian Conference of 1938 and the Bermuda Conference of April 1943 — the free world's two farcical attempts, at the initiative of the United States, to find a refuge for the Jews — proved Ben-Gurion right. Not one country opened its gates to Hitler's victims.[20]

But the Zionist solution also posed a dilemma, which intensified as Jewish misery increased: How did the individual figure in relation to the rescue of the nation as a whole? It was in January 1933, on the eve of Hitler's rise to power, that Ben-Gurion had originally presented this dilemma in all its cruelty to Mapai's council: Which came first, individual rescue or Zionist fulfillment? His answer bore all the characteristics of his political strategy and personal tenacity. "Zionism in the stage of development is not primarily engaged in saving individuals. If along the way it saves a few thousand, tens of thousands, or hundreds of thousands of individuals, so much the better." But in the event of "a conflict of interest between saving individual Jews and the good of the Zionist enterprise, we shall say the enterprise comes first." He explained, "Because Palestine is not a philanthropic enterprise" or a country of immigrants in the conventional sense, "everything must be done with an eye to history, if we are to solve the question of the Jewish people and turn Zionism into reality." In this vein he forewarned his party in 1936 that "unless Zionism provides an answer . . . to the calamity of the Jewish people, it will be struck off the Jewish agenda."

Ben-Gurion's total dedication to "historic interest," sometimes to the exclusion of the individual, found extreme expression in December 1938, when he told Mapai's Central Committee, "Were I to know that the rescue of all German Jewish children could be achieved by their transfer to England and of only half their number by transfer to Palestine, I would opt for the latter, because our concern is not only the personal interest of these children, but the historic interest of the Jewish people." Such was his custom, to state or indeed overstate his position in stark alternatives. But this brutal formulation may have been the result of his bitterness at the world's indifference to Jewish misery revealed by the Évian Conference, at Britain's betrayal of Zionism following the horrors of Kristallnacht, and at the blatant hypocrisy of Britain in claiming that the Jewish question could be solved in Angda, British Guiana, or elsewhere and refusing to allow the rescue of the ten thousand German Jewish children by sending them to Palestine. Although he very well knew that his formulation was purely theoretical and that there was no hope at all of rescuing those children, his purpose in using this wording, to which later events gave a different and unintended meaning, was to hammer home the axiom that true rescue of the Jewish people was possible only in Palestine.

His address to the June 1941 Mapai convention demonstrates that he maintained this position. "It is our duty to uphold the banner of comprehensive Zionism, which aims not for individual redress, but for the deliverance of the people as a whole." At Mapai's January 1944 council he said, "History has proved that we cannot survive as individuals." At the same time he maintained that Zionism's singularity lay in its capacity to remedy both the problem of the people and the suffering of the individual. The war and the Holocaust did not alter this view, to which he seems to have applied the finishing touches during a Mapai seminar in November 1943. "The question we face is, What is Zionism? Is it an answer to the problem of refugees — what is known, in political jargon, as rescue — or is it the solution to the historical problem, namely, redemption?" Answering his own question, Ben-Gurion said that Zionism was a synthesis, a comprehensive answer to both problems, and that Zionism would lose its rationale unless "this enterprise attends to the burning needs of the millions" facing liquidation in Europe.

Ben-Gurion was not prolific, either in his diary or in public, in expressing his feelings with regard to individual suffering, nor did he say publicly that he identified with the Nazis' victims. This sparsity of response was characteristic of other Zionist leaders, such as Weizmann, and of Jewish poets and writers. Even the most sensitive and perceptive of them, for whom Jewish life was the essence of their own life — S. Y. Agnon, Uri Zevi Greenberg, and Nathan Alterman, among others — were silent in the years of the Holocaust. Action and activation, not the baring of the soul or the epitomization of agony in prose or poetry, was expected of Ben-Gurion. This might explain his silence, which some mistook for a lack of sensitivity. Ben-Gurion knew of no way to save lives or ease the agony of European Jewry, and perhaps his

own helplessness made him prefer silence to futile verbiage. Against
this backdrop a letter to Miriam of February 1943 stands out, for it is a
rare revelation of the feelings he tried so hard to lock within.

> I cannot get away from the nightmare brought over again by fifteen peo-
> ple arrived last week from Poland. Among those arrivals is a young girl,
> she was a member of the Hechaluth in Sosnowitz. . . . A day before yes-
> terday I went to Haifa to see her, and for three hours I heard a story of
> horrors and misery, which no Dante or Poe could ever have invented, and
> you are completely helpless, and you cannot even go mad — and the sun
> shines in all her glory, and you too must go . . . on with your ordinary
> work — And I want to try to write as if we — I mean we Jews — are liv-
> ing in a normal world . . . It is not easy, believe me.[21]

Ben-Gurion probably forced himself to relate to the fate of the individual in a manner in line with his Zionist ideology: there were no
"personal" cases, no individual Jews for him; there was only "the Jewish people." He was sensitive to the suffering of individuals; his heart
went out to them in their pain; but at the same time he regarded the
people as an impersonal entity, not as a group of individuals living
their own lives. To him the people's sole deliverance was in Zionism,
and "the people" was composed of many individuals who would ultimately be saved.

A scheme to rescue children, which never materialized, sheds light
on the predicament. In December 1942 the Mandatory government
hinted that it was prepared to permit the entry of five thousand children from the Balkans and suggested the possibility of allowing the remainder of the White Paper immigration schedule — twenty-nine
thousand certificates — to be filled by rescued children. Ben-Gurion
was elated, and after taking over this matter from Henrietta Szold,
head of Youth Immigration, who worked too slowly for his taste, and
appointing a JAE committee under his chairmanship for this purpose,
he formulated a plan according to which these parentless children
would become the children of the people, which would bear the cost of
their education and of placing them in agricultural settlements. The
finest education, to be provided for them in institutions established for
this purpose — he opposed offering them for adoption, since "we know
what a stepmother is" — was to be planned by experts, to prepare
them "for any role we wish. . . . We are offered the opportunity to raise
a generation for the building of the Jewish state." In February 1943
Ben-Gurion still considered the children's immigration "a tremendous
thing," but as the weeks passed it became evident that this rescue plan,
too, was illusory. The disappointment may have made him see just how

slight was the chance of mass rescue during the war and strengthened
his conviction that he had to concentrate only on projects that were
not hopeless.[22]

By early 1943 the JAE had representatives in Istanbul who gathered
information, made contacts in Nazi Europe, and devised ways and
means of rescue, in both senses of the word. Thus the Yishuv's leaders
learned of two schemes that seemed to offer a chance of saving many
Jews. Both involved payment of ransom, one for the deportation of
Rumania's Jews outside Europe (the Transnistria plan), the other to
prevent the transportation of Slovakia's Jews to death camps in Europe
(the Europa plan). It can safely be assumed that both projects were
doomed from the start, since the Germans meant to thwart them and
the Allies had prohibited any transfer of money to the enemy. Nevertheless, the JAE had to try. In February a stormy meeting of Mapai's
secretariat, followed by a Central Committee meeting, discussed the
plans against a backdrop of harsh criticism in the party and the Histadrut and a Yishuv furious with the JAE for not doing enough rescue
work.

For the secretariat and the Central Committee, Ben-Gurion made a
distinction between "those Jews we can bring out of Europe, over here
[and] those whom we cannot bring over here." While urging that
everything possible be done to save them all, he laid down the guidelines that JAE funds be used only for rescue by immigration to Palestine, whereas rescue by assisting Jews to survive elsewhere was to be
funded solely by private and organizational donations, in Palestine and
abroad. He joined the drive to raise such donations, meeting personally
with wealthy members of the Yishuv to obtain pledges.

In August of that year, at a JAE meeting that heard a report from an
Istanbul representative claiming that the lack of funds severely restricted rescue opportunities, Ben-Gurion again spelled out his line.

> The institution called the Jewish Agency is an all-Jewish organization for
> the upbuilding of Palestine, and I do not intend to say what is more im-
> portant, building Palestine, or rescuing a single Jew from Zagreb. It may
> be that, at one time or another, the rescue of a single child from Zagreb is
> more important, but these are two different matters. . . . The Agency is
> bound to do . . . everything in the way of rescuing Jews by immigration to
> Palestine . . . This is its role. However . . . the tasks of assistance, of saving
> one more Jew, of doing all to prevent deportations, are very important . . .
> and must be assumed by another organization, to be set up and funded
> from other sources.

This distinction was agreed to by the JAE. But while it refrained
from earmarking a special budget for rescue work, it nevertheless was
quick to finance such work — by bribing Nazi officials, among other

things — hoping to be reimbursed from other sources in Palestine and abroad. In this way the JAE spent nearly a million dollars on rescue work. And despite Ben-Gurion's stated priority, he called what was done by JAE representatives holy work; in September 1943 he valued it above mere rescue. "The fact that the Jews of Palestine stand at the fore of a rescue front is an important Zionist asset." In October 1944, he asked Chaim Barlas, who had arrived from Istanbul, "Do they know there that the help comes from Palestine?"

From then on Ben-Gurion concerned himself not only with the question "How many Jews will survive?" but also with "What will the survivors want?" For the ability to exploit the disaster and the price that could be extracted from it were wholly dependent on their attitude to Zionism. "The attitude of the Jews of liberated Europe," he told Mapai's council in October 1944, "will be of great value in our political struggle," and therefore it was vital "to start preparing for the Zionist guidance of the Jews of Rumania and Bulgaria," the two countries recently freed.[23]

Sadly enough, his colleagues were not alone in dismissing his chill forebodings; Ben-Gurion himself found them hard to believe once they became reality. After the outbreak of the war, Ben-Gurion often discussed the fate of "five million homeless Jews" and now and then used an even larger number, "five or eight million displaced Jews." This meant that "Zionism now involves one thing and one thing only: seeing to their rescue." At the same time, however, he said, "No fewer than five million are being crushed and trampled in one large concentration camp [Europe] . . . pillaged and scorned, destroyed and decimated," and Hitler intended "to kill and murder and slaughter" them all. Oscillation between despair and hope characterized his estimation of the catastrophe and its dimensions. In May 1942, at the Biltmore Conference, he spoke of Palestine's capacity to absorb between three and five million Jews and conceived his project to transfer two million. Following his return to Palestine in October 1942, Ben-Gurion championed the project and spoke again and again of the immediate postwar transfer of "two million Jews, the young generation, if it survives, from Europe" to Palestine. At the Kefar Vitkin convention he explained that he used the two-million figure "for various reasons; still, it is arbitrary."[24]

His 1942 speeches and writing are marked by perplexity, reflecting the swing between hope and despair, as if echoing his was another voice that asked relentlessly whether any Jews would survive the war in Europe. At the party convention Ben-Gurion said that this gnawing doubt was "a nightmarish mystery . . . No one can tell whether there will be any Jews [in Europe] after this war." Nonetheless, in the same breath he issued a call "to provide a homeland and independence for the millions of Jews who are being destroyed, if they still exist."

By 1943 he thought there would be fewer survivors, but he still moved back and forth between fear of the worst and hope for the best. In July he told the Zionist Actions Committee, "There is only one fear for Zionism, a terrible, dreadful fear . . . If Hitler does to all the Jews of Europe what he has done to most of the Jews of Poland . . . European Jewry will be destroyed." In September he said to Mapai's Central Committee that his one fear was "Hitler. And the fear is that he will annihilate the remainder of Europe's Jews." From this point on he no longer quoted figures but spoke only of his project to transfer "many Jews." In January 1944, at the Mapai council, he coined the slogan "Maximum Jews in minimum time" and added, as if embarrassed, "A million, a million and a half . . . two million. I do not know how many." In March 1944 he said, "The question of the size of the Jewish people . . . has given me no rest this entire year. . . . None of us . . . myself included . . . knew that the catastrophe was so near and so great."

Did these ups and downs actually reflect his feelings, or were his expressions of hope born of the fear that, with no Jews remaining in Europe, Zionism would lose its raison d'être and the question would be, "A Jewish state for whom?" Was this why, consciously or not, he tended to play down the magnitude of the tragedy? This question will probably never be answered conclusively. Only on June 20, 1944, after he received authoritative information, did the harrowing truth of six million dead become entirely plain to him and a real comprehension of the Holocaust take firm hold in his mind. Like one looking back over a path recently traveled, he said, "First I thought a minimum of two million would survive; now that they are wiped out I say one million," explaining that he used this number as "a political figure," not a "statistical" one. What he pondered and what he felt, he summed up as if in shocked bewilderment. "No one in his right mind would have imagined wiping out the entire Jewish people. When we first heard it from Hitler, we did not believe him. We said, 'This is mere rhetoric.' "[25]

Ben-Gurion had realized soon after the war began that there was no possibility of massive rescue, Zionist or otherwise. The Germans would show no mercy, and there was not the slightest chance that the British would offer assistance or open Palestine to refugees. For Zionism the war was a dormant period. No rescue that could make a real difference was possible; there were only opportunities here and there for individual rescues, at a great price, which neither the JAE nor any other Jewish group had the money to pay. Moreover, even when the JAE decided to go ahead with rescue projects, they were aborted, either by the Germans (the Transnistria and Europa plans) or by the Allies

("Goods for lives," the Joel Brand affair).* Even the demand raised in the JAE and brought to Churchill by Weizmann to bomb Auschwitz and the railway lines leading to it was hopeless as far as Ben-Gurion could see, and he saw no reason to invest effort in a hopeless venture.

It seems that all his life, and particularly during times of crisis, Ben-Gurion remained true to his axiom that effort should be invested only in the achievable. In 1940 he made this axiom one of his slogans, "We shall not engage in futile efforts." This motto, intended for the war against the White Paper, was his guideline in dealing with the Holocaust. In contrast to his lack of interest in futile large-scale rescue projects during the war, his imagination soared in devising spectacular operations afterward, when, he believed, a new world order would reign. His campaign to promote the Biltmore Program and the transfer idea — "Why isn't it possible to transfer 500,000 Jews in five hundred ships departing in one day from various harbors?" he asked Mapai's 1942 convention — and to prepare the Yishuv for the absorption of the survivors — "And why isn't it possible to establish a thousand settlements" in one night? — was his sole answer to the catastrophe. Ben-Gurion had plenty of ideas for prewar and postwar mass rescue, but none for the period of the Holocaust.

Ben-Gurion's sense of destiny bound him to one mission, to which he dedicated his life: the establishment of Jewish independence in Palestine. Even after the war's outbreak and the start of the extermination, he felt certain that in leading the struggle for the state he was also making the greatest contribution to the rescue of Jews. In his view immigration and rescue were twin concepts, and rescue by immigration to Palestine was his foremost concern. This was the focus that had created in Ben-Gurion the sense of the burning ground — the fear that a historic opportunity might slip past — and generated all his political designs since his call for the conquest of Zionism.

From his point of view all his political schemes were rescue projects: declaring war on Britain in 1930 over immigration; opening the gates during Wauchope's term as high commissioner (1931–1938); "bringing over" a million Jews in 1935; bringing in four million at the time of the Peel Commission and the partition proposal in 1937; militant Zionism and the immigration revolt, declaring a state in Haifa, and opening its port for mass immigration in 1938 and 1939; the violent struggle proposed in 1940; and the one-time transfer of 1942. Ben-Gurion was thoroughly absorbed in this desperate race against time, against his colleagues, and against the harsh realities that nearly always defeated

---

* In 1944, Adolf Eichmann offered Joel Brand and the Jewish Committee in Budapest a deal, the gist of which was that, in return for American goods, especially trucks, he would spare the lives of Jews who would otherwise be sent to Auschwitz.

him. The boldest of his projects, his campaign for which ultimately
led to the split in Mapai, was the establishment of the partitioned state,
whose purpose was first and foremost the rescue of European Jewry
while there was still time. In March 1944 he told the Mapai council:

> Had a Jewish state been established seven years ago we could have
> brought over millions of Jews . . . and they would be here today. Now we
> will never bring them here . . . for they are no more. . . . Tabenkin . . . will
> believe me when I say that I would not have given up hoping for the
> whole of Palestine if I had not believed that bringing two million Jews to
> Palestine was worth more than all the fine talk in the world about one,
> whole Palestine.

Ben-Gurion's response to the Holocaust, to which he devoted all his
energy during the war years, could be manifested only after it was
over. However, the vision of the state was not only the grandest of
Ben-Gurion's rescue schemes, it was also a guarantee against another
Holocaust. The Hebrew adage "Tongs are made with tongs" — no second or third step can be taken before the first — was Ben-Gurion's favorite. A strong, cohesive ruling party was "the first tongs," without
which no "rescue" would be possible after the war, and to forge it
Ben-Gurion had to draw on all his resources. With this tongs in hand he
could frame, form, and carry through his Biltmore, or Jerusalem, Program. Therefore a last attempt to prevent the split and a reformation
of the party — not rescue — was the primary task into which he
poured all his energy. In this spirit he concluded the letter to Miriam of
the sunny, springlike February day on which he told her the nightmarish story of the young girl from Sosnowitz.

> But we must keep on, we must; perhaps in continuing to do what we
> started *here* some sixty years ago we will save a remnant who wants to be
> saved; anyhow *this* is the only thing which I can do and it is my intention
> to do it, whatever I can and as long as I can.

This remained his staunch position throughout the years of the war
and the Holocaust. In February 1944 he reiterated it to Mapai's secretariat: although "the issue of utmost urgency is that of the rescue" and
although "this issue is pressing in Rumania and in Bulgaria . . . we
must, at present, give the internal work [in the party] top priority . . .
forging the first tongs . . . The party . . . may eventually be our sole
means of rescue."[26] The marvel was not in the way he thought, but
rather in his ability — in spite of all he knew and felt — to marshal his
mind accordingly, as the burning ground erupted into a conflagration
that reduced the Jewish people to ashes, and attend to party matters as
in ordinary times. It was perhaps owing to this that after the Holocaust
there came the resurrection.

Epilogue

ALL BEN-GURION'S PLANS for action seem to have followed the same course: they were rejected when he first proposed them, then accepted and executed later. Following this pattern, his "Jaffa Professional Trade Union Alliance" and "broad-based workers' party" of 1907 emerged as Achdut ha-Avodah (1919), the Histadrut (1921), and Mapai (1930); his "conquest of Zionism" of 1928 materialized in 1935; his demand in 1939 for a Jewish army was realized in 1944; and the partition scheme, which from 1937 on was the basis of his Zionist policy and the foundation of the Biltmore Program in 1942, was also destined to be implemented well after its conception, with the UN General Assembly resolution of November 1947 and Ben-Gurion's May 14, 1948, declaration of the establishment of the State of Israel.

However, before this took place another initially rejected plan was put into effect, and had it not been, Ben-Gurion probably never would have arrived at this declaration. This was combative Zionism with the immigration revolt. What his colleagues and party had refused to do before and in the early part of the war, they carried out with extra initiative and valor when it ended. Although the world had changed beyond recognition, Ben-Gurion's formulas — "the power of adversity," "disaster means strength," and "a state is the only means of rescue" — remained unaltered. What before the fact had been only an early warning was an undeniable reality, and the Holocaust replaced "disaster" as the event to be used to advantage. The four decisive years of struggle for the Jewish people's right to a state of their own in Palestine should be seen in this context.

The struggle, no less than the establishment of the State of Israel, its War of Independence, its wars with the Arab countries and development as a Jewish state, merits a volume of its own. The actions Ben-

Gurion took to prepare for the struggle constitute the high point of his political work. Simultaneously with laying the groundwork for making the most of the Holocaust, he began working to pull his party together and make it the main engine behind his Biltmore Program. On October 18, 1942, just two weeks after his return from the United States, he informed the JAE that he "intended to devote himself" to economic planning for the absorption of millions, and that "this work would require all his time"; he would continue to chair JAE meetings, but he would be "unable to handle any . . . issues" apart from the planning. True to form, Ben-Gurion set up a special instrument for this purpose. He began suddenly to sing the praises of the Jewish Agency Executive's Economic Research Institute, headed by Arthur Ruppin, whose work he had hardly noticed hitherto — "The work of your institute is of tremendous value" — and established within it a Planning Committee composed of Eliezer Kaplan, Emil Schmorak of the JAE, and Eliezer Hoofien, a director of the Anglo-Palestine Bank, the Zionist bank which, after the establishment of the state, became Bank Leumi. Ben-Gurion himself headed this committee, and he retained this position even after resigning from the JAE in January 1943 as part of his campaign to pressure it to dismiss Weizmann.[1]

Departing from his own precedent, Ben-Gurion divided this campaign into two phases: the threat of resignation and the resignation itself. First, when the opportunity presented itself in the form of talks Weizmann was holding with the U.S. State Department, he made his threat in a letter of January 12, 1943, to the members of the JAE, in which he refused to "share the responsibility" for making Zionist policy as long as Weizmann held talks with the State Department "without our knowledge and without our authorization." To lend force to his threat, Ben-Gurion absented himself from JAE meetings in January and February in the guise of taking a vacation, writing to Miriam that he had taken "sick leave." In late February he acceded to the entreaties of a JAE delegation and returned to take part in the meetings. In mid May, however, he suffered such a fierce attack of lumbago that he was hospitalized at Jerusalem's Hadassah Hospital and, after being released on June 1, spent two weeks convalescing in a rest home in Givat Brenner. On July 25 he notified the JAE that he was no longer "associated" with it, because although the resolutions he had proposed to establish a Washington political bureau subordinate to the JAE and to convene a worldwide Zionist conference in Palestine had been adopted, they had not been carried out. Nevertheless, he continued to participate in meetings. But in September the lumbago returned and he wrote Miriam that he had to stay in bed for a week.

In October he finally acted on his threat, taking a session of the

Small Actions Committee by surprise in announcing his resignation and saying he could "not shoulder the political responsibility for the handling of our foreign affairs." The chairman of the Actions Committee flatly rejected the resignation and allowed no discussion of it. In late October and in November, Ben-Gurion said openly to the JAE what he had previously whispered only in private: the cause of his resignation was Weizmann. He first put it in writing in early November, in a letter read aloud at a JAE meeting.

> In my opinion it is imperative to ensure that Dr. Weizmann takes no political step without the knowledge and prior authorization of the Executive, and without being accompanied by members of the Executive, who will be so charged.[2]

Ben-Gurion complained that his colleagues' attempts to get him to withdraw his resignation — particularly a proposal by Rabbi Judah Leib Maimon and Schmorak that he go to London to reconcile with Weizmann — were an incessant "torture" to him. He was adamant that Weizmann come at once to Jerusalem to thrash the matter out and that a worldwide Zionist conference be held in Palestine. Weizmann, however, saw through this ploy and, using various arguments, explained that he could not come to Palestine. The JAE resolved to send a reconciliation mission of three to London.

In a clever move intended to disarm Ben-Gurion, Weizmann wired him on November 4, asking him to reconsider his resignation and come to London with Moshe Sharett, Maimon, and Schmorak, the members of the mission. Ben-Gurion replied, "Regret inability to change decision under prevailing conditions. Reasons are stated in my letter to you dated New York June eleventh 1942." In December he spent time in Tiberias taking a cure. The reconciliation mission departed for London in January 1944 and succeeded in getting from Weizmann assurances that in the future he would work in collaboration with Ben-Gurion, send fuller reports, and be more attentive to directions from Jerusalem. Ben-Gurion at length withdrew his resignation, probably because it was only one stage of the war of attrition that he knew was the sole means by which he could accomplish his design. On March 2, 1944, the JAE published an official statement on his return to his position as chairman. But this was only the quiet before the next storm. In October 1945 Ben-Gurion reverted to his 1942 tactic and wrote Weizmann, "I can no longer take part in your meetings, being unable to share in a fictitious responsibility. . . . I shall not remain in this Executive."[3]

Throughout this period, Ben-Gurion continued his work to build up the party and unify the youth organizations in preparation for their future tasks, as well as his activity on the Planning Committee, whose

meetings, he said, "are now part of the political work." In March 1944
he still believed a million surviving Jews in Europe would wish to immigrate to Palestine, and he was more hopeful about his transfer
scheme. Consequently he directed the committee in conjunction with
the Institute for Economic Research and many experts to provide him
with a "plan to settle a million Jews in Palestine, in agriculture, industry, commerce, trades — together with a plan to finance it." Weizmann, in London, learned of the committee in January 1945 and was
"amazed," he said, that it was "seriously discussing the bringing over
of a million Jews into Palestine in the course of a year or two," notwithstanding a conversation Weizmann had had with Churchill, in
which only a hundred thousand had been discussed. Moreover, Weizmann doubted the country could absorb that number.

His work on this committee brought him, Ben-Gurion told the JAE,
to take an interest in the operation's financial side, on whose resolution
the plan's success depended no less than on solving the political question. It was probably in contemplating this aspect of the issue that the
idea of reparations began to take shape in his mind. German capital
would be given in restitution to the Jewish people and directed wholly
to the building of Palestine. In January 1944 he edited a draft of three
proposals that the Planning Committee was to put on the JAE's agenda
and added a fourth in his own hand: "The committee proposes to the
Jewish Agency Executive to appoint one or more persons to investigate, in detail, the assets of the [German] enemy — movable and immovable — located in Palestine, as a source of restitution of property
to the Jewish people and to Jewish residents [for the damages caused
them by the German government]"; the clause in brackets was struck
from the letter Ben-Gurion signed as chairman of the committee and
sent to the JAE on February 17, 1944.

The innovation was that reparations were to be made to "the Jewish
people" and not exclusively to individuals and groups. Until then reparations had been discussed as compensation for the expenses of absorbing refugees, as Weizmann had proposed in November 1939, or as
"retribution and an act of vengeance" for Nazi crimes, as Eliyahu
Dobkin had moved in November 1942. Ben-Gurion's proposal, that the
JAE would accept restitution on behalf of "the Jewish people," was
new, and in June 1944 he formulated it so that his intention became
quite clear. "Who will be heir to the six million Jews who were murdered and denied help to escape their death? This is the question . . . It
has to be contemplated and for this preparations must be made . . . A
tool must be forged to speak on our behalf" — a tool to prepare for,
claim, and accept "financial restitution for the Jewish people from

Germany for the purpose of building *Eretz Israel.*" There was probably no blunter expression of turning a Jewish misfortune into a Zionist advantage. This plan, too, was destined to encounter controversy, initial rejection, and ultimate acceptance and realization in the reparations agreement signed by Germany and Israel on September 10, 1952.[4]

As the resignation drama neared its peak, Ben-Gurion requested a permit from the British Foreign Office to visit the Jewish communities of Bulgaria and Rumania, to see for himself whether his plan to bring in a million Jews had any basis in reality, and whether the conditions and attitudes of the Jews of these two countries, recently liberated by the Soviet army, would facilitate its implementation. He set himself three objectives: to discover their attitude to immigration so he would know whether they were willing to force their way into Palestine; to encourage them to do so; and to persuade the governments concerned to allow their exit. On November 23, 1944, he departed on a long and tiring journey by air and rail, via Turkey, arriving in Sofia on December 2 for a six-day stay.

In Bulgaria he found a strange situation. The Russians, having liberated it, had not yet forced upon it the Soviet regime, and the government seemed to be in the hands of the "Homeland Front," a coalition of four parties. Of its sixteen ministers only four were members of the Communist Party, but it was evident that the real power lay in the hands of the pro-Soviet minister of the interior, who controlled the "militia," by virtue of which he could extend his power throughout the country. Ben-Gurion, who met with eight members of the government, the Russian military commander, and the British consul, found "great chaos" there.

The government treated Ben-Gurion deferentially, gave him a "militiaman" bodyguard, who guided him and helped him avoid security checks, and put a special railroad car at his disposal. "Officers wanted to break into the car, but the conductor got rid of them." Various delegations were at his doorstep early every morning, and officials in border towns saluted him, as did the Russian policewomen — the prettiest, he reported, that could be found in Russia — who directed city traffic. "The Gentiles think 'the king of the Jews' has come," he wrote in his diary. Although he felt flattered, he was not fooled into thinking he was being treated so well because he was chairman of the JAE. All this "ta-ra-ram," he said, was because, for some reason, he had been mistaken for a representative of Britain and the United States.

The Jews both cheered and saddened him. In three towns on his way to Sofia they held receptions, moving him "to tears." In each, representatives of all the Jewish organizations met him at the station and brought him to the synagogue, where the entire community was gathered. He felt that most of the Jews were willing to go with him to Palestine. But a good number of the Bulgarian Jews who had been spared the Holocaust had been plunged into shocking poverty as a result of dispossession and deprivation by the Nazis and their Bulgarian collaborators. Furthermore, no hope for improving their situation was in sight for, according to Ben-Gurion, even if the government resolved to restore their property to the Jews, they would never claim it, for fear of arousing anti-Semitism. He considered it essential to save the children, who "could not last a year under such conditions. They will die." Moreover, quite a few had become Communists — many assimilated Jews supported and identified with communism — placing Zionism in "great danger." "Communism," postulated Ben-Gurion, "cannot coexist with Zionism" the way one party acknowledges the existence of another, since "with communism it is either-or."

But communism was not the only factor cooling Jewish desire to go to Palestine. Patriotism ran high in postwar Bulgaria, which called on all its citizens to put their backs into rebuilding their country and promised the Jews equal rights and restoration of their property. Jews who "ran away" to another country would bear the stigma of treason to the homeland. Ben-Gurion repeatedly heard echoes of the stock arguments of Jews opposed to immediate immigration to Palestine that "we've waited two thousand years, we can wait a little longer." His visit to Bulgaria served him as a "tiny crack" through which he could glimpse postwar Europe and "what awaits this Jewish community." What he told the Jews of Bulgaria he repeated to Mapai in Palestine. "It is clear to me that in liberated Europe there can be no waiting; either we bring them to Palestine, or the rest of European Jewry is lost . . . to the Jewish people and to Zionism. . . . Either we rescue them quickly or they are lost forever." The burning ground had not cooled in the slightest; in the aftermath of the Holocaust, it seems to have burned even hotter.

In a "huge mass meeting" overflowing with "Zionist inspiration," Ben-Gurion again trumpeted his slogan of the power of adversity, as if the Holocaust were nothing but a Zionist lesson for the future. In his speech he called for the establishment of a Jewish state in Palestine, as indicated in his notes for it.

The five years we have undergone. We are at the threshold of decisions: for the world and for us. . . . One third of our people are gone — the dead will not come back to life. The question: Will there be any guarantee, and if so what kind, that it won't happen again? They promise rights — Shall we be satisfied with that? . . . Our strength is twofold: desperation in the Diaspora and faith in the homeland.

Having been denied a Rumanian visa, he returned to Palestine on December 13, bringing thirteen Greek-language books and gifts for Paula: a robe, socks, a scarf, and handkerchiefs. His course of action with regard to Bulgaria and its Jews was now apparent to him, and he demanded of Mapai and the JAE that agents be sent to Bulgaria to organize and hasten immigration. They had to have "deep roots" in Zionism and "moral force . . . No great intellect is needed there," but one of them "must be a man of political sense [since in Bulgaria] we are within Russia's sphere. . . . She is at liberty to show us any face she wishes, but we are not. We must not appear as an enemy . . . but neither should we kneel." But the mass emigration from Bulgaria did not take place until after the founding of the state. Nearly its entire Jewish community — forty-five thousand of a total fifty thousand Jews — came to Israel in 1948 and 1949. They remembered Ben-Gurion as the man who rekindled the Zionist spark in their hearts.[5]

Before Ben-Gurion made his second trip to Europe in October 1945, to visit the Jewish survivors in the displaced persons (DP) camps in Germany, his position was greatly strengthened by the results of elections on August 1 and 6, 1944, to the Elected Assembly and to the Histadrut convention, which vindicated his insistence on the Biltmore Program despite the risk of schism in his party. Mapai won 35.9 percent of the votes in the Elected Assembly (as compared to 22.8 percent before the split) and its margin as the largest party in the assembly was greater than in the past; the breakaway Achdut ha-Avodah movement won only 10 percent. Itzhak Tabenkin's ticket suffered an even more painful defeat in the Histadrut elections, gaining only 17.5 percent of the votes, as opposed to Mapai's 52.9 percent. A comparison with the results of the previous elections, in which a united Mapai had won 69.3 percent, shows that Mapai, backing the party apparatus created by Ben-Gurion and supporting the Biltmore Program, not only retained but increased its power; the Achdut ha-Avodah movement, which endorsed Greater Palestine and called for a return to the values of the labor movement, took from Mapai not a third of the votes, as it had boasted it would, but merely a sixth.

Other events also accounted for Ben-Gurion's enhanced position. On August 12, 1944, Berl Katznelson had died of a stroke. Although his influence had gradually waned, he still had many admirers in the Yishuv and was unequaled as a balance and brake to Ben-Gurion. Ben-Gurion wrote of his grief and his appreciation of Katznelson to Miriam a month after "the lion of the pack" passed away.

The dearest and nearest friend is gon, and nothing that happened to me personally affects me so deeply. If I were able to tell you what he was — not to me only, — you certainly would thing that I am exaggerating as usual when I am talking about our people here. But I really don't know in our generation somebody like him — in wisdom, vision, truthfulness, moral and intelectual power . . . courage . . . devotion, a supreme teacher and educator a shrewd observer of events and people . . . that living miracle which was called Berl.[6]

With Tabenkin and Katznelson gone, only Ben-Gurion remained of Mapai's big three. The second rank had also dwindled. On June 11, 1945, Eliyahu Golomb, the head of the Haganah, had died of a heart attack; Moshe Beilinson had departed in 1936; and Dov Hoz had been killed in an automobile accident in 1941. Ben-Gurion remained alone at the top of the party, not only in politics but in the realm of defense as well. The opposition he would meet from then on, for a good many years, would be meek, and the criticism leveled at him would lack incisiveness. No one who counted would stand in his way in taking Weizmann apart. This was, indeed, a new Mapai, a party of nearly one voice — the Mapai of Ben-Gurion, hoisting his pennants, upholding his policies, and rolling on victoriously through all the elections.

Ben-Gurion was the first Zionist leader to visit the death and DP camps in Germany. Hosted by the American and British occupation armies, he was a personal guest of General Dwight Eisenhower. The official purpose of his visit, for which he received his pass, was to study the situation and needs of the Jewish DPs. His real intention, however, was to see for himself to what extent the power of their adversity could be used to advantage in his battle to establish the Jewish state. On his instructions, agents of the Mossad for Aliyah Bet and soldiers of the Jewish Brigade put together a plan for "armed immigration" — the fighting immigration he had proposed in 1938. Ben-Gurion envisaged the survivors of the death camps fighting their way onto the shores of Palestine, breaking through a blockade of British soldiers. He believed that the impact this battle would have on public opinion would be the ultimate achievement of the power of adversity. His examination of the skeletal survivors must have been like that of a commander reviewing his troops before battle.

As he wove this vision, Ben-Gurion was keeping in mind the first postwar Zionist Congress, scheduled for 1946. He was interested not only in the votes of the 165,000 survivors in the camps he was to visit, but also, and perhaps primarily, in becoming their representative. Their voice would be his and his would be that of the Congress. To this end he would make a second visit to the camps and act as chief spokesman at the "international" conference — later called congress — of survivors held in Munich in January 1946.

In eleven days in October 1945, Ben-Gurion visited camps near

Frankfurt, Stuttgart, Munich, Heidelberg, and Hanover, and the death camps of Dachau and Bergen-Belsen, cramming his diary with every detail. For the most part, his tone was dry and matter-of-fact. In Dachau "238,000 were burned in the crematorium. . . . I saw the ovens, the gas chambers, the kennels, the gallows, the prisoners' quarters, and the SS quarters"; in Bergen-Belsen, "Until April 15 this year 48,000 Jews were here . . . Since then 31,000 have died . . . (of typhus, tuberculosis)."

The news of his arrival in Germany on October 19 spread rapidly among Jews throughout the American zone, and everywhere he was greeted by wildly enthusiastic receptions. At Camp Zeilsheim he was asked to wait in a military car, just beyond the gates, until the final arrangements were made. One Jew happened to peer into the car and, recognizing the strong face and shock of white hair, suddenly screamed in an unearthly voice, "Ben-Gurion! Ben-Gurion!" Others gathered around the car, shouting and cheering as though a miracle had happened and Palestine itself was standing before them. The screaming crowd doubled by the minute until Ben-Gurion's escort, American army chaplain Judah Nadich, got back into the car, fearing a riot. With great difficulty he was able to direct the crowd to the camp auditorium, which was soon filled to capacity and beyond. When Ben-Gurion made his way to the front of the auditorium, the survivors broke into "Ha-Tikvah." When he arrived at Camp Feldafing, the crowd was waiting for him, and in St. Ottilien — a monastery turned into a hospital for survivors — the eight hundred patients met him with a blue and white flag wrapped in black, and orphans presented him with flowers and greeted him in Hebrew. In Camp Landsberg — the largest of the camps in Bavaria — he made his appearance in the sports stadium. In the British zone he spoke at the cemetery near Bergen-Belsen, near the great common grave where many thousands of Jews were buried.

"The tears in his eyes" testified to Ben-Gurion's feelings at the sight of the orphans in St. Ottilien, where he said, "I will not try to express the feelings within me . . . Such a thing is impossible." Perhaps this offers an additional explanation of his silence on the horror of the Holocaust. However deep his feelings, he was able to keep them concealed. In Heidelberg — on his way to Bergen-Belsen — where he had "a private bath, and what is more amazing, towels," he noted in his diary, he turned his attention to book hunting. This time, however, he was disappointed. "For the time being, they told me, no Greek books can be found here. Supply has run out."

On this visit Ben-Gurion made speeches to those just escaped from the valley of death that were similar to what he had said in the past to

He-Chalutz conventions in Poland or the Hadassah convention in Cincinnati: he praised the Zionist enterprise in Palestine and the members of the Yishuv who stood tall, as though there were no war and no Holocaust. He spoke to the survivors as if they were an abstract entity and not refugees from hell. If this was a manifestation of insensitivity or a rare aptitude for an impersonal approach, it represented another of those weaknesses which were his source of strength. Nothing better demonstrates how what detracted from him as a man enhanced him as a leader than his words to the patients of St. Ottilien.

> I can tell you that a vibrant Jewish Palestine exists and that even if its gates are locked the Yishuv will break them open with its strong hands. . . . Today we are the decisive power in Palestine . . . We have our own shops, our own factories, our own land, our own culture, and our own rifles. . . . Hitler was not far from Palestine. There could have been terrible destruction there, but what happened in Poland could not happen in Palestine. They would not have slaughtered us in synagogues. Every boy and every girl would have shot at every German soldier.

The news of a place where Jews had strength, where they could defend themselves, was the solace Ben-Gurion offered the survivors. His special instinct told him that neither caresses nor compassion was expected of him, but the bearing of a torch that lit a vision of hope for all. Astute in a way that Weizmann and every other Zionist leader were not, Ben-Gurion was capable of telling his listeners that, in exchange for the pain and suffering inflicted on each of them, the Jewish people would gain a state. It was probably precisely because his words were so plain, almost crude, that they moved and aroused his audiences. Nadich, who heard him address the DPs in Zeilsheim, wrote,

> During all the many years of their hell . . . during the years of actual physical and mental torture, that which kept them alive, that which had buoyed them up even amidst the darkest days, was the yearning, the longing, the hope for Palestine. . . . Now, after all these many years, here was Palestine right in the midst of their DP camp on German soil! For who better than Ben-Gurion personified *Eretz Israel* and its fight for freedom and independence?

In a singularly insensitive statement, Ben-Gurion told the survivors of Auschwitz and other death camps that although the European war was over, their own war was just beginning, since only Eretz Israel could guarantee that a Holocaust would never happen again. For this reason, "if necessary, we shall take on England [and] undo the White Paper . . . When Jews in Palestine do not agree, they fight . . . and not with words alone." His intent was that a single message should strike home in their hearts: the surviving remnant had to function as a "political factor" in the struggle for a state, since "what has happened . . . we cannot repair . . . and it's our duty to make sure it never happens again. There will not be another Holocaust . . . only . . . if we . . . create a reality which will not let it happen . . . Not only your children but we, whose heads are grayed with age, will yet live to see the Jewish state."

In his diary Ben-Gurion wrote that "70 percent of the survivors do in fact want to go to Palestine" and were ready to fight for that right, even at the cost of their lives. On October 31, two days after his visit ended, he summed up.

> In the struggle ahead we have on our side three major forces: the Yishuv and its strength, America, [and] the DP camps in Germany. The function of Zionism is not to help the remnant to survive in Europe, but rather to rescue them for the sake of the Jewish people and the Yishuv; the Jews of America and the DPs of Europe are allotted a special role in this rescue.

With these forces in hand, he made ready to exploit the Holocaust for the rebirth.[7]

And indeed the survivors, in whom Ben-Gurion had kindled a new flame that forged them into a "political factor," under his leadership rejected all British schemes to rehabilitate them in Europe. At their conference in Munich in January 1946, Ben-Gurion told them, "We shall not be stilled until the last of you who so wishes joins us in Palestine to build together the Jewish state," and they resolved, "Palestine is our only home!" Their voices and his became the voice of the Holocaust, and his prophecy that Hitler was not only taking but giving came true. In the name of the surviving remnant — the quintessence of the power of adversity — he set out to achieve the state.

During the years from 1940 until May 1945, fewer than ten thousand made their way into Palestine by sea illegally, and their number was deducted from the immigration schedule. On November 9, 1945, however, the total of 75,000 allocated by the White Paper was reached, and from then on the Jews had no choice but to storm Palestine by force. The figures show how great was the strength of adversity accumulated in the DP camps: between May 1945 and the establishment of the State of Israel, 74,520 Jews attempted to enter the country illegally, or 69 percent of the total of 108,000 illegals who came to Palestine by sea between 1934 and 1948.

The moment Ben-Gurion had been preparing for had arrived, and he launched the decisive battle. The Yishuv, whose hands had been tied during the war, opened its arms and, creating a powerful movement with its immigration agents and brigade soldiers, brought the survivors from the farthest reaches of Europe to Mediterranean ports, and from there to Palestine's shores. Ben-Gurion, in a sense, turned the life's breath of the lost six million into a wind that bore aloft the survivors and powered the sails of the Zionist ship, as he steered it across the waves with a sure hand to its destiny, the state.

The end of the war meant the end of the great double formula as well. Once Zionism was rid of its commitment to help the British army in the war against Hitler, combative Zionism — shelved when Italy entered the war in 1940 — burst into life, this time without opposition. The immigration war began in force, and the refugees of Hitler's death camps encountered on Palestine's shores the clubs and bullets of British soldiers. Ben-Gurion's scenario for the *Colorado*, dismissed in 1939, was enacted by a spate of ships carrying the survivors. It was they — not the British government, which locked Palestine's gates and sent its army against them — who won over public opinion in France and Italy (from whose ports dozens of illegal ships set sail for Palestine) and in Britain and the United States. The survivors killed by the British on Palestine's shores, and others who were turned away, brought Zionism added sympathy and support.

The media — indifferent in 1939 when the British had not hesitated to open fire on refugees aboard the *Aghios Nikolaus*, killing one of them — eagerly covered, in vivid detail, the survivors' struggle against the Royal Navy. The drama Ben-Gurion produced from the pent-up pressure of the survivors and the shut gates reached its peak with the *Exodus 1947*. This ship, with 4,450 illegals, including hundreds of infants, on board, all DPs, was intercepted by the Royal Navy on July 18, 1947, and escorted to Haifa. There, in a clash with the army, three illegals were killed and dozens wounded. The ship and its passengers were escorted to France, and when the illegals refused to disembark there, the ship was ordered to sail to Hamburg, in the British zone. There they were removed from the ship by force and, struggling, were returned to the DP camps in Germany before the eyes of the world press.

Illegal immigration was one of two arms of the Yishuv's great struggle. The second was armed battle within Palestine. The Palmach attacked police stations guarding the coast, blew up radar stations on Givat Olga and Mount Carmel, which were used to locate ships of illegals, and instigated diversionary clashes with the British army to enable illegals aboard the *Wingate* and other ships to get ashore. The British army responded with frequent exhaustive searches for Haganah fighters and weapons, imposing a series of curfews on the large cities. June 29, 1946 — known as Black Saturday — marked one of the peaks of that struggle: the British carried out searches and arrests throughout Palestine and besieged dozens of settlements. Five Jews were killed, dozens wounded, and some three thousand arrested and interned in detention camps. Furthermore, in a surprise operation JAE members, including Maimon, Sharett, Itzhak Gruenbaum, and Dov Joseph, were arrested.

Ben-Gurion, who was in Paris at the time, led the struggle[8] from there as he prepared for the Zionist Congress, which opened in Basel on December 9, 1946. He won a great triumph when the Congress endorsed his political line, owing in no small measure to the backing of the Hadassah representatives. This Congress did not elect a president or an Executive, but left that to the Actions Committee, which on December 29 re-elected the outgoing Executive, with Ben-Gurion as chairman. He also received the newly created defense portfolio. The Actions Committee resolved not to elect a president of the World Zionist Organization, which meant, theoretically and actually, the dismissal of Weizmann. When the state was established, Ben-Gurion, rejecting a nearly unanimous demand, refused to allow Weizmann to add his signature to the Declaration of Independence, which Ben-Gurion had composed, insisting on the technical argument that Weizmann was abroad when it was signed.

With Weizmann out of the way, Ben-Gurion, as the sole leader of Mapai, remained alone at the Zionist summit. As both captain and helmsman of the struggle, he was publicly recognized as indispensable. At this point, it seems, one Ben-Gurion ended and another was born — at the age of sixty-one — a Zionist leader, with neither partner nor rival to match him, who fearlessly and single-handedly led the struggle against the British until he could declare the State of Israel established and become its first prime minister and minister of defense. His first act was to open the gates of Palestine to the survivors of Europe and the exiled Jews of East and West. This was possible only after the long and bloody War of Independence, the costliest in human life that Israel has ever fought.

With its army still underground, not yet sworn to the flag, without air force, armor, or artillery — its major weapons the homemade Stengun and the 2.5-inch mortar — the 600,000-strong Yishuv stood its ground against the invading regular armies of Egypt, Jordan, Syria, and Iraq. The Israeli army grew in numbers and strength thanks largely to foreign Jewish volunteers — Americans prominent among them — seeking service especially in Israel's nascent air force and navy. Becoming organized and equipped and repulsing the Arab armies all at once, the army under Ben-Gurion's leadership was said to have given the Jewish people its state. At the war's end, in March 1949, Israel's troops stood on the shores of the Red Sea in the south and at the foot of the Golan Heights in the north.

Much was made of the army's heroism and of Ben-Gurion as its courageous, visionary leader. However true that is, it must be remembered that the state was truly won by the Jews who had powered the strength of adversity with their death in the crematoriums and gas chambers, giving rise to the determination, embodied in Ben-Gurion, to guarantee that never again would the ground burn beneath the Jews and never would there be another Holocaust.

NOTES
GLOSSARY
INDEX

Notes

All sources cited without reference to origin or location can be found, according to date, in the Ben-Gurion Archives at Sde Boker Campus. Additional source notes, in greater detail, appear in the three volumes of *Kin'at David*, in Hebrew.

Abbreviations in the Notes

NAMES

ABG	Amos Ben-Gurion
BK	Berl Katznelson
DBG	David Ben-Gurion
GBE	Geula (Ben-Gurion) Ben-Eliezer
RLBG	Dr. Renana Leshem–Ben-Gurion
YBZ	Itzhak Ben-Zvi
YT	Itzhak Tabenkin

INSTITUTIONS

AJC	American Jewish Congress
HEC	Histadrut Executive Committee
JAE	Jewish Agency Executive
JCA	Jewish Colonisation Association
JNF	Jewish National Fund
JTA	Jewish Telegraphic Agency
PALCOR	Palestine Correspondence, JAE's news service
WZO	World Zionist Organization
ZE	Zionist Executive

ARCHIVES

AAS	A. H. Silver Archives, Cleveland, Ohio
AJA	American Jewish Archives, Cincinnati, Ohio
AJANY	Zionist Archives and Library, New York, New York
BB	Israel Labour Party Archives, Kefar Saba, Beit Berl, Israel
CAB	Cabinet files, in the Public Record Office, Kew, England

CAHJP   Central Archives for the History of the Jewish People, Hebrew University, Jerusalem, Israel
CO   Colonial Office files, in the Public Record Office, Kew, England
CZA   Central Zionist Archives, Jerusalem, Israel
FO   Foreign Office files, in the Public Record Office, Kew, England
HECF   Histadrut Executive Committee Files, Record Group IV/208 in *L*
IDF   Military (IDF) and Defence Establishment Archives, Givatayim, Israel
ISA   Israel State Archives, Jerusalem, Israel
L   Archives and Museum of the Israel Labour Movement, Tel Aviv, Israel
LFA   Law Faculty Archives, Istanbul, Turkey
LPA   Labour Party Archives, Transport House, London, England
MBG   Ben-Gurion Archives, Sde Boker Campus, Israel
PICA   Files of the Jewish Colonisation Association, 1904–1912, by generous permission of Dorothy Rothschild, London, England
PRO   Public Record Office, Kew, England
USPZ   American Poale Zion Archives, in *L* and in *YIVO* (microfilm)
WA   Weizmann Archives, Rehovot, Israel
WO   War Office files, in the Public Record Office, Kew, England
YBZ   Yad Itzhak Ben-Zvi Historical Archives, Jerusalem, Israel
YIVO   Institute for Jewish Research, New York, New York

PRIVATE COLLECTIONS

CM   DBG's letters to Miriam Cohen, donated to *MBG* in 1987
DRH   Letters of Dov and Rivka Hoz, by permission of Tamar Gidron, Ramat Hasharon
LGR   Letters of Gusta (Strumpf) Rechev, by permission of Mrs. Rechev, Tel Aviv
LPBG   Letters of Paula Ben-Gurion (in English), Ben-Gurion estate, in *IDF*
MAY   Letters of Doris May in Arthur Lourie's papers
RK   Letters of Rega Klapholz to DBG, by permission of Dr. Rega Klapholz-Diamant, Haifa

PROTOCOLS (unpublished)

HISE   Protocols of the Histadrut Executive Committee, in the Archives of the Executive Committee of the Histadrut, Tel Aviv
HNB   Protocols of Hadassah National Board, Hadassah Archives, New York
JAG   Protocols of the Jewish Agency directorate, in *CZA*
MAP   Protocols of Mapai, in *BB*
MHEC   Protocols of the Histadrut Executive Secretariat, in the Archives of the Executive Committee of the Histadrut, Tel Aviv
PDAH   Protocols and documents of Achdut ha-Avodah, Record Group IV/404 in *L*
PHCC   Protocols of the Histadrut councils and conventions, collected in *L* and in the Histadrut Archives, Tel Aviv
ZAC   Protocols of the Zionist Actions Committee, in *CZA*
ZACS   Protocols of the Small Zionist Actions Committee, in *CZA*

PROTOCOLS (published)

SC   The Second Histadrut Convention (February 7–20, 1923), edited by Mordechai Sever, Tel Aviv, 1968
TC   The Third Histadrut Convention (July 5–21, 1927), *Davar*, Tel Aviv, bound by the *HEC*, in *L*

DIARIES (unpublished)

BKN   Berl Katznelson's Notebooks, in *BB*
YBG   David Ben-Gurion's Diaries, in *IDF*

DBG'S MEMOIRS, SPEECHES, AND ARTICLES

AE	*Autobiographical Essay, Davar,* January 10, 1961
AS	*Anahnu Ve-Shkhenenu* (We and Our Neighbors), Tel Aviv, 1931
BABG	*Beit Avi* (My Father's Home), Tel Aviv, 1975
BAMA	*Bama'arakha* (In War), 5 volumes, Tel Aviv, 1957
HAI	Biographical interview with DBG, *Ha-Aretz Shelanu,* November 16, 1963
HWH	*Ha-Poel ha-Ivri Ve-Histadruto* (The Jewish Worker and His Histadrut), Tel Aviv, 1964
IG	*Igrot* (Letters), 3 volumes (1904–1933), Tel Aviv, 1971–1974
JG	*Bi'Yehuda Uva-Galil* (In Judea and the Galilee), Ahiever Yearbook no. 2, New York, 1921
LP	*Mikhtavim Le-Paula* (Letters to Paula and the Children), Tel Aviv, 1968
MC	*Ksharai Im Itzhak Tabenkin* (My Relations with Tabenkin), *Davar,* July 16, 1971
MLA	*Mi-Ma'amad Le-Am* (From Class to Nation), Tel Aviv, 1933
PMA	*Pegishot Im Manhigim Aravim* (Meeting Arab Leaders), Tel Aviv, 1967
ZBG	*Zikhronot* (Memoirs), 6 volumes, Tel Aviv, 1971–1987

OTHER MEMOIRS, LETTERS, AND COLLECTIONS

Ben-Zvi

JC	*Jewish Chronicle,* London
JLL	Itzhak Ben-Zvi, *Ha-Gdudim Ha-Ivriyim/Igrot* (The Jewish Legion/Letters), Jerusalem, 1968
PZSA	Itzhak Ben-Zvi, *Poale Zion Ba'Aliyah Ha-Shnia* (Poale Zion in the Second Aliyah), Tel Aviv, 1950
WYBZ	Itzhak Ben-Zvi, *Kitvei Itzhak Ben-Zvi* (Writings), Tel Aviv, 1937

Katznelson

LBK	Yehuda Sharett et al., eds. *Igrot Berl Katznelson* (The Letters of Berl Katznelson), 6 volumes, Tel Aviv, 1974–1984
WBK	Shmuel Yavnieli, ed., *Kitvei Berl Katznelson* (Collected Works), 12 volumes, Tel Aviv, 1946–1950

Others

AO	Rachel Yanait, *Anu Olim* (Memoirs), Tel Aviv, 1969
BAFFY	Norman Rose, ed., *The Diaries of Blanche Dugdale,* London, 1973
DMS	Ahuvia Malkin, ed., *Moshe Sharett, Yoman Medini* (Moshe Sharett's Political Diaries), 5 volumes, Tel Aviv, 1969–1979
DV	Arieh Fialkoff, ed., *Itzhak Tabenkin, Dvarim* (Itzhak Tabenkin Collected Speeches), 7 volumes, Tel Aviv, 1967–1981
SL	Joseph Shapira, ed., *Igrot Yosef Sprinzak* (Joseph Sprinzak's Letters), 3 volumes, Tel Aviv, 1965
WJ	Eri Jabotinsky, ed., *Ktavim* (Works of Vladimir Jabotinsky), 6 volumes, Tel Aviv, 1953
WL	*The Letters and Papers of Chaim Weizmann:* Series A: Letters in 23 volumes, 1968–1980; Series B: Papers in 2 volumes, 1983–1984. Jerusalem, Israel Universities Press

SECONDARY WORKS

BGPA	Shabtai Teveth, *Ben-Gurion and the Palestinian Arabs,* New York, 1985
BGU	Bracha Habas, *David Ben-Gurion Vedoro* (Ben-Gurion and His Generation), Tel Aviv, 1952
BH	Ben-Zion Dinur et al., eds., *Sefer Toldot ha-Haganah* (History of the Haganah), 8 volumes, Tel Aviv, 1964–1972

CHR   Yemima Rosenthal, ed., *Chronologia Le-Toldot ha-Yishuv ha-Yehudi Be-Eretz-Israel* (Chronology of the Yishuv), Jerusalem, 1979

KD   Shabtai Teveth, *Kin'at David* (David's Jealousy: Biography of DBG), 3 volumes, Tel Aviv, 1977, 1980, 1987

PE   Mordechai Halamish, ed., *Sefer Płońsk Ve-Ha-Seviva* (Płońsk and Its Environs), Tel Aviv, 1963

SB   C. Ben-Yerucham, ed., *Sefer Bethar* (Bethar's History), 3 volumes, Tel Aviv, 1969

SH   Itzhak Ben-Zvi et al., eds., *Sefer Hashomer* (Hashomer Memorial Book), Tel Aviv, 1957

STRA   Shabtai Teveth, *Rezakh Arlosoroff* (The Killing of Arlosoroff), Tel Aviv, 1982

Chapter 1: Płońsk

1. Personal interview with Benjamin Ben-Gurion, Dec. 27, 1973; *BABG*, pp. 15, 16; DBG to Rachel Beit-Halachmi, Apr. 1, 1962; *ZBG*, vol. I, p. 8; Avigdor Gruen, unpublished memoirs, *IDF*.

2. DBG cited his mother's name as Broitman in his autobiographical entry for the *Encyclopedia Judaica; BGU*, pp. 32, 33; *PE*, pp. 32, 33; *BABG*, pp. 7–9, 12–14; *YBG*, Aug. 23, 1922; *AE*.

3. *ZBG*, vol. I, pp. 3–4, 7, 10; *HAI; PE*, p. 32.

4. *PE*, p. 24; Shlomo Lavi, *Aliyato shel Shalom Layish* (Haifa: Yalkut Library) pp. 15, 33; *ZBG*, vol. I, p. 8; personal interview with Benjamin Ben-Gurion.

5. *BABG*, pp. 19, 24, 30; personal interview with Itzhak Kvashna and Shlomo Yona (Taub); *IG*, letters 40, 164; *ZBG*, vol. I, pp. 5, 7, 19; *Hamelitz* Apr. 30, 1898, Jan. 12, Apr. 14, 1899.

6. *PE*, p. 34; *IG*, letters 1, 3, 4, 209; *AE*.

7. *ZBG*, vol. I, pp. 7, 10; *BABG*, p. 31; *Encyclopedia Hinukhit* (Jerusalem: The Education Office in cooperation with the Bialik Institute, 1964), vol. IV, pp. 581, 586, 587; as told by Yehezkel Rozenberg and confirmed by Mordechai Michelson; DBG to Itzhak Kvashna, Feb. 25, 1965; *PE*, pp. 27, 141, 258; *IG*, letter 2.

8. Shlomo Zemach, *Shanah Rishonah* (Tel Aviv: Am Oved, 1965), pp. 142–144; for Zemach claim that DBG had difficulty with Talmudic casuistry, see "Dapey Pinkas," *Jerusalem* (*Pirkei Sifrut Ubikoret* 9–10, Agudat Shalom, 1965); DBG to Moshe Parush, May 23, 1968; *ZBG*, vol. I, pp. 6, 8; *CZA*, file no. 21326; *BABG*, pp. 3, 18; *PE*, p. 60.

9. Lavi, pp. 50–52; *YBG*, May 26, 1915; *PE*, pp. 34, 35; as told by M. Michelson; *BABG*, p. 36; *IG*, letters 1, 3; Zemach, p. 8; G. Kressel in *Ha-Aretz*, Nov. 15, 1974; DBG to Emanuel Ben-Gurion, Aug. 11, 1968; *ZBG*, vol. I, pp. 10–11.

10. Shmuel Fox to DBG, Apr. 8, 1955; Zemach, pp. 40, 45; *IG*, letter 1; *PE*, p. 34.

11. *BGU*, p. 48; *ZBG*, vol. I, p. 11.

Chapter 2: Warsaw

1. *IG*, letters 2, 6, 11, 18.

2. *IG*, letters 1, 2, 4, 5, 6, 11, 18, 20, 32; *BABG*, p. 29.

3. *IG*, letters 11, 12, 13, 14, 15, 18, 22.

4. *IG*, letter 13; DBG letter to Shlomo Zemach, Sept. 16, 1961; *PE*, p. 31; *HAI*; *ZBG*, vol. I, p. 12.

5. *IG*, letters 2, 5, 6, 18.

6. Zvi Even-Shoshan, *Tnuat Hapoalim Be'Eretz-Israel* (Tel Aviv: Am Oved, 1963), p. 92; Moshe Mishkinsky, "National Elements in the Development of the Workers' Movement in Russia," dissertation (Hebrew), Hebrew University, 1965, p. 13; *IG*, letters 16, 17, 18, 20; *AE*.

7. *IG*, letters 19, 20; *ZBG*, vol. I, p. 13; *BGU*, p. 54; *Sefer Ussishkin*, Jerusalem, 1934, p. 105.

8. Ber Borochov, *Leshealat Zion Veteritoriah* (Ha-Kibbutz Ha-Meuchad, 1955), vol. I, p. 21 ff.; *ZBG*, vol. I, pp. 13, 14; *MC*.

9. YT, *Mi-Bifnim*, vol. 34, June 1972; *BGU*, p. 54.

10. Personal interviews with Miriam Yafeh, Abraham and Yechiel Rozenberg, M. Michelson, DBG; *SF*; reports describing violent action and robberies for party, *Wilner Volkszeitung*, June 7, 8, July 22, 1906; *HAI*.

11. As recalled by Moshe Nachmanovitz in letter to DBG, Oct. 1, 1961; *ZBG*, vol. I, p. 13; *BGU*, p. 39; *Wilner Volkszeitung*, Sept. 10, 1906; *PE*, p. 197.

12. *PE*, pp. 197, 276; *BGU*, p. 54; confirmed by Tzeira Beit-Halachmi.

13. *ZBG*, vol. I, pp. 13, 14; *IG*, letter 11.

14. *IG*, letter 11; Yehezkel Beit-Halachmi in family publication in his memory; *Yiddisher Kemfer*, May 5, Aug. 21, 1906; *ZBG*, vol. I, p. 20; *HAI*.

15. *IG*, letters 24, 25, 31; Rachel Beit-Halachmi to DBG, April 10, 1962.

16. *ZBG*, vol. I, p. 17; *BABG*, pp. 60, 61; *IG*, letters 25, 28; personal interview with Shlomo Yona (Taub).

17. Personal interview with R. Beit-Halachmi; *IG*, letters 27, 28.

Chapter 3: Jaffa

1. DBG to Israel Shochat, Jan. 15, 1956; DBG to Shlomo Zemach, Sept. 16, 1961; A. Eitan, *Asufoth*, Sept.–Oct. 1947; *JG*; *IG*, letters 30, 31, 38, 39; *BGU*, p. 63.

2. Alex Bein, *Toldot Hahityashvut Hatzionit*, Jerusalem, 1943; Joseph Gorni, "Changes in the Social and Political Structure of the Second Aliyah" in *Ha-Tzionut*, vol. I, 1970; *KD*, vol. I, p. 536 (28).

3. *ZBG*, vol. I, p. 23; *IG*, letters 29, 30, 31; *AO*, p. 4; S. Zemach, *Shanah Rishonah* (Tel Aviv: Am Oved, 1965), p. 141.

4. *IG*, letters 34, 36, 37, 40; *JG*.

5. *PE*, p. 366; in memoirs of Yehezkel and Rachel Beit-Halachmi.

6. Ze'ev Ashur, *Asufoth*, Apr. 4, 1954; K. Y. Silman, "Min Hayamim Hahem" (Hebrew), *Ha-Aretz*, May 26, 1935; *PZSA*, p. 29; *SH*, p. 11.

7. DBG to U.S. Poale Zion, Dec. 25, 1906, *Yiddisher Kemfer*, Jan. 18, 1907 (report on Succoth conference); Eitan, *Asufoth*, Sept.–Oct. 1947; *ZBG*, vol. I, p. 23; *SH*, p. 12.

8. *IG*, letter 31; *PZSA*, p. 22; *ZBG*, vol. I, p. 25; Borochov, vol. I, p. 193.

9. DBG to U.S. Poale Zion, Dec. 25, 1906, *YIVO*; *IG*, letters 34, 36, 37, 40; *JG*.

10. Shochat described dual central committee to Itzhak Ben-Zvi (*PDAH*, file no. 44) and in *SH*, p. 12; *IG*, letter 38.

11. *Ha-Poel ha-Tzair* 12, July/Aug. 1907
12. *IG*, letter 38; Z. Gluskin, Memoirs, pp. 106–107; *Hashkafah*, no. 32, 1907; *Der Yiddisher Arbeiter*, no. 25, 1907; *Asufoth*, no. 3, 1952; *BGU*; Shochat, *SH*, p. 12; *L* IV 104, YBZ file no. 45; Avi Efraim in *Ha-Poel ha-Tzair*, 2, 1907; *Pirkei Ha-Poel Ha-Tzair* (N. Twersky, 1935–1938), vol. II, p. 139.
13. *WYBZ*, vol. I, p. 43; *IG*, letter 42; *PZSA*, pp. 35–36.
14. *SC; ZBG*, vol. I, p. 33; *Hashkafah*, no. 87, 1907; DBG to Ever-Hadani, June 6, 1966, in *Toldot Agudat Hakormim*, p. 147; Abraham Krinitzi, *Bemahaneh Nahal*, Succoth, 1961.
15. *IG*, letter 44.
16. *PZSA*, pp. 49, 55; *KD*, vol. I, p. 583; *SH*, pp. 13–16; *Kovetz Hashomer* (Tel Aviv: Achdut ha-Avodah, 1938), pp. 5, 14, 16, 61.

Chapter 4: Sejera

1. On Manya see *CAHJP*, P/3/622; Shlomo Shva, *Shevet Ha-Noazim* (Merhaviah: Sifriyat Ha-Poalim, 1969); Rachel Yanait–Ben-Zvi, *Manya Shochat* (Jerusalem: Yad Ben-Zvi, 1976).
2. Manya Vilbushevitz to Judah-Leib Magnes, Sept. 9, Oct. 14, 1907, in *CAHJP*, P/3 SP/44; *SH*, p. 388; Ben-Zion Michaeli, *Sejera* (Tel Aviv: Am Oved, 1973); *ZBG*, vol. I, pp. 32, 34.
3. Shlomo Zemach, "Kibush Avodah," *Luach Ha-Aretz*, 1950–51, p. 200.
4. *IG*, letter 47; *SH*, pp. 136, 138, 388; Saadia Paz, *Memoirs* (Hebrew) (Haifa, 1962), p. 32 ff; personal interview with DBG, Nov. 29, 1968, in *L*; Shva, p. 119; Michaeli, pp. 77–78, 111; personal interview with Michaeli.
5. *IG*, letters 40, 46, 47, 50; Michaeli, p. 147.
6. *IG*, letter 49; Ever-Hadani, *Hamishim Shnot Hityashvut Bagalil*, p. 701; *JG; PICA*.
7. Kalman Marmor diary, Kalman Marmor Archive, New York; *IG*, letter 49; *BGU*, p. 141.
8. *IG*, letters 50, 51, 53; *MC*; Ever-Hadani, p. 223; *BGU*, p. 129
9. Personal interview with Yanait, Jan. 9, 1974; *AE; IG*, letter 53.
10. *IG*, letters 53, 54, 57, 59.
11. *BGU*, pp. 136–137; personal interview with Leah Cohen, widow of DBG's first Arabic teacher; *PICA*, Rozenhak to Krause, May 17, 1907; files, 9th Congress, *CZA* Z2/121; *IG*, letter 59; *ZBG*, vol. I, pp. 47–48; Ever-Hadani, p. 225.

Chapter 5: Jerusalem/Istanbul

1. *IG*, letters 60, 62; *ZBG*, vol. I, pp. 48–50; *BGU*, p. 140; personal interview with Rachel Beit-Halachmi.
2. *BGU*, pp. 139, 149; "Megamatenu," *Ha-Achdut* 1, July/August 1910, 39–40, 1911; *ZBG*, vol. I, p. 50; *AO*, pp. 198, 203, 241; *PZSA*, p. 130; Rachel Yanait to author, May 23, 1975; Gershom Schocken examined DBG's translation and compared it to Sombart's original text; R. Beit-Halachmi estate and personal interview with Hemda Polani-Avrech.
3. Succoth Conference report, *Ha-Achdut* 2/3, 4, 1910; I. Kolatt, "Ideolo-

gia Umetziut Bitenuat Ha'avoda Be'eretz Israel, 1905–1919," dissertation, Hebrew University, 1964.

4. *SH*, p. 35; *Ha-Achdut* 25/26, 27, 1911; Jacob Zerubavel letter, May 9, 1911; *PZSA*, p. 142; DBG to Zerubavel, June 13, 1911, *ISA* 105/2453; DBG to Shlomo Zemach, Sept. 16, 1961; personal interview with Polani-Avrech; *IG*, letters 46, 62, 63, 66; *L* IV 403 47; Zippora Gruen to R. Beit-Halachmi, June 18, 1911. Photographs are in Ben-Gurion House in Tel Aviv.

5. *IG*, letters 72, 73, 74, 78, 79, 81, 82, 83, 87, 89; *Saloniki — Ir Va-em Be'Israel* (Jerusalem and Tel Aviv, 1967), p. 250; *ZBG*, vol. I, p. 52; DBG to YBZ and Yanait, Jan. 21, 1912, in *CZA* A116/100; *Ha-Achdut* 11/12, Jan. 2, 1912; personal interview with Joseph Strumsa, Jan. 31, 1974.

6. *IG*, letters 82–87, 92, 93, 99, 105, 108, 110, 115, 116, 118, 122, 131, 133, 134, 135, 140; *CZA* L2/2 III; letter from dean of Istanbul University Law Faculty to Tuvia Arazi, May 15, 1952 (in DBG estate in *IDF*).

7. *BGU*, p. 208; personal interviews with Yanait, Strumsa, and R. Beit-Halachmi; *IG*, letters 28, 40, 89, 105, 109, 110, 119, 123, 128, 133, 138, 139, 140, 151–153, 155–158, 160, 162–164, 167–169, 171, 174, 176–185, on DBG and YBZ return to Palestine, see letters 185–188; DBG to R. Beit-Halachmi, Oct. 5, 1913, in R. Beit-Halachmi estate; Yanait repeatedly cautioned the author "not to forget that Ben-Gurion was supported by his father"; *Hazefirah* 69, 70, 72, 75, 77, 79, 81, particularly 84, Apr. 27, 1913; *ZBG*, vol. I, pp. 19, 66; *L* IV 403, files 16–26; *Ha-Achdut* 2/3, Oct. 1911, 44/45, 1913; *PZSA*, p. 51; *AO*, p. 338.

Chapter 6: Ottoman Patriot

1. *Ha-Achdut* 44/45, Sept. 1914, 3/4, Oct. 1914; *Ha-Cherut*, Dec. 24, 1914; A. Reuveni, *Ad Yerushalaim* (Tel Aviv, 1954), pp. 42–45, 76; E. Livneh, *Nili, Toldot Heaza Medinit* (Jerusalem and Tel Aviv: Schocken, 1961), p. 37; Magnes Collection in *CAHJP*, SP/201–204; Meir Dizengoff, *Im Tel Aviv Bagolah* (Tel Aviv, 1936), p. 13; Saadiah Paz, p. 87.

2. *PZSA*, pp. 135, 145; Alexander Chashin to Avner (*YBZ*), Feb. 1, 1912, *CZA* A116/33/1; Reuveni, p. 64 ff.; *Ha-Or* 15, Aug. 7, 1914; *AE*; *ZBG*, vol. I, pp. 66–67.

3. Efraim Cohen to Dr. Nathan, Feb. 18, 1915, *PRO* A III/15 vol. N 67/27; Reuveni, p. 81 ff.; Zerubavel diary, *PRO* 105/393; *Ha-Achdut* 14, Dec. 31, 1914.

4. YBZ and DBG student records in *LFA*; *ZBG*, vol. I, p. 69; Reuveni, pp. 178–179, 182; *L* IV 104, DBG file 2; *PZSA*, pp. 156, 158; *SH*, p. 41; *AO*, p. 358.

5. *ZBG*, vol. I, p. 71; *PMA*, p. 8.

6. *BGU*, pp. 236, 243; Blumenfeld cable to Hersh Ehrenreich, *L* III 24 (73) file 107; Magnes Archive in *CAHJP* P3/F30 L 132; *Die Zeit*, Apr. 23, 1915; *ZBG*, vol. I, pp. 73, 75; Vladimir Jabotinsky, *Autobiography* (Jerusalem: Eri Jabotinsky Publishing, 1957), p. 116 ff.; Yigal Elam, *Hagedudim Haivriim* (Hebrew), published by Ministry of Defence, pp. 11, 15–16; Shulamith Laskov, *Trumpeldor* (Haifa: Shikmona, 1972), p. 92; NYC Immigration Bureau document 76/95 4-C; *YBG*, May 3, 12, 13, 1915.

Chapter 7: New York

1. *YBG*, May 16, 17, 19, 1915; NYC Immigration Bureau document 76/95 4-C; *ZBG*, vol. I, p. 80; Nina Zuckerman to Shlomo Kaplansky, July 12, 1915, *USPZ*; personal interview with N. Zuckerman.
2. *Der Tag*, May 19, 1915; Poale Zion conference bulletin, Sept. 1915, in *USPZ*, file 128; *YBG*, May 29, 1915.
3. *YBG*, May 30, June 1, July 5, 6, 1915; personal interview with P. Cruso; *PZSA*, p. 169; Alexander Chashin to Hersh Ehrenreich, June 28, 1915, *USPZ*, file 119; Central Committee circular no. 18, June 22, 1915, *USPZ*; Shmuel Bonchek to Ehrenreich, June 2, 1915, *L* III 117/24; Third World Conference report, *CZA* Z2/934; Baruch Zuckerman to Shlomo Kaplansky, July 1915 (mistakenly dated Feb. 12, 1915), in *L* IV 104 Kaplansky file 13; *Yiddisher Nazionale Arbeiter Farband 1910–1946* (New York: National Union of the Jewish Worker, 1946), p. 39.
4. *YBG*, July 27, Aug. 2, 7, 1915; DBG to Bonchek, July 26, 1915, *L* IV 122/403; DBG to YBZ, July 28, Aug. 2, 1915, in *CZA* A116/40/1; according to *USPZ*, files 122, 124, 125.
5. Cleveland Conference bulletin, Sept. 1915, *USPZ*, files 119, 121, 122, 126, 128, 134; *PZSA*, p. 162.
6. From Comrade Mulan, July 23, 1915, *USPZ*, file 122; *He-Chalutz* regulation in *Asufoth* 6, Dec. 1959; DBG to YBZ, letters in *CZA* A116/40/1; *YBG*, May 31, June 3, July 3, 1915; memorandum to Louis Brandeis in *CZA* Z3/73; *IG*, letter 194.
7. DBG to Ehrenreich, Feb. 4, 1916, DBG cable to Bonchek from Chicago, Mar. 8, 1916, D. Fogelman to Bonchek, Mar. 6, 1916, in *USPZ*; Golda Meir, *Hayay* (Tel Aviv: Maariv Publishing, 1976), p. 44.

Chapter 8: Yizkor

1. *Yiddisher Kemfer*, May 19, 1916; M. Olgin, *Forward*, June 3, 1916; DBG to YBZ, letters in *CZA* A116/40/1.
2. According to *USPZ*, files 161, 162, 164; DBG to YBZ, letters in *CZA* A116/40/1, A116/40/2.
3. Eretz Israel Committee from Dec. 20, 1916, *USPZ*, file 179; Baruch Zuckerman, *Memoirs*, vol. II, p. 265; *ZBG*, vol. I, p. 85; *Yiddisher Kemfer*, Sept. 27, 1916; *USPZ*, Dec. 14, 1916, file 180; personal interview with Rachel Yanait.
4. Eretz Israel Committee session, May 31, 1917, in *USPZ*; *Yiddisher Kemfer*, Nov. 30, 1917; *PRO* WO 32/11353.
5. *YBG*, Nov. 23, 1917; *IG*, letter 196; *Yiddisher Kemfer*, Nov. 30, 1917; *Ha-Toren*, Dec. 17, 1917 (DBG handwritten draft in *IDF* 2443); *Die Neue Welt*, Feb. 18, 1918; Report of Action Committee, *IDF* 2450.
6. *IG*, letter 196; YBZ letter of resignation from Action Committee was published in *Yiddisher Kemfer*, May 3, 1918. Mistakenly dated Jan. 15, 1918, it is in *USPZ*.
7. *IG*, letters 245, 267; Bonchek to Ehrenreich, Feb. 14, 1918, *USPZ*; *YBZ*, 1/4/04/27; *BGU*, p. 259.

Chapter 9: Paula

1. Personal interviews with Rachel Beit-Halachmi, Eliezer Marhaim, and Nina Zuckerman; *BGU*, p. 242; *ZBG*, vol. I, p. 86; *YBG*, Dec. 5, 1917; Paula to DBG, June 5, 12, Dec. 29, 1918; *IG*, letters 205, 250.
2. Personal interviews with GBE, Pessia Munweis-Carmeli, Nina Zuckerman, Will Maslow, and Pinchas Cruso; Mira Avrech, *Paula* (Tel Aviv: Am Oved, 1965), pp. 13–14; *ZBG*, vol. I, p. 56.
3. *ZBG*, vol. I, pp. 86, 151; *IG*, letter 245; *BGU*, p. 242; personal interviews with GBE and Will Maslow; Avrech, pp. 13, 28; United States foreign resident registration no. 6074679.
4. *IG*, letter 268; War Office cable to General Wilfred White, New York, Feb. 21, 1918, *PRO* WO 32/11353; Bonchek to Ehrenreich, Mar. 3, 1918; Zvi Rozen to Ehrenreich, May 25, 1918, *USPZ*.
5. *ZBG*, vol. I, pp. 86, 104; *IG*, letters 201, 204, 207, 224, 232, 244, 250.
6. *Yiddisher Kemfer*, May 10, 1918; *Die Wahrheit*, May 28, 1918; *Der Tag*, May 30, 31, 1918.
7. Yigal Elam, *Hagedudim Haivriim*, p. 190; *PZSA*, p. 192; *Sefer ha-Aliyah Hashlishit* (Tel Aviv: Am Oved, 1964), p. 92; Paula to DBG, June 12, 15, July 16, 17, 1918; *IG*, letters 207, 228, 229, 241.
8. *IG*, letters 208, 209.

Chapter 10: Achdut ha-Avodah

1. *IG*, letter 205.
2. *YBG*, June 3, 4, 1918; *IG*, letter 207.
3. Personal interview with Lord Edwin Samuel.
4. *IG*, letter 207.
5. *IG*, letters 210, 213, 218, 228, 230; *YBG*, July 11, 1918.
6. *YBG*, Aug. 12, 1918; personal interview with Phillip Bloom, vice president, Jewish Battalion Veterans.
7. DBG at secretariat of United Kibbutz Movement, Jan. 8, 1967.
8. *YBG*, Aug. 28, 1918; *JLL*, letter 11.
9. "Toward the Future," *WBK*, vol. I, p. 66; *YBG*, Sept. 6–9, Oct. 5, 6, 10, 1918.
10. *YBG*, Sept. 6–11, 1918; *IG*, letters 234, 236; Paula to DBG, Sept. 13, 1918.
11. *YBG*, Sept. 21, 1918; *PRO* WO/95/4459.
12. *ZBG*, vol. I, p. 110; *Ha-Achdut*, no. 44/45, 1911; *"Die Kemfer Stimme,"* Sept. 1915, no. 27 (printed in *MLA*).
13. *Ha-Toren*, no. 5, written June 25, 1915, no. 14, 1916 (printed in *MLA*); *Yiddisher Kemfer*, no. 12, Mar. 1918 (printed in *MLA*); no. 41, Nov. 1917 (printed in *MLA*); *"Die Taglische Welt,"* Apr. 29, 1918.
14. *ZBG*, vol. I, p. 110.
15. *YBG*, Nov. 4, 5, 13, 14, 1918; *JLL*, letter 27.
16. *L IV* 403/23 A.
17. *YBG*, Nov. 13, 1918; *IG*, letter 242; *LBK*, vol. III, letter 281; *ZBG*, vol. I, p. 110.
18. *ZBG*, vol. I, p. 110; BK 1921 lectures, in *BB; LBK*, vol. III, pp. 81, 99; *WBK*, vol. XI, p. 198.

19. "On B. Katznelson," "Yagon Yahid" in a letter to Mapai sixth convention.
20. *JLL*, letter 31.
21. *YBG*, Dec. 4, 5, 7, 8, 10, 12, 15, 1918; *JLL*, letter 35.
22. *IG*, letter 243; personal interview with Dov Joseph; letter from A. Blumen-feld (alias of D. Bloch) to David Eder, Dec. 31, 1918, *CZA* L4/127.
23. *ZBG*, vol. I, p. 112.
24. Convention Protocol, *L* IV/403, files 28, 28A; *ZBG*, vol. I, p. 112.
25. *LBK*, vol. III, letters 28A, 298; *Ha-Poel ha-Tzair*, 3–4, Feb. 21, 1919; DBG to Shmuel Shaharia, Jan. 14, 1968.
26. Founding Convention Protocol, *L* IV/404, file no. 20A; *HWH*, p. 552; *IG*, letter 248; *Achdut ha-Avodah* (anthology), p. 14.

Chapter 11: The Elected Assembly

1. Achdut ha-Avodah resolutions, *L*.
2. Achdut ha-Avodah executive committee protocols, *L* IV/404, file no. 1A.
3. *IG*, letter 209; Paula to DBG, Apr. 11, June 15, 18, 26, July 21, Oct. 30, 1918.
4. *IG*, letters 250, 251, 257.
5. *IG*, letters 241, 257.
6. *IG*, letters 246, 258; correspondence with Cairo and Jerusalem commands, *CZA* L3/46 IV; Zionist Commission's letter to M. Lida in Migdal, Nov. 16, 1919, *CZA* L3/46 IV.
7. Paula to DBG, Dec. 27, 1918, Apr. 7, 11, 12, 15, May 10, June 13, 1919; *ZBG*, vol. I, p. 153; *IG*, letters 249, 251, 252.
8. *IDF* 4007, documents signed by British consul.
9. *ZBG*, vol. I, p. 153; *IG*, letter 257; *IDF* 2456, letter from Zionist Organization of America to H. Fineman, June 18, 1919.
10. *ZBG*, vol. I, p. 153; Jeremiah 2:2.
11. War diaries of Jewish battalions, *WO* 95; Provisional Council session (third assembly), Mar. 18, 1919, *CZA* Y1/8773; Zionist Commission bulletin, Feb. 1919, *CZA* A46/25; Achdut ha-Avodah executive committee meeting with battalion representatives, Aug. 13, 1919, *L* IV 130/36.
12. DBG to YBZ, Aug. 9, 1919, *CZA* A116/110, Oct. 5, 1919, *YBZ* 1/5/5/18; representative was Nellie Strauss. Balfouria resulted from program; *PDAH*, Aug. 13, 1919, *L*, IV 130/36; Protocol, Zionist Commission meeting with Jewish Battalion representatives, Aug. 3, 1919, *L* IV 130/36; Chaim Weizmann, *Trial and Error* (London: Hamish Hamilton, 1949), p. 284; *IG*, letter 259.
13. Trial was held Aug. 13–14, 1919. See War Diaries, note 39, *PRO* WO 95; David Eder to Provisional Council, *L* IV 130/15; *IG*, letter 262; Protocol, Provisional Council, seventh assembly, p. 40 ff., *CZA* J1/8781 I; DBG to Eder, Sept. 12, 30, 1919, *IDF* 1933; Eder to DBG, Sept. 17, 1919, *IDF*, 1933; Bezalel Yafeh to DBG, Sept. 15, 1919, *IDF*, 1933.
14. Berl Katznelson, *Kunteres* 9, July 25, 1919; DBG to YBZ, July 22, 1919, *CZA* A116/110.
15. *Kunteres* 14, Oct. 7, 1919; *Correspondence Ouvrier Juive*, Jan. 1920.
16. *MAP* Founding Convention Resolutions, p. 127; Protocol, Eretz Israel Council, Dec. 18–22, 1919, *CZA* J1/8766; election regulations accepted by

second founding meeting; Achdut ha-Avodah executive committee circular to branch committees, June 29, 1919, *IDF* 3372; Protocol, Provisional Council, seventh assembly, *CZA* J1/8781,1; *Kunteres* 15, Oct. 24, 1919; Geula Bat-Yehuda, biography of Rabbi (Fishman) Maimon in manuscript; Rabbi (Fishman) Maimon, "Teshuvah la-Rabim," *Hadshot ha-Aretz*, Apr. 26, 1920.

17. E. Almaliah, "Tragicomedy," *Doar ha-Yom*, Apr. 26, 1920; *Hadshot ha-Aretz*, Apr. 28, 1920; Ada Maimon, *50 Shnot Tenuat Hapoalot* (Tel Aviv: Am Oved, 1958), p. 207 ff.; *PDAH*, Apr. 20, 1920; *Doar ha-Yom*, Apr. 28, May 3, 6, 1920; lecture dates printed in *Kunteres*, May 8, 27, June 12, July 1, Oct. 24, 1919, Apr. 23, May 7, 1920; municipal committee elections, *Kunteres*, May 28, 1919; DBG to Jerusalem branch secretary, Mar. 30, 1920, *IDF* 3372 *CZA* I1/59; see list of votes received by Achdut ha-Avodah candidates, *PDAH* 78.

18. *BH*, vol. I, part 2, pp. 600, 950; *ZBG*, vol. I, p. 128; Chaim Weizmann diary, 1920, *WA; IG*, letter 271; correspondence and telegrams on situation in Galilee, Mar. 7–18, 1920, *IDF* 4019; *PDAH*, Apr. 20, May 21, 25, 1920; *YBG*, Apr.–June 1920; DBG cable to Foreign Office, Apr. 9, 1920, *CZA* L4/160 84.

19. YT to DBG, undated, 1920, *L* IV 104, DBG 6A.

Chapter 12: London and Vienna

1. *IG*, letters 270, 271.
2. As Chaim Weizmann said at opening of Zionist Congress on July 7, 1920, *CZA* Z4/241/17; Weizmann diary, 1920, *WA*.
3. Protocol, Provisional Council, eighth meeting, *CZA* J1/8783 II; *ZBG*, vol. I, p. 154; *WBK*, vol. I, p. 241.
4. *JC*, June 3, 1920; *L* IV 404 file 1 A.
5. *Die Zeit*, July 7, 1920.
6. Morning session, July 7, 1920, *CZA* Z4/241/17; *JC*, July 16, 1920; *Die Zeit*, July 11, 1920; *ZBG*, vol. I, p. 166; "The London Convention," *WBK*, vol. I, p. 227.
7. *LBK*, vol. IV, letter 58; Berl Katznelson, *Kunteres* 51, Sept. 2, 1920.
8. *Kunteres* 50, Aug. 27, 1920; *ZBG*, vol. I, p. 287; *Die Zeit*, Aug. 18, 1920; Poale Zion delegation deliberations, p. 37, *L;* "Die Finfte Welt Conference Bericht un Resolutzyehs," Ferlag Funim Farbandt Bureau, Vienna, 1920, p. 14, *L* III; *IG*, letter 271.
9. *Kunteres* 53; *Avangard* (Poale Zion Smol organ), no. 4, Nov. 15, 1921; circular no. 1, World Union, Sept. 1, 1920, *BB* P/8; *IG*, letter 271.
10. *IG*, letters 271, 275; according to DBG alien order certificate of registration no. 59271.
11. Reb Avigdor postcard to DBG, Sept. 5, 1920, *IDF* 4008; *IG*, letters 270, 271, 272, 274, 275, 279.

Chapter 13: The Either-Or Approach

1. Personal interview with J. Leftwich, London, the part-time employee.
2. *IG*, letter 273; Weizmann diary, 1920, *WA;* Leftwich interview.
3. Letters from Nov. 15, 26, 1920, *CZA* Z4/2017; more precisely, 778,487 she-

kels. See *CZA*, Report of the 12th Zionist Congress, London, 1922, pp. 9, 51.

4. DBG to YBZ, Dec. 11, 1920, *PDAH*, 1-A; *IG*, letter 282; E. Blumenfeld (D. Bloch) to DBG, Apr. 13, 1921, *IDF* 2456.

5. *LPA*, Mar. 1920.

6. *LPA*, LP/1AC/3I.

7. *LPA*, LP/1AC/2/108/7, 119, 120, 169; *ZBG*, vol. I, pp. 163–165; J. Pomerantz, *Die Zeit*, May 17, 1950.

8. Reader ticket no. B 16724, valid to 15 July 1921, *IDF* 4007; *IG*, letters 275, 289; Leftwich interview; DBG to YBZ and Yanait, Jan. 21, 1921, *IDF* 1427; DBG letter in circular no. 5 of Achdut ha-Avodah executive committee, Feb. 15, 1921, *PDAH* 26.

9. DBG to Rubashov (Shazar) (in Vienna), Feb. 7, 1921, *IDF* 2456; DBG handwritten list of expenses, *IDF* 2848; bills of transport and insurance from Mar. 12, 1921, *IDF* 4006.

10. *IG*, letters 289, 293; DBG to Rivka, Mar. 28, 1921, *IDF* 4008.

11. DBG to Rivka, Mar. 28, 1921; *IG*, letters 292, 293; DBG cables to Berl Locker, May 1, 3, 1921, *BB* P/8.

12. *IG*, letters 292, 297; *LPBG*, May 27, June 7, 1921.

13. Reb Avigdor to DBG, Sept. 5, 1921, *IDF* 4008; *IG*, letters 296, 302, 307, 320; personal interview with Benjamin Ben-Gurion; *LPBG*, Aug. 23, 1921.

14. Item in *Kunteres* 89; *IG*, letter 285.

15. *PDAH*, Aug. 2, 1921; DBG, *Kunteres* 4; DBG, *Kunteres* 92, Sept. 9, 1921; *IG*, letters 19, 299; Rules and Regulations of Labor Legion.

16. DBG, *Kunteres* 92, Sept. 9, 1921; *IG*, letter 301; Achdut ha-Avodah Council, Jaffa, Oct. 1, 1921, *PDAH; Kunteres* 96.

17. *IG*, letter 299.

18. *PDAH*, Nov. 18, 1922; Achdut ha-Avodah Council, Jaffa, Oct. 1, 1921, *PDAH; Kunteres* 96.

19. *LPBG*, from Płońsk, undated, *IDF* 4002.

Chapter 14: Reb Avigdor Immigrates to Palestine

1. *Kunteres* 106, Jan. 27, 1922.

2. DBG lecture in Haifa, summer 1922, *IDF* 1461.

3. *Kunteres* 102, *Pinkas* A, Jan. 1, 1922, both reported on Nov. 8, 1921, Histadrut council; *YBG*, Jan. 22, 1922.

4. *YBG*, Jan. 22, Feb. 2, 7, 1922; according to *YBG*, 1922–1925.

5. *YBG*, Feb. 28, Mar. 31, Apr. 4–7, May 6–8, 1922. Paula to DBG from Płońsk, undated, *IDF* 4002; personal interview with Pessia Munweis-Carmeli.

6. *YBG*, Mar. 9, Apr. 14, 18, 1922; *IG*, letter 307; personal interviews with Benjamin Ben-Gurion, Pessia Munweis-Carmeli, GBE, David Zakay; DBG account at executive committee fund from May 15, 1923, to July 11, 1924, *IDF* 2453.

7. Reb Avigdor to his children, Jan. 20, 1920, *IDF* 4006; *IG*, letters 274, 302, 317, 318, 320.

8. *IG*, letters 320, 322; Zippora to DBG, Sept. 27, 1922, *IDF* 4008; *YBG*, Aug., Sept., Oct. 9, 1922; Vienna Palestine office to DBG, Dec. 7, 1922, *IDF* 3453; personal interview with Emanuel Ben-Gurion.

9. *IG*, letter 375; *YBG*, Apr. 5, 1926.
10. *YBG*, July 12–13, 1925; *IG*, letter 307; personal interviews with Benjamin Ben-Gurion, Pessia Munweis-Carmeli and family; Zippora to Paula, undated and Oct. 13, 1923, *IDF* 4008; Sonia Munweis from Minsk, Jan. 3, 1924, *IDF* 4008.

Chapter 15: The Quest for Predominance

1. Histadrut council, Nov. 8, 1921; *Kunteres* 102; *Pinkas* 1.
2. *HECF* 7B.
3. Census results, *HECF* 9B; *Pinkas* 7, Dec. 1922; *ZBG*, vol. I, p. 210; *HISE*, Feb. 12, 1922 (mistakenly dated Feb. 10, 1922); *Kunteres* 111; Ramsay MacDonald to DBG, Mar. 1, 1922, *PDAH* 6A.
4. Letter from Ha-Shahar company, Dec. 4, 1921, *PDAH* 2A; A. Schochat to David Zakay and DBG, Mar. 23, 1923, *PDAH* 11B; Tel Aviv civil court ruling in favor of Haya Lutsky, Apr. 5, 1922, *PDAH* 6A; Shmuel Nativi from Amal, 1922, *PDAH* 2B; DBG to Spiegel and Luddevich, Feb. 16, 1922, *IDF* 2453; Zippora Goldberg letter, Apr. 17, 1923, *HECF* 18A; D. Zakay to Lederer, Aug. 8, 1922, *PDAH* 5A B; *YBG*, 1922: Feb. 3, 23, Mar. 29, 30, May 10, for example; Zakay notebooks, June 20, 1922 (photocopy with author).
5. *HISE*, July 3, 1921, Jan. 2, 1923; *IG*, letters 305, 407; HEC finance committee plan, June 12, 1922, *HECF* 3B; Zakay letter to Agricultural Center, Feb. 21, 1924, *HECF* 29A.
6. Personal interview with Zakay Dec. 19, 1973; Zakay to DBG, Aug. 19, 1922, *IDF* 789.
7. *SL*, vol. I; *YBG*, Mar. 23, 1922; personal interview with Zakay.
8. *IG*, letter 307; P. Schneerson, "Berlin-Moscow," in Schneerson Archives, Beit Ha-Shomer, Kefar Giladi; DBG to HEC, July 12, 1922, *HECF* 4A; *HISE*, Nov. 22, 1921.
9. Circular to labor councils, Apr. 17, 1923, *HECF* 16A; DBG to Jaffa Labor Council, Apr. 17, 1922, *IDF* 2724; HEC, signed by DBG, to Jerusalem Labor Council, Jan. 2, 1923, *L* IV 104/DBG/3; DBG letters, Feb. 16, 19, May 24, 1922, *IDF* 2453; Bank ha-Poalim to DBG, Apr. 3, 4, 1922, *L* IV 104/DBG/3.
10. Achdut ha-Avodah executive committee meeting, Nov. 5, 1921, *PDAH*; Joseph Aharonovitch to HEC secretariat, June 4, 1922, *HECF* 6A; *HISE* Apr. 26, June 5, 1923; DBG, *Kunteres* 201; HEC meeting with Agricultural Center, May 9, 1924, *IDF* 2724; *TC*, p. 26, *MHEC*.
11. DBG, *Pinkas* 7, Dec. 1922; DBG, *Kunteres* 115.
12. *SC*.
13. Histadrut council, Mar. 13, 1921; *YBG*, Jan. 13, 14, 18, 1922; David Horowitz, *Haetmol Sheli* (Tel Aviv and Jerusalem: Schocken Publishing, 1970), p. 151; *Gedud Ha-Avodah al shem Yosef Trumpeldor*, anthology (Tel Aviv: Mitzpeh Publishing, 1932).
14. Israel Shochat, "Shlichut Vederekh," *SH; BH*, vol. I, part 2, p. 123; E. Golomb to David Hacohen and Manya Shochat, Jan. 19, Feb. 13, 1922, respectively; *Hevyon Oz*, vol. I (Tel Aviv: Ayanot Publishing, 1954).
15. Anita Shapira, "Hahalom Veshivro," *Baderech* III, Dec. 1968 (Giva'at-

Havivah: Beit Baruch Lin Publishing); Labor Legion central executive committee to HEC, May 3, 1922, *HECF* 14B; *Pinkas*, Mar. 29, 1923; meeting in Tel Yosef took place Mar. 5 and reply of Legion council was received Mar. 16, 1923; *HISE*, Apr. 11, 16, 1923.

16. Referendum results, *HISE*, June 5, 1923; *HISE* May 15, 29, 1923; Legion to HEC, May 24, 1923, *HECF* 14B; *Pinkas*, Mar. 29, 1923; *Mihayeinu* 40.

17. *Pinkas*, Mar. 29, 1923; *HISE, Apr.* 11, May 15, June 5, 1923; *MHEC*, Apr. 16, 1923; *Mihayeinu* 40, memo to HEC.

18. *MHEC*, June 15, 1923; Ben-Zion Hirshowitz (Harel) notice, *Mihayeinu* 40; *TC*, p. 75; DBG, *Kunteres* 201.

Chapter 16: Messenger from the Land of Wonders

1. *MHEC*, 1923: May 14–June 17; *HISE*, 1923: July 15, Aug. 2; *YBG*, Aug. 4, 1923.

2. Power of attorney given to DBG by HEC, Aug. 2, 1923, *HECF* 12, additional copies in *IDF* 2724; permits of Trade and Industry Department and high commissioner, *CZA* 2450; report to ZE on exhibition from Jan. 4, 1924, *IDF* 2724.

3. *IG*, letters 337, 283; *YBG*, Dec. 17, 1923.

4. *IG*, letter 337; *YBG*, Aug. 4, Dec. 17, 1923; *ZBG*, vol. I, p. 223.

5. *ZBG*, vol. I, pp. 225, 226; memorandum is in *IDF* 2726; *IG*, letter 339; *YBG*, Dec. 16, 1923.

6. *YBG*, Dec. 16, 1923; *IG*, letters 342, 344; *ZBG*, vol. I, pp. 226, 229.

7. *ZBG*, vol. I, pp. 228, 229, 251, 265; *YBG*, Sept. 13, 1923 ff.; *IG*, letter 344; personal interview with Eliezer Galili.

8. *ZBG*, vol. I, pp. 237, 240, 245, 246.

9. DBG report to ZE, Jan. 4, 1924, *IDF* 2450; *ZBG*, vol. I, pp. 245, 246.

10. *YBG*, Sept. 13, 20, 1923; *ZBG*, vol. I, p. 239; *Pravda*, Sept. 4, 1923, same date DBG wrote on newspaper item, *IDF* 3345; report to ZE, *IDF* 2450.

11. *ZBG*, vol. I, p. 244; *IG*, letter 352; DBG to Bank ha-Poalim, Jan. 30, 1924, *HECF* 24 A; *YBG*, Dec. 1, 1923.

12. *ZBG*, vol. I, pp. 248, 249, 252, 253; *IG*, letter 344.

13. *ZBG*, vol. I, pp. 229, 234; personal interview with Galili; report to ZE, *IDF* 2450; *YBG*, Sept. 7, Nov. 23, Dec. 17, 1923; *LP*, p. 72.

14. Report to ZE, *IDF* 2450; personal interview with Galili; *ZBG*, vol. I, p. 269; *IG*, letter 344.

15. *ZBG*, vol. I, pp. 253, 258, 259; *YBG*, Oct. 11, 1923; articles clipped from *Pravda*, *IDF* 3345.

16. Report to ZE, *IDF* 2450; *IG*, letter 283.

17. *HISE*, Oct. 12–13, 1942; *ZBG*, vol. I, pp. 254, 268, 269.

18. Paula to DBG, Sept. 13, 1923, *IDF* 4001; DBG to Paula, Sept. 28, 1923, *IDF* 3133.

19. *YBG*, Dec. 16, 17, 1923; *IG*, letter 6; *ZBG*, vol. I, pp. 254, 268.

20. *YBG*, Dec. 16, 17, 1923; *PHCC*, Histadrut council, Dec. 22–28, 1923.

21. *YBG*, Dec. 17, 20, 1923; *Ha-Aretz*, Dec. 24, 25, 1923.

22. *PHCC*, Histadrut council, Dec. 22–28, 1923; in ZE, Dec. 4, 1923; Histadrut membership meeting, Tel Aviv, Jan. 5, 1924; *YBG*, 1924; *Pinkas* 9, vol. B, Nov. 19, 1923, *Kunteres* 143, 162, 164.

23. *Kunteres* 159; *YBG,* Dec. 16, 1923, Jan. 23, 1924; personal interview with DBG.

Chapter 17: *The Struggle for Authority*

1. *PHCC,* Histadrut council, Dec. 22–28, 1923; *Kunteres* 156, Jan. 11, 1924; *YBG,* Dec. 15, 1923.
2. DBG to Dov Hoz, Aug. 1924, *L* IV/104/Dov Hoz file 7.
3. *YBG,* Dec. 16, 1923; *PHCC,* Jan. 28–30, 1922; *Pinkas* 3–4, Mar.–Apr. 1922; HEC to wage committee, June 6, 1923, *HECF,* 29; *HISE,* Jan. 23, 1928; *Kunteres* 155, see also 129 and 135.
4. HEC to wage committee, June 18, 1923, *HECF* 29; second convention, *Kunteres* 120; *YBG,* Sept. 4, 1928.
5. *PHCC,* Histadrut council, Dec. 22–28, 1923; *MHEC,* Feb. 12, 1924.
6. *MHEC,* Feb. 12, 1924; *HISE,* Mar. 24, 1925; letters and documents in *HECF,* 27B, 16B, 208, 276.
7. *YBG,* Apr. 29, 1924; *HISE,* June 11, 1924.
8. *YBG,* May 26, June 2, 1924; *PHCC.*
9. *PDAH,* 29; *LBK,* letter 208; *YBG,* Dec. 20, 1923, June 2, 1924; personal interview with Shaul Avigur; *HISE,* June 5, 1923; Ada Golomb to Eliyahu Golomb, Mar. 12, 1934, *DRH.*
10. *HISE,* June 11, 1924, May 28, 1925; *IG,* letters 384, 390; *YBG,* May 11, Sept. 13, Oct. 11, 1924.
11. *YBG,* Dec. 23, 1924.
12. *HISE,* Nov. 26, 1922; *SC,* pp. 58–61.
13. Itzhak Laufbahn, *Ha-Poel ha-Tzair,* Dec. 26, 1924; BK to HEC, Dec. 24, 1924, DBG to HEC, Dec. 30, 1924, *HECF* 16B; *YBG,* Jan. 4, 1925; *HEC* resolutions, Jan. 4, 1925, *HECF* 16B; *IG,* letter 407; *MHEC,* Mar. 17, 1925; Joseph Sprinzak to HEC, Mar. 15, 1925, *HECF* 247.
14. *PHCC,* May 10, 1925; *HISE,* Apr. 1, 1925.
15. *HISE,* July 18, 1925.
16. Secretariat directives, Dec. 18, 1927, Dec. 14, 1928, *HECF* 154; *YBG,* Dec. 8, 1927.

Chapter 18: *Paula's Jealousy*

1. The name Renana, "joyful," was taken from Job 3:7; *YBG,* Mar., Apr.–Oct. 1925.
2. *YBG,* July 16, 17, 18, Oct. 5, 1925; Shlomo Ze'evi to DBG, Aug. 4, 1925, *IDF* 2460.
3. *YBG,* Feb. 10, May 18, Sept. 9, 10, 1926; RLBG, as told by DBG, in a personal interview.
4. RLBG in a personal interview; *YBG,* Jan. 17, June 12, Nov. 11–12, 1928; *IG,* letter 523.
5. Personal interviews with GBE, RLBG, ABG; Geula to DBG, Apr. 1, 1926, *IDF* 2040; *YBG,* Apr. 10, 1928.
6. *YBG,* Jan. 20, Apr. 22, May 29, 1926, July 8, 1927, Apr. 10, Nov. 29, 1928; *IG,* letter 552; *PHCC,* Dec. 22–28, 1923; report to third convention, p. 358;

Ha-Mashbir to DBG, Mar. 28, 1927, *L* IV/104/DBG 1; *LPBG,* Mar., Apr. 21, 1926, *IDF* 4001.

7. *LPBG,* Apr. 24, 28, 29, 1926, Aug. 10, 1930, and undated, apparently from Mar. 1926, *IDF* 4001, 4002; *YBG,* Apr. 29, May 31, 1926; personal interview with GBE; Tel Aviv municipal ledger for fiscal year 1926/27, fol. 794.

8. HEC to central control board, Feb. 22, 1931, *HECF* 276; *IG,* letter 211; Anglo-Palestine Bank to DBG, Feb. 20, 1927, *L* IV/104, DBG 1; personal interviews with GBE, ABG.

9. *LPBG,* undated and Apr. 21, 1926, *IDF* 4002, 4001, respectively.

10. *IG,* letter 229; Zippora Ben-Gurion to Paula, Sept. 13, Oct. 13, 1923, July 5, 1926, *IDF* 4008; personal interviews with ABG, GBE; *LPBG,* undated, apparently from Apr. 1926, and Apr. 2, 4, 24, 1926, *IDF* 4002; *YBG,* Dec. 17, 1923.

Chapter 19: *The Blood Wedding with Ha-Poel ha-Mizrachi*

1. Dov Hoz to Rivka Hoz, Nov. 17, 1921, *DRH;* Achdut ha-Avodah circular, Feb. 15, 1926, *PDAH* 27B; *YBG,* Jan. 19, Dec. 29, 1924; HEC to Tel Aviv Labor Council, Feb. 2, 1925, *HECF* 36; *Kunteres* 170, article by E. Ben-Naftali (Eliyahu Golomb); *MHEC,* Jan. 23, 1927; immigration and emigration figures from N. Gross lecture, "Hamitun Bameshek Hayehudi Be'eretz Israel Bishnat 1923," Jan. 16, 1979, Institute for Zionist Research.

2. Personal interview with Rachel Yanait–Ben-Zvi; *Davar,* Feb. 20, 1927; Haifa Labor Council to HEC, Mar. 6, 1926, *HECF* 31B; *HISE,* Jan. 23, 1924.

3. *IG,* letters 358, 359; DBG letter to Reb Avigdor, undated, is in Benjamin Ben-Gurion's possession.

4. Letters and documents in *HECF* 228, 125, 126; *YBG,* Jan. 15, 1929. DBG spoke by telephone with Itzhak Elam (Finkelstein).

5. *Kunteres* 115; DBG to Histadrut council, Oct. 1929; *PHCC,* Oct. 7, 1929.

6. *YBG,* May 27, 1922; force was mobilized by Hoz, perhaps with DBG's go-ahead, given in telephone call with Joseph Garfunkel, *HISE,* May 26, 1922; personal interview with Zvi Lavon, member of Tel Aviv Labor Council secretariat; see Elkanah Margalit, *Anatomiah shel Smol* (Tel Aviv: I. L. Peretz Publishing, 1977); Yehuda Sharett to Moshe Sharett and Eliyahu Golomb after second convention, *DRH.*

7. *SC,* p. 12; Margalit, *Anatomiah.*

8. *Kunteres* 129, p. 22; *SC,* pp. 57–58.

9. *HISE,* Nov. 17, 1921; *PHCC,* Nov. 8, 1921, Mar. 17–20, 1923; *Pinkas* 3, vol. II, Mar. 29, 1923; DBG, *Kunteres* 115.

10. *PHCC,* Mar. 17–20, 1923, *Pinkas* 3, vol. II, Mar. 29, 1923; *Kunteres* 136; see N. Gardy, *Pirkei Haim shel Chalutz Dati* (Tel Aviv: Ha-Poel ha-Mizrachi Publishing, 1973), p. 149 ff.

11. Ha-Poel ha-Mizrachi poster, July 6, 1923, quoted in Tel Aviv Labor Council poster, "Berur Devarim," July 9, 1923, *HECF* 11B; *Kunteres* 136; letters from Tel Aviv municipality and Tel Aviv Labor Council, July 14, 15, 1923, *HECF* 11B; *Pinkas* 7, vol. II, Aug. 1, 1928.

12. DBG to Jaffa district commissioner, July 16, 1923, *HECF* 23C; Jaffa district

commissioner to DBG, *HECF* 23C; *Pinkas* 7, vol. II, Aug. 1, 1928; DBG letter and telegram to Ramsay MacDonald and *Daily Herald,* July 21 and 25, respectively, 1923, *HECF* 23C; *Doar ha-Yom,* July 31, 1923.

13. *Kunteres* 136; *Pinkas* 7, vol. II, Aug. 1, 1928; "El Toshvey Tel Aviv," supplement to *Ha-Aretz,* July 18, 1923; Tel Aviv municipality poster, "Berur Devarim," *HECF* 11B; *Ha-Aretz,* July 25, 1923; *IG,* letter 341; DBG, *Kunteres* 204.

14. Committee decisions, July 18, 1923, *HECF* 82; *ZBG,* vol. I, p. 219.

Chapter 20: A Threat of Murder

1. *Morning Post,* May 6, 1921; Chaim Weizmann to Sir Ronald Graham in Foreign Office, July 11, 1919, *PRO* FO 371/4168; *HISE,* Dec. 30, 1920; Dov Hoz to Rivka Hoz, Apr. 30, 1921, *DRH.*

2. *YBG,* Mar. 18, May 14, 1922; *HISE,* May 14, 1922.

3. DBG to D. Bloch, July 4, 1922, *L* IV/202/54. Other committee members were J. Aharonovitch and S. Marshak; *MHEC,* July 31, 1922.

4. DBG to M. Vilner and associates in "Frakziat Poalim," Dec. 31, 1922, *IDF* 2724.

5. *Sefer Hukot Hahistadrut,* published by HEC, Oct. 1932.

6. Elkanah Margalit, p. 91; *BH,* part I, vol. II, p. 255; *YBG,* Apr. 28, 1924; *PHCC,* Apr. 27–29, 1924, *Pinkas* 8, vol. III, June 13, 1924; letter from Tel Aviv Labor Council, May 28, 1924, *HECF* 39B; Avraham Zvi appeal, Aug. 27, 1924, *HECF* 234; *HISE,* May 29, 1924.

7. *YBG,* May 29, 1924; *HISE,* May 29, 1924.

8. *Kunteres* 206, Feb. 17, 1925; *IG,* letter 414; circular with DBG signature, Aug. 25, 1924, *IDF* 2447; vicious circle is described in L. Trepper letters to Histadrut council, Nov. 24, 1925, *HECF* 239; *MHEC,* July 18, 1926; DBG to workers ousted from Histadrut, June 16, 1926, *HECF* 239.

9. On leftward tilt in Legion, see *BH,* part I, vol. II, p. 222 ff.; Anita Shapira, "Hahalom Veshivro," *Baderech* (Giva'at-Havivah: Beit Baruch Lin Publishing, December 1968), volumes C, D; *YBG,* Feb. 15, 1932, recounts Manya telling him personally; personal interview with N. Horowitz.

10. *BH,* part I, vol. II, pp. 224, 228, 229 ff., 234; Israel Shochat, *SH;* personal interview with D. Horowitz.

11. *YBG,* Apr. 6, 26, June 27, Dec. 21, 1924, Jan. 17, 23, 25, Apr. 15, 1925; *Kunteres* 200.

12. DBG, *Kunteres* 207; G. Hanoch, *Ha-Poel ha-Tzair* 24; DBG to editor, *Kunteres* 211.

13. Letter from Y. Almog (Kopelevitz) on behalf of Legion central secretariat to HEC, Apr. 2, 1926, *HECF* 53; Y. Efter and I. Marom (Mereminski) to Legion, Apr. 6, 1926, *HECF* 53; *HISE,* Apr. 7, 1926; *BH,* part I. vol. II, p. 253; Shochat, *SH.*

14. "Havaad Hapoel al Hainyanim Bagalil Haelion," *Davar,* Aug. 26, 1926; *YBG,* Oct. 16, 1925; Achdut ha-Avodah executive committee meeting with members of its faction in Histadrut council, June 17, 1926, *HISE* 18.

15. *Davar,* Aug. 26, 1926; *YBG,* July 30, 1926.

16. *Davar,* Aug. 26, 1926; *BH,* part I, vol. II, pp. 226, 251 ff.; DBG testimony to Histadrut inquiry committee shows that he was accused of blaming the Cir-

cle, *Haganah Archives*, 2274; YBZ, handwritten protocol, *YBZ* 1/4/10/28; Manya Shochat to DBG, July 23, 1926, *IDF* 794; *IG*, letter 437; P. Schneerson, *SH*, p. 292.

17. As DBG said to Shaul Avigur, afterward, Avigur to author; *YBG*, July 30, 31, 1926; *Davar*, July 27, Aug. 2, 1926; draft, in DBG handwriting, is written on Lebanon restaurant stationery, Jaffa Road, Haifa, Aug. 1, 1926, *L* IV/132/B7.

18. *HISE*, Aug. 3, 1926; *Davar*, Aug. 8, 1926; *HECF* 53; *IG*, letter 439.

19. YBZ to DBG, undated, *YBZ* 1/1/2/20; *IG*, letters 439, 442; *Davar*, Aug. 9, 1926; list of expelled, *HECF* 78; *Ha-Poel ha-Tzair* 42, Aug. 27, 1926; I. Laufbahn, "Leinyan Tel Hai Ukfar Giladi," *Ha-Poel ha Tzair* 43–44, Sept. 8, 1926.

20. "Teshuvot Vaadat Haberur Leshe'elat Haaguda," in HEC archive; *BH*, part III, vol. II, p. 1288; *HISE*, Jan. 27, 1927; *YBG*, Jan. 31, 1927.

21. J. Roznitchenko (Erez), *Kunteres* 284; public statement by delegates of right; *HISE*, Jan. 12, 23, 1927; *IG*, letter 446; Hanoch Rochel, *Derekh Haim*, laid out and printed in Tel Yosef, p. 192; *YBG*, Aug. 11, 1927, see also Apr. 2, 24, June 7; DBG, *TC*, p. 75.

22. Anita Shapira, "Hitpathuto Hapolitit shel Gedud Haavoda," *Baderech* 4, 1969; Histadrut regulations, published by HEC, 1952, p. 28.

Chapter 21: A Corpse at Sprinzak's Doorstep

1. *HISE*, May 27, 1924, Feb. 1, 26, Apr. 1, 1925.

2. *SL*, vol. I, p. 329; *HISE*, Aug. 3, 1926, Jan. 23, 1927.

3. *PHCC*, Jan. 31, Feb. 2, 1927; *Ha-Poel ha-Tzair*, Feb. 4, 1927; *Kunteres* 293.

4. Glukstein of Haifa won contract, *Davar*, Feb. 17, 1927; Jerusalem Labor Council statement in *Davar*, Feb. 25, 1927.

5. *Davar*, Feb. 17, 22, 1927; *HISE*, Mar. 16, 1927; Marom (Mereminski) report, Mar. 16, 1927, to American delegation, *HECF* 67.

6. *HISE*, Mar. 16, 24, 1927; *MHEC*, Mar. 15, 1927; YBZ notebook, Mar. 9, 1927, *YBZ* 1/8/4/3; *Ha-Poel ha-Tzair* 23, Mar. 17, 1927.

7. *Ha-Poel ha-Tzair* 23, Mar. 17, 1927; *HISE*, Mar. 16, 24, 1927; *YBG*, Mar. 19, 1927.

8. *Davar*, Mar. 11, 13, 14, 1927; *HISE*, Mar. 16, 24, 1927.

9. YBZ notebook, Mar. 9, 1927, *YBZ* 1/8/4/3; *HISE*, Mar. 16, 23, 24, 1927; *Ha-Poel ha-Tzair* 23, Mar. 17, 1927.

10. Referendum results, *HECF* 78; see Golomb handwritten notice on printed sheet of referendum results, Mar. 21, 1927, *HECF* 78; *HISE*, Mar. 16, 24, 1927; *Ha-Poel ha-Tzair* 23, Mar. 17, 1927.

11. DBG, *Kunteres* 293, Feb. 18, 1927; *HISE*, Mar. 16, 24, 1927; both versions and signatures, *HECF* 78; personal interview with I. Elam.

Chapter 22: Indispensable

1. *MHEC*, Jan. 3, Feb. 2, 1927; wage committee conclusions, May 23, 1927, *HECF* 154; HEC to wage committee, May 2, 1927, *HECF* 154.

2. Wage committee to HEC, July 3, 1927, *HECF* 154; *HISE*, May 29, 1927; *PHCC*, Jan. 20–21, 1925, *IDF* 1461.

3. *HISE*, May 29, 1927.
4. *YBG*, Sept. 4, 1928, in conversation with Isaac Nachman Steinberg.
5. *HISE*, June 24, 1927.
6. *HISE*, Jan. 23, 1928.
7. Heshel Frumkin, *Aliyah Vepituah Baderech Lemedina* (Tel Aviv: Tarbut Vehinuch Publishing, 1971), p. 12 ff.; Eliyahu Biletzky, *Solel Boneh 1924–1974* (Tel Aviv: Am Oved, Tarbut Vehinuch, 1974), p. 131.
8. *MHEC*, Jan. 1, 1923; *YBG*, Jan. 3, 1924; *Pinkas* supplement to issue 4, vol. II; HEC sessions concerning second convention, *Pinkas* 7, Dec. 1922.
9. Achdut ha-Avodah convention protocol, June 18, 1927, *PDAH* C23; *HISE*, May 24, 1924; Hillel Dan, *Bederekh Lo Selula* (Tel Aviv: Schocken, 1963), p. 51; *Davar*, June 17, 1925; E. Biletzky, p. 135; letter on behalf of Migdal Zedek group to HEC, Mar. 3, 1927, *HECF* 96.
10. Report of consortium representative, *HECF* 91; Solel Boneh to HEC, Jan. 13, 1927, *HECF* 91.
11. ZE to Bank ha-Poalim, Jan. 11, 1927, *HECF* A54; *HISE*, Feb. 23, 1927; *TC*, p. 75.
12. David Remez to Gusta Rechev, Mar. 16, 1928, *LGR*.
13. Achdut ha-Avodah council protocol, June 18, 1927, *PDAH* C23.
14. Remez to Rechev, Sept. 15, 1927, *LGR*.
15. *TC*, p. 74; *Kunteres* 289, Jan. 14, 1927; *ZBG*, vol. I, p. 308; Ada Golomb to Eliyahu Golomb, Feb. 6, 1924, *DRH*; J. Shapira to Achdut ha-Avodah executive committee, Oct. 21, 1925, *PDAH* 55; Shazar to DGB, Sept. 3, 1924, *IDF* 2037; *YBG*, Oct. 10, 1925.
16. *YBG*, Dec. 30, 1925; *Jewish Daily Forward*, Dec. 9, 1925; *Ha-Aretz*, Jan. 17, 1926.
17. *PDAH* 9; DBG, *Kunteres* 289, Jan. 14, 1927.
18. *HISE*, Mar. 24, 1927; "Hasbara," *Ha-Poel ha-Tzair* 12, 1924; C. Arlosoroff and H. Shurer reply to DBG, *Davar*, Sept. 20, 1926; *Ha-Poel ha-Tzair*, Feb. 4, 1927.
19. Letter, "On Behalf of the Expelled," to standing committee, July 5, 1927, *HECF* 43; *TC*, pp. 15, 261; DBG statements on Teachers' College conflict, *HISE*, Mar. 24, 1927; standing committee protocols, June 15, 17, 1927; *HECF* 43.
20. Report to *TC* of Histadrut by HEC, July 1927; *ZBG*, vol. I, p. 313; standing committee protocols, June 15, 17, 1927; *TC* report, p. 17.
21. *TC*; coverage in *Davar*, beginning June 7, 1927, appeared after official protocol of third convention.
22. *Davar*, Aug. 3, 1927; *YBG*, Aug. 16, 1927.
23. *TC*, p. 265.
24. S. Lavi statements, *TC*, p. 35.

Chapter 23: An Organization of Conquerors

1. Anita Shapira, *Hama'avak Hanihzav, Avodah Ivrit 1929–1939*, Tel Aviv University (Ha-Kibbutz Ha-Meuchad, 1977); *HISE*, Nov. 21, 22, Dec. 5, 1927.
2. *YBG*, Dec. 1–2, 5, 1927; *Davar*, Dec. 5, 14–15, 1927; *HISE*, Dec. 14, 1927.
3. *MHEC*, Dec. 16, 21, 1927; *Davar*, Dec. 15–16, 18, 29, 1927; *YBG*, Dec. 18,

1927; posters are in *HECF* 144; *IG*, letter 454; DBG telegram to *Daily Herald*, Dec. 18, 1927, *HECF* 144; *Times*, Dec. 19, 1927.

4. Action committee protocol, Dec. 19, 1927, *HECF* 144; *MHEC*, Dec. 16, 27, 1927; *HISE*, Dec. 14, 1927; E. Golomb to Dov Hoz and Mereminski, Dec. 22, 1927, *HECF* 144; *YBG*, Dec. 29, 1927.

5. *Ha-Aretz, Davar*, Dec. 29, 1927; *HISE*, Jan. 6, 1928.

6. *HISE*, Dec. 26, 1927, Jan. 2, 6, 1928; BK, *Kunteres* 323, Jan. 6, 1928; *YBG*, Jan. 18, 1928; DBG in National Council, Jan. 10, 1928, *MLA*, p. 250.

7. *YBG*, Jan., Feb. 3, 7, 1928.

8. DBG lecture, Haifa, Nov. 16, 1928, *IDF* 43; protocols, Nov. 20, Dec. 11, 1928, *HECF* 144; DBG to Petah Tikva agricultural committee, Dec. 5, 1928, *HECF* 144; *Davar*, Dec. 18, 1928; *CHR*, p. 173; *HISE*, Dec. 19, 1928; *Doar ha-Yom*, Jan. 10, 1929; Poale Zion Third Convention, Succoth 1907, *L* IV/104/YBG 46; *Kunteres* 25.

9. July 24, 1922, *PDAH* A1; *MHEC*, Mar. 17, 1925; *HISE*, Apr. 12, July 9, 1924; Ada Fishman (Maimon), *Ha-Poel ha-Tzair* 37, July 23, 1926.

10. *Kunteres* 289, Jan. 14, 1927; personal interview with Gerda Luft.

11. Achdut ha-Avodah executive committee session, Oct. 20, 1927, *PDAH* 9; BK platform, *IDF* 3358; *Davar*, May 27, 1928; *YBG*, May 25, Dec. 19, 1928.

12. J. Aharonovitch and I. Laufbahn to Achdut ha-Avodah, Sept. 20, 1928, *PDAH* B88; *YBG*, Nov. 8, 1928; *HISE*, Jan. 14, 1929.

13. BK platform, *IDF* 3358; *YBG*, May 28, 1929; DBG draft proposal, *IDF* 3358; *IG*, letter 483; *ZBG*, vol. I, p. 368; platform of Eretz Israel Workers' ticket, *Davar*, June 28, 1929.

14. *Davar*, Jan. 5–8, 1930.

15. *Davar*, Jan. 9, 1930.

16. *YBG*, Sept. 5, 1929; *MLA*, p. 258; paragraph 7, BK platform, *IDF* 3358.

17. *HISE*, Aug. 14, 1930; Sarah Erez, *Tekufa Aheret* (Tel Aviv: Keren David Remez Publishing, 1977), p. 101; DBG, *Kunteres* 241; *MHEC*, Nov. 29, 1922.

18. DBG, *Kunteres* 241; DBG lecture, "Irgun Hamiflaga," Oct. 10, 1925, *PDAH* 69.

19. Fishman (Maimon), *Ha-Poel ha-Tzair* 37, July 23, 1926; DBG lecture, "Irgun Hamiflaga."

20. From "Herkev Hamiflaga," *IDF* 3358.

Chapter 24: Toward a New Venture

1. *YBG*, Jan. 22, 1930; M. Beilinson, *Kunteres* 220, June 12, 1925; Young Zionist leaders, Chernovtsy, to HEC, June 7, 1926, *HECF* 76.

2. Chaim Ben-Yerucham, *SB* (Jerusalem and Tel Aviv: Hava'ad Lehotza'at Sefer Bethar, 1969), vol. I, pp. 29, 32; Vladimir Jabotinsky, "Hasmol" and "Basta," in *Basa'ar*, pp. 15, 23, respectively (Jerusalem: Eri Jabotinsky Publishing, 1953); "Oyev Hapoalim," *Ha-Aretz*, Aug. 20, 1925.

3. *SB*, p. 109; Ya'akov Shavit, *Merov Lemedina* (Tel Aviv: Yariv and Hadar Publishing, 1978); *Davar*, May 2, 1928; J. Ben-Moshe, *Kunteres* 331; *Ha-Aretz*, May 4, 1928; *YBG*, May 2, 1928.

4. *Ha-Aretz, Davar,* Oct. 7, 10, 1928; *Doar ha-Yom,* May 7, 1928; *WBK* vol. III, p. 277.

5. *Doar ha-Yom, Ha-Aretz,* July 4, 1929.

6. DBG, "Al Hakotel Veha'ikar," *AS,* p. 151; DBG at meeting of National Council, Oct. 16, 1928, *CZA,* J 1/7232; Cmd 3229, Nov. 11, 1928; *Davar,* Aug. 1, 16, 1929; *SB,* pp. 201, 205.

7. Jabotinsky, "Azhara," *Basa'ar,* p. 71; public statement by Achdut ha-Avodah and Ha-Poel ha-Tzair, *Kunteres* 380; *YBG,* Oct. 12, 1928; Jabotinsky files, *IDF* 2302, 2303, 2753; *SB,* p. 248 ff.

8. *SB,* p. 205 ff.; *Davar,* Apr. 8, 9, July 8, 1930, Dec. 20, 1932; press conference, Nov. 27, 1932; *HISE,* Apr. 15, 1929, May 9, 1932.

9. Proposal in Aba Khoushi's handwriting with corrections in DBG's handwriting, undated, *IDF* 3342; *YBG,* May 12, 24, 1932.

10. DBG's height was in his passport. He entered his weight in *YBG,* Jan. 21, 1926, after his recovery; *IG,* letters 421, 422, 423, 424, 429; *YBG,* Jan. 20, 1926, ff., and Mar.–Apr.–May 1926.

11. *YBG,* July–Aug., Sept. 1, 1927; *IG,* letter 452.

12. *Davar,* Oct. 19–27, 1927; *YBG,* Oct.–Nov. 1927.

13. *YBG,* July 8–14, 17, 1927, June 18, 21, 1928, June 6, 1929; *ZBG,* vol. I, p. 417; *IG,* letters 515, 516.

14. DBG to S. Jacobson, Mar. 5, 1964; DBG at meeting with Arabs from Ar'ara, June 8, 1970, *IDF* 1434.

15. HEC books, *L* IV/104/Dov Hoz/14; HEC pay scale, *HECF* 113; *YBG,* Feb. 23, Nov. 29, 1928, Nov. 21, 1931; according to *HECF* 110, 113, 180; *IG,* letter 212.

16. *HISE,* Nov. 17, 1930, July 28, 1931; *IG,* letters 511, 521, 525, 540; letter from Paula, Aug. 10, 1930, *IDF* 4001; *Tel Aviv Municipality Archives;* E. Golomb to Bank ha-Poalim, Dec. 31, 1930, *HECF* 161.

17. *Tel Aviv Municipality Archives;* according to *HECF* 276, 286; according to *YBG,* 1932; HEC to DBG, Apr. 26, 1933, *MBG.*

18. Report on publishing activities of *Davar,* Sept. 28, 1931, *HECF* 283; *YBG,* Aug. 12, 1932; personal interviews with GBE, RLBG, Hannah Tepper who, with her children, was a paying guest in the house; Bank ha-Poalim to DBG, Mar. 11, 1940, *IDF* 4006; DBG, *Kunteres* 118.

Chapter 25: Conquests

1. Chaim Weizmann, *Trial and Error,* p. 325; *HISE,* Nov. 26, 1922.

2. *MAP* (council), Jan. 19, 1933.

3. DBG at third convention, Achdut ha-Avodah; *Kunteres* 118; *TC.*

4. *Kunteres* 104, 110, 120, 141, 179; *MLA; YBG* (in Vienna), Aug. 20, 1925; *AS,* p. 150.

5. *IG,* letters 285, 412, 438; *ZBG,* vol. I, p. 378.

6. DBG, *Kunteres* 293; *L* IV/404/70; *ZBG,* vol. I, p. 644.

7. *YBG,* Dec. 5, 1923; Achdut ha-Avodah council, Feb. 1924, *L; IG,* letter 384.

8. *HISE,* Feb. 14, 1928, Feb. 25, Mar. 7, 25, 28, Apr. 22, 23, 30, May 6, 10, 1929; *YBG,* Feb.–Mar. 1928; *Davar,* Mar. 28, Apr. 3, 1928; *PHCC,* Mar. 1928; Achdut ha-Avodah council, Oct. 4–7, 1928, *L* IV/404/70; *YBG,* Jan. 19, 1929.

9. *Davar*, Jan. 15–16, 1929; *YBG*, Nov. 21, 1928, May 4, July 11–26, 1929; *PHCC*, Oct. 7, 1929; DBG to committees for Labor Palestine, May 14, 1929, *L* IV/208/117; *IG*, letters 477–485; *DRH*, July 23, 25, 1929.

10. Defense plan, *L* IV/208/225; *ZBG*, vol. I, pp. 362–365; *Davar*, Oct. 12, 1930; *MAP* (council), Oct. 25, 1930.

11. *HISE*, Jan. 20, Mar. 3, June 6, July 28, Aug. 9, 25, 1930; *YBG*, Apr. 17, 1930; *IG*, letters 520, 527, 530, 532, 533, 535; DBG to Mapai Central Committee, Aug. 19, 1930, *BB*, 19–3/6/22; *MAP* (enlarged secretariat), Sept. 11, 1930; DBG to E. Golomb, Sept. 1, 1930, *IDF* 1466; telegram from DBG to HEC, Sept. 11, 1930, *IDF* 2037.

12. *ZBG*, vol. I, pp. 433–488; *Davar*, Oct. 12, 13, 15, 1930; *Doar ha-Yom*, Sept. 29, 1930; *IG*, letters 539, 540, 542; *YBG*, Oct. 6, 1930; *HISE*, Oct. 20, 1930.

13. *ZBG*, vol. I, pp. 386, 462, 511, vol. II, pp. 291, 421; *MLA*, p. 276.

14. DBG to Paula from Berlin, Sept. 17, 1930; *PHCC*, Jan. 10, 1934.

15. *MAP* (Kefar Yehezkel council), July 1–4, 1932, *IDF* 2768; *LBK*, vol. VI, p. 79.

16. *ZBG*, vol. I, p. 519; *YBG*, Sept. 17, 1965; *Ha-Poel ha-Tzair* 25, pp. 30–34.

17. *YBG*, Aug. 28, 1932.

18. DBG to Rega Klapholz, undated, probably Aug. 1932, *RK;* personal interview with Rega Klapholz-Diamant, Jan. 29, 1978.

19. Personal interviews with Rivka Katznelson, Apr. 8, 1975, Oct. 2, 1977.

20. Paula to DBG, Aug. 10, 1930, *IDF* 4001.

21. *IG*, letters 559, 560; *SL*, vol. II, letter 82; *LBK*, vol. VI, letter 21; personal interview with Klapholz-Diamant; Mendel Singer diary, courtesy of his son, Uri Zimri.

22. DBG to Rega, undated, probably Aug. 1932.

Chapter 26: Victory

1. DBG to Rega, Aug. 11, 1932; *YBG*, Aug. 12, 1932.

2. DBG to Paula, Aug. 19, 1932, *IDF* 3999; DBG to Rega, Aug. 19, 1932.

3. *ZBG*, vol. I, pp. 524–529; *YBG*, Aug. 26–Sept. 3, 1932; council protocol from League for Labor Palestine, Aug. 27–28, 1932, *L* IV/208/344; *LP*, p. 80.

4. DBG to Paula, Aug. 31, 1932, *LP*; DBG to Rega, Aug. 31, 1932.

5. *ZBG*, vol. I, pp. 530–539; *YBG*, Aug. 31–Sept. 7, 1932; Locker to Weizmann, Sept. 18, 1932, *WA*.

6. *YBG*, Sept. 7–10, 1932; DBG to Rega, Sept. 7, 1932.

7. DBG expense account, Sept. 13–16, 1932; interview with Uri Zimri, Oct. 23, 1984.

8. Rega to author; *YBG*, Sept. 15–16, 1932; DBG to Rega, Feb. 15, Mar. 16, 1933.

9. Description of DBG's preparations for his trip to Poland is based on discussions at Mapai Central Committee, Sept. 12, 24, 25, Nov. 22, 1932, Oct. 1, Mar. 15, 21, 26, Apr. 20, 1933; *HEC*, Sept. 26, Nov. 15, 21, Dec. 19, 1932, Jan. 25, Feb. 9, Mar. 9, 27, Aug. 2, 1933; Histadrut council, Nov. 27, 1932; Histadrut convention, Feb. 12–18, 1933; Mapai convention, Oct. 30–Nov. 3, 1932; Hapoel national conference, Oct. 21, 1932; meeting at Beit ha-Am, Feb. 18, 1933; press conference at HEC, Nov. 27, 1932; DBG to Mapai

Central Committee; *IG,* letter 566; *YBG,* Dec. 2, 19, 1933; *Davar,* Oct. 23, Dec. 20, 1932.

10. On subject of education, *MAP* (council), Feb. 5, 1931; referendum taken on DBG proposal in Apr. 1931, *L* IV/208/326; *HISE,* Apr. 20, 1931, May 29, July 4, Oct. 3, 18, Nov. 2, 1932; *MAP* (Central Committee), Sept. 22, Oct. 9, 1932, Mar. 21, 1933.

11. Histadrut council, Nov. 27, 1932; *MAP* (Central Committee), Nov. 7, 1932.

12. *MAP* (Central Committee), Sept. 24, Oct. 27, Nov. 7, 1932; *ZBG,* vol. I, p. 540; "Hapoel Bazionut," *MLA,* 1955 edition (unabridged).

13. *MAP* (council), Jan. 19, 1933, *MAP* (Central Committee), Sept. 12, 1932.

14. *ZBG,* vol. I, p. 540; *MAP* (Central Committee), Oct. 27, 1932.

15. Information on Berit ha-Biryonim, Abba Achimeir, and Z. E. Cohen and their standing in the revisionist movement is based on *STRA.*

16. *Doar ha-Yom,* Sept. 2, 13, 1932.

17. "Tslav Hakeres Ha'adom" (The Red Swastika), published in Russian, in *Rassvet,* Oct. 23, 1932, and in Hebrew in *Hazit ha-Am,* Nov. 4, 1932; "Ken, Lishbor!" published in Yiddish in *Hajnt,* Nov. 4, 1932, and in Hebrew in *Hazit ha-Am,* Dec. 2, 1932.

18. *IDF* 2301, 2303, 3326; "Chalutzim and . . . Chalutzim," published in Yiddish in *Hajnt,* Oct. 7, 1932, and in Hebrew in *Doar ha-Yom,* Oct. 24, 1932.

19. DBG speech at Hapoel conference, *Davar,* Oct. 23, 1932; *YBG,* Dec. 20, 31, 1932, Jan. 19, 1933; Hapoel file *L* 1935/6.

20. *MAP* (Central Committee), Oct. 27, 1932, Mar. 15, 1933.

21. DBG speech at founding convention, Jan. 5, 1930, *Ha-Poel ha-Tzair* 7–8, 1930; *IG,* letters 531, 532.

22. DBG speech at meeting in Beit ha-Am, *Davar,* Mar. 21, 1933; DBG speech at Elected Assembly, *Davar,* Mar. 2, 1933.

23. *WL,* XV/292, Aug. 1, 1932.

24. Eliyahu Dobkin to Melech Noy, Nov. 9, 1932, *L* IV/208/344; in same file, Dobkin-Noy correspondence on *Hajnt* and *Moment; YBG,* Nov. 10, 1932.

25. DBG speech at press conference, Nov. 27, 1932, *IDF* 51; *YBG,* Nov. 27, 1932; *Davar,* Dec. 20, 1932, Jan. 11, 16, 24, 27, 1933; *MLA,* p. 212.

26. "Meginim Umeginim," *Moment,* Dec. 23, 1932, *Hazit ha-Am,* Jan. 6, 1933.

27. V. Jabotinsky letter to editor, *Hazit ha-Am,* May 17, 1933, Jabotinsky, *Kerech Mihtavim* (Tel Aviv: Amihai, no date), p. 331.

28. DBG to Noy, Jan. 5, 1933; "Hapoel Bazionut," *MLA,* 1955; *IG,* letter 567; *MAP* (Central Committee), Oct. 27, 1932, Mar. 15, 21, 1933; DBG to Itzhak Gruenbaum, Jan. 3, 1933, *CZA,* A127/194; *YBG,* Mar. 19, 1933; *ZBG,* vol. I, pp. 540, 559, 563.

29. *MAP* (Central Committee), Sept. 26, 1932, Mar. 15, 1933.

30. *ZBG,* vol. I, p. 559; *MAP* (Central Committee), Jan. 10, Mar. 28, 1933; DBG to Rega, Mar. 16, 1933.

31. DBG telegram from Genoa, Apr. 5, 1933; *IG,* letter 572; DBG to Rega, Apr. 25, 29, 1933; DBG to Paula from Warsaw, Apr. 11, 1933, *IDF* 3999.

32. DBG to Paula, Apr. 21, 25, 1933; DBG to Rega, June 15, 1933.

33. According to *YBG,* 1933, *ZBG,* vol. I, HEC files, and newspapers.

34. *SB; Moment,* Apr. 30, 1933.

35. "Zionut Kala veHamura," *Davar*, Jan. 11, 16, 24, 27, 1933; *YBG*, Apr. 19, 1933; *IG*, letter 572; *ZBG*, vol. II, p. 16.

36. *Davar*, Oct. 22, 1933; *MAP* (Central Committee), Mar. 21, 1933; *ZBG*, vol. II, p. 16.

37. On Arlosoroff murder, see *STRA*.

38. DBG to Geula, July 15, 1933; DBG article in *Dos Fraje Wort*, Lvov, July 2, 1933.

39. *MAP* (Central Committee), June 15, 1933; *YBG* and a letter to E. Dobkin, June 15, 1933; DBG to Central Committee, Zionist-Socialist Party, Latvia, June 30, 1933; *YBG* and letter to Meir Grabovski (Argov), July 2, 1933; DBG to Mereminski (Marom), July 7, 1933; *SB;* Aharon Weiss, *Ma'asef* 9; Gruenbaum article in *Hajnt,* translated and printed in *Davar,* Aug. 11, 1933; Levy Arie Sarid, *He-Chalutz Vetnuot Hanoar Be-Polin 1917–1933* (Tel Aviv: Am Oved, 1979).

40. For Beilisiad and Jabotinsky moves, see *STRA;* Jabotinsky to Solomon Leibovitz, *Herut* supplement, July 31, 1959; *YBG*, June 27, Oct. 16, 1933; *IG*, letters 646, 662; DBG to Paula, July 25, 1933; Dobkin to party members from Vienna, Aug. 8, 1933, *L* IV/208/2; *MAP* (Central Committee), Mar. 7, 1934.

41. DBG to Paula, May 11, 1933, *LP;* DBG to Rega, June 3, 1933.

42. DBG to Paula, June 13, 1933, *LP;* DBG to Rega, June 15, 28, 1933.

43. DBG to Rega, July 1, 7, 1933; DBG to Paula, July 15, 1933, *LP;* DBG to Paula, July 25, 1933; DBG telegram to Rega, July 26, 1933; *IG*, letters 656, 657; Dobkin letter, Aug. 8, 1933; Mendel Singer diary.

Chapter 27: The Plan

1. DBG to Paula from Prague, Aug. 24, 1933; DBG cable to HEC from Vienna, Aug. 10, 1933; DBG cable to Paula, Aug. 12, 1933; DBG to Paula from Prague, Aug. 24, 1933.

2. DBG to Paula from Prague, Sept. 2, 1933, *LP*.

3. *IG*, letters 566, 662; *PMA*, p. 18; *YBG*, Mar. 19, 1933; *Davar*, Mar. 24, 1933; *MAP* (Central Committee), Mar. 26, 1933; *ZBG*, vol. I, pp. 596, 599; DBG to Paula from Prague, Sept. 2, 1933, *LP; Ha-Aretz*, Aug. 30, 1933.

4. DBG to Paula from Prague, Sept. 2, 1933, *LP*.

5. DBG to Paula, Sept. 6, 1933, *LP*.

6. *MC;* DBG to children, Sept. 14, 1935; *ZBG*, vol. II, p. 435.

7. Personal interview with ABG; census, *L* IV/104/DBG/1; DBG to BK, Mar. 16, 1938.

8. *MAP* (Central Committee), Jan. 10, Mar. 15, 28, 1933, *MAP* (council), Jan. 19, 1933; *MAP* (secretariat), July 19, 1933; *HISE*, Feb. 9, Aug. 14, 1933; *IG*, letters 566, 622, 648, 655, 656, 657, 662; *YBG*, Aug. 8, 15, 1933; Berl Locker to Weizmann, Aug. 10, 1933, *WA;* Bankover to Mapai Central Committee, Aug. 10, 1933, *BB* 33/101; BK to Leah Katznelson, Aug. 10, 1933, *BB; BKN,* Aug. 12, 1933, *BB*.

9. Articles of Association for WZO that were ratified by twelfth congress (1921) and amended by thirteenth through twenty-first congresses (1923–1939); *Clause I* — In addition to the elected delegates, members of the Executive Committee are entitled to participate in the Congress ac-

cording to article 46 (which explains who are members of the Executive Committee); they may participate in Congress deliberations and be elected to committees with all rights and privileges accruing thereby. If they do not have a mandate as a delegate, they may not vote in the Congress or be counted among the quorum of the national societies, delegations, and factions.

10. *MAP* (Central Committee), Mar. 17, 1931, Mar. 15, 1933; DBG, *Ha-Poel ha-Tzair* 39–40, Aug. 14, 1931.

11. *MAP* (Central Committee), Jan. 10, Mar. 15, 1933; Emanuel Neumann to Louis Brandeis, Mar. 1, 1933, on his conversation with DBG, Jerusalem, Feb. 23, 1933, *AJA*, reel 99.

12. *MAP* (Central Committee), Mar. 15, 21, 1933.

13. Ibid. and Mar. 28, 1933; *Davar*, Mar. 30, 1933; *ZBG*, vol. I, p. 599; another missed opportunity to meet with Weizmann: *YBG*, Apr. 17, 1925; minutes of labor faction, Aug. 22, 1933, *BB* 33/101; Moshe Sharett to Zippora Sharett, undated, probably Aug. 1933, *DRH*.

14. *SL*, vol. II, letters 122, 123 (Aug. 20, 25, 1933); *WL* XVI/22, Aug. 13, 1933, XVI/29, Aug. 19, 1933; telegram to Weizmann from Prague, Aug. 15, 1933; Bankover to Mapai Central Committee, Aug. 10, 1933, *BB* 33/101; labor faction meeting at Congress, Aug. 26, 1933, BB 33/101.

15. *SL*, vol. II, letter 124, Aug. 27, 1933; *Davar*, Aug. 30, 1933.

16. *MAP* (Central Committee), Dec. 8, 1943; *Davar*, Jan. 14, 1934 (DBG speech at general debate at second sitting of Histadrut convention).

17. *ZBG*, vol. I, p. 663; *YBG*, Sept. 8–16, 1933; *IG*, letter 667; DBG to Paula, Sept. 16, 1933, *LP; JAG*, Oct. 4, 1933.

18. *MAP* (council), Jan. 19, 1933; *IG*, letter 648; *JAG*, Oct. 4, 1933.

19. *PMA*, p. 18.

Chapter 28: Peace Within and Peace Without

1. *IG*, letters 666, 667; *YBG*, Sept. 16–27, 1933.

2. *YBG*, Sept. 18, Oct. 6, 1933; *ZBG*, vol. I, pp. 415, 418–420, 480.

3. *Davar*, Oct. 3, 1933.

4. Ibid., Oct. 27, 1933.

5. DBG to JNF concerning his salary, Nov. 20, 1933; *YBG*, Oct.–Nov. 1933; *MAP* (Central Committee), Jan. 2, 1934.

6. DBG to Paula, Nov. 24, 25, 26, 27, 28, 1933; DBG to Rega, Nov. 24, 25, 27 (undated), 28, 1933; *YBG*, Nov. 24–28, 1933.

7. *YBG*, Nov. 28–Dec. 20, 1933; *ZBG*, vol. I, pp. 696–722; DBG to Paula, Dec. 2, 9, 14, 20, 1933; DBG to Moshe Sharett, both Nov. 29, 1933.

8. DBG to Rega, Dec. 11, 13, 1933.

9. Ibid., Dec. 18, 1933.

10. DBG to Paula, Dec. 20, 1933.

11. *YBG*, Dec. 21–27, 1933; *MAP* (Central Committee), Jan. 2, 1934; DBG to Rega, Dec. 27, 1933.

12. *Davar*, Feb. 11, 14, 15, 16, 18, 19, 1934.

13. DBG to Rega, Feb. 15, 19, 1934.

14. DBG cables to Rega, Mar. 5, 21, 1934; DBG to Rega, Mar. 5, Apr. 23, 1934.

15. DBG to Rega, July 8, 1934.

16. *ZBG*, vol. II, p. 121.
17. DBG to Rega from Larnaca, July 15, 1934.
18. *YBG*, Dec. 6, 12, 1933.
19. *Davar*, Jan. 14, 1934; *ZBG*, vol. II, p. 11; *PMA*, p. 18; *JAG*, Feb. 21, 1934.
20. BK to Mapai Central Committee, *LBK*, vol. VI, letter 59; J. Aharonovitch and S. Lavi in *Davar*, May 3 and May 19, 1933, respectively; *YBG*, Apr. 21, 1933; DBG to Dobkin, *ZBG*, vol. I, p. 626, to Joseph Sprinzak, *IG*, letter 605, to Lavi, June 3, 1933; *MAP* (Central Committee), Apr. 20, 23, 1933.
21. *Davar*, June 1, 2, 4, 1933; *Ha-Aretz*, June 1, 2, 5, 8, 1933; *Hazit ha-Am*, June 1, 1933.
22. *MAP* (Central Committee), Jan. 2, Feb. 5, 13, 1934, *MAP* (council), Mar. 21–24, 1934; *ZBG*, vol. II, pp. 17–29.
23. *MAP* (Central Committee), July 20, 1934; *ZBG*, vol. II, pp. 133–134.
24. *STRA*, p. 296; *MAP* (council), Aug. 24, 1934.
25. *BGPA*; DBG to Paula, July 30, 1934; *JAG*, Aug. 16, 1934.
26. *BGPA*.
27. *MAP* (Political Committee), Aug. 5, 30, 1934, *MAP* (Central Committee), Aug. 8, 14, 16, 19, 21, 1934, *MAP* (council), Aug. 24, 1934.
28. *BGPA*.

Chapter 29: Disappointment

1. DBG to ABG, June 9, 1933, Sept. 10, 1934; Paula to ABG, Sept. 3, 9, 1934.
2. DBG to Rega, Sept. 10, 1934; Paula to ABG, Sept. 17, 25, Oct. 9 (wrongly dated Sept. 9), 10, 1934; Geula to DBG, May 1, 1935; DBG to ABG, May 7, 1935.
3. DBG to JAE, Feb. 21, 1934; *MAP* (Central Committee), Jan. 2, 1934, *MAP* (Political Committee), Aug. 30, 1934; *JAG* (London), Sept. 13–14, 1934.
4. *YBG*, Sept. 7, 14–22, 1934; DBG telegram to Magnes, Sept. 15, 1934; *JAG*, Sept. 20–21, 1934.
5. DBG to Rega, Sept. 17, 1934; *YBG*, Sept. 22, 1934; DBG to Paula, Sept. 22, 1934.
6. *YBG*, Sept. 22–23, 1934; *ZBG*, vol. II, pp. 254, 258; *DMS*, vol. I, p. 146; *BGPA*.
7. *YBG*, Sept. 23, 1934; *La Nation arabe*, November 1934.
8. *YBG*, Sept. 24, 1934; DBG telegram to Rega, Sept. 24, 1934; photograph of DBG with Rega and Annie in Vienna, dated Sept. 26, 1934; Paula to ABG on her departure for Warsaw, Sept. 25, 1934; personal interviews with Sarah Noy, Oct. 11, 1977, Rega Klapholz-Diamant, Mar. 22, 1978, Anselm Reiss, Oct. 8, 1977; *Davar*, Oct. 3, 1934; letter from Dov Hoz, *DRH*.
9. Personal interview with GBE, Oct. 28, 1984; Paula (in Russian) to friends in Warsaw from London, Oct. 9, 1934; postcard to ABG from his parents in Warsaw, Oct. 6, 1934 (wrongly dated Sept. 7, 1934, by Paula).
10. DBG to Mapai Central Committee, *YBG*, Oct. 4, 1934; *Davar*, Oct. 3, 18, 1934; *YBG*, Sept. 27–Oct. 6, 1934.
11. *YBG*, Oct. 7, 1934; *ZBG*, vol. II, p. 181.
12. *YBG*, Oct. 8, 1934.

13. *YBG*, Oct. 15–16, 1934.
14. *JC*, Oct. 26, 1934.
15. *YBG*, Oct. 8, 1934; DBG to Mapai Central Committee, Oct. 27–28, 1934; *ZBG*, vol. II, pp. 198, 200.
16. *YBG*, Oct. 10, 1934; DBG-Jabotinsky talks according to *YBG*, Oct. 9–Nov. 11, 1934, *ZBG*, vol. II, pp. 182–271.
17. *The World Jewish Petition, Issued by the London Office of the World Union of Zionist Revisionists, Bulletin no. 2, May 1934, IDF* 2300.
18. DBG to Mapai Central Committee, Oct. 27–28, 1934; *ZBG*, vol. II, pp. 182–271.
19. Kurt Blumenfeld, *Im Kampf um den Zionismus* (Stuttgart: Deutsche Verlag-Anstalt, 1976), p. 137.
20. V. Jabotinsky to DBG, Oct. 15, 23, 29, Dec. 19, 1934, Mar. 30, May 2, 1935, see also *YBG*, July 15, 1936; DBG to Jabotinsky, Oct. 19, 28, 1934, Apr. 28, Dec. 11, 1935, Jan. 21, 1937; *LP*, p. 158; *ZBG*, vol. II, pp. 182–271.
21. DBG to Mapai Central Committee, Oct. 27–28, 1934; *ZBG*, vol. II, pp. 182–271.
22. *BKN*, Oct. 27, 1934, *BB;* BK telegram, Nov. 8, 1934, *MBG;* Sharett telegram to DBG on behalf of Eliyahu Golomb and others, Oct. 29, 1934, *ZBG*, vol. II, p. 215.
23. Geula letter, two letters from ABG, undated; DBG to ABG, Nov. 8, 1934, *ZBG*, vol. II, p. 229.
24. *YBG*, Nov. 11, 1934.
25. *JAG*, Oct. 29, 1934; *YBG*, Oct. 29, 1934.
26. *BGPA*.
27. *MAP* (Central Committee), Oct. 28, 31, Nov. 20, 1934; Itzhak Ben-Aharon to DBG, Nov. 1, 1934.
28. *MAP* (Central Committee), Oct. 31, Nov. 24, 28, Dec. 17, 20, 1934, Jan. 21, Feb. 11, 24, Mar. 4, 1935, *MAP* (convention), Mar. 24, 1935; *Ha-Poel ha-Tzair* 9, Dec. 3, 1934; YT to Mapai Central Committee, Dec. 16, 1934; *ZBG*, vol. II, pp. 216, 272–277, 290–299; *HISE*, Dec. 27, 1934, Jan. 21, 1935; *Davar*, Feb. 3, Mar. 26, 1935.
29. Jabotinsky to DBG, Mar. 3, May 2, 1935; DBG to Jabotinsky, Apr. 28, 1935.

Chapter 30: The New Executive

1. *BKN*, 1935, *BB; YBG*, Apr. 14, 1969.
2. DBG telegram to Rega from Trieste, Apr. 29, 1935; *YBG*, Apr. 29, May 3, 1935, Apr. 14, 1969; *ZBG*, vol. II, pp. 300–304; DBG to Paula from London, May 7, 1935; letter to Paula with vowel signs, written from ship, May 8, 1935.
3. Geula to DBG, May 1, June 14, 1935; DBG letter to ABG from London, May 7, 1935; DBG to Paula and children, May 8, 1935; Renana to DBG, May 9, 1935.
4. Personal interview with Rega Klapholz-Diamant; photographs of Paula and DBG in Klapholz-Diamant's possession.
5. In 1936 and 1937, Klapholz worked for Kupat Holim in the kibbutzim of Emek Yizrael, and in 1938 she was sent to Switzerland for further studies. In

1939 she worked as a general practitioner in Jerusalem, where she married Abraham Diamant, who worked for Solel Boneh and whom she had known since 1937. Abraham and Rega Diamant made their home in Haifa following Diamant's demobilization from the British army.

6. *BKN*, 1935, *BB;* Dov Hoz letter, Aug. 6, 1935, *DRH;* Eliahu Elath to author, Oct. 10, 1977; *ZBG*, vol. II, p. 308; *Memorandum on the Negev* to Louis Brandeis, June 4, 1935, *ZBG*, vol. IV, p. 321; Robert Szold to DBG June 28, 1935, to Brandeis, July 1, 1936, AJA/Brandeis/104; DBG speech at IDF parade in Eilat, Mar. 19, 1959.

7. *BKN*, 1935; *YBG*, Aug. 7, 8, 1935; BK to Leah Katznelson, Aug. 9, 1935, *LBK*, vol. VI.

8. BK to Leah, Aug. 16, 1935; *LBK*, vol. VI; *YBG*, Aug. 14, 1935; *ZBG*, vol. II, pp. 383, 410; *LP*, p. 96.

9. Rivka Hoz to Dov Hoz, Oct. 3, 1935, *DRH.*

10. *LP*, pp. 96–149; *ZBG*, vol. II, pp. 420–438; *YBG*, Sept. 1935; DBG to Paula, Sept. 22, Oct. 6, 1935; Paula telegram to DBG, Sept. 26, 1935.

11. *Der Tag*, May 15, 1935; *HNB*, Jan. 30, 1935; *ZBG*, vol. II, pp. 304, 318; *YBG*, June 1, 1935; *YBG*, Oct. 18, 1929, Dec. 7, 1930 (meeting took place on Dec. 4); *MAP* (council), Feb. 5–8, 1931; Rachel Yanait–Ben-Zvi, *AO.*

12. *HNB*, June 5, 1935; *ZBG*, vol. II, p. 315; DBG to Paula, June 10, 1935; *YBG*, Feb. 6, 1936; *LP*, p. 191; *ZBG*, vol. III, p. 77.

13. *YBG*, May 20, 1935; *MAP* (Political Committee), Mar. 3, 1934; Dov Hoz to DBG, Nov. 5, 1934, *DRH; MAP* (joint meeting of Central Committee and Ha-Shomer ha-Tzair), Nov. 22, 1934; *YBG*, Dec. 27, 1934; DBG conversation with Palcor, Jan. 17, 1935, *IDF* 1374; Locker letter, Feb. 5, 1935, *CZA* S/25/1653; Arthur Ruppin, *Pirkei Hayyai* (Tel Aviv: Am Oved, 1968), vol. III, p. 236; *MAP* (Political Committee), Feb. 14, 1935; Judge Chaim Cohen of Carlebach family, on Israel Television, Feb. 15, 1985.

14. *YBG*, Aug. 30, 1935; *ZBG*, vol. II, pp. 408–410.

15. *MAP* (Central Committee), Aug. 8, 1934, *MAP* (Political Committee), Aug. 19, 1934; *YBG*, June 21, Oct. 9, 1935; *PALCOR*, Jan. 17, 1935; Ruppin, p. 236; DBG to Moshe Sharett, Dec. 12, 1933, *ZBG*, vol. I, p. 715; DBG to Baruch Zuckerman, Dec. 12, 1933; *ZBG*, vol. I, p. 718; DBG to Geula and ABG, Sept. 8, 1935, *ZBG*, vol. II, pp. 416–420, *LP*, pp. 109–113.

16. *YBG*, Dec. 27, 1934, June 3, 5, 20, 1935; *MAP* (Political Committee), Feb. 14, 1935.

17. *MAP* (Central Committee), Aug. 5, 8, 19, 1934.

18. *MAP* (Central Committee), July 28–29, 1935; DBG letter to Geula and ABG, Sept. 8, 1935; *ZBG*, vol. II, pp. 416–420; *YBG*, Sept. 23, 1935.

19. DBG to Zuckerman, Dec. 12, 1933; *ZBG*, vol. I, p. 718; *MAP* (Political Committee), Feb. 14, 1935.

20. *MAP* (Central Committee), Mar. 26, 1935; *YBG*, June 1, 1935; *ZBG*, vol. II, p. 319.

21. *MAP* (Central Committee), Aug. 5, 1934, *MAP* (Political Committee), Dec. 21, 1935; *YBG*, Oct. 9, 10, 26, 1935; *ZBG*, vol. II, pp. 498, 550–559; *JAG*, Dec. 22, 1935; DBG to Weizmann, Oct. 13, 1935; DBG to Sharett, Oct. 13, 1935.

Chapter 31: Weizmann: A Danger to Zionism

1. *MAP* (secretariat), May 12, 1943; *PMA*, p. 70; *YBG*, Jan. 16, Feb. 12, 1936; DBG met with Sir Arthur Wauchope in Jerusalem three times during December 1935 (8, 12, 22); *MAP* (Central Committee), Jan. 19, 1936, *MAP* (Political Committee), Jan. 26, 1936; *JAG*, Jan. 26, 1936; DBG to Itzhak Schwarzbart, Jan. 28, 1936, *ZBG*, vol. III, p. 50; DBG to Lord Melchett, Feb. 4, 1936, *ZBG*, vol. III, p. 64; DBG to A. Ankorion, Mar. 5, 1936, *ZBG*, vol. III, p. 80.

2. Report on Arab agitation, Dec. 27, 1935, *ZBG*, vol. II, p. 560; *ZBG*, vol. III, p. 84 ff.; *PMA*, p. 67; Joshua Porath, *MiMehumot LeMerida* (Tel Aviv: Am Oved, 1978), p. 172; *MAP* (Political Committee), Dec. 2, 1935, *MAP* (Central Committee), Sept. 29, 1936, July 6, 1938.

3. *PMA*, p. 44; J. Porath, pp. 172, 175; the expression "appeasement of the Arabs" in DBG remarks to Weizmann, Jan. 16, 1936; *ZBG*, vol. III. pp. 23, 105.

4. *MAP* (Political Committee), Mar. 9, 1936.

5. *YBG*, Oct. 10, 30, 1935; DBG to H. Margalit, Dec. 30, 1935; *JAG*, Nov. 10, 1935; DBG to Wauchope at Apr. 2, 1936, meeting, *ZBG*, vol. III, pp. 103–109; DBG to Lord Melchett, Feb. 27, 1936.

6. *ZBG*, vol. III, pp. 103–109.

7. *ZBG*, vol. II, p. 466; DBG to Moshe Sharett, Oct. 16, 1935.

8. *ZBG*, vol. II, pp. 486–490; Wauchope's warning (Apr. 18, 1936) in J. Porath, pp. 193–194; Sharett review of debate in Parliament, *MAP* (Central Committee), Apr. 16, 1936.

9. *MAP* (Political Committee), Apr. 9, 1936.

10. DBG to Lord Melchett, Feb. 4, 27, 1936; *MAP* (Political Committee), Mar. 9, July 4, 1936, *MAP* (Central Committee), Apr. 16, 1936; *ZBG*, vol. III, pp. 78, 110; *JAG*, May 9, 1936.

11. *MAP* (Political Committee), Jan. 26, Mar. 9, 1936, *MAP* (Central Committee), Jan. 29, 1936; DBG to Schwarzbart, Jan. 28, 1936, *ZBG*, vol. III, p. 51; DBG to Zionist activists, Jan. 30, 1936, *ZBG*, vol. III, p. 52; DBG to Eliezer Kaplan, Mar. 12, 1936, *ZBG*, vol. III, p. 78.

12. *JAG*, Mar. 22, May 21, 1936; DBG to Kaplan, Mar. 12, 1936; *ZBG*, vol. III, pp. 89, 117; DBG to Zelig Brodetsky, Apr. 9, 1936, *ZBG*, vol. III, p. 115.

13. *YBG*, May 29, June 8, 10, 1936; DBG to Sharett, June 30, 1936, *ZBG*, vol. III, p. 310; Weizmann to Felix Warburg, *WL* XVII/257; *MAP* (Central Committee), July 9, 1936.

14. *MAP* (Central Committee), July 9, 1936; *YBG*, June 8–10, 1936; *PRO*, Cab. 24/263, C.P. 190, June 20, 1936; *BAFFY*, p. 21.

15. DBG to Paula, June 14, 16, 1936; *YBG*, June 14–16, 20–30, July 1, 1936; *LP*, p. 153; DBG telegram to Sharett, June 16, 1936; DBG to Sharett, June 26, 27, 30, 1936; DBG to JAE members, June 23, 1936, *ZBG*, vol. III, p. 293; *WL* XVII/268, 269, 272; protocol of interview at Colonial Office in DBG's handwriting, June 30, 1936, *PRO*, Cab. 34/263, July 4, 1936; Stephen Wise to Louis Brandeis, July 2, 1936, Brandeis Archives (microfilm), Cincinnati; *BAFFY*, July 1, 1936.

16. *MAP* (Political Committee), July 28, 1936; *YBG*, July 1–3, 1936; DBG to Sharett, July 30, 1936, *ZBG*, vol. III, p. 352.

17. *YBG*, July 2–16, 1936; *MAP* (Political Committee), July 6, 1936; *JAG*, July 6, 1936.
18. *MAP* (Central Committee), July 9, 1936, Dec. 8, 1943.

Chapter 32: Exploiting Disaster

1. Joshua Porath, p. 52.
2. Palestine Royal Commission, *Peel Report*, Cmd 5479.
3. DBG to Nahum Goldmann, Apr. 26, 1936; *ZBG*, vol. III, p. 356.
4. Three conversations with Antonius (Apr. 17, 22, 29, 1936), *MBG; PMA*, pp. 47–67; *ZBG*, vol. III, p. 130; *JAG*, Apr. 24, 1936.
5. *AS*, p. 158; *YBG*, Mar. 11, 1936; *MAP* (Political Committee), Mar. 30, 1936; DBG to JAE, June 9, 1936, *ZBG*, vol. III, p. 225.
6. *JAG*, May 19, 20, 1936; DBG-Menahem Ussishkin talk, Nov. 12, 1935, *ZBG*, vol. II, p. 509; *DMS*, vol. I, p. 133; *PMA*, p. 51; *MAP* (Political Committee), Mar. 30, 1936, *MAP* (Central Committee), Apr. 16, 1936.
7. *JAG*, May 19, 1936; *MAP* (Political Committee), Mar. 9, 30, 1936, *MAP* (Central Committee), Apr. 16, 1936.
8. *MAP* (Central Committee), Apr. 16, 1936; *MAP* (council), Jan. 23, 1937.
9. Defense program, *L* IV/208/225, IDF 794; *MAP* (Political Committee), Jan. 26, 1936, *MAP* (Central Committee), Apr. 16, 1936.
10. DBG to JAE, June 9, 1936, *ZBG*, vol. III, pp. 197, 255; *JAG*, May 19, Oct. 4, 1936.
11. DBG to Ussishkin, Nov. 11, 1936; *AS*, p. 257 (Sept. 29, 1930); *PHCC*, Feb. 8, 1937; *MAP* (Political Committee), May 4, 1936, *MAP* (Central Committee), Sept. 29, 1936; *JAG*, May 3, 1936, *ZBG*, vol. III, pp. 135, 399; *YBG*, Aug. 31, 1936.
12. *MAP* (Central Committee), May 21, June 3, Aug. 3, 1936, *MAP* (Political Committee), July 28, 1936, *MAP* (council), July 9–11, 1937; DBG to Mapai Central Committee, Aug. 11, 1936; DBG to Sharett, June 13, 1936; *ZBG*, vol. III, pp. 284, 379–389; *ZBG*, vol. III, pp. 363–368; *ZBG*, vol. III, pp. 379–389; *JAG*, May 19, 1936, *ZBG*, vol. III, p. 203; *WBK*, vol. VIII, pp. 178–209; *DV*, vol. II, pp. 283–287.
13. *MAP* (Central Committee), June 3, 1936; *WBK*, vol. VIII, p. 195; DBG to Sharett, Aug. 16, 1936, *ZBG*, vol. III, p. 371; DBG to Ha-Ihud council, Aug. 18, 1936, *ZBG*, vol. III, p. 381; DBG to Mapai Central Committee, Aug. 11, 1936, *ZBG*, vol. III, p. 364; DBG to Sharett, June 24, 1937, *ZBG*, vol. IV, p. 240.
14. *YBG*, June 26, 1937, *ZBG*, vol. IV, p. 252; DBG to Mapai Central Committee, June 18, 1936, *ZBG*, vol. III, p. 281; *PHCC*, Feb. 8, 1937.
15. DBG to JAE, June 9, 1936, *ZBG*, vol. III, p. 257; *MAP* (council), Jan. 27, 1937.
16. National Council protocol (plenum), May, 5, 1936, *ZBG*, vol. III, p. 161; DBG at Ha-Ihud council, Zurich, July 29, 1937, *ZBG*, vol. III, p. 367; *YBG*, July 10–11, 1936.
17. *YBG*, Apr. 20, 1936; assembly of Zionist parties, Jerusalem, Apr. 19, 1936, *ZBG*, vol. III, p. 122; rally organized by National Council, Tel Aviv, May 5, 1936, *ZBG*, vol. III, p. 164; *JAG*, May 15, 1936.
18. DBG to Mapai Central Committee, Aug. 11, 1936, *ZBG*, vol. III, p. 365;

rally of Yishuv representatives, Tel Aviv, Aug. 3,1938; DBG and Sharett to
Wauchope, May 14, 1936, *WA; HISE,* May 11, 21, 1936; National Council
rally, May 5, 1936; *MAP* (Central Committee), July 6, 1938, *MAP* (council),
Apr. 14, 1939; DBG letter to Zalman Shazar, May 31, 1936; argument over
havlaga (self-restraint), *MAP* (Central Committee), May 21, June 11, 1936,
MAP (Political Committee), Apr. 25, 1936; *JAG,* May 15, 17, 1936; DBG to
Mapai Central Committee, June 11, 1936.

19. *JAG,* May 17, 1936; *YBG,* July 11, 1936; DBG at Haganah meeting, Sept. 8,
1939, *IDF* 2957; *MAP* (Central Committee), July 6, 1938.
20. DBG to Shazar, July 17, 1936, *ZBG,* vol. III, p. 342; *JAG,* July 6, 1936; *MAP*
(Political Committee), July 6, Oct. 12, 1936; *YBG,* July 16, 1936; *BAFFY,*
pp. 26, 245; personal interviews with Kitty Stein, Arthur Lourie, Teddy
Kollek; letters from Blanche Dugdale, Doris May, *MBG,* 1936–1952.
21. *YBG,* Aug. 31, Sept. 1, 1936; DBG to Sharett, Sept. 2, 1936, *ZBG,* vol. III,
pp. 401, 402, 405.
22. *YBG,* Sept. 4–9, 1936.

Chapter 33: Taking On the Royal Commission

1. DBG to Zelig Brodetsky, Apr. 9, 1936; *YBG,* May 29, July 18, 1936; *JAG,*
May 3, 15, 19, 1936; *MAP* (Central Committee), May 21, 1936.
2. *YBG,* May 29, July 11, 18, 20, Aug. 30, Nov. 13, 1936; DBG to Brodetsky,
Apr. 9, 1936; DBG to Moshe Sharett, Aug. 16, 24, 1936; *JAG,* May 3, 15, 19,
Oct. 25, Dec. 13, 1936; *ZACS,* Oct. 26, 1936; *MAP* (Central Committee),
May 21, July 9, Aug. 3, 31, Sept. 29, Nov. 9, 1936; *ZBG,* vol. III, pp. 248,
363, 386, 515; *HISE,* July 9, 1936.
3. DBG to Sharett, June 29, 1936; *ZBG,* vol. III, p. 302; DBG to Dov Joseph,
Aug. 16, 1936; *WL* XVII/272, to Sir William Ormsby-Gore, July 1, 1936;
YBG, July 18, 19, 1936; Arthur Lourie to Sharett, July 20, 1936, *MBG; JAG,*
Oct. 25, 1936.
4. *YBG,* July 18, 19, 1936; DBG to Dov Joseph, Aug. 11, 1936; DBG to BK,
Oct. 19, 1936; DBG to Sharett and Eliezer Kaplan, Aug. 11, 1936; *MAP*
(Political Committee), Aug. 5, 1934, *MAP* (Central Committee), July 22,
1936; *JAG,* Aug. 9, Oct. 4, 11, Dec. 13, 1936; *ZACS,* Oct. 14,
1936.
5. DBG to BK, Oct. 19, 1936; *JAG,* Oct. 21, 1936; *LBK,* vol. VI, letter 148, Oct.
24, 1936; *MAP* (Central Committee), Oct. 25, 1936, *MAP* (Political Committee), Dec. 20, 1936; *ZBG,* vol. III, p. 352; May telegram and letter to
DBG, Oct. 28, 1936.
6. *YBG,* July 16, Nov. 6, 1936; DBG to Zalman Shazar, July 3, 1936, DBG to
Dugdale, Oct. 14, 1936; *JAG,* Oct. 11, 21, 25, Nov. 6, 1936; *MAP* (Political
Committee), Dec. 10, 1936; Dugdale to DBG, Oct. 8, 1936; *LBK,* vol. VI,
letter 147, Oct. 16, 1936.
7. *WL* XVII/336, Oct. 14–18, 1936; *WL* XVII/351, Oct. 31, 1936; *ZACS,* Oct.
13–14, 1936; *MAP* (Central Committee), Oct. 12, 1936, *MAP* (Political
Committee), Nov. 9, 1936; *LBK,* vol. VI, letter 148.
8. *LBK,* vol. VI, letter 147; *ZACS,* Nov. 10, 1942; *MAP* (Central Committee),
Sept. 29, 1936, *MAP* (Political Committee), Nov. 9, 1936; *YBG,* Nov. 16–19,
1936; *BKN,* Nov. 18–19, 1936; *Davar,* Nov. 19, 1936.

9. *LBK*, vol. VI, letter 147; *WL*, series B, vol. II, document 24; *ZACS*, Oct. 13, 26, 1936.

10. Lourie to DBG, Nov. 12, 1936; *YBG*, Nov. 20, 1936; *MAP* (Political Committee), Dec. 20, 1936.

11. *YBG*, Nov. 25, 1936; *JAG*, Nov. 22, 1936; *ZACS*, Nov. 23, 1936; *MAP* (Central Committee), Dec. 10, 1936; *WL*, series B, vol. II, documents 22, 23; *Davar*, Nov. 27, 1936; *BKN*, Nov. 26, 1936.

12. *WL*, series B, vol. II, document 23; *Ha-Aretz supplement*, July 3, 1981, "Barukh HaBa LeMalon Palace"; *BKN*, Nov. 27, Dec. 5, 1936; *YBG*, Nov. 26–Dec. 5, Dec. 9, 1936; *JAG*, Nov. 30, 1936.

13. *JAG*, Dec. 20, 23, 1936; *MAP* (Political Committee), Dec. 10, *MAP* (Central Committee), Dec. 20, 1936; *HISE*, Dec. 17, 1936; *ZACS*, Dec. 21, 1936; *YBG*, Dec. 12, 15, 17, 24, 30, 1936; DBG to Weizmann, Dec. 24, 1936; *BKN*, Dec. 12, 22, 27, 29, 30, 1936; *WL*, series B, vol. II, document 24; *ZBG*, vol. III, p. 528.

14. *YBG*, Dec. 30, 1936, Jan. 25, 1937; *ZBG*, vol. IV, p. 31, *WL* XVIII/4; *ZACS*, Jan. 13, 1937; *JAG*, Dec. 25, 1936, Jan. 3, 1937.

Chapter 34: Grappling with Partition

1. *MAP* (Central Committee), Dec. 8, 1943; *HISE*, Feb. 23–24, 1944; *JAG*, Jan. 10, 1937, Mar. 16, 1941; Histadrut councils, Feb. 7, 1937, Mar. 21–24, 1944; *BAMA*, vol. I, pp. 53–54; Knesset protocols, Jan. 4, 1950; *ZBG*, vol. IV, p. 11; DBG introduction to *Toledot Milhemet HaKommemiyut* (Tel Aviv: Ma'arakhot, 1959).

2. *Peel Report*, Cmd. 5479; *WL*, series B, vol. II, document 26.

3. *JAG*, Jan. 10, 1937; *ZACS*, Jan. 13, 1937; *MAP* (Central Committee), Feb. 5–6, 1937, *MAP* (political consultation), June 8, 1937; *Davar* (evening edition), Jan. 18, 1937; Norman Rose, *The Gentile Zionists* (London: Frank Cass, 1973), pp. 127–128; *YBG*, Feb. 4, June 26, 1937; *ZBG*, vol. IV, pp. 252, 282.

4. *MAP* (Central Committee), Feb. 5–6, Apr. 10, 1937; *ZBG*, vol. IV, pp. 282, 328; *DMS*, vol. II, pp. 62–71; *YBG*, Apr. 7, 1937; *JAG*, Jan. 3, Apr. 11, 1937; *Ha-Poel ha-Tzair* 4, March/April, 1937; *PHCC*, Feb. 8, 1937; DBG introduction to *Toledot Milhemet HaKommemiyut*.

5. *Ha-Poel ha-Tzair* 4, March/April 1937; *BAFFY*, Feb. 17, Mar. 2, 1937; *MAP* (Central Committee), Feb. 5, Apr. 10, 1937, Dec. 8, 1943; *JAG*, Apr. 11, 1937; *YBG*, June 9, 1937; DBG to ABG, July 27, 1937; *ZBG*, vol. IV, p. 329.

6. DBG to Moshe Sharett, Mar. 18, 1937; *ZACS*, Mar. 22, Apr. 20, 1937; *JAG*, Apr. 11, May 2, 1937; *WL* XVIII/77; *YBG*, May 5, 1937.

7. *YBG*, May 6–27, 29–31, June 1, 7, 9, 11, 1937; DBG to Sharett, June 1, 1937; *MAP* (Central Committee), June 8, 1937; *LBK*, vol. VI, letter 148; *BAFFY*, June 9, 1937; Rose, pp. 131–133.

8. *MAP* (Central Committee), Apr. 10, *MAP* (political consultation), June 8, 1937; *YBG*, June 9, 11, 12, 15, 1937; *BAFFY*, Apr. 27, 1937; *BAMA*, vol. I, pp. 217–221; *LP*, p. 173; colloquium on partition, June 14, 1937, attended by DBG, BK, Golomb, Weizmann, Hoz, *MBG;* *WL* XVIII/107; DBG to

Noy and Shurer, June 2, 1937; DBG to Bankover, June 13, 1937; DBG to Ussishkin, July 3, 1937; *ZBG*, vol. IV, pp. 201, 272.

9. There was a gap in Weizmann's calendar between June 21 and 28, 1937, his telegram of June 22 to Doris May is in *WA*: STAYING CLARIDGES CHAMPS ELYSEES; DBG to Paula, June 22, 1937; Weizmann to DBG, June 24, 1937 (original in Russian), *MBG*.

10. *MAP* (Central Committee), June 20–21, 1937, *MAP* (political consultation), June 23, 1937; DBG letter to ZE, Jerusalem, June 22, 1937; DBG to Sharett, June 25, 1937; *YBG*, June 11, 1937; exchange of telegrams between DBG, Bankover, and Laufbahn, *BB* 37/101; exchange of telegrams between BK, Golomb, and DBG, July 8, 1937, *MBG*.

11. DBG to Paula, June 1, 4, 12, 16 (shortened version in *LP*, p. 173), also telegram, 22, 28 (telegram), 29, 1937, *LP*, pp. 170–174; *BAFFY*, June 29, 1937; *YBG*, July 4, 1937.

12. DBG to Sharett (and Mapai council), July 3, 1937; DBG to Paula, June 29, 1937, *LP*, p. 174; *BAFFY*, June 29, July 2, 4, 1937; *YBG*, July 4, 5, 7, 1937; *ZBG*, vol. IV, p. 120.

13. Paula telegram to DBG, July 6, 1937; DBG telegrams to Paula, July 9, 12 (2), 1937; *YBG*, July 9, 13–15, 26, 29, 1937; DBG to ABG, July 28, 1937, *LP*, p. 185; Tamar (Hoz) Gidron stated that the car was a "Terraplain."

Chapter 35: First Seed

1. *Ha-Aretz*, Sept. 30, 1966; *Peel Report*, Cmd. 5379; *White Paper*, Cmd. 5513.

2. *YBG*, June 11, 1937; *The 20th Zionist Congress*, mimeographed report (WZO, JAE, Jerusalem), p. 95 ff.; *ZBG*, vol. IV, pp. 276, 385; DBG letter to Moshe Sharett, July 3, 1937.

3. *YBG*, July 4, 11, 1937; *Daily Herald*, July 9, 1937; DBG to Mapai Central Committee, July 1, 1937; DBG to Sharett, July 3, 1937; DBG speech, Ihud Council, July 29, 1937; *ZBG*, vol. IV, pp. 256, 276, 334; *MAP* (Special Central Committee), Oct. 20, 1940.

4. DBG to Mapai Central Committee, July 1, 1937; *ZBG*, vol. IV, p. 392; *YBG*, July 22, 1937; DBG to Sharett and Eliezer Kaplan, July 22, 1937, *ZBG*, vol. IV, p. 311; *MAP* (Central Committee), June 6, 20–21, 1937; *20th Zionist Congress*, p. 95 ff.; DBG to Bankover, June 13, 1937; DBG to ABG, Oct. 5, 1937; DBG to Paula, Oct. 7, 1937; *YBG*, June 26, 28, July 18, 1937; *ZBG*, vol. IV, pp. 250, 253, 256, 338.

5. *MAP* (Central Committee), June 7, 1937; *LBK*, vol. VI, letter 199; *ZBG*, vol. IV, p. 249; YT, *MiBifnim*, July 1937; personal interview with DBG (reel 5); BK to Mapai Central Committee, June 12, 1937.

6. DBG to ABG, July 27–28, 1937; *LP*, p. 175; DBG to Sharett, July 23, 1937; *ZBG*, vol. IV, pp. 318–321; DBG to Sharett and Kaplan, July 22, 1937; *ZBG*, vol. IV, p. 311; *LBK*, vol. VI, letter 223; *20th Zionist Congress*, p. 218.

7. *LBK*, vol. VI, letters 218, 219, 222; Dov Hoz to Rivka Hoz, June 30, 1937, *DRH*; *MAP* (secretariat), Dec. 4, 1942; *Forward* (Yiddish), Sept. 11, 1937; *YBG*, July 29, 1937.

8. Interview on Israel Television, Golda Meir with Yaron London, Dec. 8, 1978; DBG to Ben-Zion Katz, Sept. 1, 1957.

9. *DMS*, vol. II, p. 236; *YBG*, July 29, 1937; *ZBG*, vol. IV, p. 338; Hoz to Rivka, Oct. 7, 1937, *DRH*.
10. *20th Zionist Congress*, pp. 196, 350; *DMS*, vol. II, pp. 280, 287; Rivka Hoz to Ada Golomb, Aug. 1937, *DRH; LBK*, vol. VI, letter 222.
11. DBG telegram to Sprinzak, July 5, 1937; *MAP* (secretariat), Dec. 4, 1942; *20th Zionist Congress*, part II, 5th sitting, JA council; *SL*, vol. II, p. 346; DBG to Weizmann, Aug. 22, 1937; *ZBG*, vol. IV, pp. 422–424.
12. *BKN*, Aug. 21, 22, 1937; *LBK*, vol. VI, letters 223, 224; *SL*, vol. II, p. 344; *YBG*, Aug. 23–28, 1937.
13. *YBG*, Aug. 28–Sept. 3, 1937; DBG to Paula, Sept. 13, 1937; *LP*, pp. 188–202; Maurice Wertheim telegram to DBG and DBG reply, Aug. 29, 1937; *ZBG*, vol. IV, pp. 427, 429; *SL*, vol. II, p. 347.
14. *YBG*, Sept. 3–11, 1937; *LP*, pp. 189–202; *ZBG*, vol. IV, pp. 429–433; DBG to Paula, Sept. 13, to Kaplan, Sept. 14, to Poale Zion, America, Sept. 10, 1937; BK to Leah Katznelson, Nov. 24, 1937.
15. *Forward* (Yiddish), Sept. 9, 11, 1937; Wertheim to DBG, Sept. 14, 1937; Wertheim telegram to DBG and DBG reply, Oct. 10, 1937; DBG to Kaplan, Sept. 14–17, 1937; *LP*, pp. 202–204; BK to Leah, Nov. 24, 1937; DBG to ABG, Oct. 5, 1937.

Chapter 36: The Great Deception

1. BK and Moshe Sharett telegram to DBG, Sept. 14, 1937; Doris May telegram to DBG, Sept. 16, 1937; DBG to Paula, Sept. 17, 1937, *LP*, p. 204; *YBG*, Sept. 16, 1937.
2. *The 20th Zionist Congress*, p. 100; *DMS*, vol. II, Sept. 19, 1937; *LP*, pp. 204, 205; *YBG*, Sept. 11, 1937; Sharett to BK, Sept. 22, 1937, *BB*.
3. DBG to Paula, Sept. 24, 1937; *WL* XVIII/178; *MAP* (Central Committee), Oct. 10, 1937; Eliyahu Golomb to DBG, Oct. 11, 1937, *DRH; HNB*, Sept. 1, 16, 1937.
4. DBG to Paula, Oct. 7, 1937; *LP*, p. 214.
5. Report of Partition (Woodhead) Commission, Cmd. 5854; cabinet conclusions, *PRO* FO 371/20822 46(37); Palestine statement by His Majesty's government, Cmd. 5893; Elie Kedourie, *Islam in the Modern World* (London: Mansell, 1980), p. 167; personal interview with Malcolm MacDonald, Dec. 9, 1980; MacDonald remarks to Ambassador Ephraim Evron; Berl Locker to DBG, Aug. 7, 1938; *WL* XVIII/382.
6. *BAFFY*, Sept. 14, 1937; *WL* XVIII/290; DBG to BK, June 13, 1938; DBG to Paula, Sept. 20, Oct. 5, 1937, Mar. 16, 23, 1938; *LP*, pp. 205, 210, 223; DBG to Kaplan, Sept. 24, 1937; DBG to Sharett, Sept. 21, 1938; DBG to JAE, Oct. 3, 1938; *MAP* (Central Committee), Jan. 5, Mar. 16, June 1, 1938; *Davar*, Jan. 5, 1938; DBG article, *Davar*, Jan. 9, 1938; *JAG*, May 8, 20, June 7, 1938; *BKN*, Sept. 21, 1938; *YBG*, Nov. 8, 1938.
7. *MAP* (Central Committee), Apr. 4, 7, 16, 1936, June 8, 1938; *MAP* (convention), May 8, 1938; *JAG*, June 6, 26, 1938, Feb. 16, 1941; *ZBG*, vol. V, p. 219; *YBG*, Dec. 14, 1941; *20th Zionist Congress*, p. 107; *ZACS*, Oct. 26, 1936, Oct. 15, 1942.
8. *Forward* (Yiddish), Sept. 11, 1937; *JAG*, Jan. 30, Feb. 6, 20–22, 1938; *MAP* (Central Committee), Feb. 28, Apr. 4, May 17, 1938; DBG to Paula,

Mar. 16, 1938; *ZBG* vol. V, pp. 126, 148; *LP*, p. 222; *YBG*, Mar. 12, 1938; ZAC, Mar. 10, 1938.

9. DBG to Paula, Feb. 24, 1938; BK to DBG, Mar. 3, 31, 1938; DBG to BK, Mar. 16, 1938; *MAP* (Central Committee), Apr. 4, 1938; *JAG*, Apr. 10, 1938; *LP*, p. 219; *ZBG*, vol. V, pp. 121, 127; ZAC, Mar. 10, 1938.

10. *MAP* (convention), May 7, 1938.

11. Ibid.; DBG to JAE, Oct. 20, 1938; *ZBG*, vol. V, p. 346.

12. *JAG*, Oct. 5, 1936; *MAP* (Central Committee), Apr. 10, 1937; *YBG*, Mar. 8, Oct. 7, 1938; DBG to GBE, Oct. 1, 1938; *IG*, p. 4; *ZBG*, vol. IV, p. 423.

13. *YBG*, Sept. 13, 14, 27–28, 1938; DBG to Sharett, Sept. 20, 1938; DBG to GBE and Schwarzbart, Sept. 26, 1938; DBG to JA members, Oct. 3, 1938.

14. *YBG*, Sept. 28, 30, 1938; DBG telegrams to Sharett, Sept. 28, 1938; DBG to Renana, Sept. 30, 1938; DBG to GBE, Oct. 1, 1938.

15. *MAP* (Political Committee), Oct. 3, 1938; Dov Hoz to Rivka Hoz, Oct. 3, 1938; Rivka to Dov, Oct. 1938, *DRH; DMS*, vol. III, pp. 334, 337; *WL* XVIII/388; *YBG*, Aug. 21, Sept. 15, 1938; DBG to Sharett, Sept. 18, 1938.

16. *JAG*, Sept. 12, 1938; *YBG*, Sept. 13–15, 1938; *BAFFY*, p. 101; DBG to Sharett, Sept. 18, 20, 21, 1938; *ZBG*, vol. V, pp. 251, 256, 258, 266.

17. *YBG*, Oct. 5, 6, 13, 16, 25, 26, 30, 1938; Lourie telegram to Sharett, Dec. 4, 1938, *CZA* S25/7626; Dov Hoz to Sharett, Oct. 22, 1938, *DRH;* DBG to Malcolm MacDonald, Oct. 31, 1938; *ZBG*, vol. V, p. 377; *BAFFY*, p. 114; interview with DBG for David Lloyd George, Nov. 22, 1938; *MAP* (Political Committee), Oct. 26, 1938; *BKN*, Oct. 15, 1938.

Chapter 37: November 1938

1. *YBG*, Oct. 1, 1938; DBG to JAE members, Oct. 3, 1938.

2. Personal interviews with GBE, ABG, RLGB; DBG to GBE, Feb. 18, 28, Sept. 26, Nov. 1, 1938; GBE to DBG, Feb. 28, 1938; DBG to children, Oct. 21, 27, 1938; Israel Bar-Shira to Paula, Sept. 29, 1938.

3. DBG to Paula, June 18, Aug. 14, 22, 1936; DBG to A. Yellin, director of Department of Education, Nov. 30, 1936; DBG to Arthur Lourie, July 1, 1938; ABG to DBG, Sept. 18, 1938; personal interviews with ABG, GBE.

4. Kahana's candy store was at 47a Allenby Street and the family lived at 33 Zevulun Street; DBG to Paula, June 12, 1937; DBG to Renana, Feb. 16, Nov. 4, 1938; Renana to DBG, Feb. 6, Aug. 18, 23, Sept. 11, Oct. 28, 1938; Yonah Kahana to Paula, Aug. 25, 1938.

5. Renana to DBG, Feb. 6, 1938; DBG to Renana, Feb. 16, Mar. 1, Sept. 30, Nov. 4, 1938; DBG to Paula, Feb. 18, Mar. 16, 31, Oct. 1, 29, 1938; DBG telegrams to Paula, Mar. 22, Sept. 22, 1938; *LP*, p. 217; Paula to DBG, Oct. 3, 1938; Fodiman to DBG, Oct. 3, 1938; *BKN*, Mar. 29, 1938; DBG to GBE, Sept. 21, 26, Nov. 1, 4, 1938; DBG to Aisenberg (telegram), Sept. 14, 20, 1938; *MAP* (Political Committee), Oct. 26, 1938.

6. *MAP* (Central Committee), Apr. 25, May 17, June 29, July 6, 1938, *MAP* (council), Dec. 15–16, 1939, *MAP* (convention), May 3–5, 1938; DBG to Mapai secretariat, Oct. 28, 1938; DBG to Eliyahu Golomb, Sept. 27, Oct. 12, 1938; DBG to Moshe Sharett, Sept. 29, 1938; *Ha-Yarden*, Oct. 31, 1938; Dov Hoz to Rivka Hoz, Nov. 4, 1938, *DRH.*

7. DBG to children, Oct. 7, 1938; DBG to Itzhak Gruenbaum, Oct. 11, 1938;

DBG to Dov Joseph, Oct. 18, 1938; DBG to Paula, Oct. 7, 1937; *LP*, p. 245.

8. *YBG*, Nov. 9, 1938; *MAP* (Political Committee), Mar. 30, 1936; *MAP* (Central Committee), Apr. 16, 1936, Apr. 10, 1937; *Davar*, Nov. 15, 1938; DBG speech to council, Ha-Ihud Ha-Olami Poale Zion (Z.S.), Apr. 26, 1939; *YBG*, Feb. 22, 1938, Jan. 3, 1939; DBG to Sharett, Sept. 18, 20, 1938; *BAFFY* (Jan. 19, Sept. 19, 1938), pp. 77, 99; *ZBG*, vol. V, pp. 263, 265; DBG to JAE, Oct. 3, 1938.

9. *ZBG*, vol. V, p. 396; *PRO* Cab. 23 [38]; *YBG*, Sept. 15, 1938; DBG to JAE, Oct. 3, 1938; DBG to Sharett, Sept. 20, 1938.

10. *MAP* (Central Committee), Nov. 1, Dec. 7, 1938; *YBG*, Oct. 21, 1938; *PRO* FO 371/23223–23228, recorded from talks, Feb. 15, 20, 24–27, 1939; *DMS*, vol. IV, pp. 58, 90.

11. DBG, Yishuv rally, Dec. 12, 1938; Cmd. 6019; DBG, Tel Aviv Workers Council, July 27, 1939, *IDF* 2957 (censored version, *Davar*, July 30, 1939); *YBG*, Nov. 24, 26, Dec. 10, 1938, Mar. 24, 1939; DBG report on conversation with Malcolm MacDonald, *IDF* 2972; DBG to MacDonald, Nov. 26, 1938; *MAP* (Central Committee), Dec. 7, 1938; *DMS*, vol. IV, p. 558.

Chapter 38: The Kings of the Jews in America

1. *MAP* (Rehovot convention), May 7, 1938; DBG to Moshe Sharett, Sept. 20, 1938; DBG to GBE, ABG, and Renana, Oct. 7, 1938; *Yediot HaMercaz*, Oct. 24, 1938; Oct. 7 letter was discussed at MAP Central Committee, Oct. 26, 1938; DBG to JAE, Oct. 3, 1938; *BKN*, Nov. 27, Dec. 1, 1938; *MAP* (Central Committee), Dec. 7, 1938; *YBG*, Dec. 12, 1938.

2. *YBG*, Dec. 10, 1938, Jan. 3, 12, 1939; *JAG*, Dec. 11, 1938, Jan. 4, 1939; *MAP* (Central Committee), Dec. 15, 1938.

3. *JAG*, Dec. 11, 15, 1938; *YBG*, Dec. 10, 17, 1938, Jan. 4, 1939; *MAP* (Central Committee), Dec. 15, 19, 1938; *ZAC*, Nov. 16, 1938; Sharett telegram to DBG from London, Dec. 16, 1938.

4. *YBG*, Dec. 21–24, 1938, Jan. 3, 1939; DBG to Eliezer Kaplan, Dec. 21, 1938; DBG to Paula, Dec. 22, 1938, Jan. 1, 1939.

5. *ZACS*, Oct. 26, 1936; *PHCC*, Feb. 8, 1937, July 25–26, 1938; *The 20th Zionist Congress*, p. 107; *YBG*, Feb. 22, 1938.

6. *PHCC*, Feb. 8, 1937; G. Rivlin, ed., *La'esh ve Lamagen, Toledot Hanotrut HaIvrit* (Tel Aviv, 1962), pp. 26–28; *MAP* (Central Committee), May 4, 1936; DBG at world council, Ihud Poale Zion (Z.S.), Zurich, Aug. 4, 1937; *ZBG*, vol. IV, p. 374; DBG at Haganah meeting, Sept. 8, 1939; *BAMA*, vol. III, pp. 8, 61; *BGPA*, p. 326; *YBG*, Apr. 4, 1941.

7. *20th Zionist Congress*, p. 107; *YBG*, Feb. 22, 1938; *BGPA*, p. 326; DBG at Haganah meeting, Sept. 8, 1939; *MAP* (Central Committee), July 27, 1941.

8. Personal interview with DBG (reel 5); *BAFFY*, pp. 77, 96.

9. *YBG*, Oct. 6, 1938; *WL* XVIII/404; *MAP* (Central Committee), Dec. 7, 1938; *YBG*, Sept. 15, 22, 1938, Apr. 9, 1939.

10. Rabbi Solomon Goldman to DBG, Oct. 23, 1938, cited in Allon Gal, *David Ben-Gurion — Likrat Medinah Yehudit* (Kiriyat Sde Boker, 1985), p. 10; DBG to Goldman, Oct. 21, 27, 1938; *YBG*, Oct. 17, 1938; DBG to JAE, Oct. 20, 1938; *MAP* (Central Committee), Dec. 15, 1938; *JAG*, Dec. 11, 1938.

11. *YBG*, Jan. 1–24, 1939; DBG to Paula, Jan. 6, 12, 1939; *HNB*, Jan. 11, 1939;

Morris Hexter to Cyrus Adler, Jan. 3, 1939, Adler to Hexter, Jan. 9, 1939, cited in Gal, pp. 20, 21; DBG to Goldman, Jan. 20, 1939; Naomi W. Cohen, *Not Free to Desist — The American Jewish Committee* (Philadelphia, 1972), pp. 202–204 (cited by Gal).

12. DBG to Paula, Jan. 27, 1939.

Chapter 39: The Great Formula

1. *YBG*, Jan. 28, 29, Mar. 6, Apr. 9, 1939; DBG to Paula, Mar. 6, 1939.
2. *YBG*, Jan. 30, 31, Apr. 1, 1939; *DMS*, vol. IV, p. 107; DBG to Paula, Feb. 10, 1939.
3. DBG to Paula, Feb. 7, 9, 10, 1939; *YBG*, Feb. 10, 1939; *DMS*, vol. IV, pp. 19, 29, 41; *MAP* (Central Committee), Feb. 22, 1939; *PRO* FO 371/23223; *BKN*, Feb. 15, 1939.
4. DBG to Paula, Mar. 16, 1939; DBG to JAE, Mar. 22, 1939; *MAP* (Central Committee), Feb. 22, 1939.
5. *DMS*, vol. IV, p. 70; *YBG*, Feb. 21, 1939; DBG notation in English of "private conversation" with Malcolm MacDonald; DBG notation in English of meeting with Lord Halifax, Feb. 21, 1939.
6. *DMS*, vol. IV, pp. 89, 91, 93; *CZA* S25/7647; "General Summary," *PRO* FO 371/23227; *Davar*, Feb. 27, 1939.
7. Reuven Shiloah to Dov Hoz, Feb. 27, 1939; *L* IV 104/28; *DMS*, vol. IV, pp. 90, 94–96; *YBG*, Feb. 11, 1939; *PRO* FO 371/23226, meeting, Feb. 27, 1939; *YBG*, Feb. 18, 1939; *ZBG*, vol. VI, p. 119.
8. *DMS*, vol. IV, pp. 99, 104, 106; *ZBG*, vol. VI, p. 122; *BKN*, Mar. 3, 1939; DBG telegram to Rabbi Solomon Goldman, Mar. 3, 1939; *YBG*, Mar. 15, 19, 1939; DBG to Paula, Mar. 6, 16, 1939; DBG to JAE, Mar. 22, 1939.
9. *BAFFY*, Feb. 25, 1939, p. 125; *YBG*, Apr. 1, 1939; DBG to Paula, Feb. 7, Mar. 6, 1939; *LP*, p. 284; *DMS*, vol. IV, pp. 60, 73, 101, 135.
10. *DMS*, vol. IV, pp. 60, 117, 121, 132, 167; *WL* XIX/29 (Mar. 10, 1939), 35 (Mar. 17, 1939); *YBG*, Mar. 17, 1939; *BKN*, Mar. 8, 9, 1939; DBG to JAE, Mar. 22, 1939; Eliezer Kaplan to DBG, Feb. 24, 1939; British Intelligence, *CZA* S25/4351.
11. DBG to Paula, Mar. 16, 1939; DBG to JAE, Mar. 22, 1939.
12. *MAP* (Political Committee), Mar. 8, 1939; *YBG*, Feb. 2, 4, Mar. 10, 15, Apr. 1, 1939; notation of discussion in Mapai faction of delegation, London, Feb. 24, 1939.
13. *YBG*, Mar. 24, 1939; Meir Avizohar, *Hatzionut Halohemet* (Kiriyat Sde Boker, 1985), p. 36; DBG to Goldman, Mar. 23, 1939; Solomon Goldman-Stephen Wise telegram to DBG, Mar. 24, 1939; DBG to JAE, Mar. 22, 1939.
14. DBG to Paula, Mar. 6, 16, 1939; *ZBG*, vol. V, pp. 302–308; *MAP* (Political Committee), Apr. 5, 1939; DBG to JAE, Mar. 22, 1939; *YBG*, Apr. 9, 1939; *Official Gazette*, Apr. 12, 1939; DBG to Harold MacMichael, Apr. 13, 1939; *JAG*, May 2, 1939.
15. *YBG*, Dec. 17, 1938, Apr. 19, 21, 22, May 22, 25, 31, June 11, 1939; Economic Research Institute document, May 14, 1939; *Davar*, June 4, 1939; *MAP* (Central Committee), May 28, July 5, 1939; *JAG*, July 16, 1939; Avizohar, p. 39.
16. *YBG*, May 1, 1939; *DMS*, vol. IV, p. 91; *MAP* (Political Committee), May 4,

1936, Apr. 5, May 28, 1939; *The 21st Zionist Congress* (ZE and JAE publication, Jerusalem, 1939), p. 96 (Aug. 18, 1939) ; *MAP* (Central Committee), Sept. 12, 1939, Mar. 19, 1941; *JAG*, Sept. 17, 1939; *ZACS*, Dec. 7, 1939; DBG announcement, May 12, 1940; Golda Meir, Israel Television, Dec. 8, 1978.

Chapter 40: Struggle within a Struggle

1. *PRO* FO 371/23223–23228; DBG to JAE, Mar. 22, 1939; *ZAC*, Apr. 24, 1939; DBG to General R. H. Haining, May 19, 1939; *Sefer Hama'al* (JAE publication, 1939), May 18, 1939; *Davar*, May 19, 1939; *The Great Betrayal—Analysis of Statement of Policy* (London, 1939); *DMS*, vol. IV, p. 298; *BAMA*, vol. II, pp. 112, 121, 157, 158, 162, 167, 180; *YBG*, May 1, 1939; *ZACS*, May 3, 1939.

2. *YBG*, May 24, 25, 30, June 4, 5, 9, 13, 16, 19, July 4, 5, 7, 10, 11, Aug. 10, 1939; *JAG*, June 8, 1939; *MAP* (Central Committee), July 5, 1939; *IDF* 2008, 2045.

3. *BKN*, Oct. 6, 10, 23, Nov. 22, 1938, Jan. 29, Mar. 14, May 30, June 2, 1939; *YBG*, Oct. 26, Nov. 22, Dec. 12, 1938, Jan. 28, 29, Mar. 10, May 2, 22, June 3, 5, 6, 1939; *JAG*, Jan. 29, May 30, June 4, 1939; *MAP* (Political Committee), Apr. 5, 1939, *MAP* (Central Committee), May 28, 1939; *DMS*, vol. IV, pp. 34, 77, 176; Dov Joseph to Moshe Sharett, Jan. 30, 1939, *CZA* S25/1515; Vladimir Jabotinsky to Pinchas Rutenberg, Mar. 3, 1939, *CZA* S25/2072.

4. Figures for immigration, illegal immigration, land acquisition, and settlement according to *BH;* Mordechai Naor, *HaHa'apala 1934–1948* (Ministry of Defence publication, 1978); *YBG*, Aug. 1, 3, 4, 1939; *MAP* (council), Apr. 14–16, 1939; *JAG*, Apr. 23, 1939; DBG speech to labor faction, Zionist Congress (translated from Yiddish), *IDF* 2957; DBG to Mapai students, Jerusalem, Mar. 6, 1961.

5. *MAP* (council), Apr. 14–16, 1939; *ZACS*, June 26–27, 1939.

6. DBG to limited cadre of Haganah commanders, Sept. 8, 1939; DBG at meeting with Socialist Youth recruits, March or April 1943.

7. *JAG*, July 9, 1939; *YBG*, June 7, 8, Sept. 5, 1939, Nov. 14, 1940; Harold MacMichael to Malcolm MacDonald, Oct. 14, 1939, *PRO* FO 371/23251; *YBG*, Oct. 15, 17, 24, 1939; *BKN*, Oct. 16, 17, 1939, July 6, Nov. 7, 1941, Jan. 1, 3, 1942; *JAG*, Aug. 25, 1940; DBG to Paula from London, Sept. 8, 1940; *MAP* (Political Committee), Jan. 9, 21, Aug. 18, 1940, *MAP* (Central Committee), Nov. 2, Dec. 12, 1939, Feb. 19, 1941; *JAG*, Jan. 7, Nov. 28, 1940, Feb. 16, 1941; *HISE*, Jan. 18, 1940; see note 3.

8. *MAP* (council), Dec. 14–16, 1939; *YBG*, Nov. 23, 1939, Jan. 29, 1940; *ZACS*, Dec. 27, 1939; Sharett telegram to DBG, Dec. 25, 1939; *JAG*, Dec. 3, 26, 1939; Protocol, 21st Zionist Congress (Political Committee), Aug. 21, 1939.

9. The regulations were published in supplement 2, *Official Gazette*, special issue 988, Feb. 28, 1940; *YBG*, Jan. 29, 1940; letter from first secretary, J. MacPherson, to JAE, Feb. 26, 1940, with copy of the land regulations.

10. *Davar*, Feb. 29, 1940; *BAMA*, vol. II, p. 190.

11. *ZACS*, Feb. 29, Mar. 26, 1940; *JAG*, Feb. 4, 29, Apr. 8, 1940; *MAP* (Central Committee), Feb. 28, 1940.

12. *JAG*, Apr. 8, 1940; *BAFFY*, p. 157; *ZACS*, Feb. 29, 1940; A. Ruppin, *Pirkei*

Hayyai, vol. III, p. 324; Sharett telegram to JAE, London, Apr. 9, 1940, CZA S25/10582.

13. *JAG,* Apr. 8, 1940; *DMS,* vol. V, p. 323; *MAP* (Central Committee), Apr. 9, 1940; *Der Taglisher Yiddisher Courier,* Apr. 3, 1940; Sharett telegram to JAE, London, Apr. 9, 1940; Reuven Shiloah order, Apr. 12, 1940, CZA S35/4732; *DMS,* vol. V, p. 323; Rivka Hoz to Dov Hoz, Apr. 12, 1940, *DRH.*

Chapter 41: An Ultimatum for Weizmann

1. Golda Meir, Israel Television, Dec. 8, 1978; Abraham Katznelson remarks, *MAP* (Central Committee), Mar. 19, 1941; *HB*; *CHR*; *YBG,* June 21, 1939; "Conquering Settlement," *YBG,* June 21, 1939.

2. *JAG,* Feb. 27, Mar. 7, Apr. 21, 1940; Moshe Sharett telegram to London, Apr. 9, 1940, *CZA* S25/10582; Weizmann telegram to DBG, Apr. 13, 1940; Blanche Dugdale telegram to DBG, Apr. 13, 1940; Doris May to Sharett, Apr. 15, 1940; *MAP* (Central Committee), Apr. 14, 1940; *BKN,* Apr. 17, 1940; DBG telegram to Weizmann, Apr. 18, 1940; *ZACS,* Apr. 18, 1940.

3. *YBG,* Aug. 15, Nov. 18, 20, 1939; *SL,* vol. II, p. 394; DBG to Mapai faction, 21st Zionist Congress, Aug. 18, 1939; *MAP* (Central Committee), Sept. 12, 1939, *MAP* (Political Committee), Nov. 27, 1939; *DMS,* vol. IV, p. 510; *JAG,* Feb. 16, 1941; *BAFFY,* p. 167; DBG to Paula, May 7, 1940.

4. Broadcast in Arabic, Berlin Radio, May 8, 1940; Criminal Investigation Department reports, *CZA* S25/4351; *JAG,* Feb. 16, 1941; DBG to Paula, May 14, 1940; DBG to JAE, May 31, 1940; *MAP* (Central Committee), May 14, 1940; DBG to Eliezer Kaplan, June 11, 1940; *ZACS,* Aug. 6, 1940; *YBG,* Sept. 11, 1940; Yoav Gelber, *Toldot HaHitnadvut,* vol. I (Jerusalem: Yad Ben-Zvi Publishing, 1983), p. 71 ff.; DBG to Lord Lloyd, May 13, 1940, *CZA* Z4/14606.

5. DBG to Paula, July 1, 1940; DBG telegram to Sharett, May 15, 1940; *YBG,* June 4, 18, July 3, Aug. 26, 1940.

6. *MAP* (Central Committee), Nov. 27, 1939; Gelber, p. 78; May to Arthur Lourie, Aug. 28, 1940.

7. Gelber, p. 67 ff., 90; *YBG,* Nov. 8, 23, 1939; DBG memo, May 17, 1940; *JAG,* Nov. 8, 1939; *DMS,* vol. IV, p. 491; question-and-answer session with party members, New York, Nov. 14, 1940; DBG to Eliyahu Golomb, Nov. 23, 1939; Dudley Danby to author, Feb. 1, 1981.

8. *YBG,* Sept. 22, 26, 1940.

9. May to DBG, Sept. 7, 1939; May to Arthur Lourie, June 13, 23, July 10, 24, 31, Sept. 16, 1940.

10. May to Lourie, July 31, Sept. 2, 10, 30, 1940; Danby to author, Feb. 1, 1981; *Ha-Aretz,* Sept. 30, 1966; Plato translation from Harold North Fowler, Loeb Classical Library, vol. 167 (London: William Heinemann; Cambridge, Mass.: Harvard University Press, 1926), p. 129.

11. *YBG,* Sept. 11, 22, 1940; May to Lourie, Sept. 31, 1940; DBG to Paula, May 31, July 1, Sept. 16, 1940; *JAG,* Feb. 16, 1941; *MAP* (Central Committee), Feb. 19, 1941; *BAMA,* vol. III, p. 46.

12. Danby to author, Feb. 1, 1981; Gelber, p. 74 ff.; *WL* XX/9, 11; DBG telegram to Sharett, July 21, 1940.

13. ABG to author; *YBG*, Sept. 22, 1940; DBG to Paula, June 7, 1940; Sharett telegram to DBG, July 17, 1940; DBG telegram to Sharett, July 19, 1940; Dov Joseph telegram to DBG, Aug. 6, 1940; DBG telegram to Joseph, Aug. 8, 1940.
14. *BAFFY*, p. 174; May to Lourie, July 17, 19, Aug. 5, 28, 1940; invitation to memorial service, Aug. 6, 1940, *MBG; JAG*, London, July 19, 1940, *WA*.
15. *WL* XX/27; Gelber, pp. 76 ff., 90 ff.; May to Lourie, Sept. 2, 1940.
16. May to Lourie, Sept. 2, 6, 1940; *BAFFY*, p. 174; Weizmann to DBG, Sept. 9, 1940; DBG to Weizmann, Sept. 9, 1940; *YBG*, Sept. 11, 1940.
17. May to Lourie, Sept. 6, 10, 1940; *WL* XX/27, 37; DBG to Weizmann, Sept. 9, 1940; *YBG*, Sept. 11, 12, 1940; *BAFFY*, p. 174.
18. *YBG*, Sept. 18, 22, 1940; *WL* XX/23; protocol, Political Committee meeting, Sept. 18, 1940, taken by J. Linton, *CZA* Z4/302/24; *BAFFY*, p. 176.
19. *YBG*, Sept. 22, 1940; DBG to Paula, Oct. 2, 1940; Gelber, pp. 220, 250, 256, 259–266.
20. *YBG*, Sept. 22–28, 1940; *WL* XX/45; May to DBG, Sept. 26, 1940.

Chapter 42: Zionist Preacher

1. Doris May to Arthur Lourie, July 17, 1940; DBG to Paula, Aug. 21, Sept. 16, 1940; *JAG*, London, Sept. 18, 1940, *CZA* Z4/392/24; *Our War Programme*, Sept. 12, 1940.
2. *YBG*, Oct. 3, 9, 1940; *JAG*, Feb. 16, 1941; *MAP* (Central Committee), Feb. 19, 1941.
3. *Der Tag*, Oct. 5, 1940; *Forward*, Oct. 5, 1940; *MAP* (Central Committee), Feb. 19, 1941; *YBG*, Oct. 4, 6, 8–10, 1940.
4. DBG to Paula, Nov. 9, 1940; *MAP* (Central Committee), Feb. 19, 1941.
5. DBG to Paula, Aug. 21, Nov. 9, 1940; *YBG*, Oct. 3, 6, 7, 11, 15, 1940; *MAP* (Central Committee), Feb. 19, 1941.
6. *YBG*, Oct. 13, 15, 17, Nov. 26, 1940; DBG to Paula, Nov. 9, 1940; May cable to DBG, Nov. 29, 1940; DBG to Lourie, Jan. 14, 1941; *JAG*, Feb. 16, 1941; *PHCC*, June 7, 1941; *BAMA*, vol. III, p. 93.
7. *YBG*, Oct. 4, 6, 8, 10, 13, 1940; DBG to Paula, Nov. 9, 1940; *HNB*, Jan. 7, 1941; Gal, p. 88; *New Judaea*, Aug. 1940; *Jewish Frontier*, Nov. 1940; *Forward*, Nov. 21, 1940; *Yiddisher Kemfer*, Oct. 4, 1940; *New York Times*, Oct. 5, 1940, *YBG*, Oct. 4, 1940; press conference (Palcor, JTA), Nov. 14, 1940.
8. *YBG*, Oct. 15, 1940; *MAP* (Central Committee), Feb. 19, 1941; Gal, pp. 80–85; *JAG*, Feb. 16, 1941; *HNB*, Dec. 17, 1940.
9. *MAP* (Central Committee), Nov. 7, 10, 1940, Jan. 9, Feb. 19, 1941; *WL* XX/63, Nov. 18, 1940; DBG telegram to Weizmann, Nov. 19, 1940; *YBG*, Nov. 12, 14, 17, 19, 20, 22, 1940; Gal, p. 98; Sharett telegrams to DBG, 2837, 2844, Nov. 9, 1940; Paula telegram to DBG, Nov. 25, 1940.
10. *YBG*, Nov. 26, 1940; Gal, pp. 97–114; protocol, Winthrop Hotel meeting, Dec. 5, 1940.
11. *JAG*, Feb. 16, 1941; *MAP* (Central Committee), Feb. 19, 1941; Gal, pp. 105–119; *ZACS*, Oct. 15, 1942; Eliyahu Golomb telegram to Chaim Greenberg, Dec. 8, 1940; Sharett telegram to DBG, Dec. 9, 1940; DBG telegram

to Sharett, Dec. 11, 1940; Paula telegram to DBG, Dec. 11, 1940; DBG telegram to Paula, Dec. 13, 1940; Greenberg telegram to Golomb, Dec. 16, 1940; DBG to Rabbi Shmuel Weill, Cincinnati, Jan. 7, 1941; DBG to Mrs. John Gunther, Jan. 7, 1941; Sharett and Kaplan telegram to DBG, Jan. 10, 1941; DBG telegram to Sharett, Jan. 12, 1941.

12. DBG to Lourie, Jan. 14, 1941; DBG to Nahum Goldmann, Jan. 17, 1941; *JAG*, Feb. 16, 1941; *MAP* (Central Committee), Feb. 19, 1941; *YBG*, Jan.–Feb. 1941.

13. *BKN*, Feb. 13, May 10, 1941; *MAP* (Central Committee), Feb. 19, 1941; *JAG*, Feb. 16, Mar. 9, 16, 23, Apr. 6, 27, May 4, 16, 28, June 15, 1941; *ZACS*, May 7, 1941.

14. *MAP* (Central Committee), July 27, 1941; *BKN*, Jan. 27, 1941.

15. Tabenkin was absent from the party council in Dec. 1939 as well. In 1940 he attended only about four meetings of the Central Committee and was absent from approximately ten; he attended about four meetings of the Political Committee and was absent from about eleven. In 1941 he was absent from twenty-five Central Committee meetings (according to *MAP*); DBG meeting with representatives, United Kibbutz Movement, Mar. 18, 1941, *IDF* 1384; *MAP* (expanded secretariat), Jan. 19, 1941, *MAP* (council), Mar. 5–8, 1941; *BKN*, Jan. 22, Apr. 12, June 23, July 2, 5, 13, 1941; *Ha-Poel ha-Tzair*, Feb. 28, 1941.

16. *MAP* (secretariat), Mar. 24, 1941, *MAP* (Central Committee), Jan. 9, Mar. 19, 1941, *MAP* (council), Mar. 5–8, Apr. 27–28, 1941, *MAP* (convention at Nahalal), Mar. 9, 1941, *MAP* (month-long seminar at Rehovot), Apr. 3–4, 1941; *BAMA*, vol. III, p. 61; *MAP* (convention), June 12–13, 1941; results of the preconvention referendum and elections, May 11–13, 1941, *MBG*.

17. *JAG*, Mar. 16, 23, Apr. 6, May 4, 11, 16, 28, June 22, 1941.

18. *JAG*, Feb. 23, Mar. 16, 1941; *MAP* (Central Committee), July 27, 1941; *Davar*, Mar. 21, 1941; DBG meeting, Poale Zion Smol, Mar. 17, 1941, *IDF* 1384; DBG lecture, Histadrut Olei Germania ve Austria, *Davar*, Mar. 26, 1941; *YBG*, Apr. 21, 1941.

19. *MAP* (Central Committee), Apr. 14, June 4, July 27, 1941, *MAP* (secretariat), June 16–18, 25, July 24, 1941, *MAP* (council), Mar. 5–8, 1941, *MAP* (seminar at Rehovot), Apr. 3–4, 1941; *JAG*, Mar. 16, June 2, 1941, Jan. 25, 1942; *BKN*, May 14, June 4, 1941; DBG to Paula, Nov. 10, 1941.

20. *BKN*, June 21, 1941; *MAP* (council), Mar. 5, 1941; DBG to Paula, Aug. 1, 11, 13, 15, 1941; May to Lourie, Aug. 19, 1941.

Chapter 43: "An Act of Political Assassination"

1. *MAP* (Central Committee), Dec. 8, 1943; Doris May to Arthur Lourie, Aug. 10, 19, 1941; DBG to Paula, Nov. 11, 1941.

2. *Manchester Guardian*, Aug. 19, 1941; DBG to Paula, Aug. 19, 1941; *JAG*, Oct. 4, 1942.

3. *JAG*, Oct. 26, 1941; New Court protocol, Sept. 9, 1941; *IDF* 2928, intercepted by British Censorship when DBG left England for United States, *PRO* FO 371/27129.

4. Lord Moyne memo, Sept. 30, 1941, *PRO* FO 371/27129.

5. DBG notes, Oct. 15, 1941, and papers intercepted by British Censorship,

PRO FO 371/27129; New Court protocol, Sept. 9, 1941; memo is in *WL* XX/186, Sept. 25, 1941; May to Lourie, Sept. 18, 29, 1941; *DBG* to Paula, Aug. 19, 1941.

6. DBG to Paula, Aug. 29, 1941; *MAP* (Central Committee), Dec. 8, 1943, *MAP* (secretariat), Oct. 18, 1941; protocol, conversation with Lord Moyne, Oct. 23, 1941, *WA;* May to Lourie, Oct. 30, 1941; Berl Locker to Moshe Sharett, Dec. 2, 1941.

7. DBG to Paula, Nov. 10, 1941, read at *JAG,* Jan. 25, 1942; *YBG,* Aug. 14, 1941; May to Lourie, Aug. 27, Nov. 11, 1941; DBG to John Gilbert Winant, Sept. 5, 1941; DBG telegram to JAE, Nov. 7, 1941; DBG to Weizmann, Nov. 13, 1941; *JAG,* Oct. 4, 1942.

8. *YBG,* Nov. 24, 26–30, Dec. 23, 1941; *Der Tag,* Nov. 24, 1941; *Forward* (Yiddish), Nov. 25, 27, 1941; *New York Times,* Nov. 25, 1941; DBG to American Jewish Committee, Dec. 8, 1941; DBG to Paula, Dec. 11, 1941; *JAG,* Oct. 4, 1942.

9. *YBG,* June 19, 1939, Dec. 1, 2, 5, 1941; Weizmann to Moshe Sharett, Dec. 2, 1941, *WL* XX/222; DBG telegram to Sharett, Dec. 15, 1941; *JAG,* Dec. 21, 1941; DBG to Sharett, Feb. 8, 1942; JTA flash, Dec. 2, 1941, and DBG handwritten comments; DBG to Emanuel Neumann, Dec. 5, 1941.

10. DBG telegram to Paula, Dec. 3, 1941; *YBG,* Dec. 3–7, 21–23, 30, 1941; protocol 40, meeting, Public Relations Committee, Emergency Committee; DBG telegrams to Eliezer Kaplan, Dec. 23, 30, 1941; DBG to Lourie, Jan. 1, 1942.

11. *YBG,* Dec. 30, 1941, Jan. 2, 6, 10, 1942; Emergency Committee protocol, Jan. 5, 1942; *Yiddisher Journal,* Toronto, Canada, Jan. 9, 1942; *CZA* S25/102037; DBG to Lourie, Jan. 14, 1942.

12. DBG to Rabbi Stephen Wise, Jan. 15, 1942; DBG telegram to Berl Locker, Jan. 15, 1942; DBG telegram to Eliezer Kaplan and Sharett, Jan. 21, 1942, *CZA* S25/1495; DBG to Lourie, Jan. 27, 1942.

13. *HNB,* June 9, 1937; DBG to Lourie, Jan. 1, 1942; Emergency Committee protocol, Jan. 10, 1942; DBG to Locker, Jan. 26, 1942, *CZA* S25/1495; DBG to Sharett, Feb. 8, 1942; DBG to May, Feb. 18, 1942; personal interviews with Miriam Cohen-Taub, Nov. 11–12, 1981.

14. Cohen-Taub interviews; *JAG,* Oct. 4, 1942; *YBG,* Dec. 21, 22, 31, 1941; DBG to Sharett, Feb. 8, 1942; DBG to Felix Frankfurter, Apr. 16, 1942.

15. *YBG,* Dec. 31, 1941, Jan. 3, 6, Feb. 10, Aug. 11, 1942; *JAG,* Oct. 4, 1942; protocol, meeting with Colonel William Donovan's staff, Jan. 13, 1942, *CZA* A264/36; DBG to Ben Cohen, Feb. 6, 1942; DBG to Sharett, Feb. 8, 1942; *New York Times,* Feb. 27, Mar. 9, 10, Apr. 21, 29, May 1, 1942.

16. DBG to Sharett, Feb. 8, Apr. 16, 1942; Cohen-Taub interviews; *JAG,* Oct. 4, 1942; *BAFFY,* pp. 192, 193; DBG to Frankfurter, Apr. 14, 1942; *YBG,* Apr. 14–18, 1942; DBG telegram to Winant, Apr. 15, 1942; DBG to Frankfurter, Apr. 16, 1942; *WL* XX/192, 232, 259, 278; Franklin D. Roosevelt to Winston S. Churchill, Mar. 18, 1942, W. S. Churchill, *The Second World War,* vol. IV (London: Cassel, 1954), p. 178.

17. May to Lourie, Mar. 21, 1942; DBG to Miriam Cohen, Mar. 25, 1943, *MC,* Cohen-Taub interviews.

18. DBG to M. Cohen, Apr. 24, 25, 26, 27, 1942.

19. DBG to M. Cohen, Feb. 15, 1943; M. Cohen to DBG, Apr. 18, 1944; DBG to

M. Cohen, Nov. 1, 1942, Feb. 25, Apr. 22, May 3, 1943, Jan. 25, Apr. 25, 1944; personal interview with Feigel Broide, Paula's friend, May 22, 1974; personal interview with RLBG, Jan. 4, 1974.

20. DBG to M. Cohen, Apr. 22, 1943, Apr. 22, Sept. 20, 1944.
21. Ibid., Sept. 24, Nov. 1, Dec. 27, 1942, Feb. 15, Apr. 7, May 3, 25, July 19, Sept. 9, 1943.
22. Ibid., Mar. 25, May 3, 1943.
23. M. Cohen to DBG, Apr. 18, May 9, 1944.
24. Ibid., May 9, 1944.
25. DBG to M. Cohen, Mar. 25, Apr. 22, July 19, Sept. 19, 1943.
26. DBG to M. Cohen, Apr. 25, 1944; May to Lourie, Apr. 4, 1945; *YBG*, June 25, 1945; DBG to Cohen-Taub, June 27, 1973.
27. *YBG*, July 12, 1937; Nahum Goldmann to Wise, July 22, 1941; *HNB* July 23, 1941; *Der Tag*, May 8, 9, 1942; *Forward*, May 6, 1942; DBG telegram to JAE, Sept. 15, 1941; *WL* XX/186, 197; telegram from JAE to DBG, Dec. 4, 1941; DBG to Paula, Mar. 24, 1942; Emergency Committee protocol, Mar. 31, 1942; Meyer Weisgal telegram to Abba Hillel Silver, Apr. 23, 1942, *AAS; JAG*, June 7, Oct. 6, 1942.
28. *New York Times*, May 11, 1942; *YBG*, Dec. 18, 21, 1941, June 1, 1942; Weizmann invitation, June 1, 1942; *JAG*, Oct. 6, 1942; *WL* XX/279, 292, 295, 298, 299, 304.
29. DBG to Frankfurter, May 1, 1942; Frankfurter to DBG, May 8, 1942; DBG telegram to Linton in London, May 27, 1942; DBG telegrams to Paula, May 27, June 7, 1942; Sharett telegram to DBG, May 31, 1942; Paula telegram to DBG, June 1, 1942; Paula telegram to I. Marom, June 7, 1942; *JAG*, June 7, 1942; DBG to Sharett, Feb. 8, 1942; DBG to May, Feb. 18, 1942; Wise to delegates, Biltmore Conference, May 1, 1942; Biltmore Conference protocol, *AJANY; WL* XX/286; *YBG*, May 13, 15, 23, 29, 1942.
30. *JAG*, Oct. 4, 1942; *WL* XX/290, 312; Weizmann, *Trial and Error*, p. 524; Emergency Committee protocol, June 14, 1942; Weizmann to Roosevelt, July 2, 1942, *WA*.
31. DBG to Sharett, June 11, July 16, 1942; DBG to Weizmann, June 11, 16, 1942; Emergency Committee protocol, June 14, 16, 1942; *WL* XX/292, 295, 298; *HNB*, July 7, 1942; DBG to Wise, June 19, 25, 1942; Wise to DBG, June 22, 1942; protocol of meeting in Wise's study, June 27, 1942, *WA;* the author learned of M. Cohen's heartbreak and the epithet Pétain from Judith Epstein, Oct. 16, 1981; M. Cohen to DBG, May 9, 1944; Cohen-Taub interviews.
32. Protocol of meeting in Wise's study, June 28, 1942 *WA;* May to Lourie, Nov. 19, 1942; Weizmann, *Trial and Error*, p. 341; *WL* XX/301, 304, 306, 307, 312, 317, 321, 340; Weizmann to Berl Locker, July 15, 1942; *WA; YBG*, July 13, 1942; DBG to John McCloy, June 29, 1942; Weizmann, *Trial and Error*, manuscript pp. 398–401, *WA*.

Chapter 44: Disaster Means Strength

1. *WL* XX/292, 316, 317; Weizmann to Nahum Goldmann, Aug. 11, 1942, *WA;* DBG to Stephen Wise, June 25, July 7, 15, 1942; DBG to Goldmann,

June 30, 1942; DBG to Louis Levinthal, July 7, 1942; protocol, JAE meeting, New York, Aug. 3, 1942.

2. DBG to Felix Frankfurter, June 22, July 2, 1942; *YBG*, May 29, June 17, 24, 25, 30, July 1–3, Aug. 11, 12, 1942; *JAG*, Oct. 4, 6, 1942; DBG to Robert Patterson, June 26, 1942; DBG to John McCloy, June 29, 1942; DBG to Arthur Lourie, July 1, 1942; DBG memo to F. D. Roosevelt, July 2, 1942; *WL XX/318.*

3. DBG telegrams to Moshe Sharett, June 5, 6, 1942; Eliezer Kaplan to Lourie, June 17, 1942; *JAG*, June 14, Oct. 4, 1942; *YBG*, June 5, 1942; Weizmann, *Trial and Error, WA;* DBG to M. Wertheim, Sept. 3, 1942, *CZA* S25/1495; M. Kaufman, *Non-Zionists in America and the Struggle for Jewish Statehood 1939–1948* (Jerusalem: Hassifriya Hazionit, 1984), p. 57 ff.; Naomi W. Cohen, *American Jews and the Zionist Idea* (New York, 1975), p. 78; *American Jewish Yearbook 1947–1948*, p. 246.

4. Paula telegram to DBG, Feb. 24, 1942; DBG telegrams to Paula, Feb. 25, Mar. 28, Apr. 22, June 29, 1942; DBG telegram to Sharett, Apr. 22, 1942; Sharett telegram to DBG, Apr. 22, 1942; DBG to Paula, Mar. 24, 1942; Simon telegram to DBG, Jan. 5, 1942; Paula's will, May 19, 1942, *IDF* 3135; *KD*, vol. II, p. 578; RLBG to author, Jan. 4, 1974.

5. Dina Porath, "Rescue Efforts by the JAE 1942–1945," Ph.D. thesis (Tel Aviv University, May 1983), pp. 19, 26, 27; Emergency Committee protocol, Feb. 26, Mar. 11, 1942; *JAG*, Jan. 25, Feb. 8, 15, 22, 26, Mar. 1, 1942; Naor, *HaHa'apala.*

6. DBG to Joseph Hyman, Aug. 31, 1942; *YBG*, July 9, 1942; *JAG*, Dec. 6, 1942; *ZAC*, Oct. 15, 1942.

7. Dina Porath, pp. 21, 22; Shimon Rubinstein, *Ve'af-Al-Pi-Hen* (Jerusalem, YBZ publication, 1984).

8. *HISE*, Nov. 25–26, 1942; Emergency Committee protocol, Aug. 29, Sept. 7, 9, 17, 1942; *JAG*, Oct. 6, 1942; *MAP* (secretariat), Oct. 6, 1942, *MAP* (convention), Oct. 25, 1942, *MAP* (Political Committee), Jan. 26, 1944; *ZACS*, Oct. 15, 1942; Edvard Beneš and Papanek to Wise, Oct. 5, 1942, *AJA;* Goldmann to Itzhak Gruenbaum, Mar. 5, 1943, *CZA* S25/1234.

9. *YBG*, Sept. 18–Oct. 2, 1942; *JAG*, Oct. 13, 1944.

10. *JAG*, Oct. 4, 6, 11, Nov. 1, 8, 15, 1942; DBG to Miriam Cohen, Nov. 1, 1942.

11. *ZACS*, Jan. 17, 1943; *JAG*, Oct. 25, Nov. 1, 8, 15, 1942, Jan. 18, 31, 1943; Dina Porath, pp. 29, 30; *YBG*, Oct. 25, 1942.

12. *MAP* (convention), Oct. 25, 1942; F. H. Hinsley et al., *British Intelligence in the Second World War*, vol. II (London, 1981), p. 673.

13. *MAP* (secretariat), Nov. 24, 30, 1942; *HISE*, Nov. 25–26, 1942; *JAG*, Nov. 22, 29, 1942; DBG to M. Cohen, Nov. 23, 1942; GBE to DBG, May 19, 1942; DBG telegram to Lourie, Dec. 8, 1942; National Council protocol, Nov. 30, 1942; *BAMA*, vol. III, p. 114.

14. *JAG*, Dec. 6, 13, 1942; *ZACS*, Jan. 18, 1943; DBG telegram to Lourie, Dec. 8, 1942.

15. *ZBG*, vol. II, p. 14; *ZBG*, vol. III, p. 78; *ZBG*, vol. V, p. 377; *PHCC* (convention), Jan. 10, 1934, *PHCC* (council), Dec. 26, 1939; *ZAC*, Apr. 1, 1935; *JAG*, Nov. 27, Dec. 26, 1935, Dec. 11, 1938; DBG to Eliezer Kaplan, Mar. 4, 1936; *MAP* (Central Committee), Mar. 9, 1936, Dec. 7, 1938, *MAP* (convention), May 3–9, 1938; DBG to N. Benari, Mar. 25, 1936; *ZACS*, Oct. 26,

1936; June 26, Déc. 27, 1939; DBG to Malcolm MacDonald, Nov. 1, 1938; Mapai's Central Committee bulletin 142, Dec. 26, 1939; *To the Jewish People Throughout the World* (pamphlet published by JAE, Jerusalem-London, Feb. 1940), *CZA* S5/1022.

16. *MAP* (council), Jan. 19, 1933, *MAP* (Central Committee), May 4, 1936, Aug. 29, 1937, Mar. 19, 1941, *MAP* (convention), June 12, 1941; *ZAC*, Apr. 1, 1935; *HNB*, July 17, 1940; Biltmore Conference protocol; *HISE*, Mar. 5, 1928; *YBG*, Apr. 24, 1933; DBG to Kaplan, Mar. 4, 1936; *ZBG*, vol. III, p. 78 (Apr. 4, 1936); *ZBG*, vol. IV, p. 374; 20th Zionist Congress protocol, 1937, *JAG*, May 5, 1941; *ZACS*, May 7, 1941; "Response to the Ruler" (Mar. 24, 1943), *BAMA*, vol. II, p. 212; Zionist rally to promote unity in Yishuv, Apr. 13, 1941, *IDF* 1384.

17. *MAP* (council), Jan. 19, 1933, Mar. 5, 1941, *MAP* (Political Committee), Mar. 9, May 4, 1936, *MAP* (Central Committee), Dec. 7, 1938, Feb. 19, 1941; *YBG*, Jan. 3, 1939; *JAG*, Feb. 16, 1941.

18. *Davar*, July 30, 1939; *MAP* (convention), June 12, 1941, *MAP* (Central Committee), Mar. 19, 1941; *JAG*, May 16, 28, 1941; DBG documents intercepted Oct. 15, 1941, *PRO FO* 371/27129; *BKN*, May 10, 1941.

19. *ZACS*, Oct. 15, 1942; *MAP* (convention), Oct. 25, 1942, *MAP* (Central Committee), Dec. 8, 1943; *JAG*, Dec. 6, 1942.

20. *JAG*, Nov. 23, 1935, June 20, 1944; *ZBG*, vol. III, p. 105 (DBG meeting with Sir Arthur Wauchope, Apr. 2, 1936).

21. *MAP* (council), Jan. 19, 1933, Jan. 5, 1944, *MAP* (secretariat), Dec. 7, 1938, *MAP* (convention), June 12, 1941, *MAP* (Political Committee), Apr. 7, 1936, *MAP* (seminar at Kefar Yedidiyah), Nov. 5-6, 1943; DBG to M. Cohen, Feb. 15, 1943.

22. DBG to Felix Frankfurter, Dec. 8, 1942; *JAG*, Dec. 13, 1942, Feb. 28, Mar. 7, 1943; *MAP* (secretariat), Dec. 9, 23, 1943, *MAP* (Central Committee), Feb. 24, 1943; Dina Porath, p. 7; "Response to the Ruler" (Mar. 24, 1943).

23. Dina Porath, pp. 157, 168, 180–185; *MAP* (secretariat), Feb. 10, 1943, *MAP* (Central Committee), Feb. 24, Aug. 24, 1943, *MAP* (council), Oct. 31, 1944; *JAG*, Sept. 12, Oct. 20, 1943.

24. *JAG*, Feb. 16, 19, 1941, Oct. 6, 1942; *ZACS*, Feb. 24, 1941, Oct. 15, Nov. 10, 1942; press conference, Feb. 26, 1941; *BAMA*, vol. III, p. 46 (rough draft in MBG); Emergency Committee protocol, Sept. 17, 1942; *MAP* (secretariat), Oct. 6, 1942, *MAP* (convention), Oct. 25, 1942; *JAG*, Nov. 8, 1942.

25. *JAG*, Oct. 6, 1942, June 20, 1944; *MAP* (secretariat), Oct. 6, 1942, *MAP* (council), Mar. 6, 1943, Jan. 1, 1944; *ZACS*, Oct. 15, Nov. 10, 1942, July 5, 1943; *BAMA*, vol. III, p. 114, "El HaMatzpun Ha'Enoshi" (To the Conscience of Mankind) (Nov. 30, 1942)*HISE*, Dec. 29–30, 1943.

26. *MAP* (convention), Oct. 25, 1942, *MAP* (council), Mar. 5, 1944, *MAP* (secretariat), Feb. 22, 1944; DBG to M. Cohen, Feb. 15, 1943.

Epilogue

1. *JAG*, Oct. 18, 1942, Sept. 19, 1943.

2. DBG to JAE, Jan. 12, Nov. 3, 1943; DBG to Miriam Cohen, Feb. 15, Sept. 19, 1943; *JAG*, Feb. 28, May 10, June 27, Sept. 19, Oct. 26, Nov. 7, 1943; *ZACS*, Oct. 26, 1943; *YBG*, Feb. 18, 1943.

3. Weizmann telegram to DBG, Nov. 4, 1943, *WA;* DBG telegram to Weizmann, Nov. 8, 1943; *JAG*, Nov. 30, 1943; JAE announcement, Mar. 2, 1944; *YBG*, Oct. 10, 1945.

4. *MAP* (bureau), Jan. 13, 1944, *MAP* (Central Committee), Nov. 27, 1939, Nov. 24, 1942; *JAG*, Nov. 26, 1939, Mar. 12, May 21, June 20, 1944; *WL* XXI/260, Jan. 14, 1945; draft from Jan. 25, 1944, and DBG to JAE, Feb. 17, 1944; *DMS*, vol. IV, p. 510.

5. *YBG*, Nov. 30, Dec. 1, 9, 11, 1944; *MAP* (Central Committee) and (secretariat), Dec. 14, 1944; Vicki Tamir, *Bulgaria and Her Jews* (New York: Yeshiva University Press, 1979).

6. DBG to M. Cohen, Sept. 20, 1944.

7. *YBG*, Oct. 1, 19–31, 1945; Leo W. Schwarz, *The Redeemers* (New York: Farrar, Straus & Young, 1953), p. 175; *Unser Weg*, Oct. 21, 26, 1945; Judah Nadich, *Eisenhower and the Jews* (New York: Twayne Publishers, 1953), p. 230; personal interview with Rabbi Nadich, Oct. 15, 1981; *MAP* (secretariat), Nov. 22, 1945.

8. *YBG*, Oct. 1, 1945.

Glossary

Achdut ha-Avodah United Labour: a socialist Zionist party formed in February 1919 by the union of the Palestine Poale Zion with all other labor bodies except Ha-Poel ha-Tzair

Agricultural Committees Farmers' local representative bodies

Aliyah Bet Illegal immigration

Arab Executive Committee Representative body of Arab political parties in Palestine

Arab Higher Committee Representative body that superseded the Arab Executive Committee

Haganah Defense: the Zionist defense underground in Palestine, formed in 1920, on which the Israel Defence Army was founded in May 1948

Ha Kibbutz ha-Meuchad United Kibbutz Movement, headed by Itzhak Tabenkin

Ha-Poel ha-Tzair The Young Worker: a non-socialist Palestinian Zionist labor party, formed in 1906; Poale Zion's archrival

Histadrut Short for Ha-Histadrut ha-Klalit shel ha-Ovdim ha-Ivrim Be-Eretz Israel: the General Federation of Jewish Labour in Palestine (changed in 1965 to General Federation of Labour in Israel), formed in 1920 by Achdut ha-Avodah, Ha-Poel ha-Tzair, and minor labor bodies

IZL Irgun Zvai Leummi, Revisionists' national military organization

JAE Jewish Agency Executive, formed in 1929 as a coalition of members of the Zionist Executive and individual non-Zionists representing Jewish bodies interested in the development of the Yishuv

Jewish Agency Recognized under the British Mandate in Palestine as representative of Jewish and Zionist interests in Palestine

Lehi Splinter group of IZL

Mapai United Labor Party of Palestine, formed in January 1930 by the union of Achdut ha-Avodah, Ha-Poel ha-Tzair, and other bodies; for many years the ruling party in the Zionist Organization and in the Yishuv, and later in Israel

National Council Yishuv's representative body, chosen by Elected Assembly

Old Yishuv The religious Jewish community of Palestine prior to the establishment of the Yishuv, the anti-Zionist part of which later opposed the Yishuv

Poale Zion Workers of Zion: a world union of Zionist Marxist parties in Europe, America, and Palestine; Palestine party formed in 1906

Yishuv Community: the Jewish Community of Palestine, primarily Zionist, a term used from the end of the nineteenth century until the formation of the State of Israel in 1948

Zionist Executive A coalition elected in the Zionist biennial world congresses to head the World Zionist Organization and the Jewish Agency

Index

Abrami, Dr. Pierre, 380
Achdut ha-Avodah: DBG's idea for,
134–36, 139, 863; formation of,
139–42; DBG on executive committee and secretariat, 143–44; and settlement of ex-Legionnaires, 151; and
Kunteres, 151; and Elected Assembly, 152–55; and Haganah, 156,
213–14 (*see also* Haganah); stance
on Arab hostilities, 156–57; dispatches DBG to London, 157; delegates at 1920 Zionist Conference,
161–64; delegation at fifth World
Conference of Poale Zion, 165–69;
DBG's fund-raising efforts in Britain, 172–74; relations with British
Labour Party, 174–76; and founding
of Histadrut, 181, 183; DBG con-
centrates on, over Histadrut,
182–86; merger plans with Ha-Poel
ha-Tzair, 182, 247; DBG's labor
army concept for, 183–86; and
Labor Legion, 184, 211–13, 214,
216–17, 294; DBG shifts efforts to
Histadrut from, 187–88; and leadership of Histadrut, 208; and Great
Kvutsa, 212; conflict with Ha-Poel
ha-Tzair, 253–55; and Mops, 286;
and DBG's conflict with Zionist
Council, 322; and DBG's defense of
Solel Boneh, 336–37; representation
in Histadrut conventions, 339; cri-
tique of DBG at third Histadrut
convention, 342–43; merger with
Ha-Poel ha-Tzair, 355–62, 393–94,

404 (*see also* Mapai); unity commit-
tee for merger, 360, 361; consolida-
tion of power and strategies,
364–66; and Weizmann-Marshall
agreement, 391; and World Con-
gress for Labor Palestine, 392; and
League for Labor Palestine, 392–93;
Mapai Faction B assumes name,
843; at 1945 Elected Assembly and
Histadrut convention, 869
Achimeir, Abba, 415, 424, 462; and
Revisionist Labor Bloc, 370; and
Terrorists, 410, 411, 412
Adler, Cyrus, 686, 688
Advisory Committee on International
Affairs (British Labour Party),
175–76
AFL (American Federation of Labor),
629, 774
Aghios Nikolaus, 728, 874
Agnon, S. Y., 856
Agricultural Center (Histadrut), 200,
205, 206, 209, 301, 332; and Labor
Legion commune, 212, 215; re-
placed by Nir, 241; and Petah Tivka
labor conflict, 353
Agudat Israel, 510, 790
Aharonovitch, Joseph, 256, 270, 308;
codirector of Bank ha-Poalim,
208–9; HEC salary of, 247, 382; and
Histadrut salary advances, 326; at
third Histadrut convention, 344;
against use of violence, 461, 462
Alami, Musa, 460–61, 542; on Arab
fears, 465–66; plans meeting be-